THE YEAR'S WORK IN MODERN LANGUAGE STUDIES

THE
YEAR'S WORK IN MODERN LANGUAGE STUDIES

GENERAL EDITOR
STEPHEN PARKINSON

ASSISTANT EDITOR
LISA BARBER

SECTION EDITORS

LATIN, FRENCH, OCCITAN
LISA BARBER, M.A., D.PHIL

ITALIAN, ROMANIAN, RHETO-ROMANCE
JOHN M. A. LINDON, M.A.
Professor of Italian Studies,
University College London

ROMANCE LINGUISTICS, SPANISH, CATALAN, PORTUGUESE, GALICIAN, LATIN AMERICAN, SLAVONIC
STEPHEN PARKINSON, M.A., PH.D.
Lecturer in
Portuguese Language and Linguistics,
University of Oxford

CELTIC
DAVID A. THORNE, M.A., PH.D.
Professor of Welsh,
University of Wales, Lampeter

GERMANIC
DAVID A. WELLS, M.A., PH.D.
Professor of German,
Birkbeck College, University of London

VOLUME 63
2001

MANEY PUBLISHING
for the
MODERN HUMANITIES RESEARCH ASSOCIATION

2003

The Year's Work in Modern Language Studies may be ordered from the Subscriptions Department, Maney Publishing, Hudson Road, Leeds LS9 7DL, UK.

ISBN 1 902653 98 X

ISSN 0084-4152

Produced in Great Britain by
MANEY PUBLISHING
HUDSON ROAD   LEEDS LS9 7DL   UK

CONTENTS

ABBREVIATIONS

NAME INDEX

PREFACE

This volume surveys work, published in 2000, unless otherwise stated, in the fields of Romance, Celtic, Germanic, and Slavonic languages and literatures. An asterisk before the title of a book or article indicates that the item in question has not been seen by the contributor.

The attention of users is drawn to the lists of abbreviations at the end of the volume, which are also available on-line on the MHRA's WWW site (http://www.mhra.org.uk/Publications/Journals/ywmls.html).

Many authors, editors and publishers supply review copies and offprints of their publications. To these we and our contributors are grateful, and we would invite others to follow their example, especially in the case of work issuing from unusual, unexpected, or inaccessible sources of publication. We would ask that, whenever possible, items for review be sent directly to the appropriate contributor; where no obvious recipient can be identified, as in the case of books or journal issues relating to a number of fields, the item should be sent to one of the editors, who will distribute the contents accordingly.

The compilation of a contribution to the volume, especially in the field of the major languages and periods of literature, is a substantial research task requiring wide-ranging and specialized knowledge of the subject besides a huge reading effort accompanied by the constant exercise of critical judgement. We are deeply grateful to the authors who have devoted significant amounts of increasingly precious research time to this enterprise. The measure of their task is indicated by the number of sections for which the editors have failed to find contributors; we encourage approaches from potential contributors or groups of contributors for future volumes.

The completion of this volume would not have been possible without the contribution of Lisa Barber, Assistant Editor and compiler of the Index. Thanks are also due to the other institutions and individuals who have contributed in one way or another to the making of the volume, in particular, the secretarial and administrative staff of the Faculty of Modern Languages of Oxford University, and our printers, Maney Publishing, particularly Liz Rosindale, Caitlin Meadows, and Anna Thrush, whose expertise and patience have as ever ensured the smooth progress of this complex operation.

15 December 2002   S.R.P., L.B., J.M.A.L., D.A.T., D.A.W.

1

LATIN

I. MEDIEVAL LATIN

By Christopher J. McDonough, *Professor of Classics, University of Toronto*

1. General

Joseph Farrell, *Latin Language and Latin Culture from Ancient to Modern Times*, CUP, xiv + 148 pp., includes a liberal number of medieval writers, from Isidore to Alan of Lille, as he follows the fortunes of Latinity over two millennia. D. Ó Cróinín, 'A new seventh-century Irish commentary on Genesis', *Sac*, 40:231–65, investigates the palaeographical features and sources of the work in Munich, Bayerische Staatsbibliothek, Clm 17739, and finds them to be consistent with Bischoff's criteria for establishing its Hibernian character. J.-Y. Tilliette, 'Pour une approche littéraire des textes latins du moyen âge', *MJ*, 36:325–35, discusses Walter of Châtillon's *Alexandreis*, the *Historia Meriadoci*, and Geoffrey of Vinsauf's *Poetria Nova* in the course of defending the application of categorical concepts, provided that they were also used by the authors themselves. A. Orchard, 'The *Hisperica famina* as literature', *JMLat*, 10, 2000:1–45, argues that rhetorical and literary techniques offer a key to the work's structure and purpose. J. Ziolkowski, '*Nota bene*: why the Classics were neumed in the Middle Ages', *ib.*, 74–114, categorizes the various kinds of passages from epic, lyric, satire and drama that were sung at court and elsewhere, before he provides an inventory of MSS containing neumed texts. J. F. Domínguez Domínguez, 'Recherches sur les mots *campidoctor* et *campiductor*: de l'antiquité au moyen âge tardif', *ALMA*, 58, 2000:5–44, establishes that the predominant form *campidoctor* is strongly linked to the worlds of religion and philosophy. A. Caiazzo, 'Un commento altomedievale al *De arithmetica* di Boezio', *ib.*, 113–50, sketches the privileged place the treatise occupied in medieval education before presenting a first edition based on four MSS. A. Plassmann, 'Gildas and the negative image of the Cymry', *CMCS*, 41:1–15, examines the tradition of disloyalty and cowardice attributed to the Britons, before he argues that Gildas deployed them as part of a programme to depict a sense of Britishness distinct from Romanness. T. Gärtner, 'Zu einem Prosa-Argumentum der statianischen *Achilleis*', *Philologus*, 145:365–68, improves the text of the *accessus*. C. Schubert, 'Wie Pindar zur *Ilias*

Latina kam', *Hermes*, 129:386–93, finds that the attribution of the poem to Pindar originated in a naive reading of lines 1063–70, and conjectures that a misreading of *Pieridum* (v. 1067) evolved into the name *Pindarus*. M. Cupiccia, 'Clausole quantitative e clausole ritmiche nella prosa latina della Spagna visigotica', *FilM*, 8:25–110, applies a composite method to the prose of Julian of Toledo and Isidore of Seville, among many others, and provides tables of statistics and percentages for their use of the *cursus*. A. Bisanti, 'Note e appunti di lettura su testi mediolatini', *ib.*, 111–22, comments on texts by Paul the Deacon, Paulinus of Aquileia, a fable by the so-called *Astensis poeta* and one from *Due lotrices*, 139–41, contained in John of Garland's *Parisiana poetria*. M. W. Herren 'Bavius and Maevius: "Duo pessimi poetae sui temporis" ', *Rigg Vol.*, 3–15, reconstructs the biographies of the two critics from *testimonia*, scholia, and their appearances in literature from Vergil to Walter Map. H. Westra, 'Individuality, originality and the literary criticism of medieval Latin texts', *Fest. Dronke*, 281–92, adduces the poetry of Baudri of Bourgueil, the *Ruodlieb*, and the beast epic in a search for novel forms of expression in ML literature. J. Ziolkowski, 'The highest form of compliment: *imitatio* in medieval Latin culture', *ib.*, 293–307, surveys the high status of *imitatio* in the ancient philosophical and rhetorical traditions, before he examines the concept in later theory and practice. A. Michel, 'La rhétorique de l'amour', *REL*, 78, 2000:236–54, ranges from Homer to Thomas Aquinas, as he analyses the language of love, the forms of argumentation it adopts, the content of its thought, and the ways in which it incorporates philosophy and Christianity. C. Davidson, 'Violence and the saint play', *SP*, 98:292–314, investigates how violence in early British plays and pageants was presented and received, starting from the *Tres clerici*, suggesting that they were seen as imaginary projections of events in the lives of martyrs. E. Johnston, 'Íte: patron of the people?', *Peritia*, 14, 2000:421–28, focuses on the representation of the saint as a nurturer and mother in Latin and Irish texts. P. Russell, '*Virgilius filius Ramuth*: Irish scribes and Irish nomenclature', *ib.*, 432–33, suggests that the version of Virgilius Maro Grammaticus's name in Leiden, Bibliothek der Rijksuniversiteit, BPL 135, resulted from misreading an abbreviated form of his name that could only have occurred in an Irish milieu. T. Wünsch, 'Der heilige Bischof — zur politischen Dimension von Heiligkeit im Mittelalter und ihrem Wandel', *AKG*, 82, 2000:261–302, addresses the conditions that influenced the dynamic relationship between politics and holiness by studying the phenomenon of the holy bishop as a spiritual and worldly ruler.

2. ANGLO-SAXON

D. R. Howlett, 'The verse of Aethelweard's chronicle', *ALMA*, 58, 2000: 219–24, discerns arithmetic patterns in the poetry that mark it as part of the tradition of AS and OE metrical experimentation. N. Howe, 'An angle on this earth: sense of place in Anglo-Saxon England', *BJR*, 82, 2000: 3–27, examines cartographic knowledge in the texts of Bede, Gildas, and Aelfric, as well as bilingual charters and the *mappamundi* in London, BL, Cotton Tiberius B.v. B. Löfstedt, 'Zu den Bibelkommentaren von Theodor und Hadrian', *Eranos*, 99: 34–37, offers notes on the Latinity of the commentaries. C. M. Cain, 'Phonology and meter in the Old English macaronic verses', *SP*, 98: 273–91, argues that the Latin verses were subjected to vernacular rules of stress placement and vowel length. L. A. Garner, 'The art of translation in the Old English *Judith*', *SN*, 73: 171–83, finds that the poet elaborated scenes from the Vulgate, e.g. Holofernes's feast, so as to locate them within the vernacular poetic tradition. S. M. Pons Sanz, 'Aldredian glosses to proper names in the *Lindisfarne Gospels*', *Anglia*, 119: 173–92, establishes that the glosses provide not only lexical information, but also biblical interpretations from the patristic period. T. D. Hill, ' "When the leader is brave . . .": an Old English proverb and its vernacular context', *ib.*, 232–36, adduces *Durham Proverbs* no. 31 as a contemporary analogue to a proverb in the E version of the Anglo-Saxon *Chronicle* and reads it as an index of the tension between old heroic ideals and the pragmatic demands of war.

3. CAROLINGIAN

J. Glenn, 'Echoes of *Aeneid* 11 in Einhard's *Vita Karoli Magni*', *Classical World*, 94: 179–82, detects in Einhard's account of the battle of Roncesvalles signs of a parallel scene from Vergil's epic. M. Alberi, ' "The better paths of wisdom": Alcuin's monastic "true philosophy" and the worldly court', *Speculum*, 76: 896–910, examines the tension between Alcuin's dedication to monastic ideals, as described in the *Disputatio de vera philosophia*, and the demands of a career at Charlemagne's court. L. Bernays, 'Das sogennante "Carmen Harleianum" und seine möglichen Vorbilder', *MJ*, 36: 31–44, re-edits the poem from London, BL, Harley 2724, with a formal analysis of its composition and a discussion of the material appropriated from Horace's *Odes*. F. M. Casaretto, 'L'esordio mistico dell'"Epistola ad Grimaldum abbatem" di Ermenrico di Ellwangen: immaginario, fonti dirette e indirette', *ib.*, 205–33, discovers in Augustine's *Confessions* the source of images which led Ermenrich to link the primordial light of the cosmos with *caritas*. S. Di Brazzano, 'Cosmo-graphia Aethici, p. 161, 7–9 Prinz (= 4,2,5 p. 496 D'Avezac = 61 p. 41, 19–21 Wuttke)', *FilM*, 8:123–25, repunctuates the passage to join the phrase '*sicut in Ophir*' with the preceding clause, noting the association of Ophir in the Bible with rare and precious metals. G. P. Maggioni, 'La composizione della *Passio Zotici* [BHL 9028] e la tradizione della *Passio Getulii* [BHL 3524]. Un caso letterario tra agiografia e politica', *ib.*, 127–72, offers a critical text of *Passio Zotici* after discussing the dynamics of the two texts and the role of Pope Paschal I. T. Gärtner, 'Zu Theodulf von Orléans (?) carm. 74 Dümmler', *Maia*, 53:645–48, suggests an emendation based on an intertext from Milo of St. Amand, *De sobrietate*, I. 129–34. Id., 'Die Reaktion Karls des Grossen auf die Nachricht von der Verstümme-lung des Papstes Leo III ("Aachener Karlsepos" 441–444)', *Latomus*, 60:992–99, explores the rhetorical resonance of an idiomatic collo-quialism in an epic and finds an echo of a funerary inscription written by Theodulf of Orleans for Pope Hadrian I. M. Huglo, 'Les arts libéraux dans le "Liber glossarum"', *Scriptorium*, 55:3–33, identifies the sources of a monumental work, before he describes several MSS and edits three passages on dialectic and music not previously attested in the tradition of Isidore's *Origines*. T. Gärtner, 'Das Vogelprodigium im Helena-Epyllion des Dracontius: Antike Vorbilder und mittelalter-liches Nachleben', *Mnemosyne*, 54:345–49, notes Dracontian allusions in Ermoldus Nigellus, *In honorem Hludowici*, William of Bretone, *Philippis*, and Odo of Cluny, *Occupatio*. Id., 'Kritisch-Exegetisches zur Marcellus-Vita des Vulfinus von Die (MGH poet. lat. IV 3 p. 963–76 Strecker)', *Eranos*, 99:18–27, offers solutions to metrical problems in a text transmitted by the lacunose Codex Bononienis 1232. C. Veyrard-Cosme, 'Littérature latine du haut moyen âge et polémique antibyzantine: procédés et enjeux de la rhétorique du blâme dans les *Livres Carolins*', *REL*, 78, 2000:212–35, analyses the elements of invective in order to show how the rhetoric of blame produced a paean to a king intent on controlling the religious sphere. M. N. Todaro, 'Il commento di Rabano Mauro a Geremia', *SM*, 42:41–119, lists the sources Hrabanus appropriated, examines the preface, and describes his technique as a compiler. M. Mériaux, 'Thérouanne et son diocèse jusqu'à la fin de l'époque carolingienne. Les étapes de la christianisation d'après les sources écrites', *BEC*, 158, 2000:377–406, uses the hagiographic and diplomatic documents of Sithiu to fill the absence of an episcopal historiography of Thérou-anne. C. D. Wright, 'Bischoff's theory of Irish exegesis and the Genesis commentary in Munich clm 6302: a critique of a critique', *JMLat*, 10, 2000:115–75, points out weaknesses in recent arguments that reject Bischoff's criteria for identifying Hiberno-Latin biblical commentaries, before he assembles linguistic formulations and motifs from Irish sources that mark the Genesis commentary as belonging to the group. M. Lapidge, 'A metrical *Vita S. Iudoci* from tenth-century Winchester', *ib.*, 255–306, publishes a first edition of a poem, hermeneutic in style and based on the prose *Vita I S. Iudoci*, that was added to a collection of materials concerning the saint in London, BL, MS Royal 8.B.XIV. H. Mayr-Harting, 'Liudprand of Cremona's account of his legation to Constantinople (968) and Ottonian imperial strategy', *EHR*, 116:539–56, argues that the *Relatio de legatione* was addressed to the Dukes of Capua and Benevento, because Ottonian imperial interests required loyal allies who could act as a buffer between Byzantine southern Italy and Rome. B. M. Kaczynski, 'Bede's commentaries on Luke and Mark and the formation of a patristic canon', *Rigg Vol.*, 17–26, underscores Bede's importance in privileging the works of Ambrose, Augustine, Gregory, and Jerome by using a system of marginal attribution that identified material taken from their works. G. R. Wieland, 'The hermeneutic style of Thiofrid of Echternach', *ib.*, 27–47, discusses the style of Thiofrid's prose *Vita S. Willibrordi* ch.1–24, and its use of Grecisms that were drawn from Aldhelm and glossaries. M. Garrison, 'Alcuin, *Carmen IX* and Hrabanus, *Ad Bonosum*: a teacher and his pupil write consolation', *Fest. Dronke*, 63–78, examines the reception of Alcuin's Lindisfarne poem by his principal poetic heir, who rewrote it to reflect a different world view. M. W. Herren, 'Some quantitative poems attributed to Columbanus of Bobbio', *ib.*, 99–112, finds a congruence between the contents of *Ad Sethum*, *Ad Hunaldum*, and *Columbanus Fidolio* and the theological ideas expressed in Columbanus's prose works, reason enough not to exclude him as the author of the poems. B. K. Vollmann, 'Philosophie und Poesie — Zwei zankende Geschwister', *ib.*, 251–61, illuminates the struggle between the two modes by analysing the use of the word *poeta* in Carolingian circles, before he sketches the origin of a new, post-Carolingian conception of poetry in which ideas associated with *iocus* and *delectatio* played a central role. F. Gasparri, 'L'abbé Suger de Saint-Denis. Mémoire et perpétuations des oeuvres humaines', *CCMe*, 44:247–57, focuses on the moral vein in Suger's historical and autobiographical writings that urges the avoidance of evil through imitating exemplary lives. J. Tolan, 'Réactions chrétiennes aux conquêtes musulmanes. Étude comparée des auteurs chrétiens de Syrie et d'Espagne', *ib.*, 349–67, tracks the strategies evolved by Christians to explain Muslim success, which became increasingly polemical in an attempt to discourage apostasy.

4. The Eleventh Century

D. R. Bradley, 'The structure of the Carmen Cantabrigiense 6 ("De Lantfrido et Cobbone")', *MJ*, 36:235–48, revises the text of the preamble, and an analysis of its structure leads him to posit a gap in the narrative sequence between stanzas 4 and 5. R. Gameson, 'Hugo Pictor enlumineur normand', *CCMe*, 44:121–38, discusses the MSS that can attributed to the scribe and illustrator, whose work was widely diffused beyond Jumièges, where he spent some time. M. Frassetto, 'The writings of Ademar of Chabannes, the Peace of 994, and the "terrors of the year 1000"', *JMH*, 27:241–55, investigates the eschatological mentality of the era by studying the accounts of prodigies and signs in Ademar's universal chronicle and sermons, the language of which is indebted to the book of Revelations and Isaiah. M. Parisse, 'Le préambule d'une charte du XIe siècle, document et texte littéraire', *REL*, 78, 2000:16–25, uses a computer analysis of rare words in charters from the reign of Louis the Pious (814–840) in an effort to isolate features that could be used to detect forged charters, before he applies his findings to determine the authorship of a charter delivered by bishop Lambert of Langres in 1019. S. L. Wailes, 'Beyond virginity: flesh and spirit in the plays of Hrotsvit of Gandersheim', *Speculum*, 76:1–27, argues that the central theme of each drama concerns not sexuality, but the contest between the principles of flesh and spirit, whether in individuals or in the world, and that Hroswitha's intellectual inheritance included Augustine's commentary on Paul's ideas in *The City of God*, as mediated through the works of Hrabanus Maurus. M. Giovini, 'L'*Antapodosis* di Liutprando da Cremona alla luce delle riprese terenziane', *Maia*, 53:137–65, documents the strategic deployment of Terentian ideas, locutions, characters, and scenes to invest his history with satirical and comical themes. Id., 'Riscritture terenziane: Il motivo delle "Nozze simulate" nel *Gallicanus* di Rosvita', *ib.*, 649–73, argues that Hroswitha shaped the dramatic nucleus of her play by reinventing the opening of Terence's *Andria*. S. Boynton and M. Pantarotto, 'Ricerche sul breviario di Santa Giulia (Brescia, Biblioteca Queriniana, ms. H VI 21)', *SM*, 42:301–18, summarize the history of a very important female monastery in Brescia, before they describe the contents and provenance of the MS, which contains a number of famous hymns that are glossed and neumed.

5. The Twelfth Century

Paden, *Genres*, includes W. Wetherbee, 'The place of secular Latin lyric' (95–125), who argues on the basis of the poetry of Peter of Blois and *Carmina Burana* 67 and 88 that the learned Latin tradition adopted an ironic perspective on vernacular love poetry. The *Carmina burana*: *Four Essays*, ed. Martin H. Jones, London, Centre for Late Antique and Medieval Studies, 2000, x + 109 pp. + 22 pls, includes: A. J. Duggan, 'The world of the *Carmina burana*' (1–23), who analyses the social and intellectual events between 1150–1230 which formed the matrix for a poetic miscellany that reflects the life of a European student intelligentsia; P. Dronke, 'Latin songs in the *Carmina burana*: profane love and satire' (25–40), who investigates matters of date, provenance, and structure, before using *CB* 85, 120, 131, 165, and 177 to illustrate the international nature of the collection. D. Schaller, 'Gattungs- und Formtypen in den "Carmen Burana amatoria"', *MJ*, 36:77–93, maps a typology of ML lyric based on the coordinates of form and function, before he exemplifies his model with stanzas taken from *CB* 70, 75, 120, 121 and others. D. A. Traill, '"Mal d'amour, Joie d'amour": a new edition and interpretation of CB 60/60a', *ib.*, 95–112, offers a text, translation, notes, and discussion of the genres that were re-shaped for new expression. Id. 'Reaching the right harbour: negotiating the double entendres in *Carmina Burana* 128', *FilM*, 8:173–78, detects a homoerotic strain beneath the allegory. G. Dapelo, 'Il romanzo latino di Barlaam e Josaphat (BHL 979): preparando l'edizione', *ib.*, 179–220, presents the prolegomena, including an up-dated census of the MSS, discussion of the legend's diffusion which began in France, and a stemma. C. Wollin, 'Mutabilität in der lateinischen Dichtung des Hochmittelalters. Die Kleidermetamorphosen des Hugo Primas und des Archipoeta', *Sac*, 40:329–413, illustrates the problems presented by different versions of the same text by editing *In noua fert animus*, which he ascribes to Primas, and *Carmina Burana* 220, written by the Archpoet, who may be identified with the Galtherus mentioned in the F-version. T. Gärtner, 'Arnulf von Orléans zu Ov. rem. 777–784', *SM*, 42:319–23, emends the text of the gloss; Id., 'Zur Rekonstruktion eines mittellateinischen Kommentars zu den Heroidenbriefen Ovids', *ALMA*, 58, 2000:151–210, reconstructs the original version of the scholia, improves the text of the commentary, and discovers MS support for a conjecture by Heinsius to Ovid's text. B. Holsinger and D. Townsend, 'The Ovidian verse epistles of Master Leoninus (ca. 1135–1201)', *JMLat*, 10, 2000:239–54, edit two poems, preserved uniquely in Paris, BN, lat. 14759, which respond to the *Amores* and the *Heroides*. S. Flanagan, 'Lexicographic and syntactic explorations of doubt in twelfth-century Latin texts', *JMH*, 27:219–40, studies the semantic field of doubt words and images in order to construct a contextual definition of doubt, before he describes the emotions, metaphors, and measures of doubt. H. Pryce, 'British or Welsh? National identity in twelfth-century Wales', *EHR*, 116:775–801, concludes that while the Latin terminology used to refer to Wales and the Welsh changed (*Wallia, Wallensis* instead of *Britannia* and *Britones*), their concepts of who they were as a people did not. A. Barratt, 'Small Latin? The post-conquest learning of English religious women', *Rigg Vol.*, 51–65, examines books owned by Benedictine and Cistercian nuns and finds that some women religious were more proficient in Latin than has previously been assumed. S. Echard, 'Clothes make the man: the importance of appearance in Walter Map's *De Gadone milite strenuissimo*', *ib.*, 93–108, reads the historical narrative concerning Gado as a mixture of morality and entertainment with elements of parody. M. Winterbottom, 'William of Malmesbury *versificus*', *ib.*, 109–27, discusses William's appropriation of classical and medieval poetry as well as some unattributed verses that may be William's own. C. J. McDonough, 'Alexander Neckam: creation and Paradise in book 2 of the *Suppletio defectuum*', *ib.*, 129–48, edits two passages from the supplement to the *Laus sapientie diuine* and discusses the poetic sources that Neckam recast for his commentary on Gen. 1.1–24. G. Dinkova-Bruun, 'The story of Ezra: a versification added to Peter Riga's *Aurora*', *ib.*, 163–88, offers a diplomatic edition of the *Liber Esdre Prophete* from Cambridge, Fitzwilliam Museum, MS McClean 31. S. E. Kholi, 'Abbatissa in Lübboldesberge Hildegardi. Notizen zu den Briefen 163 und 163R Hildegards von Bingen', *Euphorion*, 95:257–62, localizes the letters in the Benedictine convent of Lippoldsberg, not to the unknown 'Lubbolzberg', and argues that the person designated in the MSS by the initial letter D. was the author of *Ep.* 163. C. Burnett, 'Learned knowledge of Arabic poetry, rhymed prose, and didactic verse from Petrus Alfonsi to Petrarch', *Fest. Dronke*, 29–62, documents the meagre evidence for prose and poetic Latin translations of verses and rhymed sayings from Arabic sources. D. Luscombe, 'Peter Abelard and the poets', *ib.*, 155–71, discusses Abelard's deft integration of Christian teaching with classical poetry and mythology in his letters to Heloise, in the *Theologia*, and in the *Carmen ad Astralabium*, despite the problematic status of pagan poetry for Christians. B. Newman, 'God and the goddesses: vision, poetry, and belief in the Middle Ages', *ib.*, 173–96, examines in what ways the treatment of female personifications in visionary and allegorical literature, Latin and vernacular, altered Christianity's concept of God. G. Orlandi, 'On the text and interpretation of Abelard's *Planctus*', *ib.*, 327–42, analyses the metrical structure of the lament for Jephtha's daughter, which leads him to suspect the probability of two *lacunae*. C. Leonardi, 'Una scheda per Ildegarde di Bingen', *ib.*, 343–48, underlines the importance of Hildegard's prophetic and authoritative tone in her correspondence with bishops and popes. A. Classen, 'Abaelards *Historia calamitatum*, der Briefwechsel mit Heloise und Gottfrieds von Strassburg *Tristan*: Historisch-biographische und fiktionale Schicksale. Eine Untersuchung zur Intertextualität im zwölften und dreizehnten Jahrhundert', *Arcadia*, 35, 2000:225–53, is persuaded that the German poet modelled Tristan and Isolde on Abelard and Heloise, even though the latter are not mentioned in *Tristan*. A. G. Rigg, 'Joseph of Exeter's pagan gods again', *MAe*, 70:19–28, divides Joseph's inconsistent attitude towards gods, omens, fate, and prophecies into five categories. A. J. Duggan, 'Classical quotations and allusions in the correspondence of Thomas Becket: an investigation of their sources', *Viator*, 32:1–22, identifies Heiric of Auxerre's *Collectanea* and the *Florilegium Gallicum* as the principal sources from which Becket's circle drew their classical citations. C. J. Mews, 'Hugh Metel, Heloise, and Peter Abelard: the letters of an Augustinian canon and the challenge of innovation in twelfth-century Lorraine', *ib.*, 59–91, discusses Hugh's interest in literary originality and its manifestation in Heloise as a writer, before he compares Hugh's prose to that of other contemporary letter-collections. R. Jakobi, 'Die *Alexandreis* vor Akkon', *FilM*, 8:221–23, argues that the late dating of Walther of Châtillon's epic poem must be abandoned after discovering that an anonymous, who described Crusader battles that occurred between 1187–90, quoted some of Walther's dedicatory verses for the archbishop of Reims in his eulogy of the archbishop of Besançon. M. Hoffmann, 'Alexander und Tydeus bei Walter von Châtillon', *MJ*, 36:249–51, connects Alexander's compulsion to conquer with the fearless anger of Statius's hero. I. Pânzaru, '*Caput mystice*. Fonctions symboliques de la tête chez les exégètes de la seconde moitié du XIIe siècle', *MA*, 107:439–53, explores the symbolism of the blows inflicted on the head of Thomas Becket, revealing how the relationship between the literal and figural was structured to illuminate the struggle between the English church and Henry II. M. Colker, 'Previously unpublished letters ascribed to Saint Jerome', *RTAM*, 62, 2000:195–217, edits from Oporto, Biblioteca publica municipal, Codex 25 (Santa Cruz 9) ten items that on linguistic grounds he classifies as medieval. F. Heinzer, '*Scalam ad coelos*. Poésie liturgique et image programmatique. Lire une miniature du livre du chapitre de l'abbaye de Zwiefalten', *CCMe*, 44:329–48, discovers that a sequence by Notker of Saint-Gall offers a key to interpreting an image of St. Benedict positioned at the head of a text of his rule, which he then sets in the context of monastic reform.

6. THE THIRTEENTH CENTURY

W. Azzam and O. Collet, 'Le manuscrit 3142 de la Bibliothèque de l'Arsenal. Mise en recueil et conscience littéraire au XIIIe siècle',

CCMe, 44:207–45, analyses the vernacular and Latin contents of the MS, whose arrangement sheds light on the interaction of various literary genres, the concept of the author, and his relationship to power. D. F. Glass, 'Otage de l'historiographie: l'*Ordo prophetarum* en Italie', *ib.*, 259–73, posits an independent Italian prophet tradition that integrated the widely diffused literature on the subject, but varied it to suit its own culture. J.-Y. Tilliette, *Des mots à la parole. Une lecture de la "Poetria nova" de Geoffroy de Vinsauf*, Geneva, Droz, 2000, 199 pp., argues that the originality of the poem lies in Geoffroy's view that the nature and function of poetry was not simply aesthetic, but a mode that gave access to knowledge of a higher reality. W.-V. Ikas, 'Martinus Polonus' *Chronicle of the Popes and the Emperors*: a medieval best-seller and its neglected influence on English medieval chronicles', *EHR*, 116:327–41, emphasizes the popularity of a work which circulated in numerous MSS in England (91 of the 437 extant), before he follows its translation into Western and Eastern vernaculars and its use by Richard of Durham, Nicholas Trevet, and Ralph Higden. A. G. Rigg, 'The long or the short of it? Amplification or abbreviation?', *JMLat*, 10, 2000:46–73, concludes from examining works by Henry of Avranches, Alexander of Ashby, and Walter of Wimborne, among others, that source criticism and structural features offer an editor useful tools for determining priority between two versions of a text. G. Dinkova-Bruun, 'Alexander of Ashby: new biographical evidence', *MedS*, 63:305–22, assembles 22 documents relating to Alexander's activities as judge-delegate and charter witness, before she edits an unpublished poetic epitaph for him from Leiden, Universiteitsbibliotheek, Vulc. 94. F. Morenzoni, ' "Sermones breues et leues composui." Les sermons d'Alexandre d'Ashby', *SM*, 42:121–64, provides a repertory of 67 sermons by Ashby, based on the discovery that certain sermons in Cambridge, UL, Ii.i.24, formerly attributed to William de Montibus, contain expressions and ideas found in Ashby's *Libellus meditationum*, a finding that confirms his interest in the practice as well as the theory of preaching. T. Gärtner, 'Zwei Textvorschläge zur metrischen *Eustachiusvita* (BHL 2768)', *AB*, 118, 2000:43–46, emends *patule* to *scapule* (v. 709) and *mortes* to *noctes* (v. 783), and unearths a Juvenalian intertext (v. 823). A. Cizek, 'Die Schulenenzyklopädie "Novus Grecismus" Konrads von Mure. Prolegomena zu einer künftigen Ausgabe des Lehrgedichts', *FmSt*, 34, 2000:236–58, summarizes the contents of a monumental reworking of Eberhard of Béthune's didactic poem, its reception and MS tradition, before he prints the two prose prologues and poetic epilogue.

7. THE FOURTEENTH AND FIFTEENTH CENTURIES

J. Usher, 'Echoes of the *Culex* in Boccaccio's *De casibus*', *GIF*, 53:237–54, argues that the series of geographical references in Boccaccio's description of the shipwreck of the Greek fleet derives from *Culex* 337–57, a copy of which he owned. N. Bisaha, 'Petrarch's vision of the Muslim and Byzantine East', *Speculum*, 76:284–314, reveals how Petrarch constructed an image of cultural decline in the East after the disappearance of Latin learning and discusses his use of examples from ancient history and literature to fashion a new approach to crusade rhetoric. D. Gade, '*Hoch in dem Lufft wirt vns erzogt ir Wunder*. Eine versifizierte "Lucidarius"-Passage in Regenbogens Langem Ton', *BGDSL*, 123:230–52, notes the presence of natural science in four vernacular poems, a tendency already visible in the 12th c. when the scientific contents of William of Conches's *Philosophia mundi* appeared in lyric poetry. M. L. Colker, 'A collection of stories in a codex of Assisi', *JMLat*, 10, 2000:176–238, edits a Franciscan collection of *exempla* preserved in Assisi, Sacro Convento di S.Francesco, MS 442, while V. P. McCarren, 'The Gloucester manuscript of the *Medulla grammatice*: an edition', *ib.*, 338–401, provides a complete list of the exclusively English MSS, before he edits the fragmentary Gloucester MS GDR/ZI/31, which offers Latin and Middle English interpretations of the Latin lemmata. *Rhetorica*, 19, ed. M. Carmargo, examines the causes for the demise of the *ars dictaminis*, and includes: C. Vulliez, '*L'ars dictaminis*, survivances et déclin, dans la moitié nord de l'espace français dans le moyen âge tardif (mil. XIIIe-mil. XVe siècles)' (141–53); G. C. Alessio, '*L'ars dictaminis* nel Quattrocento italiano: eclissi o persistenza?' (155–73); J. O. Ward, 'Rhetorical theory and the rise and decline of *dictamen* in the Middle Ages and early Renaissance' (175–223); M. Richardson, 'The fading influence of the medieval *ars dictaminis* in England after 1400' (225–47); J. R. Henderson, 'Valla's *Elegantiae* and the Humanist attack on the *ars dictaminis*' (249–68). A. Angeleri, 'L'epistola *Excusatio obiectorum* a Marsilio Santasofia di Giovanni Conversini da Ravenna', *Maia*, 53:303–49, edits a letter based on the unique MS, of the Accademia di Zagabria, with notes on the sources of Conversini's Latin. K. A. Bishop, 'The influence of Plautus and Latin elegiac comedy on Chaucer's fabliaux', *ChRev*, 35:294–317, argues that the *Pamphilus* and the *Babio*, among others, formed a bridge between the comedy of antiquity and Chaucer's comic poems. M. Kensak, 'Apollo *exterminans*: the god of poetry in Chaucer's *Manciple's Tale*', *SP*, 98:143–57, suggests that Chaucer draws upon the counter tradition of the inept Apollo invoked by Alain of Lille in the *Anticlaudianus*, and later by Dante. S. Botterill, 'Ideals of the institutional church in Dante and

Bernard of Clairvaux', *Italica*, 78:297–313, finds similarities in the views of the two writers in their discussions of the church as a socio-cultural phenomenon, although he can find no verbal parallels that could establish direct contact between them. P. G. Schmidt, '*Amor transformat amantem in amatum*. Bernhard von Waging an Nicolaus Cusanus über die Vision einer Reformunwilligen Nonne', *Fest. Dronke*, 197–215, presents a first edition of the anonymous *Epistula de quadam visione cuiusdam virginis*, a text permeated with important patristic and medieval authorities on visions. É. Wolff, 'Quelques remarques sur l'*Itinerarium* de Pétrarque', *Latomus*, 60:176–81, describes how an imaginary account of the author's pilgrimage to the Holy Land operates paradoxically as a pretext to evoke pagan antiquity. C. Pignatelli, 'Les glossaires bilingues médiévaux: entre tradition latine et développement du vulgaire', *RLiR*, 257–58:75–111, examines Latin-Italian glossaries attributed to two Tuscan teachers, Goro and Bandini, and observes their debt to Papias's *Elementarium* and Balbi's *Catholicon*, and positions the translations of the Latin lemmata within the history of the Italian language. L. Holford-Strevens, 'Humanism and the language of music treatises', *RenS*, 15:415–49, pays particular attention to the works of Paolo Cortesi and Franchino Gaffori in studying the extent to which musical writers adhered to classical standards of Latinity in style, syntax, and vocabulary. É. Séris, 'Les images de Laurent de Médicis dans la lyrique latine d'Ange Politien: une poétique de la mémoire', *Latomus*, 60:709–25, studies the mnemonic function of the poetic figures that Politian derived from classical oratory to produce the aesthetic effects of vividness, clarity, and *éclat* in depicting Lorenzo. P. Harsting, 'More evidence of Menander Rhetor on the wedding speech: Angelo Poliziano's transcription', *CIMAGL*, 72:11–34, re-edits Politian's copy of a late antique treatise on epideictic rhetoric and discusses his use of this text as a lens to read Statius's *Silvae*. W. Ludwig, 'Der dreiteilige Chor der Lakedämonier bei Plutarch und Petrus Crinitus', *Philologus*, 145:150–57, comments on the style, metre and lexicon of a Latin poem written by Politian's pupil, Pietro del Riccio Baldi. C. Ratkowitsch, 'Bukolik als Ausdruck monastischer Lebensform: Die "Adulescentia" des Baptista Mantuanus', *MJ*, 36:275–93, shows how the formal arrangement of the ten eclogues embodies Baptista's Christian transformation of Boccaccio's idea of the *vita voluptuosa*, *activa*, and *contemplativa* that was linked to the three stages of life. E. G. Whatley, 'John Lydgate's Saint Austin at Compton: the poem and its sources', *Rigg Vol.*, 191–227, relates the ME hagiographic poem to its Latin narrative source, the *Narratio mirabilis*, which he edits here for the first time. M. Martelli, 'Variazioni sul tema', *MR*, 14, 2000:49–83, includes a discussion of the metrical problems in Politian's threnody

Quis dabit capiti meo. C. S. Celenza, 'Lapo da Castiglionchio il giovane, Poggio Bracciolini e la "Vita curialis". Appunti su due testi umanistici', *ib.*, 129–43, reads the *De infelicitate principum* and the *De curiae commodis* for insights into court life and the formation of an intellectual community. S. Fiaschi, 'Prima e dopo la raccolta: diffusione e circolazione delle "Satyrae" di Francesco Filelfo. Spunti dall' epistolario edito ed inedito', *ib.*, 147–65, places the composition of the work between 1428–1450, and reconstructs Filelfo's political and cultural circles by tracking the transmission of individual satires and the collection as a whole. C. Andreasi, 'La biblioteca di frate Giovanni Battista Panetti carmelitano', *ib.*, 183–231, identifies almost 70 MSS and incunabula, which include copies of Juvenal's satires and Petrarch's letters as well as several autographs of Panetti's works as author and translator.

NEO-LATIN

POSTPONED

2

ROMANCE LANGUAGES

I. ROMANCE LINGUISTICS

By JOHN N. GREEN, *University of Bradford*

1. ACTA, FESTSCHRIFTEN

Celebrating the 30th anniversary of the American annual symposia on Romance, nostalgically held in Gainesville (*YWMLS*, 34:23), *LSRL 30* is a tidy volume of 14 papers from main sessions, again mostly monolingual in scope but less commonly embracing some items on second language acquisition, with an overview by J. Camps and C. Wiltshire, 'Romance syntax, semantics and L2 acquisition' (1–8). Papers from a parasession on phonology are to be published separately next year, as are the proceedings of the 29th meeting. Not to be outdone, the European generative Romanists offer the proceedings of their 13th meeting as D'Hulst, *Going Romance 1999*, with 15 often substantial papers, again mostly monolingual, and clustering round the themes of negatives, interrogatives, adverbials, word order, and scrambling. The proceedings of two meetings on historical linguistics make substantial use of Romance data: items from *ICHL 14* and Andersen, *Actualization*, are mentioned in the relevant sections below.

Similar in scope and appearance to an LSRL volume, *Contreras Vol.*, is an obviously affectionate tribute by pupils and colleagues, concentrating on minimalist approaches to Hispanic phonology and syntax but with a leavening of comparative material. An unusual retrospective tribute to the scholar most Romanists will associate with the (re-)discovery of the letters of Claudius Terentianus, *Giovanni Battista Pighi. Centesimo post diem natalem anno (1898–1998)*, ed. Gualtiero Calboli and Giovanni Paolo Marchi, Bologna, Pàtron, xvi + 243 pp., reveals a many-faceted œuvre well reflected in G. Calboli's evaluation 'Giovanni Battista Pighi tra linguistica e filologia' (65–88). *CatR*, 13.1–2, 1999[2001], ed. P. D. Rasico, D. M. Rogers, and C. Wittlin, appears as 'Hommage volume for Professor Joseph Gulsoy', containing a biographic interview and bibliography (11–28), from which G. emerges as a true scholar, modest to the point of self-effacement. *RRL*, 43.3–4, 1988[2001], appears as 'Hommage aux Professeurs Florica Dimitrescu-Niculescu et Alexandru Niculescu', sparse on personal details but with useful bibliographies of their writings

(127–29, 131–33 respectively). Also announced is **Hommage à Jacques Allières*, ed. Michel Aurnague and Michel Roché, Anglet, Atlantica, 660 pp.; sadly, A. did not live to enjoy the dedication, or see the publication of his own work of synthesis, **Manuel de linguistique romane*, Paris, Champion, xxii + 323 pp. (see *RLiR*, 65:313–15 and *La Linguistique*, 37.2:157–58).

2. GENERAL ROMANCE AND LATIN

The last substantive volume of the *Lexikon der Romanistischen Linguistik*, ed. Günter Holtus, Michael Metzeltin, and Christian Schmitt, Tübingen, Niemeyer, is subdivided into *Vol. 1.1. Geschichte des Faches Romanistik. Methodologie (Das Sprachsystem)*, and *Vol. 1.2. Methodologie (Sprache in der Gesellschaft / Sprache und Klassifikation / Datensammlung und -verarbeitung)*, respectively l + 1053 and xlvi + 1194 pp. (see *YWMLS*, 59:26 and Section 3 below). The sections on data analysis, library resources, and bibliography seem to me the most useful and probably the most enduring (bibliographies and journal coverage come courtesy of G. Price, M. Maiden, M. Parry, and W. Schweickard, 1.2, 1159–77, 1178–85 and 1186–94 respectively). Though *LRL* continues to be a mine of reliable information, such exhaustive coverage of 'methodology', with almost 90 contributions, some of which can do no more than illustrate a general approach with a few Romance examples, risks undermining the Romance integrity of the enterprise.

Brigitte Bauer, *Archaic Syntax and Indo-European. The Spread of Transitivity in Latin and French*, Berlin, Mouton de Gruyter, 2000, xviii + 394 pp., concentrating on structures like impersonals, dative possessives, and absolutes that are out of harmony with a nominative language, presents them as archaic residues among which impersonals are perhaps the most persistent. Also concentrating on early attestations, D. G. Miller, 'Gerund and gerundive in Latin', *Diachronica*, 17, 2000:293–349, concludes that the gerundive with concord is the older construction, while the gerund + accusative object emerged by reanalysis when avoidance of gender conflict induced a gerundive to agree (invisibly) with a nearby masculine or neuter NP or determiner. Calboli, *Papers V*, includes: J. Herman, 'Morphologie pronominale et évolution syntaxique' (95–107), on the distinctive dative forms of ILLE; A. Orlandini, 'Les pronoms indéfinis et la négation' (151–78), contrasting the common /n-/ forms with the rarer ones; and H. Rosén, 'On pro-nouns, pro-verbs and pro-sentences in Latin' (179–97). C. Bodelot, 'Grammaire du texte et style', *REL*, 78:26–43, catalogues the surprising range of complement types in Latin which, even after balancing grammatical requirements with discoursal preferences, left ample room for speaker spontaneity.

The reversal of Determinatum and determinans order (as in Fr. *un jus vert* [Dd] > *verjus* [dD]) leads R. de Dardel, 'Précisions sur l'ordre des termes d'origine germanique', *ZRP*, 117:1–22, to the uncharacteristic conclusion of Germanic adstrate influence, since it began in the area he delimits as 'Proto-Romance C' and later spread to much of continental Romance. D. also contributes 'Éléments de rection verbale protoromane', *RLiR*, 65:341–68, avowedly an initial sketch of a vast potential field taking in transitivity, valency, and complementation; in the hybrid object-marking of P-R, [animacy] was the driver of the prepositional accusative, which spread from exclusive reference to people in P-R zone A to animate common nouns in zone B, until its progress was checked by the gradual fixing of word order. Pouring rather old wine into not very new bottles, G. Salvi attributes 'La formazione del sistema V2 delle lingue romanze antiche', *LS*, 35, 2000:665–92, to variation already present in Latin, with optional V-initial structures reinforced by the continuing 'Wackernagel effect' on weakly stressed elements. And an idea first launched by B. Schlieben-Lange but greeted with some scepticism is refloated by S. Goyette, 'From Latin to Early Romance: a case of partial creolization?', McWhorter, *Language Change*, 103–31: there was indeed massive loss of mediopassive inflection and little new grammaticalization, but it also matters whether the forms eliminated were in frequent use and had a range of acceptable substitutes — they weren't, and had!

3. HISTORY OF ROMANCE LINGUISTICS

The first part of *Lexikon der Romanistischen Linguistik*, I,1 (see Section 2 above) boasts 21 main chapters on the history of Romance linguistics, several with subsections. Among them, the major reviews of the earliest periods are particularly valuable: J. Lüdtke, 'Romanische Philologie von Dante bis Raynouard' (1–35), on some key figures like Celso Cittadini, often unjustly overlooked; P. Swiggers, 'Linguistique et grammaticographie romanes' (36–121), pinpointing 19th-c. professionalization and the 'canonization' of the discipline alongside the early emergence of normativity and (pre-)sociolinguistic awareness; and P. Wunderli, 'Die romanische Philologie von Diez bis zu den Junggrammatikern' (121–75), again linking personalities to themes, notably the critical edition of texts and the challenge posed to sound laws by the systematic investigation of dialect . Later sections tend to alternate between careful (but sometimes overlapping) surveys by non-practitioners and short, propagandist accounts by devotees; an honourable exception being M. Herslund's sober assessment of 'Glossématique' (314–21) as more a general semiology than a theory of natural language. Some of the models covered have only tenuous links to Romance data and only one contribution, R. Posner's 'Histoire des grammaires romanes comparées' (532–43), explicitly tackles the comparative dimension. The second volume of another compendious survey, *History of the Language Sciences*, ed. Sylvain Auroux et al. (HSK, 18.2), Berlin, de Gruyter, xxiv + 1095–2005 pp. (see *YWMLS*, 62:18), contains only one Romance item: P. Swiggers, 'Les débuts de la philologie romane au XIXe siècle, surtout en Allemagne' (1272–85), which sees the characteristic techniques as radiating outwards from Germany. It is, however, salutary to note from Giorgio Graffi's *200 Years of Syntax. A Critical Survey* (SHLS, 98), Amsterdam, Benjamins, xiv + 551 pp., how little impact early work on Romance syntax had on the wider development of that field.

Frank-Rutger Hausmann, '*Vom Strudel der Ereignisse verschlungen*'. *Deutsche Romanistik im 'Dritten Reich'* (Analecta Romanica, 61), Frankfurt, Klostermann, 2000, xxiv + 741 pp., inspires awe before this unflinching exercise in *Vergangenheitsbewältigung*; the culmination of years of research, it juxtaposes chronological narrative, personal histories of survivors and victims, and sober assessment of the scarring of German Romanistik during this period. Absorbing but less painful is the second volume of *History of Linguistics in Spain*, ed. E. F. K. Koerner and Hans-Josef Niederehe (SHLS, 100), Amsterdam, Benjamins, xxii + 463 pp., with an introduction by H.-J.N. (ix-xxii), and 21 articles spanning the Renaissance and Golden Age to the present day, including a further sharp reassessment of Menéndez Pidal by J. del Valle: 'La historificación de la lingüística histórica' (367–87). E. Burr, 'Grammatikalisierung und Normierung in frühen Grammatiken des Französischen, Italienischen, Portugiesischen und Spanischen', *ZRP*, 117:189–221, traces early Romance normative rules back to the models of Donatus and Priscian; but soon the process took on a life of its own, with gender concord assuming a high profile, and Nebrija specifying a natural order of expression and categorizing mishaps into *phrasis*, *schema*, and *solecismo* — respectively normal, venial, and unforgivable.

W. Mańczak, 'Badania Romanistyczne w Latach 1945–1998', *KN*, 46, 1999[2000]:23–29, reports more activity in literary studies than linguistics, and more of the latter in synchronic than historical, with French taking the lion's share and M. Gawełko deserving special mention; in some cases, the borderline between Romance and general linguistics is hard to draw. *La Linguistique*, 37.1, ed. Colette Feuillard, is a memorial to Martinet, including F.'s 'Le fonctionnalisme d'André Martinet' (5–20), A. Tabouret-Keller, 'Pour une vision dynamique des situations linguistiques complexes' (21–28), and J. Morais Barbosa, 'Être martinetien' (115–23), endorsing both the continuing validity of M.'s functionalism and Hagège's specific claim that M. — despite differences on diachrony — was nevertheless the most Saussurean of contemporary linguists. Another free spirit is chronicled, with an excellent bibliography, by P. Swiggers, 'Albert Dauzat et la linguistique (romane et générale) de son temps', *RLiR*, 65:33–74; described as 'un flâneur solitaire', D.'s opinions naturally evolved over an extraordinary 60-year career, but he saw himself primarily as a contributor to French linguistics, founding *FM* and pioneering the study of regional varieties.

4. PHONOLOGY

In 'Quantity or stress?', *Journal of Quantitative Linguistics*, 8:81–97, stochastic modelling of a corpus of classical hexameters leads A. Pawłowski and M. Eder to conclude that quantity could not have been the chief determinant of rhythmicity in Latin; rather, basic requirements of memory and recitation favoured a regular pattern of stress in consecutive metrical feet. Examining mismatches of syllable weight and syllable structure, especially in contexts of diphthong-ization, hiatus, and syncope, B. E. Bullock, 'Double prosody and stress shift in Proto-Romance', *Probus*, 13:173–92, claims that quantity was unstable in early Romance, with covert lengthening as well as shortening. Similarly iconoclastic, A. Cser, 'Diphthongs in the syllable structure of Latin', *Glotta*, 75, 1999[2001]:172–93, argues that conservative syllable structure required /aj, oj, aw/ to be analysed as biphonemic V + C sequences; they were not diphthongs at all. In 'Análisis contrastivo de la alternancia monoptongo / diptongo en los verbos del español y del italiano', *RELing*, 30, 2000:383–95, R. A. Martín Vegas shows how minor syllabic differences produce divergent outcomes from very similar phonolo-gical processes; in both languages, morphologization, internal level-ling, and denominal coinings have led to ever greater opacity.

Unconvinced by the current fashionability of prosodic tiers, P. M. Bertinetto, 'Boundary strength and linguistic ecology', *FLin*, 33, 1999[2000]:267–86, uses intervocalic /s/ voicing and other lenition processes to plead for a return to a hierarchy of morpheme boundaries in the explanation of phonological change. In a well illustrated study drawing eclectically on earlier work, E. Casanova rejects 'cultismo' as an explanation for 'La conservació de les vocals posttòniques internes en català, occità i castellà', *CatR*, 13, 1999[2001]:73–106, claiming instead that when there is a weakness in the system, perhaps bolstered by odd consonantism, native words can undergo popular influences favouring the survival of forms that are socially stronger. Taking Romance palatalization as a case study, J. M. Aski, 'Multivariable reanalysis and phonological split', *ICHL 14*, 31–47, shows that neither traditional explanations of internal developments allied to dialect borrowing nor Labov's two-stage model will adequately account for the exceptionally complex criss-crossing patterns in full lexemes and derivational affixes; she believes that an intermediate stage must be postulated.

5. MORPHOLOGY

A. Carstairs-McCarthy, 'Grammatically conditioned allomorphy, paradigmatic structure and the ancestry constraint', *TPS*, 99:223–45, draws on Latin verbal morphology to show that 'ancestry' in structural trees defining cyclic processes might explain why outward sensitivity relates to categories while inward sensitivity relates to individual properties of 'descendants'. Admitting to some remaining mystery, M. Maiden, 'A strange affinity: perfecto y tiempos afines', *BHS(L)*, 78:441–64, makes use of Aronoff's notion of 'morphome' to account for the regularity and persistence of the *tuve, tuviese, tuviera, tuviere* pattern in Ibero-romance. A. Nocentini, 'La genesi del futuro e del condizionale sintetico romanzo', *ZRP*, 117:367–401, recognizing threefold anomalies (synthesis, postposed auxiliary, and arhyzotonic stress), argues that the new paradigms are instances of contingent 'preadaptive change', which involves fairly minor restructuring of old forms to fit new functions, in contrast to the permanent grammaticalization of the new HABĒRE-past forms. Seeking to overthrow Raposo's influential analysis, A. M. Martins, 'On the origin of the Portuguese inflected infinitive', *ICHL 14*, 207–22, finds that the O Ptg. infinitives had nominative case-assigning properties and were more finite-like than their modern equivalents, which would support the rehabilitation of the older hypothesis of development from the imperfect subjunctive. Not what you might suppose, according to D. Bentley, 'On the origin of Sardinian *áere a* plus infinitive', *MedRom*, 23, 1999[2001]:321–58, the prepositional link ousts the bare infinitive from the 13th c. onwards, but is an indigenous development that does not go back to HABĒRE AD. Similarly, D. Bentley and T. Eythórsson argue that 'Alternation according to person in Italo-Romance', *ICHL 14*, 62–74, began as straightforward avoidance of homonymy but has led to reanalysis: auxiliary selection is still driven by the need to mark unaccusativity, normally by HABĒRE, so dialects using ESSE in transitive or unergative verb paradigms have reanalysed the forms as person markers, to avoid the apparent conflict.

Heteronymy rules, it seems. N. La Fauci, 'Quel pasticciaccio brutto della declinazione scomparsa', *VR*, 60:15–24, rejects the traditional categories used to explain the loss of the case system in favour of [± extra-nuclear], [± adnominal], [± adverbal]; the undermining of [adnominal : adverbal] was the first catastrophic change, leading to an uneasy nominative : accusative opposition which was itself quickly undermined by serialization, although the prepositional accusative nearly gave alternative relief. The sheer variety of oddities — from prepositional accusatives, to dative experiencers and 'having' hunger and cold — intrigues M. Haspelmath in 'Non-canonical marking of core arguments in European languages', Aikhenvald, *Marking*, 53–83. Almost sketching a new paradigm of research, M. Saltarelli, 'The realization of number in Italian and Spanish', *Contreras Vol.*, 239–54, harnesses optimality to reconcile grammatico-semantic with articulatory-perceptual axes, postulating right-edge [coronality] as central to the expression of number. But, on a lighter note, M. Fanfani, 'Il plurale dell'*euro*', *LN*, 62 : 101–06, notes that current usage fails to match the confusing EU directive of October 1998, which attempted to distinguish between plural marking on determiners and on the word itself; the injunction to pluralize in French, Spanish, and Portuguese but not in Italian would only be valid if *euro* were still a prefix(oid), which it clearly is not.

6. Syntax

Two items explore constraints on extraction: C. Tellier, 'Definite determiners in French and Spanish', *Contreras Vol.*, 279–92, updates Chomsky's 'specificity effect' to take in Romance demonstratives and possessives, but rather spoils the description by postulating twin, homophonous determiners (one purely expletive!) as the explanation; while M. A. Depiante, 'On null complement anaphora in Spanish and Italian', *Probus*, 13 : 193–221, more plausibly proposes to distin-guish between deep and surface anaphora for VP-ellipses like *Juan las puede ver* **y María las quiere Ø*. J. B. Bernstein, 'Focusing the "right" way in Romance determiner phrases', *ib.*, 1–29, examines right-periphery properties of determiners and possessives, arguing that prenominal position for such elements is neutral, whereas DP-final position (as in *un libro mío*) conveys focus. M.-L. Rivero, 'On impersonal reflexives in Romance and Slavic', *LSRL 30*, 169–95, ascribing both similarities and differences (notably the absence of SE-intransitives in Polish) to parametric semantic variation, treats SE-impersonals as syntactic simplex anaphors with an implicit [human] feature repairing a referential deficiency — not unlike more tradi-tional accounts. In 'What do "prepositional complementizers" do?', *Probus*, 13 : 155–71, R. D. Borsley reviews Kayne's recent proposal that PCs cause other elements to move around them, but shows good reasons to prefer the traditional approach, in which PCs originate in surface position and do not push anyone around.

Andersen, *Actualization*, contains, in addition to H. Andersen's 'Introduction' (1–20), and 'Position paper' (21–57), tying the explanation of grammatical conditioning to a cognitive theory of markedness, applications to Romance data by J. C. Smith, 'Markedness, functionality, and perseveration in the actualization of a morphosyntactic change'(203–23), on the loss of object concord from compound tenseforms; and by L. Schøsler, 'From Latin to Modern French' (169–85), who examines contradictory tendencies in subordinate clauses (conservative in retaining bicasual marking and rejecting V2; innovative in eliminating Pro-drop and accepting stylistic inversion), concluding that Andersen's schema is an imperfect explanation. Careful longitudinal research on the acquisition of object omission by N. Müller and A. Hulk, 'Crosslinguistic influence in bilingual language acquisition', *Bilingualism, Language and Cognition*, 4:1–21, with peer comment (23–48) and response (49–53), leads them to conclude that while the children clearly understand the structure and have no difficulty in keeping Germanic and Romance distinct, there is still some carryover when mapping universal principles on to particular syntactico-pragmatic systems.

Drawing on extensive medieval and modern data, R. Sornicola, 'Stability, variation and change in word order', Sornicola, *Stability*, 101–15, infers from the consistently dominant SVO order of medieval Romance texts that Latin must already have moved away from basic SOV order; more surprisingly, she claims that medieval Spanish and Italian had hardly more freedom than French, with OVS and OSV attested as minor variants, but still far from frequent. Focusing on the categorial shift of weak pronouns as phrases in Latin to heads or affixes in Romance, G. Salvi, 'La nascita dei clitici romanzi', *RF*, 113:285–319, relates the evolution to word order and the loss of the case system, which led to a greatly increased incidence of adverbal weak pronouns in early Romance, in turn undermining their phrasal properties and precipitating reanalysis as adverbal heads. R. Simon and D. Cerbasi, 'Types and diachronic evolution of Romance causative constructions', *ib.*, 441–73, establish that Latin had all the necessary forerunners of the Romance *faire faire / far fare* constructions, but that the strength gradient of the causative lexemes has changed, from IUBĒRE > SUADĒRE > FACĔRE/EFFICĔRE in Latin to *facere* > *laxare* > *ponere* in Romance.

7. DISCOURSE AND PRAGMATICS

Acknowledging the elusiveness of the concept and the need for an onomasiological approach, Baron, *Possession*, includes five Romance items: I. Bartning, 'Towards a typology of French NP *de* NP structures'

(147–67), and H. H. Müller, 'Spanish N *de* N structures from a cognitive perspective' (169–86), both struggling with nexi that resemble but are not prototypical possessives; M. Riegel, 'The grammatical category "possession" and the part-whole relation in French' (187–200), largely on the semantic ambiguity of *posséder*; A.-M. Spanoghe, '(In)alienability and (in)determination in Portuguese' (227–42), on the link between inalienability and subjective extralinguistic experience; and A. M. Bolkestein, 'Possessors and experiencers in Classical Latin' (269–83), stressing the grammatical discrepancies between possessive and 'sympathetic' datives and true possessive genitives. Continuity from Latin is a mirage, claims D. G. Miller, 'Innovation of the indirect reflexive in Old French', *ICHL 14*, 223–39, tracing the emergence and syntactic consequences of the novel *il se lave les mains* construction alongside the long-established *il lui lave les mains* and now increasingly unacceptable *il lave ses mains*. Contrasting Germanic and Romance, B. Lamiroy, 'Grammaticalisation et possession inaliénable', Schøsler, *Valence*, 82–97, believes that dative exponency is the loser in a gradual actantial shift favouring nominative / agentive functions; hence, languages in both families can be situated on a cline, the productivity of the dative possessive in southern Romance signalling a lower degree of grammaticalization than in French. Notwithstanding, E. Lavric, 'Parties du corps actives et passives', *RLiR*, 65:145–68, believes that the full onomasiological schema proposed by B. J. Andrews in 1987 can be simplified, at least for French: parts of the body viewed as active in the event are introduced by a definite article or possessive, whereas those perceived as passive recipients are expressed by the dative + definite construction (*elle lui lave les mains*).

Behind P. Koch's daunting title 'Les métataxes actancielles entre expérient et phénomène', Schøsler, *Valence*, 59–81, lies an interesting comparison of means of expressing 'liking', whether by a transitive verb or some kind of dative periphrasis; diachronic shifts along a continuum are quite possible, but syntactic, propositional, and informational factors all contribute to the mechanism. Frajzyngier, *Reflexives*, includes two Romance items: R. Maldonado, 'Conceptual distance and transitivity increase' (153–85), on Spanish 'optional' reflexives, and R. Waltereit, 'What it means to deceive yourself' (257–78). Comparing clitic clusters in Spanish and Italian, E. C. García, 'The cognitive implications of unlike grammars', *NMi*, 102:389–417, finds ample proof for the 'common sense' view that the more grammaticalized system of Spanish leads to the avoidance of complex combinations while the looser system of Italian — with, crucially, the extra forms *gli* and *ci* — allows speakers to take greater liberties.

Proposing a convincing discoursal account of subjunctive usage, with some similarities to iconicity, J. Quer, 'Interpreting mood', *Probus*, 13:81–111, views mood shifts as signals of a change in the speaker's evaluation of the proposition or property expressed in the embedded clause. T. Móia, 'Temporal location of events and the distribution of the Romance counterparts of *since*-adverbials', *LSRL 30*, 137–52, distinguishes between inclusive and durative reference, claiming that Romance *desde* ∼ *da* ∼ *depuis* constructions, unlike their English equivalents, are not usually compatible with the description of events within an envisaged timeframe. Viewing Romanian as a compromise between the conflicting preference of general Romance for prenominal determiners and the prevalence of postposed in Balkans, M. M. Manoliu, 'The conversational factor in language change', *ICHL 14*, 187–205, proposes a discoursal explanation in which appositive demonstratives were first used as conversation markers and then subject to cyclic bleaching. On a lighter but still informative note, G. Scurtu and A. Rădulescu, 'Énoncés portant sur les échanges de nature rituelle (salutations et souhaits)', *IG*, 91:20–21, compare French and Romanian greetings and politeness expressions, showing that parallel origins do not guarantee suitability in the same range of social contexts.

8. Lexis

In 'Le vocabulaire de la crainte en latin', *REL*, 77, 2000:216–33, J.-F. Thomas studies usage among 1st-c. AD writers, reminding us that METUS is the neutral term, with TIMOR indicating an anticipated danger, FORMIDO an overwhelming dread, PAUOR a fear capable of paralysing the subject, and TERROR acute anxiety before some transforming event; these generalizations, however, are not wholly reliable.

Langages, 143, ed. Xavier Blanco, assembles seven interesting if disparate items on 'Lexicologie contrastive espagnol-français', including B.'s 'Dictionnaires électroniques et traduction automatique' (49–70), on the evident value of searchable databases; A. Desporte and F. Martin-Berthelet, 'Noms d'animaux et expressions en français et en espagnol' (71–90), contrasting directly equivalent similes and set phrases (*être une tortue/vipère* ∼ *ser una tortuga/víbora*) with semantic but not formal matches (impatience or anxiety symbolized by *puces* ∼ *pulgas*) and yet others with no apparent connection (*vachement* ∼ **vaca*); and B. Lamiroy, 'La préposition en français et en espagnol' (91–105), on infinitival connectors, where French has grammaticalized only *de* and *à*, while Spanish retains a wider range only partly bleached. In similar vein, L. Groza, 'Créations phraséologiques parallèles', *RLiR*, 65:223–28, contrasts Fr. *arriver comme mars/marée en carême* with Rom. *ca martie/nunta în post* whose matching form and denotation of inevitability mask the negative connotation of *ca nunta în post* (turning up 'like a bad penny').

Extraordinary in its context, G. Longobardi, 'Formal syntax, diachronic minimalism and etymology', *LI*, 32:275–302, laments the divorce of etymology from theoretical linguistics and uses the history of Fr. *chez*, with its irregular phonetism and change of categorial status, to illustrate his proposed Inertia Theory, a means to connect minimalism with the messy data of historical linguistics. Of which there is no lack; for instance. . . Taking up an idea of Jud's and sifting new data, R. Liver, 'Die Etymologie von fr. *trouver* und die bündner-romanischen Reflexe von TROPUS und TROPARE', *VR*, 60:117–27, reluctantly concludes that nothing new is revealed about the development of French, though the data do prove that reflexes of TROPA/US were quite widespread, with two meaning strands — finding and arranging. Meanwhile, G. Colón Domènech, 'Discordia concors: a reply to J. Gulsoy's articles on Cat. *inxa*, Cast. *hincha*, and Port. *incha*', *CatR*, 13, 1999[2001]:107–15, believes that in this instance the gentlemanly loyalty of the dedicatee towards his irrascible master Coromines was misplaced, for the two groups of meanings simply cannot be reconciled in a single history; 'punch, awl, scion, reed/wind instrument' are compatible with INFLARE and attested in 13th-c. Castilian, but 'hatred, anger' must have a different source, perhaps cognate with Gallo-Romance *enche/anche*. Moreover, H. J. Wolf, 'Die italienische Parallele zu frz. *denrée*. Erbwörter und Erstbelege', *ZRP*, 117:82–98, is unconvinced by the conventional etymology of *DENARIATA < DENARIU even though Romance congeners apparently support the reconstruction, preferring as the model O. Tuscan *dinaiata*, originally 'the amount of land one could buy for one denarius', which uses the more frequent, older suffix but may have been blended later. And finally, E. Grab-Kempf, 'Ein Berberismus im Altspanischen: *aves acedes* (f. pl.) "Zikaden"', *ib.*, 444–48, retracts an earlier etymology relating *acedes* to Gk. ἀχέτα(ς), a good phonetic and semantic match which still leaves the puzzle of *aves*; instead, she proposes a Berber etymon mislearned in popular Arabic as **ab az-zīz* and metanalysed in Romance; grasshoppers ever were flighty and misunderstood.

'What kind of thing is a derivational affix?', *YM*, 1999[2001]:25–52, ponders M. Maiden, answering — with Romanian and Spanish evidence — that it is a classic Saussurean sign, biunique and arbitrary but with a signans that is intramorphological, so differentiating it from 'other' lexical morphemes. J.-C. Anscombre, 'A propos des mécanismes sémantiques de formation de certains noms d'agent en français et en espagnol', *Langages*, 143:28–48, praises the flexibility of Spanish, after examining the constraints on the distribution of *-(d)or/eur* and noting that *-dor* is not compatible with ergatives. Lastly, to bolster Malkiel's purely derivational account of the suffix of misfortune, A. G. Areddu develops ingenious 'Nuove ipotesi su *ASTRUCUS*', *RPh*, 54:325–30 — there could be influence from the name of the prophet of doom Hhabaqqûq, who may survive in thin disguise in Late Latin *bacuceas* and certainly in Italo-Romance *bacucco* 'stupid'.

9. SOCIOLINGUISTICS AND DIALECTOLOGY

Verbum, 22.2, 2000, ed. Fernand Carton, on the theme 'Géolinguistique en Europe', assembles five principal articles on innovations in dialectology — conceptual, investigative, and technical — hoping to persuade the sceptical that an old discipline still has much to offer. At the greatest time-depth, M. Alinei promotes his Continuity Theory as 'An alternative model for the origins of European peoples and languages', *QS*, 21, 2000:21–50, and 'European dialects: a window on the pre-history of Europe', *LS*, 36:219–40, rejecting major Bronze Age invasions as the cause of 'Indo-Europeanization' (*à la* Gimbutas and Renfrew) and arguing instead for continuity back into antiquity on the grounds of massive persistence of Palaeolithic genetic material. Reuniting dialectology and historical phonology, P. Videsott uses 'La palatalizzazione di CA e GA nell'arco alpino orientale', *VR*, 60:25–50, as the criterion to delimit the northern extent of Italo-Romance at the end of the first millennium.

LS, 36.2, 'Eurotaal: le lingue d'Europa', ed. Sergio Scalise, brings together 14 contributions on variety, bilingualism, maintenance, and aspects of language (and dialect) policy, with thoughtful Romance contributions by H. Walter, 'Langue française, langues régionales et francophonie' (267–74), and J. M. Blecua and S. Varela, 'Las lenguas de España' (275–90). Roland Bauer, *Sprachsoziologische Studien zur Mehrsprachigkeit im Aostatal* (*ZRP*, Beiheft 296), Tübingen, Niemeyer, 1999, xviii + 518 pp., combines a useful external history with an exemplary attitudinal survey of current usage and maintenance across 24 census points in bilingual communities. In a neighbouring zone, G. Iannàccaro and V. Dell'Àquila, 'Elementi per lo studio delle frontiere linguistiche in Val di Fassa', *Géolinguistique*, 8, 1999:3–49, find that perceptions of native speakers and 'objective' researchers do not always coincide, with natives acutely aware of the symbolic value of language use and switching. J. L. Hayes, 'The integration of Romance vocabulary in Maltese', *RPh*, 54:393–405, ostensibly a review article of a 1995 PhD by M. Mifsud, is a pretext for a sketch of the cultural and linguistic history of the island, the vigour of its language and the boost given to its Romance content and productivity by alignment with Tuscan; but also some less optimistic inferences from recent attitudinal research appearing to favour English as the language of higher education and social aspiration.

II. FRENCH STUDIES*

LANGUAGE

By GLANVILLE PRICE,
University of Wales Aberystwyth

1. GENERAL AND BIBLIOGRAPHICAL

Wendy Ayres-Bennett and Janice Carruthers with Rosalind Temple, *Problems and Perspectives: Studies in the Modern French Language*, London, Longman, xix + 406 pp., is an excellent and much needed work surveying critically, and on the basis of sound scholarship and an admirable familiarity with previous work in the field, a number of fundamental and, in many cases, controversial topics. Part I, 'Preliminaries' covers, *inter alia*, the definition of French in terms of register, discourse type, geographical variation, and sociolinguistic variables, outlines the bases for a description of the sound system, morphology, syntax, and lexis of the language, and discusses the origins and methodology of a number of theoretical approaches to the analysis of the language. Part II, 'Choice of topics and approaches', which accounts for some 85% of the volume, examines how such varied problems as word-final consonants, nasal vowels, the French schwa, verb morphology, aspect, past tenses, the subjunctive, pronominal verbs, declarative word order, relations between clauses, negation, neologism, and word creation have been tackled by scholars of different theoretical persuasions. Dominique Maingueneau, Jean-Louis Chiss, and Jacques Filliolet, **Introduction à la linguistique française, 2*, Hachette, 160 pp.

Le Français de référence: constructions et appropriations d'un concept, ed. Michel Francard, 2 vols (*CILL*, 26 (2000) and 27), Leuven, Peeters, 409, 240 pp., publishes the *Actes du colloque de Louvain-la-Neuve, 3–5 novembre 1999*; the first four papers itemized below are grouped under the heading 'Constructions d'un concept' while the remainder come under the heading 'Appropriations d'un concept'; vol. 1 includes P. Swiggers, 'Le français de référence: contours méthodologiques et historiques d'un concept' (13–42), D. Blampain, 'Aux origines du français de référence, la traduction' (43–54), J.-P. Saint-Gérand, 'Sentiment national, constructions et représentations linguistiques au XIXe siècle. Les travaux des frères Bescherelle à l'aune du concept de "français de référence"' (55–73), A. Goosse, 'Le bon usage comme référence' (75–85); (under the subheading 'Dans le domaine

* The place of publication of books is Paris unless otherwise stated.

phonétique') Y. C. Morin, 'Le français de référence et les normes de prononciation' (91–135); (under 'Dans le domaine lexical') C. Poirier, 'Le français de référence et la lexicographie différentielle au Québec' (139–55), P. Rézeau, 'Le français de référence et la lexicologie/lexicographie différentielle en Europe' (157–85), A. Paquot, 'Architecture du français, français de référence et lexicographie périphérique' (187–95), C. Frey, 'Français de référence et français en Afrique et à Madagascar. Théories, idéologies et pratiques' (197–211), K. Boucher, 'Français de référence et inventaire lexical: l'exemple du Gabon' (213–24), D. Latin, 'Dictionnaire "francophone" et français de référence. Quelques inférences de la variation géolinguistique sur la métalangue du dictionnaire de la langue française' (225–42), F. Berdal-Masuy, 'Le français de référence dans les langues de spécialité: mythe ou réalité?' (243–61); and (under 'Dans le domaine syntaxique') F. Gadet, 'Français de référence et syntaxe' (265–83), M. Bilger, 'Autour du projet "Corpus de référence du français parlé"' (285–96), G. Ledegen and V. Quillard, 'Quelle référence pour l'interrogation totale? Réponses syntaxiques et pragmatiques' (297–312), D. Van Raemdonck, 'La description fonctionnelle du français de référence. De la révérence orthographique à la préférence systématique' (313–24), L. Rosier, 'Les "bâtards" du discours. De la nomenclature, des discours grammaticaux et des pratiques de référence en matière de discours rapporté en français' (325–43), and A. C. Simon, 'Français de référence et segmentation du discours oral. L'exemple de la phrase' (345–58); vol. 2 has (under 'En sociolinguistique') N. Gueunier, 'Le français de "référence": approche sociolinguistique' (9–33), T. Bulot, 'La construction de la coherence communautaire. Le français de référence au centre-ville' (35–42), J. Hatungimana, 'Français d'Afrique: de la norme pédagogique à la norme francophone' (43–55), C. Noyau, 'Le français de référence dans l'enseignement du français et en français au Togo' (57–73), F. Benzakour, 'Français de référence et la diffusion du français en usage au Maroc' (75–87), A. Valdman, 'Le français de référence et la diffusion du français en Amérique du Nord et aux Antilles françaises' (89–110), A. Boudreau, 'Le français de référence entre le même et l'autre. L'exemple des petites communautés' (111–22), P. Martel, 'Le français de référence et l'aménagement linguistique' (123–39), B. Pöll, 'Français de référence et pluralité identitaire: un antagonisme inconciliable?' (141–51); and (under 'En didactique') É. Charmeux, 'Le français de référence et la didactique du français langue maternelle' (155–66), J.-P. Simon, 'Essai de définition de la notion de "français de référence" dans le cadre d'une socio-didactique du français' (167–78), O. Dezutter and F. Thyrion, 'Quel(s) français de référence pour les étudiants qui entament des études universitaires?' (179–92), M. Delforge, ' "Fais gaffe, le prof t'écoute." Le contexte scolaire en tant que situation formelle pour approcher le français de référence' (193–206), and C. Ronveaux, 'Que dire pour apprendre à parler? Le français de référence à travers les programmes belges de français' (207–20), with a closing summing-up by M. Francard, 'Le français de référence: formes, normes et identités' (223–40). Pascale Certa, *Le français d'aujourd'hui*, Balland, 128 pp. Daniel Péchoin and Bernard Dauphin, *Dictionnaire des difficultés du français d'aujourd'hui*, Larousse, 688 pp.

L'Expansion du français dans les Suds (XVe–XXe siècles), ed. Colette Dubois et al., Univ. de Provence, 2000, 348 pp., publishes papers given at a conference in 1998.

Haut Conseil de la Francophonie, *État de la francophonie dans le monde: données 1999–2000 et 6 études inédites*, Documentation française, 639 pp. Délégation générale à la langue française, *Langue française et francophonie: répertoire des organismes et associations œuvrant pour la promotion de la langue française*, 5th edn, Documentation française, 184 pp. Xavier Deniau, *La Francophonie* ('Que sais-je?', 2111), PUF, 128 pp. Bernhard Pöll, *Francophonies périphériques: histoire, statut et profil des principales variétés du français hors de France*, L'Harmattan, 231 pp. *Francophonie et polynomie*, ed. Claudine Bavoux and François Gaudin, Mont-Saint-Aignan, Rouen U.P., 194 pp. Pierre Dumont, *L'Interculturel dans l'espace francophone*, L'Harmattan, 224 pp. *Variations et dynamisme du français: une approche polynomique de l'espace francophone*, ed. Foued Laroussi and Sophie Babault, L'Harmattan, 209 pp. Stélio Farandjis, *Philosophie de la francophonie*, L'Harmattan, 1999, 216 pp. *Recherches africaines. La francophonie: l'indispensable mutation du paternalisme vers un multilatéralisme équilibré*, L'Harmattan, 133 pp. *Arabofrancophonie*, ed. Monique Pontault, L'Harmattan, 319 pp.

L. Schena, 'Études de linguistique française en Italie. Guide bibliographique, 1960–1997. Grammatologie', *LInv*, 23, 2000:77–114, is a critical review article.

Though dealing specifically only with two French problems (infinitives introduced or not by a preposition; the expression of inalienable possession), L. Schøsler, 'La valence verbale dans une perspective diachronique: quelques problèmes méthodologiques', Schøsler, *Valence*, 98–112, is also of general methodological interest (the need for a big enough corpus, the need to ensure one is comparing like with like).

2. History of Grammar and of Linguistic Theory

Colette Demaizière's critical edition of Pierre de la Ramée, *Grammaire (1572)*, Champion, 167 pp., reproduces the text letter by letter, as closely as is possible in modern typography; the editor's contribution consists principally of an introduction and some hundreds of footnotes elucidating references in the text and, in particular, points of linguistic interest. She also edits Antoine Cauchie (Caucius), *Grammaire française (1586)*, Champion, 544 pp., which includes the original Latin text of the last edition of the *Grammatica gallica* published in the author's lifetime (the first edition dates from 1570) together with an annotated French translation and indexes of place names and of nouns, verbs, and adjectives quoted by Cauchie in his examples. M. Glatigny, 'Les jugements d'acceptabilité dans *Le Courrier de Vaugelas* (1868–1881)', *FM*, 69 : 129–60, deals with a periodical of apparently little significance edited by E. Martin. Anja Klein-Zirbes, **Die 'Défense de la langue française' als Zeugnis des französischen Sprachpurismus: linguistische Untersuchung einer sprachnormativen Zeitschrift im Publikationszeitraum von 1962 bis 2000*, Berne, Lang, 238 pp.

3.   HISTORY OF THE LANGUAGE

W. Ayres-Bennett, 'Socio-historical linguistics and the history of French', *JFLS*, 11 : 159–77, offers a critical and informative, if inevitably brief, survey of work in the field, draws attention to the problems involved in collecting and interpreting the data, and stresses 'the value of looking at variation in the past'.

Sylvie Bazin-Tacchela, **Initiation à l'ancien français*, Hachette, 160 pp.

IG, 90, a commemorative tribute to Guy Serbat (1918–2001) under the title 'La langue française du XIXe siècle et son histoire', includes: J.-P. Saint-Gérand, 'L'histoire de la langue française au XIXe siècle. Ambitions, contradictions et réalisations' (5–18); M. Glatigny, 'L'éternel retour de la norme au XIXe siècle' (19–23); Y. Portebois and M. Fournier, ' "La langue est au peuple et la grammaire chez les écrivains." La revue critique des livres nouveaux, ou *Trente années de comptes rendus linguistiques (1833–1863)*' (24–31); É. Bordas, 'Un stylème dix-neuviémiste. Le déterminant discontinu *un de ces . . . qui . . .*' (32–43); F. Martin-Berthet, 'L'histoire des composés. *Grand magasin, tranche de vie*' (44–49); I. Turcan, 'Mémoire de préverbes passés. Usages linguistiques et littéraires, et témoignage de quelques dictionnaires de langue française jusqu'au XIXe siècle' (50–61); P. Blumenthal, 'Le *Dictionnaire des synonymes* de Pierre-Benjamin Lafaye' (62–67); D. A. Kibbee, 'Le patois dans l'histoire de la langue française selon le dictionnaire de Littré' (68–72); and G. Wolf, 'Gaston Paris, Michel Bréal, et les études linguistiques' (73–79).

4. TEXTS

In two articles on Robert de Boron's *Merlin*, J.-C. Herbin, *IG*, 88:33–39, discusses regional graphies in BNF MS fr. 747, and E. Oppermann, *ib.*, 40–43, considers a use of the so-called 'présent de narration'. F. Duval, 'Les *melliflux termes nouveaux* du *Séjour d'Honneur*', *RLiR*, 65:397–448, is on a late 15th-c. text by Octovien de Saint-Gelais.

5. PHONETICS AND PHONOLOGY

Aidan Coveney, *The Sounds of Contemporary French: Articulation and Diversity*, Exeter, Elm Bank, x + 214 pp., provides a detailed analysis of all the phonemes of French, with the help of numerous diagrams based on tracings from films taken from A. Bothorel et al., *Cinéradiographie des voyelles et consonnes du français*, 1986 (see *YWMLS*, 49:29); a substantial chapter is devoted to 'Intersegmental coordination' (covering a wide range of types of coarticulation, allophonic variation, and assimilation), and due attention is paid throughout to regional European French and Canadian pronunciations; comparisons and contrasts are helpfully drawn with English (including regional varieties of English) and, occasionally, other languages. J.-P. Chevrot, L. Beaud, and R. Varga, 'Developmental data on a French sociolinguistic variable: post-consonantal word-final /R/', *LVC*, 12:295–319, is based on the language of children aged 6–12. A. B. Hansen, 'Les changements actuels des voyelles nasales du français parisien: confusions ou changement en chaîne?', *Linguistique*, 37.2:33–47, concludes that the system is undergoing an as yet unfinished 'processus de réaménagement'. R. Sampson, 'Liaison, nasal vowels and productivity', *JFLS*, 11:241–58, demonstrates that, beside the types *bon ami* and *mon ami*, one must take account of the possibility of ' "ZERO-liaison" ' or the non-use of a distinct liaison alternant' in such contexts as *fin observateur, mignon objet d'art*.

Corine Astésand, *Rythme et accentuation en français: invariance et variabilité stylistique*, L'Harmattan, 336 pp. F. Poiré discusses 'L'accent focal et l'accent d'emphase dans la description de l'intonation en français', *CanJL*, 45, 2000:275–302.

6. ORTHOGRAPHY AND PUNCTUATION

Nina Catach, *Histoire de l'orthographe française*, Champion, 425 pp., has chapters on Old French (from the Strasbourg Oaths onwards) and Middle French, followed by others on each later century. The doctrines and practice of a number of 16th-c. and 17th-c. grammarians and lexicographers are analysed, after which attention is focused mainly on successive editions of the Academy's dictionary and reactions thereto, with a 'Postface' by Renée Honvault on the ninth edition (1986–) and the proposed *Rectifications* of 1990. We are fortunate that Honvault, in collaboration with Irène Rosier-Catach, was able so skilfully to select and assemble the more or less finished or, in some cases, unfinished drafts of the different chapters left by the author at her death and make available to us in coherent form this important work. Many of the contributions to *Variations sur l'orthographe et les systèmes d'écriture: mélanges en hommage à Nina Catach*, ed. Claude Gruaz and Renée Honvault, Champion, 401 pp., could equally figure in other sections of this survey (grammar, lexicography, lexicology, or dialects); they include (in addition to four not relating specifically to French): V. Gak, 'A propos du système graphique français: quelques problèmes à discuter' (23–34); C. Gruaz, 'Du plurisystème à la grammaire homologique' (35–42); R. Honvault, 'Une histoire d'*e*' (43–59); J.-P. Jaffré, 'Écritures et acquisition: retour sur la mixité graphique' (61–72); V. Lucci, 'Orthographe française, mixité, fixité et "pureté"' (73–81); L. Catach, 'L'informatique comme miroir de la recherche' (85–99); M. Tournier, '"Madame la marquise"' (101–18), on the feminization of titles, etc.; J.-C. Rebejkow, 'La réforme de l'orthographe et le problème des pluriels réguliers dans les dictionnaires' (119–27); M. Matthey, 'Variation orthographique, enseignement et changement' (129–37); M. Lenoble-Pinson, 'Noms en asyndète. Comment s'écrivent-ils? Précédés ou non d'un trait d'union? Sous quelle forme au pluriel?' (139–46); J. Picoche, 'Quelques nouveautés dictionnairiques' (147–56); G. Ouy, 'A propos des orthographes du moyen français' (195–206); R. Martin, 'Quelles graphies en nomenclature dans un dictionnaire de moyen français?' (207–15); N. Andrieux, 'En termes d'archigraphème: la lettre *O* dans le français écrit au moyen âge' (217–28); S. Baddeley, 'La "parolle tresnée" au XVIe siècle: témoignages sur la perception de la longueur vocalique' (229–39); J.-C. Pellat, 'Repères pour l'histoire de l'orthographe française: le XVIIe siècle' (241–56); R. Wooldridge, 'Les consonnes aspirées dans la première édition du *Dictionnaire de l'Académie françoise* (1694)' (257–73); L. Pasques, 'Vers une théorie de la prosodie du français (du XIIIe au XVIIIe siècle)' (275–94); J. Chaurand, 'Les étymologies de Gilliéron' (311–28); J.-M. Eloy, 'Génétique textuelle en picard: orthographe populaire et travail de langues' (329–45); M.-R. Simon, 'Patois et morale. Les enjeux d'une écriture' (347–56); F. Jejcic, 'Du manuscrit au livre: les états d'un texte écrit en sarthois (1993)' (357–73); and a classified 'Bibliographie générale de Nina Catach' by J.-P. Jaffré (387–98).

Bernard Traimond, *Une cause nationale: l'orthographe française?*, PUF, 287 pp. *Orthographe*, ed. Alain Bentolila, Nathan, 320 pp. Maxime de Cadigan, *La Ponctuation française*, L'Isle-Adam, Saint-Mont, 39 pp.

7. GRAMMAR

OLD AND MIDDLE FRENCH

P. Blumenthal, 'Valence ontologique en diachronie', Schøsler, *Valence*, 13–33, covers the whole period of the language from the 12th to the 20th cs, dealing in particular with the verbs *connaître,savoir, voir, sentir, constater, réaliser* and *se rendre compte.* M. Herslund, 'L'actant fondamental et les verbes symétriques et réfléchis de l'ancien français', *ib.*, 34–42, looks *inter alia* at verbs such as *(s')aprochier, (se) monter, (se) taisir.* M. Goyens, 'L'origine des verbes français à construction dative', *ib.*, 43–58, traces from Latin to Modern French the evolution in the syntax of verbs like *obéir* and *ressembler.* A. Valli, 'Étude des constructions à verbe support en moyen français: contribution au débat sur la notion de locution verbale', *ib.*, 113–31, looking in particular though not exclusively at locutions based on *faire, avoir,* or *donner,* is a follow-up to the work of M. Wilmet and others.

Sophie Prévost, *La Postposition du sujet en français aux XVe et XVIe siècles: analyse sémantico-pragmatique*, CNRS, 325 pp. Luigi Catalani, *Die Negation im Mittelfranzösischen*, Berne, Lang, 537 pp. E. Torterat reflects on '*Et* en emploi "syndético-hypotactique"': hypothèses sur une *jonction implicite* en ancien et en moyen français', *BSLP*, 95, 2000: 183–202.

MODERN FRENCH

Sophie Aslanides, *Grammaire du français: du mot au texte*, Champion, 243 pp., is a reference grammar that, within its limited compass, covers an impressive amount of ground with commendable clarity; in addition to discussing in a more or less conventional manner the form and function of the parts of speech and basic syntactical constructions, and although addressed specifically at native-speakers and teachers of French, it addresses informatively a number of topics that are particularly puzzling for foreign learners, even advanced learners (e.g. *mon père est oenologue* or *un oenologue?*, *une foule envahit* or *envahissent la place?*); a useful chapter on 'La grammaire du texte' goes beyond what many other grammars offer. Henri Bonnard, *Les Trois Logiques de la grammaire française* (Champs linguistiques), Brussels, Duculot, 251 pp., is a further addition to this important series; 'Logique référentielle' deals broadly speaking with parts of speech; 'Logique propositionnelle' analyses the ways in which these are linked 'selon quelques schèmes reçus', thereby covering principally complements (of verbs, nouns, pronouns, adjectives, and adverbs), voice, and subordinate clauses; 'Logique phrastique' examines how the resulting 'chains' are adapted to new needs, thereby covering *inter alia* theme and rheme, negation, 'la phrase sans la proposition' (interjections, constructions such as *Ne pas fumer, Où me cacher?, Doucement!*, etc.), 'la phrase propositionnelle' (declarative clauses, the passive, impersonal constructions, interrogative, exclamatory and imperative clauses, parataxis, direct and indirect speech, detachment, etc.); those who may perhaps recoil in alarm at seeing a few formulae and diagrams *à la* Gustave Guillaume on first opening this book may take heart — there are not too many of them. *Grammaire alphabétique*, ed. Alain Bentolila, Nathan, 384 pp. F. Marty, 'Les signaux morphologiques du français parlé', *FM*, 69:211–40, has little that is new to say. M. Plénat reviews 'Quelques thèmes de recherche actuels en morphophonologie française', *CLe*, 77, 2000:27–62.

M. Nielsen, 'Les groupes nominaux $N^1 + Prép. + N^2$ et $N^1 + Prép. + N^2$ *déf.* et la notion de *synapsie*', *RevR*, 36:20–40, distinguishes between such types as (to take the simplest kinds of examples) *coup de fil* and *grève de la faim*.

E. Lavric, 'Parties du corps actives et passives', *RLiR*, 65:145–68, studies the use of the possessive and of the definite article (with or without a dative pronoun) with reference to parts of the body. M. Salles, 'Lorsqu'un SN indéfini n'introduit pas un référent nouveau', *IG*, 91:9–12, on the type 'Tu as trompé *Marie*, tu as déçu *une femme* qui t'adorait', asks 'Pourquoi présenter comme nouveau quelque chose qui ne l'est pas?' — the reason is to be found in 'une modification du point de vue'. A. Carlier, 'Les articles *du* et *des* en synchronie et en diachronie', *RevR*, 35, 2000:177–206, offers 'une analyse de leur résistance à l'interprétation générique'. M.-N. Gary-Prieur, 'GN démonstratifs à référence générique: une généralité discursive', *JFLS*, 11:221–39, disputes the widespread assumption that the demonstratives are incompatible with a generic interpretation.

A. Rabatel discusses 'La valeur de *on* pronom indéfini / pronom personnel dans les perceptions représentées', *IG*, 88: 16–22.

M. Salles, 'Hypothèse d'un continuum entre les adjectifs "modaux" et les adjectifs qualificatifs', *IG*, 88:23–27, deals with adjectives whose meaning, either generally or in combination with certain nouns (e.g. *un gros fumeur, un fumeur gros*), differs according to whether they precede or follow the noun. C. Molinier, 'Les adjectifs de couleur en français. Éléments pour une classification', *RevR*, 36:193–206, distinguishes between 'adjectifs de couleur catégorisateurs' and 'adjectifs de caractérisation générale des couleurs'. S. Roggenbuck, 'Zur Stellung des Adjektivs im modernen Französisch', *ZRP*, 117:430–43, argues that the position of the adjective is a multifactorial problem — whatever criterion one may decide to adopt, doubts remain. C. Schnedecker, '*Premier, second* et *dernier*: des ordinaux peu ordinaires', *FM*, 69:21–38, concludes (unsurprisingly) that the class of so-called 'ordinal adjectives' 'n'a ni le comportement syntaxique ni le rôle sémantique des adjectifs qualificatifs' and, more interestingly, that the ordinals do not constitute a homogeneous group; she again assures us (cf. *YWMLS*, 62:39) that she has not yet said her last word on the subject of ordinals.

Le Présent en français, ed. Pierre Le Goffic, Amsterdam, Rodopi, vi + 116 pp., includes the following: J.-M. Fournier, 'L'analyse du présent dans les grammaires de l'âge classique' (1–26), which devotes particular attention to Nicolas Beauzée's *Grammaire générale* (1767) and to J. Harris's *Hermes* (1751); S. Mellet, 'Valeur aspectuelle du présent: un problème de frontière' (27–39); H. Chuquet, 'Présent, discours rapporté et repérage composite dans les textes de presse' (41–60), contrasting passages from *Le Monde diplomatique* with the English translations thereof; A. Jaubert, 'Entre convention et effet de présence, l'image induite de l'actualité' (61–75); P. Le Goffic and F. Lab, 'Le présent "pro futuro"' (77–98), identifying eight different types of example; and O. Soutet, 'De la double représentation du subjonctif présent en psychomécanique' (99–116). P. Dendale, 'Le futur conjectural *versus devoir* épistémique: différences de valeur et de restrictions d'emploi', *FM*, 69:1–20, has interesting insights but lacks the space here to develop them adequately. D. M. Engel, 'Absolutely perfect? What is the status of the "futur antérieur"?', *JFLS*, 11:201–20, concludes that it is 'a tense-aspect with additional modal functions'.

Les Verbes modaux, ed. Patrick Dendale and Johan van der Auwera (Cahiers Chronos, 8), Amsterdam, Rodopi, iv + 173 pp., includes (in addition to one item on Latin and two on English): A. Ouattara, 'Modalités et verbes modaux dans les écrits de Bernard Pottier' (1–16); N. Le Querler, 'La place du verbe modal *pouvoir* dans une typologie des modalités' (17–32); B. Defrancq, 'Que peuvent bien *pouvoir* et *bien*?' (33–46); H. Kronning, 'Pour une tripartition des emplois du modal *devoir*' (67–84); C. Marque-Pucheu, 'Valeurs de *devoir* dans les énoncés comportant *selon N*' (85–101); J.-P. Desclés and Z. Guentchéva, 'La notion d'abduction et le verbe *devoir* "épistémique"' (103–22); and A. Schrott, 'Le futur périphrastique et l'allure extraordinaire' (159–70) (on the type *aller faire*). P. Skårup, 'Les valeurs temporelles des verbaux du français moderne et ancien', *RevR*, 36:207–34, takes account of four 'points', viz. 'le point narratif, le point perspectif, le point visé et le point narré'.

Olivier Soutet, *Le Subjonctif en français*, Gap, Ophrys, 161 pp.

K. Hölker, 'Lexikalische Variation der Zeitschemata bei einwertigen Verben im Französischen', *ZRP*, 117:50–81, covers the expression of 'activities', 'accomplishments', 'achievements', and 'states' (the English terms are the author's own) and modifications to the pattern brought about by metaphor, metonymy, and synecdoche.

R. Veland, 'Deux siècles d'évolution d'un microsystème grammatical en français: la concessive d'indétermination à structure *Pro être Adj*', *ZRP*, 117:255–64, discusses the types *tout boiteux qu'il est, si bonne soit-elle*, and variants thereon in the 19th and 20th cs. C. Schapira, 'La phrase tautologique', *LInv*, 23:269–86, is exclusively on French.

M. Siri-Sami, 'Distribution et valeurs des infinitifs prépositionnels', *IG*, 88:3–9, concludes that *à* and *de* before infinitives are not empty prepositions but 'des marqueurs d'opérations énonciatives'.

J. Bacha, 'Le déterminant *pas mal de*', *IG*, 88:16–22, seeks to 'définir son identité sémantique, en l'opposant systématiquement aux autres quantificatifs indéfinis'. L. Pop, *IG*, 91:13–19, discusses a category of adverbs that she terms 'adverbes de texte'. E. Moline, '*Elle ne fait rien comme tout le monde*: les modifieurs adverbiaux de manière en *comme*', *RevR*, 36:171–92, argues that the constructions in question should be considered as adverbial modifiers rather than as comparatives.

Pierre Larrivée, *L'Interprétation des séquences négatives: portée et foyer des négations en français* (Champs linguistiques), Brussels, Duculot, 216 pp., presents a closely argued and by no means easily accessible thesis, in which however each step is backed up by examples (drawn from texts or constructed) and the reader is not left floundering in a morass of obfuscatory jargon; two chapters dealing in general terms with 'la notion de portée, sa description intuitive, les marques morphosyntaxiques auxquelles elle s'associe et ses rapports avec les négations' are followed by four on focalization, with particular reference to the ways in which it functions in relation to negation and complements and quantifiers in negative constructions. W. J. Ashby, 'Un nouveau regard sur la chute de *ne* en français parlé tourangeau: s'agit-il d'un changement en cours?', *JFLS*, 11:1–22, finds that, in Tours at least, *ne* was dropped more frequently in 1995 than in 1976 and that his question is probably to be answered in the affirmative.

Adeline Nazarfenko, *La Cause et son expression en français*, Gap, Ophrys, 169 pp. M. Piot, 'Les conjonctions doubles — coordination-subordination', *LInv*, 23, 2000:45–76, is specifically on French. M. Olsen, '*Puisque*: syllogisme caché', *RevR*, 36:41–58, argues that *puisque* 'évolue dans un domaine logique plutôt que causal'.

TrL, 42–43, ed. Lucien Kupferman, Eva Katz, and Maria Asnès, publishes, under the title 'La préposition française dans tous ses états', the proceedings of a colloquium held at Tel Aviv in September, 2000; the contents are grouped under two headings: 'Syntaxe du groupe prépositionnel' includes: L. Melis, 'La préposition est-elle toujours la tête d'un groupe prépositionnel?' (11–22); D. Gaatone, 'Les prépositions: une classe aux contours flous' (23–31) (an abridged version of a forthcoming article); L. Kupferman, 'Les déplacements des syntagmes en *de*: un regard du troisième type' (33–41); V. Lagae, 'Le pronom *en*: des compléments adnominaux aux syntagmes quantificateurs' (43–57); D. Van Raemdonck, 'Adverbe et préposition: cousin, cousine?' (59–70); M. Piot, 'Relations entre prépositions et conjonctions? L'apport de la comparaison en langues romanes' (71–81) (mainly on French, despite the title); C. Blanche-Benveniste, 'Préposition à éclipses' (83–95); B. Kampers-Manhe, 'Le statut de la préposition dans les mots composés' (97–109); A. Dugas, 'Une analyse des constructions transitives indirectes en français' (111–20); and C. Cortier, 'Les syntagmes prépositionnels prédicatifs dans les grammaires universitaires: un observatoire de la place accordée aux prépositions' (121–40); 'Formes et sens des prépositions' includes: A. Borillo, 'Il y a prépositions et prépositions' (141–55); S. Adler, 'Les locutions prépositives: questions de méthodologie et de définition' (157–70); S. Porhiel, '*Au sujet de* et *à propos de* — une analyse lexicographique, discursive et linguistique' (171–81); J.-C. Anscombre, 'L'analyse de la construction *en tout N* par D. Leeman: quelques remarques' (183–97); F. Lefeuvre, '*Pour quoi*' (199–210); F. Martin and M. Dominicy, '*À travers, au travers (de)* et le point de vue' (211–27); P. Dendale, 'L'emploi spatial de *contre*: propositions pour un traitement unifié' (229–39); and D. Leeman, '*Tout contre* vs *très contre*' (241–52). L. Iordanskaja and N. Arbatchewsky-Jumarie, 'Quatre prépositions causales du français: leur sémantisme et cooccurrence', *LInv*, 23, 2000:115–53, discuss *à cause de, sous l'effet de, de*, and *par*. G. Longobardi considers 'Formal syntax, diachronic minimalism, and etymology: the history of French *chez*', *LI*, 32:275–302.

F. Drijkoningen and B. Kampers-Manhe, 'On the interpretation of postverbal subject positions', *RLFRU*, 20:29–42, seek to present a brief overview of 'facts of French pertaining to issues with respect to (in)definiteness effects and semantic and pragmatic differences in postverbal positions'. S. Cummins considers 'The unaccusative hypothesis and the impersonal construction in French', *CanJL*, 45, 2000:225–51, while S. Katz looks at 'Categories of *C'est*-cleft construction', *ib.*, 253–73.

CPr, 34, includes six articles on 'L'interjection en français'.

Isabel Gonzales Rey, **La Phraséologie du français*, Toulouse, Univ. de Mirail-Toulouse, 224 pp.

8. LEXICOGRAPHY

The *FEW*, vol. 25 ('refonte du tome 1er'), has reached fasc. 158 (2000), covering AUSCULTARE — AUTÓS; fasc. 159 completes vol.22, part 2, 'Matériaux d'origine inconnue ou incertaine', which began appearing in 1973, while fasc. 160, 36 pp., consists of a 'Table des matières et index des concepts' of volumes 21 to 23. Kurt Baldinger's *Dictionnaire étymologique de l'ancien français* (now published 'sous la direction philologique de Frankwalt Möhren'),Tübingen, Niemeyer — Quebec, Laval U.P., has reached fasc. I 1, 188 columns, covering I — INCREPATION.

CD-ROM versions of **Dictionnaires des XVIe et XVIIe siècles* (ten dictionaries from Robert Estienne to Thomas Corneille) and of **Les Dictionnaires de l'Académie française 1687–1798 (toutes les éditions des XVIIe et XVIIIe siècles)* have been issued by Champion Électronique. **Pour informatiser le 'Dictionnaire universel' de Basnage (1702) et de Trévoux (1704): approche théorique et pratique*, ed. Chantal Wionet and Agnès Tutin, Champion, 128 pp. **Le Grand Robert de la langue française*, new edn, Le Robert, 6 vols.

The contributions to *Les Dictionnaires de langue française*, ed. Jean Pruvost, Champion, 331 pp., are grouped under three headings: under 'Les dictionnaires d'apprentissage' are P. Corbin, 'Des imagiers aux dictionnaires: cadrage d'un champ de recherche' (15–66), J. Pruvost, 'Les dictionnaires d'apprentissage monolingues de la langue française (1856–1991): problèmes et méthodes' (67–95); J. Rey-Debove, 'De quelques utopies lexicographiques concernant l'apprentissage des langues' (97–103), J. Picoche, J.-C. Rolland, and M.-L. Honeste, 'Un dictionnaire d'apprentissage du français' (105–13), R. Galisson, 'Une dictionnairique à géométrie variable au service de la lexiculture' (115–38), M. Cormier, C. Ouimet, and J.-C. Boulanger, 'A propos de la néobienséance dans les dictionnaires scolaires: les prénoms dans les exemples' (139–68), R. Jacquenod, 'Une approche du dictionnaire étymologique du collégien à l'adulte' (169–72); under 'Les dictionnaires spécialisés de la langue' are M. Arrivé, 'Une grammaire en forme de dictionnaire?' (175–83), L. Biedermann-Pasques, 'Un dictionnaire spécialisé d'histoire de l'orthographe française, le *DHOF*' (185–96) (on the *DHOF*, see *YWMLS*, 56:40), C. Gruaz, 'Nouveaux aspects théoriques du dictionnaire synchronique de familles de mots français' (197–214), D. Delas, 'Pour un dictionnaire analogique moderne' (215–22);

under 'Les dictionnaires de spécialité' are L. Depecker, 'Les vocabulaires spécialisés: nouvelles perspectives d'aménagement' (225–29); A. Clas, 'Les dictionnaires bilingues de spécialité' (231–45); J.-C. Boulanger, 'L'aménagement des marques d'usage technolectales dans les dictionnaires généraux bilingues' (247–71); M. Tournier, 'Un dictionnaire de fréquences syndicales' (273–90).

Nina Catach, *VARLEX: variation lexicale et évolution graphique du français actuel: dictionnaires récents, 1989–1997*, CILF, 237 pp. *Dictionnaire des homonymes*, ed. Christine Ouvrard, Larousse, 304 pp.

Catherine Zavatta, *Les Mots du cirque*, Belin, 350 pp., is the latest addition to the series 'Le Français retrouvé' to which we have often drawn attention (most recently, *YWMLS*, 60 : 39); the 800 or so entries (many of them a page and more in length) in this encyclopedic dictionary cover not only lexical items (some of them familiar enough, such as *échasses, éléphant, propriété artistique*, and others much more specialized, including *bouteillophone, diaboliste* and *rola-rola*) but also personalities and places associated in one way or another with the circus (*la Goulue, Grock, Cirque Médrano, Musée des arts forains, Saintes-Maries-de-la-Mer*, etc.); a book to be consulted with profit and pleasure.

The third edition, ed. Jean-Benoit Ormal-Grenon and Natalie Pomier, of *The Oxford-Hachette French Dictionary*, ed. Marie-Hélène Corréard and Valerie Grundy, OUP, xxxviii + 912 + 93 + 1948 pp., (see *YWMLS*, 56 : 49), has been redesigned and is stated to include over 3000 new words and meanings; a number of 'boxes' explaining aspects of life and culture (e.g. *agrégation, département, colonie de vacances, Matignon, American dream, eisteddfod, English Heritage, Received Pronunciation*) are also added.

9. LEXICOLOGY

Marie-Françoise Mortureux, *La Lexicologie entre langue et discours*, Armand Colin, 192 pp., consists of eight chapters usefully and clearly defining and exemplifying aspects of the scope and methodology of lexicological studies, followed by some 60 pages of 'exercices commentés' and 'textes commentés' and a bibliography that is supplemented by bibliographical notes to each chapter. Malcolm Offord, *French Words: Past, Present and Future*, Clevedon, Multilingual Matters, viii + 125 pp., is a multifaceted presentation of the vocabulary of French; two chapters illustrating from French more generally applicable features of lexicological study (morphemes, stems, lexemes, collocation, synonyms, antonyms, homonyms, etc.) are followed by three that investigate the origins of French words, dealing respectively with 'Words with a long history' (mainly on the Latin element in

French, including the phonetic evolution of inherited words), words of foreign origin, and neologisms.

Loïc Depecker, *L'Invention de la langue: le choix des mots nouveaux*, Armand Colin–Larousse, 720 pp., is an original and thoroughly researched and documented volume describing and analysing the work of a score of French *Commissions ministérielles de terminologie* (CMTs) during the period 1970–1993; rather more than half of the text traces the history of the CMTs (covering such diverse fields as transport, defence, telecommunications, tourism, sport, agriculture, nuclear engineering, education, the 'féminisation des titres', etc.) and comments on the numerous *arrêtés* emanating from them; another substantial chapter deals with their organization and functioning while shorter chapters assess the principles and methods adopted in their work, the reaction of the Académie and other bodies to their recommendations, the success or failure of the terms adopted, press reactions, and lessons to be learned. *CPr*, 36, 'Linguistique de la dénomination', includes: G. Kleiber, 'Remarques sur la dénomination' (21–41); J.-C. Anscombre, 'Dénomination, sens et référence dans une théorie des stéréotypes nominaux' (43–72); A. Collinot, 'Dénomination d'un objet social dans un discours encyclopédique' (73–91); G. Petit, 'Pour une conception lexicologique de la dénomination' (93–115); J. Humbley, 'Quelques enjeux de la dénomination en terminologie' (117–39); C. Boisson, 'Dénomination et "vision"' (141–68); H. Constantin de Chanay, 'La dénomination: perspective discursive et interactive' (169–88); and P. Siblot, 'De la dénomination à la nomination. Les dynamiques de la signifiance nominale et le propre du nom' (189–214).

Majid el-Houssi, *Les *Arabismes dans la langue française (du Moyen Âge à nos jours)*, L'Harmattan, 217 pp.

R. Liver, 'Die Etymologie von fr. *trouver* und die bündnerromanischen Reflexe von TROPUS und TROPARE', *VR*, 60:117–27, takes up Jud's suggestion that evidence from Romansch might cast light on the problematic etymology of *trouver*, but finds the results of her investigation disappointing. D. A. Trotter, 'Le *clou tillart*: régionalisme normanno-picard en ancien français?', *RLiR*, 65:369–80, takes a case of problematic etymology to stress the importance of archival evidence. C. Tetet, 'Notes de lexicologie sportive', *CLe*, 77, 2000:189–200, studies *sport* and its derivatives in 19th-c. and 20th-c. texts. H. Walter, 'Les "faux amis" anglais et l'autre côté du miroir', *Linguistique*, 37.2:101–12, looks in particular at lexical parallels between English and French that are not in fact *faux amis* and may, indeed, in many cases be *bons amis*. C. Vandeloise, 'Verbes de changement, de transformation et de génération', *CLe*, 77,

2000:117–36, offers a lexical analysis of verbs such as *devenir, se transformer, naître, mourir, geler,* and *s'évaporer.*

C. Marque-Pucheu, 'La sélection des noms dans la locution *au bord de N* et le concept analytique de "crise"', *FM,* 69:183–98, expatiates on concrete and figurative usages.

G. Petit, 'Un hybride sémiotique. Le nom déposé', *LInv,* 23, 2000:161–92, discusses words of the type *Kleenex, Walkman, Cocotte-Minute.*

R. Martin considers the morphology, semantics and vitality of 'Le préfixe *a-* /*ad-* en moyen français', *Romania,* 119:289–322. D. Corbin, 'Préfixes et suffixes: du sens aux catégories', *JFLS,* 11:41–69, argues for a new interpretation of the 'capacité catégorisatrice' of affixes. Towards the end of a long and difficult article, G. Petit, 'Dénomination et lexique', *ib.,* 89–121, tells us that 'conclure ne peut être que prématuré et partiel' — his words.

10. ONOMASTICS

Jacques Chaurand and Maurice Lebègue, *Noms de lieux de Picardie,* Bonneton, 2000, 224 pp., is not a dictionary but a historical and thematic survey that is both scholarly and readable. A first part, 'Construction d'une toponymie', includes chapters on pre-Roman, Gallo-Roman, and Germanic elements, on 'l'hagiotoponymie', and on 'Quelques reflets de la société médiévale dans la toponymie', while a second section deals with names based on words for, respectively, trees and other plants, animals, and topographical features; the volume is completed by a bibliography and an index of names covered. E. Siegrist discusses the etymologies of the place name *Vevey* and the river name *la Veveyse, BNF,* 36:239–47, and in a second article, *VR,* 60:205–09, associates these names with the tribal name of the (Bituriges) Vivisci.

11. SEMANTICS

S. Mejri looks at 'La structuration sémantique des énoncés proverbiaux', *IG,* 88:10–15.

12. DIALECTS AND REGIONAL FRENCH

Mélanges sur les variétés du français de France, d'hier et d'aujourd'hui, III, ed. J.-P. Chambon et al., Champion, 206 pp. *Dictionnaire des régionalismes de France,* ed. Pierre Rézeau, Brussels, De Boeck Duculot, 1140 pp., is an excellent work that constitutes a major and indispensable accession to the field of French lexicography. Far more than just a dictionary, it fully lives up to the promise of its subtitle, *Géographie et histoire d'un patrimoine linguistique*. Each of the thoroughly documented articles, all of them going into considerable detail and some running to two or more pages, gives precise definitions for the headword and precisely located examples, and specifies (in over 300 cases with the aid of a map) its geographical range, with bibliographical references, and, as and where necessary, reference to derivatives and/or synonyms, and a commentary on points of pronunciation, syntax, and etymology. This admirable volume is completed by an extensive bibliography and a well-classified index. (On this work, see also *YWMLS*, 62:47.)

Jules Corblet, **Glossaire étymologique et comparatif du patois picard ancien et moderne; précédé de Recherches philologiques et littéraires sur ce dialecte*, Cœuvres-et-Valséry (Aisne), Ressouvenances, 2 vols, 619 pp., is a facsimile reprint of a work first published in 1851. J. Chaurand traces 'L'entrée du mot *gamin* dans les parlers de l'est picard', *RLiR*, 65:229–44. In a well documented and convincing article, R. Lepelley, 'Particularités phonétiques et romanisation du domaine gallo-roman "nord-occidental"', *ib.*, 33–74, argues that the existence of a north-western Gallo-Romance area is to be attributed not to the influence of the Germanic invasions but to 'une romanisation intense de cette région à l'époque gallo-romaine'. René Morley, **Patois du bocage normand*, Saint-Jean-de-Mauvrets, Petit pavé, 114 pp. Michèle Benoit and Claude Michel, **Le Parler de Metz et du pays messin*, Woippy, Serpenoise, 237 pp. Robert Lesigne, **Mots et figures des trois provinces: Champagne, Lorraine, Franche-Comté*, L'Harmattan, 184 pp. Jean-Paul Colin, *Expressions familières de Franche-Comté*, Bonneton, 159 pp., usefully supplements M. and G. Duchet-Suchaux's *Dictionnaire du français régional de Franche-Comté* (see *YWMLS*, 55:62); over 400 idiomatic expressions are explained and characterized and the volume is completed by a bibliography and a 'répertoire thématique'. P. Blanchet reports on recent 'Enquêtes sur les évolutions générationnelles du français dans le pays vannetais (Bretagne)', *FM*, 39:58–76. Roger Verdier, **Dictionnaire du patois du haut Maine*, Le Coudray-Macouard (Maine-et-Loire), Cheminements, 300 pp. Jean-Baptiste Luron, **Glossaire rural du Centre*, Sury-en-Vaux, A à Z Patrimoine, 75 pp.

13. Channel Islands French

Hellmut Lösch, *Die französischen Varietäten auf den Kanalinseln in Vergangenheit, Gegenwart und Zukunft* (Beihefte zu *Quo Vadis, Romania?*, 9), Vienna, Praesens, 2000, xi + 191 pp., is, within its limits, both comprehensive and informative; a historical overview ranges from prehistoric times to the present, devoting special attention to the period from the 18th c. onwards; discussion of dialectal variations between and within the islands and of the literary use of Guernsey and Jersey French is inevitably somewhat schematic; coverage of the recent and contemporary situation deals, *inter alia multa*, with the (now very limited) use of the different varieties in such fields as the media, education, and the cultural life of the islands, the evidence of official and unofficial language censuses, societies and institutions concerned to foster the languages or traditions of the islands, and the role (now vestigial) of standard French; there is a good bibliography of some 250 items; this is a book that deserves to be translated into French or, better, English (the one-page English abstract provided is quite inadequate).

Mari C. Jones, *Jersey Norman French. A Linguistic Study of an Obsolescent Dialect* (Publications of the Philological Society, 34), Oxford, Blackwell, xvi + 239 pp., is a wide-ranging and thorough survey, based on a thorough knowledge of primary and secondary sources and on field-work (in particular, a questionnaire administered to 50 native speakers), which achieves its aim of giving 'a comprehensive account of the situation of Jèrriais at the beginning of the twenty-first century'. It covers, *inter alia*, the sociolinguistic setting of Jèrriais, its phonology (with due attention to regional variation and its relationship to other varieties of insular and mainland Norman French), attitudes towards the language, language planning on Jersey, and linguistic developments within the language, including the influence of standard French and, even more so, English. The pessimistic, but doubtless realistic, conclusion is that 'despite the efforts of the revitalizers, [. . .] the survival of Jèrriais is by no means assured', though it is perhaps still too early to abandon all hope.

N. Spence surveys 'The language changes in Jersey', *Annual Bulletin of the Société Jersiaise*, 28:133–42, citing evidence from 1694 onwards, and 'Le sort de la francophonie à Jersey', *Revue de l'Avranchin et du Pays de Granville*, 78:165–77. Id., 'Diphtongaisons supplémentaires dans les parlers normands de l'est de Jersey', *RLiR*, 65:25–31, draws attention to types of diphthongization that do not occur in the west of the island or on the mainland of Normandy.

14. FRENCH IN NORTH AMERICA AND THE CARIBBEAN

Le Français au Québec: 400 ans d'histoire et de vie, ed. Michel Plourde, Saint-Laurent, *Bellarmin*, 186 pp.

P. Martin et al. look closely at 'Les voyelles nasales en français du Québec', *Linguistique*, 37.3:49–70. E. Nikièma discusses 'Government-licensing and consonant cluster simplification in Quebec French', *CanJL*, 44, 2000:327–57.

Annick Farina, *Dictionnaires de langue française au Canada. Lexicographie et société au Québec*, Champion, 445 pp., is admirably successful in being at the same time historical, descriptive and critical; three descriptive and critical chapters deal, each in chronological order, with respectively 'les dictionnaires de curieux', 'les dictionnaires d'éducateurs' and 'les dictionnaires de lexicographes'; a 60-page bibliography of some 250 items (mainly dictionaries and other books together with a few articles), ranging in date from 1752 to 1999, is supplemented by an alphabetical list (by compiler) of dictionaries, a bibliography of *comptes rendus*, and sets of *fiches historiques d'articles lexicographiques* reproducing the entries for 11 words from different dictionaries.

Offord, *Francophone Literatures*, consists of literary extracts from different parts of the francophone world with a commentary on each; two of the four parts are devoted respectively to the Caribbean (seven extracts) and to Canada (seven extracts, including one relating to Nova Scotia); M. Offord contributes to each chapter a commentary on the language and style thereof.

15. French in Africa and the Indian Ocean

Two sections of Offord, *Francophone Literatures*, are devoted respectively to North Africa (seven extracts) and to Black Africa (seven extracts from West African writers, including one by a Réunionnaise); M. Offord again provides commentaries on language and style.

16. Sociolinguistics

Jean-Marie Klinkenberg, **La Langue et le citoyen: pour une autre politique de la langue française*, PUF, 192 pp. Nigel Armstrong, **Social and Stylistic Variation in Spoken French: A Comparative Approach*, Amsterdam, Benjamins, ix + 278 pp.

17. Special Registers

A. Condamines examines the use of '*Chez* dans un corpus de sciences naturelles', *CLe*, 77, 2000: 165–87.

18. Pragmatics, Discourse Analysis, and Textual Analysis

Monique L'Huillier, Bronwen Martin, and Raynalle Udris, *French Discourse Analysis*, Dublin–London, Philomel, 2000, 349 pp., serves both as an introduction to the subject, setting out its fundamental linguistic concepts (and drawing on the work of, in particular, M. A. K. Halliday, D. Maingueneau, and the Paris School of Semiotics), and as a workbook; Part I, 'Cohesion', deals with grammatical features such as (co)reference, connectors, aspect and modality, and with lexical cohesion, while Part II, 'Coherence', brings in notions such as the presence of the speaker, situational reference (including cultural assumptions), narrative and argumentative models, and register and genre; a final section 'Putting it all together', is largely devoted to the analysis of titles and to a selection of other texts for analysis; the practical value of the volume is enhanced by the fact that it is most attractively produced. A. Rabatel considers 'La valeur délibérative des connecteurs et marqueurs temporels *mais*, *cependant, maintenant, alors, et* dans l'embrayage du point de vue', *RF*, 113:153–70, while C. Rossari and J. Joyez discuss '*Du coup* et les connecteurs de conséquence dans une perspective dynamique', *LInv*, 23:303–26.

Guy Achard-Bayle, *Grammaire des métamorphoses: référence, identité, changement, fiction*, Brussels, Duculot, 300 pp., the latest volume in the 'Champs linguistiques' series, is a work of great erudition based on profound reflection; however, it makes such demands on and so few concessions to its potential readers that it is unlikely to have the intellectual appeal or the practical utility of most of the other volumes in the series, to many of which a warm welcome has been reserved in these pages (see for example *YWMLS*, 61:36 and 45, 62:50, and pp. 34 and 37 above).

M.-B. Mosegaard Hansen, 'L'importance de l'analyse des interactions pour l'étude grammaticale de la langue', *RevR*, 36:115–31, takes issue with C. Blanche-Benveniste's claim that the 'comportements des locuteurs' have no effect on grammar. K. Beeching, 'Repair strategies and social interaction in spontaneous spoken French: the pragmatic particle *enfin*', *JFLS*, 11:23–40, investigates the rules concerning the syntactic and pragmatic properties of the use of *enfin*. A. Grobet, 'L'organisation informationnelle: aspects linguistiques et discursifs', *ib.*, 71–87, is a foretaste of work to come.

19.   CONTRASTIVE STUDIES

L. Beheydt et al., **Recherches contrastives néerlandais-français/Contrastief onderzoek Nederlands-Frans*, Leuven–Paris, Peeters, 248 pp. J.-M. Dewaele, 'Une distinction mesurable: corpus oraux et écrits sur le continuum de la déixis', *JFLS*, 11:179–99, analyses the relative proportions of different parts of speech in the spoken and the written language in 21 French, Dutch, and Italian corpora. R. Porquier, ' "*Il m'a sauté dessus*", "*je lui ai couru après*": un cas de postposition en français', *ib.*, 123–34, includes a brief 'confrontation avec l'anglais'. O. Eriksson, 'Adjectif et apposition. Étude contrastive sur une construction controversée', *RevR*, 35, 2000: 207–32, contrasts French (and to some extent Italian) with Swedish.

EARLY MEDIEVAL LITERATURE

By Sara I. James, *Honorary Research Fellow, University of Hull*, and Adrian P. Tudor, *Department of French, University of Hull*

1. General

Jacques Monfrin, *Etudes de philologie romane* (PRF, 230), 1035 pp., will be of great interest to all medievalists. This volume reprints a selection of M.'s articles, speeches, and lectures, published from 1954 onwards on a variety of topics. The subjects treated include Paul Meyer and his legacy to philological studies; philology itself; epic, romance, and other lyric texts; medieval culture; translation; and historiography.

Simon Gaunt, *Retelling the Tale: An Introduction to Medieval French Literature* (New Readings. Introductions to European Literature and Culture), London, Duckworth, 160 pp., is an attractive, and fairly novel, book which places the emphasis firmly on enjoyment and accessibility, and realistically addresses the needs of students reading medieval French texts for the first time. G. offers strategies for reading different types of texts (including epic, romance, and lay) rather than a conventional literary history. He demonstrates that although many early texts allude to oral sources when retelling a story, they actually belong to a sophisticated written culture which enjoyed competing interpretations of the same story. There is a useful *mise en contexte*, followed by seven brief chapters tackling issues such as 'oral' style, orality, cyclicity and continuation, intertextuality, and originality / *remaniement*. Quotations are in OF and English. William Chester Jordan, *Ideology and Royal Power in Medieval France: Kingship, Crusades and the Jews*, Aldershot, Ashgate, x + 276 pp., is a collection of articles published throughout J.'s career.

Richard Trachsler, *Disjointures—Conjointures: étude sur l'interférence des matières narratives dans la littérature française du Moyen Age* (RHel, 120), 2000, 429 pp., explores works that find themselves at the confluence of the three narrative traditions commonly identified by modern scholarship: *matière de France, matière de Bretagne, matière de Rome*. Elizabeth Archibald, *Incest and the Medieval Imagination*, OUP, xv + 295 pp., situates Latin and vernacular incest stories in their literary and cultural contexts; OF texts are central to A.'s project. This impressive study explains medieval incest laws, surveys classical stories and their medieval adaptations, and examines in detail various relationships: mother-son (Gregorius legend), father-daughter (*La Manekine*), sibling (Arthurian legend). It equally considers the ambiguous position of the Virgin. Jean-Jacques Vincensini, *Motifs et thèmes du récit médiéval* (Fac Littérature), Nathan, 2000, vi + 154 pp., is a slim but meaty volume intended for *DEUG, Licence,* and *classe préparatoire* students. Concentrating on romance, lay and *fabliau,* Vincensini traces the development of motifs, discusses what they reveal of morals and aesthetics, and offers strategies for understanding and exploring this vital aspect of the medieval literary world. A. Varvaro, 'Elaboration des textes et modalités du récit dans la littérature française médiévale', *Romania,* 119:1–75, challenges received views on the transmission of literary texts, performance, and *mouvance.* V.'s conclusions have implications for editors of a wide variety of OF texts. E. Baumgartner, 'Sur quelques constantes et variations de l'image de l'écrivain (XIIe–XIIIe siècles), Zimmerman, *Auctor,* 391–400, examines the terminology used by writers such as Jean de Meun, Chrétien, Guernes de Pont-Sainte-Maxence, Wace, and Benoît de Sainte-Maure, to describe their activity. M. Gally, 'Invention d'une langue et signature', *ib.,* 523–30, addresses the development of vernacular language and its *mouvance,* as seen in Marie de France and Wace. Id., 'Etre ou ne pas être *oiseus.* Lecture de quelques prologues du XIIIe siècle', *BDBA,* 19:101–10, examines the ways in which authors depict their work as virtuous because it seeks to provide 'useful' reading material (as opposed to the more frivolous 'poésie aristocratique', in G.'s terms, preceding it). M. Perret, 'Les types de fins: modèles et déviances', *ib.,* 181–200, seeks to create a typology of endings in an extremely broad range of texts, distinguishing between epilogue and closure. R. Wolf-Bonvin, 'Un vêtement sans l'être: la chemise', *Senefiance,* 47:383–94, contrasts the *chemise* as a profoundly ambivalent symbol: it is both an article of clothing and a signifier of nudity. It also represents both spiritual repentance and erotic possibility. P. Ménard, 'L'heure de la méridienne dans la littérature médiévale', *Tyssens Vol.,* 327–38, discusses the use of the hour and its relevance in Latin, French, and English poetry, mentioning in passing four lays: *Lanval, Graelent, Guigemar,* and *Tydorel.* A. Varvaro, 'Ipotesi per una nuova storia della letteratura francese medievale', *ib.,* 573–84, provides, in an all too brief article, an intriguing (if 'utopistica') view of the development and dissemination of literature, from the oral to written traditions. T. Venckeleer, 'Quelques réflexions sur le style formulaire', *ib.,* 585–94, announces a project at the University of Antwerp which will, like this article, use instances of formulae to further modern knowledge of OF vocabulary. Charles Ridoux, **Evolution des études médiévales en France de 1860 à 1914* (Nouvelle Bibliothèque du Moyen Age, 56), Champion, 1168 pp. Fabienne Pomel, **Les Voies de l'au-delà et l'essor de l'allégorie au Moyen Age* (Nouvelle Bibliothèque du Moyen Age, 57), Champion, 656 pp. **Les Traducteurs au travail: leurs manuscrits et leurs méthodes,* ed. Jacqueline Hamesse (Textes et Etudes du Moyen Age, 18), Turnhout, Brepols, 530 pp.

2. Epic

Huguette Legros, *L'Amitié dans les chansons de geste à l'epoque romane*, Aix-en-Provence, Provence U.P., 445 pp., studies 14 *chansons de geste* (including two versions of *Ami et Amile*) in a study that includes not only friendship and military companionship, but also the relationships between uncle and nephew, king and subject, and religious foes. This work is broken up into several small chapters, on topics ranging from the origins and meanings of words linked to friendship, and the socio-historical and cultural contexts in which friendships developed in the Middle Ages, to the Classical tradition. The rigid separation of different aspects of friendship, while useful for creating a typology, nevertheless means that analysis of epic friendship is restricted to descriptions of episodes illustrating a particular point, rather than a fully developed study.

ROLAND AND CHARLEMAGNE. John L. Grigsby, *The Gab as a Latent Genre in Medieval French Literature: Drinking and Boasting in the Middle Ages*, Cambridge, MA, Medieval Academy of America, 2000, ix + 255 pp. This study uses the *Voyage de Charlemagne* as a hook upon which to hang a pan-European study of the etymology and social customs of drunken boasting. G. claims the 'gab' is a genre in and of itself, of which the *Voyage de Charlemagne* is the hapax. H. Braet, 'Le *Voyage de Charlemagne* et le lecteur', *Tyssens Vol.*, 103–08, proposes that the plot is set in motion at various points by misunderstandings — the queen's, Charlemagne's, Hugues's — that cast doubt upon the ability of the 'reader'.

M. de Combarieu du Grès, 'Aiquin et Charlemagne: deux figures royales dans la *Chanson d'Aiquin*', *ib.*, 121–32, emphasizes the unusual status of the Saracen Aiquin, who in this poem is given equal consideration to that of his opponent, Charlemagne. A. Labbé, '"Fontayne riche et de moult grant beauté": la source scellée de Quidalet dans la *Chanson d'Aiquin*', *ib.*, 299–318, sees the episode in question as one of great intertextual and metaphoric significance.

A. Taylor, 'Was there a Song of Roland?', *Speculum*, 76:28–65, relates the history of scholars' attempts to trace the tale of Roland and Charlemagne before Francisque Michel's 1835 discovery, as well as discussing the extent to which the poem itself (and the tradition it represents) has been superseded by its nationalistic significance. S. Kinoshita, ' "Pagans are wrong and Christians are right": alterity, gender, and nation in the *Chanson de Roland*', *JMEMS*, 31:79–111, is part of a special issue on race and alterity in the Middle Ages. K. rightly points to difference in this work as primarily religious and cultural, rather than racial, warning against both 19th-c. and later (anachronistic) readings that either gloss over difference (as with

Gautier's dismissal of women in epic) or give it disproportionate significance (certain contemporary critics on race). Furthermore, the threat posed by differentiation is negligible as long as differentiation is religious and conversion always possible. As a point of comparison, K. also assesses Western Europeans' attitudes to their Eastern counterparts, encountered during the Crusades. H. M. Adrien, ' "Baligant" ou l'effet paratextuel du *Roland*', *DFS*, 57 : 3–9, analyses the Baligant episode, arguing that it is in itself the element that makes the *Roland* a *chanson de geste* and confers on it its generic status. W. van Emden, 'Où sont les morts de Roncevaux? La quête des morts et le stemma du *Roland rimé*', *Tyssens Vol.*, 559–71, revisits the question of whether the relatively young Cambridge MS may in fact be closer to the original than some older MSS.

GUILLAUME D'ORANGE AND THE GARIN CYCLE. *La Chanson de Guillaume*, ed. and trans. Philip E. Bennett (CGFT, 121.II), 2000, 209 pp., provides a lucid English prose translation (at the bottom of each page of verse) of the single MS (London, BL Add. 38663). The introduction and notes are solid, informative, and accessible, making this a valuable resource for the student audience for which it is intended. This work is complemented by Id., *La Chanson de Guillaume and La Prise d'Orange* (CGFT, 121.I), 2000, 134 pp. This slim volume provides a rigorous, thorough, and original analysis of key themes, characters, and episodes in both works. Of particular interest are the interpretation of Guillaume's physical and moral absence, the epic style of *La Prise d'Orange* and its ramifications for claims of the work as 'parody', and the use of a broad range of European epic heroes and traditions as counterpoints to the French. Id., 'Guillaume au court nez et Mimi-Nashi-Hoïchi: variations sur un thème folklorique', *Tyssens Vol.*, 77–87, defends Guillaume's 'court nez' as a defining physical characteristic, analogous to Hoïchi's missing ears in the Japanese epic. In both cases, the physical markings are those of heroic encounters with the otherworld and its dangers.

Les Epopées romanes: la Geste des Narbonnais, ed. Madeleine Tyssens and Jeanne Wathelet-Willem (GRLM, 3), Heidelberg, Winter, 176 pp., provides brief summaries of all 24 poems comprising the cycle (also known as the *geste de Monglane* or the *cycle de Guillaume d'Orange*), including comparative analyses of the texts as they relate to each other. The only caveat is that the Table of Contents would be more informative if it listed all the poems analysed rather than grouping them under 'Geste des Narbonnais'.

A. Corbellari, 'Le dehors et le dedans dans *La Prise d'Orange*', *MA*, 107 : 239–52, discusses the theme of 'woman and city'. M. Houdeville, 'Le jeu du nu et du vêtu à travers le déguisement du chevalier',

Senefiance, 47 : 179–85, examines how episodes of disguise and discovery in *Le Charroi de Nîmes* and *La Prise d'Orange* not only further the plot but also reveal the social and cultural signification of clothing. A. Moisan, 'L'habit monastique: de la plaisanterie au texte littéraire', *ib.*, 243–54, analyses the social and spiritual aspects of Guillaume's robing in the *Moniage Guillaume*. J. Raidelet, ' "Le cuer n'est mie en l'ermin engoulez." Revêtir une identité dans *Aliscans*', *ib.*, 313–24, observes the discrepancy between fine clothing and good character present in the poem (e.g. Rainouart, Blanchefleur). Such a discrepancy is all the more significant for being rare in a tradition that all too often equates the external appearance with internal attributes. F. Bogdanow, 'Un nouveau manuscrit d'*Aliscans* et de la *Bataille Loquifer*', *Romania*, 119 : 357–413, briefly surveys some of the textual implications of these two newly-discovered fragments. B. Guidot, 'Le *Siège de Barbastre*: une idéologie ambigüe', *Tyssens Vol.*, 208–25, considers that the Christian-Saracen conflict has become slightly more nuanced than in the *cycle du roi* poems: there are instances of personal sympathy between opponents, the Saracens become more eloquent in debate, and the theological points are less starkly promoted. E. A. Heinemann, 'Réalisations de l'art métrique de la chanson de geste: le cas des *Charroi de Nîmes*', *ib.*, 227–41, contains reflections upon the versions A, B, C, D, and the Vulgate of the poem, favouring heavily the work of the AB group for its poetic and literary merits. F. Suard, 'Autour de Vivien: sur quelques personnages de la *Chevalerie Vivien*', *ib.*, 487–98, is a brief evocation of the other characters in the poem, with Guichardet (among Vivien's other contemporaries) the central focus of the article. J. Subrenat, 'Vivien est-il un héros suicidaire?', *ib.*, 499–510, meanwhile examines Vivien himself, and his death, from the audience's perspective. Recalling that Guillaume questions Vivien's vow and his adherence to it, S. gives a measured consideration to this question — which has no definitive answer — based on readings of the *Enfances Vivien* and the *Chevalerie Vivien*. L. T. Ramey, 'Role models? Saracen women in medieval French epic', *RoN*, 41 : 131–42, seeks to uncover a message for Christian women in the target audience, attentive to the genre's portrayals of characters such as Orable/Guibourc.

EPICS OF REVOLT. M. Careri, 'Codici facsimilati e tradizione attiva nella *Geste des Loherains*', *Romania*, 19 : 323–56, is a broad survey of the manuscript tradition of the cycle, as well as of the approaches taken by its editors. J.-P. Martin, 'Notes sur le manuscrit de Bruxelles de *Garin le Lorrain*', *Tyssens Vol.*, 318–26, discusses two distinguishing points of this MS (traditionally denoted as Q, containing also *Girbert de Metz*): its versification is of particular interest when compared with

MS S; and it alone specifically locates the relic named in the poem at the Cathedral of St Pierre in Troyes.

OTHER EPICS. J.-P. Martin, 'Notes lexicographiques sur *Orson de Beauvais*', *Tyssens Vol.*, 231–41, continues the tradition stated in the first line, analysing the poem more for its linguistic content than for any literary points of interest. J. H. M. Taylor, 'The lure of the hybrid: *Tristan de Nanteuil*, chanson de geste arthurien?', *ArLit*, 18:77–88, studies a little-known branch of the *Doon de Mayence* cycle, suggesting that the 'Arthuricity' of *Tristan de Nanteuil* should be regarded as an attempt to breathe new life into the *chanson de geste*. S. B. Edgington, ' "Sont çou ore les fems que jo voi la venir?" Women in the *Chanson d'Antioche*', Edgington, *Crusades*, 154–62, analyses various episodes of female involvement in the First Crusade, concluding that Graindor de Douai's depictions are intended both to amuse and inspire the audience.

3. ROMANCE

Micheline Dessaint, *La Femme médiatrice dans de grandes œuvres romanesques du XIIe siècle* (Essais sur le Moyen Age, 24), Champion, 203 pp., analyses women who help the male heroes in their quest for self. Centring on Marie de France's *Lais*, the anonymous lays, the Tristan legend, and Chrétien de Troyes, the study suggests that whether lady, queen or fairy, women who play this key role in 12th-c. romances force the heroes to confront the inner self. These texts thus form a bridge between epic and prose romance. Anne Wilson, *Plots and Powers. Magical Structures in Medieval Narrative*, Gainesville, Florida U.P., xvi + 234 pp., is an unusual and unorthodox book which continues W.'s previous work of identifying texts produced by a hitherto unrecognized system of irrational thinking. Romance texts, including *Lanval*, *La Manekine*, and the *Tristan* stories, are examined via an attempt to distinguish the thought-making processes used to produce them. Magic is demystified and magical and non-magical versions of a same plot are compared and contrasted. A. Corbellari, 'De la représentation médiévale. Fantasme et ressemblance dans l'esthétique romanesque du Moyen Age central', *Poétique*, 127:259–79, suggests that in a number of plastic portraits described in 12th-c. and 13th-c. romance may be seen the embryo of representation intended to resemble its subject, encountered in art some two centuries later. This fascinating hypothesis is ably supported by evidence from Thomas' *Tristan*, the *Roman d'Alexandre*, the *Continuation Gauvain*, *Hunbaut* and the prose *Lancelot-Graal*. F. Mora, 'Remploi et sens du jeu dans quelques textes médio-latins et français des XIIe et XIIIe siècles: Baudri de Bourgueil, Hue de Rotelande, Renaut de

Beaujeu', Zimmermann, *Auctor*, 219–30, identifies a ludic conception of rewriting, which was vital in the establishment of vernacular literature. Although key works such as *Ipomédon* pay homage to the wisdom and knowledge of their predecessors, their *auctoritas* comes from themselves. W. Paden, 'The lyric lady in narrative', Krause, *Heroine*, 107–22, challenges traditional views of courtly love as exclusively extramarital and necessarily involving a socially superior woman. Examining lyric insertions in Jean Renart's *Roman de la rose* and Gerbert de Montreuil's *Roman de la violette*, Paden argues that since these passages were considered suitable to depict love between an unmarried man and woman, the *fin'amor* witnessed may be identified purely as desire. The lyric could therefore sing of love leading to marriage. J.-G. Gouttebroze, 'Entre le nu et le vêtu: le transparent', *Senefiance*, 47:153–64, mischievously considers evocations of transparent items worn by romance heroines; these evocations reveal that in the opening up of an imaginary space, romance affords its authors and audience a degree of liberation. J.-M. Pastré, 'Valeur mythique de la nudité dans quelques romans médiévaux de France et d'Allemagne', *ib.*, 271–82, studies the Indo-European myth of Indra's combat againt Vritra as reflected in Chrétien's *Yvain*, *Le Roman d'Yder*, *La Vie du Pape Grégoire*, and a number of German texts. J. Hamilton, 'Ruses du destin: blessures et guérisons dans l'univers chevaleresque', Grodek, *Ruse*, 261–69, describes how a group of *topoi* related to the figure of the wounded knight in the *Tristan* poems, *Le Conte du Graal*, and Marie de France converge around the notion of fecundity: impossible for the wounded knight, dreamed about by the woman healer. S. Schaller, 'Ekphrasis et lumière', *PRIS-MA*, 17:123–41, studies light and luminescent objects in texts including *Eneas*, *Partonopeu de Blois*, and *L'Escoufle*.

CHRÉTIEN DE TROYES. Joseph J. Duggan, *The Romances of Chrétien de Troyes*, New Haven, Yale U.P., 408 pp., situates Chrétien within the social and intellectual currents of his time. Chapters focus on major issues in Chrétien's romances rather than on individual works, with topics ranging from the importance of kinship and genealogy to standards of secular moral responsibility, and from Chrétien's art of narration to his representation of knighthood. *Cligès*, trans. Ruth Harwood Cline, Athens–London, Georgia U.P., 2000, xxvii + 217 pp., and *Erec et Enide*, trans. Id., Athens–London, Georgia U.P., xxv + 225 pp., both provide verse translations seeking to reproduce Chrétien's wit and wordplay, to punctuate the narrative by rhyme, and to alter pace through metre. *Cligès* is quite idiomatic and in particular would seem to make the long monologues easier for the modern ear. In *Erec*, C. wants to recreate the style and substance of Chrétien's original octosyllabic couplets. The introduction posits that Chrétien was an aristocratic clergyman with a benefice who travelled to Brittany and Britain in noble and royal entourages before returning to Troyes to write for a family with extensive kinship networks in Britain. In both volumes notes are rather sparse, but the texts themselves are an attractive read and will provide students unable to read OF with a useful, and provocative, study tool. **Le Chevalier au lion*, trans. Jean-Pierre Foucher and Dominique Trouvé (La Bibliothèque Gallimard, 65), 252 pp.

A. Guerreau-Jalabert, 'Le cerf et l'épervier dans la structure du prologue d'Erec', Bagliani, *Chasse*, 203–20, considers the values lent to hunting in the social symbolism of the Middle Ages and in the milieu which produced romance. Hunting in *Erec* always functions as a symbolic element which combines with other narrative details to give an episode its vital *senefiance*. M. Bolduc, 'Images of romance: the miniatures of *Erec et Enide* and *Le Roman de Silence*', *Arthuriana*, 12:101–12, argues that if the manuscript illuminations of chivalric romance are typically active and courtly, those of the *Roman de Silence* visually highlight the romance's preoccupation with language and gender. C. W. Carroll and M. C. Timelli, '*L'Extrait du Roman d'Erec et Enide* de La Curne de Sainte-Palaye', *ArLit*, 18:89–124, present the text prepared by the 18th-c. scholar La Curne de Sainte-Palaye, indicating the MSS he had access to and explaining his working methods. A. de Mandach, 'Les modèles anglo-normands de Chrétien. Chrétien en Angleterre', *RZLG*, 25:283–93, sets forth common points between *Erec* and the Welsh *Gereint ac Enid* in order to postulate a significant early corpus serving as source to these legends.

J. T. Grimbert, 'On Fenice's vain attempts to revise a romantic archetype and Chrétien's fabled hostility to the Tristan legend', Krause, *Heroine*, 87–106, demonstrates the degree to which standard ideas about medieval literary love in fact reflect late 19th-c. assumptions about women and gender. A new synthesis of modern and medieval is required in order to rework our critical consideration of *fin'amor*. *Cligès* was not written as an anti-*Tristan* since what Chrétien shows is the extent of Fenice and her mother's delusions about controlling their love lives.

S. N. Brody, 'Reflections of Yvain's inner life', *RPh*, 54:277–98, reads the events following Yvain's public humiliation by Laudine's messenger as a struggle between Y.'s Christian virtues and the vices he succumbed to in abandoning Laudine for Gauvain. J. M. Sullivan, 'The Lady Lunete: literary conventions of counsel and the criticism of counsel in Chrétien's *Yvain* and Hartmann's *Iwein*', *Neophilologus*, 85:335–54, credits Chrétien with a distinctly 'romance' type of counsel, distinguished by an emphasis on private counsel between individuals. Chrétien problematizes the positive nature of counsel, whereas temporal and geographical considerations lead Hartmann to view both public and private counsel as singularly positive. E. Burle, 'Nudité, dépouillement, création: une figure de fous', *Senefiance*, 47:59–73, studies *Yvain* alongside *Majnûn Laylâ* and *Le Fou d'Elsa*.

D. Piraprez, 'Chrétien de Troyes, allégoriste malgré lui? Amour et allégorie dans *Le Roman de la rose* et *Le Chevalier de la charrette*', Dor, *Conjointure*, 83–94, posits that Chrétien's text encourages an allegorical reading. This is because his apparent uncertainty about courtly love, and the conflicting interpretations his text seems to express and allow, reveal him as an artist very much aware of the fictionality and artificiality of his work. S. Feinstein, 'Losing your head in Chrétien's *Knight of the Cart*', *Arthuriana*, 9:45–62, shows the importance accorded to speech and to the head as the locus of potentially destabilizing speech, invoking religious iconography such as saints' beheadings. F. rejects as simplistic both the Freudian equation of beheading with castration, and the view of women's roles in instigating beheadings as decisive.

M. Vauthier, 'Les paradoxes du Prologue du *Conte du Graal*. "Vers de nouvelles perspectives"', *BDBA*, 19:225–39, regards the prologue as a statement of the author's project at the time he composed the text, hence his use of the future tense. Other uses of the future suggest a secret idea the author will seek to realize through his writing. The prologue equally has an appeasing function. B. N. Sargent-Baur, 'Le jeu des noms de personnes dans le *Conte du Graal*', *Neophilologus*, 85:485–99, views naming as a vital element of Chrétien's last romance. The hero's name is a constant motif, and Gauvain's revealed or concealed identity forms an important psychological element. Naming more generally can also have a bearing on how a character comes to self-knowledge. C. Deschapper, 'Keu l'ambigu', Dor, *Conjointure*, 35–51, is a useful rethinking of the role of Keu, paying particular reference to the *Conte du Graal*. D. examines the character's narrative role and a seneschal's historic role, concluding that both have been treated less than fairly by modern scholarship. K. Stierle, '*A te convien tenere altro vïaggio*: Dantes *Commedia* und Chrétiens *Contes del Graal*', *RZLG*, 25:39–64, reads the former text as a comment on the latter, more specifically on the theme of quest and movement both physical and metaphorical.

OTHER ARTHURIAN. Helen J. Nicholson, *Love, War and the Grail. Templars, Hospitallars and Teutonic Knights in Medieval Epic and Romance* (History of Warfare, 4), Leiden, Brill, xiii + 273 pp., is an ambitious and enlightening study which exploits French, German, and English texts. It examines the knights' religious and warrior roles and carefully considers the role of 'Templars' in the Grail romances. The frequent appearance of the military orders in fictional literature gives an insight into how they were viewed by the noble knightly classes for whom these texts were composed and who supported these knights. There is evidence for a continued belief in military service as a religious vocation. Mireille Séguy, **Les Romans du Graal ou le signe imaginé* (Nouvelle Bibliothèque du Moyen Age, 58), Champion, 512 pp. P. McCracken, 'Chaste subjects: gender, heroism and desire in the Grail quest', Burger, *Queering*, 123–42, shows how romance re-envisions gender and sexual conventions. A chaste heroism, standing outside a normative sexual economy, is in a tense relation to the conventional masculinity of knighthood. The queer hero is an outsider essentially through his desire not to desire. D. K. E. Crawford, 'Saint Joseph and Britain: the Old French origins', *Arthuriana*, 11 : 1–20, notes that the association of Joseph of Arimathea with the Grail and Britain in early Arthurian romance was caused by the identification of the Grail as a blood relic. A further association with Joseph would have been virtually automatic, since Joseph and the Crucifixion story were already part of popular tradition. Patricia Terry and Nancy Vine Durling, **Finding the Grail. Retold from Old French Sources*, Gainesville, Florida U.P., 2000, 128 pp. Annie Combes and Annie Bertin, **Ecritures du Graal (XIIe–XIIIe siècles)* (Etudes Littéraires), PUF, 128 pp. P. Le Rider, 'A propos de costumes: de Girard de Barri au *Conte du Graal* et à *Fergus*', *MA*, 107 : 253–82, refines her 1977 study of the same subject. The three texts offer different images of barbarians, *Fergus* being the most fictive. M. Séguy, 'Le sceau brisé. L'impossible fin de la *Troisième continuation du Conte du Graal*', *BDBA*, 19 : 213–23, posits that the 'impossible epilogue' offers itself as a complex, metadiscursive commentary on the act of writing, reflecting the aesthetic principles which organize the composition of the work. Stoyan Atanassov, *L'Idole inconnue. Le personnage de Gauvain dans quelques romans du XIIe siècle* (Medievalia, 31), Orleans, Paradigme, 2000, 141 pp., studies Gauvain in the first, second, and third *Continuations*, *La Vengeance de Raguidel*, *Le Chevalier aux deux épées*, and *L'Atre périlleux*. These works have been misjudged: they in fact show a remarkable coherence when an intertextual and intratextual semantic approach is applied. Gauvain is a type rather than an individual; he is 'l'idole inconnue' since his name, fame, and eventual nickname do not necessarily operate on the same level. A. seeks to rehabilitate some of these works by arguing that, in the 13th c., their subject was no longer the character of Gauvain but the narrative itself.

J. Benito de la Fuente, 'Le nu et le vêtu dans les romans arthuriens du XIIIe siècle', *Senefiance*, 47 : 127–38, considers passages where the naked body is the reflection of the divine, and others where it is an instrument of damnation. In particular, women, whether richly dressed or dangerously naked, are the texts' great losers. Thierry Delcourt, *La Littérature arthurienne* (Que sais-je?, 3578), PUF, 128 pp.

Joseph of Arimathea, Merlin, Perceval. The Trilogy of Prose Romances attributed to Robert de Boron, trans. Nigel Bryant (Arthurian Studies, 48), Cambridge, Brewer, 172 pp., is a translation of these capital texts telling of the origins of the Grail quest, recounting subsequent adventures, and offering a resolution to the Arthurian story. B. uses the version found in MS E.39 of the Biblioteca Estense in Modena, one of only 2 MSS containing all three texts, but it is not clear if his base is the MS itself or Cerquiglini's 1981 Modern French translation. In a frustratingly brief introduction, B. states his belief that Robert knew the contents of Chrétien's *Perceval* and deliberately christianized it. The translations appear quite readable, but notes are extremely scarce, and the lack of any line references is a serious flaw. Emmanuèle Baumgartner, *Robert de Boron: Le Merlin en prose. Fondations du récit arthurien* (Etudes Littéraires), PUF, 128 pp.

M. Séguy, 'Hippocrate victime des images: à propos d'un épisode déconcertant de *L'Estoire del saint Graal*', *Romania*, 119:440–64, concludes that the *Estoire* echoes the latest avatars of scared iconography, thereby reaffirming its importance as a rewriting of Christian history. E. A. Angresano, 'Modeling narrative authority and constructing the subject in the Prose-*Lancelot*', *RoN*, 41:143–52, identifies a 'formal switch' as evidence that the text can be read not only as a chivalrous diversion but also a treatise of didactic intent. The narrator's hidden techniques offset the polarity between literal truth and untruth, situating the text's true identity in the dynamic relationship between them. M. de Combarieu du Grès, 'Lancelot entre nu et vêtu dans le *Lancelot* en prose', *Senefiance*, 47:87–103, carefully traces the history of Lancelot through the clothes he wears, or does not wear. Annie Combes, *Les Voies de l'aventure: réécriture et composition romanesque dans le Lancelot en Prose* (Nouvelle Bibliothèque du Moyen Age, 59), Champion, 528 pp. M.-L. Meneghetti, 'Lancelot, Guenièvre e Rigaut de Berbezilh (per la fonte della *razo* di PC 421,2)', *Tyssens Vol.*, 338–47, links the episode of the false Guinevere in the former text to the latter's Occitan work. Andrea M. L. Williams, *The Adventures of the Holy Grail: A Study of 'La Queste del saint Graal'*, Oxford–Berne, Lang, 206 pp., explains the link between metaphor and structure by means of a detailed analysis of a number of key narrative sections. W. concludes that the author has carefully constructed a hierarchy of characters, and that he intentionally places the sometimes confused reader in a position analogous to the questing knight. This incisive study of the literary technique of structuring a text by means of metaphor, in which W. insists upon narrative content as sets of relationships which place elements within a defining framework, has broad implications for other didactic and fictional texts. O. Errecade, 'L'autre armure ou le vêtement de foi dans la *Queste del saint Graal*', *Senefiance*, 47:115–26, views descriptions of clothing in the *Queste* as key to understanding a protagonist's final reconciliation with God.

Le Livre du Graal, I: *Joseph d'Arimathie, Merlin, Les Premiers faits du roi Arthur*, ed. and trans. Daniel Poirion et al. (Bibliothèque de la Pléiade, 476), lxxv + 1918 pp., edits and translates the texts from MS B. The scholarly apparatus is extremely rigorous, including detailed notes on the MSS and texts, long lists of variants, and a substantial introduction dealing with authorship, themes, and motifs. The impressive team of scholars (P. Walter, A. Berthelot, R. Deschaux, I. Freire-Nunes, G. Gros) have produced a volume destined to become a standard work of reference for all researchers working on the *Lancelot-Graal*.

A. Berthelot, 'Merlin, ou l'homme sauvage chez les chavaliers', *Senefiance*, 47:17–28, identifies Merlin as the sole male character in the *Lancelot-Graal* whose physical appearance occupies the medieval narrators. Unlike other characters, whose physical aspect requires no gloss, descriptions of Merlin's constantly changing appearance are necessary to distance him from his true nature. Danièle James-Raoul, *Merlin l'Enchanteur*, Livre de Poche, 126 pp., is a collection of translations into Modern French of brief extracts from sources such as Myrddin, *Saint Kentigern et Lailokern*, Geoffrey of Monmouth, Wace, Robert de Boron, and the *Suite-Vulgate*. It is a 'no frills' budget volume which may appeal to lecturers seeking an affordable set text for an introductory, survey-type course. *Merlin, roman du XIIIe siècle*, ed. Danielle Quéruel and Christine Ferlampin Archer, Ellipses, 128 pp., is a collection of essays tracing the development of the character Merlin. R. Trachsler, 'Merlin chez Jules César. De l'épisode de Grisandole à la tradition manuscrite de la *Suite du Merlin*', *SFr*, 45:61–70, considers the Grisandole episode as a *récit bref* inserted into the *Estoire de Merlin*. However, given the MS and textual evidence based on an examination of the 31 MSS of the *Suite Vulgate*, the episode cannot be said to be wholly autonomous. Id., **'Pour une nouvelle édition de la *Suite-Vulgate du Merlin*', *VR*, 60:128–48. S. Lowson, 'Madness in Arthurian romance', Dousteyssier-Khoze, *(Ab)Normalities*, 77–86, finds that for Daguenet le Fol and Merlin madness becomes the constantly adapting vehicle which carries them. R. Lendo, 'Du *Conte du Brait* au *Baladro del sabio Merlín*. Mutation et réécriture', *Romania*, 119:414–39, attempts to unravel developments following the *Post-Vulgate*, in particular in Hispanic romance.

A. L. Furtado, 'The questing beast as emblem of the ruin of Logres in the *Post-Vulgate*', *Arthuriana* 9:27–48, studies the similarities and differences between the mythic questing beast before the Middle Ages (e.g., Scylla, Biblical instances), their sources as punishment for illicit love, and their role as harbingers of doom for kingdoms.

D. Maddox, 'Epreuves et ambiguïté dans *Le Bel inconnu*', Dor, *Conjointure*, 67–82, examines the heroic test of the *fier baiser*, which is centrally located between a prior qualifying phase and an ensuing series of 'specular encounters'. These momentous instances offer an overall heroic profile that is ultimately quite ambivalent. S. Sturm-Maddox, 'The Arthurian romance in Sicily: *Floriant et Florete*', *ib.*, 95–107, is a sensitive study of the Arthurian ending of a text which recalls the troubled history of Sicily under the Normans. F. Carapezza, 'Le fragment de Turin de *Rigomer*. Nouvelles perspectives', *Romania*, 119:76–112, challenges a number of *idées reçues*: the 'Jehan' of the text is not the author but more probably the source of the main narrative action; the episode found in the Turin fragment should be considered an authentic 'continuation'; the work should be known simply as *Rigomer*; Chrétien, and especially *Yvain*, play a vital role as thematic source; and *Rigomer* may be a northern extension of the legend of *Chapalu*. Jean-Claude Marol, **Le Fier baiser. Aux sources de l'amour chevaleresque*, Éditions du Relié, 188 pp.

TRISTAN AND ISEUT. Emile Lavielle, *Béroul: Tristan et Iseut* (Connaissance d'une Œuvre, 60), Rosny-sous-Bois, Bréal, 2000, 127 pp., is a student-friendly guide that promises to be a useful starting point for introductory courses. L. comments on authorship, historical and literary context, sources and influences, gives suggestions for further reading, and offers a commentary on the text, characters, themes, and motifs. R. N. Illingworth, 'The composition of the *Tristan* of Béroul', *ArLit*, 18:1–76, builds on more strictly philological work to cast new light on the relationship between authorship and source. The text can be characterized by a process of gradual accretion, up to and including the modifications made by the final redaction.

P.-Y. Badel and N. Harano, 'Fragments du *Tristan en prose* (version III)', *Romania*, 119:219–30, edit the Takamiya fragments for the first time. These fragments tell of Palamède's meeting with Galehondin, and the arrival and adventures of Perceval and Hector at the Île de Joie.

ROMANS D'ANTIQUITÉ. V. Gontero, 'La clarté de l'escarboucle dans les romans antiques', *PRIS-MA*, 17:57–72, examines the carbuncle's place as the 'gem of gems' in early medieval literary texts. A. Petit, 'Nu et nudité dans les romans antiques', *Senefiance*, 47:283–98, is a global study of the adjective 'nu' in the four *romans antiques*. The study underlines links with *chansons de geste*, and more specific instances in which nudity is key to the substance of the *roman antique*, such as the discovery of incest in *Thèbes* and the love and funerary themes of *Eneas* and *Troie*. C. Desprès Caubrière, ' "Le nu sous le vêtu'', dans quelques extraits du roman antique', *Senefiance*, 47 : 105–14, examines *Thèbes, Eneas, Troie*, and *Alexandre*, discovering successive modifications of the Romanesque vision of seduction and sexuality. A. Petit, 'Le premier portrait féminin dans le roman du Moyen Age. Les filles d'Adraste dans le *Roman de Thèbes*', *Tyssens Vol.*, 376–88, studies both the Classical influences upon this purely physical description and sets it forth as the model for that of future romance heroines. Id., 'Les chefs-d'œuvre à l'épreuve de la traduction: le *Roman de Thèbes* et le *Roman d'Eneas*', *MA*, 107 : 481–502, highlights the translation and adaptation skills of the medieval authors. When considered as historiographical documents in the humanist context of the 12th-c. renaissance, *Thèbes* and *Eneas* must be held as masterpieces of history, romance, adaptation, translation, epic, science, and even science-fiction.

V. Gontero, 'Le corps paré du défunt. Les rites funéraires dans le *Roman d'Eneas*', *Senefiance*, 47 : 139–52, judges the text's treatment of the dead worthy of the title *mirabilia*. There is also a specular quality to the narrative, between Pallas and Camille, and between the Latin source and the medieval vernacular adaptation. V. Dang, 'De la lâcheté du guerrier à la maîtrise du prince: Eneas à la conquête du pouvoir', *MA*, 107 : 9–28, explores the message of *Eneas* as read through a study of the text's structure and intratextual links: unlike in *Thèbes* and *Troie*, the narrator does not state his intentions in the prologue. Eneas in fact offers examples of good and bad government, where real power is based on knowledge of self.

A. Petit, 'Prologues du *Roman de Thèbes*', *BDBA*, 19 : 201–11, examines the sections common to all MSS — the duty to transmit knowledge, the desire for posthumous glory, the selection of a noble and clerical public — and the developments of the long version, which acknowledges the laicisation of clerical culture. D. Battles, 'Trojan elements of the *Roman de Thèbes*', *Neophilologus*, 85 : 163–76, argues, in the light of the numerous echoes of *Troie*, that the *Thèbes* poet attempts to re-fight the Trojan war, inverting winners and losers. This inversion can be accounted for by the poem's historical and political context within the Angevin empire.

U. Mölk, 'Alberics Alexanderlied', *CN*, 61 : 7–24, is of interest in as much as it cites excerpts of the *Roman d'Alexandre* as points of comparison with the Latin text that is its primary focus.

Piramus et Tisbé, ed. Penny Eley (*LivOS*, 5), <http://www.liv. ac.uk/www/french/LOS>, offers a substantial introduction, a critical edition, detailed notes, an English translation, and four diplomatic transcriptions (MSS R, C, B and A). M.-M. Castellani, 'La réalisation du projet initial dans *Athis et Prophilias*', *BDBA*, 19 : 45–56, examines the different endings of the two versions. The Tours version is in complete harmony with the initial project, as set out in the prologue; the long version, in breaking with the spirit of the prologue, reveals the author's interest in the east, the *roman antique,* the *chanson de geste,* and writing romance. C. Ruby, 'Un nouveau fragment d'*Athis et Prophilias*', *Romania,* 119 : 518–33, edits 120 lines from the short version: vv. 2607–68 (ed. Hilka), then 58 new lines.

OTHER ROMANCES. P. Price, 'Confessions of a godless killer: Guy of Warwick and comprehensive entertainment', Weiss, *Romance,* 93–110, considers the contradictory views on marital violence in the AN *Gui de Warewic* and the various English romances which followed. P. demonstrates how all the Guy narratives invite the audience to enjoy without reserve the hero's chivalric feats before his confession, and then to admire his penitence for shocking past sins (which he has not actually committed). Corinne Pierreville, **Gautier d'Arras, l'autre Chrétien* (Nouvelle Bibliothèque du Moyen Age, 55), Champion, 384 pp. S. Menelgado, 'Quand le narrateur est amoureux: prologues et épilogues "lyriques" dans le roman de chevalerie en vers aux XIIe et XIIIe siècles', *BDBA,* 19 : 149–66, studies dedications to a lady, explicitly and amorously linked to the narrator, in *Partonopeu de Blois, Florimont, Le Bel inconnu, Floriant et Florete, Joufroi de Poitiers* and *Le Castelain de Couci.* M. Jeay, 'Ruser avec la mort: trois lectures médiévales d'une séquence topique', Grodek, *Ruse,* 283–96, examines *La Manekine, Le Roman du comte d'Anjou* and *La Belle Hélène de Constantinople.* J. describes the movement of *topoi* between texts and traditions and suggests a heuristic value for the notion of the *topos,* using as example that of the ruses employed by a heroine to escape death. **Essays on the Poetic and Legal Writings of Philippe de Remy,* ed. Sarah-Grace Heller and Michelle Reichert, NY–Lampeter, Mellen, 316 pp. A. Cowell, '*Gautier d'Aupais,* courtly love and the dangers of the tavern', *RoN,* 41 : 273–80, reads the tavern scene as a meditation on the declining values of the aristocracy and on the problematic status of the subject in romance. This short romance is in fact a parody of the tavern scene: the ideology of courtly love which dominates the text's conclusion can be read as an echo of, and reaction to, the poetics and economics of the tavern, market, and profit.

A. Strubel, 'L'allégorie et la description: le début du *Roman de la rose* de Guillaume de Lorris', *Hicks Vol.,* 121–32, considers the function of the descriptive discourse, in particular its place in the author's poetic strategy. The opening 1,500 lines of the *Rose* reflect both a simple transition towards the dreamworld of fiction, and a text to be read beyond the words of the author. D. Kelly, 'The implications of age and ageing in the *Roman de la rose*', *ib.,* 91–104, concludes that the *Rose* illustrates the multiple ways in which readers may interpret a text in the light of their own experience. Ambiguity invites us to read the romance *apo koinou*: is the text concerned with the fact of ageing, or the scale of ages through which we all pass? The age *topos* opens the text to multiple readings. S.-G. Heller, 'Light as glamour: the luminescent ideas of beauty in the *Roman de la rose*', *Speculum*, 76:934–59, revealing the material importance of light-producing attire, situates the text in a Gothic world where beauty required the possession of light. She suggests that the remarkable way in which Guillaume de Lorris consistently and repeatedly employs luminescent objects may constitute one of the major factors which attracted Jean de Meun to the text as a basis for a continuation in which he repeatedly deals with optics, mirrors, and rainbows.

B. Guidot, 'Le style enjoué de Jean Renart dans *L'Escoufle*', *TL*, 33:11–27, analyses briefly the generic and stylistic traditions evoked by Jean Renart in a work perhaps unfavourably compared with Arthurian romance and *chanson de geste*. G. particularly appreciates Jean Renart's use of brisk rhythm, selective description, intertextuality, and characterization.

LAIS. E. Archibald, 'The Breton lay in Middle English: genre, transmission and the Franklin's Tale', Weiss, *Romance*, 55–70, discusses lays circulating in both English and French in Anglo-Norman England. In particular, she considers how the notion of the 'Breton lay' might have been understood from the earliest texts through to Chaucer. K. Mottershead, 'Le scénario de l'épreuve chez Marie de France et Chrétien de Troyes: une ruse du destin?', Grodek, *Ruse*, 271–81, shows how the typical trial scenario associated with popular tales has been refocussed by Marie and Chrétien. Some characters break with the constraints imposed by the trial narrative in order to challenge their fate, thereby striving to control it. S. I. Sobecki, 'A source for the magical ship in *Partonopeu de Blois* and Marie de France's *Guigemar*', *NQ*, 246:220–22, suggests that Marie's account bridges the development of the motif from Benedeit's *St Brendan* to Melior's ship in *Partonopeu*. L. Gemenne, 'Comment des élèves de l'enseignement secondaire lisent-ils le lai de *Bisclavret* de Marie de France?', Dor, *Conjointure*, 53–65, describes an experiment in teaching Marie de France to 16-year-olds. J. V. Molle, 'La nudité et les habits du "garulf" dans *Bisclavret* (et dans d'autres récits de loups et de louves)', *Senefiance*, 47:255–69, gathers evidence for the existence of a preexisting werewolf legend. Chapter Four ('Shape and Story') of Carolyn Walker Bynum's *Metamorphosis and Identity*, NY, Zone, 280 pp., includes a sub-chapter entitled 'Some stories about werewolves: Marie de France's *Bisclavret*'. In this analysis, metamorphosis is the ultimate metaphor for Marie. J. H. McCash, ' "Ensemble poënt bien durer": time and timelessness in the *Chevrefoil* of Marie de

France', *Arthuriana*, 9 : 32–44, demonstrates that *Chaitivel, Chevrefoil,* and *Eliduc* illustrate a spectrum of models of love, from 'superficial', staged, pseudo-courtly love to doomed courtly love, all finally transcended by divine love and charity. S. Malatrait, 'Zeitlose Märchen? Anmerkungen zur Zeit in den *Lais* der Marie de France', *RJ*, 51 : 108–27, studies the role of time in structuring narrative and signifying change. C. R. Houg, 'Trickery and betrayal in the *Lais* of Marie de France', *MedP*, 16 : 50–62, examines incidents found in all 12 *lais*, the motives underpinning such behaviour, and the consequences.

4. Religious Writings

Jocelyn Wogan-Browne, *Saints' Lives and Women's Literary Culture, c. 1150–1300: Virginity and its Authorizations*, OUP, xvi + 314 pp., focuses on women's uses and adaptations of the ideal of virgin sanctity in Anglo-Norman England. A study of biographical, theological, and historiographical texts indicates a rich and complex literary culture, especially in the vernacular. The requirements and responses of the audience and the authority of the producers suggest that hagiography was perhaps *the* major form of representing women. D. Robertson, '*Cume lur cumpaine et lur veisine*: women's roles in Anglo-Norman hagiography', Krause, *Heroine*, 13–25, concentrates on vernacular writings connected with the Abbey of Barking. Relationships develop between the heroines of legend and the women writers and readers, thereby establishing a true female *communitas*. These texts can be read as women speaking to women about women.

'The Life of St Alexis', trans. Nancy Vine Durling, Head, *Hagiography*, 317–40, is preceded by a short introduction and very brief notes. The translation is based on Storey's 1968 edition of MS L. M. Burrell, '(Dis)closure in *La Vie de Saint Alexis*', *AUMLA*, 95 : 1–12, proposes a revision of Hatcher's bipartite structure of the poem, focussing on the instances of what B. calls closure/disclosure (with emphasis on relationships between individuals). In a somewhat anachronistic conclusion, B. condemns Alexis for 'closing off' secular life, thereby becoming (in her interpretation) a poor intercessor. S. O. Malicote, 'The illuminated *Geste de Saint Gille*: questions of genre', *RR*, 90 : 285–300, states that this particular work, which contains both *Aiol* and *Elie de saint Gille*, has been illustrated by the same artist in the single extant MS. M. studies how the artist glossed, structured, and emphasized elements of both texts with illuminations, and concludes by warning scholars against basing strict generic divisions on a work's illuminations. *Deux versions de la Vie de saint Georges*, ed. Yvette Guilcher (CFMA, 138), 156 pp., offers a fascinating glimpse of the development

of medieval hagiography. The late 12th-c. or early 13th-c. Tours MS
927 gives a vernacular version of the legend very close to the Latin
prototext, whereas the 14th-c. MS (refered to throughout as Chelten-
ham MS 3668) presents a new version in which the combat against
the dragon appears. Both texts are short but full of merit. The OF *Vie
de sainte Agnès* is one of the core texts examined by A. B. Thompson in
'The legend of Saint Agnes: improvisation and the practice of
hagiography', *Exemplaria*, 13:355–98. Misrecognition can create the
space for an open-ended textual practice in the hagiographic tradition
and help disguise a poet's departure from cultural dispositions that
might otherwise seem troubling to him and his audience. Clara
Strijbosch, **The Seafaring Saint: Sources and Analogues of the Twelfth-
Century Voyage of Saint Brendan*, Dublin, Four Courts, 2000, 336 pp.

D. L. Pike, ' "Le dreit enfer vus mosterruns": Marie de France's
Espurgatoire Seint Patriz', *Viator*, 32:43–58, is a useful study which
contends that the *Espurgatoire* is a significant work of literary value.
Marie's enigmatic translation, dependent upon a complex web of
intertextuality, uses the frame of descent simultaneously to bracket
the realm of poetry from, and weld it to, everyday reality. Catherine
Deschapper, *Je veux mes amis saluer . . . Etude et comparaison des traductions
des 'Vers de la mort' d'Hélinand de Froidmont* (Les Cahiers du Théâtre-
Poème, 12), Brussels, Ambedui, 1999, 166 pp., is a rather innovative
study of a medieval text packed with *realia* and other complex
obstacles to a modern reader, through four translations into Modern
French. Such an analysis is an unexpectedly rich way of reinvesting
the *Vers de la mort* with the cultural and poetic values of its author and
the society within which he lived and worked. J. M. Smeets, 'Sept
vers d'un manuscrit perdu', *Romania*, 119:534–42, offers variants
from the margins of BNF, f.fr.789 for Gautier de Belleperche and
Pieros de Riés's *La Chevalerie de Judas de Machabee*.

'Gautier de Coincy, *Miracles of the Virgin*', trans. R. Blumenfeld-
Kosinski, Head, *Hagiography*, 627–53, translates into prose and from
Koenig: 1 Mir 12, 1 Mir 17, 1 Mir 20, 1 Mir 21, 1 Mir 26, 1 Mir 33,
1 Mir 35 and 11 Mir 27. M.-G. Grossel, 'Prologues et épilogues dans
les *Miracles de Nostre Dame* de Gautier de Coinci', *BDBA*, 19:111–22,
examines the author's reflections on his own work. The prologues
suggest a certain pride on the author's part, whilst flourishes in the
epilogues suggest that Gautier is loath to finish his splendid work.
K. M. Krause, 'Virgin, saint and sinners: women in Gautier de
Coinci's *Miracles de Nostre Dame*', Krause, *Heroine*, 26–52, is a broad
examination of Gautier's female characters in each of the three
categories of the title. K. in particular highlights three ambiguities:
the Virgin as a woman; contrasting fates of male and female sinners;
and gender questions in *l'Impératrice de Rome*. The assumption

underlying Gautier's discourse is that women are fundamentally sinful and deceitful. A. Drzewicka, 'Gautier de Coincy et la *povre fame*', *Tyssens Vol.*, 149–60, for her part concludes that Gautier, while very much a product of his time and culture, nevertheless exhibits a sympathy for and respect of women, especially those who are poor and/or victims.

G. Hasenohr, 'Les prologues des textes de dévotion en langue française (XIIIe–XVe siècles)', Hamesse, *Prologues*, 593–638, explores what a medieval author may have considered a prologue, and its function, to be. She concludes that, particularly in the case of prose texts, the presence or absence of a prologue is determined more with regard to reception than to writing. Editions of OF verse and prose prologues are appended to this rich study. G. Gros, 'Vierge de lumière et *Miserere*: étude sur la prière mariale du Reclus de Molliens', *PRIS-MA*, 17:73–90, closely examines this prayer to the Virgin, which follows a sermon on the misery of man and is one of the earliest OF verse versions. M. Zink, 'Le Cantique des Cantiques et le *Vilain ânier*', *Tyssens Vol.*, 631–41, studies the *fabliau* (found, alongside religious writings, in MS 173 of the Bibliothèque municipale de Mans) as a commentary on the Song of Songs and an edifying work in its own right.

5.   OTHER GENRES

LYRIC.   *Songs of the Women Trouvères*, ed. Eglal Doss-Quinby et al., New Haven, Yale U.P., 2000, 328 pp., is an anthology of works by women *trouvères* in northern France in the 12th and 13th cs. The volume presents songs attributed to eight named female *trouvères* along with a selection of anonymous compositions in the feminine voice that may have been composed by women. The book includes the OF texts of 75 compositions, extant music for 18 monophonic songs and 19 polyphonic motets, and English translations. D. Kelly, 'The poem as art of poetry: the rhetoric of imitation in the *grand chant courtois*', Paden, *Genres*, 191–208, argues convincingly that both the *canso* and *grand chant courtois* functioned in terms analogous to Latin rhetoric. Like Latin poetry, they were founded upon treatises, models and imitation; there is therefore no ironic gloss in the relation of Latin to vernacular in figures such as the Châtelain de Couci and Thibaut de Champagne. E. Aubrey, 'Genre as determinant of melody in the songs of the troubadours and the trouvères', *ib.*, 273–96, casts troubadour and trouvère song within a rhetorical perspective in order to analyse the relation between word and melody. While the text provides matter, the melody offers form. Matter and form are conceived inseparably in relation to the song's theme, and since theme is the basis of genre, genre determines the song's structure, language, function, and melody. S. Huot, 'Intergeneric play: the pastourelle in thirteenth-century French motets', *ib.*, 297–316, explores the interaction between the *pastourelle* and the newly developing motet. The motet highlights the contrast between the sexuality of the *pastourelle* world and the restraint of the courtly *chanson*, between variations on the plot of the traditional *pastourelle*, and between secular and sacred. This interaction is one example of 13th-c. experimentation with lyric forms.

I. Hardy, ' "Nus ne poroit de mauvaise raison" (R1887): a case for Raoul de Soissons', *MAe*, 70:95–111, examines the textual history of this (purportedly anonymous) song, its style, and lexicon to attribute it to Raoul de Soissons. R. Crespo, 'Conon de Béthune (R. 303, 19–24) e Gautier de Dargies (R. 1290, 21–22); Chrétien de Troyes, *Yvain*, 2533–2534', *Tyssens Vol.*, 133–38, suggests influences arising from a close reading of the three extracts. L. Rossi, 'Carestia, Tristan, les troubadours et le modèle de saint Paul: encore sur *D'Amors qui m'a tolu a moi* (RS 1664)', *ib.*, 403–19, posits not only Chrétien's *D'Amors qui m'a tolu a moi* but also his *Amors tençon et bataille* (RS 121) as poetically and ideologically significant — the poet-lover may not have his heart's desire, but he gains spiritually through learning to appreciate what he does have. L. Spetia, 'Il *corpus* delle pastorelle francesi: una questione ancora aperta', *ib.*, 475–86, debates the generic divisions between *pastourelle* and other lyric forms (e.g. *chanson de mal mariée, ballade*). Marie-Noëlle Toury, **Mort et fin'amor dans la poésie d'oc et d'oil aux XIIe et XIIIe siècles* (Nouvelle Bibliothèque du Moyen Age, 60), Champion, 352 pp.

ROMAN DE RENART. R. Anthony Lodge and Kenneth Varty, *The Earliest Branches of the Roman de Renart* (Synthema, 1), Louvain, Peeters, 193 pp., is a study and edition of branches II-va in Turin, Biblioteca Reale, MS Varia 151. The editors test Foulet's theory that these branches form a primitive, single narrative, concluding that despite some strong evidence, the unity hypothesis has rightly been challenged over the past 20 years. There are abundant notes, a detailed glossary, and a meaty introduction that places the text within the larger literary, linguistic, and artistic context of the *Roman de Renart*. The section on 'Sources and Analogues' is particularly rich. Noburu Harano and Shinya Shigemi, *Concordance du Roman de Renart d'après l'édition gamma*, Hiroshima, Keisuisha, 1362 pp., uses the 1983–85 edition of Fukumoto, Harano, and Suzuki to offer a 1265-page alphabetical listing, plus tables of frequency of use. R. Bellon, 'Editer le *Roman de Renart*: bilan, problèmes et perspectives', *Reinardus*, 14:23–38, is a detailed discussion of the manuscript evidence concerning Branche XX following the completion by Lecoy of Roques' edition of the Cange MS (B). The division of MSS into classes (structural criteria) does not always correspond with their division into families (textual criteria), indicating a need for critical editions of the ten as yet unedited *RdeR* MSS. A. Strubel, 'Editer Renart', *IL*, 53 : 32–38, argues the case for broadening the already wide corpus of editions available. M. Bonafin, 'Les joyeuses funérailles de Renart', *Reinardus*, 14 : 89–98, studies the burial and 'three deaths' of Renart in the context of both the Goliardic tradition and agricultural festivals. In Branche XVII a jubilant victory is won by a body which is both grotesque (sexual and exuberant) and injured (mutilated, castrated). Such a triumph, with its mixture of tears and laughter, is rooted in pagan folklore rather than Christian doctrine. M. Lawrence, 'Parole, pouvoir, plaisir et déguisement du goupil dans "Renart jongleur" ', *ib.*, 173–88, notes that in Branche Ib Renart is unrecognizable since he hides his distinctive characteristics. This gives the modern reader a clearer indication of the author's understanding of Renart's identity, in particular that of Renart as storyteller. The author identifies Renart by his language and defines him as the master of words. Renart's successful disguise represents the triumph of words, and his ultimate aim is to enjoy the power and pleasure conferred by language. Y. Takana, 'La parodie des chansons de geste dans le *Roman de Renart*. L'imitation des "laisses" dans l'épisode de la plainte des coqs de la branche I', *ib.*, 255–65, applies a statistical and comparatist approach to discern the author's parodic intention in dramatising Renart's change of fortune. C. Zemmour, 'Le *Roman de Renart*: l'écriture d'une domestication illusoire', *ib.*, 287–310, examines the branches of the Cange MS and suggests that, when taken together, literary fiction and social anthropology can inform our knowledge of self. J.-H. Grisward, 'Loki, Renart et les sarcasmes de Maupertuis', *Hicks Vol.*, 293–306, rejects Roger Bellon's reading of Renart's boastings during the Maupertuis siege as 'une reprise bestournée' of the pagans' words in the *Chanson de Roland*, in favour of the motif belonging to an older, Indo-European mythology. The argument is supported with evidence from the 11th-c. Scandanavian *Lokasenna*.

FABLIAUX. Ian Short and Roy J. Pearcy, *Eighteen Anglo-Norman Fabliaux* (ANTS Plain Texts Series, 14), London, ANTS, 2000, 41 pp., is a modest but important booklet that raises a number of fundamental questions concerning genre. The edition includes four Marie de France fables dealing with human protagonists, and seven tales from *Le Chastoiement d'un pere a son fils*. The editors note that the great collections published by Legrand d'Aussy, Barbazan, and Méon in fact imitate the content of *fabliaux* manuscripts. In publishing these 18 texts under the title '*fabliaux*', S. and P. make a significant contribution to the debate concerning the nature, if not the definition, of a *fabliau*. *Chevalerie et grivoiserie*. *Fabliaux de chevalerie*, I (Textes et Traductions des Classiques Français du Moyen Age, 7), ed. and trans. Jean-Luc Leclanche, Champion, 282 pp., offers an edition and prose translation of *Le Prêtre et le chevalier* (MS F), *Bérénger au long cul* (MS D), *La Mégère émasculée* (MS G), *Guillaume au faucon* (MS D) and *Le Fouteur* (MS D). L. highlights the tales' reflection of a courtly setting and of courtly conventions, suggesting that they conform to contemporary social attitudes. He also includes texts of *Le Dit des putains et des jongleurs* and *Le Lai du libertin* which are key to our understanding of courtly humour. R. J. Pearcy, 'Fabliau and romance: three notes', *RoN*, 41:267–72, offers instances from *Les Chevaliers*, *Les Clers et les vilains*, *Le Sacristain*, and *Le Pescheor de Pont seur Saine* which demonstrate that the authors of *fabliaux* and romance operate within the same cultural milieu, and that their writings reflect the same attitudes towards phenomena which might have been supposed capable of generating distinctive responses.

M.-T. Lorcin, 'Le nu et le vêtu dans les fabliaux', *Senefiance*, 47:231–41, reflects, with her usual perspicacity, on everyday nudity, women tested with nudity, men punished by nudity, erotic scenes, and disguises. A. Cobby, 'Langage du pouvoir, pouvoir du langage: *Constant du Hamel* et *Les Trois Aveugles de Compiègne*', *Reinardus*, 14:131–51, is an illuminating study of the interdependence of language and power in these two texts. In *Constant* the weak resist and subvert the domination of the strong through words, and the author is able to establish a network of echoes which serve to reinforce the plot. The rhetorical games of *Les Trois Aveugles* underline the vital importance of language: each protagonist carefully chooses his language relative to his interlocutor, and again the narrator's language echoes these choices.

MORAL, DIDACTIC, AND ALLEGORICAL WORKS. A. Corbellari, 'L'haleine vierge du loup. Quelques réflexions autour d'une fable de Marie de France', *Romania*, 119:196–218, examines the wolf in *Du loup qui fut roi* alongside bestiary and animal epic representations. The fable can be read as a denunciation of the tyrant who 'devours' his people, but must also be placed in a broader, timeless context: the loss of language is the prelude to barbarism. R. Trachsler, 'Les *Fables* de Marie de France. Manuscrits et éditions', *CCMe*, 44:45–63, is a meticulous and thoughtful reconsideration of the numerous, varied, and generally stemma-resistant *Fables* MSS. T. suggests a project similar in spirit to the *NRCF*, publishing perhaps three or four editions of a same fable, and applying *ad hoc* solutions to individual problems. However it is achieved, a detailed examination of the textual tradition of the *Fables* is now a pressing need. M. Léonard, 'Le *dit* médiéval: de l'écriture à la conception du livre', *TLit*, 14:17–26, studies the interventions of the author as he becomes an editor entering into a dialogue with his reader. The movement from oral to written culture implies a new role for the author and new demands of the reader. A. Smets, 'L'image ambiguë du chien à travers la littérature didactique latine et française (XIIe–XIVe siècles)', *Reinardus*, 14:243–53, suggests that the reason why Latin bestiaries tend to accentuate the positive aspects of the dog, whereas French texts are more negative, may be explained by their sources. 13th-c. encyclopedias are generally more neutral than the moralized works which followed.

DRAMA. **The Medieval European Stage, 500–1550*, ed. William Tydeman, CUP, 782 pp. T. Revol, 'Nudités théâtrales au Moyen Age', *Senefiance*, 47:325–37, is a brief but sensitive analysis of the possibility and role of nudity in medieval drama. J. Tolmie, 'Framing persuasion: Eve and the fall of the verbal order', *Mediaevalia*, 20:93–118, applies Freudian analysis to the *Jeu d'Adam*. The play describes a reversal in the 'natural' order of things, where Eve becomes the dominant partner. Feminine counsel is read as a form of male ventriloquism: the marital state must model woman's verbal and educative relationship to man on man's relationship with God. Monique Lagarde and Claude Lachet, *Aucassin et Nicolette*, L'École des Loisirs, 2000, 116 pp., is a Modern French adaptation. The prose sections closely follow the OF text, but the verse sections are translated more freely: L. and L. seek to preserve the spirit of the verse by respecting metre and rhyming patterns.

HISTORIOGRAPHY AND CHRONICLE. C. Hanley, 'Reading the past through the present: Ambroise, the Minstrel of Reims, and Jordan Fantosme', *Mediaevalia*, 20:263–82, examines the circumstances prevailing at the time of composition of three chronicles pertaining to a same theme: warring kings (the Third Crusade, 1187–92, and the war between Henry II of England and the Young Henry, 1173–74). It is vital to consider the 'hidden agenda' of a work of historiography in order to grasp more fully details and patterns of emphasis whose significance would otherwise be lost. M. Thiry-Stassin, 'Ygerne entre Geoffroy de Monmouth et Wace', Dor, *Conjointure*, 109–21, highlights the divergent depictions in the *Historia regum Britanniae* and *Brut* which result from the differences in both period and audience. C. Croizy-Naquet, 'Prologues et épilogues dans quelques textes historiques du XIIIe siècle', *BDBA*, 19:77–90, addresses the ways in which these writings use the division between Latin and vernacular, verse and prose to create new criteria for relating the past. C.-N. further develops this line of enquiry in 'Deux représentations de la troisième croisade: l'*Estoire de la guerre sainte* et la *Chronique d'Ernoul et de Bernard le*

Trésorier', *CCMe*, 44:313–27, which analyses how Ambroise, in writing the former, gives a partial account in verse, compared with Ernoul's dispassionate prose.

LATE MEDIEVAL LITERATURE

By NICOLE LASSAHN, *University of Chicago*

1. NARRATIVE GENRES

A. Allen, 'La mélancolie du biographe: *Le Roman du Castelain du Couci et le deuil de la voix*', *Neophilologus*, 85 : 25–41, examines the relationship of this narrative to the trouvère voice through an analysis of lyric insertions. U. Jokinen, 'Vice, vertu, jouissance: réflexions sur les *Cent Nouvelles Nouvelles*', pp. 293–99 of *Langage et référence*, ed. H. Kronning et al. (AUU, SRU, 63), 712 pp., looks at vice, virtue, and *jouissance*; C. Azueilsa, 'L'avant dernier récit des *Cent Nouvelles nouvelles*: une anti-Griselda du XVe siècle', *CN*, 61 : 361–81, argues that *nouvelle* 99 in this *c.* 1492 manuscript version is an intertextual game in dialogue with Boccaccio's Griselda, questioning the idea of adding morals to literary tales. H. White, *Nature, Sex, and Goodness in a Medieval Literary Tradition*, OUP, 2000, 278 pp., re-examines the consensus that the medieval Nature is automatically connected with a Christian God or with Reason. The work as a whole is comparative; the two French chapters (4 and 5) concentrate on the *Rose* and the 15th c. *querelle* over it. M. Szkilnik, 'Nourriture et blasons dans *Jehan de Saintré* d'Antoine de la Salle (1451)', *FCS*, 26 : 183–99, re-examines the opposition between the two men of the love triangle as an opposition between the two places of the *roman*: the abbey and the court; G. Angelo, 'Author and authority in the *Evangiles des quenouilles*', *ib.*, 21–41, re-examines the relationship of orality to written text by comparing the earlier version of this text with the later version which includes a male authority and a move toward the written.

Work in gender and queer studies includes S. Carden, 'Poetic justice: the revenge of La Guignarde in the *Livre des Cent Ballades*', Krause, *Heroine*, 133–51, who reassesses the role of La Guignarde beyond the conventions of her source in the *Rose*'s La Vieille, and sees her, rather, as challenging the foundations of courtly language convention, exposing its fundamental inconsistencies; A. Pairet, 'Melusine's double binds: foundation, transgression, and the genealogical romance', *ib.*, 71–86, argues that genealogical narrative reflects the political instability of the 100 years war; the foundation of the fortress by Melusine makes her both transgressive and stable since she is the founding mother; D. Wrisley, 'Women's voices raised in prayer: on the "epic credo" in Adenet le Roi's *Berte as grans piés*', *ib.*, 53–68, claiming that their status as prayer renders these women's voices universal, and argues that female vernacular speech, especially prayer, provides both exemplary female protagonists and Adenet's own vernacular voice; and C. Lucken, 'Woman's cry: broken language, marital disputes, and the poetics of medieval farce', *ib.*, 152–79, examines misogynistic conventions of women in medieval farce: although the farce always paints them in a bad light, it cannot exist as a genre without this stock character. L. locates the fundamental idea as the farcical woman's noisiness, which is opposed to the courtly woman as a 'tower of silence'.

F. Sautman, ' "Just like a woman": queer history, womanizing the body, and the boys in Arnaud's band', Burger, *Queering*, 168–89, argues against the role of women as heteronormative figures in 'traditional' queer readings in the treatment of Baudouin de Sebourc, Froissart's account of Despenser, and the story of Arnaud de Vernoille found in Inquisition records. Id., 'What can they possibly do together? Queer epic performances in *Tristan de Nanteuil*', pp. 199–232 of *Same Sex Love and Desire among Women in the Middle Ages*, ed. Francesca Canade Sautman and Pamela Sheingorn, NY, Palgrave, 312 pp., explores two late-medieval examples of cross-dressed women whose marital and sexual bonds with another woman are normalized when one woman becomes a biological man and gets an heir. F. Jurney, 'Secret identities: (un)masking gender in *Le Roman de Silence* by Heldris de Cornouaille and *L'Enfant de sable* by Tahar Ben Jelloun', *DFS*, 55:3–10, compares the *Roman de Silence* to the 1985 novel in terms of transvestism both as socio-political phenomenon and part of the protagonists' identity formation.

M. Colombo-Timelli, '*Le Purgatoire des mauvais maris* et *l'Enfer des mauvaises femmes*', *Romania*, 119:483–505, is a detailed textual history of these two texts in terms of the relationship between them created in part by that textual history. J. Boro, 'The textual history of *Huon of Burdeux*: a reassessment of the facts', *NQ*, 48:233–37. D. Burrows, '*Do Con, do vet et de la soriz*: édition d'un texte tiré de Berne 354', *ZRP*, 117:23–49, is a critical edition, with commentary on its closest sources, of this brief piece from a manuscript compiled in the first half of the 14th century. *La Chanson de Croissant en prose du XVeme siecle*, ed. M. Raby, NY, Lang, 141 pp., is a critical edition of the prose version of this continuation of Huon de Bordeaux; it uses early printed copies as base texts. Bernard Ribémont has re-edited Nicole de Margival's dream poem, the *Dit de la Panthère* (CFMA), Champion, 2000, 152 pp. *Chevalerie et grivoiserie: fabliaux de chevalerie*, ed. and trans. J.-L. Leclanche (CFMA), Champion, 283 pp., is a critical edition of five fabliaux of this sub-genre which engages the courtly narrative, all with facing-page modern French translation. *Les Trois Fils de rois*, ed. G. Palumbo (CFMA), Champion, 633 pp. Four volumes have also appeared in the TLF series: *Perceforest. Deuxième partie*, II, ed. G. Roussineau, 784 pp.; Octovien de Saint-Gelais, *Le Séjour d'honneur*, ed.

F. Duval, 534 pp.; *Histoire de la Reine Berthe et du Roy Pépin: mise en prose d'une chanson de geste*, ed. P. Tylus, 348 pp.; and Jean Wauquelin, *La Belle Hélène de Constantinople*, ed. M. C. de Crécy, 800 pp. René d'Anjou, *The Book of Love Smitten Heart*, ed. and trans. K. Karczewska and S. Gibbs, NY, Garland, 228 pp.

2. POETRY

Studies of Christine de Pizan include M. Amsler, 'Rape and silence: Ovid's mythography and medieval readers', pp. 61–96 of *Representing Rape in Medieval and Early Modern Literature*, ed. Elizabeth Robertson and Christine M. Rose, NY, Palgrave, 453 pp., who argues that medieval readers of Ovid, especially of the *Ovide moralisé*, tend to elide or erase his explicit accounts of rape by allegorizing them; M. Desmond and P. Sheingorn, 'Queering Ovidian myth: bestiality and desire in Christine de Pizan's *Epistre Othea*', Burger, *Queering*, 3–27, who examine Christine's visually-centered adaptation of Ovid as a queering of his idea of metamorphosis.

I. Bétemps, 'La figure du poète dans le *Voir Dit*: du cœur d'amant au testam(a)nt', *Littératures*, 45:5–22, reconsiders the figure of the poet within the *Voir Dit* using a link between love and poetic creation with respect to the narrator as *fin amant*. There is also a new translation of Machaut's *Capture of Alexandria* by J. Shirlet, Hampshire, Ashgate, 218 pp. R. Boenig, 'Musical instruments as iconographical artifacts in medieval poetry', pp. 1–15 of *Material Culture and Cultural Materialisms in the Middle Ages and Renaissance*, ed. C. Perry, Turnhout, Brepols, 246 pp., treats Machaut's *Remède de Fortune*. K. Krause, 'The material erotic: the clothed and unclothed female body in the *Roman de la violette*', *ib.*, 17–39, presents a feminist approach to eroticism in Gerbert de Montreuil.

Two very differing studies of Charles d'Orléans are A. E. B. Coldiron, 'Toward a comparative New Historicism: land tenures and some fifteenth-century poems', *CL*, 53:97–116, who, arguing against monolingual assumptions within previous historicist criticism, focuses on the tri-lingual poet Charles d'Orléans, finding that the poetic sequences in French and English are politically different when read in a trans-cultural context; and G. Gros, 'Le Livre du prince et le clerc: édition, diffusion et réception d'une œuvre (Martin le Franc lecteur de Charles d'Orléans)', *TLit*, 14:43–58, who uses the terms *clerc* and *prince* to examine Martin le Franc's relationship as reader of Charles d'Orléans.

H. Dell, 'Voices, "realities" and narrative style in the anonymous *chansons de toile*', *Parergon*, 18:17–33, examines female voice in 16 anonymous *chansons de toile* in order to test D. Earnshaw's hypothesis about the female voice in lyric poetry. P. Michon, 'Une édition manuscrite d'Eustache Deschamps: le double lay de la fragilité humaine', *TLit*, 14:27–41, compares the version of this poem in Paris, BNF, f. fr. 20029, a collected works manuscript compiled posthumously, with that in BNF, f. fr. 840, a presentation copy for the King of France. N. Bordessoule, ' "Fine words on closed ears": impertinent women, discordant voices, discourteous words', Krause, *Heroine*, 123–32, argues for new representations of women in the late middle ages (*c.* 1275–1500), representations in which the courtly heritage of these characters is challenged and even subverted. B. takes the *Rose*'s La Vieille as a starting point, and examines in particular Jehan Acart de Hesdin's *La Prise Amoureuse* (1322) and Chartier's *La Belle Dame sans merci*.

Musicologists continue to contribute to textual studies of lyric poetry in the period: D. Humphreys, 'A study in emulation: Philip van Wilder's *En despit des envyeulx*', *EMus*, 29:93–106; and A. Stone, 'A singer at the fountain: homage and irony in Ciconia's 'Sus une fontayne', *MusL*, 82:361–90, which examines the relationship of this French work to its quoted source, Filippetto de Caserta.

Two studies treat larger questions of literary period and development: J. Cerquiglini-Toulet, 'A la recherche des pères: la liste des auteurs illustres à la fin du Moyen Age', *MLN*, 116:630–43, argues for a new kind of power in the 14th c. based on personal glory and poetic renown, which is related to extant concepts of sovereignty, and uses both lyric and narrative poetry in her analysis; while A. Armstrong, 'Paratexte et autorité(s) chez les grands rhétoriqueurs', *TLit*, 14:61–89, considers the authority of these late poets, especially Jean Lemaire de Belges and Jean Bouchet, in terms of the visual and paratextual resources available with the coming of mechanical reproduction and the printing press.

3. DRAMA

K. Schoell, 'Actor, scene, and audience of the fifteenth-century French farce: the farce in the light of the semiotics of performance', *FCS*, 26:158–68, reconsiders French farce as a genre, using a semiotic approach to the historical question of their performance. G. Runnalls, 'Les mystères à Paris et en Île-de-France à la fin du moyen âge: l'apport de six actes notariés', *Romania*, 119:113–69, examines textual evidence and evidence about historical performance for some very late mystery plays in order to address the question of why the flourishing 15th-c. dramatic life of Paris has left so little written documentation. S. Pietrini, 'Medieval ideas of the ancient actor and

Roman theater', *Early Drama, Art, and Music Review*, 24:1–21, treats medieval acting and staging.

Les Mystères de la Procession de Lille: 1: *La Pentateuque*, ed. Alan E. Knight, Geneva, Droz, 632 pp., contains 12 pieces from the 72 mystery plays performed for the procession at Lille which began about 1270. The single manuscript from which they have been edited is of the 15th century.

4. HISTORICAL AND POLITICAL LITERATURE

N. Black, '*La Belle Hélène de Constantinople* and crusade propaganda at the court of Philip the Good', *FCS*, 26:42–51, examining this 15th-c. translation of a 14th-c. *chanson de geste* as historical fiction, argues that the version found in Brussels, Bibliothèque Royale, 9967, promotes Philip of Burgundy's political and religious crusade agenda. J. Cohen, 'On Saracen enjoyment: some fantasies of race in late medieval France and England', *JMEMS*, 31:113–46, uses psychoanalytic theory, especially that of Kristeva, to discuss the construction of the idea of race in late medieval France and England, especially the concept of the Muslim as Saracen. Though most English examples are of the 14th c., the French sources (e.g. Benoît de Sainte-Maure and the *Chronique des ducs de Normandie*) are somewhat earlier. N. Hochner, '*Pierre Gringore*: une satire à la solde du pouvoir', *FCS*, 26:102–120, investigates the paradox whereby Louis XII is portrayed favourably even while a substantial critique of misrule and abuse is simultaneously offered. E. DuBruck, 'Pope Joan: another look upon Martin le Franc's *Papesse Jeanne* (*c.* 1440) and Dietrich Schernberg's play *Frau Jutta* (1480)', *ib.*, 75–85, compares German and French accounts, claiming that Martin le Franc's version rehabilitates Joan using terms like those from the *querelle des femmes*.

Three works have appeared on Froissart's historical writing: G. Diller, 'Romanesque construct in Froissart's *Chroniques*: the case of Pierre de Craon and Louis d'Orléans', *FCS*, 26:66–74, argues that Froissart grafts an Arthurian, romanesque structure on to his narrative of Charles VI's frenzy in 1392; C. Sponsler, 'The king's boyfriend: Froissart's political theater of 1326', Burger, *Queering*, 143–67, argues that Froissart narrates the events of 1326 as a contest between Hugh Despenser and Queen Isabella even though other contemporary accounts describe it mostly as a matter of Edward's mishandling of patronage; and L. Stock, 'What gets lost in translation: the "Englishing" of Froissart's *Chroniques* from the sixteenth century to the present', *MedP*, 16:117–34, argues that the two English translations currently used — usually cited uncritically by literary scholars looking to historical context — reflect the Tudor and

Victorian mores of their translators as much as those of Froissart's own culture.

Four essays have been published on Christine's non-literary work: D. Bohler, 'Un regard sur Christine de Pizan', *Clio*, 13:117–23, examines Christine as a female intellectual in a male world; B. considers both her relationship to her father as Pygmalion figure and how her female status affects her fit into public-private dichotomy; J. Ruud, 'Medieval woman writing medieval woman: Christine de Pizan's *Ditié de Jehanne d'Arc*', pp. 73–88 of *Proceedings of the Eighth Annual Northern Plains Conference on Earlier British Literature*, ed. Robert J. De Smith, Sioux Center, Dordt College, 98 pp., argues for adding this text to English survey courses on the grounds that it provides a more accurate view of medieval literature's international quality in two ways: the engagement of the female voice with the authority of the clerk and with that of women's visionary literature provide a background for works like the Wife of Bath's prologue and Margery Kempe's book; C. Le Brun-Gouanvic, 'Christine de Pizan et l'édification de la cité éternelle', *EF*, 37:51–65, considering her didactic works, examines how Christine integrates the political and religious thinking of her time into an original treatment; she uses the Christian doctrine of the eternal to rework the secular ideas of posthumous glory emerging in nascent humanism; and E. Lanz, 'Las enseñanzas de *Le Livre des trois vertus* à l'enseignement des dames de Christine de Pizan y sus primeras lecturas', *CN*, 61:335–360, uses the manuscript tradition, especially Christine's dedications to Isabelle de France and Marguerite of Bourbon, as a guide to 15th-c. readership and interpretation.

Philippe de Commynes, *Lettres*, ed. J. Blanchard (TLF), 335 pp. Marco Polo, *Le Devisement du monde*, 1: *Départ des voyageurs et traversée de la Perse*, ed. P. Ménard et al. (TLF), 285 pp. F. Duval, *La Traduction du 'Romuleon' par Sébastien Mamerot. Etude sur la diffusion de l'histoire romaine en langue vernaculaire*, Geneva, Droz, 480 pp., is a study of the translation relationship between Latin and vernacular versions.

5. Religious, Moral, and Didactic Literature

A. Hedeman, *Of Counselors and Kings: The Three Versions of Pierre Salmon's Dialogues*, Urbana, Illinois U.P., 123 pp., reads these dialogues in the context of Charles VI. I. Black, 'The theatricality of marriage in two late medieval narrative texts', *DFS*, 56:6–16, claims that Deschamps's *Miroir de Mariage* and the anonymous *XV Joies de Mariage*, though both narrative works, use dramatic techniques to portray 'real' marriage through the filter of theatricality. A. Cowell, 'Advertising, rhetoric, and literature: a medieval response to contemporary theory', *PoetT*, 22 : 795–827, argues against the idea that advertising is fundamentally 'unpoetic' by connecting it with rhetoric. C. Vulliez, 'L'ars dictaminis, survivances et déclin, dans la moitié nord de l'espace français dans le Moyen Age tardif (mil. XIIIe–mil. XVe siècles)', *Rhetorica*, 19 : 141–53, is on manuals of rhetoric in the later middle ages.

Medieval conduct books are discussed by K. Ashley, 'The *Miroir des bonnes femmes*: not for women only?', Ashley, *Conduct*, 86–105, who compares the actual readers and owners of the *Miroir des bonnes femmes* with the hypothetical audience (the books are explicitly written for women); A. argues that this engenders not a reflection of these actual audiences but rather a part of the formation of a bourgeois ethos; R. Clark, 'Constructing the female subject in late medieval devotion', *ib.*, 160–82, argues that we can determine something about female subjectivity from conduct books despite the seemingly passive attitude they ask of their audience, because the conduct books consistently 'overreach' simple practice, showing a negotiation of the idea of subjecthood; R. Krueger, ' "Nouvelles choses": social instability and the problem of fashion in the *Livre du chevalier de La Tour Landry*, the *Ménagier de Paris*, and Christine de Pizan's *Livre des trois vertus*', *ib.*, 49–85, explores the simultaneous rise of conduct books and ideas of women's fashion to argue that both attempt, in different ways, to 'navigate ambivalence of social identity' during a period of social change.

Three essays on French Boethian literature and translations are printed in *Carmina Philosophiae*, 10: K. Atkinson, 'A *dit contre Fortune*, the Medieval French Boethian *Consolatio* contained in MS Paris, Bibliothèque Nationale, fr. 25418' (1–22), argues that this verse translation is an abridgement of Renaut's *Roman de Fortune et de Felicité*; G. Cropp, 'An Italian translation of *Le Livre de Boèce de Consolacion*' (23–30), argues that this Italian version is based on the unglossed French version; and J. Evans, 'Peter de Rivo and the problem of future contingents' (39–55), argues that the 15th-c. Rivo's political situation affects his solution of the Boethian problem of free will.

F. Meltzer, *For Fear of the Fire: Joan of Arc and the Limits of Subjectivity*, Chicago U.P., 248 pp., sees Joan as a liminal figure at the very beginning of the modern age and of subjectivity; S. Richards, 'Keeping up with the Maid of Orléans: Joan of Arc in literature and film', *PhilP*, 47 : 37–43, traces the ways Joan has been used in the later historical periods in which she was received and remade.

Marguerite Porete is the subject of two works: A. Hollywood, *Sensible Ecstasy: Mysticism, Sexual Difference, and the Demands of History*, Chicago U.P., 371 pp.; and J. Robinson, *Nobility and Annihilation in Marguerite Porete's 'Mirror of simple souls'*, Albany, SUNY, 178 pp.

THE SIXTEENTH CENTURY

By GILLES BANDERIER, *Basle*

1. GENERAL

An indispensable guide from henceforth, for all those who study French 16th-c. poetry, will be Jean Paul Barbier's life achievement, *Ma bibliothèque poétique*, Part 4, vol. 2: 'Contemporains et successeurs de Ronsard. De Desportes à La Boétie', Geneva, Droz, 600 pp. The volume is lavishly illustrated. The most renowned writer in this new volume is Philippe Desportes, and the 22 oldest editions of his works (all in the possession of the Genevan book lover) are minutely described, but we can also meet such highly estimable poets as Robert Garnier, Jacques Grévin, and Amadis Jamyn.

Half a century after its first edition, the long awaited overhaul of the comprehensive *Dictionnaire des lettres françaises — le XVIe siècle*, Librairie Générale Française, 1218 pp., has been brought to completion by the late lamented Michel Simonin. It is not a mere reprint, but a complete revision, containing 2,400 separate entries. The articles on major writers (such as Marot, Rabelais, Ronsard, d'Aubigné) or literary genres (epic, sonnet, novel, etc.) have been brought up to date. This is a highly important tool of reference, which should always be to hand.

Madeleine Lazard, *Les Avenues de Fémynie*, Fayard, 438 pp., is an eminently readable book on a still hardly known and often caricatured subject. Under headings such as 'La femme théorique', 'Le regard de la société', 'L'union conjugale', 'Misères de la vie conjugale', this magisterial synthesis deals with topics as different as love, marriage, work, pregnancy, childbirth, prostitution, the religious life, education and writing, with queens as well as with whores.

The complete *Correspondance* of Théodore de Bèze continues on its way, and volume 23, ed. Alain Dufour, Béatrice Nicollier, and Hervé Genton (THR, 346), 302 pp., gathers the letters written during the year 1582. One may then read 'Le dit et le non-dit dans la correspondance de Théodore de Bèze', *L'Epistolaire*, 135–39, by A. Dufour, the greatest authority on Bezean studies.

2. HISTORY OF THE BOOK

Book history most often concerns the description of printed books, yet we must not forget the huge quantity of manuscripts produced during the 16th century. M. D. Orth, 'French Renaissance manuscripts and *L'Histoire du Livre*', *Viator*, 32:245–78, deals mostly with secular illuminated manuscripts from 1515 to 1547.

Rodolphe Peter, Jean-François Gilmont, and Christian Krieger, *Bibliotheca Calviniana. Les livres de Jean Calvin publiés au XVIe siècle* (THR, 339), 2000, 680 pp., is the third volume of this paragon of bibliographical precision and describes the editions and translations (into e.g. Latin, Spanish, Dutch, German) which appeared from Calvin's death up to the end of the 16th century. Five indexes (printers and stationers, proper names, places and two for titles) complete this magnificent research tool.

L. Van Delft, 'Le concept de théâtre dans la culture classique', *RZLG*, 25:73–85, discusses the point that titles given to books have much to do with the *Weltanschauung* of an age. After Curtius, there is no point in insisting on how important the metaphor of *theatrum* could be. Numerous books include the polysemic word on their title pages and this may be a key to the Renaissance mind.

Several studies are devoted to the Estienne dynasty of printers and lexicographers. B. Boudou, 'Henri Estienne éditeur d'historiens, ou comment écrire l'histoire?', *NRSS*, 19.1:37–50, studies Estienne as a printer of historical works, with a predilection for Greek historians (see also Id., 'Le *Commentariolus* de Henri Estienne sur la *Correspondance* de Cicéron', *L'Epistolaire*, 33–49). But Estienne was also a man of his time, concerned about contemporary events, and an avid reader of *canards*, as we read in Id., 'Le chroniqueur du temps présent dans l'*Apologie pour Hérodote*', *Dubois Vol.*, 51–62. The lexicographical activity is studied by M. Furno, 'Le mariage de Calepin et du *Thesaurus*, sous l'olivier de Robert Estienne, à Genève, en 1553', *BHR*, 63:511–32. Stating that '[Henri] Estienne has been [. . .] one of the most injustly neglected figures in early modern intellectual history', J. Considine devotes an article to 'The lexicographer as hero: Samuel Johnson and Henri Estienne', *PQ*, 79:205–24.

Another stationers' dynasty, which published for instance Montaigne and Du Bartas, is studied by M. Simonin, 'La culture d'un couple de marchands-libraires: les L'Angelier au premier pilier du Palais (1574–1620)', *RFHL*, 106–09, 2000:49–70, and J. Balsamo, 'Les étrennes d'Abel L'Angelier. Quelques remarques d'histoire du livre et d'histoire littéraire', *Bertaud Vol.*, 107–20.

Bibliography has a history too and A. Cullière, 'Pour une préhistoire littéraire. La Croix du Maine et la rumeur', *Bertaud Vol.*, 81–90, reminds us of a time long ago, when compiling a bibliography was not a purely scientific task. What did men of the Renaissance read and how did they read? New insights are provided by J.-M. Chatelain, 'Humanisme et culture de la note', *Revue de la B.N.F.*, 1999.2:26–36, and L. Lobbes, 'Les recueils de citations au XVIe siècle: inventaire', Roig Miranda, *Transmission*, 127–37. Looking through these collections of authoritative quotations, L. distinguishes between adage, proverb, maxim, and *apophthegmata* properly speaking.

3. Humanism, Theology, and the History of Ideas

Florence Vuilleumier Laurens, *La Raison des figures symboliques à la Renaissance et à l'âge classique. Etudes sur les fondements philosophiques, théologiques et rhétoriques de l'image* (THR, 340), 2000, 542 pp., will be an essential for every well-supplied research library, and for those studying the 16th c., even if a part of this fascinating synthesis concerns the 17th c. It considers the theory of images through devices, emblems, inscriptions, and ceremonies such as funerals or entries, and deals with theoreticians like Masen, Caussin, and Tesauro.

Poétiques de la Renaissance. Le modèle italien, le monde franco-bourguignon et leur héritage en France au XVIe siècle, ed. Perine Galand-Hallyn and Fernand Hallyn, foreword by Terence Cave (THR, 348), 788 pp., is an invaluable and also massive book, exploring the transition between the 15th and 16th centuries. 'L'hypothèse de départ [. . .] est que la poétique renaissante française doit sa constitution à un double héritage. A la faveur des échanges entre l'Italie et la France, que viennent intensifier les guerres d'Italie, les poètes du XVIe siècle français voient se rejoindre et se fondre, non sans débats parfois ardents, une tradition nationale, d'origine médiévale, aujourd'hui couramment désignée sous le nom de rhétorique seconde, et l'héritage humaniste du Quattrocento italien, lui-même issu [. . .] de la redécouverte et de l'exploitation des doctrines poétiques et rhétoriques de l'Antiquité gréco-romaine.'

Documents oubliés sur l'alchimie, la kabbale et Guillaume Postel offerts, à l'occasion de son 90e anniversaire, à François Secret par ses élèves et amis, ed. Sylvain Matton (THR, 353), 470 pp. This *Festschrift* for a great scholar, who devoted his life to the dark side of the Renaissance (esotericism and the Kabbala), includes among other papers five studies on Guillaume Postel, by C. Gilly, J.-F. Maillard, J.-P. Brach, W. Kirsop, and V. Neveu. In his introductory note, Sylvain Matton observes that François Secret has always attached the greatest importance to 'le document (souvent oublié ou inconnu) plutôt que la glose, les faits plutôt que les interprétations, et les études ponctuelles, mais très précises, plutôt que les vues générales prétendument synthétiques qui se révèlent trop fréquemment prématurées et infondées.' These words should be remembered by every Renaissance scholar and might become a lapidary inscription at the pediment of research institutes.

Following *Pré-histoires* (*YWMLS*, 61:96–97) and published in the same series edited by M. Jeanneret and M. Engammare, Terence Cave's *Pré-histoires II. Langues étrangères et troubles économiques au XVIe siècle*, Geneva, Droz, 216 pp. is not only a book on Rabelais. It is nevertheless clear that the first part relies chiefly on Rabelaisian materials, while the second is based on economic theories, with a fine interpretation of Jean Bodin's *Response à M. de Malestroit*.

Jean Calvin, *Sermons sur la Genèse*, ed. Max Engammare (*Supplementa Calviniana*, XI.1 and 2), 2 vols, Neukirchen-Vluyn, Neukirchener Vlg, 2000, lxviii + 1182 pp., deserves inclusion here, although pulpit oratory is not usually regarded as literature. This excellent edition displays an impressive breadth of scholarship and provides an in-depth commentary on almost 100 sermons preached by the Genevan reformer. Editing his preaching is not easy, and the city of Geneva can hardly be proud to have sold 45 manuscript volumes of Calvin's sermons as old paper for bookbinders or booksellers in 1805! The editor has based his work on Bodleian Library MS 740. Another study on Calvin's preaching is that of Wilhelmus H. Th. Moehn, '*God calls us to his service*'. *The Relation between God and his Audience in Calvin's Sermons on Acts* (THR, 345), 280 pp. (See also p. 80.)

According to J. Céard, 'Nature et culture à la Renaissance: quelques réflexions sur la naissance du concept de culture', *RZLG*, 25:65–72, the opposition between *nature* and *culture* (which belongs essentially to the Age of Enlightenment) is not relevant for Renaissance studies. It would be better to distinguish *physis* (nature) and *thesis* (convention), nature and custom, or nature and art.

U. Langer, 'Vertus du sujet, vertu du prince à l'aube de l'absolutisme en France', pp. 117–28 of *Fonder les savoirs, fonder les pouvoirs (XVe–XVIIe siècles)*, ed. D. de Courcelles, Ecole des Chartes, 2000, 144 pp., studies the relations between ethics and rhetoric in eulogies of the King. On a related field, see J. Vignes, 'Inspiration poétique et faveur du prince chez Marot, Du Bellay et Ronsard', *Gendre Vol.*, 35–48; and M. Bideaux, 'La libéralité du prince: entre chevalerie et humanisme', *Dubois Vol.*, 257–67.

Literary salons were not a 17th-c. invention and they already played an important part in Renaissance France, though little is known about them. G. Schrenck, 'Marguerite de Valois et son monde, ou la chambre bruissante', Marchal, *Salons*, 167–72, makes his contribution to our knowledge of the famous Queen's intellectual life.

4.   POETRY AND PROSE

Is it a sign of the times that memoirs are given great critical attention? N. Kuperty-Tsur, 'Le moi, sujet de l'histoire', *NRSS*, 19.1:63–81, provides an interpretation of 'le genre dans son ensemble', in order to define a taxonomy. In a further article, 'Argumentation, facteurs sociaux et politiques à l'origine du genre des mémoires à la Renaissance en France', Wild, *Genre*, II, 199–216, she also remarks that 'les Mémoires s'écrivent dans une visée apologétique pour redorer un blason terni par la diffamation'. C.-G. Dubois's contribution, 'L'individu comme moteur historiographique: formes de la biographie dans la période 1560–1600', *NRSS*, 19.1:83–105, is a revision of a paper first published in the *Histoire comparée des littératures de langues européennes*, Amsterdam–Philadelphia, Benjamins, 2000, vol. IV, 271–83, and provides a rare study of French memoirs from a comparative viewpoint. The memoirs of Philippe Duplessis-Mornay's wife, born Charlotte Arbaleste, are examined by N. Kuperty-Tsur, 'Rhétorique des témoignages protestants autour de la Saint-Barthélemy. Le cas des *Mémoires* de Charlotte Duplessis-Mornay', *Elseneur*, 17:159–78, and by P.-L. Vaillancourt, 'Charlotte de Mornay dans la tourmente de la Saint-Barthélemy', *Dubois Vol.*, 127–36.

On the Renaissance short story in general and how it managed to win acclaim thanks to its didactic side, see K. Blaïech-Ajroud, 'La nouvelle française de la Renaissance: un souci de légitimation', Wild, *Genre*, II, 95–106.

5. Theatre and Rhetoric

Comedy was a neglected genre in Renaissance France. O. Millet, 'La comédie française de la Renaissance comme jeu parodique avec la tragédie et les genres littéraires élevés', *Bertaud Vol.*, 449–66, points out how it tried to define itself in relation to the high genre of tragedy, by the means of parody. This process reached its highest point in the invention of tragi-comedy.

J.-D. Beaudin, 'Formes de la beauté scénique dans le théâtre de Robert Garnier', *NRSS*, 18.2, 2000:93–112. It has frequently been said that humanist tragedies were for reading only. Even if this statement is true for a dramatist like Du Monin, it is not so for Garnier, who took care over the representation of his tragedies. The article by A. Osawa, 'Considérations sur l'expression du regard dans *Bradamante* de Robert Garnier', *RevAR*, 14:35–50, is unfortunately (for non-Japanese readers) in Japanese, with an alluring French summary.

M. Cassan, 'La tragédie *Regulus* (1582) au miroir des guerres de religion', *BHR*, 63:87–103, is a political interpretation of the Roman tragedy by J. de Beaubrueil. A more thematic analysis is given by C. de Buzon, 'Action et passions: l'amour de la patrie et le pathétique dans *Regulus*', *Dubois Vol.*, 63–77.

J. Braybrook, 'Remy Belleau's *La Reconnue* and Niccolò Machia-velli's *Clizia*', *RenS*, 15:1–16, is a study on Renaissance processes of imitation. Belleau probably never read a single line by Machiavelli, but both imitate Plautus's *Casina*.

6. EMBLEMATICA

On relationships between literature and emblems, the article by P. Eichel-Lojkine, '*Seneca se necans*', *NRSS*, 19.1:107–47, studies how the death of the Roman philosopher is presented in Boissard's *Theatrum vitae humanae* (1596) and Thevet's *Vrais pourtraits et vies* (1584).

Relations between emblem collections and printers' marks are seldom analysed. A. Adams, 'Georgette de Montenay and the device of the Dordrecht printer François Bosselaer', *BHR*, 63:63–72, shows the link between Montenay's eighth emblem and the devices of the Dutch printer, who has obviously taken them from Montenay's collection (for she was a Protestant writer); see also Id., 'Georgette de Montenay's *Emblemes ou devises chrestiennes*, 1567, new dating, new context', *ib.*, 567–74. On the fringe of emblematic studies, T. Tran Quoc examines the engravings of 'Le *Marquetis* d'Antoine du Saix: du recueil comme mosaïque à l'emblème comme signature', *ib.*, 575–95. However instructive the article may be, the poor quality of illustrations has to be deplored.

7. INDIVIDUAL AUTHORS

D'AUBIGNÉ. The year's major event is unquestionably Gilbert Schrenck's bibliography on *Agrippa d'Aubigné*, Memini, 244 pp., which, under headings such as 'Manuscrits', 'Editions', 'Etudes biblio-graphiques', 'Etudes générales', 'Lectures critiques', lists more than 1000 precise references of books and articles, each with a few lines of commentary. This is a valuable guide in an ever-growing forest.

Agrippa d'Aubigné is the only great 16th-c. writer whose work is not completely available in print today. Recently some new texts or new versions of already known pieces have come to light, mainly from the Tronchin collection kept in the Geneva Public and University Library, and have been dealt with in a series of articles by G. Banderier: 'Une lettre d'A. d'A.' *BSHPF*, 145, 1999:475–84, concerns a long letter to Henri de La Tour, duke of Bouillon, which as well as its biographical value, sheds light on the writing of the *Tragiques*; Id., '"À la France delivrée" d'A. d'A.: quelques variantes inédites', *BHR*, 62, 2000:647–51; Id., 'A. d'A. et Louis XIII: un texte inédit', *FSB*, 79:4–8, presents the first sketch of a never printed and caustic satire against the King; Id., 'A. d'A. et la Valteline: un texte inédit', *PFSCL*, 28, 54:141–51, edits a report on a planned military raid against Spain; Id., 'En marge du *Traitté sur les guerres civiles*: un texte inédit d'A. d'A.', *BSHPF*, 147:285–303, deals with a political treatise written at the beginning of his Genevan exile; Id., 'A. d'A. et la bataille du Pertuis-Breton', *AHSA*, 55:257–84, discusses an ironical narration of a forgotten battle; (see also *TWMLS* 61:111–12). G. Banderier has also briefly studied d'Aubigné's political conceptions in 'Henri IV et la paix: Du Bartas, d'Aubigné, Jeannin', *Paix des armes, paix des âmes*, ed. P. Mironneau et I. Pébay-Clottes, Imprimerie Nationale, 2000, 381–94.

A famous page of the *Tragiques* depicts the soul of Coligny, after his beheading, gazing from heaven at the slaughter and laughing. G. Nakam, 'Le rire de l'amiral Coligny dans l'architecture des *Tragiques*', *Charpentier Vol.*, 203–24, stresses the importance of this episode. The violent description may be a recollection from Prudentius's narration of the martyrdom of St Agnes (d'Aubigné was an avid reader and familiar with Latin poetry). The influences of Prudentius and Vida on the *Tragiques* are studied in G. Banderier, ' "Quelque chose qui se puisse appeler Œuvre": les *Tragiques* d'A. d'A. et leurs modèles', *SN*, 73:197–210. On the links between the *Tragiques* and the *Histoire Universelle*, we may read A. Hamada, 'Du sang et de l'eau dans le livre "Les Fers" des *Tragiques*', *RevAR*, 14:93–102.

Albineana, 13, 262 pp., is devoted to the prose works, with studies by M.-H. Prat, 'L'écriture des *Lettres de poincts de science*' (15–33); C.-G. Dubois, 'De l'étrange au surnaturel' (35–51); M.-M. Fragonard, 'Les *Missives et discours militaires*' (53–70); B. Ertlé, 'A. d'A. et ses destinataires dans la correspondance' (71–83); M. Soulié, 'Le surnaturel dans l'*Histoire Universelle*' (87–96); G. Banderier, 'A propos de la deuxième édition de l'*Histoire Universelle*: une lettre adressée à A. d'A.' (97–104), and Id., 'La réception d'A. d'A. hier et aujourd'hui' (241–55), concerning the discovery in Oxford, Bodleian Library, MS Tanner 260 of the first (and only) English translation of the *Histoire Universelle*, undertaken by William Whiteway (1599–1635); N. Kuperty-Tsur, 'Aspects de la rhétorique d'A. d'A. dans *Sa Vie à ses enfants*' (105–18); V. Ferrer, 'Derniers feux d'un genre: les *Méditations sur les Pseaumes*' (119–31); G. Mathieu-Castellani, 'L'imaginaire judiciaire dans le traité *Du debvoir mutuel des roys et des subjects*' (135–51); E. Kotler, 'De quelques aspects de l'argumentation dans la *Confession du sieur de Sancy*' (153–68); G. Schrenck, 'Aspects de la réception du *Sancy*' (169–78); C. Fantoni, 'Narration et narrateurs dans *Les Aventures du baron de Faeneste*' (179–89); H. Weber, 'Les tapisseries du *Faeneste*' (191–205); J.-R. Fanlo, 'Argumentation et jeu carnavalesque dans les écrits politiques d'A. d'A.' (207–23); and I. Dubail, 'D'A. controversiste: pédant ou gentilhomme?' (225–38).

Other studies on d'Aubigné's prose works are: P. de Lajarte, 'Récit autobiographique et récit historique dans *Sa Vie à ses enfants* d'A. d'A.', *Elseneur*, 17:85–105, which suggests an equivalence between d'Aubigné's own life and the fate of the whole Protestant community. D'Aubigné hated former Protestants who converted to Catholicism and wrote a witty but biting lampoon against one of them, showing the fairly disreputable reasons he had for his conversion, and this is treated by G. Schrenck, 'A. d'A. et la *Confession de Sancy*: une histoire de l'apostat au creux du pamphlet', *Dubois Vol.*, 147–56. M.-M. Fragonard skims through Agrippa's letters in 'Editer une correspondance. Sur l'exemple des lettres d'Agrippa d'Aubigné', *L'Epistolaire*, 53–66. When d'A. wrote his *Avantures du baron de Faeneste*, Henri IV already belonged to history. The King's sentimental (or sexual) life was no secret and d'A. depicts him as a comical lover, a subject discussed by C. Fantoni, 'Henri IV burlesque dans *Les Avantures du baron de Faeneste*', *NRSS*, 19.2:69–81. G. Banderier, 'Un mot russe chez d'Aubigné', *FSB*, 75, 2000:4–8, considers why it may be that although it is accepted that d'Aubigné did not know Russian, yet a Russian noun can be found in his works.

DU BARTAS.   G. Banderier, 'Le séjour écossais de Du Bartas: une lettre inédite d'Henri de Navarre à Jacques VI', *BHR*, 63:305–09, presents an important document from London, BL, MS Additional, 38846.

Before falling into oblivion, Du B.'s *Sepmaine* was an astonishing bestseller, going through *c.* 200 editions (200,000–300,000 copies) and being translated into almost every European language. This success may have been partly due to the encyclopedic knowledge displayed by the poem, as discussed by G. Banderier, 'Une poétique de l'encyclopédie. Sciences et transmission du savoir dans la *Sepmaine* de Du Bartas', Roig Miranda, *Transmission*, 239–64. Id., 'Un "heureux phénix"? Renaissance et mort de l'*hexaméron* (1578–1615)', Wild, *Genre*, I, 181–97, studies how Du B.'s masterwork marked the renewal of an old Christian genre, the *hexameron*, a poetical paraphrase of the first chapter of Genesis; the unabridged version is published in *Nmi*, 102:251–67. Until the very end of his life, Du B. also amplified other Biblical texts, for instance those presenting Solomon, as discussed in J. Dauphiné, 'Des "recherches infiniment belles" de Du Bartas dans *La Magnificence*', *Dubois Vol.*, 359–65.

DU BELLAY.   *La Deffence, et illustration de la langue françoyse*, ed. Jean-Charles Monferran (TLF, 543), 416 pp., is a new edition of Du B.'s treaty, which provides an interesting 'dossier critique', including the Italian text of the *Dialogue delle lingue* by Speroni Sperone and its French translation by Claude Gruget, and several polemical texts by Sébillet, Aneau, Des Autels, and Du B. himself, in the framework of the *querelle* raised by the *Deffence*. J.-C. M. has restored its original novelty and freshness to Du B.'s theoretical treaty. See also G. Defaux, 'Du Bellay, Ronsard, Sainte-Beuve et le mythe humaniste du progrès', *Dubois Vol.*, 314–25.

Françoise Argod-Dutard, *L'Écriture de Joachim Du Bellay*, Geneva, Droz, 536 pp., studies the spelling of Du Bellay from his preserved letters and provides a linguistic interpretation of both letters and poetical collections, suitable mostly for well-informed specialists in linguistics. Id., 'Les *Regrets* de J. Du Bellay: du temps de l'histoire au temps de la poésie', *Dubois Vol.*, 339–58, is a rich study on the passage from chronology to poetry.

J.-F. Courouau, 'La *Deffence* de Du Bellay et les apologies de la langue occitane, XVIe–XVIIe siècles', *RHR*, 53:9–32, studies the influence of the 'premier manifeste littéraire français' (Saulnier) upon Occitan writers and shows how Du B.'s work was paradoxically employed against French literary hegemony. In practice, the relations between different languages were intricate and Du B. did not consider it beneath him to translate and sometimes imitate Virgil or Homer, a subject discussed by O. Millet, 'Présence de Virgile dans *L'Olive* de Du Bellay', *Gendre Vol.*, 105–18, and P. Ford, 'Du Bellay et les mythes homériques', *Dubois Vol.*, 327–38. C. Bené, 'La poésie religieuse en France. Ses liens avec l'Europe humaniste. L'exemple de Du Bellay', *SFr*, 134:211–21, is a ambitious study of the diffusion of French devotional poetry beyond its national, denominational, and linguistic borders.

A. Tripet, 'De quelques usages de Rome après Du Bellay', *Gendre Vol.*, 345–55, shows how Du B.'s lukewarm description of Rome has of course not prevented other writers, for instance Grévin, Castiglione, and Sponde, from seeing the *Urbs* through their own eyes. A brief survey of the poet's critical reception is given by W. J. A. Bots, 'Joachim Du Bellay entre l'histoire littéraire et la stylistique au cours du XXe siècle', *Bertaud Vol.*, 73–79.

MARGUERITE DE NAVARRE. A complete edition in 13 volumes of the Queen's work is in progress, under the direction of Nicole Cazauran and published by Champion. The first three volumes have already appeared: Sabine Lardon has edited the *'Pater Noster' et 'Petit Œuvre dévot'* (*Œuvres complètes*, I), 152 pp., respectively a short verse dialogue (an adaptation of Luther's *Kurtz begreiff*), and a poem revealing the influence of Dante. Simone De Reyff has edited *Le Triomphe de l'Agneau* (*Œuvres complètes*, III), 304 pp., and Michèle Clément La *'Complainte pour un detenu prisonnier' et les 'Chansons spirituelles'* (*Œuvres complètes*, IX), 318 pp. These minor pieces of devotional poetry were published for the first time by Jean de Tournes in the 1547 edition of the *Marguerites de la Marguerite des Princesses*, and Clément has

also used Paris, BNF, MS fr. 24498. All three volumes come with
lengthy introductions, several indexes (biblical quotations and allusions, proper names) and glossaries. The initial reception of the
Queen's poetry is studied by J. Lecointe, 'L'idole de la reine: les
rapports entre M. de N. et la Pléiade d'après *Le Tombeau de Marguerite
de Valois* (1551)', *Gendre Vol.*, 95–103.

J. Miernowski, 'L'intentionalité dans l'*Heptaméron* de Marguerite de
Navarre', *BHR*, 63:201–25, is a clever theological enquiry, demonstrating that the collection of short stories is not a profane or worldly
hapax in a work in other respects entirely devoted to God. Despite
appearances, there is no rupture between the *Heptaméron* and religious
moralities. An opposing view is taken by R. Regosin, 'Death's desire:
sensuality and spirituality in Marguerite de Navarre's *Heptaméron*',
MLN, 116:770–94, which gives a secular if not psychocritical
interpretation. The storytellers are torn between on the one hand
sexual desire 'that overcomes death in the generation of life' and 'that
also engenders death', and, on the other hand, the hope of a very
unsure and probably selective salvation. M. Tetel, 'La froideur des
couvertures', *Dubois Vol.*, 137–46, sees how sexual desire comes veiled,
whereas P. de Lajarte, 'Amour et passion amoureuse dans l'*Heptaméron*: perspective éthique et perspective pathologique', *Charpentier
Vol.*, 369–87, sees it as one facet of love, this terribly vexed and
complex notion.

The last short story of Marguerite's collection owes much to a
medieval poem. G. Eckard, 'Temps et espace dans *La Chastelaine de
Vergi* et la LXXe nouvelle de l'*Heptaméron*', *Gendre Vol.*, 79–94,
compares 'la manière dont l'auteur anonyme de la nouvelle versifiée
du XIIIe siècle, puis M. de N. agencent les coordonnées spatio-
temporelles où ils situent la même intrigue.' G. Banderier examines
an enigmatic turn of phrase in ' "Bailler les Innocens" (*Heptaméron*,
45)', *FSB*, 81:2–3.

L. Middlebrook, ' "Tout mon office": body politics and family
dynamics in the verse *Epîtres* of Marguerite de Navarre', *RQ*,
54:1108–41, examines the *Epîtres* (of moderate literary interest)
exchanged by the Queen with her mother Louise de Savoie and her
brother François I and focuses on the representation of feminity.

MAROT. The organization of Marot's two books of epigrams
(1538) is analysed by F. Rouget, 'Marot épigrammatiste: l'épigramme
et la virtuosité en liberté', *Gendre Vol.*, 15–34. T. Mantovani traces the
influence of Martin Le Franc's *Champion des Dames* on Marot's *Temple
de Cupido* in 'Martin Le Franc et Clément Marot', *Charpentier Vol.*,
19–36. J.-C. Monferran, 'Père et fils dans l'*Adolescence clémentine*', *ib.*,
125–40, reveals again how difficult it seems to be to study Marot

without the background of his family and contemporaries (see on this also *YWLMS*, 60:105, and 61:114).

MONTAIGNE. A new edition of the *Essais* is always a scholarly event. As is well known, the text of Montaigne's masterwork is usually established following either the *exemplaire de Bordeaux* (a example of the 1588 edition published by L'Angelier with abundant autograph *marginalia*) or the 1595 edition, printed under the supervision of Marie de Gournay by L'Angelier and Sonnius, from another and now lost manuscript or copy with *marginalia*. The critical edition recently produced by André Tournon has followed very closely the *exemplaire de Bordeaux* (*YWMLS*, 60:95), and we now have the *Essais* edited by D. Bjaï, B. Boudou, J. Céard, and I. Pantin, Librairie Générale Française, 1854 pp., published according to the 1595 edition. There are no paragraphs and the editors have dropped the distinction between the different stages A, B, and C. (One may observe that, without these, it will not be possible to study a point like 'L'évolution de la pensée de Montaigne devant celle de son temps', by W. J. A. Bots, Wild, *Genre*, II, 189–97). The spelling is modernized. The editors have reprinted the 'Pages du sieur de Montaigne', a kind of thematic index which appeared for the first time in a 1602 edition. The editions of the *Essais* given by Villey-Saulnier, Tournon, and the present team are in fact complementary and have to be used together.

Many things, most of them silly, have been written on Montaigne and La Boétie's friendship, but it is not flattery to say that Gérard Defaux's impeccably erudite yet at the same time lively book: *Montaigne et le travail de l'amitié. Du lit de mort d'Etienne de La Boétie aux 'Essais' de 1595*, Orléans, Paradigme, 376 pp., will stay on our shelves for many years. The expression 'travail de l'amitié' recalls the fashionable turn of phrase 'travail du deuil', but far from any reductionist interpretation, G. Defaux shows how Montaigne made recesses for his late friend within his heart, his library, and the *Essais*, in order to answer the dying lament: 'Mon frère! mon frère! Me refusez vous donques une place?'. In subsequent work, 'Une leçon de scepticisme: Montaigne, le monde et les grands hommes', *MLN*, 116:644–65, D. shows how Montaigne escaped some Renaissance illusions, for 'la Renaissance', writes the author, 'dont nos manuels d'histoire littéraire nous rebattent les oreilles est une Renaissance elle aussi avortée, une Renaissance qui se défait dans l'horreur et la boue des guerres civiles'.

J. Balsamo, 'L'histoire des Turcs à l'épreuve des *Essais*', *Dubois Vol.*, 221–36, studies the originality of M., neither a religious fanatic nor a simple inquiring mind, in his treatment of Turkish subjects.

We know that Montaigne was a good and faithful friend, but what sort of husband might he have been? M. Simonin, 'Françoise (de la

Chassaigne) et (son?) Michel: du ménage chez Montaigne', *Charpentier Vol.*, 156–70, publishes a MS deed copied out by a solicitor in order to settle a problem raised by the dowry of Montaigne's wife. T. Cave examines the Aristotelian and Senecan substrata of 'L'analyse des passions chez Montaigne'. *ib.*, 389–406.

Montaigne was viewed by 19th-c. critics as a *moraliste* and every *moraliste* worthy of the name should blame idleness (see the quotations from Gruget and La Primaudaye cited in the article below), but nevertheless he seemed to praise it. V. Krause, 'Montaigne's art of idleness', *Viator*, 31, 2000: 361–80, sees in his self-proclaimed idleness an attempt to restore Roman *otium*.

E. Macphail, 'Montaigne and the Trial of Socrates', *BHR*, 63:457–75, studies, as did G. Defaux rather differently (see p. 89 above), how Montaigne's reading of Socrates's trial and death are intended to 'advance an aristocratic critique of some of the most cherished if illusory ideals of Renaissance humanism'. The author focuses her attention especially on 'De la phisionomie' (III, 2). M. Gauna, 'Montaigne et l'éthique séculaire', *Dubois Vol.*, 173–83, introduces us to a Montaigne free from 'tout le bagage idéologique de son époque et de sa religion', a very questionable point of view. Philosphers will find an ontological interpretation of the *Essais* in A. Tournon, 'Le principe de privation', *Charpentier Vol.*, 171–84.

Had Montaigne written an account now lost of Henri d'Anjou's election to the throne of Poland, is a theory discussed by C. Magnien, 'Montaigne historien de "l'expédition" de Henri d'Anjou en Pologne? Hypothèses . . .', *Dubois Vol.*, 195–206.

A. Szabari, ' "Parler seulement de moy": the disposition of the subject in Montaigne's essay "De l'art de conferer" ', *MLN*, 116:1001–24, is a close analysis of *Essais*, III, 8, and of Montaigne's project of representing himself. Even if Montaigne's body was not the doleful *corpusculum* of Erasmus, he was not on friendly terms with it, as F. Lestringant reminds us in 'Montaigne et le corps en procès', *Charpentier Vol.*, 91–107. Therapeutic aspects of the Italian pages of Montaigne's diary are studied by M. Viallon-Schoneveld, '*Ricordati della boletta*', *Dubois Vol.*, 185–93. Finally, the ideological stakes of Montaigne's biographies are explored by M. Simonin, 'Un enjeu de l'histoire littéraire des XIXe et XXe siècles: la construction de la *Montani Vita*', *Bertaud Vol.*, 91–105.

RABELAIS. Vol. 39 of the *Etudes rabelaisiennes* (THR, 344), 2000, 176 pp., is a *miscellanea* with contributions by F. Rigolot, W. Kemp, G. Milhe Poutingon, C. Clavel, C. Seutin, P. Walter, B. de Cornulier, L.-G. Tin, and F. Cornillat. Far more impressive and to a certain extent definitive, vol. 40 is entirely devoted to a work of much debated authenticity, *Le Cinquiesme Livre*, ed. Franco Giacone (THR, 354), and publishes the *Proceedings* of an October 1998 symposium held in Rome. 37 communications from noted scholars deal with editorial questions, zoology, medicine, music, etc., and the volume will be indispensable for any future examination of this mysterious novel. V. Zaercher, 'L'incise dans le dialogue rabelaisien: un discours incident', *NRSS*, 18.2, 2000: 7–22, is an *addendum* to her dissertation on Rabelaisian dialogue (*YWMLS*, 62:88). M. Marrache, 'Enthousiasme et inspiration dans les contes de Panurge', *ib.*, 23–35, studies enthusiasm, the link between ebriety and narration. H. Glidden subtly explores the fifth chapter of *Pantagruel* and the link between autobiography and novel in 'Lieux de mémoire et passion de l'ami chez Rabelais', *Charpentier Vol.*, 141–53.

RONSARD. Denis Bjaï, *La 'Franciade' sur le métier. Ronsard et la pratique du poème héroïque* (THR, 350), 512 pp., studies the composition of this stillborn epic and several themes such as 'Troie contrefaite', 'La fortune de mer', 'Dans les erreurs de Crète'. A section deals with the reception of the poem. The copious bibliography will be useful for every Ronsard specialist.

Pierre Martin and Gérard Milhe Poutingon, *'Odes' de Ronsard*, Neuilly, Atlande, 288 pp., will prove a useful asset to a rarely frequented aspect of Ronsard's poetry. It is intended in particular for advanced students, and includes both literary and grammatical chapters. These *Odes*, torn between inspiration, divine gift, and intimate lyrism, as seen by D. Ménager, 'Passion et fureur poétique dans les *Odes*', *Charpentier Vol.*, 317–30, exalt poetic energy, and are close to the *Amours* (describing erotic love), as J. Rieu points out in 'Fureur et passion dans les *Amours* de Ronsard', *ib.*, 73–89. On the *Odes* also, J. Céard has published a valuable bibliography and a list of *errata* and *addenda* to the Laumonier edition in *NRSS*, 19.2: 104–20.

It is hard to give a satisfactory definition of the French elegy, a blending of epistolary forms and rhetorical themes. R. wrote elegies throughout his life, and B. Andersson, 'Un genre et ses fonctions: l'exemple de l'élégie ronsardienne', *ib.*, 49–68, provides an interesting study of this corpus. The poem entitled 'La Lyre' is lavishly commented upon by O. Pot, 'Variations sur une lyre. De Ronsard à Poussin', *Versants*, 39:5–30.

N. Bochenek, 'Au seuil des *Discours politiques* de Ronsard', *RevAR*, 14:51–67, studies Ronsard's editorial strategy during the religious wars, through four polemical pieces of poetry. One may also try F. Lestringant, 'Ronsard, Prométhée et les protestants: physique et théologie des *Discours*', *Gendre Vol.*, 223–36.

The *Hymnes* have been somewhat neglected, with only one study, by J. Céard, ' "Au travers du voile": l'*Hymne de l'hyver* de Ronsard', *Gendre Vol.*, 209–22.

Even if Ronsardian epic, elegies, and odes are enjoying renewed favour, Ronsard remains the poet of Cassandre, Marie, and Hélène. C. Hayashi, 'La vision du monde néo-platonicien dans "Sur la mort de Marie"(1578)', *RevAR*, 14:1–16, is in Japanese but a French summary informs us that this article tries to show how the poet used the myth of Protesilaus. Poetical rhythm is studied by M.-M. Fontaine, 'Les fidélités de l'oreille. Ronsard, Marot et Rabelais', *Gendre Vol.*, 137–51. In the same *Festschrift* are also the articles by N. Cazauran, 'Cassandre en 1552 ou l'invention d'un personnage' (167–75), O. Pot, 'Les *Amours* de 1552–1553 ou la tentation du monodrame lyrique' (177–93), and G. Mathieu-Castellani, 'Jeux de miroirs et écriture précieuse dans *Les Amours* de Ronsard' (195–208).

Ronsard's reception is a complex matter. A new element is provided by A. L. Gordon, 'Lire Ronsard en 1610: la rhétorique restreinte de Pierre de Deimier', *Bertaud Vol.*, 121–30.

8. Minor Writers

POETRY.   Although Ernst Robert Curtius' *European Literature and the Latin Middle Ages* was published decades ago, *Toposforschung* has still not won acclaim in French universities; all the more reason for noticing two articles: D. Ménager, 'Le *Nox erat* de Virgile et la poésie de la Renaissance', *Gendre Vol.*, 1–13, is a comparative study (Ariosto, Tasso, Ronsard, etc.) of a Virgilian pattern; and P. Galand-Hallyn, ' "Pourquoi les roses sont rouges": la couleur du mythe, d'Aphtonius à Ronsard', *ib.*, 153–66, presents a remarkably detailed inquiry.

James Helgeson, *Harmonie divine et subjectivité poétique chez Maurice Scève* (THR, 349), 160 pp., is an interesting study on the relationship between Scève and music which, in the Renaissance mind, had to be divided into *musica practica* (real and audible) and *musica speculativa* (musical philosophy or metaphysics). S. was most interested in the second of these, embodied in the myth of Orpheus. S. is regarded by a long critical tradition as a mere Petrarchist poet, writing and publishing love poetry, but G. Defaux, '(Re) visiting *Délie*: Maurice Scève and Marian poetry', *RQ*, 54:685–739, proves that he is a Christian poet too, if not more than a worldly love poet. He imitated fixed-form poems for poetical competitions such as the *Puys*. There is no clear separation between devotional and profane poetry in *Délie*. A prosodic analysis of this same work is made by T. Cave, 'Rime et structure du dizain dans la *Délie*', *Gendre Vol.*, 49–57. H. Weber, 'Diane-Hécate chez Scève, Jodelle et d'Aubigné', *ib.*, 59–64, is like a footnote to Jean Seznec's book on the survival of Pagan gods.

A single study has been published on J. Peletier du Mans's canzoniere *L'Amour des Amours*: I. Pantin, 'Après une lecture de Dante', *Gendre Vol.*, 259–73, dealing with the influence of Dante. F. Rigolot, 'Quand Ovide devient Sapho: Louise Labé, héroïne de l'héroïde', *ib.*, 65–78, deals with Ovidian influence on Louise's poetry. Olivier de Magny is often denounced by critics as a mere plagiarist of Italian poets. Y. Giraud, 'Traducteur servile ou adaptateur intelligent: Olivier de Magny et ses modèles italiens', *ib.*, 247–57, is an useful reappraisal. The problem of translation is also at the centre of G. Demerson, 'Belleau au travail: l'exemple de Sapho', *ib.*, 275–87. Jean-Antoine de Baïf is not usually considered an 'écrivain engagé', but Y. Roberts, 'The regency of 1574 in the *Discours merveilleux* and in the poems of J.-A. de Baïf', *BHR*, 63:261–75, shows that the political attitude of this former supporter of Catherine de Médicis evolved swiftly.

2001 was a sparse year for Desportes studies, after the previous blooming (see *YWMLS* 62:101). To be noted are a study of a little known prose collection by B. Petey-Girard, 'Remarques sur le formulaire de prières de Philippe Desportes', *SFr*, 133:3–17, and J. Rieu's 'Le corps du poète dans *Les Amours de Diane* de Desportes', *Gendre Vol.*, 303–20. Some early editions are exhaustively described in Jean Paul Barbier, *Ma bibliothèque poétique*, 4.2, 9–109 (see p. 79 above), with a minutely detailed and indispensable 'Tableau chronologique des œuvres poétiques de P. Desportes' (pp. 471–545).

H. Marek, 'De la roue d'Ixion à la "divine Sphère". Le mythe antique au service de la philosophie platonicienne dans les *Erreurs amoureuses* de Pontus de Tyard', *NRSS*, 18.2, 2000:55–77, examines the use of mythological imagery in Tyard's almost cryptic poetry. His whole work seems to stand between Neoplatonic tradition (Pico) and mannerist aesthetic, as R. E. Campo sets out to prove in 'Tyard's graphic metamorphoses: figuring the semiosic drift in the *Douze Fables de fleuves ou fontaines*', *RQ*, 54:776–800. For the lover as servile martyr, see S. Perrier, 'Le sujet "passionnaire" dans la poésie de Tyard', *Charpentier Vol.*, 37–55.

Some unnoticed poems by Du Monin cast a new light on the student years of another poet, Lazare de Selve, chancellor of Catherine de Bourbon, as discussed by G. Banderier, 'La jeunesse de Lazare de Selve', *BHR*, 63:81–85. Id., 'Notes sur Jean-Edouard Du Monin', *ib.*, 61, 1999:57–70, brings new material on Du Monin's tragic death. The linguistic interests of his mixed but coherent work are described by Id. in 'Babel à l'œuvre: Du Monin et le plurilinguisme', pp. 241–64 of *Babel à la Renaissance*, ed. James Dauphiné and

Myriam Jacquemier, Mont-de-Marsan, Editions InterUniversitaires, 1999.

Alumnus of Du Bartas and encyclopedic poet, Joseph Du Chesne was involved in a obsure Genevan criminal affair discussed by D. Kahn, 'Inceste, assassinat, persécutions et alchimie en France et à Genève', *BHR*, 63:227–59. The minutely detailed study by L. Petris, 'Unité et ruptures dans les *Sonnets de la mort* de Jean de Sponde', *Gendre Vol.*, 357–71, provides the text of these 12 sonnets, for A. Boase's edition seems to be faulty. Even if it is a prose treatise, *L'Art poëtique françois* by Pierre Laudun d'Aigaliers, ed. Jean-Charles Monferran et al., STFM, 2000, cx + 244 pp., must be included in this section. Published at the end of the 16th c., after decades of poetic experiments, some of them successes and most of them failures, this faultlessly edited book appears to be a kind of appraisal, attempting to unite Ronsard and Marot.

PROSE. Jean Lemaire de Belges, *Des anciennes pompes funeralles*, ed. Marie-Madeleine Fontaine, STFM, xc + 186 pp., is a first edition from two MSS of the Bibliothèque Nationale. This curious work is an ethnological inquiry into sepultural practices. It deserves to be compared to Henri de Sponde's *Cimetieres sacrez*, a text which is overdue for a modern edition.

The work attributed to Madeleine de L'Aubespine, *Cabinet des saines affections*, ed. Colette H. Winn, Champion, 136 pp., is a little book of moral meditations, impregnated with Stoicism, and was issued five times between 1584(?) and 1600. Marie Le Gendre, *L'Exercice de l'âme vertueuse*, ed. Colette H. Winn, Champion, 200 pp., presents 12 discourses, with a dialogue and several pieces of poetry, which were originally published in 1596.

W. Schleiner studies the chivalric novel and laughter in a work not especially recognised as humorous in 'Laughter and challenges to the Other in the French *Amadis de Gaule*', *SCJ*, 32:91–107. D. Duport, 'Le beau paysage selon Pierre Belon du Mans', *RHR*, 53:57–75, examines B.'s attitude towards landscape during his travels. He was one of the first to admire landscape for itself. P. Demarolle, 'La place des apprentissages dans la littérature et dans la vie d'après l'œuvre de Philippe de Vigneulles', Roig Miranda, *Transmission*, 13–26, examines the culture of a draper of Lorraine.

On Renaissance dialogue, see two studies by R. I. Vulcan, 'Le dialogue humaniste, un instrument idéal de diffusion du savoir', Roig Miranda, *Transmission*, 229–38, and 'Les nouveautés du dialogue humaniste: exégèse et conversation', Wild, *Genre*, 1, 41–50.

J.-E. Girot, 'Une version inconnue du *Discours de la servitude volontaire* de La Boétie', *BHR*, 63:511–65, discusses how, according to

Montaigne, La Boétie's pamphlet was read before being printed, and some manuscript copies were taken. The two MSS examined in this article are to be found in Chambéry and Milan.

A special issue of *RHR* (51–52) is devoted to the work and style of Etienne Tabourot des Accords, with contributions by M.-L. Demonet, 'Le statut de l'écrit et du visible dans les genres traités par T.' (11–28), J.-M. Messiaen, 'Les *Bigarrures* de T.: une conception originale du signifiant' (29–41), M. Paquant, 'T. dans la lexicographie traditionnelle' (43–56), V. Mecking, 'A propos du vocabulaire de T. et de son intérêt pour le français préclassique' (57–72), N. Dazord, 'La mesure de T.' (73–90), M. Clément, 'Les ruses du rationalisme dans "des faux sorciers, et de leurs imposture"' (91–102), E. Naya, 'T., songeur drolatique' (103–20), G.-A. Pérouse, 'Le dialogue de la prose et des vers dans l'œuvre de T.' (121–34), S. Peytavin, 'T. a-t-il écrit des "essais"?' (135–51), H. Glidden, 'Epigramme et joutes d'esprit: les *Touches* de T.' (153–63), C. Clavel, 'T. et la pratique de l'apophtegme' (165–86), B. C. Bowen, 'La rhétorique des *Escraignes dijonnoises*' (209–15), and M. Simonin, 'Enquête sur les *Escraignes*' (217–30), with an afterword by F. Goyet.

Pierre de L'Estoile's diary is an invaluable source of information for the reigns of Henri III and Henri IV. G. Schrenck regards it as a literary text, by a clever use of narratological concepts in 'La poétique du seuil dans le *Registre-journal du règne de Henri III*', *Bertaud Vol.*, 493–502. To what genre does this text belong? It is neither memoirs nor an historical account. F. Marin, 'Les *Registres-journaux* de Pierre de L'Estoile: étrangeté et écriture du moi problématique', Wild, *Genre*, II, 217–30, considers the influence on L'Estoile of Montaigne's *Essais*.

L. Gris-Renucci, 'Savoirs, énigmes, "fantasie": le "Songe du curieux" dans le *Cabinet de Minerve* de Béroalde de Verville', *RHR*, 53:77–95, asks whether Verville was an alchemist using allegorical symbols or an allegorist dealing with alchemical conceits.

M.-M. Fragonard, 'E. Pasquier, les passions et l'histoire dans *Les Recherches de la France*', *Charpentier Vol.*, 187–202, discusses the bibliophile and polemicist, Estienne Pasquier, who was also an avid reader of historical books, as examined by C. Magnien, 'Pasquier historien', *NRSS*, 19.1:51–62. See also M.-L. Demonet, 'Langue naturelle et langue coutumière chez E. Pasquier et Montaigne', *Dubois Vol.*, 207–20.

Two articles on an important Protestant prose writer are H. Daussy, 'La correspondance de Philippe Duplessis-Mornay: inventaire et typologie', *L'Epistolaire*, 211–26, and Id., with the assistance of P. Gourdin, 'Livres et papiers de Philippe Duplessis-Mornay', *BSHPF*, 147:629–53.

Since Leonard C. Jones's monograph of 1917, numerous studies have been devoted to Simon Goulart, a friend of Agrippa d'Aubigné and commentator of Du Bartas, but only a few new documents have been discovered. G. Banderier, 'Documents sur Simon Goulart', *BSHPF*, 146, 2000:571–606, publishes the critical edition of 18 hitherto unknown letters written by the Genevan minister, from 1598 to 1627.

A booklet printed in 1584 and quoting lines from Du Bartas' *Seconde Semaine* (published a few weeks before) may be ascribed to a Catholic dignitary, the future bishop Jacques Davy Du Perron, as noted by G. Banderier, 'Le *Paradoxe de la Discorde*: un opuscule du jeune Du Perron?', *AnN*, 50, 2000:409–32. On his youth, see Id., 'Le roman d'une ascension sociale sous les derniers Valois: les années de jeunesse de Jacques Davy du Perron (1556–1587)', *Mémoires de l'Académie des Sciences, Arts et Belles-Lettres de Caen*, 39:71–121.

THE SEVENTEENTH CENTURY

By J. Trethewey, *University of Wales, Aberystwyth*, and J. P. Short, *formerly Senior Lecturer in French at the University of Sheffield*

1. General

Mark Bannister, *Condé in Context: Ideological Change in Seventeenth-Century France*, Oxford, Legenda, 2000, 240 pp., is, as B. suggests, an example of *histoire des mentalités*: an examination of successive definitions, offered by a variety of writers throughout the 17th c., of Le Grand Condé, firstly as a military hero, but one with taste and enthusiasm for the arts, then, during the Fronde, a rebel, and finally once again 'a great example to the nation, with his days of rebellion well nigh forgotten', and adulation of him as a courtier, patron, and *honnête homme* added to praise of his prowess as a warrior. J. Wollenberg, 'Richelieu et le système européen de sécurité collective. La bibliothèque du Cardinal comme centre intellectuel d'une nouvelle politique', *DSS*, 53:99–112, refers to the works R. wrote or commissioned to further this aim. Myriam Yardeni, *Repenser l'histoire: aspects de l'historiographie huguenote des guerres de religion à la Révolution française* (Vie des Huguenots, 11), Champion, 2000, 224 pp., collects articles previously published between 1964 and 1997, in which Palma Cayet and Pierre Du Moulin figure prominently among polemicists at the beginning of the 17th c., and Bayle and Jacques Basnage at the end.

DFS, 56, Fall, has a 'Special Issue' on *Le Mariage sous l'Ancien Régime*, ed. Claire Carlin: K. Perry Long, 'The alchemical wedding in the works of Clovis Hestau de Nuysement' (27–35), finds in N. a forerunner of those who in more recent times have questioned 'traditional distinctions on which gender roles are based'; K. A. Hoffmann, 'The strange bodies of married women' (36–45), peruses 17th-c. and 18th-c. pieces by demonologists, physicians, compilers of pamphlets and marriage manuals, setting out beliefs about married women and sex; H. claims that female bodies then were 'slippery narrative spaces'; M. M. Houle, 'The marriage question, or the *Querelle des hommes* in Rabelais, Molière and Boileau' (46–54), scrutinizes Rabelais's *Tiers Livre*, Molière's *L'École des femmes* and *Le Mariage forcé* and Boileau's *Satire X* for their ways of asking 'whether it is better for a man to marry or to remain single'; A. E. Zuerner, 'Disorderly wives, loyal subjects: marriage and war in Early Modern France' (55–65), looks at Jean-Marie de Vernon's *L'Amazone chrétienne ou les aventures de Madame de Saint-Balmon*, and Catherine Meurdrac's autobiography, *Mémoires de Madame de la Guette*, in order to 'explore the various effects of war on gender dynamics within marriage'; C. H.

Winn, 'Portraits d'épouses exemplaires dans l'*Apologie pour les dames* de Jacqueline de Miremont (1602)' (66–77), summarizes this polemical work written in verse; K. Wine, 'Honored guests: wife and mistress in "Les Plaisirs de l'île enchantée"' (78–90), examines the 'balancing act' performed by Louis XIV in using the festival to honour not only Queen and Queen Mother but also his mistress Louise de La Vallière; C. Carlin, 'Gérer son mariage au XVIIe siècle: l'exemple de Jeanne de Schomberg' (91–97), demonstrates how this modest, devout Jansenist produced a treatise on marriage 'qui met en valeur les capacités, les talents et le pouvoir féminins, tout en prétendant les cacher'.

Patricia Francis Cholakian, *Women and the Politics of Self-Representation in Seventeenth-Century France*, Newark, Delaware U.P. — London, Associated U.P., 2000, 219 pp., reads the memoirs of Marguerite de Valois, Mlle de Montpensier, Hortense and Marie Mancini, Jeanne Guyon, and the Abbé de Choisy as 'case studies in the representation of victimization, internalized oppression, and strategies of resistance'. F. E. Beasley, 'Altering the fabric of history: women's participation in the classical age', Stephens, *Women's Writing*, 64–83, shows how women 'used' political struggles, such as the Fronde, to further their own cause and increase their role in literary and other intellectual activities. *Homosexuality in Early Modern France, a Documentary Collection*, ed. Jeffrey Merrick and Bryan T. Ragan, Jr., OUP, xvi + 256 pp., collects documents, legal, medical, pious, and satirical, dating from the 1530s to the Revolution, all here translated into English. Frank Greiner, *Les Métamorphoses d'Hermès: tradition alchimique et esthétique littéraire dans la France de l'âge baroque (1583–1646)* (BLR, 3.42), 2000, 663 pp., lists and describes the many alchemical texts available in France in the period, Béroalde de Verville figuring prominently.

LitC, 43 prints papers on *Le Temps au XVIIe siècle*, ed. Pierre Pasquier, covering all the arts in Europe. The following relate to French literature: B. Chédozeau, 'L'histoire religieuse au XVIIe siècle. L'histoire de l'Église, ou histoire ecclésiastique et les *collectiones conciliorum*' (163–80), studies 17th-c. views on the power of the Pope in relation to the Councils; C. Belin, 'L'espace-temps de la méditation' (227–39), is concerned with a variety of European thinkers from Ignatius Loyola onwards, but particularly with Bossuet, Agnès Arnauld, Pascal, Bérulle, and Hopil; T. Verdier, 'Le temps de la promenade' (257–68), writes of gardens, courtliness, and *promenades* in literature, and also of appreciative or disgruntled depicters like Mlle de Scudéry and Saint-Simon; F.-X. Cuche, 'À la fin du règne de Louis XIV: le temps introuvable' (269–84), notes the clash of pessimism and optimism on the subject of time among Anciens and Modernes. J. Rohou, 'L'anthropologie pessimiste des "classiques":

tentative de distinction et d'explication', *RHLF*, 101 : 1523–50, offers 'une hypothèse historique' suggesting that until 1683 literature inspired by the 'système louis-quatorzien' blamed human problems on 'la nature de l'homme', whereas later writers blamed 'ses conditionnements socio-idéologiques'.

Méchoulan, *Vengeance*, has the following papers of 17th-c. interest: C. Biet, 'Douceur de la vengeance, plaisir de l'interdit. Le statut de la vengeance au XVIIe siècle' (11–32), views the subject as treated by Corneille (*Le Cid* and *Horace*), the authors of *histoires tragiques*, and Racine (*Britannicus* and *Mithridate*); A. Gaillard, 'Vengeances héroïques, vengeances libertines. La structure de l'échange entre offenseur et offensé dans quelques récits de Montaigne à Louvet' (33–48), points out that 'l'offenseur (et non pas seulement l'offensé) attend, espère une réponse à son affront', and illustrates the point with M.'s cannibals, Tristan's *Page disgracié*, Racine's *Bajazet* and some 18th-c. works; S. Chisogne, 'La fin d'un consensus. Vengeance et conscience dans les *Histoires tragiques*' (49–67), notes that, unlike earlier collections of *contes*, where the *facétieux* was the norm, these *histoires* (from Boaistuau to Camus) 'privilégient, de manière presque exclusive, les vraies vengeances, ces crimes sanglants dont la cruauté et la violence ostentatoires semblent justifier à elles seules le qualificatif de "tragiques"'.

DSS, 53.3, prints ten articles on *Les Entrées royales*, concerned as much with the political and social history surrounding such celebrations as with the contributions of the arts to their splendour and effectiveness. Published descriptions of these events are considered, as in D. Moncond'huy, 'Galerie et livre d'entrée (à propos de l'entrée de Louis XIII à Paris en 1628)' (441–55), and, of a more general nature, in M.-F. Wagner, 'De la ville de province en paroles et en musique à la ville silencieuse ou la disparition de l'entrée royale sous Louis XIII' (457–75), where the evolution away from outdoor ceremony towards celebration of a more literary or theatrical nature is charted; M.-C. Canova-Green, 'L'entrée de Louis XIII dans Marseille le 7 novembre 1622' (521–30), reproduces a hitherto unpublished account of this event. V. Schröder, 'Entre l'oraison funèbre et l'éloge historique: l'hommage aux morts à l'Académie française', *MLN*, 116:666–88, looks at the 'éloge funèbre' in the 17th c. in order to define 'les pratiques commémoratives en usage sous l'Ancien Régime, et les différentes notions de "grandeur" qu'elles impliquent'.

Sellier Vol. prints contributions covering literary, philosophical, polemical, linguistic, artistic, and architectural topics: H. Bouchilloux, 'La querelle de l'amour: Pascal, Malebranche, Fénelon' (95–108), considers three representative views, all 'augustiniennes', put forward by the three writers, all of which, B. asserts, are 'à la fois cohérentes et incompatibles'. Other essays are reviewed *passim* below.

TLit, 14, is devoted to *L'Écrivain éditeur, 1. Du Moyen Âge à la fin du XVIIIe siècle*, ed. François Bessire. Six papers cover the 17th c.: G. Saba, 'Georges de Scudéry et Jean Mairet éditeurs de Théophile de Viau' (189–203), examines S.'s three-part edition of T.'s *Œuvres* and M.'s 1641 edition of the *Nouvelles Œuvres*; B. Barbiche, 'La première édition des *Œconomies royales* de Sully (1638–1640)' (205–14), reproduces and comments on the contract signed in 1638 between S. and Jacques Bouquet of Auxerre, the printer of this clandestine edition of his memoirs, together with Bouquet's *quittance* on completion of the work; D. Donetzkoff, 'Défense et illustration d'une orthodoxie spirituelle: Robert Arnauld d'Andilly éditeur des lettres de Jean Duvergier de Hauranne, abbé de Saint-Cyran' (215–32), reproduces and comments on A.'s own account of how he approached the task of introducing and editing the prison letters written between 1638 and 1643; A. Niderst, 'Madeleine de Scudéry, Ménage et Pellisson éditeurs de Sarasin' (233–42), gives details of the friendship between the *romancière* and the poet (Amilcar in *Clélie*) which, soon after his death, led to her preparing with Ménage the *Œuvres de M. Sarasin* (1655), for which P. wrote the preface; J. Lafond, 'Un duc et pair de France éditeur' (243–55), considers how a 17th-c. *honnête homme* (his example is La Rochefoucauld) could bring himself to publish his works, order the material, and make revisions for later editions; M. Maître, 'Éditer, imprimer, publier: quelques stratégies féminines au XVIIe siècle' (258–76), revisits problems created by assumptions about feminine modesty and quotes *stratégies* resorted to by Mlle de Scudéry, Mme de Villedieu, and Mlle de Montpensier.

Marianne Closson, *L'Imaginaire démoniaque en France (1550–1650): genèse de la littérature fantastique* (THR, 341), 2000, 544 pp., enthusiastically explores all the highways and byways of human credulity concerning sorcery, witches' sabbaths, satanism, demonic possession, 'pactes diaboliques', and related phenomena which appear in the literature of this period when 'la chasse aux sorcières' was at its height, the literature dwindling away as the pursuit was discredited in the second half of the 17th c. From all this, C. claims, there was later born 'une littérature fantastique consciente d'elle-même et par-là même érigée en genre'. Laura Verciani, *Le Moi et ses diables: autobiographie spirituelle et récit de possession au XVIIe siècle* (Lumière classique, 33), Champion, 208 pp., studies four texts, by Jeanne Féry, Jeanne des Anges, Jean-Joseph Surin, and Madeleine Bavent, all personal accounts of the experience of demonic possession, all 'très imitatifs, et en même temps fortement subjectifs, où s'affrontent — en se heurtant souvent — le savoir théologique et la singularité de l'expérience'. V. emphasizes the rarity of such texts in which the ex-possessed recounts at first hand instead of having recourse to a third party. V. is desirous to 'suivre les traces de la subjectivité du "je" écrivant', and is therefore engaged in an 'analyse littéraire et linguistique' rather than in the commoner exercise of studying 'les composantes historiques, religieuses, anthropologiques et psycho-pathologiques'. *La Querelle des Anciens et des Modernes, XVIIe–XVIIIe siècles*, ed. Anne-Marie Lecoq (Folio classique, 3414), Gallimard, 893 pp., is an anthology covering the entire debate from Mersenne's *Questions inouïes* (1634) to Augustin-Simon Irailh's *Querelles littéraires* (1761). Nearly all the writers are French, though Swift, Pope, Vico, and Antonio Conti are allowed a translated word in edgeways. The anthology is preceded by an essay: M. Fumaroli, 'Les abeilles et les araignées' (7–218), outlining the history of the *Querelle*, and followed by a postface: J.-R. Armogathe, 'Une ancienne querelle' (801–49), delving into its prehistory and ramifications. R. Worvill, 'Roger de Piles' theory of art and new techniques for opening scenes in Molière, Landois and Diderot', *BJECS*, 24:77–89, reports P.'s advice to artists to produce an immediate strong visual effect, advice taken by the three dramatists in opening scenes (in M.'s case, *Le Malade imaginaire*).

LitC, 40, 2000, prints papers on *Droit et littérature*: A. Viala, 'Le statut de l'écrivain à l'âge classique: notes et remarques' (77–86), starts from Furetière's definition of the word *auteur*, and then traces the progress in the 17th c. of notions foreshadowing the modern concepts of *droits d'auteur* and *propriété littéraire*; E. Méchoulan, 'La dette et la loi: considérations sur la vengeance' (275–94), cites Corneille, Racine, Pascal, and Rosset; S. Requemora, 'Les voyageurs à la découverte du droit naturel' (347–64), looks at utopian writings and those of real travellers, all contributors to the *rêve exotique* and to the notion of *droit naturel*.

Bérangère Parmentier, *Le Siècle des moralistes, de Montaigne à La Bruyère*, Seuil, 2000, xi + 345 pp., introduces the works of four major authors, Montaigne, La Rochefoucauld, Pascal, and La Bruyère, and three minor ones, Nicole, Saint-Évremond, and La Fontaine, places them in their evolving social and historical contexts, studies the 'formes brisées, formes brèves' that characterize them, and surveys their common themes. Jean-Pierre van Elslande, *L'Imaginaire pastoral du XVIIe siècle 1600–1650*, PUF, 1999, 214 pp., studies mainly *L'Astrée* and its derivatives (adaptations, imitations, satirical reactions), and the input of piety ('l'Arcadie dévote') or *libertinage* ('l'Arcadie libertine').

Bertaud Vol. covers literature from the Middle Ages to the present day of several European countries besides French: J. Balsamo, 'Les Étrennes d'Abel L'Angelier (1600): quelques remarques d'histoire du livre et d'histoire littéraire' (107–20), reveals the riches among L'A.'s latest publications and in his backlist; C. Rizza, 'Baroque: une notion heuristique pour la littérature française du XVIIe siècle' (131–41), expresses doubts about the term as an identifier of either a 'cadre chronologique' or a style, but then points to the richness of the research it has engendered; R. Duchêne, 'L'imposture biographique: de Mme de Sévigné à Ninon de Lenclos' (209–20), uses his own studies of these two women as pegs on which to hang observations on the biographer's craft. F. Deloffre, 'Quelques réflexions sur la critique d'attribution' (247–71), cites examples mainly concerning Robert Challe.

There is a discussion of the terms 'baroque' and 'classique' in *Racine et/ou le classicisme*, ed. Ronald W. Tobin (Biblio 17, 129), Tübingen, Narr, 505 pp.: J.-C. Vuillemin 'Baroque: pertinence ou obsolescence?' (480–96), reaffirms his faith in a word that evokes 'l'incertain' and the 'chimérique'; J. D. Lyons, 'What do we mean when we say "classique"?' (497–505), surveys evolving usage from the early 19th c. and then shows how the term is now variously used as a period marker by both 'exalters' and 'debunkers', and advises us to 'limit the *dégâts*' by accepting the term 'in its broadest sense without otherwise projecting backwards the myth of a self-conscious, mature, and calculating classicism'. N. Doiron, 'Paroles du cœur', *Beugnot Vol.*, 183–93, reviews all the meanings attached to the word 'cœur' throughout the 17th c.

Delcourt, *Bibliothèque bleue*, collects papers covering various countries and periods. Those concerning 17th-c. France are: J.-D. Mellot, 'La Bibliothèque bleue de Rouen: l'émergence d'une production indésirable et très demandée (fin XVIIe-début XVIIIe siècle)' (23–39), using Rouen as an example of an authority moving from indifference to hostility, then to attempts to control for social purposes; H. Blom, 'La présence de romans de chevalerie dans les bibliothèques privées des XVIIe et XVIIIe siècles' (51–67), scrutinizes catalogues from 1630 to 1750 to reveal the presence of romances in the series; S. Baudelle-Michels, 'La révolte des *Quatre Fils Aymon* dans les livrets de colportage' (69–77), looks at versions of this *roman de chevalerie*, seeing in it 'non pas une quelconque démonstration antimonarchiste, mais le tableau animé et haut en relief de situations morales et politiques aussi héroïques que pathétiques'; L. Andries, '*Mélusine* et *Orson*: deux réécritures de la Bibliothèque bleue' (79–92), reviews the *remaniements* of these tales in their passage from the Renaissance to the Bibliothèque bleue in the 17th and 18th cs; V. Milliot, 'La ville à travers la littérature de colportage (XVIe-XIXe): images urbaines et "usages" du livre' (93–108), finds Paris above all a 'motif majeur d'inspiration'; H. Bouquin, 'L'illustration du roman de *Mélusine* dans la Bibliothèque bleue (XVIIe-début XVIIIe siècle)' (139–47), notes that the illustrations, from being depictions of episodes in the story, eventually become unrelated to it; he puts this evolution down to increasing illiteracy.

Paolo Carile, *Huguenots sans frontières: voyage et écriture à la Renaissance et à l'âge classique* (Les Géographies du Monde, 3), Champion, 319 pp., reprints, revised, previously published studies. French 17th-c. writers studied include Henri Duquesne (Réunion), Marc Lescarbot (Nouvelle France), Jean-Baptiste Tavernier, François Leguat and Guillaume de Laujardière (southern Africa), and Charles de Rochefort (West Indies). D. Sangsue, 'Le récit de voyage humoristique (XVIIe–XIXe siècle)', *RHLF*, 101:1139–62, starts his European survey with Chapelle and Bachaumont's *Voyage* and La Fontaine's *Relation* in his redefinition of this genre. Galibert Nivoelisoa, *Chronobibliographie analytique de la littérature de voyage imprimée en français sur l'océan Indien (Madagascar-Réunion-Maurice) des origines à 1896* (Histoire du Livre et des Bibliothèques, 4), Champion, 2000, 231 pp., has 42 entries for the period 1600–1715.

French 17. An Annual Descriptive Bibliography of French Seventeenth-Century Studies, 48, ed. Suzanne C. Toczyski, Rohnert Park, CA, Sonoma State Univ., 2000, 196 pp., has a new editor and place of publication, but remains unchanged in form and comprehensive coverage.

2.   POETRY

V. Adam, 'Les *topoi* du temps dans la poésie baroque', *LitC*, 43:11–25, examines the *topoi* used by baroque poets to express their obsession with time and change. These are images of man passing through life to death, the seeds of which are in him from birth, and include the phoenix and, unusually, wax and thread which symbolize inconstancy and fragility. M. Clément, 'Le temps mystique dans la poésie spirituelle du XVIIe siècle', *ib.*, 195–204, attempts to make clear the problem of time as expressed in the spiritual works of some early 17th-c. poets who saw it as a means of understanding eternity and the notion of a god. A. Génetiot, 'Fonctions du dialogue dans quelques genres lyriques au XVIIe siècle', *PFSCL*, 54:9–30, discusses the eclogue, satire, *conte*, and fable and shows that the use of dialogue in these genres differs according to the aims of the specific lyric form. It is most powerful in the fable and its use in those of La Fontaine is thoroughly analysed. M. Jeanneret, 'Sonnets luxurieux: de l'érotique à l'obscène', *Gendre Vol.*, 385–400, examines the erotic poems of Malherbe amongst others and teases out the relationship between the wish to write such poems and the political and ideological background of the early 17th century. The conclusion is that writing such poems constitutes a desire to protect freedom and uphold the right to rebel against authority. J.-P. Chauveau, 'Variations sur un thème:l'hiver vu par quelques poètes du XVIIe siècle', *ib.*, 401–10, considers several poems which evoke winter by, amongst others, Boisrobert, Saint-Amant, and Agrippa d'Aubigné. In an age when the seasons made more impact, winter was particularly testing for many and the images in these poems can be seen as comments on contemporary human issues.

CANTENAC. *Satyres Nouvelles*, ed. Anne-Marie Clin-Lalande, Exeter U.P., 100 pp., is the first publication since the 17th c. of this little-known text. The introduction has useful details of the life of B. de C. and interprets the *Satyres*.

CONRART. R. Zuber, 'Pour Arnauld d'Andilly; une épître inédite de Conrart', *Sellier Vol.*, 477–85, prints this hitherto unpublished *épître* written *c.* 1645. Z. examines the circumstances of its composition and points out the contribution it makes to understanding the literary and political background of this pre-Fronde period.

JACQUES. J. Plantié, 'Un poète provincial, Jacques Jacques. Défenseur des Jésuites', *Sellier Vol.*, 557–68, is a spirited account of the burlesque poem *Le Faut Mourir* (1655) by the comparatively unknown poet from the Alps, Jacques Jacques, which gives a favourable view of the Jesuits.

LA FONTAINE. Maya Slater, *The Craft of La Fontaine*, London, Athlone, 2000, 256 pp., sets out to prove that La F. is 'acutely aware of the value of suggestion, even insinuation, rather than bold statement'. She does this by subjecting the *Fables* to a detailed analysis in which she shows that the deceptive simplicity of La F. is anything but simple. By a series of extremely subtle and perceptive readings of individual fables S. proves that if the full beauty of La F.'s art is to be savoured all the implications of even one word must be understood. As she puts it 'his writing needs to be "decoded" if its full impact is to be appreciated'. The book has chapters on 'Style', 'Imagery', 'Animals', 'Creating a world', and each one adds a 'layer' to the uncovering of the art of La F. which must make those who already like this author even more enthusiastic. Randolph P. Runyon, *In La Fontaine's Labyrinth: A Thread Through the 'Fables'*, Charlottesville, Rookwood, 2000, 210 pp., is a voyage through the *Fables* in search of clues which will allow the problem of whether La F. had a plan in the ordering of his fables to be solved. R.'s analyses of individual fables are detailed and he finds echoes and repetitions which go backwards and forwards through the whole work allowing him to conclude that La F. did indeed impose a clear structure on the work which proves that there is 'more intelligence at work in the arrangement of the *Fables* than we had thought'. Andrew Calder, *The 'Fables' of La Fontaine*,

Wisdom Brought down to Earth, Geneva, Droz, 220 pp., takes a number of themes and explores them with reference to the *Fables*. He sets out to show the very deep foundations on which La F. built the structure of his work. Well versed in the writings of ancients and moderns such as Plato and Montaigne, La F. was able to draw on this well of knowledge when creating his world inhabited as it is by men and animals representing men. C. goes into great detail on those aspects of La F. which he wishes to highlight and, indeed, there is very little that does not come under his scrutiny. The result is a very thorough, very detailed, and very learned reading of the *Fables* which opens many windows into their meaning.

M. O. Austin, 'Marianne Moore's translation of the term *galand* in the *Fables* of La Fontaine', *PFSCL*, 54:81–92, examines M.M.'s flexibility and insight in translating *galand* and, in so doing, makes many pertinent observations about the style and the depiction of characters in the *Fables*. J. Gallucci, 'La Fontaine: exemple et prophétie', *Sellier Vol.*, 463–75, investigates the role of prophecy in the *Fables* and suggests that, like that of the oracle at Delphi, the message of the *Fables* is not clear but is worth probing. R. Francillon, '"Les Obsèques de la Lionne": un concentré de la poétique de La Fontaine', *Gendre Vol.*, 433–43, analyses this fable and points out the veiled criticism of contemporary institutions, including the monarchy, which it contains, and suggests that there are parallels with some of Pascal's attitudes. O. Leplatre, '"Le Songe de Vaux" de Jean de La Fontaine: les métamorphoses de l'inachevé', *Rivara*, *L'Œuvre inachevée*, 83–92, uses the fact that the château de Vaux was incomplete when La F. wrote this work to draw parallels between the unfinished building and the unfinished poem. Paradoxically a dream being by its nature unfinished the poem achieves a completeness of sense which otherwise it might not.

NOSTREDAME.   *Œuvres spirituelles*, ed. Lance K. Donaldson-Evans, Geneva, Droz, 199 pp. In a long introduction the editor describes the life of César de Nostredame (1553–1629), son of the famous Nostradamus, and claims that he is one of the most representative religious poets of the baroque period and deserves to be put on a par with Sponde and La Ceppède although he does not, like them, write sonnets. He is a painter as well as a poet and this emerges in his writings as so many of his descriptions seem like descriptions of portraits. The editor analyses and comments on the poems *Les Perles ou les larmes de la Magdeleine*, *Dymas ou le bon larron* and *La Marie dolente*.

PERRAULT.   *Les Murs de Troye ou l'origine du burlesque, Livre* I, ed. Yvette Saupié (Biblio 17, 127), Tübingen, Narr, 121 pp., is the first publication of this work of the Frères Perrault (with their friend Beaurain) since the original edition of 1653. The very full introduction describes the circumstances in which it was composed in a period when the burlesque was very much in fashion. The interest of the text lies in the possible relationship between the systematic mocking of gods and heroes which characterize the genre and the events of the Fronde which was just coming to an end at that date. Not as effective as the much better known *Le Virgile travesty* of Scarron, this text merits its revival if only for the light it throws on the preoccupations of the Perrault brothers at this time, preoccupations which were to become more apparent when they wrote their famous *Contes* much later in the century.

RACINE. J. Dubu, 'Entre le vide et l'événement pur', *Sellier Vol.*, 415–23, is an examination of Racine's early poems *Le Paysage, ou les promenades de Port-Royal*, showing the intricacies of the metre used and the relevance of this to the tragedies written later.

SAINT-AMANT. G. Peureux, 'Lire le tableau, voir le poème: Poussin et Saint-Amant', *SFr*, 133:18–29, is a detailed account of the relationship between Poussin's paintings and the poems of Saint-Amant, treating particularly the *Moyse sauvé* bringing out the pictorial qualities of Saint-Amant's descriptions which correspond to Poussin's treatment of the same subjects.

TRISTAN L'HERMITE. J. C. Shepard, *Mannerism and Baroque in Seventeenth-Century French Poetry. The Example of Tristan l'Hermite*, Chapel Hill, North Carolina U.P., 188 pp., has very pertinent chapters which attempt to define the concepts of mannerism and the baroque in a clear and useful way. These concepts are then used to suggest readings of Tristan's poems which are illuminating. The overall conclusion which S. proposes is that 'Tristan is primarily a mannerist poet of love and a baroque poet in his heroic, philosophical, and religious poems'. A. Génétiot, 'Harmonie et tragédie: le lyrisme mélancolique de "l'Orphée"', *CTH*, 23:5–32, is a detailed analysis of this poem in which G. explores T.'s expression of the passions and shows how it is similar to the exploration of these in contemporary tragedy. G. Peureux, '*Les Plaintes d'Acante* et leurs annotations: Tristan à la recherche de son public', *ib.*, 33–50, points out the importance of the annotations for understanding the change in attitude of poets in the early 17th c. T.'s *Plaintes* mark a turning point from 'learned' to 'galant' poetry. L. Philipps, 'Les annotations des "Plaintes d'Acante": le commentaire de son poème', *ib.*, 51–60, sees the annotations as an ambiguous text which is not all it seems. T. seems deliberately to be drawing the reader on into areas of understanding which are not always clear but which prolong the directions the poem itself seems to be taking. L. Grove, 'Emblèmes d'amour dans "Les Plaintes d'Acante"', *ib.*, 61–72, examines the links between the *Plaintes* and some 17th-c. books of emblems published in the Low Countries showing the, at times, very close relationship between the scene depicted in the emblem and the description by Tristan and concludes that the *Plaintes* reveal a mentality mixing text and image, narration and description. J.-P. Chauveau, 'Tristan et les plaisirs de Monsieur', *ib.*, 73–74, is a commentary on two extracts of *vers de ballet: Monsieur, représentant une Sultane* and *Monsieur, représentant un Africain*. G. Banderier, 'Notes sur la réception de Tristan', *ib.*, 78–81, cites references to T. in Naudé's *Mascurat* in 1650 and Villiers de l'Isle-Adam in 1886.

3. DRAMA

Hélène Baby, *La Tragi-comédie de Corneille à Quinault*, Klincksieck, 306 pp., tackles the question of the tragi-comedy with the aim of pinning down its distinctive characteristics which made its contribution to 17th-c. drama unique. By examining more than 120 examples of the genre dating from the period 1628–1642, B. explores the relationship between the world of the tragi-comedy and reality as it was then envisaged with particular reference to the social structures of this period. Somewhat bogged down by the mass of material examined, this theme does nevertheless emerge and makes its point. Ziad M. Elmarsafy, *The Histrionic Sensibility. Theatricality and Identity from Corneille to Rousseau* (Biblio 17, 124), Tübingen, Narr, 243 pp., is a thoughtful survey of those aspects of the works of Molière and the two Corneilles which brings out the links between them and their way of interpreting the world around them while at the same time throwing light on the relationship between these interpretations and the reality of 17th-c. France. Sabine Chaouche, *L'Art du comédien. Déclamation et jeu scénique en France à l'âge classique*, Champion, 454 pp., analyses the rules of rhetoric in order to illustrate the art of acting and demonstrates how acting and oratory were allied. C. examines many texts and by choosing examples of movement and declamation taken from plays themselves is able to illustrate how the actor changed the rules in order to produce something new. A perceptive and very thoroughly researched work which brings to light many new facets of the art of acting in the 17th century. Alan Howe, *Le Théâtre professionnel à Paris, 1600–1649*, Centre historique des Archives Nationales, 2000, 454 pp., presents a collection of documents from the Minutier central des notaires de Paris, the majority of which have not been published before, and is extremely valuable because of the information they yield. In his rich and rewarding study of the documents H. is able to shed much new light on the lives of actors and on the composition of the *troupes* and their activities in Paris in the period surveyed. He interprets the documents and shows how they can be used so that it will be difficult from now on to study the history of the theatre, *troupes*, and actors themselves in the first half of the 17th-c. without having recourse to this immensely rich compilation and its illuminating commentary.

Tomlinson, *Theatre*, includes C. E. J. Caldicott, 'For the non-classical in seventeenth-century French theatre' (27–38), which discusses the problems raised by the meaning of the word 'classicism'; W. Brooks, 'Decrypting the chronology of early French opera' (39–52), which points out how dangerous it is to accept statements concerning the performances of opera whch are not based on firm evidence and how difficult it is to obtain this; C. Mazouer, 'Comment écrire une histoire du théâtre au XVIIe siècle' (53–69), describing his approach to this project, defining his aims, and justifying the choice of those that he has made; K. Cameron, 'The critical edition: the editor's incubus?' (71–79), which discusses the *raison d'être* of the critical edition and, with all his experience as General Editor of the Exeter *Textes littéraires*, offers his thoughts on the responsibilities involved; J. Dunkley, 'Old plays; modern editions' (81–97), underlines the importance, and difficulty, of scientific editing to make sure that what is presented to the public is as accurate as it can be made to be; C. Guillot, 'La recherche en iconographie théâtrale aujourd'hui: quelques réflexions sur l'utilisation de l'image du livre du XVIIe siècle' (101–16), analyses some contemporary illustrations of Mairet's *La Silvanire* and the *Mirame* of Desmarets and shows the interest and profit of iconography for the study of 17th-c. drama; A. E. Zanger, 'Betwixt and between print and performance: a new approach to studying Molière's body at/of work' (117–38), discusses eight images published in editions of Molière produced between 1661 and 1669 with reference to the function they serve and what can be learned from them; J. Clarke, 'The Hotel Guénégaud auditorium according to the theatre's account books' (139–53), deduces important information about the size and capacity of this theatre from a careful analysis of the account books, a source hitherto not used for this purpose; C. Williford, 'Computer modelling classical French theatre spaces: three reconstructions' (155–64), provides, with illustrations, computer-generated tours of the Hôtel de Bourgogne, the Palais Cardinal theatre, and the Palais-Royal theatre; C. Biet, 'L'interprétation des classiques sur la scène française contemporaine' (249–69), surveys the great variety of interpretations of Corneille, Molière, and Racine on the French stage today and makes a plea for widening the repertoire to include plays of dramatists who are never performed; B. Russell, 'Theatre scholarship in the age of electronics' (273–83), explores the enormous potential of the computer in making available texts and other theatre material online; G. Spielmann, 'Spectacles du Grand Siècle: du projet épistémologique au projet éducatif'

(285–300), is a description of a course given by S. to introduce students to the importance of 'spectacle' as a component of studying 17th-c. literature.

Marc Vuillermoz, *Le Système des objets dans le théâtre français des années 1625–1650*, Geneva, Droz, 2000, 333 pp., is a very detailed examination of the role of objects, understood in the widest sense of the word, in the elaboration of the drama in the theatre of the period. Objects such as letters, swords, chains, doors, torches, crowns, sceptres, etc. are shown to be used either to enhance the presentation of a character or a situation or to suggest ways in which the action should be viewed by the spectator. The work contains many tables and enumerations, the importance or significance of which are not clear but as a whole the immense amount of work which has gone into the preparation of this volume does illuminate an aspect of the theatricality of the drama of this period which is novel and stimulating.

J.-L. Backès, 'Le spectre de Plutarque', *RLC*, 298 : 214–19, discusses the meaning of 'influence' and 'parallelism' with reference to Plutarch and questions the value of these concepts and the way they are used. M.-N. Casals, 'La vérité comme indice dans trois poétiques du premier XVIIe siècle: Jean Vauquelin de La Fresnay, Pierre de Deimier, Jean Chapelain', *DSS*, 210 : 19–33, looks at the attitudes of these three theoreticians towards the role of reality in poetry and drama concentrating on the difference between *vrai* and *vraisemblable*. B. Louvat-Molozay, 'Le traitement du temps dans la tragi-comédie et dans la pastorale (1628–1632): les enjeux dramatiques du débat autour de la règle des vingt-quatre heures', *LitC*, 43 : 117–45, discusses the treatment of time in the two specified genres and comes to the conclusion that it poses insoluble problems for them because of the incompatibility of the subject-matter with the objective of compressing the action into 24 hours. C. Kintzler, 'Temps expérimental de théâtre, temps empirique d'opéra: la question du spectacle', *ib.*, 117–25, claims that one of the differences between tragedy and opera springs from the use of time which has completely opposite functions in each genre, because in tragedy spectacle is not to the fore whereas in opera it is all-important. P. Pasquier, 'L'ombre du temps: réflexion sur le statut du temps dramatique dans le discours esthétique du XVIIe siècle', *ib.*, 89–116, is a very thorough and detailed examination of texts relating to the unity of time showing how this evolved between 1628 and 1663 and its importance in understanding the subtle change of perspective on time in plays of the earlier period and those of the later period. G. Revaz, 'La "veuve captive" dans la tragédie classique', *RHLF*, 101 : 213–26, examines the role of the captive widow in tragedy and relates it to political undercurrents where power and love come into conflict. L. Van Delft, 'L'idée de théâtre (XVIe–XVIIIe siècles)', *ib.*, 1349–65, is an examination of the change undergone by the designation *Theatrum* showing how its meaning from being all-embracing has considerably narrowed and provides a vast bibliography using the term from 1539 to 1783, most of which are relevant to the 17th century. J.-C. Vuillemin, 'Quelques réflexions sur l'enseignement du théâtre classique', *RHT*, 211 : 125–46, deals with the relative importance of the dramatic (i.e. linguistic) text and the performance (i.e. semiotic) text and makes cogent points.

AUBIGNAC. Abbé d'Aubignac, *La Pratique du théâtre*, ed. H. Baby, Champion, 758 pp. This new edition of the *Pratique* has an introduction placing it in context, notes illuminating the text, and a long section entitled *Observations sur la Pratique du Théâtre* in which B. discusses all the important points raised by the text. This new edition makes this seminal text available once more in an edition which will be definitive for a long time to come.

CORNEILLE. Pierre Ronzeaud, *Corneille/Le Cid*, Klincksieck, 206 pp. This anthology in the collection 'Parcours critique', introduced by R., brings together twelve articles on *Le Cid* by P. Bénichou, P. Sellier, J. Serroy, M. Margitic, R. Pintard, P. Voltz, M. Bertaud, S. Doubrovsky, M. Vuillermoz, J. Garagnon, P. Pavins, and R. Albanese Jr. To have these articles, each with a distinctive point of view to put forward, united in one volume is exceptionally useful for any study of *Le Cid*. Claire L. Carlin, *Women Reading Corneille. Feminist Psychocriticisms of "Le Cid"*, Berne, Lang, 2000, 166 pp. By basing chapters on the works of five writers of works of feminist psychoanalytic criticism, C. explores *Le Cid* from this point of view. She uses these theories to demonstrate how Chimène can be seen to represent the female who refuses to accept the rules of society laid down by men and thus highlights the problems of a society in transition towards the triumph of absolutism. J.-Y. Vialleton, *Lectures du jeune Corneille: "L'Illusion comique" et "Le Cid"*, Rennes U.P., 166 pp., is a collection of nine articles which look at these two plays under three headings: 'comédie, tragédie et tragi-comédie: la question du genre dramatique', 'rhétorique et poétique dramatique', and 'contextes, significations'. The points of view expressed provide an excellent introduction to modern interpretations not only of these plays but of 17th-c. drama as a whole.

Corneille, *Horace*, ed. M. Escola, GF Flammarion, 212 pp., is an edition having an exceptional quality of presentation and supplementary material. N. Ekstein, 'Uncertainty in Corneille's *Héraclius*', *NFS*, 40.2 : 3–13, investigates the tangled relationships in this play in order to examine questions of identity and the problems that arise when deliberate attempts are made to disguise reality. G. Banderier,

'Corneille et les Jésuites: un poème inédit', *DSS*, 212:545–49, publishes a poem which is a translation by C. of an epigram addressed to Anne d'Autriche and is significant because it shows the strong relationship between C. and the Jesuits in 1659–1660 at the moment when his career was beginning again with the production of *Œdipe*.

DU RYER. *LitC*, 42, 'Pierre Du Ryer dramaturge et traducteur', is devoted entirely to articles on Du Ryer introduced by Dominique Moncond'huy. It includes J.-P. Chauveau, 'Deux générations de poètes: Isaac Du Ryer, père de Pierre' (13–28), an examination of the poetry of Isaac Du Ryer, pointing out its affinities with the poets of the early 17th c.; O. Bousquet, 'Pierre Du Ryer dramaturge: une stratégie de l'oubli' (29–58), which discusses the reasons why the plays of Du Ryer failed to survive and concludes that it was because they reflect a political situation more suited to the early part of the 17th c.; D. Blocker and D. Ribaud, 'Du Ryer ou l'écriture indirecte' (67–97), use Du R.'s occasional writings to explain why he seems to detach himself from his work; H. Baby, 'Pierre Du Ryer et la tragi-comédie, 1628–1638: le tournant d'un génie?' (101–20), analyses the 11 tragi-comedies of Du R. and shows how they differ from his tragedies, and insists on emphasizing the completely different conceptions which separate the two genres; L. Picciola, 'L'adaptation scénique de l'histoire d'Argénis et Poliarque: les dramaturgies de Du Ryer et de Calderon' (121–36), compares two adaptations of Barclay's novel and makes many points concerning the different approaches of the French and Spanish playwrights; G. Conesa, 'Comique et enjouement dans *Les Vendanges de Suresnes*' (137–44), claims that the *poétique* which supports this play echoes the profound changes in the social life of the early 17th c.; V. Steinberg, '*Les Vendanges de Suresnes* et la modernité comique' (145–63), suggests that Du R. by combining pastoral elements with realistic elements creates a play which reflects the values of its time and is comic; A. Duroux, '*Lucrèce ou* le renouveau de la tragédie. Eléments pour une dramaturgie de la tragédie des années 1630–1640' (167–79), compares Du R.'s *Lucrèce* with Chevreau's play of the same name and claims that the former uses new principles of dramatic writing then coming into vogue and thus composes one of the first 'regular' tragedies; V. Narcisse, '*Alcionée* ou le théâtre de la soumission' (181–96), is a discussion of the political implications of this tragedy, treating as it does the problem of how far a ruler ought to keep his word, an interesting subject in the time of Richelieu; M. Escola, 'Simplicité d'*Alcionée*. Notes sur une notion difficile' (197–219), is a very dense investigation of the meaning of *simplicité* not only in *Alcionée* but in many plays of Corneille and Racine also; S. Chaouche, '*Alcionée*: une tragédie du pathétique tendre?' (221–44), looks at the evidence for labelling *Alcionée* thus, and in the course of the discussion probes fruitfully into many aspects of the development of tragedy in the mid-17th c.; D. Moncond'huy. '*Thémistocle*, tragédie désinvolte ou (dé)cousue?' (245–54), discusses the shortcomings of the play because of its attempts to be too many things at once. Its weakness suggests a reason why Du R. turned to writing tragi-comedies; B. Louvat-Molozay, '*Saul* de Du Ryer: entre La Taille et la Bible, le double défi d'une tragédie biblique moderne' (257–76), sets out to prove that in this tragedy Du R. treats in a modern way a subject taken from a different tradition; M. Papapetrou-Miller, '*Esther* ou de l'obscurité à la lumière' (277–94), is a very detailed analysis of this play based on the opposition of light and darkness which P.-M. sees as a theme running through the play; R. Ganette, 'Méthodes en phraséométrie. Application à des fragments de l'*Esther* de Du Ryer et celle de Racine' (295–325), scrutinizes many examples of 'phrase' in Du R. and R. and concludes that this method shows up the difference in style in the two dramatists — eloquence in Du R. and poetry in Racine; C. Guillot, 'Les éditions illustrées du théâtre de Pierre Du Ryer: image et contexte éditorial' (329–45), discusses the frontispieces of four plays and analyses them in detail. These illustrations must be 'read' as well as 'looked at' as then they contribute greatly to the comprehension of the text.

MAIRET.   P. Tomlinson, 'Jean Mairet and Henri II de Montmorency, or what's a poet worth? Some new evidence', *PFSCL*, 54:31–44, analyses receipts given by Mairet for payments made to him by Montmorency in 1630, draws conclusions about his relative prosperity, and makes some interesting comments about the social situation of dramatists and poets at this time based on the generosity of their patrons.

MOLIÈRE.   Joseph Pineau, *Le Théâtre de Molière. Une dynamique de la liberté*, Minard, 2000, 226 pp. In this dense and stimulating discussion of the plays of Molière, P. sets out to prove that there is a development in the progression of his comedies which shows M. striving to come to terms with the obstacles and frustrations, both external and internal, which meet men as they go through life. M.'s dynamism comes from the unusual power with which he confronts reality and makes it explode by his choice of characters and the motives that drive them, reflecting the agitation and difficulties of a society on the move. In the course of his journey through the plays of M., P. reveals an extensive knowledge of Molière criticism which he puts to excellent use.

C. Bourqui, 'Molière interprète de tragédies hagiographiques', *RHLF*, 101:21–35, discusses in detail the relationship between Molière's repertory in *L'Illustre Théâtre* and plays dealing with the lives of saints particularly *L'Illustre comédien* of Desfontaines. B. puts forward, in a note, a tentative theory that M. himself might be the author of this play.

M. Gutwirth, '*Maître Jacques ou le sourire de Molière*', *Van den Heuvel Vol.*, 95–114, sets out to define 'humour' in the widest sense and then narrows it down to the difference between 'sourire' and 'rire' which is then exemplified in *Le Malade imaginaire* and *L'Avare*.

F. Rouget, 'Molière lecteur d'Etienne Pasquier? Réflexions autour du libertinage de *Dom Juan*', *DSS*, 211:257–67, is a detailed and convincing investigation of the similarities between Don Juan's praise of inconstancy and that elaborated by Philopole in the *Monophile* of Etienne Pasquier (1554). No attempt is made to claim Pasquier as a direct source of M. but the evidence for such a claim is very convincing. C. Cagnat-Debœuf, ' "Le tambour du petit Colin": les noms propres dans *Dom Juan*', *ib.*, 210:35–47, is a penetrating analysis of the significance of names in *Dom Juan* showing that Molière was playing on a wide variety of possibilities in his choice of names which, when looked at carefully, are very revealing about the characters thus designated.

A. Calder, '*Le Misanthrope*: from ideas to shared experience', Tomlinson, *Theatre*, 167–77, suggests ways of teaching *Le Misanthrope* and in so doing raises the question of laughter and its function especially in relation to Alceste.

C. Kintzler, '*Les Femmes savantes* de Molière et la question des fonctions du savoir', *DSS*, 211:243–56, is a complicated and difficult study of the philosophical questions raised by this play, particularly with regard to the man/woman relationship as a reflexion of the body/mind division as seen in the three *savantes*. L. Riggs, 'Reason's text as palimpsest: sensuality subverts "sense" in Molière's *Les Femmes savantes*', *PFSCL*, 54:93–103, argues that because language is a means used by those in power to impose their will on others, the *Femmes savantes* can be interpreted as an example of this which utterly fails.

PUGET DE LA SERRE. C. Guillot, 'Les illustrations du *Martyre de Sainte Catherine* de Puget de La Serre: des images à référence scénique', *DSS*, 211:307–22, scrutinizes the illustrations of this play published in 1643, of interest because of the detailed description of the scenery they give which throws light on the significance and symbolism of the action described in the text.

QUINAULT. A. Cullière, '*La Fille généreuse*, tragi-comédie en quête d'auteur', *DSS*, 212:535–44, shows that the play is not, as often supposed, by Madame de Balmon, and brings forward evidence which does not, however, claim to be irrefutable, that Q. is, indeed, the author of this tragi-comedy.

RACINE. *Racine et/ou le classicisme,* ed. R. W. Tobin (Biblio 17, 129), Tübingen, Narr, 505 pp., prints the *Actes* of the 1999 Santa Barbara Conference, with an introduction by R. W. Tobin: G. Declercq, 'Poéticité *versus* rhétoricité; pathos et logos dans les tragédies de Racine' (19–53), argues that, far from destroying *poéticité,* the *rhétoricité* which is part of R.'s dramatic approach to his subjects is indispensable for the development of the expression of passion; G. Forestier, 'Editer Racine aujourd'hui: choix, enjeux, significations' (55–71), explains why in his edition of the works of Racine (Pléiade, 1999) he chose to use the punctuation Racine used in the first editions of his plays rather than that of the final collected edition of 1697, used by almost all other editors. He shows that the earlier punctuation throws light on the way R.'s verses were declaimed on the stage, as punctuation was used, not in a grammatical way, but in order to guide the speaker not the reader; C. Kintzler, 'L'opéra, révélation et trahison du théâtre' (73–89), discusses the relationship between the tragedy and opera and shows how they interact with each other, thus illustrating unsuspected aspects of both genres; B. Bolduc, '*Iphigénie*: de la vaine éloquence à l'artifice efficace' (93–112), examines this tragedy as symbolizing, to a certain extent, the triumph of artifice because of its first performance in the gardens of Versailles; R. Racevskis, 'The time of tragedy: *Andromaque, Britannicus, Bérénice*' (113–23), draws conclusions about R.'s methods of denoting time in these three tragedies especially *Bérénice;* R. Albanese Jr., '*Britannicus:* une dramaturgie de l'espace' (125–35), argues that the concept of space in the tragedy can affect the interpretation of the roles of Néron, Agrippine and Junie; L. F. Norman, 'Racine's "other eye": history, nature and decorum from ancient to modern' (139–50), is a discussion of R.'s attitude towards ancient history and concludes that 'ancient history is exploited by R. for its very otherness'; E. Bury, 'Racine historiographe: théorie et pratique de l'écriture historique' (151–68), claims that when R. became *historiographe du roi* he was already well prepared through his meticulous study of ancient historians and that there is no discrepancy in the tragic poet becoming a historian; S. M. Guénoun, 'Coupures et recoupements: une histoire en lambeaux. Etudes des *Notes et fragments* de Racine' (169–94), argues convincingly that there is much to be gleaned on R.'s modes of thought from a study of these; E. Limbrick, 'Racine: the historian in the text' (195–205), sees the *Abrégé de l'Histoire de Port-Royal* as an attempt by R. to blame the Jesuits for Louis XIV's hostility to the Jansenists; N. Ekstein, '*Le Change* in Corneille and Racine' (209–21), traces the history of *change* from its role in the early plays of C. and R. to its fuller expression in the later tragedies; S. R. Baker, 'Sounds of silence: faltering speech in Racine's *Bérénice* and Corneille's *Tite et*

Bérénice' (223–32), examines what can be learned from the silences in both plays and concludes that 'tragic misunderstandings of the Racinian type do not occur in Corneille's version: the *dramatis personae* understand each other all too well'; L. W. Riggs, 'The sovereign eye and the empty throne. Chimène silent, Junie invisible' (233–45), discusses the ways in which *Le Cid* and *Britannicus* exemplify in their own ways the idea of a 'state' and the exercise of power in conflict with assertions of the individual; J. Campbell, ' "Enseigner Racine", *mission impossible?'* (249–60), outlines the decline in the study of R. in French schools and universities and discusses possible remedies; P. Bayley, 'Let's dump classicism' (261–64), pleads for the study of R. unencumbered by outdated notions of classicism which only hinder the student tackling this author for the first time; W. Brooks, 'Racine; or the triumph of irrelevance' (265–74), describes how R. can be introduced into an undergraduate course by using comparisons with comedy which provide unexpected insights into both genres; M. Hawcroft, 'Racine through pictures' (275–307), analyses very perceptively the contents of some illustrations which accompany R.'s text in editions from the 17th to the early 19th c.; M. S. Koppisch, ' "Tout fuit, tout se refuse à mes embrassements"; can we continue to teach Racine?' (309–19), is a discussion of the function and aims of University teaching of literature using R. as the peg on which to hang the arguments; S. C. Toczyski, 'Teaching *Phèdre*: desire and the phenomenology of action' (321–32), offers an exploration of the meanings of 'to act', 'to do', and 'to perform' in understanding *Phèdre*; L. MacKenzie, 'Phèdre makes the scene: opening (the) signals and semantics' (333–40), probes the significance of some of the terms in Phèdre's opening speech; J. Emelina, 'Le bonheur dans les tragédies profanes de Racine' (343–67), sets out to bring to the fore some aspects of Racinian criticism which E. thinks are being neglected at the expense of what he calls 'une critique "technique" sur la génétique, la dramaturgie ou la rhétorique'. He does this by examining R.'s treatment of love both unrequited and, particularly, requited; P. Zoberman, 'Ethics, politics, and metaphysics: representations of power in Racine's theater' (369–88), examines the way R.'s tragedies, especially *Iphigénie*, reflect the way power in 17th-c. France was exercised through absolute monarchy; L. Van Delft, ' "Philosophie" et "comédie": nature — ou condition — humaines?' (389–92), suggests directions which research on R. could take under the headings 'moraliste' and 'anthropologique'; G. Cowart, 'Sappho's Cythera: the *fête galante* vs. the *fête monarchique* in seventeenth-century France' (395–408), looks at some opera-ballets at different periods of the reign of Louis XIV; M. Delcroix, 'Katachronismes raciniens' (423–35), explains the title by looking at aspects of the language of *Phèdre* and its use of words like *séduire* which are multi-layered and, when carefully dissected, reveal meanings not immediately apparent; D. Course, 'Pourquoi Racine n'a-t-il jamais écrit de pièce sur Judith?' (437–48), argues that, although Judith was a favourite 17th-c. heroine, R. considered Esther a more attractive subject for a tragedy. P. Gethner, 'Pros and cons of human sacrifice in French mythological plays' (449–58), discusses plays other than *Iphigénie* which involve human sacrifice, especially the *Endymion* of Françoise Pascal; M.-F. Hilgar, 'L'héroïne de Racine a-t-elle franchi le pas?' (471–75), demonstrates, by examining the tenets of casuistry, that Œnone's accusation of Hippolyte fits neatly into one of its categories and hence illustrates the responsibility of Phèdre; J.-C. Vuillemin, 'Baroque: pertinence ou obsolescence?' (479–96) is a spirited discussion of the thorny problem of the 'baroque' and suggests that 'classicism' is, possibly, 'un baroque à la française'; J. D. Lyons, 'What do we mean when we say "classique"?' (497–505), takes up the argument and goes on to say that the terms *'classicisme'* and *'classique'* should be used with extreme caution.

V. Desnain, *'Les Faux Miroirs*: the good woman/bad woman dichotomy in Racine's tragedies', *MLR*, 96:38–46, describes the contrast between the female characters in R., claiming the existence of a 'bad' woman to counteract 'the good woman'. The characteristics of these are explored showing that the'good' woman is the one who fits in most easily to a male-dominated society while the 'bad' woman is she who does not accept it and therefore pays the price. Ead., ' "Fille de Jézabel": female genealogies in Racine', Tomlinson, *Theatre*, 191–203, raises the very important question of the contribution feminist theory can make to 17th-c. studies using examples of female characters in Racine's tragedies.

R. Albanese, Jr., 'Silence et parole dans *Britannicus'*, *AJFS*, 38:179–89, examines the role of silence and speech in the tragedy emphasizing the different forms this takes and its importance both for moving the action forward and bringing out the tragedy of the situation.

D. Berry, ' "Rough magic": Ted Hughes's translation of Jean Racine's *Phèdre'*, Tomlinson, *Theatre*, 207–28, discusses this translation with much insight, demonstrating how H., while translating R.'s tragedy superbly, nevertheless 'transmutes and metamorphoses it [. . .] into an English poetic drama'.

A. T. Delehanty, 'God's hand in history: Racine's *Athalie* as the end of salvation historiography', *PFSCL*, 54:155–66, takes two views of history, narrative history and 'salvation' history, and argues that *Athalie* is dealing with the clash of these two interpretations, thus producing a tragedy which is specially relevant to the period in which it was written.

C. Smith, 'Racine in the modern Modern Languages curriculum', Tomlinson, *Theatre*, 179–89, looks at the place of tragedy and Racine in particular in modern University French courses and makes the case for persisting in teaching this subject.

SCARRON. *Le Jodelet Duelliste*, ed. J. Carson, Geneva, Droz, 2000, 208 pp., is a most welcome edition of this comedy of Scarron with informative introduction and notes.

URFÉ. Honoré d'Urfé, *La Sylvanire (1627)*, ed. L. Giavarini, Toulouse, Société de Littératures Classiques — Paris, Champion, 178 pp. This first modern edition of *La S.* has a very full introduction which is not only useful as a history of the pastoral in the early 17th c. but also for its discussion of d'U.'s work showing how *La S.* fits into it although it was not published until after his death. The text is well presented and adequately annotated. The *Avis au lecteur* is valuable for its explanation of the role of rhyme in plays and because it contains a declaration by d'U. that his aim was to 'plaire et par accident profiter'.

4. PROSE

Jacques Berchtold, *Les Prisons du roman (XVIIe–XVIIIe siècle). Lectures plurielles et intertextuelles de 'Guzman d'Alfarache' à 'Jacques le fataliste'* (HICL, 386), 784 pp., studies a double theme, 'la menace d'être emmené en prison' and 'le séjour en prison', and its treatment in the 'romans proto-réalistes' of Spain (those of Alemán and Quevedo) and France (Sorel's *Francion*, Claireville's *Gascon extravagant*, Cyrano's *États et empires du soleil*, and works by Préfontaine, Dassoucy, Courtilz de Sandras, and others). Giorgi, *Perspectives*, contains the following: E. Bury, 'À la recherche d'un genre perdu: le roman et les poéticiens du XVIIe siècle' (9–33), which points to the fact that 'l'évolution du roman au XVIIe siècle en France a constamment pris en défaut l'élaboration théorique des poéticiens', so that prose fiction evaded the efforts of theorists to fix it according to the precepts of Aristotle and his Italian Renaissance disciples; G. Giorgi, 'Les poétiques italiennes et françaises du roman au XVIe et au XVIIe siècles' (35–52), also writes of attempts to codify the novel; A. Capatti, 'L'ivrognerie enfantine dans le roman burlesque' (145–62), looks at *Le Roman comique, Le Page disgracié, Francion*, and d'Assoucy's *Aventures burlesques*; B. Bray, 'Le roman par lettres, ou la fiction dénoncée' (187–211), claims that, if *vraisemblance* means anything, this form is 'un genre hybride, au point d'en être proprement inconcevable [. . .]: qui dit roman entend fiction, et qui dit lettres suppose authenticité';

G. Berger, 'Histoire et fiction dans les pseudo-mémoires de l'âge classique: dilemme du roman ou dilemme de l'historiographie?' (213–26), looks at the 'techniques d'illusion' used in *pseudo-mémoires* to deceive readers, and also at the dubious 'valeur scientifique' of history in the period; F. Piva, 'Crise du roman, roman de la crise. Aspects du roman français à la fin du XVIIe siècle' (281–303), pinpoints interesting and significant trends.

N. Grande, 'Le temps dans la fiction, les fictions du temps. Réflexions sur le temps et ses représentations dans quelques œuvres de fiction narrative en prose du XVIIe siècle', *LitC*, 43 : 147–59, picks out Rosset, d'Urfé, Mlle de Scudéry, and Mme de La Fayette for their different attitudes to time. L. Plazenet, 'Origine de la fable ou alibi romanesque? Les vicissitudes du manuscrit trouvé chez les imitateurs d'Héliodore en France aux XVIe et XVIIe siècles', Herman, *Manuscrit trouvé*, 47–60, notes how several French authors of romances imitate H.'s use of the topos with variations in the details. Id., 'Révolution ou imposture? De l'imitation à l'invention du roman grec en France aux XVIe et XVIIe siècles' Bessière, *Commencement*, 23–47, covers the same period more widely.

Isabelle Trivisani-Moreau, *Dans l'empire de Flore: la représentation romanesque de la nature de 1660 à 1680* (Biblio 17, 126), Tübingen, Narr, 509 pp., covers all forms of fiction in this fertile period which also saw a development of interest in gardens like those of Versailles. T.-M. concludes that the notion of a garden as a *locus amoenus* tends to prevail. 'Nature originelle' is less valued than that 'imitée et recréée par l'homme'. Christian Leroy, *La Poésie en prose du XVIIe siècle à nos jours: histoire d'un genre* (Unichamp essentiel, 2), Champion, 192 pp. is more interested in the genre and its derivations than in periods. Tragedy is considered, and also epic, Fénelon's *Télémaque* being classified among the latter and given particular attention.

Elizabeth C. Goldsmith, *Publishing Women's Life Stories in France, 1647–1720: from Voice to Print*, Aldershot–Burlington, Vt., Ashgate, vii + 172 pp., introduces us to a group of innovative women autobiographers who betray in different ways 'a more subversive and personal agenda' than traditional male memorialists. The lives chosen are those of Marie de l'Incarnation, Jeanne des Anges, and Jeanne Guyon (religious lives), Hortense and Marie Mancini (courtly lives), and Mme de Villedieu (a 'scandalous' life). C. Abraham, 'Comment peut-on être femme?', *PFSCL*, 28 : 135–40, considers literary portraits of 'la plus haute aristocratie', and what writers wished to achieve in them, using the *Gallerie* of Mlle de Montpensier as his main example. C. L. Carlin, 'Imagining marriage in the 1690s', *ib.*, 167–76, looks at the variety of polemical texts written during this decade as a reaction to the *Traité du mariage* of 1670 — misogynistic satires, repressive demands from theologians, and on the other hand works of fiction by Villedieu, d'Aulnoy, and Anne Bellinzani Ferrand attacking arranged marriage and advocating personal choice.

Thierry Pech, *Conter le crime. Droit et littérature sous la Contre-Réforme: Les Histoires tragiques (1559–1644)* (Lumière classique, 24), Champion, 2000, 480 pp., studies a vogue for tales of 'le scandale, le châtiment et les passions qu'ils suscitent', and sees their popularity as a reaction to the desire felt by the authorities to 'renforcer le secret des procédures criminelles'.

E. Dubois, 'Quelques aperçus sur l'épître spirituelle au XVIIe siècle', *TLit*, 13, 2000 : 101–11, reviews letters by eminent clerics and nuns advising, instructing, consoling, reprimanding colleagues, relatives, and friends about matters pious and practical. J.-P. Landry, 'Éléments pour une histoire littéraire de la prédication en France au XVIIe siècle', *Bertaud Vol.*, 143–52, notes recent neglect of 17th-c. pulpit oratory, but considers this to be no more than 'un épiphénomène passager'. To help repair this neglect he recalls for us the more interesting names associated with oratory, and reminds us of its variety, its *genres* and *sous-genres*. R. Baustert, 'Les thèmes homériques dans les lettres de consolation de la première moitié du XVIIe siècle', *ib.*, 555–71, quotes Louys Richeôme, Cyrano, Claude-Barthelémy Morisot, Etienne Bachot, and Guillaume de Rebours. Francine Wild, *Naissance du genre des ana (1574–1712)* (Études et essais sur la Renaissance, 29), Champion, 781 pp., delves into the origins and evolution of the genre. Carole Martin, *Imposture utopique et procès colonial: Denis Veiras — Robert Challe* (EMF Critiques), Charlottesville, Rookwood, 2000, 268 pp., studies first the *Histoire des Sévarambes*, then *Les Illustres Françaises*, with a third section, on 'Utopisme et libertinage', comparing them.

AULNOY. Jean Mainil, *Madame d'Aulnoy et le rire des fées: essai sur la subversion féerique et le merveilleux comique sous l'ancien régime*, Kimé, 291 pp., seeks to show how this author 'effectue une subversion idéologique et narrative à partir des termes culturels et littéraires qui ont été assignés à la femme et à la femme auteur précisément par l'idéologie qu'elle subvertit'. He claims that A. 'inaugure [. . .] une écriture ironique de la femme auteur sous l'Ancien Régime'. R. Guichemerre, 'Une émule inattendue de Scarron: Madame d'Aulnoy', *Van den Heuvel Vol.*, 69–76, notes A.'s use of frame narrative for three sets of her *contes*, and is struck by the resemblance of the last of these, *Le Nouveau Gentilhomme bourgeois*, with its six inserted *contes*, to Scarron's *Roman comique*.

BALZAC. *Beugnot Vol.* prints five contributions on B.: R. Zuber, 'Sur une lettre de Guez de Balzac: du manuscrit à l'imprimé' (37–43), shows us how the raw material of a manuscript letter, when it comes to publication, 'peut se raccourcir, se scinder, s'alléger', and may serve as a basis for letters to new recipients; R. Arbour, 'La première édition du *Prince* de Guez de Balzac' (45–55), throws light on the order of publication of the two earliest editions by reproducing and commenting on the *contrat d'impression* found in the Minutier central; J. Jéhasse, 'Guez de Balzac et les trois *Discours à Monsieur Descartes*' (57–70), examines each *discours* in turn and accounts for its place in B.'s works; P. Dandrey, 'Guez de Balzac paradoxal: l'éloge satirique du Barbon' (71–82), comments on 'œuvres pseudo-encomiastiques', and defines B.'s point of view as that of a Cartesian who believed that 'l'on ne saurait avoir raison ni être sage tout seul'; E. Méchoulan, 'Les deux plus rares choses du monde: être vrai et paraître vrai' (83–95), starts with B., and ranges over 17th-c. views on this relationship.

BÉROALDE DE VERVILLE.   D. Mauri, 'L'écriture "alchimique" de Béroalde de Verville romancier', Giorgi, *Perspectives*, 53–77, reviews the several thousand pages published by B. between 1592 and 1610, to bring out his most significant characteristics — the role of the narrator, the status of the characters, and their 'approfondissement psychologique', and finally tackles 'quelques problèmes relatifs aux intrigues, aux structures et aux thèmes'. P. Servet, 'Béroalde de Verville, *Le Moyen de parvenir* ou les vertiges de l'inachèvement', Rivara, *L'Œuvre inachevée*, 61–69, praises this 'livre contre toutes les formes de savoir, toutes les formes de clôture, toutes les formes de définition', which 'déconstruit méthodiquement tous les processus narratifs et dialogiques que les XVe et XVIe siècles avaient mis en place'.

BOSSUET.   *Sermons: Le Carême du Louvre 1662*, ed. Constance Cagnat-Debœuf (Folio classique, 3458), Gallimard, 384 pp. C.-D. in her preface introduces us to the circumstances surrounding 'la réforme de la prédication', to the notion of 'le sermon classique' and to the salient themes of court life and its shortcomings and *libertinage*.

CAMUS.   *L'Amphithéâtre sanglant*, ed. Stéphan Ferrari (Sources classiques, 27), Champion, 419 pp., reproduces the 1630 edition of this collection. F.'s introduction includes a biography, a history of the genre, and a study of the stories, revealing them always to have an identical 'schéma narratif'. A. L. Franchetti, 'Les travestissements romanesques de J.-P. Camus', Giorgi, *Perspectives*, 107–28, reappraises the 17th-c. practice of using fiction to discredit fiction, and analyses some of C.'s techniques of subversion. M. Cox, 'The bishop's secret: Jean-Pierre Camus's unacknowledged source', *FSB*, 77, 2000: 5–7, reveals that C. owes much to Simon Goulart's *Thresor d'histoires admirables et memorables*.

CYRANO DE BERGERAC. *Œuvres complètes, 1: L'Autre Monde ou les États et Empires de la Lune, Les États et Empires du Soleil, Fragment de physique*, ed. Madeleine Alcover (Sources classiques, 15), Champion, 2000, ccix + 615 pp., is accompanied by an introduction which displays A.'s commitment to accuracy and completeness. *Œuvres complètes, II: Lettres, Entretiens pointus, mazarinades*, ed. Luciano Erba and Hubert Carrier (Sources classiques, 34), Champion, 512 pp. *Lettres satiriques et amoureuses précédées de Lettres diverses*, ed. Jean-Charles Darmon and Alain Mothu, Desjonquères, 1999, 256 pp., modernizes spelling and punctuation. M. Botto, 'Le monde fictionnel de Cyrano de Bergerac', Giorgi, *Perspectives*, 163–86, assembles recently expressed opinions on 'l'organisation des textes cyraniens en tant que récits'. L. Petris, 'Figures, fonctions et sens de l'inversion dans *Les Estats et Empires de la Lune* de Cyrano de Bergerac', *DSS*, 53:269–83, asserts that C.'s work is a 'dialogue philosophique baroque, par son goût de l'irrégularité, du changement et de l'inattendu, par une odeur d'inconstance et d'incertitude qui pèse sur toute théorie'.

DU PLAISIR. J. Mesnard, 'Lumières sur le sieur Du Plaisir', *Beugnot Vol.*, 275–91, convincingly demonstrates that Du P. and 'Paul-Roger Sibour' were the same person.

DU RYER, PIERRE. E. Bury, 'Note sur Pierre Du Ryer traducteur', *LitC*, 42:59–65, raises questions, and seeks to 'indiquer quelques éléments de réponse' about Du R.'s translations and their relation to his times, his contemporaries, and his dramatic works.

FÉLIBIEN. U. Dionne, 'Félibien dialoguiste: les *Entretiens sur les vies des peintres*', *DSS*, 53:49–74, finds F. following a late-17th-c. trend by presenting his ideas in dialogue form rather than as a 'discours savant'.

FURETIÈRE. *Le Roman bourgeois*, ed. Marine Roy-Garibal (GF, 1073), Flammarion, 399 pp., is furnished with a thorough 'présentation' discussing the novel's themes, language, and literary and social context. Id., 'Furetière et le droit bourgeois de la langue' *LitC*, 40, 2000:103–18, studies F.'s *factums* against the Académie Française's efforts to suppress his dictionary.

GOURNAY. H. Fournier, 'S'approprier l'autorité de la voix de l'autre: Marie de Gournay et la traduction de l'Ode III, IX d'Horace', Wilson-Chevalier, *Fémynie*, 41–50, surveys G.'s theories on translation, and examines how she put them to use in her version of this ode; G. is also referred to in S. Steinberg, 'Le mythe des Amazones et son utilisation politique de la Renaissance à la Fronde', *ib.*, 261–73, as one of the writers using the myth as an image to inspire women in their quest for freedom and equality, while others, such as Mlle de Montpensier, Mme de Chevreuse, and Mme de Longueville during the Fronde, use it to denote women who distinguish themselves in warlike situations.

GUILLERAGUES.   T. Lassalle-Maraval, '*Les Lettres portugaises*: œuvre inachevée?', Rivara, *L'Œuvre inachevée*, 93–102, points to the remarkable number of sequels inspired by this work, reviews them, and then questions 'la pertinence de tels ajouts en examinant la cohérence de l'œuvre ainsi complétée'.

LA BRUYÈRE.   *La Bruyère: le métier du moraliste*, ed. Jean Dagen et al. (Moralia, 5), Champion, 261 pp., prints conference papers which study La B.'s reactions to his literary predecessors and contemporaries, and discuss the editions of the *Caractères*, their form, rhetoric and style. L. van Delft, 'La mémoire du théâtre chez La Bruyère', *Beugnot Vol.*, 293–301, pursuing a subject which he had already broached in the above conference, seeks the theatrical in the style and content of *Les Caractères*, and in the life of the author. Claire Badiou-Monferran, *Les Conjonctions de coordination ou 'l'art de lier ses pensées' chez La Bruyère* (Bibliothèque de grammaire et de linguistique, 5), Champion, 2000, 645 pp., presents a study which is in part about co-ordinating conjunctions in general, and in part about such conjunctions in the *Caractères*.

LA FAYETTE.   R. Francillon, 'Madame de La Fayette: au carrefour des esthétiques du roman', Giorgi, *Perspectives*, 269–80, admires the narrative method adopted by the novelist who employs the voice of an objective historian but nevertheless gives the impression of having lived in the times and known the characters featuring in the novel.

LA ROCHEFOUCAULD.   Q. M. Hope, 'La Rochefoucauld and the vicissitudes of time', *PFSCL*, 28.1 : 105–20, rapidly reviews the *Maximes* and *Réflexions diverses*, to show how they can be taken to represent the 'journey through life'. R. Hodgson, 'La sagesse humaine face à une "souveraine puissance": la prudence et la fortune chez La Rochefoucauld', *DSS*, 53 : 233–42, emphasizes La R.'s views on the limitless power of 'la fortune'. J. Lafond, 'La Rochefoucauld: le moi, l'autre et les autres', *Sellier Vol.*, 425–34, qualifies the views expressed by T. Todorov in *Poétique*, 53, 1983 : 37–47 (see *YWMLS*, 45 : 115). P. Force, 'De l'utilité et de l'honnêteté dans les *Maximes* de La Rochefoucauld', *ib.*, 435–47, places the Augustinianism of the *Maximes* 'dans le contexte du débat antique et moderne sur les rapports de l'utile et de l'honnête'.

MONTPENSIER.   Vincent J. Pitts, *La Grande Mademoiselle at the Court of France 1627–1693*, Baltimore–London, Johns Hopkins U.P., 268 pp., is biography.

MORGUES.   Seung-Hui Lim, 'Mathieu de Morgues, bon français ou bon catholique?' *DSS*, 53 : 655–72, finds this 'pamphlétaire de

Marie de Médicis' a 'bon catholique', and no admirer of the centralized France that Cardinal Richelieu sought to establish.

PASCAL, FRANÇOISE DE. *Le Commerce du Parnasse*, ed. Deborah Steinberger (Textes littéraires, 111), Exeter U.P., xiii + 49 pp., is a sequence of letters in prose and verse by P. herself or by unidentified correspondents of hers. S. notes in her introduction the development of 'une intrigue principale' in which 'de véritables personnages s'esquissent', and claims credibly that the work is an early representative of the fictional *genre épistolaire*. S. proposes Guilleragues as one of P.'s correspondents.

PERRAULT, CHARLES. C. Velay-Vallantin, 'Les vies singulières du *Chat botté* en Angleterre: métamorphoses d'un conte de Perrault dans le colportage anglais du XVIIIe siècle', Delcourt, *Bibliothèque bleue*, 235–50, follows changes to the original wrought by adaptation for the theatre.

RETZ. Y. Le Bozec, 'La mise en place du vraisemblable dans les *Mémoires* du Cardinal de Retz', *PFSCL*, 28.1:61–79, sees the work as one written according to 'les règles du *vraisemblable* littéraire' where *le vrai* came second.

ROHAN, HENRI DE. Solange and Pierre Deyon, *Henri de Rohan, huguenot de plume et d'épée, 1579–1638*, Perrin, 2000, 224 pp., is a study of R.'s life and writings.

SCARRON. J. Serroy, '*Le Roman comique*, roman carrefour', Giorgi, *Perspectives*, 129–44, shows how S. makes use of the town of Le Mans and its Tripot de la Biche as a *carrefour* for 'personnages divers venus d'horizons différents' and also for 'deux veines romanesques: [. . .] la tradition comique, satirique et picaresque' and 'la veine romanesque, sentimentale et héroïque'. J.-P. Landry, '*Le Roman comique* ou le nécessaire inachèvement', Rivara, *L'Œuvre inachevée*, 71–82, emphasizes that S.'s novel is 'de bout en bout ironique', that it is at once a *roman* and an *anti-roman*. He wishes to assuage our 'malaise et frustration' at S.'s failure to complete his novel by suggesting another way of looking at its incompleteness, noting a 'mélange de rigueur dans la composition et de désinvolture dans l'expression' which makes the novel hard for a *continuateur* to complete. Perhaps, L. suggests, S. did not intend it to end.

SCUDÉRY, GEORGES DE. R.-G. Pellegrini, 'Les œuvres de Georges de Scudéry dans la critique contemporaine: quelques réflexions', *Bertaud Vol.*, 179–90, defends S. against his detractors and surveys recent work on him. E. Dutertre, 'Les palais de Monsieur de Scudéry', *ib.*, 573–601, suggests that S. may have collaborated with his sister on devising the plot of *Ibrahim*, and written the description in it of Ibrahim's palace which has much in common with other descriptions by him in prose and verse.

SCUDÉRY, MADELEINE DE. C. Morlet-Chantalat, 'Le théâtre dans le roman. Aspects du comique dans la *Clélie*', Giorgi, *Perspectives*, 251–67, finds in episodes and characters (particularly Amilcar) 'tout ce qui provoque le rire par les moyens du théâtre'. SÉVIGNÉ. M.-C. Killeen, 'Loin des yeux, près du cœur: Madame de Sévigné et le supplément de l'écriture', *PFSCL*, 28.1 : 121–34, depicts S. writing to 'conjurer la présence de sa fille en son absence', though 'il s'agirait pour elle non point tant de compenser une séparation physique passagère d'avec la destinataire mais bien plus de nier, avec un acharnement forcené, la séparation première d'avec elle'. C. Cartmill, 'Madame de Sévigné et les maximes du mariage' *DFS*, 56 : 98–107, discovers 'plusieurs exemples de discours généralisant relevant de différents genres sentencieux [. . .] qui se rapportent souvent à l'amitié et qui s'appliquent au mariage', and particularly examples betraying a distrust of *amour-passion* and also a conviction that in marriage 'le bien constitue un critère encore plus important que la naissance'. M. Gérard, 'Madame de Sévigné et le souvenir de Pascal', *Sellier Vol.*, 449–62, claims that there is 'un énorme dossier' which 'reste à établir'.

SOREL. *LitC*, 41, is devoted to *Francion*: J. Morgante, 'La réécriture de la première partie de *Francion*: techniques d'écriture libertine' (13–30), counsels 'une triple lecture' of all three versions of the novel in order to appreciate the 'travail de dissimulation' undertaken by S.; A. Suozzi, 'La bourgeoisie à la recherche de la noblesse: le libertinage de l'*Histoire comique de Francion*' (31–40); Y. Giraud, ' '"Mais j'étais un grand trompeur . . .". Franchise et tromperie ou le double jeu de Francion' (41–48), attacks those who see in Francion a libertine hero rather than (in G.'s view) a 'faussaire' and a hypocrite; M. Debaisieux, 'Sous le signe de Mercure: de la thématique du vol à la fraude littéraire dans le *Francion*' (49–61), tackles the question of how far 'la figure ambivalente de Mercure répond de la représentation du protagoniste', and how far 'l'identification à un dieu dont les principaux attributs sont ruse, mensonge et vol s'accorde avec la thématique de l'histoire comique'; P. Ronzeaud, 'L'imagination dans l'*Histoire comique de Francion*: l'autre Naïs' (63–82), studies the third and final version, and finds above all in 'la personnalité vivante et créatrice de Francion' a form of perfection — 'une autre Naïs'; F. Assaf, '*Francion*: une étude carnavalesque' (85–95), considers the first version of *Francion* to be as *carnavalesque* as Rabelais; C. Mazouer, 'Le théâtre dans l'*Histoire comique de Francion* de Charles Sorel (Livres I à VIII)' (97–107), compares S.'s evocation of aspects of theatre with the reality of the time, and points to the author's awareness of the link between 'l'esthétique du roman et celle de la comédie'; G. Verdier, ' '"Femmes-objets"? Femmes de tête? L'indécidable sexe féminin dans l'*Histoire comique de Francion*' (111–21), probes 'les signifiants par lesquels se construisent les "personnages" féminins'; J. Serroy, 'La P ... irrespectueuse: l'histoire de la vieille dans le *Francion* de Sorel' (123–31), concentrates on Agathe's story, her role in the 1623 version, and the contrast between her and 'l'image idéale de l'Autre' — Naïs; F. Dumora-Mabille, 'Logiques du sens dans le songe de Francion' (133–52), examines the Book III narration, placing it in progressively widening contexts, concluding with that of the 'vulgate freudienne'; C. Zonga, 'Les mots et les choses dans l'*Histoire comique de Francion*' (155–66), reveals a 'vérité à facettes' produced by the 'rapports problématiques et multiples' between 'le signe et son référent', leading us to reflect on language, on literature, and the writer's place in society; E. Desiles, 'Des signes à la littérature: problèmes de langage dans l'*Histoire comique de Francion*' (167–86), examines allusions to speech, gesture, and style; N. Fournier, 'Langage, discours, métadiscours, style dans l'*Histoire comique de Francion*' (187–212), surveys the varieties of language S. refers to and uses.

H. Tucker, ' "Une autre de vostre ventre": parodic musicality in Charles Sorel's *Histoire comique de Francion* and *Le Berger extravagant*', *FrF*, 24, 1999:303–14. W. De Vos, 'Les personnages dans *Polyandre* de Charles Sorel: manuscrits ambulants?', Herman, *Manuscrit trouvé*, 61–72, points to S.'s mockery in *Francion* and *Polyandre* of the fashion of noting down *lieux communs*.

D'URFÉ. S. Poli, '*L'Astrée*, les fleuves bucoliques et les heureuses terres de l'Ancien Régime', Giorgi, *Perspectives*, 79–106, notes the way in which U. suggests *correspondances* between the moods of his characters and natural phenomena, and contrasts them with the settings established in the *incipits* of earlier Italian, Spanish, and French pastoral romances. P. Berthiaume, 'Psychodoxie du personnage dans *L'Astrée*', *DSS*, 53:3–18, is harsh with U., claiming that 'les personnages se réduisent [. . .] à des abstractions soumises à des codes, à des essences, figés qu'ils sont dans l'image que le discours donne d'eux'.

VALINCOUR. *Lettres à Madame la Marquise *** sur le sujet de la Princesse de Clèves*, ed. Christine Montabetti (GF 1114), Flammarion, 174 pp. Extracts from the Abbé de Charnes's *Conversations sur la critique de la Princesse de Clèves* are also given.

VILLEDIEU. R. Harneit, '*Le Portefeuille* de Mme de Villedieu: édition et réimpression des *Œuvres meslées* au XVIIe siècle', *RHLF*, 101:1455–62, finds many more editions of the collection than have hitherto been listed. A. Defrance, 'Vengeances d'amour dans les nouvelles historiques et/ou galantes de Madame de Villedieu', Méchoulan, *Vengeance*, 97–129, shows how, in V.'s view, the strength of the *passion amoureuse* 'fait la faiblesse de l'homme, son universalité celle des sociétés, à toute époque et en tous lieux'. B. Vanhouck, 'Henriette et Madeleine: jeux et enjeux de la réécriture au XVIIe siècle', *DSS*, 53:673–87, sees in the anonymous *Mémoires de la vie de Mlle Delfosses ou le Chevalier Baltazar* (1695) an imitation of V.'s *Mémoires de la vie d'Henriette-Sylvie de Molière*, and an implicit commentary on its form and content.

5. THOUGHT

Moreau, *Scepticisme*, contains papers on 16th-c. and 17th-c. European philosophers, scholars and scientists of which seven are on French 17th-c. writers and reviewed under their names below. One is of a general nature: C. Borghero, '*Cartesius scepticus*. Aspects de la querelle sur le scepticisme de Descartes dans la seconde moitié du XVIIe siècle' (391–406), which studies texts by various European scholars arguing for and against the claim, the most notable Frenchman in the debate being Huet.

Philippe Sellier, *Port-Royal et la littérature, II: Le siècle de Saint-Augustin, La Rochefoucauld, Mme de Lafayette, Racine* (Lumière classique, 34), Champion, 2000, 294 pp., prints 18 papers and articles, all but one published elsewhere between 1969 and '2001' (*sic*). The one *inédit* is 'Qu'est-ce que le Jansénisme (1640–1713)?' (43–76), which concentrates on 'le jansénisme attribué à Port-Royal, c'est à dire un ensemble de positions sur la théologie de la grâce divine', following the evolution of these from the *Augustinus* to the bull *Unigenitus*.

CPR, 50, prints colloquium papers on *Port-Royal et l'Oratoire*: D. de Courcelles, 'Pour une archéologie spirituelle: Thérèse d'Avila dans l'histoire de l'Oratoire et de Port-Royal' (47–62), affirms that 'la conjonction de l'Oratoire et de Port-Royal [. . .] due à la volonté de trois personnes, Bérulle, la Mère Angélique Arnauld et Saint-Cyran [. . .] s'effectue autour de la personnalité et de l'œuvre de Thérèse d'Avila'; B. Delahaye, 'Les relations épistolaires du cardinal Pierre de Bérulle avec les amis de Port-Royal: le père Charles Maignart' (63–80), introduces us to M., and reproduces a hitherto unpublished letter from him to B.; D. Donetzkoff, 'Saint-Cyran et Condren' (81–99), traces their association from 1620 to its rupture in 1636; M. Dupuy, 'Sous l'influence de l'Oratoire, une redéfinition de la vie religieuse' (119–27), notes the influence of Bérulle on the 'constitutions de quelques congrégations dans la mouvance de Port-Royal'; A. Ferrari, 'L'inspiration oratorienne dans les débuts de Port-Royal' (129–40), traces similarities, mutual interests, and friendships; F. Vanhoorne, 'Entre Oratoire et Jansénisme: politiques de Quesnel et de Duguet' (195–208), proposes to 'situer les politiques élaborées' [by Q. and D.] 'dans le cadre d'une tradition bérullienne et dévote';

R. Hermon-Belot, 'La politique chrétienne de Duguet à Grégoire: du prince chrétien à la souveraineté du peuple' (209–27), notes in both, despite the distance in time that separated them and the vast social evolution that had taken place, an 'accent augustinien' and a 'besoin d'unir [. . .] politique, morale et piété'; R. Cadoux, 'La question anthropologique chez Bérulle et chez Saint-Cyran' (315–23), finds the latter to be the 'fidèle disciple' of the former in rejecting humanism and embracing the Bérullian notion of 'servitude' to Christ; A. Levi, 'Gibieuf, Zamet, Saint-Cyran et Jansen: alliances et incompatibilités théologiques et spirituelles' (325–41), looks at the teaching, careers, and personal relations of these four; I. Noye, 'Fractures entre des disciples du P. de Condren' (343–53), is concerned with the public differences evident in the early 1650s between the *père* Desmares and the *abbé* Olier, due, claims N., to the increasing animosity of the latter towards Port-Royal; J.-R. Armogathe, 'Port-Royal et l'Oratoire: l'affaire Séguenot (1638)' (367–81), seeks to 'mettre en valeur les enjeux doctrinaux de cette "affaire" et son lien avec l'évolution politique de Port-Royal'; P. Magnard, 'L'homme entre rien et tout' (433–45), finds differences between the Oratoire and Port-Royal in the 'reprise de l'un à l'autre du langage néantiste'; H. Michon, 'Bérulle et Pascal: de l'anéantissement' (447–62), makes subtle comparisons; H. Bouchilloux, 'Le statut de l'amour-propre chez Pascal et Malebranche' (513–24), inquires how the positions of these two on the subject 'diffèrent en fonction de leurs théologies respectives'; M. Moriarty, 'Imagination et rapports sociaux chez Pascal et Malebranche' (525–39), looks at their respective analyses of the 'puissances trompeuses'; M.-A. Robert, 'Connaissance de l'histoire et morale chrétienne à l'Oratoire et à Port-Royal (Bernard Lamy, Louis Thomassin, Pierre Nicole)' (557–76), compares the pedagogical works of the two Oratorians L. and T. with the *Traité de l'éducation d'un Prince* by N.

A. McKenna, 'Les *Pensées* de Pascal: une ébauche d'apologie sceptique', Moreau, *Scepticisme*, 348–61, links the 'pari' with 'la logique de la "Machine" qui est celle de notre seconde nature' and which will constitute 'un détournement du scepticisme de Montaigne'. N. H. Courtès, 'Le temps de la méditation chez Descartes et Malebranche', *LitC*, 43:205–25, finds the influence of the Oratoire in the *Méditations* of both.

Michel Terestchenko, *Amour et désespoir de François de Sales à Fénelon*, Seuil, 2000, 414 pp., studies a 17th-c. tension between the notion of 'une humanité vouée par nature au mal et à l'enfer éternel' and that of those who were 'confiantes dans la raison et les pouvoirs de la volonté' allied to 'l'amour désintéressé de Dieu'. This debate over the 'mystère de la justice divine' is pursued by T. through theologians and philosophers, within and outside the Catholic Church, culminating in 'le pur amour chez Fénelon [. . .] présenté comme un *antipari* pascalien, comme un refus de calculer nos chances de salut'. Alain Faudemay, *Le Clair et l'obscur à l'âge classique* (Travaux des universités suisses, 8), Geneva, Slatkine, 583 pp., compares two centuries of artists, philosophers, theologians, lexicographers, and grammarians, and concludes that, whenever these two terms are confronted, 'il arrive que les textes flottent quelque peu entre la continuité qui solidarise et le contraste qui exclut'. Sylvia Giocanti, *Penser l'irrésolution. Montaigne, Pascal, La Mothe Le Vayer: trois itinéraires sceptiques* (BLR, Série 3, 45), Champion, 732 pp., starts from the assertion that M.'s scepticism 'ne réside [. . .] pas dans les discours théoriques [. . .] mais dans sa mise en exercice [. . .]. Le sceptique est sceptique en ce qu'il fait l'essai de sa pensée irrésolue, et non en ce qu'il l'expose avec résolution'. P. and La M. consider M. 'comme un sceptique en acte dont le scepticisme se traduit par la pratique de l'essai [. . .] de la pensée'.

Tullio Gregory, *Genèse de la raison classique de Charron à Descartes*, trans. Marilène Raiola, PUF, 2000, 366 pp., reprints essays, all previously published between 1964 and 1992, on 'le libertinisme', on C., on Gassendi, and on D. Muriel Bourgeois, Olivier Guerrier, and Laurence Vanoflen, *Littérature et morale 16e-18e siècle: de l'humaniste au philosophe* (U. Lettres), Armand Colin, 192 pp., aim to avoid a 'découpage séculaire' and emphasise a continuity across the ages. R. W. Serjeantson, 'The passions and animal language', *JHI*, 62:425–44, surveys views on the subject from Montaigne to Claude Perrault.

ANTOINE ARNAULD.   *Textes philosophiques: Conclusions philosophiques, Dissertation en deux parties sur la vision des vérités en Dieu et l'amour de la vertu, Règles du bon sens . . ., De la liberté de l'homme*, ed. Denis Moreau (Épiméthée), PUF, xi + 332 pp. M. urges us to neglect A. the polemicist for the A. of the *Logique* 'qui fournit les clés d'accès à ses œuvres', particularly, here, the *Dissertatio bipartita* (translated by M.), and the *Règles*, which are the longest work in this volume.

CHARRON.   N. Stricker, 'Le sage de Charron: une réévaluation', Moreau, *Scepticisme*, 164–73, takes issue with those who see C. as a *libertin*, and claims that 'si *Les Trois Veritez* se fondaient sur la première injonction augustinienne: *Credo ut intelligas*, la *Sagesse* renvoie à la seconde: *Intellige ut credas*, dans la mesure où la sagesse humaine prépare à recevoir la foi'.

COTON.   B. Petey-Girard, 'De l'oraison mentale au sermon intérieur: la petite rhétorique méditative du révérend père Coton', *PFSCL*, 28.1:45–60, presents this Jesuit's *Sermons sur les principales et plus difficiles matières de la foy* (1617), and places them in their Counter-Reformation context and in that of a tradition dating back to St. Augustine.

DESCARTES. *Descartes et la Renaissance*, ed. Emmanuel Faye (Centre d'études supérieures de la Renaissance, *Le Savoir de Mantice*, 5), Champion, 1999, 453 pp., prints conference papers. Daniel Gerber, *Descartes Embodied: Reading Cartesian Philosophy through Cartesian Science*, CUP, xii + 337 pp., collects previously published essays. J. Bourg, 'The rhetoric of modal equivocacy in Cartesian transubstantiation', *JHI*, 62:121–40. A. Christofidou, 'Descartes' dualism: correcting some misconceptions', *JHP*, 39:215–38, concentrates on what is 'standardly' referred to as 'the argument from doubt'. J. Brody, 'Descartes, *Discours de la méthode*: essai de lecture philologique', *Beugnot Vol.*, 211–27, wishes to demonstrate how 'la révolution accomplie par Descartes dans le domaine des idées est inséparable des vicissitudes de son langage et des complexités de sa rhétorique'. T. Shiokawa, 'Pourquoi le bon sens est-il la chose du monde la mieux partagée?', *Sellier Vol.*, 143–60, takes D.'s opening assertion in the *Discours de la méthode* to be irony, 'badinage sérieux', 'une sorte de proverbe', and refers us back to Montaigne for a similar usage. Edouard Mehl, *Descartes en Allemagne 1619–1620: le contexte allemand de l'élaboration de la science cartésienne*, Strasbourg U.P., 367 pp., concentrates on D.'s early stay in south Germany, and the scientific and philosophical trends and traditions that might have exerted their influence on him there. V. Aucante, 'La démesure apprivoisée des passions', *DSS*, 53:613–30, studies D.'s *Traité des passions de l'âme*. J.-P. Cavaillé, 'Descartes et les sceptiques modernes: une culture de la tromperie', Moreau, *Scepticisme*, 334–47, seeks to fill gaps in the history of the subject, and to examine the *Recherche de la vérité par la lumière naturelle* in order to 'appréhender quelques traits du scepticisme exploité et réfuté par Descartes'.

DUGUET. H. Savon, 'Jacques-Joseph Du Guet: des Pères de l'Église au figurisme', *CPR*, 50:157–75, looks at the *Règles pour l'Intelligence des Saintes Écritures* which he claims is a 'manifeste du figurisme'. G. Aventurier, M. Grange, and A. Collet, 'La correspondance de la famille Duguet (1683–1750): une découverte récente', *ib.*, 177–93, introduce us to 168 newly discovered letters.

FORTIN DE LA HOGUETTE. G. Ferreti, 'The *Testament* of La Hoguette and its sources', *French History*, 15:123–38, introduces and contextualizes F.'s 'conseils fidelles d'un bon père à ses enfans'.

GASSENDI. J.-C. Darmon, 'Le jardin de la loi: de l'utilité comme fondement du droit et du politique chez Gassendi', *LitC*, 40, 2000:53–73, tackles the question: 'En quel sens peut-on parler d'une politique, voire d'une théorie de la justice proprement épicurienne au seuil de l'Âge classique?' and finds the answer in G.'s reflections on *utilitas*, and, more succinctly, in François Bernier's *Abrégé de la philosophie de M. Gassendi*. Id., 'Sortir du scepticisme, Gassendi et les signes', Moreau, *Scepticisme*, 222–38, seeks, in Book 2, chapter 5 of the *Syntagma*, 'le moment essentiel du "dépassement" gassendien du scepticisme'.

GOULAS.   N. Hepp, 'Nicolas Goulas: un solitaire *extra muros*', *Sellier Vol.*, 487–94, discusses in particular G.'s preface to his *Mémoires*.

LA BARDE.   J. Lesaulnier, 'L'oratorien Léonor de La Barde lecteur de Saint Augustin et de Descartes (1607–1672)' *Sellier Vol.*, 495–511, provides details, particularly on La B.'s relations with D., and also with Antoine Arnauld.

LA MOTHE LE VAYER.   S. Giocanti, 'La Mothe Le Vayer: scepticisme libertin et pratique de la contrariété', Moreau, *Scepticisme*, 239–56, examines the 'deux figures de la contrariété [. . .] privilégiées par La Mothe Le Vayer: la Fortune, qui nous contrarie en nous infligeant ses revers, l'Opiniâtre, qui nous contrarie en nous contredisant systématiquement'.

LAMY.   C. Noille-Clauzade, 'Bernard Lamy, ou la Rhétorique de Port-Royal', *CPR*, 50:541–55, regards L.'s *Rhétorique* as being 'sous l'égide de *La Logique ou L'Art de penser*'.

LA PEYRÈRE.   F. Parente, '"Du tort qu'ont les Chrétiens de persécuter les Juifs": quelques observations à propos du "philosémitisme" d'Isaac de La Peyrère', Tollet, *Textes*, 51–66, wishes to correct misunderstandings dating from La P.'s lifetime, claiming that he was less *philosémitique* than has been supposed.

LE MAISTRE DE SACY.   G. Banderier, 'Note sur l'*Imitation* traduite par Le Maistre de Sacy', *FSB*, 80:2–3, makes corrections to the extensive article in *RFHL*, 1996, by M. Delaveau on translations of Thomas à Kempis's manual.

MALEBRANCHE.   A. Robinet, 'Malebranche et Port-Royal', *CPR*, 50:503–12, wonders how far an author as original and independent-minded as M. would be respectful towards the 'édits oratoriens, notamment anti-cartésiens, aussi bien que des formulaires anti-jansénistes signés d'office', but also 'dans quelle mesure ces règlements prennent en compte ses propres apports'.

MERSENNE.   N. Malcolm, 'Six unknown letters from Mersenne to Vegelin', *SCen*, 16:95–122, introduces us to these autograph letters on music and musical instruments, dating from September 1641 to January 1644, addressed to Philip Ernst Vegelin, now among the Vegelin papers in the Provincial Archive of Friesland at Leeuwarden. B. Joly, 'La figure du sceptique dans *La Vérité des sciences* de Marin

Mersenne', Moreau, *Scepticisme*, 257–76, finds M. not so much anti-sceptical as willing to use scepticism as 'une attitude à adopter, un moment nécessaire dans la recherche de la vérité'.

MONTFAUCON DE VILLARS. P. Sellier, 'Un palimpseste pascalien: *Le Comte de Gabalī*', *Beugnot Vol.*, 247–53, reviews this attack of 1671, by the Abbé M. de V., on the *Pensées*, and points to its debt to the *Provinciales* for its strategy.

NICOLE. B. Guion, 'Nicole lecteur de Pascal', *Sellier Vol.*, 369–98, examines the various, often contradictory, judgments expressed by N. on P.

PASCAL. *Œuvres complètes*, II, ed. Michel Le Guern (Bibliothèque de la Pléiade), Gallimard, 2000, 1710 pp., completes the edition begun with vol. I in 1998 (see *TWMLS*, 60:136). It contains the letters, *Opuscules*, *Écrits sur la grâce*, *Œuvres mathématiques d'Amos Dettonville (sur la roulette)*, *Les Carosses à cinq sols*, the *Pensées*, and the *Vers et propos attribués à Pascal*. The *Pensées* are regrouped to juxtapose 'les textes portés par le même papier', which has necessitated a new numbering, and consequently the inclusion of a concordance with the editions of Brunschvicg, Lafuma, and Sellier.

Sellier Vol. contains the following essays on P.: A. Bord, 'Pascal: essai de biographie spirituelle' (259–70), which ponders on the influence of the 'Carmes déchaussés' on P.; J. Mesnard, 'Le double Mystère de Jésus' (271–88), which comments on the unity or otherwise of Sellier frs. 749 and 751; C. M. Natoli, 'Les *Provinciales*: ruse contre ruse, force contre force?' (289–99), who wishes to understand the impact of P.'s attack: 'son désir d'agréer au grand public [. . .] a-t-il abouti à la séduction de ceux qu'il voulait désabuser?'; G. Ferreyrolles, 'De la causalité historique chez Pascal' (309–32), discusses P.'s views on the relationship manifested in history between natural and divine causality; P. Magnard, 'Un corps plein de membres pensants' (333–40), shows P., in his *Pensées*, faithful to the spirit of St. Augustine, adhering to traditional views of society, of the relationship between the classes, and between the king and his subjects; L. Thirouin, ' "Transition de la connaissance de l'homme à Dieu": examen d'une liasse des *Pensées*' (351–68), offers a thought-provoking reading. E. Gilby, 'Reflexivity in the *Pensées*: Pascal's discourse on discourse', *FS*, 55:315–26, asserts that 'the object of Pascal's thought is the elusive nature of the thought itself'. M. Philonenko, 'Pascal, lecteur et adaptateur du *Quatrième Livre d'Esdras*', *Bertaud Vol.*, 643–49, looks at Sellier fr. 425 and at the circumstances of its composition. Régine Pouzet, *Chronique des Pascal. "Les affaires du monde" d'Étienne Pascal à Marguerite Périer (1588–1733)* (Lumière classique, 30), Champion, 696 pp., is a meticulously researched and documented history of the Pascal-Périer family. Dominique Descotes,

'Port-Royal et les indivisibles', *Sellier Vol.*, 185–99, considers the reception of the *Lettres de A. Dettonville* by P.'s Port-Royal friends.

QUESNEL.   H. Schmitz du Moulin, 'Quesnel et Port-Royal', *CPR*, 50:249–64, writes of Q.'s relations with Antoine Arnauld, his attitude to the *Formulaire* drawn up by the 'Assemblée du Clergé', and his eventual exile.

SIMON, RICHARD.   S. Ben Massaoud, 'La *Bibliothèque critique* de Richard Simon', *CPR*, 50:101–18, comments on this 'recueil de notes, mémoires et correspondance'.

THE EIGHTEENTH CENTURY

By ROBIN HOWELLS, *Reader in French, Birkbeck College, London*; RUSSELL GOULBOURNE, *Lecturer in French, University of Leeds*; HEATHER LLOYD, *Senior Lecturer in French, University of Glasgow*; SHEILA MASON, *Senior Lecturer in French Studies, University of Birmingham*; and KATE E. TUNSTALL, *Fellow in French, Worcester College, Oxford.*

1. GENERAL

L'Atlantique, ed. Marcel Dorigny (*DhS*, 33), PUF, 759 pp., seeks, following Anglo-Saxon precedents, to confirm the reality of 'une civilisation atlantique des lumières'. Four areas of enquiry are addressed: the Atlantic as forum of exchange, the geopolitics of maritime power, the circulation of knowledge, representations and sociability. The subject matter is preponderantly historical, but as S. Marzagalli, 'Sur les origines de l' "Atlantic History" ' (17–32), argues, deciding whether the ocean was a basin conjoining cultures or a ditch dividing them is a prerequisite of analysing the formation of identity. J. Gury, 'Le philosophe et la morue' (81–100), discerns Raynal's influence in the European Enlightenment's endorsement of the Newfoundland fisheries' moral wholesomeness. M. Belissa, 'Les Lumières contre la guerre de course' (119–31), reviews the fruitless denunciations of buccaneering in Mably, Linguet, and Condorcet. F. Regourd, 'Les Antilles et les Lumières' (182–99), adduces the evidence of the indigenous and transatlantic booktrade, notarial inventories of private libraries, and the existence of learned and literary societies to reverse, particularly in relation to San Domingo, stereotypical pictures of the 'milieu créole' as anti-intellectual, venal, and debauched. N. Wulf and E. Marienstras, 'Traduire, emprunter, adapter la Déclaration d'indépendance des États-Unis' (201–18), investigate the authorship and the linguistic and conceptual hurdles of translating the Declaration for French consumption. Pointing to the shift from Lockian contractualism to ideas of natural society, they demonstrate the tenacity of cultural matrices in construing the modern nation-state. P. Cheney, 'Les économistes français et l'image de l'Amérique' (231–45), traces the conflict between the Montesquieu-Hume assessment of commerce as the progenitor of civilisation and physiocratic denunciations (inspired by American agrarianism) of the regressive features of modern Continental fiscality, thus illuminating the colonial process as domination, exploitation, and plantation. A. Potofsky, 'La Révolution transatlantique des émigrés' (247–63), contrasts the innovative observational methodology, influenced by Arthur Young, of Liancourt's *Voyages aux États-Unis* (1798) with the retrogressive imperialist thematics of other *émigré* accounts. This brings out the polarizations of exiled opinion, despite a common core of centralist assumptions, which are conveniently shared with the current Federalist regime but uncomfortably at odds with the Jacobin citizenry. Y. Bénot, 'L'internationale abolitionniste et l'esquisse d'une civilisation atlantique' (265–79), illuminates the constituent elements of transnational abolitionist opinion and activism prior to the Revolution. It sees the secularist French tradition emerging from Montesquieu that culminated in the propaganda of Brissot and L. S. Mercier pitted against royal obduracy, while English piety capitalized on legal rulings. S. Albertan-Coppola, 'Un Atlantique des Lumières? D'après *l'Histoire générale des voyages*' (302–16), discerns an embryonic scientific conception of geography and its linkage of history and territory in Prévost's skilful distillation and synthesis of detail from primary sources in vols XII-XV of the work. Of linked interest is M. Cardy, 'Place and space in two eighteenth-century French texts', pp. 49–59 of *Frontières flottantes: lieu et espace dans les cultures francophones du Canada / Shifting Boundaries: Place and Space in the Francophone Cultures of Canada*, ed. Jaap Lintvelt and François Paré, Amsterdam, Rodopi, 257 pp., which compares and contrasts the treatment of America and native Americans in Pierre-Jacques Payen de Noyan's *Variétés littéraires* and Pierre Pouchot's *Mémoires sur la dernière guerre de l'Amérique septentrionale, entre la France et l'Angleterre.*

MLN, 116.4:627–769, 'Le culte des grands hommes', ed. Jacques Neefs, includes two articles summarizing substantial research. J.-C. Bonnet, 'Le culte des grands hommes en France au XVIIIe siècle ou la défaite de la monarchie' (689–704), argues that the rising cult of patriotism (beginning with Fénelon's *Télémaque* and then the abbé de Saint-Pierre, but developing principally after about 1760) reflects a decline in the status of the Crown. D. A. Bell, 'Canon wars in eighteenth-century France: the monarchy, the Revolution and the "Grands Hommes de la Patrie"' (705–38), offers a more complex (and more fully referenced) account. In his view the patriotic cult, which drew not only on classical antiquity but even on religious aspiration, was encouraged by the Crown. Close to the values of the High Enlightenment, it was reoriented by the popular and insistently contemporary radicalism of the Revolutionary period. Bonnet's article draws on twenty years of research, and especially his *Naissance du Panthéon* (1998), while Bell digests from his book *The Cult of the Nation in France: Inventing Nationalism 1680–1800*, Cambridge, MA, Harvard U.P., xiv + 304 pp.

Le Mariage sous l'ancien régime, ed. Claire Carlin (*DFS*, 56), 166 pp., contains several articles on the 18th century. The editorial introduction points to broad changes in the status of marriage in the early modern period. A religious and communal bond for procreation gradually becomes, primarily on the Protestant side and among the bourgeoisie, a legal and sentimental bond for social order. R. Davison, 'Happy marriage: myth or reality in eighteenth-century France?' The case of Madame d'Epinay and her family' (116–24), recounts the marriages of this companion of the 'philosophes', her daughter (whom she wed at 15 to a provincial noble of 35), and her granddaughter for whom she wrote the *Conversations d'Emilie*. R. P. Thomas, 'Marriage as theatre in the novels of Madame Riccoboni' (125–32), summarizes the account of sentimental relations in four novels. N. Bérenguier, 'D'un mémoire judiciaire à une *Cause célèbre*: le parcours d'une femme adultère' (133–43), provides a fascinating sketch of this period subgenre and a reading of its presentation of a 1773 adultery case. G. Verdier, 'Olympe de Gouges et le divorce sur la scène révolutionnaire: adieu au mariage d'ancien régime?' (154–64), looks principally at de Gouges's play on this topic, one of half-a-dozen following the (short-lived) legitimation of divorce in 1792. J. Whatley, 'Dissoluble marriage, paradise lost: Suzanne Necker's *Réflexions sur le divorce*' (144–53), considers with refreshing moral intelligence the differing views of Suzanne and her daughter Mme de Staël.

J. Hellegouarc'h, 'Salons du XVIIIe siècle: problèmes de sources', Marchal, *Salons*, 29–37, explores the problems of dealing with documentary evidence about *salons* which is both limited and biased. A. Lilti, 'Le salon de Mme Geoffrin: salon philosophique ou sociabilité mondaine', *ib.*, 137–46, carefully reassesses the make-up and significance of Mme Geoffrin's *salon*, calling into question some of the grand claims made by recent feminist critics, and highlighting the ambivalent role of Mme Geoffrin herself. M. Crogiez, 'La duchesse d'Enville (1716–1797): relations et réseaux d'une aristocrate influente', *ib.*, 147–54, paves the way for a worthy resurrection of this neglected aristocrat. C. Cazenobe, 'Atypique et significatif: le petit salon de Madame d'Epinay', *ib.*, 155–64, describes what life was like in this *salon*. I. Vissière, 'Lausanne: un laboratoire littéraire au XVIIIe siècle', *ib.*, 233–41, shows how Lausanne's unusually cultivated and cosmopolitan status is reflected in contemporary works as diverse as Voltaire's letters and Edward Gibbon's memoirs. L. Versini, 'Les salons littéraires nancéiens de 1760 à 1789', *ib.*, 243–49, argues in favour of the cultural importance of Nancy by focusing on a number of *salons*. On the same subject, J. T. Pekacz, 'Gendered discourse as a political option in pre-revolutionary France', Cossy, *Progrès*, 331–46, offers a timely critical reassessment of some feminist revisionist and Habermas-inspired assumptions about the role of Parisian *salons* and the women running them in the 18th c.

SVEC 2001 : 12 contains five substantial articles on women: M. Gut-wirth, 'The "Article Genève" quarrel and the reticence of French Enlightenment discourse on women in the public realm' (135–66), demonstrates how Rousseau's *Lettre à d'Alembert* and the addressee's response embed relatively brief texts about women's nature and place in society within arguments that have only slight connections with their major themes; C. R. Montfort, 'Mme de Sévigné and the Jesuits in the *siècle des Lumières*' (167–77), examines the impact religion had in influencing the reception of S.'s letters in the 18th c.; E. Russo, 'From *précieuse* to mother figure: sentiment, authority and the eighteenth-century *salonnière*' (179–98), traces shifts in the gendering of the public sphere through an analysis of representations of the authority of the *salonnière*; P. Stewart and M. Ebel-Davenport, 'Dossier Claude Crébillon — Henriette Marie Stafford' (199–231), includes a substantial appendix of documentary material; and M. Trouille, 'Conflicting views of marriage and spousal abuse in pre-revolutionary France: the separation case of Jeanne Fouragnan (Toulouse 1782)' (233–65), offers a fascinating insight into the separation suit brought by the wife of a prominent merchant of Toulouse who accused her husband and adult stepson of physical abuse.

Anne Coudreuse, *Le Refus du pathos au XVIIIe siècle*, Champion, 270 pp., explores the problematic relationship between passion and representation in the 18th c., showing how writers like Voltaire have recourse to irony, and writers like Sade have recourse to apathy, as a way of denying pathos for both aesthetic and ethical reasons: despite its evident popularity amongst 18th-c. novel-readers and theatre audiences, pathos came to be seen as an obscene and useless failing in good taste. Servanne Woodward, *Explorations de l'imaginaire de la représentation au dix-huitième siècle français: Chardin, Vigée-Lebrun, Diderot, Marivaux*, Lewiston NY, Mellen, 255 pp., is a wide-ranging treatment of the well-worn problem of representation in the 18th c., taking in, and suggesting fruitful intellectual relationships between, aesthetics, visual arts, painting, autobiography, and theatre.

Pucci, *Sites*, fruitfully examines texts as apparently diverse as Marivaux's *Le Spectateur français* (17–62), Diderot's *Salons* (63–102), literature of the exotic (103–33), and the *théâtre de la foire* (134–82), focusing throughout on the polysemic figure of the spectator and tracing a suggestive cultural shift in the course of the 18th c. from the silent spectator to one more vocal and self-conscious. Ziad Elmarsafy, *The Histrionic Sensibility: Theatricality and Identity from Corneille to Rousseau*, Tübingen, Narr, 243 pp., is concerned in its second half with the evidently fluid (and not always clearly defined) notion of theatricality in the 18th c., considering in particular questions of identity and 'self-construction' in some of Marivaux's plays and novels and the novels of Crébillon *fils*, and lastly 'Rousseau's project of auto-deification', with particular reference to the *Confessions* and the *Lettre à d'Alembert*.

Jeanne Charpentier and Michel Charpentier, *Le Mouvement des Lumières au XVIIIe siècle*, Nathan, 128 pp., combines annotated extracts from key philosophical texts with clear critical discussion to provide a useful introductory guide for university students.

L'Ecrivain éditeur 1. Du Moyen Age à la fin du XVIIIe siècle, ed. François Bessire (*TLit*, 14), Adirel, 402 pp., entitles its 18th-c. section 'L'affirmation de l'auteur'. F. Deloffre, 'L'écrivain éditeur posthume dans la littérature clandestine' (279–98), offers an account of the strategies employed by Challe to make his *Difficultés sur la religion* acceptable to future readers. L. Versini, 'Diderot éditeur de soi-même et des autres' (299–307), looks at D.'s attempts in his last years to organize a posthumous edition of his works (many of course unpublished) to appear in Holland, or France (less likely), or Catherine's Russia (more likely). R. Marchal, 'Des satyres parmi les nymphes: *Contes moraux et nouvelles Idylles* de Diderot et Salomon Gessner' (309–19), considers the apparently surprising appearance of two of Diderot's short fictions among the works of Gessner, in editions overseen and illustrated by the latter. Marchal argues convincingly that the French freethinker and the Swiss pastoralist have several 'Romantic' traits in common. M.-E. Plagnol-Diéval, 'Editer le théâtre de société: le cas de Carmontelle' (321–34), shows how these works commissioned for private performance reflect their origins. V. Sarrazin, 'L'auteur éditeur de ses œuvres à la fin du XVIIIe siècle: aspects légaux et économiques' (335–60), is a substantial and valuable analysis of the relations between publisher and author. 'Publication' may be understood as an intellectual act (by the author), a material undertaking (by the publisher) or a technical procedure (the printer). In the second category, the publisher-printer's legal monopoly through the 'privilège' was weakened by the Crown in the 1770s, and authors including Sedaine and Florian attempted to market their works independently. The practice of soliciting subscriptions is examined in the final article by P. Gray and W. Kirsop, 'L'art du prospectus: l'écrivain éditeur et son public' (361–74), who show how the publication of more substantial works through advance subscription spread from England and Holland to France (where the author still had to work through the publisher), while the prospectus also served the ends of publicity and even on occasions of research collaboration.

Geneviève Artigas-Menant, *Lumières clandestines: les papiers de Thomas Pichon*, Champion, 425 pp., offers the first thoroughgoing analysis of the library of this 18th-c. collector of clandestine libertine texts, including a catalogue (201–80). Id., *Du secret des clandestins à la propagande voltairienne*, Champion, 440 pp., brings together the author's articles over the last 20 years on clandestine writing, with a new introduction (9–16), and arranging them effectively around different centres of interest, including six articles on Robert Challe and nine on Voltaire; the volume also has a comprehensive bibliography and a good index. O. Mostefai, 'La violence pamphlétaire et ses stratégies en France à l'époque des Lumières', Cossy, *Progrès*, 281–95, proceeds from a useful definition of 'pamphlet' in the 18th c. to an examination of the symbolic and real violence that pamphlets imply and provoke: symbolic violence done to the targets of attack, and real violence to the texts themselves and, sometimes, their authors.

Máire Kennedy, *French Books in Eighteenth-Century Ireland* (SVEC 2001:07), x + 253 pp., is a thorough account of the presence in Ireland of Europe's dominant verbal culture (from the most popular authors and works in private libraries — headed respectively by Voltaire, no less, and *Télémaque* — to the location of teachers of the language). Already important, French received a very ambiguous boost at the start of the period with the Huguenot arrivals, but really expands with trade and literacy after the mid-century. J. Schøsler, 'L'*Essai sur l'entendement* de Locke et la lutte philosophique en France au XVIIIe siècle: l'histoire des traductions, des éditions et de la diffusion journalistique (1688–1742)', *SVEC 2001:04*, 1–259, is a monograph-length, impressively scholarly, and seemingly exhaustive study of the reception in France of the *Essay Concerning Human Understanding*, demonstrating convincingly how the text made a great impact on areas of metaphysical and religious debate outside its own immediate scope.

2. DIDEROT

Andrew Curran's excellent *Sublime Disorder. Physical Monstrosity in Diderot's Universe* (SVEC 2001:01), xi + 171 pp., explores what the monster means for D.'s views of nature, materialism, generation, and the notions of order and disorder. He shows that if in D.'s universe monsters are often accidents of nature, in his texts they are, on the contrary, creatures carefully crafted with a specific end in mind. Curran challenges the view that monsters are always used by D. as emblems of the godless universe, and reveals instead their polyvalence. He argues that monsters occupy an ambivalent place in D's thought: while they are naturalized in the materialist universe, representing nothing more than an extreme difference within an unbroken continuum of forms, they are not normalized and retain a transgressive dimension. Curran traces an evolution in D.'s thought from his reading of Shaftesbury, revealed to be a more likely source for his early view of monsters than the debates at the Académie royale des sciences, to the *Lettre sur les aveugles* in which monstrosity does indeed function as a means of accusing Providence, to *Le Rêve de d'Alembert* in which, materialism now a given, monsters become an object of knowledge in themselves. Yet whilst in *Le Rêve*, the birth of a monster is an almost prosaic event, simply an accident in the complicated process of generation, Curran shows that the birth of the moral monster, a congenitally evil individual, is far more threatening to D. He explores this in relation to *Le Neveu*, and is careful to show that *Le Neveu* is a staging of the problem of the moral monster rather than a portrait of one in the character of Lui. A highly stimulating study.

Hisashi Ida, *Genèse d'une morale matérialiste. Les passions et le contrôle de soi chez Diderot*, Champion, 400 pp., is a careful study of the centrality of the twin notions of enthusiasm and sensibility in D.'s thinking on matters aesthetic, medical, and moral, in which their fundamental ambivalence is made clear. The study is impressive for the way in which Diderot's ideas are explored in relation to a wide range of early modern texts, from medical works by Robert Burton and Philippe Hecquet, to aesthetic writings by Le Brun, de Piles, Burke, and to moral and philosophical texts by Hobbes, Hume, the Cambridge Neo-Platonists. The argument for the influence on D. of writers in English is of particular interest.

In Béatrice Didier's *Diderot dramaturge du vivant*, PUF, 213 pp., we are given an exploration of drama and biology in D.'s œuvre. D.'s interest in these seemingly unrelated fields spans his career — from his agreeing to translate James's *Medical Dictionary* in 1743 to the writing of *Eléments de physiologie* in 1780s, and from his early plays of the late 1750s to *Est-il bon, est-il méchant* which he was still amending in the last year of his life. Insightful links between them are suggested by Didier as she analyses the ways in which D. both insists on the place of the physical body in his dramaturgy and dramatizes biology and the workings of matter in *Le Rêve de d'Alembert*.

RDE, 30, takes as its theme the line from *Jacques le fataliste*: 'Celui qui prendrait ce que j'écris pour la vérité serait peut-être moins dans l'erreur que celui qui le prendrait pour une fable'. P. Quintilli, 'De la vérité comme *adequatio* à la vérité comme processus dans la philosophie de D.' (17–33), explores this in relation to the *Pensées sur l'interprétation de la nature* and *Le Neveu de Rameau* to argue that for D. truth is functional and bound up with time and narrative: 'c'est une fable (ou affabulation) qui a besoin du temps pour s'expliquer et se déployer'. In the same volume, A. Strugnell, 'Fable et vérité: stratégies narrative et discursive dans les écrits de D. sur le colonialisme' (35–46), fruitfully compares the line from *Jacques* with the assertions in *Supplément au voyage de Bougainville* — 'A. Est-ce que vous donneriez dans la fable de Tahiti? B. Ce n'est point une fable; et vous n'auriez aucun doute sur la sincérité de Bougainville, si vous connaissiez le supplément de son voyage' — to explore how D. weaves truth and fiction together in the latter text to arrive at a vision for the future liberation of both the Tahitians and the French. In 'Le pouvoir des fables ou la vérité selon *Jacques*' (47–64), P. Chartier reminds us of the relationship between the word 'erreur' in the line quoted and 'errance' and 'errement', activities central to the novel, and further analyses the structure of the line which, with its conditional tenses and its 'peut-être', avoids stating anything indubitably. He argues that this holds true for D.'s novel as a whole in which 'rien n'échappe au doute', and argues that it demands that we adopt a sceptical reading strategy. Included also in the volume is A. Arbo, 'D. et l'hiéroglyphe musicale' (65–80), which offers an original contribution to the study of D.'s notion of the musical hieroglyph by comparing it to the sketch, and arguing that in their non-mimetic mode of representation both suggest images to the listener's/viewer's imagination. L. Y. Mock also gives us the second instalment (the first appeared in *RDE*, 29) of his work on politics and the *parlement* in the *Encyclopédie*, 'D. et la lutte parlementaire au temps de l'*Encyclopédie*' (93–126).

L. Versini, 'Cycles, séries et liaisons chez Diderot conteur', *AJFS*, 38:99–106, is a modest piece which offers an inventory of themes and refrains in D.'s contes, listing the presence of parallelisms, pendants, ternary rhythms, series of five dialogues, meteorological motifs, and geographical locations.

Pucci, *Sites*, contains a chapter on spectating in D.'s *salons*: 'Keeping the image honest. The narrator as Spectator in tableaux in D.'s *Salons*' (63–102). She engages with Fried's seminal work on the *salons* and nuances it by treating D.'s art criticism as a first-person narrative, arguing that Fried's notion of D. as an enthralled beholder, whose presence is neutralized, is one-sided; it ignores the theatrical aspects of the narrative voice with its shifting perspectives and multiple guises. K. E. Tunstall, 'D.'s "promenade Vernet"', or the *salon* as landscape garden', *FS*, 55:339–49.

3. Montesquieu

Montesquieu du Nord au Sud: Actes de la table ronde organisée à Paris les 29 et 30 janvier 1999 avec le soutien de la Maison des sciences de l'homme, ed. Jean Ehrard (CM, 6), 203 pp., studies the diffusion of M.'s writings and the varied means facilitating it through Eastern and Northern Europe. *L'Atelier de Montesquieu. Manuscrits inédits de la Brède*, ed. C. Volpilhac-Auger and C. Bustaret (CM, 7), 320 pp., makes available in a scholarly edition the manuscript residue primarily of M.'s editorial work on the *Lois* transferred in 1994 from La Brède to the Bordeaux Archive.

RMon, 5, contains C. Jacot-Grapa, 'L'économie du détail chez Montesquieu' (23–39), which investigates the pedigree and status, epistemological and aesthetic, of the 'detail' or 'particular case' in M.'s writings, demonstrating, against Classical precedent, its methodological indispensability to his anthropological vision; C. Martin, 'L'institution du sérail. Quelques réflexions sur le livre XVI de *L'Esprit des lois*' (41–57), which examines the contradictions implicit in M.'s analysis in *Lois* XVI of oriental polygamy, in the wake of its assessment by Bourdieu as mythology built on socially conditioned fantasy, primarily of female concupiscence; B. Binoche, 'Comment suivre la nature? Tracy, lecteur de Montesquieu' (59–91), which scrutinizes T.'s transformation of the *Lois* in order to engage with the axes of liberty, sovereignty, work, class structure, and civilization, so formulating a retroactively attributable 'social science', in the post-revolutionary cause of promoting political stability and the proper use of wealth; B. Bomel-Rainelli, 'Les rapports de Bossuet et de Montesquieu dans les manuels d'histoire de la littérature de 1841 à 1992' (125–42), which skilfully exploits a detailed parallel examination of the evaluation of B. and M. as Roman historians at the hands of educational vulgarizers, to expose the linkage to confessional conformism — providentialist imitation cedes to authentically secular determinism only in the 1890s, when M. as inventor of historical sociology eclipses B. altogether, simultaneously liberating the 18th c. as a self-sufficient sphere of study; J. Ehrard, 'Montesquieu dans le monde en l'an 2000' (147–53), who gives a overview of recent scholarship; and 'Actualité et modernité de Montesquieu', ed. C. Larrère and M. Porret (175–81), reporting conversations with Jean Starobinski and offering illuminating comparisons between M. and Rousseau as writers, setting M.'s pluralism against today's globally trivializing cultural commercialism.

O. Kenshur, 'Virtue and defilement: moral rationalism and sexual prohibitions in *Lettres persanes*', *SVEC 2001: 12*, 69–112, rehabilitates M. as a practitioner of Enlightenment rationalism rather than of the currently modish post-absolutist epistemology of variability. Stressing contextualization as an essential tool, he marshals the evidence that contradictory 'knowledge claims' in the *Lettres persanes* uniformly bear the taint of sensory or superstitious fallibility; thereby subjecting the conceptual apparatus of revealed religion to a rationally driven critique, harnessed to the value of moral autonomy, which effectively unifies the seraglio narrative with the letters on demography.

E. Badinter, 'Six lettres inédites de Mme Geoffrin à Martin Folkes', *DhS*, 33:319–38, sheds new light on Montesquieu's inhibiting relationship with his son, J.-B. de Secondat, and confirms the status of G.'s salon in the 1740s.

4. ROUSSEAU

The Cambridge Companion to Rousseau, ed. Patrick Riley, CUP, xii + 453 pp., is a collection of essays oriented mainly towards R.'s thought. The opening piece by G. A. Kelly, 'A general overview' (8–56), is extraordinarily good (though it seems to date from the 1960s — no proper bibliographical references are provided). M. Hulliung, 'Rousseau, Voltaire, and the revenge of Pascal' (57–77), finds this revenge in R.'s confirmation, *pace* Voltaire, that self-interest and virtue cannot be merged. P. Riley, 'Rousseau, Fénelon, and the Quarrel between the Ancients and the Moderns' (78–93), proposes that R.'s ideal social models, pastoral and civic, are indebted respectively to the Bétique and Salente of *Télémaque*. C. Brooke, 'Rousseau's political philosophy: Stoic and Augustinian origins' (94–123), argues carefully that R. draws on Stoicism (right will, and republicanism), but also on the opposed Augustinian tradition (condemning the concupiscent self-love which Enlightenment liberalism legitimized), while saving *amour de soi* which becomes not part of original sin but of original goodness. P. Riley now on home territory locates 'Rousseau's general will' (124–53), between theology and Kant. J. Shklar, 'Rousseau's images of authority (especially in *La Nouvelle Héloïse*)' (154–92), begins with characteristic trenchancy but the piece tries to cover too much. Then we have several accounts of central topics: V. Gourevitch, 'Rousseau's religious thought' (193–246), uses the early *Lettre sur la Providence* to develop a wide review. G. Parry, '*Emile*: learning to be men, women, and citizens' (247–71), concludes that the first and last goals are not easily reconciled. S. M. Shell, '*Emile*: nature and the education of Sophie' (272–301), broadly defends R.'s position on Woman in Book 5 in relation to his wider philosophy. C. Kelly, 'Rousseau's *Confessions*' (302–28), mainly proposes as elsewhere that R.'s account of himself illustrates his philosophy of man. C. N. Dugan and T. B. Strong, 'Music, politics, theatre and representation in Rousseau' (329–64), argue that music, unlike theatre, offers the emotional identification which R. thinks necessary in the good polity. (This focus on persuasion is perhaps a trend in Rousseau criticism.) J. Starobinski, 'The motto *Vitam impendere vero* and the question of lying' (365–96), offers in translation much of the text of a piece which appeared (the volume fails to mention) in *ASocRous*, 42, 1999 (see *YWMLS*, 62:144).

T. Kavanagh, 'Rousseau's *The Levite of Ephraim*: synthesis within a "minor" work' (397–417), provides another version of his persuasive reading of this strange work as both personal myth and political thought. The literary and philosophical approaches to R., he suggests, too often proceed independently. R. Wokler, 'Ancient postmodernism in the philosophy of Rousseau' (418–43), lets off a few squibs before offering a clear historical evaluation and a generous defence of R.'s political thought.

James Swenson, *On Jean-Jacques Rousseau Considered as one of the First Authors of the Revolution*, Stanford U.P., xiii + 320 pp., is a mildly deconstructionist exploration of this familiar formula. Thoroughly researched and slowly developed, its argument is that ambiguities in R.'s works (notably the *Inégalité, Julie*, and *Du Contrat social*) and in the concept of 'authorship' are reproduced in the discourse of the Revolution. Raymond Birn, *Forging Rousseau: Print, Commerce and Cultural Manipulation in the Late Enlightenment* (SVEC 2001:08), ix + 281 pp., puts a new-historical title on an old-historical account of the publication of the posthumous *Collection complète* of the Master's works (Geneva, 1780–82) by Du Peyrou and Moultou. A preliminary section attributes to R. a new position on intellectual property rights.

Jean-Jacques Rousseau, politique et nation. Actes du IIe Colloque international de Montmorency (27 septembre-4 octobre 1995), ed. Robert Thiéry, Champion, xxiv + 1163 pp., comprises a mammoth retrospective and tribute to post-war Rousseau scholarship, as well as a major re-evaluation of the axes of his political thought, consequent upon the recent opening of a fault line in democratic ideology between liberalism and egalitarian socialism. 95 papers, grouped in a thematic framework, address the multiple tensions between the abstractions of universalist theory and perceptions of specificity: anthropological, historical, linguistic, and cultural, often highlighting lesser known texts, particularly within the musical corpus. Jean Terrel, *Les Théories du pacte social: droit naturel, souveraineté et contrat de Bodin à Rousseau*, Seuil, 423 pp., is a valuable primer but also a revisionist history. Systematic and closely-argued, it affirms that the association of all three titular elements emerges only in Hobbes, and then in Rousseau who inflects it towards a newly egalitarian republicanism. F. Moulin, 'Les trois formes du contrat dans la *Nouvelle Héloïse*', *IL*, 53:13–21, reveals how this novel is dramatically and structurally underpinned by the idea of pact, and shows how in counterpoint creative imagination integrates its premises into emotional experience. G. Ansart, 'Rousseau, Bataille et le principe de l'utilité classique', *FS*, 55:25–35, examines the resonances of the notion of gratuitous expenditure in R. and B., seeing R.'s condemnation as a failure of anthropological insight.

ASocRous, 43, continues the renaissance of the *Annales* under the editorship of J. Berchtold and M. Porret. It begins with a magisterial overview of R.'s first *Discours* by J. Starobinski, who treads a typically sinuous and enlightening path between R.'s thought and his subjectivity (9–40). T. Todorov, 'La morale sociale de Rousseau' (41–57), adopting the convenient principle that 'certaines des formules les plus célèbres de Rousseau ne sont pas à prendre à la lettre', finds that he is a proponent of human fraternity. M. Fabien, 'Rousseau et le mal social' (59–106), takes us over familiar territory in the *Inégalité*. S. Labrusse, 'Le droit de vie et de mort selon Jean-Jacques Rousseau' (107–28), seeks to rescue R. from his espousal in *Du contrat social* of the death penalty. P. Hartmann's 'Enquête sur le terme "philosophie"' in the early works (129–79), establishes rather elaborately the opposed significations of the term, then hails R. as a prescient opponent of economic liberalism. J. Berchtold (181–203), reprints his perceptive piece on monstrous self-images in the *Dialogues* (see *YWMLS*, 62: 146). F. Lestringant, 'Musset et Rousseau' (205–40), traces Musset's shift from mockery to imitation of *Julie*, and the repetition in his relations with George Sand of Rousseau's œdipal triangles. A. Gür prefaces and publishes 15 previously unknown letters of 1704 from David Rousseau (R.'s grandfather) to a servant of the Duke of Savoy (241–78). David's sympathy for the 'popular' party in Geneva — hostile to the Genevan oligarchy and its pro-French policies — will be those of R. This is confirmed in the text of a letter of 1754 to R. from J.-F. Deluc regarding the dedication of the *Inégalité*, also newly discovered by A. Gür (347–53). M. Porret prefaces and republishes the pious but clear-eyed posthumous account of R. during his last years in Paris by Corancez (279–346). Finally a note by J. Cormier shows that Rousseau knew the Filleau-Challe Continuation of *Don Quixote* (355–57).

EJJR, 12, 'Rousseau et l'exclusion', begins with ten papers around this interesting topic. The first three articles, by S. Faessel (9–23), J. Boulad-Ayoub (25–37), and Y. Vargas (39–47), reflect in different ways upon exclusion as R.'s fate but also his choice. P.-M. Vernes (49–57), then argues that his exclusion reflects the logic of his pessimistic political thought. T. L'Aminot (89–117), reviews the unsympathetic treatment throughout R.'s writings of the figure of the prostitute. I. Cseppentô (131–49), compares the exiled state of Saint-Preux with the rather different condition of exile depicted in 'romans de l'émigration' following 1789. L. Spaas (151–54), ends nicely with a kind of 'plaidoyer pour Thérèse' drawn from the 1978 film about R. by C. Goretta. Other studies consider R. and the abbé de Saint-Pierre (Y. Charara, 157–68); Jean-Baptiste Rousseau (P. Adamy, 169–87); the anticipation of R.'s 'Copernican revolution' in education by the remarkable 16th-c. Czech bishop Comenius (E. Krotky, 189–203); R.'s resistance to the philosophy of Condillac and especially Helvétius through a partial return to Locke (J. Schøsler, 219–26); R.'s claims for the instinctual behaviour of animals in the light of the findings of Konrad Lorenz (C. Elmquist, 227–43); and 'myth' in the sense of Socratic illustration — but not regressive desire? — in R.'s writings (J. Roussel, 205–13). A 'Chronique du musée J.-J. Rousseau de Montmorency' (253–62), details recent acquisitions and activities. This is followed by a 50-page bibliography of recent work on, nearby, or possibly relevant to R., reviewed principally by this journal's indefatigable editor Tanguy L'Aminot.

Jean-Louis Cornille, *La Lettre française de Crébillon fils à Rousseau, Laclos, Sade*, Leuven, Peeters, 131 pp., has a good chapter on R.'s letter-novel. *Julie* is seen as R.'s imperialistic takeover of the previous female tradition of epistolary passion, which he refocuses on virtue, the topos of writing, and himself. P. Stewart, 'On the translation of *Julie*', *SVEC 2001:04*, 309–16, discusses some problems that he and Jean Vaché encountered in their translation (New England U.P., 1997). F. S. Eigeldinger, 'Nécessité et vertu dans les *minora* de Rousseau', *ib.*, 319–39, looks at *Emile et Sophie*, the *Lettres à Sara* and the *Lévite*. M. O'Dea, 'Philosophie, histoire et imagination dans le *Discours sur l'origine de l'inégalité* de Jean-Jacques Rousseau', *ib.*, 340–60, identifies tensions in this work (and among critics) between the first two approaches, partially resolved by the third.

5. VOLTAIRE

WORKS. Two volumes augment the corpus of the modern critical edition of V.'s works. *Œuvres de 1711–1722* (I) (Œuvres complètes de Voltaire, 1A), Oxford, Voltaire Foundation, xxx + 477 pp., is of particular importance, presenting as it does *Œdipe*, the work that first brought V. fame. It is here edited, with a substantial introduction, by David Jory, who also presents and edits in the same volume *Lettres sur Œdipe* and the much lesser known *Artémire*. These are preceded in the volume by a preface by W. H. Barber giving a brief outline of the period covered, and by an edition by John Renwick of 43 lines surviving of *Amulius et Numitor*, believed to have been written by V. when a schoolboy. *Œuvres de 1762* (I) (Œuvres complètes de Voltaire, 56A), Oxford, Voltaire Foundation, xxi + 567 pp., after a preface by Haydn Mason, contains *Testament de Jean Meslier*, ed. Roland Desné; *Balance égale, Extrait de la Gazette de Londres*, and *Petit avis à un jésuite*, all three edited by Diana Guiragossian Carr; *Eloge de M. de Crébillon*, ed. Jeroom Vercruysse; *Saül*, ed. Henri Lagrave and Marie-Hélène Cotoni; and *Poetry of 1762*, ed. Simon Davies.

THOUGHT AND INFLUENCE. F. Bessire, 'Beaumarchais éditeur de Voltaire', *RHLF*, 4, 2000: 1125–38, is an enthralling account of the vicissitudes — technical, commercial, and organizational as well as ideological — surrounding Beaumarchais' great project, the *édition de Kehl* of V.'s complete works which, in Bessire's view, inaugurates the concept 'homme et œuvre'. Alongside this it is interesting to read W. H. Barber, 'Voltaire after Besterman', *SVEC 2001: 12*, 3–14, a lecture delivered in Oxford on 1 March 2001 to commemorate the 25th anniversary of Besterman's death, and which illustrates the importance of Besterman's decision, as first modern editor of V.'s *Complete works*, to present them in chronological order of composition, thus enabling us to appreciate the diversity of V.'s intellectual and artistic preoccupations at any one time in his career. G. Santato, 'Le *Contre Voltaire* d'Alfieri: la satire *L'Antireligionería*', *ib.*, 15–43, discusses Alfieri's 1796 satire and other writings, demonstrating his extreme hostility to V. whom he had previously sought to emulate, but through whom he eventually mounts an attack against the spirit of the Enlightenment itself. S. Pierse, '*Le silence des passions?* Rousseau and Voltaire on the sciences and the arts', *ib.*, 451–57, while admitting it unlikely that V. was writing in direct reaction to Rousseau's *Discours sur les sciences et les arts*, sees in chapters 31–34 of *Le Siècle de Louis XIV* a broad though very different response to the same themes.

SVEC 2001: 10 is devoted in part to items on the *Lettres philosophiques*: T. E. D. Braun, 'Voltaire, the English connection' (219–25), examines the impact of V.'s stay in England on the English, focusing on the wide range of influential people that he knew there and cataloguing those of his works that were translated into English in the ten years following his departure; N. Cronk, 'The *Letters concerning the English nation* as an English work: reconsidering the Harcourt Brown thesis' (226–39), concludes that no part of the *Lettres anglaises* was originally composed by Voltaire in English; J. P. Lee, 'The unexamined premise: Voltaire, John Lockman and the myth of the *English letters*' (240–70), shows convincingly that the *Letters concerning the English Nation* were translated by Lockman, whose various reflections on translation are contained in an appendix to the article. The welcome renewal of interest in *Lettres philosophiques* is complemented elsewhere: N. Cronk, 'Lord Hervey and Voltaire's *Letters concerning the English Nation*', *NQ*, n.s. 48:409–11, presents evidence from Hervey's correspondence strengthening the argument that the *Letters concerning the English Nation*, although published before the *Lettres philosophiques*, were a translation from the French and not part of V.'s original redaction; and G. Gargett, 'Oliver Goldsmith and Voltaire's *Lettres philosophiques*', *MLR*, 96:952–63, argues that Goldsmith was strongly influenced by V.'s text early in his career.

Cirey dans la vie intellectuelle: la réception de Newton en France, ed. François de Gandt (SVEC 2001 : 11), vi + 253 pp., after an introduction by the editor, 'Préambule: un moment de grâce' (1–5), provides a mix of articles both of specifically scientific and of more general interest, with Cirey as a backdrop: R. Pomeau, 'Voltaire et Mme Du Châtelet à Cirey: amour et travail' (9–15); G. Haroche-Bouzinac, 'Voltaire à Cirey, poète et philosophe, d'après sa correspondance, 1735–1738' (16–25); B. E. Schwarzbach, 'Les études bibliques à Cirey' (26–54); A. Firode, 'Locke et les philosophes français' (57–72); P. Hamou, 'Algarotti vulgarisateur' (73–89); R. Locqueneux, 'La physique expérimentale vers 1740: expérience, systèmes et hypothèses' (90–111); W. H. Barber, 'Le Newton de Voltaire' (115–25); F. de Gandt, 'Qu'est-ce qu'être newtonien en 1740?' (126–47); V. Le Ru, 'La conception sceptique de la matière au temps de Cirey' (148–58); and E. Vamboulis, 'La discussion de l'attraction chez Voltaire' (159–70). The same volume contains four articles under the general title of 'La physique de Mme Du Châtelet' including B. Joly, 'Les théories du feu de Voltaire et de Mme Du Châtelet' (212–37).

U. Janssens, 'Blake, Pope and Voltaire, or the art of imitation', *SVEC 2001 : 10*, 271–86, is a clever and convincing comparison between V.'s *Vers sur la mort de Mlle Lecouvreur, fameuse actrice*, and the poem by Pope on which it was modelled, *Elegy to the memory of an unfortunate lady*, each of which, it is argued, Blake was alluding to in the ornamentations of his paintings of V. and Pope respectively. R. Quintero, ' "Serious and merry by turns": the Pope-Swift *Miscellanies*', *ib.*, 287–95, suggests that V. drew lessons from Pope's strategies in relation to the appearance of three of the four volumes of the *Miscellanies* between 1727–28, a period overlapping with his stay in England.

Mining a rich seam, the legacy of V., which has recently become a focus of scholarly interest, Raymond Trousson, *Visages de Voltaire (XVIIIe - XIXe siècles)*, Champion, 461 pp., offers a series of fairly discrete studies of how V. was viewed by, among others, the prince de Ligne, Isabelle de Charrière, l'abbé Barruel, Stendhal, Lamartine, Michelet, Delacroix, Comte, Balzac, Nerval, Louis Blanc, Barbey d'Aurevilly, Louis Veuillot, the Goncourts, Taine, and Brunetière. This readable volume illustrates how the figure of V. continued throughout the 19th c. to obsess detractors and admirers alike.

M. S. Rivière, 'Women's responses to Voltaire's writings in the eighteenth century: "a silencing of the feminine" ', *NZJFS*, 22 : 5–27, is a detailed exploration of the relationship between V. and the influential women of his day, concluding that, with notable exceptions such as the Electress of Saxony and Catherine II, he used influential women as sounding-boards or as go-betweens providing access to powerful men, and that such women offered him and his works generally uncritical acclaim. Id., 'Voltaire, women and reception: Racine in the eighteenth century', pp. 135–54 of *Racine: the Power and the Pleasure*, ed. Edric Caldicott and Derval Conroy, Dublin, University College Dublin Press, xiv + 250 pp., discusses how V., to serve his own ends as a propagandist for Racine, distorts the commentaries of both Mme de Sévigné and Mme de Caylus and argues that, in promoting Racine, V. was also fuelling his own reputation as a dramatist among female devotees.

Stanislaw Fiszer, *L'Image de la Pologne dans l'œuvre de Voltaire* (SVEC 2001:05), xv + 188 pp., is an exhaustive and extensively documented exploration of V.'s often sardonic attitude to and depiction of Poland; his typically Enlightenment etiology of political paralysis, chronic anarchy fed by aristocratic republicanism, and intolerance served effectively to demystify the country's history. *Voltaire et Henri IV*, Editions de la Réunion des Musées Nationaux, 104 pp., is a copiously illustrated *catalogue raisonné* accompanying an exhibition of the same name (at the musée national du château de Pau, 27 April–30 July 2001) and including three articles, one by M. Delon, 'Voltaire, chantre du plus juste des princes' (10–12), and two by P. Mironneau, 'La Henriade, foyer d'une iconographie nationale' (13–20), and 'Henri IV et Voltaire : parallèle et paradoxes' (21–24).

G. Artigas-Menant, 'De l'austérité au sourire : Voltaire et les manuscrits philosophiques clandestins', *Van den Heuvel Vol.*, 1–17, discusses how, in his crusade against 'l'infâme', V. edited and aided the dissemination of some of the anti-religious writings that had been circulating clandestinely since the early years of the century. J.-J. Robrieux, 'Aspects rhétorico-argumentatifs de l'ironie chez Voltaire', *ib.*, 221–58, analyses a large number of examples of irony culled from a wide range of V.'s writings.

RV, 1, 'Hommage à René Pomeau', ed. S. Menant, was the very fitting launch volume of the Société des Études Voltairiennes's new periodical. In addition to the proceedings of the memorial session held on 17th June 2000, it contains a bibliography of Pomeau's works, reprints of six of his harder-to-find articles, and one unpublished essay, 'Voltaire et Paris' (69–73), charting V.'s fraught relationship with the metropolis. C. Mervaud, 'La perception voltairienne de l'autre et de l'ailleurs dans l'*Histoire de l'Empire de Russie sous Pierre le Grand*' (27–38), combines assessment of V.'s method and approach to the 'raw' documentation deriving from contemporary Russian sources, and of the paradoxes rooted in Enlightenment assumptions investing his philosophy of history. Thus, while the Russian 'other' intrigues, V. strives to accommodate it within the universalist compass of the civilized West, just as anthropological relativism fails to dim his commitment to the cult of the great leader. R. Mortier, 'Le concept de lumière(s) chez Voltaire' (39–43), explores V.'s usage of the term particularly in the *Correspondance*, highlighting his preference for 'raison' when defining his century. M.-H. Cotoni, 'Bible et création littéraire' (53–67), relates the contrasting use of Biblical sources in *Le Taureau blanc* and *Saül* to generic parameters, projecting the surrealist affinities of V.'s rationally-motivated decanonisation of figures and motifs.

6. Non-Fiction

GENERAL

'La Gazette d'Amsterdam'. Miroir de l'Europe au XVIIIe siècle, ed. P. Rétat (SVEC 2001:06), vii + 295 pp., collectively researched from the Centre lyonnais de recherche sur le XVIIIe siècle, is a major contribution to the historiography of European periodicals. It utilizes the unrivalled and ready-indexed archival collection of the contemporary French Ministry of Foreign Affairs, and offers statistical analysis as well as illustrative syntheses. The *Gazette*'s lifespan from 1691–1796 as the major news source of the reading public frames the study of its fortunes as printed object, item of merchandise, vector of public opinion, channel of influence on national and international politics, and as mirror of events, foreign cultures, and political, juridical, and religious fora. Documentary appendices on typographical features and the Genevan reimpression together with an exhaustive bibliography complete the volume.

INDIVIDUAL AUTHORS

BERNARDIN DE SAINT-PIERRE. 'Actes du colloque de Dijon (mars 1999): de Bernardin de Saint-Pierre à Jean-Jacques Rousseau', *DhS*, 33:493–548, include two articles which engage with Rousseau's thought: M. Soëtard, 'Fin, finalité, finalisme. Le rôle de l'imaginaire chez Rousseau et Bernardin de Saint-Pierre' (528–38), showing that Bernardin, through his providentialist educational theory of harmonization with nature, unconsciously breaks with Rousseau's naturalistic teleology, prompted by its dynamic of autonomization in the name of liberty; and A.-M. Drouin-Hans, 'Rapport au savoir et utopie en éducation chez Rousseau et Bernardin de Saint-Pierre' (548–58), which similarly explodes their apparently united scepticism towards knowledge and their valorization of ignorance. While the cautionary factor in B. is the non-generic value of altruism, for R. it is proper mental competence; but in both, utopian theory is dissolved by an education of suffering fictionally portrayed.

BUFFON. Jeff Loveland, *Rhetoric and Natural History: Buffon in Polemical and Literary Context* (SVEC 2001:03), 214 pp., rejects the traditional view that literature and science are incompatible and uses rhetoric as an analytical tool to assess how Buffon seeks to persuade the reader of his multi-volume *Histoire naturelle*, showing convincingly how scientific rhetoric becomes a crucial complement to intellectual history.

DU BOS. J. C. O'Neal, *'Nature's culture in Du Bos's *Réflexions critiques sur la poésie et sur la peinture*', Goodman, *Art*, 15–27.

LE MAITRE DE CLAVILLE. P. Naudin, 'Un pédagogue enjoué: Le Maître de Claville, l'auteur du *Traité du vrai mérite de l'homme*', Van den Heuvel Vol., 147–55, offers insights into how L. makes a pedagogical treatise a fun read, avoiding the dogmatic and the didactic.

MABLY. Y. Charara, 'Droit et vertu dans la pensée de Mably', *DhS*, 33:384–98, relates M.'s thought to political and social conditions. Following Pocock, it is shown to reflect the advance from a juridical morality bequeathed by the School of Natural Law, focused on the use of power, to a civic morality inspired by Classical republicanism, and focused on citizen equality.

RAYNAL. C. Fortuny, 'La troisième édition de l'*Histoire des deux Indes* et ses contrefaçons: les contributions de Genève et Neuchâtel', *SVEC 2001:12*, 269–97, offers important new bibliographical information. S. Aravamudan, 'Progress through violence or progress from violence? Interpreting the ambivalences of the *Histoire des deux Indes*', Cossy, *Progrès*, 259–80, demonstrates how R.'s text manages to juggle topics as implicitly contradictory as slave plantation management, emancipationist philosophy, European national expansion, and the independence of the colonies.

SUARD. E. Francalanza, 'Mondanité et cosmopolitisme dans la seconde moitié du XVIIIe siècle: l'exemple de Jean-Baptiste-Antoine Suard (1733–1817)', Marchal, *Salons*, 83–94, is a timely and impressively scholarly reappraisal of S.'s life and works in the context of *salon* culture and better known figures such as Diderot.

7. PROSE FICTION

GENERAL. *Transformations du genre romanesque au XVIIIe siècle*, ed. English Showalter, a special issue of *ECentF*, 13.2–3, is a substantial collection of articles by some very distinguished hands. G. May, 'La réhabilitation du roman français: souvenirs et conjectures' (147–54), notes that 18th-c. prose fiction, a low and marginal genre in its own time, has only recently become the critical fashion in ours. J. DeJean, 'Was the eighteenth century long only in England?' (155–62), is less modest about her own early contribution. P. Stewart, 'The rise of *I*'

(163–81), argues that the key to 18th-c. fiction is not 'realism' but 'interiority'. J. Sgard, 'Le mot "roman"' (183–95), finds the term repeatedly buried but re-emergent. The legitimacy of compartment-alizing 18th-c. fiction by subgenre or periodization, denied by both these articles, is convincingly exemplified in M. Cook, 'La fiction courte en France, 1790–1800' (197–211). F. Deloffre, 'Une "œuvre fondatrice", *Les Illustres françaises*' (213–34), celebrates one of the several notable works which he himself first made available to us through a modern critical edition. C. Labrosse, 'Nouveauté de *La Nouvelle Héloïse*' (235–46), brings out remarkably the new phenomenon of reader-identification with the fiction. H. Coulet, 'Destin du conte moral' (247–58), notes how Marmontel around 1760 yoked this adjective to a generic term whose implications had long been rather immoral. M. Delon, 'Variations du roman-liste: du temps individuel au temps vécu' (259–77), ambitiously attempts to trace the trans-formation of the functions of the narrative review or 'list' — most frequently of women — from the baroque 'galerie' through the rococo and libertinism to the 'lived experience' of a narrating subject. Analogously, M. Moser-Verrey, 'Le langage du corps romanesque des *Illustres françaises* (1713) à *La Sorcière de Verberie* (1798)' (349–78), carefully considers examples of corporeal description — yes, women again — from the classical 'portraits' in Challe to the animated and eroticised 'tableaux' in late 18th-c. writers such as Restif. J. Terrasse, 'La contamination des genres chez Diderot: contes, nouvelles, entretiens ou dialogues philosophiques?' (279–300) examines the hybrid characteristics of Diderot's tales. R. Trousson, 'La *Dolbreuse* de Loaisel de Tréogate: du roman libertin au "roman utile"' (301–13), offers a critical account of this Rousseauistic novel of 1783. L. Spaas, '*Paul et Virginie*: the shipwreck of an idyll' (315–24) calls on her edition of Bernardin's correspondence with his sister to confirm a 'monstrous' subtext in Bernardin's fiction. The theme of this volume is less than evident here; similarly in J. G. Altman, 'Strategic timing: women's questions, domestic servitude, and the dating game in Montesquieu' (323–48). T. M. Kavanagh, 'Coupling the novel: reading bodies in La Morlière's *Angola*' (389–413), finds fiction (texts, mirrors, portraits) to be a stimulus to shared corporeal pleasures in much of this novel of 1747, but their negation in the new cult of the unrealizable which will be established by Rousseau in *Julie*. J. H. Stewart, 'Reading Lives "à la manière des romans de Crébillon"' (415–35), deals with the ambivalent perception of sexual desire in older women, mainly through allusions in the correspondence between Horace Walpole (whose homosexuality Stewart never mentions) and Mme du Deffand. H. Lafon, 'Le roman au miroir du dramatique' (437–59), informat-ively surveys the new relations (texual and paratextual) between novels and their stage adaptations 1750–1800. E. Showalter, 'Mme de Graffigny, reader of fiction' (461–76), shows (from G.'s voluminous correspondence) that she read widely and judged energetically but not predictably, especially in view of the qualities of her own *Péruvienne*. N. K. Miller, 'Cover stories: Enlightenment libertinage, postmodern *recyclage*' (477–99), reflects on modern images of 18th-c. French culture.

AJFS, 38, contains a number of articles on 18th-c. fiction in general. R. L. Frautschi, 'Par monts et par vaux: Enlightenment French prose fiction in Eastern and Central European collections' (16–24), uses empirical evidence to demonstrate that reading French fiction in the 18th c. was a truly pan-European phenomenon; J. Sgard, 'La classification des romans' (25–35), is an entertaining review of (seemingly flawed) attempts to classify the novel into sub-genres; P. Clancy, 'The literary *conte de fées*: a tale of survival and revival' (36–53), charts the changing popularity of this woman-dominated literary phenomenon from the late 17th c. to the present day, popularity exemplified by the reception of Mme Le Prince de Beaumont's *La Belle et la bête*; P. Brady, 'From chaos to control: the subversive structure of desire' (69–78), uses the complex language of control theory to compare and contrast Marivaux's *La Vie de Marianne*, Diderot's *Le Neveu de Rameau*, and Laclos's *Les Liaisons dangereuses*, focusing in particular on the dynamics of desire in the three novels and concluding, not unexpectedly, that 'whereas Marianne subverts class barriers and the Nephew subverts conventional morality, Merteuil subverts male dominance by refusing to become Valmont's mistress again'; F. Moureau, '*L'Infidélité de Lucinde, ou l'Amour outragé*: un roman inédit du début du XVIIIe siècle' (79–93), offers a fascinating insight into this anonymous, unpublished novel, explaining its historical allusions and setting in its generic context, showing how it fluctuates suggestively between *roman* and *mémoire*; and W. Kirsop, 'Canonical novels for gentlemen's libraries' (166–76), surveys a number of 18th-c. works which advise the educated male reader on which books he should have in his library, showing how these works reflect changing attitudes to the novel, in particular a growing desire to control and classify the suspect genre.

K. Astbury, 'National identity and politicization in fiction up to the Revolution: the example of the moral tale', *LitH*, 10:6–17, argues that this new exemplary subgenre emerges around 1760, espousing virtue and then patriotism.

SVEC 2001:04 includes a number of brief articles addressing the general theme of the translation and reception of English fiction in France: L. Asfour, 'Theories of translation and the English novel in France, 1740–1790' (269–78), surveys universalist views of language in France, the rising tide of translations after *Pamela*, resistance to English vulgarity and then to foreign influence, but also a shift towards 'Romantic' translation — truer to the original — at the end of the century; S. Soupel, 'Laurence Sterne, ses traducteurs et ses interprètes' (291–98), focuses primarily on versions of *A Sentimental Journey*; and M. Lévy, 'La traduction du roman noir' (299–308), introduces some examples of French versions of the Gothic novel, including the abbé Morellet's translations of Ann Radcliffe.

Mathilde Cortey, *L'Invention de la courtisane au XVIIIe siècle dans les romans-mémoires des "filles du monde" de Madame Meheust à Sade (1732–1797)*, Arguments, 307 pp., is a clear, detailed, and rigorous analysis of the representation of the ambivalent figure of the *courtisane* in more than 40 memoir novels. Peter Cryle, *The Telling of the Act: Sexuality as Narrative in Eighteenth- and Nineteenth-Century France*, Newark, Delaware U.P., 433 pp., examines the emergence of 'a new thematic regime' in the second half of the 18th c. as representations of sexuality undergo a process of narrativization: erotic literature, including works by Diderot, Sade, and Crébillon *fils*, comes to thematize utterance as the direct emergence of sexual truth.

INDIVIDUAL AUTHORS

BERNARDIN DE SAINT-PIERRE. J. Steigerwald, 'Arcadie historique: *Paul et Virginie* de Bernardin de Saint-Pierre, entre classicisme et préromantisme', *RGI*, 16:69–86, analyses the pastoral structure of the novel, considering how B. combines quotations from classical writers like Horace and Virgil with broader allusions to contemporary intertexts.

CHALLE. A. de Sola, 'Traduction et trafic d'influences: *The Illustrious French Lovers* de Penelope Aubin et *Les Illustres françaises* de Robert Challe', *FS*, 55:327–38, is a general account. S. Charles, 'Fortune des *Illustres*: la traduction anglaise des *Illustres françaises*', *ECentF*, 14:95–109, covers similar territory more closely, using but also criticising Sola's edition (NY, Mellen, 2000) of Aubin.

CRÉBILLON *fils*. *Lettres athéniennes*, ed. Ernest Sturm, Saint-Genouph, Nizet, 468 pp., is an excellent critical edition of this neglected 1771 text, set in the time of Alcibiades, offering a sound analysis of the genesis and significance of the text and an impressive bibliography.

DESFONTAINES. F. Weil, 'L'abbé Desfontaines et le roman', *AJFS*, 38:94–98, offers a brisk overview of D.'s career as a writer and translator of novels. E. Nye, 'Modernity in Desfontaines's translation of *Joseph Andrews*', *SVEC 2001:04*, 279–84, stresses D.'s unusual fidelity to the English original and interprets his slight divergences as lip-service to contemporary literary practice.

DUCLOS.   P. Berthiaume, 'Exercices spirituels et quiétisme dans *Les Confessions du comte de **** de Charles Pinot Duclos', *SVEC 2001: 12*, 57–68, focuses on the representation of love in the novel and on the Comte's ontological difficulties, setting these in the context of contemporary religious thought.

GALLAND.   Lethuy Hoang, **Les Mille et une nuits: à travers l'infini des espaces et des temps. Le conteur Galland, le conte et son public*, NY, Lang, 201 pp.

GENLIS.   J. C. Schaneman, 'Rewriting *Adèle et Théodore*: intertextual connections between Madame de Genlis and Ann Radcliffe', *CLS*, 38:31–45, is a careful and convincing intertextual analysis, based in part on an account of the reception of G. in England, of Radcliffe's *The Romance of the Forest*, highlighting the striking parallels between its plot and characters and those of G.'s epistolary novel. D. Yim, 'Madame de Genlis's *Adèle et Théodore*: its influence on an English family's education', *AJFS*, 38:141–57, analyses G.'s influence on one Margaret Chinnery and the education of her children in 18th-c. Essex.

GRAFFIGNY.   S. Cornand, 'La lettre d'indignation ou l'éloquence dans la correspondance de Mme de Graffigny', *RHLF*, 101:37–56, looks rather diffusely at chatty register, occasional indignant eloquence, and literary reference in the copious *Correspondance*. C. Simonin, 'Mme de Graffigny et les amertumes de la passion, ou un cruel autoportrait dans *Les Saturnales*', *SVEC 2001: 12*, 467–76, suggests that in G.'s play of 1752 the role of Servilie, in love with the younger and inconstant César, reflects G.'s own earlier relationship with Demarest. R. Howells, 'The *Péruvienne* and pathos', *FS*, 55:453–66, argues that the work is centred on Zilia's writing of her own pathos.

LA PLACE.   W. McMorran, 'Fielding in France: La Place's *Tom Jones*', *SVEC 2001: 04*, 285–90, demonstrates how La P.'s adaptation seeks to neutralize the supposed Englishness, and in particular the picaresque qualities, of the original.

LESAGE.   Frédéric Mancier, *Le Modèle aristocratique français et espagnol dans l'œuvre romanesque de Lesage: 'L'Histoire de Gil Blas de Santillane'*, un cas exemplaire, Paris-Sorbonne U.P., 528 pp., is a major and wide-ranging study offering much more than its title might suggest, notably new perspectives on the generic status of the text (theatrical novel, picaresque novel, *roman d'apprentissage*, memoir novel), with some particularly pertinent pages on style and self-representation in the text (325–58); the book ends with a well-informed and informative bibliographical essay. J. Wagner, *'L'Orient voilé de Raphaël dans *Gil Blas'*, *Tangence*, 65 : 33–51.

MARIVAUX. Marivaux's *Journaux* have been well served by being on this year's *agrégation* syllabus. *Etudes sur les 'Journaux' de Marivaux*, ed. Nicholas Cronk and François Moureau (Vif), Oxford, Voltaire Foundation, 172 pp., is a well-rounded volume which contains some essential reading: M. Gilot, 'Introduction' (1–23), is a collage of earlier publications and serves as a valuable critical and bibliographical *entrée en matière*; F. Moureau, 'Journaux moraux et journalistes au début du XVIIIe siècle: Marivaux et le libertinage rocaille' (25–45), sets M. in the context of the periodical press in the 18th c. and brings out the key features of M.'s distinctive contribution; P. France, 'Société, journalisme et essai: deux spectateurs' (47–73), is a French translation of an invaluable article first published in English in 1991, offering a detailed generic analysis of M.'s texts; M.-H. Cotoni, 'Usage du *distinguo* et art du dédoublement dans le *Cabinet du philosophe*' (75–93), is a meticulous analysis of structures and themes of exchange and reversibility, notions more familiar in studies of M.'s novels and plays; J. Mander, 'L'écriture personnelle dans les *Journaux*', is a French translation of a chapter from her 1999 monograph, *Circles of Learning: Narratology and the Eighteenth-Century French Novel* (*StV*, 366); N. Cronk, ' "Ecoutez, mon lecteur futur": la narration romanesque et le rôle du lecteur dans *L'Indigent philosophe*' (121–30), traces M.'s search for a voice in his text, comparing him both with Voltaire in the *Lettres philosophiques* and with English writers like Addison, and drawing attention to proto-Diderotian aspects of M.'s self-reflexivity; F. Bessire, ' "Je ne sais pas faire de lettres qui méritent d'être imprimées": la lettre dans *Le Spectateur français* et *Le Cabinet du philosophe*' (131–39), examines the organic relationship between letter and journal in the 18th c.; C. Gallouët-Schutter, 'L'invitation au voyage, ou la dynamique du double registre dans les *Journaux*' (141–44), is a reprint of an article first published in 1992 (*StV*, 304 : 1203–07); F. Deloffre, 'Les "repentirs" de Marivaux' (145–59), skilfully examines the significance of M.'s editorial modifications to his texts; Fréron, 'Le Spectateur ou le Socrate moderne, et le *Spectateur français*' (161–68), is the review of M.'s work that first appeared in the *Année littéraire* in 1755, glossed here by A. Julia; C. Seth, 'Bibliography' (169–72), is an up-to-date list.

Jean-Paul Sermain and Chantal Wionet, *Journaux de Marivaux*, Neuilly, Atlande, 220 pp., is a clear and scholarly book divided into three sections: 'Repères' (17–44), setting the *journaux* in the context of M.'s life and works, contemporary aesthetic debates and other genres, notably theatre; 'Problématiques' (47–133), focusing in particular on the moral stance of the work and its literary structure; and 'Le travail du texte' (137–205), a very detailed analysis of M.'s lexicon, syntax, and style. Catherine Gallouët, *Marivaux: journaux et fictions*, Orléans, Paradigme, 168 pp., is made up of (slightly) revised versions of articles published over the last ten years: the first six chapters are about the *Journaux*, the last seven are about the novels, but they all highlight M.'s constant self-conscious reflection on the art of writing in his texts. Françoise Gevrey, **Marivaux, 'Journaux'*, SEDES, 128 pp.

Littératures, 45, contains four useful articles, all focusing in different ways on the role of the authorial self: J.-P. Sermain, 'Désir d'écriture et amour de soi dans les *Journaux* de Marivaux' (95–103); J.-P. Grosperrin, 'Le "tour" des mouvements dans les *Journaux* de Marivaux' (105–31); C. Martin, ' "Microlectures": sujets mineurs et finesse de perception dans les *Journaux* de Marivaux' (133–49); K. Bénac, 'Marivaux disciple de Pascal? Les "deux ordres" du divertissement dans *L'Indigent Philosophe*' (151–67). The online version of *RMar*, <www.revuemarivaux.org>, includes seven articles on the *Journaux*: J.-C. Abramovici, ' "Penser en homme": le sourire du spectateur de la cinquième feuille'; C. Costantin, 'Ecriture moralistique et philosophique du langage dans *Le Spectateur français*: contribution marivaudienne au décodage critique de "la langue qui parle l'amour-propre" '; R. Démoris, 'Aux frontières de l'impensé: Marivaux et la sexualité'; A. Zagamé, 'Le partage de la parole dans *Le Spectateur français* de Marivaux'; M. Escola, 'L'école des lecteurs: effets de fiction, fictions de l'effet dans la douzième feuille du *Spectateur français*'; E. Lièvre, 'Lecture à double sens: la leçon herméneutique de la première feuille du *Spectateur français*'; and J.-P. Sermain, 'Amour et solitude dans les *Journaux* de Marivaux'. A. F. Grenon, 'La formulation de la loi morale dans *Le Spectateur français* de Marivaux', *RHLF*, 101 : 1163–80, focuses on *L'Histoire de l'inconnu*, the last five *feuillets* of *Le Spectateur français*, showing how M. creates a polyphonic fictional world which becomes the context for a self-conscious reflection on the universality of moral law, founded on individual conscience.

MARMONTEL. R. L. Dawson, 'Marmontel Made in Britain', *AJFS*, 38 : 107–23, examines the history of M.'s publication and reception in Britain.

PRÉVOST. *Histoire du chevalier Des Grieux et de Manon Lescaut*, ed. Claire Jaquier, Gallimard, 279 pp., is an extremely useful edition of the 1753 edition, with abundant explanatory notes, all based on modern research. G. Ansart, 'Jansenist themes and influences in Prévost's *Cleveland*', *SVEC 2001 : 12*, 47–55, argues that Augustinian theology constitutes a significant part of the ideological make-up of the novel, influencing not only its 'neo-tragic structure' but also its view of fallen man living in solitude in an unstable and corrupt world. V. Papadopoulou Brady, * ' "Manon Lescaut, c'est lui": a study of point of view in Prévost's *Manon Lescaut*', *Intertexts*, 5:156–67. Jonathan Walsh, *Abbé Prévost's 'Histoire d'une Grecque moderne': Figures of Authority on Trial*, Birmingham, AL, Summa, 179 pp., is a useful critical account of the novel.

RESTIF DE LA BRETONNE. D. Coward, 'Restif de la Bretonne and time', *AJFS*, 38:129–40, explores R.'s proto-Proustian fascination with time in his novels, setting these in the context of 18th-c. conceptions of time.

RICCOBONI. *Histoire des amours de Gertrude*, Indigo–Côté-femmes, 82 pp., is a completely uncritical edition, with no editorial material whatsoever, of R.'s 1780 novel, set at the end of the reign of Charles VII.

SADE. John Phillips, *Sade: The Libertine Novels*, Pluto, 204 pp., is an excellent up-to-date introductory study for English-speaking readers, focusing on S.'s four main novels (*Les 120 Journées de Sodome*, *La Philosophie dans le boudoir*, *Justine*, *L'Histoire de Juliette*) and setting them in their historical, political, philosophical, and literary contexts. It also opens up new perspectives of interest to scholars of S., most notably the thesis that S.'s quest can best be understood as an unconscious desire for transcendence of the body. C. Bauer-Funke, 'Aline et Léonore ou les effets de la violence: violence et progrès dans *Aline et Valcour* ou le roman philosophique du marquis de Sade', Cossy, *Progrès*, 167–86, shows how S. exploits the polyphony of his novel to create a contrast between optimistic and violent world-views.

8.　THEATRE

GENERAL. Maurice Lever, *Théâtre et Lumières: les spectacles de Paris au XVIIIe siècle*, Fayard, 394 pp., is a very welcome overview of the 18th-c. theatrical world in Paris, focusing in turn on theatres, actors, plays, and social attitudes. Pierre Jourda, *Le Théâtre à Montpellier, 1755–1851* (SVEC 2001:02), 268 pp., is the fruit of archival research into Montpellier's first permanent theatre, though the paucity of sources means that only two chapters are devoted to the 18th c.: the first examines the construction of the playhouse in 1755 (11–19), the second issues of repertory, personnel, finances, and critical response (20–38). M.-E. Plagnol-Diéval, 'Fournisseurs et commanditaires: le cas des théâtres du duc d'Orléans', Marchal, *Salons*, 303–13, offers a fascinating account of one man's *théâtromanie* in the broader context of 18th-c. *théâtres de société*. J. S. Ravel, 'Theatre beyond privilege: changes in French play publication, 1700–1789', *SVEC 2001:12*, 299–347, excitingly explores a new approach to 18th-c. drama based not on performance figures, but on publication history, an approach which serves in part to highlight a shift in the cultural and political significance of publication from the beginning to the end of the 18th c: in 1700 printed play texts served primarily to memorialize the theatrical event, but by 1789 the texts allowed people to incorporate drama into the new, post-*ancien régime* cultural practices.

INDIVIDUAL AUTHORS

AUTREAU. D. Quéro, '*Platée*, "drame satyrique"?', *Van den Heuvel Vol.*, 195–220, provides a very rich and probing analysis of *Platée*, a 1745 *ballet bouffon* with music by Rameau, highlighting in particular its debt to the pastoral tradition as well as to ancient Greek theatre and the *Cyclops* of Euripides.

BEAUMARCHAIS. *Le Mariage de Figaro*, ed. Guy Bourbonnais, Laval, Beauchemin, 285 pp., is a serviceable student edition of the play. S. Menant, 'Beaumarchais, la méchanceté, la solitude et le comique', *Van den Heuvel Vol.*, 125–45, offers a careful analysis of B.'s comic technique, showing how the traditional aim of making audiences laugh is combined with more modern and specifically contemporary themes, in particular wickedness (Bartholo in *Le Barbier de Séville*, the Comte in *Le Mariage de Figaro*, Bégearss in *La Mère coupable*) and solitude, the latter understood in both the social and moral senses of the term. R. Andrews, 'From Beaumarchais to Da Ponte: a new view of the sexual politics of *Figaro*', *MusL*, 82:214–33, is a clear and scholarly comparison of B.'s play and Mozart's opera, casting new light on the characterization of the Comte and the Comtesse, and throwing into sharp relief the problematic confrontation that the play stages between the attitudes and goals of male and female characters, particularly in the area of marital, and therefore erotic, relationships.

GENLIS. M.-E. Plagnol-Diéval, 'Du mot d'esprit au mot d'enfant dans les théâtres d'éducation', *Van den Heuvel Vol.*, 179–93, provides a cogent analysis of verbal wit and irony in the theatre of Mme de G., showing how they are pressed into the service of the moral aims of *théâtre d'éducation*.

DE GOUGES. G. S. Brown, 'The self-fashionings of Olympe de Gouges, 1784–1789', *Representations*, 34:383–401, offers a scholarly reassessment of de G., and in particular of her 1788 play *Zamore et Mirza*, which in 1792 became the now more famous *L'Esclavage des noirs*, focusing on her engagement with, rather than marginality from, *ancien régime* cultural institutions; in doing so he usefully calls into question some of the *idées reçues* about de G.'s status as a late 18th-c. woman writer.

MARIVAUX. Micheline Boudet, *La Comédie italienne: Marivaux et Silvia*, Albin Michel, 261 pp., reconstructs the fruitful relationship —

professional and otherwise — between M. and Silvia Balletti, the *prima amorosa* of the Italian troupe in Paris.

MONVEL. *Théâtre, discours politiques et réflexions diverses*, ed. Roselyne Laplace, Champion, 382 pp., includes briefly annotated editions of three plays: *L'Amant bourru* (1777), a reasonably funny character comedy; *Les Amours de Bayard* (1789), a *comédie héroïque*; and *Les Victimes cloîtrées* (1791), an anti-religious satirical *drame*.

PIRON. S. D. Nell, *'Trading places: dialogical transvestites and monological gender politics in Alexis Piron's *Tirésias* and *La Métromanie*', *ESJ*, 17–18:131–46.

9. POETRY

GENERAL. C. Seth, 'La poésie de salon ou l'impossible œuvre complète', Marchal, *Salons*, 293–301, offers a critical overview of so-called *poésie fugitive* in the 18th c., with particular reference to Delille and Gentil-Bernard. Christian Leroy, *La Poésie en prose française du XVIIe siècle à nos jours: histoire d'un genre*, Champion, 223 pp., casts its net wide, sometimes confusingly so, to include an inconsistent section on early modern prose tragedy (13–57), a largely well-focused chapter on *Télémaque* and its imitations (59–77), and a much broader discussion of 18th-c. 'prose lyrique' and, less satisfyingly, 'le lyrisme pré-romantique' (79–124); the bibliography is disappointingly thin (211–12).

INDIVIDUAL AUTHORS

CHÉNIER. D. Millet-Gérard, 'Résonances virgiliennes chez André Chénier', *CAIEF*, 53:213–34, is a learned and insightful analysis of C.'s debt in the *Bucoliques* to Virgil, focusing on themes and style, the latter topic embracing sentence structure, versification, and sound patterns. E. Guitton, 'L'inspiration poétique d'André Chénier et le milieu ambiant', Marchal, *Salons*, 39–46, tries to deconstruct the image of C. as a bookish, Virgilian poet by searching in the *Bucoliques* for traces of the influence of friends, acquaintances, and the poet's own experiences, which is a difficult task given that so little is known about C.'s life. J. Millner, 'André Chénier's astonishing revolutionary language in the iambs', *DFS*, 57:10–24, claims that C.'s poetic language has much in common with that of his revolutionary enemies, particularly in terms of what she sees as its oratorical excesses and its heroic imagery.

DULAURENS. M. Bokobza-Kahan, 'Une conscience écartelée: Dulaurens', *RHLF*, 101:1367–82, looks beyond D.'s comic novel *Le Compère Mathieu* to his neglected poetry, in particular *Le Balai* (1762), an anti-religious *poème héroï-comique*, and explores the organic links between the writer's thought and style, showing how the self-derision which characterizes his style becomes part of his sceptical vision which is linked to his views on tolerance.

THE ROMANTIC ERA

By JOHN WHITTAKER, *University of Hull*

1. GENERAL

M. Bacholle, 'Women in their apartment: the trespassing gaze', *PhilP*, 48: 18–28, places Delacroix's *Femmes d'Alger* within the literary context of Romantic Orientalism. J. Neefs, 'La "haine des grands hommes" au XIXe siècle', *MLN*, 116: 750–69, notes that 19th-c. writers did much to develop and maintain the concept of the great man, though they treated it with increasing unease and ambiguity as the century progressed.

Napoléon: de l'histoire à la légende, ed. Bernard Devaux, In Forma, 2000, 448 pp., is the proceedings of a conference held at the Musée de l'Armée on 30 November and 1 December 1999. It contains: J. Delmas, 'Histoire et légende' (11–14), introducing the theme of the construction of the 'Légende napoléonienne'; B. Gainot, 'La légende noire du Directoire' (15–25), on the myth of Brumaire, mainly of N.'s creation; J.-P. Clément, 'Un émigré face au coup d'état de brumaire: Chateaubriand' (27–45), explaining C.'s position during the period 1800–04, between his return from exile and his resignation from the Rome embassy; P. Gourmen, 'La seconde campagne d'Italie' (47–57), on N.'s military strategy; M. Arrous, 'Stendhal, Napoléon et l'Italie' (59–74), showing the importance of the figure of N. in S.'s work; J. Garnier, 'Iéna, une victoire exemplaire' (75–86); T. Bodin, 'Les batailles napoléoniennes de Balzac' (87–115), on the attempts to write the novel entitled *La Bataille*, and noting that N. is the most frequently cited name in *La Comédie humaine*; F. Dartois-Lapeyre, 'Napoléon, l'opéra et la danse' (117–53), on his desire to encourage France's supremacy in these arts; C. Helfrich, 'L'Empereur et l'Hôtel des Invalides' (155–65), on his plans for an institution that he admired; C. Gué, 'Russie 1812, les limites du système napoléonien' (167–96), explaining the failure of the campaign; M. Cadot, 'Tolstoï contre Napoléon' (197–209), showing that, though T. remained resolutely opposed to N., he had some admiration for his greatness; G. Bodinier, 'Officiers et soldats de l'armée impériale face à Napoléon' (211–32), on the evolution of N.'s relationship with the army; F. Lacaille, 'Deux peintres de la légende, Delaroche et Meissonnier' (233–50), on two portraits of the Emperor painted in 1814; F. Laurent, 'Car nous t'avons pour Dieu sans t'avoir eu pour maître!' (251–77), on Hugo's attitude to N. and the images of him which are found in his work; F. Lagrange, 'Le sabre et la pierre: les bas-reliefs du tombeau de Napoléon entre légende et récupération politique' (279–314), observing that these images place little emphasis upon military glory; J.-C. Yon, 'La légende napoléonienne au théâtre, 1848–69' (315–44), tracing the progress of a persistent fashion on the French stage, which extends from 1830 to 1900; J. Tulard, 'Napoléon dans le roman populaire' (345–48), referring to the period 1870–1920; S. Vielledent, 'Le retour du "petit chapeau" en 1830' (351–72), on the revival of plays dealing with N. after the abolition of censorship; Id., 'Anthologie du napoléonisme dramatique en 1830' (373–436), a fascinating collection of 71 extracts from the plays; G. Pompidou, 'Le génie de Napoléon domine notre histoire, comme il préfigure l'avenir de l'Europe' (437–44), the text of the speech made in August 1969 in Ajaccio.

Elvire de Brissac, *O dix-neuvième*, Grasset, 394 pp., is a personal appreciation of the culture and society of the 19th c. as seen through the lives of two contrasting figures: Alphonse de Lamartine and Eugène Schneider, the industrialist and owner of Le Creusot. Although it is fair to say that there is no new information on the life of L., that of S. merits attention, and the contrast between the two is an apt reminder of the world beyond literary history, allowing a new perspective of L.'s achievements. Pierre Laforgue, *Romanticoco, fantaisie, chimère et mélancolie (1830–1860)*, Vincennes U.P., 246 pp., invents a new word to describe divergent forms of Romanticism. The first part identifies a poetic change in Romanticism following the July Revolution, to do with the vision of the world, the importance of feelings, the stability of symbols and beliefs, melancholy, travel, Bohemian existence, and chimaerae. The second part studies examples of the phenomenon: Balzac's *La Femme de trente ans* and *Illusions perdues*, George Sand's *Lettres d'un voyageur*, Musset's *La Nuit de mai*, Vigny's *La Flûte*, Michelet's *L'Oiseau*, *L'Insecte*, *La Mer*, and *La Montagne*, and ending with Baudelaire. Corinne Pelta, *Le Romantisme libéral en France 1815–1830*, L'Harmattan, 302 pp., examines Romanticism's radical shift in direction from ultra-Royalist beginnings, prior to 1826, towards a new vision of the individual and of society. Beginning with the changes witnessed in both, we then move to questions of artistic representation: the search for a hidden truth; the continuing fascination with vivid images of violence. A chapter on the social role of the theatre is of particular interest. Finally, we are shown the role of the writer as educator and economist, concluding that Romanticism is fundamentally the spirit of freedom.

Whitney Walton, *Eve's Proud Descendants*, Stanford U.P., 2000, 308 pp., is concerned with Marie d'Agoult, Hortense Allart, Delphine Gay de Girardin, and George Sand, all four being successful authors in the same Parisian literary milieu at roughly the same time. It combines a biographical study of each with historical analysis of

French literary and political culture, particularly under the July Monarchy. There are two chapters on the articulation of their republicanism, and the way in which they transformed it by proposing sweeping changes in gender and family relations. Unfortunately, the 1848 Revolution did not achieve the changes they sought, though their lives proved that equality of the sexes would be possible in the future.

The manner of two brief introductions to the period, aimed at students, gives a measure of the progress which has been achieved over the last 30 years in the understanding of Romanticism. Patrick Marot, *Histoire de la littérature française du XIXe siècle*, Champion, 185 pp., offers a broad overview, giving particular attention to the evolution of æsthetics and to key issues, rather than to movements, generations or authors. The three sections of the book begin with a consideration of the social environment of the time, before moving to an effective definition of the Romantic æsthetic, then providing a broad perspective of the full range of genres. Christian Chelebourg, *Le Romantisme*, Nathan, 121 pp., takes a similar direction. Three chapters give an overview of the history of Romanticism, before moving to æsthetic considerations, and then to an effective summary of the principal topics found in Romantic literature. The sheer accuracy of the perspective, and the concentration of considerable detail in a slender volume, are admirable characteristics which may turn this introduction into a work of ready reference.

2. CONSULATE WRITERS

K. Sainson, ' "Le régénérateur de la France": literary accounts of Napoleonic regeneration, 1799–1805', *NCFS*, 30:9–25, traces the earliest stages of the development of the 'Légende napoléonienne' in the work of writers such as Mouton and Lamontagne, and with particular reference to Grainville's *Le Dernier Homme*.

CHATEAUBRIAND. J. F. Hamilton, 'Connecting *Atala* and *René*: the *senex* and *puer* archetypes', *RoQ*, 48:239–49, suggests that the Chactas-René dyad enables an expanded meaning which would not otherwise be available, for they represent two aspects of the same personality, while presenting an archetypal split in the age-youth polarity. C. Moscovici, 'Hybridity and ethics in Chateaubriand's Atala', *NCFS*, 29:197–216, leads us from the simple contrast, at the beginning of the story, between savage nature and European culture, towards the more complex appreciation of the nature of cultural difference and hybridity which is fundamental to the work as a whole. F. Bassan, 'Une amitié littéraire: Chateaubriand et Dumas père', *ib.*, 217–25, presents the details of this unlikely friendship, their initial meeting when in voluntary exile in Lucerne in 1832, the political views they shared, and the profound admiration of D. for C., though they came from different generations and social backgrounds.

Enfance et voyages de Chateaubriand, Armorique, Amérique, ed. Jean Balcou, Champion, 141 pp., contains the proceedings of a conference held in Brest in September 1998. It includes: P. Le Guillou, 'Introduction au colloque' (7–13), noting C.'s affinity with Brittany and the sea, and his taste for nostalgia; J. Balcou, 'René et la Révolution: "orgie noir d'un cœur blessé"' (15–22), on the works C. published and re-edited in 1826; J.-P. Clément, '1826, un tournant de la pensée politique de Chateaubriand: l'édition critique de L'*Essai sur les révolutions*' (23–34), showing how C.'s changing political views affected his annotations; M. Blain-Pinel, 'Marines et paysages marins' (35–46), examining C.'s skill with seascapes; P. Antoine, 'Le paysage américain chez Chateaubriand' (47–59), showing that the images of wild solitude in the New World are linked to the imagination of C.'s early period; C. Montalbetti, 'Écritures de l'Amérique: les aventures de la matière américaine: identité, variante et variation' (61–74), on the epic and poetic inspiration which America provided, and the evolution of the texts initially composed there; C. Bayle, 'Ce que dit René aux jeunes gens d'aujourd'hui' (75–82), finding that the personal themes of solitude and inner conflict commend themselves to young people of every generation; A. Seite-Salaun, 'De Loaisel de Tréogate à Chateaubriand' (83–98), on the work of a minor 18th-c. novelist and playwright, whose *Florello* may possibly be a source of *Atala*; J. Balcou, 'Chateaubriand à Brest: janvier juin 1783, genèse d'une aventure, génétique d'un texte' (99–123), on a text written by C. at the age of 14 and which closely resembles a passage from the *Mémoires d'outre-tombe*.

Chateaubriand visionnaire, ed. Jean-Paul Clément, Fallois, 152 pp., contains the proceedings of a conference held at the Fondation Singer-Polignac on 28 June 2000. It includes: Id., 'Présentation' (11–22), introducing the topic of the prophetic pages at the end of the *Mémoires d'outre-tombe*; B. Heudré, 'Chateaubriand visionnaire du catholicisme' (23–32), showing the modernity of C.'s religious attitudes, as expressed here; J. Julliard, 'Chateaubriand et le socialisme' (33–43), examining the references to socialism from the perspective of 1841, and concluding that C.'s belief in the future of democracy, provided it did not infringe upon personal liberty, was essentially Christian; J. Cluzel, 'Chateaubriand, champion de la liberté, "la presse, l'électricité sociale"' (45–54), on C.'s resolute support for the freedom of the press; P. Bénichou, 'Chateaubriand et son siècle, d'après *René* et *Le Génie du christianisme*' (55–70), finding that these early works exerted a considerable and complex influence on

19th-c. literature and religious attitudes, but that it was no more than temporary and partial; G. Berger, 'Chateaubriand et la mondialisation' (71–88), showing C.'s remarkably prescient awareness of the beginnings of globalization; G. de Broglie, 'Chateaubriand ou la messe de la langue française' (89–103), on the celebration of the French language, a common theme in his work, and his ideas on the evolution of languages; J.-P. Clément, 'Conclusions' (107–17), linking his predictions to present-day conditions; A. Damien, 'Chateaubriand et la course aux honneurs' (119–43), the text of a lecture given at the Maison Chateaubriand in April 2000, an account of the various honours he received.

Agnès Verlet, *Les Vanités de Chateaubriand*, Geneva, Droz, 367 pp., is a study of the theme of vanity which runs through C.'s work, and which is particularly evident in the *Mémoires d'outre-tombe*. Traced from biblical and classical sources, by way of a range of artistic representations in which it is associated with melancholy, we are shown that the theme becomes central to C.'s philosophy of life, representing the human being's relationship with death. The analysis reveals the richness and the complexity of C.'s treatment of the concept of vanity, enabling a fuller understanding of his writing.

MME DE STAËL. *Mme de Staël*, ed. Michel Delon and Françoise Mélonio, Paris-Sorbonne U.P., 2000, 137 pp., contains the proceedings of the conference held at the Sorbonne in November 1999. It includes: V. Rambaud, '*Corinne* ou le roman des adieux' (7–16), observing that one of the particular features of the novel is in the importance attached to farewells, and not only in the three major scenes which punctuate the story; A. Minski, 'La niche vide du Panthéon: monuments et beaux-arts de Rome' (17–30), investigating the genre of *Corinne* and indicating the balance between description and narrative; F. Bercegol, 'Mme de Staël portraitiste dans *Corinne ou l'Italie*' (31–54), explaining that, though S. was usually reticent when it came to descriptions of people, the prevalence of portraits demonstrates the development of her skill as a novelist; C. Garry-Boussel, 'L'homme du Nord et l'homme du Midi dans *Corinne* de Mme de Staël' (55–66), considering the north-south paradigm in the novel and the organization of S.'s geographical and imaginary space; J. Huchette, 'Le comte d'Erfeuil et la représentation du caractère français (67–74), finding that S.'s idea of national character has more to do with a dynamic process of historical and geographical determination than with a fixed classification; M. Delon, 'Du vague staëlien des passions' (75–83), on a conception of the passions which combines awareness of individual human suffering, of the needs of the community, and of momentary pleasure with a perception of the infinite; M. Brix, 'Les sources mystiques de Corinne: la femme, l'amour et le sacré' (85–97), showing the confusion between art, love and religion, which is probably due to the evolution of attitudes towards all three; C. Seth, ' "Une âme exilée sur la terre". *Corinne*: un mythe moderne de la transgression' (99–129), on the numerous unspoken boundaries which Corinne oversteps in the story, and the reasons why she does so. Angelica Goodden, *Madame de Staël, Delphine and Corinne*, London, Grant and Cutler, 2000, 83 pp., is a brief introduction for students which gives a number of aids to understanding and a clear notion of the thematic links between the two novels.

3. POETRY

DESBORDES-VALMORE. O. Bivort, 'Les "vies absentes" de Rimbaud et Marceline Desbordes-Valmore', *RHLF*, 101 : 1269–73, identifies the influence of D.-V. on R., firstly in the line from 'C'est moi' quoted in *Une Saison en enfer*, then in his evident familiarity with her work, and in the way that he took up certain of her metrical innovations.

GAUTIER. Martine Lavaud, *Théophile Gautier, militant du romantisme*, Champion, 638 pp., begins with the familiar red waistcoat of the *Hernani* opening night, and the satirical journalism of the *Jeunes-France* period, but goes on to show that the ready caricature of the militant Romantic is a cliché which is not easily reconciled with G.'s later standpoints, for example his approval of the Second Empire. This thorough account of the whole of G.'s writing, poetry, fiction, and journalism, shows three phases of his militancy: polemical and anti-bourgeois; pedagogical, addressing the modern world; æsthetic and subdued. Due emphasis is placed on his versatility and his originality, and the complexity of his views and techniques. *Victor Hugo par Théophile Gautier*, Champion, 2000, 264 pp., contains a range of texts, introduced and with notes by F. Court-Perez.

GUÉRIN. *Maurice de Guérin et le romantisme*, ed. Marie-Catherine Huet-Brichard, Toulouse, Le Mirail U.P., 2000, 224 pp., contains the proceedings of a conference held at Toulouse and the Chateau du Cayla in May 1999. It includes: C. Gély, 'Moïse, Charon, Glaucus: l'eau et les rêves dans le *Cahier vert*' (11–22), examining the use of water imagery to represent the source of life and of poetry; B. Benneteau, 'Les paysages du *Cahier vert*, transcription littéraire d'un regard pictural' (23–34), on the visual arts as a source of inspiration, and the use of visual imagery, in particular colours, in the poems; K. Schärer, 'Les romantiques et le temps-flux' (35–43), on the distinctive nature of Romantic temporality, particularly a heightened awareness of the fleeting moment; J.-M. Le Lannou, 'L'immensité de la vie: être selon Maurice de Guérin' (45–63), taking G.'s work as a demonstration of how we may escape the constraints which are placed on existence, and how poetry may transform and liberate the soul; M.-T. Mathet, 'Ombres et mystères: les secrets d'une écriture romantique' (65–75), considering the crucial paradox which is central to G.'s work, that poetry of its very nature contains secrets, yet the poet is committed to revealing them to his audience; M. Schärer-Nussberger, 'Parole et silence' (77–90), on G.'s idea of the poet having an intimate relationship with nature, yet one which was potentially false if nature was not seen with an inner eye, and if an appropriate essential language was not sought with which to speak of it; J.-P. Zubiate, 'Écriture et appréhension de l'immensité chez Maurice de Guérin' (91–113), on the difficulty of finding language which is appropriate to describe the infinite, though G. distinguishes himself as a modern writer by combining a sincere effort in this direction with a recognition of his limitations; J. M. Vest, 'Maurice de Guérin et les mages: un retour aux sources' (115–22), linking the use of the Magus image with the Breton period of 1832–34 and identifying its sources in the work of Hugo, Lamartine, and Vigny; X. Ravier, 'Maurice de Guérin et l'horizon mythique' (123–36), on G.'s extensive knowledge of the mythology of Ancient Greece and its influence on *Le Centaure* and *La Bacchante*; D. Millet-Gérard, '*Sublimitas et profundum*: l'énigme du catholicisme romantique chez Maurice de Guérin' (127–64), leading to the conclusion that, however hazardous the friendship with Lamennais may have been to G.'s religious attitudes, *Le Centaure* and *La Bacchante* are at least more Catholic than *Paroles d'un croyant*; J. Burgos, 'De la création, du créateur et du *Centaure*' (165–76), showing that *Le Centaure* is not merely a stylistic exercise, but profoundly anchored in the poet's universe and his imagination; M.-C. Huet-Brichard, 'Guérin et la nouvelle école imaginaire et poétique' (177–87), on an article of 1834 in *La France catholique*, in which G. defines his position on the threshold of neo-Catholicism and of Romanticism; P. Brunel, 'Maurice de Guérin et l'idylle romantique' (189–200), on the complex influences to be observed in the idyllic passages of Le *Cahier vert*; P. Berthier, 'Jules et Maurice: un *De Amicitia* romantique' (201–18), on the important early friendship with Barbey d'Aurevilly.

HUGO. Louis Aguettant, *Victor Hugo, poète de la nature*, ed. Jeanne and Jacques Lonchampt, L'Harmattan 2000, 511 pp., preserves a very detailed account of the importance of nature in the work of H., compiled from the notes and unpublished manuscript of a lecturer who died in 1931. Max Gallo, *Victor Hugo*, 2 vols, XO, 493, 510 pp., is an extensive and well-written biography, aimed primarily at the general reader. For the H. expert, most of the information will be familiar, though the careful linking of the life with the poetry, and the sheer amount of detail, make it a potentially useful guide for students.

Emmanuel Godo, *Victor Hugo et Dieu, bibliographie d'une âme*, Cerf, 281 pp., is an effective theological analysis of H.'s religious views, as expressed in his writing and, for the most part, in the poetry. The usual trap of attempting to capture him within a particular form of Catholicism has, fortunately, been avoided. We are led to a clear conclusion that, though H.'s spirituality was profoundly influenced by Christianity, his religious attitudes were personal and original, and one may not define them in terms of denominational orthodoxy. Jean-François Kahn, *Victor Hugo, un révolutionnaire, suivi de de L'Extraordinaire Métamorphose*, Fayard, 953 pp., combines two works in a single volume, the first consisting of new material, the second a revised version of that published in 1984. The two are very closely connected and should be read as one. How did H., a viscount and monarchist, become a public enemy under the Second Empire, and then the revolutionary of the Paris Commune? The answer is in the radical transformation of his social and political views during the period 1847–51.

SAINTE-BEUVE. M.-C. Huet-Brichard, 'Sainte-Beuve à la lumière de Baudelaire: "la pointe extrême du Kamchatka romantique"', *RHLF*, 101 : 263–80, begins with the lines of appreciation in S.-B.'s article, 'Des prochaines élections à l'Académie', and traces the numerous elements of affinity between the work of the two poets, with particular emphasis on their combination of lyricism and irony.

4. THE NOVEL

A. Lascar, 'La courtisane romantique (1830–1850): solitude et ambiguïté d'un personnage romanesque', *RHLF*, 101 : 1193–1215, presents a sweeping panorama of the many works in which the figure of the courtesan appears, but ends by identifying Esther, Marguerite Gautier, and Dumas *Père*'s Fernande as the most striking examples. Laure Lévêque, *Le Roman de l'histoire 1780–1850*, L'Harmattan, 402 pp., is not only concerned with the historical novel, but with the history of the novel's evolution into a new and dominant genre, the links between literature and society, and novelists' changing historical perspectives. Attention is given to the work of Balzac, Chateaubriand, Constant, Custine, Mme de Duras, Hugo, Las Cases, Sainte-Beuve, Senancour, Mme de Staël, and Stendhal.

BALZAC. D. Aranda, 'Originalité historique du retour de personnages balzaciens', *RHLF*, 101 : 1573–89, notes that, though B. may not have been the first to employ the technique, his particular manner of using it, and in particular his approach to temporality, became archetypal, extending the potential resources of the Realist novel. A.-P. Durand, 'Lucien Chardon-de Rubempré: champion du monde en titres', *RoQ*, 48:250–56, shows how Lucien's search for an identity, in *Illusions perdues*, may be explained by the theories of Althusser. M. Lastinger, 'The CAPital letter: Balzac's *Le Colonel Chabert* and the names of a rose', *NCFS*, 30:39–57, investigates the interplay of phonemes, sememes, and subtext, and finds that there is, beyond the verbal narrative, a representation of profound human fears and desires. N. B. Rogers, 'De 93 à *L'Histoire des treize*: la Terreur de (Marie-)Antoinette de Langeais', *RHLF*, 101:51–69, demonstrates the impact upon *La Duchesse de Langeais* of the scandalous revolutionary tribunal and the subsequent execution of the Queen, representing a crystallization of B.'s political, erotic, social, and æsthetic anxieties, and ultimately resulting in something resembling a Restoration of the authority of the narrator. R. Shuh, 'Madness and military history in Balzac's "Adieu"', *FrF*, 26.1:39–51, shows that, although in *La Comedie humaine* B. abandons the overtly historical mode of the novels of his youth, certain of his works continue to grapple with the past, even though, as in the case of this short story of 1830, they conclude resolutely in the present.

Envers balzaciens, ed. Andrea Del Lungo and Alexandre Péraud, Poitiers, La Licorne, 250 pp., contains the proceedings of the conference held at Bordeaux in November 1999. It includes: M. Milner, 'Ouverture' (5–7); S. Vachon, ' "L'envers est l'endroit de l'auteur" ' (9–18), introducing the themes of the conference with phrases from *Splendeurs et misères des courtisanes* and from a letter to Madame Hanska; A. Péraud, 'Scénographies de l'envers dans *L'Envers de l'histoire contemporaine*' (21–38), stressing the importance of this key novel, which definitively establishes the coherence of *La Comédie humaine*; T. Stöber, 'Du voir au savoir, du sens au sens: le regard de la modernité et ses figures chez Balzac' (39–50), which examines the perspective of hidden essence in *La Comédie humaine* and the relationship between the metaphysical and the physical; E. Cullmann, 'Le parcours de l'envers à l'endroit' (51–62), which considers the role played on stage and behind the scenes by the character Jacques Collin, alias Vautrin; B. Lyon-Caen, 'L'envers en pli, l'envers à plat: forme et signification dans le texte balzacien des années 1840' (63–83), showing how far the ambitions of the 'Avant-propos' of 1842 are achieved in four works of 1844: *Les Petits Bourgeois*, *Modeste Mignon*, *Les Paysans*, and *Les Employés*; A. Del Lungo, 'Fenêtres à l'envers (perversions, effractions, pénétrations)' (87–102), demonstrating the various functions of window imagery, as a point of access between interior and exterior, as a means to delimit the view, and even as a magic mirror; B. Milcent, 'Effets de la réversibilité dans les lettres d'adieu des personnages balzaciens' (103–15), noting the dramatic ambiguity of these letters, but observing that they enable the revelation of the human dimension; I.-K. Kim, 'Balzac-Janus: sociocritique du bilatéral' (117–30), beginning with B.'s innovative use of the word 'bilatéral' in *Illusions Perdues*, and finding that the frequent motif of revealing two sides of a character or situation emphasizes an ambivalence of meaning, which may have precedence over an inner truth; C. Barel-Moisan, 'Brouillages narratifs: l'intertextualité ou l'envers du roman' (133–50), considering internal and external intertextuality, the former giving the novel a new status by destabilizing the continuum between reality and fiction, the latter permitting a means of escape from a hermetically-sealed fictional world; C. Couleau, 'L'ironie, principe de réversibilité du récit' (151–64), seeking to define the manner of ironic notation as a hermeneutic tool, as a means to introduce doubt or to perturb, and as a principle of reversibility; A. Déruelle, 'Sujet et hors-sujet dans *Ferragus* de Balzac' (165–80), covering the technique of digression in the novel, which blurs the boundary between foreground and background; J.-D. Ebguy, ' "Ce que racontent les romans": "mise en scène" des situations dans *La Fausse Maîtresse*' (181–98), analysing the narrative technique of a story which B. said he found difficult to write; S. Pietri, 'Le don de l'envers: *Une Passion dans le désert* de Balzac et *Un Artiste de la faim* de Kafka' (201–19), identifying K.'s debt to B. and describing the differences between the philosophical and authorial stance of the two stories; I. Michelot, 'Le roman au risque du théâtre: théâtralisation et réversibilité dans *La Duchesse de Langeais*' (221–32), noting the importance of the theatre in the novel, and B.'s use of dramatic techniques; V. Bui, ' "L'escriptoire à double goddet": *Les Contes drolatiques* envers de *La Comédie humaine* et endroit du désir féminin' (233–44), suggesting that B. suppressed the theme of female desire from the *Contes* in order to avoid the accusation of obscenity, though in so doing he removed an important feature distinguishing them from the novels.

Marcel Boisvert, *L'Éducation de la jeune fille de province dans Balzac*, Montréal, Guérin, 2000, v + 242 pp., is based on the numerous portraits of provincial girls in *La Comédie humaine*, and is in three parts. The first deals with physical appearance, moral status, and the girls' place in society. The second is concerned with girls' education in the early 19th c., both in schools and in the family. The third considers their destiny, the role which society then offered to women, marriage and motherhood, or remaining single. The conclusion is that B.'s representation of provincial girls is realistic and an integral part of his attempt to portray the society of his time in *La Comédie humaine*. Ketty Kupfer, *Les Juifs de Balzac*, NM7, 366 pp., shows that B.'s numerous Jewish characters derive from his ambition to paint a realistic portrait of society. Having gained full rights of citizenship with the Revolution, the Jewish sector of the population was a new element of considerable economic importance. B.'s representation of them is ambivalent: men and women are seen differently, as are 'authentic' Jews who accept their origins and 'inauthentic' Jews who hide them; they display superiority in some contexts and inferiority in others. Torn between recognition of their virtues and stock prejudice against them, we see that B. is representative of his time. Alexandra K. Wettlaufer, *Pen vs. Paintbrush: Girodet, Balzac and the Myth of Pygmalion in Postrevolutionary France*, NY, Palgrave, xi + 323 pp., notes G.'s intimate association with Romantic poets, taking the evident rivalry between him and B. as a representative case study of the relationship between painting and literature in the first half of the 19th c., associated with a struggle for artistic identity. Particular attention is given to *La Maison du chat-qui-pelote*, *Sarrasine* and, inevitably, the representation of the painter in *Le Chef-d'œuvre inconnu*.

DUMAS PÈRE. K. Vassilev, 'Vengeance et récit dans *Le Comte de Monte-Cristo*', *FrF*, 26.2:43–66, considers the manner in which the theme of vengeance provides the structure of the story, enabling the metamorphosis of Edmond Dantès into the hero, yet remains firmly anchored in the world of fiction. J.-M. Salien, **La subversion de l'orientalisme dans *Le Comte de Monte Cristo* d'Alexandre Dumas', *EF*, 36, 2000:179–90.

DURAS. Chantal Bertrand-Jennings, *D'un siècle l'autre: romans de Claire de Duras*, La Chasse au Snark, 141 pp., sets out to demonstrate the originality and the modernity of D.'s three novels, *Ourika*, *Édouard*, and *Olivier ou le secret*, and to evaluate their role in the transition from Classicism to Romanticism. Features which are shown to be of particular importance include the representation of nature, England and the English way of thinking, and the themes of unrequited love and of exile. Not least is the emphasis which is given to feelings, representing a move to more feminine values and opening up new opportunities for the feminine voice.

HUGO. K. M. Grossman, 'From classic to pop icon: popularizing Hugo', *FR*, 74:482–95, argues that H. was at least in part responsible for his metamorphosis into a media star, and that the Disney *Hunchback of Notre-Dame* or the stage musical *Les Misérables* are not corruptions of his novels, but evidence of a hypertextual web joining élite and popular culture.

MÉRIMÉE. J. S. Patty, 'Prénom Carmen, or the charms of etymology', *RoN*, 42:35–41, returns to the etymology of the heroine's name, concluding in favour of a source in Santa María del Carmen, though M. would undoubtedly have been aware of the various meanings of the Latin word. C. Requena, 'Autour de *La Venus d'Ille* et de *Carmen* de Prosper Mérimée: le thème de l'eau et de l'altitude',

RHLF, 101 : 1591–1610, examines the very close links between the two figures, the imagery and mythology of altitude and water, and a memory of La Giralda of Seville.

SAND. E. Ender, ' "Une femme qui rêve n'est pas tout à fait une femme": *Lélia* en rupture d'identité', *NCFS*, 29 : 226–46, links the 1833 version of the text, by means of the phenomenological work of the philosopher Denise Riley, to broader issues concerned with the construction of gender differences, representing S. as a precursor of modern feminist thought. D. Laporte, ' "Ne m'appelez donc jamais femme auteur": déconstruction et refus du roman sentimental chez George Sand', *ib.*, 247–55, describes S.'s resolute rejection of the sentimental tradition of women's writing, to the extent that she engaged in parody and deconstruction of the genre, disowning those of her own works which could be said to fall within it. In so doing, she gained a reputation for being subversive, but nevertheless failed to adhere to the feminist principles of her time. *George Sand, jenseits des Identischen, au-delà de l'identique*, ed. Gislinde Seybert and Gisela Schlientz, Bielefeld, Aisthesis, 2000, 471 pp., contains the proceedings of the 13th Internationale George Sand Kolloquium, held in Hanover in July 1997. It includes 30 papers on the way S. established both her personal identity and that of her characters, her contribution to the development of autobiography, the social perspectives of her novels, style, gender identity, and the reception of her work outside France. Janet Hiddleston, *George Sand, Indiana, Mauprat*, Glasgow U.P., 2000, iv + 88 pp., is an introduction for students covering, for *Indiana*, context, narrative voice, characterization, plot, Realism, and Symbolism, and for *Mauprat*, context, education, romance, socialism, and narrative frame. Emphasis is placed on the composite nature and possible alternative readings of *Indiana*, and of the greater importance of the moral message in *Mauprat*. Cam-Thi Doan Poisson, *Poétique de la mobilité: les lieux dans 'Histoire de ma vie' de George Sand*, Amsterdam, Rodopi, 2000, 260 pp., is a detailed analysis of the use of space in the autobiography, and of the evidence it presents of a need for movement, a journey which is either real or symbolic. Particular attention is given to the theme of borders which must be crossed, and the consequent transition from culture to culture. Love is also a journey, and death is perceived as the ultimate border.

STENDHAL. P. Seys, 'Taine, inventeur de Stendhal', *LR*, 54 : 13–31, shows that T., in an article of 1864 on *Le Rouge et le noir*, may have been the first fully to appreciate S.'s superior skill as a writer, and also to identify the novel as a major work.

VIGNY. M. Cambien, 'Vérité de l'art et rhétorique du vraisemblable: une (re)lecture de *Cinq-Mars*', *NCFS*, 30 : 26–38, examines closely the relationship between the theory of truth in art, as outlined in the preface of 1829, and the precise manner of the narrative. Though the novel is shown to move from the historical to the philosophical, emphasis is given to its strict semiotic coherence.

5. DRAMA

MÉRIMÉE.   O. Mandel, 'Nouveau regard sur Mérimée dramaturge', *RHLF*, 101 : 1217–31, 1383–98, shows that, despite his success as a writer of novels and short stories, M. had begun his literary career by writing plays, and continued to do so. Seeking to rehabilitate M. as a playwright, Mandel pleads both for the production and for the edition of the plays, though he stresses that a rigorous process of selection is necessary in both areas.

6. WRITERS IN OTHER GENRES

Encyclopedia of Life Writing, ed. Margaretta Jolly, 2 vols, London–Chicago, Fitzroy Dearborn, xlvii + 537, xxxv + 539–1090 pp., includes: M. Sheringham, 'Chateaubriand' (195–96), noting that the revival of critical interest in the last 30 years has led to greater recognition of the importance of the *Mémoires d'outre-tombe*; J. R. Whittaker, 'France: 19th-century auto/biography' (337–38), observing the significant development in the status of biography and autobiography, the increase in its volume and the diversification of types of life writing; D. A. Powell, 'Sand, George' (776–78), on *Histoire de ma vie*, the arduous and lengthy process of writing it, and the nature of the emotions and the events it portrays, *Lettres d'un voyageur* and the *Journal intime*, as well as the works of fiction with a strong autobiographical element, *Un Hiver à Majorque, Elle et lui, Journal d'un voyageur pendant la guerre*, and the 26 volumes of correspondence; P. Wagstaff, 'Stendhal' (844–45), considering the strategies of *La Vie de Henry Brulard*, the neglect of sequential chronology, the spontaneous pursuit of memories, the technique of delaying the narration of what matters most to the author, the privileged place he affords to childhood experience; S. L. Jones, 'Tocqueville, Alexis de' (877–78), on the autobiographical content of his theoretical writing, *Voyage en Amérique, Quinze jours au désert*, and his diary of 1848, *Les Souvenirs*.

COMTE.   Raquel Capurro, *Le Positivisme est un culte des morts: Auguste Comte*, Epel, 156 pp., is a precise and thorough summary of C.'s life and the origins and evolution of Positivism. From his early years, the beginning of his career and the mental breakdown he experienced in 1826, we move quickly to the death of Clotilde de Vaux and the consequent mourning, eventually transformed into the cult of the dead. The final chapter, on the impact of C.'s work in Latin America, reflects the author's location, though it also leads to reflection on his European heritage.

FOURIER. Michel Brix, *L'Héritage de Fourier, Utopie amoureuse et libération sexuelle*, La Chasse au Snark, 219 pp., concentrates on F.'s advocacy of free love in Utopia. Following a reminder that he was not the first to propose such a thing, the first part outlines his theories, identifies the importance he attached to the passions, and links his ideas to Romanticism in general. The second part traces the influence of his theories on succeeding generations, from the Surrealists to the present, by way of *Lady Chatterley's Lover*, Wilhelm Reich, and May 1968.

MAISTRE. Bastien Miquel, *Joseph de Maistre, un philosophe à la cour du Tsar*, Albin Michel, 2000, 255 pp., is concerned with the period 1802–17, when M. was the Sardinian ambassador to the court of Alexander I in St Petersburg. It is based extensively on unpublished material from family archives, giving an interesting and informative account of the life of the author and of the environment in which the *Soirées* were written.

NAPOLÉON. *Napoléon Bonaparte, œuvres littéraires et écrits militaires*, ed. Jean Tulard, 3 vols, Bibliothèque des Introuvables, 387, 351, 458 pp., is essential reading for those who seek to understand the personality of the Emperor, and of considerable interest for all students of the period in which he lived. We are reminded that, in his youth, N. seemed more interested in achieving success as a writer than in a military career. The style is distinctive and the range of different kinds of material is striking. There are poems, the beginnings of a novel, journalism and, perhaps most important, the extensive notes taken when reading the work of others. On more familiar territory, there are pamphlets, speeches, strategic theory, and accounts of military action. The edition is organized chronologically, from 1785 to the abdication of the 25 June 1815.

NERVAL. H. Mizuno, 'Le travail de l'écriture dans *Le Voyage en Orient*. Le "Catéchisme des Druses" à la façon de Gérard de Nerval', *RLC*, 75:511–25, identifies probable sources of the 12 texts which were intended as appendices, making a convincing argument in favour of their inclusion in all editions.

TALLEYRAND-PÉRIGORD. Eberhard Ernst, *Talleyrand in Amerika, 1794–1796: Ein Emigrantenschicksal zur Zeit der französischen Revolution*, Frankfurt, Lang, 2000, 185 pp., begins with T.'s exile in England, before describing his sea voyage from Falmouth to Philadelphia. There follows an account of his meetings with Alexander Hamilton and his journeys to Maine and Albany, then his return to Hamburg.

TOCQUEVILLE. S. Weiner, 'Terre à terre: Tocqueville, Aron, Baudrillard, and the American way of life', *YFS*, 100:13–24, begins with *De la démocratie en Amérique*, T.'s original evaluation of the differences between the American and the French way of thinking, and considers his influence on later writers, though noting that there have subsequently been considerable changes in perspective. Manning Clark, *The Ideal of Alexis de Tocqueville*, Carlton South, Melbourne U.P., 2000, xiv + 185 pp., is a previously unpublished thesis submitted in 1949. It considers T.'s work, the attraction of the ideal which he defined, and the conditions that he placed on its achievement, before putting it to the test and reflecting on the limits of the liberal creed. Eric Keslassy, *Le Libéralisme de Tocqueville à l'épreuve du pauperisme*, L'Harmattan, 2000, 285 pp., considers an aspect of T.'s writing which is rarely given due consideration, his socio-economic thinking on the poverty of his time. His true political position is shown to be somewhere between state socialism and economic liberalism, his views on the role of the state depending on the context. French politicians are said to have tended to misappropriate his views, and to describe him as a liberal can never be more than partially true. Cheryl Welch, *De Tocqueville*, OUP, x + 284 pp., demonstrates the relevance of T.'s ideas to the concerns of the present day, not least his deep anxieties about the operation of democracy. Having placed him in his historical and intellectual context, we are offered a perspective of the evolution of his thinking on revolution, freedom, history, slavery, religion and gender. Separate chapters deal with his major writings on the United States and France, before a conclusion explaining why he remains one of the most debated figures in political and social theory.

TRISTAN. Evelyne Bloch-Dano, *Flora Tristan, la femme-messie*, Grasset, 350 pp, is a sound and accessible biography which treads a careful path through evidence and myth concerning the life of the author of *Pérégrinations d'un paria*, *Promenades dans Londres* and *Union ouvrière*. We are given a clear perspective of the originality and the modernity of her ideas, involving the emancipation both of women and of the working class. A good deal of attention is given to her writing, the well-chosen quotations inviting one to read further.

THE NINETEENTH CENTURY
(POST-ROMANTIC)

By LARRY DUFFY, *Lecturer in French, University of Ulster at Coleraine*

1. GENERAL

P. Larousse, **Grand Dictionnaire universel du XIXe siècle*, CD-ROM, Champion, 2000.

Province-Paris. Topographies littéraires du XIXe siècle. Actes du colloque de Rouen, 19 et 20 mars 1999, ed. A. Djourachkovitch and Y. Leclerc, Rouen U.P., 2000, 261 pp., has an introduction by A. Djourachkovitch (5–7), and is then divided into two main sections, 'Figures de France' and 'Normandismes'. The first section includes an overview of the title's opposition by J. George, entitled 'Paris-Province: un mouvement du capital' (15–25), and a discussion of the evolution of the understanding of provinciality by O. Pétré-Grenouilleau, 'De la "province" à la "région"', les enjeux historiques d'une transfiguration académique' (27–40), before proceeding to the literary representation of aspects of the divide. A substantial number of articles are on the first half of the century (including a subsection on Balzac); those which deal with our period are as follows: V. Dupuy, 'Province et mémoire: l'espace et le temps dans *Sylvie* de Gérard de Nerval' (145–58); S. Champeau, 'La province dans le *Journal* des Goncourt' (159–205); F. Court-Perez, 'Brouillage et mirage: Paris-Province dans *Numa Roumestan* de Daudet' (207–29); A. Montandon, 'La province dans l'œuvre de Champfleury' (231–50); C. Becker, ' "On s'enferme à Aix, mais [à Paris] l'on marche" — Zola' (251–60); F. Lacoste, 'Paris, la province et le chef-lieu: tradition et progrès dans *Le Moulin du Frau* et *Jacquou le croquant* d'Eugène Le Roy' (261–69). The second section, which perhaps appears unnecessarily reductive in classifying Flaubert, Maupassant, and Barbey as Norman writers (the depiction of Normandy as 'province' being a specific theme lending itself more to a conference in Rouen than to the collective work emerging from it), includes H. Celdran-Johannessen, 'La province comme espace de parole: la rumeur dans *Un Prêtre marié* (1864) de Barbey d'Aurevilly' (297–314); A. Néry, 'Valogne et Paris: le non-lieu dans *Le Bonheur dans le crime* de Barbey d'Aurevilly' (315–20); M. Durel, 'Fictionnalisation des clichés sur l'opposition Paris-Province: une préfiguration du *Dictionnaire des idées reçues* dans les brouillons de *Madame Bovary*' (323–30); M. Desportes, 'Paris perdu' (331–40), dealing with Flaubert's relationship with M. Du Camp; S. Dord-Crouslé, 'L'écart provincial dans *Bouvard et Pécuchet* (341–54); E. Vincent, 'Paris-Province: Maupassant passé en revues' (357–71); S. Deboskre, 'La mère-province dans l'œuvre de Maupassant' (381–90); S. Spandonis, 'L'introuvable province: de l'opposition réaliste à l'indétermination décadente. La représentation de la province dans l'œuvre de Jean Lorrain' (393–412). The work ends with a Postface by Y. Leclerc (431–34), and a short anthology of texts on the eponymous dichotomy, including extracts from Flaubert, Maupassant, Larousse, Bourdieu (435–43). The whole volume is diverse and entertaining. See also C. Ippolito, 'Paris 1890: la décadence au miroir alexandrin', *RoS*, 18, 2000: 125–33. *Paris au bal. Treize physiologies sur la danse*, ed. A. Montandon, Champion, 2000, 496 pp.

Alison Finch, *Women's Writing in Nineteenth-Century France*, CUP, 2000, xvi + 316 pp., is a thorough survey of women's writing in the period. It is divided into three chronological sections (1800–1829, 1830–1869, 1870–1899), the second of which is devoted to Sand and her contemporaries and explores the issue of women and politics, and the last of which, 'Naturalism and symbolism: the beginnings of a new era', features, after an overview, discussion of Tinayre, Ackermann, Gyp, Krysinska, Michel, and Rachilde. Finch argues that although women writers 'do not always fit easily into the major trends of nineteenth-century literature', they can be repositioned fruitfully within other traditions. R. Lloyd, 'The nineteenth century: shaping women', Stephens, *Women's Writing*, 20–46, presents a survey of women's writing contextualized in the legal, constitutional, and social conditions of the period and their implications for women. R. Sauvé, *De l'éloge à l'exclusion. Les femmes auteurs et leurs préfaciers au XIXe siècle*, Saint-Denis, Vincennes U.P., 2000, 250 pp., is an analytical study of prefaces to works by women, based on a corpus of over 200 'préfaces allographes'. N. Edelman, 'Représentation de la maladie et construction de la différence des sexes. Des maladies de femmes aux maladies nerveuses, l'hystérie comme exemple', *Romantisme*, 110, 2000: 73–87, is a useful survey of 19th-c. medical and other discourses on women's bodies, and in particular on hysteria, seen as the defining female malady. It argues that the period 1857–59 is pivotal for hysteria not only in terms of the shift in emphasis from the female genitals to the nervous system as its seat (thus raising the possibility of the male hysteric), but also in terms of its literary representation, notably in the work of Flaubert. J. Yee, *Clichés de la femme exotique: un regard sur la littérature coloniale française entre 1871 et 1914*, L'Harmattan, 2000, 368 pp. N. A. Haxell, ' "Ces dames du cirque": a taxonomy of male desire in nineteenth-century French literature and art', *MLN*, 115, 2000: 783–800, examines the figure of the female circus performer in various roles in a range of texts from Balzac to Huysmans.

Symbolism, Decadence and the 'Fin de Siècle'. French and European Perspectives, ed. P. McGuinness, Exeter U.P., 2000, x + 340 pp., contains an introduction by P. McGuinness (1–18), and then includes P. Dyan, 'Mallarmé and the 'siècle finissant' (19–28); J. Birkett, 'Disinterested Narcissus: the play of politics in decadent form' (29–45); A. Finch, 'Experiments in women's writing in the *fin de siècle*' (46–56); C. Scott, 'The poetry of symbolism and decadence' (57–71); M. Holland, 'The difficult distance: Mallarmé, symbolism and the stage' (72–89); D. Reynolds, 'The kinesthetics of chance: Mallarmé's *Un coup de dés* and avant-garde choreography' (90–104); I. Christie, 'Villiers, Verne, Lumière: film and the business of immortality' (105–21); P. Cooke, 'Text and image, allegory and symbol in Gustave Moreau's *Jupiter et Sémélé*' (122–43); J. Stubbs, 'Between medecine and hermeticism: the "unconscious" in *fin-de-siècle* France' (144–74); S. Ashley, 'Primitivism, celticism and morbidity in the atlantic *fin de siècle*' (175–193); P. Laude, 'Belgian symbolism and Belgian literary identity' (194–208); S. W. Vinall, 'French symbolism and Italian poetry: 1880–1920' (244–63); P. McGuinness, 'From Mallarmé to Pound: the "Franco-Anglo-American" axis' (264–79). See also A. Cousseau, 'Ophélie: histoire d'un mythe fin de siècle', *RHLF*, 101 : 81–104, who examines the autonomous status of Shakespeare's heroine in the second half of the 19th c.

E. Emery, *Romancing the Cathedral. Gothic Architecture in fin-de-siècle French Culture*, Albany, SUNY Press, vii + 234 pp., provides an account of the French Gothic revival from an architectural perspective, and explores how this is represented in the works of e.g. Hugo, Zola, Huysmans, and Proust.

J. de Palacio, **'Le paysage fin-de-siècle'*, pp. 175–82 of *Paysages romantiques*, ed. Gérard Peylet, Pessac, Bordeaux U.P., 2000, 497 pp.

Romantisme, 112, is devoted to 'La Collection', and includes: J.-P. Guillerm, 'Les maisons de l'art. L'imaginaire du musée de peinture au XIXe siècle' (31–43); V. Long, 'Les collectionneurs d'œuvres d'art et la donation au musée à la fin du XIXe siècle: l'exemple du musée du Louvre' (45–54); F. Hamon, 'Collections: ce que disent les dictionnaires' (55–70); D. Pety, 'Le personnage du collectionneur au XIXe siècle: de l'excentrique à l'amateur distingué' (71–81); B. Vouilloux, 'Le discours sur la collection' (95–108). The issue also contains a bibliography of contemporary texts and modern criticism on the idea of the collection. See also J. Simpson, **'Symbolist aesthetics and the decorative image/text'*, *FrF*, 25, 2000 : 177–204.

Dieu, la chair et les livres. Une approche de la décadence, ed. S. Thorel-Cailleteau, Champion, 2000, 666 pp. + 10 pl., is an enormous collective study of decadence (with its substantial thematic appendices, almost an encyclopedia), and contains an introduction by

S. Thorel-Cailleteau, 'Décadence — inanité sonore' (11–27); V. Jankélévitch, 'La décadence' (33–63); S. Ballestra-Puech, 'Les "pauvres dieux en décadence": les mythes antiques dans la littérature fin-de-siècle' (65–82); P. Tortonese, 'Gautier: la sainte écriture' (83–142); N. Arambasin, 'Le sacre d'une esthétique: Rodin et la décadence' (143–57); D. Millet-Gérard, 'Théologie de la décadence' (159–201); A. Gonzalez-Salvador, 'Morbide' (207–30); P. Jourde, 'Le monstre' (241–63); J. Noiray, 'Eros, machines et modernité 1900: l'exemple du Surmâle' (265–80); L. Bermudez, ' "La coulée huileuse d'un regard . . ." ' (281–94); C. Grivel, 'Luxures' (295–334); J. de Palacio, 'La postérité de *Salammbô* ou Carthage fin-de-siècle' (339–66); J.-L. Cabanès, 'L'écriture artiste: écarts et maladie' (367–93); J. Prungnaud, 'Le roman gothique' (395–419); E. Stead, 'Encore Salomé: entrelacs du texte et de l'image de Wilde et Beardsley à Mossa et Merlet' (421–57, + 10 pl.); D. Sangsue, 'L'excentricité fin-de-siècle' (459–82); A. Fernandez-Zoïla, 'L'œuvre d'art entre dégénérescence et décadence' (487–507); P.-H. Castel, 'L'hystérie, des Goncourt à Huysmans, entre littérature et histoire de la médecine' (509–49); C. Jamain, 'La fibre et l'onde (sur l'imaginaire de la musique chez le décadent)' (551–66); C. Coquio, 'Le vilain petit détail et le grand méchant tout' (567–608); B. Lafargue, 'La feinte décadence de l'art (post)moderne' (611–29).

T. Unwin, *Textes réfléchissants: réalisme et réflexivité au dix-neuvième siècle*, Oxford, Lang, 2000, 216 pp., is an exploration of texts as 'reflexive' accounts of the relationship between reality and its representation, examining works by Flaubert, Verne, Barbey d'Aurevilly, and Maupassant.

C. Becker, *Lire le réalisme et le naturalisme*, Nathan, 2000, viii + 213 pp., presents a very clear and accessible discussion of realism, naturalism, and mimesis, exploring the *grands courants* while examining works by Stendhal, Balzac, Champfleury, Flaubert, Zola, Huysmans, the Goncourts, etc.

History of European Literature, ed. Annick Benoit-Dusausoy and Guy Fontaine, trans. Michael Wooff, London, Routledge, 2000, xxviii + 731 pp. (originally published by Hachette Éducation in 1992), includes H. Marmarinou, 'The second half of the nineteenth century: realism and naturalism' (447–90), which, although covering these genres in a Europe-wide context, perhaps inevitably deals for the most part with French realism and naturalism. This section contains J. E. Jackson, 'Poetry and the birth of modernism' (472–75), an essay on the poetry of the period, and articles by G. Fontaine (476) and M. Gosselin (477–80), respectively on Hugo and Baudelaire. This is followed by A. Varty, 'The "fin de siècle" ' (492–529), which features the following sub-sections: C. Purkis, 'Eros in literature'

(513–16), G. Fontaine, 'Verlaine and Rimbaud' (516–17), M. Otten, 'Maeterlinck' (527–29). L. R. Koos, 'Executing the real in *fin de siècle* France', *DFS*, 57:36–46, explores the problematics of the real as an organizing principle of truth, through a reading of *À Rebours*, and a consideration of critical reaction to the wax figures of the Musée Grevin. See also J. Dubois, *Les Romanciers du réel. De Balzac à Simenon, Seuil, 2000, 360 pp.

B. Vouilloux, 'L'"impressionnisme littéraire"': une révision', *Poétique*, 121, 2000:61–85, reassesses the traditional assimilation to impressionist painting made of authors such as the Goncourts, Vallès, Daudet, Loti, Flaubert, Zola, Maupassant, Verlaine, Laforgue, Rimbaud, and Mallarmé. N. Savy, 'Un flou impressionniste. Sur un malentendu sémantique et iconographique', *Romantisme*, 110, 2000:27–37, examines the semantic history and misuse of the term 'impressionnisme' in relation to both visual and written cultural production.

D. De la Motte, *'Making news, making readers: the creation of the modern newspaper public in nineteenth-century France', pp. 339–49 of *Nineteenth-Century Media and the Construction of Identities, ed. and introd. L. Brake, B. Bell, and D. Finkelstein, NY, Palgrave, 2000, xv + 387 pp. J.-Y. Mollier, 'Diffuser les connaissances au XIXe siècle, un exercise délicat', *Romantisme*, 108, 2000:91–101, situates firmly in the Third Republic the eventual progressive revolution in the area of publishing concerned with the dissemination of factual and scientific knowledge. Id., *'Littérature et presse du trottoir à la Belle Époque, *EF*, 36.3, 2000:81–94.

B. de Margerie, S.J., *Du péché, de la grace et du pardon. Du confessional en littérature*, Bar-le-Duc, Saint-Paul, 2000, 246 pp., is an account (written primarily from a theological point of view) of the role played by the 'sacrement du pardon' in a range of authors, divided into two main sections, 'Auteurs laïques et modernes' (Chateaubriand, Lamartine, Vigny, Verlaine, Huysmans, Claudel), and 'Auteurs prêtres et classiques' (François de Sales, Bossuet). P. Terrone, 'Sataniques, mon Père . . .', *RTr*, 58, 2000:121–39, examines the role of the priest in texts by Barbey, Villiers, Huysmans, Mirbeau, Zola, and others.

EsC, 41.2, a special issue on genetic criticism ('Devenir de la critique génétique'), contains, after a preface by R. Pickering (3–8): A. Grésillon, 'La critique génétique, aujourd'hui et demain' (9–15); C. Bustarret, 'Paper evidence and the interpretation of the creative process in modern literary manuscripts' (16–28); É. Le Calvez, 'Génétique, poétique, autotextualité (*Salammbô* sous la tente)' (29–39); D. Désormeaux, 'Le mythe de l'original: la main de Flaubert' (40–52); P. Gifford, 'Tracking anti-teleology: is there an "end" in sight?' (53–67). É. Marty, 'Pourquoi la génétique?', *Textuel*, 37, 2000:53–60, addresses the decentring of theory by genetic studies.

Mélodrames et romans noirs, 1750–1890, ed. S. Bernard-Griffiths and J. Sgard, Toulouse, Mirail U.P., 2000, 534 pp. + 4 pl., sets out to examine the links between the two overlooked genres of the title, from the starting point of the 'connotation de mauvais goût' of which they are held to be emblematic. The volume is introduced in a preface by J. Sgard (7–13), and includes the following: Angels Santa, '*Le Bossu de Paul Féval, passage du roman au mélodrame*' (235–45); H. Millot, 'Utilisation, récupération et détournement du roman noir dans *Les Chants de Maldoror*' (461–77); S. Disegni, 'La trilogie de Jules Vallès. Du roman populaire à l'autobiographie' (479–97); F. Marotin, 'L'inspiration noire et mélodramatique de Jules Vallès' (499–513); P. Jonchière, 'Gothique et histoire: l'écriture du sens chez Barbey d'Aurevilly' (515–29).

J. Rigoli, *Lire le délire. Aliénisme, rhétorique et littérature en France au XIXe siècle*, Fayard, 650 pp., is an enormous study of the rhetoric of psychiatric discourse on madness, and its representation in literature. M. Lavaud, ' "Grotesque XIXe siècle": le vertige relativiste des exhumations littéraires', *Romantisme*, 114:41–49, explores the idea of the grotesque in numerous fictional and critical writings.

La Nature dévoilée. French Literary Responses to Science, ed. L. Duffy and C. Emerson, Hull, Hull Univ. French Dept., 2000, vi + 200 pp., has a section entitled 'Naturalist responses to science', containing: L. Duffy, 'Flaubert traduit Carnot? *L'Éducation sentimentale* and the structure of thermodynamic revolutions' (61–78); N. Cotton, 'A jaundiced view of physiognomy in Zola's *La Fortune des Rougon*' (79–93); W. Gallois, 'Industrial culture and alienation in Zola's *La Bête humaine*' (95–104); J. Patrick, 'Des esseintes/des essences?: Huysmans, chemistry and nature' (105–18).

David Baguley, *Napoleon III and His Regime. An Extravaganza*, Baton Rouge, Louisiana State U.P., 2000, xxii + 425 pp., has an original structure, divided between history of the period, a biography of Louis Napoléon, and representation of Emperor and Empire. S. Aprile, ' "Qu'il est dur à monter et à descendre l'escalier d'autrui". L'exil des proscrits français sous le Second Empire', *Romantisme*, 110, 2000:89–100. J. Neefs, 'La "haine des grands hommes" au XIXe siècle', *MLN*, 116:750–69, addresses the paradoxical relationship between greatness and anonymity in the 19th c., and its representation and ironization in texts by Balzac, Michelet, Baudelaire, Flaubert (in particular *Bouvard et Pécuchet*).

L. Corbin, ' "Cette frontière où se perdent les limites strictes entre le même et l'autre": discourses of nineteeenth-century French colonisation', *RoQ*, 47, 2000:131–44.

G. Leroy, 'La réception littéraire de l'Allemagne en France (1870–1899)', *L'Amitié Charles Péguy*, 90, 2000:131–49.

L. Tack, 'Relations interculturelles belges dans les revues littéraires (1869–1899)', *RLC*, 75:379–96, discusses the bicultural specificity of *fin-de-siècle* Belgium.

M. Wolff, *'Western novels as children's literature in nineteenth-century France', *Mosaic*, 34.2:87–102.

2. POETRY

Six French Poets of the Nineteenth Century. Lamartine, Hugo, Baudelaire, Verlaine, Rimbaud, Mallarmé, ed. with introd. E. H. and A. M. Blackmore, OUP, 2000, 384 pp., contains a substantial introduction and notes, with parallel translations by E. H. and A. M. Blackmore (Lamartine, Hugo, Mallarmé), James McGowan (Baudelaire), Martin Sorrell (Verlaine, Rimbaud). *Dictionnaire de Poésie de Baudelaire à nos jours*, ed. M. Jarrety, PUF, xiv + 896 pp., contains extensive, well-documented and usefully cross-referenced articles on poets and themes, from the mid-19th c. onwards, e.g. S. Meitinger's article on Mallarmé (461–67), which presents detailed readings of M.'s major works, and lists most recent editions, has a substantial bibliography of scholarly criticism, and a list of themes, individuals, and publications covered elsewhere in the volume. P. Loubier, 'Le poète dans sa mansarde', *CRITM*, 21, 2000:37–53, explores the *topos* of the garret as stereotypical habitat of the poet, referring to a range of late-19th-c. poets. A. M. Paliyenko, '(Re)placing women in French poetic history: the Romantic legacy', *Symposium*, 53, 2000:261–82, surveys the poetry and critical writings of Ackermann and others in the context of mainstream critical invective against women poets. G. Cacciavillani, *L'Oggetto poetico*, Rimini, Panozzo, 2000, 140 pp.

BANVILLE.　*Œuvres poétiques complètes, édition critique*, ed. P. J. Edwards, vol. VIII, Champion, iv + 814 pp., contains *Dans la fournaise* (ed. P. S. Hambly) and previously unpublished poems (ed. P. J. Edwards and P. S. Hambly). E. Souffrin-Le Breton, 'Banville and his three sonnets on the mythical Amazons', *MLR*, 95, 2000:72–84, examines the evolution of the figure of the Amazon in B.'s work. Ead., 'Théodore de Banville and his predilection for jewellery', *AJFS*, 37, 2000:359–84.

BARBEY D'AUREVILLY.　P. Auraix-Jonchière, *'Un palais dans un labyrinthe'. Barbey d'Aurevilly, Poèmes*, Champion, 296 pp, consists of a critical edition of the poems and a commentary.

BAUDELAIRE.　*Nouvelles lettres*, ed. C. Pichois, Fayard, 2000, 125 pp., contains 75 new letters. Ulrich Baer, *Remnants of Song. Trauma and the Experience of Modernity in Charles Baudelaire and Paul Celan*,

Stanford U.P., 2000, xi + 343 pp., is a comparative study of 'the first poet, and the last poet, of [. . .] modernity'. B. Bowles, 'Poetic practice and historical paradigm: Charles Baudelaire's anti-semitism', *PMLA*, 115, 2000: 195–208, starting from a remark made in *Mon Cœur mis à nu* apparently advocating the extermination of the Jews, considers an aspect of B. which has strangely been overlooked, and suggests that B.'s anti-semitism is a 'modern' racial one rather than a 'theological' one rooted in Catholic tradition. J.-L. Cloët, ' "Le spectre de la rose" ou Baudelaire et son "fantôme" . . .' *RSH*, 264: 67–98, explores flower imagery and antiquity in B.'s poetry. M. Finck, 'Portrait de Baudelaire en guitariste espagnol: lecture d'une page des Paradis artificiels', *CRITM*, 21: 55–74, examines the figure of the poet as musician, with references to Hoffmann, Wagner, etc. P. Maillard, 'L'allégorie Baudelaire. Poétique d'une métafigure du discours', *Romantisme*, 107, 2000: 37–48, discusses allegory and *ekphrasis* in B.'s work. C. Pichois, 'Entre Jouve, Daumier et Baudelaire', *RZLG*, 25: 123–27, examines the disputed attribution to D. of a portrait of B., and that of a poem wrongly attributed to B. by Jouve. C. Samina-dayar-Perrin, 'Baudelaire poète latin', *ib.*, 113: 87–103, assesses the relevance of B.'s classical education to his poetry. M. Scott, 'Super-fluous intrigues in Baudelaire's prose poems', *FS*, 55: 351–62, challenges, through its reading of *Le Spleen de Paris*, the widespread attribution to B. of views expressed in B.'s poems, and argues that the 'explicit message' of prose poems conceals their 'oblique message'. J. Starobinski, '*Les Chats* de Baudelaire. Une relecture', *RZLG*, 25: 105–22, revisits B.'s poem, starting from a 1962 reading by Lévi-Strauss and Jakobson, and examining several versions.

Y. Bonnefoy, **Baudelaire: la tentation de l'oubli*, BNF, 2000, 55 pp. P. Labarthe, **Patrick Labarthe présente 'Petits poèmes en prose' de Charles Baudelaire*, Gallimard, 2000, 241 pp. P. Laforgue, **Ut Pictura Poesis. Baudelaire, la peinture et le romantisme*, Lyons U.P., 2000, 216 pp. G. Cacciavillani, **La Malinconia di Baudelaire*, Naples, Liguori, 2000, 197 pp. B. Schlossman, *'La nuit du poëte: Baudelaire, Benjamin et la passante', *DFS*, 53, 2000: 12–26. M. Richter, *'Chez Baudelaire, la pitié ricane: lecture de "La servante au grand cœur . . ." (Fleurs du mal, C)', *RLMC*, 13, 2000: 295–306. P. Dayan, *'De la traduction en musique chez Baudelaire', *RoS*, 18, 2000: 99–111. D. A. Monson, *'Baudelaire, toujours pareil à lui-même', *Neophilologus*, 85: 355–68. C. Pichois, *'Baudelaire entre Catulle Mendes et Leconte de Lisle', *RHLF*, 100, 2000: 1581–84.

COPPÉE. Y. Mortelette, 'François Coppée et la poétique de l'horizon: de la promenade en banlieue au voyage imaginaire', *SFr*, 135: 542–53.

KRYSINSKA. F. Goulesque, '"Le Hibou" qui voulait danser: Marie Krysinska, une innovatrice du vers libre doublée d'une innovatrice de la poésie moderne', *Symposium*, 53, 2000:220–33, introduces the rediscovered works of the Symbolist poet and *chansonnière*.

LAFORGUE. A. Corbellari, 'Orgues et pianos. Le sacré et le profane dans la poésie de Jules Laforgue', *Romantisme*, 107, 2000:49–58. H. Scepi, **Poétique de Jules Laforgue*, PUF, 2000, 210 pp. Id. and J.-P. Saint-Gérand, *Les Complaintes de Jules Laforgue*, Neuilly, Atlande, 2000, 190 pp.

LAUTRÉAMONT. *Les Chants de Maldoror. Poésies*, Poche, 446 pp., contains a dossier by J.-L. Steinmetz.

LECONTE DE LISLE. H. Lindler, 'Intellectualität und Pathos. Zur Rezeptionslenkung bei Leconte de Lisle', *ZFSL*, 110, 2000:136–59, looks at L.'s rhetorical strategies for influencing readers, through examination of 'L'incantation du Loup'.

LOUYS. A. Jansen, 'Pierre Louys (1870–1925): poète méconnu ou inconnu?', *Revue Générale*, 135.1, 2000:53–62.

MALLARMÉ. É. Benoit, 'Un enjeu de l'esthétique mallarméenne: la poésie et le sens du monde', *Romantisme*, 111:107–20, argues that the essential question to be asked about poetry is that of what poetry is, and that for M. it is a means of expressing the mysteries of existence, through transition from inessential to essential language. F. Chatelain, 'La mise en scène de la fiction: réflexions autour de la structure du recueil des *Poésies* de Mallarmé', *ib.*, 89–105, addresses the notion of the *receuil*, with its ambivalence over order and disorder. *Mallarmé on CD-ROM. Un Coup de dés jamais n'abolira le hasard*, trans., introd., and ed. Penny Florence, Oxford, Legenda, 2000, reproduces M.'s typography and layout. Multiple ways of reading the poem are possible. R. Lloyd, 'Mallarmé and the bounds of translation', *NFS*, 40:14–25, approaches the difficulties and pleasures of translating Mallarmé, taking into account both translations of Mallarmé and Mallarmé's translations of other poets. Ead., 'Mallarmé at the millennium', *MLR*, 95, 2000:674–83. J.-M. Maulpoix, 'Portrait du poète en araignée', *CRITM*, 21:75–82. B. Vibert, 'La sœur et la rivale. Sur Mallarmé, la musique et les lettres', *Poétique*, 123, 2000:340–52, argues against consideration of M.'s approach to music as part of general philosophical/aesthetic theory. C. Lyu, **Stéphane Mallarmé as Miss Satin: the texture of fashion and poetry', *EsC*, 40.3, 2000:61–71.

NERVAL. H. Mizuno, 'Le travail de l'écriture dans *le Voyage en Orient. Le "Catéchisme des Druses"* à la façon de Gérard de Nerval', *RLC*, 75:511–25, examines the poetic form of N.'s account of Druze belief. Meryl Tyers, *Critical Fictions. Nerval's 'Les Illuminés'*, Oxford, Legenda, 1999, xvi + 122 pp.

RIMBAUD. G. Robb, *Rimbaud*, London, Picador, 2000, xvii + 522 pp., is an exhaustive account of R.'s life and works, with quotations given in English. *Collected Poems*, trans. with introd. and notes by Martin Sorrell, OUP, xi + 337 pp., is a parallel text edition. P. Grouix, *Étude sur Rimbaud, 'Une saison en enfer', 'Illuminations'*, Ellipses, 128 pp., is a concise critical guide. A. Fongaro, 'A propos de *Marine*', *RLMC*, 14:285–94, offers a reading which suggests R. is mocking his reader. G. Macklin, 'Defamiliarization and discontinuity: Rimbaud's "Parade", "Angoisse", "Soir historique"', *NFS*, 39, 2000:163–76. G. Moulaison, *'"Alchimie du verbe" ou le catch spirituel d'*Une Saison en enfer*', *DFS*, 53, 2000:27–41. M. Murat, *'Rimbaud et le vers libre: remarques sur l'invention d'une forme', *RHLF*, 100, 2000:255–76. K. Ross, *'Rimbaud and the transformation of social space', *YFS*, 43, 2000:123–42. N. Watteyne, *'Temps labile et sujet vacillant dans les *Illuminations* de Rimbaud: "Matinée d'ivresse"', un exemple éloquent', *LR*, 54, 2000:33–49.

SAINTE-BEUVE. M.-C. Huet-Brichard, 'Sainte-Beuve à la lumière de Baudelaire: "la pointe extrême du Kamtchatka romantique"', *RHLF*, 101:263–80, examines *Joseph Delorme* as a potential influence on Baudelaire's poetry.

3. FICTION

W. Guentner, 'Representations of women and the sketch in nine-teenth-century French prose fiction', *RLMC*, 14:27–57, looks at the depiction of women (as artists' models) and the sketch (as opposed to the finished work) in a range of texts (by Balzac, Feydeau, Zola, Mérimée, Flaubert, Bloy, et al.).

BARBEY D'AUREVILLY. J.-M. Jeanton Lamarche, *Pour un portrait de Jules-Amédée Barbey d'Aurevilly: regards sur l'ensemble de son œuvre, témoignages de la critique, études et documents inédits*, L'Harmattan, 2000, 511 pp. Y. Clavaron, *Étude sur Barbey d'Aurevilly, 'Les Diaboliques'*, Ellipses, 2000, 112 pp. A. Frémiot, *'(Im)pudeur en jupons et (dés)honneur du galon', *EsC*, 39.4, 1999:90–100.

BERTRAND. *Œuvres complètes*, introd. and annot. H. H. Poggenburg, Champion, 2000, 1184 pp.

BOURGET. D. C. J. Lee, 'Bourget's debt to Herbert Spencer: *Le Disciple* and the self-adjusting watch', *MLR*, 95:653–73, explores the tensions between the excessive regulation of Sixte's life, and the vital, unpredictable world that everywhere confronts him, in relation to the positivist thought of Spencer.

DAUDET. G. Brault, 'Reflections on Daudet's "La Dernière Classe: récit d'un petit Alsacien" ', *Symposium*, 53, 2000: 67–76.

FLAUBERT. Y. Leclerc's Centre Flaubert website, ⟨http://www.univ-rouen.fr/flaubert/⟩, online since May 2001, provides access to books, manuscripts, correspondence, discussions, and current research, and is the platform for the first edition of *La Revue Flaubert*, with the following articles in PDF format: C. Gothot-Mersch, 'Flaubert dans les lettres de la cinquantaine'; A. Djourachkovitch, 'En fait de nouvelles'; P.-J. Dufief, 'La place de l'échange Flaubert-Goncourt dans le t. IV de la Pléiade. De la correspondance à trois à une correspondance à deux'; R. M. Palermo di Stefano, 'Les itinéraires textuels d'une correspondance'; M. Martinez 'La "phrénésie" de l'idéal'; Y. Leclerc, 'Sept années noires'.

G. Wall, *Flaubert. A Life*, London, Faber, viii + 413 pp., is a substantial, well-documented, straightforward chronological account of F.'s life and works. *Œuvres de jeunesse. Œuvres complètes*, 1, ed. Claudine Gothot-Mersch and Guy Sagnès, Gallimard, lxxxiv + 1667 pp., is the opening instalment of the long-awaited Pléiade edition of F.'s works. G. Sagnès's 'Préface' (xi-xxxv) presents a general overview of F.'s life and writings; C. Gothot-Mersch's 'Introduction' to the volume (xxxvii-lxvi) takes a biographical approach, arguing that 'les écrits de jeunesse [de F.], très largement conservés, offrent l'occasion exceptionelle de suivre pas à pas la formation d'un artiste'. The volume contains, along with everything written by F. between the ages of 10 and 25 (arranged in chronological order) and the usual *notices*, *notes*, and *variantes*, substantial appendices of genetic material. A. Tooke, *Flaubert and the Pictorial Arts. From Image to Text*, OUP, 2000, xii + 316 pp., is a thorough reading of Flaubert's art commentaries, of the representation of pictorial art and artists in his fiction, and of the 'tension between image and text' throughout his works, which, argues Tooke, 'enact a continually repeated pattern of invocation and repression of the image'. S. Laüt-Berr, *Flaubert et l'antiquité, itinéraires d'une passion*, Champion, 375 pp., charts F.'s journey, by way of examination of the published fiction and the correspondence, from 'la découverte de l'antiquité au collège' to 'l'écriture des chefs-d'œuvre de sa maturité'. U. Schulz-Buschhaus, 'Flauberts Poetik des *deus absconditus* und die Erzähltraditionen auktorialer Autorität und auktorialer Kontingenz', *RZLG*, 25: 129–48, examines the problematics of authorship. M. Orr, *Flaubert. Writing the Masculine*, OUP, 2000, x + 239 pp., examines all F.'s major fiction, with a view to analysing 'the formation and reformulation of "masculinity" and "manhood" in its complex and evolving nineteenth-century and French contexts'. Orr argues that F.'s fiction is concerned with differences between men more than with those between men and women. *Réceptions créatrices de l'œuvre de Flaubert*, ed. P. Chardin, Tours U.P., 2000, 189 pp.

L'Éducation sentimentale, Flammarion, GF, 606 pp., contains a dossier (including maps, manuscript facsimiles, and transcriptions) by S. Dord-Crouslé. T. Poyet, *Le Nihilisme de Flaubert. 'L'Éducation sentimentale' comme champ d'application*, Kimé, 304 pp., is a straightforward study, based on (and indeed suitable for) an undergraduate lecture course, dealing with F.'s novel in its social and historical context as apotheosis of F.'s 'dénonciation générale de l'existence', with the usual references to Schopenhauer etc. T. Williams, 'Dussardier sur les barricades: naissance d'un "héros de juin"', *RHLF*, 101:71–80, presents a genetic reading of a significant aspect of the depiction of June 1848 in *L'Éducation sentimentale*, indicating a pessimistic view of humanity and of the possibility of political progress. G. Cacciavillani, *La Coscienza immaginante nell'Educazione sentimentale*, Rimini, Panozzo, 2000, 105 pp.

The Nineteenth-Century Novel. Identities, ed. D. Walder, London, Routledge, vii + 368 pp., contains M. Brooks and N. Watson, 'Madame Bovary: a novel about nothing' (9–28), and 'Madame Bovary: becoming a heroine' (29–47). These two articles examine *Madame Bovary* in the context of key themes represented in the 19th-c. novel (the other texts studied in the volume are in English). The first deals with realist detail, cliché and *ennui*, the second with Emma's identity; the approach is a didactic one, with frequent questions aimed at undergraduate readers. E. J. Gallagher, 'Flaubert's *Madame Bovary* and Mauriac's *Thérèse Desqueyroux*: influence with no apparent anxiety', *DFS*, 57:25–35, examines parallels between the two novels and between their respective heroines. A. Raitt, 'Emma Bovary's pyramid', *FS*, 55:37–46, discusses the pyramidal structure of F.'s novel; while H. Laroche, 'Être au parfum: la pyramide de Flaubert', *Romantisme*, 107, 2000: 23–36, examines the recurrent motif of the pyramid in F.'s work.

Salammbô, Flammarion, GF, 468 pp., contains a dossier and other documentation by G. Séginger. S. D. Kropp, 'Language dynamics: the Carthaginian exploitation of the mercenaries in Flaubert's *Salammbô*', *DFS*, 53, 2000:42–48.

S. Dord-Crouslé, *'Bouvard et Pécuchet' de Flaubert: une "encyclopédie critique en farce"*, Belin, 2000, 139 pp., is a clearly laid out study of F.'s novel, addressing questions of science, knowledge, and belief.

V. Provenzano, '"Hérodias", or the self-annihilation of the absolute work', *MLN*, 115, 2000:761–82, considers notions of space and time in F.'s story. M. Black, *'Félicité and the imperfect of repetition in "Un Cœur simple"'*, *NFS*, 39, 2000:149–62. E. J. Gallagher, *'Monsieur Bournisien: Flaubert's Curé de campagne'*, *DFS*,

51, 2000:45–57. C. Ippolito, *'Flaubert's pearl necklace: weaving a garland of images in the reader's memory', *Symposium*, 54, 2000:169–87.

FROMENTIN. Barbara Wright, *Eugène Fromentin: A Life in Art and Letters*, Oxford, Lang, 2000, 616 pp. + 28 pl., is an exhaustive account of F.'s life, interdisciplinary in approach, drawing largely on his correspondence and writings. Eugène Fromentin, *Dominique*, Poche, 320 pp., has a preface by P. Dufour entitled 'Les fantômes de Fromentin' (5–38), and a 'Dossier' (277–311), incorporating 'Fromentin à l'œuvre' (278–84), 'Réception du roman' (285–93), 'La bibliothèque de Dominique' (294–308), and 'Deux portraits de Fromentin' (from the Goncourt *Journal* and Maxime du Camp's *Souvenirs littéraires)* (309–11). A.-M. Christin, 'Eugène Fromentin peintre et écrivain', *Textuel*, 38, 2000:37–49, argues that F.'s inclination towards writing was informed primarily by his receptivity to the visual.

GONCOURT. *RSH*, 259, 2000, is devoted to the G. brothers, and contains: J.-L. Cabanès, 'Présentation' (7–12); C. Grivel, 'En 18.. le jour est fait dans la question' (13–26); J. de Palacio, 'Le silence des Goncourt: du livre brûlé au livre interdit' (27–39); J.-P. Guillerm, '*Notes sur l'Italie/ L'Italie d'hier*: la fabrique interdite' (41–54); M. Dottin-Orsini, 'Les frères Goncourt et le "roman des actrices"' (55–74); M. Donaldson-Evans, 'Écriture et transformation: sur quelques intertextes inexplorés de *Madame Gervaisais*' (75–90); J. Noiray, 'Tristesse de l'acrobate. Création artistique et fraternité dans *Les Frères Zemganno*' (91–110); D. Pety, 'Les peintres-poètes de *L'Art du XVIIIe siècle*' (111–26); J.-L. Cabanès, 'Le *Journal* des Goncourt: du document intime au document d'art' (127–51); P.-J. Dufief, 'Les Goncourt et l'antiquité' (153–69); P. Tortonese, 'Le kaléidoscope des frères Goncourt' (171–95); É. Bordas, 'Les imparfaits des Goncourt, ou les silences du romanesque' (197–216); B. Vouilloux, 'L'"écriture artiste": enjeux et présupposés d'un manifeste littéraire' (217–38); D. Pety, 'Un inédit des Goncourt: le compte-rendu de l'exposition du boulevard des Italiens de 1860' (239–61).

V. Partensky, 'Entre ébauche et débauche: le corps étranger ou la passion des Goncourt', *Textuel*, 38, 2000:85–96, examines the relationship between visual art and writing in the work of the Goncourts. É. Roy-Reverzy, 'La passion religieuse: les Goncourt, Zola et la question anticléricale', *Romantisme*, 107, 2000:59–70, examines anticlericalism and misogyny in the work of the G. brothers. Z. P.-J. Dufief, *'La lettre dans les romans des Goncourt: de l'effet de réel à la fétichisation de l'autographe', *EsC*, 40.4, 2000:58–67.

GYP. W. Z. Silverman, *'Gyp and Flammarion: a marriage of love or convenience', *FR*, 73, 2000:910–20.

HUYSMANS. A. Gamot, 'Glose pour des Esseintes. Lecture de la *Notice* d'*A rebours*', *Poétique*, 123, 2000, 321–37, approaches the *Notice* (predating the celebrated *Préface* by 20 years) from the point of view of etymology, intertextuality, decadence, and spirituality. P. Glaudes, 'L'espace et le symbole dans *La Cathédrale* de Huysmans', *RTr*, 58, 2000: 111–20, discusses medieval symbolism in H.'s novel. G. Peylet, **Huysmans, la double quête. Vers un essai synthétique de l'œuvre*, L'Harmattan. G. Bonnet, **L'alchimie amusante: les fuyants secrets du romanesque huysmanien'*, *Modernités*, 14, 2000: 85–111.

LOTI. V. Magri-Mourgues, **Aux marges de la prose: Loti, *Le Désert* (1895)', *TLit*, 13, 2000: 247–60.

MAUPASSANT. R. Lefebvre, **Horreur et ressemblance dans les contes et nouvelles de Maupassant: du semblable à l'innomable', *TLit*, 13, 2000: 227–45. F. Place-Verghnes, **Maupassant porno-graphe', *Neophilologus*, 85: 501–17. M. Prévost, **Le cadavre de Schopenhauer dans le cercueil d'Edgar Poe. Notes sur *Auprès d'un mort* de Guy de Maupassant', *ib.*, 83, 2000: 371–83. J. van de Stadt, 'Seeing "amiss" or misreading "a miss": imperfect vision in Maupassant's "Les Tombales"', *DFS*, 51, 2000: 37–44.

MIRBEAU. C. Herzfeld, **Le Monde imaginaire d'Octave Mirbeau*, Angers U.P., 103 pp.

RACHILDE. M. J. Anderson, 'Writing the non-conforming body: Rachilde's *Monsieur Vénus* (1884) and *Madame Adonis* (1888)', *NZJFS*, 21, 2000: 5–17, looks at *fin-de-siècle* non-conformity to preordained gender roles as depicted in R.'s novels, with particular reference to the respective cases of the heroines Raoule and Marcelle. S. L. F. Richards, 'Perversion as diversion: the female gaze in the novels of Rachilde', *PhilP*, 48: 37–42, is a Freudian reading of scopophilia in *Monsieur Vénus* and *Madame Adonis*. A. Montandon, **La vieille femme et la guerre: Rachilde face au désordre', *EsC*, 40.2, 2000: 15–24.

ROD. N. White, 'Divorce and political scandal in Édouard Rod's *Michel Teissier* novels', *MLR*, 96: 667–78, reads R.'s two Teissier novels as long-overlooked texts which are however key documents in relation to the history of family life.

RODENBACH. R. Ziegler, 'The text as suitcase and coffin: traveling beyond decadence in Georges Rodenbach's *Le Rouet des brumes*', *DFS*, 48, 1999: 35–43, reads R.'s short stories as illustration of the argument that 'decadent works are often constructed as containers without contents'.

SCHWOB. P. M. W. Cogman, 'Marcel Schwob and the railway story', *AJFS*, 37, 2000: 22–39, reads S.'s two tales of supernatural events on trains in the light of prevalent late 19th-c. fears of contagious disease, and within the tradition of travel narrative.

SÉGUR. P. Brown, 'Gustave Doré's magical realism: the *Nouveaux Contes de fées* of the Comtesse de Ségur', *MLR*, 95, 2000:964–77 (incl. 8 pl.), identifies affinities between D.'s illustrations for the 1857 edition of S.'s collection of fairy tales, and his later and earlier work, arguing further that the collaborative text is testimony to the status of children's literature during the period.

VALLÈS. C. Saminadayar-Perrin, *'L'Enfant' de Jules Vallès*, Gallimard, 2000, 234 pp.

VILLIERS DE L'ISLE-ADAM. I. Rosy, *'Hadaly/idéal/idole: une réécriture "artificielle" du mythe de Pygmalion par Villiers de l'Isle-Adam', *RevR*, 35, 2000:101–20.

ZOLA. *AJFS*, 38.3, a special issue entitled 'Zola: modern perspectives', contains: D. Baguley, 'An *état présent* of Zola studies (1986–2000)' (305–20); H. Mitterand (trans. F. Neilson), 'Zola, "ce rêveur définitif"' (321–35); H. Thompson, 'Berthe's "dessous douteux": the body stripped in *Pot-Bouille*' (336–48), examining 'images of dress and undress' in Z.'s novel; C. Dousteyssier-Khoze, 'Zola and *Le(s) Chat(s) Noir(s)*' (349–64, incl. 3 pl.), a discussion of parodies of Z. by such *fumistes* as Salis, Allais etc.; J. J. Duffy, Jr, 'The aesthetic and the political in Zola's writing on art' (365–78), which argues that for Z., 'realist art always implies a politics of meaning'; C. Pierre-Gnassounou, 'Un personnage décevant: le sergent de ville Poisson dans *L'Assommoir*' (379–92), an analysis of texts featuring the character in the light of Huysmans's critical response to Z.'s novel; J. Beizer, *'Au* (delà du) *Bonheur des dames*: notes on the underground' (393–406), looking at desire in the department-store novel in relation to a Deleuzian model of repetition; B. Nelson, 'Nana: uses of the female body' (407–29), which considers the body from various perspectives (as spectacle, as text, as body politic, as Freudian or Lacanian construct); G. Chaitin, 'Transposing the Dreyfus affair: the trauma of identity in Zola's *Vérité*' (430–44).

CNat, 75, contains articles on Z. from three perspectives. The first of three corresponding sections, 'Formes de la fiction', is devoted to 'les lignes de force qui composent l'unité des *Rougon-Macquart*', and contains: P. Pellini, '"Si je triche un peu": Zola et le roman historique' (7–28); A. Fonyi, 'La femme, son propriétaire et le voleur. Premières élaborations du scénario œdipien dans l'œuvre de Zola' (29–50), a psychoanalytic reading of representations of the Oedipal narrative in Z.'s early work; S. Collot, 'Rythmes dans *Les Rougon-Macquart*' (51–55); O. Got, 'Le regard de la "Bête" (57–70), examining the 'coup d'œil' as a key motif in *La Bête humaine*; F. Wagner, 'Nana en son miroir' (71–86), addressing the disputed problematics of linearity in narrative; M. Gantrel, 'Zola et ses doubles: les instances d'autoreprésentation dans *Pot-Bouille* et *L'Œuvre*'

(87–98); S. L. F. Richards, 'Le sang, la menstruation et le corps féminin' (99–107), arguing for a resituation of Z. in relation to contemporary medical and scientific discourse on female reproductive biology. The middle section of the volume, 'Questions fin de siècle', includes: K. Haavik, 'Le Saint Martyr du deux décembre' (111–20), exploring religious aspects of *La Fortune des Rougon*; T. Ozwald, 'Un remède contre le mal du siècle. *Le Docteur Pascal*, ou l'évangélisme thérapeutique de Zola' (121–38), exploring the interplay of scientism and mimesis in *Les Rougon-Macquart*; A. Carol, 'Zola et la combustion spontanée: de l'usage d'un mythe en médecine' (139–55), examining, in relation to Macquart's death in *Le Docteur Pascal*, Z.'s reading of contemporary medical discourse on spontaneous combustion; I. Delamotte, 'Maurice de Fleury et Zola' (157–71); B. Laville, '*Paris*, un roman de formation' (173–81); J.-M. Seillan, 'L'Afrique utopique de *Fécondité*' (183–202). The volume's final section, entitled 'Traductions et transpositions', contains S. Saillard, 'La première traduction espagnole de *Germinal*' (217–42), which sees the 1885 appearance of the novel in Spanish translation as a landmark in the history of Z.'s reception in Spain; Y. Lemarié, '*Nana*, un film de Dorothy Arzner' (243–54); C. Duboile and J. Sonntag, 'De Zola à Carné. L'adaptation de *Thérèse Raquin*' (255–64).

Henri Mitterand, *Zola.* II. *L'homme de Germinal, 1871–1893*, Fayard, 1192 pp. + 32 pl., is the second of three eventual volumes of a so far exhaustive biography, dealing with the period during which the *Rougon-Macquart* cycle was produced. Significantly, this volume is based largely on research for M.'s previous editions of Z.'s works, so diverges at least to some extent from a conventional biography, in that the texts are foregrounded. W. Gallois, *Zola: The History of Capitalism*, Berne, Lang, 2000, 296 pp., offers a systematic dialectical reading of *Les Rougon-Macquart* as history of capitalism which argues for the cycle's continued political relevance. K. H. Haavik, *In Mortal Combat. The Conflict of Life and Death in Zola's Rougon-Macquart*, Birmingham, Al., Summa, 2000, x + 178 pp., argues, through discussion of *La Fortune des Rougon*, *La Faute de l'abbé Mouret*, *L'Assommoir*, *Une Page d'amour*, *Germinal*, and *Le Docteur Pascal*, that far from existing in symbiosis, life and death function as bitterly opposed forces in Z.'s cycle. É. Lemirre and J. Cotin, 'D'un paradis l'autre: la mort-fleur', *RSH*, 264:111–36, examines the idea of the forest, along with flower imagery, principally in *Les Rougon-Macquart*, referring to preparatory manuscript material as well as to published text.

Pot Luck, trans. Brian Nelson, OUP, 1999, xxii + 393 pp., has a critical introduction by the translator, pp. vii-xiv. E. J. Ahearn, 'Monceau, Camondo, *La Curée*, *L'Argent*: history, art, evil', *FR*, 73, 2000:1100–15, explores the associations between Zola's novels and a Jewish family resident in the rue Monceau, in the context of banalized anti-semitism. S. Harrow, 'Exposing the imperial cultural fabric: critical description in Zola's *La Curée*', *FS*, 54, 2000:439–52. E. M. Knutson, 'The natural and the supernatural in Zola's *Thérèse Raquin*', *Symposium*, 55:140–54, explores the problematic relationship between scientific discourse and the supernatural in Z.'s novel.

O. Lumbroso, 'De la palette à l'écritoire. Pratiques et usages du dessin chez Émile Zola', *Romantisme*, 107, 2000:71–85, examines aspects of the relationship between Z.'s (graphic) sketches and his fiction. Id., *'Quand détruire, c'est créer. Censure et autocensure dans la genèse de *L'Assommoir*', *Poétique*, 125:68–83. T. E. Mussio, 'Anticommunity and chaos: the role of free indirect discourse in Zola's *Germinal*', pp. 71–88 of *Caverns of Night: Coal Mines in Art, Literature and Film*, ed. and introd. W. B. Thesing, Columbia, South Carolina U.P., 2000, 343 pp. M. Schmid, 'From decadence to health: Zola's Paris', *RoS*, 18, 2000:99–111. G. Woollen, 'Zola's Halles, a *Grande Surface* before their time', *ib.*, 21–30. J. McNair, 'Zolaizm in Russia', *MLR*, 95, 2000:450–62, discusses the significance of Zola and French naturalism in late-19th-c. Russian literary criticism.

Y. Lemarié, **Ventre et manducation dans l'œuvre de Zola*, Villeneuve d'Ascq, Septentrion U.P., 2000, 545 pp. M.-A. Voisin-Fougère, **L'Ironie naturaliste. Zola et les paradoxes du sérieux*, Champion, 271 pp. See also HUYSMANS.

4. NON-FICTIONAL PROSE

C. Avlami, 'L'écriture de l'histoire grecque en France au XIXe siècle: temporalités historiques et enjeux politiques', *Romantisme*, 113, 61–85, charts the political considerations determining the teaching of Athenian democracy in 19th-c. France.

ACKERMANN. D. Jenson, 'Louise Ackermann's monstrous nature', *Symposium*, 53, 2000:234–48, considers the charge of 'monstruosité' levelled against A.'s poetry in the light of her critical writings on women as writers.

BASHKIRTSEFF. S. Wilson, 'Making an exhibition of oneself in public: the preface to Marie Bashkirtseff's *journal intime*', *FS*, 55:485–97, argues that the very fact that the previously unpublished B. wrote a preface to her *journal intime* sets it apart from other 19th-c. women's diaries, and considers its claim to the status of 'document humain' in relation to E. de Goncourt's disquisition on that concept in the preface to *La Faustin*.

BAUDELAIRE. T. Dolan, **Manet, Baudelaire and Hugo in 1862', *WI*, 16, 2000:145–62. K. O. Mills, **Le Peintre de la vie moderne* reconsidered: the Albatross takes flight', *RoQ*, 47, 2000:19–33.

BOURGET. J. Simpson, 'Bourget, Laforgue and impressionism's inside story', *FS*, 55:467–83, examines B.'s and L.'s presentation, in their art criticism, of Impressionism as metaphor for cultural as well as aesthetic transformation, and their reliance in this connexion on contemporary evolutionary theories.

GAUTIER. S. Moussa, 'Éloge du divers: anthropologie et esthétique dans les *Voyages méditerranéens* de Gautier', *Romantisme*, 114:51–60, examines notions of barbarism, savagery, and exoticism in G.'s travel writings.

GONCOURT. S. Champeau, *La Notion d'artiste chez les Goncourt (1852–70)*, Champion, 2000, 558 pp., identifies the various ideas associated with the term 'artiste' by the Goncourts, primarily in their *Journal*, but also in *Charles Demailly* and *Manette Salomon*. P.-J. Dufief, **'Les Goncourt moralistes', *TLit*, 13, 2000:217–26. See also BASHKIRTSEFF.

HUYSMANS. E. Emery, 'Écrire la fin: *Sainte Lydwine de Schiedam* de J.-K. Huysmans', *CNat*, 75:203–14, explores the apparent tension between the apocalyptic imagery of the opening chapter of H.'s hagiography and H.'s naturalist concern for authentic documentary detail.

LAFORGUE. See BOURGET.

MAETERLINCK. P. Gorceix, 'L'image de la germanité chez un Belge, Flamand de langue française: Maurice Maeterlinck (1862–1949)', *RLC*, 75:397–409, argues for the influence of M.'s *milieu* on his work.

MAUCLAIR. E. Kearns, 'Mauclair and the musical world of the *Fin de Siècle* and the *Belle Époque*', *MLR*, 96:334–46, presents an overview of M.'s music criticism.

RENAN. J. Coates, 'Renan and Pater's *Marius the Epicurean*', *CLS*, 37, 2000:402–23, traces the waning of P.'s enthusiasm for R., and assesses P.'s challenge to R.'s view of Marcus Aurelius as expressed in *Marc-Aurèle et la fin du monde antique* (1882).

SAINTE-BEUVE. *Romantisme*, 109, 2000, a special edition on 'Sainte-Beuve ou l'invention de la critique', includes: A. Ubersfeld, 'Sainte-Beuve dans le *Journal* des Goncourt' (23–31); G. Antoine, 'Pour ou contre Sainte-Beuve?' (33–44). P. Nelles, **'Sainte-Beuve between Renaissance and Enlightenment', *JHI*, 61, 2000:473–92. P. Laforgue, **'Sainte-Beuve, Baudelaire et Proust, ou Saturne et sa postérité', *RHLF*, 100, 2000:107–23.

TAINE. Hilary Nias, *The Artificial Self. The Psychology of Hippolyte Taine*, Oxford, Legenda, 1999, xii + 260 pp., resituates the development of T.'s thought within the distinct intellectual and institutional context of the Second Empire, partly basing its argument on a substantial body of previously unpublished writings. B. Donatelli,

'Taine lecteur de Flaubert. Quand l'histoire rencontre la littérature', *Romantisme*, 111:75–87, examines T.'s criticism of F.'s fiction, which reveals an admiration of F. as 'historian'. P. Whyte, 'Ethnocentrisme et pragmatisme relativiste. L'Angleterre, l'Italie et l'Allemagne selon Taine', *ib.*, 114:79–88, looks at aesthetic aspects of T.'s determinism. A. Lavernhe-Grosset, 'Fleur et affleurement du corps imaginaire dans le *Voyage en Italie* de Taine', *RSH*, 264:99–109, examines flower imagery as bodily metaphor in T.'s travelogue.

5. THEATRE

FLAUBERT. B. Vibert, ' "Élu-foutu: l'être ou ne pas être". Sur *Le Candidat* de Flaubert', *RTr*, 59:43–53, discusses the critical reception and political context of F.'s play.

GONCOURT. R. de Felici, 'Fantaisie et naturalisme dans la poétique dramatique d'Edmond de Goncourt', *RHLF*, 101:1399–1422, argues that E. de G.'s fascination for the theatre has been overlooked, and that there is much of interest in both his criticism and his adaptation of fiction for the 'naturalist' stage.

MAETERLINCK. Patrick McGuinness, *Maurice Maeterlinck and the Making of Modern Theatre*, OUP, 2000, x + 270 pp., explores Maeterlinck's innovative contribution to Symbolism and the development of static theatre, and its impact not only in his immediate literary context but also, significantly, elsewhere. P. Gorceix, *'Maeterlinck ou la poétique du mystère', *Modernités*, 14, 2000:221–43. N. V. Marusiak, 'Moris Meterlink v Rossii 90-kh gg. XIX — nachala XXv.: K probleme literaturnoi retseptsii', *VMUF*, 2000, no.3:98–104, examines M.'s reception in Russia at the turn of the 20th century.

VILLIERS DE L'ISLE-ADAM. G. Jolly, 'La didascalie chez Villiers de l'Isle-Adam. Un autre lieu de l'écriture théâtrale', *Poétique*, 128:447–62, argues that while V.'s theatre is not 'naturalist', nor can it be seen unproblematically as a herald of symbolism.

THE TWENTIETH CENTURY 1900–1945
POSTPONED

THE TWENTIETH CENTURY SINCE 1945
POSTPONED

FRENCH CANADIAN LITERATURE

By CHRISTOPHER ROLFE, *Senior Lecturer in French, University of Leicester*

1. GENERAL

Lise Gauvin, *Langagement. L'écrivain et la langue au Québec*, Montreal, Boréal, 2000, 254 pp., is a vital text that seeks to come to terms with Quebec literature's apparent obsession with 'une problématique de la langue'. Of particular note are the following chapters: 'De *Speak White* à *Speak What*: du côté des manifestes' (49–70); 'Michel Tremblay et le théâtre de la langue' (123–41); and, underlining the growing importance of immigrant writers, 'L'écriture nomade' (181–207). For an excellent discussion of popular oral language in contemporary Quebec drama, see also J. Moss, '"Watch your language!" The special effects of theatrical vulgarity', *CanL*, 168 : 14–29. Klaus-Dieter Ertler, **Der frankokanadische Roman der dreissiger Jahre: eine ideologieanaly-tische Darstellung*, Tübingen, Niemeyer, 2000, x + 436 pp. Jacques Allard, *Le Roman du Québec: histoire, perspectives, lectures*, Montreal, Québec Amérique, 2000, 446 pp. *Métamorphoses et avatars littéraires dans la francophonie canadienne*, ed. Louis Bélanger, Vanier, Interligne, 2000, 153 pp., is a collection of essays that does not really coalesce into the intended critique of '[le] caractère fictif, non seulement de la création littéraire elle-même, mais d'une littéraire elle-même cloisonnée par les communautés qu'on prétend lui faire représenter', but which does offer insight into a range of writers including A. Maillet, G. Miron, H. Aquin, L. Conan, and S. Kokis. *Diffractions. Romans et nouvelles du Québec. Etudes*, ed. François Gallays, Orléans–Ontario, David, 2000, 378 pp., features essays on G. Roy, L. Conan, A. Langevin, G. Bessette, M. Bosco, J. Poulin, R. Ducharme, A. Hébert, and C. Matthieu, and generally repays reading. Jaap Lintvelt, *Aspects de la narration. Thématique, idéologie et identité*, Quebec, Nota bene, 2000, 306 pp., has valuable sections on A. Hébert and J. Poulin. Norbert Spehner, *Le Roman policier en Amérique française*, Quebec, Alire, 2000, 418 pp., will be of immense value not only to those interested in the topic but to students of Quebec literature in general. It incorporates an excellent critical essay and a detailed *recensement* of the *polars* published in Canada. Suzanne Giguère, *Passeurs culturels. Une littérature en mutation*, Quebec, Laval U.P., 263 pp., adds considerably to our understanding of migrant literature in Quebec. It consists of inter-views with eleven authors, including E. Ollivier, N. Kattan, M. Latif-Ghattas, and R. Robin, and has a typically thoughtful introduction by Pierre Nepveu. Lucie Hotte, *Romans de la lecture, lecture du roman. L'inscription de la lecture*, Quebec, Nota bene, 183 pp., addresses the question of 'Qu'est-ce que lire?' via the analysis of a number of novels that present 'des personnages lecteurs'. These include Aquin's *Trou de mémoire*, Bessette's *Le Libraire*, Ducharme's *Le Nez qui voque*, Godbout's *Salut Galarneau!*, Robert Lalonde's *L'Ogre de Grand Remous*, and Daniel Poliquin's *L'Ecureuil noir*. Very dense and very dull. Mary Jean Green, *Women and Narrative Identity: Rewriting the Quebec National Text, Montreal, McGill–Queen's U.P., xi + 197 pp. *Poésie et politique. Mélanges offerts en hommage à Michel van Schendel*, ed. Paul Chamberland *et al.*, Montreal, L'Hexagone, 511 pp., contains at least two essays of interest to Quebec specialists: J. Allard, 'Le voyage américain de *Volkswagen blues*' (315–29), and D. Saint-Jacques, 'Déterminations internationales de la nationalisation de la littérature au Québec' (331–44). Maurice Lemire, *Les Ecrits de la Nouvelle-France*, Quebec, Nota bene, 2000, 191 pp., is a short but compelling study that sheds light not only on relatively well-known material (the Jesuit *Relations*, to take an obvious example), but also on 'unknown' writings such as those emanating from the Seven Years War. Thoroughly recommended.

VI, 26.3, has a dossier on 'Généalogies de la figure du patriote 1837–1838', which, directly or indirectly, will be of interest to literature specialists. For example, D. Vaillancourt, 'Les têtes à Patriote: une figure retorse au XIXe siècle' (456–73) makes some useful comments on Pierre-Joseph-Olivier Chauveau's *Charles Guérin*. This novel is also discussed, along with Honoré Beaugrand's *Jeanne la fileuse*, novels by Marie-Claire Daveluy, and Louis Caron's *Le Canard de bois* in M. Randall, 'Plus patriote que ça . . . Fictions du Patriote 1847–1981' (516–38). Also recommended is R. Major, 'Le patriote pathétique. (Le patriote de la Révolution tranquille)' (539–55), which examines narratives of the 1960s depicting revolutionary patriots and concludes they are generally wimpish. He discusses, amongst others, Aquin, Claude Jasmin, and the sadly neglected *A perte de temps* by Pierre Gravel.

M. Olscamp, 'Un air de famille. Entre *La Relève* et *Refus global*: la génération cachée', *Tangence*, 62, 2000:7–33, investigates 'le sort d'une *constellation* de penseurs et de créateurs que réunit une même vision de la culture.' M. Cambron, 'Les récits du *Canadien*. Politique, fiction et nation', *ib.*, 63, 2000:109–34, usefully explores the famous newspaper's role in promoting a national literature. *EF*, 37.3, has a dossier on 'Ecriture et judéité au Québec'. François Ouellet and François Paré, *Traversées. Lettres*, Ottawa, Le Nordir, 2000, 182 pp., presents the correspondence between these two respected critics during the period from May 1998 to June 2000. If the exchange of letters seems self-conscious and even pretentious, it does provide a refreshingly different perspective on contemporary literature.

Conteurs franco-canadiens, ed. Peter Klaus, Stuttgart, Reclam, 2000, 168 pp., is an anthology of short stories that includes some old favourites and some interesting new ones (by Stanley Péan, a Haitian immigrant, for example). *Sous les mâts des Prairies. Anthologie littéraire fransaskoise et de l'Ouest canadien*, ed. Bernard Wilhelm, Regina, La Nouvelle Plume, 2000, 294 pp., contrives to suggest that Prairie francophone literature is alive and kicking but, hardly surprisingly, of little universal consequence. René Dionne, *Bibliographie de la littérature franco-ontarienne 1610–1993*, Ottawa, Vermillon, 2000, 619 pp., is a valuable research tool.

La Poésie d'expression française en Amérique du nord. Cheminement récent, ed. Laurent Lavoie, Beauport, Publications MNH, 2000, 182 pp., is an eclectic collection of papers from a conference of the same title held at the Collège universitaire du Cap-Breton in 1998. The pages on Quebec and Acadian *chansonniers* such as François Charron and Daniel Bélanger and the group 1755 offer some fresh perspectives, whilst I. Oore's piece on Marie-Claire Blais (127–37) sheds light on the novelist's poetic output. Gilles Marcotte, *Le Lecteur de poèmes*, Montreal, Boréal, 2000, 210 pp., has articulate, jargon-free essays on Grandbois, Anne Hébert, Rina Lasnier, Miron, Fernand Ouellette, Robert Melançon as well as René Char, Robert Marteau, and Pierre Jean Jouve. Jacques Blais, *Parmi les hasards. Dix études sur la poésie québécoise*, Quebec, Nota bene, 276 pp., offers, to begin with, two essays on the beginnings of 'modern' poetry in Quebec (one revisits *Le Nigog*), and follows these with sensitive readings of specific poems by Nelligan, Saint-Denys Garneau, Anne Hébert, Jean-Guy Pilon, Paul-Marie Lapointe, Gatien Lapointe.

Le Théâtre québécois 1975–1995, ed. Dominique Lafon, Montreal, Fides, 527 pp., is volume x of the *Archives des lettres canadiennes* published under the aegis of the Centre de recherche en civilisation canadienne-française at the University of Ottawa, and is a comprehensive, authoritative collection of essays covering all aspects of Quebec theatre during a period which witnessed an almost incredible creative effervescence. Absolutely indispensable.

2. INDIVIDUAL AUTHORS

BABINEAU. C. Filteau, ' "His mind like a flippant bastard": culture et hétéroglossie dans une nouvelle de l'auteur acadien Jean Babineau', *Littérature*, 121:76–100, considers issues such as code switching in B.'s *La Foulée*.

BEAULIEU. G. Baril, 'L'immonde comme dessein, mobile et délit d'écriture', *VI*, 26, 2000:40–59, focuses on B.'s *Un Rêve québécois* as the metaphor of a dream of writing turned to nightmare.

BLAIS. V.-L. Tremblay, '*La Belle Bête* de Marie-Claire Blais: du conte éponyme à l'histoire familiale', *CanL*, 169:13–30, seeks to explore narrative structures and themes 'en ouvrant l'œuvre à un jeu dialogique entre l'intertexte féerique qui l'a inspirée [et] l'ordre familiale dont elle s'est nourrie.' M. Couillard, 'La politique et l'écriture de dé-raison: *Les Manuscrits de Pauline Archange* de Marie-Claire Blais et *La Maison aux esprits* d'Isabel Allende', *EtLitt*, 32.3–33.1:77–93, compares and contrasts the narrative and discursive strategies adopted by the two writers.

BROSSARD. Susan Knutson, *Narrative in the Feminine. Daphne Marlatt and Nicole Brossard*, Waterloo, Wilfred Laurier U.P., 2000, 233 pp., firstly explores how these two experimental writers have contributed to feminist theory, and then goes on to offer narratological readings of M.'s *How to Hug a Stone* and B.'s *Picture Theory*. An important study, not least for the way it brings Canadian writers from the two linguistic backgrounds together. K. Conley, 'Going for baroque in the twentieth century: from Desnos to Brossard', *QuS*, 31:12–23, discusses *Baroque d'aube* and its links with the surrealism of the 1920s.

BUIES. Micheline Morisset, *Arthur Buies, chevalier errant*, Quebec, Nota bene, 2000, 208 pp., is a stimulating 'biography' that transcends time by bringing B. back to life in 1995 to confront the crucial issues of the time: an original, and successful way of bringing out the importance of his thought.

CHAUVEAU. V. Roy, 'La réception critique de *Charles Guérin* de Pierre-Joseph-Olivier Chauveau au XIXe siècle. De l'émergence d'une littérature nationale', *VI*, 26:339–58, analyses C.'s novel with a view to identifying the prevailing aesthetic standards of the time.

CHIASSON. T. Bissonnette, 'Hybrider, dit-il', *Nuit blanche*, 80, 2000:22–25, constitutes a slim but useful introduction to this important Acadian poet.

CONAN. M. Lemire, 'Félicité Angers sous l'éclairage de sa correspondance', *VI*, 26, 2000:128–44, sheds further light on the private life of C. via her unpublished correspondence.

DANDURAND. L. Saint-Martin, 'Playing with gender, playing with fire: Anne Dandurand's and Jeanne Le Roy's feminist parodies of *Histoire d'O*', *NFS*, 40:31–40, asks to what extent parody can really succeed in challenging and subverting the traditional distribution of gender roles and power.

DELAHAYE. Robert Lahaise, *Guy Delahaye. Poète-psychiatre*, Montreal, Lidec, 2000, 62 pp., is a basic biography with lots of rather interesting illustrations and photographs.

DESAUTELS. *VI*, 26.2, has a substantial dossier on the author best known perhaps for her 1998 autobiographical narrative *Ce fauve, le Bonheur*.

DUCHARME. Pierre-Louis Vaillancourt, *Réjean Ducharme. De la pie-grièche à l'oiseau moqueur*, L'Harmattan, 2000, 254 pp., succeeds in both elucidating a rich but frequently baffling *œuvre* and demonstrating its essential modernity. The titles of the chapters are as captivating as that of the volume. E. Nardout-Lafarge, 'Ducharme, du sale et du propre', *VI*, 26, 2000: 74–94, explores the significance of dirt in D.'s nine published novels and, at the same time, how dirt is resisted by the purity and emptiness embodied in specific characters. Nardout-Lafarge has also published **Réjean Ducharme: une poétique du débris*, Montreal, Fides, 312 pp.

FERRON. A. Brochu, 'Recto-verso: le Québec dans le *Ciel de Québec* et *Les Pays étrangers*', *CEB*, 2, 1999: 29–41. Luc Gauvreau, *Index onomastique de l'œuvre de Jacques Ferron, suivi d'une chronologie complète*, Montreal U.P., 2000, 248 pp., is a research tool that is light years away from the vitality and enchantment of F.'s work. Jacques Ferron and François Hébert, *'Vous blaguez sûrement . . .'*, ed. François-Simon Labelle, Outremont, Lanctôt, 2000, 155 pp., presents the judiciously edited correspondence between F. and H. from May 1976 to April 1984. Letter writing was extremely important to F. — he would habitually use letters to elaborate ideas for his work — and this exchange is therefore of major significance. Jacques Ferron, *Textes épars (1935–1959)*, ed. Pierre Cantin, Luc Gauvreau, and Marcel Olscamp, Outremont, Lanctôt, 2000, 226 pp. R. Patry, 'Le gentil-homme allemand et les voleurs d'âme: "Loutiquenne" et les "(de) Quéclin" dans l'univers ferronien', *VI*, 26, 2000: 145–65, is an erudite but at times off-putting study of foreign words and, in particular, two terms that are gallicised by F. B. Bednarski, 'Translating Ferron, Ferron translating: thoughts on an example of translation within', *Meta*, 45, 2000: 37–51, revolves around F.'s insertion of a poem by Samuel Butler into his *Les Confitures de coings*. Interesting for the light shed on the act of translation and on F.'s text itself. S. Marcotte, ' "Je n'écris que pour écrire". Lettres de Jacques Ferron à ses sœurs (1933–1945)', *VI*, 26: 585–95, examines the importance of F.'s letters in triggering a literary persona for himself.

FRÉCHETTE. Louis Fréchette, *Contes de Jos Violon*, ed. Aurélien Boivin, Montreal, Guérin, 1999, 119 pp., is a fine critical edition based on the last published version whilst F. was alive.

GARNEAU, ST-D. Michel Biron, *L'Absence du maître. Saint-Denys Garneau, Ferron, Ducharme*, Montreal U.P., 2000, 322 pp., is a Victor W. Turner inspired re-reading of the work of the three writers that asks 'la modernité québécoise est-elle caractérisée par une absence du maître?'. France Gascon, *L'Univers de Saint-Denys Garneau, le peintre, le critique*, Montreal, Boreal, 200 pp., presents a selection of the poet's paintings. Although a far better poet than he was painter, these works do demonstrate a real talent (especially his sense of pictorial space) and are a vital adjunct to his poetry. A must for G. specialists. K. Larose, 'Saint-Denys Garneau et le vol culturel', *EF*, 37.3 : 147–63, seeks to establish the structural coherence of the final prose pieces, often judged unreadable, that announced G.'s final silence.

GAUVREAU. J. Paquin, 'Voyage au cœur de l'immonde ou la fouille exploratrice de Claude Gauvreau', *VI*, 26, 2000:95–106, revolves around a figure that looms large in G.'s work — and especially *Pétrouchka* — i.e. the disembowelled woman.

GÉLINAS. Anne-Marie Sicotte, *Gratien Gélinas. Du naïf Fridolin à l'ombrageux Tit-Coq*, Montreal, XYZ, 173 pp., is yet another lively biography in the *Grandes figures* collection.

GODIN. *Gérald Godin. Un poète en politique*, ed. Lucille Beaudry, Robert Comeau, and Guy Lachapelle, Montreal, L'Hexagone, 2000, 154 pp., is a collection of papers from a conference on G. held in Trois-Rivières in 1997. The volume is divided into three sections that correspond to the major aspects of G.'s career: poet, journalist, politician. The latter section is significant in that it stresses his conception of a *new* Quebec, 'une nation qu'il a voulue à l'aune de l'altérité'. André Gervais, *Petit glossaire des 'Cantouques' de Gérald Godin*, Quebec, Nota bene, 2000, 169 pp., lists and explains the *québécismes* and *godinismes*, and also the proper names, found in G.'s ground-breaking poems. Of immense value. Gérald Godin, *Ils ne demandaient qu'à brûler*, ed. André Gervais, Montreal, L'Hexagone, 573 pp., is a welcome edition that brings together all the major collections and various hitherto unpublished poems.

GRANDBOIS. Yves Laliberté, *Les Rituels de l'absolu. Essai sur la poésie d'Alain Grandbois*, Ottawa, David, 331 pp., is an intelligent but dense essay that brings out the erudition that accompanies G.'s philosophical and spiritual explorations.

GUÈVREMONT. D. Décarie, 'Le relais des survenants chez Germaine Guèvremont', *VI*, 26:359–83, follows up some of the strands of meaning prompted by the similarities between the *Survenant* and the *Acayenne* in G.'s *Le Survenant* and *Marie-Didace*.

HÉBERT. *Lectures d'Anne Hébert. Aliénation et contestation*, ed. Pierre Hébert and Christiane Lahaie, Montreal, Fides, 1999, 121 pp., is the inaugural number of a new yearly journal devoted to H. Robert Harvey, *Poétique d'Anne Hébert. Jeunesse et genèse. Suivi de lecture du 'Tombeaux des rois'*, Quebec, L'Instant même, 2000, 344 pp., is a well-crafted study. The analysis of *Tombeaux des rois* is particularly persuasive. *'Le Torrent' d'Anne Hébert*, ed. Claude Cassista and Jean Simard, Montreal, Leméac, 66 pp., is one of a series of enterprising *manuels d'étudiant* published by Leméac which 'se propose[nt] d'entrer dans l'univers des grandes œuvres de la littérature québécoise en empruntant des chemins qui l'entourent.' (See entries under HÉMON and POULIN. All are thoroughly recommended for their stimulating contextualization.)

HÉMON. '*Maria Chapdelaine*' *de Louis Hémon*, ed. Gilles Perron, Montreal, Leméac, 2000, 71 pp.

HERTEL. *CEB*, 3, 2000, has a dossier on Hertel which does something to rehabilitate a writer who is now all but forgotten (but who was a major influence on Jean Ethier-Blais).

JACOB. L. Saint-Martin, 'Infanticide, suicide, matricide, and mother-daughter love: Suzanne Jacob's *L'Obéissance* and Ying Chen's *L'Ingratitude*', *CanL*, 169:60–83, is a powerful study of two novels with much in common.

LAFERRIÈRE. Dany Laferrière, *J'écris comme je vis. Entretiens avec Bernard Magnier*, Outremont, Lanctôt, 247 pp., presents the transcripts of a series of wide-ranging interviews from 1999. Immensely useful for an understanding of L., his work, and his views (on *négritude*, feminism, other writers, etc.).

LANGUIRAND. Jacques Languirand, *Presque tout Jacques Languirand*, Montreal, Stanké, 892 pp., is a most welcome collection of the plays of one of Quebec's most distinctive voices. The edition may perhaps prompt the sort of academic attention that L.'s ability to create moments of high dramatic tension, his sense of the comic, his taste for ambiguity and black humour deserve but have not yet received.

LA ROCQUE. K. Meadwell, 'L'œuvre en devenir: une lecture des dossiers génétiques scénariques de *Serge d'entre les morts*, *Les Masques* et *Le Passager* de Gibert La Rocque', *CanL*, 168:105–18.

LEPAGE. *Theater sans frontières. Essays on the Dramatic Universe of Robert Lepage*, ed. Joseph Donohue and Jane Koustas, Michigan State U.P., 2000, 269 pp., is a high quality collection that tackles all facets of L.'s work in a scholarly fashion, although the absence of an index will inhibit its use as a research tool.

MAILLET. M. Boehringer, 'En guise de roman, une auto/biographie acadienne: *Les Confessions de Jeanne de Valois* par Antonine Maillet', *IJFS*, 3, 2000:18–24. Marie-Andrée Michaud, *La Voie du cœur*, Montreal, Fides, 2000, 230 pp., is a collection of interviews broadcast on Radio-Canada in 1997–98 including one with M. (17–28).

MIRON. Pierre Vadeboncœur, *L'Humanité improvisée*, Montreal, Bellarmin, 2000, 187 pp., is a disconcerting critical analysis of postmodernism whose opening 30 pages are devoted to a celebration of M.

MONETTE. J. Ricouart, 'Violence et désir dans l'œuvre de Madeleine Monette', *IJFS*, 2, 1999:68–75.

MORIN. H. Marcotte, '*Le Paon d'émail de P. Morin*: l'exploration des lointains', *Tangence*, 65:82–90, seeks to demonstrate how M. cultivates an aesthetic of emancipation from a hegemonic ideal and yet, paradoxically, has recourse to traditional Orientalism.

OLLIVIER. *LQu*, 102, has a valuable section on O.

POULIN. P. Socken, 'Jacques Poulin's *Le Cœur de la baleine bleue*: a rewriting of Gabrielle Roy's *Alexandre Chenevert?*', *IJFS*, 2, 1999:106–11, argues that P.'s novel grapples with the same fundamental issues as R.'s and that he is, in a sense, her literary and spiritual heir. Isabelle L'Italien-Savard, '*Les Grandes Marées' de Jacques Poulin*, Montreal, Leméac, 2000, 78 pp. M. Leduc, 'Le bonheur autrement. L'héritage décrié de Robinson Crusoé dans *Les Grandes Marées* de Jacques Poulin', *VI*, 26:569–84, argues that P.'s novel denounces and subverts Crusoe's capitalist values and explores more profoundly humane attitudes.

PROULX. D. Rochat, 'Le corps dérobé: handicap et condition postmoderne dans *Homme invisible à la fenêtre* de Monique Proulx', *QuS*, 31:113–27.

ROY. *Le Pays de 'Bonheur d'occasion'*, ed. François Ricard, Sophie Marcotte, and Jane Everett, Montreal, Boréal, 2000, 160 pp., comprises nine hitherto unpublished or unobtainable autobiographical pieces by R. Essential reading. L. Saint-Martin, 'Les sœurs ennemies: Gabrielle et Adèle Roy', *Tangence*, 62, 2000:50–72. François Ricard, *Introduction à l'œuvre de Gabrielle Roy (1945–1975)*, Quebec, Nota bene, 199 pp., is a solid overview, with, in particular, some useful pages on R.'s journalism. S. Marcotte, 'Correspondance, autobiographie, et journal personnel chez Gabrielle Roy', *QuS*, 31:76–96. T. M. Carr, 'Separation, mourning, and consolation in *La Route d'Altamont'*, *QuS*, 31:97–112. L. Brotherson, 'Odours as metaphor in *Bonheur d'occasion'*, *AJFS*, 38:272–84, is thoughtful but limited in scope.

SOUCY. *LQu*, 97, 2000, has a useful dossier on S. B. Gervais, 'L'art de se brûler les doigts. L'imaginaire de la fin de *La Petite Fille qui aimait trop les allumettes* de Gaétan Soucy', *VI*, 26:384–93, attempts to explain the questions raised by a young girl who, although about to give birth, persists in the belief she is a boy.

THÉORET. B. Havercroft, 'Fragments d'un parcours remémoré: *Journal pour mémoire* de France Théoret', *QuS*, 31:36–49.

THÉRIAULT. R. Bérubé, 'Raconter des histoires de père en fille: portraits d'Yves et Marie José Thériault', *Tangence*, 62, 2000:84–99.

TREMBLAY. Luc Boulanger, *Pièces à conviction. Entretiens avec Michel Tremblay*, Montreal, Leméac, 179 pp., presents 18 interviews with the playwright by the well-known drama critic of *Voir*. Each interview deals with one of the major plays and is interesting for the light shed on how T. himself views his works, their creation and reception, the interview (no.17, pp. 157–63) on *Messe solennelle pour une pleine lune d'été* particularly so for the light shed on T.'s response to the critics' initial thumbs down. *Emblématiques de l'époque du joual. Jacques Renaud, Gérald Godin, Michel Tremblay, Yvon Deschamps*, ed. André Gervais, Outremont, Lanctôt, 2000, 196 pp., presents a series of important essays that address various aspects of the work of the four writers who, between them, established *joual* as a vital literary tool in the 1960s. Of particular value for the coverage of T. and Godin whose works have stood the test of time rather better than the others. Craig Stewart Walker, *The Buried Astrolabe. Canadian Dramatic Imagination and Western Tradition*, Montreal, McGill–Queen's U.P., 467 pp., has an engaging, thoughtful chapter on T. entitled 'Michel Tremblay: existential mythopoeia' (201–63), that convincingly sets out and explores 'an elaborate, idiosyncratic mythology extending through his work.' J. Cardinal, 'Exorciser l'immonde. Parole et sacré dans *Sainte Carmen de la Main* de Michel Tremblay', *VI*, 26, 2000 : 18–39, analyses how T. creates a 'theatre of exorcism' in order to fend off that which threatens the order that speech brings. L. Gauvin, 'L'imaginaire des langues: du carnavalesque au baroque (Tremblay, Kourouma)', *Littérature*, 121 : 101–15, is a stimulating comparison of, on the face of it, two unlikely bedfellows.

VADEBONCŒUR. A. Caumartin, 'Pierre Vadeboncœur et la rhétorique de l'extrême', *EtLitt*, 32.3/33.1, 27–39, examines how V.'s *Trois essais sur l'insignifiance* partake of both the lyrical/meditative essay and the polemical pamphlet.

CARIBBEAN LITERATURE

By MARY GALLAGHER, *University College Dublin*

1. GENERAL

Dominique Chancé, *L'Auteur en souffrance: Essai sur la position et la représentation de l'auteur dans le roman antillais contemporain (1981–1992)*, PUF, 2000, 224 pp., resonates with the many studies that have similarly identified the self-reflexive focus of much French Caribbean writing as central. The study concentrates more or less exclusively on the five most prominent novelists from Martinique and Guadeloupe, namely Glissant, Chamoiseau, Confiant, Condé, and Maximin and includes a revealing interview with Patrick Chamoiseau. The often tense, and — the author would argue — painful, relation between writing and Caribbean culture (especially oral culture) is the one examined by Chancé, whose clarity of viewpoint is partly founded on the relative homogeneity of one of the projects cherished by all five novelists studied, namely an exploration of the specificity of writing and of authorship. Biringanine Ndagano, *Nègre tricolore: Littérature et domination en pays créole*, pref. Jacques Chévrier, Maisonneuve & Larose, 2000, 210 pp., is a particularly welcome study in that it concentrates on the relatively neglected domain of Guyanese writing in French. The principal authors studied in some detail are Damas, Stéphenson, Patient, and Taubira-Delannon, whose work is scoured for signs of 'une abolition et une décolonisation bâclées'. Attentive to the important questions of Guyanese cultural specificity, and to writing in Creole and writing by women, the study includes interviews with Élie Stéphenson, Rosange Blérald, Serge Patient, and Christiane Taubira-Delannon. Delphine Perret, *La Créolité: espace et création*, Martinique, Ibis Rouge, 313 pp., is a very thorough and quite sympathetic textbook covering the issues and the writing associated with the *créolité* movement. A first chapter situates the movement historically and theoretically. The next six chapters examine Martinique as it enters the 21st c., the history of the term 'creole', the linguistic philosophy of the *créolité* movement, the question of the relation between orality and writing, and the idea of collective identity explored in part through the meaning of the pronoun 'nous', ending with a chapter entitled 'vers une anthropologie de la créolisation'. H. Adlai Murdoch Jr., *Creole Identity in the French Caribbean Novel*, Gainesville, Florida U.P., 320 pp., is a rich and searching study of how 'creoleness' or the creolization process has been less conceptualized than articulated in a 'complex concatenation of history, politics, ethnicity, and discourse'. In a study that pays close attention to sites of ambivalence, heterogeneity, and ambiguity, Murdoch bases his approach on readings of the function and effects of narrative in five novels: Glissant's *La Lézarde*, Condé's *En attendant le bonheur*, Maximin's *L'Isolé Soleil*, Dracius-Pinalie's *L'Autre qui danse*, and Chamoiseau's *Solibo Magnifique*. The corpus is a rich one and, while the first and fourth of these texts have probably never been as well or as thoroughly analysed and appreciated, all of Murdoch's readings are fresh and genuinely illuminating. Anne Marty, *Haïti en littérature*, Maisonneuve & Larose, 2000, 222 pp., is prefaced by Régis Antoine and is less a straightforward historical account of the representation of Haiti in Haitian literature from 1804 to the present than a study which identifies as central to that representation the literary treatment of gender, specifically female characters, by both women and men writers. After a historical overview, and following a chapter on the literary articulation of the polarization of nationalism into conservative and socialist strands following the American Occupation of 1915, Marty studies patterns of representation of women by male authors from 1885 to 1925; the relative and perhaps related treatment of female characters in Haitian and Quebec novels between 1938 and 1980; and, finally, the treatment of women characters by some Haitian women novelists. The study closes with a series of interviews with six contemporary (male) novelists: Dorsinville, Ollivier, Lahens, Frankétienne, Denis, and Caillard.

2. INDIVIDUAL AUTHORS

CÉSAIRE. D. Kanaté, 'Aimé Césaire et Paul Chamberland: le pays sous le regard de la subversion', *Francofonia*, 9, 2000:121–37, compares the subversive use of the image of the native land in the writing of two poets, one Québecois, the other Martiniquan.

CHAMOISEAU. V. Maisier, 'Patrick Chamoiseau's novel *Texaco* and the picaresque genre', *DFS*, 57:128–36, studies the extent to which *Texaco* corresponds to the picaresque model. Without denying the limits of that correspondence, Maisier sheds interesting light on the cross-cultural and transhistoric generic echoes awoken by the novel's treatment of themes such as social marginality and dehumanization. S. L. Shelly, 'Addressing linguistic and cultural diversity with Patrick Chamoiseau's *Chemin d'école*', *FR*, 75:112–26, shows how 'standard and non-standard systems come together on the page' of C.'s text, presenting 'very real challenges for the classroom' and 'an opportunity to address cultural diversity and to foster critical thinking skills through foreign language study'.

R. C. Caldwell, Jr., 'Creole voice, Creole time: narrative strategies in C.'s *Chronique des sept misères*', *RoQ*, 47, 2000:103–11, shows how, in C.'s writing, the 'path to the Creole identity lies in the excavation of the past', concluding by asking how 'the true Martinican identity sought by Chamoiseau [. . .] in a past of resistance and suffering [. . .] can be sustained today in a comfortable world of social security checks and televised football'. J. Nnadi, 'Mémoire d'Afrique, mémoire biblique: la congruence des mythes du nègre dans *Texaco* de Patrick Chamoiseau', *PF*, 15:75–91, claims that two 'mémoires mythiques — de la Bible et de l'Afrique' come together in C.'s novel. In this study, the term 'congruence' is crucial, and the article concludes, indeed, by noting not just that *Texaco* underlines the 'interdépendance des races différentes dans la créolité du futur', but that C.'s *créolité* fuses with *négritude*, integrating it rather than exorcizing it, thus proving itself to be based on 'la rencontre des différences'. M. McCusker, 'Translating the Creole voice: from the oral to the literary tradition in Patrick Chamoiseau's *Texaco*', pp. 117–27 of *Reading Across the Lines*, ed. Chris Shorley and Maeve McCusker, Dublin, Royal Irish Academy, 2000, 232 pp., provides a succint study of the relentless dominance of textuality in C.'s writing, and notes the creative dissonance between the author's prose fiction and his theoretical pronouncements on orality.

CONDÉ. A. R. Munoz, 'Une conversation avec M. Condé', *RoQ*, 47, 2000:157–64, following a more wide-ranging conversation, is divided into sections concentating on several of C.'s best-known novels. R. H. McCormick Jr., 'A new conception of identity: an interview with Maryse Condé', *WLT*, 74, 2000:519–28, is largely devoted to questions arising from *Desirada*, which C. identifies as her favourite of all her own novels.

MAXIMIN. Christiane Chaulet-Achour, *La Trilogie caribéenne de Daniel Maximin: analyse et contrepoint*, Karthala, 2000, 230 pp., is a close and insightful study of M.'s three textually and intertextually very dense novels. The first chapter considers the question of the enunciation of each of the three novels; the second considers their narrative structure; the third the dialogical or intertextual dimension of the writing. The fourth chapter explores the traces of folktale enunciation. The author then devotes four chapters to the imprint of history, myth, femininity as resistance, and geographical space. This is a most welcome study of some of the more poetic writing to emerge in recent years from the French Caribbean. Regrettably there is no bibliography or index.

F. Lagarde, 'Entre histoire et poésie: Maximin romantique', *PF*, 15:135–50, studies how Maximin's writing, particularly in *L'Isolé Soleil* and *Soufrières*, raises the question of the balance suggested in his work between writing, imagination, and reality, and also between magic, poetry, music, and art, on the one hand, and history, on the other.

PINEAU. F. Mugnier, 'La France dans l'oeuvre de G. Pineau', *PF*, 15:61–73, concludes that metropolitan France plays an important role in the creolization of Caribbean society, thus contributing to the deconstruction of outmoded notions such as race, nationality, and territory.

SAINT-JOHN PERSE. In *Modernité de Saint-John Perse?*, ed. Catherine Mayaux, Besançon, Presses universitaires franc-comtoises, 460 pp., two articles treat the question of the poet's Caribbean posterity. M. Sacotte, 'Quelques usages contemporains du texte de Saint-John Perse' (351–62), studies the ironic, even comical parody and pastiche of Saint-John Perse's writing in novels by Maryse Condé and Raphaël Confiant, while M. Gallagher, 'Saint-John Perse: créole, donc moderne?' (363–76), considers the relation or contradiction between the *créolistes'* integration of the Saint-John Perse intertext, on the one hand, and the claims that they make regarding the modernity of their writing or aesthetic, on the other.

AFRICAN AND MAGHREB LITERATURE
POSTPONED

III. OCCITAN STUDIES

LANGUAGE

By KATHRYN KLINGEBIEL, *Professor of French, University of Hawai'i at Mānoa*

1. BIBLIOGRAPHICAL AND GENERAL

Bibliographie des adhérents depuis 1985 (BAIEO, 15), Montpellier, AIEO, 2000, 345 pp., *MLAIntBibl*, 3, 2000[2001]:213–14, includes C. Bonnet on 'Occitan Language' (8825–71), and 'Old Provençal' (8872–81). K. Klingebiel, 'Occitan linguistic bibliography for 2000', *Tenso*, 16:130–94. M. Westmoreland, 'Current studies in occitan linguistics', *CRLN*, 50:32–40. A new web-based critical bibliography for the medieval language is available at <www.arnaut.it>, created and directed by Massimiliano De Conca; the first instalment covers 1998–2001. Jean Fourié, *Bibliographie des ouvrages, œuvres, études et articles en langue d'oc ou intéressant la langue et la littérature d'oc, publiés en 1998* (*Lou Félibrige*, 232–33, supp.), 1999, 56 pp. Id., *Bibliographie des ouvrages, œuvres, études et articles en langue d'oc ou intéressant la langue et la littérature d'oc, publiés en 1999* (*Lou Félibrige*, 234–35, supp.), 2000, 52 pp. A. Rieger, 'Provenzalistik, Altokzitanisch und Okzitanisch. Geschichte und Auftrag als Subdisziplin der Romanistik', *RZLG*, 24, 2000:214–17. Henri Boyer and Philippe Gardy coordinate a sweeping look at **Dix siècles d'usages et d'images de l'occitan: des troubadours à l'Internet*, postface by Robert Lafont, L'Harmattan, 469 pp.

2. MEDIEVAL PERIOD (TO 1500)

PHONETICS AND PHONOLOGY. W. Manczak, 'Développement phonétique irrégulier dû à la fréquence en ancien occitan', *AIEO 6*, 232–35. Beyond regular phonetic development and analogical levelling, irregular development due to frequency of usage provides a third factor in explaining word forms.

MORPHOSYNTAX. P. Skårup, 'Cataphore en ancien occitan, étudiée dans les poèmes de Bernard de Ventadour', *RLR*, 104, 2000:271–316, shows that cataphoric words need not precede the clause to which they refer, the subordinate clause being most frequently introduced by *que, car, don, per que, com*.

LEXIS AND LEXICOLOGY. P. T. Ricketts, *Concordance de l'occitan médiéval/A Concordance of Medieval Occitan*, 2 vols + CD-ROM, Turnhout, Brepols, 16 + 16, 62 pp. The CD-ROM, complete with viewing software, is accompanied by a bilingual printed *Guide* and a *Bibliography*. Each successive *tranche* will offer updates as well as additional materials on non-lyric texts in verse, texts in prose, and, if funding materializes, the troubadour *chansonniers*. Kurt Baldinger, with Nicoline Hörsch, *Dictionnaire onomasiologique de l'ancien occitan. Supplément*, Fasc. 7, Tübingen, Niemeyer, 2000, 80 pp., runs from 1234 *évacuer les excréments* to 1275 *âne*. *DOM, Fasc. 3 (*adenan-afermat*), ed. Wolf-Dieter Stempel et al., Tübingen, Niemeyer, 80 pp. J.-P. Chambon welcomes *DOM* in *RLR*, 104, 2000:439–58, as an eminently successful middle ground between the *Petit Levy* and a full-scale philological dictionary of Old Occitan; Chambon also provides here (448–52) a substantial section of complementary materials. M. Perugi, 'La linguistique des troubadours: quelques réflexions', *AIEO 6*, 123–32, contains background material, case histories, and conclusions based on P.'s on-going work directing the *Lessico dei trovatori del periodo classico (LTC)*, described in *SM*, 31, 1990:481–544.

PARTICULAR SEMANTIC FIELDS. R. Toscano, 'Fruchier, òrt, jardin', *GS*, 33, no. 478, 2000:489–92, clarifies *verdier* (v. 1, *Las Novas del papagay*) as 'garden', not 'orchard' or 'kitchen garden'.

TEXTS. L. Borghi Cedrini, 'Recuperi linguistici nella tradizione manoscritta dei trovatori (per l'edizione critica dell'opera di Peire Milo)', *AIEO 6*, 171–79, concludes that choice of 'good' variants can no longer be based on Occitan grammars, but must be reworked after careful review of MS traditions. C. Van der Horst, 'Traits caractéristiques des *Documents linguistiques* de Paul Meyer vérifiés dans des documents d'autres régions', *ib.*, 270–77, discusses a database of texts from the Alps, Marseille, and Avignon that prove helpful for localizing dialect traits. G. Tavani, **Il plurilinguismo nella lirica dei trovatori*', pp. 123–42 of *Documenti letterari del plurilinguismo*, ed. Vincenzo Orioles, Roma, Il Calamo, 2000, 426 pp., shows how each multilingual text can yield evidence to support or refute claims of cultural unity or linguistic interchangeability within the medieval Romance domain.

DIALECTS

GASCON. Xavier Beltour, **Le Particularisme aquitain-gascon au Moyen-Âge*, Belin-Beliet, Princi Neguer, 1999, 200 pp. A. Cauhapé continues his series on 'Moulins et meuniers en Béarn', parts 5–9: 'De la structure et du fonctionnement d'un moulin à eau', *PG*, 196, 2000:10–12 (texts from 1570, 1601); 'Ces "moulins" qui ne sont pas des moulins à grains', *ib.*, 197, 2000:7–9 (texts from 1332, 1783, 1603); 'De la propriété des moulins à eau', *ib.*, 198, 2000:3–4 (texts from 1544, 1388, 1323, 1491); *ib.*, 199, 2000:7–9 (texts from 1544, 1384, 1415, 1441); *ib.*, 200, 2000:6–7 (texts from 1548, 1540, 1480); 'Du droit et obligation de banalité au droit de mouture et la *pugnère*', *ib.*, 201, 2000:5–6 (texts from 1319, 1571, 1352, 1395); and *ib.*,

202:7–8. J. Lafitte, '*Que* enonciatiu en los tèstes vielhs', *LDGM*, 15, 2000:18–20, is useful primarily for its review of medieval attestations. Id., '*Que* enonciatiu en lo Fòr d'Aspa', *ib.*, 16, 2000:18. F. Galès, 'Petit glossaire béarnais des termes d'architecture', < www.societes-savantes-toulouse.asso.fr / samf / grmaison / globearn.htm >, 2000, presents 120 terms extracted from a study of the 14th-c. counts of Foix and Béarn.

LANGUEDOCIEN (INCLUDING S. PÉRIG.). P. A. Clément, 'La délimitation de la baronnie d'Hierle par les mesures à grain', *LiCC*, 117, 1999:6–7. Id., 'La règlementation d'un four banal', *ib.*, 18, offers a reading from charter 421 of the *cartulaire de Maguelone* (2 mai 1226). E. Demaille, 'Plan de Lodève en 1401', *ib.*, 118, 1999:19, reconstructs Lodève from modern sources. G. Caillat, 'Les "hommes" de 1407', *ib.*, 119, 1999:11–18, gives lists of inhabitants, taken from the *compoix* of Rousses [Lozère], 1558.

PROVENÇAL. G. Barruol, 'Voies antiques de Haute-Provence: état des recherches', *PrH*, 50, no. 201, 2000:251–56.

AUVERGNAT. J. Vesòla, 'Sus le priorat d'Agriffolia (quauques actes en lenga nòstra)', *Lo Convise*, 31, 2000:14–15, edits acts of April 1252, June 1408, and the early 15th c., from a Cantal priory built in 1120. Id., 'Un acòrdi de 1474 en lenga d'òc', *ib.*, 33:13, edits a text dated 27 September 1474 (Archives Départementales du Cantal, MS 3 E 50, f.58v). Id. 'Reglament per l'aiga d'una fònt en 1465', *La Cabreta*, 159, 2000:9–10, is an edition and glossary of a legal agreement dated June 1465 (Archives Départementales du Cantal, MS 3 E 28, 4, f. 64).

PROVENÇAL ALPIN. H. P. Kunert, 'Le dialecte de Guardia Piemontese, les Vaudois et l'occitan alpin du XIVe siècle', *AIEO 6*, 222–31. The dialect of Guardia Piemontese can serve as a witness of Occitan spoken in the Alps in the 14th and 15th centuries.

3. POST-MEDIEVAL PERIOD

GENERAL. D. Grosclaude, 'L'IEO qu'ei l'occitanisme', *Occitans!*, 100:v–vi, discusses how, after more than 50 years of the IEO, pan-Occitanism remains the sole possibility for Occitan language and culture to survive. Jòrgi Peladan edits the *Actes de l'Université d'Été 1998*, Nîmes, MARPOC, 2000, 234 pp., containing several items of general interest: P. Grau, 'Les relations occitano-catalans dans les années trente et le panoccitanism' (15–45), reviews differences and similarities up to 1939 and the death of the pan-Occitanist movement; J. Escartin, 'La pensada identitària provençalista e occitanista' (158–79), hopes for renewed Occitan identity based on the new 'Euròregions'; for E. Cestor, 'La musique occitane: entre tradition et grand marché' (211–34), music provides an optimal vehicle for cultural and linguistic reintegration into the mainstream; M. Van Den Bòssche, 'Occitan e internet' (112–23), reviews a wide variety of websites for Occitan culture. Peladan also edits *Actes de l'Université d'Été 1999*, Nîmes, MARPOC, 151 pp., offering: F. Carbona, 'Notas sus l'istòria de l'occitanisme' (5–17), an *historique* largely inspired by L. Abrate (see below); C. Barsotti, 'Lo moviment politic occitan deis annadas 1930 a uèi' (18–36), traces the dialectic between Occitan political party and national political party, politics and culture; F. Giroussens, 'L'occitan a l'escola primaria: una disciplina impossibla? De 1947 à 1973, une "longa paciéncia" — Analisi de las revistas pedagogicas occitanistas' (37–61); J. D. Estève, 'Las novas capitadas de l'occitan' (62–68), describes MED'Oc, a student movement at the Univ. of Montpellier; G. Dazas, 'A prepaus de dialèctes' (69–77), sends a clear message about dialect variety: 'normalizar es pas uniformisar'; M. Chapduelh, 'Coma èsser Lemosin?' (78–94), finds no need for an Occitan 'centralisme' on the model of France or Catalonia; D. Mallet, 'Le CIRDOC, qu'est-ce que c'est?' (95–103), in which the dynamic director of the CIRDOC in Béziers describes the genesis of this national library of Occitania and its place in the new Europe; M. Stenta, 'La femna al temps dels trobadors' (104–21), concludes that the position of women in the world of *fin'amor* is like a 'pan de nas al poder de la Glèisa'; P. Pasquini, 'Le rôle des femmes dans l'abandon de la langue' (122–37); believes that Occitan-speaking women must reclaim the use of their language 'pour dire quelque chose, et non pour qu'on se réjouisse du maintien de ce beau parler'.

J.-P. Dalbera, 'La linguistique occitane moderne. Etat des recherches, innovations théoriques et méthodologiques', *AIEO 6*, 71–101, reviews work done in atlases (1970–2000), structural analyses, phonology, morphology, generative analyses, diachronic studies, interferences between systems in contact, diatopic considerations, syntheses, lexical studies, dictionaries, etymology, and various areas of innovation. Id., **'Nouvelles technologies et perspectives: Nouvelles en géolinguistique', *Verbum* (Nancy), 22, 2000:135–55. M. C. Alén-Garabato, 'Le débat sur la norme au sein de la "communauté occitane virtuelle"', *AIEO 6*, 512–21, analyses some 5500 electronic messages received in three years on the website 'listoc', finding lack of agreement within the virtual Occitan community regarding the desirability of linguistic and graphic norms. R. Bistolfi, 'Langues régionales: l'impulsion corse?', *LSPS*, 146:36–37, is a call to preserve both the basic unity of Occitan and dialect diversity. G. Behling, 'Transmettre l'occitan en l'an 2000: quels enjeux, quelle perspective?', *AIEO 6*, 522–29, concludes that only by finding a popular base can

Occitan assure its existence, since competence in Occitan does not necessarily imply use of the language, and use of the language does not imply its transmission. M.-C. Coste-Rixte, 'La traduction, un acte militant au service de l'occitan', *ib.* 530–34, reviews potential advantages of modern Occitan translations, such as their use in schools to replace French versions of foreign works, or their usefulness to local tourist offices. Laurent Abrate, *Occitanie 1900–1968, des idées et des hommes. L'émergence et l'histoire de la revendication occitane*, Puylaurens, IEO, 622 pp., offers the most clear-eyed, pointed analysis to date of the Occitan movement.

Jean-François Courouau presents *Premiers combats pour la langue occitane: manifestes linguistiques occitans XVIe–XVIIe siècles*, Biarritz, Atlantica–IEO, 192 pp.

J.-L. Fossat, 'La description de l'occitan en question', *AIEO 6*, 546–52, proposes a method for unifying linguistic description of language structures with pedagogical applications for the language learner. P. Cichon, 'Aspects de l'enseignement de l'occitan aux XIXe et XXe siècles', *ib.*, 813–20, asks whether the single-minded orientation of French public education has moved beyond its original goal of integrating French citizens into a single nation. If so, the author offers suggestions centering on the social and pragmatic roles to be played by Occitan. E. Leitzke-Ungerer, '"L'Occitanie? Connais pas." Enseigner une culture régionale de la France au second cycle du lycée allemand', *ib.*, 821–37, discusses how the latest German manuals of FLE (Français langue étrangère) show a marked preference for non-Parisian characters and scenarios, despite their lack of explicit information about French regional language and culture. L.-A. Skupas, 'L'enseignement du provençal moderne à l'Université de Vilnius (Lituanie)', *ib.*, 854–56, is an account of the author's adventures in teaching Provençal in Lithuania and of various activities linking the two languages and cultures. Sabine Schick, *Die Calandreta-Bewegung zwischen Okzitanismus und Reformpädagogik: eine empirische Untersuchung zur bilingualen Erziehung in Südfrankreich*, Berne, Lang, 2000, xx + 336 pp. Peter Cichon, *Einführung in die okzitanische Sprache*, Bonn, Romanistischer Vlg, 1999, 146 pp.

B. Giély, 'La lengo dins l'an 2000. Cèntre internaciounau de l'escrich en lengo d'Oc', *PrA*, 141, 2000:4, reminds his readers (among other things) that all of Mistral has now been digitized, and that a new multilingual dictionary of computer vocabulary is being prepared at the CIEL d'Oc in Berre–L'Étang (<www.lpl.univ-aix.fr/ciel>). P. Berengier, 'Nostro lengo numerisado', *ib.*, 6, describes the integrated databases (text, graphics, phonetics, sound, grammar, dictionary, atlas) available by subscription through the university in Toulouse site (<www.univ.tlse2.fr/erss/clid/occitan>). E. Possenti reviews 'La lengo dins l'an 2000. Cèntre de l'Ouralita en lengo d'Oc', *ib.*, 5, and *ib.*, 143, 2000:8–9, further describes the COL'Oc in Aix, inaugurated in February 2000, with its mission to preserve Occitan culture. P. Berengier describes Montolieu, northwest of Carcassonne, the first town in the Midi devoted to booksellers, and their web-searchable catalogues, in 'Lou païs dóu libre', *ib.*, 144, 2000:13.

R. Lafont, 'Eurocongrès 2000 des espace occitans et catalans', *BIO*, 29–30, 2000:2–4, presents the nine domains of the 15-month congress that opened in January 2001: language and socialization, teaching, history, research, press, environment, culture, institutions. L. Durand, 'Un coulòqui pèr li lengo d'Europo à l'UNESCO. Diversita culturalo e plurilinguisme', *PrA*, 146, 2000:3, reviews an April 2001 colloquium organized by the BELMR (Burèu Euroupen di Lengo li Mens Espandido). E. Hammel, 'L'action publique en faveur de l'occitan. Paramètres et contraintes', *AIEO 6*, 102–15, reports on the fruits of his 13 years of work in the Languedoc-Roussillon region. E. Ros, 'L'occitan dins la vita publica', *PN*, 89, 2000:3–4, reviews various manifestations of Occitan in the public sector, e.g., the home page of the Lycée Montaigne in Bordeaux and the *Servici de la lenga occitana* run by the Université Paul-Valéry in Montpellier. According to R. Bistolfi, 'Langues régionales: l'enlise-ment?' *LSPS*, 142, 2000:54–55, some 79% of the French public appeared ready to accept a modification of their constitution to permit application of the Charter for Regional Languages. H. Stroh, 'L'Occitan e la cultura francesa', *Canta Grelh* (Rodez), 43, 2000:6–9, concludes that knowledge of French alone does not ensure knowledge of French culture.

ORTHOGRAPHY. Jacques Taupiac, **L'Occitan moderne*, Puylaurens, IEO Sector de linguistica–the author, 127 pp., despite its title, is a look at Alibert's norm for '*e* de sosteniment', allowed in learned words but disallowed in popular words, e.g. *mond modèrn*, as against *monde modèrne* preferred by Taupiac, Teulat, and others. Anon., 'Per l'unitat grafico de la lengo d'Oc', *Lou Païs* (Montpellier), 359 suppl., 2000:11, presents details of Jean-Claude Bouvier's new 'Grafio Unitario', based on Alibert for consonants, Mistral for vowels. J. Taupiac discusses spelling readjustments in 'Les événements qui avoient lieu', *L'Occitan*, 151:8, and concludes in 'Nòrma e prestigi d'una lenga', *ib.*, 152:8, that spelling should indeed be aligned on pronunciation. Id., 'Règlas d'accentuaction', *ib.*, 153:11, reviews cases in which the tonic syllable is penultimate, ultimate (i.e., consonant final), and exceptions. T. differentiates homophones, homographs, and homonyms in 'Los ononims (prononciatz [lous oumounims])', *ib.*, 154:7. M. Audoièr, 'Grafia e ideologia', *ib.*, 152:6, calls for a change in the attitude of the Conselh de la Lenga Occitana, and a spelling for the language that is 'nacionala, englobanta, fonetica'. J. Lafitte, 'Autes toponimes (1). Occitania o Occitània? [*Occitania*]; Auvèrnia o Auvèrnha?[*Auvèrnia*]', *LDGM*, 16, 2000:41–42. C. Rapin, 'Nòstra lenga: Grecismes simplificats', *Lo Lugarn* (Agen), 72, 2000:2, summarizes the principles for spelling words from Greek, e.g., *crestian, idraulic*.

PHONETICS AND PHONOLOGY. T. Meisenburg, 'À propos des caractéristiques prosodiques de l'occitan', *AIEO 6*, 553–60, studies stress in Occitan within its Romance context, both diachronic and synchronic.

MORPHOSYNTAX. R. Teulat looks at 'Las variantas dins l'occitan federal', *GS*, 33, no. 474:301–06 and *ib.*, no. 478:493–98, as he proposes three categories of acceptable variants in verb morphology. A. Lagarda, 'La répétition', *Camins d'Estiu* (Hautefage-la-Tour), 79, 2000:27–28, examines various types of reinforcement through repetition of noun, pronoun, verb, and adverb, e.g., *lèu-lèu* 'bien vite'. Id., 'La préposition *per*', *ib.*, 80, 2000:29–30, sees how usage, e.g., *un ostal per vendre*, frequently differs from French. C. Rapin, 'Nòstra lenga: los distributius', *Lo Lugarn*, 74, 2000:20, contrasts gasc. *qu'avem sengles frairs* with lang. *avèm cadun un fraire*. C. Laux, '*Un desenat, un quinzenat*', *L'Occitan*, 150:7, points out that for quantities and units of measure, two suffixes are available, e.g., *un ponhat/una ponhada*. Id., 'Falses amics', *ib.*, 151:7, details various uses of *tornar* vis-à-vis Fr. *tourner*, with further discussion in '*Virar, escotar*', *ib.*, 152:7. F. Carbona, 'Ont cal plaçar les pronoms?', *GS*, 33, no. 482:132–35, argues eloquently for *te vòli dire que . . .*, as against *vòli te dire*. Florian Vernet, **Dictionnaire grammatical de l'occitan moderne*, Montpellier, Université Paul Valéry, 400 pp.

LEXIS AND LEXICOLOGY. M. Grosclaude, 'Jorn, dia . . .', *PG*, 198, 2000:5–6, proposes a sample article for a possible pan-Occitan dictionary, his encyclopedia approach covering variants, geographical distribution, etymology, days of the week and their derivatives, synonyms, antonyms, and astronomical equivalents. J. Fay, 'Segonda lenga romana', *La Cabreta*, 159, 2000:3–5, presents a glossary of general Occitan neologisms for today's living, e.g., *la dimenjada* for 'weekend'. C. Laux briefly reviews typical uses of diminutives in various lexical fields, e.g., clothing, food, body in 'Diminutius', *L'Occitan*, 146, 2000:7. Id., '*Lac, laus, laux*', *ib.*, 155:7.

In his series 'L'Occitan blos', J. Taupiac details a number of lexical items: 'L'arma', *ib.*, 152:8; 'L'eurò', *ib.*, 153:8; 'Los mòrts e dimarts', *ib.*, 154:8, both words in which [r] is final; 'L'èuro e lo deute', *ib.*, 155:8, pointing out that stress and post-vocalic position make a true consonant of the 'u' of *èuro*.

PARTICULAR SEMANTIC FIELDS. G. Bonifassi, 'Le vocabulaire guerrier dans *Toloza* et dans la *Chanson de la Croisade*. Etude comparative', *FL*, 131, 2000:9–34. Félix Gras was evidently familiar with the original version of the *Chanson de la Croisade* when he composed *Toloza* (1881).

ONOMASTICS. A. Lagarda, 'Les noms de famille occitans', *GS*, 478, 2000:483–88, provides a sample entry from the author's work-in-progress, a pan-Occitan dictionary of personal names. Georges Gibelin, *Que signifie votre nom? Étude onomastique des noms de famille originaires des pays d'oc*, Spéracèdes, TAC Motifs, 2000, 216 pp.

SOCIOLINGUISTICS. P. Martel, 'La grand paur dels ben-parlants', *RevO*, 8, 1999:81–97, asks what will happen to the 1000-year-old tradition of linguistic 'unity' in France, and says that many fear the answer. N. Sano, 'Un regard sur le francitan — une brève enquête', *AIEO 6*, 597–610, considers diglossia and code-switching, giving a presentation of the current situation of *francitan* 'contact des langues entre le français et l'occitan', focusing here on vocabulary collected in Montpellier in 1997. A. Rafanell and A. Rossich, 'La langue occitane dans la Catalogne du XVIIIe siècle', *Lengas*, 48, 2000:45–65, study Antoni de Bastero (1700–1750) and his vision of Catalan, Provençal, *lemosi*, and *valenciana* as a single language. L. Fornés, 'Lo filològ Michel Ventura Balanyà, una nòrma per lo diasistèma occitanò-roman', *AIEO 6*, 535–54, describes the little-known work of Ventura Balanyà (1878–1930), to whom is dedicated the first volume of Perbòsc's *Revista Occitana* (1903), and who taught Romance languages at Cornell, among other posts. A. Penella i Ramon, 'El dialecte romànic ilerdo-valentí i la seua relació amb el diasistema occitano-romànic', *PdO*, 4:7–19, concludes that 'el català sembla ser una evolució tardana del llenguadocià convergent amb l'ilerdo-valentí'.

TEXTS. J.-L. Pouliquen reflects on Jacques Audiberti's final novel, *Dimanche m'attend*, with the novelist's claims to 'Un *oc* à soi', *Oc*, 334–35, 2000:64–66. M. Poitavin describes the playful aspects of 'Le feuilleton parodique de Florian Vernet', *Lengas*, 48, 2000:67–88.

4. GASCON AND BÉARNAIS

GENERAL. I. Loubère, 'De la grand-mère à la scène: formes de tradition de la langue occitane en Gascogne', *Garona*, 15, 1999:127–38. In this survey, male subjects' attitude toward their Occitan identity was linked to language. J. Antoine asks, 'Comment peut-on être gascon?', *Lou Païs*, 66:6–8. Patrice Poujade, *Identités et solidarités dans les Pyrénées. Essai sur les relations humaines, XVI-XIXe siècle*, Aspet, PyréGraph, 2000, 202 pp.

ORTHOGRAPHY. J. Lafitte and J. Ensergueix, 'Toponimes gascons (3)', *LDGM*, 15, 2000:31–33, details spellings for Hautes-Pyrénées, Ariège, and Gers. This is continued in part 4, *ib*., 16, 2000:37–41 (Comminges, Couserans; Médoc). J. Lafitte, 'Noter le –[n] des 3èmes et 6èmes personnes', *ib*., 15, 2000:34–40, argues further for use of 'nn' (as in *Jann*, *Agenn*, etc.). Id. proposes to clarify the use of 'x' in the Gascon of Médoc, *ib*., 42–43, through the study of older texts. Id., 'Grafia e lo gascon', *ib*., 44–46, continues his reaction to various solutions proposed for Gascon spellings, e.g., accentuation of third-person plurals. Id. muses further on *ò* or *òc*? *Felibridge* or *Felibritge*?, in 'Autes punts de grafia', *ib*., 46–48, then treats *pèrcha*, *gallés*, *Gertz*, *pèd* in *ib*., 16, 2000:45–48. G. Nariòo presents 27 examples of 'L'utilisation du trait d'union dans les mots composés', *PG*, 200, 2000:99–10.

PHONETICS AND PHONOLOGY. J. Lafitte, 'Les consonantas amudidas en finau atòne', *LDGM*, 15, 2000:40–41.

MORPHOSYNTAX. C. D. Pusch, 'Aperçu de la subordination relative en gascon: variation morphologique et particularités fonctionnelles', *AIEO 6*, 571–82, concludes that certain hesitations in Gascon relative subordination, e.g., *de que/ de qui* are usefully clarified by diachronic and synchronic comparison with Spanish and other Romance languages. M. Grosclaude, 'Deux pronoms compléments de la 3e personne qui se suivent', *PG*, 199, 2000:11–12, discusses the parallel Gascon systems in *–ac* and *–i* (*que l'ac balhi/ que li balhi* 'je le lui donne'), which continue to resist neat formulation. G. Nariòo, 'Que serí poduda entrar en quauque banca', *ib*., 198, 2000:7, recommends gasc. *en*, not **dins*, the latter reserved for use within a limited time or space. Id., 'Branas totas esperlits', *ib*., 199, 2000:13, outlines the pan-Occitan rule of agreement, e.g., *tota sola*. Id., 'Que parla tostemps de si medish', *ib*., 200, 2000:11, rules for *si medish* after preposition, but *eth medish* elsewhere, e.g., *que s'ac hè eth medish*. Id., 'Que cau que bévias vin tot dia', *ib*., 201, 2000:14, studies *caler* followed by noun, infinitive, or subjunctive mood. J. Lafitte, '*–ra()*, desinéncia deu "futur deu passat"', *LDGM*, 15, 2000:30, notes that this tense, e.g., *que's demandava se vengora* 'il se demandait s'il viendrait', is not included in Michel Grosclaude and Gilabèrt Narioo's *Répertoire des conjugaisons occitanes de Gascogne*, 1999 (see *YWMLS*, 62:208). J. Lafitte, 'Tornar ta la nòrma: *escade-s'i*', *ib*., 16, 2000:43–44, looks at various cases of enclisis with personal pronouns, e.g., *que sabossetz separar-ve'n*.

LEXIS AND LEXICOLOGY. J. Lafitte, 'Lexic gascon e lexic occitan', *LDGM*, 16, 2000:8–9. Id., 'Sus un escanilh de l'"enciclopedia occitana"', *ib*., 10–14. Id., 'Pecas deu *Palay*', *ib*., 15–17. Id. discusses various problems asociated with translations into Gascon in 'Vocabulari mesclat. (i) *espèr*, *espèrr*, *esper[r]*, *ahida/hida/hisa*; (ii) *envielhir* 'vieillir'; (iii) *gal[l]ès* 'gaulois/gallois', *ib*., 23–35.

PARTICULAR SEMANTIC FIELDS. J. Lafitte, '*La cot*: "la peau, la couenne"', *LDGM*, 15, 2000:11, corrects Lespy's reading of *cot* as 'unit of measure'. Id., '*Lo cot, lo code*: "le coude, le coin, la coudée"', *ib.*, 12–18; and further thumbnail sketches of Gascon vocabulary, *ib.*, 22–29. Id., 'Un glossari d'arquitectura religiosa', *ib.* 16, 2000:19–22, reflects on possible additions to the 84-item Gascon vocabulary of religious architecture presented by M. Grosclaude in 'Entà visitar ua glèisa', *PG*, 199, 2000:6.

ONOMASTICS. N. Rei-Bèthvéder, 'Artics, ciutat bilingua', *Reclams*, 779, 2000:5–7, gives the background to the all-Occitan sign-posting of Artix. B. Casenave proposes 41 terms for street names and roadsigns as used in Artix and Bordes: 'Senhalizacion occitana: vocabulari, toponimia, istòria', *PG*, 201, 2000:2. M. Grosclaude, 'Le *Pont-Long*', *ib.*, 9–10, proposes PONTUM LONGUM as etymon for this unusual geographical depression near Pau airport. Michel Grosclaude and Jean-François Le Nail, **Dictionnaire toponymique des communes des Hautes-Pyrénées*, Tarbes, Ràdio País Bigòrra–Conseil Général des Hautes-Pyrénées, 2000, 348 pp. Osmin Ricau, **Histoire des noms de famille d'origine gasconne: l'exemple de la Bigorre*, Pau, Princi Néguer, 2000, 137 pp. Nicolas Rey-Bèthbéder, **Noms des lieux-dits de Saint-Lys*, Saint-Lys, Assoc. País de Catinou e Jacouti NS Loubatières, 2000, 60 pp.

SUBDIALECTS. 'Aran, vallée occitane', *BIO*, 29–30, 2000:5. Immigrants to the Val d'Aran, now more than 50% of the population, must learn the language if it is to be preserved.

5. SOUTHERN OCCITAN

LANGUEDOCIEN (INCLUDING S. PÉRIG.)

GENERAL. **Atlas du Parc National des Cévennes*, Florac, Atelier Technique des Espaces Naturels-Edater, 1999, 72 pp.

LEXIS AND LEXICOLOGY. Christian Laux, *Diccionari occitan-francés (lengadocian)*, Puylaurens, IEO-Tarn, 624 pp., provides, in addition to its 36,000 lexical entries, a table of proper names by Serge Granier (605–21), rules for pronunciation, an abridged grammar of the modern language, conjugation tables, and maps. This is a fitting complement to the late author's *Diccionari francés-occitan*, 2nd ed., 2000 (see *YWMLS*, 62:210). **Trésor de notre langue de Lacaune-Murat, dictionnaire occitan-français*, Nages (Tarn), Centre de Recherche du Patrimoine de Rieumontagné, 1999, 84 pp. Rémy Chastel and Emile Tichet present their new **Dictionnaire français-occitan-dialecte gévaudanais*, St-Sauveur-de-Peyre, L'Escolo Gabalo, 2000, xix + 360 pp.

PARTICULAR SEMANTIC FIELDS. J. Fulhet, 'Pichòt bestiari roergas, a basa d'expressions idiomaticas' (1), *Oc*, 336, 2000:33–35; (2), *ib.*

337, 2000 : 36–37; (3), *ib.*, 338 : 38–39, draws on the linguistic atlas of the Massif Central, several dictionaries, and personal surveys.

ONOMASTICS.   A. Lagarda, **Rivel (Aude) et ses environs, les noms de lieux, la géographie, la tradition et l'histoire*, Carbonne, the author, 96 pp.

SOCIOLINGUISTICS.   P. Gardy and J.-F. Courouau, *'Une signalisation bilingue français-occitan dans un village languedocien: mise en oeuvre et réception', pp. 251–69 of *Noms et re-noms: la dénomination des personnes, des populations, des langues et des territoires*, Rouen, Publications de l'Université de Rouen, 1999, 287 pp. G. Caillat, 'L'usage du français en Cévennes à l'époque moderne', *LiCC*, 116, 1999 : 1–6, sees that while Occitan and Protestantism go hand-in-hand in this area, the Réforme actually furthered the spread of French in the Midi.

TEXTS.   Christian-Pierre Bedel continues the series 'Al Canton' published in Rodez by the Mission Départementale de la Culture: **Bèlmont, Montlaur, Monés-Proencós, Murasson, Reborguil, Sent-Sever*, 1999, 256 pp. **Peiralèu, La Cressa, Mostuèjols, Ribièira, La Ròca, Sent-Andriu, Vairau*, 1999, 270 pp. **Laissac, Bertolena, Cossèrgas, Cruèjols, Galhac, Palmàs, Severac, Vimenet*, 2000, 312 pp. **Requistar, Connac, Durenca, Ledèrgas, Rutlac, La Sèlva, Sent-Jan.* / *Réquista, Connac, Durenque, Lédergues, Rulhac-Saint-Cirq, Saint-Jean-Delnous, La Selve*, with preface by Dominique Azam, 2000, 310 pp.

PAREMIOLOGY.   M. Dussol, 'Moun paire disié', runs through four successive issues of *Lou Païs*: 362, 2000 : 65; 363, 2000 : 89; 364, 2000 : 120; 365, 2000 : 145. Anon., 'Prouvèrbis agricolos', *ib.*, 19.

PROVENÇAL

GENERAL.   G. Achard-Bayle, 'Y a-t-il une ou plusieurs Provence(s)? Représentations ordinaires et discours savants', *AIEO 6*, 497–511, examines multiple world views of Provence, using lexical, orthographical, and morphosyntactic markers in well-known literary works. A. Compan, opining that not all Jacobinism comes from Paris, offers a short pro-Provençal piece on 'Lènga e dialèite', *L'Astrado*, 35, 2000 : 105–15.

ORTHOGRAPHY.   P. Pessemesse, *AIEO 6*, 561–70, studies 'Evolucion dei grafias e dei mentalitats (1840–1890) vista a travèrs deis òbras deis escrivans provençaus d'Ate' within the totality of writings published in *Le Mercure Aptésien* (1839–1925).

LEXIS AND LEXICOLOGY.   Reinat Toscano, **Biais de dire — Façons de parler*, Belin-Beliet, Princi Néguer, 2000, 36 pp.

PARTICULAR SEMANTIC FIELDS.   J.-L. Domenge, 'Vocabulaire provençal du ver à soie', *AVEPB*, 96.2, 2000 : 39–40.

SUBDIALECTS. H. Barberis, 'Le vocabulaire du boucher en dialecte mentonasque', *OPM*, 94, 2000:27. R. Mari-Gastaldi, 'Proverbes du vieux Menton', *ib.*, 95, 2000:22. J. Chirio details words in Nissart for the millenium, e.g., *mile/mila, darrié sècoulou/siècle*, in 'D'un milenari à l'autre', *LSPS*, 139, 1999:45. J. Garavagno, *'Lu bastian countrari*. De l'importance de l'accent tonique', *ib.*, 140, 2000:49, further illustrates phonemic word stress in *nissart*, e.g., *coulera* 'colère' vs *coulerà* 'choléra', with additional instalments in *ib.*, 145:47; and *ib.* 146:47.

TEXTS. R. Bertrand, 'Un discours en provençal à Gardanne', *PrH*, 50, no. 202, 2000:471–73, gives the text of a short speech apparently given in June 1793 by a *commissaire de la paix* travelling through Provence on behalf of the *mouvement sectionnaire de Marseille*.

6. NORTHERN OCCITAN

LIMOUSIN (INCLUDING N. PÉRIG.)

GENERAL. Christian Bonnet edits *La Lenga d'aur. L'occitan, patrimoine linguistique de Poitou-Charentes. Etudes sur la langue et la littérature*, La Couronne, Conversa occitana–IEO-Charente, 155 pp., with bibliographies of Limousin language (146–49) and civilization (150–53); L. Jagueneau, 'L'occitan de Charente: principaux traits linguistiques' (25–39); and previously published papers by Bonnet, G. Gonfroy, J. Roux, Y. Lavalade, and others. The volume appeared in connection with a colloquium at Chabanais in May 2001 devoted to François Rempnoux. J.-F. Vinhau interviews I. Lavalada in '30 Ans d'accion occitana en Lemosin', *Occitans!*, 98, 2000:6–7. J. Nouillac, 'Histoire de Tulle (1). Les origines de Tulle et de son monastère', *Lemouzi*, 155, 2000:6–18, continued in (2) *ib.*, 156, 2000:51–62, with a selection of reprinted writings by P. Maureille, R. de Cosnac, and others (63–65).

MORPHOSYNTAX. Jean Roux, **Per aprener l'occitan: précis de conjugaison (limousin)*, is a special number of *PN*, 2000.

LEXIS AND LEXICOLOGY. Gilbert Pasty, *Glossaire des dialectes marchois et haut limousin de la Creuse*, Châteauneuf-sur-Loire, Brezenty, 1999, 253 pp.

ONOMASTICS. Yves Lavalade, *Dictionnaire toponymique de la Haute-Vienne*, Saint-Paul, Lucien Souny, 2000, 680 pp., details more than 10,000 toponyms from 200 communes. E. Théron, 'L'histoire de Tulle à travers ses fontaines (X), Le Trech (1), 'La fontaine Villeneuve', *Lemouzi*, 154, 2000:108–10; (2) 'La "fontaine des amoureux"', *ib.*, 155, 2000:19–27. J. Ros, 'Périgueux', *PN*, 89, 2000:21–22, proposes 'Perigüers' to continue attested spellings from the Renaissance. See also Id., 'La fòrma occitana dau nom de *Périgueux*', *Lo Bornat*, 2000, no. 4:26–28.

AUVERGNAT (INCLUDING N. PÉRIG.)

PAREMIOLOGY. J. M. Maurí presents 25 proverbs in 'Biais de dire del Nòrd-Cantal', *Lo Convise*, 29, 2000:16; *ib.*, 30, 2000:19; *ib.*, 31, 2000:19. A. Vermenosa, 'Relevat d'expressions e aforismes', *ib.*, 31, 2000:26–27, presents sayings collected by the founder of the Auvergnat Felibrige. R. Toscano, 'Comptinas', *ib.*, 32, 2000:16, gives two children's rhymes on the subject of hares, with an accompanying version in Nissart. Z. Bòsc, 'Los provèrbis sus la castanha e lo castanhièr', *L'Esquilon* (Rodez), 66, 2000:7–9.

PROVENÇAL ALPIN

ONOMASTICS. Marziano Di Maio, **Guida dei toponimi di Bardonecchia e frazioni. Dran k'lä sië tro tar. Bardonecchia* (I Quaderni di Bardonecchia, 2), Pinerolo, Alzani, 2000, 151 pp., lists more than 850 toponyms in the area of *Bardunàicë* alone.

SUBDIALECTS. J.-C. Rixte, 'Le dictionnaire de Louis Moutier: sa genèse et la question de son utilisation par Mistral', *AIEO 6*, 583–96, gives an *historique* of this still-unpublished dictionary, supplemented by the 33 pages of bibliography for Moutier (186–218) listed in R.'s *Textes et auteurs drômois de langue d'oc*, IEO-Drôme and Daufinat-Provença, Tèrra d'òc, 2000, 311 pp. Charles Botton, Jean Gaber, and Albert Bianco, **Eu saoueudjinn. Le Parler de Saorge: mots, expressions, dictons, traditions, anecdotes, recettes*, Breil-sur-Roya, Cabri, 2000, 261 pp., with CD. **Atlante linguistico ed etnografico del Piemonte occidentale*, Vol. 4, *Bibliografia* [part 1, to 1996], ed. Paola Tirone, Alessandria, dell'Orso, 1999.

SOCIOLINGUISTICS. Pierre Pasquini, **Des immigrés au croisement des langues. Entre dialetto, occitan provençal et français: les italiens de Noves au XXe siècle*, Canet, Llibres del Trabucaire, 2000, 200 pp.

PAREMIOLOGY. Paola Dessolis, **Raccolta di proverbi e detti popolari nella conca di Bardonecchia* (I Quaderni di Bardonecchia, 1), Pinerolo, Alzani, 2000, 206 pp.

LITERATURE

By MIRIAM CABRÉ, *Universitat de Girona*, and SADURNÍ MARTÍ, *Universitat de Girona*

1. RESEARCH TOOLS

W. Pfeffer, 'Bibliography of Occitan literature for 1999', *Tenso*, 16:97–129, follows an author/topic classification. *Arnaut: rassegna di filologia occitana*, ed. Massimiliano De Conca, <www.arnaut.it>, includes annotated lists of recent scholarship arranged by broad topics. Two CD-ROMs generate concordances of the full lyrical troubadour corpus: *Trobadors: concordanze della lirica trobadorica*, ed. Rocco Distilo, Rome, Sismel–Galluzzo; and Peter Ricketts et al., *Concordance de l'Occitan Médiéval (COM)*, Turnhout, Brepols. Two further projects on Access troubadour databases are presented by S. Asperti and F. Zinelli, 'Bibliografia elettronica dei trovatori (BedT), *Le Médiéviste et l'ordinateur*', 39, <irht.cnrs-orleans.fr/meto/MO39_musique_et_poesie1.htm>; and K. Klingebiel, 'Littérature perdue des troubadours', *AIEO 6*, 213–21. *Rialto*, <www.rialto.unina>, bears the first tests of a full-text repertoire, with some ad hoc editions. Original or corrected Occitan editions are also found in the *Biblioteca* of the *Repertorio informatizzato dell'antica letteratura catalana* <www.rialc.unina.it>.

2. EDITIONS AND TEXTUAL CRITICISM

Paolo Gresti, *Il trovatore Uc Brunenc: edizione critica con commento, glossario e rimario*, Tübingen, Niemeyer, xlviii + 150 pp., complements the edition of Uc's *cansos* (turn of the 12th c.) with Daude de Pradas' *planh* for his death. Miquel Pujol, *Poesia occitanocatalana de Castelló d'Empúries: recull de poemes de final del segle XIII i primer terç del XIV*, Figueres, Institut d'Estudis Empordanesos — Girona, Patronat Francesc Eiximenis, 382 pp., edits 21 poems (some extremely fragmentary) found in notary books. *Contributions à l'étude de l'ancien occitan: textes lyriques et non-lyriques en vers*, ed. Peter T. Ricketts, Birmingham, AIEO, 2000, 118 pp., critically edits some *COM* texts (see above), notably the corpus of Peire Lunel and the *Novas de l'heretge*. The usefulness of *COM* as an editorial tool is exemplified in Id., 'Peire Bremon Ricas Novas, problèmes lexicologiques', *FL*, 129, 1999:161–69. J. Gourc, 'Le retour d'Azemar', *AIEO 6*, 405–10, adds a new poem from MS z to his 1991 edition. C. Di Girolamo, 'Pir meu cor allegrari', *BCSS*, 19:5–21, includes a new edition of the *cobla* PC 461.97. A. Wanono,

'Où l'on reparle de la reine Esther: essai d'interprétation lexico-logique à partir d'une parodie hébraïco-provençale de Crescas du Caylar (c. 1327)', *FL*, 129, 1999:349–78, reinterprets obscure passages by rethinking transliteration problems. L. Barbieri, 'Pour une nouvelle édition du troubadour Arnaut de Maruelh', *AIEO 6*, 141–56, focuses on assessing doubtful attributions on metrical grounds. W. Mèliga, 'Une nouvelle édition du troubadour Gaucelm Faidit', *ib.*, 236–43, announces a forthcoming Lachmannian edition and discusses poem order. L. Milone, 'Contini filologo: per un capitolo de la cultura italiana del secondo doppoguerra', *Humanitas*, 56.1:734–46, exemplifies ecdotic discussion with excerpts from his forthcoming edition of Raimbaut d'Aurenga.

Other articles on specific aspects of textual transmission include M. Perugi, 'Variantes de tradition et variantes d'auteur dans la chanson XII (BdT 29,8) d'Arnaut Daniel', *FL*, 129, 1999:115–50; M. De Conca, 'Raimbaut d'Aurenga ed Arnaut Daniel nel ms. C (BN, Paris, fr. 856): alcuni spunti lessicologici', *RPh*, 54:57–70; G. Vallín, 'Lo vers del novel chan', *Romania*, 475–76:506–17; and I. de Riquer and M. Gómez Muntané, 'La *desdansa* de Sant Joan de les Abadesses: édition philologique et musicale', *Tyssens Vol.*, 389–401, who complete this collection of *dansas* thanks to the recovery of a manuscript lost in the 1930s.

Several articles focus on a single manuscript: S. G. Nichols, 'L'orgueil du manuscript: sur un chansonnier des troubadours', Berchtold, *Dragonetti*, 73–88, on the layout of MS N, which results in a dialogue between William IX and the *trobairitz*; G. Noto, 'Il canzoniere provenzale P: problemi e prospettive di studio', *AIEO 6*, 244–53, highlights the filiation of *vidas* and the relationship of MSS P and S as fruitful lines of research; A. Touber, 'Troubadours — siciliens — Minnesänger: le manuscrit P (Firenze, BML, Pl. xli 42)', *ib.*, 254–69, finds clues to suggest Dante knew this manuscript. I. Zamuner, 'Le fonti della sezione V2 del canzoniere provenzale marciano', *ib.*, 278–97, attributes this section to a 14th-c. Italian scribe. *Canzonieri iberici*, ed. Patrizia Botta, Carmen Parrilla, and Ignacio Pérez Pascual, 2 vols., Corunna, Toxosoutos, 358, 399 pp., has three articles on troubadour Catalan MSS: M. Cabré, 'Un cançoner de Cerverí de Girona?' (I, 283–99), S. Ventura, 'Le scelte d'autore operate dal compilatore del ms. Sg' (I, 271–82) and A. Alberni, 'Notes per a una reconstrucció codicològica del *Cançoner Vega-Aguiló* (BdC, mss. 7 i 8)' (I, 301–11).

One of the articles in 'Miscellanea occitanica' (*RLaR*, 105.2, 2000) reconstructs the original fascicle structure of the *Flamenca unicum*: N. Togni, 'Les lacunes du manuscrit de *Flamenca*' (379–97). M.-A. Bossy, 'Alphonse le Sage et la compilation des oeuvres de Guiraut

Riquier', *AIEO 6*, 180–88, investigates the aims and sources of Riquier's songbook.

3. CULTURAL AND HISTORICAL BACKGROUND

Boitani, *Produzione*, II, maps the cultural output of Catalan-Occitan courts in three very useful studies: W. Mèliga, 'L'Aquitania trobadorica' (201–51), S. Vatteroni, 'Le corti della Francia meridionale' (353–98), and A. Espadaler, 'La Catalogna dei re' (873–933). Fredric L. Cheyette, *Ermengard of Narbonne and the World of the Troubadours*, Ithaca, Cornell U.P., xiii + 474 pp., describes the political and social context of Ermengard's court, focusing on the language of feudal love. R. Harvey, 'Occitan extravagance at the court assembly of Beaucaire in 1174', *CN*, 61:55–74, reinterprets this festival as a public political gesture by the count of Toulouse. Nicole M. Schulman, *Where Troubadours Were Bishops: The Occitania of Folc of Marseille (1150–1231)*, NY–London, Routledge, 256 pp., sketches contemporary society while following Folquet de Marselha's twisted career. R. Lafont, 'Les trois espaces de l'épique occitane médiévale: essai de synthèse', *AIEO 6*, 448–57, investigates the role of Cluny monasteries in epic creation. *Cahiers de Fanjeaux*, 35, 2000, is devoted to 'Église et culture en France méridionale (XII-XIV siècles)': of especial note is G. Passerat, 'L'église et la poésie: les débuts du Consistori del Gay Saber' (443–73), who vindicates Molinier as a capable and learned author. Also on the impact of religious culture on troubadours is B. Saouma, 'L'humilité et l'orgeuil chez Saint Bernard et les troubadours', *FL*, 129, 1999:339–48; and N. Unlandt, 'Sur les rapports entre l'ordre de Cîteaux et les troubadours', *AIEO 6*, 487–93. L. Paterson, 'Gender negotiations in France during the central Middle Ages: the literary evidences', Linehan, *Medieval World*, 246–65, includes troubadour texts as lay sources.

4. POETRY

Paden, *Genres*, reconsiders the validity of genre studies and includes W. D. Paden, 'The system of genres in troubadour lyric' (21–67), who surveys diachronic diversity; E. W. Poe, 'Coblerai car mi platz: the role of the *cobla* in the Old Occitan tradition' (68–94); R. T. Pickens, 'The Old Occitan arts of poetry and the early troubadour lyric' (209–41), who focuses on the genre system of pre-1180 troubadours; J. Dagenais, 'Genre and demonstrative rhetoric: praise and blame in the *Razos de trobar* and the *Doctrina de compondre dictats*' (242–54), discussing the role of demonstrative rhetoric in troubadour reception; D. Kelly, 'The poem as art of poetry: the rhetoric of imitation in the grand chant courtois' (191–208), analysing *canso* as a mock dialectic case; E. Aubrey, 'Genre as determinant of melody in the songs of the troubadours and the trouvères' (273–96), emphasizing the *trivium* tradition. *John L. Grigsby, *The Gab as a Latent Genre in Medieval French Literature: Drinking and Boasting in the Middle Ages*, Cambridge, Mass, Medieval Academy of America, 2000, ix + 255 pp., includes discussion on some Occitan *gabs*.

Several articles in *Il genere tenzone nelle letterature romanze delle origini (Atti del convegno internazionale, Losanna, 1997)*, ed. Matteo Pedroni and Antonio Stäuble, Ravenna, Longo, 1999, 533 pp., are concerned with Occitan texts: P. Allegretti, 'Il sonetto dialogato due-trecentesco: l'intercisio e le sue origini gallo-romanze' (73–109); M. Gally, 'Entre sens et non sens: approches comparatives de la *tenso* d'oc et du *jeu-parti* arrageois' (223–35); D. Billy, 'Pour une réhabilitation de la terminologie des troubadours: tenson, partimen et expressions synonymes' (237–313); F. Zufferey, 'Tensons réelles et tensons fictives au sein de la littérature provençale' (315–28); M.-C. Gérard-Zai, 'La forme dialogique dans *Las Novas del papagay* occitanes' (329–39); P. Gresti, 'Un nuovo trovatore italiano? Osservazioni sul partiment tra Aycard de Fossat e Girard Cavalaz, *Si paradis et enfernz son aital* (BdT 6a.1)' (341–54); M. Cabré, 'Du genre débat dans l'oeuvre de Cerverí de Girona' (363–77). Pierre Bec, *La Jouste poétique: de la tenson médiévale aux débats chantés traditionnels*, Paris, Les Belles Lettres, 2000, 521 pp., sets Occitan debates within world literature. Other articles focus on a specific troubadour genre: M. Brea, '"E a vos aug son escondig / comtar" (*Judici d'amor*, vv. 1387–88)', *AIEO 6*, 334–42, discusses the meaning of *escondig*; I. de Riquer, 'La *mala dona* chez les troubadours provençaux et les poêtes catalans', *FL*, 129, 1999:171–88; M. de Winter-Hosman, 'Un texte peut en cacher un autre. Intertextualité chez quelques troubadours autour de 1200', *AIEO 6*, 248–54, also deals with *mala canso*; C. Franchi, 'Le procedure della soggettività nelle pastorelle di lingua occitanica', *AION(SR)*, 42, 2000:71–108; P. G. Beltrami, 'Giraut de Borneil, la pastorella "alla provenzale" e il moralismo cortese', *ZFSL*, 111:138–64; P. Uhl, '*Devinalh*: subtradition médiévale ou métatradition médiévistique?', *RevR*, 36:283–96; G. Vallín, 'El estribote románico y una cantiga de Pero da Ponte', *Tyssens Vol.*, 537–47. N. Henrard, 'La Passion d'Augsbourg: un texte dramatique occitan?', *ib.*, 243–56, rereads the *Passion* as the oldest extant fragment of a vernacular Sybil song. G. Tavani, 'Il plurilinguismo nella lirica dei trovatori', Orioles, *Plurilinguismo*, 123–42, analyses this corpus of four Occitan poems.

Métriques du Moyen Age et de la Renaissance', ed. Dominique Billy, Paris, L'Harmattan, 1999, 392 pp., contains several methodological approaches: P. Canettieri, 'Strutture modulari e intertestualità nella lirica dei trovatori' (53–70); R. Pelosini, 'Contraffazione e imitazione metrica nel genere del compianto funebre romanzo' (207–32); and M. Perugi, 'La "licence excusée par la rime"' (233–49). C. Phan, 'Imitation and innovation in an anonymous French contrafactum of Bernart de Ventadorn's *Ara no vei luzir solelh*', *Tenso*, 16:66–96, shows metre and music variations in original and *contrafactum*. Several articles provide identifications, attributions, and intertextual analysis: L. Paterson, 'Syria, Poitou and the reconquista (or tales of the undead): who was the count in Marcabru's *Vers del lavador?*', Phillips, *Second Crusade*, 133–49, can reinterpret and redate the piece by proposing Baldwin of Marash as the 'count' and Occitania as the place of composition. L. Lazzerini, 'Un'ipotesi sul dittico dell'Estornel (con alcune osservazioni in merito d'una nuova edizione di Marcabruno)', *SMV*, 46, 2000:121–66, analyses concomitant Latin texts and interprets Marcabru's as an anti-William IX piece. L. Gizzi, 'Un tassello per *Sobre·l viell trobar e·l novel* (BdT 323, 24): Peire d'Alvernhe e Guglielmo IX', *AION(SR)*, 42, 2000:307–13, detects a strong influence of William IX. M. Bardell, 'The allegorical landscape: Peire Vidal's "Ric Thesaur"', *FS*, 55, 51–65, locates this piece within Peire's debate with the Marquis of Lancia. A. Espadaler, 'El final del *Jaufre* i, novament, Cerverí de Girona', *BRABLB*, 1999–2000: 321–34, proposes new arguments for his 1272–74 dating. S. Guida, 'Trobairitz fantomatiche? I casi Alamanda ed Escaronha', *AIEO 6*, 411–33, researches their relationship with contemporary troubadours. S. Asperti, 'Per "Gossalbo Roitz"', *Tyssens Vol.*, 49–62, identifies this troubadour on the basis of a MS C variant. L. Rossi, '*Carestia*, Tristan, les troubadours et le modèle de saint Paul: encore sur *D'Amors qui m'a tolu a moi* (RS 1664)', *ib.*, 403–19, revisits the identity of *Carestia*. E. Schulze-Busacker, '*Si tots temps vols viure valens e pros* (P.-C. 335, 51a)', *ib.*, 441–57, finds a didactic context that forbids attribution to Cardenal. Sergio Vatteroni publishes the two versions of 'Si tots temps' in <www.rialc.unina.it/obis.si_tots_temps.htm>. G. E. Sansone, 'Una difficile paternità: la tenzone di Peire Duran', *AIEO 6*, 478–86, confirms Peire's authorship by intertextual analysis with his *cansos*. F. Gambino, 'Osservazioni sulle attribuzioni "inverosimili" nella tradizione manoscritta provenzale (I)', *ib.*, 372–90, and her 'Caso, intenzione, parodia: osservazioni sulle attribuzioni 'inverosimili' nella tradizione manoscritta provenzale (II)', *SMV*, 46, 2000:35–84, confirm or discard a number of doubtful attributions. Marie-Noëlle Toury, *Mort et fin'amor dans la poésie d'oc et d'oïl aux XIIe et XIIIe siècles*, Paris, Champion, 346 pp., surveys the evolution of both terms and the emergence of alternative motifs to death by love. S. Gaunt, 'A martyr to love: sacrificial desire in the poetry of Bernart de Ventadorn', *JMEMS*, 31:477–506, uses psychoanalytical tools to explore the interaction of death by love in troubadour and religious texts. V. Bertolucci Pizzorusso, 'La mort de la dame dans les genres lyriques autres que le *planh*', *AIEO 6*, 327–33, surveys this motif; while her 'Strategie testuali per una morte lirica: Belh Deport', *Tyssens Vol.*, 89–102, focuses on Guiraut Riquier's elaboration. G. Gouiran, 'Le Papagai de Flaubert. Réfléxions à propos de la dame de la *Novas del Papagai*', *AIEO 6*, 391–404, critically reviews previous readings. Michael Bernsen, *Die Problematisierung lyrischen Sprechens im Mittelalter: eine Untersuchung zum Diskurswandel der Liebesdichtung von den Provenzalen bis zu Petrarca*, Tübingen, Niemeyer, vii + 366 pp., analyses the stages of subjective self-consciousness in troubadour lyrics (58–167).

5. SCIENTIFIC, DOCTRINAL AND OTHER PROSE TEXTS

C. Léglu, 'Savaric de Mauléon: entre *vidas* et biographies', *AIEO 6*, 458–63, draws the biographic pattern of *vidas* close to private anecdote. E. Schulze-Busacker, 'Les proverbes dans la lyrique occitane', *FL*, 129, 1999:189–210, establishes stages in the use of proverbs from *ornatus* to metareflection. P. T. Ricketts, 'L'éthique de Matfre Ermengaud dans le *Breviari d'Amor*', *AIEO 6*, 464–68, guides us through a comprehensive moral Franciscan reading; and Id., 'Le *Breviari d'amor* de Matfre Ermengaud de Béziers: un texte et une passion', *BSASLB*, 5:17–20, gives a report on the ongoing edition. V. Galent-Fasseur, 'Mort et salut des troubadours: le *Breviari d'amors* de Matfre Ermengaut', *Cahiers de Fanjeaux*, 35, 2000:423–41, views it as a spiritual reinterpretation of the troubadour tradition. G. Hasenohr, 'Un *Donat* de dévotion en langue d'oc du XIIIe siècle: le *Liber divini amoris*', *ib.*, 219–43, analyses a mystical treatise structured by conjugation models. L. Badia, 'Pour la version occitane du *De rerum proprietatibus* de Barthélemy l'Anglais (XIVe siècle)', *AIEO 6*, 310–26, discusses the treatise as part of a vernacular translation programme at Foix. J. Ducos, 'L'écrit scientifique au Moyen Age — langue d'oc et langue d'oïl', *Garona*, 15, 1999:55–71, surveys Occitan translations and finds them a less coherent corpus than the French. Two articles on Boysset's treatises are P. Gautier Dalché, 'Bertrand Boisset et la science', *Cahiers de Fanjeaux*, 35, 2000:261–85; and S. Thiolier-Méjean, 'Arnaut de Villeneuve comme auctoritas dans l'oeuvre de Bertran Boysset d'Arles', *FL*, 130, 2000:7–39.

MODERN PERIOD

POSTPONED

IV. SPANISH STUDIES

LANGUAGE

By STEVEN DWORKIN, *University of Michigan*, and
MIRANDA STEWART, *University of Strathclyde*

1. GENERAL

Introducción a la lingüística española, ed. Manuel Alvar, B, Ariel, 2000, 628 pp., is an uneven collection of chapters on traditional areas such as grammar, syntax, and lexis with few of the developments of the last 30 years included. There is little reference to any linguistics above the level of the sentence and, where there is, it sits uneasily in inappropriate rubrics, for example, text linguistics is touched upon under syntax. Ana María Rodríguez Fernández, *Bibliografía fundamental de la lengua española*, M, Castalia, 2000, 223 pp., is a useful research tool for those working in traditional linguistics. Miranda Stewart, *The Spanish Language Today*, London, Routledge, 1999, 237 pp., takes a sociolinguistic approach to variation and change in the contemporary Spanish language. José Ignacio Hualde, Anton Olarrea, and Anna María Escobar, *Introducción a la lingüística hispánica*, CUP, 371 pp., have provided an introductory text aimed at the US University market covering cognitive approaches to linguistics, phonetics and phonology, morphology, syntax, history of the Spanish language, and language variation. Within the academic writing perspective, Carolina Figueras, *Pragmática de la punctuación*, B, Octaedro, 180 pp., provides a communicatively-based student guide.

Josse de Kock at the University of Salamanca continues to add volumes to his excellent series *Gramática española: enseñanza e investigación*: Rocío Caravedo, *Lingüística de corpus: cuestiones teórico-metodológicas aplicadas al español*, Salamanca U.P., 1999, 286 pp., provides an overview of corpus-building and relevant analytic principles and illustrates these with a selection of studies of different variables. *Lingüística con corpus, 14 aplicaciones al español*, ed. Josse de Kock, Salamanca U.P., 402 pp., is an up-to-date volume bringing together researchers from Spain and abroad who are currently working with a variety of corpora of written and spoken texts. Goedele de Sterck, *II Gramática*, Salamanca U.P., 2000, 381 pp., takes a critical corpus-based approach to looking at *-se, -ra, -ría, -re* in the educated Spanish of seven cities and is consequently able to confirm or deny certain impressionistic views of their use. She shows, for example, that it is often not useful to oppose the Spanish of Spain to that of Latin America and that other variables such as register and mode can be more powerful in explaining usage. Another, more inconclusive, corpus-based study is that of Francisco Fernández and Luz Gil Salom, *Enlaces oracionales y organización retórica del discurso científico en inglés y español*, Valencia U.P., 2000, 132 pp. José R. Gómez Molina, *El español hablado de Valencia: materiales para su estudio 1. Nivel sociocultural alto*, Valencia U.P., 474 pp., provides a transcribed corpus of 24 semi-directed interviews. From the same Val.Es.Co group there is *¿Cómo se comenta un texto oral?*, ed. Antonio Briz, B, Ariel, 2000, 313 pp., which uses one extract from a naturally-occurring corpus to investigate conversational structure, lexis, syntax, prosody, and language contact. This builds on an earlier volume by the same author, *El español coloquial en la conversación*, B, Ariel, 1998, 225 pp., which characterizes naturally-occurring conversation and, using approaches from Europe and America, analyses mainly pragmatic phenomena such as discourse connectors, politeness strategies, and turn management. Leonor Ruiz, *La fraseología del español coloquial*, B, Ariel, 1998, 126 pp., follows an approach broadly grounded in Spanish linguistics in examining the syntax and pragmatics of a similar corpus of naturally-occurring conversations. Santiago Alcoba, *La expresión oral*, B, Ariel, 2000, 203 pp., includes a CD and provides a very useful introduction to pronunciation and intonation as well as illustrating several standard varieties of Spanish.

2. DIACHRONIC STUDIES

Historical Spanish linguistics is paying growing attention to the study of linguistic variation in earlier stages of a language's history. In addition to Ralph Penny's major book (see *YWMLS*, 62 : 218), specialists now have available a study focusing on variation in the early modern language: Kormi Anipa, *A Critical Examination of Linguistic Variation in Golden-Age Spanish*, NY, Lang, 254 pp., uses data culled from 16th-c. and 17th-c. grammars of Spanish and from selected literary texts (especially picaresque novels) to study such variables in verbal morphology as *do/doy/*, *so/soy*, etc; *cayo/caigo*, *trayo/traigo*, etc.; syncope, metathesis, and epenthesis in future stems, plural imperatives (*mirá/mirad*), as well as the opposition *haber/tener* and various address forms (*tú, vos, el/ella, vuestra merced*). D. Tuten, 'Modeling koineization', *ICHL 14*, 325–36, criticizes the models of koineization proposed by J. Siegel and P. Trudgill. Using the history of *leísmo*, he seeks to show that koineization can involve the introduction of new features not found in any of the contributing dialects. The discussion of *leísmo* occupies less than two pages of this paper.

Methodological issues concerning the role of textual parameters (genre, configurations, etc) in diachronic linguistic analysis are the main concern of two important papers: R. Eberenz, '*Los regimientos de peste* a fines de la Edad Media: configuración de un nuevo género textual', Jacob, *Lengua medieval*, 79–96, describes the construction as a textual genre of manuals dealing with the plague as a prelude to the linguistic analysis of these texts and their place in the history of the Spanish language; J. Kabatek, '¿Cómo investigar las tradiciones discursivas medievales? El ejemplo de los textos jurídicos castellanos', *ib.*, 97–132, seeks to define the relation between the creation of new discursive traditions and language change, taking as his data base three different categories of Castilian juridical texts from the 12th and 13th cs. The relevant linguistic distinctions lie in the lexicon, textual markers, sentence types, and their degree of syntactic integration. The paper focuses on methodological considerations more than on linguistic analysis. W. Oesterreicher, 'La "recontextualización" de los géneros medievales como tarea hermenéutica', *ib.*, 199–231, is a dense theoretical and methodological reflection on the hermeneutics of the recontextualization as written language of discourse and the independence of the written text (a process O. labels 'autonomización' from the original oral communicative event). Both processes are essential for a proper diachronic analysis of texts. M. Alvar, 'Historia y lingüística: los *Repartimientos* de la Provincia de Málaga (1485–1496)', *BRAE*, 71:5–44, discusses how these documents can be used to re-examine the spread in the late 15th c. in the Province of Málaga of the linguistic norms radiating from Seville. The *Repartimientos* show that many of the settlers in reconquered Málaga came from western Andalusia. M. Quilis Merín, 'Lectura, escritura y enseñanza en la época de orígenes', Aleza, *Estudios*, 159–71, describes how changes in education and reading and writing practices and techniques impact on textual production in the High Middle Ages in Spain.

3. DIACHRONIC PHONETICS AND PHONOLOGY

C. Pensado, 'Sobre la historia del ensordecimiento final', *ER*, 22, 2000:29–57, examines closely, within a pan-Romance framework, issues relating to the history of devoicing of word-final obstruents in Hispano-Romance. K. Wireback, 'A gradual approach to sibilant + /j/ metathesis in Hispano-Romance', *La corónica*, 30:159–203, examines in great detail the articulatory and acoustic aspects of sibilant + palatal glide metathesis in Spanish, Portuguese, and Catalan and provides evidence to support the analysis of metathesis as a gradual shift. He deals with the divergence of the Portuguese developments of the sequences at issue *vis-à-vis* the situation in Spanish and Catalan. The studies by Pensado and Wireback offer fine examples of the value of applying the insights provided by general phonetics to specific problems in the history of Spanish and Romance. J. M. Chamorro Martínez, 'Los germanos "hermanos" conversos de Sevilla: historia de un cambio fonético-fonológico peninsular', *ALH*, 14:91–117, suggests that the orthographic *h*- of *hermano* represents an aspiration derived from the initial consonant of GERMANUS. Id., 'Cambios fonológicos en las hablas del mediodía peninsular', *RFE*, 81:403–414, presents cases of late medieval and early modern documentation of aspiration of /s/ and consonant gemination. J. Vázquez Obrador, 'Diacronía vocálica en la toponimia de Sobre-monte, Sobrepuerto y Tierra de Biescas (Huesca)', *Alazet*, 12, 2000:201–42, examines the Aragonese evolution of vowels as reflected in local toponymy.

4. DIACHRONIC MORPHOLOGY

M. J. López Bobo, '¿ Por que *suçidió*? Sobre la supuesta inalterabilidad del vocalismo átono', *Verba*, 27, 2000:175–203, studies the evolution of unstressed stem vowels in -*er* verbs in texts ranging from the 13th to 17th cs. Such verbs were subject to unstressed vowel raising by analogy with -*ir* verbs until the 17th c. C. Pensado, 'De nuevo sobre *doy*, *estoy*, *soy* y *voy*', Borrego, *Cuestiones*, 187–96, revisits the question of the offglide observable in these verb forms, which the author had earlier explained as the result of the addition of a paragogic -*e* to avoid an oxytonic verb ending. This study examines and rejects the hypothesis that these forms result from agglutination of the subject pronoun through spreading of the palatal, as in *so yo* > *soy yo* > *soy*. J. Rini, 'The extraordinary survival of Spanish *veía*; another facet of analogy revealed', *HR*, 69:501–25, seeks to explain why imperfect *veía* (based on the O Sp. infinitive *veer*) won out over *vía* (based on *ver*). R.'s solution involves the following analogical chain: *creo : creía*, *leo : leía*, *veo : X* where X = *veía*. R. views this as an example of the analogical retention of an historically older form. K. Anipa, '*Tomad* and *tomá*, etc.: change and continuity in a morphological feature', *MLR*, 95, 2000:389–98, studies the coexistence of formal variants of the second person plural imperative forms as reflected in selected Golden Age grammars and literary texts which attempt to reproduce colloquial usage. This is essentially one of the chapters of his previously cited book. M. Maiden, 'A strange affinity: "perfecto y tiempos afines"', *BHS(L)*, 78:441–64, invokes M. Aronoff's concept of the 'mor-phome' in an effort to explain why so-called Spanish 'irregular' verbs show the same root in the preterite, past subjunctive, and (now obsolete) future subjunctive. The uniformity of the roots at issue reflects an attempt by speakers to render morphological complexity more systematically predictable.

5. DIACHRONIC SYNTAX

The most important contribution of the year is Rolf Eberenz, *El español en el otoño de la Edad Media. Sobre el artículo y los pronombres*, M, Gredos, 486 pp. This excellent book uses a large corpus of late medieval texts to trace and describe the syntactic evolution of the selected constructions in the transition from the medieval to the early modern language. Topics treated include the form of the article before nouns beginning with a vowel, the grammaticalization of *nosotros, vosotros*, forms of address (*tú, vos, vuestra merced*), the use of the so-called neuter *ello*, clitic pronoun placement, pronoun duplication, *leísmo, laísmo, loísmo*, and questions concerning possessives, demonstratives, and indefinite pronouns and adjectives.

The role of grammaticalization processes in language change continues to receive deserved attention. Rena Torres Cacoullos, *Grammaticalization, Synchronic Variation, and Language Contact. A Study of Spanish Progressive –ndo Constructions*, Amsterdam–Philadelphia, Benjamins, 252 pp., uses data from Old Spanish and contemporary Mexican and New Mexican Spanish to develop a grammaticalization account of variation and change over time in progressive constructions. Two excellent studies by C. Company Company illustrate how Romance diachronic studies can advance through the application of insights provided by recent work on language change. Her 'Gramaticalización, debilitamiento semántico y reanálisis. El posesivo como artículo en la evolución sintáctica del español', *RFE*, 81 : 49–87, offers a detailed study of the grammaticalization processes by which possessives in Spanish underwent a weakening of their anaphoric and deictic values and became mere clitic determiners, becoming essentially functional equivalents of the definite article. This functional equivalency led to the end of the typical medieval construction *el mi libro*. In 'Multiple dative-marking grammaticalization. Spanish as a special kind of primary object language', *StLa*, 25 : 1–47, C. seeks to provide diachronic evidence from Spanish on how a language acquires primary object properties. Spanish has been undergoing a series of syntactic changes by which a grammaticalization process reinforces dative object marking as a prime argument in the history of Spanish. Spanish is passing from being a direct object–indirect object language to becoming a primary object–secondary object type language.

The role of textual parameters in diachronic linguistic analysis is the subject of several essays, all of which appeared in Jacob, *Lengua medieval*: M. Castillo Lluch, 'El desarrollo de las expresiones de excepción en español antiguo: el caso de la tradición jurídica' (29–44), seeks to demonstrate how the study of an appropriate textual genre (in this case 13th-c. Spanish legal texts) can throw light on a set of syntactic relations, specifically expressions denoting exceptions. R. Cano Aguilar, 'La construcción del discurso en el siglo XIII: diálogo y narración en Berceo y *el Alexandre*' (133–51), analyzes the growing use of juxtaposition and subordination rather than coordination as clause-linking devices in the selected texts, a process of linguistic elaboration and refinement in the written language. He leaves open the origin in written Castilian of these constructions. D. Jacob, '¿Representividad lingüística o autonomía pragmática del texto antiguo? El ejemplo del pasado compuesto' (153–76), questions the degree to which medieval texts represent the linguistic reality of the moment. Discursive practices and textual genre may prevent the appearance of a given construction in a given corpus. The author illustrates these important issues with the example of the relative rarity of the present perfect (*he amado*) in medieval texts. He calls into question some long-held notions concerning the use of this verb form in the medieval language, noting that in many early texts this verb form had a deontic value and was rarely used with a non-personal subject. M. Barra Jover, 'Corpus diacrónico, constatación e inducción' (177–97), offers a theoretical meditation on the value and treatment of data culled from a linguistic corpus. He offers as a concrete illustration of the relevant issues the genesis and diffusion in medieval Hispano-Romance of subordinators involving a preposition or adverb followed by *que*, e.g. *sin que*, *siempre que*.

The loss of the O Sp. adverbial clitics *y* and *ende* continues to arouse interest. D. Wanner, 'La pérdida del clítico adverbial *y* en castellano', Jacob, *Lengua medieval*, 1–28, uses a large electronic data base (*ADMYTE*) to trace the rivalry of the adverbial clitic *y* 'there' with its rivals *ay* and *allí* and to identify the various factors responsible for its loss in the not fully developed system of clitics of late Medieval Spanish. C. Sánchez Lancis, 'The evolutions of the Old Spanish adverbs *ende* and *y*: a case of grammaticalization', *CWLP*, 9:101–18, attributes their loss to a double process of grammaticalization. *Ende* became grammaticalized in the phrase *por ende* when it lost its locative meaning; adverbial *y* morphologized and disappeared as an independent lexical adverb when it began to express 'pure' reference to a place.

Using a corpus of 15th-c. Castilian texts from the Crown of Aragon, Paloma Arroyo Vega, *La diátesis verbal en el castellano del siglo* XV (Cuadernos de Filología, Anejo 39), V, Facultat de Filologia, Univ. de València, 182 pp., affirms the existence in late medieval

Spanish of an opposition between the active and the middle voice. She also claims that the restructuring of compound tenses with *auer/ ser* + participle, as well as the uses of constructions with *se* observable in the texts analyzed, point the way to the modern uses of these constructions. Manuel Mosteiro Louzao, *Los esquemas causales en castellano medieval*, Santiago de Compostela U.P., 211 pp., examines the choice of verbal tense and mood in causal clauses. S. Hurtado González, 'El pretérito anterior en castellano medieval', *Verba*, 27, 2000:205–21, describes and analyses the syntactic structures in which forms such as *hube amado* appear in the medieval language. J. G. Moreno de Alba, 'Los pretéritos de indicativo en el *Poema del Cid*', *NRFH*, 48, 2000:275–97, studies the use of all verb forms employed to express past time in the *Cid*. The most frequent are the preterite, historical present, imperfect, and compound past.

M. Batllori and F. Roca, 'The value of definite determiners from Old Spanish to Modern Spanish', Pintzuk, *Diachronic Syntax*, 241–54, seeks to demonstrate that in Old Spanish the behaviour of *el, la los, las* can be best explained by positing two grammatical subsystems: an innovative grammar in which these forms function as discourse anaphors and a traditional grammar in which these items continue to express deictic meanings. Historically, the evolution of Latin ILLE, ILLA, ILLUD involves their reanalysis as functional heads lacking all the syntactic and semantic properties of demonstratives. L. Silva-Villar, 'Verbless derivation in historical syntax: a case study in northwestern Iberian languages', Gutiérrez-Rexach, *Spanish Syntax*, 309–46, examines within the Minimalist Program such constructions as *dolo/ulo* 'where is X?' in Spanish, Galician, and Asturo-Leonese. The author seeks to demonstrate that historical syntax and language variation can provide insights into questions of synchronic productive syntax. J. L. Girón Alconchel, 'Sintaxis y discurso en el español del Siglo de Oro (Contribución a la historia del discurso indirecto libre)', *VLet*, 11, 2000:93–113, studies free indirect discourse in narrative texts from the Siglo de Oro as a sequel to his earlier studies of the same phenomenon in the medieval language. Although the texts at issue are written in what appears to be Medieval Latin, F. González Ollé, 'Tuteo y voseo en documentos navarros altomedievales', *Lamíquiz Vol.*, 435–44, is relevant to the study of the uses of *tú* and *vos* in medieval Hispano-Romance.

6. DIACHRONIC LEXICOLOGY

With the publication of fascicle 21, Bodo Müller's *Diccionario del español medieval* has reached the word *albudecal*. Lloyd A. Kasten and Florian Cody, *Tentative Dictionary of Medieval Spanish*, NY, Hispanic Seminary of Medieval Studies, 745 pp., is a greatly expanded second edition of the identically titled dictionary issued in 1946. This version contains over 26,000 entries based on data culled from 86 texts covering the period 1140–1489. Each entry provides text locations (often based on antiquated editions) and a Spanish gloss of the headword. Xosé Lluis García Arias, *Propuestes etimoloxiques (1975–2000)*, Oviedo, Academia de la Llingua Asturiana, 2000, 352 pp. gathers together previously published studies on diachronic issues of Asturian lexicology. A substantial portion of the book is written in Bable. M. Ariza Viguera, 'Diccionario histórico e historia de la lengua', Ruhstaller, *Tendencias*, 57–74, offers a diachronic analysis of the raw material presented in various entries found in Vol. 1 of the Academy's *Diccionario histórico de la lengua española*. I. Pujol Payet, 'Algunas cuestiones acerca del cambio semántico en el mundo de los numerales', pp. 817–30 of *Cien años de investigación semántica: de Michel Bréal a la actualidad. Actas del Congreso Internacional de Semántica, Universidad de La Laguna, España, 27–31 de octubre de 1997*, ed. Marcos Martínez Hernández et al., 2 vols, M, Ediciones Clásicas, 2000, xxiv + 1758 pp., studies the semantics of derivatives in *-ario/-ero* formed from bases which are numerals.

STUDIES OF INDIVIDUAL WORDS. I.-X. Adiego, 'En torno al origen de la voz *guillarse* 'irse, huirse'' *BRAE*, 71:45–55, argues that this verb is of Gypsy origin rather than a blend of slang *guiñarse* 'huir' and *escullar/-ir* 'escabullirse', as proposed by Corominas. E. Grab-Kempf, 'Ein Berberismus im Altspanischen: *aves acedes* (f. pl.) "Zikaden"', *ZRP*, 117:444–48, seeks to show that O Sp. *aves acedes* 'cicada' is of Berber origin and not Greek as suggested by the author herself in *Diccionario del español medieval*, fasc. 6, 359a. B. Pastor, 'El origen de la Madeja de Seda', *ib.* 449–52, deals with *madeja*, a Hellenism which entered Spanish through Latin METAXA. Y. González-Aranda, 'Algunas notas sobre la evolución semántica de *bajar* en español', *ALH*, 14, 2000:169–192, is a systematic chronological study of that verb's semantic evolution. J. W. Albrecht, 'Is there another pattern of origin for the word *pícaro*?', *RoN*, 41:153–60, proposes that this longstanding crux of Spanish etymology derives through some form of popular etymology from the family of Fr. *piquer, pique, piqueron*. The arguments presented are far from convincing.

7. SYNTAX

Los marcadores del discurso, ed. María Antonia Martín Zorraquino and Estrella Montolío Durán, Arco Libros, 1998, 286 pp., attempts to set out an eclectic range of linguistic approaches in the first section of the volume and these are subsequently applied in a series of empirical studies looking, for example, at discrete discourse markers such as

que, si, es que, en cambio/por el contrario, en cualquier caso/en todo caso.
Estrella Montolío, *Conectores de la lengua escrita*, B, Ariel, 173 pp., takes
a relevance-theoretical approach to discourse connectors which
would benefit from a properly corpus-based approach. S. A.
Schwenter, 'Expectations and (in)sufficiency: Spanish *como* conditionals', *Linguistics*, 39:733–60, on the basis of four corpora, provides
a persuasive description of this non-canonical conditional construction and shows that the complex pragmatic information referred to
in the use of *como* can throw light on more basic conditionals. He
makes a compelling case for further research into 'counter-
expectation' in semantic and pragmatic analyses. G. de Mello,
'['Lo' + adjetivo = 'es que'] seguido de indicativo/subjuntivo: 'lo
importante es que tienes/tengas amigos', *HR*, 67, 1999:489–503,
uses PILEI data from 12 capital cities and finds that when this
structure is used with an evaluative expression the indicative is used;
predictably the subjunctive tends to occur to hypothetical events.
When the structure is used to refer to real events, the use of the
subjunctive obeys pragmatic considerations. C. Pountain, 'Pragmatic
factors in the evolution of the Romance reflexive (with special
reference to Spanish)', *JHR*, 1, 2000:5–25, examines the extension
of functions of the reflexive and argues that pragmatic factors play an
important role in accounting for this development. J. Harris, 'Spanish
imperatives: syntax meets morphology', *JL*, 34, 1998:27–52, takes
issue with the assertion that morphological mood correlates directly
with logical mood (citing, for example, the syntactic subjunctive
hágalo, used as a semantic imperative), yet does not develop the
pragmatic consequences of this argument. T. Jiménez Juliá, 'Tema
en español y en inglés', *BHS(G)*, 78, 2000:153–79, starts from the
contrast between the relatively variable word order in Spanish,
essentially a topic-prominent language, and the syntactic constraints
of English where S-V (-complement) is the principal word order, to
analyse the very different ways in which topic functions in each
language. T. Morris, 'Topicity vs. thematicity: topic-prominence in
impromptu Spanish discourse', *JP*, 29, 1998:193–203, looks at how
fronted topics such as *líderes, hay muchos . . .*, or *pues, yo por la de Conchita
Martínez* function as signalling devices, pragmatically motivated by
the need of the speaker to establish conversational agendas. Francisco
Yus, *El uso del lenguaje en Internet*, B, Ariel, 271 pp., takes relevance
theory as his main approach to some very interesting internet data
but it does not prove as relevant as some other approaches
(conversational analysis, politeness) that he also applies. Similarly,
Heraclia Castellón Alcalá, *El lenguaje administrativo*, Granada, La Vega,
2000, 366 pp., uses interesting data but would have benefited from a

more appropriate frame of analysis. I. Mackenzie, 'Marginal codification in Spanish', *JHR*, 1, 2000:215–27, looks at Alarcos's model
of predication structure and finds that verb phrases do not conveniently divide into different functional categories, and, on occasion,
resist classification altogether.

8. Morphology

E. Feliu, 'Output constraints on two Spanish word-creation processes', *Linguistics*, 39:871–91, shows that trisyllabic nominal truncation e.g. *analfa* < *analfabeto* and *-ata/-aca* suffixation (*bocata* <
bocadillo, *mensaca* < *mensajero*) are closely related word-creation
processes. Ramón Almela Pérez, *Procedimientos de formación de palabras
en español*, B, Ariel, 1999, 253 pp., is more interested in the mechanisms of word creation e.g. affixation and their definition than in their
product and how it is used. C. E. Piñeiros, 'Prosodic and segmental
unmarkedness in Spanish truncation', *Linguistics*, 38, 2000:63–98,
examines hypocoristics as truncated forms which preserve segmental
material from the initial syllables of the source form (*Beatriz-Bea*) or
from the final syllables (*Armando-Mando*). R. Pellen, 'Phraséologie et
phraséographie en espagnol: de la typologie à l'inventaire des
ressources', *BH*, n.s. [2001]:607–74, looks at the lexicographic
metalanguage used in Spanish dictionaries and identifies inconsistencies within dictionaries, (e.g. in the DRAE, CD-ROM, 1995, why
should *sin consuelo* be presented as expr. adv. fig. while *en abanico* is
referred to as loc. adv.) and between them (he looks at DRAE, DUE,
DIGILE, GDLE). He proposes a framework based on collocation
(*crisis interna (grave, institucional . . .)*), set phrases or *lexie (tener lugar, hora
punta*) and idioms or *locutions (tira y afloja, de pelo en pecho)*. María
Angeles Calero Fernández, *Sexismo lingüístico*, M, Narcea, 1999,
206 pp., has an extensive chapter on misogyny and androcentrism in
the Spanish language and in authorities on the Spanish language (e.g.
DRAE). J. England, 'Analogical feminines in Modern Spanish:
pressures on the peninsular standard', *BHS(G)*, 76, 1999:415–39 uses
a corpus of written Spanish dating back to 1976 and provides a
wealth of attested examples to chart the gradual acceptance of some
analogical feminine forms. For example, *abogada* has virtually completely ousted *abogado* to refer to a woman lawyer; however, in the
case of *medico/médica*, competition is still unresolved. Spain continues
to produce predictable outbursts about the alleged parlous state of
the language, e.g. B. Pastor, *Las perversiones de la lengua*, B, Planeta,
205 pp.

9. SOCIOLINGUISTICS AND DIALECTOLOGY

Carmen Silva-Corvalán, *Sociolingüística y pragmática del español*, Washington, DC, Georgetown U.P., 367 pp., is an extremely welcome re-edition (extensively revised and expanded) of S.-C.'s 1989 work *Sociolingüística: teoría y análisis* (M, Alhambra). It proves a rigorous theoretical introduction to sociolinguistics and has the signal advantage using copious examples taken from naturally-occurring Spanish. However, its coverage of pragmatics is less comprehensive and less well illustrated. María José Serrano, *Estudios de variación sintáctica*, M, Vervuert, 1999, 260 pp., contains a very useful, well-documented, introduction by S. reviewing work on syntactic variation in Spanish, 'Nuevas perspectivas en variación sintáctica' (11–50), followed by a series of well-chosen articles, mainly by established scholars, examining case studies in Spain and Latin America: M. Sedano, '*¿Ahí o allí? Un estudio sociolingüístico*' (51–64), S. Schwenter, 'Evidentiality in Spanish morphosyntax: a reanalysis of *(de)queísmo*' (65–88), M. T. Poblete, 'La variación en la construcción de textos orales ligada al uso de marcadores discursivo-conversacionales' (89–102), G. Cepeda, 'La variación pragmático-discursiva, entonacional y sociolingüística de los conectores conjuntivos en el habla de Valdivia, Chile' (103–20), D. Ranson, 'Variación sintáctica del adjetivo demostrativo en español' (121–42), N. Alturo, 'El papel de la anterioridad y de la perfectividad en la representación de estados y eventos' (143–72), J. L. Blas Arroyo, ' "Están ahí *bajo*": un caso de variación grammatical en una situación de contacto de lenguas' (173–96), F. Klein-Andreu, 'Variación actual y reinterpretación histórica: *le/s, la/s, lo/s* en Castilla' (197–220), P. M. Butragueño '¿Es funcional la variación lingüística?' (221–36), M. Casanovas Catalá, 'La identidad semántica en la variación sintáctica: un estudio empírico' (237–60). Marina Díaz Peralta, *La expresión de futuro en el español de Las Palmas de Gran Canaria*, Las Palmas de Gran Canaria, Cabildo de Gran Canaria, 2000, 247 pp., is a rigorous study examining variation and change in the use of the present, morphological future, and *ir a* + infinitive. Amongst other findings she argues that when these forms are used for concrete time reference there is evidence of a change in progress towards the morphological future. C. Pollán, 'The expression of pragmatic values by means of verbal morphology: a variationist study', *LVC*, 13:59–89, uses VARBRUL 2S to investigate a variable context in the use of two Galician verb forms (*cantei* and *cantara*) and three Spanish verb forms used in Galicia (*canté, cantara*, and *había cantado*). She finds that variation is constrained by pragmatic linguistic factors and that while the forms *cantei* and *canté* are preferred, contexts with low discourse focalization favour *cantara* and *había cantado*. R. Cameron, 'A variable syntax of speech, gesture and sound effect: direct quotations in Spanish', *ib.*, 10, 1998:43–83, provides a variationist account of how direct quotations are framed in the Spanish spoken by 62 socially stratified speakers from San Juan, Puerto Rico. He finds evidence of both social and stylistic patterning, and, in the case of the latter, that topic-triggered attention to form is a better explanatory model than that of audience design. R. Torres Cacoullos, 'Variation and grammaticization in progressives. Spanish *–ndo* construction', *Studies in Language*, 23.1, 1999:00–000, finds that frequency of use can play an important role in semantic generalization. For example, it could account for the erosion of the progressive meaning of *estar trabajando* and its extension to habitual situations. Ana María Cestero Mancera, *El intercambio de turnos de habla en la conversación*, Alcalá de Henares U.P., 2000, 308 pp., takes a variationist approach to applying conversational analysis to a corpus of naturally-occurring Spanish data finding that in mixed-age pairs the older speaker interrupts/overlaps more frequently.

Clare Mar-Molinero, *The Politics of Language in the Spanish-Speaking World*, London, Routledge, 2000, 242 pp., is an important contribution to work on language planning and policy and provides excellent coverage of this area locating case studies from both sides of the Atlantic within a closely argued frame. L. Williams, 'Política lingüística en la España actual', *BHS(L)*, 78:1–15, reviews language planning in Spain since the 1978 Constitution concluding that if minority language autonomous communities wish to retain their co-official language they will need to follow the example of Catalonia and impose its use. Miquel Siguan, *Bilingüismo y lenguas en contacto*, M, Alianza, 368 pp., is a very well-documented overview of issues concerning bilingualism and language planning with many examples, case studies and bibliographical references taken from Spain and elsewhere in the Spanish-speaking world. See also *La educación bilingüe: veinte años del seminario sobre Lengua y Educación*, ed. Miquel Siguan, B, ICE–Univ. de Barcelona, 2000, 218 pp. *El Español en el Mundo. Anuario del Instituto Cervantes 2001*, M, Instituto Cervantes, 357 pp., contains the following articles some of which are particularly helpful in charting the position of Spanish in the United States. L. Morales, 'El español en la Florida: los cubanos de Miami' (13–63), C. Silva-Corvalán, 'La situación del español en Estados Unidos' (65–116), G. Gómez Dacal, 'El español en las enseñanzas primaria y secundaria de Estados Unidos' (117–96), F. Moreno Fernández, 'El español en Brasil' (197–227), T. Fisac, 'La enseñanza del español en Asia Oriental' (229–98), F. Marcos Marín, 'La lengua española en Internet' (299–357), D. Martín Mayorga 'El español en la sociedad de la información' (359–74).

M. Altaber, 'The effect of dominant discourses on the vitality of Judeo-Spanish in the Turkish social context', *JMMD*, 19, 1998:263–81, focuses on the Turkish Jews living in Istanbul and uses data from the mid 1990s to show how they have internalized a negative evaluation of Judeo-Spanish, an attitude which may prevail over current preoccupations with ethnicity and which may hasten the demise of this variety. *IJSL*, 142, 2000, 'Language spread policy, III: languages of former colonial powers and former colonies: the case of Puerto Rico', ed. C. M. Ramírez González and Roamé Torres, has the following articles which relate to the use of Spanish: J. A. Vélez, 'Understanding Spanish language maintenance in Puerto Rico: political will meets the demographic imperative' (15–24), S. Clampitt-Dunlap, 'Nationalism and native-language maintenance in Puerto Rico' (25–34), A. Morales, '¿Simplificación o interferencia?: el español en Puerto Rico' (35–62), A. Pousada, 'The competent bilingual in Puerto Rico' (103–18). *IJSL*, 149, 'Between koineization and standardization: New World Spanish revisited', ed. M. Hidalgo, includes the following articles: M. Hidalgo, 'One century of study in New World Spanish' (9–32), C. Parodi, 'Contacto de dialectos y lenguas en el Nuevo Mundo: la vernacularización del español en América' (33–53), M. Hidalgo, 'Social stratification in New Spain' (55–78), A. M. Escobar, 'Contact features in colonial Peruvian Spanish' (79–93), G. de Granda, 'Procesos de *estandarización revertida* en la configuración histórica del español americano: el caso del espacio surandino' (95–118), M. Niño-Murcia, 'Late-stage standardization and language ideology in the Colombian press' (119–44), F. D. Althoff, 'Hispanic and Afro-Hispanic languages in the Americas' (145–55).

Estudios de dialectología dedicados a Manuel Alvar: con motivo del XL aniversario de la publicación de El español hablado en Tenerife, ed. Cristóbal Corrales and Dolores Corbella, La Laguna (Tenerife), Instituto de Estudios Canarios, 2000, 256 pp., is a mainly lexicographical tribute to Alvar's pioneering work in the 1950s focusing on subsequent developments in Canarian dialectology. Samper Padilla and Trapeco contribute interesting new work on *popular* vs *culto* lexis and some uses of diminutives and augmentatives respectively. Manuel Alvar continues to publish posthumously with *El español en Venezuela: estudios, mapas, textos*, ed. Antonio Alvar Esquerra and Florentino Paredes, M, Agencia española de Cooperación Internacional; *El español en el sur de los Estados Unidos: estudios, encuestas, textos*, M, La Goleta, 2000, 504 pp., *El español en la República dominicana: estudios, encuestas, textos*, Alcalá de Henares U.P., 2000, 481 pp. E. Mendieta, *El préstamo en el español de los Estados Unidos*, Lang, 1999, 180 pp. uses data from the above to identify and analyse borrowing whether through loanwords (pure or blends), semantic extension, and calquing. Chapter 6 relates these to user variables (ethnic group and sex) showing that the Puerto Rican community is the most innovative especially compared to the more conservative Mexican Americans, and that the sex of the speaker has little effect on the type of frequency of borrowing preferred. Felice Coles, *Isleño Spanish*, Munich, Lincom Europa 278, 1999, 79 pp., provides a rather haphazard description of the phonology/phonetics, morphology and syntax of this Louisiana variety of Spanish undergoing 'gradual death'. Luis Ortiz López, *El Caribe hispánico: perspectivas lingüísticas actuales*, M, Vervuert, 1999, 350 pp., brings together a series of chapters covering morphosyntax, lexis, and language contact phenomena: J. Lipski, 'El sufijo –ico y las palabras ague/awe y aguora/ahuora: rutas de evolución y entorno dialectológico' (17–42); J. Holm, G. Lorenzino, and H. de Mello, 'Diferentes grados de reestructuración en dos lenguas vernáculas: el español caribeño y el portugués brasileño' (43–60); K. Green, 'The preverbal marker a in a semi-creolized variety of non-standard Dominican Spanish' (61–75); A. Morales, 'Anteposición de sujeto en el español del Caribe' (77–98); A. T. Pérez Leroux, 'Innovación sintáctica en el español del Caribe y los principios de la gramática universal' (99–118); R. Núñez Cedeño, 'En torno a la neutralidad genérica del pronombre "él"' (119–29); G. de Granda, 'Léxico marinero en el español dominicano' (131–46); H. López Morales, 'Anglicismos en el léxico disponible de Puerto Rico' (147–70); A. Schwegler, 'El vocabulario africano de Palenque (Colombia)' (171–253); M. Vaquero et al., 'El léxico de las noticias televisadas de Puerto Rico' (255–70); W. Megenny, 'El español afrocaribeño: ¿mito o realidad?' (271–94); L. Ortiz López, 'El sistema verbal del español haitiano en Cuba: implicaciones para las lenguas en contacto en el Caribe' (295–315); I. Pérez Guerra, 'Contacto lingüístico dominico-haitiano en República Dominicana: datos para su estudio' (317–31); M. and E. Alvar, 'Un manuscrito sobre la evangelización en español en Chibcha (1582–1586)' (333–41).

Julio Calvo Pérez, *Teoría y práctica del contacto: el español de América en el candelero*, M, Vervuert, 2000, 211 pp., contains an introduction and nine chapters written from a variety of theoretical perspectives on, for example, aspect (Jorques Jiménez), Spanish/Nahuatl (Hernández Sacristán), Spanish/Aymara, Spanish/Quechua (Calvo Pérez), Spanish/Guaraní (Pruñonosa, Palacios Alcaine), Spanish/English (Roca), Papamiento, Palenquero and *Bozal* (Bartens) and a variety of Mexican indigenous languages (Flores Farfán). J. Diego Quesada, 'On language contact: another look at Spanish-speaking (Central) America', *JHR*, 1, 2000:229–42, distinguishes between 'interference' and 'influence' when examining contact between Spanish and the Amerindian languages and provides a useful interpretive model of language contact phenomena. R. E. Vann, 'Aspects of Spanish deictic expressions in Barcelona: a quantitative examination', *LVC*, 10, 1998:263–00, examines cross-linguistic pragmatic transfer from Catalan to Spanish in a corpus of elicited data and argues that the resulting innovative variety provides a potential resource for expressing Catalan identity. A. J. Toribio, 'Language variation and the linguistic enactment of identity among Dominicans', *Linguistics*, 38, 2000:1133–59, examines the strong affinity of the islanders to their particular variety of Spanish; its covert prestige means that Dominican immigrants are unlikely to relinquish it in favour of a Pan-hispanic standard or of English. Amanda Castro, *Pronominal Address in Honduran Spanish*, Lincom Europa, 2000, 133 pp., through a quantitative study of 347 speakers, examines the Honduran pronominal address system which has conserved three variants, *vos*, *usted* and, principally in the written language, *tú*. Particularly interesting is the examination of *usted* as potentially encoding both distance and solidarity/intimacy and of the pragmatic motivations for pronominal switching. B. Bailey, 'Social/interactional functions of code-switching among Dominican Americans', *Pragmatics*, 10, 2000:165–93, reanalyses the situational, metaphorical, and contextualizing functions of code-switching as a multifunctional, interactional phenomenon and concentrates on the latter, under-researched function, interpreting it within conversational management and specifically the achievement of repair. María Antonia Martín Zorraquino and José María Enguita Utrilla, *Las lenguas de Aragón*, Zaragoza, Caja de Ahorros de la Inmaculada, 2000, 96 pp., provides a basic introduction with written textual examples. *Las hablas andaluzas: problemas y perspectivas*, ed. María Auxiliadora Castillo Carballo and Juan Manuel García Platero, Seville, Signatura, 237 pp., provides mainly lexicographical chapters on this variety with useful bibliographical references. John McWhorter, *The Missing Spanish Creoles*, London–California, Univ. of California Press, 2000, 281 pp., is a stimulating and controversial work arguing that Creole genesis arose from pidginization in West African trade settlements. As Spain, unlike France, Portugal, and Holland, had no such settlements, this would explain why there was no Spanish pidgin to bring to the New World.

10. DISCOURSE ANALYSIS AND PRAGMATICS

There is a homage to the pioneering Latin American linguist, Beatriz Lavandera, in *DisSoc*, 12, which includes the following articles principally on discourse analysis: E. Traugott et al., 'Beatriz Lavandera 1942–98' (5–8), M. García Negroni et al., 'A homage to Beatriz R. Lavandera: an overview of political discourse analysis from the approach of Lavandera and her students' (9–21), A. Bolívar, 'Changes in Venezuelan political dialogue: the role of advertising during electoral campaigns' (23–45), L. Berardi, 'Globalization and poverty in Chile' (47–58), T. Carbó, 'Regarding reading: on a methodological approach' (59–89), M. Pardo, 'Linguistic persuasion as an essential political factor in current democracies: critical analysis of the globalization discourse in Argentina at the turn of the century' (91–118).

Interactional pragmatics, and notably politeness theory, has produced a lively body of work in very recent years. M. Placencia, 'Inequality in address behaviour at public institutions in La Paz, Bolivia', *AnL*, 43:198–217, uses linguistic politeness to argue persuasively that there exists discriminatory behaviour in the treatment of indigenous persons in service encounters. Id., 'Pragmatic variation: Ecuadorian Spanish vs. Peninsular Spanish', *SAL*, 2, 1998:71–106, argues that Ecuadorian Spanish is characterized, amongst other features, by greater indirectness, formality, deference and the use of certain forms (e.g. the future tense) for strategic politeness when compared with Peninsular Spanish where economy through ellipsis and absence of request formulae is a frequent strategy. Rosina Márquez Reiter, *Linguistic Politeness in Britain and Uruguay*, Amsterdam––Philadelphia, Benjamins, 2000, 225 pp., is a cross-cultural study of requests and apologies in Southern British English and Uruguayan Spanish (US). Using parallel data derived from open role-play, she argues, for example, that users of US use less conventional and non-conventional indirectness and they are less concerned with reducing the level of coerciveness in requests. N. Hernández-Flores, 'Politeness ideology in Spanish colloquial conversation: the case of advice' *Pragmatics*, 9, 1999:37–49, redefines notions of face for a Spanish context and argues that the giving of unsolicited advice can fulfil the face wants of self-affirmation and *confianza* valued by that society. N. Lorenzo-Dus, 'Compliment response among British and Spanish university students: a contrastive study', *JP*, 33:107–27, uses a corpus collected by means of a Discourse Completion Test and a framework derived from politeness theory to point up potential cross-cultural miscommunication; for example, the use of ironic upgrades by Spanish males in response to compliments may lead to their characterization as excessively boastful by British counterparts. C. García, 'The three stages of Venezuelan invitations and responses', *Multilingua*, 18, 1999:391–433, looked at a group of male and female Venezuelan Spanish speakers and found that female participants strongly favoured deference strategies in making an invitation and responding to a refusal and solidarity strategies when parting, males being less deferential. Females were more verbose and used more strategies than males and both groups actively sought to respect the interlocutor's positive face throughout the interaction. M. Stewart, 'Pronouns of power and solidarity: the case of the Spanish first person plural *nosotros*', *ib.*, 20 : 155–69, argues, within a politeness framework, that the indeterminacy inherent in speaker-hearer reference functions as a strategic resource. Id., 'Hedging your bets — the use of *yo* in face-to-face interaction', *WJMLL*, 2000, argues that an explanation for the high occurrence of *yo* with verbs of cognition can be found in the interactional need for speakers to hedge their opinions and that the use of *yo* as a hedge to the Gricean maxim of quality can serve simultaneously to protect the speaker's face and to allow the construction of self. J. L. Blas Arroyo, 'Mire usted St. González . . . Personal deixis in Spanish political-electoral debate', *JP*, 32, 2000 : 1–27, analyses personal pronominal reference in the speech of a Prime Minister and leader of the opposition in Spain and attempts to describe the principal fields of meaning activated by the different pronouns in the discourse of electoral debate. D. A. Koike et al., 'Spanish *no*, *sí*: reactive moves to perceived face-threatening acts', *ib.*, 33 : 701–23, 879–99, investigate the pragmatic functions of these particles in four discourse contexts and demonstrate their face-saving potential both for speaker and hearer within a politeness framework. V. Savala, 'Borrowing evidential functions from Quechua: the role of *pues* as a discourse marker in Andean Spanish', *ib.*, 999–1023, demonstrates how, in this variety of Spanish, the particle *pues* serves as a discourse marker to clarify assumptions by speakers and hearers of what constitutes given or assumed knowledge. She then links this particle to the Quechua suffix *–mi* which functions as a validational marker and argues that the Andean Spanish *pues* is used differently from the standard Spanish form. S. Blackwell, 'Anaphora interpretations in Spanish utterances and the neo-Gricean pragmatic theory', *ib.*, 32, 2000 : 389–424, tests one of Stephen Levinson's neo-Gricean submaxims against the results of an oral comprehension test for anaphora interpretations in Spanish and finds that while certain sub-maxims obtain, e.g. that of referential parsimony, others, e.g. the more 'minimal' the form, the stronger the preference for a coreferential reading, are not borne out by the data. S. Hale, 'How are courtroom questions interpreted? An analysis of Spanish interpreters' practices', pp. 21–50 of *Triadic Exchanges*, ed. Ian Mason, Manchester, St. Jerome, 208 pp., investigates the formulation of questions in Spanish and English. While pragmatic equivalence can be achieved between both languages, speakers must draw on different resources in each language to create the same illocutionary force.

MEDIEVAL LITERATURE
POSTPONED

ALJAMIADO LITERATURE
POSTPONED

LITERATURE, 1490–1700
(PROSE AND POETRY)
By Carmen Peraita, *Villanova University*

1. General

Kormi Anipa, *A Critical Examination of Linguistic Variation in Golden Age Spanish*, NY, Lang, 254 pp., compares the linguistic thought of Renaissance Spanish and English grammarians such as Nebrija, Valdés, Correas, John Sanford, and others, with the spoken language as it appears in contemporary fiction (*Lozana, Guzmán* 1, *Lazarillo, Rinconete, Buscón*, etc.). *Palabras para el pueblo. Vol.* 1. *Aproximación general a la Literatura de Cordel*, ed. Luis Díaz G. Viana, M, CSIC, 2000, 486 pp. *Prosa y poesía. Homenaje a Gonzalo Sobejano*, ed. Christopher Maurer et al., M, Gredos, 462 pp., includes A. Egido, 'Voces y cosas. Claves para la poesía del Siglo de Oro' (105–22); L. López Grigera, 'Algo más sobre el Caso de *Lazarillo de Tormes*' (221–30); F. Márquez Villanueva, 'La picaresca, Cervantes y *Moll Flanders*' (255–66); F. Rico, 'Polvos y paja' (311–23); E. L. Rivers, 'Cantar de Cantares: espíritu de la letra' (323–30); and M. L. Welles, 'Felicitous fabrications: Ovid according to Jorge de Bustamante' (451–59). Antonio Cortijo Ocaña, *La evolución genérica de la ficción sentimental de los siglos* xv *y* xvi, London, Tamesis, 349 pp. John W. O'Malley, *Trent and All That. Renaming Catholicism in the Early Modern Era*, CUP, 2000, 219 pp., is a concise overview of 50 years of scholarship on Catholicism in early modern Europe. Rogelio Reyes Cano, *Estudios sobre Cristóbal de Castillejo*, Salamanca U.P., 2000, 158 pp., studies a variety of facets of C.'s work and influences.

2. Printing, Reading, Libraries, and Bibliography

Imprenta y crítica textual en el Siglo de Oro, ed. Pablo Andrés and Sonia Garza (Centro para la Edición de los Clásicos Españoles), Valladolid U.P., 2000, 301 pp., presents studies by J. Moll, 'La imprenta manual' (13–27); P. Andrés et al., 'El original de imprenta' (29–64); S. Garza, 'La cuenta del original' (65–95); T. J. Dadson, 'La corrección de pruebas (y un libro de poesía)' (97–128); D. W. Cruikshank, 'Los 'hurtos de la prensa' en las obras dramáticas' (129–50); J. M. Micó, 'Mateo Alemán y el *Guzmán de Alfarache*: la novela, a pie de imprenta' (151–69); G. Di Stefano, 'El pliego suelto: del lenguaje a la página' (171–85); J. Martín Abad, 'Soporte, texto y noticia bibliográfica' (187–222); F. Rico, 'Crítica textual y transmisión impresa (para la edición de *La Celestina*)' (223–41); R. Chartier, 'La pluma, el papel y la voz. Entre crítica textual e historia cultural' (243–57). It includes two appendices, Cristobal Suárez de Figueroa, 'De los impresores' (259–66), and Juan Caramuel, '*Syntagma de arte typographica*' (267–87). María Carmen Álvarez Márquez, *El libro manuscrito en Sevilla (siglo XVI)*, Seville, Ayuntamiento, 2000, 317 pp., is a well-documented and detailed investigation of the production and circulation of manuscripts. Fernando Bouza, *Corre manuscrito. Una historia cultural del Siglo de Oro*, M, Marcial Pons, 359 pp., gathers a fascinating collection of essays on topics such as the circulation of manuscripts in Spain and Portugal in the 16th and 17th cs: 'Tocar las letras. Cédulas, nóminas, cartas de toque, resguardo y daño en el Siglo de Oro' (85–108), 'Escribir en monipodio. De los libelos de vecinos a las críticas al rey' (109–36), 'Cartas secas y cartas de nuevas. Lo que hay de nuevo que avisar es . . .' (137–78), 'La estafeta del bufón. Cartas de gente de placer en la Corte de los Austrias' (179–214), 'Vidas de palacio. Las biografías manuscritas como manual de corte' (215–40), 'De memoria, archivos y lucha política en la España de los Austrias' (241–88), '*Propio Marte*. Majestad y autoría en la alta edad moderna' (289–312). Hipólito Escolar Sobrino, *Manual de historia del libro*, M, Gredos, 2000, 423 pp., surveys the development of the book from the origin of writing to the 'galaxia Marconi'.

François Géal, *Figures de la bibliothèque dans l'imaginaire espagnol du Siècle d'Or*, Paris, Champion, 1999, 944 pp., is an exhaustive and outstanding examination of ways in which libraries were represented in the *imaginaire* social, focusing on actual libraries, treatises on libraries — such as *De las librerías*, Diego de Arce (1608), *De bene disponenda bibliotheca*, Francisco de Araoz (1631), *Musei sive bibliothecae libri quattuor*, Claude Clément (S.J.) teacher of 'erudition' at the Colegio Imperial of Madrid (1635) — as well as libraries in literary, poetic, autobiographic texts (*Don Quixote*, *Criticón*). The study begins with the project of the Escorial library (1563) and ends in 1716 with the foundation of the new Royal Library by Philip V. Alicia Cordón Mesa, *Pliegos sueltos poéticos en castellano del siglo XVII de la Biblioteca de Catalunya. Catálogo* (Colección Repertorios Bibliográficos, 3), Alcalá de Henares U.P., 220 pp.

3. HUMANIST AND RHETORICAL THOUGHT

Benito Arias Montano, *Libro de la generación y regeneración del hombre o acerca de la historia del género humano. Primera parte de la Magna Obra, esto es, Alma*, ed. Fernando Navarro Antolín, pref. Luis Gómez Canseco, trans. Fernando Navarro Antolín et al. (Biblioteca Montaniana), Huelva U.P. — Junta de Andalucía, 1999, 694 pp., is an erudite

edition of M.'s explanation of God as a philologist, concerned with
being correctly understood and busy inventing languages.
M. emphasizes the Christian humanist task of copying, transmitting,
and explaining God's message and the role of Hebrew as divine
language. He claims that his text — which begins with the creation of
man and ends with the redemption by Christ — is patterned after
God's plan for the human race. Antonio Cortijo Ocaña, *Teoría de la
historia y teoría política en Sebastián Fox Morcillo. De historiae institutione
dialogus, Diálogo de la enseñanza de la historia*, Alcalá de Henares U.P.,
2000, 311 pp.

V. Moreno Gallego, J. Solana Pujalte, and I. J. García Pinilla, 'Dos
memoriales de Juan Ginés de Sepúlveda a Felipe II y otra documenta-
ción inédita', *BRAH*, 118:131–54, contains three previously
unknown documents. Fernando de Herrera, *Tomás Moro*, ed.
Francisco López Estrada, Seville U.P., 177 pp. *España y América en una
perspectiva humanista. Homenaje a Marcel Bataillon*, ed. Joseph Perez, M,
Casa de Velázquez, 211 pp., includes A. Egido, 'Erasmo y la Torre
de Babel. La búsqueda de la lengua perfecta' (11–34); J. Canavaggio,
'Las reflexiones de Marcel Bataillon sobre Juan de la Cueva, sesenta
años después' (35–44); A. Villanova, 'Don Quijote, loco entreverado
con lúcidos intervalos' (45–68); R. García Cárcel, 'Bataillon y las
corrientes espirituales periféricas' (69–78); J. I. Tellechea Idígoras,
'1559 ¿Crisis religiosa española o europea?' (79–92); J. Pérez de
Tudela y Bueso, 'Letra y espíritu de la ley en el padre Las Casas'
(93–106); A. Saint-Lu, 'Bartolomé de las Casas en sus escritos'
(107–22); T. Hampe Martínez, 'De cronistas, rebeliones y polémicas:
Marcel Bataillon frente a la conquista del Perú' (123–40); A. Milhou,
'América frente a los sueños orientales (1492–principios del siglo
XVII)' (141–211). *Latin and Vernacular in Renaissance Spain*, ed. Barry
Taylor and Alejandro Coroleu (Cañada Blanch Monograph, 3;
Manchester Spanish and Portuguese Studies, 8), Manchester, Depart-
ment of Spanish and Portuguese, 1999, 160 pp., presents articles by
E. Gómez Sierra, 'Home and away in Paris: Pedro Sánchez Ciruelo
and his *Disputatio dyalogus*' (83–104); J. Pascual, 'Bilingual cultures:
the learned and the vernacular in Renaissance Seville and ancient
Rome' (113–20); and A. Coroleu, '*Aliena scripta retexere*: Francisco
Sánchez de las Brozas's poetry commentaries' (121–30). Miguel
Ángel González Manjarrés, *Entre la imitación y el plagio. Fuentes e
influencias en el Dioscórides de Andrés Laguna*, Segovia, Caja Segovia, 2000,
191 pp.

BIBLE. *La Biblia del Oso, según la traducción de Casiodoro de Reina,
publicada en Basilea en el año 1569*, M, Alfaguara, 4 vols, 554, 962, 1148,
698 pp., is a much-needed edition of this key translation. Natalio

Fernández Marcos and Emilia Fernández Tejero, *Biblia y humanismo. Texto, talantes y controversias del siglo* XVI *español*, M, FUE, 1999, 293 pp.
RHETORIC. *Retóricas y poéticas españolas, siglos* XVI-XIX, ed. Isabel Paraíso, Valladolid U.P., 2000, 216 pp., includes three articles on Golden Age rhetorical theory, A. Martín Jiménez, 'La retórica clásica al servicio de la predicación: los seis libros de la *Retórica eclesiástica* (1576) de fray Luis de Granada' (11–46); I. Paraíso, 'Fundación del canón métrico: el *Arte Poética Española* (1592) de Juan Díaz Rengifo' (47–94); J. García Rodríguez, 'Retórica y educación: el *Epítome de la Elocuencia Española* (1692) de Francisco de Artiga' (95–148). Manuel López Muñoz, *Fray Luis de Granada y la retórica*, Almería U.P., 2000, 222 pp. *Rhetoric and Law in Early Modern Europe*, ed. Victoria Kahn and Lorna Hutson, New Haven–London, Yale U.P., 355 pp., includes the noteworthy 'The duty to love: passion and obligation in Early Modern political theory' (243–68). José Aragüez Aldaz, *Deus Concionator. Mundo predicado y retórica del exemplum en los Siglos de Oro*, Amsterdam–Atlanta, Rodopi, 1999, 344 pp.

4. CULTURAL STUDIES

Luis Zapata, *Miscelánea o Varia Historia*, Llerena, Editores Extremeños, 1999, 362 pp., is a welcome edition of this seminal reference text. Gabriel de Sarabia, *Coplas en loor de Carlos V [Pliego de cordel] Impreso en Salamanca en la Calle de Moros por Rodrigo de Castañeda*, ed. José María Sanz Hermida, Salamanca, Diputación, 2000, 61 pp. Bernardino Montaña de Montserrate, *Libro de la anothomia del hombre* (1551), pref. Ginés Doménech Ratto, Murcia U.P., xvii + 133 ff., 1999, is a facsimile of the first anatomical treatise in Spanish by a Galenic physician of Philip II, written when the influence of Vesalius's anatomy started to grow in Spain. Montaña includes 'Sueño del Marqués de Mondejar' and a 'Declaración del sueño' between the Marqués and the author, which focuses on 'la compostura del cuerpo humano'. Baltasar Porreño, *Dichos y hechos del Señor Rey don Felipe Segundo. El prudente, potentíssimo y glorioso monarca de las Españas y de las Indias*, ed. Antonio Álvarez-Ossorio Alvariño, M, SECCFC, 164 pp. Juan Christóval Calvete de Estrella, *El felicísimo viaje del muy alto y muy poderoso príncipe don Phelippe*, ed. Paloma Cuenca, M, SECCFC, 755 pp., includes also Vicente Álvarez's 'Relación del camino y buen viaje que hizo el príncipe de España don Phelipe', the illustrations 'Arcos triunfales de la entrada de Amberes' from Cornelius Schryver's *Spectaculorum in susceptione Philippi Hisp. Princ. Divi Caroli V Caes.*, and studies by, among others, J. Martínez-Millán, F. Checa, and A. Álvarez-Ossorio. Simón Contarini, *Estado de la monarquía española a principios del siglo* XVII, Algazara, Málaga, 82 pp., presents an interesting document on Philip III and Lerma by the ambassador of Venice in Madrid. Carlos Álvarez Nogal, *Sevilla y la monarquía hispánica en el siglo XVII* (Biblioteca de Temas Sevillanos), Seville, Ayuntamiento, 2000, 163 pp.

Sebastián de Covarrubias, *Suplemento al Tesoro de la Lengua Española Castellana*, ed. Georgina Dopico and Jacques Lezra, M, Polifemo, xxviii + 390 + ccciv pp., the last part containing a 'biografía documental'. Sydney Anglo, *The Martial Arts of Renaissance Europe*, New Haven–London, Yale U.P., 2000, 384 pp., situates in its European context Gerónimo Sánchez de Carranza's *Philosophia de las armas*, Francisco Lórenz de Rada's *Nobleza de la Espada*, as well as Pacheco de Narváez's *Enseñanza de la filosofía y destreza de las armas*, and the work of three of his disciples, Gaspar Agustín de Lara, Miguel Pérez de Mendoza and Francisco Antonio Ettenhard. *Charles Quint et la monarchie universelle*, ed. Anne Molinié-Bertrand and Jean-Paul Duviols, Paris-Sorbonne U.P., 288 pp., includes A. Merle, 'L'empereur et le tyran. La lutte contre le pouvoir ottoman selon Juan Ginés de Sepúlveda' (183–92); A. Molinié-Bertrand, 'Don Juan d'Autriche, héros de roman' (193–204); S. Roubaud, 'De la cour d'Arthur à la bibliothèque de Charles Quint: la longue errance des chevaliers de roman' (239–50); and A. Condé, 'Le diable et la femme: du discours des traités de démonologie aux aveus des accusées. L'exemple de la diocèse de Cuenca (XVIe–XVIIe siècles)' (265–78).

In *Carlos V y la quiebra del humanismo político en Europa (1530–1558)*, ed. José Martínez Millán, M, SECCFC, 4 vols, 626, 432, 472, 502 pp., the following articles stand out amongst those included: J. M. Headley, 'The emperor and his chancellor: disputes over empire, administration and Pope (1519–1529)' (I, 21–36); J. A. Fernández Santamaría, 'Juan Ginés de Sepúlveda y la guerra' (I, 37–92); F. Márquez Villanueva, 'Nuevas de Corte. Fray Antonio de Guevara, periodista de Carlos V' (II, 13–28); A. Redondo, 'El *Discurso sobre Europa* del doctor Laguna (Colonia, 1543), entre amarguras y esperanza' (III, 261–76); B. Cuart Moner, 'Juan Ginés de Sepúlveda, cronista del emperador' (III, 341–68); A. Sarrión Mora, 'La religiosidad de la mujer en Castilla durante la época pretridentina' (IV, 103–18); M. Andrés Martín, 'La espiritualidad española en tiempo de Carlos V' (IV, 157–80); J. I. Tellechea Idígoras, 'Lo que el Emperador no supo. Proceso de Paulo IV a Carlos V y a Felipe II' (IV, 181–96); J. C. Nieto, 'Herejía en la Capilla Imperial: Constantino Ponce de la Fuente y la imagen del Diablo' (IV, 213–26); R. Pieper, 'Cartas, avisos e impresos: los medios de comunicación en el imperio de Carlos V' (IV, 231–42).

Estudios sobre iglesia y sociedad en Andalucía en la Edad Moderna, ed. Antonio Luis Cortés Peña and Miguel Luis López-Guadalupe,

Granada U.P., 1999, 535 pp., is a collection of noteworthy studies on the Inquisition, the Church, devotion, and religious art in Andalusia. It includes also fascinating essays on the history of reading such as F. Bouza on 'La legibilidad de la experiencia religiosa' (389–408). Sara Tilghman Nalle, *Mad for God. Bartolomé Sánchez, the Secret Messiah of Cardenete*, Charlottesville–London, Virginia U.P., 228 pp. Joseph Bergin, *The Seventeenth Century*, OUP, 265 pp. Victoria González de Caldas, *El poder y su imagen. La Inquisición Real*, Seville U.P., 263 pp. Mercedes Maroto Camino, *Practising Places: Saint Teresa, Lazarillo and the Early Modern City*, Amsterdam–Atlanta, Rodopi, 189 pp. Lynette M. F. Bosch, *Art, Liturgy and Legends in Renaissance Toledo. The Mendoza and the Iglesia Primada*, University Park, Penn State U.P., 2000, 292 pp., studies liturgical manuscripts commissioned by members of the Mendoza family for the cathedral of Toledo, investigating ritual, ideological, and political roles played by such manuscripts in the complex life of the cathedral. Lauriane Fallay d'Este, *L'art de la peinture. Peinture et théorie à Séville au temps de Francisco Pacheco (1564–1644)*, Paris, Champion, 829 pp., surveys painting in Andalucia in P.'s time and aspects such as patronage, art collections, relationships between painters and patrons, painters' economic status, foreign influences, the importance of art treatises, mainly those of Pablo de Céspedes and Pacheco. Antonio Urquízar Herrera, *El Renacimiento en la periferia. La recepción de los modos italianos en la experiencia pictórica del Quiniento cordobés*, Cordoba U.P., 384 pp. José Luis Cano de Gardoqui García, *Tesoros y colecciones. Orígenes y evolución del coleccionismo artístico*, Valladolid U.P., 166 pp. Ann Rosalind Jones and Peter Stallybrass, *Renaissance Clothing and the Materials of Memory*, CUP, 2000, 368 pp., includes 'Arachne's Web: Velázquez's *Las Hilanderas*' (89–103). Carmen Bernis, *Los trajes y los tipos sociales en el Quijote*, M, El Viso, 229 pp., is beautifully and profusely illustrated (with almost 700 illustrations), and is an erudite and indispensable study of the history of clothing; it describes in depth and reconstructs every aspect of dress codes in *Don Quixote*: 'El camino', 'Las armas y las letras', 'La corte de los duques', 'La caza', 'Los vestidos y las armas de don Quijote', 'Artesanos y otros hombres del común', 'El ama y la sobrina. El traje de las mujeres comunes', 'Los villanos', 'El mundo del cautivo'. B.'s investigation of roles played by clothing is invaluable for understanding the implications of dress codes in Early Modern Spain. *La transmission du savoir dans l'Europe des XVIe et XVIIe siècles*, ed. Marie Roig Miranda, pref. Francine Wild, Paris, Champion, 2000, 542 pp., edits the papers of a conference held in November 1997 and has sections on 'Les types du savoir', 'La mise en savoir', and 'La circulation du savoir', and includes noteworthy essays by C. Vaíllo, 'La formation culturelle de la personne chez Antonio López de Vega' (69–80); C. Bouzy 'Des

Hierogliphica de Valeriano au *Tesoro de la Lengua*: de la somme symboliste à l'encyclopédisme didactique' (139–60); A. S. Trueblood, 'Le savoir transmis par l'emblème; répercussions expressives chez Lope de Vega et Cervantés' (161–70); M. Zuili, 'Alejo Venegas, moraliste tolédan du XVIe siècle, ou la diffusion de la connaissance par le livre' (399–412); M. A. Etayo-Piñol, 'Lyon, plaque tournante de la culture espagnole en France à l'époque moderne' (451–68); E. Marigno, 'Les jácaras de Quevedo: la transmission de la *germanía* par le théatre de Quevedo' (469–82). Roberto J. González-Casanovas, *Autodescubrimiento y autodominio de Colón a Calderón: Discursos renacentistas de autoridad y experiencia (Interpretaciones fenomenológicas y sociosemióticas)*, Potomac, Scripta Humanistica, 2000, 160 pp. Thomas Austin O'Connor, *Love in the 'Corral'. Conjugal Spirituality and Anti-Theatrical Polemic in Early Modern Spain*, NY, Lang, 2000, 395 pp. Rocío Sánchez Rubio and Isabel Testón Núñez, *El hilo que nos une. Las relaciones epistolares en el Viejo y el Nuevo Mundo (Siglos* XVI-XVIII), pref. Antonio Domínguez Ortíz, Mérida, Junta de Extremadura, 1999, 693 pp.

EMBLEMS.   *Del libro de emblemas a la ciudad simbólica, Actas del III Simposio Internacional de Emblemática Hispánica*, ed. Víctor Mínguez, Castellón de la Plana, Universitat Jaume I, 2000, 2 vols, 536, 537–1050 pp., includes among others, F. Rodríguez de la Flor, 'La imagen corográfica de la ciudad penitencial contrarreformista: El Greco, Toledo (h. 1610)' (59–94); A. Castillo, 'Artificios epigráficos. Lecturas emblemáticas del escribir monumental en la ciudad del Siglo de Oro' (151–68); C. Bouzy, '*Pegma* o las imágenes de la entrada en Amberes de Alberto e Isabel, archiduques de Austria (Ioannes Bochius, *Pompa Triunphalis at spectaculorum*, Antverpiae, Ex officina Plantiniana, 1602' (343–60); G. Ledda, 'Proyección emblemática en aparatos efímeros y en configuraciones simbólicas festivas' (361–76); J. Enrique Viola Nevado, 'El ciudadano bibliófilo. Ciudad y *ex-libris*' (435–52); S. López Poza 'Variantes en las portadas y en las *picturae* de las dos versiones de las *Empresas Políticas* de Saavedra Fajardo' (621–46); J. M. González de Zárate 'Hendrik Goltzius. Les *culbuteurs*. Los cuatro humillados vencidos por su arrogancia. Otra imagen del rey prudente' (819–46); P. Pedraza, 'La *Hypnerotomachia* cumple medio milenio' (1037–42).

WOMEN'S STUDIES.   Renée Levine Melammed, *Heretics or Daughters of Israel? The Crypto-Jewish Women of Castile*, OUP, 1999, 256 pp., explores the lives of several *conversas* resorting to Inquisitorial trials, and includes 'Judaizing heresy, the Inquisition, and the conversas', 'Jew and conversas. The first century of crypto-judaism', 'The lives of judaizing women after 1492', 'Messianic turmoil circa 1500', 'Castilian conversas at work', 'The López-Villarreal family: three convicted judaizers (1516–1521)', 'The López women's *tachas*', 'The Inquisition and the mid-wife', 'The judaizers of Alcázar at the end of the sixteenth century: corks floating on water', 'Conclusio. Heretics or daughters of Israel?'. Georgina Dopico Black, *Perfect Wives, Other Women. Adultery and Inquisition in Early Modern Spain*, Durham, Duke U.P., 307 pp. *A Wild Country out in the Garden. The Spiritual Journals of a Colonial Mexican Nun*, ed. and trans. Kathleen A. Myers and Amanda Powel, Bloomington–Indianapolis, Indiana U.P., 1999, 386 pp. María de Zayas y Sotomayor, *La traición en la amistad. Friendship Betrayed*, trans. Catherine Larson, Lewisburg, Bucknell U.P., 1999, 197 pp.

5. POETRY

Fernando de Herrera, *Anotaciones a la poesía de Garcilaso*, ed. Inoria Pepe and José María Reyes, M, Cátedra, 1134 pp. Baltazar del Alcázar, *Obra poética*, ed. Valentín Núñez Rivera, M, Cátedra, 716 pp. José María Ferri Coll, *La poesía de la Academia de los Nocturnos*, Alicante U.P., 363 pp.

Poética silva. Un manuscrito granadino del Siglo de Oro, ed. Inmaculada Osuna, Seville U.P.–Córdoba U.P., 2000, 2 vols, 292, 278 pp. José Manuel Pedrosa, *Tradición oral y escrituras poéticas en los siglos de oro*, Sendoa, Oiartzun, 1999, 204 pp, explores the influence of popular songs in Golden Age poetry and ways in which Camoens, Góngora, Quevedo, Calderón, and Claramonte adapted popular songs, and is a key study for comprehending techniques of writing and re-writing poetry in Golden Age Spain. R. John McCaw, *The Transforming Text: A Study of Luis de Góngora's Soledades*, Potomac, Scripta Humanística, 2000, 175 pp.

6. PROSE

Several publications by the Centro de Estudios Cervantinos, Alcalá de Henares, are noteworthy: *Libro segundo de don Clarián de Landanís*, 2000, 374 pp. *Libro segundo de don Clarián de Landanís* (Guía de lectura), 2000, 134 pp. *El Baldo* (Guía de lectura), 2000, 104 pp.

Lía Schwartz, 'La retórica de la cita en las *Novelas a Marcia Leonarda* de Lope de Vega', *Edad de Oro*, 19, 1999:265–86, examines the use of *iudicia, sententiae*, and *exempla* by L. de V. to give moral authority to his text.

PICARESQUE AND *LAZARILLO DE TORMES*. *The Life of Lazarillo de Tormes*, trans. David Rowland (1586), ed. Keith Whitlock, Warminster, Aris & Phillips, 2000, 168 pp. *Vida del Lazarillo castigado o Lazarillo de la Inquisición*, ed. Gonzalo Santonja, M, España Nuevo Milenio, 2000, 71 pp. *Edad de Oro*, 20, 2000, focuses on 'Revisión de la picaresca', and includes among other articles: F. Cabo Aseguinolaza, 'La novela picaresca y los modelos de la historia literaria' (23–38);

M. Cavillac, 'La figura del mercader en el *Guzmán de Alfarache*' (69–84); E. Cros, 'La noción de novela picaresca como género desde la perspectiva sociocrítica' (85–94); A. Rey Hazas, 'El bestiario emblemático de *La pícara Justina*' (119–46).

7. INDIVIDUAL AUTHORS

CERVANTES. *Don Quijote de la Mancha*, ed. T. Lathrop, 2 vols, Newark, Juan de la Cuesta, 871, vi + 150 pp., is a superb edition for English speaking readers, which focuses on linguistic and cultural vagaries; the second volume is a most useful DQ dictionary, Spanish-English. *Don Quijote*, trans. Burton Raffel, ed. Diana de Armas Wilson, NY, Norton, 1999, 858 pp. *Don Quixote*, trans. John Rutherford, ed. Roberto González Echevarría, Harmondsworth, Penguin, 2000, 1023 pp. José Ortega y Gasset, *Meditations on Quixote*, trans. Evelyn Rugg and Diego Marín, ed. Julián Marías, Urbana–Chicago, Illinois U.P., 2000, 192 pp.

David R. Castillo, *(A)wry Views. Anamorphosis, Cervantes, and the Early Picaresque*, West Lafayette, Purdue U.P., 182 pp. includes studies on the *Lazarillo*, *Guzmán de Alfarache*, *La pícara Justina*, *Don Quixote*, *Persiles*, and the honour system in Cervantes's theatre. *Echoes and Inscriptions. Comparative Approaches to Early Modern Spanish Literatures*, ed. Barbara Simerka and Christopher B. Weimer, Lewisburg, Bucknell U.P., 2000, 277 pp. Frederick A. De Armas, *Cervantes, Raphael and the Classics* (CSLAIL), 1998, 241 pp. *Cervantes for the 21st Century / Cervantes para el siglo XXI. Studies in Honor of Edward Dudley*, ed. Francisco La Rubia Prado, Newark, Juan de la Cuesta, 2000, 238 pp., includes A. J. Cruz, 'Redressing Dorotea' (11–32); E. Friedman, 'Guzmán de Alfarache, Don Quijote, and the subject of the novel' (61–78); E. M. Gerli, 'Truth, lies, and representation: the crux of *El curioso impertinente*' (107–22). Henry W. Sullivan, *Grotesque Purgatory. A Study of Cervantes's Don Quixote*, Part II, University Park, Penn State U.P., 1999, 216 pp. Hans-Jörg Neuschäfer, *La ética del Quijote. Función de las novelas intercaladas*, M, Gredos, 1999, 122 pp. Jean Canavaggio, *Cervantes entre vida y creación*, Biblioteca de Estudios Cervantinos, Alcalá de Henares, 2000, 253 pp. Charles D. Presberg, *Adventures in Paradox. Don Quixote and the Western Tradition*, University Park, Penn State U.P., 250 pp.

GRACIÁN. *Obras completas*, ed. Luis Sánchez Laílla, pref. A. Egido, M, Espasa, 1700 pp. *El Criticón*, ed. Carlos Vaíllo, pref. José Manuel Blecua (Biblioteca Universal), M, Círculo de Lectores, 2000, 953 pp. *El Héroe*, ed. Aurora Egido, Zaragoza, Institución Fernando el Cátólico, 48 pp., is a facsimile edition of the autograph manuscript in the National Library in Madrid. *Oráculo manual y arte de prudencia*, ed. Aurora Egido, Zaragoza, Institución Fernando el Católico, xl + 210 ff., is a wonderful facsimile of this 'libro menino' printed in Huesca by Juan Nogués in 1647. *Libros libres de Baltasar Gracián, catálogo de la exposición bibliográfica*, Zaragoza, Gobierno de Aragón, 314 pp., includes F. Bouza, 'Aun en lo material del papel y impresión'. Sobre la cultura escrita en el siglo de Gracián' (11–50); A. Egido 'Gracián y sus libros' (51–86); J. Moll, 'Hacia una bibliografía estructurada de las obras sueltas de Gracián' (87–93); F. Asín Remírez de Esparza, 'La imprenta en Huesca en la época de Gracián' (95–110). Malcom K. Read, *Transitional Discourses: Culture and Society in Early Modern Spain* (Ottawa Hispanic Studies, 21), Ottawa, Dovehouse, 1998, 274 pp., includes 'Saving appearances: language and commodification in Baltasar Gracián' (91–120). Miguel Grande Yáñez, *Justicia y ley natural en Baltasar Gracián*, M, Comillas U.P., 2000, 410 pp. Aurora Egido has also published *Humanidades y dignidad del hombre en Baltasar Gracián*, Salamanca U.P., 182 pp., and *Las caras de la prudencia y Baltasar Gracián*, M, Castalia, 2000, 258 pp. *Gracián Hoy, Boletín de la Fundación Federico García Lorca*, includes A. Egido, 'En el nombre de Baltasar Gracián y Morales' (17–22), F. Rodríguez de la Flor, 'El corazón celado. Baltasar Gracián y las figuras de la disimulación barroca' (53–69), and M. G. Profeti, 'Sobre intertextualidad y red teórica en la *Agudeza*' (107–09). *Baltasar Gracián: estado de la cuestión y nuevas perspectivas*, ed. Aurora Egido and María Carmen Marín, Zaragoza, Gobierno de Aragón–Institución 'Fernando El Católico', 229 pp., includes studies on individual works by Gracián, such as C. Vaíllo on *El criticón*, A. Montaner on *El político don Fernando el Católico*; J. Moll surveys editorial problems, 'En busca de las primeras ediciones de Gracián' (161–63).

QUEVEDO. *Historia de la vida del Buscón llamado don Pablos, ejemplo de vagamundos y espejo de tacaños*, ed. Victoriano Roncero López, M, Biblioteca Nueva, 1999, 279 pp. *La musa Clío del Parnaso español de Quevedo*, ed. Ignacio Arellano and Victoriano Roncero, Pamplona, EUNSA, 212 pp., is a profusely annotated edition and scholarly study of a key part of Q.'s poetic *corpus*. S. López Poza, 'Agudeza simbólica aplicada al vituperio político en cuatro sonetos de Quevedo', *RFLI*, 3, 2000: 197–223.

SAN JUAN DE LA CRUZ. Birgitta Mark, *Mysticism and Cognition. The Cognitive Development of John of the Cross as Revealed in his Works*, Aarhus U.P., 2000, 299 pp. Hein Blommestijn, Jos Huls, and Kees Waajman, *The Footprint of Love. John of the Cross and Guide in the Wilderness*, trans. John Vriend, Louvain, Peeters, 2000, 211 pp.

LITERATURE 1490–1700 (DRAMA)
POSTPONED

LITERATURE, 1700–1823

By GABRIEL SÁNCHEZ ESPINOSA, *Lecturer in Hispanic Studies,*
The Queen's University of Belfast

1. BIBLIOGRAPHY

F. Aguilar Piñal, *Bibliografía de autores españoles del siglo* XVIII. X: *Anónimos II*, M, CSIC, 736 pp., contains 5,227 entries relating to anonymous legal and normative works — always so difficult to trace — ordered chronologically. This last volume of the series means the successful culmination of this exemplary research tool for *dieciochistas*.

2. THOUGHT AND THE ENLIGHTENMENT

M. Bolufer, 'Los intelectuales valencianos y la cultura británica del siglo XVIII', *Estudis*, 27:299–346, centres on British travellers in the Valencia region, the British correspondents of G. Mayans, and A. Ponz's 1783 journey to England.

A. Jardine, *Cartas de España*, Alicante U.P., 442 pp., contains a useful study and well annotated translation by J.-F. Pérez Berenguel of the Spanish section of the *Letters from Barbary, France, Spain, Portugal* (London, 1788), written by an artillery officer who became British consul in Corunna between 1793 and 1796, and maintained in those years a significant correspondence with G.-M. de Jovellanos. In the early 1790s, Jardine had moved in the radical circles of William Godwin and the Philomathian Society in London.

La imagen de Manuel Godoy, ed. I. Rose-de Viejo and E. Laparra López, Badajoz, Junta de Extremadura, 193 pp., is a useful book published on the occasion of the 150th anniversary of the death of Manuel Godoy, the *Príncipe de la Paz*, main minister during the reign of Charles IV (1788–1808), that goes further towards the necessary revision of this important figure in the crisis period of the Spanish Enlightenment. E. La Parra's 'El mejor servidor del Rey, Manuel Godoy (1767–1851)', *ib.*, 55–116, studies among other topics Godoy's difficult and ambiguous dealings with the main intellectuals and *ilustrados* of his period in government; I. Rose-de Viejo's article 'Una imagen real para el favorito: galería retratística de Manuel Godoy', *ib.*, 119–73, approaches *inter alia* the topics of his book collecting and his sponsoring of books.

J. Santos Puerto, '*La Sinapia*: luces para buscar la utopía de la ilustración', *BH*, n.s. [2001]:481–510, argues convincingly that the Benedictine Martín Sarmiento (1695–1772) could be the author of this 'utopia' that up to now has been attributed to an unknown *novator* in the first half of the 18th century. A. Úbeda de los Cobos, *Pensamiento artístico español del siglo XVIII. De Antonio Palomino a Francisco de Goya*, M, Aldeasa–Museo del Prado, 443 pp.

E. Velasco Moreno, *La Real Academia de la Historia en el siglo XVIII: una historia de sociabilidad*, M, Centro de Estudios Políticos y Constitucionales, 2000, 342 pp., approaches this fundamental institution of Spanish Enlightenment from the point of view of Habermas's concept of the public sphere. Chapter 3 studies the legal structure and day to day functioning of the Academy. Chapters 4 and 5 are dedicated to the characterization of the academicians, their privileges and obligations. Chapter 6 chronicles the different literary projects in which the Academy was involved in the course of the 18th c. and focuses on its relevant role as a consultative institution in cultural matters. Appendix 3 provides a very useful biographical inventory of academicians.

3. LITERARY HISTORY

GENERAL. M. Boixareu and R. Desné, *Recepción de autores franceses de la época clásica en los siglos XVIII y XIX en España y en el extranjero*, M, Uned, 380 pp., gathers together the papers delivered at a conference that took place in Ávila in Autumn 1997. The following articles stand out amongst those included: J. Checa Beltrán, 'Fuentes francesas de la teoría literaria española del siglo XVIII' (51–58), G. Sánchez Espinosa, 'Madame de Sévigné y la carta familiar en España durante el siglo XVIII' (111–23), A.-C. Tolivar, 'La réception de Racine dans l'Espagne du XVIIIe siècle' (127–37), A. Saura, 'Recepción en España de las tragedias de Prosper Jolyot de Crébillon' (171–89), N. Bittoun-Debruyne, 'Le théâtre de Marivaux en Espagne (XVIIIe et XIXe siècles)' (191–204), and M.-J. Alonso Seoane, 'Una novela inédita de Olavide y su original francés' (247–52).

J. Checa Beltrán, 'Apuntes sobre poética y machismo', *Salina*, 12:70–75, reviews some Spanish 18th-c. *poéticas* from what is an unusual critical perspective as regards this kind of texts.

M. Meléndez, 'Eighteenth-century Spanish America: historical dimensions and new theoretical approaches', *REH*, 35:615–32, aims to correct the usually scarce attention paid to the literary and cultural production of this socially very dynamic century, offering an informative panorama of the most relevant contributions published in the past decade from the perspective of new theoretical approaches.

España festejante. El siglo XVIII, ed. M. Torrione, Málaga, Diputación de Málaga, 2000, 559 pp., is mainly devoted to the study of 18th-c. literary sub-genres and ephemeral literature. The following articles stand out: C. Gilard, 'Reyes y bandidos: el arte de morir en el pliego

de cordel narrativo' (85–94), M. Coulon, 'Representación y significación de la fiesta en el sainete de la segunda mitad del siglo XVIII'
(165–72), L. Domergue, 'Nipho canta las glorias de los Borbones: el
periodista y la literatura de circunstancia' (249–55), F.-J. Campos y
Fernández de Sevilla, 'Ciclo literario en el convento madrileño de
San Felipe el Real con motivo de la coronación de Carlos IV'
(257–65), M. Torrione, 'El real coliseo del Buen Retiro: memoria de
una arquitectura desaparecida' (295–322).

F. Uzcanga Meinecke, 'Ideas de la sátira en el siglo XVIII: hacia
una nueva función en el marco de la ideología ilustrada', *RLit*,
126:425–59, undertakes a diachronic survey of 18th-c. Spanish
comments on the theory of satire, focusing on Luzán, the polemics
around *Fray Gerundio de Campazas*, the statements of neoclassical
authors such as Nicolás Fernández de Moratín, and the satirical press.
The rehabilitation of this genre in the 18th c. ran parallel to the
process of secularization in which Spanish society was immersed.

NARRATIVE.   Segunda Martínez de Robles, *Las españolas náufragas
o Correspondencia de dos amigas (1831)*, ed. M.-A. Sánchez Sánchez,
Salamanca, GES XVIII, 2000, 138 pp., is an edition of a short
Byzantine novel narrated through the correspondence of two female
friends who sign their letters DSM and NDS. The author must have
been the daughter of an absolutist army officer in the Spain of
Ferdinand VII.

Ana Rueda, *Cartas sin lacrar. La novela epistolar y la España ilustrada,
1789–1840*, M, Iberoamericana, 524 pp., chronicles and analyses
this hitherto neglected genre that succeeded in presenting Spanish
contemporary society to its readers. Rueda's study will undoubtedly
contribute to a revision of the origins of the 19th-c. Spanish realist
novel.

PERIODICAL LITERATURE.   *El Pensador*, Lanzarote, Universidad de
Las Palmas de Gran Canaria–Cabildo de Lanzarote, 1999, 7 vols, is
a facsimile edition of one of the most important and imitated
periodicals of the Spanish Enlightenment, originally published
between the years 1762–67 by J. Clavijo y Fajardo following the
model of Addison's *Spectator*. This work is indispensable for all
interested in this period. Vol. I contains a very light introduction to
the work.

THEATRE.   J.-J. Berbel Rodríguez, 'La tragedia *Ataúlfo* de Monti-
ano y el concordato de 1753', *RLit*, 125:115–28, situates this tragedy
based on the first Visigothic king of Spain in its political context: the
peaceful reign of Ferdinand VI and the positive ending in January
1753 of the negotiations between the Spanish *regalista* government
and Rome. *Ataúlfo* was never written to be performed — contrary to
the opinion of R. Andioc, who thought it was banned from the stage,

because of its risky political motifs, which he associated with the Esquilache riots — but to be read by a selected readership of poets and intellectuals linked to the political establishment.

L. D. Harney, 'Carnival and critical reception in the *sainete* tradition', *MLN*, 117:310–30, addresses the polarization characteristic of criticism and scholarship regarding the composition and reception of 18th-c. *sainete* and late 19th-c. *género chico*.

4. Individual Authors

AZARA.   G. Sánchez Espinosa, 'La relación de las exequias de Carlos III en Roma y el nuevo gusto neoclásico', *Goya*, 282:169–77, studies the non-venal, luxury publications — some of them by the printer G. Bodoni — that recorded Charles III's funerals in the Neo-classical Rome of Pope Pius VI and looks at how this baroque literary genre was used as a vehicle for new ideas of the Enlightenment and Neo-Classicism.

CADALSO.   A. C. Graf, 'Necrophilia and materialist thoughts in José Cadalso's *Noches lúgubres*: romanticism's anxious adornment of political economy', *JSCS*, 2:210–30, sees morbid romantic sentimentalism as a function of a dynamic relationship between early modern psychosexual conventions (as recorded by Petrarch) and the late 18th c.'s crisis of political economy (Adam Smith's labour valuation of wealth).

CIENFUEGOS.   R. Froldi, 'Nicasio Álvarez de Cienfuegos, dramaturgo', *Salina*, 15:133–37, studies his tragedies *Idomeneo, Pítaco, Zoraida,* and *La condesa de Castilla.* In his opinion, the moral conflict, which is the main element in Cienfuegos's thought and works, shapes the dramatic action of these plays written during the crisis period of the Spanish Enlightenment. Cienfuegos's despair cannot be identified with Romanticism. Politically he is very close to the liberalism that will bear fruit in the 1812 Cadiz Constitution. In his writing Cienfuegos avoids the rigidity of classical tradition.

CLAVIJERO.   R. Froldi, 'Una carta inédita de Francisco Javier Clavijero, en torno a la supresión de la Compañía de Jesús', *RLit*, 126:517–33, edits an unknown letter of *c.* 1776 by the exiled author of the *Storia antica de Messico* and the *Storia della California* in which he sternly criticizes Pope Clement XIV and the secular powers in Europe for the suppression of the Jesuits.

CLAVIJO Y FAJARDO.   *Prólogo a la traducción de la Historia Natural del Conde de Buffon*, ed. J.-L. Prieto, La Orotava (Tenerife), Fundación Canaria Orotava de Historia de la Ciencia, 90 pp., is a well-prologued edition that is aimed more at the general public than the specialist reader.

FORNER. P. Álvarez de Miranda, 'Una carta inédita de Juan Pablo Forner y su contexto polémico', pp. 21–29 of *Homenaje a Elena Catena*, ed. F. Sevilla Arroyo, M, Castalia, 576 pp., shows Forner's intervention as an arrogant polemicist for hire in a forgotten literary quarrel between second rank writers that took place in Madrid in 1790 in the pages of the periodicals *Correo de Madrid* and *Diario de Madrid*.

FUERTE HÍJAR. A. Acereda, *La marquesa de Fuerte Híjar, una dramaturga de la Ilustración (estudio y edición de La sabia indiscreta)*, Cadiz U.P., 2000, 279 pp., presents in its literary and social context a one-act play by a hitherto little-known female writer, the Marchioness of Fuerte Híjar (1748–1817?), a friend of the poet N. Álvarez de Cienfuegos, who presided over a literary salon and was a member of the Junta de Damas of the Economic Society of Madrid.

IRIARTE. Tomás de Iriarte, *Recurso jurídico del zagal Dorido (1784)*, Rimini, Panozzo–Bologna U.P., 2000, 75 pp. is a new addition by Maurizio Fabbri to the Spanish 18th-c. series published by the Centro di Studi sul Settecento Spagnolo of the University of Bologna. The anonymous satirical poem *Recurso jurídico que ante el tribunal de Apolo y a nombre de los ingenios de Madrid hace el zagal Dorido en defensa y desagravio del desprecio que se ha hecho de sus obras*, originated in the wake of the scandal of the 1784 play-writing competition organized by Madrid city council, which gave the prize to C.-M. Trigueros's *Los menestrales* and J. Meléndez Valdés's *Las bodas de Camacho*. Throughout his introduction M. Fabbri defends the hypothesis of T. de Iriarte's authorship of this polymetric, 1000-line poem, that proves to be in need of a final polish, and was written in the tradition of Cervantes's *Viaje de Parnaso*. His main argument for the attribution is the inclusion of Iriarte's sonnet, '¡Oh *Bodas de Camacho*, oh sin ventura . . .', in the body of the poem (vv. 712–25). Nevertheless, this attribution does not match well with the fiercely anti-neoclassical spirit that is dominant throughout this satirical poem.

LUZÁN. R. Hill, 'Modern science as emergent culture: Luzán's *Juicio de París renovado: fábula épica*', *Hispanófila*, 132:53–68, analyses this poem, written for the festivities celebrating King Ferdinand VI's entry into Madrid in 1746, as a significant example of I. Luzán's interest in Newton's theories and experimental science in general.

SAMANIEGO. Félix María de Samaniego, *Obras Completas*, ed. Emilio Palacios, M, Fundación José Antonio de Castro, 663 pp., contains not only his fables written for the Real Seminario Bascongado, but also his complete erotic poetry and his version of the *Arte poética* by Horace.

TRIGUEROS. Cándido María Trigueros, *Teatro Español Burlesco o Quijote de los teatros (1802)*, ed. M.-J. Rodríguez Sánchez de León, with a prologue by F. Aguilar Piñal, Salamanca, GES xviii, 2000, 157 pp., and by the same editor, *El académico Cándido María Trigueros (1736–1798)*, M, Real Academia de la Historia, 267 pp., are two valuable additions to our knowledge of this very active figure in the literary life of the Spanish Enlightenment. The latter book focuses on Trigueros's activities as a member of different Academies or learned societies and gathers together various studies published by F. Aguilar Piñal in the last 20 years.

LITERATURE 1823–1898

POSTPONED

LITERATURE, 1898–1936

By K. M. SIBBALD, *McGill University*

1. GENERAL

BIBLIOGRAPHY. *Artículos periodísticos (1900–1998)*, ed. Francisco Gutiérrez Carbajo, M, Castalia, 1999, 328 pp., anthologizes significant excerpts by the Generation of 1898, Blasco Ibáñez, Ortega y Gasset, and Francisco Ayala, as well as the lesser known Zamacois, Carmen de Burgos, and Corpus Barga from our period; the texts deal with anarchism, ethics, World War I, the Church, and the Second Republic in 20th-c. life and letters. Elisabel Larriba, *Dictionnaire de la littérature espagnole*, Paris, Champion, 158 pp., attempts to atone for perceived neglect by offering a concise, historical compendium replete with individual bibliographies for student use; of slight interest here, it contains potted accounts of familiar material on the now classic members of the Generations of 1898 and 1927, although, curiously, Maeztu and Gerardo Diego are omitted, while José María Cossío and María Teresa León get a mention apiece, and Pérez de Ayala is misspelt. 'Bibliografía', *NRFH*, 49:581–670, see particularly 'Siglo XX' (640–70), is a real treasure trove for further study, with important bibliographic additions on Alberti, Dámaso Alonso, Azorín, Benavente, García Lorca, Juan Ramón, Antonio Machado, and Unamuno; while C. Byrne, 'Review of miscellanies', *BHS(G)*, 78:411–20, lists other items of interest on the Generation of 1898, Dámaso Alonso, Diego, and Antonio Machado.

PERIODICAL LITERATURE. M. A. González López, 'Índice de la revista *Raza española* (1919–1930)', *RLit*, 63:535–82, documents the editorial policy, contributors, and contents of this nationalist magazine that reflected the distinctly conservative taste of its founder, Blanca de los Ríos, in art, history, and literature. L. Estepa, 'Manuel Machado, la revista *Manolita* y la tertulia de Cansinos Asséns', *CHA*, 613–14:197–212, recounts the fun and games surrounding the gestation in 1916 in La Campana tavern of two issues of a forgotten little review whose motto was 'picardía, frivolidad', with input from Cansinos Asséns, Juan Cascales Muñoz, Manuel Machado, José Andión, and Antonio Sánchez, as well as details of two poems by Machado and an account of Juan Ramón's wedding. María Teresa García-Abad García, *Perfiles críticos para una historia del teatro español: 'La Voz' y 'La Libertad' 1926–36*, SSSAS, 2000, 367 pp., documents thoroughly the complex web of ideas about the theatre between the two World Wars, with very useful bibliographies of articles and reviews published in these major newspapers by such distinguished critics as *Andrenio*, Manuel Machado, Alberto Ínsua, Melchor Fernández Almagro, Enrique de Mesa, and Luis Aranjo-Costa, as well as noted practitioners in the theatre arts such as Max Aub, Azorín, Ramón J. Sender, Cipriano Rivas Cherif, Jacinto Grau, and Benjamín Jarnés, among others. J. M. Barrera López, 'De las *Primeras vanguardias* al núcleo central del 27: el corpus de revistas', *Ínsula*, 649–50: 2–6, reprints some earlier ideas in a comprehensive listing, together with the plea for a complete set both of the facsimiles of these now impossible-to-find little magazines and an epistolary archive that would illustrate and explicate such work. Patricia Bolaños-Fabres, *El 27 lúdico: los suplementos de 'Carmen' y 'Gallo'*, Valladolid, Universitas Castellae, 2000, 96 pp., looks at the new literature espoused by the 1927 Generation, recording the buzz words *gurrinica, catoblepa, putrefacto*, and *Antofagasta* in the generational slang, and situating the two reviews alongside other contemporary periodical literature (see also *YWMLS*, 53: 349).

LITERARY AND CULTURAL HISTORY. *La generación del 98 frente al nuevo fin de siglo*, ed. Jesús Torrecilla, Amsterdam–Atlanta, Rodopi, 2000, 301 pp., makes the neat division between the essays on the relation of this group to the larger context of European Modernism, and those concentrating on differences between the centre and the periphery in the power base(s) of Spanish society. This can be read with profit alongside the intelligent collection of essays in *Spain's 1898 Crisis. Regenerationism, Modernism, Post-Colonialism*, ed. Joseph Harrison and Alan Hoyle, MUP, 2000, 293 pp., in which of special interest are the first two of three parts: Unamuno and Maeztu are the main focus in the different perspectives on the regenerationist debate in J. Harrison, 'Tackling national decadence: economic regenerationism in Spain after the colonial *débâcle*' (55–67), S. G. H. Roberts, 'Unamuno and the restoration political project: a re-evaluation' (68–80), G. Minter, '*Amor y pedagogía*: an object lesson in biography' (81–90), N. G. Round, 'Horrible children' (91–104), on Galdós, Unamuno and Pérez de Ayala, and, taking the international view, A. Hennessy, 'Ramiro de Maeztu: *hispanidad* and the search for a surrogate imperialism' (105–17); loosely grouped under modernism in Part II are J. Blasco, 'El "98" que nunca existió' (121–31), questioning the very notion of the 1898 Generation altogether; A. Sinclair, 'Authority or authenticity? The battle of the cultures at the millennial crossroads' (132–45), on such a clash as evinced in the writings of Baroja and Unamuno and its relevance today; S. Kirkpatrick, 'The "feminine element": *fin-de siècle* Spain, modernity, and the woman writer' (146–55), righting the sexual balance by reference to María Martínez Sierra; R. A. Cardwell, 'Deconstructing the binaries of *enfrentismo*: José María Llanas Aguilaniedo's *Navegar pintoresco* and the finisecular novel' (156–69), rescuing a neglected figure in order to blur distinctions between the Generation and *modernismo*; A. Longhurst, 'Noventaiocho y novela: lo viejo y lo nuevo' (170–80), identifying the fiction of the generation within the wider European definition of modernism, while A. Hoyle, 'The function of landscape in Baroja's *La lucha por la vida*' (181–94), supports the usefulness of the more conventional grouping; J. Macklin, 'Constructing the 98: Pérez de Ayala's 1942 prologue to *Troteras y andanzas*' (195–204), reveals the retrospective view from a literary legatee, G. Gullón, 'La percepción sensorial y el texto modernista' (205–15), deconstructs the whole 1898 edifice, while P. McDermott, 'Modernism and imperialism' (216–26), focuses on Machado to show how he reaches beyond nationalism to post-imperialism. The whole is rounded off by five more essays dealing with the repercussions of the Spanish-American War still felt in Latin America.

Cambio de siglo. Ideas, mentalidades, sensibilidades en España hacia 1900, ed. Patrick Collard and Eric Storm, Amsterdam–Atlanta, Rodopi, 2000, 148 pp., brings together general essays on the intellectuals and their dealings with the clergy, the *pueblo*, and the 'problema de España' by Julio de la Checa Merino and Diego Núñez, and on women's writing at the turn of the century by Elizabeth Munson; while specific authors of this period are taken up most competently in E. I. Fox, 'Azorín, periodista público'; F. Peyrègne, 'Antonio Machado, deseo y frustración'; R. Lefere, '*Hacia otra España*: hacia un compromiso total'; and J. Goode, 'La contradicción como arma: Ortega y Gasset y el concepto español de la modernidad'. Francisco Javier Díez de Revenga, *La poesía de Vanguardia*, M, Laberinto, 206 pp., provides a useful 'Cronología' (9–11) and some graphic illustrations from the relevant little poetry magazines, focuses on the Spanish poets of *ultraísmo*, *creacionismo*, and surrealism, and selects the necessary bibliography (204–14) for their study.

The contribution of a peripheral figure attracts attention: R. Quance, 'Un espejo vacío: sobre una ilustración de Norah Borges para el ultraísmo', *RO*, 237:134–47, complemented by S. Bauer, 'Norah Borges, musa de las vanguardias', *CHA*, 610:87–96, an account of 'los hermanos ultra', Jorge Luis Borges and his sister Norah, in *Grecia* and *Proa*, and appreciative comments by Isaac del Vando Villar, Adriano del Valle, Guillermo de Torre, and Gómez de la Serna.

In an on-going review, J. Issorel, 'Note (no. 3) sur les anthologies de la génération de 1927', *BH*, 102, 2000:249–59, relentlessly continues to document the collections and anthologies, here those published between 1993–99 by Gaspar Garrote Bernal, Antonio Gómez Yebra, Manuel Cifo González, Miguel Casado and Olvido

García Valdés, Francisco Moreno Gómez, Víctor de Lama, Víctor de la Concha, and Emilio Miró (see also *YWMLS*, 47:373, 56:384); while F. M. Soguero, 'Las antologías de prosa de 1927', *Ínsula*, 649-50:31-33, gives details of the less-celebrated prose writings collected since 1997 by Domingo Ródenas and Ana Rodríguez Fischer, with a tip of the hat to the earlier commentaries and texts collated by Díaz-Plaja (1956) and Ramón Buckley and John Crispin (1973); and, despite the title, María Victoria Utrera Torremocha, *Teoría del poema en prosa*, Seville U.P., 1999, 395 pp., concentrates on concrete practice rather than abstract theorizing, particularly with regard to Juan Ramón, the 1927 Generation in general, and Luis Cernuda in particular.

As a preview to the centenary celebration, Javier Pérez Bazo, in collaboration with Carmen Valcárcel, edits, with an introductory study and suitable annotations, Juan Chabás, *Literatura española contemporánea (1858–1950)*, M, Verbum, cxiv + 703 pp., the highly personal, but still useful, literary history first published in Cuba in 1952; Id. compiles the special number of *Ínsula*, 657, 'De la fábula a la vida. Juan Chabás (1900–1954)', containing Id., 'Juan Chabás en la literatura de su tiempo' (3–6), an overview of the author's long trajectory through *ultraísta* verse, vanguard novels, and later poetry of social commitment, that highlights the critical essay as Chabás's *forte*, and pays tribute to his connections with the major reviews of the day; J. L. Bernal Salgado, 'Reflejos vanguardistas: *Espejo* de Juan Chabás' (6–7), a commentary on the curious mixture of *ultraísmo* and tradition in the echoes of Jiménez and Antonio Machado along with those of Huidobro; F. J. Díez de Revenga, 'La poesía de Juan Chabás en las revistas de la primera vanguardia' (8–11), quoting extensively from the 'hibridismo' of the poems published 1921–22 in *España*, *Ultra*, *Índice*, and *Horizonte*; J. M. Barrera López, 'De *Ultra* a *La joven literatura*: Chabás en su generación' (11–15), sets his sights on one of the 'estrellas diminutas' (with Garfias and Hinojosa) of the 1927 Generation, and adds some useful documentation from the local newspapers *El Liberal*, *El Correo de Andalucía*, and *El Noticiero Sevillano*; D. Ródenas de Moya, 'Notas sobre los primeros pasos novelísticos de Juan Chabás' (15–17), indicates the Levantine influence of Azorín and Miró; M. Aznar Soler, 'Juan Chabás y las vanguardias teatrales: sus colaboraciones en *Diario de Barcelona* (1929–1930)' (18–20), documents well how the 'Arte y Letras' section began on 24 January 1929 as an undefined miscellany open to 'las palpitaciones de la actualidad' but soon became a definite 'programa' and then a serious 'boletín de noticias' marking genuine literary innovation in the work of Aub, Valentín Andrés Álvarez, Gómez de la Serna, and Claudio de la Torre; G. Morelli, 'Juan Chabás y la Generación del 1927' (21–23), justifies Chabás's relation to the group as a critic; J. D. Cuadriello, 'El exilio de Juan Chabás en Cuba' (23–26), gives details of Chabás's work for *Nosotros*, *Hoy*, and *Luz*, university teaching, and semi-clandestine life in Batista's right-wing Havana, all framed by Chabás's three marriages to Simone Téry, Lydia de Rivera, and Aída Valls; J. García Gabaldón, 'Del ensayo crítico a la historiografía literaria' (26–29), concentrates on Chabás's 'crítica concéntrica', arguing that he is a worthy contemporary of José Bergamín, Dámaso Alonso, Giménez Caballero, and Antonio Espina in the Vossler-Spitzer-Croce-Rémy de Gourmont tradition; C. González, ' "Olvidado de su sangre": el enigma de un cuento de *Fábula y vida*, de Juan Chabás' (29–32), is a close reading of a difficult prose piece describing the recurrent nightmares about action in the field long after the Spanish Civil War had ended; and A. Dubost, 'Sombras y luces de la vida de Juan Chabás' (33–36) is a graphic account of Chabás's bitter isolation and exile in Cuba despite the consolation offered by wife Aída Valls and friend Juan Marinello.

A curious pair from opposite ends of the spectrum: Miguel Ángel Lozano Marco, *Imágenes de pesimismo. Literatura y arte en España 1898–1930, Alicante U.P., 2000, 119 pp., collects work published on the symbolist aesthetic since 1987, with reference to the topic of 'la España negra', José Gutiérrez Solana and Valle-Inclán, and Azorín as a literary critic between 1912–15, *Lecturas españolas* and resignation in the Azorinian vision of reality; while J. A. Llera, 'Poéticas del humor: desde el novecentismo hasta la época contemporánea', *RLit*, 63:461–76, includes short entries of interest here on 'los novecentistas' Ortega, Gómez de la Serna, and Wenceslao Fernández Flórez, as well as the 'other' Generation of 1927 that includes Jardiel Poncela, Miguel Mihura, and Edgar Neville. J. Whiston, ' "República y paz": monarchy and militarism in Azaña's writings on Primo de Rivera's *coup d'état* of 1923', *BHS(G)*, 78:775–91, is a well-researched assessment of Azaña's call for new solutions to counterbalance the disastrous combination of the monarchy and the military in Spain since 1814, that pays proper tribute to this important modernizer who made such good use of invective and gallows humour in the clarity and cogency of his critique of the take-over by Primo de Rivera.

Some overdue revisionism is practised from the woman's point of view. Catherine G. Bellver, *Absence and Presence: Spanish Women Poets of the Twenties and Thirties*, Cranbury, NJ, Bucknell U.P., 294 pp., not only provides the necessary amplification of the literary panorama in the early 20th c. but also a valuable addition to the theoretical discussion of contemporary Spanish poetry; a feminist take is given on the 'athletic personality' of Concha Méndez, Josefina de la Torre's female discourse, Rosa Chacel's linguistic virtuosity, Carmen Conde's innovative change of course, and the sexual basis of Ernestina de Champourcín's *jouissance*, all in a well-stocked arsenal of anecdotes, bibliographic sources, and feminist writing. Breaking with the traditionally all-male identification of the 1927 Generation, Gregory K. Cole, *Spanish Women Poets of the Generation of 1927*, Lewiston, NY, Mellen, 2000, 189 pp., picks out six women worthy of further study, Pilar de Valderrama, Elisabeth Mulder, Rosa Chacel, Josefina de la Torre, Concha Méndez, and Ernestina de Champourcín, but gives only basic introductory overviews and some bio-bibliographical information. *Mujeres novelistas en el panorama literario del siglo XX*, ed. Marina Villaba Álvarez, Cuenca, Castilla-La Mancha U.P., 2000, 437 pp., collects papers from the 1998 international conference on Spanish narrative, with notable interventions on mothers and daughters in Spanish literature, epistolary autobiography, as well as some specific work on Rosa Chacel of interest here. *Breve historia feminista de la literatura española (en lengua catalana, gallega y vasca*, VI, ed. Iris Zavala, Rubí, Anthropos, 2000, fleshes out the general picture.

The often difficult relationship between the two art forms is highlighted in a special number of *ALEC*, 26, dedicated to 'Teatro y cine' containing D. Dougherty, 'Pensándolo bien: el teatro a la luz del cine (1914–1936)' (9–25), which uses writings of Antonio Espina, Benjamín Jarnés, Antonio Machado, Unamuno, and Pérez de Ayala to elucidate how, after World War I, the *revista de gran espectáculo* and a revised Aristotelianism, principally embodied in García Lorca's tragedies, were the theatrical answers to the challenge posed by the cinema; M. T. García-Abad García, '*Viaje a la luna*: del texto ΌΣΤΡΑΚΟΝ a la imagen onírica' (27–44), exploring the mesh between the work of painter Frédéric Amat and dramatist García Lorca in this hybrid art form; A. L. Hueso, 'El referente teatral en la evolución histórica del cine' (46–61), citing a motley cast that includes Max Reinhardt, Brecht, Marcel Pagnol, Tennessee Williams, Arthur Miller, and Kenneth Branagh, to show how often the theatre has been the referent for the more important moments in the history of the cinema; J. M. del Pino, 'Poéticas enfrentadas: teatro y cine en Antonio Espina y la *Revista de Occidente*' (91–112), which shows how two articles, theorizing on the then newest art form and published in 1925 and 1927, respectively, were fundamental documents in the evolution of the Spanish vanguard given the formal enunciation of the crisis in the theatre and the future direction of fiction to be found therein; R. Utrera Macías, '*La Lola se va a los puertos*: una obra teatral con dos versiones cinematográficas' (147–73), sets up a triangle between the theatre play and a first film version made in 1947 for a nationalist audience and the very different socio-political context of the second shot in 1993; C. B. Morris, 'Los Quintero ante los "cambios y mudanzas" de su época' (175–97), recovers the humour of these dramatists' deliberate celebration of the voice and its registers in the early years of the silent cinema; M. P. Holt, 'Jardiel Poncela's dark Hollywood comedy: anticipating postmodernism' (199–211), looks at the kaleidescope of verbal and visual intetextuality in *El amor sólo dura 2.000 metros*, finding similarities in *Singin' in the Rain*, *The Day of the Locust*, and Charles Busch's plays of the 1980s in the postmodern parodic case of the replayable art form; while J. A. Pérez Bowie, 'Teatro en verso y cine: una relación conflictiva' (317–35), makes some valuable observations on work by Pérez de Ayala, the Machados, Pedro Muñoz Seca, and Jardiel Poncela which has been adapted for the cinema. In a similar vein, María Asunción Gómez, *Del escenario a la pantalla. La adaptación cinematográfica del teatro español*, Chapel Hill, NC, North Carolina U.P., 2000, 231 pp., selects various theatrical works adapted to the silver screen; of interest here are her comments concerning Carlos Saura's filmic version of *Bodas de sangre*, the ideological distance between Arniches's *La señorita de Trevélez* and Juan Antonio Bardem's *Calle mayor*, and a feminist reading of changes in plot and character in the film *Divinas palabras*. More specifically, M. Ribar, 'Surrealism, *tremendismo*, love and sexuality in turn-of-the-century Spanish film: images from the cinema of Luis Buñuel', *HisJ*, 22 : 349–56, rehearses some standard opinions about Buñuel's forceful tactics in denouncing all that opposes human freedom.

2. POETRY

A sound overview, A. Acereda, 'La poética del modernismo: una hermenéutica de la modernidad existencial', *CA*, 85 : 85–103, provides some revisionist critical thinking about *modernismo* and Modernism, with interesting comments on Rosalía de Castro's role and the transatlantic connections in modern Spanish poetry. Héctor Martínez Ferrer, *Ultraísmo, creacionismo, surrealismo. Análisis textual (AMal*, Anejo 26), Malaga, Fac. de Filosofia y Letras, Malaga Univ., 1999, 262 pp., contains some careful, extended thematic and stylistic analyses of 17 poems by ten authors of our period; *ultraísmo* is almost too well represented with six poems by five different poets, in sad contrast are the two poems, both by Gerardo Diego, on *creacionismo*, while only the most canonical poets, García Lorca, Alberti, and Cernuda, exemplify surrealism in eight well-known poems, all without imput from the likes of Juan Larrea, Rogelio Buendía, Juan José Domenchina, Giménez Caballero, or José María Hinojosa; the whole study is also sold short by the author's decision not to give any final recapitulation or set of conclusions.

Didactic in approach, Gregorio Torres Nebrera, *Entendimiento del poema. De Rubén Darío a Claudio Rodríguez*, M, de la Torre, 1999, 319 pp., offers a selection from 11 poets, of interest here: Unamuno, Antonio Machado, Alberti, Guillén, Dámaso Alonso, Salinas, and Cernuda, together with a complete textual analysis that students may find helpful. A useful facsimile sheds light on our period, José María Barrera López provides editorial apparatus and Miguel de Torre a preliminary study to Guillermo de Torre, *Helices 1918. Poemas 1922*, Malaga, Centro Cultural de la Generación del 27, 2000, 40 + 130 pp. Of somewhat marginal interest here is M. L. Canfield, 'Un siglo de poesía: balance y perspectivas', *Hispamérica*, 85, 2000: 3–36, focusing primarily on writing in the Americas, but showing how Juan Ramón's poetic ideals, Jorge Guillén's version of pure poetry, and Gerardo Diego's *creacionismo* intersect and have effect on the work of the Colombians Eduardo Carranza, Jaime Jaramillo Escobar, and Giovanni Quessep, the Cuba of José Lezama Lima and Mariano Brull, and the much touted rehumanization of Pablo Neruda et al. in *Caballo verde para la poesía*.

A. López Castro, 'Luis Cernuda: poeta y crítico', *Salina*, 15:203–10, situates the Spanish writer along with Baudelaire, Ezra Pound, T. S. Eliot and Juan Ramón Jiménez, as practitioners who recreate in their criticism the original authenticity of the poetry under scrutiny. M. Garbisu Buesa, 'La poesía según Jorge Guillén y Giuseppe Ungaretti. Un punto en común: Paul Valéry', *Ínsula*, 654:9–13, rather naively pinpoints Valéry, and even T. S. Eliot, and possibly Eugenio Montale, as mediators between the members of a truly *European* generation. J. Salvatierra, '*Miguel Hernández*: el reto de la poesía en el teatro', *PAc*, 289:57–60, takes a look behind the curtain at the award-winning production. M. Juliá, 'Ámbitos americanos en el simbolismo del último Juan Ramón Jiménez', *HR*, 69:53–71, finds a change in attitude between the nuptial visit of 1916 and long-term exile after 1936, and concentrates on the lyric vision of New York, the Florida Everglades, and the Atlantic Ocean in the complex later poetry. H. López González de Orduña, 'Hacia una definición de *Orbe* de Juan Larrea', *BHS(G)*, 78:361–70, runs along the treadmill of tradition and innovation, vainly seeking the 'voluntad iconoclasta' essential to the vanguard poet. N. R. Orringer, 'Superseding temporality in Antonio Machado's *Soledades*: a quest for the Golden Age', *ib.*, 335–59, takes an unusual critical stance by concentrating on borrowings from not only Verlaine and Darío, but also Góngora, Fray Luis de León, and San Juan de la Cruz, in the attempt to detain linear time in this Silver Age collection. José Moreno Villa, *Jacinta la pelirroja*, ed. Rafael Ballesteros and Julio Neira, M, Castalia, 2000, 138 pp., makes a welcome appearance in a readily available form. A. A. Anderson, 'Lucía Sánchez Saornil, poeta ultraísta', *Salina*, 15:195–202, usefully documents the life and work of *ultraísmo*'s only woman poet, exploring the play between poetry signed with her real name and her masculine *alias*, Luciano de San-Saor, and reading with appreciation her sparse but complex *corpus* published in the literary magazines of the 1920s. J. Andújar Almansa, '*La copa del rey de Thule* de Francisco Villaespesa: manifiesto poético del modernismo español', *RLit*, 63:129–56, celebrates uncritically the centenary of this publication by 'el paladín, el cruzado, el pujil del modernismo' some time before the appearance of the better-known examples of Jiménez's *Ninfeas* and *Almas de violeta*, or *Alma* and *Soledades* by the Machado brothers.

INDIVIDUAL POETS

ALBERTI. H. Lange Hansen, 'Escultura y rayo. Cumbre y ocaso del neogongorismo en la "Soledad tercera" de Rafael Alberti', *ALEC*, 26:553–72, provides close readings that concentrate on the erotic, *creacionista*, and metaphorical elements, in order to highlight A.'s experimental play rather than any slavish homage to an earlier model. M. Thompson, 'The interplay of theatrical codes in Rafael Alberti's *De un momento a otro*', *BHS(L)*, 78:355–65, re-examines the only full-length play previously banned by Francoist censorship not to have been featured in a high profile production on the return to democracy, and explicates well A.'s impassioned exploration of the ideological implications of four different theatrical strategies in this modest 'Drama de una familia española'.

ALEIXANDRE. The correspondence lends itself to literary criticism: *Correspondencia a la generación del 27 (1928–1984)*, ed. Irma Emiliozzi, M, Castalia, 383 pp.; A. Duque Amusco, '"Queriendo contra la ausencia." (Cartas de Vicente Aleixandre a Pedro Salinas: 1948–1951)', *Ínsula*, 649–50:7–9, documents a friendship dating from 1930, and reproduces five letters from the Salinas archive in the Houghton Library, dated from March 1948 to October 1951, that tell of the re-editing of 'Cero' in 1944, mutual friends in 'los Dámasos' who acted as intermediaries, news of Jorge Guillén in Madrid in the early 1950s, and an interest in Salinas's theatre. J. L. Campal Fernández, 'Bibliografía "de" Vicente Aleixandre', *BH*, n.s. [2001]:307–12, provides a useful but incomplete history of the Nobel laureate's literary production according to the basic poetry and prose divisions, including both hard cover and paperback editions but neither the translations nor the *artículos sueltos*. M. A. Márquez, 'La rima en la poesía última de Vicente Aleixandre', *HR*, 69:337–53, is a detailed examination for the specialist.

DIEGO.　Reviving interest in an important event is *Gerardo Diego y el III centenario de Góngora (correspondencia inédita)*, ed. Gabriele Morelli, V, Pre-Textos, 235 pp. *Ínsula*, 649–50, shows interest in the collecting of the prose work of this poet: F. J. Díez de Revenga, 'Gerardo Diego: la memoria de un poeta' (15–17), documents the publication process of the three volumes entitled *Memoria de un poeta* (1997), *Prosa literaria* (2000), and the forthcoming *Prosa musical*, whetting our appetite with extensive quotation on painters and painting, bull-fighting, the spiritual life, language, and the teaching of literature; J. L. Bernal, 'La prosa literaria de Gerardo Diego' (17–22), encourages revisionist readings of D. and his generation; all rounded off with the text of two lectures D. gave at the University of Buenos Aires in 1928, 'El valor de los recuerdos' (23–25), reprinted from *Arriba* (1979), and 'La nueva arte poética española', reprinted from *Síntesis* (1929), with some interesting contemporary views of a young generation of poet-friends that are still of interest today.

GARCÍA LORCA.　*Fire, Blood and the Alphabet: One Hundred Years of Lorca*, ed. Sebastian Doggart and Michael Thompson (Durham Modern Language Series, 6), Durham U.P., 1999, 282 pp., distils the essence of a three-day fiesta in Newcastle upon Tyne designed to open up Lorcan criticism by reassessing the impact of his work, eliciting some creative responses, and considering some of the translations, but, sadly, it covers much familiar ground and is of limited appeal; while *Federico García Lorca, clásico moderno. 1898–1998*, ed. Andrés Soria Olmedo, María José Sánchez Montes, and Juan Varo Zafra, Granada, Diputación de Granada, 2000, 72 pp., is another late flurry of activity left over from the centenary celebrations. Drawing upon anthropology, psychoanalysis, and literary theory, Sarah Wright, *The Trickster-Function in the Theatre of García Lorca*, London, Tamesis, 2000, 149 pp., is an excellent treatment of the liminal realm in G.L.'s most challenging theatrical texts; highlighting androgyny, male fantasy, masochism, masquerade, and the carnivalesque results in some innovative readings, and among the best is her account of 'The Body in Pain' in Chapter V, dedicated to *El público*. Scraping the bottom of the barrel, A. Correa Ramón, 'El poema "Elegía": una reinterpretación lorquiana de los prototipos femeninos de fin de siglo', *BHS(L)*, 78:47–56, is a close reading of the poem written in 1918 that decries the usual Virgin Mary — sinful Eve binary division of womanhood by the Judeo-Christian patriarchy, and exemplifies, in Maravillas Parejas, the combination of passion and spirituality that would inspire the many female protagonists who denounce restriction and repression. J. Salazar Rincón, 'Rocío y escarcha: dos símbolos afines y contrapuestos en la obra de Federico García Lorca', *RHM*, 44:63–79, uses Bachelard to justify G.L.'s particular predilection in a painstaking meander through multiple examples of literary culture from the Bible and early Greece, to medieval bestiaries and Fernán Caballero; while M. Cruz Rodríguez, 'El yo poético frente a la agonía existencial en el *Diván del Tamarit* de Federico García Lorca', *HisJ*, 22:357–64, concentrates on *gacelas* ii, vii, viii, and ix, and *casidas* ii, vi, and ix, to remark on the black pessimism and profound anguish G.L. experienced during poetic creation.

Taking a novel approach, W. A. Dobrian, ' "Muerto de amor" de Lorca: ¿un tercer *Camborio*?', *His(US)*, 84:399–405, takes up the trail of the real-life gypsy Luis Heredia Cortés from Chauchina in *romances* other than the two compositions that name him in the *Romancero gitano*, and, first, finds oblique references in 'Encrucijada' and 'Sorpresa' of the *Poema del cante jondo*, in order to explicate the poetic details of the embalming and wake held after the mysterious death of the prototype of Antoñito el Camborio; while S. G. Polansky, 'Lorca and Salinas in New York: mannequins and the modern landscape', *ib.*, 451–61, explores intelligently the vanguard representations of mannequin-like forms that speak of the coldness and captivity of modern life in this unusual pairing of the oldest and youngest members of the 1927 Generation.

On the theatre: C. Karageorgou-Batea, 'Discurso y escenificación del deseo en *Amor de don Perlimplín con Belisa en su jardín* de Federico García Lorca', *BH*, n.s. [2001]:191–223, makes good use of earlier criticism to analyse the dramatic mechanisms employed by García Lorca to stage desire and communicate the evolutionary nature of his characters. A. Bugliani, 'Pharisaism: the Biblical subtext in *La casa de Bernarda Alba*', *RHM*, 44:80–87, is a close textual reading designed to show how the teachings of Jesus are subverted and become merely a Pharisaical simulacrum in which maintaining appearances is of primary importance; while B. Contez, 'Sadomasoquismo y travestismo en *El público* de Federico García Lorca: un reto al heterosexismo compulsivo', *Hispanófila*, 133:31–42, questions heterosexual suppositions in an alternative analysis that goes beyond the usual sexist and patriarchal conventions.

GARFIAS. *Ínsula*, 653, is a substantial *homenaje* containing J. M. Barrera López, 'En *El diván lírico* de *Ultra*: Cansinos y Garfias' (3–5), a biographical note on the vicissitudes in the relationship in the vanguard and in exile among the cohort of 'literatos puros y poetas virginales que encienden una vela a la República y otra a la Compañía de Jesús', fleshed out in Id., 'Pedro Garfias / Cartas a Rael Cansinos-Assens (1918–1920)' (13–16), a selection of the correspondence, together with explanatory notes, addressed to the 'Querido Maestro' who held court in his *tertulia* at the Colonial; J. M. Díaz de

Guereñu, 'Coalición de bolcheviques: amistades fugaces de la primera vanguardia' (5–7), documents the more fleeting friendship between G., Diego, and Larrea in the early 1920s; F. J. Díez de Revenga, ' "Mi corazón temblando en el ala del sur": Pedro Garfias en la órbita del 27' (8–10), situates G.'s publication of 1926 in the aesthetic of *Horizonte*, founded in 1922 and coordinated by the triumvirate G., José Rivas Panedas, and Juan Chabás; G. Morelli, 'Pedro Garfias y la *Antología* de Diego' (10–12), examines the *casus* Garfias and disinters the reasons for Diego's literary vengeance in his bitterness over the failure of *Horizonte* to publish *Manual de espuma*, even after 500 pesetas were paid cash down for the enterprise; R. Reyes Cano, 'El taurismo de Pedro Garfias en el contexto de su generación' (17–19), highlighting G. and Gerardo Diego as serious *aficionados*; S. Salaün, 'Pedro Garfias, poeta de vanguardia' (19–24), which explores at length differences between the aesthetic and the political vanguard that go beyond generational limits to include both war poetry and that written in exile, in order thereby to acclaim G. as a 'poeta-soldado'; J. Pérez Bazo, 'Una primavera en Eaton Hastings: el primer exilio del poeta Pedro Garfias' (24–28), a close reading of the poems written in Farringdon House between April and May 1939, focusing on nostalgia, solitude, and loss; while J. M. Barrera López, 'Bibliografía de Pedro Garfias (Salamanca, 1901 — Monterrey, Mexico, 1967)' (16), has some useful detail. The above are complemented by the centenary re-edition of *Héroes del sur (Poesías de la guerra), ed. José María Barrera López, Cordoba–Seville, Ayuntamiento de Pozoblanco-Renacimiento.

SALINAS. Some clever interpretations of the poetry are provided in: L. F. Bonner, 'Sobre "Underwood Girls" de Pedro Salinas', *RHM*, 44:238–41, a close analysis of S.'s felicitous rendition of the Mallarmean art of writing; R. Katz Crispin, ' "¡Qué verdad revelada!": the poet and the absent beloved of Pedro Salinas's *La voz a ti debida*, *Razón de amor* and *Largo lamento*', *ib.*, 108–25, a re-reading of the trilogy in the light of, and with substantial quotation from, the biographical documentation available since 1995 in the 355 letters housed in the Houghton Library concerning S.'s *affaire* with Katherine Rue Reding Whitmore; and A. Acereda, 'Del amor a la angustia: *Todo más claro y otros poemas* (1949) de Pedro Salinas', *HisJ*, 21, 2000:9–24, which places S. in the trajectory that runs from Rosalía de Castro, *via* Unamuno and Darío, to the 1927 Generation, to find hope even in S.'s final work marked by existential anguish and ironic horror in the face of never-ending exile. (See also GARCÍA LORCA above and PROSE below.)

3. PROSE

Ignacio Soldevila Durante, *Historia de la novela española (1936–2000)*, M, Castalia, 579 pp., is the updated version of this handy overview. J. E. Serrano Asenjo, 'Ideas sobre la novela en los años veinte. Metanovelas y otros textos doctrinales', pp. 129–41 of *La novela en España (siglos XIX y XX)*, ed. Paul Aubert (Collection de la Casa de Velázquez, 66), M, Casa de Velázquez, 303 pp., concentrates on Gómez de la Serna's *El novelista* (1923), Jarnés's *El profesor inútil* (1926), and Unamuno's *Cómo se hace una novela* (1927); while M. T. Pao, 'The view from the wheel: de Torre, Salinas, and Hinojosa', *RHM*, 44:88–107, illustrates how literary sensibility was changed irrevocably by the increased velocity of the motor car, with reference to the vanguard texts 'Al volante', 'Entrada en Sevilla', and 'Los guantes del paisaje' and their authors' individual engagement with modernity.

D. Viñas Riquer, 'Francisco Ayala: ideas sobre la novela', *CHA*, 612:79–89, serves as the overview; while C. Richmond, 'De mitos y metamórforsis: las constantes vanguardistas en la obra narrativa de Francisco Ayala', *His(US)*, 84:774–84, outlines the literary epic stretching from *El boxeador y un ángel* (1929) and *Cazador en el alba* (1930), through *Los usurpadores* (1949), until *El jardín de las delicias* (1971 and 1999). J. Maurice, 'Azorín y la Andalucía trágica: ¿una nueva escritura de lo social?', *ECon*, 13, 2000:99–107, convincingly illustrates how Azorín uses language to smooth the rough edges of reality in the Spanish tradition; while R. Johnson, 'El método arqueológico en la novelística de Azorín', *His(US)*, 84:767–73, starts at *La voluntad* (1902), and works through *Antonio Azorín* (1903), *Don Juan* (1922), *Doña Inés* (1925), *El caballero inactual* (1928), to *María Fontán* (1943) and *Salvadora de Olbería* (1944), to document Azorín's view of history as the reconstruction of the past within a preoccupation for Spain and the causes of national suffering.

Pío Baroja, *Libertad frente a sumisión*, ed. Miguel Angel García de Juan, M, Caro Raggio, 266 pp., is a collection of journalistic contributions published in 1938. A. García, 'Blasco Ibáñez en México', *Ínsula*, 654:7–8, documents the polemical reception in Mexico of Blasco Ibáñez both during his visit in 1920 and after the subsequent publication, first in the US and later in the novel *La reina Calafia*, of his opinions on Mexican militarism. M. T. Pao, 'Still(ed) life: the ekphrastic prose poems of Ernesto Giménez Caballero', *RCEH*, 25:469–88, takes an intelligent look at the 'fichas textuales' of the final section of *Yo, inspector de alcantarillas* (1928) in conjunction with art criticism by Murray Krieger and Wendy Steiner to show how vanguard writing produces a form of virtual space in which to engage the reader's imagination. I. Arellano, 'Aspectos satíricos en las novelas de Ganivet', *BH*, n.s. [2001]:155–67, compares a similar structure and point of view found in both *La conquesta del reino de Maya* and *Los trabajos del indefatigable creador Pío Cid*, but highlights the very different ironic perspective and satirical treatment of education and politics in the latter novel; while M. J. Marr, '(Anti)heroism in Ángel Ganivet's *Los trabajos del indefatigable creador Pío Cid'*, *RHM*, 44:231–37, finds neither a classical model nor yet the prototype for a contemporary anti-hero, but rather a curiously ambivalent literary creation which prefigures a prominent archetype of literary modernity.

For the collector, L. Estepa, 'Las greguerías ilustradas de Ramón Gómez de la Serna', *CHA*, 608:47–48, comments upon some vintage pieces first published in *Lecturas* in 1927–28 and reproduced here (49–60); while G. Roof Nunley, 'Gómez de la Serna as travel writer', *RHM*, 44:46–62, explicates the process of Ramón's deliberate self-detachment from his surroundings that led to a sense of isolation in both Spain and Argentina. Benjamín Jarnés, *El profesor inútil*, ed. Francisco Miguel Soguero García, Zaragoza, CSIC, 2000, 315 pp.; and J. J. Lanz, 'La novelística de Benjamín Jarnés en el primer exilio; hacia *La novia del viento'*, *BH*, 102, 2000:133–67, analyses this 1940 novel in order to establish connections between the so-called 'dehumanized' writings published before the Civil War and the later literary production in exile. Emilio Palacios Fernández introduces and contextualizes a rich collection of prose, theatre, and political essays of Ramiro de Maeztu, *Obra literaria olvidada (1897–1910)*, M, Biblioteca Nueva, 2000, 524 pp., a worthy companion volume to his earlier 1982 critique (*YWMLS*, 45:367); and José Luis Villacañas, *Ramiro de Maeztu y el ideal de la burguesía en España*, M, Espasa Calpe, 2000, 494 pp., clarifies Maeztu's thesis that medieval scholasticism lasts through the 18th c. in Spain and leads to decadence and backwardness in the 20th c., which, compounded by bourgeois liberalism, thwarts progress. Through some painstaking research, Margarita Nelken, *La trampa del arenal*, ed. Ángela Ena Bordonada, M, Castalia, 2000, 215 pp., uses letters and personal archives to contextualize the definitive biography and explicate the feminism and politics in the novel that first appeared in 1923. J. C. Ara Torralba, 'Ocasión del vacío: la escritura de Ramón J. Sender (1901–1982)', *CHA*, 612:117–26, marks the centenary with some general comments. E. Moffatt, 'Reinscribing the fantastic in Eduardo Zamacois' *El otro'*, *BHS(L)*, 78:339–54, rescues this early 20th-c. example of the vibrant development of the fantastic in narrative fiction by reference to cultural source material in symbolism and decadentism, and documents both sultry erotic desire and the then fashionable fascination with the supernatural.

AUB. Ignacio Soldevila and José Pérez Bowie edit with full critical apparatus and a two part introductory study, Max Aub, *Obras completas. El laberinto mágico I*, V, Biblioteca Valenciana, II, 652 pp. José-Carlos Mainer writes an introductory study (11–37) and annotates (299–329) the 56 portraits of friends and contemporaries written between 1944–70 collected in *Cuerpos presentes*, Segorbe, Fundación Max Aub, 333 pp. Ignacio Soldevila Durante edits with an introduction (6–17) and useful footnotes, *Max Aub-Francisco Ayala. Epistolario 1952–1972*, V, Fundación Max–Biblioteca Valenciana, 213 pp., providing some interesting facsimiles and a moving testimony to friendship in exile.

ORTEGA Y GASSET. José Luis Abellán, *Ortega y Gasset y los orígenes de la transición democrática*, M, Espasa Calpe, 2000, 378 pp., is based on a rich store of personal documentation; divided into three parts, the first, 'Hacia una biografía del protagonista (1883–1945)', identifies O.'s family circle, masters and friends of his youth, his profound attachment to El Escorial, his love for the intensely Spanish institutions of the *corrida* and the *tertulia*, his Hamlet-like suffering in exile, and his return to Spain; Part II deals with the 'década ominosa', 1945–55, while Part III, 'La muerte de Ortega y Gasset y los orígenes de la transición (1955–1975)' is a (largely autobiographical) account of O.'s continuing presence inspiring the Generations of 1956 and 1968 in their work for democracy in Spain. Concentrating on O.'s influence on post-war Germany, Franke Jung-Lindemann, **Zur Rezeption des Werkes von José Ortega y Gasset in den deutschsprachigen Ländern*, Frankfurt, Lang, 211 pp.

RO, 241, celebrates the 75th anniversary of the publication of *La rebelión de las masas* and *La deshumanización del arte*, with a brief introduction by José Luis Molinuevo (5–6) and V. Bozal, 'Ortega y Gasset: el ver del arte, proximidad y distancia' (6–20), explaining how relevant O.'s discussion of 'ejecutividad' in yesterday's vanguard is to the contents of the contemporary art collections in today's museums; R. Rodríguez, 'La dimensión cultural de la universidad' (21–43), making the case for a revival in the 21st c. of the University's primary role in the transmission of culture, seen by O. as more important than either professional training or scientific research; I. Couso, 'Educar: la responsabilidad de humanizar la vida' (44–55), reflecting on O.'s pioneering views on education; I. Sánchez Cámara, 'De la rebelión a la degradación de las masas' (56–71), providing a new reading, *via The Screwtape Letters* and 'the Historical Point of View', and good company in Alain Finkielkraut, Allan Bloom, Alasdair MacIntyre, and George Steiner; and E. Trías, 'Pensar en compañía de Ortega y Gasset' (72–86), pressing T. S. Eliot into service to explain how O. 'accompanies' us in our contemporary way of thinking rather than demonstrating the usual *pro* or *contra* reaction to this philosopher. John T. Graham, **The Social Thought of Ortega y Gasset: A Systematic Synthesis in Postmodernism and Interdisciplinarity*, Missouri U.P., 616 pp.

UNAMUNO. More personal correspondence becomes available: J. M. Martínez Cachero, 'Epistolario Rafael Altamira–Miguel de Unamuno (1896–1934)', *Salina*, 15:267–95; and María de las Nieves Pinillos, **Delfina, la enamorada de Unamuno*, M, Laberinto, 1999, which recounts the one-sided *romance* conducted by the Argentinian Delfina Morina y Vedia in some 160 letters that document both personal sentiment and a vision of Spain and Argentina between 1907 until 1936. M. P. Rodríguez, '¿Qué desastre? ¿Qué nación? ¿Qué problema? Revisiones del nacionalismo español y del nacionalismo vasco a la luz de Miguel de Unamuno', *Inti*, 51, 2000:3–16, projects U.'s vision of colonialism and his controversial relations with the 'bizcaitarristas' on to present day discussion of Euzkadi. E. Núñez, 'Criatura y creador en *Niebla* de Unamuno', *ETL*, 28, 1999–2000:133–44, reflects on the three levels of reference in Augusto Pérez, Unamuno, and God; while V. Guerrero, 'Diégesis y realidad en *Niebla*', *RevR*, 36:255–64, relies heavily on Genette's terminology and multiple diagrams with only partial success. In comparative vein: Anna Wieczorek Gray, **Introducción a un estudio comparativo entre Miguel de Unamuno y León Tolstói*, M, Pliegos, 168 pp.; D. Perrot, 'Georges Bernanos et Miguel de Unamuno: deuz écrivains devant l'absolu', *RLC*, 298:257–62, outlines a methodology to study the shared commitment to explaining human destiny; while J. G. Ardila, 'El "hacer político" de Unamuno y el punto de vista platónico-kierkegaardiano', *BH*, n.s. [2001]:169–90, traces U.'s involvement in public debate and sets him up as one of the first real democrats of the 20th century.

VALLE-INCLÁN. P. Ríos Sánchez, 'Valle-Inclán: mistificación de textos bíblicos en *Divinas palabras*', *RLit*, 63:157–83, insists that evil is not conquered nor order restored in the 'burla engañosa y subversión satánica' and *esperpento*-like interpretation of Biblical teaching. A. Cortijo Ocaña, 'Ideología y edad media en *Cuento de abril* de Valle-Inclán', *BHS(L)*, 78:27–46, explicates various *leitmotifs* to show how V.-I. incorporates medieval Spanish literature into 19th-c. symbolism. W. de Rafols, 'Recreating the lost object: images of the hand in *Sonata de otoño*', *RHM*, 44:31–45, suggests that such ubiquitous references are rooted in V.-I.'s own physical loss and the resulting narcissistic melancholy. Increased critical interest produces some new reviews: *ALEC*, 26, brings out a new *Anuario Valle-Inclán*, 1, containing:

D. Dougherty, 'La crisis del personaje en el teatro de Valle-Inclán: Montenegro y Máximo Estrella' (9–27), incorporating fellow travellers Maeterlinck, Pirandello, and Kaiser in a journey from the Baroque to cubism; I. Fernández Peláez, 'Las contradicciones de *La lámpara maravillosa*' (29–57), documenting V.-I.'s juggling with a romantic world view and a modernist sensibility; R. C. Spires, 'Postcolonial discourse in *Sonata de estío*' (59–73), on the postmodern subversion of the Don Juan myth; D. Troncoso, 'Técnicas narrativas en las *Comedias bárbaras*' (75–98), plays with the trilogy 'sub specie theatri'; L. M. Fernández, '*Romance de lobos* en el cine: ¿un proyecto frustrado de Valle-Inclán' (99–109), quotes *El Diario de Pontevedra* of 13 February 1919 to document V.-I.'s early interest; V. Milner Garlitz, 'Valle-Inclán y la gira de Valencia de 1911' (111–41), details fully accounts of V.-I.'s lecture tour in *El Diario de Valencia*; M. Á. Gómez Abalo, 'Cinco contribuciones de Valle-Inclán en la prensa' (143–74), adds useful information on variants and glosses; L. T. González-del-Valle, '*Del Cesarismo*: a forgotten intertextual antecedent of *Tirano Banderas*' (175–82), traces links with the Dominican writer Rafael Damirón; R. Macato Rey, 'Valle-Inclán y Anglada Camarasa: una conferencia de 1916' (183–96), scours the press for light on V.-I.'s lecture in El Retiro; C. Míguez Vilas, '*El Correo Español*: apostilla a la polémica sobre *El embrujado*' (197–203), dishes the dirt on in-fighting between V.-I., Galdós, María Guerrero, and Fernando Díaz de Mendoza; X. Núñez Sabarís and M. P. Veiga Grandal, 'Ecos en la prensa de un homennaje a Valle-Inclán en Madrid (1922)' (205–18), celebrates the banquet at Fornos; M. Santos Zas, 'Valle-Inclán y la prensa cubana: el viaje a la Habana de 1921' (219–53), unearths some new material of difficult access; M. Vidal Maza, 'Valle-Inclán y la I Guerra Mundial: declaraciones a *El Radical* (1916)' (255–62), attests well to V.-I.'s vociferous denunciation of Spanish neutrality; C. Villarmea Álvarez, 'Las versiones de "El íncubo" en la prensa periódica' (263–76), usefully collates various revisions and variants; finally J. Serrano Alonso and A. de Juan Bolufer, 'Bibliografía sobre Ramón del Valle-Inclán (1995–2000)' (277–311), present a neatly organized update on their earlier general bibliography (1995), that incoporates news of various centres of research on V.-I., theses, and an ever-increasing critical output. Newly on-line at < http//www.el pasajero.com >, *El Pasajero. Revista de estudios sobre Ramón del Valle-Inclán*, has useful information on conferences, publications, television programmes, and discussion groups. *HTe*, 1, begins publication with an issue dedicated to V.-I. containing: M. C. Bobes Naves, 'El marido engañado y vengador en *Los cuernos de don Friolera*' (13–34), reviewing antecedents and variations on the theme in order to emphasize the enormous difference between female and male adultery and work out the new twist here on the triple sequence 'Traición–Venganza–Consecuencias' in the absence of any infidelity, the death of the daughter and not that of the wife, and the important dramatic part given the representative of society (doña Tadea Calderón, don Fermín, or the Cuerpo de Carabineros), all played out in three different versions (*bululú*,   *esperpento*, and *romance de ciego*); R. Espejo Saavedra, 'Entre el mito y la desilusión: el discurso histórico simbolista de *Águila de Blasón* y *Romance de lobos*' (37–53), exploring the play between bourgeois, positivist official history and the antidote found in an alternative symbolist discourse; L. T. González del Valle, 'Valle-Inclán ante la tragedia' (55–75), examining briefly the classic tragic code and illustrating V.-I.'s innovations in his use of the 'tragedia de ensueño' in *Voces de gesta*, *El embrujado*, and *Luces de Bohemia*; V. Holloway, 'Monstruos paganos, primitivos y populares en el teatro de Ramón del Valle-Inclán' (77–94), describing in detail the monsters in *Romance de lobos* (1908), *El embrujado* (1913), and *Divinas palabras* (1920); J. M. Martín Olalla, 'La "divagación estética" de *La enamorada del rey*' (95–113), illustrating well the aesthetic fun and games of Maese Lotario in which the national tragedy is converted and subverted in farce; S. Salaün, 'Valle-Inclán y la pintura' (115–35), documenting the close links between the plastic arts and the realization of V.-I.'s innovative theatre; K. M. Sibbald, '¿Cuento de hadas, farsa infantil o código particular teatral?: *La cabeza del dragón* de Valle-Inclán y su aportación al desarrollo del teatro infantil al finalizar el siglo xx en España' (137–57), considering the nonsense canon and children's literature to find evidence of V.-I.'s exemplarity in the genre and his on-going influence on the social realism of Alfonso Sastre, Lauro Olmo, and Carlos Muñiz in the midst of Francoist censorship, and even on the progressive institutionalization of children's literature with the advent of democracy in spectacles put on by Jesús Campos, Luis Matilla, and José Luis Alonso de Santos; R. de la Fuente Ballesteros, 'Algunos autógrafos valleinclanianos y la Academia Española de Bellas Artes en Roma' (159–81), analysing V.-I.'s bitter disillusion with his failure to secure this political appointment before 1934, reproducing two letters sent to Pérez de Ayala, and six written to Gregorio Marañón to be found in the Rodríguez Porrero Collection in the archives of Bartolomé March.

4. Theatre

Critical work on the drama of the period is also noted above under garcía lorca, salinas, unamuno and valle-inclán.   K. Aggor and C. J. Harris, 'El drama español del siglo xx: bibliografía selecta del año 1999', *Estreno*, 27.1 : 52–66, if not quite synchronized with this bibliographic compilation, is worth consulting for details on editions, doctoral theses, and reviews not recorded here, as well as other items on Alberti, Max Aub, and García Lorca. Tony A. Harvell, *Index to Twentieth-Century Spanish Plays: In Collections, Anthologies and Periodicals*, Lanham, MD, Scarecrow, 2000, fills some gaps. *En torno al teatro breve*, ed. Margot Versteeg, Amsterdam–Atlanta, Rodopi, 2000, 136 pp., contains two essays by the editor of interest here, her 'Introducción: una placentera exploración por el variopinta panorama del texto breve', and 'Currinches, garbanzos y fusiladores: escribir para el género chico'. Michael Kidd, *Stages of Desire. The Mythological Tradition in Classical and Contemporary Spanish Theater*, University Park, Pennsylvania State U.P., 1999, 266 pp., has comments in Chapter 3 on Unamuno's *Fedra* and Grau's *El Señor de Pigmalión*. *Teatro universitario en Zaragoza 1939–1999*, ed. Jesús Rubio Jiménez, Zaragoza U.P., 1999, 376 pp., is a little broader in scope than the title suggests and usefully documents, and attractively illustrates, the circumvention of Francoist censureship in quality productions for the stage by reference to cast lists, programmes, photographs of various scene sets, and details of costume design.

M. P. Yáñez, 'La *noche del sábado* de Jacinto Benavente: ¿intento modernista o reflexión literaria?', *Salina*, 15:191–94, opts for a modern, rather than a narrowly defined *modernista*, reading of the 1903 play and underscores Benavente's scepticism about renovation and innovation in the theatre. Juan Aguilar Sastre and Manuel Aznar, *Cipriano Rivas Cherify el teatro español de su época (1891–1967)*, M, Publicaciones de la Asociación de Directores de Escena de España, 1999, 593 pp., note particularly the European influences on Rivas's ideas on the theatre in this record of his life and achievements in pre-Civil War Spain and after in exile in America; the mammoth 57-page bibliography, including details of original plays, librettos for ballet and opera, relevant translations, and editions is especially welcome. A. Sobejano-Morán, 'La función metatextual del signo dramático en *El Señor de Pigmalión*', *Gestos*, 30, 2000:71–82, deftly illustrates Grau's use of distancing to break with the traditional separation of stage and audience in realist theatre. In preparation for the centenary, Fernando Valls and David Roas collect with bio-bibliographic details, Enrique Jardiel Poncela, *Máximas mínimas y otros aforismos*, B, Edhasa, 2000; and they both coordinate the homage, 'La literatura inverosímil de Enrique Jardiel Poncela', *Ínsula*, 660, offering a prefatory study to counterbalance more official celebrations (2); L. López Molina, 'Jardiel Poncela y Ramón' (2–5), documenting the friendship enjoyed since 1922 in Pombo and *Buen Humor*; D. Roas and F. Valls, 'Jardiel Poncela en la revista *Gutiérrez*' (5–9), incorporating fascinating details about Jardiel Poncela's satirical contributions on misogyny, the middle class, tourist guide books, sentimental drama, and auto-propaganda into a study of the major outlets for contemporary humour in, first, *Buen Humor* and *Gutiérrez*, and, in the postwar period, in *La Codorniz* and *La Ametralladora*; J. M. Barrera López, 'Dos novelas cortas de Jardiel Poncela: *La sencillez fragante* y *La defensas del cerebro*' (9–11), pinpointing the techniques and innovations of the 'novela rosa' and the 'novela de suspenso y misterio' used in Jardiel Poncela's later work; E. García Fuentes, 'Tratamiento de lo literario en *¡Espérame en Siberia, vida mía!*' (12–16), explicating the literary nature of Jardiel Poncela's authorial pact with his readership; D. Ródenas de Moya, 'El humorismo violento de Jardiel en *La Tournée de Dios*' (17–20), returning to Juvenal, the Archpriest of Hita, Quevedo, and Padre Isla in order to trace Jardiel Poncela's humour as 'acre, violento, descarado' and typical in its pessimistic world view; M. J. Conde Guerri, 'Los locos egregios de Jardiel' (20–22), identifying the other vanguard members of the 'Neurópatas Club' of the 1920s and Jardiel Poncela's use of the comic side of mental illness; M. de Paco, 'Jardiel Poncela en el teatro español de la vanguardia' (23–24), revisiting the phenomenon of *jardielistas* and *jardielófobos*; while A. A. Gómez Yebra, 'Mujer *versus* hombre en las *Máximas mínimas* de Jardiel' (24–27), finds Jardiel Poncela and Gómez de la Serna worthy emulators of Seneca and Cato in abundant examples of their shared *machista* misogyny. A. Domínguez Leiva, 'En el centenario de Jardiel Poncela', *CHA*, 609:105–16, provides a postscript summary high-lighting Jardiel Poncela's eroticism, black humour, and attention to language.

LITERATURE, 1936 TO THE PRESENT DAY

By IRENE MIZRAHI, *Boston College*

1. GENERAL

El papel de la literatura en el siglo XX, ed. F. Lopéz Criado, Corunna U.P., 500 pp., is a collection of essays written by different scholars who participated in the first *Congreso Nacional: Literatura y Sociedad* at Corunna in April 2000. The following are of relevance to this section: J. Romera Castillo, 'Tres tipos de discurso autobiográfico sobre la guerra (in)civil española (Portela Valladares, Azaña e Indalecio Prieto)' (7–10), who argues that most testimonies about the Civil War are different types of autobiographical discourse, analysing three in particular: 'el autodefensivo de un impotente (Portela Valladares), el manipulado descaradamente (Manuel Azaña) y el apologético de sus ideas (Indalecio Prieto)'; G. Torres Nebrera, 'Crónica de teatros (1940–1965): conservadores, renovadores' (55–76), an overview of the Spanish theatre during the 25 years embraced by the title, taking into consideration the antinomies between 'conservadores' and 'renovadores' that have often polarized the history of Spanish drama; C. Oliva, 'Teatro y sociedad en la España del siglo XX' (77–96), dividing the theatre of the 20th c. into three stages, arguing that the important changes of the last period reveal the existence of an abyss between the theatre that initiated the century and that which ended it; J. M. Balcells, 'Mujer y poesía española: 1980–2000' (97–118), analysing the language, tendencies, and themes of poets such as A. Amorós, C. Borja, A. Salas, M. J. Flores, E. Otero, J. Castillo, A. M. Navales, and P. Canelo, pointing out that the unusual increase of poetry written by women in the last 20 years of the 20th c. has not acquired recognition because it continues to be excluded from many anthologies; I. Vázquez Fernández, 'El personaje del anciano en la novela de Miguel Delibes' (135–44), who studies the character of the old persons, in particular their solitude and fear of death, in D.'s *La hoja roja* (1959) and *Cartas de amor de un sexagenario voluptuoso* (1983); E. J. Gil López, 'La voz femenina en la narrativa española contemporánea' (165–76), focusing on Matute's *Olvidado Rey Gudú* (1996), Soler Espiauba's *La mancha de la mora* (1998), Grandes's *Atlas de Geografía Humana* (1998), Sánchez's *El misterio de todos los días* (1999), and Mayoral's *La sombra del ángel* (2000), arguing that, apart from their thematic and formal diversity, these novels unite 'ingredientes tan atractivos como la magia, la reflexión sobre temas de plena actualidad [y] el retrato de las múltiples facetas de la vida íntima y social de nuestros días'; G. Vásquez Rodríguez, 'Erotismo y androginia en la

narrativa española contemporánea' (177–98), analysing the image of
the androgynous in novels by Spanish and Latin American authors
such as Vincent's *Balada de Caín* (1987), García Hortelano's *Muñeca y
Macho* (1990), and Sampedro's *El amante lesbiano* (2000), and claiming
that 'el andrógino [. . .] agita la pulsión erótica en esa marea que
entrelaza lo femenino y lo masculino, bien para ironizar esas formas
esquemáticas [. . .], o bien para cuestionar los afectos y deseos de los
cuerpos desde una efervescencia de lo sexual imposible'; B. L. Felipe,
'La poesía en prosa en España: 1939–1975' (195–208), an important
contribution to the seldom studied genre of poetic prose that focuses
on both the authors who cultivated it and its forms and tendencies
during the years indicated in the title; A. Domínguez Rey, 'La
retracción en la poesía de José Ángel Valente' (247–64), who studies
V.'s *Breve son* (1953–68), *El inocente* (1967–70), *Interior con figuras*
(1973–76), and *Tres lecciones de tinieblas* (1977–79), using the concept
of 'retracción' which, according to D.R., implies a phenomenological
attitude of critical revision and a rhythmic fundament at the same
time; M. Carbayo Abengozar, 'Significación social de las novelas de
Carmen Martín Gaite en cuanto al desarrollo de la conciencia
feminista en la España del siglo xx' (361–76), claiming that the
development in the treatment of feminine characters from M.G.'s
first novels of the 1950s to the last, *Irse de casa* (1998), corresponds to
the evolution of Spanish feminism, a movement that has also been
influenced by M.G.'s writings; J. I. González Urtado, 'La soledad en
la obra de Javier Tomeo' (389–400), who examines T.'s novels, *El
cazador de leones* in particular, and shows how solitude is a recurrent
theme communicated through brevity, fragmentation, absurdity, and
the aesthetic of the grotesque; I. Torres Rivas, 'Parodia y novela
policiaca en *La hija del caníbal* de Rosa Montero' (401–14), who uses
the concept of parody developed by L. Hutcheon and M. Rose to
demonstrate how M.'s novel constitutes a parody of the detective
novel as defined by J. Madrid's *La novela policiaca española*; E. Martínez
Rico, 'Los umbrales de Umbral. Primeros pasos novelescos de
Francisco Umbral' (415–28), who aims at demonstrating the coherence of U.'s work from his first to his last publication; C. J. Morales
Villanueva, 'La realidad virtual de la sociedad actual: La narrativa
de José Ángel Mañas' (429–36), arguing that M.'s *Historias de Kronen*
(1994) constitutes a faithful representation of hyperrealism as defined
by Baudrillard; J. Navarro Benítez, 'Una periodización literaria de la
poesía española del siglo xx' (437–50), attempting to incorporate
poets of the last 20 years into the history of 20th-c. Spanish literature
following the scheme of disposition of movements and authors
proposed by J. Hierro's 'Taller de creación literaria' in 1998, and
using anthologies of poetry published since 1980; C. Chao Mata, 'El

camino de Santiago y la literatura' (451–62), on travel memories and novels published since the 1980s that deal with the subject of peregrination. Among the titles considered are: *En camino a los cuarenta*, *Nunca llegaré a Santiago*, *Endrina y el secreto del peregrino*, *Los peregrinos a Santiago*, *La espada y la rosa*, *El bordón y la estrella*, and *El peregrino*, which is analysed briefly in the second part (457–60); M. J. Olaziregi Alustiza, 'Bernardo Atxaga o la seducción de los lectores vascos' (463–74), describing the present system of Basque literature in order to explain the unusual place occupied by A., whose production has had an extraordinary repercussion among both literary critics and Basque writers; J. Frau, 'Análisis de un fracaso poético: la idea del poeta como guía de la sociedad' (475–86), who argues that poetics such as León Felipe's (which claim the moral superiority or special clairvoyance of the author) are condemned to failure, and discusses the motives leading to this defeat; C. Peinado Elliot, 'La muerte del sujeto en *El canto del Llanero Solitario* de L. M. Panero' (487–500), seeing the dissolution of the subject and its insertion in a space of absolute solitude in P.'s poem as an evocation of the myth of the eternal return of man to the undifferentiated or, in F.'s words, 'el regreso de lo humano a lo inhumano, mito que se cumple y se actualiza, según Panero, en la literatura y se encarna en el poeta'.

F. Umbral, *Los alucinados: personajes, escritores, monstrous. Una historia diferente de la literatura*, M, La Esfera de los Libros, 196 pp., has a prologue, 'Manual de instrucciones para leer a Umbral' (9–24), by J. A. Marina, and includes brief essays (generally written in a very personal tone) about authors from Darío to Gimferrer. Of particular importance here are the sections dedicated to the following writers: 'Los prosistas de la Falange' (121–24), A. de Foxá (125–28), L. Rosales (133–36), J. M. Pemán (137–40), Á. Cunqueiro (145–48), A. Buero Vallejo (149–52), C. J. Cela (173–76), J. Hierro (177–80), M. Delibes (181–84), 'La generación de los 50' (185–88), 'Los Adonáis' (winners of the Adonáis poetry prize such as C. Rodríguez, J. Á. Valente, F. Brines, and C. Sahagún) (189–92), and F. Gimferrer (193–96).

N. E. Richardson, *Postmodern 'Paletos': Immigration, Democracy, and Globalization in Spanish Narrative and Film, 1950–2000*, Lewisburg, Bucknell U.P., 260 pp., is an excellent book on the development of the city/country dynamics in narrative and film of the second half of the 20th c., taking into consideration the problematic nature of texts and 'reality'. R. illustrates this development with a detailed analysis of a film and a novel in each chapter: *Surcos* and *Los bravos* (ch.1, the 1950s), *La ciudad no es para mí* and *Tiempo de silencio* (ch.2, the 1960s), *La prima angelica* and *El cuarto de atrás* (ch.3, the 1970s), ¿*Qué he hecho yo para merecer esto?* and *Juegos de la edad tardía* (ch.4, the 1980s), and *Vacas* and *Calzados Lola* (ch.5, the 1990s); R. concludes that, whatever may be the future struggles of Spanish society, 'the richly layered constructs of city and country will continue to work side by side in Spanish culture and society, often blinding those who would see but always at the same time giving voice to the culturally silenced'. *A Twice-Told Tale: Reinventing the Encounter in Iberian/Iberian American Literature and Film*, ed. S. Juan-Navarro and T. R. Young, Newark, Delaware U.P., 301 pp., is an interesting collection of essays written by various scholars who aim at exploring 'contemporary reconstructions of the age of "discovery", exploration, and conquest vis-à-vis 15th-c. and 16th-c. sources (histories, chronicles, and *relaciones*)'. The contributors discuss 'the problem of interpreting encounters between historical periods that foster radically different perspectives ("the imperial eye" of European colonial discourse and the historical revisionism of contemporary culture)'. For our section special attention should be paid to the following two essays: W. Fraser de Zambrano, 'Transhistorical and transgeographical seductions in Rosa Montero's *Te trataré como una reina*' (91–108), demonstrating how the novel's fictive and mythic sexual paradigms 'show themselves to be rooted in gender difference and to have contributed to the construction of masculinity, femininity, subjectivity, desire, and a culture of violence over the last five hundred years, best witnessed in the colonial discursive dynamic of the couple'; and S. P. Berardini, '*La isla amarilla*: (re)vision and subversion of the discovery' (275–84), showing how P. Pedrero's play is 'an inversion of the historical events of the conquest in that it allows the Pacific Islanders to "discover" and explore the "civilized" world'. For B., this drama constitutes 'a comic (re)vision of Spain as a colonizing country in the modern era'.

Dale J. Pratt, *Signs of Science: Literature, Science, and Spanish Modernity since 1868*, West Lafayette, Indiana, Purdue U.P., 226 pp., is composed of six chapters in which P. traces out 'the fortunes of cultural modernity in Spain between the Glorious Revolution of 1868 and the Franco years by tracking the changing aesthetic and ideological values of literary images of science'. Ch.1 is on the ideological aftermath of the 'Gloriosa' and its relevance in the history of science and literature in Spain. Ch. 2 explores science's place in realist writings. Chs. 3 and 4 study images of science in the work of Ramón y Cajal. Ch. 5 examines the attitudes toward science of the Generation of 1898 and its potential as a cultural force for the country's modernization. Ch. 6 shows how Ortega y Gasset, Laín Entralgo, and Martín-Santos 'rejected nineteenth-century valorizations of science as they formulated new ways of looking at scientific activity and rhetoric'.

2. PROSE

GENERAL.   M. Bertrand de Muñoz, *Guerra y novela: la Guerra española de 1936–1939*, Seville, Alfar, 365 pp., contains a series of essays (some in French but the majority in Spanish) published during the author's academic career. G. Gullón, 'Contexto para el estudio de la narrativa del nuevo milenio', *ETL*, 29:6–22, is an overview of the cultural situation in which the book exists in the present century, reviewing the role played by those who have a direct interest in it: authors, editors, salespersons, critics, reviewers, and readers. P. Nieva de la Paz, 'Éxitos de la narrativa española de mujeres durante la transición política (1975–1981)', *Hispanófila*, 131:31–42, discusses the novels of four authors which obtained commercial success during the transition period — M. Salisachs's *La gangrena* and *La presencia*, C. Conde's *Soy la madre*, R. Montero's *Crónica del desamor* and *La función delta*, and M. Roig's *La hora violeta* — , and claims that these novels exemplify two tendencies in the general panorama of post-war Spanish narrative: the first tendency emphasizes plot while using different sub-genres and simple narrative techniques (Salisachs and Conde); the second introduces themes of contemporary interest while adopting a perspective of feminine testimony involved with present times (Montero and Roig). S. Kingery, 'Memories of love: Ana María Moix and Esther Tusquets remember', *Mester*, 30:52–63, discusses how M. and T. fictionalize their common autobiographical experiences in *Julia* and *El mismo mar de todos los veranos*, and argues that, although these authors differ in their vision of the future for their respective protagonists, in their novels 'lesbian love appears as a briefly liberating, but in the long run, unsustainable option'. S. A. Oropesa, '*Los misterios de Madrid* (1992): Crónicas literarias', *RHM*, 54:220–30, establishes a comparison between Mendoza's *El misterio de la cripta embrujada* and *La verdad sobre el caso Savolta* and Muñoz Molina's *El jinete polaco* and *Los misterios de Madrid*, and claims that these novels complement each other as vehicles to narrate Spanish reality through different techniques, and also that they are 'intencionadamente, lecturas desviadas, extrañadas, del género negro para conseguir el efecto deseado: atrear la atención del lector mediante el extrañamiento'.

INDIVIDUAL AUTHORS

ATXAGA.   N. E. Rodríguez, 'La palabra está en otra parte: escritura e identidad en *Obabakoak*', *RHM*, 54:176–90, discusses the novelist's epilogue to his Spanish translation of this book (1989), initially published in the Basque language (1988), in which A. indicates the lack of a Basque literary language (labelled 'el antecedente'). According to R., 'el gesto de Atxaga de remarcar el lenguage [euskera] como el eje de su proyecto literario responde a una voluntad disuasiva que consiste en desviar la atención del lector castellanohablante de una lectura ideológica de la novela recalcando al contrario el proyecto literario que la anima.'

AUB. S. Faber, 'Un pasado que no fue, un futuro imposible: juegos parahistóricos en los cuentos del exilio de Max Aub', *ETL*, 29:82–9, investigates the strategies used by A. to confront the issues of exile in 'El remate', 'De los beneficios de las guerras civiles', and 'La verdadera historia de la muerte de Francisco Franco'.

BENET. R. Espejo-Saavedra, 'La desterritorialización del detective: en torno a *El aire de un crimen*', *ALEC*, 26:483–98, establishes a parallel between the aesthetic theory proposed by B. in this novel and the effort to develop a vocabulary capable of doing justice to the multiple nature of existence suggested by Deleuze and Guattari in *A Thousand Plateaux: Capitalism and Schizophrenia*.

ESPINA. J. M. del Pino, 'Poéticas enfrentadas: teatro y cine en Antonio Espina y *Revista de Occidente*', *ALEC*, 26:91–112, explores E.'s essays on cinematography published in *Revista de Occidente*, 'Las dramáticas del momento' (1925) and 'Reflexiones sobre cinematografía' (1927) in particular, and convincingly shows how E. judges the filmic phenomenon from the perspectives of both formalism and Ortega's theories in *La deshumanización del arte*.

GOYTISOLO. E. Cibreiro, 'Apocalipsis y ecologismo, muerte y posteridad: de *Paisajes después de la batalla* a *La saga de los Marx* de Juan Goytisolo', *ALEC*, 26:433–64, analyses the moral, intellectual, and social implications of G.'s perspective on the subject of death and other related themes in *Paisajes después de la batalla* (1993), *La cuarentena* (1991), and *La saga de los Marx* (1993). S. J. Black, 'Mysticism, postmodernism and transgression in *La cuarentena* by Juan Goytisolo', *BHS(G)*, 78:241–58, uses this novel to illustrate the idea that G.'s latest work engages with aspects of mysticism and postmodernism in ways which raise questions about the precise nature of his social critique which, so claims B., 'has remained unchanged since the early sixties, in spite of the new departures taken by recent novels'.

GRANDES. C. Arkinstall, 'Mothers and daughters in Almudena Grandes' short fiction', *ALEC*, 26:409–32, employs a sophisticated theoretical apparatus to analyse the theme of the 'good-enough' mother and daughter in two short stories by G.: 'La buena hija' and 'Amor de madre'.

JIMÉNEZ LOZANO. F. J. Higuero, 'Las fisuras estructurales del desmantelamiento subversivo en *Las señoras* de Jiménez Lozano', *BHS(L)*, 78:383–94, highlights the textual strategies used in this novel to prevent stable interpretations, emphasizing 'la crítica incisiva que contra el discurso de la modernidad triunfante se detecta a lo largo de lo relatado en *Las señoras*, narración en donde parece no quedar resquicio alguno desde el que poder asentarse inequívocadamente en una complacencia tranquilizadora'.

MARÍAS. C. J. García, 'Imágenes como palabras y *Corazón tan blanco* de Javier Marías', *RHM*, 54: 191–202, indicates the complex relationships that exist in this novel between the written or spoken word, the visual, and the face-to-face encounters between characters, and examines how the articulation of different communicative mediations (verbal or visual) shapes the desire to capture the truthful identity of the subject.

MARTÍN SANTOS. Á. Cueva Puente, 'La novela de tesis: *El combate de Santa Casilda*, de Luis Martín Santos', *AlAm*, 20: 491–500, uses the ideas of Genette and Suleiman as theoretical support for the study of this novel, in which, according to C.P., M.S. 'se nos muestra como un sociólogo y novelista que desde un humanismo dialéctico [. . .] enjuicia, con pasión, un periódo controvertido de la historia del país, el enfrentamiento entre la Ilustración y el Antiguo Régimen.'

MENDOZA. C.-Y. Yang, '*El misterio* y *El laberinto* de Eduardo Mendoza: la presencia del género policiaco', *CH*, 23: 245–54, does not provide many new insights in this examination of how the detective genre operates in *El misterio de la cripta embrujada* (1979) and *El laberinto de las aceitunas* (1982).

PÉREZ-REVERTE. C. A. Durham, 'Books beyond borders: intertextuality in Arturo Pérez-Reverte's *El Club Dumas*', *ALEC*, 26: 465–82, claims that, in this novel, 'complex acts of travel and of translation function together as both strategy and metaphor in what might be described as a (meta)fictional journey beyond historical, linguistic, and geographic borders: the *intertextual* becomes the bridge to the *international*.'

DE PRADA. M. A. Gómez, '*Las mascaras del héroe* de Juan Manuel de Prada: una reescritura del esperpento', *ALEC*, 26: 519–36, shows how this novel, rich in intertextual allusions to historical and literary characters and documents, constitutes a rewriting of Valle-Inclán's *esperpento*, particularly *Luces de Bohemia*.

RIERA. A. Tsuchiya, 'Discourse and the strategies of power in Carme Riera's *En el último azul*: a cultural analysis of the Inquisition', *JILAS*, 7: 77–84, argues that this novel, a complex hybrid of history and fiction, presents 'an analysis of the Inquisition, and the function of discourse in the production of its disciplinary regime'.

ROIG. C. Dupláa, 'Los lugares de la memoria en la Barcelona de Montserrat Roig', *RHM*, 54: 166–75, is a brilliant paper on R.'s work, specifically her archaeological search for feminine traces in Barcelona's history in 'De finestres, balcons i galeries'.

THIEBAUT. F. J. Higuero, 'Logros y límites de la modernidad en la escritura ensayística de Carlos Thiebaut', *AlAm*, 20:465–82, focuses on T.'s essays *Historia del nombrar, Los límites de la comunidad, Vindicación del ciudadano,* and *De la tolerancia,* in which H. finds not only the recognition of the successes of modernity, but also an acknowledgement of its limits.

TUSQUETS. D. Casado, 'From the modern to the postmodern novel: the case of Esther Tusquets', *Hispanófila,* 133:43–52, is on the issue of the genre of T.'s *Siete miradas en un mismo paisaje* (1981). C. contends that this work constitutes a postmodern novel, in contrast with *El mismo mar de todos los veranos* (1978), *El amor es un juego solitario* (1979), *Varada tras el último naufragio* (1980), and *Para no volver* (1985), which constitute a modern novelistic tetralogy.

3. POETRY

GENERAL. J. Á. Sánchez Ibáñez, *La edición de la poesía en Aragón 1962–2000: aproximación bibliográfica* (supplement to *Poesía en el Campus,* 50), 139 pp., is a bibliographical repertory exclusively oriented towards the poetic production published in Aragon during these years. C. Ferradáns, 'De seducción, perfume y ropa interior: poesía y publicidad en la España contemporánea', *ALEC,* 26:499–518, studies F. Rubio's 'Paco Rabanne: In Memoriam' and A. Rossetti's 'Calvin Klein, Underdrawers', concluding that these poems constitute 'poemas *plurales* que entran en el juego seductor de las apariencias (Rossetti) para denunciar el lenguaje publicitario que construye y confirma las bases ideológicas de nuestra cultura finisecular (Rubio)'. J. Letrán, ' "Tócala otra vez, Sam": tradición y poesía española en los umbrales del tercer milenio', *BHS(L),* 78:71–87, uses Genette's concept of hypertextuality to show both how poets of the end of the 20th c. such as L. A. de Cuenca, L. García Montero, and J. L. García Martín rewrite literary tradition and how this rewriting coincides with the establishment of the paradigm of postmodernism.

INDIVIDUAL AUTHORS

BIEDMA. A. Armisén, 'Lecciones, lecturas y juegos *según sentencia del tiempo.* Aspectos de lo lúdico en la poesía comprometida de Jaime Gil de Biedma', *VLet,* 12:89–128, analyses the sources of the opposition of game v. tragedy in B.'s compromised poetry, in which, so claims A., it is incorporated within the vital and theoretical assimilation of diverse systems of thought.

BRINES. J. L. Gómez Toré, 'El exilio y el reino en *Palabras a la oscuridad* de Francisco Brines: la búsqueda de un espacio', *ALEC*, 26:519–36, argues that, in this collection of poetry, travelling refers to symbols such as 'exile' and 'realm' (or the lost paradise and the search for it), from which it is possible to comprehend the roots of two of B.'s basic themes: childhood and love.

OTERO. M. Camarero, 'Preludio de poesía social en *Ancia*, de Blas de Otero', *Salina*, 15:215–21, finds striking evidences of social poetry in O.'s first two books, and thereby proposes to reconsider the concept of 'poesía desarraigada' not only as an existentialist concept but also a social one.

4. DRAMA

GENERAL. H. Yim, 'El tema del muchacho afeminado en el teatro y el cine españoles', *Ojáncano*, 19:55–71, discusses the development of the effeminate protagonist in several works. According to the critic, the characters of J. Calvo Sotelo's *Una noche de lluvia* (1968) and R. Romero's *Acelgas con champán* (1969) overcome the accusation of effeminate by showing their attraction to feminine characters; in T. Luca de Tena's *Hay una luz sobre la cama* (1969), the protagonist refuses to demonstrate that this accusation is false; the protagonist of V. Aranda's *Cambio de sexo* (1977) proves that he has a natural inverted sexuality; while, finally, in E. de la Iglesia's *El pico* (1983), the protagonist presents the modality of the Anglo-Saxon gay. J. A. Zachman, 'El placer fugaz y el amor angustiado: metateatro, género y poder en *El suplicio del placer* de Sabina Berman y *Noches de amor efímero* de Paloma Pedrero', *Gestos*, 31:37–50, approaches these two plays from a feminist perspective to show that, even though one can find some differences at the stylistic and dialectic levels, 'las obras son excepcionalmente parecidas en cuanto a la estructura, los temas y las técnicas que utilizan para presentar, cuestionar e invertir las cargas de género, identidad y poder en las relaciones íntimas'. K. Aggor and C. J. Harris, 'El drama español del siglo xx: bibliografía selecta del año 1999', *Estreno*, 27:52–66, offer a wide bibliographical panorama that includes dramatic texts, critical books and articles, interviews, doctoral dissertations, and reviews.

INDIVIDUAL AUTHORS

ARAÚJO. C. Evans-Corrales, 'The dramatic use of artifice in Luis Araújo's *Las aventuras y andanzas del Aurelio y la Constanza*', *Estreno*, 27:16–22, is a superb article that shows how in this play A. uses multiple dramatic devices and disparate experimental elements that react with each other to reveal unexpected levels of understanding for an audience of both children and adults.

BUERO VALLEJO. As homage to this author, *Estreno*, 27, includes the following articles: V. Dixon, ' "Pintar de otra manera": art in the life and work of Antonio Buero Vallejo' (13–21), which seeks to show how art is a constant presence in B.V.'s life and work; M. T. Halsey, 'El tiempo y la historia: *Misión al pueblo desierto* desde el contexto del teatro de Buero' (22–29), who sees both the presence of previous plays and the evolution of B.V.'s thought in his last work mentioned in the title; M. P. Holt, 'Remembering Antonio, the misteries of chance' (29–34), who discusses the enigmas of chance whose workings inspired P.H.'s carrer-long dedication to B.V.'s theatre; J. López Mozo, 'Buero Vallejo y los autores españoles de hoy' (34–37), focusing on the significance of B.V.'s theatre for the following generations of Spanish dramatists; E. Pajón Macloy, 'Un alegato contra el poder. *El concierto de San Ovidio*, de Antonio Buero Vallejo' (37–38); J. Cross Newman, 'Mission as constant in Antonio Buero Vallejo' (38–43), who argues that the play reiterates a recurring element in Buero's plays: 'The element of mission, the call to rescue or recover a lost entity, whether the integrity or mental wholeness of an individual or of a nation, or to save a painting from destruction'; P. W. O'Connor, '*La señal que se espera* de Antonio Buero Vallejo: el espíritu milenario y el mundo como texto' (43–47), who deals particularly with the transcendental meaning of the so-called 'coincidencias significativas' in this play; V. Serrano and M. de Paco, 'Las últimas obras de Antonio Buero Vallejo: principio y fin de una búsqueda' (47–52), focusing on *Las trampas del azar* and *Misión al pueblo desierto*, which are considered 'una especie de brillante compendio de lo que significa la producción de uno de los dramaturgos señeros de la historia de nuestra escena y del teatro occidental contemporáneo'.

CABAL. G. Torres Nebrera, 'El primer teatro de Fermín Cabal', *Salina*, 15:229–45, is on C.'s theatre from the end of the 1970s until *Caballito del diablo* (1985), emphasizing its moral — even 'profundamente ética' — dimension.

JUNYENT. A. Hughes, 'La mujer y el lenguaje patriarchal en el teatro de Sebastián Junyent', *BHS(L)*, 78:367–82, establishes a contrast between feminine protagonists — the traditional and the emancipated — in J.'s *Hay que deshacer la casa* and *Señora de . . .*, concluding that the attitude of the latter does not seem convincing as a positive alternative: 'Si la mujer tradicional se encuentra atrapada en el patriarcado, con todos los abusos que ello supone, la vida de la protagonista feminista no parece ni más feliz ni más libre que la de su colega tradicional.'

LÓPEZ MOZO.   E. J. Doll, 'La intermedialidad del teatro de López Mozo: de lo visual a lo textual', *Estreno*, 27:8–15, shows a parallel in the transformation of both L.M.'s style and way of using painting and sculpture through a chronological study of his theatre from *Cuatro Happenings* (1967–70) to *Yo, maldita India . . .* (1988).

NIEVA.   A. D. Hitchcock, 'A theater posed against itself: Nieva's metadramatic *Tórtolas crepúsculo y . . . telón*', *Gestos*, 32:75–89, shows the consequences of the play's status of 'overwhelming metatheatricality': 'to beg for its own theatrical actualisation [. . .] in a way that a more literary work such as *Salvator Rosa*, a much later Nieva composition, does not'.

PEDRERO.   S. P. Berardini, 'Huellas mitológicas en el teatro de Paloma Pedrero', *Gestos*, 31:51–64, uncovers the mythological references present in P.'s *El color de agosto* and *Besos de lobo*, and reveals how these references influence the interpretation of the plays while adding textual depth at the same time.

V. CATALAN STUDIES

LANGUAGE

By Jordi Cicres, *Universitat de Girona*

1. General

Ll. López del Castillo, *Qüestions bàsiques del català actual: lèxic i semàntica, fonètica i ortografia*, B, Edicions 62, 205 pp., is divided into two parts. The first discusses lexical problems of the linguistic norm, the second approaches Catalan phonetics from the point of view of linguistic variation (language registers and levels) and proposes a standard pronunciation, and explains the orthographic system taking into account the criteria and assessment which guided its structure. *Llengua catalana IV*, ed. M. A. Martí, B, UOC, 30 pp., is a university handbook on computational linguistics and university education. C. Vilà, *La llengua catalana com a sistema*, B, UOC, provides an introduction to linguistics in the form of an invitation to reflect on the language as a system, and on Catalan in particular. *Llengua i ràdio*, ed. J. Julià, B, PAM, 206 pp. is a selection of articles which reflect on the role of language in the mass media and specifically radio. It focuses on the role of radio regarding the normalization of Catalan. F. Vallverdú, *El català estàndard i els mitjans audiovisuals: escrits elaborats des de la Comissió de Normalització Lingüística de TVC (Coorporació Catalana de Ràdio i Televisió)*, B, Edicions 62, 150 pp., is an analysis of the presence and use of Catalan language in the mass media. J. Julià, *L'inici de la lingüística catalana: Bernhard Schädel, Mn. Antoni M. Alcover i l'Institut d'Estudis Catalans. Una aproximació epistolar, 1904–1925*, B, Curial – PAM, 411 pp., contains the correspondence between Catalan and non-Catalan linguists in the first decades of the 20th century. The most important correspondence is that between Schädel and Alcover. This period corresponds to the beginnings of the linguistic science for the Catalan language. *La lingüística de Pompeu Fabra*, ed. J. Ginebra, R. Martínez, and M. Pradill Alacant, IIFV — Universitat Rovira i Virgili, 412 pp., joins the works presented at the International Colloquium 'La lingüística de Pompeu Fabra' in Tarragona, on 14–16 December 1998. Lexicology, grammar, norm theory and practice of normalization, standardization, history, etc. are treated in this work. A. Vila, *Una llengua entre cinc mil: el català*, B, PAM, 201 pp., takes Catalan as the starting point and by comparing its morphology, lexis, syntax, phonetics, and other areas of grammar with other languages (71 languages), he describes the nature of

Catalan sentences, words, lexical combinations, sound characteristics, which are as arbitrary as in any other language. In A. Cros,
M. Segarra, and A. M. Torrent, *Llengua oral i llengua escrita a la televisió*,
B, PAM, 196 pp., the oral and written language in TV is analysed:
news programmes, TV series, educational programmes, TV spots,
etc.

M. Fuentes, 'Los numerales en la lengua de signos catalana',
Sintagma, 12 : 19–35, describes the subsystem of the cardinal numerals
in Catalan Sign Language (LSC), according to the variety used in
Barcelona. Subsystems of numerals are relatively independent of the
other subsystems of a language, so this allows them to be described in
a relatively independent way without detracting from language unity.

2. PHONETICS AND PHONOLOGY

P. Prieto et al., 'Anàlisi acústica de la resolució de xocs accentuals en
català', *EFE*, 11 : 11–40, examine the process of production of two
syllables in a clash context and describe the stress clash resolution
strategies used in Catalan. The results show that duration and
amplitude are not robust acoustic correlates of the perception of
deaccenting; conversely, the F_0 contour seems to be the main cue of
destressing in such clash contexts. J. Carrera, 'Algunes consideracions
generals sobre l'anàlisi acústica de [e] i de [a] àtones', *ib.*, 67–88, is a
minor contribution to the spectrographic study of non-stressed vowels
from North-Western Catalan. It focuses on the vowels [a] and [e] in
absolute initial position and establishes a connection between Catalan
stressed and unstressed vowels while presenting some of the effects of
coarticulation through comparison with other Romance languages.
F. Gutiérrez, 'Estudio acústico de la entonación de enunciados con la
función de acuerdo y reserva en inglés y catalán', *ib.*, 143–58, is the
report of an acoustic study of the intonational exponence of the
meanings 'agreement' and 'reservation' in English and Catalan.
Three examples were constructed for English and then projected into
Catalan. All the examples were read by 3 informants for each of the
two languages. The data for English confirm the use of falling
intonation for agreement and falling-rising intonation for reservation.
The initial point of the falling tones was higher for reservation that
for agreement. As regards Catalan, a fall is used for both agreement
and reservation, with limited use of the fall-rise for the latter meaning,
the initial point of the fall, though, is higher for reservation than for
agreement.

M. Badia, *Diftongs i africats, dues qüestions polèmiques de fonologia catalana*, B, Curial Edicions Catalanes – PAM, 215 pp., is a comprehensive work about diphthongs and affricative sounds. B. distinguishes between systematic and non-systematic diphthongs. Their difference is in their phonetic context (into or outside of the word). With regard to affricative sounds, Badia defends the monophonematic character of the sounds [tʃ] and [dʒ], and the diphonematic character of [ts] and [dz].

P. Prieto, *Fonètica i fonologia catalanes*, B, UOC, is a university handbook of Catalan general phonetics and phonology. A complement to this work is the *Laboratori virtual de pràctiques*, CD-ROM, which includes practical exercises, a multimedia course called *Speech Production and Perception I*, animations, a program for acoustic analysis — ANETO — and a corpus of the Catalan dialects.

3. SYNTAX, MORPHOLOGY, AND PRAGMATICS

C. Riera, 'Repetició i elisió de preposicions', *Llengua nacional*, 30:22–27, analyses the repetition or elision of prepositions in Catalan linked phrases. Three groups are described: first, with obligatory repetition; second, preferably with repetition; and third, preferably with elision. But these divisions are not clear-cut, because some examples can be distributed in more than one group. J. Vallcorba, 'Les interferències en els adverbials *en* i *hi* i les substitucions esgarriadores', *ib.*, 30:13–21; 31:23–29; 32:15–20; and 37:13–15 (multiple parts), analyses the differences between Catalan and Castilian usage in which the Catalan solution is the pronouns *en* or *hi* and the Spanish one is another construction, for example in partitive clauses, anaphoric clauses, etc. In A. Jané, 'Sobre el complement del nom', *ib.*, 33:19–25, the previous works of J. Vallcorba on the use and abuse of the pronoun *en* are analysed, but from the point of view of the modern language rather than Old Catalan. J. analyses the pronoun *en* as a partitive, as a complement of the accusative, and as a complementary subject. L. Escobar and A. Gavarró, 'The acquisition of clitics and strong pronouns in Catalan', pp. 161–80 of *Clitics in Phonology, Morphology and Syntax*, ed. B. Gerlach and J. Grijzenhout, Philadelphia, Benjamins, 2000, 441 pp., analyses the differences in the acquisition of clitics and strong pronouns in Catalan. J. Ramos, 'El verb "haver-hi": evolució dels usos sintàctics', *ER*, 23:123–46, examines the syntactic evolution of the verb *haver-hi* through a large number of texts written in Catalan from the 13th c. until the present day. Linguistic analysis focuses on three basic features of this verb which have not been much studied from a diachronic perspective: the grammaticalization of the locative clitic *hi*, the syntactical features of the post-verbal subject and the concord between the verb and this subject. A. Saragossà, 'Sobre la coherència lingüística del superlatiu aplicat a circumstancials ("vine al més tost que pugues")', *ib.*, 92–122, seeks to show that the Catalan linguistic ruling about superlatives is not very coherent (explicit rejection of the Castilian *lo* and hidden use of it). This contradiction can be solved by resorting to living popular constructions. M. Llinàs-Grau and M. Coll-Alfonso, 'Telic verbs in early Catalan', *Probus*, 13:69–79, focus on child speech sequences which diverge from their corresponding adult counterparts in terms of the order of their constituents. They analyse the OV sequences and show how these only show up co-occurring with telic verbs. Another part of the analysis of the OV constructions implies noticing that the morphological make-up of the verbal elements is not always non-finite. The alternation observed between VO-OV constructions seems to be determined by the verb type.

M. Pascual, 'A syntactic analysis of instrumental prepositional phrases', *CWPL*, 9:53–68, deals with those Catalan and Spanish prepositional phrases (PP) introduced by the prepositions *amb* (Catalan) — *con* (Spanish), that designate the instrument used to carry out the action expressed by the verb, analysing them as a small clause that has a dyadic predicate: the proposition. P. proposes that the instrumental PP forms an independent derivation that must merge with a verbal syntactic derivation in order to get licensed. G. Rigau, 'The role of the quantifier *tot* in some Catalan temporal phrases', *ib.*, 85–100, analyses two kinds of Catalan temporal adjuncts headed by the quantifier *tot* 'all': the intensive *tot* XP ('all XP') and the extensive *tot XP que* ('all XP that'), and offers an explanation for their different behaviour. X. Villalba, 'The right edge of exclamative sentences in Catalan', *ib.*, 119–35, argues that certain exclamative constructions apparently involving right-dislocation of an adjective must be analysed as having it *in situ*, forming a small clause with a null exclamative operator. Moreover, it is suggested that the obligatory appearance of the marker *de* ('of') and the partitive clitic *en/ne* in this construction, follows from the presence of the null exclamative operator.

The following works are brief studies of specific grammar problems: X. Rull, 'La construcció *ser* + participi en els temps perfets', *Llengua Nacional*, 35:28–29, analyses the construction with the verb *ser* plus participle in perfect tenses vs. the standard construction with *haver* plus participle (e.g. *són vistos* vs. *han vist*); A. Jané, 'El pronom *ell* (i flexió) referit a inanimats', *ib.*, 29:23–25, collects some examples that prove that the use of the pronoun *ell* does not result from Spanish influence, because in Old Catalan there are a lot of examples; J. Ginebra, 'Nota sobre els possessius', *ib.*, 35:21–22, analyses, from the point of view of the norm, some structures with a possessive;

J. Vallcorba, 'La invasió dels verbs en condicional', *ib.*, 18–19, analyses the misuse of the conditional tense as opposed to periphrases with the verb *deure*; A. Jané, 'Sobre l'omissió indeguda i l'ús abusiu del pronom "hi"', *ib.*, 36: 12–16, analyses the use of the pronoun *hi*; J. Ruaix, 'Abús de "només"', *ib.*, 37: 21–23, examines the different uses of the adverb *només* and proposes some contexts in which it should not be used; A. Jané, 'Un cas de concordança: "Ell és un dels qui va(n) dir que sí"', *ib.*, 16–20, examines the concord in examples with a singular noun phrase incorporating plural reference.

M. J. Cuenca, *Sintaxi catalana*, B, UOC, is a university handbook of Catalan syntax, for students of the Universitat Oberta de Catalunya. J. Bastardas, *Substantius usats en sentit figurat com a qualificadors de persona*, B, Societat Catalana de Llengua i Literatura, 68 pp., analyses some words on the borderline of nouns and adjectives, like *plom*, *bleda*, *sabatot*, *rata*, etc. These words — initially nouns — are used as adjectives describing people. F. Ordóñez, *The Clausal Structure of Spanish: A Comparative Study*, NY, Garland, 209 pp. focuses its investigation in Spanish structures, but Catalan and other languages are present in the comparative study.

M. Bassols, *Les claus de la pragmàtica*, Vic U.P., 256 pp., provides introductory accounts of pragmatics, with theoretical information and practical examples.

4. LEXIS

Ll. López del Castillo, *Gran diccionari 62 de la llengua catalana*, B, Edicions 62, 1236 pp., is a dictionary of usage which includes many terms which are not admitted by the linguistic norm, but used normally by speakers. Also, it has little specific scientific and technical vocabulary. There are also abridged versions of this work. Another usage dictionary is J. Lacreu, *Diccionari bàsic d'ús del valencià*, València, Bromera, 815 pp., based on the Valencian dialect. A. M. Alcover, *Mostra de diccionari mallorquí*, ed. M. P. Perea, B, PAM, 368 pp. IEC, *Diccionari manual de la llengua catalana*, B, IEC, 1435 pp., is a reduced version of the official normative Catalan dictionary. The 10th volume of J. Coromines, J. Ferrer, J. Ferrer, and J. Pujadas, *Diccionari etimològic i complementari de la llengua catalana*, B, Curial–'la Caixa', 1020 pp., with the indexes of the complete work, has appeared. A. Rico and D. Paloma, *Diccionari de pronunciació en català*, B, Edicions 62, 309 pp., is a list of more than 2000 words presenting phonetic difficulties. The work is conceived as a quick-reference dictionary. J. Lacreu et al., *Diccionari valencià de pronunciació*, València, Bromera, 959 pp. is a more complex pronunciation dictionary, based on the Valencian dialect; J. Bruguera, *Diccionari de dubtes i dificultats del català*, B, Enciclopèdia

Catalana, 279 pp., includes the most usual doubts in Catalan grammar. J. Badia, *Diccionari escolar: dubtes, incorreccions i barbarismes*, B, Castellnou, 419 pp. is a school dictionary which includes doubts, barbarisms, and other grammar mistakes. E. Franquesa et al., *Nou diccionari de neologismes*, B, Edicions 62, 503 pp. M. T. Cabré and J. Feliu, *La terminología científico-técnica*, B, Univ. Pompeu Fabra, 302 pp., collects the contributions of the IULATERM members on the automatic recognition of pertinent terminological items of a specialized field and their delimitation when they are phrasal units, and with the representation of the specialized knowledge of a text on the basis of the establishment of the conceptual junctions that synthesize them and their relationships. M. S. González, *Frases fetes al nord de la llengua: diccionari de les comarques de Castelló*, Castelló, Servei de Publicacions, Diputació de Castelló, 125 pp., is a collection of the typical proverbs of the Castelló region. C. de Arce, *Sinònims i antònims: diccionari català*, B, Seuba, 350 pp., is a synonym and antonym dictionary. *Lexicologia catalana: semàntica del mot i semàntica de l'oració*, ed. M. T. Espinal et al., B, UOC, is a university handbook on lexis.

Bilingual dictionaries include *Diccionari bàsic català-castellà, castellà-català*, B, Enciclopèdia Catalana, 505 pp.; *Diccionari escolar: català-castellà, castellano-catalán*, B, Biblograf, 415 pp. (a school dictionary); *Larousse pocket dictionary: Catalan-English, English-Catalan*, B, Larousse, 444 pp.; and *Larousse diccionari compact: català-anglès, English-Catalan*, B, Larousse, 551 pp. D. Nosell, *Diccionari suec-català*, B, Enciclopèdia Catalana, 809 pp.; A. Alkuwaifi and M. Torres, *Diccionari infantil il·lustrat català-àrab: 3–6 anys*, B, Punt d'Intercanvi: Associació Socio-cultural, 30 pp. J. Willis and M. Ashby, *Diccionari Oxford pocket català per a estudiants d'anglès: català-anglès, anglès català*, OUP, 683 pp. with a diskette with exercises; M. Mayer et al., *Llatí-català, català-llatí*, B, Spes, 161 pp.; A. Febrer, *Diccionari menorquí, espanyol, francès i llatí*, B, IEC, 431 pp. (critical edition and study by M. Paredes). 'False friends' dictionaries include C. Castellanos and F. Lenoir, *Diccionari de paranys de traducció: francès català. Faus amis*, B, Enciclopèdia Catalana, 334 pp.; I. Turull, *Diccionari de paranys de traducció italià-català: falsi amici*, B, Enciclopèdia Catalana, 205 pp.

M. T. Espinal, 'On the semantic status of n-words in Catalan and Spanish', *Lingua*, 110, 2000:557–80, provides some arguments to claim that Catalan and Spanish n-words are not lexically ambiguous. They are intrinsically negative expressions, in the sense that they are indefinites incorporated into a numeral meaning $\|0\|$, and they are weak quantifiers, inasmuch as they are underspecified for quantificational force. It suggests the relevance of a hierarchy of negative items (negative quantifiers / minimizers, n-words, and polarity items)

determined by the position of these items within a scale of quantifica-
tional force. G. Colón, 'Aprovechamiento nebrisense en el contraste
léxico español vs. catalán y "valenciano" ', *QS*, 21.1 : 81–125, analyses
many pairs of lexical items in Catalan and Spanish, which appear in
different editions of Nebrija's *Introductiones latinae* and translations of
this work. The aim of this work is not to analyse these items but to
supply examples to lexicologists and language historians.

Works establishing the terminology of different specialized fields
include: J. Pla, *Diccionari Pla de literatura*, ed. V. Puig, B, Destino,
920 pp.; Ll. de Yzaguirre and O. Comas, *Diccionari oficial de l'scrabble
en català*, B, Enciclopèdia Catalana, 597 pp.; A. Gassiot and J. Ramon,
Diccionari de ciències ambientals, B, Edicions 62, 311 pp.; TERMCAT,
Diccionari de química analítica, B, Enciclopèdia Catalana, 252 pp.;
Diccionari visual de la construcció, B, Departament de Política Territorial
i Obres Públiques – TERMCAT, 310 pp.; TERMCAT – INK
Catalunya, *Diccionari d'auditoria i compatibilitat*, B, TERMCAT, optical
disk; TERMCAT, *Diccionari de la negociació col·lectiva*, B, TERMCAT –
Departament de Treball, 157 pp.; TERMCAT, *Diccionari d'economia i
empresa*, B, Gestió i Edició de Mitjans, 263 pp.; J. Tusón, *Diccionari de
lingüística*, B, VOX, 396 pp.; M. Foz, E. Llauradó, and J. Ramis,
Diccionari enciclopèdic de medicina, B, Acadèmia de Ciències Mèdiques
de Catalunya i de Balears – Enciclopèdia Catalana, 2024 pp.;
TERMCAT, *Diccionari de trànsit*, B, Enciclopèdia Catalana – TERM-
CAT, 245 pp.; *Societat de la informació; noves tecnologies i internet*, B,
TERMCAT, 288 pp.; E. Domènech *et al.*, *Diccionari bàsic de prehistòria*,
Alacant U.P., 60 pp.; R. Escolano *et al.*, *Diccionari juridicoadministratiu*,
Alacant U.P., 162 pp.; J. M. García, *Diccionari d'arqueologia*, Alacant
U.P., 95 pp.; TERMCAT, *Diccionari d'Internet*, B, Enciclopèdia Cata-
lana, 189 pp.; J. Melendres, *La direcció dels actors: diccionari mínim*, B,
Institut del Teatre, 144 pp.; X. Favà, *Diccionari dels noms de ceps i raïms:
l'ampelonímia catalana*, B, IEC, 455 pp.; F. Ruiz *et al.*, *Diccionari de
sociolingüística*, B, Enciclopèdia Catalana, 328 pp.; *Diccionari de saneja-
ment*, B, Generalitat de Catalunya. Departament de Medi Ambient:
Agència Catalana de l'Aigua, optical disk; Ll. M. de Cisneros *et al.*,
Diccionari de la qualitat, B, Enginyers Industrials de Catalunya,
Marcombo Boixareu, 124 pp.; E. Franquesa *et al.*, *Diccionari d'assegu-
rances: terminologia i fraseologia*, B, TERMCAT, 214 pp.; E. Franquesa
et al., *Diccionari de la neu*, B, Enciclopèdia Catalana – TERMCAT,
348 pp.; A. Fargas, *Diccionari de la francmaçoneria*, B, Edicions 62,
239 pp.; X. Brotons, *Diccionari casteller*, B, Diputació de Barcelona,
81 pp.; *Diccionari d'otorinolaringologia*, B, TERMCAT, 194 pp.; *Diccionari d'oftalmologia*, B, TERMCAT, 184 pp.; E. Albacar, *Diccionari jurídic
per a infermeria*, B, Marrè, 201 pp.; J. Civit et al., *Treballem en català*, B,

La Terra, 60 pp. (about cattle raising); and *Diccionari d'hoteleria i turisme*, B, Edicions 62–TERMCAT, 201 pp.

5. DIALECTOLOGY

J. Veny and L. Pons, *Atles lingüístic del domini català*, B, IEC, is a selection of maps with information about different language features in the different areas of the Catalan Countries. F. X. Llorca, *El llenguatge mariner de la Marina*, Alacant U.P., 196 pp., describes sailors' terminology in la Marina, a Valencian region. S. Romero, 'Notes per a la caracterització de la parla de la Conca de Tremp', *Sintagma*, 13:55–77, adds to and updates the data on oral use in la Conca de Tremp, a language community of intradialectal transition between the ribagorçano-pallaresa and the lleidatà areas, presenting the specific linguistic features placing it in the dialect continuum and illustrating tendencies in present-day speech. J.-P. Escudero, 'Le Catalan septentrional, un dialecte partagé entre deux désinences: *Parli/firmo* (je parle/je signe)', *RECat*, 3:199–209, analyses the development of first person singular inflection in the Northern dialect of Catalan. C. Camps, 'Noms de peixos de mar i d'estany a Catalunya Nord', *ib.*, 191–97, is a compilation of terms for sea and pond fish in N. Catalonia. J. Sotgiu, 'Mestres de paleta, palaus i cases', *L'Alguer*, 73:9–18, studies the vocabulary of bricklaying, palaces, and houses in Alghero; Id., 'Fraïlis, frailarjos i mascarjos', *ib.*, 72:16–20, is a compilation of names related to ironmongery, also in Alghero; Id., 'Sabates i sabaters', *ib.*, 68:9–16, compiles vocabulary related to shoemaking; and Id., 'Tubistes, gas, aigua i energia elèctrica', *ib.*, 70:17–20, includes the specific terminology of gas, water, and electricity in Alghero.

J. Monturiol and E. Domínguez, *El parlar de la Garrotxa*, Olot, Ràdio Olot, 179 pp., is a brief study of the linguistic features of the Catalan area of la Garrotxa, covering phonetics, morphology, syntax, and lexicon. O. Cubells, *El parlar de la Palma d'Ebre: Riera d'Ebre*, Palma d'Ebre, Associació Cultural l'Espona, 186 pp., is a similar study, focused on the town of Palma d'Ebre. J. Corbera, *Caracterització del lèxic alguerès*, Palma, Univ. de les Illes Balears, 325 pp., is a characterization of the lexical items of the Sardinian town of Alghero.

6. HISTORY OF THE LANGUAGE AND DIACHRONIC STUDIES

J. Argenter, 'Code-switching and dialogism: verbal practices among Catalan Jews in the Middle Ages', *LSo*, 30:377–402, analyses data from the records of communicative practices left behind by Catalan Jewish communities of the 14th and 15th centuries. It analyses two of the verbal genres, which themselves must be viewed in the context of a broader Hispano-Arabic cultural tradition. In this analysis of the functions that code-switching played in these verbal practices, a contrast emerges between the use of code-switching and lexical borrowing in both verbal genres. J. Armangué, 'Sis segles en català', *RFR*, 17, 2000:217–28, analyses the refined and semi-refined, literary and public, Catalan language in Sardinia from the 14th to the 20th century. It concludes with a excursus on Algherese in modern Alghero.

C. Martínez, *La llengua catalana a Mallorca al segle XVIII i primer terç del XIX*, Palma de Mallorca, Univ. de les Illes Balears, Departament de Filologia Catalana i Lingüística Genera – PAM, 407 pp. is a description of the Catalan language in Mallorca during the 18th c. and the first third of the 19th century. F. Bernat, *Gramàtica històrica catalana* II: *l'evolució del sistema*, B, UOC de Catalunya, is a university handbook on the history of the Catalan language. It is divided into three units: phonetics (F. Bernat and M. Massanell); morphology (the same authors), and syntax (J. Martí). V. Pitarch, *Llengua i església durant el barroc valencià*, V, IIFV – PAM, 382 pp., is an analysis of the sociolinguistic situation in Valencia during the 16th and 17th centuries. The ecclesiastical use of the language is analysed. J. Miralles, *Entorn de la història de la llengua*, Palma, Univ. de les Illes Balears, 201 pp., is an analysis of the history of the language from a variety of points of view (historical, sociolinguistic, grammatical, etc.).

7. Sociolinguistics

J. M. Blecua, and S. Varela, 'Las lenguas de España: presente y futuro', *LS*, 36:275–87, digresses about the situation of the variety of languages in Spain (Catalan, Basque, Castilian, and Galician). They suggest education and respect to reach a peaceful coexistence of the different languages of Spain. They are optimistic because the statistics demonstrate that society is respectful of other languages. F. Munar, 'Unes dades d'ensenyament en català esperançadores a les illes Balears', *Escola catalana*, 384:30–32, analyses the evolution of the Catalan language in the Balearic education system since the government change in 1999. Some of the measures adopted by the new government were to demand the C level of Catalan for teachers, to increase the number of teachers of the Catalan language, etc. J. Solé, 'De la sobirania nacional a la sobirania sociolingüística', *ib.*, 381:19–21, suggests national sovereignty as the previous stage of sociolinguistic sovereignty in the Catalan countries. A. Bastardas, 'Normalització lingüística i globalització: l'escola catalana en el segle XXI', *ib.*, 24–26, analyses the state of the linguistic normalization of the Catalan language — not as a standardization and literacy phenomenon but as an effective bilingualization process.

B. Montoya, *Els alacantins catalanoparlants: una generació interrompuda*, B, IEC, 200 pp., is a study of phonetic, morphological, and lexical features in different groups of speakers living in the city of Alacant (one group speaking Catalan as their mother tongue, another speaking Catalan as their second language); important differences have been verified between the two groups. The phenomenon of linguistic atrophy is also analysed. *Societat, llengua i norma: a l'entorn de la normativització de la llengua catalana*, ed. M. À. Pradilla et al., Benicarló, Alambor, 284 pp., is an anthology of the lectures in the series 'Societat, llengua i norma: a l'entorn de la normativització de la llengua catalana', organized in Tarragona in November 1999. C. Castellanos, *Llengua, dialectes i estandardització*, B, Octaedro, 125 pp., is an approach to the concepts of language, dialects, and standardization from the point of view of sociolinguistics. *Llengua i ús a les terres de Ponent: criteris i àmbits d'aplicació*, ed. J. Julià, Lleida, Pagès, 103 pp., is a sociolinguistic study of the use of the Catalan language in the area of Lleida. *Llengua i mitjans de comunicació: actes del Congrés de Llengua i Mitjans de Comunicació: Lleida, 17–18 de desembre de 1999*, ed. I. Creus, J. Julià, and S. Romero, Lleida, Pagès, 358 pp., are the proceedings of this congress about language and mass media.

VARIATION. J. L. Blas Arroyo, and D. Tricker, 'Principles of variationism for disambiguating language contact phenomena: the case of lone Spanish nouns in Catalan discourse', *LVC*, 12, 2000:103–40, determines the status of ambiguous lone Spanish-origin nouns in Catalan discourse using the comparative variationist method. It analyses their distribution and conditioning and it compares them to their counterparts in unmixed Spanish or in multiple-word code-switches. The main conclusion is that Spanish-origin nouns in an otherwise Catalan context present grammatical variability similar to that of Catalan nouns, and that they behave differently from Spanish nouns in a monolingual context.

8. PSYCHOLINGUISTICS AND LANGUAGE ACQUISITION

À. Colomé, 'Lexical activation in bilinguals' speech production: language-specific or language-independent?', *JMemL*, 45:726–36, discusses whether the language that bilinguals are not using is nonetheless activated, using an adaptation of the phoneme monitoring task for speech production. Three experiments were conducted in which highly fluent Catalan-Spanish bilinguals had to decide whether a certain phoneme was in a picture illustrating a Catalan noun. Phonemes could be either part of the Catalan word, part of its Spanish translation, or absent from both nouns. Results showed that participants took longer to reject the phoneme appearing in the Spanish word than the control one. A fourth control experiment involving monolinguals indicated that these results were not due to specific characteristics of the material. The same pattern was replicated at different SOAs, which leads us to conclude that both the target language and the language not in use are simultaneously activated. M. Prat-Sala, R. Shillcock, and A. Sorace, 'Animacy effects on the production of object-dislocated descriptions by Catalan-speaking children', *JCL*, 27, 2000:97–117, presents an experiment that examined two related questions, first the effects of animacy on the production of different syntactic structures and word orders by Catalan-speaking children, and second the relationship between age and the production of different syntactic structures by these children. Participants (children aged 4 to 11) tended to produce more object-dislocated descriptions when the patient was animate than when it was inanimate. It argues that frequency of exposure to a particular syntactic structure is an important factor that contributes to the acquisition of that syntactic structure. It also suggests that the effects of animacy on the production of object-dislocated descriptions can be explained by means of conceptual and lexical accessibility. M. Juan-Garau, and C. Pérez-Vidal, 'Mixing and pragmatic parental strategies in early bilingual acquisition', *ib.*, 28:59–86, investigate the relationship between a child's degree of bilingualism and features of parental input, seeking to demonstrate that parental discourse strategies have a direct bearing on the levels of mixing present in child's utterances in his weaker language, English. The longitudinal study of a Catalan/English bilingual child shows that whereas the Catalan-speaking mother negotiates a bilingual context of interaction with her son, the English-speaking father endeavours to impose a monolingual context, a change of strategy which clearly favours the child's increasing use of the minority language, entailing a sharp decline in rates of mixing. J. Cebrian, 'Transferability and productivity of L1 rules in Catalan-English interlanguage', *SSLA*, 22:1–26, examines the interference of L1 (Catalan) neutralization rules in the acquisition of a marked L2 (English) phonological feature. The voicing contrast in final position in Catalan is neutralized by voicing or devoicing rules, depending on the environment. The results of an experiment testing the production of target final obstruents in different environments indicate a very high incidence of devoicing, which confirms the prevalence of final devoicing in second language acquisition and points to the joint effect of transfer and universal tendencies.

J. Julià, *L'ensenyament del català com a L2. De la teoria a la pràctica*, Lleida U.P., 227 pp., has a dozen works divided into two blocks, on the teaching of Catalan as a second language. The first block provides theoretical contributions on the application of linguistics to language teaching, and to Catalan in particular; the second block provides particular experiences on the teaching of Catalan as a second language. F. Tolosa et al., *Material lingüístic en català per a exploracions logoaudiomètriques*, Palma, Univ. de les Illes Balears, 102 pp., provides linguistic materials in Catalan to facilitate logoaudiometric exploration.

MEDIEVAL LITERATURE

By Lola Badia, *Professor of Catalan Literature at the Universitat de Girona* and Miriam Cabré, *Researcher at the Universitat de Girona*

1. General

BIBLIOGRAPHY AND HISTORICAL BACKGROUND. *BBAHLM*, 14:1–63, provides an annotated list of studies on medieval Catalan for the year 2000. Gabriel Ensenyat Pujol, *Història de la Literatura Catalana a Mallorca a l'Edat Mitjana*, Palma, El Tall, 206 pp., dedicates special attention to Llull and Lullism, but also comments on Turmeda, lyric poetry, and the first printed editions. Xavier Luna-Batlle, *Textos històrics catalans (segles XII al XVIII)*, Bellaterra, UAB U.P., 1999, 196 pp., is an anthology of non-literary texts (legal, administrative, religious, chronicles, memories, treatises, cookbooks) using existing editions. Giuseppe E. Sansone, *Poesia catalana del Medioevo: antologia*, Novara, Interlinea, 253 pp., is a wide-ranging anthology, from Llull to Pere Serafí, which uses the best available editions and provides Italian verse translations and occasional notes. A. Espadaler, 'La Catalogna dei re', Boitani, *Produzione*, II, 873–932, surveys the impact of royal patronage on 12th-c. to 15th-c. literature. J. Turró, 'Una cort a Barcelona per a la literatura del segle XV', *RCat*, 163:97–123, argues that 15th-c. Catalan literature is not alien to the royal court since the departure of King Alfons el Magnànim to Naples did not obliterate mainland Trastamara courts.

COLLECTED ESSAYS. Two homage volumes to Pere Bohigas make accessible some of his classic articles: *Mirall d'una llarga vida: a Pere Bohigas, centenari*, ed. Antoni M. Badia Margarit, Germà Colón, and Josep Moran Ocerinjauregui, B, IEC, 799 pp., and his *Inventario de códices miniaturados o iluminados de procedencia catalana o existentes en bibliotecas catalanas*, ed. Vinyet Panyella and Joana Escobedo, B, Biblioteca de Catalunya, 2000, 110 pp. Other extremely useful facsimile editions of seminal studies are: Antoni Rubió i Lluch, *Documents per a la història de la cultura catalana medieval*, 2 vols, B, IEC, 2000, 486, 454 pp., and Id., *Diplomatari de l'Orient català (1301–1409): col·lecció de documents per a la història de l'expedició catalana a Orient i dels ducats d'Atenes i Neopàtria*, B, IEC, 798 pp.

ARCHIVAL RESEARCH AND READERSHIP. Volume II.1 of *Repertori de Manuscrits Catalans (1474–1620)*, ed. Eulàlia Duran, offers codicological and bibliographic data for two further library holdings: *Barcelona, Biblioteca Pública Episcopal i Biblioteca de la Universitat*, ed. Eulàlia Miralles and Maria Toldrà, B, IEC, 2000, 411 pp. I. Padrosa Gorgot, 'Catàleg de manuscrits llatins de la Biblioteca del Palau de Perelada',

Annals de l'Institut d'Estudis Gironins, 40, 1999:309–79, lists, among others, two Lullian manuscripts. Christian Guilleré edits and studies the *Llibre verd de la ciutat de Girona (1144–1533)*, B, Fundació Noguera–Pagès, 2000, 746 pp. J. Hernando Delgado has added two contributions to his valuable series of studies on book circulation in medieval Barcelona: 'El llibre de gramàtica a la Barcelona del segle XIV segons els documents dels protocols notarials', *AST*, 71, 1998:359–78, and his 'Crèdit i llibres a Barcelona, segle XV: els contractes de venda de rendes (censals, morts i violaris) garantits amb vendes simulades de llibres; el llibre, instrument econòmic i objecte de cultura', *Estudis Històrics i Documents dels Arxius de Protocols*, 18, 2000:7–22.

2. LYRIC AND NARRATIVE VERSE

LYRIC POETRY AND MS TRANSMISSION. Two new issues of *Materials de l'Arxiu Informatitzat de Textos Catalans Medievals*, Bellaterra, Seminari de Filologia i Informàtica de la UAB: volume 1.A is by Anna Alberni, *Cançoner Vega-Aguiló. Barcelona, Biblioteca de Catalunya, ms. 7* (14 microfiches), and volume 4 is by Francesc J. Gómez and Marta Vilaseca, *Cançoner de l'Ateneu. Barcelona, Biblioteca de l'Ateneu Barcelonès, ms. 1* (16 microfiches). G. Borriero, 'Il tópos dell'ineffabile nella retorica medievale e nella lirica trobadorica', *MedRom*, 23, 1999:21–65, includes Berenguer de Palol, Cerverí de Girona, and Guillem de Cabestany in his survey. Miquel Pujol, *Poesia occitanocatalana de Castelló d'Empúries*, Girona, Patronat Francesc Eiximenis — Figueras, Institut d'Estudis Empordanesos, 382 pp., edits 19 poems with troubadour roots, found in archival documents dated between 1288 and 1328. G. Avenoza, '*Ai espiga novela!* Estudi i edició d'una pastorel·la catalana del segle XIV', *Orduna Vol.*, 53–71, edits a recently discovered pastourelle which represents one of the earliest Catalan examples of the genre. *Canzonieri iberici*, ed. Patrizia Botta, Carmen Parrilla, and Ignacio Pérez Pascual, 2 vols, Padua U.P. — Noia, Toxosoutos — Corunna U.P., 358, 399 pp., contains several articles on specific Catalan manuscripts including A. Alberni, 'Notes per a una reconstrucció codicològica del *Cançoner Vega-Aguiló* (BdC, mss. 7 i 8)' (I, 301–11); M. Cabré, 'Un cançoner de Cerverí de Girona?' (I, 283–99); J.-L. Martos, 'La génesis de un cancionero de autor: Joan Roís de Corella y el *Cançoner de Mayans*' (I, 313–28); and S. Ventura, 'Le scelte d'autore operate dal compilatore del ms. Sg' (I, 271–82). Another contribution offers annotated editions of newly found or little-known texts: O. Grapí and E. de La Marnierre, 'Al marge dels cançoners (1): alguns textos poètics catalans inèdits o poc coneguts' (I, 219–65). L. Gimeno Betí, 'Català i occità: a l'entorn de la llengua del *Cançoner dels Masdovelles*', *RLiR*, 253–54, 2000: 119–65, systematically describes the linguistic features of this MS. M. Garcia Sempere, 'L'edició de 1539 de l'obra d'Ausiàs March: algunes dades noves', *Actes* (Barcelona), 177–98, studies Romaní's translation, considering a new copy. Pere Serafí, *Poesies catalanes*, ed. Josep Romeu i Figueras, ENC, B21, 482 pp., offers an annotated critical edition of Serafí's corpus of 159 poems.

NARRATIVE POETRY. A. M. Compagna, 'Epica catalana perduta ed epica in Catalogna', Luongo, *Epopée*, 645–54, surveys diverging studies on the existence of prose renderings of epic poems and the circulation of French and Spanish epics in Catalonia. A. G. Hauf, ' "Artús, aycell qui atenon *li bretó*?"': *La Faula*, seducció o reivindicació políticomoral?', *Bolletí de la Societat Arqueològica Lul·liana*, 56, 2000: 7–24, revisits the problems posed by a sebastianist interpretation of *La Faula*.

3. DOCTRINAL AND RELIGIOUS PROSE

RAMON LLULL AND LULLISM

The *Base de Dades Ramon Llull (= Llull DB)*, ed. Antoni Bonner, B, Departament de Filologia Catalana i Biblioteca de la Universitat de Barcelona, <http://orbita.bib.ub.es/llull/> makes available online all known data (title, incipit, explicit, MSS, catalogues, bibliographies, cross-references) on L.'s works and those wrongly attributed to him. Two new critical editions of L.'s Latin treatises: *Arbor Scientiae*, ed. Pere Villalba, 3 vols (CCCM, 180A-C = ROL, 24–26), Turnhout, Brepols, 2000, 360, 830, 1430 pp., and *Liber de Est Dei, Liber de cognitione Dei, Liber de homine, Liber de Deo*, ed. Fernando Domínguez Reboiras (CCCM, 112 = ROL, 21), Turnhout, Brepols, 2000, 424 pp. Carles Llinàs, *Ars angelica: la gnoseologia de Ramon Llull*, B, IEC, 2000, 381 pp., is a general introduction to L.'s theology and angelology. The first volume of the Col·lecció Blaquerna, Jocelyn N. Hillgarth, *Diplomatari lul·lià: documents relatius a Ramon Llull i a la seva família*, Barcelona U.P. — Palma, Univ. de les Illes Balears, 105 pp., gathers and translates into Catalan all known documents about L. and his immediate family. M. Greiner, 'La piété de Jacques II de Majorque et les ordres mendiants: une tradition revisitée', pp. 33–115 of *A travers de l'histoire du Roussillon: de l'empreinte chrétienne à l'humanisme contemporain*, Perpignan, Société agricole, scientifique et littéraire des Pyrénées-Orientales, 410 pp., analyses the relationship of one of L.'s royal sponsors with spiritual mouvements. L. Cabré, 'Homilètica lul·liana: context i públic a l'ombra de l'Art', *SLu*, 40: 3–22, studies L.'s sermons in the light of popular preaching; two other articles are concerned with L.'s Figures: J. E. Rubio, 'Com és la vertadera figura

X de l'*Ars compendiosa inveniendi veritatem?*', *ib.*, 47–80, and Y. Dam-
bergs, 'Elemental figure symmetry', *ib.*, 81–110. J. Santanach, 'Notes
per a la cronologia del cicle de l'*Ars compendiosa inveniendi veritatem*', *ib.*,
23–46, proposes a new date for several early Lullian works. C. Lohr,
'The Arabic background to Ramon Lull's *Liber chaos* (ca. 1285)',
Traditio, 55, 2000: 159–70, detects new borrowings from the works of
Ibn-al'Arabî. F. Domínguez Reboiras, 'El discurso luliano sobre
María', Piastra, *Mariologia*, 277–303, discusses the background of L.'s
mariological arguments. J. Santanach, 'Les definicions lul·lianes del
ms. 11559 de la biblioteca Nacional de Madrid', *LlLi*, 12:203–38,
edits a didactic Lullian vocabulary; and Id., 'Perduts, amagats i
retrobats: història de dos manuscrits de la *Doctrina pueril*', *EMarg*, 68,
2000: 106–15, reconstructs the circulation of two Lullian MSS.

ARNAU DE VILANOVA AND OTHER SCIENTIFIC TEXTS

ATCA, 20, is chiefly concerned with Vilanova: J. Mensa Valls,
'Observacions sobre l'autoria i la finalitat del *Tractatus quidam in quo
respondetur obiectionibus que fiebant contra "Tractatum Arnaldi de adventu
Antichristi"*' (403–51), discusses the context and authorship of a
Latin treatise, for which J. Perarnau Espelt provides an edition
(201–348). Perarnau devotes three further articles to edit V.'s treatises
and study their historical and doctrinal context: 'L'*Apologia de versutiis
atque peruersitatibus pseudotheologorum et religiosorum ad magistrum Jacobum
Albi, canonicum dignensem*, d'Arnau de Vilanova' (7–199); 'Sobre la
primera crisi entorn el *De adventu Antichristi* d'Arnau de Vilanova:
París 1299–1300' (349–402); and 'Sobre l'estructura global del *De
tempore adventus Antichristi* d'Arnau de Vilanova' (561–74). A. Carré
and L. Cifuentes, '*Quesits* (Barcelona, Pere Posa, 1499): una traducció
catalana desconeguda del *Liber de homine (Il Perchè)* de Girolamo
Manfredi amb filtre napolità' (543–60), analyse the Catalan version
of this Italian treatise on healthcare and physiognomy. L. Cifuentes,
'La medicina en las galeras de la Corona de Aragón a finales de la
Edad Media: la caja del barbero y sus libros', *Medicina & Historia*, 4,
2000: 1–15, shows what books were used by late medieval ship
surgeons.

FRANCESC EIXIMENIS AND OTHER MORAL TEXTS

M. D. Bailey, 'From sorcery to witchcraft: clerical conceptions of
magic in the later Middle Ages', *Speculum*, 76:960–90, deals with
Nicolau Eimeric and his *Directorium inquisitorum* and *Contra demonum
invocantores*. C. Wittlin, 'Francesc Eiximenis and the "sins of the
tongue": observations on a semantic field', *CatR*, 13, 1999:255–76,

surveys the treatment of this sin in E.'s *Terç* and his *Llibre de les dones*. Two articles in *Actes* (Barcelona) are concerned with Eiximenis: D. J. Viera, 'Sinners, repenters and saints: Adam and Eve in the Catalan Works of Eiximenis' (495–508); and C. Wittlin, 'Eiximenis i la destitució dels reis Pirro, Trocus de Pèrsia, Torpeius, Salopí i Lleó: crítiques encobertes del rei Pere en el *Dotzè*' (509–27). J. de Puig, 'Més textos catalans antics de la "Biblioteca Capitular y Colombina" de Sevilla', *ATCA*, 20:453–510, discusses the contents of an Eximenian anthology and a miscellaneous manuscript that copies, among other texts, a new version of the *Història d'Apol·loni*. Juan Fernández de Heredia, *Rams de flores o Libro de actoridades*, ed. Conrado Guardiola Alcover, Zaragoza, IFC, 1998, 492 pp., is a critical edition and study of the sources for this sapiential treatise. A. Carré, 'Nova terminologia mèdica medieval', *ELLC*, 42 9–17, is a lexical contribution based on the Catalan translation of Hippocrates' *Aphorisms*.

4. HISTORICAL AND ARTISTIC PROSE, ROMANCE

HISTORIOGRAPHY. J. M. Pujol, '¿Cultura eclesiàstica o competència retòrica? El llatí, la Bíblia i el rei en Jaume', *ER*, 23:147–72, is concerned with King Jaume as an author and his ability to use Latin and Biblical sources, some of which are identified here. A. Ferrando Francès, 'Aproximació dialectològica al *Llibre dels fets* de Jaume I', *ATCA*, 20:512–31, draws King Jaume's linguistic profile. Ramon Muntaner, *Crònica*, ed. Vicent Josep Escartí, 2 vols, V, Institució Alfons el Magnànim, 1999, 648 pp., provides an introduction to the chronicle and an edition based on those of Casacuberta and Soldevila. M. Alvira Cabrer, 'La Cruzada Albigense y la intervención de la Corona de Aragón en Occitania: el recuerdo de las crónicas hispánicas del siglo XIII', *Hispania*, 60, 2000:947–76, analyses the different accounts of the defeat at Muret found in several chronicles. M. Zaragozà, '*Libre dels conquists de la illa de Sicília*', *Actes* (Barcelona), 529–60, studies manuscript witnesses that copy this chronicle, especially MS 2084 in Madrid, Biblioteca Nacional. J. D. Garrido Valls, 'Un nou manuscrit de la *Crònica dels reis d'Aragó i comtes de Barcelona*: el ms. ventimigliano 1/83 de la Biblioteca Regionale Universitaria de Catània', *ELLC*, 42:19–36, discusses a 15th-c. Catalan translation of the *Crònica de Sant Joan de la Penya*. M. Josepa Arnall Juan, *Lletres reials a la ciutat de Girona (1293–1515)*, 2 vols., Girona, Ajuntament — B, Fundació Noguera, 2000, 1022 pp., edits 700 royal letters in Catalan, Latin, and Spanish. Anna Cortadellas, *Repertori de llegendes historiogràfiques de la Corona d'Aragó*, PAM, 243 pp., offers a thematic classification of motifs found in chronicles, revealing a wealth of legendary materials.

BERNAT METGE. J. Butinyà, 'Al voltant dels conceptes de gentilitat i profetisme a *Lo somni* de Bernat Metge i la font del *Secretum*', *LlLi*, 12:47–75, interrelates some of M.'s sources, especially on the notion of gentility. S. M. Cingolani, 'Bernat Metge vindicat', *RCat*, 166:113–34, proposes an all-encompassing interpretation of M., based on his previous work and a forthcoming edition of *Lo somni*.

TIRANT LO BLANC AND CURIAL E GÜELFA. R. Beltrán, 'Huellas de las oraciones de *Los tres reyes de oriente* y *Las cuatro esquinas* en *Tirant lo Blanc*', Alvar, *Lyra*, 415–24, deals with folk sources in *T.*, while his '*Aspera et inurbana verba*: la ira de Melibea y Carmesina y la lección desoída de Andreas Capellanus', *Orduna Vol.*, 73–89, detects common cultural roots in *T.* and *Celestina*. B. Morros Mestres, 'La difusión de un diagnóstico de amor desde la antigüedad a la época moderna', *BRAE*, 79, 1999:93–150, studies lovesickness in *T.* from both literary and medical points of view; Id., 'El Tirant lo Blanc y la égloga II de Garcilaso', *VLet*, 12.1:3–22, suggests that the first part of Garcilaso's eclogue II is influenced by *Tirant*. J.-A. Aguilar Avila, 'Xenofont, Anaxàgores i l'emperador: sobre dues anècdotes del *Breviloqui* al *Tirant lo Blanc*', *ELLC*, 42:61–75, deals with *T.*'s sources. D. Azorin Martínez, 'Nova intenció de Joanot Martorell en l'episodi del cavaller Espèrcius', *Actes* (Barcelona), 85–119, and H. Gonzàlvez Escolano, 'Els models cavallerescos en el *Curial e Güelfa*', *ELLC*, 42:37–60, reflect on models of chivalry in *T.* and *C.*, respectively. G. Sabaté, 'La concepció de l'heroi al *Curial e Güelfa*', *ŽK*, 13, 2000:7–20, discusses Curial as a hero.

JOAN ROÍS DE CORELLA. The edition of *Les proses mitològiques de Joan Roís de Corella*, ed. Josep Lluís Martos, Alacant, IIFV-PAM, 477 pp., discusses dating, style, language, and manuscripts. Its brief analysis of C.'s sources is completed by Id., *Fonts i seqüència cronològica de les proses mitològiques de Joan Roís de Corella*, Alacant U.P., 317 pp. Martos also focuses on the use of Ovid's *Heroides* in 'El epitafio de Hero y Leandro en la obra de Joan Roís de Corella', pp. 85–94 of *Proceedings of the 9th Colloquium*, ed. Andrew M. Beresford and Alan Deyermond (PMHRS, 26), 2000, 238 pp.; and in his 'El género popular de los *goigs* y Joan Roís de Corella: *La vida de la sacratíssima verge Maria* y la *Oració*', Alvar, *Lyra*, 85–97, M. reflects on oral sources in two of C.'s lyrics. Joan Roís de Corella, *Prosa profana*, ed. Vicent Martines Peres, M, Gredos, 314 pp., is a Spanish translation of C.'s non-religious works. A. G. Hauf, 'De l'*Speculum humanae salvationis* a l'*Spill* de Jaume Roig', *ER*, 23:173–219, studies the role of the religious mirror metaphor in *Spill*. A. I. Peirats Navarro, '*De no concepta*: debat *versus* veritat a l'*Spill*', *LlLi*, 12:7–45, analyses immaculist mariology in the manuscript and editions of *Spill*. T. Martínez Romero, 'Joan Roís de Corella interpretat des d'Ausiàs March', *CN*,

61:159–94, discusses March as a model for C.'s use of classical sources.

5. TRANSLATIONS AND OTHER GENRES AND TEXTS

The volume *Essays on Medieval Translation in the Iberian Peninsula*, ed. Tomàs Martínez Romero and Roxana Recio, Castelló de la Plana, Universitat Jaume I, 350 pp. offers an array of papers on Catalan topics: G. Avenoza, 'Antoni Canals, Simon de Hesdin, Nicolas de Gonesse, Juan Alfonso de Zamora y Hugo de Urriés: lecturas e interpretaciones de un clásico (Valerio Máximo) y de sus comentaristas (Dionisio de Burgo Santo Sepulcro y Fray Lucas)' (45–73); L. Cifuentes, 'Las traducciones catalanas y castellanas de la *Chirurgia Magna* de Lanfranco de Milán: un ejemplo de intercomunicación cultural y científica a finales de la Edad Media' (95–127); S. Cingolani, 'Traducció literària i traducció cultural' (129–52); G. Colon, '*Traduir* i *traducció* en catalán, con una ojeada a los romances vecinos' (153–71); D. de Courcelles, 'Traduire et citer les Évangiles en Catalogne à la fin du XVe siècle: quelques enjeux de la traduction et de la citacion dans la *Vita Christi* de sor Isabel de Villena' (173–90); A. G. Hauf, 'Fray Hernando de Talavera, O.S.H., y las traducciones castellanas de la *Vita Christi* de Fr. Francesc Eiximenis, O.F.M.' (203–50); T. Martínez Romero, 'Sobre la intencionalitat del *Valeri Màxim* d'Antoni Canals' (251–68); R. Recio, 'Petrarca traductor: los cambios de traducción peninsular en el siglo xv a través de la historia de Válter y Griselda' (291–308); N. Roser Nebot, 'Trujamán: intérprete comunitario y traductor para fines específicos en la baja Edad Media' (309–23); and C. Wittlin, 'Tipología de los errores cometidos por traductores medievales' (341–50). Jesús Alturo Perucho, *Studia in codicum fragmenta*, Bellaterra, UAB, Seminari de Paleografia, Diplomàtica i Codicologia, 1999, 31 pp., assembles manuscript data on several Catalan versions of religious texts, such as the *Moralia in Job* and the *Vita sancti Antonii*. F. Crosas, 'El testimonio "perdido" de Jaume Conesa y sus *Històries troianes*', *Signo*, 8:295–99, identifies a lost manuscript of Conesa's translation. Marinela Garcia Sempere, *La versió catalana medieval dels tractats de falconeria Dancus rex i Guillelmus falconarius*, Alacant U.P., 1999, 234 pp., provides an edition, study, and concordances. T. Martínez Romero, 'Algunas consideraciones sobre la *Tabulatio Senecae* y su traducción catalana', *Evphrosyne*, n.s. 29:95–110, deals with the circulation of Manelli's compendium and analyses its Catalan translation. Germà Colón, *Les Regles d'esquivar vocables: autoria i entorn lingüístic*, B, IEC, 112 pp., is a thorough revision of Badia Margarit's recent edition.

6. DRAMA

J. Romeu Figueras, 'Joglaria: espectacle i incidència en el teatre a la Catalunya medieval', pp. 21–25 of *El teatre popular a l'Edat Mitjana i al Renaixement. Actes del II Simposi Internacional d'Història del Teatre (Barcelona, 1988)*, B, Institut del Teatre, 1999, 515 pp., surveys the impact of jongleurs on medieval theatre. P. Vila, 'A fragment of a fifteenth-century mystery play in Catalan about the Resurrection', *Mediaevalia*, 22, 2000:183–208, edits (with an English translation) a play copied in MS U-180 of the Arxiu Diocesà de Girona.

MODERN LITERATURE
POSTPONED

VI. PORTUGUESE STUDIES

LANGUAGE
POSTPONED

MEDIEVAL LITERATURE
POSTPONED

LITERATURE 1500 TO THE PRESENT DAY
POSTPONED

VII. GALICIAN STUDIES

LANGUAGE

By Francisco Dubert García, *Universidade de Santiago de Compostela*,
David Mackenzie, *University College, Cork*, and
Xulio Sousa Fernández, *Universidade de Santiago de Compostela*

1. Bibliographical and General

A. Santamarina Fernández produces a most useful computer-
generated *Diccionario de diccionarios*, Corunna, Fundación Pedro Barrié
de la Maza, 62 pp. + 1 CD-ROM, which allows the user to consult
11 dictionaries of Galician published between 1873 and 1961, with
all the usual flexibility of this format, and including reproductions of
the title-pages. X. M. Carballeira Anllo is the general editor of a *Gran
diccionario Xerais da lingua*, Vigo, Xerais, xvi + 2027 pp., whose
100,000 entries document both standard and non-standard varieties
of the language. M. Neira and X. Riveiro, *Vocabulario gallego-castellano
de Juan Manuel Pintos*, SC, RAG, 154 pp., is a critical edition of this
early dictionary of 1865, with 7,000 entries. X. R. Varela Pérez, 'O
estatus do galego na bibliografía lingüística escrita en inglés', *CadL*,
21, 2000:103–21, shows that English-speaking linguists are generally
ignorant about Galician. A. Santamarina Fernández, 'Os lexicógrafos
galegos. Historia dunha profesión', *Rodríguez González Vol.*, 7–21, is a
brief outline of Galician lexicography before the establishment of the
standard. M. Álvarez de la Granja and E. González Seoane, 'A
elaboración do *Diccionario Enciclopédico Gallego-Castellano*', *ib.*, 23–212,
examine the compilation process used for this dictionary. F. García
Gondar, 'La presencia del gallego en la filología española
(1914–1970): análisis de algunas revistas', *CISEHL 2*, 435–46,
provides details of elements of Galician interest in the Spanish
journals *BRAE*, *RFE*, and *RDTP* between 1914 and 1970. E. López
Varela, *Unha casa para a lingua: A Real Academia Galega baixo a presidencia
de Manuel Murguía (1905–1923)*, Corunna, Espiral Maior, 208 pp.,
details with impressive documentation the beginnings and the early
years of the Royal Galician Academy. M. D. Sánchez Palomino, 'El
primer diccionario gallego y sus motivaciones: relación con las ideas
de su tiempo', *CISEHL 2*, 847–57, looks at the regionalist motives
that lay behind F. J. Rodríguez's compilation of his dictionary and
A. de la Iglesia's publication of it. X. González-Millán, *O diccionario
enciclopédico de Eladio Rodríguez, a canonización lexicográfica da literatura
galega*, Vigo, Xerais, 190 pp., is an interesting and detailed study of
the sources used and the selection criteria for the dictionary,

suggesting that they represent the establishment of a canon of authors and literary works; and Id., 'Os diccionarios de autoridades: a antoloxización lexicográfica da literatura medieval', *Madrygal*, 4:61–69, analyses the role of the principal Galician dictionaries in the formation of a canon and in the legitimation of a collective identity. M. X. Bugarín López and B. González Rei, 'Achegamento ós diccionarios galegos do século xix', Regueira, *Estudios*, 47–58, is a brief overview of lexicographical work in the 19th c., in which B.L. and G.R. note the cumulative process of dictionary compilation, the practical nature of the works produced (Galician-Castilian) and their encyclopaedic tendencies. V. Álvarez Ruiz de Ojeda, 'Eladio Rodríguez González e a Real Academia Galega. Crónica e epistolario', *BRAG*, 362:9–67, gives an account of R.G.'s work in the Academy, and edits his correspondence with leading figures of the day. A. Fachal Fraguela et al., 'Proxecto dun diccionario bilingüe castelán-galego', Regueira, *Estudios*, 107–17, give an account of the Royal Galician Academy's Castilian-Galician dictionary currently in progress.

2. HISTORICAL AND DIALECTOLOGY

X. H. Costas González, 'Tipoloxía das falas do Val do río Ellas', *APL* 15, 1, 293–310, after a brief introduction, attempts to claim these varieties as Galician (which is odd in a dialectologist). J. A. Souto Cabo's edition of Ruy Vásques, *Crónica de Santa Maria de Íria*, SC, Cabido da SAMI Catedral, Seminario de Estudos Galegos, should have had us dancing in the streets, but the Lusist bogey combines with Capitular distortions of history to get in the way, with the result that the introduction is skewed to favour the Santiago connection and the editorial criteria are hopelessly confused, leading to the production of a philologically inept and therefore useless edition. Another opportunity lost. X. M. Suárez Fernández, 'Primeiros usos escritos de -y- < -LJ-, C'L-, -G'L- en gallego-asturiano', *LLA*, 75:99–110, charts the dialectal distribution of palatal reflexes of these Latin groups in the Galician of Asturias, discerning two areas, one with a voiced palatal lateral, the other with a voiced lateral fricative, and goes on to review the representation of these reflexes in Asturian texts. R. Mariño Paz, 'Cronoloxía da regularización dos temas de perfecto dos verbos *valer* e *doer* en galego', *Carvalho Vol.*, 1, 699–711, documents the reflexes *valv-* > *val-* and *dolv-* > *do-*. Id., 'As liñas en galego do *Theatro Moral y Político de la Noble Academia Compostelana* (1731) de Pablo Mendoza de los Ríos', *RGF*, 1, 2000:35–65, provides an edition and linguistic study of the Galician part of this 19th-c. text. M. Recalde, 'Le parcours socioculturel du galicien du Moyen Âge au XXe siècle', *Leng(T)*, 47, 2000:11–39, undertakes a brief account of the external history of Galician, made more interesting by the addition of the author's acute critical *aperçus*. F. Romero Lema, *Vocabulario de Soneira*, ed. X. M. Rei Lema (*CadL, Anexo* 6), 194 pp., contains an edition and study of a MS containing a word-list from this region in NW Galicia. C. Silva Domínguez, '*Aver seu acordo, fazer sua oraçõ*: a participación do posesivo na construcción de lexías complexas no galego medieval', Regueira, *Estudios*, 249–64, is an interesting study of possessives functioning as determiners and/or modifiers in the medieval language. J. A. Souto Cabo, 'Sobre (falsos) testemunhos galegos de *dezir* e *recebir*: dous documentos de Ribas de Sil', *Carvalho Vol.*, 1, 937–62, deploys philological and linguistic arguments to justify the attribution to Castilian influence of the changes of conjugation in Galician of *viver* > *vivir*, *dicer* > *dicir* and *receber* > *recibir*. D. Suárez Vázquez, 'As autoridades no *Diccionario gallego-castellano* (1913–1928) da Real Academia Galega', *CadL*, 21, 2000:67–102, lists the sources of the citations in the first Galician Academy Dictionary, and examines the criteria used in their selection. X. Varela Barreiro, 'A emerxencia de *Vario(s)*', *RGF*, 2:53–67, in an original study, looks at the sudden appearance of the quantifier *varios* in the written language, and in dictionaries and grammars, concluding that it is probably a Castilianism. X. Viejo Fernández, 'Sobre el latín astur-galaico: afinidad y fragmentación lingüística en el noroeste peninsular', *CIEG 6*, 257–66, considers the linguistic fragmentation of the Roman province of Gallaecia. J. Diéguez, 'Manutenção dos ditongos *ai, au* face a *ei, ou* na área galego-portuguesa: uma proposta explicativa', *APL 15*, 1, 335–57, attempts to provide a history of the diphthongs *au* and *ai* in varieties of Galician in Lugo and Ourense, but the absence of any theoretical framework takes force from his arguments. J. L. Rodríguez, 'Para um perfil das formas de tratamento: *vostede / vosté . . ., você*', *Carvalho Vol.*, 1, 847–83, offers an etymological study of the pronouns *vostede, vosté*, and *você* whose objective is to show that the first two are Castilian in origin. P. Pitta and I. Vázquez, 'Correspondências no uso de *usted* (esp.), *vostede* (gal.), *vosté* (cat.) e *você* (pt.) segundo a norma padrão peninsular', *Losada Vol.*, 582–87, look at the question from a different and more productive standpoint. C. Hermida Gulías, 'Valentín Lamas Carvajal, catapulta do Rexurdimento', *Xornadas Lamas*, 11–29, considers LC one of the principal Galicianists of the 19th c., and asserts that the 'Rexurdimento' was especially significant for the recuperation of the language. I. Seoane, 'Eladio Rodríguez e o primeiro diccionario da RAG', *BRAG*, 362:97–133, describes the elaboration of the Academy dictionary and the effects on it of the various changes in the administration of the Academy, with an interesting appendix of correspondence. F. Fernández Rei, 'A lingua medieval e a súa importancia na elaboración do galego moderno', Cortijo, *Estudios*, 17–42, considers the relevance of lexical archaisms in the elaboration of a literary code, and shows that the period at the end of the 19th c. marked the beginning of this phenomenon in Galician. A. Santamarina Fernández, 'O *Diccionario enciclopédico gallego-castellano* de don Eladio Rodríguez González. Algunhas reflexións sobre a súa historia externa e o seu significado na lexicografía galega', *Grial*, 39:233–49, examines the social and historical context in which the dictionary was compiled, and describes the process.

3. GRAMMAR

S. Bragado Trigo, 'Relacións sintáctico-pragmáticas diverxentes en galego e portugués', *CadL*, 22, 2000:71–80, is a contrastive analysis. A. Cereixo Silva, 'A marcaxe do complemento indirecto na *Crónica Troiana*', *Losada Vol.*, 253–59, deals with the relationship between the use of the preposition *a*, word-order and the use of dative clitics as indirect object markers in the language of the *Crónica troiana*. Id., 'O complemento indirecto cos verbos de dicción. Marcaxe e colocación', *CIEG 6*, 1:143–55, studies the collocation of the indirect object with verbs of saying in medieval Galicia, noting its markedness and its position after the verb and before the direct object. X. Soto Andión, 'Algunhas estruturas de verbo causativo en galego moderno', *CILPR 22*, VI, 467–80, is a somewhat superficial account of the syntax of a miscellany of 'causal' verbs extracted from literary works of the 20th century. Id., 'Algunhas estruturas co verbo *andar* en galego moderno', Veiga, *Verbo*, 177–89, describes 12 kinds of different constructions with 'andar'. M.-C. Flaux, 'Notas sobre a expresión da futuridade en galego', *Le Gonidec Vol.*, 151–60, lists the verbs whose present indicative may be used with future sense in Galician, and presents an extension of her work in 'Achega á expresión da futuridade verbal nas gramáticas galegas ata 1980', *CadL*, 23:69–88, and she is properly critical of grammars before that of Álvarez Blanco et al., 1986, in their treatment of this aspect. A. Alonso Núñez, 'Os sufixos nominais diminutivos do galego actual', *Verba*, 27:133–74, undertakes a critical review of the area, and offers a list of productive diminutive suffixes, together with a detailed functional description and an examination of its use in modern Galician. R. Álvarez Blanco, 'O redobro de *a* + fn en galego moderno', *APL 15*, I, 75–93, examines the reduplication of the clitic pronoun and the corresponding direct/indirect object clauses, pointing out the extension of the pleonastic construction to the direct object and the marker function assumed by the clitic. In '¡Vivan eles, vivan elas!', *Losada Vol.*, 149–55, she contributes to the study of modes of address in Galician with an analysis of the use of the pronouns *el* and *ela*, to which she assigns an intermediate position between *ti* and *vostede*. The same author's '*El vai ben* así: pervivencia e construcción de *el* invariable', *CadL*, 23:5–33, is a superb analysis of this phenomenon, with a delineation of eight environments in which this optional resource may be used, and an accurate, clear, and concise statement of conclusion. A model study by one of Galicia's finest scholars. X. R. Freixeiro Mato, *Gramática da lingua galega* III. *Morfosintaxe*, Vigo, A Nosa Terra, 2000, 358 pp., is flawed in the same ways as the earlier volumes. Id., 'Interferencias e niveis de uso dalgunhas construccións con pronome posesivo en galego', *RGF*, 2:69–88, emits oddly prescriptive opinions on various Galician possessive constructions, and his *Manual de Gramática Galega*, Vigo, A Nosa Terra, 269 pp., is likewise a curiously old-fashioned, prescriptive grammar. D. García Represas, 'L'expression du doute en galicien', *CILPR 22*, VII, 269–76, is a concise examination of the various grammatical resources available for the expression of doubt in Galician. Id., 'A necesidade e maila obriga en galego', *CadL*, 23:89–116, moves on to the expression of need and obligation, doing, as he implies, the spadework necessary for a language in the process of broadening its domains. E. Holt, 'Comparative optimality-theoretic dialectology: singular/plural nasal alternations in Galician, Mirandese (Leonese) and Spanish', pp. 125–43 of *Hispanic Linguistics at the Turn of Millenium: Papers from the 3rd Hispanic Linguistics Symposium, Georgetown University, October 1999*, ed. H. Campos et al., Somerville, MA, Cascadilla, 2000, offers an interesting diachronic and synchronic analysis of the reflexes of –ANUM/-ANAM from the OT viewpoint, although his data for Galician appear somewhat inaccurate. X. C. Lagares, 'Algunhas consideracións sobre o xénero gramatical e o sexismo lingüístico en galego', *RGF*, 1, 2000:67–96, in addition to dealing with interesting grammatical aspects of gender, allows himself a somewhat strange excursus on 'sexism' in grammar in which he proposes some odd ways of avoiding it. Id., 'O xénero gramatical: entre o léxico e a gramática', Regueira, *Estudios*, 173–83, allowing that gender in nouns may express lexical content beyond the purely grammatical, wonders whether gender variation in certain nouns should be considered a flexional or derivational process. V. M. Longa and G. Lorenzo, 'Universal constraints on "superfluous" elements: the case of Galician "Arb. CHE"', Gutiérrez-Rexach, *Spanish Syntax*, 173–91, attempt to discover what place in Universal Grammar is appropriate for the Galician ethical dative, but their judgement of the grammaticality of certain Galician sentences appears faulty and this compromises their findings. The same authors look at 'Movimiento nuclear y economía: valor de la concordancia y movilidad de los clíticos en los romances occidentales', *Verba*, 28:101–24, comparing the position of clitics in infinitive constructions in Galician, Portuguese, and Asturian. M. A. Sobriño Pérez, 'Análise comparativa da posición dos clíticos en galego e asturiano', Regueira, *Estudios*, 265–77, notes the similarity of clitic placement in these varieties. A. Rodríguez Guerra, 'Os esquemas causais en galego medieval', *ib.*, 225–47, examines the frequency and the diachronic evolution of causal prepositional phrases in notarial, narrative, and literary texts between the 13th and the 15th centuries, and briefly deals with the prepositive collocation of the clitic pronoun in these constructions. Id., 'Conxuncións temporais e locucións conxuntivas temporais en galego medieval', *Verba*, 28:207–58, is a detailed study of time relators in the medieval period, concluding that, although the proportions vary, the same relators are predominant in both the medieval and the modern language. X. L. Regueira Fernández, 'A construcción causativa "facer" + infinitivo na gramática funcional', Regueira, *Estudios*, 209–23, examines causative constructions in the light of functional grammar and points to two aspects of Galician — the double dative and the dative with infinitive — which cannot be dealt with by it. F. A. Cidrás Escáneo, 'Construccións medias e impersoais con "se" como construccións sintácticas distintas en galego (e noutras linguas)', *ib.*, 71–81, is a characteristically thoughtful contribution from this stimulating young scholar, which studies the semantic proximity of certain middle and impersonal constructions with *se* in Galician, and demonstrates the unfortunate consequences of the application to the Romance languages of descriptions of English middle constructions.

4. Lexis and Semantics

R. Álvarez Blanco and X. Xove, 'Contribución ó estudio do léxico de J. M. Pintos', *Carvalho Vol.*, 1, 369–409, study the language of P. and his sources in a comparison of his dictionary with later ones. M. X. Bugarín López and B. González Rei, 'O *Diccionario gallego-castellano* de Porto Rey', *CadL*, 21, 2000:25–66, provide a detailed evaluation of this dictionary, published in 1900, and provide a critical edition of the MS in F. Porto Rey, *Diccionario gallego-castellano*, Corunna, RAG, 2000, 492 pp. B. Castaño Torrado, 'Algúns procedementos para chegar a unha solución terminolóxica. Casos prácticos', Regueira, *Estudios*, 59–70, after a brief theoretical introduction, provides illustrative case studies. F. Fernández Rei, 'Dialectalismos, arcaísmos e empréstimos portugueses na construcción da lingua literaria de Ramón Cabanillas', *Carvalho Vol.*, 1, 507–25, examines the lexis of Cabanillas, and points to his importance in the construction of the modern Galician literary code. M. Álvarez de la Granja, 'Transgresión da fixación fraseolóxica', *CILPR 22*, VI, 19–26, assesses the syntactic flexibility of certain phrases in Galician, noting the extent of their fossilization and the degree to which they are susceptible to semantic analysis. E. Rivas Quintas, *Rega e outros servicios*, [Ourense], Grafodos, 2000, 253 pp., is a chaotically organized but useful study of the vocabulary associated with agricultural irrigation: he locates the various forms, and lists place and river toponomy. He also compiles a lexicon of water terminology, *A auga na natureza*, [Ourense], Grafodos, 2000, 460 pp., again including toponomy and specialized regional vocabulary. C. Cambre García et al., 'A achega de material léxico ó diccionario da Real Academia Galega (1913–1928)', *CIEG 6*, 1, 35–53, provide a list of the sources used in the compilation of the Academy's first dictionary. I. Diz Gamallo, '*Matar, matarse / morrer*: semellanzas e diferencias entre as distintas formas de expresión do elemento intransitivo da relación sintáctico-semántica "causa-resultado"', Regueira, *Estudios*, 83–90, after a brief theoretical discussion of the distinct realizations of the causative and resultative senses of an identical verbal lexeme, goes on to analyse the semantic differences between the resultatives *morrer* and *matarse*. M. González González, 'A terminoloxía galega: un labor normalizador', *ib.*, 157–72, underlines the necessity for a unified approach to terminological matters, and gives examples of the work of the terminological service *Termigal*. R. A. Martínez Seixo, *Diccionario fraseolóxico galego: unha achega desde o galego vivo*, Vigo, A Nosa Terra, 2000, 207 pp., coordinates the compilation of a 'dictionary' of various types of phrases and sayings, with 1263 entries. However, he is outdone by X. A. Pena, *Diccionario Cumio de Expresións e frases feitas castelán-galego*, Vigo, Cumio, 927 pp., who produces a more complete compilation. A. Vidal Meixón, 'Estudio do léxico en Galicia: un achegamento á sinonimia', *CIEG 6*, 69–84, studies verb phrases referentially identical to single lexemes and notes the degree of synonymy. C. González Orejón, 'Los nombres de flores y plantas en el diccionario de Cuveiro', *RevLex*, 7:63–75, lists the sources used by J. Cuveiro Piñol in the elaboration of the entries for flowers and plants in his 1876 dictionary. M. García Ares, 'As unidades léxicas compostas na lexicografía galega', Regueira, *Estudios*, 143–56, is a thoughtful examination of the way in which seven standard dictionaries of Galician deal with locutions, in which she correctly notes the lack of any clear criterion denoting awareness of the need to treat these elements of discourse in a coherent fashion.

5. Etymology, Onomastics, and Toponymy

E. Bascuas López, '*Rego* y *requeixo*. Una pervivencia hispana de la raíz indoeuropea *er*- «moverse»', *Verba*, 27, 2000:359–78, is an etymological study of these two words. F. Cabeza Quiles, *Os nomes da terra: topónimos galegos*, Noia, Toxosoutos, 2000, 480 pp., is an etymological and historical study of some 2,000 place-names. X. M. Lema Suárez, 'Cambios onomásticos nunha parroquia rural galega ó longo dos séculos XVII, XVIII e XIX', *CIEG 6*, I, 235–55, deals with his stated theme. A. I. Boullón Agrelo, 'Galician female names in the Middle Ages (from 13th to 15th century)', Kremer, *Onomastik*, II, 122–35, studies the use of female names in notarial documents of the 13th, 14th, and 15th cs, classifies them by region, and notes the relatively high frequency of María (25%). F. R. Tato Plaza, 'Personal names in Rianxo (Galicia) in the 15th century', *ib.*, 136–42, is a statistical study of the occurrence of both male and female names in a Rianxo document of 1457, in which T.P. concludes that the frequency is similar to that of other areas. X. Frías Conde, 'O elemento árabe en galego (I)', *RGF*, I, 2000: 157–71, examines words and toponyms of Arabic origin, and propounds the thesis that Galician forms are earlier than their Portuguese equivalents. B. F. Head, 'A etimologia de *saudade*', *Carvalho Vol.*, I, 595–627, in a closely-argued and well-documented analysis of this Galician-Portuguese word, assembles new data to show that it is indeed of Latin origin. G. Sacau Rodríguez, *Os nomes da ría de Vigo: Libro Segundo (O Berbés — Oitavén — Verdugo)*, Vigo, Instituto de Estudios Vigueses, 2000, 311 pp., lists the toponyms of the *ría*, and adds a short etymological study. N. Ares Vázquez, 'Toponimia do concello de Monterroso', *Lucensia*, 10:259–76, undertakes an etymological study of over 100 toponyms in this Lugo district. M. C. Fernández López, 'Gal. *amoado, butelo, lacazán*: helenismos comunes', Regueira, *Estudios*, 119–26, studies the etyma of these words and their occurrence in Latin and Romance.

N. Ares Vázquez, 'Toponimia do Concello da Fonsagrada', *Lucensia*, 11:317–36, offers an overview of toponymic studies of this Lugo area, placing special emphasis on origins. Id., 'Toponimia do concello de Chantada', *ib.*, 71–96, does the same for Chantada, also in Lugo. J. J. Moralejo Álvarez, 'Hidronimia galaica preromana', Villar, *Religión*, 501–09, proposes an investigation of the pre-Roman hydronomy of Gallaecia which would take into account the latest work on the extension of the pre-Roman languages and peoples of the area.

6. PHONETICS

F. Dubert García, 'A alomorfia do artigo definido galego á luz da fonoloxía prosódica', Regueira, *Estudios*, 91–105, attempts to explain which types of phonetic rules should be used to describe the morphology of the definite article, on what grammatical level they operate, and the kind of prosodic unit they produce. Id., 'Sons e letras nas *Gramáticas clásicas* do galego', *Carvalho Vol.*, 1, 463–75, shows how the traditional grammars of Galician attempt to describe the sounds of the language based on the orthographic alphabet. S. Labraña Barrero, 'A fonética galega: da articulatoria tradicional ás tecnoloxías máis actuais', *CIEG 6*, 157–76, gives an overview of Galician phonological studies, from its origins through its achievements to the tasks ahead. C. Martínez Mayo, 'Descrición acústica de tres fricativas galegas: [ş], [θ], [ʃ]', *CadL*, 22, 2000:81–99, consists of an acoustic study of the coronal fricatives of 'galego común'. X. L. Regueira, 'As vocais nucleares nos ditongos galegos *ei* e *ou*: algúns datos acústicos', *Verba*, 28:339–54, provides an acoustic description of tongue height in the production of the nucleic vowels represented by the letters *e* and *o* in the sequences *ei* and *ou*. V. Formoso Gosende, 'Análise acústica das sibilantes de dúas parroquias no concello de Ordes', *CadL*, 23:53–67, distinguishes an alveolar and a palatal, though the degree of separation is minimal in the final analysis.

7. SOCIOLINGUISTICS AND PSYCHOLINGUISTICS

M. C. Alén Garabato, 'Le galicien piégé par l'histoire? La question de la norme', *Leng(T)*, 47, 2000:67–95, discusses competition between norms in the context of the process of normativization. C. Álvarez Cáccamo, 'Para um modelo do "code-switching" e a alternancia de variedades como fenómenos distintos: dados do discurso galego-português/espanhol na Galiza', *ESoc*, 1, 2000:111–28, in an interesting study, proposes a theoretical distinction between variation and code-switching, based on Galician data. S. Alonso Pintos, 'O ideal de lingua na *Gramática* de Carballo Calero', *Grial*, 38, 2000:461–74, looks at the development of C.C.'s grammar through successive editions, and shows how the changes reflect the social standing of the language. T. Verdelho, 'Uma polémica sobre "la lengua lusitana, ò gallega" no século XVIII', *Carvalho Vol.*, 1, 759–806, discusses a contemporary rejoinder to Feijóo's affirmation of the superiority of Galician over Portuguese, and identifies the author as the Portuguese Martinho de Mendoça. A. X. Pereiro Rozas and O. Juncos Rabadán, 'Referencia cohesiva no discurso narrativo na vellez', *Verba*, 27, 2000:317–39, analyse the use of endophoric elements in the discourse of adults and note the relationship between cognitive deterioration and the use of referential elements in stories. H. Monteagudo Romero, 'Ideas de Manuel Murguía sobre o idioma galego', *BRAG*, 361:197–220, after a detailed analysis, concludes that M.'s view of language reflects contemporary Galicianist thinking.

F. Dubert García, '¿Norma galega, sistema galego-portugués? Aplicación dos termos de Coseriu ó "galego" e ó "portugués"', *CadL*, 22, 2000: 101–22, reviews Coseriu's definitions of 'sistema', 'norma', and 'fala', and goes on to demonstrate how these terms are frequently misused in Galician (socio)linguistics.

M. A. Fernández Rodríguez, 'Cuando los hablantes se niegan a elegir: multilingüismo e identidad múltiple en la modernidad reflexiva', *ESoc*, 1, 2000:47–58, after proposing a definition of linguistic identity distinct from national or ethnic identity, goes on to ponder the linguistic identity of multilingual individuals and the possibility of using linguistic identity to construct identity in the modern world. F. Fernández Rei, '¿Existe ou non unha lingua galega moderna? O ILG e o debate sobre a norma do galego', *ATO*, 42, 2000:205–13, is the text of a lecture in which F.R. sets out the sociolinguistic justification for regarding Galician as a language distinct from Portuguese, and argues that an agreement on a standard would always be possible among people who sustain this view. Id., 'A proposta de acordo normativo do 2001. Notas e documentos sobre a *Questione della lingua* galega', *ib.*, 48:97–120, is a historical document in that this participant details the negotiations which led up to the current agreement on norms, and sets out what has been changed and gives an appreciation of the significance of the achievement. M. C. Pazos Balado, 'O tratamento do nivel de lingua nos diccionarios', Regueira, *Estudios*, 197–207, is critical of the lack of information on register and sociolect in dictionaries of Galician. X. L. Regueira Fernández, 'Un modelo de estándar oral para a lingua galega', *CIEG* 6, 19–33, proposes a standard for pronunciation, then — wisely perhaps — ponders the practical viability of such schemes. G. Rei Doval, 'Matériaux pour une histoire de la sociolinguistique galicienne: antécédents et études macrosociolinguistiques empiriques (1967–1997)', *Leng(T)*, 47, 2000:159–91, describes and categorizes the work of the leading Galician sociolinguists. U. Tenreiro López, 'As etiquetas non gramaticais nos diccionarios', Regueira, *Estudios*, 293–300, studies three Galician dictionaries from the point of view of their presentation of information on usage. J. del Valle, 'Monoglossic policies for a heteroglossic culture: misinterpreted multilingualism in modern Galician', *Language & Communication*, 20, 2000: 105–32, shows that the preponderant linguistic currents in Galicia give rise to monoglossic sociolinguistic descriptions, which contrast with the heteroglossic attitude of the majority of Galician speakers as between Galician and Castilian. M. Fernández Rodríguez, 'Entre castellano y gallego: la identidad lingüística del gallego', pp. 81–105 of *Identidades lingüísticas en la España autonómica*, ed. G. Bossong and F. Báez de Aguilar González, Frankfurt, Vervuert — Madrid, Iberoamericana,

2000, offers a most interesting (because of his position as linguist and participant) personal view of the Galician norm controversy. J. E. Gargallo Gil, 'Aranés, Mirandés, ¿Valego? Tres enclaves romances de fronteira, tres retos de supervivencia e preservación da identidade na Europa do novo milenio', *ATO*, 47 : 61–75, examines the situation of Aranese, Mirandese, and the contact vernaculars of Spanish Extremadura. C. Hermida Gulías, 'The Galician speech community', pp. 110–40 of *Multilingualism in Spain: Sociolinguistic and Psycholinguistic Aspects of Linguistic Minority Groups*, Clevedon, Multilingual Matters, is a short external history of the language and a contemporary sociolinguistic overview. M. Barajó Calvo and X.-H. Costas González, 'Posibilidades legais de equilibrio lingüístico no Bierzo occidental e as Portelas. Breve referencia á terra Eo-Navia e ó Val do río Ellas', *ATO*, 47:91–104, review the linguistic legislation governing the Galician spoken in León, Zamora, and Extremadura, and reflect on Galician's chances of survival in these areas. S. Rivas Barrós, 'Aproximación histórica ao galego nas escolas (1900–1936): un saber ausente e unha voz silenciada', *RGF*, 2:167–79, is a short but most interesting description of language-teaching techniques in Galician schools in the first third of the 20th c., based on the personal experience of pupils. M. C. Alén Garabato, 'A textualización dos *funcionamentos diglósicos* nas cancións do *Rock bravú* e no discurso que acompaña este movemento', *Verba*, 28:305–35, studies the lyrics of rock songs and shows that they reflect current popular attitudes to language. M. C. Núñez Singala, 'Algunhas reflexións verbo da elaboración de plans de política lingüística', *CadL*, 23:35–52, makes sensible proposals, but is perhaps ingenuous in thinking that bad practice will cede to good theory.

LITERATURE

By Dolores Vilavedra, *Departamento de Filoloxía Galega, Universidade de Santiago de Compostela*, and Derek Flitter, *Senior Lecturer in Modern Spanish Language and Literature, University of Birmingham*

1. General

The presence of sociologically founded systems theory is becoming increasingly evident in studies of Galician literature. One key example is Antón Figueroa, *Nación, literatura, identidade. Comunicación literaria e campos sociais en Galicia*, Vigo, Xerais, 171 pp., a lucid and intellectually rigorous study of the problematic emergence of a Galician literary system. Equally, X. González-Millán, 'Producción, clasificación e comercialización da literatura. Os catálogos de Edicións Xerais de Galicia', *AELG*, 2000: 11–42, examines the institutionalization of Galician literary discourse within the last two decades using as a primary focus the Xerais catalogue for those years. There are two further volumes in an ongoing encyclopaedic study of Galician literature: Vol. 32 of *Galicia. Literatura*, is entitled *O século XX. A literatura anterior á guerra civil*, ed. Anxo Tarrío, Corunna, Hércules, 495 pp., and includes the following: R. Nicolás, 'Problemática do Modernismo en Galicia: Cabanillas, Noriega e epígonos do Rexurdimento' (26–83); A. Casas, 'A poesía galega entre 1916 e 1936' (84–211), a boldly revisionist reading of poetry of that period; J. Ventura, 'A narrativa na Época Nós' (214–77); A. Abuín and E. Ruibal, 'O teatro galego entre 1900 e 1936' (278–355); I. Soto, 'O ensaio e a crítica na Época Nós' (356–81); X. L. Axeitos, 'Literatura e cultura na emigración' (448–80). Vol. 33 of the same series, *A literatura desde 1936 ata hoxe: poesía e teatro*, ed. Anxo Tarrío, Corunna, Hércules, 543 pp., contains C. Rodríguez, 'Escritores galegos ante a guerra civil' (24–111), a densely catalogued biographical and bibliographical survey; R. Raña's study of post-Civil War verse in 'A xeración da República. Promoción de Enlace' (112–99), and 'A xeración dos 50 e a poesía social' (200–39); X. M. Dasilva, 'Do epigonismo da poesía social-realista ós inicios da renovación estética' (240–84); I. Cochón, 'Unha proposta de superación da orde xeracional. Oitenta/noventa' (288–363), and Id., 'A poesía de fin de milenio. O reaxuste dos anos noventa' (364–417); X. M. González, 'As relacións literatura-arte' (418–41); L. Tato, 'O teatro desde 1936' (442–511); L. Pérez, 'O teatro na emigración' (512–28).

Estudios sobre humor literario, ed. J. Figueroa, Vigo U.P., contains the following: A. Herrero, 'Pranto paródico en *Os vellos non deben de namorarse.* Castelao, ironista' (313–20); C. Larkin, 'Dickens y Cunqueiro: aproximaciones críticas en humor' (321–28); B. M. Vázquez, 'El humor literario gallego' (329–40). The theme of emigration figures in M. X. Lama and D. Vilavedra, 'La emigración a la Argentina en la literatura gallega', pp. 279–303 of *La Galicia austral. La inmigración gallega en la Argentina*, ed. X. M. Núñez, Buenos Aires, Biblos, 320 pp.

2. NARRATIVE

D. Vilavedra, 'Huellas de la Postmodernidad en la narrativa gallega', pp. 225–38 of *Matrices del siglo XX: signos precursores de la postmodernidad*, ed. A. Conde et al., M, Univ. Complutense, 560 pp., gives a panoramic survey of elements of postmodernism in contemporary Galician narrative. The same writer's 'A narrativa galega, ás voltas co presente', Suárez, *Letras galegas*, 23–32, has the same focus in its analysis of works by a new generation of writers. O. Rodríguez, 'As primeiras novelas galegas editadas en Cuba', *CIEG 6*, 277–88, uncovers early examples of narrative fiction written by Galician émigrés in Cuba.

3. POETRY

S. Bermúdez, '¿Sen a *ansiedade da influencia?* Rosalía de Castro, Harold Bloom e as poetas galegas do século XX', *AELG*, 2000:135–58, studies the indebtedness to Rosalía and the desire for self-affirmation in work by four contemporary women poets: Xohana Torres, Pura Vázquez, Luz Pozo, and Ana Romaní. M. do C. Rábade, 'Límites e posibilidades dun estudio tipolóxico das antoloxías', *ib.*, 205–24, is a thoroughgoing attempt to mark out a typology for such collections and to determine their function in the emergence of a Galician literary system. The same writer's 'An introduction to the history of Galician poetry', pp. 41–69 of *Poetry is the World's Great Miracle*, Pen Clube de Galicia, 210 pp., provides a rapid overview. Similarly inclusive is A. Casas, 'Público e empresas editoras na poesía galega entre a fundación das Irmandades da Fala e a Guerra Civil', *Varela Vol.*, 107–20. A further panoramic view of Galician poetry of the last 50 years is to be found in X. L. García, 'Os últimos cincoenta anos da poesía galega', *NovR*, 19, 1999:369–412. A. Acuña, 'Poesía galega en Madrid: o grupo poético Bilbao', *CIEG 6*, 515–32, examines the Madrilenian group's contribution to Galician verse.

4. THEATRE

M. F. Vieites, 'Cronoloxía e temporalidade na literatura dramática galega. A periodización. Unha proposta de traballo', *BGL*, 25 : 51–90, taking V.'s previous work at least one stage further, proposes a chronological classification of the history of Galician theatre. J. M. Paz, 'O Antroido no teatro galego contemporáneo', Suárez, *Letras galegas*, 45–58, examines the presence of Carnival and its literary codification.

5. POPULAR LITERATURE

D. Schubarth, 'O simbolismo na lírica popular galega', *AELG*, 2000 : 225–48, considers symbolic components of the popular lyric related to everyday life and to representations of the feminine.

6. MEDIAEVAL LITERATURE

T. López, 'De lírica trovadoresca na Galiza decimonónica: Teófilo Braga e Antonio de la Iglesia', *NovR*, 19, 1999 : 281–90, confirms the role played by the Portuguese cultural historian in widening knowledge of the mediaeval lyric within Galicia. J. A. Souto's edition of the *Crónica de Santa María de Iria*, SC, Cabido da S.A.M.I. Catedral–Seminario de Estudos Galegos, 284 pp., contains an extensive introduction (11–48). M. Arbor, *O Cancioneiro de Afonso Sanchez: edición e estudio*, Santiago de Compostella U.P., 392 pp., is an edition with critical study based upon the writer's doctoral thesis.

7. WOMEN'S STUDIES

CIEG 6 includes M. Buongiorno, 'Destierros físicos e imaginarios: la identificación con Galicia y la recuperación de la identidad femenina' (491–99); and H. González, 'Crítica feminista en Galicia. Relecturas baixo o paraugas totalizador' (501–14).

8. INDIVIDUAL AUTHORS

BLANCO AMOR. A. B. Martínez Delgado, '*A esmorga*' de Blanco Amor e '*Parranda*' de Gonzalo Suárez, Sada, O Castro, 165 pp., is a comparative study of the literary and filmic structures of these works.

BOUZA-BREY. In the collected volume *Xornadas sobre Fermín Bouza Brey*, SC, Xunta, 186 pp., the following articles stand out: X. M. Dasilva, 'A canonicidade literaria de Bouza-Brey' (13–42), an analysis of the reasons underlying the rapid incorporation of B.-B.'s work into the Galician canon; T. López, 'Os liños do pensamento: a poesía de F. Bouza-Brey' (43–54), a lucid examination of the multiplicity of voices in B.-B.'s verse.

CARRÉ ALDAO. M. Romero's edition, *Obra narrativa en galego*, SC, CILLRP, 167 pp., surveys C.A.'s fiction in an expansive introduction (3–54).

CASTELAO. The proceedings of the *Congreso sobre Castelao*, SC, Xunta, 480 pp., include the following highlights: M. Rosales, 'Aspectos estilísticos da prosa narrativa de Castelao' (67–74), an extension of R.'s ongoing work on C.'s style; X. M. Dasilva, 'Creación autóctona e literatura traducida en Castelao' (75–102), appraises C.'s detached view of the literary translations published in his time; R. García, 'Castelao con Valle-Inclán' (103–30), documents known relations between the two writers; D. Vilavedra, 'As ideas literarias de Castelao' (131–44); C. P. Martínez, 'Para a avaliación (est)ética de *Os vellos non deben de namorarse* (Por volta de tres reservas básicas)' (145–68), an attempt to bring critical study of C.'s drama up to date; H. Monteagudo, 'Castelao ensaísta. As primeiras *Verbas de chumbo*' (175–200), evaluates C.'s contribution, in these pieces, to the historical development of the Galician literary essay; M. C. Noia, 'Notas para unha tipoloxía de Castelao escritor' (249–60) revisits some of the characteristics commonly felt to define C.'s profile as a writer.

CASTRO, LUISA. I. Sobrino, 'O imposible (contra)discurso da anterioridade. A representación da infancia en *Baleas e baleas* de L. Castro', *Varela Vol.*, 553–64, examines how this work strives to recreate the discourse of the child.

CASTRO, ROSALÍA. X. M. Dobarro and L. Rodríguez, 'O contexto. Ramón Otero Pedrayo e Roberto Vidal Bolaño arredor de Rosalía', pp. 49–123 of R. Otero Pedrayo, *Rosalía*, SC, IGAEM, 206 pp., undertakes a wide-ranging analysis of the depiction of Rosalía in Vidal Bolaño's version of Otero's text. There are three studies of Rosalía in *CIEG 6*: M. Esturo, 'Una aproximación a la narrativa de Rosalía de Castro: *El caballero de las botas azules*' (467–72); A. López, 'Rosalía na escrita feminina nos anos 1991–1999' (473–90); A. Pociña, 'Avances da investigación sobre Rosalía nos anos 1991–1999' (451–66). R. Carvalho, 'Falta um capítulo em *El Caballero de las botas azules*', *NovR*, 19, 1999:13–20, asks questions about the textual integrity of the novel.

CUNQUEIRO. E. González, *El mundo clásico en la literatura española: de Guevara y Cervantes a Álvaro Cunqueiro', *Moenia*, 6, 2000:319–39. In *CIEG 6* can be found R. Rodríguez, 'Bilingüismo e estilo na escrita cunqueiriana' (367–76), an analysis of the consequences of bilingualism in C.'s style; A. Santana, 'Sinbad o los sueños de la ficción producen . . . la ficción como eje de la escritura en Álvaro Cunqueiro' (377–85), an examination of the mechanisms that underpin the structure of C.'s novels.

CURROS ENRÍQUEZ. The sesquicentenary of C.E.'s birth was marked by the appearance of numerous publications, including X. Alonso, 'O poeta Curros Enríquez contra Franco', *BRAG*, 362:137–68, dealing with anti-Franco material alluding to or invoking C.E.'s own life and work; and A. López-Casanova, 'Poética e poesía de Curros Enríquez (claves para unha lectura de *Aires da miña terra)*', *ib.*, 169–98, making an exhaustive appraisal of that work's thematic and structural concerns. X. M. Dasilva, 'Curros Enríquez, traductor de Camões: as endechas "A Bárbara escrava" en galego', *Grial*, 39:405–20, considers C.E. as literary translator.

DÍAZ CASTRO. A. Requeixo, 'Xosé María Díaz Castro, poeta de preguerra', *Madrygal*, 4:99–110, looks at D.C.'s poetry published prior to the Civil War.

GONZÁLEZ TOSAR. L. Fraga, 'Luís G. Tosar: a palabra na procura da eternidade', *AELG*, 2000:159–84, examines the cognitive function of memory within G.T.'s poetics.

LAMAS CARVAJAL. *Xornadas sobre Lamas Carvajal*, SC, Xunta, 234 pp., includes the following: C. Hermida, 'V. Lamas, catapulta do Rexurdimento' (11–29), evaluates L.C.'s contribution to the success of the Galician cultural revival; V. Álvarez, 'O *Catecismo do labrego*: textos e contextos' (53–67), compares L.C.'s poetic text with contemporary catechisms of the Church; X. L. Axeitos, 'Agrarismo e redención do *Catecismo do labrego*' (77–86), appraises the same text's reception in its own time; M. P. García, 'O asubío espertador na poesía de Lamas Carvajal e o seu tempo' (87–104), locates L.C.'s work within the Galician tradition, especially in its formulation of thematic motifs; A. Tarrío, 'O asubío espertador na poesía de Lamas Carvajal e o seu tempo' (105–32), considers progressive elements in the poetry. Three articles: A. Gómez, 'Lamas xornalista: o contributo d'o *O tío Marcos da Portela á divulgación da literatura galega decimonónica*' (133–43), M. Queixas, 'Lamas xornalista' (145–51), and M. Valcárcel, 'As claves do xornalismo de V. Lamas' (153–75), are dedicated to L.C.'s journalism, a key element in his writing and in his contribution to the historical development of literary Galician.

LUGRÍS FREIRE. T. López, 'Cuba nas orixes do teatro galego', *CIEG 6*, 269–76, appraises the role played by the Galician community in Cuba, most particularly by L.F., in the beginnings of Cuban theatre.

MANUEL ANTONIO. F. Casal, 'O habitáculo suspenso. *De catro a catro:* literatura galega e modernidade', *NovR*, 19, 1999:233–48, assesses the role of this text in the dialogue between Galician literature and modernity. *Xornadas sobre Manuel Antonio*, SC, Xunta, has the following among its more significant pieces: P. Vázquez, 'Ruptura e tempo na poesía de M. Antonio' (13–28), which seeks to connect the aesthetic and ideological underpinning of M.A.'s verse with Nietzschean nihilism; R. Raña, 'As sínteses de M. Antonio' (51–60), views M.A.'s poetry as a series of discrete elements acting in synergy; C. L. Bernárdez, 'O contexto M. Antonio. A renovación poética galega e a vangarda internacional' (109–15), locates M.A. within the wider European avant-garde; M. Forcadela, 'O tempo narrativo nun poeta eterno' (125–38), studies underlying narrative structures in the poetry of M.A. and Ramón Cabanillas; X. M. Dasilva, 'O máis acá do manifesto *¡Máis alá!*' (139–85), examines the context in which the manifesto appeared, its active response to that context, and subsequent critical interpretations of its content.

MANUEL MARÍA. *Manuel María*, ed. A. Blanco, Lugo, Asociación cultural Xermolos–Ophiusa, 609 pp., is an uneven collection containing work by a diversity of contributors.

MONTES. *Xornadas sobre Eugenio Montes*, SC, Xunta, 230 pp., contains the following significant essays: F. J. Díez, 'E. Montes, en la primera vanguardia' (39–56), an appraisal of M.'s contacts with and place within the avant-garde; J. Gutiérrez, 'La prosa del 27: Eugenio Montes' (121–56), which seeks to locate M. within the wider Spanish 'Generation of 1927'; J. M. Bonet, 'E. Montes, ultraísta' (221–30), highlights specific tendencies within M.'s verse.

MURGUÍA. E. López, *Unha casa para a lingua. A RAG baixo a presidencia de Manuel Murguía (1905–1923)*, Corunna, Espiral maior, 201 pp., is a history of the Galician Academy in its early phase under M.'s presidency. Among the proceedings of the *Congreso sobre Manuel Murguía*, SC, Xunta, 322 pp., the following, testifying to M.'s broad intellectual range, are the most noteworthy: E. Mariño, 'Un novelista precoz e laureado: *desde el cielo*' (69–88), considers an early novel; I. Cabano, 'Murguía e o seu *Diccionario de escritores galegos*' (155–68), analyses M.'s criteria for selection; J. L. Forneiro, 'Mais textos para a produçao de Murguía en língua galega: o seu romanceiro apócrifo' (169–88), provides an assessment of ballad texts collected or composed by M.; A. B. Fortes, 'O proxecto literario de Murguía' (315–20), evaluates M.'s contribution to the conceptual patterning of Galician literary discourse. M. Fernández, 'O celtismo literario galego dende Manuel Murguía. A relixión dos verdes vales', *Cahiers Galiciens/Cadernos Galegos/Kaieroù Galizek*, 1 : 39–50, uses M. as a point of departure for his consideration of Celtic elements in Galician literature.

NEIRA VILAS. C. Son, *X. Neira Vilas y 'Memorias dun neno labrego'. Acercamiento a la novela gallega más popular de la segunda mitad del siglo XX*, Sada, O Castro, 222 pp., is a monograph dedicated to N.V.'s novel.

OTERO. X. M. Dasilva, 'Camões interpretado por Otero Pedrayo: unha conferencia (1940) en galego e un artigo (1953) en portugués', *Grial*, 39:165–208, supplies a transcription with critical study of two key texts in the historical reception of the Portuguese poet in Galicia. C. Patterson, 'Otero Pedrayo e a *Decadencia de Occidente*: morte, resurrección, manipulación', *AELG*, 2000:43–68, is a rigorous study of points of convergence and divergence between O.P. and Oswald Spengler. Among the essays in *CIEG 6* can be found J. Ventura, 'Modelos femininos nas novelas de formación de preguerra de Otero Pedrayo' (345–53). Worth consulting also is the special issue of *Raigame*, 12, dedicated to O.P.

PATO. S. Bermúdez, '*Festa da palabra* y el canon literario gallego contemporáneo: la labor (des)mitificadora de Chus Pato y Ana Romaní', Suárez, *Letras galegas*, 33–44, evaluates the journal's role in the assimilation of both writers into the Galician literary canon.

PESQUEIRA. M. T. Araújo, *Relatos e outras prosas de Roque Pesqueira Crespo*, SC, CILLRP, has a thoroughgoing introduction (3–76).

RISCO. O. Rodríguez, *Estética e teoría da cultura en Vicente Risco*, Vigo, Galaxia, 263 pp., is an impressive study that probes the European origins of R.'s thought.

RIVAS. *CIEG 6* contains D. Asorey, 'A literatura galega en tempos de posmodernidade: aproximación á obra narrativa para adultos de M. Rivas' (397–426); M. C. Lamela and M. X. Nogueira, 'Emigración, estranxeiría e palabras da tribo. Aproximación á obra poética de M. Rivas' (427–46), an assessment of R.'s poetry founded upon theories of identity.

RODRÍGUEZ GONZÁLEZ. The latest honorand of the *Día das Letras Galegas* attracted numerous testimonies to his intellectual versatility. On R.G. as creative writer are C. Delgado, 'A estrea de E. Rodríguez como participante nos xogos florais', *BRAG*, 362:69–79, a critical survey of the poems contributed by R.G. to such contests; Rodríguez, 'A poesía de Eladio Rodríguez', *ib.*, 81–95, attempts a thematic classification of R.G.'s verse. *Xornadas sobre E. Rodríguez González*, SC, Xunta, 290 pp., includes one particularly incisive piece: X. M. Domínguez, 'Mística e relixiosidade da terra en *Oraciós campesiñas*' (245–62), an analysis of the poetic elements that codify religiosity within the collection. X. M. Dasilva, 'O vello E. Rodríguez González e o manifesto *¡Máis alá!*', *BGL*, 25:7–34, elucidates R.G.'s connections with Manuel Antonio.

RODRÍGUEZ MOURULLO. T. Bermúdez's wide-ranging introduction (7–92) to Gonzalo Rodríguez Mourullo, *Nasce un árbore.
Memorias de Tains*, Vigo, Galaxia, analyses R.M.'s narrative production.

ROMANÍ. See PATO.

ROMPENTE. A. Avendaño, 'O meu Rompente', *Madrygal*,
4:25–32, is a personal addition to the history of this group of poets
from the pen of one of its original members. A. also supplies 'Estéticas
da poesía e signos de ruptura. Unha nova ollada ó Grupo de
Comunicación poética Rompente', *ib.*, 89–94, a survey of the most
innovative features of the grouping within the Galician literary
context; and '*De catro a catro*: a música da modernidade', *Xornadas sobre
Manuel Antonio*, 61–70, a study of this work's contribution to the
discourse of modernity in Galicia and its influence upon the
Rompente group.

RUIBAL. *Teatro, cerimonia e xogo. A traxectoria teatral, literaria e
cinematográfica de Euloxio R. Ruibal*, ed. A. Abuín, Lugo, TrisTram,
325 pp., is a collective volume that constitutes the most comprehensive critical coverage to date of R.'s work. It includes A. Abuín,
'Euloxio R. Ruibal: glosario' (9–27), which identifies the principal
literary thrust of R.'s production; L. Tato, 'A obra dramática de
Euloxio R. Ruibal' (27–41), which supplies a broad overview of the
drama; M. Pérez, 'Aspectos populares no teatro de Euloxio R. Ruibal'
(41–57), elucidating the influence of popular culture in R.'s theatre;
C. Fernández, 'Hermeneuse de *Zardigot*: traxedia, existencialismo e
sicoanálise' (57–102), which, as the title suggests, undertakes a
hermeneutical study of the work; D. Vilavedra, 'Apuntes para unha
análise da recepción de *Zardigot*' (103–12), analysing critical responses
to this play from the standpoint of reception theory; C. Blanco,
'Achegas para a comparación entre *Madre Coraxe e os seus fillos* e
Zardigot' (113–38), a comparative study with a view to specifying the
impact of Brecht on R.'s work; M. Vieites, '*O cabodano*: comunicacións
patolóxicas e conflicto dramático. Notas dispersas para unha drama-
turxia posible' (155–208), an interpretation that leads to a view of the
play's stage production as a form of psychotherapy; C. Becerra, 'O
mito do poder nunha farsa de Euloxio R. Ruibal' (139–54),
examining R.'s treatment of the myth of power as defined by Mircea
Eliade in *A sonada e proveitosa enchenta do Marqués Ruchestinto*; I. López,
'*O son da buguina*: xogos de ficción ou a novidade saudosa' (209–30),
which assesses this piece as a synthesis of diverse recurring features of
R.'s overall production; S. Sánchez, 'O xogo dramático no teatro
infantil de Ruibal' (231–46), which scrutinizes R.'s plays written for
children; T. Vilariño, 'De 'Cartel de cego' a *Casarriba*. A *fantástica
viaxe* narrativa de Euloxio R. Ruibal', (247–82), a study of R.'s
narrative fiction.

SEOANE. X. L. García, 'A muller na obra poética de L. Seoane', *Madrygal*, 4:45–60, assesses key examples of the representation of women in S.'s verse. M. F. Vieites, 'Erwin Piscator, Peter Weiss, Augusto Boal e Luis Seoane. A propósito do *Esquema de farsa*, unha proposta inaugural e visionaria, entre o teatro popular e a performance', *Grial*, 39:251–76, approaches the cited text in line with the theories of Piscator and Brecht and in the light of new trends in the theatre in the second half of the 20th century.

TORO. B. Mitaine, 'Quebra de identidade e proceso de autohistorización na obra de Suso de Toro', *AELG*, 2000:185–204, analyses those narrative mechanisms that provide connections between the crises of identity experienced by T.'s fictional creations and wider Galician society.

VIDAL BOLAÑO. I. López, 'R. Vidal Bolaño na (re)construcción do teatro galego. De *Abrente* a *Mar revolto*', pp. 45–134 of R. Vidal, *Mar revolto*, SC, IGAEM, 293 pp., is an exhaustive and well-documented study of the role of V.B. in the recent renovation of Galician theatre.

VIII. LATIN AMERICAN STUDIES

SPANISH AMERICAN LITERATURE
THE COLONIAL PERIOD
POSTPONED

THE NINETEENTH CENTURY

By Annella McDermott, *Department of Hispanic, Portuguese and Latin American Studies, University of Bristol*

1. General

Cuban Studies, 29, 1999, is a literary issue in Spanish which contains two articles on Martí and two on Julián del Casal: C. Ripoll and M. A. Tellechea, 'Seis crónicas inéditas de José Martí' (1–65), consists of the texts themselves, published by M. in the New York *Sun*, preceded by an explanation of their previous neglect; R. Rojas Gutiérrez, 'José Martí: la República escrita' (66–82), explores the relationship between politics and poetics in M.'s work; F. Morán, 'Dos crónicas inéditas de Julián del Casal' (115–200), contains the text of the articles and a short explanatory introduction; E. de Armas, 'Julián del Casal: el poeta en sus cartas' (121–28), contains the text of the letters and a brief introduction. I. Schulman, 'El otro modernismo: el caso de Darío Herrera', *RevIb*, 196:389–98, stresses the diversity within *modernismo* and the dangers of an overly schematic view of literary movements, and examines three writers generally marginalized: Juana Borrero (Cuba), Rafael Ángel Troyo (Costa Rica), and Darío Herrera (Panamá). Id., 'Sobre los orientalismos del modernismo hispanoamericano', *CAm*, 223:33–43, argues against the view that the *modernistas*' interest in the Orient was of a purely exoticist nature. Reference is made in particular to Enrique Gómez Carrillo, Julio Herrera y Reissig, José Martí, and Juan José Tablada. A. Vigne Pacheco, 'El padre Las Casas entre los modernistas', *CMHLB*, 76–77:475–83, compares two short prose pieces, one by José Martí, the other by Amado Nervo, which have Las Casas as their subject. T. Ward, 'Rumbos hacia una teoría peruana de la literatura: sociedad y letras en Matto, Cabello y González Prada', *BHS(L)*, 78:89–101, examines literary theories elaborated by these three authors, and relates them to attempts to establish Peru's cultural independence from Spain.

INDIVIDUAL AUTHORS

BELLO, ANDRÉS. Iván Jaksić, *Andrés Bello: Scholarship and Nation-Building in Nineteenth-Century Latin America*, CUP, xxiv + 254 pp., is an intellectual biography of B., which focuses on issues of nation-building, identity, and language.

CABELLO DE CARBONERA, MERCEDES. O. Voysest, 'El naturalismo de Mercedes Cabello de Carbonera: un ideario ecléctico y de compromiso', *RHM*, 53, 2000:366–87, stresses the particularities of this Peruvian novelist's response to Zola and naturalism.

CARRASQUILLA, TOMÁS. E. Neira Palacio, 'El contexto regional de Tomás Carrasquilla', *Hispamérica*, 89:87–93, demonstrates that Carrasquilla was striving to escape in his writing what he saw as a false dichotomy between regional and universal concerns.

CASAL, JULIÁN DEL. O. Monteros, 'Casal y Maceo en La Habana elegante', *CAm*, 225:57–70, recalls the circumstances of the meeting of the two men in Havana, probably in April/May 1890, and proposes that the stereotyped contrasts of warrior/poet, Bronze Titan/decadent bard, and so on must be questioned, since they have been used to exclude Casal from the Cuban imagined community.

ECHEVERRÍA, ESTEBAN. J. C. Mercado, 'Articulación del discurso histórico y ficcional en *El matadero*', *BHS(L)*, 78:531–37, examines possible sources for parts of the story in contemporary prints and paintings, and in the work of a relatively little-known French author, Louis Sébastien Mercier.

GUTIÉRREZ NÁJERA, MANUEL. J. M. Martínez, 'El público femenino del modernismo: de la lectora figurada a la lectora histórica en las prosas de Gutiérrez Nájera', *RevIb*, 194–95:15–29, traces the figure of woman as reader through a wide variety of genres explored by G.N., in order to demonstrate the importance to the evolution of *modernismo* of its female readership.

MANZANO, JUAN FRANCISCO. J. Branche, 'Mulato entre negros (y blancos): writing, race, the anti-slavery question, and Juan Francisco Manzano's *Autobiografía*', *BLAR*, 20.1:63–87, discusses M.'s presenta-tion of himself as a mulatto and a 'good slave', seeing this as a version of himself that M. was obliged to construct in order to appeal to whites.

MARTÍ, JOSÉ. J. L. Camacho, 'Los límites de la transgresión: la virilización de la mujer y la feminización del poeta en José Martí', *RevIb*, 194–95:69–78, looks at two areas in M.'s work: criticism of manly women and identification of the figure of the poet with passivity, beauty, and fragility. M. appears to seek a mythical androgynous beauty, attributed to superior beings, whom the poet strives to imitate. *Re-Reading José Martí One Hundred Years Later*, ed.

Julio Rodríguez-Luis, NY U.P., 1999, ix + 155 pp., originated in a conference held at the University of Wisconsin-Milwaukee in 1995 to re-evaluate in the centenary year of his death the significance of M.'s writing for Cuban and Latin American history and culture. Around half of the articles included here are revised versions of papers presented at the conference, the others were written for the book. Susana Rotker, *The American Chronicles of José Martí: Journalism and Modernity in Spanish America*, Hanover, NH, New England U.P., 2000, x + 144 pp., is the English translation of a book originally published by Casa de Las Américas, Cuba, in 1992, and now difficult to obtain.

OLMEDO, JOSÉ JOAQUÍN. C. Conway, 'Gender, Empire and Revolution in *La Victoria de Junín*', *HR*, 69:299–317, reads the poem alongside O.'s earlier pro-Spanish and monarchist writing, to show both emergent and residual elements in this work.

RODÓ, JOSÉ ENRIQUE. *CAm*, 222, has three articles to mark (a few months late) the centenary of the publication of *Ariel*: H. Achugar, '¿Quién es Enjolrás? *Ariel* atrapado entre Víctor Hugo y *Star Trek*' (75–84), is initially a rather idiosyncratic essay, which goes on, however, to suggest that the importance of *Ariel* is that it proposes a form of cultural resistance. A. Melis, 'El vuelo atormentado de *Ariel*' (72–75), is especially concerned with responses to the work, particularly those of José Carlos Mariátegui and Julio Antonio Mella. P. Rocca, 'La lección de Próspero: Rodó, la enseñanza de la literatura y los *Apuntes inéditos*' (84–97), focuses on R.'s activities as a journalist, literary critic, and teacher, seeing them as an approach, albeit timid, to the democratization of culture.

SARMIENTO, DOMINGO FAUSTINO. L. Area, 'Geografías imaginarias: el *Facundo* y *Campaña en el Ejército Grande* de Domingo Faustino Sarmiento', *RevIb*, 194–95:91–103, contrasts S.'s attitudes to the Pampa in the two works, and attributes the differences to the particular political circumstances in which each work was written.

VILLAVERDE, CIRILO E. Guizar Villaverde, '*Excursión a Vueltabajo* de Cirilo Villaverde: viaje hacia la emergencia de la nación cubana', *RevIb*, 194–95:219–38, ties these descriptions of travel to the project of creating an imagined community in Cuba.

THE TWENTIETH CENTURY

POSTPONED

BRAZILIAN LITERATURE

By MARK DINNEEN, *Spanish, Portuguese and Latin American Studies,*
University of Southampton

I. GENERAL

Maria Angélica Lopes Guimarães, *A coreografia do desejo: cem anos de
ficção brasileira*, Cotia, Ateliê, 231 pp., is a collection of 14 essays
previously published in journals. A comparative literary approach is
used to discuss the work of such writers as Machado de Assis, Aníbal
Machado, Clarice Lispector, and Oswald França Junior. *De sertões,
desertos e espaços incivilizados*, ed. Ângela Mendes de Almeida, Berthold
Zilly, and Eli Napoleão de Lima, R, Mauad, 301 pp., contains a
series of analyses of the central role that the civilization/barbarism
dichotomy has played in Brazilian thought. Reference is made to the
work of Gilberto Freyre, Caio Prado Júnior, Sérgio Buarque de
Holanda, and Manoel Bomfim, among others. Indursky, *Discurso*,
consists of 50 essays, originating from conference papers, on a wide
range of literary, cultural, and linguistic topics, loosely linked by a
central concern with language and its use. It includes studies of such
writers as Alencar, Cecília Meireles, Guimarães Rosa, Ferreira
Gullar, Rubem Fonseca, Augusto dos Anjos, and Erico Veríssimo.
L. Camargo, 'A poesía infantil no Brasil', *RCLL*, 53:87–94, reviews
poetry written for children from the late 18th c. to the present, tracing
the transition from a poetry of moral education to one of entertainment, humour, and imagination. B. Resende, 'Brazilian Modernism:
the canonised revolution', pp. 199–216 of *Through the Kaleidoscope: The
Experience of Modernity in Latin America*, ed. Vivian Schelling, London,
Verso, 2000, 312 pp., seeks to show how modernist literature became
canonized, resulting in the exclusion from literary studies of other
forms of writing, much of which, like the novels of Benjamin
Constallar, enjoyed a wide readership. *Brazilian Feminisms*, ed. Solange
Ribeiro de Oliveira and Judith Still, Nottingham U.P., 1999, 190 pp.,
is a collection of essays, wide ranging in their scope, which makes a
valuable contribution to feminist criticism of Brazilian literature. In
addition to essays on feminist theory, the volume includes studies of
Clarice Lispector, Patrícia Galvão, and Lygia Fagundes, and essays
examining the representation of women in Brazilian writing of the
16th, 19th and 20th centuries. Mark Curran, *História do Brasil em
cordel*, SPo, EDUSP, 288 pp., is a survey of Brazilian popular poetry
written during the last hundred years, examining how it has recorded
major events in Brazilian history. Maria do Carmo Campos, *A matéria
prima: o Brasil de longe e de perto e outros ensaios*, Porto Alegre, Mercado

Aberto, 1999, 308 pp., contains 20 essays on contemporary literature, analysing poetry, with reference to Drummond de Andrade and Melo Neto; prose, particularly dealing with Clarice Lispector, Graciliano Ramos, and Veríssimo; and the relationship between poetry and music in the work of Mário de Andrade and Murilo Mendes.

2. COLONIAL

H. J. Vizeu Araújo, 'Á margem fria do pátrio rio: licença poética e circumstância mineira na poesia de Claudio Manuel da Costa', Indursky, *Discurso*, 459–71, traces the development of C.'s poetry through a study of its themes and language and highlights the tension within it between European influences and concern for local issues and environment.

3. NINETEENTH CENTURY

João Roberto Faria, *Idéias teatrais: o século XIX no Brasil*, SPo, Perspectiva–FAPESP, 685 pp., gives a detailed overview of the development of Brazil's 19th-c. theatre, centring on the different theories of dramatic production that were produced. Concise accounts of major phases, works, and dramatists are followed by an extensive collection of essays and letters on the theatre written by some of Brazil's best known writers of the period. See also Sábato Magaldi and Maria Thereza Vargas under TWENTIETH CENTURY: DRAMA. S. Chalhoub, 'What are noses for? Paternalism, Social Darwinism and Race Science in Machado de Assis', *JLACS*, 10.4:171–91, focuses on M.'s *Memórias póstumas de Brás Cubas*, examining the narrator's philosophical musings in order to demonstrate the impact that European scientific theories of the late 19th c. had on M.'s thought. L. Perrone-Moisés, 'Machado de Assis y Borges; nacionalismo y color local', *CHA*, 618:53–64, compares the two writers' approaches to the issue of national identity, with particular reference to M.'s *Instinto de nacionalidade*, and argues that irony is the fundamental tool that both use to confront the contradictions they encounter. Massaud Moisés, **Machado de Assis: ficção e utopia*, SPo, Cultrix, 152 pp. Maria de la Concepción Piñero Valverde, *'Cosas de España' en Machado de Assis e otros temas hispano-brasileiros*, SPo, Giordano, 2000, 158 pp., deals with cultural exchanges between Spain and Brazil in the 19th century. It includes two studies on M., one identifying Spanish elements and references to Spain in his novels, and the other discussing the influence of Cervantes in *Quincas Borba*. Gilberto Pinheiro Passos, *O Napoleão de Botafogo: presença francesa* *em Quincas Borba*, SPo, Annablume, 2000, 96 pp., discusses the incorporation of French elements into Machado's novel and how they relate to the author's use of irony. R. Howes, 'Race and transgressive sexuality in Adolfo Caminha's *Bom Crioulo*', *LBR*, 38.1:41–62, studies the sources used by C. in the novel as the basis for discussing its treatment of homosexuality and miscegenation. (See TWENTIETH CENTURY: POETRY for studies of Gonçalves Dias and Cruz e Sousa.) Eunice Moreira et al., *Falas diversas: quatro estudos sobre Joaquim Norberto*, Porto Alegre, Universidade Católica do Rio Grande do Sul, 98 pp., analyses the varied work of Joaquim Norberto de Sousa e Silva, seen as a forgotten writer whose role in the development of Brazilian literature deserves recognition. Fernando Antonio Mencarelli, *Cena aberta: a absolivação de um bilontra e o teatro de revista de Artur Azevedo*, Campinas, Unicamp, 1999, 323 pp., is a detailed study of A.'s *teatro de revista* within its social context, focusing on one particular example, *O bilontra*. The author convincingly demonstrates that, although essentially a form of light-hearted entertainment, the *teatro de revista* played an important role in the development of modern Brazilian drama and had serious social repercussions. Maria Cecília Queiroz de Morães Pinto, *Alencar e a França: perfis*, SPo, Annablume, 1999, 275 pp., studies A.'s novels *Lucíola*, *Diva*, and *Senhora*, to examine how his fiction was marked by his reading of French romantic literature. The study highlights the tension in A.'s work between French influences and his project for a national literature.

4. TWENTIETH CENTURY

POETRY

Luiza Franco Moreira, *Meninos, poetas e heróis: aspectos de Cassiano Ricardo do Modernismo ao Estado Novo*, SPo, EDUSP, 195 pp., studies R.'s best known poetic work, *Martim Cererê*, alongside examples of his essay writing and activity as a journalist in an attempt to shed light on the relationship between his politics and his writing. *O poema: leitores e leituras*, ed. Viviana Bosi et al., Cotia, Ataliê, 184 pp., consists of eight essays on different poets, studied in the light of a wide range of cultural theory, but most incorporating close readings of particular poems. Manuel Bandeira, Mário de Andrade, Jorge de Lima, and Carlos Drummond de Andrade are among the poets studied, along with Antônio Gonçalves Dias and João da Cruz e Sousa from the 19th century. Toninho Vaz, *Paulo Leminski: o bandido que sabia latim*, R, Record, 377 pp., is the first full biography of L., thoroughly researched, showing in detail the development of his work but not analysing his poetry. Betina Ribeiro Rodrigues da Cunha, *A poética da natureza na obra de Eluard e Bandeira*, SPo, Annablume, 2000, 242 pp., is a comparative study of Paul Eluard and Manuel Bandeira, with particular emphasis on the vision of the natural world conveyed in their work. Ruy Espinheira Filho, *Tumulto de amor e outros tumultos: criação e arte em Mário de Andrade*, R, Record, 316 pp. C. A. Perrone, 'Resource and resonance: a story of transamerican poetics and Brazilian song in global and cultural perspective', *LBR*, 38.2:75–83, relates Brazilian popular song of the 1990s to earlier currents of poetry in a discussion of texts with a transnational prespective. M. Perloff, 'Concrete prose in the nineties: Haroldo de Campos's *Galáxias* and after', *ConLit*, 42.2:270–93, makes particular reference to C.'s theories on literature in a discussion of the relationship between verse and prose in concrete poetics. Leila V. B. Gouvêa, *Cecília em Portugal: ensaio biográfico sobre a presença de Cecília Meireles na terra de Camões, Antero e Pessoa*, SPo, Iluminuras, 128 pp. *Mais poesia hoje*, ed. Celia Pedrosa, R, Sette Letras, 2000, 195 pp., is a series of essays by poets and critics based on conference papers. Wide in scope, if somewhat uneven, the volume offers new perspectives on such issues as poetry and politics, poetry and memory, and national and regional identity.

DRAMA

Jane Milling and Graham Ley, *Modern Theories of Performance: From Stanislavski to Boal*, Basingstoke, Palgrave, 198 pp., contains a concise and informative chapter on Boal's theories, outlining their evolution and highlighting their most contentious elements. Sábato Magaldi and Maria Thereza Vargas, *Cem anos de teatro em São Paulo*, SPo, Senac, 438 pp., is a history of the theatre in São Paulo from the late 19th to the late 20th century. C. Overhoff, 'Incorporando o pensamento ocidental: dramaturgos brasileiros nos anos noventa', *LATR*, 34.2:55–72, argues that in the 1990s a new tendency emerged in the Brazilian theatre which sought to challenge Western cultural tradition through the use of Brazilian elements of African and indigenous origin. Plays by Luis Alberto de Abreu and Alcides Nogueira are discussed as examples. K. da Costa Bezerra, 'Amores de Abat-jour: a cena teatral brasileira e a escrita de mulheres nos anos vinte', *ib.*, 35.1:75–87, seeks recognition for the work of the forgotten dramatist, Maria Eugênia Celso. Focusing on her first play, dating from 1925, the article highlights how the playwright problematizes representations of male and female that were common at the time.

PROSE

Jorge Amado: New Critical Essays, ed. Keith H. Brower, Earl E. Fitz, and Enrique Martinez-Vidal, NY–London, Routledge, 291 pp., is a collection of 18 thought-provoking essays covering numerous aspects of A.'s work. Of particular interest are those contributions that address the most controversial issues arising from his novels, such as his portrayal of women, in essays by Ellen Douglass, Elizabeth Lowe, and Susan Canty Quinlan; of the Brazilian working class, discussed by Earl E. Fitz; and of racial issues, dealt with by Nelson Vieira.

Earl E. Fitz, *Sexuality and Being in the Poststructuralist Universe of Clarice Lispector: The Différance of Desire*, Austin, Univ. of Texas Press, 272 pp., is a study of impressive scope, with chapters on the structure, style, and sociopolitical and psychoanalytical dimensions of L.'s work, and with references to examples from all areas of her fiction. It argues that, because L. wrote what were essentially poststructural texts, poststructural analysis provides the most thorough understanding of her writing. Ricardo Iannace, *A leitora Clarice Lispector*, SPo, EDUSP, 218 pp., examines the ways in which L.'s reading of other writers, such as Monteiro Lobato, Chekhov, and Katherine Mansfield, may have influenced her own work. Carlos Mendes de Sousa, *Clarice Lispector, figuras de escrita*, Braga, Universidade de Minho, 2000, 506 pp. H. Owen, 'Masculine impostures and female ripostes: Onetti and Clarice Lispector', pp. 133–143 of *Onetti and Others: Comparative Essays on a Major Figure in Latin American Literature*, ed. Gustavo San Román, Albany, SUNY, 1999, 119 pp., uses Cixous's theory of *écriture féminine* to contrast the construction of sexuality in O.'s *Bienvenido Bob* and L.'s *A partida do trem*. D. Coli, 'Clarice Lispector y la economía andrógina de *Agua viva*', *RCEH*, 26:199–210, discusses how L. makes use of androgynous elements within her novel in order to express her philosophical concerns. M. Collette, 'El reconocimiento de la identidad corporal femenina en *La pasión de GH*, de Clarice Lispector', *ib.*, 211–23, examines the novel's exploration of female subjectivity, focusing on the protagonist's discovery of repressed dimensions of her identity. C. A. Sloan, 'The social and textual implications of the creation of a male narrating subject in Clarice Lispector's *A hora da estrela*', *LBR*, 38.1:89–102, analyses the narrative form of the novel in the light of Hélène Cixous's theory of libidinal economies.

R. da Silveira Lobo Sternberg, 'Celebrating the celebration', *RCEH*, 26:241–53, discusses how Ivan Angelo's *A festa* not only deals with the theme of political oppression, as experienced in Brazil in the 1970s, but also seeks to highlight to the reader the 'ideological underpinnings' within all narratives. Ana Cristina Chiara, *Pedro Nava: um Homem no limiar*, R, EDUERJ, 139 pp., is a study of N.'s memoirs which focuses particularly on his attempts to confront death. His treatment of the subject is discussed in the light of the thought of such philosophers as Henri Bergson and Edgar Morin. Odalice de Castro e Silva, *A obra de arte e seu intérprete*, Fortaleza, Universidade Federal de

Ceará, 2000, 322 pp., is a study of both the fiction and the literary criticism produced by Osman Lins. Nilce Sant'Anna Martins, *O léxico de Guimarães Rosa*, SPo, EDUSP, 536 pp., is an extensive dictionary of the vocabulary used in R.'s fiction, which, for the specialist, is a useful guide to the regionalisms, neologisms, and archaic expressions he employs. The derivation of each entry is given, followed by an example of it taken from one of R.'s works. *Outras margens: estudos da obra de Guimarães Rosa*, ed. Lélia Parreira and Maria Theresa Abelha Alves, SPo, Autêntica, 367 pp., contains over 20 essays on R.'s fiction, which include discussion of its reception beyond Brazil, analyses of narrative technique and comparative studies. João Adolfo Hansen, *o O: a ficção da literatura em 'Grande sertão: veredas'*, SPo, Hedra, 2000, 198 pp., offers an in-depth discussion of the linguistic originality of the novel. Osvando J. de Morais, *'Grande sertão: veredas': o romance transformado*, SPo, EDUSP–FAPESP, 2000, 276 pp., raises many interesting issues about the relationship between literature and film. It examines how R.'s novel was adapted for television by Walter George Durst, focusing on the difficulties involved and the solutions sought, and discussing the complexities of the narrative. P. Armstrong, 'Guimarães Rosa in translation: *scrittore, editore, traduttore, traditore*', *LBR*, 38.1 : 63–87, discusses aspects of R.'s philosophy of literary creation and translation through a study of his personal involvement in the translation of his major works into various languages. Pascoal Farinaccio, **'Serafim ponte grande' e as dificuldades da crítica literária*, Cotia, Ateliê, 235 pp., claims to be the first major study of the novel by Oswald de Andrade. *Identidades e representações na cultura brasileira*, ed. Rita Oliveira Godet and Licia Soares de Souza, João Pessoa, Ideia, 230 pp., is a collection of conference papers dealing mainly with issues of cultural memory and identity, and which make particular reference to North Eastern writers such as Graciliano Ramos and José Lins do Rego. Maria Alzira Brum Lemos, *O doutor e o jagunço: ciências, mestiçagem e cultura em 'Os sertões'*, SPo, Arte e Ciência–UNIMAR, 2000, 224 pp., is a thoroughly researched analysis of da Cunha's epic work, studied in relation to scientific thought of the period, with sections on the impact of racial and environmental determinism, positivism and evolutionism. The study argues that certain concepts evident in *Os sertões* can still be found in the work of present day scholars and writers. Luiz Fernando Valente, 'Brazilian literature and citizenship: from Euclides da Cunha to Marcos Dias', *LBR*, 38.2 : 11–27, discusses changing views of citizenship in Brazil in the course of the 20th c. through a comparison of C.'s *Os Sertões* and poetry by D. from the 1990s. D. E. Butler, 'The national territory and the state in *Facundo* and *Os sertões*', *BHS(L)*, 78 : 103–10, compares the two works by Sarmiento and Da Cunha as responses to the consolidation of the control of the state over national territory. *Leituras cruzadas: diálogos da história com a literatura*, ed. Sandra Jatahy Pesavento, Porto Alegre, Universidade Federal do Rio Grande do Sul, 2000, 287 pp., examines the relationship between literature and history by studying work by Dyonélio Machado, Érico Veríssimo, Cassiano Ricardo, Monteiro Lobato, and Ciro dos Anjos in the light of the ideas of Sérgio Buarque de Holanda and Antônio Cândido. Cleudene de Oliveira Aragão, *Xosé Neira Vilas e Rachel de Queiroz: fabuladores artífices*, Corunna, do Castro, 2000, 216 pp., is a comparative study of the works of the two writers, written in Galician, which stresses the cultural links between their native regions. J. Courteau, 'A feminização do discurso nacional na obra de Raquel de Queiroz', *His(US)*, 84:749–57, focuses particularly on Q.'s last novel, *Memorial da Maria Moura*, in order to show how she attempts to affirm the role of women in Brazilian history and in the development of the nation. R. M. Levine, 'Different Carolinas', *LBR*, 38.2:61–73, is an interesting discussion of the diaries of Carolina Maria de Jesus, focusing on the process of editing involved in their production and the caustic criticism made of them by some Brazilian intellectuals. José Ramos Tinhorão, *A música popular no romance brasileiro. II: século XX*, SPo, Editora 34, 2000, 415 pp., is the second volume of a trilogy examining how and with what objectives popular music is used by Brazilian novelists in their writing. Lima Barreto, Jorge Amado, Erico Veríssimo, and Afonso Schmidt are among the writers discussed. Elizabeth A. Marchant, *Critical Acts: Latin American Women and Cultural Criticism*, Gainesville, Florida U.P., 1999, 144 pp., includes a chapter on Lúcia Miguel Pereira, examining how the treatment of gender issues in her novels contrasts with that found in her literary criticism. Edu Teruki Otsuka, **Marcas de catástrofe: experiência urbana e indústria cultural em Rubem Fonseca, João Gilberto Noll e Chico Buarque*, SPo, Nankin, 223 pp. Idilva Maria Pires Germano, *Alegorias do Brasil: Imagens de Brasilidade em 'Triste fim de Policarpo'*, SPo, Annablume, 134 pp., examines the vision of Brazil conveyed in Lima Barreto's novel and João Ubaldo Ribeiro's *Viva o povo brasileiro*, concentrating particularly on how both writers use allegory to ironic effect. Fernando C. Gill, *O romance da urbanização*, Porto Alegre, EDIPUCRS, 1999, 148 pp., identifies, through the study of novels by Dyonélio Machado, Graciliano Ramos, and Cyro dos Anjos, a new current of fiction emerging in the 1930s, which began to explore the contradictions inherent in the transition from a rural to an urban, industrialized society. It concludes that the study of such texts highlights the need for a reassessment of the notion of modernity as applied to Brazil. On a similar theme, T. Pellegrini, 'A ficção brasileira hoje: os caminhos da cidade', *RCLL*, 53:115–28, briefly surveys Brazilian novels of the last two decades to show how the long-standing dichotomy between rural and urban fiction has been replaced by works which use urban themes to debate social, political and cultural issues.

IX. ITALIAN STUDIES

LANGUAGE

By ADAM LEDGEWAY, *Lecturer in Romance Philology, University of Cambridge,* and ALESSANDRA LOMBARDI, *Research Assistant, University of Manchester*
(This survey covers the years 2000 and 2001)

I. GENERAL

Lorenzo Renzi, one of the leading figures in the field of (Italo-) Romance linguistics in Italy over recent decades, receives a much-deserved tribute in the form of two separate collections of essays written by colleagues and former pupils highlighting R.'s wide-ranging interests in such areas as syntax, phonology, historical linguistics, and philology: *Il tempo, i tempi: omaggio a Lorenzo Renzi,* ed. Rosanna Brusegan and Michele Cortelazzo, Padua, Esedra, 1999, x + 310 pp., and *Renzi Vol.* The central position occupied by R. in Italian linguistics is also reflected by his pioneering work on the *ItalAnt* research project, which will lead to a much-awaited grammar of early (Tuscan) Italian bringing together the expertise of many leading figures in the field along lines similar to those of his very successful project on modern Italian which produced the monumental three-volume *Grande grammatica italiana di consultazione* (Bo, Il Mulino, 1988–95). Preliminary results and pilot studies conducted for *ItalAnt* are now published in two collections of papers: *Italant: per una grammatica dell'italiano antico,* ed. Lorenzo Renzi, Padua, Centrostampa Palazzo Maldura, 1998, 89 pp., and a special issue of *LS,* 'Linguistica e italiano antico', ed. Lorenzo Renzi and Antonietta Bisetto, 35, 2000:537–743. M. Barbera and C. Marello, 'L'annotazione morfo-sintattica del *Padua Corpus*: strategie adottate e problemi di acquisizione', *RevR,* 36:3–20, gives a detailed account of the Turin *ItalAnt* group's plan to part-of-speech tag the Padua Corpus for the benefit of all participants in the *ItalAnt* project.

Conference proceedings of particular interest include *La preistoria dell'italiano. Atti della tavola rotonda di linguistica storica, Università Ca' Foscari di Venezia 11–13 giugno 1998,* ed. József Herman and Anna Marinetti, Tübingen, Niemeyer, 2000, 279 pp.; *I confini del dialetto. Atti del convengo Sappada/Plodn (Belluno), 5–9 luglio 2000,* ed. Gianna Marcato, Padua, Unipress, ii + 349 pp.; *L'italiano oltre frontiera. Quinto convegno internazionale, Leuven, 22–25 aprile 1998,* ed. Serge Vanvolsem, 2 vols, F, Cesati, 2000, 548, 525 pp.; *Fonologia e morfologia dell'italiano e dei dialetti d'Italia. Atti del 31. congresso della società di linguistica italiana,*

Padua, 25–27 settembre 1997, ed. Paola Benincà, Alberto Mioni, and Laura Vanelli, Ro, Bulzoni, 1999, iii + 637 pp. The continuing importance of dialectal evidence in challenging and developing general issues in linguistic theory is confirmed by two important monographs by Cecilia Poletto and Adam Ledgeway dealing respectively with the syntax of northern and southern dialects (see relevant sections), and the recent collection of outstanding articles contained in Repetti, *Phonological Theory*, an important contribution to both Italian dialectology and phonological theory, serving as an excellent introduction to the phonological structures of the dialects (northern, central, southern) while at the same time presenting the reader with a number of sophisticated analyses of complex and often poorly understood and under-studied phonological phenomena.

2. HISTORY OF THE LANGUAGE, EARLY TEXTS, AND DIACHRONIC STUDIES

**Un volgarizzamento tardo duecentesco fiorentino dell'Antidotarium Nicolai*, ed. Lucia Fontanelle, Alessandria, Orso, 2000, xxxviii + 321 pp. Maria Antonietta Passarelli, **La lingua della patria: Leon Battista Alberti e la questione del volgare*, Ro, Bagatto, 1999, 95 pp. M. Tavoni, 'Storia della lingua e storia della coscienza linguistica: appunti medievali e rinascimentali', *SGI*, 18, 1999:205–31, traces the emergence in Italy of an awareness of the value of the native vernacular vis-à-vis Latin and other dialectal varieties from the time of Dante through 14th-c. humanists to the debates of 16th-c. grammarians. T. Matarrese, 'Alle soglie della grammatica: imparare a leggere (e a scrivere) tra Medioevo e Rinascimento', *ib.*, 233–56, reviews a number of medieval Latin and, in particular, Renaissance vernacular grammars, illustrating their significance as valuable tools of learning employed in the teaching of reading and writing in 16th-c. Italy. M. Lieber and R. Teichner, 'Altre retrodatazioni della terminologia grammaticale italiana in base alla Grammatichetta di Trissino', *ZRP*, 116, 2000:279–304, examines in detail Trissino's use of grammatical terminology in his 1529 grammar, investigating in particular his translation equivalents of terms used in Priscian's Latin grammar, and concludes with an alphabetical list of grammatical terms coined by Trissino. A. Scarano, 'Storia grammaticale dell'aggettivo. Da sottoclasse di parole a parte del discorso', *SGI*, 18, 1999:57–90, charts the various treatments and conceptions of the grammatical class of adjective in the history of linguistics, focusing principally on Italian grammars from the 15th to the 20th centuries. G. Mattarucco,

'Alcuni punti critici nelle grammatiche italiane da Fortunio a Buonmattei', *ib.*, 19, 2000:93–139, offers a comparative analysis of 15 Italian grammars from the 16th c. to the first half of the 17th c., examining such topics as the classification of parts of speech, the status of the article, the number and definition of conjugational classes, tenses, and moods, and the problem of verbal allomorphy. Alessandro Manzoni, *Scritti linguistici inediti*, ed. Angelo Stella and Maurizio Vitale, 2 vols, Mi, Centro Nazionale Studi Manzoniani, 2000, xx + 437, xlii + 1247 pp. Stephane Oppes, *Dalla intuizione all'espressione della parola: la filosofia del linguaggio nel primo Novecento italiano*, Ro, Pontificium Athenaeum Antonianum, 2000, 263 pp.

The buoyant state of research into the internal history of the language is confirmed by the appearance of a number of new volumes dedicated to this topic: *Studi di storia della lingua italiana offerti a Ghino Ghinassi*, ed. Paolo Bongrani, F, Le Lettere, 578 pp.; Gianfranco Lotti, *L'aventurosa storia della lingua italiana*, Mi, Bompiani, 2000, 256 pp.; Riccardo Tesi, *Storia dell'italiano: la formazione della lingua comune dalle origini al Rinascimento*, Ro, Laterza, vii + 325 pp.; Umberto Panozzo, *Storia della lingua italiana*, Rimini, Panozzo, 1999, 382 pp.; Paolo D'Achille, *Breve grammatica storica dell'italiano*, Ro, Carocci, 126 pp.; Alberto Zamboni, *Alle origini dell'italiano. Dinamiche e tipologie della transizione dal latino*, Ro, Carocci, 2000, 225 pp. Of particular interest is Arrigo Castellani, *Grammatica storica della lingua italiana*, 1, *Introduzione*, Bo, Il Mulino, 2000, xxxviii + 618 pp., the first of four projected volumes dealing respectively with the formation of the literary language, phonology, morphology, and syntax. This first volume brings together six chapters, the first five of which represent substantially modified and enlarged versions of previously published articles, focusing on classical and spoken Latin; Germanic, Gallo-Romance, and northern dialect influences on Tuscan; dialectal variation in medieval Tuscany; and the formation of the *lingua poetica*. Though the prose often proves quite dense in places, the author's exceptional knowledge and manipulation of the textual evidence, together with the high degree of detail characterizing his presentation, promise to make this a 'classic' of Italian linguistics. L. Renzi, ' "ItalAnt": come e perché una grammatica dell'italiano antico', *LS*, 35, 2000:717–29, presents the rationale behind the *ItalAnt* project and makes a persuasive case for a comprehensive grammar of old Italian, while discussing some of the problems in defining old Italian (ultimately taken to be old Florentine) and highlighting a number of the principal phonological, morphological, and syntactic differences between Tuscan on the one hand and northern and central-southern varieties on the other. Similar issues regarding the validity of a grammar of old Italian, its organization and periodization, and the question of choosing appropriate texts are addressed in a companion article by N. Vincent, 'Il progetto "ItalAnt": una presentazione e alcune considerazioni', *ib.*, 731–43, an abridged version of an earlier article by the same author entitled 'A new grammar of old Italian', Lepschy, *Dictionaries*, 91–110. L. Renzi, 'Teorie linguistiche antiche e moderne davanti allo studio dell'italiano antico', *LS*, 35, 2000:537–45, surveys the impact of various linguistic paradigms and methodological approaches on the study of old Italian, concluding on a positive note with regard to the new possibilities offered by electronic resources.

N. Vincent, 'Competition and correspondence in syntactic change: null arguments in Latin and Romance', Pitzuk, *Diachronic Syntax*, 25–50, applies the optimality-theoretic notions of constraints and constraint ranking to Lexical Functional Grammar to explain in an illuminating way the changes in null argument licensing from Latin to Italian. For example, V. maintains that the loss of Latin null objects is to be related to the development of a system of object clitics, the emergence of which can, in turn, be interpreted as a consequence of a re-ranking of a set of universal constraints applying to pronominals whose different rankings in Latin and Italian correlate with the observed differences in pronoun inventory. A. M. Martins, 'Polarity items in Romance: underspecification and lexical change', *ib.*, 191–219, draws heavily on Italian and dialectal evidence, in addition to other Romance varieties, to trace the behaviour and distribution of negative and positive indefinites, the development of which, it is argued, lends support to the lexical revision process underlying language acquisition. Two articles dealing with relative pronouns in early texts are O. Merisalo, 'L'omissione del relativizzatore nel toscano del fine trecento alla luce delle lettere di Francesco Datini', *NMi*, 101, 2000:279–85, which observes on the basis of a corpus of 116 letters the frequent omission of the relativizer in subject and object functions in early Tuscan; and F. Sestito, 'Sull'alternanza *che/il quale* nell'italiano antico', *SGI*, 18, 1999:5–30, which surveys treatments of both pronominal relative forms in 15th- and 16th-c. grammars of Italian that consider the pair to be freely interchangeable, although S. observes on the basis of an examination of 16th-c. literary texts that *il quale* is most frequently employed in subject or (in)direct object function in explicative relatives. R. Ambrosini, 'Sulla sintassi del verbo nella prosa toscana del Dugento ovvero tempo e aspetto nell'italiano antico', *LS*, 35, 2000:547–71, investigates the relationship between narratological and syntactic structures in 13th-c. Tuscan prose, noting how, for example, the constant use of the *passato remoto*, required by the narration, entails that the presentation of themes is marked by means of the perfective tenses. M. Squartini, 'Filogenesi e ontogenesi del futuro italiano', *AGI*, 86:194–225, is an enlightening comparison of the semantic functions of the future tense in 13th- and 14th-c. Italian and modern standard Italian, focusing on the epistemic functions of the paradigm. While in modern Italian the future tense is increasingly specialized as an evidential and concessive marker (e.g. *avrà telefonato* 'he must have rung'), early Italian is shown to rarely use the future with this value, although employing it with a wide range of other non-factual values as witnessed by its frequent use in rhetorical questions. A. Lobodanov, 'L'uso in coppia dei verba dicendi e dei verbi di moto nell'italiano antico', *SGI*, 19, 2000:41–50, is a brief examination of a peculiar old Tuscan paratactic pattern involving two finite verbs of saying or motion (e.g. *e 'l figluolo rispuose e disse*; *si mosse e andò in Egitto*), where the first verb expresses the initial intention of movement or the initiation of a speech act and the second verb the realization of the movement or speech act. S. Vegnaduzzo, 'Il congiuntivo nelle frasi subordinate in italiano antico', *LS*, 35, 2000:693–713, offers a valuable corpus-based investigation of subjunctive usage in old Italian, highlighting how the subjunctive mood has a more limited distribution in old Italian than in contemporary Italian. S. Telve, 'Aspetti sintattici del discorso indiretto nella prosa fra tre- e cinquecento e nelle "Consulte e pratiche" fiorentine', *SGI*, 19, 2000:51–91, analyses a corpus of Italian chancery and chronicle texts to examine indirect speech in relation to the usage of verbal and nominal introductory elements, coordination, infinitives, and verbal tenses. C. Robustelli, 'La sintassi dei verbi percettivi *vedere* e *sentire* nell'italiano antico', *ib.*, 5–40. C. Di Meola, 'Synchronic variation as a result of grammaticalization: concessive subjunctions in German and Italian', *Linguistics*, 39, 133–49, draws on contemporary written texts to demonstrate that different stages of an ongoing process of grammaticalization can coexist synchronically, noting striking parallels in the development of German and Italian concessive subordinators. M. Barbera, M. Mazzoleni, and M. Pantiglioni, 'Costrutti concessivi fattuali in italiano antico', *LS*, 2000, 35:573–603, observe a number of differences in the formation of concessive clauses in early Tuscan and modern Italian: morphosyntactically, both contemporary Italian and early Tuscan make use of hypotactic structures (introduced by subordinating conjunctions) and paratactic structures (connected by coordinating conjunctions and/or adverbial elements), but only the latter makes recourse to so-called parahypotaxis where the concessive value is marked by the reversed order main clause + dependent clause (the latter introduced by a coordinating conjunction). Further differences arise in the choice of the morpholexical items employed to mark the concessive value, especially in hypotaxis. G. Frenguelli, ' "Senza che" nella prosa italiana dalle origini ai giorni nostri', *LN*, 62 : 7–39, makes expert use of the philological evidence to demonstrate two distinct uses of the complex subordinating conjunction *senza che*, which functioned both as a coordinating conjunction and a negative privative subordinator. While the latter function survives to the present-day, F. highlights how the former coordinating use was almost entirely lost by the beginning of the 17th century. V. Egerland, 'Frasi subordinate al participio in italiano antico', *LS*, 2000, 35 : 605–28, explores a number of differences in the syntax of past participles in modern and early Italian. In contrast to modern Italian, E. highlights how in absolute participial clauses in 13th-c. Tuscan the participle could be of the unergative class, be associated with both active and passive value, and occur in a variety of positions with respect to other elements of the clause. Significantly, these properties are also shown to surface in the periphrastic *avere* + participle + object construction, which ambiguously allows of both a resultative reading ('I have got the book read') alongside of a past tense reading ('I have read the book'). G. Salvi, 'La formazione del sistema V2 delle lingue romanze antiche', *ib.*, 665–92, is a highly convincing account of medieval Romance V2, which S. argues to have arisen from an original Latin verb-initial word order.

3. PHONETICS AND PHONOLOGY

L. Turchi and P.-M. Bertinetto, 'La durata vocalica di fronte ai nessi /sC/: un'indagine su soggetti pisani', *SILTA*, 29, 2000: 389–421, attempts to shed new light on the syllabification of /sC/ clusters, traditionally considered heterosyllabic, through an examination of the duration of vowels preceding such clusters. Interestingly, the results highlight considerable variation among speakers, inasmuch as the cluster is treated as heterosyllabic by some speakers and as a tautosyllabic sequence by others, whereas in many other speakers no discernible tendency could be detected at all. B.-M. Bertinetto, 'Boundary strength and linguistic ecology (mostly exemplified on intervocalic /s/-voicing in Italian)', *FLin*, 33, 1999: 267–96, rejects current prosodically-based phonological analyses of Italian /s/-voicing in favour of an analysis based on a scalar interpretation of morpheme boundaries. T. Cravens, 'Sociolinguistic subversion of a phonological hierarchy', *Word*, 51, 2000: 1–19, maintains that sound change is selective within specific classes and that the relative propensity of class members to undergo change in specific environments is constant within a given language. Although Tuscan spirantization appears to violate these basic principles, C. argues that detailed analysis of change in progress suggests, in contrast, that sociolinguistic factors operative during the variation phase of implementation can disrupt a system-internal implicational directionality. E. Pickett, S. Blumstein, and M. Burton, 'Effects of speaking rate on the singleton/geminate consonant contrast in Italian', *Phonetica*, 56, 1999: 135–57, reports on the results of a production and perception experiment to investigate the effect of speech rate on the short/long consonant contrast in words spoken in isolation and in a sentential string. In terms of production, it was found that while closure duration discriminated between the two consonantal types within a given speaking rate, the ratio between consonant duration and preceding vowel duration discriminated between short and long consonants both within and across speaking rates. In terms of perception, manipulation of the consonant to vowel ratio was demonstrated to directly affect the perception of the long/short distinction, although there was considerable variation among speakers. Rodney Sampson, *Nasal Vowel Evolution in Romance*, OUP, 1999, xv + 413, provides a much-needed account of the development of nasality in Italo-Romance, with two clearly written and detailed chapters dedicated to Italo-Romance (though dealing, of course, predominantly with northern Italian dialects) and Sardinian-Corsican. J. Aski, 'La sonorizzazione variabile e esiti multipli. Lo sviluppo de /sj/ dal latino all'italiano', *ZRP*, 117: 265–96, examines the phonetic variants of the outcome of intervocalic /sj/ in a corpus of 37 medieval Tuscan documents, which are interpreted as attestations of variable voicing (voiceless vs voiced palatal affricate), a variation which she observes in many modern dialects of Tuscany and central Italy. M. Mancini, 'Tra dialettologia latina e dialettologia italoromanza: sul trattamento di lat. -kt-', *ib.*, 116, 2000: 107–40, is a thoroughly unpersuasive attack on the traditional thesis which takes Lat. -KT- to have developed regularly into central-southern *-tt-* (FACTUM > *fatto*), maintaining instead that pre-4th-c. AD Roman data support a different development in which the occlusive margin in the ancient cluster -KT- weakened first to *-ht-* and then *-t-* through contact with northern Italic dialects. M. Maiden, 'Phonological dissimilation and clitic morphology in Italo-Romance', Repetti, *Phonological Theory*, 169–89, scrutinizes rival pairs of phonologically distinct but functionally non-distinct clitic pronouns in the history of a wide range of dialects (e.g. northern 3rd person dative pronouns *li* vs *ga/ge*), noting that typically just one of the clitic pair is grammaticalized to the exclusion of the other in those cases where the other variant would have given rise to a sequence of phonologically identical segments (as in the case of two 3rd person *l*-clitics). M. interprets this as strong evidence for a symbiotic relationship between morphological variations which present fortuitously dissimilatory effects and a general phonological preference for dissimilated structures.

M. D'Imperio and S. Rosenthall, 'Phonetics and phonology of main stress in Italian', *Phonology*, 16, 1999: 1–28, demonstrates in the speech of central and southern Italians the duration of stressed vowels in open penultimate syllables to be significantly greater than that of stressed vowels in all other lexical positions: a case of phonological lengthening which the authors interpret from an optimality-theoretic perspective to be subject to a constraint ranking best satisfied by a bimoraic monosyllabic foot, whereas antepenultimate open-syllable stress corresponds to a bimoraic disyllabic foot. E. Cresti, 'Force illocutoire, articulation topic/comment et contour prosodique en italien parlé', *FLa*, 13, 1999: 168–81, explores intonation contours of colloquial Italian utterances, noting that in contrast to conventional intonation patterns which are associated with specific illocutionary functions, the falling-rising contour associated with a topic/comment segmentation lacks independent illocutionary value. F. Rossi, 'Non lo sai che ora è? Alcune considerazioni sull'intonazione e sul valore pragmatico degli enunciati con dislocazione a destra', *SGI*, 18, 1999: 145–93, offers an insightful comparison of the key prosodic and pragmatic properties of left and right dislocation structures drawn from a corpus of six films. M. D'Imperio, 'Acoustic-perceptual correlates of sentence prominence in Italian', *OSUWPL*, 54, 2000: 58–77, reports on the results of an experiment using synthetic speech to test which of fundamental frequency, duration, and intensity is the most influential in the perception of prominence structure at the sentence level, and whether there are differences between questions and statements. Id., 'Focus and tonal structure in Neapolitan Italian', *SpC*, 33: 339–56, investigates the acoustic and perceptual characteristics of focal and post-focal accents in yes/no interrogatives in the Italian variety spoken in Naples. D's findings demonstrate that when focus is early, this produces a post-focal accent which aligns with the last stressed syllable of the intonation phrase, though not with the nuclear accent of the intonation phrase despite being final, and which is acoustically much reduced in contrast to the focal accent.

4. MORPHOLOGY

M. Maiden, 'Some reflections on the place of morphology in the history of Italian', Lepschy, *Dictionaries*, 53–72, draws on a number of examples of idiosyncratic morphological patterning in the history of the Italian verbal paradigm in support of the view that recurrent, albeit synchronically unmotivated, patterns of inflectional morphology should be considered in some sense the characteristic structural 'signature' which marks the language out against all others. Id., 'Di un cambiamento intramorfologico: origini del tipo *dissi dicesti*, ecc., nell'italoromanzo', *AGI*, 85, 2000 : 137–71, argues against traditional explanations of the idiosyncratic pattern of allomorphy characteristic of the Italian *passato remoto* (e.g. *dissi / -e / -ero* vs *dicesti / -emmo / -este*) which consider such allomorphy an accidental side-effect of phonological or semantic-morphological changes involving, for example, the analogical extension of allomorphic patterns created by regular phonological change to all verbs, or an arrested process of analogical levelling where in certain cases levelling would have otherwise produced homophony with the present indicative. M. maintains, instead, that the relevant allomorphs (in his terms 'morphomes') became associated historically with stress and were therefore subject to a type of 'intramorphological' regularization arising from their reanalysis as inherently stressed forms. M. Ippolito, 'On the past participle morphology in Italian', *MITWPL*, 33, 1999 : 111–37, is an unconvincing analysis within the framework of distributive morphology of the *-t-* participial formative that appears both in verbal environments (*parlato*) and denominal or deverbal nominalizations (*pedata / uscita*). Essentially, I. argues that when not immediately dominated by CP, the (aspect/voice) I node associated with the verbal/nominal participle is defined as a default I in the absence of a [+ continuous] feature and hence is filled by a default *-t-* formative. E. Mangi, 'Questioni di semantica nella morfologia derivazionale dell'italiano: il suffisso *-oso*, fra sincronia e diacronia', *AGI*, 86 : 3–24, highlights a number of weaknesses in Scalise's analysis of the word formation rules applying to the denominal adjectival suffix *-oso*, as well as his semantic treatment of the suffix which M. demonstrates in fact to be polysemous. It is argued that the present-day semantics of the latter can only be understood by making reference to the diachronic evidence, noting, in particular, that already in Latin the derivational suffix -osus was subject to a degree of polysemy. Evaluative suffixes form the topic of discussion in two articles by N. Grandi, 'Su alcune presunte anomalie della morfologia valutativa: il rapporto con il genere ed il numero', *ib.*, 25–56, exploring the impact of evaluative suffixes on gender and number distinctions, and 'I suffissi valutativi tra derivazione e flessione: uno studio interlinguistico', *ib.*, 129–73, which highlights the common properties of evaluative suffixes in (Italo-)Romance, modern Greek, and Southern Slavonic languages. M. Maiden, 'Il sistema desinenziale del sostantivo nell'italo-romanzo preletterario. Ricostruzione parziale a partire dai dialetti moderni (il significato storico di plurali del tipo *amici*)', pp. 167–79 of *La preistoria dell'italiano*, noted above, presents some very persuasive evidence gleaned from medieval texts and the modern dialects in support of the thesis that the nominal systems of preliterary Italo-Romance operated according to a binary (nominative vs oblique) case system. Significant evidence to this effect is adduced from velar-final masculine nouns derived from the Lat. 2nd declension where, in contrast to the general tendency to preserve the non-palatalizing oblique plural inflection -os > *-oi (*fuoco* / *-chi*), an original nominative plural inflection -i > -i has exceptionally been retained in: i) nouns with a semantically unmarked plural (*porco* / *-ci*, *asparago* / *-gi*), where the relative infrequency of the velar-stem of the singular would not have consequently favoured the non-palatalized oblique form at the expense of the palatalized nominative form, as happened with those nouns with a semantically marked plural (e.g. *fuoco* / *-chi*); and ii) nouns denoting animates (*amico* / *-ci*) which would presumably have occurred most frequently as sentential subject or have been used as vocatives. Vito Pirrelli, **Paradigmi in morfologia. Un approccio interdisciplinare alla flessione verbale dell'italiano*, Pisa, IEPI, 2000, xix + 217 pp.

5. Syntax

P. Acquaviva, 'La grammatica italiana: il lavoro comincia adesso', *LS*, 35, 2000:249–71, is an original contribution which questions whether all Italian speakers are native speakers of the same cognitive system in the light of recent syntactic research which has unearthed a number of areas where speakers present different acceptability judgments. Richard Kayne, *Parameters and Universals*, OUP, 2000, xiv + 369, brings together a number of previously published papers by this renowned scholar dealing principally with theoretical issues in Romance and Germanic. As has always been typical of K.'s work, many of the articles in this volume draw predominantly, if not almost exclusively, on Italian and the dialects and hence will prove of particular interest to Italianists with an interest in such topics as auxiliary distribution, past participial agreement, clitic placement, imperatives, and complementizers. P. Acquaviva, 'Syntactic intervention effects on Italian polarity items', *Renzi Vol.*, 1–18, demonstrates that negative polarity items (e.g. *niente*) and dependent items (e.g. *qualcosa*) are subject to a constraint that requires them to occur adjacent to their licensing operator by LF. A. Belletti, 'Speculations on the possible source of expletive negation in Italian clauses', *ib.*, 19–37, makes the original, though highly speculative, claim that comparative *più* and expletive *non* in comparative sentences such as *era più bello di quanto non pensassi* should be formally identified with the negative discontinuous sequence *non ... più* in such sentences as *non balla più*. Caterina Donati, **La sintassi della comparazione*, Padua, Unipress, 2000, 220 pp. L. Lonzi, 'Either "subject-oriented" or merely sentential', *Renzi Vol.*, 213–32, refutes the existence of a class of subject-oriented sentence adverbs, arguing instead that the different uses of adverbs like *intelligentemente* in *Intelligentemente, Maria ha istruito Giovanni* and *Giovanni si è comportato intelligentemente* should be clearly distinguished. In the first example, the adverb receives a subject-oriented interpretation and is subject to the structural condition that it enter into a c-command control relation with the agent subject (hence its general incompatibility with passive sentences), whereas in the second sentence the adverb has the value of an evaluative sentence adverb involving sentential scope but not c-command. F. Travisi, 'Morfosintassi dei pronomi relativi nell'uso giornalistico contemporaneo', *SGI*, 19, 2000:233–86, charts the use of relative pronouns in journalistic prose from the 1950s to the late 1990s, noting a general increase in relative clause usage and in the overall use of *che*, in contrast to the increasingly less frequent *il quale* and the indirect relative *cui*. C. Cecchetto, 'Doubling structures and reconstruction', *Probus*, 12, 2000:93–126, proposes a unified movement analysis of clitic left-dislocation (ClLD) constructions and clitic doubling, arguing that the unexpected absence of parasitic gaps and weak cross over effects under the movement analysis of ClLD is a consequence of a particular kind of trace left by left-dislocated DPs. Mara Frascarelli, **The syntax-phonology interface in focus and topic constructions in Italian*, Dordrecht, Kluwer, 2000, 224 pp. The fine structure of the left periphery of the clause is explored in three thought-provoking articles in *Renzi Vol.*: P. Benincà, 'The position of topic and focus in the left periphery' (35–64), provides an excellent detailed discussion of the ordering and semantico-pragmatic interpretation of elements occurring in the CP space. Building on Rizzi's seminal study, B. makes a convincing case for a modified structure consisting of a single Topic projection above FocP, a Disc(ourse)P above ForceP hosting hanging topics, and identifies wh-exclamatives with the specifier position of ForceP. C. Poletto, 'Complementizer deletion and verb movement in standard Italian' (265–86), exploits the split-CP hypothesis to explain a number of complementizer deletion phenomena in standard Italian and northern Italian dialects, proposing that in such cases the finite verb, attracted by an irrealis feature (subjunctive clauses) or an operator feature (disjunctive clauses), raises to at least one of two possible complementizer positions. L. Rizzi, 'On the position "Int(errogative)" in the left periphery of the clause' (287–96), is an important revision to the author's earlier influential work on the CP space, proposing a further functional projection 'Int(errogative)P' sandwiched between both topic projections, whose head and specifier positions are argued to host the indirect interrogative complementizer *se* and the *wh*-phrase *perché*, respectively. S. Suzuki, 'I costituenti a sinistra e la constrastività in italiano antico e moderno', *AGI*, 86: 57–78, is a truly enlightening discussion and comparison of the syntactic, semantic, and pragmatic differences characterizing left-dislocated and focused structures in early Tuscan and modern Italian.

Nunzio La Fauci, *Forme romanze della funzione predicativa: teorie, testi, tassonomie*, Pisa, ETS, 2000, 142 pp., is a collection of six revised essays. P.-M. Bertinetto, ' "Propulsive" tenses in modern Italian fictional prose', *Renzi Vol.*, 97–115, questions the continued dominance of the *passato remoto* as the unmarked narrative tense in 20th-c. fictional prose, noting how it is frequently replaced by the "epic" present, the compound past, and even the pluperfect. Giancarlo Buoiano, *Tempo, aspetto e azione verbale in italiano, inglese e danese*, Pescara, Libreria dell'Università, 1998, 315 pp. F. Benucci, 'Aspect prefixes in verbal periphrases in Italian and other Romance languages', *Renzi Vol.*, 65–96, draws a parallel between clitic placement (e.g. *voglio vederlo* vs *lo voglio vedere*) and that of aspectual prefixes (e.g. *voglio rivederlo* vs ??*lo rivoglio vedere*) in terms of Cinque's highly articulated clause structure. G. Cinque, ' "Restructuring" and the order of aspectual and root modal heads', *ib.*, 136–55, continues C.'s research into the functional structure of the clause, adducing evidence from Italian restructuring constructions as to the precise position and ordering of modal and aspectual projections. P. Stichauer, 'Su alcune costruzioni con verbo supporto in italiano', *LPr*, 10, 2000: 37–50, discusses the notions of operator and argument in terms of an analysis of support verbs and nominal verbs, drawing on Italian constructions with the support verbs *avere*, *fare*, *dare*, and *prendere*. A. Giorgi and F. Pianesi, 'Sequence of tense phenomena in Italian: a morphosyntactic analysis', *Probus*, 12, 2000: 1–32, explores the availability of the so-called double access reading in the temporal interpretation of complement clauses: whereas the embedded indicative verb in *Gianni ha detto che Maria è incinta* is interpreted as simultaneous both with respect to the time of the utterance and the time of the saying, the embedded subjunctive verb in *Gianni credeva che Maria fosse incinta* is interpreted as simultaneous only with the matrix. Such behaviour, and the possibility in certain cases to delete the complementizer, lead the authors to conclude that Italian has two different complementizers exhibiting distinct morphosyntactic properties. M. Manzini, 'Sentential complementation', pp. 241–67 of *Lexical Specification and Insertion*, ed. Peter Coopmans, Martin Everaert, and Jane Grimshaw, Amsterdam, John Benjamins, 2000, xvii + 476 pp., maintains that a subjunctive in general is an indefinite T bound by an intensional operator in a syntactic dependency, which like other syntactic dependencies, proves sensitive to islands and parasitic gap configurations, concluding that the selection of the subjunctive by certain classes of lexical predicates follows as a consequence of their ability to embed intensional operators.

Guido Mensching, *Infinitive Constructions with Specified Subjects. A syntactic analysis of the Romance Languages*, OUP, 2000, xiv + 267 pp., traces in considerable detail the distribution and syntactic properties of infinitival constructions with overt subjects in the history of Italian and the dialects, and attempts to explain the licensing of overt nominative subjects in terms of a compositional approach ($\pm$Agr, $\pm$Tns) to verbal inflection. G. Longobardi, ' "Postverbal" subjects and the mapping hypothesis', *LI*, 31, 2000:691–702, examines the interpretation and distribution of indefinites in support of the claim that post-verbal subjects may occupy one of two possible positions: either a VP-internal position or a focus or dislocation position within the left-periphery (accompanied by remnant movement). L. concludes that the behaviour of Italian indefinites lends further support to Diesing's mapping hypothesis, according to which presuppositional NPs must vacate the VP. A. Cardinaletti, 'A second thought on *emarginazione*: destressing vs. "right dislocation" ', *Renzi Vol.*, 117–35, proposes on the basis of the distribution of quantified constituents, binding phenomena, and agreement patterns two distinct structural derivations for Italian VSO (*ha comprato* GIANNI*, il giornale*) and VOS (*ha comprato* IL GIORNALE*, Gianni*) orders, despite similar prosodic and pragmatic properties, analysing the former as a case of *emarginazione* of the object (remaining *in situ*) and the latter a case of right-dislocation of the subject. C. Tortora, 'Evidence for a null locative in Italian', *ib.*, 313–26, presents persuasive evidence for recognizing a subclass of unaccusative predicates that subcategorize for an implicit GOAL argument. These predicates, in contrast to other unaccusatives, force a speaker-oriented GOAL reading whenever the overt subject is post-verbal (*È arrivata una ragazza* 'a girl has arrived (here)' vs *Una ragazza è arrivata* 'A girl has arrived (somewhere)'), a structure which finds a striking parallel in the Piedmontese dialect of Borgomanero where the thematicized implicit GOAL argument is overtly realized in the locative clitic *ghi*, namely *ngh è rivà-gghi na fjola*. These facts are explained by proposing that in the case of a post-verbal subject the vacant preverbal subject position is targeted by the subcategorized (null) locative argument. Post-verbal subjects of unergatives receive a quite different explanation in A. Belletti, ' "Inversion" as focalization', pp. 60–90 of *Subject Inversion in Romance and the Theory of Universal Grammar*, ed. Aafke Hulk and Jean-Yves Pollock, OUP, vii + 215 pp., who, observing that post-verbal subjects tend to carry new information, argues for a lower FocP within the IP space where such subjects can be licensed. On this interpretation, the ungrammaticality of VSO orders follows as a consequence of a minimality violation triggered by the subject intervening between the base position and the Case-licensing position of the object.

6. SEMANTICS

C. Andorno, 'Avverbi focalizzanti in italiano. Parametri per un'analisi', *SILTA*, 28, 1999:43–83, provides an excellent overview of the principal semantic properties of focus particles like *anche, solo, proprio, almeno*, paying particular attention to such notions as informativeness, quantification, scalar implicature, presupposition, and pragmatic entailment. A. Ferrari, 'Tra rappresentazione ed esecuzione: indicare la "causalità testuale" con i nomi e con i verbi', *SGI*, 18, 1999:113–44, focuses on the question of the semantic nature and pragmatic effects of textual causality as expressed by nouns and verbs in contrast to grammatical words or discourse markers, as well as addressing related issues such as the distinction between directive and representative meanings/connectives and their pragmatic effects, and the communicative salience of causal relations. E. Jezek, 'Classi verbali e composizionalità: il caso della doppia inaccusatività nell'italiano', *SILTA*, 29, 2000:289–310, proposes a lexical split between two classes of unaccusative predicate (e.g. simplex *svenire* vs pronominal *dissolversi*), which in aspectual terms can be interpreted as the syntactic counterpart of two different kinds of telic event. M. Lo Duca, 'Proprietà valenziali e criteri di descrizione lessicografica: un caso di alternanza argomentale', *ib.*, 219–42, explores the most appropriate lexicographic classification of verbs with variable valencies (e.g.

transitive/intransitive, transitive/ergative alternations). H. Siller-Runggaldier, 'Fra semantica e formazione delle parole: i cambiamenti di valenza verbale', *ItStudien*, 21, 2000:233–68, asks whether changes in verb valency, and hence changes in argument structure (e.g. transitive *Il contadino brucia la paglia* vs intransitive *La paglia brucia*), should be treated as a purely semantic phenomenon or as a productive word-formation process, concluding that they involve a marginal type of conversion with semantic characteristics largely comparable to those found with prefixation. A. Giorgi and F. Pianesi, 'Imperfect dreams: the temporal dependencies of fictional predicates', *Probus*, 13:31–68, demonstrates that the interpretative properties (the availability of temporal anchoring, presence/absence of a speaker-oriented propositional attitude) of indicative complement clauses embedded under *sognare* are largely determined by the choice of embedded tense, a generalization which the authors propose to capture at the syntactic level by assuming some degree of interaction between the temporal features of T and those of C. U. Wandruszka, 'Über die Bedeutung des romanischen Konjunktivs und die Geburt des Nebensatzes', *ZRP*, 116, 2000:56–71, considers the distribution of the indicative and subjunctive moods, concluding that the choice of mood in subordinate clauses be interpreted as a type of morphosyntactic government between main and dependent verbs. M. Moneglia, 'Cambiamenti semantici palesi e nascosti nel lessico verbale italiano: le transizioni di possesso', *LS*, 2000, 35:629–63, explores the semantic changes evident in the differing uses of the two verbs of possession transition, *prendere* and *togliere*, in 13th- and 14th-c. Tuscan and contemporary Italian. P. Koch, 'Indirizzi cognitivi per una tipologia lessicale dell'italiano', *ItStudien*, 21, 2000:99–117.

7. PRAGMATICS AND DISCOURSE

Jacqueline Visconti, *I connettivi condizionali complessi in italiano e in inglese: uno studio contrastivo*, Alessandria, Orso, 2000, 265 pp., provides an excellent comparative analysis of the semantic and pragmatic properties of complex conditional connectives in English and Italian, such as *supposing* or *a condizione che*. Reflecting on such theoretical concepts as 'connective', 'context', and 'lexical entry', the discussion raises important issues both from a lexical-semantic and a text-linguistic perspective. Bice Mortara Garavelli, **Le parole e la giustizia: divagazioni grammaticali e retoriche su testi giuridici italiani*, T, Einaudi, 264 pp. Luciano Vitacolonna, **Principi e contributi di semiotica del testo*, Ro, Bulzoni, 2000, 236 pp. Ugo Volli, **Manuale di semiotica*, Ro, Laterza, 2000, 278 pp. Alessandro Perissinotto, **Il testo multimediale: gli ipertesti* *tra semiotica e didattica*, T, UTET, 2000, 247 pp. Alessandro Capone, **Dilemmas and Excogitations: An Essay on Modality, Clitics and Discourse*, Messina, Siciliano, 2000, 189 pp., and 'Dilemmas and excogitations: considerations on modality, clitics and discourse', *LS*, 35, 2000:447–69, both explore the semantic-pragmatic interpretation of clitic *lo* in conjunction with verbs of propositional attitude. D. Porietti, ' "Comunque": dalla frase al testo', *SGI*, 19, 2000:175–231, traces the development of *comunque* into a textual connective through an examination of its use and meaning in 19th- and 20th-c. literary texts. A.-M. De Cesare, 'Fra teoria e pratica: sintassi, semantica e traduzioni inglesi dell'avverbio "proprio" ', *SILTA*, 30:143–69, undertakes a detailed analysis of the semantic and syntactic properties of the intensifying use of *proprio* and the two similar adverbs *davvero* and *molto* in spoken discourse. S. Bruti, ' "In fact" and "infatti": the same, similar or different', *Pragmatics*, 9, 1999:519–33, investigates the degree of equivalence between English *in fact* and Italian *infatti*, observing that, although both terms satisfy the same syntactic criteria and their respective lexical meanings both appear to contribute to illocutionary focus, English *in fact* occurs more naturally in declaratives, whereas Italian *infatti* tends to occur more frequently in second-speaker responses, either alone or in conjunction with other words. C. Aslanov, 'Interpreting the language-mixing in terms of code-switching: the case of the Franco-Italian interface in the Middle Ages', *JP*, 32, 2000:1273–81, analyses a number of cases of code-switching between French and Italian in two medieval texts, which are shown to be motivated by both extralinguistic and intralinguistic factors. G. Nardini, 'When husbands die: joke-telling in an Italian ladies' club in Chicago', *Pragmatics*, 10, 2000:87–97. M. Pagan, 'Le allocuzioni nelle commedie di Goldoni (1738–1751)', *SGI*, 19, 2000:141–73, surveys the various forms of address used in 32 early Goldoni plays, interpreting the attested forms in relation to 18th-c. social divisions and exploring their use in relation to alternative expression of second-person reference.

8. LEXIS

G. Nencioni, 'Il "rovesciamento" del primo vocabolario della Crusca (1612)', *IJL*, 14:21–22, reports on recent work which has now made the Accademia's 1612 *Vocabolario* available on CD-ROM and which will also shortly lead to its general availability on the Internet. **Glossario degli antichi volgari italiani*, ed. Giorgio Colussi, Foligno, Editoriale Umbra, 2000, 664 pp. P. Beltrami, 'Il *Tesoro della lingua italiana delle origini* ovvero "Il vocabolario del CNR" ', Lepschy,

Dictionaries, 33–49, reports on the progress of ongoing work on a dictionary of old Italian, which can be consulted at <www.csovi.fi.cnr.it.>. F. Sabatini, 'La grammatica delle valenze e la dimensione testuale della lingua nel *DISC*', *ib.*, 111–27, highlights the innovations employed by Sabatini and Coletti in their *Dizionario italiano Sabatini Coletti*. G. Lepschy, 'About new dictionaries', *ib.*, 3–9, provides an excellent, albeit brief, comparative survey of a number of modern monolingual dictionaries. C. Cirillo, 'Gender and feminine agentives in Italian dictionaries: 1612–1917', *ib.*, 11–23, charts the main developments in the treatment of gender and agentive nouns through three centuries of Italian lexicography, concentrating on such issues as the criteria used in classifying nouns according to their gender, how such information is indicated, and the arrangement of entries in the case of derivatives referring to women. J. Visconti, 'Dictionaries as research tools: *casomai* and other conjunctions', *ib.*, 25–32, evaluates the usefulness of dictionaries as a tool in linguistic analysis through an examination of conditional conjunctions. G. Rovere, 'Gradi di lessicalizzazione nel linguaggio giuridico', *SILTA*, 28, 1999:395–412. Federico Faloppa, **Lessico e alterità: la formulazione del diverso*, Alessandria, Orso, 2000, 167 pp. Emilio D'Agostino, **Le forme lessicali del parlare: analisi quantitativa e qualitativa del parlato italiano*, Na, Editoriale Scientifica, 209 pp. Bruna Monica Quartu, **Dizionario dei modi di dire della lingua italiana: 10.000 modi di dire ed estensioni figurate in ordine alfabetico per lemmi portanti e campi di significato*, Mi, Rizzoli, 2000, xiii + 714 pp. Marco Zanni, **Ditelo con gli insulti e non accontentatevi di un semplice vaffanculo. Dizionario completo degli insulti italiano–inglese*, Reggio Emilia, Tecnograf, 1999, 269 pp. M. De Boer, 'Le cazzate di Coliandro: osservazioni sintattiche, semantiche e pragmatiche sulle parolacce italiane', *ItStudien*, 21, 2000:35–64, explores the use of *cazzo*, its derivatives (e.g. *cazzata, cazziare, scazzare*), and other *parolacce* as used in a novel by Carlo Lucarelli.

F. Crevatin, 'Note etimologiche italoromanze', *ILing*, 22, 1999:177–79. H. J. Wolf, 'Die italienische Parallele zu frz. *denrée*. Erbwörter und Erstbelege', *ZRP*, 117:82–98, surveys a large number of lexicographic records and early Italo-Romance texts, comparing and contrasting cognates of the French *denrée*. O. Valikangas, '*Ja ja, ja déjà* et *già già* en français et en italien au XVIe siècle', *NMi*, 101:365–72, sketches the development, distribution, and mutual influence of the rival adverbial pairs *ja (ja)/déjà* and *già (già)/di già* in 16th-c. literary French and Italian. F. Rainer, 'Juristenlatein und Handelssprache: It. *cambiale* "Wechsel"', *ZRP*, 116, 2000:591–3, investigates the origins of the Italian terms *lettera di cambio* and *cambiale*, noting how the former, which had been in use since the Middle Ages, began to be replaced by the latter in the 18th century. F. Rainer, 'L'origine di *alco(o)lismo*', *LN*, 62:42–3, concludes that Italian *alco(o)lismo* is most probably a calque of a neo-Latin term *alcoholismus*, rather than a calque of the corresponding German or French terms. Id., 'Tarantismo', *ib.*, 58. Edoardo Bianchini, **Italiano straniero: piccolo repertorio storico dei barbarismi e dei significati che mutano nella lingua italiana*, Perugia, Guerra, 1999, 180 pp. Tullio De Mauro and Marco Mancini, **Parole straniere nella lingua italiana*, Mi, Garzanti, xvi + 800 pp. F. Casadei, 'Le locuzioni preposizionali. Struttura lessicale e gradi di lessicalizzazione', *LS*, 36:43–79, presents a detailed syntactic analysis of prepositional compounds such as *a causa di* and *al termine di*, which are demonstrated to exhibit differing degrees of morphosyntactic cohesion which can, in turn, be mapped on to a cline of lexicalization. M. Conenna, 'Structure syntaxique des proverbes français et italiens', *Langages*, 139, 2000:27–38, applies Maurice Gross's lexical-grammatical model to the study of proverbs.

9. SOCIOLINGUISTICS

Two valuable articles dealing with Italian sociolinguistics from a diachronic perspective are: M. Dardano, 'Ist eine historische Soziolinguistik des Altitalienischen möglich?', *Soziolinguistica*, 13, 1999:4–16, a general overview of the state of research into the sociolinguistic situation in early Italy; and C. Giovanardi, 'Soziolinguistik und italienische Sprachgeschichte: einige Betrachtungen zur Debatte im 16. Jahrhundert', *ib.*, 17–26, which surveys the work of 16th-c. Italian philologists and grammarians to investigate the relationship between Italian language history and sociolinguistics. Arturo Tosi, *Language and society in a changing Italy*, Clevedon, Multilingual Matters, xii + 288 pp., organized into three sections dealing with 'everyday language', 'special languages', and 'language contacts', provides a comprehensive survey of the relationship between language and society in contemporary Italy, with extensive overviews of linguistic diversity, social variation, special codes, and language varieties within Italian society, and in situations of language contact both within and outside Italy. As an up-to-date account of the Italian sociolinguistic situation, this book will prove a rich source of information for both students and scholars alike. Immacolata Tempesta, **Varietà della lingua e rete sociale*, Mi, Angeli, 2000, 123 pp., presents empirical research on the interrelation between linguistic behaviour and social environment. R. Casapullo, 'Qualche appunto su norma e uso nell'italiano contemporaneo', *FBS*, 30, 2000:19–31, is a fascinating exploration of some of the problems of linguistic unity in contemporary Italy, including the role, if any, of such bodies as the Accademia della Crusca, the excessive influence of the spoken language on the written language, the incorporation of geographical and social variation, and prescriptive concerns about the high number of current Anglicisms in the language. G. Berruto, 'La sociolinguistique européenne: le substandard et le code switching', *Sociolinguistica*, 14, 2000:66–73, proposes that the term 'substandard', increasingly frequent in Italian and German sociolinguistics since the 1980s, be reserved as a preliminary analytic concept embracing everything that deviates from the standard form of the language, while adducing examples of code-switching between Swiss German and Italian and between Italian and Sicilian to argue against Myers-Scotton's universal code-switching model. J. Vizmuller-Zocco, 'Il sostrato dialettale nella deriva dell'italiano neo-standard', *Italica*, 76, 1999:469–79, evaluates the influence of the dialects on the development of contemporary spoken standard Italian, highlighting 14 examples of variability in contemporary spoken Italian attributable to the dialectal substrate. M. Cortelazzo, 'L'italiano e le sue varietà: una situazione in movimento', *LS*, 36:417–30, identifies a number of areas where grammatical structures and features (e.g. indicative substituting subjunctive, *lui/lei* substituting *egli/ella*), which were previously defined as substandard, have now been fully integrated into the standard language. F. Cleis, ' "Anche la mia capa è stata apprendista". La sessuazione del discorso: lingua italiana e Canton Ticino', *BSLA*, 72, 2000:81–106, surveys essays by Marina Mizzau and Patrizia Violi that raise issues regarding gender-equal language usage in Italian, sketching the history of non-sexist language as a political issue in Italy and various academic and political attempts to change traditional sexist usage. C. concludes with an examination of the impact of language feminization in the Canton Ticino, which is claimed to be lagging behind the rest of Switzerland in gender-equal usage. C. Robustelli, 'Lingua e identità di genere. Problemi attuali nell'italiano', *SILTA*, 29, 2000:507–27, identifies a number of unresolved problems in the choice between masculine and feminine forms of titles, agreement phenomena, and agentive nouns in current usage. M. Bicio, 'Forme e modelli di italiano radiofonico: Radio Onda Ligure', *RID*, 23, 1999[2000]:203–34. P. Diadori, 'The language of Italian TV sales', *CJIS*, 23, 2000:123–46. *Corpus di italiano parlato, ed. Emanuela Cresti, 2 vols, F, Accademia della Crusca, 2000, 282, 389 pp. + 1 CD-ROM. G. Antonelli, 'Moduli sintattici e contesti funzionali nella narrativa italiana degli ultimi quarant'anni', *ASNSL*, 237, 2000:305–37, makes a convincing case for the increasing influence of the syntax of spoken Italian on narrative style over the last 40 years, as witnessed by the growing use of such phenomena as dislocation, parataxis, nominalizations, and repetition. Stefan Schneider, *Il congiuntivo tra modalità e subordinazione: uno studio sull'italiano parlato*, Ro, Carocci, 1999, 207 pp. *La variazione linguistica: tra scritto e parlato*, ed. Ines Loi Corvetto, Ro, Carocci, 2000, 175 pp. Claudia Dinale, *I giovani allo scrittoio*, Padua, Esedra, 240 pp. Pietro Trifone, *L'italiano a teatro: dalla commedia rinascimentale a Dario Fo*, Pisa, IEPI, 2000, 179 pp. Daniela Forapani, *L'italiano dell'economia*, Perugia, Guerra, 2000, 151 pp. + 1 CD-ROM, 1 audiocassette and 1 videocassette. Giovanni Ragone and Emiliano Laurenzi, *Analogie: introduzione al linguaggio della pubblicità*, Na, Liguori, ix + 222 pp. Fabio Rossi, *Le parole dello schermo: analisi linguistica del parlato di sei film dal 1948 al 1957*, Ro, Bulzoni, 1999, 548 pp.

10. PSYCHOLINGUISTICS AND LANGUAGE ACQUISITION

Giacomo Stella, *Sviluppo cognitivo: argomenti di psicologia cognitiva*, Mi, B. Mondadori, 2000, xiv + 142 pp. P. Bottari, P. Cipriani, A.-M. Chilosi, and L. Pfanner, 'The Italian determiner system in normal acquisition, specific language impairment, and childhood aphasia', *BL*, 77:283–93, compares the development of the Italian determiner system in aphasic and SLI children with that found in normally developing children. E. Bates, P. Marangolo, L. Pizzamiglio, and D. Frederic, 'Linguistic and nonlinguistic priming in aphasia', *BL*, 76:62–69. Donella Antelmi, *Fisiologia e patologia dell'apprendimento linguistico*, Mi, Arcipelago, 1999, 128 pp.

Il suono delle parole: percezione e conoscenza del linguaggio dei bambini, ed. Margherita Orsolini, Mi, La Nuova Italia, 2000, xiv + 353 pp. L. D'Odorico, S. Carubbi, N. Salerni, and V. Calvo, 'Vocabulary development in Italian children: a longitudinal evaluation of quantit-ative and qualitative aspects', *JCL*, 23:351–72, charts the rate of lexical acquisition in children from 1;0 until the 200 word stage, placing particular attention on the referential-expressive distinction and the timing of vocabulary spurts. Stefania Ferraris, *Imparare la sintassi: lo sviluppo della subordinazione nelle varietà di apprendimento di italiano L1 e L2*, Vercelli, Mercurio, 1999, 303 pp. M.-T. Guasti and G. Chierchia, 'Backward versus forward anaphora: reconstruction in child grammar', *LaA*, 8, 1999–2000:129–70, unifies under Principle C of the Binding Theory a number of seemingly unrelated cases of backward and forward anaphora, the latter involving LF reconstruc-tion effects. The fact that Italian-speaking children develop an early mastery of both constructions is argued by the authors to provide direct evidence of a biologically-determined mechanism subsuming both standard Principle C effects and cases of reconstruction. Cecilia Andorno, *Focalizzatori fra connessione e messa a fuoco: il punto di vista delle varietà di apprendimento*, Mi, Angeli, 2000, 294 pp. M. S. Barbieri and E. Bascelli, 'La comprensione dei verbi modali epistemici e deontici in età evolutiva', *GIP*, 27, 2000:529–48, reports the results of an experiment designed to compare the acquisition of deontic and epistemic modality in children aged between three and nine years, demonstrating that comprehension of deontic modal forms precedes that of epistemic modal forms. Jeannette Schaeffer, *The Acquisition of Direct Object Scrambling and Clitic Placement: Syntax and Pragmatics*, Amsterdam, Benjamins, 2000, xii + 187 pp., concludes from experimental data that Italian clitic placement and Dutch direct object scrambling are similar syntactic processes, both proving optional in early grammar as a result of their acquisition being largely determined by pragmatic factors.

11. Dialectology

L. Savoia, 'Note sulla formazione degli studi linguistici e dialettologici in Italia', *SGI*, 19, 2000:363–421, traces the development of Italian linguistics and dialectology as a discipline in Italy since the beginning of the 19th c., stressing the overwhelming influence of Ascoli's strictly empirical descriptive model and the strong idealistic influence of Benedetto Croce on Italian linguistics since the early 20th c. M. Loporcaro, 'Dialect variation across time and space and the explanation of language change', *Sprachwissenschaft*, 25, 2000:387–418, reconsiders the relationship between the study of dialect variation and external explanations of language change, highlighting the relevance of dialectology and the use of dialect data in diachronic linguistics through the example of a case study of variation over time and space in the pronominal clitic systems of a number of Italo-Romance dialects. M. Manzini and L. Savoia, 'The syntax of object clitics: *si* in Italian dialects', *Renzi Vol.*, 233–64, investigates within a minimalist framework the variable ordering of object clitics in relation to indefinite *si/se* in a wide-range of northern, central, and southern dialects.

NORTHERN DIALECTS. Cecilia Poletto, *The Higher Functional Field. Evidence from Northern Italian Dialects*, OUP, 2000, xii + 207 pp., represents a truly impressive initial sketch of the finer structure of the higher portion of the clause, the structural space situated between the functional projections traditionally labelled IP and CP, through an in-depth examination of the distribution and behaviour of subject clitics in one hundred different northern dialects. Evidence from the latter leads P. to recognize four distinct classes of subject clitic, two situated within the CP space (invariable and deictic clitics) and two within the IP space (number and person clitics) forming what she terms the agreement field. In addition to providing an original and appealing analysis of subject clitics, the proposed analysis of the agreement field, together with a richly-articulated split CP space, is demonstrated to have significant implications for related issues such as subject positions (for example, QP and DP subjects are argued to occupy distinct positions), interrogatives, which apparently exploit an 'interrogative field' within the CP space, V-second phenomena, complementizer deletion, and various types of subjunctive clause (the latter two both derived via V-movement to positions within the CP space). Pietro Monti, *Vocabolario della Gallia cisalpina e celtica*, Pavia, Liutprand, 2000, xi + 139 pp. L. Begioni, 'L'approccio microdialettometrico: verso una nuova definizione delle frontiere linguistiche nel continuum dialettale dell'Italia settentrionale', *RID*, 23, 1999[2000]:65–86, provides a linguistic description of the principal phonological and morphological microvariations found in a transitional area of the Apennines situated within the Emilia-Romagna region but displaying significant influences from the bordering Ligurian dialects. J. Hajek, 'How many moras? Overlength and maximal moraicity in Italy', Repetti, *Phonological Theory*, 111–35, challenges the traditional assumption of a maximal bimoraic structure for syllables in the light of evidence from standard Italian, Lombard, Friulan, and, in particular, Bolognese dialects which present some significant cases of trimoraicity manifested in three degrees of vowel quantity (e.g. Milanese /a/ 'at', /aː/ 'has; ah', and /aːː/ 'aah; yes'). J.-P. Montreuil, 'Sonority and derived clusters in Rhaeto-Romance and Gallo-Italic', Repetti, *Phonological Theory*, 211–37, compares complex word-initial onsets in some dialects of northern Italy and eastern Switzerland, demonstrating that the properties of derived clusters are quite different from those of underlying clusters.

PIEDMONT. Franco Castellani, *Dizionario del dialetto di Cascinagrossa*, Alessandria, Orso, 1999, xiv + 295 pp. Luciano Gibelli, *Dnans ch'a fàssa neuit: angign e ròbe dël passà salvà de la dësmèntia. Prima che scenda il buio: oggetti e cose del passato raccolte per non dimenticare*, Ivrea, Priuli & Verlucca, 1999, 679 pp. H. Goebl, 'Langues standards et dialectes locaux dans la France du sud-est et l'Italie septentrionale sous le coup de l'effet-frontière: une approche dialectométrique', *IJSL*, 145, 2000:181–215, draws on the evidence of the *ALF* and the *AIS* to highlight the impact of the national and para-national borders between France, Italy, and Switzerland on the dialectal make-up of south-eastern France and northern Italy. L. Zörner, 'La dittongazione nei dialetti francoprovenzali della Valle Orco: un confronto coi dialetti altoitaliani, occitanici e col francese antico', *RID*, 24, 2000[2001]: 111–24, undertakes an examination of diphthongization in the Franco-Provençal dialect of Noasca to determine its relationship to surrounding Occitan, French, and northern Italian dialect varieties. R. Bauer, 'Piemontesisch im Aostatal', *Linguistica*, 40, 2000: 117–30, examines the position of Piedmontese in the linguistic mix of the Aosta Valley, discussing the communicative functions and domains of usage of the dialect in relation to Italian, French, and Franco-Provençal. B. argues, on the strength of a survey exploring contemporary linguistic usage, that, whereas a century ago Piedmontese was perceived as a threat to Italian and French, today the position of the dialect is increasingly threatened by the pervasive presence of Italian.

LIGURIA. *Dizionario italiano–pietrese*, ed. Giacomo Accame, Genoa, De Ferrari, 1999, 196 pp. F. Toso, 'Contatto linguistico e percezione. Per una valutazione delle voci d'origine sarda in Taberchino', *Linguistica*, 40, 2000: 291–326, considers the considerable influence of Sardinian on the lexis of the Genoese dialects spoken on the islands of Carloforte and Calasetta situated to the southwest of Sardinia.

LOMBARDY. G. Sanga, 'Il dialetto di Milano', *RID*, 23, 1999[2000]: 137–64, embarks on a brief history of the dialect of Milan, which is considered in terms of three distinct chronological periods, namely archaic Milanese (unattested), modern Milanese (ancient, middle, classical), and contemporary Milanese, before providing a detailed description of the orthography, phonetics, and morphology of so-called classical Milanese, which S. identifies with the language of Porta and Cherubini. P. Prieto, 'Vowel lengthening in Milanese', Repetti, *Phonological Theory*, 255–72, proposes within an optimality-theoretic framework three constraints (Foot Binarity, High-Sonority-Nucleus, and Fill) to account for the restricted distribution of long vowels to word-final stressed syllables. Aldo Pola and Dante Tozzi, *Voci e locuzioni idiomatiche del dialetto tiranese (con profilo del dialetto di Tirano)*, Tirano, Poletti, 1998, 218 pp. Gian Battista Salvadori, *Vocabolario del dialetto di Roncone: ghe pàrlo àla mè set. Oltre 7600 lemmi dialettali con pronunzia, forme grammaticali, toponimi, dialoghi, filastrocche, cenni entografici ed espressioni gergali*, Roncone, Comune di Roncone, 1999, 523 pp.

VENETO. Marisa Milani, *El pì bel favelare del mondo: saggi ruzzantiani*, ed. Ivano Paccagnella, Padua, Esedra, 2000, xix + 200 pp. Manlio Cortelazzo, *Itinerari dialettali veneti*, Padua, Esedra, 1999, 175 pp. Rino Grandesso, *Strasse ossi e ferovecio … La tradizione orale nella civiltà contadina veneta del 20. secolo*, Camposampiero, Noce, 144 pp. Giuseppe Calò, **Veneziando*, Venice, Filippi, 1999, 162 pp. Giuseppe Brancale, **Istria: dialetti e preistoria*, Trieste, Italo Svevo, 1998, 142 pp. R. Zanuttini and P. Portner, 'The characterization of exclamative clauses in Paduan', *Language*, 76, 2000: 123–32, is an enlightening account of the properties of exclamative structures in Paduan, which are demonstrated to differ in many significant respects from their Italian equivalents.

EMILIA-ROMAGNA. L. Repetti, 'Uneven or moraic tronchees? Evidence from Emilian and Romagnol dialects', Repetti, *Phonological Theory*, 273–88, presents data from a number of dialects of Emilia-Romagna to provide support for the hypothesis that the (HL) trochaic foot is uneven. Pietro Mainoldi, **Manuale dell'odierno dialetto bolognese: suoni e segni, grammatica-vocabolario*, Bo, Forni, 2000, vii + 126 pp. Luigi Vitali, **Dizionario bolognese: italiano–bolognese, bolognese–italiano*, Mi, Vallardi, 2000, 570 pp. Libero Ercolani, **4500 modi di dire e 280 indovinelli in dialetto romagnolo*, Forlì, Marzocchi, 2000, xi + 687 pp.

CENTRAL AND SOUTHERN DIALECTS. Adam Ledgeway, *A Comparative Syntax of the Dialects of Southern Italy: A Minimalist Approach*, Oxford, Blackwell, 2000, xvi + 329 pp., a much-welcomed addition to an increasing body of work on the dialects of southern Italy, which have traditionally been a poorly understood and unexplored area of Italian dialectology, explores and brings together, for the first time in many cases, a large number of significant and hitherto unexplored syntactic phenomena in a wide range of dialects numbering nearly two hundred in total. While appealing to both traditional descriptive dialectologists and Romanists for the range and quantity of data it presents, it will also be of interest to theoretical linguistics for its generative analyses of such topics as object marking (dative shift, prepositional accusative), control, finiteness, infinitival complementation, and auxiliary selection. Id., 'Dialect syntax and generative grammar', Lepschy, *Dictionaries*, 73–89, highlights through an analysis of the prepositional accusative in the dialects of southern Italy the significance, unfortunately too frequently overlooked, of dialect data for issues in generative syntactic theory. L. Renzi, 'I dialetti italiani centro-meridionali tra le lingue romanze. Uno sguardo alla sintassi', *LS*, 36: 81–96, compares and contrasts four key areas in the syntax of the noun phrase in the dialects of Italy with an examination of the distribution of the definite article in conjunction with proper nouns and possessive adjectives (northern, Tuscan *la Maria* vs central-southern *Maria*), the pre- vs post-nominal positioning of the latter (northern, Tuscan *il mio amico* vs central-southern, Sardinian *l'amico mio*), the inventory and position of the quantifier 'many' (northern,

Tuscan *tanta frutta* vs central-southern *frutta assai*), and the form and position of focalizing adverbs meaning 'also' (northern, Tuscan *anche loro* vs central-southern *loro pure*). R. concludes that while Tuscan and northern dialects often coincide in many respects, dialects of the Centre-South show greater affinities with Romanian. J. Trumper and G. Chiodo, 'La pertinenza degli eventi catastrofici naturali per la dialettologia e la linguistica romanze', *RID*, 23, 1999[2000]:9–38, claims that the present state of the dialects of southern Italy has been shaped by demographic dynamics caused by seismic disasters over the last thousand years, with the exception of the archaic Lausberg zone which, on account of its exclusion from catastrophic seismic events, apparently represents the true southern linguistic type. M. Loporcaro, 'Stress stability under cliticization and the prosodic status of Romance clitics', Repetti, *Phonological Theory*, 137–68, noting that Italo-Romance strings consisting of verb + enclitic(s) present variable stress placement patterns (Italian: stress placement unaffected; Neapolitan: stress reassigned under adjunction of two or more enclitics; Stabiese: stress reassigned under adjunction of just one enclitic), rejects previous accounts based on the assumption that clitics subcategorize for different prosodic categories (Prosodic Word, Phonological Phrase, or Clitic Group), demonstrating instead that clitics invariably form part of the Prosodic Word. In contrast, L. argues that the variable patterns of stress placement derive from a parametric option allowing or forbidding stress to be reassigned post-lexically.

TUSCANY. *Nuovi testi pratesi dalle origini al 1320*, ed. Renzo Fantappiè, 2 vols, F, Accademia della Crusca, 2000, xxi + 573, 401 pp. Alessandro Bencistà, *Vocabolario del vernacolo fiorentino: con esempi delle principali voci da Dante a Benigni*, F, Libreria Chiari, 394 pp. L. Giannelli, 'Dare nomi alle cose. Percezione della realtà e verbalizzazione nell'ambiente di macchia', *RID*, 23, 1999[2000]: 235–64. Giulio Maffii, *Lessico della memoria d'un fiorentino*, F, Polistampa, 2000, 159 pp. G. Marotta, 'Oxytone infinitives in the dialect of Pisa', Repetti, *Phonological Theory*, 191–210, examines the aberrant rhythmical pattern of oxytone infinitival forms in the vernacular speech of Pisa and their interaction with such processes as *raddoppiamento fonologico*, concluding that Pisan should be analysed as having left-headed and right-headed feet. Gianluca Biasci, *L'evoluzione del dialetto pisano in un carteggio mercantile del 15. secolo*, Pescara, Libreria dell'Università, 1998, v + 276 pp. Guido Guidi, *Grammatica storica del vernacolo pisano*, Ospedaletto, Offset Grafica, 2000, 327 pp. Emilio Tolaini, *Pisano antico: le parole del mare. Termini volgari e mediolatini attinenti alle attività marinare pisane nel Medioevo*, Pisa, Nistri-Lischi, 1999, 143 pp.

CORSICA.   Alexandra Jaffe, **Ideologies in Action: Language Politics on Corsica*, Berlin, Mouton de Gruyter, 1999, x + 323 pp., presents an ethnographic study of language use and language planning on Corsica, where there has been a language shift away from the now minority language, Corsican, towards the official language French.

LAZIO.   **Roma e il suo territorio: lingua, dialetto e società*, ed. Maurizio Dardano, Ro, Bulzoni, 1999, 343 pp. Maurizio Trifone, **Lingua e società nella Roma rinascimentale*, F, Cesati, 1999, 717 pp., provides an in-depth historical linguistic analysis of late 15th-c. and early 16-c. Roman society through numerous unpublished documents by 355 writers of different social extraction. Ezio Urbani, **Il vernacolo viterbese: glossario viterbese–italiano, italiano–viterbese con note di grammatica e accenni di fonetica, morfologia e sintassi*, Viterbo, Sette Città, 1999, 203 pp.

ABRUZZO.   Antonio Sorella, **Studi linguistici abruzzesi*, Pescara, Libreria dell'Università, 2000, 129 pp. L. Marra, E. Villante, and M. Lolli, **Dizionario italiano aquilano italiano*, L'Aquila, Colacchi, 2000, 212 pp.

CAMPANIA.   B. Bullock, 'Consonant gemination in Neapolitan', Repetti, *Phonological Theory*, 45–58, considers Neapolitan *raddoppiamento sintattico* (RS) to be a lexically-determined phenomenon, triggered in conjunction with a restricted class of functional words endowed with a final bimoraic syllable that provides an additional timing slot which surfaces in RS under appropriate syntactic conditions. Interpreted within an optimality-theoretic framework, B. thus derives RS as a compromise between two competing constraints which require that i) certain syllables be bimoraic; and ii) final vowels remain short. Nicola De Blasi and Luigi Imperatore, *Il napoletano parlato e scritto. Con note di grammatica storica*, Na, Libreria Dante & Descartes, 2000, 236 pp., provides an excellent overview of the internal history of the dialect, with detailed sections on phonology, morphology, syntax, lexis, and orthography. A. Ledgeway, 'I tempi sovraccomposti nel napoletano antico', *ID*, 60, 1997–99:105–23, explores the origins of double compound perfective forms of the type *erano stati venuti* in early Neapolitan through an examination of the distribution of such forms in the 14th-c. *Libro de la destructione de Troya*, concluding that their emergence is linked to semantic and morphological changes in the reorganization of the passive voice in the passage from Latin to Romance. Early Neapolitan compound perfective forms are also the topic of inquiry in V. Formentin, 'L'ausiliazione perfettiva in antico napoletano', *AGI*, 86:79–117, which identifies a structural pattern in the gradual extension of auxiliary *avere* to unaccusative predicates in early Neapolitan texts. In particular, the first occurrences of auxiliary *avere* with unaccusatives are demonstrated to initially affect only verbs in the pluperfect subjunctive and the conditional perfect (e.g. *avesse / averria venuto*), whereas auxiliary *essere* is retained in conjunction with verb forms from other paradigms. B. Naddeo, *'Urban Arcadia: representations of the dialect of Naples in linguistic theory and comic theater, 1696–1780', *ECS*, 35:41–65. Two articles that explore the mix of spoken Italian and Neapolitan dialect in the films of the late actor Massimo Troisi are S. Bertucci, 'Il parlato cinematografico di Massimo Troisi', *RID*, 23, 1999[2000]: 165–202, and C. Stromboli, 'La lingua di *Ricomincio da tre* di Massimo Troisi', *ib.*, 24, 2000[2001]:125–66. Renato De Falco, *Del parlar napoletano: manualetto per tutti*, Na, Colonnese, 2000, 111 pp., contains some interesting notes on phonetics, morphology, and lexis. Francesco D'Ascoli, **La filosofia popolare napoletana: locuzioni tipiche del dialetto. Significato e origine*, Na, Gallina, 1999, 155 pp. Mario Del Noce, **Racconti napoletani: storia ed origine di antichi detti napoletani*, Lago Patria, Pironti, 1999, 182 pp. P. Como, 'Usi e funzioni del tipo verbale *fo-* a Monte di Procida', *RID*, 23, 1999[2000]:113–36, explores the distribution of two competing variants of the imperfect indicative of *essere* (*er-/fo-*) in the peripheral Neapolitan variety of Monte di Procida, noting how both occur with equal frequency in her oral corpus but are distributed unequally in the speech of individual speakers, though apparently not in accordance with particular semantic, stylistic-pragmatic, or sociolinguistic factors. P. Del Puente, 'Nuove colonie galloitaliche in Campania', *ILing*, 23, 2000:133–42, reports on the results of recent fieldwork investigations into the phonological structures of three dialects spoken in the villages of Torraca, Casalletto Spartano, and Vibonati, which, on the basis of the data presented, are demonstrated to be Gallo-Romance.

APULIA. Matteo Gioiosa, *Grammatica del dialetto sannicandrese*, San Nicandro Garganico, Gioiosa Editrice, 2000, 223 pp., despite its traditional scholastic approach, offers a surprisingly detailed and thorough treatment of the phonology, morphology, and syntax of the dialect of San Nicandro Garganico. Pasquale Ricciardelli, **La parlata di Torremaggiore*, Foggia, Leone, 1999, 399 pp. Vito Barracano, **Vocabolario dialettale barese*, Bari, Adda, 2000, 203 pp. Terry Brian Mildare, **Aspetti della fonologia e della morfologia del molese, un dialetto pugliese dell'Italia sud-orientale*, Bari, Levante, xv + 190 pp. A. Calabrese, 'The feature [Advanced Tongue Root] and vowel fronting in Romance', Repetti, *Phonological Theory*, 59–88, proposes within the constraint-and-repair model of phonology an explanation for the fronting rule /u/ > [y] in Altamurano (and Romance more generally) in terms of a feature [ATR]. F. D'Introno and R. Weston, 'Vowel alternation, vowel/consonant assimilation and OCP effects in a Barese dialect', *ib.*, 89–110, describe the complex patterns of atonic vowel retention, centralization to schwa, and raising in the dialect of Corato, which they variously ascribe to the place of articulation of the unstressed vowel, of any adjacent consonants, and of the following stressed vowel, and to the position of the unstressed vowel within the phrase. Raffaele Di Giulio, *La nostra parlata: ulteriore contributo al recupero e salvataggio del linguaggio dialettale brindisino. Dizionario fraseologico dialettale brindisino–italiano, italiano–brindisino*, Fasano, Schena, 1999, 684 pp. E. Tamborrino, 'Metaplasmo di genere e plurale in -*ure* intorno a Maglie (Lecce)', *RID*, 24, 2000[2001]: 29–52, investigates the vitality of gender differences in contemporary dialect and regional Italian (e.g. dialect *apu* 'ape', regional Italian *la comune*), and plural formations in -ORA > -*ure* in dialect (e.g. *càpure* 'teste d'aglio'). While the former phenomenon is demonstrated to be recessive in the modern dialects, the latter is shown to have fallen almost entirely out of use, now only occurring residually in a few isolated areas in a small number of lexicalized cases. A. Sobrero and A. Mighetta, 'I tanti nomi della ceramica in Salento: questione di confini o vaghezza semantica?', *QS*, 22:67–92.

CALABRIA. S. Iemmello, 'Italiano regionale e scolarizzazione: un case-study calabrese mediano', *RID*, 24, 2000[2001]: 97–110, assesses the extent of dialect interference on the regional Italian of Montepaone in the speech of four distinct groups of speakers distinguished by their differing degrees of education. Whereas morphological features are found to be particularly resilient to dialect interference, the phonology and syntax of the local variety of Italian exhibit considerable influence from the dialect substrate, particularly in the speech of the least educated. Bruno Tassone, *Grammatica e dizionario del dialetto crotonese*, Soveria Mannelli, Calabria Letteraria, 2000, 492 pp. Romano Napolitano, *Toponimi urbani ed extraurbani di Paola: saggio di toponomastica storico-linguistico-topografico*, Cosenza, Progetto 2000, 1999, 96 pp. Alessandro De Theis, *Spiegazione etimologica de' nomi generici delle piante*, Castrovillari, Prometeo, 2000, 186 pp. Francesco Cosco and Anna Maria Cosco, *Nella lingua ... la storia: vocabolario etimologico del dialetto della provincia di Crotone*, Soveria Mannelli, Calabria Letteraria, 2000, liii + 355 pp. Bruno Tassone, *Grammatica e dizionario del dialetto crotonese*, Soveria Mannelli, Calabria letteraria, 2000, 492 pp.

SICILY. L. Amenta, 'Tra lingua e dialetto: le perifrasi nell'italiano regionale di Sicilia', *RID*, 23, 1999[2000]:87–112, is a valuable comparative study of a number of gerundival, infinitival, and paratactic aspectual periphrases in standard Italian, Sicilian regional Italian, and Sicilian dialect, highlighting their differing aspectual meanings, morphological properties, and degrees of grammaticalization. Gaetano Cipolla, *Introduction to Sicilian Grammar*, NY, Legas, xiv + 225 pp. Mariano Fondacaro, *Vocabolario del dialetto ennese*, Enna, Il Lunario, xv + 549 pp. Massimo Genchi and Gioacchino Cannizzaro, *Lessico del dialetto di Castelbuono*, Palermo, CSFLS, 2000, xxvi + 409 pp. Giovanni Ruffino and Nara Bernardi, *Per una ricerca sulla cultura alimentare e sul lessico gastronomico in Sicilia: appunti e materiali*, CSFLS, 2000, 111 pp.

12. SARDINIAN

Gian Paolo Bazzoni, *Elementi di grammatica sassarese*, Sassari, Stampacolor, 1999, 88 pp. Giovanni Casciu, *Vocabulariu sardu campidanesu-italianu*, Dolianova, Grafica del Parteolla, 1999, 461 pp. Antonio Lepori, *Gramàtiga sarda po is campidanesus: daus obras in d-unu libru*, Cagliari, Quartu Sant'Elena, 253 pp. Shortly to be followed by a second volume is Massimo Pittau, *Dizionario della lingua sarda: fraseologico ed etimologico*, Cagliari, Gasperini, 2000, 1007 pp. Enzo Espa, *Dizionario sardo–italiano*, Sassari, Delfino, 1999, xix + 1430 pp. Mario Puddu, *Ditzionàriu de sa limba e de sa cultura sarda*, Cagliari, Condaghes, 2000, xxiii + 1828 pp. *La lingua sarda: l'identità socioculturale della Sardegna nel prossimo millennio. Pro loco di Senorbì. Atti del convegno di Quartu Sant'Elena, 9–10 maggio 1997*, ed. Roberto Bolognesi and Karijn Helsloot, Cagliari, Condaghese, 1999, 191 pp.

13. ITALIAN ABROAD

M. Russo, 'Orientalismi in un anonimo *Dictionnaire* della lingua franca (1830)', *ZRP*, 117:222–54, discusses the *lingua franca*, a predominantly Italian-based pidgin spoken on the Mediterranean coast from the Middle Ages to the early 20th c., against the valuable evidence contained in the 19th-c. anonymous *Dictionnaire de la langue franque* which, as highlighted in this work, also provides a large number of examples of common terms of Arabic and Turkish origin. S. Covino, 'Lingua e identità nazionale: un binomio problematico. La questione dell'italiano a Malta in alcuni studi recenti', *RID*, 23, 1999[2000]: 265–92, charts the history of the Italian language on the island of Malta as documented in a number of poorly-known recent studies, observing how for centuries Italian was the language employed in schools, courts, and by the clergy until the advent of English colonialism in the early 19th-c., which gave rise to the so-called *questione della lingua maltese*, a core political controversy that divided the pro-British imperialists and the pro-Italian nationalists for many decades. A. De Fina and F. Bizzoni, 'Un estudio sobre el deterioro del italiano hablado en la comunidad italiana residente en la ciudad de México', *EstLA*, 17, 1999–2000: 30–31, 253–70, investigates the influence of Spanish on the speech of first generation Italian immigrants living in Mexico City, highlighting the frequent phenomenon of copying and meaning extension.

DUECENTO AND TRECENTO I
DANTE

By CATHERINE M. KEEN, *Lecturer in Italian, University of Leeds*

1. GENERAL

Besides some valuable monographs, 2001 has seen the publication of a number of volumes that collect the studies of individual scholars into a single place. It seems appropriate to start the survey with one such volume, which deals with the early years of D.'s career as a writer. Guglielmo Gorni, *Dante prima della Commedia*, Fiesole, Cadmo, 299 pp., gathers essays providing valuable insight into D.'s early output of poetry and prose. A number of the essays have appeared elsewhere; their re-issue in a single collection emphasizes the continuity of G.'s concerns and the rigour of his philological method, where minute attention to details within the texts discussed proves, again and again, to have wide-ranging implications for our understanding of D.'s practice as a writer. The book has three main sections: the first is dedicated to D.'s personal and literary relationships with representatives of the early Tuscan tradition (especially Guittone); the second section is dedicated to the *VN*, and is particularly valuable in bringing together many of G.'s essays on editorial practice relating to his own edition (1996), as well as on issues of content; the final section includes essays on the *Cvo* and the *Fiore*, as well as additional essays on D.'s lyric practice, notably in the post-exile period. Article-length studies that deal with the progress from early works to later ones include: D. S. Cervigni, 'From beginning to end: Dante's Judeo-Christian fourfold mytho-poiesis', *AnI*, 18, 2000:143–74. It traces D.'s concern as author to mark his own creative presence in his texts — from *VN* to *DC* — and to show how this in turn emulates and points towards the presence of God's creative stamp on all creation, in accordance with Judeo-Christian tradition. The essay outlines how D.'s *œuvre* engages with the archetypal myths of creation, fall, redemption, and rebirth that shaped his cultural universe, working in different ways in different texts, yet collectively painting a coherent picture that is both distinctively individual and also universally applicable to the intertwined notions of end and beginning. O. Holmes, 'Dante's two beloveds: ethics as erotic choice', *ib.*, 19:25–50, investigates Dante's concern in several works — notably the *VN* and *Cvo*, besides the *DC* — with exploring the ethics of choice between vice and virtue, represented in the two favourite metaphors of choice between different paths, and choice between different women. The antecedents for both figures in classical and in scriptural tradition are explored in some detail, and H. shows how the turn towards vice is often figured as seduction. While D. does explore apparently straightforward binary oppositions — notably in the *VN*'s *donna gentile* episode, or in *Inf.*'s image of the *via smarrita* — H. shows that he often shifts the choice to selection between good and better, rather than bad and good, presenting a hierarchized continuum of choice rather than absolute oppositions. The essay suggests that this sense of continuity may inform D.'s predilection with three-part structures, where a preliminary choice leads on towards a further and more enlightened one, allowing mistaken choices of path or love to be corrected back towards the right, rather than leading to irreparable rupture. Another study that follows developments from the *VN* through to the *DC* is W. Pötters, ' "Ella era uno nove": rapporti geometrici fra la *Vita Nova* e la *Commedia*', *LIA*, 2 : 27–60. The article proposes an analysis of various numerological elements in the *VN* and *DC*, starting from the association of Beatrice with the number nine in *VN*, but also including, for instance, the DXV conundrum of *Purg.* xxxiii, as well as other episodes. P. suggests that numerical elements may constitute another portion of the allegory of the poem, and that careful correspondences must be assumed to link numerological and geometric references within and between the *VN* and *DC*. To follow the detailed argument requires, however, a better understanding of mathematics and geometry than the present reviewer possesses.

Two volumes of essays by Zygmunt Barański have appeared in the past two years: while often dealing with material he has treated in earlier publications, the essays have always been substantially reviewed and extended since their previous appearances, and considerable new material has been introduced, enhancing the scope and stimulus of two very coherent volumes. *Dante e i segni. Saggi per una storia intellettuale di Dante Alighieri*, Na, Liguori, 2000, x + 231 pp., is primarily concerned with exploring D.'s intellectual and artistic relationships with medieval hermeneutic and semiotic traditions, arguing for the need to recognize the equal, or greater, importance to D. of Neoplatonic as well as Aristotelian-Thomistic thinking. The opening chapters deal with general themes, and discuss developments in D.'s intellectual outlook over different phases of his career, from the early lyrics and the *VN*, through the *Cvo*, to the *DC*. The middle chapters are dedicated to the *DC*, offering detailed analysis of selected canti from the *Inf.* and the *Par.*, and investigating how D. uses the single narrative components of the poem to highlight themes and issues that have far wider significance for the comprehension of the whole. The final chapter turns to the *Questio*, arguing that in form and in content, this apparently scholastic, Aristotelian work actually points towards Neoplatonist conclusions. This final essay emphasizes B.'s broader critique, sustained throughout the volume, of the modern critical tendency to try to force D.'s work into a rationalist mould that appeals to 20th-c. intellectual assumptions, but which can often prove out of key with the medieval realities of the texts themselves. Id., '*Chiosar con altro testo*'. *Leggere Dante nel Trecento*, Fiesole, Cadmo, 181 pp., picks up on some of the same points as the 2000 volume regarding the importance of detaching ourselves from modern critical assumptions in understanding medieval texts. In this case, the majority of the texts under review are the Trecento commentaries on the *DC* — a broad category which includes the *Ep. a Cangrande*, Petrarch's *Triumphi*, and Boccaccio's *Trattatello*, as well as the more formal exegetical works of Benvenuto and Maramauro. The first chapter (a new essay which serves in part as an introduction to the following, more detailed, discussions of individual works) discusses the shortcomings of conventional modern approaches to the commentaries, arguing that critics often fail to understand the generic conventions and the critical methodologies of the medieval commentators; the following essays offer vivid illustrations of the new insights that can be gained by approaching the commentaries on their own terms. The readings of Boccaccio and Petrarch, in particular, cast some fascinating light onto the personal, poetic, and intertextual relationships between D.'s work and that of the other *due corone*; although the essay on P., perhaps due to the poet's notorious ambiguity regarding his knowledge and use of D., has less to say on the subject of D. reception than the others. The discussions of Benvenuto and M. (the latter again a previously unpublished study) provide insights into the mindset of those facing the challenge of applying — or in the case of M. creatively misapplying — traditional scholarly methods to the new text of the *DC*. The volume overall makes a valuable contribution to a field that B. shows to be ripe for new exploration, that of establishing how D. was read by his first audiences, in the century following his death. Issues relating to the reading of medieval texts — in this case back to D.'s own — are also addressed by Guy P. Raffa, *Divine Dialectic: Dante's Incarnational Poetry*, Toronto U.P., 2000, xii + 254 pp. The book focuses mainly on the *DC*, though it also considers the *VN* in some detail, arguing that the Incarnation occupies a cardinal position in D.'s approach both to history and to poetry. The term 'Incarnation' as used by R. takes on a rather specialized meaning, with roots both in theology (medieval and later) and in modern dialectical thought, to indicate an ability to 'have it both ways' or to present a 'both–and structure' (6) on issues normally seen as implying singular choice: humanity and the divine, action and contemplation, material and intellectual/spiritual desire, and so on. Similarly, pairs of souls from the *DC* can be viewed as examples of 'Incarnational' challenge: not only in the case of such obvious otherworldly neighbours as Ulisse and Diomede or Saints Francis and Dominic, but also, for instance, with Cacciaguida and Brunetto or Virgil and D.-character, R. emphasises that D. simultaneously embraces contradiction and resolution between the individuals, and the ideas or experiences that they represent. Similarly, in the *VN*, the protagonist's failure to understand Beatrice's Christological role in mediating between the human and the divine is classed as an Incarnational failure on the author's part (whether intentional or not). As these examples indicate, the terminology of the Incarnation covers a wide range of usage in the book, at times drifting towards jargon; but there is considerable satisfaction and subtlety in the volume's thesis that D.'s central hermeneutic insists on the continuity between apparent opposites, and that he invites his readers to bring this insight to bear in their strategies of reading not only his poem, but also the historical and the spiritual realities of the world(s) outside it.

An intriguing study that brings together questions of natural science and of hermeneutics is Alison Cornish, *Reading Dante's Stars*, Yale U.P., 2000, ix + 226 pp. C. argues that D. uses astronomical references throughout the *DC*, and elsewhere, to explore the questions of how to read, and how to represent, the realities of the universe, showing that allusions to stars and planets in D. repeatedly draw attention to issues of rhetoric, reception, and interpretation. The main focus of her study is the *DC*, but the introductory chapter also examines astrological and hermeneutic lore from the *VN* and *Cvo*, and the later chapters often cross-refer fruitfully to passages from the minor works. A small number of clear and helpful diagrams provide illustration for some of the less familiar or more abstruse aspects of medieval and Dantean cosmological thinking, and the text also offers clear explanations of the various scientific points. The range of reference extends from questions about the dating of the journey, to the practical application of astronomy in areas such as farming or navigation, to the more elevated areas of textual and scientific scholarship and to medieval semiotics: that is, the interpretation of astral and textual signs. Proceeding mostly by close readings of selected passages, the author provides detailed illustration of her thesis that D.'s interest in reading and interpretation is ethical in nature, and that astronomical references offer no mere rhetorical ornament but are fundamental to his poetics, throughout the *DC* providing visual parallels to his strategies of narrative representation.

The essays collected in Pinchard, *Pour Dante*, represent the proceedings of at least two conferences held in Paris during the past decade, to discuss a number of aspects of D. and a wide range of his works. Several of the articles are discussed in the appropriate sections below, where their matter deals strictly with a single work or part thereof, or with D.'s later *fortuna*, but two comparative articles are worth considering here. C. Trottmann, 'A propos des "duo ultima": de la *Monarchie* au *Banquet* et retour' (215–36), addresses the issue of D.'s view of the relationship between the spiritual and temporal powers, noting how his arguments fit the context of medieval debate over papal-imperial hierarchy, which also touched controversies regarding the beatific vision, and the relationship between moral philosophy and theology, addressed in D.'s philosophical treatises and elsewhere. T. opposes those critics who view the *Mon.* and *Cvo* as discontinuous in their attitude towards the two powers, stressing how D. avoids philosophical extremism in his contention that the two beatitudes identified in the closing pages of *Mon.* are conceived not as Averroistically opposed to one another, but rather as two linked phases on the same spiritual journey. B. Faes de' Mottoni, 'Il linguaggio e la memoria dell'angelo in Dante' (237–54), also draws out complementary ideas from different works, in this case *DC* and *DVE*. In the latter text, D. asserts that angels have no need of language, and in *Par.* xxix, of memory either: the critic shows these two statements to be fundamentally interconnected. The essay explores D.'s statements on these two angelic absences in relation to the pronouncements of Albert the Great and Aquinas on angelic intellection, suggesting that D.'s deliberate divergence from such authorities indicates a polemic with 'un esempio di vane e inutile discussioni terrene' (249). These polemical intentions seem only emphasized by D.'s technique of borrowing evidence from the scholastics' lists of refuted *auctoritates*, which he uses to bolster his own arguments for the opposite case.

The most recent volume of *DaSt*, 118 (2000), marks the transition to the new millennium by reprinting a number of important essays from the journal's first century of existence (1882–1982). The essays cover a diverse range of topics, and the roll-call of authors represents some illustrious names in the American history of D. studies. The selection furthermore allows the reader both to track different phases of interest in particular topics — for instance, questions about allegory, or about politics — and to access swiftly and easily a number of essays that have had a significant impact on the way that D. is read by scholars and students alike. The first three essays focus on the early years of the Dante Society of America, with two reprints of 19th-c. sketches of Dante scholars, and one excerpt from D.-inspired fiction. C. E. Norton, 'Remarks of Mr Norton at the Annual Meeting held on May 16, 1882' (1–6), offers tribute to the Society's founder, H. W.

Longfellow; biographical material is also covered in T. W. Koch, 'Dante in America: a historical and bibliographical study' (7–56); while M. Pearl, 'From *The Dante Club*' (57–84), provides an enjoyable extract from P.'s forthcoming historical novel, set in the milieu of a precursor body to the Society, Longfellow's 'Dante Club'. It provides vivid portraits of leading contemporary *dantisti*, intertwining an account of their critical and cultural activities with elements of a murder mystery, where the methods of a gruesome series of homicides imitate the punishments of *Inf.*: the present extract focuses on a 'Simoniac' murder victim. The remainder of the essays present purer examples of literary and cultural analysis: C. H. Grandgent, '*Quid ploras?*' (85–94); E. H. Wilkins, 'Reminiscence and anticipation in the *Divine Comedy*' (95–108); E. Williamson, 'De beatitudine huius vitae' (109–28); D. H. Gillerman, 'Trecento illustrations of the *Divina Commedia*' (129–66); C. S. Singleton, 'In exitu Israel de Aegypto' (167–88); J. Freccero, 'Dante's prologue scene' (189–216); G. Cambon, 'Dante's presence in American literature' (217–42); C. T. Davis, 'Dante's vision of history' (243–60); R. Hollander, 'Dante *theologus-poeta*' (261–302); and M. P. Simonelli, 'L'inquisizione e Dante: alcune osservazioni' (303–22). The final essay, G. Mazzotta, 'Reflections on Dante studies in America' (323–30), provides an appropriate counter-balance to the opening three, focusing as it does on American D. studies in the 20th c. M. offers criticism of the tendency to categorize European and North American approaches to D. in polarized terms, assigning philology to Europe and exegesis to the United States, and stresses rather that a highly creative tension often subsists between the scholarly outlooks of the two continents. His reflections on the contributions to American criticism by such European refugee scholars as Auerbach, Spitzer, and Leo provides a reminder of the very immediate and personal manner in which cross-fertilizations between schools and traditions can occur, producing valuable new insights to the texts. Among the postwar critics whose work M. singles out for praise are both critics represented among this number's selection of reissued essays, such as Hollander (for his inventive work on allegory) and Freccero (for his interpretation of D.'s figuralism), and those whose names were surely omitted only for reasons of space, such as Barolini and Durling, both notable for their work on linguistic issues. This year's *RMS*, 27, includes a special issue, 'Current trends in Dante Studies', with six Dantean essays (three reviewed in separate sections below). Z. G. Barański, 'Three notes on Dante and Horace' (5–37), discusses textual minutiae in a number of D.'s citations of H. that prove to cast significant light on his engagement with the *Ars poetica* and on the status of *DVE* as a manual directed specifically towards poetic, rather than more general prose/

dictaminal composition. The issues of D.'s attitude in the treatise towards the textual division of the Horatian *Ars*, his approach to *inventio*, and his citation of exemplary classical prose writers — with the notable omission of Cicero — are subjected to comparative investigation with the standard conventions of medieval rhetorical *artes*. B. shows that they mark deliberate divergences from the norm on D.'s part, part of a strategy that signals his own innovative, and highly specialized, undertaking. S. Gilson, 'Medieval science in Dante's *Commedia*: past approaches and future directions' (39–77), provides a valuable survey of critical approaches to scientific material in the *DC*. The essay's first section provides an assessment of what constitutes Dantean 'science', given that modern usage of this term has no exact medieval equivalent. A second section explores the different ways in which critics from the Renaissance to the present day have approached such material, and stresses the problems that arise from the tendency to consider it as a separate category, without contextualizing scientific passages with regard to their place both in the poem and in the wider medieval intellectual framework. The third section urges the importance of re-integrating consideration of D.'s science in the *DC* with that of its poetic presentation and function, investigating the different fashions in which D. deploys scientific lexis and imagery, and culminating with the brief but stimulating analysis of three passages from *Par.* where scientific references 'form part of a larger interlocking textual network' (54) that also produces literary, scriptural, and theological resonances. A valuable appendix provides brief notes on the available critical studies on various scientific topics, ranging from astronomy to alchemy or mathematics. C. M. Keen, 'The language of exile in Dante' (79–102), explores different aspects of the theme of exile in D.'s *œuvre*. A first section explores the spiritual significance of the themes of exile and *peregrinatio* in D.'s youthful *VN*, while further sections discuss the impact of historical exile on D.'s self-representation as author/ protagonist in the *Cvo* and in the *DC* in relation to both classical and Christian models. Linguistic thought and poetic practice in *DVE* and *DC* are placed in relation to both Ovidian and Babelic conceptions of how exile produces linguistic barbarism, concluding with the suggestion that St John the Baptist represents a compellingly Florentine, yet also scriptural, model for the enterprise of achieving appropriate exilic utterance.

2. Fortune

A fascinating insight into Dante's *fortuna* among visual artists is offered by Corrado Gizzi, *Dante istoriato: vent'anni di ricerca iconografica dantesca*,

Mi, Skira, 1999, 413 pp. The handsome volume provides a survey of the exhibitions organized over two decades at the Casa di D. in Abruzzo, covering artists from the Renaissance to the 20th c. as various as Botticelli, Michelangelo, Raphael, Blake, Flaxman, Dante Gabriel Rossetti, Dalì, and Guttuso (to name but a few), illustrated with numerous high quality colour plates. The accompanying essays provide contextual and interpretative material that stresses the perennial attraction felt by figurative artists towards illustrating and interpreting D.'s life and works over the centuries. A closing 'Antologia critica' (355–405) presents extracts from the writing of a number of distinguished art historians and critics on various of the works illustrated, and an appendix (411–13) gives full bibliographical details for the catalogues of each of the separate exhibitions surveyed in the main text. R. Owen, 'Dante's reception by 14th- and 15th-c. illustrators of the *Commedia*', *RMS*, 27: 163–225, explores a more restricted, but fascinating, aspect of the visual interpretation of the *DC*, focusing on early MS illustration. The essay provides useful insights into the way that iconographic traditions for illustrating the new poem rapidly emerged and became established, and into the working methods of the illustrators, and their relationships to the text. Two major approaches are identified: one option was to provide a single image at the start of each *cantica*, normally featuring the figure of D. as author and including some emblematic reference to the matter of the *cantica*. Other MSS provide individual illustrations to each canto, sometimes offering crowded scenes depicting different stages of the canto narrative, at others picking out a single representative element or cluster of elements. The essay culminates with some reflections on the Botticelli illustrations and stresses that their approach is essentially very traditional, showing that appreciation of the high quality of B.'s draughtsmanship should not bias critical judgement into ignoring how strongly rooted is their iconographical scheme in conventions that had become well established during the previous century.

Early written commentary is the subject of P. Procaccioli, 'Cronache di una disaffezione: la memoria del primo Giubileo nei commenti danteschi dal Tre al Cinquecento', Esposito, *Dante*, 183–99. The article reviews Jubilee *loci* in the early commentary tradition for the evidence they can provide about their authors' recognition and evaluation (or lack thereof) of the theme of Jubilee in the *DC*, which in turn casts light on their conception of their critical endeavours *in se*. P.'s chosen episodes are *Inf.* XVIII and *Purg.* II, and he discusses in some detail commentary by a range of authors from the first two centuries of D. criticism, tracing shifts not only in their conceptual and aesthetic interests, but also in the approach they bring to the

formal enterprise of D. criticism itself, with the move from the forms
of medieval scholastic exegesis to those of Renaissance humanism.
M. Seriacopi, 'Due chiose inedite di Filippo Villani alla *Commedìa*',
L'Alighieri, 41.2 : 114–17, notes the presence of two clearly identifiable
comments in V.'s hand on the Laurenziana 'Santa Croce' MS of the
DC, following the opening rubrics of *Inf.* VI and XI. The full text of
both is provided, and careful analysis of each stresses, firstly, the
additional evidence they provide of V.'s detailed knowledge of the
DC as a whole, and secondly, his interest in the allegorical interpretation of these passages, both of which cast an interesting light on his
readiness to use the text to find parallels with the socio-political
realities of his own time, given the condemnatory tone of his
comments on the problems of greed and of tyranny. Id., 'Un
commento anonimo inedito della Laurenziana all'*Inferno* e al *Purgatorio*. Parte prima: *Inferno*', *LIA*, 1, 2000:69–188, opens with a brief
presentation of the commentary notes on the *DC* in the Laurenziana's
MS Pluteo XL 37, which are based on a vulgarization of Benvenuto's
commentary, but which offer a very personal selection from the
original that differs strongly from both B.'s own and the Talice
versions of the text. Elements are cut, lengthened, and altered to suit
the interpretative interests of the anonymous 15th-c. reader, who
shows a taste for both lexical analysis and historical-literary commentary. A detailed description of the MS (70–72) is followed by the
presentation of the edited text of the notes to the whole of the *Inf.* The
edition is continued and completed in Id., 'Un commento inedito
della Laurenziana all'*Inferno* e al *Purgatorio*. Parte seconda: *Purgatorio*',
LIA, 2:99–156, taking us to the end of canto XXIV, where the
commentary ends. Several essays in Pinchard, *Pour Dante*, also deal
with medieval and Renaissance D. reception and commentary.
D. Parker, 'Edizioni e interpretazioni della *Commedia* nel Rinascimento' (295–304), picks up on the importance of considering how the
material production of Renaissance books affected their interpretation and diffusion, in relation to editions of the *DC* produced between
1472 and 1502. By considering issues such as size and format,
inclusion of commentary and/or illustrations, typeface, etc.,
P. reaches valuable conclusions about the way in which the *DC* was
presented to the public as a 'contemporary classic'. Reviewing a large
number of editions produced in very different forms, P. stresses that,
given how much the material form of a book can say about its
symbolic function with regard to its readers, the very variety of early
print editions of the *DC* tells much about its perennial appeal within
rapidly changing cultural, social, and political milieus. M. Dozon,
'Poésie et mythologie: les *Esposizioni* de Boccacce à la *Divine Comédie*'
(305–16), provides an analysis of B.'s exegetical methods and interests

that suggests that, in spite of B.'s 'medieval' concern to elucidate moral values and occasional encyclopaedist touches, the *Esposizioni* emerge as very 'humanist' readings, showing both scholarly concern over D.'s exactitude and historicity vis-à-vis classical sources, and an open, dialogic approach to the relationship between author and commentator which highlights the educational and initiatory importance of poetry in widening the readers' moral and critical horizons. F. La Brasca, 'Préambules d'un effacement: de quelques lieux théologiques dantesques dans trois commentaries humanistes de la *Divine Comédie*' (345–74), analyses the different approaches to D. as both poet and theologian in the commentaries of Serravalle, Landino, and Vellutello. Arguing that the attitude of each reflects assumptions and prejudices of contemporary significance, the essay examines passages where commentary on D.'s doctrinal assumptions reveals the humanist critics' different emphases and interests. It focuses especially on evidence about attitudes to the papacy, the classification of heresy, and D.'s hierarchy of sins, in commentary on *Inf.* IX and XI, and moves on to discuss the assumptions that all three make about author–reader qualifications and relationships with regard to *Inf.* I-II and, especially, *Par.* II. C. Vasoli, 'Ficin et Dante' (375–87), notes how F.'s dedication of his vulgarization of the *Mon.* to Antonio di Tuccio Manetti and Bernardo del Nero places it within very a particular cultural and political context, in which Lorenzo de' Medici and the leading Florentine intellectuals were rediscovering D. and the *stilnovisti* as part of their assertion of Florentine cultural hegemony in the context of struggles with Rome, and were also bringing humanistic *theologia platonica* to the interpretation of the *DC*. The essay discusses Dantean echoes and influences in F.'s own work, as well as his critical activity both with the translation of the *Mon.* and with his celebration of the lavish 1481 Florentine edition of the *DC*, which hails D. as the initiator of the humanist, neo-Platonist tastes and traditions of F.'s own Florentine milieu. R. Cooper, 'Dante sous François Ier: la traduction de François Bergaigne' (389–406), opens with a brief investigation of D.'s *fortuna* in 15th- and 16th-c. France, noting that early interest in his linguistic and conceptual achievement was increasingly succeeded by a more anecdotal approach, and later found D. the target of considerable hostility, over both his denigration of French rulers (especially Hugh Capet) and accusations of dependence on medieval French and Occitan vernacular innovations. However, C. also highlights a more positive and learned 16th-c. interest in D. among a relatively small court circle, to which the translation of B. bears witness. The essay provides a useful analysis of B.'s technique — he uses *terza rima* and inserts verse quatrains as rubrics to each canto — and of the printed and MS copies of the text, with a detailed discussion of the accompanying illustrations.

The reception of D. among both critics and creative writers in the more modern period has, as always, produced a fertile crop of studies. A single-volume collection of critical essays by practising poets of the 20th-c. provides an insight into D.'s enduring appeal to fellow artists. *The Poet's Dante*, ed. Peter S. Hawkins and Rachel Jacoff, NY, Farrar Straus and Giroux, xxvi + 406 pp., is divided into two sections, the first presenting reprints of short essays or extracts from longer studies by those whom the editors term 'the Illustrious Dead' (xvi), predominantly Anglo-Saxon but also including a small selection in translation by European writers. This first set of essays comprises: E. Pound, 'From *Dante*' (3–11); W. B. Yeats, 'From *A Vision*' (12–15); C. Williams, 'From *The Figure of Beatrice*' (16–27); T. S. Eliot, 'What Dante means to me' (28–39); O. Mandelstam, 'Conversation about Dante' (40–93); E. Montale, 'Dante, yesterday and today' (94–117); J. L. Borges, 'The *Divine Comedy*' (118–35); W. H. Auden, 'From *The Vision of Eros*' (136–43); R. Fitzgerald, 'Mirroring the *Commedia*: an appreciation of Laurence Binyon's version' (144–70); R. Lowell, 'Dante's actuality and fecundity in the Anglo-Saxon world epics' (171–85); R. Duncan, 'The sweetness and greatness of Dante's *Divine Comedy*' (186–209); H. Nemerov, 'The dream of Dante' (210–26); J. Merrill, 'Divine Poem' (211–37). The second part of the volume presents specially-commissioned essays by living poets, all writing in English, some already well-known for their involvement with D., including those such as Pinsky or Heaney who have also undertaken translation from the *DC*; others were asked to contribute 'simply because we wanted to know what they would have to say on the subject' (xvii), and their Dantean musings draw out sometimes unexpected, but always fertile, considerations of the poet and his text. The essays in part II comprise: S. Heaney, 'Envies and identifications: Dante and the modern poet' (239–58); C. Wright, 'Dantino mio' (259–64); J. Osherow, 'She's come undone: an American Jew looks at Dante' (265–76, see below); J. D. McClatchy, 'His enamel' (277–91); W. S. Merwin, 'Poetry rising from the dead' (292–305); R. Pinsky, 'The pageant of unbeing', (306–18); G. Hill, 'Between politics and eternity' (319–32); R. Warren, 'Words and blood' (333–42); W. S. Di Piero, 'Our sweating selves' (344–53); D. Halpern, 'Dante in Perpignan' (354–58); A. Williamson, 'The tears of Cocytus' (359–69); M. Doty, 'Rooting for the damned' (370–79); C. K. Williams, 'Souls' (380–82); M. Baine Campbell, 'Wrath, order, paradise' (383–94), E. Hirsch, 'Summoning shades' (395–402).

Elsewhere, E. Bufalchi, 'Lezioni dantesche di Arturo Graf tra i manoscritti di Ferdinando Gabotto', *L'Alighieri*, 41.1, 2000:59–116, draws attention to the rediscovery of the transcription (by Gabotto and Cesare Damilano) of Graf's university lectures on D., Petrarch, and Boccaccio, a comparative series that treated all three as representatives of a single historical/literary movement. The article highlights Graf's interest in D.'s cultural concern with the classical tradition, and in considering the poet within his medieval artistic and philosophical context; also his appreciation, despite the condemnations of De Sanctis, of D.'s rhetorical and philosophical strategies and of the *VN*. The appendix allows us to sample the flavour of the essays, supplying the full text of the first eight *Lezioni su Dante*. The reprints are continued in a second article by the same author, 'Arturo Graf, "Lezioni dantesche"', *L'Alighieri*, 42.1:59–113, where twelve more essays appear. Another 19th-c. D. critic is the focus of H. Heintze's essay, *'Karl Witte zum hundertsten Todestag und zum zweihundertsten Geburtstag', *DDJ*, 76:23–42. A different aspect of the 19th-c. reception of D. is discussed by V. R. Jones, 'Dante the popular *cantastorie*: Porta's dialect translation of the *Comedy*', *The Italianist*, 20, 2000:44–57, which provides an intriguing study of the broad political and cultural implications of P.'s decision to translate sections of the *Inf.* into Milanese dialect, and offers a number of telling (often very funny!) citations from P.'s version. She stresses the significance of P.'s presentation of the work as *travestito* into Milanese, drawing attention to the change in metre, the interpolations and excisions, and the modernizing and humorous effect of what is more an interpretation than a translation. J. argues that P.'s changes turn D. from the authoritative and unapproachable *vates* of a literary classic into a jocose *cantastorie*, with many of the attributes of Maggi's Meneghino character from the dialect theatre. While the effect of these manipulations is superficially deflating, such intertextual reference to dialect tradition aligns P.'s new text within its own canon of Milanese classics; it also allows P. to present himself as engaged in a faithfully Dantean enterprise, that of developing a language and a literary tradition that will move away from the cautious elegance of a moribund high culture — whether that of medieval Latin, or of Enlightenment Tuscan — towards the vigour and authenticity of a modern vernacular culture. M. Lentzen, *'Denkmäler und Dichtung', *DDJ* 76:57–88, discusses well-known Dante monuments (S. Croce, Piazza S. Croce, Trento, New York) in relation to poems by Leopardi, Carducci, and Pascoli. M. Rusi, 'La fortuna americana di Dante e un mediatore italiano', *AFLLS*, 39, 2000:263–76, in the course of discussing correspondence between the family of H. W. Longfellow and Giacomo Zanella, one of his Italian translators, mentions the latter's receipt of some autograph MS lines from L.'s translation of

Par. xxx, in posthumous acknowledgement of his translation activities. (Z.'s own apparent lack of interest in D. suggests that he might have been more gratified by, than appreciative of, the gesture.) A darker side of Dante reception, in the 20th-c., emerges in Thomas Taterka's impressive *Dante Deutsch: Studien zur Lagerliteratur*, Berlin, Erich Schmidt, 1999, 227 pp. The all-too-vivid understanding of D. generated in the mid 20th century by the infernal experience of the Nazi concentration camp regime provides the tragically compelling theme of the study. The volume examines not only the production of numerous *Lagertexte*, but also the emergence of a *Lagerdiskurs* which has been developed in a number of different languages and over several decades to meet the needs of those who survived the camps and of those (ex-inmates or otherwise) who have tried to interpret that experience, offering reflections on a huge number of more or less prolific and well-known commentators, including Imre Kertész, Ruth Klüger, Primo Levi, Jorge Semprun, and Peter Weiss. T. suggests that the framework of D.'s hell offers not merely an ornamental resource to these writers, with its eminently literary and cultural resonances, but provides them with a central element in any attempt at describing or — more importantly — understanding the world of the Lager. Further German reception of D., and specifically of the *DVE*, is examined by H. Stammerjohann, *'Die rezeption von Dantes Traktat *De vulgari eloquentia* im Deutschen Sprachraum', *DDJ*, 76 : 129–75. J. Osherow, 'She's come undone: an American Jew looks at Dante', *Western Humanities Review*, 55 : 27–36, provides an engaging personal account of a poet's encounter with a poet — one mediated by yet another poet, as the opening paragraph recalls O.'s first, unrecognized reading of a line from D. as occurring through Eliot's *Wasteland*. The article provides illuminating reflection on the attractions of *terza rima* and its practical challenge to the composer, or to the translator of D. (including a brief personal example); and on D.'s incorporation into his own text of other languages and poetries, analysing the example of *Purg.* II's citation of *Ps.* 114, which strikes this author through its blend of Jewish and Christian, Hebrew Latin and Italian, and medieval and modern resonances. The last three essays of Pinchard, *Pour Dante*, discuss 19th- and 20th-c. criticism and reception of D. among writers and philosophers: N. Mineo, 'Foscolo e la riscoperta di Dante' (429–46); J.-F. Marquet, 'Dante dans l'idéalisme allemand' (447–56), who focuses particularly on the Dantean interests of Fichte, Schelling, and Hegel; and D. Millet-Gérard, 'Claudel poète-théologien: la référence dantesque' (457–78).

COMPARATIVE STUDIES. G. Armstrong, 'Dantean framing devices in Boccaccio's *Corbaccio*', *RMS*, 27 : 139–61, produces an intriguing investigation of B.'s use of Dantean reference and allusion, suggesting that the *C*, rather than the *Decameron*, is the text that displays the most dense and characteristic pattern of engagement with D., embracing both the *VN* and the *DC*. A.'s analysis not only demonstrates the *C*'s high concentration of lexical *dantismi*, but stresses that B.'s allusions are always contextually, structurally, and thematically charged. Thus the opening narrative of *innamoramento* draws heavily on the *VN*, while opening phases of the dream vision allude to *Inf.* v and xiii to draw together allusions to lust and to suicide; B. operates a deliberate ironic reversal of the *VN*'s concluding promise of (delayed) celebration of Beatrice's splendour, in the *C*'s closing promise to publish the beloved's perfidy. This latter type of allusion, A. argues, allows B. to challenge audience expectation, precisely because of the contextual appropriateness of the placing of his *dantismi*; and thus establishes an intriguing dialogic relationship between author and reader in which D.'s intertextual presence plays a central, but ambiguous, part. D. Gibbons, 'Tasso "petroso": beyond Petrarchan and Dantean metaphor in the *Gerusalemme Liberata*', *ISt*, 55, 2000:83–98, explores T.'s use of metaphor and suggests that it displays strong traces at times of the *asprezza* of D.'s *petrose*, notably *Così nel mio parlar*. Combining detailed lexical analysis of passages from the *GL* with discussions of a broader and more theoretical nature, G. shows that T.'s practice in his epic shows rhetorical debts to D.'s lyric practice in the *petrose* at least, and that this encounter with D. may have helped him to reassess the contribution lyric could make even to the sterner generic and formal enterprise of the epic. The work of one of D.'s earliest *cultori* is discussed by G. Marrani, 'Fra Cecco Angiolieri e Dante: Nicolò de' Rossi comico', *De Robertis Vol.*, 281–304. The essay offers detailed analysis of a number of De R.'s sonnets and canzoni, identifying the traces of two different models of 'comic' writing that shaped the Trevisan's practice: that of D. and that of A. The study shows that De R.'s reception of D. is not confined solely or primarily to the explicitly satirical or critical comic tone of the *DC* or the *petrose* (not to mention the *Fiore*, of which M. identifies a number of echoes), but also reveals an interest in the comicity of the narrative and of the allegorical lyrics of the *VN*, and of a range of other *stilnovisti*, including Cavalcanti and Cino. Although primarily dedicated to Petrarch, there are references to D. and *VN*'s 'stile della loda' in C. Molinari, 'Petrarca e il *gran desio*: poesia della lode nel *Canzoniere*', *ib.*, 305–44. In an article co-authored by D. Robey, A. Cipollone, and P. Nasti, 'Rhythm and metre in Renaissance narrative poetry', *The Italianist*, 20, 2000:21–43, the *DC* makes several appearances for comparative purposes, although the article is primarily concerned with the computer analysis of features of narrative poetry from the Cinquecento. Several comparative studies of D. and medieval or Renaissance writers also appear in Pinchard, *Pour Dante*. C. Cazalé Bérard, 'Autour du chant v de l'*Enfer*: les réécritures boccaciennes de l'*Amor Gentile*' (317–32), discusses B.'s lifelong engagement with D., as scholar-critic, as imitator and author, and as (sometimes parodic) rewriter. Focusing on the Francesca episode, the article analyses the nuances of this literary relationship in B.'s *Esposizioni*. Rather than treating F. as the allegorical 'type' of lust, B.'s interests involve extensive intertextual engagement with vernacular and classical tradition in the novella-like account of her love story in the mode of courtly *amore dilettevole* (with obvious resonances with D.'s *VN* and B.'s own *Filocolo*). Even his interpretation of moral meanings in the episode displays less interest in the general typology of sin than in producing yet another new text, in B.'s rhetorically-polished diatribe against Florentine frivolity and conspicuous consumption. The essay suggests that B.'s strategies of narration and interpretation should be viewed as marking a shift in cultural typology: D. was able to allow his roles as *actor* and *auctor* in the *VN* and *DC* to converge without any moral anxiety, confident that Beatrice could come to represent salvation; for B., narratological and interpretative responsibility is an ambiguous issue, and *amore dilettevole* can scarcely ever be transcended into *amore onesto*. M. Picone, 'Riscritture dantesche nel *Canzoniere* di Petrarca' (333–43), argues against the tradition that takes P.'s reception of D. to be largely passive. Rather, the essay suggests that D.'s example is a fundamental point of reference throughout the *Canzoniere*: albeit as a point of contrast and opposition. Where D.'s love story allows him to make an allegorical journey of Christian *renovatio* from the despair of Good Friday to the redemptive joy of Easter, P.'s emotional journey follows an emblematically circular path from one despondent Good Friday (his first encounter with Laura) to another (her death). A microtextual illustration of this macrotextual trend is provided in the example of P.'s madrigal LIV, which rewrites the theme of Dantean-Augustinian *peregrinatio* into an amorous *erranza* that remains estranged from the City of God. B. Pinchard, 'De Dante à Rabelais: enquête sur l'idée "comique"' (407–25), sets out an intriguing series of proposals that link the notions of comicity of the medieval D. and the humanist R. at a deep level, despite the wide divergences apparent in the respective seriousness and humour of their two great works. P. outlines their shared interest in defending the viability of the vernacular for literary composition and their concern with formal and stylistic aspects of comicity within the framework of debates over the status of vernacular culture and of the proper occupations of scholars and writers; even their subject matter, despite its obvious differences in type, reveals a common interest in the representation of questions concerning the proper conduct of human life: all of which makes R. an eminently serious writer and D. an eminently comic one.

The prominence that D. has held for a great 20th-c. writer is impressively explored in Lucia Boldrini's *Joyce, Dante and the Poetics of Literary Relations: Language and Meaning in Finnegans Wake*, CUP, xi + 233 pp. This is a dense study based on highly detailed textual analysis of parallel passages from D. and J., particularly focused on matters of linguistic practice; the opening chapter introduces further comparative resonances by examining Beckett's ideas on both writers. B. discusses the concepts of Babelic fall and creative refinement (particularly in relation to the *volgare illustre*) raised by the *DVE*, and the questions of interpretation and 'layered' meaning addressed in the *Cvo* and the *Ep. to Can Grande*, in relation to J.'s creative practice in *FW*, with a wealth of convincing illustrative citations from the two authors. The impressive, if occasionally overwhelming, abundance of textual analysis makes this a scrupulous and challenging comparative investigation. The same authors are discussed in T. Pisanti, 'Appunti su Dante in Joyce e Beckett', *CLett*, 29:627–36. The essay investigates the rediscovery of the medieval by these two pre-eminently modern writers, discussing their variations on Dantean themes, with particular reference to J.'s *Ulysses* and to B.'s *Echo's Bones* (focusing on the figure of Malacoda) and *More Pricks than Kicks* (focusing on Belacqua). Irish reception of D. is also analysed in detail by R. de Rooy, 'Dante e la *Divina Commedia* nell'opera poetica di Seamus Heaney', *RELI*, 16, 2000:51–79. The essay opens with an investigation of H.'s first encounters with D. — both through the *DC* (in English) and through the critical writings of Eliot and Mandelstam — at around the period of his withdrawal (self-exile) from a city torn by political violence, tracing fruitful parallels with D.'s exile from Florence. This is followed by detailed analysis of passages from works where H. translates, mentions or alludes to the *DC*, underlining the politico-ethical immediacy that H. found in D. De R. makes clear the strength of H.'s personal response to D. — but stresses also that he engages closely with only a relatively limited number of passages from the *DC*, often combining elements from different parts of the *DC* (e.g. Brunetto Latini with Cacciaguida), and also that he makes essentially areligious interpretations of these chosen episodes that create new poetic effects often ultimately un-Dantean in feeling. An impressive programme of research is presented in Maria Sabrina Titone, *Cantiche del Novecento: Dante nell'opera di Luzi e Pasolini*, F, Olschki, xxxi + 226 pp. The volume highlights the engagement of two figures of considerable stature in modern Italian culture with the work of D., including transcriptions of interviews that each has given on the subject. The paradigmatic position that the *DC* is shown to hold in the work and thought of these two much-admired artists is impressive, but their visions of D. are shown to be almost opposite in kind. For P., D. brings an all-too-vivid reality to the descent into Hell of a life of daring, often scandalous, experimentation — linguistic, narrative, and/or biographical — which colours and influences both the cinema and the poetry of P. himself; for L., D. is rather an inspiration towards hope and illumination. The study is illustrated with numerous comparative readings of the poems (and in P.'s case, also the films) alongside passages from the *DC*, which provide telling illustration of how D. is used by the two authors, while two opening chapters contextualize this use by exploring the evidence about P.'s and L.'s own readings of D., and their response to the language, imagery, and poetics of the *DC* and other works. L. Gattamorta, 'Luzi e Dante: figure e trame di una intertestualità', *StCrit* 15, 2000: 193–218, opens with remarks on the absence of any sustained study of L.'s *dantismo* that may well have been superseded by the appearance of Titone's study. The short essay takes a necessarily limited approach, investigating Dantean intertextualities in L.'s two post-war collections, *Primizie del deserto* and *Onore del vero*, stressing that L.'s engagement with D. tends to be 'riflessivo', based on *aemulatio*, rather than 'integrativo', based on *imitatio* (194). An American reader of D. is discussed by M. Chiamenti, 'Dante & LF', *De Robertis Vol.*, 79–89, who investigates intertextual relationships between D. and Lawrence Ferlinghetti, revealing some intriguing recastings of the *DC* in particular among what F. terms his 'allusions or references or rip-offs' (80) to D. Another strand of modern D. reception is discussed by D. Kämper, *'Dante im Musiktheater des 20. Jahrhunderts. Luigi Dallapiccolas Bühnenwerk Ulisse', *DDJ*, 76:89–102.

3. TEXTUAL TRADITION

New editions of D.'s works are always welcome, providing fresh insights into the textual tradition and editorial history of the poet's works. Unquestionably the most significant textual contribution of this year — and probably for years to come — is Federico Sanguineti's substantial new edition of the *DC*: *Dantis Alagherii Comedia*, F, SISMEL-Galluzzo, lxxxviii + 582 pp. A meticulous application of Lachmannian method has permitted S. to draw up a new *stemma codicum* which, while providing a place for the many hundreds of MS copies of the whole or parts of the *DC*, identifies a compact set of just seven authoritative MSS as the working foundation for his edition. His α branch comprises one Bolognese MS, two Pisan, and three Florentine (or from within the Florentine ambit), the β branch a single Emilian MS (Vat. Urbinate Lat. 366), which in fact provides the basis for this

edition, with corrections checked against the α MSS: this allows him
to privilege the textual evidence in cases where Petrocchi and others
have, in the absence of an authoritative *stemma*, run into editorial
difficulties. The resulting text is, naturally enough, sometimes unset-
tling, overturning many of the readings to which 40 years of
Petrocchian authority have accustomed us. The weight given to a
non-Florentine MS (although S. has intervened to correct the most
obvious non-Florentine features), and the rigorous application of
Lachmann's criteria, both features based on strict adherence to the
MSS, can seem almost simplistic after the conventional lengthy lists
of variants and justificatory glosses, but have the striking merit of
allowing the texts closest to the archetype to speak for themselves:
although this in turn can raise its own questions, for instance over the
accuracy of the archetype and the linguistic origins of its copyist.
While reliance on a non-Florentine MS may be criticized, S. makes a
persuasive case for the importance of recognizing that the Urbinate
is closer to the earliest copies of the *DC* than any other surviving
copy — and of course those who wish to return specifically to the
earliest full Florentine reading are well served by Lanza's recent
(1996) edition of the Trivulziano 1080 (one of S.'s α texts). Altogether,
S.'s work represents a magisterial achievement, and in challenging us
to re-read the text with fresh eyes, and to re-assess our critical
judgements when faced with changing textual evidence, has made a
valuable contribution to the wider field of D. studies, as well as an
impressive stride forwards in philological and editorial terms. Further
discussion of his editorial practice appears in Id., 'Testo e esegesi
della *Comedia*', Marietti, *Dante*, 17–33. The article sets out some of the
criteria used in establishing the working critical *corpus* of MSS, and
discusses the characteristics of the α and β traditions; the question of
Florentine versus other regional usage is also reviewed. To give an
insight into his working method, S. provides discussion of a selection
of *loci* where divergences within the MSS *corpus* has required nice
editorial decision — especially in the case of *adiaforia* or of linguistic
judgments. The essay closes with a sample from the new edition, of
'Capitulum 5' — where the new form 'Nullo è maggior dolore | ca
ricordarsi...' (121–22), for instance, indicates something of the kind
of divergences away from the Petrocchian *vulgata* towards new critical
readings with which the full edition is packed. A. Antonelli and
R. Pedani, 'Appunti sulla più antica attestazione dell'*Inferno*', *SPCT*,
63:29–41, provides a fascinating insight into the culture of the
Bolognese notarial class in the very early Trecento. Ultraviolet
scanning of the cover of a notarial register in the Bolognese *Archivio di
Stato* dating from 1304, has revealed the presence of a single *DC*
terzina, *Inf.* v 103–05. The authors discuss a number of similar

discoveries on this and other public documents, where the covers are scribbled with snippets of poetry, proverbs, signatures, and sketches of figures and animals, that attest the rich verbal and symbolic culture possessed by the Comune's administrators. Its traces survive in the public-private twilight zone of the paratextual, appropriating the instruments of the Comune's official and impersonal authority to articulate, with strong individual self-consciousness, their own personal tastes, humour, and verbal/visual idiosyncrasies. M. Boschi Rotiroti, 'Accertamenti paleografici su un gruppo di manoscritti danteschi', *MR*, 14, 2000: 119–28, discusses aspects of the different types of hand adopted by the earliest copyists of the *DC*, using these data to trace patterns of construction and diffusion of the text, which in some milieus settles swiftly into highly stable channels and in others followed varied paths of development. A key stage in the development of such changes is identified as occurring once professional scribes became involved in copying, as exemplified by the standardization of palaeographic and generic conventions in the so-called 'Danti del Cento' MS group, which established a model that, even after the shift to a predominant *littera textualis*, retained considerable influence over later copyists.

On the subject of textual questions relating to minor works, it is worth drawing attention to Luca Carlo Rossi's edition of the *Vita Nova*, Mi, Mondadori, 1999, lxiii + 262 pp., which presents, in accessible and affordable form, the text established in Gorni's recent critical edition (1996), which has so radically transformed understanding of the *libello*; the long introductory essay by G. highlights many of the most important aspects of the new text. F. La Brasca, 'Essai de bilan provisoire sur la tradition textuelle des *Rime* de Dante et en particulier des *Petrose*', Marietti, *Dante*, 217–51, is a densely packed article that highlights some of the problems attendant on establishing editorial approaches to the *Rime*, starting indeed from the very question whether D.'s lyric output should be classed a *Canzoniere* or more simply *Rime*: titles that have considerable implications for editing and interpretation. Tracing the problems 'backwards' from the selections, arrangements, and titles of various modern editions familiar to the scholarly public, to the MS tradition, La B. notes what divergences there are between different early collections of small or large numbers of D.'s lyrics, whose heterogeneity provides little guidance for modern editors. The micro-corpus of the *Petrose* is then examined in more detail, showing how even this small and closely-linked group of lyrics is differently presented by early copyists, in a symptomatic example of the editorial challenges of the *Rime* at large. The transmission history of the *Cvo* receives attention from N. Bianchi, 'Le prime quattro edizioni del *Convivio* di Dante: appunti per una ricerca', *MR*, 14, 2000:233–41. She describes and analyses the first four editions produced before Bembo's edition established its absolute textual pre-eminence, examining the texts carefully for the light they shed on contemporary Dantean interests and editorial practice, as well as for the readings they have furnished to fuel 20th-c. editorial debates.

4. MINOR WORKS

On the *VN*: Joseph F. Privitera, *A Reference Grammar of Medieval Italian according to Dante, with a Dual Language Edition of the Vita Nova*, Lewiston, Mellen, 2000, vii + 114 pp., is presumably aimed primarily at a student audience. The Reference Grammar (1–26) and Lexicon (27–38) do indeed provide useful if somewhat schematic guidance on the recognition and comprehension of the forms of the *VN*'s prose and verse. A student readership should however approach the edition provided in the second part of the volume (40–113) with considerable caution. The introductory page heralds this as a 'critical edition', but the term is misleading: based throughout on the Hoepli 1992 edition of Barbi's text, the prose parts have been drastically cut, following the author's view that they are 'dull and uninteresting except as they serve as *explications de texte*' (v), to produce a curiously garbled text. The title (*Vita Nova*) and the altered chapter sequence (31 sections, each based around — in some cases simply reduced to — an individual lyric, have been produced) superficially recall the revisions to the standard text made in Gorni's 1996 critical edition, but the author appears unaware of G.'s work, or of the textual and interpretative debates which it has generated. The translations follow the abbreviated Italian, but are in themselves very fair: it is a shame that a potentially useful student tool should be vitiated by the curious decisions taken over the presentation of the text itself. D. Ferraris, '*Vita Nova*: le livre comme Dichtung', Marietti, *Dante*, 195–217, explores the novelistic aspects of the *VN*. It opens with an examination of the Pauline theme of conversion in the text, with its narrative of the moral transformation of the protagonist from corporeally-driven *homo vetus*, through introspection and self-examination, into *homo novus*. F. notes how rhetorical devices such as personification and *psychomachia* stress the interiority of the love story, and how the theme of literary conversion accompanies the erotic and intellectual themes, making the *prosimetrum* collation of lyric *disjecta membra* outline a coherent novelistic narrative of self-discovery and self-transformation. G. Ferrero, 'In lode di Dante: sapere astronomico pubblico e tradizione sapienziale nella data di morte di Beatrice', *CLett*, 28, 2000:418–38, returns to the much-debated issue of the brevity of

D.'s treatment of B.'s death. The calendrical and numerological references in the relevant passage are reviewed in relation to a number of astronomical texts translated from Arabic in contemporary circulation, and also to traditional Ptolemaic/Sapiential astronomy. Their respective accounts of celestial motion have a theological function in relation to establishing the dates, in the latter case of Pentecost, in the former, of the death of Mohammed (which falls, like that of Beatrice's death, on 8 June). The article suggests that the date of M.'s death plays a pivotal role in D.'s account of human history, suggesting that B. herself should be viewed as 'una geniale costruzione letteraria' (434) enabling D. to link the importance of knowledge of the cosmos with that of knowledge of tradition and history, and to stress their mutual interdependence. G. Gorni, 'Per la *Vita Nova*', *SFI*, 58, 2000: 29–48, reviews the reception of his critical edition in its first five years, providing a useful summary of the points of greatest contention, with their various solutions, and supplying a useful bibliography covering both review articles and more substantial essays, plus edition references (47–48). Reflections on his own methodology, and analysis of his practice as regards spelling, paragraphing, etc., brings us up close to his philological practice. A fascinating section of discussion also deals with the status of the *VN* as a *prosimetrum* and its place among other Latin and vernacular examples of the genre. G.'s survey of the *libello*'s relationship with Ovid and Boethius, with Brunetto Latini's *Tesoretto* and *Rettorica*, with the Occitan poets' *vidas* and *razos*, and with letters by Guittone and D. himself, reveals a wealth of possible precedents for the enterprise of compilation and exegesis represented by the *VN*. This survey again offers several occasions for philological discussion (for instance, over D.'s use of the term *ragione* in relation to Occitan *razos* or to Brunetto's preferred term *cagione*) that open intriguing lines of enquiry. M. Guglielminetti, 'Beatrice acheropita', Marietti, *Dante*, 131–45, suggests that D. consistently represents B. in the *VN* under an angelic, Marian, or Christological guise. Through a deliberate strategy of allusion to scriptural texts, this representation provides an *imagine acheropita* of the beloved that appears to have been written not by a human but a divine hand (that of the Scriptures or that of Love/God) — all of which allows D. to assert the elevated status of the book he figures himself from the outset as copying, rather than (or as well as) creating. C. Libaude, 'Le coeur et le sang: la première vision de la *Vita nuova*', Pinchard, *Pour Dante*, 127–59, investigates the dream episode of the *VN*'s first sonnet and accompanying prose, focusing on the meanings of two symbolic elements: the *drappo sanguigno* covering B.'s naked body, and her ingestion of D.'s flaming heart. The former element is analysed in relation to the theme of blood (*sangue/sanguigno*) and of body, concealed beneath the *drappo*, in scriptural and in secular tradition, drawing out their symbolic associations with the processes of generation and birth, with baptism and with martyrdom, and especially with Christ's Last Supper and Passion, to show how B. is cast as a Christological figure who will convey revelation, redemption, and rebirth to D. through her salvific life and death. The second motif is examined in relation to the rather grisly courtly tradition of the eaten heart, where a cannibalistic ritual features as a symbol of amorous loyalty (though often in stories of adultery) and of trans-formations of love and courage. Further motifs of ingestion and digestion from D.'s other works and from the scriptures are explored, to show how D. transforms the eaten heart tradition into a symbol of his reinventions of courtly language and idea. L. suggests that by placing a motif associated with the end of profane love at the beginning of his own narrative of spiritualized love, in conjunction with the Christological overtones of the symbolic *drappo sanguigno*, D. draws attention to his rewriting of the courtly experience: the themes of transformation and rebirth symbolized in both the scriptural and the secular elements of both motifs are explicitly heralded from the outset of the narrative, and invite the reader in turn to ingest and digest D.'s own *libello* with appropriate care and attention. M. Picone, 'Il *prosimetrum* della *Vita Nova*', *LIA*, 2:17–26, addresses questions about genre. The essay offers a probing investi-gation both of possible textual models for the *VN*'s prose-poetry combination, and of the way that D. presents himself as author. As regards form, P. surveys two models also reviewed by Gorni (above): Boethius — whose *Consolatio* P. finds to be essentially an *anti*-model for the *VN* — and the Occitan *vidas* and *razos*. While the Occitan model, or more specifically, those Italian MSS that present this prose material alongside the lyrics, offers some intriguing parallels, P.'s final conclusion is that a classical source, Ovid's *Remedia Amoris*, is D.'s principal model. Here too, the model is strictly related to medieval MS presentation conventions, and P. notes that D.'s presence within his own text takes on different aspects, each related to medieval processes of MS production and reception. By the way that he presents his work on the page, and comments on his fashioning of it, D. casts himself not only as the mechanical *scriptor* and editorial *compilator*, but also as the scholarly *commentator* who expounds the verse texts' hidden meanings, and also, most significantly, as a poetic *auctoritas* whose work merits the prestigious treatment that his authors will recognize through visual stimuli as ranking him alongside the elevated *auctoritates* of the classical world. The essay also appears in Marietti, *Dante*, 177–94.

On the *Cvo*: G. Inglese, 'Sul testo di *Convivio* (1) "da providenza di propria natura" (I. i. 1)', *La Cultura*, 38, 2000:247–61, opens both philological and conceptual questions in discussing his title quotation. In choosing 'propria natura' rather than 'prima natura', he opts for a reading rejected by Ageno (1995) in her critical edition, but one well represented in a branch of the transmission history. The two phrasings suggest rather different philosophical consequences, too, and in opting for 'propria natura', I. leads us towards a specifically Thomist view of the differences and/or convergences between universal Nature and the particular nature of the individual human being. Detailed analysis of passages from Aristotle, Avicenna, Albertus Magnus, Aquinas, and several others helps cast light on the much-disputed question of how the *Cvo* (and later the *Mon.*) conceives the pursuit and realization of happiness by human beings, both individually and collectively. S. Marchesi, 'La rilettura del *De Officiis* e i due tempi della composizione del *Convivio*', *GSLI*, 178:84–107, proposes evidence of a break in composition between the first three books of the *Cvo* and Book IV, based on examining the number and quality of D.'s citations from the *De Off.* In M.'s view, the extensive reference to Cicero's treatise in the last completed book of the *Cvo* reveal the enthusiasm of a neophyte, suggesting that D.'s first full reading of it filled the break in composing his own work. The arguments are supported by detailed comparative discussions of passages with a Ciceronian flavour in Book I, which M. suggests are all (bar one) sufficiently different in context, structure, or terminology from the supposed original that they must in fact depend on a secondary source — in several cases, this appears to be Brunetto Latini's *Tresor*. When analogous comparisons are conducted in the case of Book IV, the *De Off.* is always closely and appropriately followed (though details from L. may also be present). Further evidence supporting the theory of D.'s recent encounter with *De Off.* is supplied in M.'s closing analysis of D.'s interest in the highly Ciceronian virtue of magnanimity in both *Cvo* IV and *Inf.*, and of both these works' distinction between vices of force and of fraud, that once again recalls the *De Off.*

Two essays in the first section of the Pinchard, *Pour Dante*, collection deal with the *Mon.* J. Quillet, 'La *Monarchia* de Dante Alighieri' (25–38), focuses on the assertions in Book I regarding the emperor's Providential appointment, and in Book III regarding imperial responsibility for the 'beatitudine huius vitae'. She looks to the *Cvo* to cast light on D.'s ideas about imperial functions in relation specifically to Italy, noting some shared interests with such pre-humanist political philosophers as Mussato and Marsiglio. The essay argues the close relationship between the *Cvo*'s depiction of the emperor as 'cavalcatore de la ragione umana' and the philosophical activity envisioned at the end of *Mon.* III, stressing that the treatises' interest in humanity's dual mortal/immortal nature gives the role of emperor towards 'la partie corruptible' (30) a sanctified eschatological function. R. Lambertini, 'La monarchia prima della *Monarchia*: le ragioni del *regnum* nella ricezione medioevale di Aristotele' (39–76), seeks to establish the background (though not necessarily the precise sources) for D.'s presentation of the *rationes* for empire in *Mon.* I. The article offers a detailed survey of Scholastic commentaries on the *Ethics* and the *Politics*, and of various works in the mirror-for-princes genre, to provide the background against which to evaluate D.'s originality. L. suggests that D.'s views, while often using familiar-sounding allusions, show less interest in establishing the virtues needed by a ruler, but rather focus on defining the nature and limits of the imperial office itself, which by virtue of its universality eliminates any personal defect of cupidity in its holder. L. stresses that D.'s approach to questions of power and hierarchy is articulated consistently through an engagement with human nature, rather than through the analogies with nature or art typical of medieval Aristotelianism, suggesting that D.'s anthropocentric approach offers a foreshadowing of humanist attitudes.

On the *Rime*: M. Cursietti, 'Dante e Forese alla taverna del Panìco: le prove documentarie della falsità del tenzone', *L'Alighieri*, 41.2, 2000:1–22, returns once again to the thesis that the *tenzone* is a literary forgery, perpetrated in C.'s view by 'lo Za' (Stefano di Tommaso Finiguerri). The article reviews the arguments for a later dating of the crucial Chigiano MS that provide a philological basis for the forgery hypothesis, while a comparative analysis of various allusions in the *tenzone* with Lanza's edition of lo Za's *Poemetti* (1994) offers additional evidence for C.'s identification of the real correspondents as Bicci Castellani and Giovanni Gerardi da Prato. Id., 'Ricorriamo alla fine e messer Giano: una nuova ipotesi sulla "pulzelletta" a messer Brunetto', *Romania*, 118, 2000:519–29, similarly raises questions of authenticity: C. urges the necessity of considering the text on its own terms, without any pro-Dantean prejudice occasioned by the traditional attribution. Analysis of textual elements provides C. with 'double' readings of the sonnet, one conventional, one obscene and sodomitical. The investigation, illustrated with frequent and detailed lexical discussion, concludes that this, as in C.'s view the *tenzone*, is a witty literary fraud from a later period, ascribed to D. and Brunetto in knowing allusion to the sodomitical implications of *Inf.* XV. D. Gibbons, ' "Com più vi fere Amor coi suoi vincastri": its metaphors, influences and dating', *The Italianist*, 20, 2000:5–20, offers a survey of a number of important questions regarding the place of the title lyric within the Dantean corpus, which prove in turn to raise wider issues of considerable importance about the poet's development. The question whether and, if so, how far the sonnet's recherché metaphors reveal direct influence from Occitan has long occupied critical attention, and G. opens with a useful survey of the hypotheses and their significance. His scrupulous analysis stresses that, while Occitan influence cannot be ruled out, this is not a lyric that shows strong influence from the master of *trobar clus*, Arnaut Daniel, in style or structure. G. argues persuasively, with a wealth of illustrative evidence, that D. did not need the encounter with A. to "become" metaphorical in the *petrose* or the *DC*: an interest in metaphor is present even in this clearly early pre-*stilnovo* lyric, suggesting that D.'s reading of A. should be viewed as prompting rather the extension of pre-existing tendencies than the introduction of radical changes to D.'s use of figural language. C. Perrus, 'Énonciation et construction du sujet dans les *Petrose*', Marietti, *Dante*, 251–67, offers a dense and stimulating close reading of the *Petrose* sequence, which focuses especially on the 'io' who speaks in the lyrics, and this figure's function as both protagonist and enunciator of the text. The analysis highlights the distinctive characteristics of the *Petrose* within D.'s larger *œuvre*, standing out not only on obvious formal and linguistic grounds, but also for their resistance to allegorization and their disengagement from courtly discourse.

On the *Epistle to Cangrande*: E. Cecchini, 'C'è falso e falso (Dante, *Epistola a Cangrande*)', *Maia*, 53:171–78, takes fierce issue with Brugnoli's recent publications on the *Ep.*, especially those critical of C.'s own (1995) edn of the text. To clarify the dispute with B., C. provides numerous detailed examples in support of his own editorial choices, and offers a useful analysis of the editorial method pursued when establishing his text. The debate over authenticity naturally provides a further major point of dissent between the two scholars: C. argues that his edition offers a text with the flavour of authenticity to which — if the *Ep.* be false — any decent forger would aspire, reproving B. for his 'voler privilegiare incoerenze di contenuto e disarmonie formali [...], perché ha deciso in partenza che siamo di fronte a un falso totale o parziale' (174). A detailed comparative analysis of his own and B.'s readings of § 12–13 provides some illustration of the type of case over which the two critics dissent, and a shorter, but equally polemical, discussion of § 22 brings the essay to a close. R. Hollander, 'Il dibattito odierno attorno all'*Epistola* a Cangrande', Pinchard, *Pour Dante*, 255–68, offers a calmer survey of recent contributions to the debate over authenticity (with a valuable bibliography for those who wish to pursue the issue further). The main bulk of the essay is dedicated to summarizing, with admirable clarity, some of the key points in the debate, and the opinions of the principal participants, on the questions about the authenticity of the first part of the *Ep.* versus that of its later paragraphs; the question of its use and/or attribution in early commentary; the use of the *cursus*; and the issue of allegory. H. closes with a modest but confident reaffirmation of his own view that the *Ep.* is authentic, and with the reminder that though it was probably written 'frettolosamente, e con lo scopo primario di ottenere vitto e alloggio' (265), its suggestions about how to read the *DC* should not be dismissed lightly. T. Ricklin, 'Struttura e autenticità dell'*Epistola* a Cangrande', *ib.*, 269–78, also argues for the authenticity of the text, focusing on formal analysis of individual paragraphs. The arguments proceed neatly: stressing that many critics are happy to accept the authenticity of § 1–13, R. offers a detailed formal and conceptual analysis of § 88, which he shows to relate closely to the acceptably Dantean § 13. By showing that § 88 in turn presents material closely interwoven with that of preceding paragraphs, he extends his argument to embrace them as authentic; and suggests that, in that case, § 89–90 are credibly authentic too. R.'s methodical assessment of the evidence uses analysis of § 88 to show the futility of arguing that § 14–87 are forgeries if § 1–13 are accepted as genuine; and his closing remarks usefully contextualize the probable circumstances of the *Ep.*'s composition in the light of D.'s *Cvo* pronouncements on authorial activity in exile.

5. COMEDY

A major study of some formal characteristics of the *DC* is provided by David Robey's research into *Sound and Structure in the Divine Comedy*, OUP, 2000, x + 204 pp. The book sets out to construct a systematic description and analysis of the sounds of the *DC*, bringing R.'s expertise in computer-assisted textual analysis to bear on the poem's metrical and phonological aspects, and examining numerous large sections of text in detail. In the four main chapters, R. analyses the features of alliteration/assonance, rhyme, syllable divisions, and accent, making comparisons not only between the *DC*'s three *cantiche*, but also between the *DC* and D.'s lyric verse (and even prose), and between the *DC* and later medieval and Renaissance lyric and narrative verse, to examine how — or indeed whether — sound features in Dante's great narrative poem achieve particular functions or effects. The results are analysed with considerable subtlety in R.'s prose, but are also presented visually via a large number of tables which break the results down to an impressive level of detail. At the same time, R. is disarmingly ready to admit the limitations of his method: indeed, he urges that one of the advantages of being able to process large quantities of data is that it may reveal negative or contradictory results, as well as positive ones, thus performing a useful function in clearing the critical decks, so to speak. This is not to say that the book lacks conclusions: the cumulative results of the investigation tend to show that sound features in the *DC* are largely autonomous from context, thus dispelling a long-cherished critical commonplace; it also highlights just how distinctive many of the *DC*'s formal features are, showing some marked differences from works by other medieval and Renaissance authors. The book's opening and closing chapters are more contextual in their approach, chapter 1 presenting an analysis of previous studies of sound features in the *DC*, and chapter 6 offering a discussion of the fortunes in Italy of the theoretical tools of formalism, structuralism, and semiotics.

Structure is also a central focus for discussion in Francesco Tateo, *Simmetrie dantesche*, Bari, Palomar, 252 pp. All but one (chapter 6) of its ten essays have been published separately elsewhere, but have been adapted to fit the shape of a continuous argument in the new volume, and the bibliography has been sensibly updated throughout to include the more recent publications of greatest pertinence to T.'s chosen topics. The *simmetrie* of the volume's title are long-recognized structural and linguistic devices in the *DC*: the verbal reprises, and the examples of repetition, variation, and opposition, with which D. links together the different parts of the poem's complex architecture. The majority of the essays take the form of *lecturae* of single canti (though the ninth chapter offers a comparative investigation of parallel canti — in each case the twentieth — from the three *cantiche*), with analysis of their key rhetorical and conceptual points, focusing on the *dispositio* of each unit both as a whole and in the context of its place within the journey narrative. For instance, *Inf.* IV (chapter 1) introduces the theme of comparison between pagan and Biblical antiquity, while *Purg.* XXIV (chapter 8) explores coincidences and divergences between the natural and the spiritual, and their respective place in poetry. In all of the essays, T. discusses the functioning of systems of symmetry, whether based on likeness or unlikeness, in relation to D.'s other-worldly topographies and encounters, to the poetic and rhetorical structures of different episodes, and to the use of number and numerology. The essays stress how correspondences between the elements in different systems — be they figural and typological, scientific and cosmological, or ethical and spiritual — and the fruitful intermeshing of the systems themselves create patterns of balance and symmetry that are fundamental to both the ethical and the aesthetic core of the *DC*.

Article-length studies on topics relating to the *DC* in general include a number from Esposito, *Dante* (which also offers a number of canto- or *cantica*-specific studies reviewed in the relevant sections below). The problematic question of D.'s presence in Rome in 1300 is covered by E. Plebani, 'Tra devozione e mercatura: Fiorentini a Roma nell'anno del primo Giubileo' (69–85), who provides a brief discussion of the relevant data, and of the critical assessments over the likelihood of a Dantean Jubilee pilgrimage; the essay also provides considerations about the motivations and activities of other Florentine visitors to Rome in 1300. M. Cursietti, 'Memorie topografiche di Roma giubilare nell'opera di Dante (con una nuova ipotesi su *Par.* ix, 40: *questo centesimo anno ancor s'incinqua*)' (103–13), likewise returns to the question of a possible Jubilee pilgrimage on D.'s part, evaluating the reliability of contemporary evidence on this point, and the significance of the reference to the Jubilee in *Inf.* xviii. Moving on to the *Par.* citation in his title, C. offers convincing arguments in support of interpreting the reference in terms of millennia rather than centuries and of placing the year 1300 at the mid-point of a temporal arc leading from Creation to Last Judgement. R. Mercuri, 'Significati simbolici e metaforici del Giubileo nell'opera di Dante' (115–40), stresses the links between the theme of salvific pilgrimage fundamental to the *DC* (and indeed foreshadowed in the *VN*) and the Jubilee concept, showing how the poem combines the themes of individual and universal *renovatio* and engages with the ideas of political exile, heroic quest, and Christian *peregrinatio*. The article goes on to provide close analysis of episodes from the *DC* where content and/or lexis provide clear evidence of such thematic concerns, predominantly taken from *Purg.* and *Par.* Another edited collection, Marietti, *Dante*, provides a further crop of general studies. I. Abramé-Battesti, 'Fonction poétique et fonction d'autorité dans *La Divine Comédie*' (35–47), investigates changes in D.'s manipulation of classical, and even theological, *auctoritates* between the *VN* or *Cvo* and the *DC*, notably in cases where words or opinions are attributed to such authors. Where the earlier works formulate such utterances in hypothetical or prosopopeic form, the *DC* operates a 'transvocalisation' (37) whereby the texts are appropriated by D. to create his own new texts and combinations of texts in the vernacular framework of the poem, often creating tensions between the referential or rhetorical function and the exemplary function of the allusion. The essay shows how D. uses the fiction of the journey, with its providential sanction, to short-circuit the normal process of authorization by citation, when it places D. and his text at the beginning rather than at the end of the chain of intertextual relationships, making the truths of his own text validate those of his authorities rather than, or as well as, the reverse. L. Pertile, 'Dante popolare' (67–91), offers a dense and stimulating investigation of the extent to which D. drew on, and spoke to, popular culture in composing the *DC*. The essay starts with an investigation of Minos, noting how *Inf.* transforms the dignified patrician judge imagined by Virgil into a grotesque figure, whose tail makes him immediately recognizable as one of the devils any medieval Christian would expect to encounter in hell. The example allows P. to extend his investigation, showing how D. deliberately employs, at least for much of *Inf.* and *Purg.*, imagery and narrative styles that would strike an immediate chord with uneducated readers, echoing popular preaching traditions in his use of vivid novelistic detail and conformity to traditional cultural categories, that make his moral accessible. Only the *Par.*, P. argues, uses style and matter that assume an educated and specialist audience. P. urges the importance of returning to popular culture in assessing D.'s practice, and achievement in the *DC*, reminding us that much of the experimentalism and polysemy that critics recognize in D. signal not the sophisticated textual and conceptual manipulations of a coolly detached theorist, but an urgent and committed attempt to deliver a message to an audience found on the piazza, rather than in the university or seminary alone. A. Lavau, 'Métrique et narration dans *La Divine Comédie*: les cent vers de clôture de chant' (111–28), investigates a formal and structural issue: whether particular characteristics can be identified for the closing line of each canto of the *DC*. Given the metrical structure of *terza rima*, the final line always occupies a somewhat isolated position, which may give its content a special prominence. The analysis is pursued methodically, and some useful conclusions achieved: that the line is normally in the 'voice' of D.-poeta, and addressed to the reader; and that it normally deals either with matter relating to the development of the journey or with didactic matter, the former especially in *Inf.* and the latter especially in *Purg.* and *Par.*; all of which casts interesting light on the communicative and narrative strategies of the *DC*. D. Bisconti, 'Cordeliers et cordelières dans *La Divine Comédie*' (271–304), constructs an investigation of D.'s attitude towards Franciscan spirituality, and of his stance in the debates between Conventuals and Spirituals, through the investigation of two Franciscans from the *DC*: Guido da Montefeltro (*Inf.* xxvii) and Piccarda Donati (*Par.* iii). The encounter with G. is shown to highlight D.'s interest not only in the questions of Church unity and Church poverty that are so often associated with the citation of Boniface VIII in this episode, but also with the intellectual and theological implications of the Franciscans' acceptance or otherwise of the conventual infrastructure that facilitates scholarship, demonstrated in *Inf.* through the devil's mastery of quasi-Conventual or Oxfordian theological and logical insights. P. on the other hand articulates some of the mysticism of St Clare, in discourses that emphasize a feminine religiosity focused on mystical love and on the interiority of conversion and chastity.

Other articles on the *DC* as a whole include: B. D. Schildgen, 'Dante's Utopian political vision, the Roman empire, and the salvation of pagans', *AnI*, 19:51–69, which investigates the criteria that D. may have used in deciding which pagans might be granted a place in *Purg.* or *Par.* She argues that the choice is related intimately to both political considerations — the engagement of the individual pagan with the Roman empire, and the symbolic qualities of justice, liberty, and happiness that it represents according to D.'s *Mon.* — and theological ones, in particular with the virtue of hope. The majority of D.'s pagan writers and thinkers failed to recognize the providential mission of empire, and hence they are relegated to Limbo: but the illuminated commitment of Cato, Statius, Ripheus, and Trajan (and, S. speculates, perhaps of Augustus and Livy) to liberty, justice, and a humble appreciation of the Roman destiny, allows D. to award them a place among the redeemed. R. Fasani, 'L'altro stilnovo: ammonizioni e invettive nella *Commedia*', *RELI*, 16, 2000:83–98, takes the form of a meticulous analytical list of the episodes where particularly striking passages of admonition or invective occur in the *DC*, from *Inf.* VII to *Par.* XXX. The essay suggests that these passages constitute an 'altro stilnovo', dedicated to the poetry not of praise but of condemnation, stressing that the forms and language of this inverted *stilnovo* are as varied and original as those of the canonical 'stile de la loda'. The detail in the list, and its comprehensive compilation from a careful reading of all three *cantiche*, highlights with almost mathematical accuracy how the narrative of the *DC* works counter-intuitively not to reduce but increase the doses of harsh condemnation, in number and in frequency, culminating in the *Par.* with stronger and stronger denunciations of human negligence, as D.-*personaggio* gains greater and greater understanding of the breadth of divine love. M. T. Lanza, 'A proposito di Dante e Stazio', *EL*, 36.3:3–11, provides an intertextual investigation of reminiscences of both the *Achilleid* and the *Thebaid* in the *DC*. The essay draws attention in particular to a possible Statian element overlooked by previous criticism in the episode of the *messo da ciel* in *Inf.* IX, which she relates to two encounters with other-worldly messengers in S., the infernal Tisyphone and the divine Mercury. She also discusses how S.'s representations of motherhood — especially in the tragic story of Hypsipyle — may have left traces in a number of different passages, ranging from direct citation of Statius in the *Cvo* to more elusive possible echoes in *Par.* XXXII. Linguistic questions are the focus of attention in L. Peirone, '*Frate* e *fratello*, *suora* e *sorella* nella *Divina Commedia*', *ib.*, 36.1:67–72. The essay proposes to investigate whether clear patterns can be identified in D.'s choices between the various terms to designate literal (blood), professional (monastic), or figural (sympathetic) brotherhood and sisterhood. In the case of the feminine terms, D.'s practice is relatively restricted, and the figural category in particular remains relatively little used. The terms *frate* and *fratello*, on the other hand, are used in a variety of contexts; P. especially highlights the use of *frate*, especially in the *Purg.*, as a kind of ceremonial title when D. wishes to indicate a bond of sympathy and affection between speakers: a masculine solidarity which finds no equivalent in his representation of relationships involving women. G. Tardiola, ' "Ancor nel libro suo che *Scala* ha nome": in occasione della traduzione italiana dell'*Escatologia* di Asín Palacios', *LIA*, 1, 2000: 59–68, offers reflections on the fortunes of A. P.'s proposals regarding intertextual relationships between the *DC* and the Muslim dream-vision journey of the *Libro della Scala*, paying particular attention to work by Corti, Moraldi, Saccone, Segre, and Zolla from the 1980s and 1990s. The essay emphasizes the importance of the original study, and of the work recently produced by the Italian scholars reviewed, hailing the arrival of an Italian translation of A. P.'s monograph (a mere 75 years after its original publication!) as likely to provide a stimulus to yet more contributions to the field.

A number of essays address issues that bear on the dating of the *DC*'s fictional journey. G. Brugnoli, 'Nel mezzo del cammin di nostra vita', Esposito, *Dante*, 87–102, recalls how the opening lines of the poem offer links with Old Testament calls to penitence and absolution (in *Ezekiel* and *Isaiah*). Drawing on calendrical and narrative data from the same canto, and from elsewhere in the *DC*, B. investigates numerological aspects of the *DC* that help link it to the Hebraic tradition of calculations for the Jubilee proclamation of phases of repentance and forgiveness, that were also strategically used by Boniface in proclaiming the Christian Jubilee of 1300 (the final page of the article provides the text of this proclamation). The article further investigates the quarrels over dating and anniversaries caused by the multiplicity of calendars in use in medieval Italy (Boniface dating the Jubilee *a nativitate* with a start date of 25 December, Florentine convention beginning the year *ab incarnatione* on 25 March). Id., 'L'astrologia in Dante e la datazione del "viaggio" dantesco', *L'Alighieri*, 41.1, 2000: 25–57, discusses similar themes, addressing D.'s interest in contemporary attempts to reconcile pagan astrological lore into the Christian system of belief. Proponents of such attempts drew analogies between Christ and the Sun, and stressed the calendrical prominence of Sun-day as holy day. Conflict ensued between those (including notably Boniface VIII) who took Christ's birth to have occurred on a Saturday, and those who made it match the Resurrection in occurring on a Sunday (as implied by the Florentine calendar). The essay offers detailed astrological references to allocate the start-date for the *DC*'s journey, suggesting that D.'s choice was intended to polemicize Boniface VIII's calendrical preferences. The dating of the journey is also the central concern of A. Mitescu, 'La *Divina Commedia* quale itinerario pasquale nel Santo Sepolcro in Gerusalemme', *L'Alighieri*, 42.1 : 37–57. The essay opens with a detailed discussion of the dating question, where M., like Brugnoli, rejects the conventional hypothesis that *Inf.* opens on Good Friday 1300. She reaches very different conclusions to B., however: using evidence about D.'s calendrical calculations based on study of the *VN* and *Cvo* as well as the *DC*, she finds the start date to be 28 March 1298 of the Florentine *calendario comune*. In accordance with the assumption that the Crucifixion occurred on a date when stars and planets matched their astronomical positions on the date of the Creation established by the traditional Hebrew calendar, and corroborated by Bede and Dionysius, this would fit D.'s own journey within the same astronomical framework of exact Jubilee recurrence, if M.'s interpretation of astronomical and calendrical references in the *DC* is correct. The action of the journey is thus allocated to the period between the eve of Palm Sunday, 28 March, and Easter Day, 6 April 1298, with its various phases — marked by ritual and liturgical performances in many stages of *Purg.* and *Par.* — corresponding to the liturgical celebrations that punctuate Holy Week, as celebrated both in Jerusalem at the church of the Holy Sepulchre and at St Peter's in Rome. Highlighting the emphasis paid to correspondences between the celebrations of Rome and Jerusalem in the first Jubilee year, 1300, M. suggests that D.'s dating allows him to outline still purer correspondences between the sacred timing of the *DC*'s journey and the mysteries of Fall and Redemption, an argument that she further supports by identifying various topographical parallels between the sacred and symbolic architecture of the Holy Sepulchre shrine and the structures of D.'s afterworld. Broader issues relating to chronology and periodization are addressed in two essays from Pinchard, *Pour Dante*. A. Calvet, 'Dante et les joachimismes' (77–98), stresses the diversity of Joachimite writings, but also their common concern with the idea of *renovatio* and interest in identifying Ages of spiritual progress or decline, and outlines a number of passages where D.'s concerns with change and prophecy may echo Joachimite thought. Passages from the *Mon.* as well as the *DC* are discussed; the analysis of the theme of poverty, and of possible Jubilee-related allusions, in *Par.* IX stand out particularly. N. Mineo, 'Gli spirituali francescani e l'*Apocalisse* di Dante' (99–126), addresses similar themes, in this case paying particular attention to elements in the Earthly

Paradise sequence that recall the writings of Olivi. M. however is more sceptical than Calvet over the extent to which Joachimite influence is detectable in D.: although M. grants that borrowings from millennial literature can be identified, he stresses that D. uses them to support very different lines of argument and interpretation to those intended by their original proponents. J. Hein, 'Concept et image du temps dans la *Divine Comédie*' (161–80), investigates tensions in the *DC*'s conception of the functioning of time, and the problematic relationship between the time-bound realm of history and the timelessness of eternity that emerges from the text. H. identifies an initial clash, in the realm of history, between a linear, messianic conception of time (expressed especially in D.'s pronouncements on Henry VII and the Veltro prophecy) and the circularity of history stressed by Stoic classical thinkers. Both models are in a sense pre-empted or overturned by the eternity of the Godhead, whereby cases such as the salvation of Ripheus interfere with expectations based on futurity and conditionality and provide a direct challenge to both systems of time measurement.

INFERNO

The whole enterprise of reading the *Inf.* — or even the *DC* as a whole — comes under review in F. Finotti, 'Il poema ermeneutico (*Inferno* I-II)', *LItal*, 53:489–508. The essay investigates what F. urges to be the peculiarly self-reflexive hermeneutic of the poem. Characterization and narrative concerns in *Inf.* I introduce the risk of failure into the poem from the start, a risk that strengthens on every occasion where D.-character is tempted to succumb to the sinful example of the damned: F. stresses that the sole weapon used to combat such dangers is that of poetry. Only with the appearance of Virgil, the *poeta* whose *parola ornata* will guide D.-character, does the journey become physically and conceptually possible; and when V. speaks of Beatrice, the journey's promoter, as 'loda di Dio vera', he recalls the *VN*'s conviction that the 'stile della loda' has a salvific function: V. and B. are no mere allegories of reason and faith, but living examples of the fundamental importance of poetry. A detailed investigation of parallels and inversions between cantos I and II illustrate F.'s contentions about the *DC*'s 'carattere autointerpretativo' (495), folding patterns back on themselves intratextually, and implanting intertextual allusion (to the *Aeneid* and the Bible) into even small details. The question of allegory is investigated carefully, stressing that rather than seeking to identify separate layers of allegory, the poem often draws attention to ambiguity and interpretative error, making hermeneutics not an external tool applied to the text, but an integral element in its textuality. G. Ledda, 'Su una *lectura* zurighese dell'*Inferno*', *RELI*, 17 : 105–14, primarily a detailed and useful review of the *Inferno* volume reviewed last year, also offers reflections on the practice of *lectura Dantis* in general, in all its changing forms, as we enter the 21st c. R. J. Quinones, 'Dante's *Inferno* in our time', *Della Terza Vol.*, 47–59, opens with a discussion of the preference much Modernist criticism has shown for *Purg.*, presenting a plea for revival of interest in *Inf.* and discussing some of the characteristics that make a return to the first *cantica* worthwhile for 21st-c. readers. After examining organizational, linguistic, and philosophic aspects of the *Inf.*, Q. offers an evaluation of the *cantica*'s arts of dissuasion and divestment. The essay suggest that the *Inf.* may have peculiar appeal for the readership of our times, offering a vision of 'radicalized evil' (59) that has an all-too-immediate relevance to our own era's confrontations with the issues of guilt and violence. A. A. Iannucci, 'Dante's intertextual and intratextual strategies in the *Commedia*: the Limbo of the children', *ib.*, 61–87, discusses D.'s selection and use of sources, and his structuring of the *DC*, stressing the care he takes to bring his reader's attention repeatedly to a tightly-linked set of core concerns relating to faith and reason, baptism and original sin, free will and predestination, and the relationships between divine and human justice. The essay focuses on D.'s Limbo, showing that its location, and its occupants and the extent of their punishment, reflect elements borrowed eclectically from Abelard, Albert the Great, Aquinas, and Virgil, but above all from Bonaventure. Besides these intertextual elements, it highlights the intratextual evidence that makes *Inf.* IV a 'structurally determining episode' (83): *Inf.* focuses on the adult virtuous pagans, but D. returns to the fate of its infant inhabitants as late as *Par.* XXXII, where the final pronouncements on the salvation of baptized and unbaptized infants close questions about sin, faith, and predestination that have been live issues with regard to both adults and children ever since *Inf.* IV.

Single-canto studies include, on *Inf.* III: A. Heil, ' "Che fece per viltade il gran rifiuto ...": Ein Akrostichon in Dantes *Commedia* (*Inf.* 3, 58–60)?', *RF*, 113:227–32, focuses on the famous problem of identifying the unknown sinner that the essay's title cites, whose name as one of the *ignavi* in *Inf.* cannot be mentioned in view of the Virgilian warning that 'fama di loro il mondo esser non lassa' (49). H. suggests that D.'s solution is to construct an acrostic: the terzina referring to the 'gran rifiuto' provides, through the opening letter of each hendecasyllable (P, V, C), the initial letters of the sinner's name and title: taken together with the contextual information in the canto, this allows the reader to identify 'Coelestinus V Papa' (232). Corroboration for the hypothesis seems confirmed by the evidence in commentary and illustration that the earliest readers of the *DC*, well-versed in deciphering such textual clues, did almost unanimously identify the allusion as referring to Pope Celestine. On *Inf.* IV: S. Vazzana, ' "Orazio satiro"?', *RCCM* 43:91–102. The essay queries whether the adjective 'satiro' should be interpreted as indicating an especial interest in or influence from Horace's *Satires*, suggesting that the *DC* shows only one or at most two instances where a direct debt to them can be identified. Echoes of H.'s other works are considerably more numerous (a number of persuasive examples are provided), and the *Epistles* — including the *Ars poetica* — stand out as most influential, providing D. with both verbal and conceptual material for his pronouncements on moral and rhetorical questions (the latter often themselves ethically coloured in Horatian mode). H. therefore seems to be named as satirist in *Inf.* in order to widen the spread of genres represented by D.'s classical *auctoritates* rather than to mark his primary area of activity, thus heightening the implicit claim that D. himself, with the new linguistic and generic form of the *DC*, has left the whole span of pre-Christian literary achievement behind. On *Inf.* VII: N. Cacciaglia, 'I guerci in miniera (considerazioni sul c. VII dell'*Inferno*', *FoI*, 35: 67–79, suggests that many elements, both linguistic and conceptual, in the punishments of Hell's fourth circle may have been modelled on the activities of mining for metal in the Sienese Maremma. Echoes of 14th-c. mining terminology and of aspects of mine work (bearing heavy weights, division into work-teams, etc.) provide linguistic and visual analogies with the gruelling work of mining for precious metals — an apt frame of allusion for the punishment of the canto's money-driven sinners. The interpretation also throws up an intriguing hypothesis regarding the nonsense language of Pluto, which C. suggests may have been suggested to D. by the presence of German overseers in the Tuscan metal-extraction industry — figures of notoriously harsh and irascible authority whose utterance would have been scarcely intelligible to their Tuscan underlings. On *Inf.* XIV: S. Vazzana, 'Il canto XIV dell'*Inferno*', *L'Alighieri*, 41.2, 2000:23–52, focuses on the structure of the canto, tracing a careful symmetry between its different elements, which V. compares to the architectural interconnection in the lyric canzone form of themes, language, and imagery between *fronte*, *piedi*, *sirima*, and *commiato*. Analysis of the Veglio and of Capaneo reveals the intertextual subtleties in D.'s negative reworkings of heroic figures from classical literary tradition. On *Inf.* XVIII: A. Lanza, 'Note testuali a *Inferno* XVIII', Esposito, *Dante*, 141–48, provides a philological survey of the canto (occasioned by its famous reference to the Jubilee pilgrims traversing the Ponte Sant'Angelo), listing and commenting on a number of cases where his own edition (*Commedìa*, 1996), based on the strongly Florentine Trivulziana MS 1080, produces divergent readings from the Petrocchian standard *vulgata*; the full text of L.'s edition of the canto appears on pp. 145–48. On *Inf.* xx: M. Palma de Cesnola, 'Teseo, Creonte e la morte di Tiresia (*Inf.* xx 58–59)', *L'Alighieri*, 41.1, 2000:117–25, discusses the divergence between ancient and modern commentators over the interpretation of the reference to Thebes's enslavement after the death of Tiresias, which early commentators all relate to the period of domination by Theseus of Athens. The essay offers a detailed reconstruction of modern divergence, originating with Scartazzini, from this account: this provides an intriguing demonstration of the ease with which errors become accepted unquestioningly into a tradition of exegesis and criticism. On *Inf.* xxvi: M. Corti, 'Bilan des études dantesques, et quelques considérations sur Ulysse', Pinchard, *Pour Dante*, 203–14, traces antecedents for D.'s assertion that U.'s *curiositas* impelled him on into a final journey beyond the pillars of Hercules, and outlines the traditions which, especially in Muslim Spanish lore, came to associate them with the 'non plus ultra' dictum. Bringing these considerations to bear on the canto, C. highlights how elements in U.'s *orazione* echo the language and ideas of what she has long termed 'radical Aristotelianism' and, more specifically, the work of Boethius of Dacia. She suggests that by placing such allusions into U.'s speech, D. signals his definitive break in the *DC* with an intellectual milieu that had fascinated him (and Guido Cavalcanti) in youth, but also admits the allure of the ideas by making the great orator and hero of the classical world, U., their exponent. G. Gorni, 'I "riguardi" di Ercole e l'"arto passo" di Ulisse', *LIA*, 1, 2000:43–58, sets out to shed light on the passage as a whole by opening a new investigation of the two key words quoted in the article title: the results suggest that this canto may have a more precise nautical context than is normally supposed. G.'s asks two questions in the article: where *exactly* are the 'riguardi' of Hercules? And was the 'passo' of U. and his companions 'alto' (as Petrocchi's *vulgata* reads) or 'arto'? Investigation of the geographical lore of medieval Italy — using Pliny, Isidore, and Brunetto Latini's *Tresor* as primary sources — suggests that the pillars of H. were located not at the Straits of Gibraltar but at the Isthmus of Cadiz, while a detailed examination of the marine references in U.'s speech produces the suggestion that, alongside the mention of the 'foce stretta', U. is likely to have designated the Isthmus an '*arto* passo', thus giving a technical and correct description of the coastal features defining these distant European waters. Geographical precision also contributes to the thesis in Id., ' "Quando | mi diparti' da Circe", ou les sirènes d'Ulysse', Marietti, *Dante*, 51–66. A close examination of the rhetorical features of U.'s account of his last journey highlights echoes of both Ovid and Virgil, and suggests the

importance of reading the sequence intertextually, alongside both the
Ovidian account of Circe, and the Virgilian figure of Aeneas with his
divinely-sanctioned sea voyages, whose name is cited at *Inf.* XXVI, 93
in connection with C.'s island. G. suggests that later in the canto,
'viver come bruti' carries direct reference to C. and her dangerous
allurements: U. is urging his companions to avoid returning to her
island, making their onward journey a rejection of Circean sensory
corruption, as well as an evasion of the patriotic and familial *pietas*
that will come to be associated with the island by Aeneas's renaming
it after his nurse Gaeta; although U.'s failed landfall on another
island, Mount Purgatory, confirms his final anti-Aenean flaws, as he
attempts to force a way into the afterlife that A., like D., accepts can
only be undertaken under divine sanction. A. Kablitz, 'Il canto di
Ulisse agli occhi dei commentatori contemporanei e delle indagini
moderne', *LIA*, 2:61–92, confronts two of the perennial critical
controversies over the canto: is U. a positive or a negative figure? And
for what precise fault is he condemned? A detailed study of scriptural
and patristic authorities casts light on the question of U. as *consigliere
frodolente*. K. stresses the importance of U.'s reference to pursuing
knowledge until the end of 'questa piccola vigilia d'i nostri sensi'. The
liturgical form *vigilia* suggests that U. is concerned with earthly, sense-
based knowledge alone, pertaining to life as the *vigilia* of death: in
other words, U. is contradicting his own rhetorical exhortations and
advocating a sensory goal that has to do with 'viver come bruti',
rather than with eternity and the afterlife. U. deliberately blinds
himself to intellectual and spiritual truth in establishing such a goal
for his quest: whereas D.-character, in contrast, is participating in a
quest for rational truth and knowledge about the world beyond the
vigilia of sensory life. In K.'s view, the episode as a whole serves to
provide a deeper initiation of D.-character into the full meaning of
his own journey, through his encounter with U. and his sin against
truth. M. Picone, 'Il contesto classico del canto di Ulisse', *StCrit*, 15,
2000:171–92, argues for the importance of appreciating the careful
construction of the U. episode, based on a double programme that
both returns to authoritative classical sources regarding U.'s experiences and imbues them with Christian allegorical significance.
Among sources, P. notes the significance of Virgilian material, but
emphasizes the pre-eminence of the *Metamorphoses* in establishing
U. as the master-orator and exemplar of pagan virtue; but also
master-fraudster, condemned to this *bolgia* for the Trojan horse
stratagem. This fraud can be seen as a *felix culpa*, cause of Aeneas's
exile and hence of the foundation of Rome; further Adamic elements
in the canto are identified in the crucial issue of free will and the
decision to transgress sacred limits in pursuit of knowledge. The

Ovidian resonances in the canto extend beyond simply the characterization of U. himself: his exhortation not to live 'come bruti' gains
satirical force from the Circean episode, while echoes of the journeys
of Icarus and Phaeton enrich the description of U.'s 'folle volo',
providing a rich framework of impressive but sacrilegious inverse
parallels to D.-character's Christian quest.

PURGATORIO

Lectura Dantis Turicensis: Purgatorio, ed. Georges Güntert and Michelangelo Picone, F, Cesati, 515 pp., is the second volume of the stimulating
lectura series promoted by the University of Zurich. This volume
follows close on the heels of the *Inf.* essays published last year, and
brings together an equally impressive cast of international contributors. Once again, the two editors each provide a number of the
essays themselves: G. is responsible for the essays on cantos III, VIII,
X, XVII and XVIII, and P. for cantos II, V, VII, IX, XV, XIX, XXII, XXVI
and XXIX, thus providing a substantial and coherent backbone for the
volume. Two others have contributed serially: M. Perugi (canti VI,
XXXII), A. Stäuble (XX, XXX); the remaining single studies come from
a wide range of scholars, giving the volume a stimulating element of
diversity: Z. G. Barański (XXV), J. Bartuschat (I), S. Bellomo (XXXIII),
C. Bologna (XXXI), A. Cipollone (XVI), R. Fasani (XXVII), A. Ghisal-
berti (IV), B. Guthmüller (XIV), A. Kablitz (XIII), B. König (XXVIII),
V. Panicara (XXIII), L. C. Rossi (XXI) — not to be confused with
L. Rossi (XXIV), K. Stierle, (XI), and J. A. Scott (XII).

Elsewhere, a general survey of themes fundamental to Antipurgatorio as a whole, extending beyond the two canti mentioned in the title,
emerges in M. Aversano, 'Le opere di misericordia tra il V e il VI
canto del *Purgatorio*', Esposito, *Dante*, 153–82. The essay suggests that
the message of conversion — in its technical, theological sense —
associated with the 1300 Jubilee produces an emphasis, in the
Antipurgatorio sequences, on the importance of performing acts of
compassion. Using Biblical and theological *auctoritates*, philology, and
intratextual comparisons with the *Inf.*, A. outlines a precise line of
conversional behaviour in the acts of mutual assistance and the
expressions of sympathetic emotion exchanged between the souls of
cantos V and VI, and highlights the contrast between the active and
loving compassion of these souls, with the cupidity, pride, and envy
that makes 'serva Italia' a place of absolute selfishness, the antithesis
of Purgatorial love or pity. J. Bartuschat, 'Dante voyageur dans le
Purgatoire', Marietti, *Dante*, 147–73, investigates the theme of the
journey in *Purg.*, investigating its multiple functions in the structure
and the meaning of this part of the poem, where the motif of change

associated with the idea of travel plays a particularly prominent part. D.'s notion of journeying is placed in a comparative context through consideration of other texts such as Latini's *Tesoretto*. B. goes on to explore various episodes from the *Purg.*, establishing two axes to the narrative function of the journey theme: a syntagmatic axis, where narrative progress is achieved through the structured theme of ascent; and a paradigmatic axis, where the motif of the journey invokes other layers of meaning in the *cantica*, such as exile, pilgrimage, conversion, or the act of writing itself. A. Ruschioni, *‘La poetica della luce nel *Purgatorio*’, *Archivio storico lodigiano* 119, 2000 [2001]:177–224. R. Stella, ‘La critique narrativisée de la poésie dans le *Purgatoire*’, Marietti, *Dante*, 91–110, focuses on episodes in the *Purg.* where D. encounters poets, and where he cites from his own lyric *œuvre*. S. notes that the numerous encounters with vernacular and Latin poets for which the *cantica* is famous are each constructed in a distinct manner, a variety that is no mere rhetorical *varietas* but a carefully constructed narrative ‘effet du réel’ (95). This realism in turn heightens the ‘effet d’autorité’ (98) achieved by the citation of external texts — with their pre-established historicity and authenticity — within another text; and makes the encounters of D. with individual poets who cite poetic works and traditions metonymic of D.'s encounter with his own poetry. This makes the process of creation of the new text self-reflexive, and inscribes poetic historiography and criticism into the broader narrative of regeneration and reconquest of *Purg.* as a whole.

Single-canto studies include, on *Purg.* I: G. Muresu, ‘Il “sacrificio” per la libertà (*Purgatorio* I)’, *RLI*, 105:357–403. The essay offers a lengthy and detailed discussion of several important strands of thought in the canto. The opening two sections examine the canto's language, and also the indications it provides about the physical structures of Mount Purgatory, and of the other realms of the afterlife, in a series of close analyses that stress how carefully D. demarcates the poetic and ethical differences between the *Inf.* and the other two *cantiche*. Scrutiny, for instance, of the canto's astrological references reveals a rich hinterland of allusion that stresses the difference between the northern, earthly, and sinful hemisphere where both the inhabited continents and the abyss of hell are located, from the southern, illuminated, and beatified hemisphere where all souls are guaranteed final salvation. The essay's following four sections examine different aspects of the figure of Cato and the perennial conundrums his presence in *Purg.* presents. The evidence presented here all stresses C.'s appropriateness as the first spirit encountered in the realm of salvation: his physical appearance, for instance, assimilates him to the Biblical patriarchs with whom he was (presumably) rescued from Limbo at the crucifixion, while his virtuous suicide recalls the divinely sanctioned self-destruction of the Church's early virgin martyrs; his refusal to accept the Roman empire is equally explained by his virtue, which left him no need of the constraining authority of D.'s imperial *remedium peccati*. Rather than seeing C. as a gatekeeper, M. suggests that his presence is symbolic, showing D.-*personaggio* that all whom he will encounter henceforth have freely chosen to reject Satan — C.'s beloved 'libertà' is not merely political, but also spiritual. Similarly, M. suggests that the exchanges between C. and Virgil, often taken to indicate defective understanding in one or both, are performed for the benefit of the pilgrim, who through the words and the ritual actions of these two classical heroes is pointed towards a rebirth of his own free will towards a new humility in the worlds beyond sin. On *Purg.* ii: L. Cassata, 'L'indulgenza giubilare nell'episodio di Casella (*Purg.* ii, 91–105)', Esposito, *Dante*, 149–51, discusses the theological peculiarity of the claim that Casella did not profit immediately from the Jubilee indulgence to embark for Mount Purgatory as soon as the Jubilee year began. The critic stresses that D. appears to be following orthodox theological convention in assuming that C. — in death perfectly attuned to the demands of Christian humility — voluntarily withheld from embarking on his purification until he had completed a proper penitence, and shows the Thomistic authority for drawing such a distinction between 'volontà assoluta' (C.'s desire to proceed) and 'volontà relativa, condizionata' (151), expressed in his acceptance of the need to wait. On *Purg.* iii: L. Scorrano, 'Dall'abbandono alla bontà riconquistata', *L'Alighieri*, 41.2, 2000:53–71, emphasizes two themes in the canto: the importance of the role of the mountain as almost another protagonist in the *Purg.*, forming a line of connection between the souls who ascend its terraces; and the fear of abandonment and solitude, highlighted in the encounter with Manfredi, which introduces an anticipation of the feelings of isolation induced by Virgil's disappearance at the mountain summit. S. argues that the introduction of these themes in the opening canti of the new *cantica* highlight issues that will prove fundamental to the subsequent structural and stylistic procedures in the *Purg*. On *Purg.* vii: T. Santelli, '*Purgatorio* canto vii', *L'Alighieri*, 41.2, 2000, 73–98, takes up the question of the position of Sordello, whom critics variously allocate a place among those who died by violence or the negligent princes of the valley. S. suggests that rather than belonging definitively to either of these groups, Sordello's importance in the sequence derives from his role as poet. His solitude in *Purg*. reflects the solitude appropriate to poetic genius in life and makes him an apt mirror-image for D., the exile-pilgrim whose earthly fate will impose political and social solitude on him but will also thereby promote his poetic and spiritual development towards a level of merit worthy of inclusion in the new and perfect community of the heavenly *patria*. On *Purg.* XII: A. Tartaro, 'La pedagogia di Virgilio e i segni della superbia (*Purgatorio* XII)', *La Cultura*, 39:19–34, analyses the canto's linking position between the terraces of pride and envy, and focuses attention onto the phenomenon of the sculpted *exempla* of pride that pave the pathway. T. suggests that the canto achieves a balance between the harsh immediacy of the sculptures, with their uncompromising message about sin and punishment, and the gentleness of the pedagogical care with which V. soothes the anxieties they raise for the protagonist. Fruitful reflections on the physical structures described in the canto demonstrate the significance of the reliefs' position on the path: this forces the viewers (D. and the sinners) to bend down humbly to learn their moral lesson (and also represses artistic pride by placing God's own masterpieces beneath their passing feet), while also pulling them onwards in their circular progress round the terrace. The timing of this canto's action at the sixth hour provides another reminder of the dangers of pride: Adam will later tell D. (*Par.* XXVI) that the Fall occurred at the sixth hour, while the Bible records that this was also the time of the death of Christ at the Crucifixion. On *Purg.* XIV: G. A. Camerino, '*Purgatorio* XIV: corrispondenze simbologiche, strutturali e stilistiche', *L'Alighieri*, 41.2, 2000:99–121, investigates how the structuring of the canto, in conjunction with canto XIII, provides unitary progression throughout the encounter with the envious, whilst at the stylistic level, D. maintains a counterpoint between high and low register that reinforces the symbolic significance of the cantos' evocation of degenerate contemporary reality versus a past of civilized *cortesia*. On *Purg.* XX: T. Santelli, 'Canto XX del *Purgatorio*', *L'Alighieri*, 42.1:7–35, opens with a discriminating and detailed discussion of 20th-c. critics' *lecturae* of the canto, drawing attention to the diversity of their interpretations and, especially, of their assessment of D.'s view of its central figure, Hugh Capet. The essay highlights the episodic structure of the canto, where linguistic and conceptual differences clearly distinguish the opening and closing sections, with a lyrical tone dedicated to prayer and praise, from the violence and invective that characterizes the central encounter with H. It further investigates the antecedents for D.'s choice of language and imagery in his depictions of poverty and humility, and contextualizes his concern with avarice (on the part both of H. and of his descendants) by placing the canto's central spiritual and political material in close relation both to the prophecy of the Veltro and to the political *Ep.s* occasioned by Henry VII's Italian campaigns. S. emphasizes that D. is concerned less with strict factual accuracy in his political pronouncements (whether relating to the long-dead H. or to recent events between Boniface VIII and Philip IV) than with party concerns — even when they are those of a solitary 'parte per [se] stesso' of moral righteousness, rather than those of Guelf or Ghibelline faction bias. On *Purg.* XXII: M. d'Ettore, 'I gradini e la poesia nel canto XXII del *Purgatorio*', *CLett*, 29:3–14, examines the intersection in the canto's treatment of the theme of ascent in physical terms (that of D.-character and his companions) and in poetic ones (that of D.-poet as his narrative grows ever more elevated), both aspects highlighted by the prominent presence of the classical tragic writers Virgil and Statius and by the use of the image of the steps that lead up the mountain. Intertextual allusions are identified with the symbolic spiritual ascents of the Dream of Jacob and the *Libro della Scala*, and the symbolic steps towards God outlined by St Bernard's sermon on the *Cantica*. The allegories of physical and spiritual ascent evoked by these allusions are supplemented by the network of references to poetic achievement in the exchanges between V. and S. on their ancient compeers: all tending to support D.'s concern with the elevation of style and content that he consistently pursues as he approaches the earthly, and the heavenly, paradise. On *Purg.* XXIV: M. Aversano, 'Sulla poetica dantesca nel canto XXIV del *Purgatorio*', *L'Alighieri*, 41.2, 2000:123–38, proposes a dense application to the canto of a system of minute analysis of single *luoghi* according to their verbal structure and their intratextual correspondences within the canto and within the *DC*, widening out to pursue intertextual allusion to various macrotexts, most notably to the Bible. The essay focuses primarily on D.'s presentation of the theme of poetic excellence, and the question of personal/textual relationships between poets and schools of poets, paying considerable attention to Virgil as well as to the canto's engagement with vernacular lyric traditions. On *Purg.* XXIX: M. Picone, *'Dantes dichterischer Triumph: eine lectura von *Purg.* XXIX', *DDJ*, 76:103–28.

PARADISO

F. Tateo, *'Percorsi agostiniani in Dante', *DDJ*, 76:43–56. S. Botterill, 'Ideals of the institutional Church in Dante and Bernard of Clairvaux', *Italica*, 78:297–313, takes as its starting point a divergence between the references to St B. in Benvenuto's commentary between the Talice version of 1375 and the Imolan's own 1380 edition. The earlier version states that St B. had not been officially canonized: fruitfully, this error forces the commentator to justify D.'s choice of final guide, which leads to an emphasis on St B.'s interest in ecclesiastical decadence, and the need for reform, which of course was also an urgent concern for the poet. The main body of the article is devoted to a probing and finely-nuanced examination of issues of influence (that critical bugbear), questioning whether direct connections can be identified between the Cistercian and D., perhaps mediated via Joachimite lines of transmission: it sensibly concludes that direct influence, in the 21st-c. sense, is impossible to prove — but that D.'s utterances on ecclesiastical corruption and on reform do display a Bernardine cast, probably absorbed as part of a broader cultural patrimony, suggesting that the presence of St B. in *Par.* may hint at D.'s awareness of a debt to the Saint's thinking. D. Gibbons, 'Alimentary metaphors in Dante's *Paradiso*', *MLR*, 96:693–706, considers a single class of metaphors from across the whole *cantica*: those terms that relate to hunger, thirst, taste, and digestion. An illuminating discussion of traditional uses of such metaphors in both sapiential and scholastic theology is followed by an examination of departures from such traditions on D.'s part, especially in matters of lexical choice, formal position, and combinations of terms. The article ends with a closer analysis a set of alimentary metaphors from Aquinas's speeches in cantos X and XI, each dramatizing the problem of excess — metaphorical gluttony — with regard to the human intellect. Strikingly, D. makes the great scholastic thinker condemn his followers and draw a subtle but essential distinction between forcing the intellectual appetite on forbidden matters and a more proper attendance of the manna of divine revelation. M. Marietti, 'Les cris et les silences du Ciel de Saturne', Marietti, *Dante*, 305–31, stresses the structural and thematic symmetries between cantos XXI and XXII. She notes how the prevailing silence of the Heaven, interrupted by the contemplatives' deafening shout at the end of XXI, focuses the reader's attention on to words: especially, those of the two principal speakers of the sequence, Benedict and Peter Damian. Analysis of the rhetorical and structural forms of their two speeches shows an elegant symmetry between the two, creating continuity of discourse despite the disruption of the shout, and also establishing verbal and thematic connections with preceding and following canti. J. Mazzaro, '*Paradiso* XX, the missing Virgin, and absent presence', *FoI*, 35:5–22, despite its ostensible concern with a single canto, casts the net of its dense investigation across much of the *Par.* (and beyond); particular attention is paid to *Par.* II and XXXIII, for instance. The article investigates patterns of repetition and intertextuality from throughout the *DC*, noting the importance of 'absent presences' in many of D.'s allusions to his own or others' texts, where omissions or reworkings of expected detail provide a hermeneutic challenge to the reader. The missing Virgin of *Par.* XX is of course Mary: but, in the canto of justice, is also Astrea, whose place in the classical myth of the

Golden Age intertwines with the Marian/Biblical themes of Fall and Redemption. The (absent) reference also leads to reflections on the middle ground lying between these two poles — the Iron Age of a post-Lapsarian epoch — and M.'s discussion of the two paradisal references to the myth of the Argonauts highlights the interest of D.'s conceptual and poetic procedures, where patterns of interconnection between episodes in the narrative constantly invite the reader to cross-refer and seek deeper meaning by discovering changes, and challenges, in the components of the text. M. Morrison, 'Looking at God: imagery for the divinity in Dante's *Paradiso*', *FoI*, 35:307–17, considers the two visions of God experienced by D.-*personaggio* in *Par.* xxviii and xxxiii, respectively as a 'punto' and a circle-pattern. M. investigates the probable Dionysian origins of these symbols, and shows that the imagery and doctrine of the angels' amorous encircling of the divine in xxviii provides a direct anticipation of what the protagonist experiences in the final canto, as he too is absorbed into the circular motion of love. P. Nasti, 'The wise poet: Solomon in Dante's heaven of the sun', *RMS* 27:103–38, investigates the representation of Solomon, whom she shows to be in many ways the most prominent and most complex of the figures encountered in the Sun. His uniqueness is underscored in many ways: he is sole political figure among the contemplative religious of this heaven; he is praised as the wisest of men; most significantly for this essay, language associated with the Solomonic books of the Old Testament permeates the entire sequence, making him a poetic and theological *auctoritas* who functions 'to celebrate D.'s idea of divinely inspired human poetry' (109). The article shows how language in this sequence draws heavily on the theme of marriage, and underlines the sweetness and the joy of corporeal and amorous experience, in terms that recall the language of the *Song of Songs* and which seem strongly influenced by the mystical exegetical tradition that viewed the *Song* as allegorizing relationships between Christ and the Church, the Virgin, and Christ, or the individual Christian and his God, creating a complex web of intertextual allusion that gives Solomon a pivotal role as poetic interpreter of the divine to the human — and thus an authority for and precursor to D.'s own enterprise in the *Par.*, and the *DC* as a whole. C. Trottmann, 'Communion des saints et jugement dernier dans les chants xix-xx du *Paradis*', Pinchard, *Pour Dante*, 181–99, explores both the imperial and the eschatological themes introduced via the symbol of the eagle in the sphere of Jupiter. The communion of saints in the eagle mirrors the unity promised to mankind by the empire on earth, where the collective actuation of human intellection under imperial rule ought to echo the unity of intellection expressed in the eagle's single form and voice. The essay's discussion of the questions about salvation and predestination raised by the presence of Ripheus seeks to find theological supports for D.'s audacious gesture among the writings of Aquinas. The presentation of political issues in these same cantos are examined by P. Caye, 'La prothèse aquiline ou de la résolution de l'antimonie du Pouvoir chez Dante', *ib.*, 279–92.

Single-canto studies include, on *Par.* II: M. Picone, 'Il corpo nella/ della luna: sul canto II del *Paradiso*', *L'Alighieri*, 41.1, 2000: 1–23. The article stresses the importance of this canto to the *DC*'s central, and audacious, claim that D.-character's journey is a corporeal one. P. argues that this claim permits D.-poet — despite the numerous protestations of ineffability — to make a genuine attempt to achieve concrete descriptions of *Par.*, by emphasizing how the protagonist's presence brings temporal historicity into the ahistorical realm of heaven. He shows that the first two cantos of *Par.* establish the narratological premises for the *cantica* as a whole; and provides some important reflections on D.'s use of the myth of the Argonauts as the emblem of his poetic and spiritual enterprise. On *Par.* III: J. Freccero, 'Moon shadows: *Paradiso* III', *Della Terza Vol.*, 89–101, discusses the ideas about light, optics, reflection, and refraction raised by the similes D. uses to introduce the shadowy faces of the souls, referring to water, pearl jewellery, and the myth of Narcissus. The article identifies D.'s use in the similes of the rhetorical figures of *prosopopoeia* and *hypographein*, which intensify both the effectiveness, and the elusiveness, of his evocation of *Par.*'s insubstantial phenomena. A comparative survey of later authors' engagement with the simultaneously reflective and refractive qualities of glass and water underscores how significant a contribution the imagery makes to D.'s paradisal poetics — among F.'s selection of authors are Petrarch, Bacon, Frost, Wordsworth, Donne, and Galileo. On *Par.* X: G. Tulone, 'Gli "invidiosi veri" nella *Commedia* e nelle fonti dantesche', *LItal*, 52, 2000: 345–78, ranges well beyond the limits of Canto X in its consideration of the implications of D.'s allusion to Sigier's 'invidiosi veri'. An exhaustive survey of the use of the terms *invidia* and *verità* (plus its opposite *menzogna*) takes us into the midst of 13th-c. theological discussion, tracing etymologies, authorities, and interpretations from their Biblical sources, through the Patristic authorities, notably Augustine, and forward to more contemporary medieval usage in Peter Lombard, Aquinas, and others. The essay highlights the importance of the terms *invidia* and *verità* to accounts of the irreconcilable differences between Christ and Lucifer, the father of lies, and the significance of the affinities between envy and hypocrisy, where consciously-chosen subversion of the truth is disguised as truth. S. thus becomes an emblematic defender of the truths neglected by the very Church that condemned him, whose frivolous equivocations contrast with S.'s painstaking devotion to 'pensieri | gravi' and the pursuit of God's wisdom.

DUECENTO AND TRECENTO II
(EXCLUDING DANTE)

By ROBERTA CAPELLI and ATTILIO MOTTA, *Padua*

I. GENERAL

Arrigo Castellani, *Grammatica storica della lingua italiana*, I: *Introduzione*, Bo, Il Mulino, 2000, xxxviii + 631 pp. (to be followed by three vols respectively devoted to phonology, morphology, and syntax) is of fundamental importance, not only for historians of the language. The work falls into six chapters: 'Latino volgare e latino classico'; 'L'elemento germanico'; 'L'influsso galloromanzo'; 'Mode settentrionali e parole d'oltremare'; 'Le varietà toscane nel Medioevo'; 'Cenni sulla formazione della lingua poetica'. This last section is particularly interesting, offering, as it does, fresh data useful for the study of early Italian lyric poetry. P. Cherchi, 'Filologie del 2000', *RELI*, 17:135–53, assesses the position of present-day philological disciplines, which are seen as threatened by a 'culto per la edizione critica' (137); it also examines new tendencies (the so-called New Philology) and the application of new computer techniques to philology. A. Pioletti, 'Pluralità dell'antico nelle culture europee del Medioevo', *Siculorum Gymnasium*, 52, 1999[2001]:813–22, reflects upon the concept of 'antiquity' and on the influence exerted by the 'ancient' in Romance literature. G. Murano, 'Opere diffuse per *exemplar* e pecia. Indagini per un repertorio', *IMU*, 41, 2000:73–100, presents a preliminary report on his planned exhaustive compilation of works circulated in the form of an *exemplar* or 'pecia': the project will be founded on all lists discovered to date, on the statutes and documents relating to universities' publishing activity, and on extraction of data from catalogues of MSS. C. Del Popolo, 'Un paragrafo di critica testuale: *emendatio ex fonte*', *SPCT*, 63:5–28, with particular reference to lyric poetry, opens a methodological discussion aiming to demonstrate that, with texts transmitted by a single witness, *emendatio* becomes necessary once one can determine, with some degree of certainty, that the error is attributable to the copyist or even to the author. A survey conducted by R. Stillers, 'La letteratura italiana prima del 1500. Rassegna degli studi nei paesi di lingua tedesca (1995–2000)', *EL*, 26.1:89–98, shows that the 13th c. represents 'the Cinderella of German Italian studies' (89) and that critical interest is overwhelmingly concentrated on the *Trecento* masters, Dante, Petrarch, and Boccaccio. F. Dolbeau, 'Critique d'attribution, critique d'authenticité. Réflexions préliminaires', *FilM*, 6–7, 1999–2000:

33–62, from an initial distinction between anonymity, pseudo-epigraphy, and pluri-attribution, traces the course of authenticity criticism and the genesis of 'attributive' criticism, from 15th-c. origins with Lorenzo Valla to 17th-c. controversy over the *Imitatio Christi* with its consequent pursuit of — and expertise in — manuscripts, and down from there through the Golden Age of triumphant positivism to present-day relativization in intermediate situations (rewritings, revisions, interpolations, etc.) and to the rule of caution in the use of internal criteria.

2. DUECENTO AND TRECENTO EXCLUDING BOCCACCIO AND PETRARCH

Attention must be drawn, at the outset, to the four volumes devoted to photographic reproductions of the three fundamental manuscripts of the earliest Italian lyric poetry, which were compiled in Tuscany at the end of the 13th c.: *I canzonieri della lirica italiana delle origini*, ed. Lino Leonardi, 4 vols, F, SISMEL-Galluzzo, 2000–01: I, *Il canzoniere Vaticano*, cxiv + 368 pls, Vatican MS Vat. Lat. 3793; II, *Il canzoniere Laurenziano*, lxviii + 312 pls, MS Redi 9 at Florence's Biblioteca Laurenziana; III, *Il canzoniere Palatino*, xxxviii + 172 pls, MS Banco Rari 217, ex Palatino 418a, at Florence's Biblioteca Nazionale Centrale; IV, *Studi critici*, x + 458 pp. This last volume is devoted to a close examination of strictly philological, paleographical, and linguistic questions. For the Sicilian school, M. De Paolis, 'La scuola siciliana', *EL*, 26.2:99–102, updates the bibliography and outlines the critical debate of recent years. The poetic output of Giacomo da Lentini and the setting in which he worked are the theme of the volume edited by R. Arqués, *La poesia di Giacomo da Lentini. Scienza e filosofia nel XIII secolo in Sicilia e nel Mediterraneo occidentale*, Palermo, Centro di Studi Filologici e Linguistici Siciliani, 2000, 254 pp. The volume gathers the proceedings of a conference on the subject which took place at Barcelona's Universitat Autònoma in October 1997. S. Bianchini, 'Lacrime e diamanti. Per Giacomo da Lentini, *(S)ì alta amanza à pres'a lo me' core*', *CrT*, 3, 2000:803–6, asserts that the comparison between the heart of the beloved woman, which is as hard as diamond but softened by the tears of the poet, is not supported by the tradition of the *lapidari* (in which diamond can only be dissolved by blood). Tears' miracle-working power is, however, attested in the *Dialogue de Placide et Timéo*, an anonymous work in *langue d'oïl* and encyclopaedic in character, from the end of the 13th c. With exemplary rigour, Giuseppina Brunetti, *Il frammento inedito 'Resplendiente stella de albur' di Giacomino Pugliese e la poesia italiana delle origini*, Tübingen, Niemeyer, 2000, viii + 400 pp., publishes Giacomino's

Sicilian *canzone* contained in a MS to be found at Zurich's Zentralbib-liothek. The edition of this poetic fragment is inserted within a wider discourse concerning the circulation of lyric poetry at the origins and the figure of Giacomino in history and poetry. Another high-quality work is the critical edition Federico di Svevia, *Rime*, ed. Letterio Cassata, Ro, Quiritta, 156 pp., which consists of an introduction, a philological, historical, and linguistic commentary, and a rhyming dictionary. The volume includes the three poems securely attributable to Frederick (*Dolze meo drudo, De la mia didianza e Misura, Providentia*) and the four (*Oi lasso, Poi ca voi piace, Per la fera menbranza* and *Amor voglio blasmare*) of uncertain attribution. G. Desideri, ' "Et orietur vobis timentibus nomen meum sol iustitiae". Ripensare l'invenzione del sonetto', *CrT*, 3, 2000:623–64, maintains that the sonnet might have originated from ideological factors in the political and cultural context of the court of Frederick II. M. Spampinato Beretta, 'Discussione di alcuni *loci critici* in una nuova edizione del *Contrasto* di Cielo d'Alcamo', *Siculorum Gymnasium*, 52, 1999[2001]:1017–27, analyses some of the most disputed passages of this poetic text and puts forward hypotheses for their reconstruction, giving an account of the most important emendations that have been proposed over the years.

M. Santagata, 'Appunti per una storia dell'antica lirica profana', *NRLI*, 4.1, 2001:9–40, presents a socio-political analysis of the birth of the *stilnovo*, the factors which determined its flowering, and the cohesive factors of what later became a poetic school. A contribution of a general character is L. Ballerini, '*Colui che vede Amore*: per un prelievo di poetica da Guido Cavalcanti', *LItal*, 53:165–92, which seeks, within the *stilnovo*, evidence of what is defined an 'ascertainment syndrome' or 'quell'ansia di appurare se il rimatore che operi […] nell'ambiente dei fedeli d'Amore, sia o non sia sincero nelle proprie effusioni, e, soprattutto, se intenda che cosa si celi veramente sotto la *sottiglianza*' (57), a quality to which Guido Cavalcanti lays claim. A considerable group of essays focus on Cavalcanti in *CrT*, 4.1, a monographic issue, entitled 'Alle origini dell'Io lirico: Cavalcanti o dell'interiorità', which comprises: R. Antonelli, 'Cavalcanti o dell'interiorità' (1–22); G. Gorni, 'Una silloge d'autore nelle rime di Cavalcanti' (23–40); P. Cherchi, 'Cavalcanti e la rappresentazione' (41–58); C. Bologna, 'Fisiologia del Disamore' (59–88); M. Auciello, '*Spiriti* e *fiammette*: dalla metonimia alla metafora' (89–136); F. San-guineti, '*Loco* e *dimoranza*: Guido fra averroismo e platonismo' (137–40); G. Inglese, 'Dubbi d'amore' (141–54); F. Brugnolo, 'Cavalcanti "cortese". Ancora su Donna me prega, vv. 57–62' (155–72); R. Mercuri, 'Il poeta della morte' (173–98); G. Desideri, 'Sed rideret Aristotiles si audiret... "Da più a uno face un sollegismo" ' (199–222); D. Bonanno, 'Guido in Paradiso. Donna me prega e l'ultimo canto della Commedia' (223–44); L. Formisano, 'Cavalcanti e la pastorella' (245–62); I. Maffia Scariati, 'Tra l'Amico di Dante e il "primo amico" ' (263–304); and L. Cassata, 'Un'ipotesi per *Pg.* 24, 61–62' (305–10). C. Giunta, 'Sul *mottetto* di Guido Cavalcanti', *SFI*, 58, 2000: 5–28, argues that 'di un genere *mottetto* nella poesia italiana delle origini non è davvero il caso di parlare' (28) and reaches this conclusion by way of an analysis of the 'first' motet of the Italian tradition, Guido Cavalcanti's poem, *Gianni, quel Guido salute*, which was written in reply to Gianni Alfani's sonnet, *Guido, quel Gianni ch'a te fu l'altr'ieri*. S. Sarteschi, '*Donna me prega – Vita Nuova*: la direzione di una polemica', *RELI*, 15, 2000: 9–35, reverts to the age-old problem of the chronology of the *Vita nuova* and the Cavalcanti *canzone*, maintaining the priority of the latter. R. Scrimieri, 'Dante y Cavalcanti: a propósito de la balada del capítulo XII de la *Vita Nuova*, *Tenzone*, 2: 67–103, shows how Dante moves beyond Cavalcanti's love philosophy and poetic (present throughout the *Vita Nuova* and, more specifically, in the themes of the *ballata* of ch. XII) through 'una medida anticavalcantiana como es la *matera nuova* de la *lode*' (68): he embarks on an independent development which brings him to the 'reconocimiento del principio de realidad [que] tiene, por tanto, repercusiones en la poesia de la *Vita Nuova* y constituye el primer paso hacia la poetica de la *Commedia*' (88). N. Tonelli, ' "De Guidone de Cavalcantibus physico" (con una noterella su Giacomo da Lentini ottico)', *De Robertis Vol*, 459–508, shows that — according to a gloss by Dino del Garbo, who was a doctor-philosopher, teacher, and commentator of scientific texts destined to exert a wide influence — the sentiment analysed by Cavalcanti in *Donna me prega* is *hereos* or *heroicus* love, which medieval medicine regarded as pathological. On the basis of this evidence T. re-examines the *canzone* focusing mainly on the third and fourth *stanze* (485–508). The digression on Giacomo da Lentini (480–84) and the theories of vision on which *Or come pote* is based affords further proof of the interaction of poetic practice and scientific curiosity. We note the two monographs Antonio Gagliardi, *Guido Cavalcanti: poesia e filosofia*, Alessandria, Orso, 188 pp., and Id., *Cino da Pistoia: le poetiche dell'anima*, Alessandria, Orso, 187 pp. R. Leporatti, 'Il "libro" di Guittone e la *Vita Nuova*', *NRLI*, 4.1: 41–150, investigates the relationship between the *stilnovo* poets and Guittone d'Arezzo, arguing that the arrangement of Guittone's complete output in a form similar to that contained in MS Laurenziano Rediano 9 may have been the model for the *Vita Nuova*. M. Picone, 'Guittone, Guinizzelli e Dante', *L'Alighieri*, 18: 5–19, puts forward the hypothesis that the two 'Guidi' of *Purg.* XI, 94–99, are not Cavalcanti and Guinizzelli, but Guinizzelli and Guittone d'Arezzo (the 'Guidonem Aretinum' of the *De Vulgari Eloquentia*). To support his thesis, Picone analyses the exchange of *tenzoni* between the two poets and also the one between Guinizzelli and Bonagiunta. Also the author agrees with M. Papahaghi's hypothesis that the poem sent by Guinizzelli to Guittone together with *O caro padre* is not *Lo fin pregi'avanzato* (as maintained by Contini) but *Al cor gentil rempaira sempre amore*. H. W. Storey, 'Sulle orme di Guittone: i programmi grafico-visivi del codice Banco Rari 217', *Velli Vol.*, 1, 93–105, focusing on the figure of Guittone, defines the characteristics of the Banco Rari MS (formerly Pal. 418) which contains a number of sonnets and *canzoni* by the poet and, additionally, an interesting graphic apparatus. The frequent absence of correspondence between miniature and poetic text leads Storey to formulate the hypothesis that the transcription of the poems and the decoration of the manuscript were carried out by two distinct hands working at different times and using different methods.

On comic-realistic verse: S. Buzzetti Gallarati, 'Alle origini di un linguaggio: la poesia satirica di Rustico Filippi (I)', *MedRom*, 24, 2000: 346–84, via an analysis of various passages of Rustico's satirical sonnets resorting to an ambiguous erotic lexis, stresses the poet's 'dynamic idea of language' (348) and puts forward the hypothesis that 'il Filippi sperimenti […] una lingua equivoca, allusiva e metaforica, in fase di elaborazione all'interno dei nuovi idiomi romanzi, in parte evidente ma in gran parte da decifrare' (346). M. Pampinella, 'Influssi classici nei sonetti dialogati di Cecco Angiolieri?', *LIA*, 2:93–98, suggests that the structure of the two dialogical sonnets of Cecco and Becchina (*'Becchina mia!' 'Cecco, nol ti confesso'* and *'Becchin'amor!' 'Che vuo', falso tradito?'*) may reveal a 'comic matrix' (94) deriving from Terence, an author well known in the Middle Ages and included in school *curricula*. F. Alfie, 'One year — or two decades — of drunkenness? Cecco Angiolieri and the Udine 10 Codex', *Italica*, 78:18–35, analyses the sonnet *Tutto quest'anno ch'è, mi son frustato* (transmitted only by the 15th-c. MS Udine 10), providing a diplomatic transcription and confirming Angiolieri's authorship on the basis of references to be found within the poet's *œuvre*. Id., 'Wolves in sheep's clothing: Jean de Meun, Durante and Bindo Bonichi', *RStI*, 18.1, 2000:34–59, starts from the relationships between Guillaume de Lorris / Jean de Meun, authors of the *Roman de la Rose*, and Sir Durante, author of the *Fiore*, and between Sir Durante and Bindo Bonichi (who borrows and adapts the first four lines of sonnet 97 of the *Fiore*: *Chi della pelle del monton fasciasse*), in order to disclose the mechanism of reciprocal influences that links author, translator, and scribe during the medieval period.

Religious literature holds a special place. *Santità ed eremitismo nella Toscana medievale. Atti delle giornate di studio (11–12 giugno 1999)*, ed. Alessandra Gianni, Siena, Cantagalli, 150 pp., gathers seven contributions which explore the title theme from a hagiographical, historical, and above all art-historical point of view: E. Susi, 'San Mamiliano eremita nelle fonti agiografiche dell'Alto Medioevo'; M. Pellegrini, 'La cattedra e il deserto. L'episcopato di Siena e la chiesa di San Leonardo al Lago (secc. XI–XIII)'; F. Marcelli, 'Appunti di lavoro sull'iconografia di un "santo senza abito": Guglielmo da Malavalle'; A. Gianni, 'Iconografia delle sante cellane: Verdiana, Giovanna, Umiltà'; M. Corsi, 'Il ciclo eremitico di S. Marta a Siena'; E. Catoni, 'Dai Padri del deserto ad Agostino: iconografia degli affreschi del chiostro di Lecceto'; and I. Gagliardi, 'Santa Maria alla Sambuca presso Livorno: un eremo gesuato tra fine '300 e '500'. In *Gli studi di mariologia medievale: bilancio storiografico. Atti del I Convegno Mariologico della Fondazione Ezio Franceschini (Parma, 7–8 novembre 1997)*, ed. Clelia Maria Piastra, F, SISMEL–Galluzzo, xv + 362 pp., we note the contributions of F. A. Dal Pino, 'Culto e pietà mariana presso i frati minori nel Medioevo' (159–92), and L. Gaffuri, 'La predicazione domenicana su Maria (il secolo XIII)' (193–216). The first essay shows how, from St Francis's works onwards, an increasingly institutionalized cult of the Virgin Mary developed; the second essay, on the other hand, examines the characteristics of the Marian cult within the Dominican setting of the 13th c., concentrating on its growing importance in relation to the institutional history of the Order. *San Francesco e il francescanesimo nella letteratura italiana dal XIII al XIV secolo. Atti del Convegno nazionale (Assisi, 1–2 dicembre 1999)*, ed. Stanislao Da Campagnola and Pasquale Tuscano, Assisi, Accademia Properziana del Subasio, 300 pp. G. Pozzi, 'Lo stile di San Francesco', *IMU*, 41, 2000: 7–72, looks at the stylistic features specific to the work of St Francis, underlining the inadequacy of the traditional definition, *sermo humilis*, for a production which in fact is based on cultured models. A. D'Angelo, 'Metafisica e teologia. Le oscillazioni di Tommaso d'Aquino', *La Cultura*, 39: 411–64, looking at the relationship between metaphysics and theology in Aristotle and Thomas Aquinas, concentrates on the figure of the theologian with a view to answering the question: 'C'è, e se c'è in che cosa consiste e come si fonda, un "passaggio" logico che conduce dal concetto di "ente in quanto ente" a Dio inteso come "persona"?' (411). *Les sermons et la visite pastorale de Federico Visconti archevêque de Pise (1253–1277)*, ed. Nicole Bériou and Isabelle Le Masne de Chermont, with the collaboration of P. Bourgain and M. Innocenti, Ro, École Française de Rome, xi + 1185 pp., is a valuable edition of the famous collection of sermons (preserved in a single MS), which includes an introduction, a commentary on the texts, a linguistic study, and a glossary. F. Troncarelli, ' "Ke la malonta ve don Dé". Herneis le Romanceeur, Bartolomeo Guiscolo e lo scandalo dell'*Evangelium Aeternum*', *QMed*, 51:6–34, supplies new and interesting information on the scandal triggered in Paris in 1254 by the circulation of *Introductorius in Evangelium Aeternum* by the Italian Franciscan Gerardo di Borgo San Donnino. Examining the two manuscripts which bear traces of the influence of Gerardo, Vat. Ott. Lat. 190 e il Dresden Sächs. Land. A 121, T. argues that they both originated in Paris, but whereas the former is a luxury product (unfinished) from the *atelier* of the bookseller-publisher Herneis le Romanceeur, the latter is the handiwork of a group of non-professional scribes, assisted for the miniatures by Fra Bartolomeo Guiscolo, Fra Gerardo's closest collaborator. C. Del Popolo, 'Nomi in alcuni testi di poesia religiosa', *Il nome nel testo*, 2–3, 2000–2001:253–62, offers some examples of etymology and interpretation of names drawn from the scrutiny of some 300 *laude* dating from between the 13th and 15th-c. Giovanni De Galerijs, *Laudario dei Battuti*, ed. Mahmoud Salem Elsheikh Bologna, CTL, lvii + 172 pp., also includes an interesting apparatus of linguistic notes and a glossary. M. Morrison, 'A mystic's drama: the paschal mystery in the visions of Angela da Foligno', *Italica*, 78:36–52, focuses on 'the influence of certain religious activities (sacred dramatic *laude* and liturgical observances) on particular visions' (36) which are narrated in the *Memoriale* of the Franciscan tertiary. For Iacopone we draw attention to: *Iacopone da Todi. Atti del XXXVII Convegno storico internazionale (Todi, 8–11 ottobre 2000)*, Todi, CISAM, x + 393 pp. The anthology *Iacopone da Todi e la poesia religiosa del Duecento*, ed. Paolo Canettieri, Mi, Rizzoli, 260 pp., as well as the main section devoted to Iacopone, includes texts by St Francis, Garzo, Frate Guittone, the Veronese *lauda*, and the prayer of the Virgin's servants. The essay-length preface can be divided into three parts, the first devoted to the relationship between religious and troubadour poetry, the second concentrating on the figure of Iacopone, and the third concerning aesthetics in mystical poetry. M. Aversano, 'Alle origini del teatro italiano: personaggi, luoghi e scene in *Donna de Paradiso* di Iacopone da Todi', *CLett*, 29:211–61, examines Iacopone's famous *lauda* to demonstrate that Iacopone anticipates Dante in the use of a poetic language based on the authority of the patristic Bible. V. Abbruzzetti, 'La *Donna de Paradiso* de Jacopone da Todi: un exercice spirituel', *ChrI*, 63–64, 2000:17–28, rereads the *lauda*, comparing it directly with the story of the Passion as related in the Gospels.

Among contributions devoted to Marco Polo, the following are certainly worth noting: *Milione*, ed. Lucia Battaglia Ricci, F, Sansoni, lx + 256 pp. The editor's introduction is followed by a section of critical essays gathering contributions by Luigi Foscolo Benedetto, Attilio Momigliano, Jacques Le Goff, Sergio Solmi, Leonardo Olschki, Franco Borlandi, Valeria Bertolucci Pizzorusso, Gianfranco Contini, and Ugo Tucci. P. Ménard, 'Marco Polo en Angleterre', *MedRom*, 24, 2000[2001]: 189–208, describes the fragment contained in the British Library MS Cotton, Othon D V (ff. 92v and 93r-v); read under ultraviolet light, its Anglo-Norman character becomes apparent on linguistic grounds, against Benedetto's view that it belongs to the Franco-Italian branch of the MS tradition. The article falls into six sections: a paleographical examination, a linguistic analysis, the edited text, an apparatus of notes and commentary, a glossary, and a study of the MS's relationship with the rest of the tradition.

On medieval Latin writing: A. Bisanti, 'Note e appunti di lettura su testi mediolatini', *FilM*, 8: 111–22, identifies echoes of classical *auctores* in Paul the Deacon's elegiac hymn, in Paolino d'Aquileia's *Versus de Herico duce*, in the tale *Novus Avianus* by the so-called 'Astensis poeta', and in a passage of the medieval tragedy *exemplum* (*Due lotrices*) included by Giovanni di Garlandia into his *Parisiana poetria*. P. G. Schmidt, 'Perché tanti anonimi nel Medioevo? Il problema della personalità dell'autore nella filologia mediolatina', *ib.*, 6–7, 1999–2000: 1–8, reflects upon the question of anonymity in medieval Latin production, pointing out some of the possible reasons for this widespread phenomenon. G. Dapelo, 'Il romanzo latino di Barlaam e Josaphat (BHL 979): preparando l'edizione', *ib.*, 8: 179–220, anticipates some of the results of his research into the second and successful Latin translation of this work, providing an update of the census of MSS (which now number 95, following the discovery of 12 new witnesses) and presenting some of the most significant data to have emerged during the work of *recensio*.

A considerable number of contributions elude classification by thematic categories since they address specific themes or minor authors of the 13th-c. literature. Taking up a long-standing question of interpretation, F. Beggiato, '*Sequenza di Sant'Eulalia* v. 15: "adunet" non "aduret"', *CrT*, 3, 2000: 563–86, rejects the reading *aduret* given by Henry Dexter Learned in 1941 and confirms the validity of the previously accepted *adunet* on the basis of precise paleographic and linguistic arguments. A. Carrega, '*Il Gatto lupesco' e 'Il Mare amoroso*', Alessandria, Orso, 2000, 99 pp., publishes the two texts with facing translation and a lengthy commentary which attempts to sum up what has been written on these two problematic early works down to the present day. P. Chiesa, 'Varianti d'autore nell'Alto Medioevo fra filologia e critica letteraria', *FilM*, 8: 1–24, underlines that multiple authorial redaction is probably quite common in early medieval literature but in most cases difficult to demonstrate; an examination of some autograph MSS can also yield interesting indications as to the degree of critical awareness with which the author refines his text. S. De Laude, 'Artù, re dei morti, e Andrea Cappellano', *ParL*, 51, 2000:102–16, shows that the story of the Breton knight introduced by Andrea Cappellano in the *De Amore* as an *excursus* possessing *auctoritas*, 'combina tratti del nucleo mitico celtico alla base di tanti romanzi arturiani' (109) and emphasizes interesting elements of 'culti legati al viaggio estatico nel mondo dei morti' (113) of Celtic literary origin. M. Fumagalli, 'L'ordito intertestuale del *Libro de li exempli*', *Velli Vol.*, I, 63–92, preparatory to a critical edition of the work, casts new light on the various stages in the text's genesis, the *auctoritates* used by the compiler, the originality of this literary product, and the kind of socio-cultural context which brought it into being. *Magistri Guidonis Fabe Rota nova, ex codice manuscripto oxoniensi 'New College 255' nunc primum prodit*, curantibus Alphonso P. Campbell et Vergilio Pini. / Virgilio Pini, *La tradizione manoscritta di Guido Faba dal XIII al XV secolo*. / Antonio Saiani, *La figura di Guido Faba nel Prologo autobiografico della 'Rota Nova'. Una rilettura*, Bo, Istituto per la Storia dell'Università di Bologna, 2000, xix + 515 pp., contains Guido Faba's *Rota nova* (a manual of rhetoric written around 1225–26) in an edition left unfinished at the death of Virgilio Pini and now published, together with related material, thanks to Antonio Saiani. His essay on Faba, which is nothing less than an *excursus* on the history of the *ars dictaminis*, also analysing the personality and activity of the Bologna *magister* against the political and cultural situation of his time, is very interesting. C. Giunta, 'Due poesie probabilmente duecentesche dal codice Mezzabarba', *MedRom*, 24, 2000[2001]:321–45, publishes two very early poems from the MS Mezzabarba for the first time and analyses their style and metre. G. puts forward the hypothesis that the author of *Messer lo conte Guido* may be a friend of Guittone, or even Guittone himself, while, with regard to the anonymous *Gentil messer, la virtù sottile*, he suggests a dating 'within the first century of Italian poetry'. M. Petoletti, 'Il *Diversiloquium* di Bonaiuto da Casentino, poeta di curia ai tempi di Bonifacio VIII', *Aevum*, 75:381–448, publishes the work by a papal chaplain (a collection of occasional verse and a prose treatise on the virtues and vices) contained in MS Vat. Lat. 2854. L. Petrucci, 'Astrologia alcandreica in volgare alla fine del Duecento', *SLeI*, 17, 2000:5–26, points out that the *Trattazione* contained in Magliabechi MS XX.60, ff. 56–57, derives from the *Liber Alchandrei*. The article borrows from, and develops, S. Bertelli, 'Un manoscritto di geomanzia in volgare della fine del secolo XIII', *SFI*, 57, 1999:5–32. P. Rinoldi, 'Nota al v. 198 della '*Morte di*

Carlomagno', *MR*, 14, 2000:111–18, suggests emending this difficult-to-decipher passage of the Franco-Italian poem in MS Canoniciano 54 at the Bodleian: the proper name contained in the line is said to be 'Lohier': perhaps Charlemagne's grandson Lothar since he is said in l. 197 to be heir to a kingdom. More historical than literary in character is P. C. Begotti, 'Il patriarcato di Aquileia nel Medioevo. Temi e problemi di una ricerca', *Ce fastu?*, 77:261–72, where the various stages in the development of the ecclesiastical province of Aquileia are examined in the light of the growing importance of the patriarch. Straddling art and literature is D. P. Lackey, 'Giotto's mirror', *StD*, 66:243–53, which investigates Giotto's possible sources in the monochrome frescoes of the Vices and Virtues in the Scrovegni Chapel in Padua, suggesting the possibility of a relationship between the painter and Dante.

Moving on to the 14th c., we draw attention to two contributions on religious poetry. A. Andreose, 'Censimento dei manoscritti del Pianto della Vergine ("Lamentatio beatae Virginis") di Enselmino da Montebelluna conservati alla Biblioteca Nazionale Marciana', *QVen*, 33:7–28, describes the eight mid-14th-c. Marciana MSS of the poem, whose vast MS tradition poses many editorial problems. The article shows how study of the MS material can produce important information on the ways a work circulated, on its reception, and on attributional criteria. C. Del Popolo, 'Una tessera iacoponica in Passavanti', *LItal*, 53:397–400, detects the presence of the refrain of Iacopone's *lauda*, *Quando t'alegri*, for 'the memory of death', in chap. IV of the 'Trattato sull'umiltà' in the *Specchio di vera penitenza*. At the border between prose and poetry, C. Giunti, 'Il *Reggimento* di Francesco da Barberino: prosa ritmica o versi sciolti', *SPCT*, 63:43–74, starting from a close analysis of the *scriptio continua* of apograph Barb. lat. 4001, criticizes the attempt made by the most recent editor (Sansone) to distinguish between blank verse and ornate, 'numbered' prose on the basis of the complex 'paragraphematic' system of the MS, and in the place of his hypothesis of authorial evolution suggests that the work is simply unfinished.

Prose narrative, even without the *Decameron*, attracts a goodly crop of contributions. A. Fontes Baratto, 'Narrateur, *beffatore*, nécromancien: les avatars de l'homme de cour dans le Novellino', *ChrI*, 63–64, 2000:29–40, in a Deleuzian perspective looks at the evolution of the courtier's characteristics from an itinerant figure (later the merchant) in search of social recognition (N4) to the *beffatore* aware of the 'urbane' effect of controlled narrative (N84, 86, 89), and even the necromancer of an overwhelming illusory perturbation (N21). L. Zarker Morgan, 'The *Reine Sibille* – *Macario* story and the Charlemagne cycle throughout Europe: a re-examination of the

Franco-Italian *Macario*, *Italica*, 78 : 1–17, summarizes the plot of the late *chanson de geste* — which narrates the false accusation of adultery, exile, and rehabilitation of Charlemagne's wife — comparing it with the Alberic and Old French fragment precedents and with the German, Spanish (*Noble Cuento*), and Andrea da Barberino (*Nerbonesi*) versions. F. G. B. Trolese, 'Un lezionario trecentesco del monastero di S. Giustina in Padova', *IMU*, 42 : 63–90, describes an illuminated parchment MS in *littera textualis* (Berlin, Staatsbibliothek, MS. lat. fol. 480) containing an anthology of hagiographic narratives for liturgical use (*Passiones*, *Vitae*, *Legendae*), including the rites of Saints Giustina and Prosdocimo and the translation (i.e. transfer) of Saints Luke and Mathias. In contrast, T. Pesenti, 'The *Libri Galieni* in Italian universities in the fourteenth century', IMU, 42 : 119–48, investigates this group of medical texts from the point of view of their transcription in *quaterni* as opposed to *pecia*, and of their circulation and price. Of a more historical and art-historical than literary character is A. Dunlop, 'Masculinity, crusading, and devotion: Francesco Casali's fresco in the Trecento Perugian *Contado*', *Speculum*, 76 : 315–36, which, starting from a Sacchetti novella whose protagonist is the devotional anxiety of the Lord of Cortona (whom the author identifies with the client portrayed in an Orvieto-school fresco at Santa Maria delle Grazie, Magione, near Perugia), explores the link between chivalry and devotion in the minor nobility of the late 14th c.

3. BOCCACCIO

Some of the latest volumes on B. to have been published are the fruits of 'long fidelity', starting with the substantial monograph Luigi Surdich, *Boccaccio*, Ro–Bari, Laterza, 335 pp., which in nine chapters traces his entire biographical and literary career, from his transfer 'Da Firenze a Napoli' and poetic–*galant* début (ch. 1), 'La narrazione amorosa ed epica del *Filocolo*' (ch. 2), and the amalgam of 'armi e amori' in *Filostrato* and *Teseida* (ch. 3), to his 'ritorno a Firenze' which accounts for the allegorical register of *Comedia* and *Amorosa visione* (ch. 4) and his output 'all'ombra di Ovidio' (the *Elegia* and *Ninfale*, ch. 5). The *Decameron*'s 'tempo storico' and 'ragioni narrative' are summarized in ch. 6, the articulation in 10 Days analysed in ch. 7, and the work's linguistic and structural 'varietà e ordine' assessed in ch. 8. Ch. 9 looks at B.'s concluding phase, divided (with the *Epistole*, *Carmen*, *Genealogie* and *Corbaccio*) between 'erudizione, misoginia, e culto di Dante'. Similarly, Vittorio Zaccaria, *Boccaccio narratore, storico, moralista e mitografo*, F, Olschki, xv + 268 pp., gathers 30 years' work on the *De Mulieris*, *De Casibus* e *Genealogie*, from the textual and linguistic studies that already accompanied his critical editions to his exploration of B.'s persistent narrative urge in the Latin writings and the presence in them of the Italian (Dante e Petrarch) and Latin (Tacitus e Pliny) classics. Again, Victoria Kirkham, *Fabulous Vernacular: Boccaccio's Filocolo and the Art of Medieval Fiction*, Ann Arbor, Michigan U.P., xii + 317 pp., gathers the results of a decade's research into the most ambitious European prose narrative of the time, where B. takes up his lady's invitation to remove the story of Florio e Biancifiore from the 'fabulosi parlari degli ignoranti', asserting the 'epic' aspect of the 'little book' without denying its derivation from popular archetypes. The study reconstructs the *Filocolo*'s links with the classical–romance inheritance (Chrétien de Troyes, the Sicilian school, the *stilnovo* and Dante, though not yet Petrarch), and the strategies of the author's assertion of identity, from the summoning-up of a female figure who is a synthesis of amorous metaphors from the Virgin Mary to Beatrice (ch. 1), to the choice of a signature — Giovanni da Certaldo — analogous to the 'geographical' epithets of illustrious predecessors (ch. 2), and on to the masterly construction of the autobiographical myth of a 'forced canonization' (ch. 3). B.'s legal training casts light on his recontextualization (analysed in the last three chapters) of the 'popular' plot in the world of contemporary social events. Bound up with B.'s *fortuna* are *Le Annotazioni e i discorsi sul 'Decameron' del 1573 dei deputati fiorentini*, ed. Giuseppe Chiecchi, Ro–Padua, Antenore, lxv + 553 pp. The introduction to this critical edition reconstructs the work's compositional history, which ran parallel to the difficult task of reordering the *Decameron* carried out, in relation to the *Lettera*, by Vincenzo Borghini and the other members of the deputation (Antinori, Benivieni, Guicciardini). Torn between censorial imperatives and the philological nature of the task, his empirical vocation prevailed over Bembo's theories in his defence of Florentine and Dantean usage; and with an extraordinary restorative — almost therapeutic — passion he sought to resist the corrupting power of textual tradition, whose phenomena he registered with a precision and detail worthy of modern editorial scholarship, in 'abbozzi' that were to become widely known. The edition has full critical apparatus, a list of MSS and glosses, a bibliography, and indexes.

Numerous articles are devoted to themes or to individual novelle of the *Decameron*: R. Ambrosini, 'Sull'onomastica nel Decameron', *RELI*, 16, 2000:13–32, stresses the ambiguous authenticating function of naming in the deliberate and dialectical mingling of historical reality (surnames) and imagination (first names) on which the entire work rests from Ser Ciappelletto to Griselda. B. Porcelli, 'Abbinamenti di novelle nel *Decameron*', *Italianistica*, 29:205–8, points out two pairings of novelle according to the principle of the unlike in the like — in one case in successive stories (IV 6–7), in the other at a distance (VII 3 and 10). Intense Swiss-school activity has been directed at Day I: M. Canova, 'Ciappelletto e il progetto di Dio: lettura di *Decameron* I.1', *RELI*, 17:9–32, identifies a symmetrical structure in the opening novella, whereby a concentric series of frames, beginning with the relationship between the *brigata* and God, encloses the protagonist's confession; M. Picone, 'Una scheda per Ciappelletto', *ib.*, 33–40, on adjacent ground, underlines the macro-textual function of the self-satisfied and mystificatory *virtus elocutionis* of Ciappelletto (a *figura auctoris*) in his parody (*en abyme*), and surpassing, of the *narratio brevis* of a saint's life. Id., 'Lettura intertestuale della novella della marchesana di Monferrato (*Dec.* I.5)', *ChrI*, 63–64, 2000: 71–80, analyses the 'intellectual' adaptation of the opening story of the *Book of Sindbad* or *of the Seven Wise Masters* (oriental version), 'The lion's footprint', in Juan Manuel's *Conde Lucanor* and in B., showing how it shifts attention from the sexual quest of the king (unhappy heir to Jaufré's *amor de lohn*) to the metaphorical competence of the woman in preparing the banquet and in the decisive verbal skirmish. Id., 'Le "merende" di maestro Alberto (*Decameron* I.10)', *RELI*, 16, 2000: 99–110, points out the parodic reversal of the *gabbo* (*Vita Nuova*, 18), and of *fin'amor* orthodoxy, in the victorious counter-witticism of old Alberto to Malgherida, who is a model both of the *mulier loquens*, as proposed by Pampinea, and of Bolognese female docility. M. Taylor, 'The fortunes of Alatiel: a reading of *Decameron* 2,7', *FoI*, 35:318–31, stresses the 'metanarrative' character of the suspension of patriarchal tutelage and the inversion of gender roles *vis-à-vis* the Homeric model in the erotic odyssey of a princess fatal to almost all her lovers. Two articles on the longest novella of the *Decameron* close the series of specific contributions: L. Marcozzi, ' "Passio" e "ratio" tra Andrea Cappellano e Boccaccio: la novella dello scolare e della vedova (*Decameron* VIII, 7) e i castighi del *De Amore*', *Italianistica* 30:9–32, measures the gap between the allegorical system of *amoenitas, humiditas*, and *siccitas* in Cappellano's code of courtly precepts and its iconic survivals in the novella of Elena and Rinieri: bourgeois survivals confined to the moral *intentio* at the margin of the *narratio*. M. Schonbuch, 'Elena, donna Petra', *ChrI*, 63–64, 2000: 109–18, on the basis of a number of parallelisms and textual correspondences, proposes to extend the allusive nature of the Infernal overtones of the punishment to those features of the protagonist Rinieri himself which most closely correspond to the Dante of the *Trattatello*, whose revenge, aspired to in the *petrose*, he (Rinieri) is said to achieve.

Other contributions variously relate to the *fortuna* of the *Decameron*: M. Gagliano, 'Le *Trecentonovelle* et le *Décaméron*: emprunts et effets intertextuels', *ib.*, 95–107, in Sacchetti's borrowings from B. identifies, in addition to ones that serve the purposes of comic and recreative accentuation, those of Domenichi, Bergamino, Cavalcanti, and Gianfigliazzi, which are marked by the same parodic taste as is sometimes applied to historical events and which points to the 'decay' of the world represented in the *Decameron*. F. Bausi, 'Boccaccio a Macondo. Spunti decameroniani nella narrativa di Gabriel Garcìa Màrquez', *RStI*, 18.1, 2000:127–44, starting from *Nessuno scriva al colonnello* (1961), whose rationalistic and programmatically committed structure is said to owe something to the adoption as model of the novella of Federigo degli Alberighi, points out that B. also left his mark on *La prodigiosa sera di Baltazar* and *I funerali della Mamà Grande* (1962), and on *Cent'anni di solitudine* (1967).

The characteristics and *fortuna* of B. illustrations occupy a place of their own in B. studies. Here, of course, the field is dominated by V. Branca's 'Boccaccio visualizzato' project. Id., 'Il narrar boccacciano per immagini e la pittura veneta', *AIV*, 158, 2000:361–408, points out the influence which B.'s pluri-expressive vocation — a realization (notably in MSS Hamilton 90 at Berlin and in It. 482 at Paris) of the Augustinian nexus between *pictura* and *litterae* — exerted on Tuscan and Venetian art: the *Teseida* on Carpaccio, Ghismonda's suicide on Cima da Conegliano and Bachiacca, Cimone's contemplation of Ephigenia on miniatures and chests, on Botticelli (thanks to the mediation of Poliziano), and, through the illustrations of printed editions of the work, on the iconography of Venus in the Veneto Renaissance. Also, L. Bolzoni, 'Note in margine al "Boccaccio visualizzato"', *GSLI*, 178:270–73, citing Poe's *The Purloined Letter* a propos of the denial of centrality to the image in literary texts, points to the new visual capacity expressed in the project directed by Branca, starting from the experience of Aby Warburg and the importance of the image in B.'s *œuvre* and the B. MS tradition and for an understanding of his reception. Leading us into the next sub-section, J. Bartuschat, 'La *De vita et moribus Domini Francisci Petracchi* de Boccace', *ChrI*, 63–64, 2000:81–94, sees the originality of the encomium to lie in the type and character of the biographical writing, which is far from any possible models (*vidas, accessus ad auctorem*, St Jerome's *De viris illustribus*) and in the prevalence of the literary profile over the 'philosophical' *Mavortius Miles*, and especially the poetic portrait of the new Apollo, a paragon of good sense, whose physical description is also allocated a surprising amount of space.

4. PETRARCH

The seventh centenary celebrations of the poet's birth are inaugurated by a reprint of Francesco Petrarca, *Rerum Vulgarium Fragmenta*.

Anastatica dell'edizione Valdezoco Padova 1472, ed. Gino Belloni, Venice, Marsilio–Regione del Veneto, pp. lxvi + 380 pp. The introduction reconstructs the commercial and university background of Paduan publishing and the pro-Florentine linguistic and cultural context which directed its initial choices of vernacular texts: the *Fiammetta* and *Guerrin Meschino*, and what was only the third printing anywhere of the *Canzoniere*, embellished from the autograph (the present-day MS Vat. Lat. 3195, from which the innovative title derives), which at that time belonged to the Paduan Santasofia family, and accompanied, as was starting to be traditional, by the *Triumphi*, the table of poems, the *Nota de Laura*, and Bruni's *Vita del Petrarca*, which here, like the two sonnets in praise of Petrarch, was anonymous. A synthetic, but accurate and full, introduction to *RVF* is Serena Fornasiero, *Petrarca: guida al Canzoniere*, Ro, Carocci, 125 pp., which summarizes the collection's overall characteristics, its compositional history (with particular reference to its different 'forms'), its narrative thread and 'characters', its metrical structures, and its linguistic features. Different in its aims is Ugo Dotti, *Petrarca civile. Alle origini dell'intellettuale moderno*, Ro, Donzelli, 240 pp., which emphasizes the 'militant' nature of P.'s attitude to his historical and cultural context by identifying, in an analysis of his correspondence, three basic tendencies: a 'narrative' project divided between everyday life and an exemplary vocation, the convergence of a vast moral and cultural patrimony gained from his studies, and his constant confrontation with the pressing problems and troubled institutions of the contemporary world (from the challenge to the feudal class to the waning Empire, from the 'captive' Church to the nascent Signorie), a confrontation constantly prompted, despite inevitabile conditioning, by an 'Enlightened' spirit.

Turning to articles and moving from the general to the particular: N. Bisaha, 'Petrarch's vision of the Muslim and Byzantine East', *Speculum*, 76:284–314, an extremely topical piece, underlines the articulated and yet 'integralist' nature of the welding wrought by P. between classical thought and crusading revanchism (tinged with apocalyptic thought in the *Carolus redivivus* of *RVF* 27 and 28) in his sanction of the representations of Islam and orthodox Christianity in fashion in the 14th c. and beyond. 'Aesthetic' problems are at the heart of C. Cabaillot, 'Nature et fonction de la poésie chez F. Pétrarque', *ChrI*, 63–64, 2000:53–70, lamenting scant interest for P.'s poetic theory which, given his aversion to scholasticism, was not systematic. Adopting the necessary functional distinction (the formal distinction is inadequate), an evolution can be observed from a reproductive to an artificial and anti-naturalistic conception of poetry, which is a divine instrument of knowledge and one of the highest means of spiritual progress and of access to truth through an articulated (and also allegorical) interpretation of texts. A somewhat similar theme is addressed *in re* by G. Bardin, 'Una dimora poco stabile: lo spazio poetico in *RVF* 23, 126, 323', *RStI*, 18.1, 2000:26–33, which reconstructs the history of P.'s attempt to create a poetic universe, from the *canzone delle metamorfosi*, where poetry means salvation, through poetry of memory where memory proves insufficient for an enduring transfiguration, to the poetry of the allegorical vision of the double death of Laura and poetic inspiration. G. Polezzo Susto, 'La lingua delle canzoni del Petrarca nel testo del Sachella', *SPCT*, 62:5–36, examines MS Braidense AD, XVI.20 (which contains the canzoni and *Trionfi*) listing omissions and variants vis-à-vis the autograph, Italian and Latin marginalia, and the characteristics, in spelling, phonetics, morphology, of Sachella's transcription which, though not devoid of northern features and Latinisms, does substantially respect P.'s language. Still on the *Canzoniere*, but moving to another poetic genre, L. Polino, 'Ancora qualche nota sui madrigali di Petrarca (*RVF* 52, 54, 106, 121)', *Italianistica*, 30:307–23, reconstructs the origin, and the revision and contextualization mechanisms, at the outset of the *Canzoniere*, of the poems occasioned by P.'s encounter with the *ars nova* of the Po Valley courts and conceived for figures other than Laura. A thematic approach is taken in D. Bonanno, 'Appunti sulla fantasia del "piede" nel *Canzoniere* di Petrarca', *Italianistica*, 30:69–84, which, among the various bodily metaphors registered by Curtius, follows that of the soul's wings in its growing complication from Phaedrus, via Augustine and Dante (Matelda), in the linking of eye, foot, and voice. The combination crops up repeatedly in *RVF* representing by turns Laura's miracle-working powers, the instruments of the poet's confusion, or their complex interplay.

Moving on to individual poems, the first issue of *Stilistica e metrica italiana*, a new journal of stylistics directed by P. V. Mengaldo, contains a particularly significant concentration of contributions, opening with S. Albonico, 'Per un commento a RVF 50. Parte prima', *SMI*, 1:3–30, which points to the presence, in every stanza of the strategic canzone 50, of a syntactic scheme going back not so much to Dante's sestina as to the common source, *Aeneid* iv: *Nox erat...*, here multiplied in a web of references. The *vecchiarella* is identified as heir to the *vetula-anicula* figure, symbolizing empirical wisdom and the faith of the *simpliciores*, who appears elsewhere in Petrarch. P. V. Mengaldo, 'Ancora sulla doppia redazione di un sonetto di Petrarca', *ib.*, 31–44, points out how the transformation of 'Nel tempo, lasso, de la notte, quando' in *Tutto 'l dì piango* is informed not merely by atomization of the original Dante *tessere* but by the principles of lexical *variatio* and *dissimilatio* of timbre, and by an overall tonal shift, from dramatic to contemplative and analytical, confirmed by the ritual appearance of Laura for the sonnet's insertion in *RVF* (216). Finally, in the 'Notes and discussions' section, A. Afribo, 'Sulla sintassi dei *Rerum vulgarium fragmenta*', *ib.*, 337–50, underlines that Contini's judgement on P. led to a dearth of stylistic, and especially syntactic, studies before Tonelli's antidogmatic operation, which reveals subordination to the third and fourth degree in half the sonnets, with syntactic cohesion particularly in the *fronte* thanks to hypothetical and 'long' consecutive clauses. L. Zuliani, 'Una possibile correzione interpuntiva al *Canzoniere* di Petrarca', *CrT*, 3, 2000 : 807–16, proposes (in the wake of Cozzo and Melodia, but against Contini and Santagata) attaching v. 7 ('per lagrime ch'i' spargo a mille a mille') of *ballata* LV (*Quel foco ch'i' pensai che fosse spento*) to the preceding sentence despite the punctuation of MS Vat. lat. 3195 (at this point idiographic) and in keeping with P.'s *usus* and the tendency usually to respect even 'weak' metrical divisions which prevailed down to Bembo. Significantly, it is to Bembo that we owe the received punctuation of the passage in question. T. E. Mussio, 'The phoenix narrative in Canzone 323', *RStI*, 18.2, 2000 : 14–31, champions the *figura Christi* interpretation of the phoenix and the meaning of rebirth in the otherwise 'Laurian' allegorical sequence of six visions of death in *Standomi un giorno solo alla finestra*. On the final canzone of *RVF*: A. Musumeci, 'Petrarca e l'opera aperta', *ib.*, 1–13, points out how, in the very text in which P. concludes his amorous experience and rejects its value, all the attributes of the Virgin (*bella, dolce, pia, pura, santa, sola*) come from the constellation of Laura (except 'stabile in eterno' which corrects her fickleness) and put forward her contradictory presence *ad infinitum*.

Focusing on P.'s letter-writing activity, R. J. Lokaj, 'La Cleopatra napoletana: Giovanna d'Angiò nelle *Familiares* di Petrarca', *GSLI*, 177, 2000 : 481–521, points out the subtle web of references and the retrospective narrative coherence of the letters on the *egitia monstra* of Roberto's daughter, whom P. represents as opposed to her pious father and to the mysterious *virgo bellatrix* Maria of Pozzuoli (V,3) and, together with the court (primarily Roberto di Mileto), as responsible for the Babylonian decadence of the kingdom. Two other contributions look at historical-philological problems relating to this area of P.'s output: U. Dotti, 'Il quindicesimo delle *Senili*: sul libro e la datazione di alcune lettere', *GSLI*, 177, 2000 : 522–33, investigates the composite character of the book, in which the anti-scholastic polemic and the proposed humanist synthesis of theology and poetry stand out (with letters to Marsili, Boccaccio, and Benvenuto da Imola); he dates to 1371 the reply to Lombardo della Seta (III) and postpones to 1372 the first letter to Cabassoles (XIV). Similarly,

B. Martinelli, 'Petrarca e l'epistola del ventoso: i diversi tempi della scrittura', *RLettI*, 19.1:9–57, extends the letter's period of composition well beyond the traditional limit of 1353, setting its genesis in the summer of 1336 and attributing to its Milanese revision a substantial amplification which conflates various passages of St Augustine's *Confessions*.

Last but not least, M. Ciccuto, 'Copisti e filologi', *ParL*, 51.1, 2000:16–23, commenting on Santagata's narrative divagation on the *Copista* Malpaghini, points to its compatibility with the P.'s development in maturity, as Bettarini has also noted, while G. Dell'Aquila, 'La Crusca e Petrarca', *RLettI*, 19.1:59–78, a lexicographical contribution, tabulates the Petrarchan occurrences cited for a number of headwords in the Crusca's first *Vocabolario*: the fact that they are set in secondary positions is seen as reflecting, embryonically, the mistrust that was to develop in the second half of the Cinquecento and lead eventually to Tassoni's *Considerazioni*.

HUMANISM AND THE RENAISSANCE

By PAOLO L. ROSSI, *Senior Lecturer in Italian Studies, University of Lancaster*, and
NADIA CANNATA SALAMONE, *Lecturer in Italian, University of Reading*

1. GENERAL

Aby Warburg, *The Renewal of Pagan Antiquity*, trans. David D. Britt, Los Angeles, Getty Research Institute, 1999, 859 pp., is the first English version of the German text edited by Gertrud Bing in 1932. This long overdue translation will make more accessible one of the great landmarks in the study and interpretation of art and culture. The introduction by K. W. Forster highlights the importance and the original nature not only of Warburg's writings but also of his way of writing. It reassesses: Warburg's contribution to our understanding of the nature of communication and the transformation of signs; the complexity of cultural processes and transitions; his methodology and preoccupations, and the influence of Karl Lamprecht and Hermann Usener. Hellmut Wohl, *The Aesthetics of Italian Renaissance Art. A Reconsideration of Style*, CUP, 1999, xii + 376 pp., argues that discussions of art in Renaissance texts, far from empty rhetoric, are reliable guides to understanding both the making and the appreciation of such works in their time. Focusing on two key words, *rilievo* and *ornato*, and using texts by Alberti, A. Caro, Manuel Chrysoloras, Angelo Decembrio, Doni, Ficino, Firenzuola, G. Gilio, Manetti, Poliziano, A. Traversari, and Vasari he suggests that shifts in style were primarily dictated by the rhetorical *ornato* tradition that had analogies with the *ornatio* of classical rhetoric. *The Place of the Antique in Early Modern Europe*, ed. Ingrid D. Rowland, Chicago U.P., 1999, viii + 109 pp., comprises five essays to form the catalogue to an exhibition at the Smart museum: I. Rowland examines what the antique meant for Sigismondo Malatesta, Athanasius Kircher, and Antonio Magliabechi; A. Terry's concerns are the images of metamorphoses from Ovid to Ariosto; M. Matsubara looks at the Renaissance re-evaluation of the Graeco-Roman legacy of allegory in portrait medals; M. Pereira investigates how a classical tradition supported Christian concerns and beliefs, and goes into the antiquarian activities of Cassiano dal Pozzo. Floriana Mauro, *La rinascita dell'antico e riutilizzo dei monumenti classici nel medioevo*, Ro, EDUP, 123 pp., focuses on the amphitheatre in Lucca, the mausoleum of Cecilia Metella on the Via Appia, and the fortress at Velia.

Roy Eriksen, *The Building in the Text. Alberti to Shakespeare and Milton*, University Park, Pennsylvania State U.P., xxi + 194 pp., is an original study arguing that 'Renaissance aesthetic theory and practice reveal an impulse to control the various systems of signification that reproduce and communicate the artist's initial idea'. It opens up new perspectives on how writers 'designed' their works, and how 'Renaissance writing and artistic theory share a common ground in a small body of formal devices ultimately originating in periodic rhetoric'. Texts by Alberti, Ariosto, Vasari, Giulio Camillo Delminio, and Tasso are examined. *Studi di letteratura, critica e linguistica offerti a Riccardo Scrivano*, pref. Franco Salvatori, Ro, Bulzoni, 2000, 210 pp., comprises eight essays including: R. Mordenti's review of critical theory and the application of 'categorie critiche di seicentismo' to the 15th c., particularly the works of the Leccese preacher Fra Roberto Caracciolo; A. Gareffi on the literary strategems and moral hierarchies in Tasso and Ariosto. Giovanni Bárberi Squarotti, *Selvaggia dilettanza. La caccia nella letteratura italiana dalle origini a Marino*, Venice, Marsilio, 2000, 379 pp., is a valuable in-depth study that examines the many complex implications of this topos. It covers courtly pursuits, moral considerations, and the positive and negative dialogues with classical sources. Writers examined include Alberti, Doni, Tasso, Erasmo di Valvasone, and Bruno. The study encompasses the hunt as symbol, allegory, and metaphor in poetry, dialogues, and treatises. *Cinquecento capriccioso e irregolare. Eresie letterarie nell'Italia del Cinquecento*, ed. Paolo Procaccioli and Angelo Romano, Ro, Vecchiarelli, 1999, 246 pp., contains studies on: Giovanni Giustiniani; Doni and the Accademia Pellegrina; virtue and theft in Lodovico Domenichi; the *Dialoghi piacevoli* of Niccolò Franco; the *volgare* and Ortensio Lando; and Aretino's cultural milieu. *L'umana compagnia. Studi in onore di Gennaro Savarese*, ed. Rosanna Alhaique Pettinelli, Ro, Bulzoni, 1999, 441 pp., has 22 essays including: L. Bolzoni on the links between rhetoric, dialectic, and images in late 16th-c. Italy; C. Cieri Via on Piero Valeriano's *Hieroglyphica* and decoration in Rome for Leo X and Clement VII; V. De Caprio on Valla's *Elegantie*; L. Fortini on Bembo, Trifon Gabriele, and the debate on literature and language; M. Miglio's reconstruction of the library of 63 volumes belonging to Giacomo Bovio (1489–1522); A. Quondam on Paolo Cortesi's *De Cardinalatu*; and C. Bologna on Agnolo Colocci's interest in measurement and classification.

Panizza, *Women*, an extraordinarily rich and stimulating collection, in addition to the three items also relevant to the 17th-c. noted last year (*YWMLS*, 62:436) comprises a further 26 essays, the specifically literary noted in the sub-sections that follow, the rest listed here: under 'Women and the Court', D. Knox, 'Civility, courtesy and women in the Italian Renaissance' (2–17); E. S. Welch, 'Women as patrons and clients in the courts of Quattrocento Italy' (18–34); F. Daenens, 'Isabella Sforza: beyond the stereotype' (35–56); under

'Women and the Church', G. Zarri, 'Christian good manners: spiritual and monastic rules in the Quattro- and Cinquecento' (76–91); V. Primhak, 'Benedictine communities in Venetian society: the convent of S. Zaccaria' (92–104); under 'Legal constraints and ethical precepts', M. Graziosi, 'Women and criminal law: the notion of diminished responsibility in Prospero Farinaccio (1544–1618) and other Renaissance jurists' (166–81); C. Meek, 'Women between the law and social reality in early Renaissance Lucca' (182–93); B. Richardson, '"Amore maritale": advice on love and marriage in the second half of the Cinquecento' (194–205); J. Bridgeman, '"Pagare le pompe": why Quattrocento sumptuary laws did not work' (209–26); and under 'Female models of comportment', M. Ajmar, 'Exemplary women in Renaissance Italy' (244–64); P. Tinagli, 'Womanly virtues in Quattrocento Florentine marriage furnishings' (265–84); S. F. Matthews Grieco, 'Persuasive pictures: didactic prints and the contruction of the social identity of women in sixteenth-century Italy' (285–314). The sections 'Women and the stage' and 'Women and letters' are covered below, under POETRY, DRAMA, or PROSE, with the exception of N. Cannata Salamone, 'Women and the making of the Italian literary canon', 498–512, which reflects on the passive role played by women, in the late Quattrocento and early Cinquecento, as 'a substantial and established component of the public for which vernacular literature was produced', and C. Fahy, 'Women and Italian Cinquecento literary academies', 438–52, which argues that academies were already just as much male strongholds in the Cinquecento as they were to be in the following century: 'women writers and intellectuals . . . operated outside, or at the best on the margins of, the literary academy, which as an institution did little or nothing to encourage the literary activities of women or enhance their intellectual status'. Gerardo Cioffari, *Bona Sforza. Donna del Rinascimento tra Italia e Polonia*, Bari, Levante, 2000, 418 pp., covers the artists, writers, musicians, poets, and sculptors attracted to the Polish court. The appendix has an essay by M. Werner, 'L'immagine di Bona Sforza nella letteratura italiana del Cinquecento'. J. Bryce, 'Performing for strangers: women, dance, and music in *Quattrocento* Florence', *RQ*, 54 : 1074–1107, points to the role of patrician women in entertaining visiting notables and uses 'modern concepts of gendered performance and the performance of gender to speculate on the nature of that experience for the women involved'.

The project to publish all the evidence of Columbus's voyages nears completion. *Oviedo on Columbus. Repertorium Columbianum IX*, ed. Jesús Carrillo, trans. Diane Avalle-Arce, Turnhout, Brepols, 2000, 224 pp., has an introduction that delves into the political and propaganda motives for Gonzalo Fernández de Oviedo's portrait of

Columbus and shows how, by giving Columbus the central role in discovering the New World, he projected a message intended to justify the Spanish Crown's policy of imperial expansion. Oviedo's importance as a natural historian is also highlighted with an assessment of his interests and his erudite classical models. *Las Casas on Columbus. The Third Voyage. Repertorium Columbianum XI*, ed. Geoffrey Symcox and Jesús Carrillo, trans. Michael Hammer and Blair Sullivan, Turnhout, Brepols, 333 pp., covers the period 1458–1500 which saw the trips to Trinidad, the Gulf of Paria, and Hispaniola, and completes the coverage of Columbus's voyages in this series, though another volume on Italian narrative accounts is still to come. Bartolomé de Las Casas presents the most complete account we have of Columbus. The work is also to be noted for its erudition and concern for moral and political issues, particularly the fate of the indigenous peoples. This is in great contrast to Oviedo's starting point and shows how in both cases there is a socio-political agenda behind the history. *Italian Reports on America 1493–1522. Letters, Dispatches, and Papal Bulls, Repertorium Columbianum*, x, ed. Geoffrey Symcox and Giovanna Rabitti, trans. Peter D. Diehl, Turnhout, Brepols, 161 pp., shows how religion was used to justify the journeys. It reveals the delicate nature of papal involvement, the powerful role of Italian merchant capital, and the inventive nature of reports which conflated the real and the imaginary. The introduction discusses the question of authorship, the context of the writings, and the diplomatic practices of Italian states which appear to have been very ad hoc. Luigi Monga, *Due ambasciatori veneziani nella Spagna di fine Cinquecento. I diari dei viaggi di Antonio Tiepolo (1571–1572) e Francesco Vendramin (1592–1593)*, Moncalieri, CIRVI, 2000, 295 pp., studies two diaries which, as well as commenting on political events, give us a window into what interested the writers, and the language and images they used to express their experiences. They make observations about topography, economic matters, agriculture, and the different languages encountered. Although some of these themes were linked to strategic and military matters, the writings convey a sense of wonder at the real regional variations experienced by the early-modern traveller. Paolo Santonino, *Itinerario in Carinzia, Stiria e Carniola (1485–1487)*, Pisa–Ro, IEPI, 1999, 239 pp., relates the details of a journey made in the retinue of Bishop Pietro Carlo and others, and touches on economic matters, geography, climate, natural history, music, ailments, and remedies.

La table et ses dessous. Culture, alimentation et convivialité en Italie (XIVe – XVIe siècles), ed. Adelin Charles Fiorato and Anna Fontes Baratto, Paris, Sorbonne Nouvelle, 1999, 364 pp., contains 13 essays investigating the relationships between food and culture including: S. Lazard on how to conduct oneself at table in Francesco da Barberino's *Reggimento e costume di donna*; L. D'Eramo on the *mensa divina* in the letters of Catherine of Siena; N. Bianchi Bensimon on food and melancholy in Ficino's *De vita*; J.-P. Garrido on over-indulgence in Luigi Pulci's *Morgante*; A. Fontes Baratto on Giovanni Sabadino degli Arienti's *Porretane novelle*; J.-C. Zancarini on food in *Ruzante*, the *Pastoral*, and the *Dialoghi*. Other texts investigated include Pontormo's *Diario*, Anton Francesco Grazzini's *Cene* and *Rime burlesche*, Moderata Fonte's *Il merito delle donne*, Aretino's *Cortigiana*, and Francesco Liberati's *Perfetto maestro di casa*.

Il Perfetto capitano. Immagini e realtà (secoli XV e XVII), ed. Marcello Fantoni, Ro, Bulzoni, 531 pp., has an extensive introduction on history and mythography which assesses the methodology and problems in examining symbolism and ideology; there follow 14 essays in three sections: 'Il gran capitano e il potere', with studies of the imagery of Alessandro Farnese as duke and captain in Caprarola, and of the Medici Grand Dukes and the images of war; 'Il gran capitano e la letteratura politica', which examines the place of the captain and the prince as captain; 'L'iconografia', which includes studies on representing the perfect captain in literary portraits, the iconography of Ferrante Gonzaga, and images of the perfect captain in medals and the audience to whom these were directed. *Carlo V e l'Italia*, ed. Marcello Fantoni, Ro, Bulzoni, 2000, 269 pp., has 10 essays in two sections which reveal economic designs, the stability resulting from imperial presence, and the social impact of imperial grants of land, titles, and honours. It investigates how Charles became the object of prose and poetry and how humanist learning directed at Roman imperial themes created a complex Italian iconography of imperial majesty. *Carolus V Imperator*, ed. Pedro Navascués Palacio, Barcelona, Lunwerg, 1999, 457 pp., is a beautifully produced volume which covers the social, political, and cultural world in which Charles V struggled to exert his imperial authority in both Europe and the New World. The studies offer an impressive wealth of visual, literary, and documentary material. Of particular interest is the essay by B. Mitchell, 'Carlos V como triunfador' (213–15), which uses woodcuts, armour, paintings, and literary works to investigate 'spectacular demonstrations of the Emperor's power and pretensions' and the great impact such images had on a largely illiterate society.

Stefano Telve, *Testualità e sintassi del discorso trascritto nelle Consulte e Pratiche fiorentine (1505)*, Ro, Bulzoni, 2000, 349 pp., examines the effects of the process of transcription as the proceedings of the Consiglio of the Florentine republic were transformed from the spoken into the written word, and as the individual Latin forms were superseded by the use of the early 16th-c. *volgare*. The study concentrates on syntactic and textual structures and provides 'una doppia angolatura storico-linguistica e insieme pragmatico-testuale'. Marco Pellegrini, *Congiure di Romagna. Lorenzo de' Medici e il duplice tirannicidio a Forlì e a Faenza nel 1488*, F, Olschki, 1999, 190 pp., is linked to the project to edit the letters of Lorenzo, and it expands the epistolary evidence with further documentation to examine the events leading to the destabilization of the Romagna, the assassination of Girolamo Riario and Galeotto Manfredi, and the capture of Giovanni Bentivoglio. *Archivi di Stato di Firenze Inventario XIII (1564–67): Mediceo del Principato filze 515–529A*, ed. Marcella Morviducci (*Carteggio Universale di Cosimo I de' Medici*, vol. 9, part 13), F, Regione Toscana, 608 pp., continues the project to publish inventories to some 100,000 letters from 1537 to 1574.

Leonardo da Vinci: i documenti e le testimonianze contemporanee, ed. Edoardo Villata, Mi, Ente Raccolta Vinciana, 1999, xx + 320 pp., discusses the publishing tradition of documents relating to Leonardo with a critique of Luca Beltrami's *Documenti e memorie*, Milan 1919. There follow 346 texts from a wide range of sources which give substance to his projects, journeys, and life. The project to translate Leonardo's MSS into English will be a welcome contribution to scholarship. *The Manuscripts of Leonardo da Vinci in the Institut de France: Manuscript A*, trans. John Venerella, Mi, Ente Raccolta Vinciana, 1999, xlvii + 347 pp., gives a full description of the folios followed by a glossary of particular or idiosyncratic words and images. *The Manuscripts of Leonardo da Vinci in the Institut de France: Manuscript I*, trans. John Venerella, Mi, Ente Raccolta Vinciana, 2000, xxix + 203 pp., assesses contributions to L.'s studies in Latin and geometry, and in flow and transport phenomena. *The Manuscripts of Leonardo da Vinci in the Institut de France: Manuscript M*, trans. John Venerella, Mi, Ente Raccolta Vinciana, xxxvii + 124 pp., has detailed descriptions of the MS and its contents, and an assessment of scholarship on L.'s work in geometry and mechanics. There are notes on the problems of translating *forza* and the phrase *Sta (a) stilli*. David Alan Brown, *Leonardo apprendista*, F, Giunti, 19 pp. + 17 pls, deals with a computer reconstruction of the *Ginevra de' Benci*. Robert Zwijnenberg, *The Writings and Drawings of Leonardo da Vinci. Order and Chaos in Early Modern Thought*, CUP, 1999, 232 pp., puts forward the thesis that L.'s notebooks, far from containing a chaotic collection of data, were organized in a 'special order and structure to L.'s own needs'. This study addresses the fundamental question of why he continually filled notebooks with drawings and writings, and concludes that these were the daily necessities of his intellectual activity and an integral part of his thinking, aimed at stimulating scholarly study. Michael White, *Leonardo. The First Scientist*, London, Little Brown, 2000, 370 pp., gives a useful synthesis of his scientific ideas and of the notebooks, but a lack of rigour in the use of terminology and rather loose judgements on his activities do not help to clarify his activity as a scientist or his place within the socio-intellectual structure of his age. Valerie Shrimplin, *Sun Symbolism and Cosmology in Michelangelo's Last Judgement*, Kirksville, Truman State U.P., 2000, xv + 375 pp., uses a lecture on Copernicus (1523), early Christian iconography, literary works including Dante and Vittoria Colonna, the writings of Ficino, and Neoplatonic and Hermetic writings to propose that Michelangelo envisaged a cosmology of a circular universe with God as the Sun at its centre. W. Wallace, 'Michelangelo's *Leda*: the diplomatic context', *RenS*, 15:473–99, suggests that the work should be seen as playing a part in Florentine-Ferrarese political relations and that it was a diplomatic gift to Alfonso d'Este. *Pictorial Composition from Medieval to Modern Art*, ed. Paul Taylor and François Quiviger, London, Warburg Institute, 2000, 256 pp., has 11 essays including: C. Hope on the term *composizione* and its variants in Cennino Cennini's *Libro dell'arte*, Alberti's *De pictura*, and the two editions of Vasari's *Vite* to show the restricted application of the term; F. Quiviger on the 'methods of imagining human bodies which inform Renaissance compositional practices'.

BIBLIOGRAPHY, PRINTING AND PUBLISHING. *Gli incunaboli e le Cinquecentine della Biblioteca Comunale di Ala*, ed. Anna Gonzo, Trento, Provincia Autonoma di Trento, 2000, 350 pp., has an introduction that discusses the formation of the collection followed by a list of 360 works with critical apparatus and indexes. *Incunaboli e Cinquecentine del Fondo Trentino della Biblioteca Comunale di Trento*, ed. Elena Ravelli and Mauro Hausbergher, Trento, Provincia Autonoma di Trento, 2000, xxxiii + 401 pp., includes an essay by Marco Bellabara, 'Mercanti di libri, librerie, biblioteche e lettori a Trento fra Quattro e Cinquecento: prime note', which makes a contribution to our understanding of the place of books in society. This is followed by a catalogue of 518 items with critical apparatus, indexes, and the oft-ignored details of the bindings. Donato Giri, *Le Cinquecentine della Società Letteraria di Verona*, Verona, Società Letteraria di Verona, 91 pp., lists 106 items with full bibliographical descriptions. Patrizia Bellardone, *Tipografi lessonesi a Venezia nel Cinquecento*, Vigliano Biellese, Gariazzo, 1999, 163 pp., has three essays that examine the activities of the printers Joanne, Albertino, and Bernardino Trubeus in Venice. It details the editions published and examines Bernardino's role in publishing works on agricultural matters. The study stems from a collaborative project between the Lessona Biblioteca Civica and the Biella Biblioteche Civiche. The same scholar, in *Da Lessona a Venezia: i Viano nei documenti d'archivio*, Lessona, Biblioteca Civica Grosso, 2000, 14 pp., provides a short resumé of recent research into the history of the Viano publishing concern in Venice.

Giorgio Vercellin, *Venezia e l'origine della stampa in caratteri arabi*, Padua, Il Poligrafo, 126 pp., enables us to appreciate the spread of Arabic learning and religious works in its different phases. It offers a detailed account of the first appearance of Arabic characters in Bernard von Breydenbach's *Peregrinatio in terram sanctam* followed by detailed catalogue entries for 14 early texts. Giuseppina Zappella, *Il libro antico a stampa*, I. *Studio, tecniche, tipologie, evoluzione*, Mi, Bibliografica, 682 pp., is indispensable for those interested in the techniques and procedures of early printing. It fulfils its declared aim to be a 'summa delle conoscenze acquisite e delle problematiche emergenti nello specifico settore disciplinare'. The material is set out in five sections: 'Il supporto' deals with all aspects of paper manufacture (watermarks, the trade, costs, how paper was used); 'L'allestimento' covers type and fonts, printing manuals, the organization of the shop, and the processes of printing; 'La struttura' examines format, the size of pages, and the way they were bound to form a book; 'L'identità' discusses the terminology for describing the initial pages of books and their purpose, and deals with titles, colophons, and printer's marks. All the topics are backed up by a wealth of bibliographical information. Lorenzo Baldacchini, *Il libro antico*, Ro, Carocci, 173 pp., is a wide-ranging study covering: production (the shift from MS to print, costs, paper, type, ink, and press); readers; libraries; booksellers; the appearance of the book (frontispiece, colophon, size, fonts, illustrations, binding); the methodology for describing old texts; the intricacies of collation. It also lists a number of useful web sites. *Antichi tesori di inchiostro. Documenti e volumi dall' XI al XIX secolo*, ed. Gianluca Popolla, Susa, Centro Culturale Diocesano, 142 pp., has a useful array of plates and diagrams which set out clearly, with the standard nomenclature, the physical structure of MS documents and the construction of early printed books. Lodovica Braida, *Stampa e cultura in Europa*, Ro–Bari, Laterza, 2000, 162 pp., is a useful synthesis. *Bibliofilia*, 103, gathers a number of studies in the field: B. Richardson, 'A series of woodcut borders in early sixteenth-century Venetian title pages and the career of Pietro Bembo' (136–64); M. Gazzini, 'Scuola, libri e cultura nelle confraternite milanesi fra tardo Medioevo e prima età moderna' (215–61); C. Fahy, 'La carta nelle edizioni aldine del 1527 e del 1528' (263–89), is concerned with problems relating to paper, its sourcing, its purchase, and the difficulties of identification. We also note U. Motta, 'L'Ambr. S77 sup. e l'inventario dei libri di Antonio Querenghi: antichi e moderni nell'erudizione di fine Cinquecento', *IMU*, 41, 2000: 243–400.

The Renaissance Computer. Knowledge, Technology in the First Age of Print, ed. Neil Rhodes and Jonathan Sawday, London, Routledge, 2000, 212 pp., comprises 12 essays that deal with the problems of understanding how printing delivered knowledge, and the relationship between new technology and the promotion of old knowledge. Themes examined include: the overlap of different technologies; memory systems; networks of knowledge; the relationship between mathematics, the order of words, and the order of things; the complex functions of illustrations; user-friendliness in both Renaissance texts and contemporary electronic media; national and international boundaries; early-modern attempts at the organization and re-ordering of knowledge.

2. HUMANISM.

Ronald G. Witt, *In the Footsteps of the Ancients. The Origins of Humanism from Lovato to Bruni*, Leiden, Brill, 2000, xiii + 562 pp., proposes that the 'advent of humanism was intimately connected with the broad, long-term changes in Italian political, economic, social, and cultural life . . . the movement served, first of all, to promote the transformation and second to validate the new society's achievements'. The study emphasizes the importance of the French experience from the late 12th c. as a source of vernacular models and philosophical innovations. It traces the beginnings of humanism in poetry and gives reasons why humanism spread only gradually, and with attendant stylistic changes, to other forms of Latin writing. It explains the leading role of Florence in the humanist movement by investigating the translations of Latin works into the vernacular, which created a demand from the learned patriciate for instruction in ancient Latin literature. This is a persuasive account which demands and deserves attention as its conclusions, if accepted, will have far reaching repercussion for Quattrocento scholarship. Riccardo Fubini, *L'umanesimo italiano e i suoi storici. Origini rinascimentali, critica moderna*, Mi, Angeli, 347 pp., is a collection of 13 essays all with a strong historiographical slant. The volume is in three parts: 'L'umanesimo italiano: profilo storico' revisits the problem of defining the terms humanist and humanism; 'Leonardo Bruni e Lorenzo Valla' covers Bruni's radical philosophical stance and both his link to, and his break from, medieval scholasticism, it assesses Valla's contribution to philosophical and philological methodologies, and it gives a reappraisal of the *Dialectica*; 'L'umanesimo e il Rinascimento nella storiografia moderna' investigates the contributions of Burckhardt and Hans Baron. David Nicholas, *The Transformations of Europe 1300–1600*, London, Arnold, 1999, 486 pp., offers useful perspectives on the nature of humanism, its effect on attitudes towards language and education, and on civil society and the development of printing. It also covers literature and art, Leonardo and the scientific spirit, political thought, the spread of humanism, university education, the information revolution, and the reaction against humanism. Leonardo Bruni, *History of the Florentine People*, i. *Books 1–4*, ed. and trans. James Hankins, Cambridge, MA, Harvard U.P., xxi + 520 pp., is the first of three projected volumes which will also include a new edition and translation of the *Rerum suo tempore gestarum commentarius*. The introduction to the volume reviews the importance of this text in considering Bruni's biography and his scholarship. It sees 'his powerful recasting of the broad outlines of Etruscan, Roman and medieval history' as a means to enhancing the status of the republican government in Florence, and gives an assessment of his concept of political liberty and the legacy of his conceptual framework. Matteo Palmieri, *La vita di Niccolò Acciaioli*, ed. Alessandra Mita Ferraro, Bo, Il Mulino, liii + 114 pp., is a translation with commentary of the *Vita di Nicolai Acciaioli*, an important text for the development of biography. The introduction examines P.'s cultural strategies and their political significance, particularly his aim to praise the civic duty of the *vita activa*. The work's sources are assessed, and a biography of Acciaioli is followed by a translation, with excellent notes, using the text established by Gino Scaramella (Bologna 1918–34). In *Giulio Cesare Scaligero e Nicolò d'Arco. La cultura umanistica nelle terre del Sommolago tra XV e XVI secolo*, ed. François Bruzzo and Federica Fanizza, Trento, Provincia Autonoma di Trento, 1999, 253 pp., B.'s introduction assessing the cultural milieu in the area of Riva del Garda is followed by 13 scholarly essays. Topics include: Scaliger's origins; humanist culture at Riva and N. d'Arco; the difficulties of assessing Scaliger's character and his many activities; Paolo Giovio, Andrea Alciato, and N. d'Arco; Tasso's *postille* to Scaliger; Scaliger and the theory of *imprese*; Veronese humanists in the *Carmi* of Piero Valeriano; Scaliger's interest in science. M. Poli, 'Sur la fortune du *De familia*, des *Intercenales* et du *Momus* d'Alberti avant leur première édition', *REI*, 47:167–78, examines the MSS and printed editions and warns of the pitfalls of blindly accepting that MSS, which had limited circulation at the time, could exert much influence. J. Richards, 'Assumed simplicity and the critique of nobility: or how Castiglione read Cicero', *RQ*, 54:460–86, proposes that a study of Cicero's use of dissimulation, or 'assumed simplicity', in *De oratore* helps us to interpret Ludovico da Canossa's *sprezzatura* in the *Cortegiano*. L. Holford-Strevens, 'Humanism and the language of music treatises', *RenS*, 15:415–49, looks at innovations in the use of Greek pitch-names, the attempts at achieving a classical style, and the use of pseudo-antique vocabulary, and reveals the influence and lasting importance of traditional terminology.

Rinascimento e Classicismo. Materiali per l'analisi del sistema culturale di Antico regime, ed. Amedeo Quondam, Ro, Bulzoni, 1999, 487 pp., presents a selection of texts aimed at providing essential points of reference for understanding what we call the Renaissance (in terms of the rebirth of antiquity). The material is presented under five headings: 'Antichi e moderni'; 'L'imitazione'; 'Il sistema estetico e letterario del Classicismo. I fondamenti della legge'; 'Il sistema letterario del Classicismo. Le leggi della poesia'; 'Il sistema classico letterario del Classicismo. I generi della poesia'. 'Gasparino Barzizza e la rinascita degli studi classici: fra continuità e rinnovamento', *AION (FL)*, 21, a monographic issue ed. Lucia Gualdo Rosa, 316 pp., gathers articles by V. Brown on B.'s interest in Virgil, R. Gualdo on B.'s role in promoting elementary Latin grammar studies, and a number of essays on individual texts by G. Albanese, S. Marcucci, G. Barbaro, L. Gualdo Rosa, and A. Piscitelli. Matteo Venier, *Per una storia del testo di Virgilio nella prima età del libro a stampa (1469–1519)*, Udine, Forum, xxi + 158 pp., is more than a catalogue of editors. In the first part of the study meticulous philological scholarship is applied to examine the textual histories which indicate the use of a large number of MSS. The second part examines Virgil incunabula published in 1469–1475 from a strictly textual point of view. For the period 1476–1500 only a partial survey is attempted. The third part examines in detail three texts from the Aldine press published in 1501, 1505, and 1507 and the one edited by Benedetto Riccardini and published by Giunti in 1510. This study gives an insight into humanist scholarship and the painstaking care taken by editors to produce a 'correct' text. Scholars will welcome the facsimile reprint Vladimiro Zabughin, *Vergilio nel rinascimento italiano da Dante a Torquato Tasso*, 2 vols, ed. Stefano Carrai and Alberto Cavarzere, Trento U.P., 2000, xxxix + 403, 496 pp., of a work first published by Zanichelli in 1921–23. The editors have provided useful indexes to the Virgil quotations, to MSS, and to writers and artists. They have also provided accurate bibliographical references to the works cited.

Cetty Muscolino, *Il tempio Malatestiano di Rimini*, Ravenna, Longo, 2000, 99 pp., investigates Alberti's contribution to the Tempio and the iconography of its interior decorations. These reflect humanism in the themes of the Muses and liberal arts, and in the use of astrology and botanical symbolism. The text is accompanied by quite excellent illustrations. Charles Dempsey, *Inventing the Renaissance Putto*, Chapel Hill, North Carolina U.P., xvii + 277 pp., contributes to our understanding of the concepts of Renaissance, humanism, and humanist activities. The analyses of Botticelli's *Mars and Venus* and Poliziano's

Stanze per la Giostra, and the interpretation of the figure of the Renaissance putto, explore the interaction between vernacular and classical forms of expression in the Quattrocento. *Il parato di Niccolò V per il Giubileo del 1450*, ed. Beatrice Paolozzi Strozzi, F, SPES, 2000, 155 pp., draws on Vespasiano da Bisticci's and Giannozzo Manetti's humanist writings on Nicholas to discuss his cultural interests and the preoccupation with painted portraits, portraits on humanist tombs, medallic portraits of the pope and his contemporaries, and the decorative arts. Maria Losito, *Pirro Ligorio e il casino di Paolo IV in Vaticano. L''essempio' delle 'cose passate'*, Ro, Palombi, 2000, 175 pp., shows how humanist and antiquarian studies manifested themselves into material objects. It traces the transformations of the *casino* of Paul IV into a *villa all'antica* complete with nympheum, which fulfilled the functions of a museum of antiquities, a place for hosting the meetings of an academy, and a setting for a *coenatio*.

PHILOSOPHY AND HISTORY OF IDEAS. Nicola Cusano, *Il gioco della palla*, introd. and trans. Graziella Federici Vescovini, Ro, Città Nuova, 147 pp., gives a trans., with detailed notes, of the *Ludo globi*. The introduction points to how Cusanus differed from contemporary humanists in his attitude towards scholasticism. This dialogue written shortly before his death gathers together themes from his previous works and adopts the metaphor of the game to investigate and explain the tensions between human qualities and potential and the absolute. Marsilio Ficino, *Platonic Theology*, I: *Books 1–4*, ed. James Hankins and William Bowen, trans. Michael J. B. Allen and John Warden, Cambridge, MA, Harvard U.P., xviii + 341 pp., is the first of five volumes which will translate the complete text with a planned comprehensive index of names and subjects, an index of sources, and a concordance covering the Basel edition of 1576 and the edition produced by Raymond Marcel, Paris 1964–70. The introduction to this text reviews the main themes of Ficino's religious thinking, his philosophical endeavours, and the complexity of the themes and positions taken and how they mirror the preoccupations of his age. Antonio Persio, *Trattato dell'ingegno dell'Huomo*, ed. Luciano Artese, Pisa–Ro, IEPI, xii + 312 pp., gives the text, with notes on sources, of a work which develops Bernardino Telesio's theory of *spiritus* with its echoes of stoicism, Neoplatonism, and Ficino. The scholarly introduction sketches Persio's biography, tracing the points of divergence from Telesio. The appendix gives the text of *Del bever caldo*, Venice 1593, in facsimile. Though concentrating on the philosophy of antiquity, Anthony Gottlieb, *The Dream of Reason. A History of Philosophy from the Greeks to the Renaissance*, London, Penguin, ix + 469 pp., gives a clear account of the main themes and protagonists on which and whom Renaissance developments in the study of Plato, Neoplatonism, and nature were founded. Antonella Romano, *La Contre-réforme mathématique. Constitution et diffusion d'une culture mathématique jésuite à la Renaissance*, Ro, École Française de Rome, 1999, xi + 691 pp. + 22 pls., systematically investigates the relationship between the diversity of activity in the periphery and the norms set out in the centre. It points to the difficulties of arriving at a balanced view because of the extreme positions of both the anti-Jesuit camp and the Society's own defenders and hagiographers. The study compares and contrasts theory and practice, what should have been taught as against what was taught. It seeks to identify the concerns preoccupying the Collegio Romano and others at the centre of Jesuit culture, and how these concerns were promoted, mitigated, and accepted within the wider intellectual context of late-16th-c. Europe, while also exploring the social context in which new methodologies and a new epistemology were being forged. *Le sezioni coniche di Maurolico*, ed. Rocco Sinisgalli and Salvatore Vasola, F, Cadmo, 2000, 153 pp., gives the text of a translation of Apollonius by Francesco Maurolico. The introduction traces the antecedents in the geometry writings of Dürer and Leonardo and in Lorenzo Valla's translation of extracts from Apollonius.

Irma Naso, *Università e sapere medico nel Quattrocento. Pantaleone da Confienza e le sue opere*, Cuneo, Società per gli Studi Storici, Archeologici ed Artistici, 2000, 315 pp., examines Pantaleone's role and fame as a doctor, his teaching activities at the Studio in Turin, his love of books which led to his involvement in the establishment of printing presses at Turin and Pavia, and his political and diplomatic activities on behalf of Ludovico of Savoy and Galeazzo Maria Sforza of Milan. Giovanni Ceccarelli, *La salute dei pontefici nelle mani di Dio e dei medici*, Mi, Ancora, 204 pp., chronologically lists the popes from Alexander VI to Leo XIII with details of their election, illnesses, and death and some delightful anecdotal data. 'Medicine in the Renaissance city', *RenS*, 15.2, is a special number, edited by Vivian Nutton, which includes studies by: K. Park on the important role played by itinerant snakehandlers known as the *pauliani* (104–20); M. A. Katritszky on the image of the early modern mountebank (121–53); J. Cherry on the continuation of medical attitudes to the healing properties of jewellery in the Renaissance (154–71). Christian D. von Dehsen, *Lives and Legacies. An Encyclopedia of People who changed the World. Philosophers and Religious Leaders*, Chicago–London, Fitzroy Dearborn, 1999, x + 246 pp., has entries on Machiavelli and Savonarola.

BRUNO. *Rinascimento*, 40, 2000, a special number devoted to Giordano Bruno, includes: S. Bassi, 'Struttura e diacronia nelle *Opere Magiche* di Giordano Bruno' (3–18); L. Bolzoni, 'Note su Bruno e Ariosto' (19–44); M. Ciliberto, 'Bruno e l'*Apocalisse*. Per una storia interna degli *Eroici furori* (45–74); M. Matteoli, 'L'arte della natura nei primi scritti mnemotecnici di Bruno' (75–122); R. Sturlese, 'Arte della natura e arte della memoria in Giordano Bruno' (123–42); and M. Zonta, 'Due note sulle fonti ebraiche di Giovanni Pico e Giordano Bruno' (143–53). *BrC*, 6, 2000, carries 'L'individualità tra divino e umano', the papers of the fourth 'Letture bruniane' gathering in Rome, which include: F. Mignini, 'La dottrina dell'individuo in Cusano e Bruno' (325–50); S. Toussaint, 'L'individuo estatico. Tecniche profetiche in Marsilio Ficino e Giovanni Pico della Mirandola' (351–80); E. Canone, 'Il fanciullo e la fenice. L'eterna essenza umana e gli innumerabili individui secondo Bruno' (381–406); P. F. Mugnai, 'Una proposta di lettura per un brano del primo dialogo degli *Eroici Furori*' (407–16); M. Fintoni, 'Figure dell'umanità di Bruno' (417–36); G. Paganini, 'Umano e divino in un contemporaneo di Bruno: l'antropologia di Giusto Lipsio' (437–52). The same issue also has D. Quaglioni, '"Ex his quae deponet iudicetur". L'autodifesa di Bruno' (299–319), L. Albanese, 'Bruno e gli *Oracoli dei Caldei*' (539–46), and the two other essays noted below. *BrC*, 7, continues with Id., 'Bruno e le linee indivisibili' (201–208); F. Beretta, 'Giordano Bruno e l'Inquisizione romana. Considerazioni sul processo' (15–50); and M. Palumbo, 'Un "introvabile" Bruno casanatense' (245–54). C. Vasoli, 'Bruno e l'"arte della memoria"', *Il Veltro*, 44, 2000: 299–312. S. Ricci, '"Fede" e "dissimulazione". Bruno lettore di Machiavelli nella crisi delle guerre di religione', *FC*, 25, 2000: 245–62.

Aspects and moments of B.'s reception and influence are studied in: C. Lüthy and W. R. Newman, 'Daniel Sennert's earliest writings (1599–1600) and their debt to Giordano Bruno', *BrC*, 6, 2000: 261–80; C. Buccolini, '*Contractiones* in Bruno: potenza dell'individuo e grazia divina nell'interpretazione di Mersenne', *ib.*, 503–35; B. Ferraro, 'Gl'*infiniti mondi* di Giordano Bruno e la letteratura "lunare"', *CLett*, 29: 273–92, with special reference to Kepler, Francis Godwin, and Cyrano de Bergerac. A. Savorelli, 'Le ultime paginee bruniane di Felice Tocco', *BrC*, 7: 259–68. Stock is taken of the present in H. Gatti, 'The state of Giordano Bruno studies at the end of the four-hundredth centenary of the philosopher's death', *RQ*, 54: 252–61. To mark the loss (in August 2001) of the *doyen* of B. scholars: Giovanni Aquilecchia, *Giordano Bruno*, T, Aragno, 140 pp., appeared posthumously, with a bibliography of his writings compiled by T. Provvidera.

RELIGIOUS THOUGHT AND THE CHURCH. *Pier Paolo Vergerio il Giovane, in problema attraverso l'Europa del Cinquecento*, ed. Ugo Rozzo, Udine, Forum, 2000, viii + 375 pp., gathers 15 essays celebrating the 500th anniversary of Vergerio's birth and which make use of new material from the Archivi del Sant'Uffizio. The essays cover biographical matters, his meeting with Luther, his contacts with family and friends during his exile, his religious conversion, his influence in Slovenia and Istria, the enmity of Marcello Cervini and Girolamo Muzio, his links with Italian reforming circles, his commentary on Della Casa's 1549 catalogue of prohibited books, and the religious and literary links between Vergerio and Francesco Negri. *Presenze eterodosse nel Viterbese tra Quattro e Cinquecento*, ed. Vincenzo De Caprio and Concetta Ranieri, Ro, Izzi, 2000, ix + 293 pp., gathers 11 studies covering the anxieties, hopes, and controversies engendered by religious tensions and thoughts of reform, and such topics as: the activities of Giovanni Mercurio da Correggio; new biographical data for, and the recreation of the intellectual interests of, Ludovico Lazzarelli; the strange story of Lucia Brocadelli da Narni (a possible source for Ariosto's Melissa); Ercole I of Ferrara and the city of Viterbo; myth and history in Annius of Viterbo; the theme of heterodoxy in mid 16th-c. lists of literati; philosophy and classical myth in Egidius of Viterbo (an excellent study); humanist and reforming circles; the religious ideas of Vittoria Colonna; and Vittoria Colonna's poetry and the Ecclesia Viterbiensis (1541–46). Caterina Vigri, *Le sette armi spirituali*, ed. Antonella Degl'Innocenti, F, SISMEL-Galluzzo, 2000, xliii + 73 pp., is an ann. critical edition of a work first circulated in 1438, which is both a spiritual autobiography and a pious tract addressed to nuns to teach them the path to salvation. Peter Martyr Vermigli, *The Oxford Treatise and Disputation on the Eucharist 1549*, ed. and trans. Joseph C. McLelland, Kirksville, Truman State U.P., 2000, xlvi + 306 pp., is the text of Vermigli's first public debate as a protestant theologian. The introduction points to the biblical, patristic, and medieval sources, and the difficulties Vermigli experienced in coming to terms with his exile in England. *L'apertura degli archivi del Sant'Uffizio Romano*, ed. Adriano Prosperi et al., Ro, Accademia dei Lincei, 2000, 194 pp., comprises eight essays and six shorter notes by some of the foremost scholars in this field that indicate the accessibility and nature of the new source material and offer fresh perspectives and avenues for research. Specific topics covered include: the Roman Inquisition; the Congregation of the Index; the Inquisition, the Index, and Machiavelli. G. Fragnito, 'L'applicazione dell'Indice dei libri proibiti di Clemente VIII', *ASI*, 159:107–49, investigates the complex power struggles within the Church and the difficulty of exerting control with regard to publishing and reading. Samuele Giombi, *Libri e pulpiti: letteratura, sapienza e storia religiosa nel Rinascimento*, Ro, Carocci, xii + 307 pp., includes studies on: Bolognese humanism and Giovanni and Gian Francesco Pico, investigating letter-writing, Erasmian humanism, and astrology; the

Carmelite humanist Giovanni Battista Spagnoli and his attitude to
Church reform, his religious poetry in Latin, and the image of the
Turk in his writings; new perspectives on the figure of Erasmus in
Bolognese culture; Achille Bocchi, 16th-c. rhetoric, and Nicodemism;
Ciceronianism in Bolognese humanism; encyclopaedism, curiosities,
and religious propaganda; and Tomaso Garzoni and the fate of the
Piazza universale at the hands of the preachers.

SAVONAROLA.   *Girolamo Savonarola da Ferrara all'Europa*, ed. Gigliola
Fragnito and Mario Miegge, F, SISMEL–Galluzzo, xix + 553 pp.,
with 29 essays falling into three sections, *inter alia* includes: a
comparative study by I. Lazzarini of Este holdings and those of other
states to identify salient features of the political structures and to
arrive at a methodology for interpreting the available evidence;
M. Folin on the problems of communication between rulers, the role
of the diplomat, the preoccupations of foreign policy, and *politica di
prestigio*; R. Rusconi on images of preaching in Renaissance art and
their possible influence on Savonarola; G. Zarri on the problems
inherent in the study of S.'s influence on women and the reactions of
institutions and individuals to his teaching before and after his death;
T. Matarrese on the language used by S. to address his Florentine
audience and how preparing the text of his sermons for printing was
a deliberate act in which S. collaborated with the notary Lorenzo
Violi; A. M. Fioravanti Baraldi on the 16th-c. editions of Ludovico
Pittorio and the iconography of the illustrations; A. Ghinato on the
journey of the Bibbia di Santa Maria degli Angeli from its original
home in Ferrara and its fate in the hands of Savonarola when his
marginalia transformed it 'da un incunabolo in un prezioso
manoscritto'; G. Tamani on Jewish culture in late Quattrocento
Ferrara and the activities of copyists; E. Barbieri's detailed analysis of
the printing of S.'s works by Florentine and Venetian printers, with
the texts of the dedications. U. Rozzo comments on the prolific
nature of Savonarola publishing and the complex pattern and
character of the official prohibitions in the various Roman and foreign
Indexes of prohibited books; A. Barzazi focuses on the Savonarolan
texts mentioned in the inventories of religious libraries submitted to
the Congregation of the Index; and R. Campioni reports on the first
results of a survey into Savonarolan texts in the Emilia Romagna. I
also note, from the second part, entitled 'Dirigenti religiosi nelle città
libere (1494–1548)': a historiographical essay by G. C. Garfagnini
pointing to lacunae in Savonarola scholarship, problems in interpreting the evidence, including his writings, and the dangers of ignoring
contemporary belief systems; G. Chiottolini on relationships and
tensions between the city and its ecclesiastical institutions in Central
and Northern Italy; and a comparison by B. Hamm of three different

styles of preaching before the Reformation. *Una città e il suo profeta. Firenze di fronte al Savonarola*, ed. Gian Carlo Garfagnini, F, SISMEL–Galluzzo, xvi + 575 pp., comprises 30 essays, which include: C. Vasoli's elegant and meticulous review of S. scholarship since Pasquale Villari's *History* of 1859–61; essays by M. Scudieri, S. Pini, and G. Rasario on relics and images of S.'s presence today in San Marco; G. C. Garfagnini on the political dimension to S.'s religious message; M. Miglio on the reaction of Rome to S.'s refusal to bow before authority; C. Leonardi on the problems of assessing S.'s spirituality; M. Martelli on S.'s poetry; D. Delcorno Branca on the adoption and adaptation of Dantesque images and language in the poetry of Poliziano; P. Viti on S. between elite and popular culture; A. F. Verde on S.'s attitude to the Bible; R. Rusconi on how S. used his sermons; L. Polizzotto's call for a more balanced, fact-based attitude to S. research; A. Valerio on S.'s attitude to women and their role in his vision of society; K. Eisenbichler on how S.'s view of widows resulted from a consideration of morality and contemporary demographic trends; and G. Cattin et al. on S.'s active interest in music and the lack of any lasting legacy after his death. *I processi di Girolamo Savonarola 1498*, ed. Ida Giovanna Rao, Paolo Viti, and Raffaela Maria Zaccaria, F, SISMEL–Galluzzo, cxix + 211 pp., is nothing less than a complete overhaul of the texts first edited by Pasquale Villari in 1861. The introduction points out the problems in Villari's text and criticizes the methodology adopted by later historians whose lack of philological and historical rigour has led to real misinterpretations and facile judgements. This is a volume concerned with textual reconstruction rather than interpretation, and a full discussion of the sources is followed by a critical text with exhaustive notes, which will surely become the basis for new interpretations of Savonarola's trial. Gian Carlo Garfagnini, '*Questa è la terra tua*'. *Savonarola e Firenze*, F, SISMEL–Galluzzo, 2000, xxvi + 458 pp., is a collection of 20 studies which reflect Garfagnini's wide-ranging interests and expertise. The topics covered include: S.'s historiography and Florence; transferring sermons into printed texts; S. and prophecy between myth and history; Giorgio Benigno Salviati and Savonarola; S. and Lorenzo de' Medici within the context of the political, historical, and cultural dynamics of the city; political and religious polemics in Florence; S. and astrology; S. and Giovanni and Gianfrancesco Pico della Mirandola; S. and Domenico Benivieni; S. and the Fathers of the Church; literature and literati in S.'s writings; and S. and Domenico Buonvicini. Many of these essays are accompanied by previously unpublished documents and texts. *Il Santuario di Santa Maria del Sasso di Bibbiena dalla protezione Medicea al Savonarola*, ed. Armando Felice Verde and Raffaella Maria Zaccaria,

F, SISMEL–Galluzzo, 2000, xxii + 126 pp., has 11 essays in three sections. The section 'Religione e letteratura' has essays by: M. Martelli on Lorenzo de' Medici's religious poetry within the context of political and cultural considerations; F. Bausi on Latin epigrams in praise of the Madonna in the religious poetry of Ugolino Verino; P. Viti on Piero Dovizi's escapades for Lorenzo de' Medici against Savonarola and his use, before Machiavelli, of the expression *caccasangue* in a letter. The printing history of popular editions of Savonarola in the Quattro and Cinquecento is traced by P. Scapecchi. The other sections are 'Storia e documenti' and 'Devozione e arte'.

INDIVIDUAL CENTRES. Paul A. Merkley and Lora L. M. Merkley, *Music and Patronage at the Sforza Court*, Brepols, Turnhout, 1999, xxx + 514 pp., is a study firmly embedded in documentation and is much more than a book about music. It sets out the innovative methods used by Francesco Sforza to both establish political hegemony and promote his court. It points to significant factors that contributed to intellectual and humanistic achievements and the humanist education of the members of the administration. It shows how singers were part of embassies and were sometimes used as diplomats, and how liturgical music was a vehicle for statecraft. It points to Sforza's aggressive diplomatic activity, which involved luring musicians from other courts with attendant political repercussions, and to the internal dissent resulting from lavish patronage as one reason for the assassination of Galeazzo Maria Sforza. It traces the close links between patronage and historiography and the importance of Greek studies, and calls for a reassessment of humanism at the Milanese court. Monica Ferrari, *'Per non manchare in tuto del debito mio'. L'educazione dei bambini Sforza nel Cinquecento*, Mi, Angeli, 2000, 272 pp., touches on all things linked to the schooling of these important children. This is a well researched study based on documents in Milan, Pavia, Mantua, and Modena, and it offers a rare and fascinating insight into the activities of teachers, governors, and doctors, the nature of parental advice, and theories on education and on the formation of a prince. Hans Semper, *Carpi una sede principesca del Rinascimento*, ed. Luisa Giordano, Pisa, ETS, 1999, 483 pp., though first published in German in 1882, is still an important source of data for Carpi's humanist activity and its links to an international circle of scholars and writers, and also to Roman publishing and culture.

3. POETRY

'Le donne, i cavalier, l'arme, gli amori'. Poema e romanzo: la narrativa lunga in Italia, ed. Francesco Bruni, Venice, Marsilio, 448 pp., focuses on

narrative poetry and contains essays ranging from Dante's *Comedy* to the *Teseida, Morgante, Inamoramento de Orlando, Orlando Furioso, Baldus* and to contemporary literature. *Il prosimetro nella letteratura italiana*, ed. Andrea Comboni and Alessandra di Ricco, Trento, Dipartimento di Scienze Filologiche e Storiche, 2000, 574 pp., contains 14 articles, mostly concerned with Renaissance poetry, which include: P. Vecchi Galli on *Nicolosa Bella*; O. Besomi on *Pamphilia*; C. Vecce on the prosimetrum in Renaissance Naples; A. Albonico on a hitherto unknown *prosimetro pastorale*; C. Berra on Niccolò Liburnio's *Selvette*; G. Dilemmi on Muzzarelli and Landolfi; B. Grazioli on Minturno; and A. Comboni on *L'Aura Soave* by Ascanio Centorio degli Ortensi. O. Besomi, 'Un nuovo testimone di *Pamphilia* a Wolfenbüttel', *FC*, 25, 2000:165–78, as well as describing the new MS, discusses the hypothesis that the work was by Antonio Ivani (1430–82).

Giorgio Dilemmi, *Dalle corti al Bembo*, Bo, CLUEB, 2000, ix + 358 pp., is a collection of already published work designed to lead the reader through the various forms of Quattrocento poetry into the canon and beyond. Thus the book is divided into three parts: 'Corti e poesia' deals with Boiardo, A. Phileremo Fregoso, Guidotto Prestinari, Matteo Bandello; 'Esercizi di lettura' focuses on Boiardo and Ariosto; 'Al cospetto del Bembo' moves from Bembo the courtier to his relationship with Veronica Gambara and closes with Della Casa.

Nadia Cannata, *Il canzoniere a stampa (1470–1530). Tradizione e fortuna di un genere fra storia del libro e letteratura*, Ro, Dipartimento di Studi Romanzi–Bagatto Libri, 2000, 476 pp., provides a detailed study of the verse collections published in print during this period, which includes a complete catalogue and the bibliographical descriptions of nearly half the editions still extant. By the same author, an historical and linguistic survey of the terminology used over time to describe verse collections, which illustrates the origins and the reasons for the generalized use of the term *canzoniere*, is: 'Dal *ritmo* al *canzoniere*: note sull'origine e l'uso in Italia della terminologia relativa alle raccolte poetiche in volgare (secc. XIII-XX)', *CrT*, 4: 397–429. C. Bologna, 'La copia colocciana del Canzoniere Vaticano (Vat. Lat. 4823)', pp. 105–52 of *I canzonieri della lirica italiana delle origini*, ed. Lino Leonardi, F, SISMEL–Galluzzo, is an overdetailed analysis of the manuscript copy of Vat. Lat. 3793, which however is an important witness for 16th-c. vernacular philology applied to early medieval poetry and relevant for the study and development of lyric poetry in the early Renaissance.

La lirica rinascimentale, ed. Roberto Gigliucci, introd. Jacqueline Risset, Ro, IPZS, 1030 pp., is an anthology which groups extracts from the works of 70 poets, from both Quattro and Cinquecento from a variety of different geographical areas and poetic schools. Each author is prefaced by a short biographical and bibliographical note. The aim of the collection is so-called 'divulgazione di qualità', although one cannot but wonder about the use of such an expensive book, unlikely to enter private homes and not really useful to a scholar either. A reprint of one of the first of an important series of mid-Cinquecento poetic anthologies in now available: *Rime diverse di molti eccellentissimi autori: Giolito 1545*, ed. Franco Tomasi and Paolo Zaja, RES, S. Mauro Torinese, xlviii + 475 pp., equipped with notes, biographical and other, and a lengthy introduction. Not noted earlier was Antonio Marzo, *Note sulla poesia erotica del Cinquecento, con appendice di testi*, Lecce, Adriatica, 1999, 192 pp., in which the texts outweigh the notes. W. Theodor Elwert, *La poesia dialettale d'arte in Italia*, Ro, Biblioteca Nazionale Centrale Vittorio Emanuele, 2000, 78 pp., is the only translation of Elwert's essay discussing Ferrari's and Croce's conflicting theses on Italian dialect literature through a detailed examination of it, with particular attention to poetry.

S. Ritrovato, 'Forme e stili del madrigale cinquecentesco', *SPCT*, 62 : 119–54, looks at a number of madrigals, starting from translations of one by Pontano attributed to Ariosto, Strozzi, and Marino, and sets them against the background of the rich Cinquecento tradition of the genre in an attempt (advertised in the title) to establish the forms and styles, which are many and varied, of the metrical genre. Ottaviano Petrucci, *Frottole libro nono*, ed. Francesco Facchin and Giovanni Zanovello, Bo, CLUEB, 1999, 255 pp., continues the project to publish P.'s settings from between 1504 and 1514: a valuable source for assessing taste within different cultural *milieux* and the importance and diffusion of specific poets and poems. The poets featuring in this volume are Evangelista Maddaleni Capodiferro, Petrarch, Antonio Cammelli, Cornelio Castaldi, Serafino Aquilano, Niccolò da Correggio, Antonio Tebaldeo, and Cariteo.

G. Frezza, 'Sul concetto di "lirica" nelle teorie aristoteliche e platoniche del Cinquecento', *LItal*, 53 : 278–94, moves from the lack of proper theorization on lyric poetry during the Cinquecento — to note that poetry itself functioned as the only real obstacle to the acritical reception of Aristotle's *Poetics*. From discussions on poetry (Riccoboni, Varchi, Minturno, Castelvetro, and Tasso) the idea emerged for the first time that Aristotle's authority could not suffice as a guide to the modern experience of poetry. S. Jossa, 'Ordine e casualità: ideologizzazione del poema e difficoltà del racconto fra Ariosto e Tasso', *FC*, 25, 2000 : 3–39, deals with the heated discussions which took place between 1547 and 1558 on the model for writing narrative poems. A. Bettinelli, 'Le postille di Bernardo e di Torquato Tasso al commento di Francesco Robortello alla *Poetica* di Aristotele',

IMU, 42:181–284. Micaela Rinaldi, *Torquato Tasso e Francesco Patrizi: tra polemiche letterarie e incontri intellettuali*, Ravenna, Longo, 117 pp. Very late Cinquecento poetics are represented by: M. Slawinski, 'La poetica di Giulio Cortese tra Campanella e Marino', *BrC*, 7:127–54, which relates to S.'s edition of Cortese's *Prose* (see *YWMLS*, 62:428).

R. Sodano, 'Intorno ai *Coryciana*: conflitti politici e letterari in Roma dagli anni di Leone X a quelli di Clemente VII', *GSLI*, 178:420–50, a further study of a well-known and well-researched collection now discussed in the context of the early Roman Renaissance, reveals that its progressive restyling was due to the harsh polemics in which Roman and northern humanists were engaged. Under the aegis of the statues for which they wrote, their acrimonious debates focused on religion and ideology. S. Jossa, 'L'eroe nudo e l'eroe vestito. La rappresenta-zione di un gesto da Omero a Cervantes', *Intersezioni*, 21:5–36, discusses — from Homer to the Chanson de Roland, Chrétien de Troyes, Ariosto, Trissino, Alamanni, Tasso, and Cervantes — the recurrence and representation of the act of the dressing and undressing of the hero. Useful information on a not too well known topic can be found in M. Savoretti, 'L'*Eneide* di Virgilio nelle traduzioni cinquecen-tesche in ottava rima di Aldobrando Cerretani, Lodovico Dolce e Ercole Udine', *CLett*, 29:435–57.

Among the many studies of individual poets the following seem of a certain interest: C. Del Popolo, 'Il petrarchismo di Matteo Caldo', *GSLI*, 178:47–56, discusses Caldo's popular *poemetto*, six books of narrative verse (*sestine* linked through *rimalmezzo*) entitled *Vita Christi Salvatoris eiusque Matris Sanctissimae*, which, despite belonging to a non-lyrical genre, was influenced by Petrarch's language and style. M. Frapolli, 'Un micro-canzoniere di Domenico Venier in antologia', *QVen*, 33:29–38, studies the little *corpus* of 33 lyric poems by Venier contained in *Il sesto libro delle rime di diversi* (Venice, 1553) and is able to identify a *canzoniere* structure for them. An Italian translation of another Venier's poetry is available in Maffio Venier, *Poesie diverse*, ed. Attilio Carminati, pref. Manlio Cortelazzo, Venice, Corbo e Fiore, 259 pp. A preparatory study for a critical edn is Massimo Castoldi, *Per il testo critico delle rime di Girolamo Verità*, Verona, Biblioteca Civica, 2000, 192 pp. A. Vallunga, 'Petrarchismo di Lorenzo Regozza notaio bellunese tra '500 e '600', *Archivio Storico di Belluno, Feltre e Cadore*, 72, 2000:112–14. Orsatto Giustinian, *Sonetti alla moglie*, ed. Simone Mammana, F, Le Càriti, 65 pp. A. Macchioni, 'Il dantismo "osser-vante" di Marino Ionata', *Italianistica*, 29, 2000: 27–44, analyses *El giardino poema in terza rima*, a journey through the afterworld published posthumously in 1490. Marino, an imitator of Dante of considerable cultural depth, came from the marginal Molise, and combines Dante with his own Franciscan culture.

Hitherto unpublished verse texts have been brought to light in A. Lanza, 'El libro de' ghiribizzi di Giovanni Betti', *LIA*, 2:157–326, which edits the major work of a Quattrocento Florentine surviving in two MSS — 12,248 hendecasyllables in quatrains — which is of considerable linguistic interest; and M. Moxedabo Lanza, 'Il *Liber pamphilianus* di Tommaso Baldinotti', *ib.*, 359–414, which edits a *canzoniere* of 250-odd poems, almost all sonnets, from the MS at Florence's Biblioteca Nazionale Centrale. N. Cacace Saxby, 'Il codice 240 della Biblioteca di Classe (Ravenna)', *ib.*, 327–50, catalogues the verse contained in the Ravenna MS. D. Maestri, 'Un manoscritto con probabili inediti del Firenzuola', *LItal*, 53:63–78, proposes attributing to F. the unattributed verse contained in a 16th-c. MS recently acquired by the Biblioteca Nazionale Centrale in Florence. C. Del Popolo, 'Sacchetti, *Rime*, 107, vv. 14–15', *FC*, 25, 2000:109–13, examines S.'s references to 'the confusion of tongues', here and elsewhere in his verse.

On individual women poets I note: R. Russell, 'Chiara Matraini nella tradizione lirica femminile', *FoI*, 34, 2000: 415–27, which adds some useful material to the recent important contributions on this poet by arguing about her belonging to a tradition of women poets. Isabella Morra's poetry is enjoying an important revival. Last year her *Rime* appeared in a critical edition. Now the *acta* of a 1999 conference devoted to her have come out: *Isabella Morra e la poesia del Rinascimento Europeo*, ed. Nerla De Giovanni, Alghero, Nemapress, 175 pp. A theoretical approach in the study of women's poetry of the Renaissance is attempted by S. Ruffo Fiore, 'A critical approach to feminine presence in early modern Italian poetry: genre and gender', *RStI*, 18.1, 2000:60–67, which however, for the Cinquecento, contains nothing substantial, mentioning Gaspara Stampa and Veronica Franco only in passing.

General bibliographical reviews include: G. Forni, 'Rassegna di studi sulla lirica del Cinquecento (1989–2000), II: Dal Tansillo al Tasso', *LItal*, 53:422–61; P. Diffley, 'Some recent translations of Renaissance works', *ItS*, 56:148–59, a review article which among other translations into English looks at Joseph Tusiani's *Morgante* and Joscelyn Godwin's *Hypnerotomachia Polyphili*; G. D'Agostino and M. Lettieri, 'La letteratura italiana del Quattrocento, Cinquecento e Seicento nell'ottica nordamericana (1987–1999)', *EL*, 25.2, 2000: 95–111, a detailed review of American critical literature which could be a useful tool with which to monitor North American work on Italian Renaissance poetry. The bibliography of a great student of Renaissance culture, Giancarlo Breschi, *L'opera di Gianfranco Contini. Bibliografia degli scritti*, F, SISMEL–Galluzzo, 2000, 126 pp., is relevant, directly or indirectly, to Italian Renaissance poetry.

ARIOSTO. Ludovico Ariosto, *La novella di Fiordispina*, ed. Stefano Giovannuzzi, F, Le Càriti, 64 pp., rather unconvincingly presents the *novella* as a metaphor for the uses of literature (of lack thereof) and of its relationship with reality. M. Villa, 'Tra "inchiesta" e "profezia": Bradamante nel *Furioso*', *Acme*, 54:141–73, studies the figure of Bradamante and its role as a unifying device in the narrative. The author contrasts Bradamante's 'sane' love and amorous quest — which will meet with Ruggiero's pursuit of virtue, resulting in the perfection of both — with the insane quest that will lead Orlando to his ruin. This allows the author an intelligent and illuminating insight not only into several episodes of the poem and into its characters, but also into their function and ultimately into the very structure of the poem. A. Casadei, 'Nomi di personaggi nel *Furioso*', *Il nome nel testo*, 2–3, 2000–2001: 229–37, discusses Ariosto's criteria in choosing names for the poem, his preference towards the Tuscan forms of names originating from the chivalric tradition, the refined cultural allusiveness of the names he invented, and his sensitivity for sound and cultural reminiscences which, merely by means of names, he succeeds in evoking. Magic and the deceptions suffered by both characters and readers of the *Orlando Furioso* are investigated in L. Giannetti Ruggiero, 'L'incanto delle parole e la magia del discorso nell'*Orlando Furioso*', *Italica*, 78:149–75, a short essay which focuses on interplay between poetry and reality. M. Cerrai, 'Una lettura del *Furioso* attraverso le immagini', *StCrit*, 16:99–134, discusses the illustrated edition of the *Furioso* published by Giolito in 1542, where the 46 woodcuts amount to a sort of textual exegesis providing a key to the complexity of the text and its interpretation, and demonstrates that for the historian and the critic these images represent an extremely valuable insight into the readership of the *Furioso*. On images as well, and in particular on a much discussed topic, L. Freedman, 'Titian's *Ruggero and Angelica*: a tribute to Ludovico Ariosto', *RenS*, 15:287–300. S. Dal Bianco, 'Ritmi e toni negli episodi del *Furioso*', *SMI*, 1:159–206, is a detailed study of rhythm, sound, and sense and their relationships in the *Furioso*. A. D'Orto, 'Criteri e tecniche di imitazione nelle *Satire* dell'Ariosto', *CLett*, 29:419–35, discusses Ariosto's debts to the language and style of the Quattrocento *cantari* in writing his *Satire*. On A.'s biography, see M. Paoli, ' "Appetiva le rape": les *appunti* dits "de Virginio" à la lumière des premières biographies de l'Arioste', *ChrI*, 63–64, 2000: 217–47.

BOIARDO. F. Berardi, 'Il libro di Orlando', *EL*, 26.2:39–59, discusses the four passages in which Boiardo uses the word 'libro' in the *Innamorato* and the significance of this term in the poem. T. Matarrese, '*L'inamoramento de Orlando*: osservazioni sul testo e sulla lingua', *LItal*, 53:401–12, comments on, and adds further relevant material to, what is an important edition of Boiardo's poem. G. Masi, 'Cronaca (nera) e letteratura: Apuleio, Sigismondo Pandolfo Malatesta e la novella boiardesco di Stella e Marchino', *StIt*, 25:87–102.

BRUNO. Patrizia Farinelli, *Il 'Furioso' nel labirinto. Studio degli 'Eroici furori' di G. Bruno*, Bari, Adriatica, 2000, 342 pp., is a detailed monographic study of Bruno's petrarchism in the *Eroici Furori*.

BURCHIELLO. M. Zaccarello, 'Rettifiche, aggiunte e supplemento bibliografico al *Censimento* dei testimoni contenenti rime del Burchiello', *SPCT*, 62:85–117, provides a series of MS descriptions, to be added to Messina's census of Burchiello MSS and early printed books, which have emerged from preparatory work for a critical edition of Burchiello. MSS and early printed books are described, dated, and as far as possible given a place of origin. A study of B.'s art is: Id., 'Indovinelli, paradossi e satira del saccente: "naturale" ed "accidentale" nei *Sonetti del Burchiello*', *RELI*, 15, 2000:111–28.

CARITEO. P. Morossi, 'Il primo canzoniere di Cariteo secondo il codice Morocco', *SFI*, 58, 2000:173–98, studies the MS, previously known as De Marinis, described by Contini in 1964 and now housed at the Fondazione Antonio Maria and Mariella Marocco in Turin. It contains the text (very close to the *editio princeps*) of a verse collection divided into three sections and loosely imitating Propertius's elegies. According to Morossi, the MS, a dedicatory copy for Ferrandino d'Aragona, was written by a private amateur and not by Ferrandino or Cariteo himself as suggested by Contini. It could be defined a *canzoniere* not because it affords a narrative development, but as a 'canzoniere situazionale'.

CELLINI. A general revival of interest for Cellini's *Rime* is testified to by a series of new contributions: Benvenuto Cellini, *Rime*, introd., comm. Vittorio Gatto, Ro, Izzi, xviii + 220 pp., which reprints Maier's 1968 edition and equips it with a new commentary. P. Paolini, 'Le rime di B. Cellini', and G. Dell'Aquila, 'Benvenuto Cellini lirico' both in *RLI*, 8, 2000. Vittorio Gatto, *Benvenuto Cellini. La protesta di un irregolare*, Na, Liguori, iv + 68 pp., re-addresses, among other things, the issue of Cellini's position in the debate about the arts and his conception of the role of the artist-intellectual.

COLONNA. A. Brundin, 'Vittoria Colonna and the Virgin Mary', *MLR*, 96:61–81, studies the selection of poems by Colonna (MS Ashb. 1153 at the Laurenziana) sent in 1540 to Marguerite d'Angoulême, Queen of Navarre. It remained unpublished as such, yet combined unpublished and published material in an interesting and innovative way. A. Bullock, 'Il canzoniere di Vittoria Colonna: nuove prospettive e discussioni', *RELI*, 16, 2000:111–32, is a review article which responds to the publication, by T. Toscano in 1998, of a group of unknown poems marking the death of F. D'Avalos. From the point of view of gender studies, Colonna's poetry is discussed by S. M. Adler, 'Strong mothers, strong daughters: the representation of female identity in Vittoria Colonna's *Rime* and *Carteggio*', *Italica*, 77, 2000:311–30. G. Rabitti, 'Vittoria Colonna as role model for Cinquecento women poets', Panizza, *Women*, 478–97.

DELLA CASA. Giovanni Della Casa, *Rime*, ed. G. Tanturli, Parma, Fondazione Pietro Bembo – Ugo Guanda, 244 pp., is a valuable new edition of the poems.

FOLENGO. Simona Gatti Ravedati published a critical edition of the poem in ottave *La umanità del figliuolo di Dio*, Alessandria, Orso, 2000, 474 pp., previously available only in the collection 'Scrittori d'Italia' and in its one very rare Cinquecento edition (1533). The volume includes notes and indexes and a very substantial introduction.

MICHELANGELO. A. Maggi, 'L'immagine del concetto d'amore: una lettura del frammento michelangiolesco *Ben fu, temprando il ciel tuo vivo raggio*', *REI*, 46, 2000:259–68, analyses a fragment from M.'s *Rime* as an example of why his rhetoric should be seen as the most direct and genuine expression of neoplatonic thought.

POLIZIANO. D. Delcorno Branca, 'Lucrezia, Poliziano, Lorenzo: note su alcune convergenze fra lirica sacra e lirica profana', *Interpres*, 19, 2000:57–73, inscribed *Per Rossella Bessi. In Memoriam* identifies some influences of the devotional poems by Lucrezia Tornabuoni on Lorenzo's and Poliziano's poetic language.

PULCI, LUCA D. Bisconti, 'La *Pistola I* de Luca Pulci entre louange courtisane et poésie pastorale', *ChrI*, 63–64, 2000:119–38, argues that the *Pistola I* is an introduction and key to all the others. The *Pistola* is published with a rich commentary.

PULCI, LUIGI D. Puccini, 'Una fonte per Margutte', *GSLI*, 177, 2000:534–39, identifies the *Cantare di Geta e Birria* as a hitherto unknown literary source for the encounter between Morgante and Margutte.

SANNAZARO. S. Monti, 'La dedica del *De Partu Virginis*, di Jacopo Sannazaro nelle vicende della sua genesi', *Aevum*, 75:629–40, traces the various stages undergone by the epigram by which the 1526 *editio princeps* of the work was dedicated to the then pope, Clement VII. Rosangela Fanara, *Strutture macrotestuali nei Sonetti e Canzoni di Jacobo Sannazaro*, Pisa, IEPI, 2000, 93 pp., seeks to identify a *canzoniere* structure in Sannazaro's *Rime*. On the *Arcadia*: Marina Riccucci, *Il neghittoso e il fier connubio: storia e filologia nell'Arcadia' di Jacopo Sannazaro*, Na, Liguori, 228 pp.

TANSILLO. M. T. Imbriani, 'Intertestualità tra le *Lagrime* di Luigi Tansillo e di Torquato Tasso', *CLett*, 29:15–32, analyses the relationships between Tasso's *Stanze* and Tansillo's *Lagrime di S. Pietro*, a source for many similar poems in the late 16th c. On his lyric poetry E. Milburn, '*Come scultor che scopra/ grand'arte in picciol'opra*: Luigi Tansillo and a miniature *canzoniere* in the *Rime di diversi* of 1552', *ItS*, 56:4–29.

TASSO. E. Stoppino, '"Onde è tassato l'Ariosto". Appunti sulla tradizione del romanzo nella *Gerusalemme liberata*', *StCrit*, 16:225–44, explores the ambivalent relationship (with its mixture of censure and emulation) that links Tasso to Ariosto. Emanuele Scotti, *I testimoni della fase alfa della 'Gerusalemme Liberata'*, Alessandria, Orso, 140 pp., traces the first stages of the composition of the *GL*, which have hitherto been virtually unknown. Loredana Chines, *I veli del poeta. Un percorso fra Petrarca e Tasso*, Ro, Carocci, 2000, 112 pp., explores the significance of the veil in Petrarch's poetry — the semantic allusiveness of the word to both the lady and the poetry which describes her — and in turn considers its relevance for the poetry of Tasso, its *velamen*, and its complex sources. Franco Fortini, *Le rose dell'abisso. Dialoghi sui classici italiani*, T, Bollati Boringhieri, 2000, 120 pp., his readings of the *GL* for Italian radio, is an interesting and valuable acquisition. F. Pignatti, 'La morte di Sveno (*Gerusalemme Liberata*, VIII, 5–40) e la tradizione epico-cavalleresca medievale', *GSLI*, 177, 2000:363–403, discusses the death of Sveno episode, derived from William of Tyre's chronicle of the first crusade, and the problem of its relation to the the poem as a whole. This allows the author to advance some interesting considerations on the medieval sources of modern epic. An interesting study of Tasso's Armida and her representation in the poem and in contemporary art is to be found in A. Di Benedetto, 'Lo sguardo di Armida (un'icona della *Gerusalemme Liberata*)', *LItal*, 53:39–48.

C. Gigante, 'Dal Tasso al Bargeo, dal Bargeo al Tasso. Per un'interpretazione del ventesimo libro della *Gerusalemme Conquistata*', *EL*, 26.2:61–72, examines the relationship between the dream created by Tasso in the 20th canto of the *Gerusalemme Conquistata* and its most significant precedent in Cinquecento literature: the dream of Godfrey of Bouillon in Pier Angelo da Barga's *Syrias*, Book VI; C. Gigante, 'Nel cantiere della *Gerusalemme Conquistata*. Lettura del ms. autografo del poema', *FC*, 26:161–86, conducts an investigation of the making of the *Conquistata* on the evidence of a Neapolitan MS which carries its pre-1593 version. M. Cataudella, 'Le sette stanze sulla vita di S. Benedetto di T. Tasso', *EL*, 26.1:41–49, argues that the *stanze* are to be considered as the project of an unfinished poem rather than fragments of his late poetry.

An analysis of Tasso's use of metaphor in his poetic practice and theoretical writings is conducted in D. Gibbons, 'Tasso "petroso":

beyond Petrarchan and Dantean metaphor in the *Gerusalemme Liberata*', *ItS*, 55, 2000:83–98.

S. Miano, 'Le postille di T. Tasso alle *Annotazioni* di Alessandro Piccolomini alla *Poetica* di Aristotele', *Aevum*, 74, 2000:721–50, is an initial study of Tasso notes which reveal that he attentively read earlier commentaries by Francesco Robortello, Vincenzo Maggi, Pietro Vettori, and Lodovico Castelvetro, and that Aristotle's *Poetics* was of interest to him especially for the relationship between poetry, historical subject-matter, and the unity of the poem.

Bibliographical contributions include: E. Ardissino, 'Rassegna degli studi per il quarto centenario tassiano', *LItal*, 52, 2000:624–61; a useful tool for study of all aspects of Tasso's activity is to be found in B. Basile, 'La biblioteca del Tasso. Rilievi ed elenchi di libri dalle *Lettere* del poeta', *FC*, 25, 2000:222–44.

4. THEATRE.

A. Concolino Mancini Abram, 'Tradizione e innovazione nella commedia del Cinquecento', *ChrI*, 65:27–47, analyses some of the most representative Cinquecento comedies (*La Calandria*, *La Mandragola*, *La Cortigiana*, *La Lena*) with the intent of identifying the peculiarities of each text in its relationship with the Latin tradition on the one hand and the Tuscan *novella* on the other. In this connection A. Guidotti, 'Novellistica e teatro del Cinquecento', pp. 395–418 of *Favole parabole istorie. La forma della scrittura novellistica dal Medioevo al Rinascimento*, ed. Gabriella Albanese, Lucia Battaglia Ricci, and Rossella Bessi, Ro, Salerno, 2000, 600 pp., comes back to the much-debated general relationship between the two genres, while a particular instance is examined in A. Mongatti, 'Il *Filosofo* di Pietro Aretino e la riscrittura della novella di Andreuccio (*Decameron*, II 5)', *StIt*, 23, 2000:27–46.

In Panizza, *Women*, the section 'Women and the stage', comprises: R. Andrews, 'Isabella Andreini and others: women on stage in the late *Cinquecento*' (316–33); M. Günsberg, 'Gender deceptions: cross-dressing in Italian Renaissance comedy' (334–49); and R. E. Bancroft-Marcus, 'Attitudes to women in the drama of Venetian Crete' (350–65). The Andreini (including Giovan Battista), as well as Tristano Martinelli and Silvio Fiorilli, loom large in Siro Ferrone, *The Travelling Invention: Italian Actors between 1580 and 1630*, London, UCL Centre for Italian Studies, 2000, 18 pp., which views the birth of the modern theatre as the work of *commedia dell'arte* actors who 'deserve credit for having founded the discipline of theatrical performance which has come down to us today'.

Giovanna Romei, *Teoria, testo e scena. Studi sullo spettacolo in Italia dal Rinascimento a Pirandello*, ed. Giorgio Patrizi and Luisa Tinti, Ro, Bulzoni, 328 pp., collects the author's last work, ranging from Cinquecento theatre and pastoral genre to the Commedia dell'Arte and Pirandello.

A. M. Testaverde, 'Stanze pubbliche e accademia privata nel viaggio di un testo scenico tra Italia e Spagna', *MR*, 14, 2000:243–71, traces the history of a *pièce* entitled *Spada dannata* which contains a repertoire of scenes written by the actor Stefanello Bottarga of the company of authors which went to Spain with the famous Zan Ganassa. The source of the play — which must be connected with the practices of the *comici dell'arte* — is contrasted with other versions from different times and contexts. T. Megale, 'I padroni di Arlecchino', *ib.*, 273–81, is an interesting profile of the comic actor Arlecchino Martinelli, active in Mantua at the beginning of the Seicento. T. Montone, '*Il Magico legato*: una pastorale italiana ad Anversa nel 1607', *FC*, 26:263–77, deals with a very rare but nonetheless important comedy in verse which must be seen as one of the jewels of the literature produced by the Italian merchants active in Antwerp during the 16th and 17th c. Across theatre and cultural studies lies M. Bregoli Russo, 'L'attore Tommaso Inghirami (Fedra) e l'Accademia Romana', *CLett*, 29:263–72, which investigates Inghirami's central role in the cultural policy of the papacy of Leo X in relation to theatre. B. Pesca, 'L'intreccio mancato della *Venexiana*, ovvero: le vie dell'amore a Venezia', *ItQ*, 38, 1–2:5–14, discusses some peculiarities in the structure of the comedy and of its scenes which makes it an *unicum* in Italian Cinquecento theatre. W. Sahlfeld, 'Bacchantes et bacchanales dans la littérature italienne de la Renaissance et du baroque', *REI*, 46:189–208, refers to texts from Poliziano's *Orfeo* to Marino's *Adone*. *La resurressioni*, ed. Concetto Del Popolo, Alessandria, Orso, 2000, 94 pp., provides a critical text for a 15th-c. Sicilian play. K. Eisenbichler, 'Un'opera sconosciuta (e autografa) di Giovan Maria Cecchi: "Atto recitabile da fare avanti che nella Compagnia si dieno li panellini benedetti"', *SPCT*, 63:75–106, presents and edits a one-act religious text that has come to light in a MS recently acquired by the Beinecke Library at Yale.

Apparati funebri medicei per Filippo II di Spagna e Margherita d'Austria, ed. Monica Bietti, F, Sillabe, 1999, 208 pp., in 16 essays reconstructing the diverse cultural manifestations with which Medici Florence marked the death of Philip II in 1598 and his wife in 1612, shows how expertise in scenography and stage machinery could be turned to the service of the state and testify to the wide range of cultural exchanges between Florence and Madrid which reinforced close economic and political ties.

For bibliographical information see V. Gallo, 'La tragedia del Cinquecento: ancora una rassegna (1995–2000)', *EL*, 26.1: 99–104, and — on Italian translations of the Celestina — R. C. Melzi, '*Celestina* Italian style', *RStI*, 18.2, 2000: 32–43.

ARIOSTO. Giuseppe Coluccia, *L'esperienza teatrale di L. Ariosto*, Lecce, Manni, 288 pp., traces the development of Ariosto's theatre from *La cassaria* and *I suppositi* to *Il negromante* and *La lena*.

DELLA PORTA. Giovanbattista Della Porta, *Teatro*, 1: *Tragedie*, ed. Raffaele Sirri, Na, ESI, 2000, 444 pp., in the Edizione Nazionale delle Opere, contains new editions of *La Penelope*, *Il Georgio*, *L'Ulisse*, all provided with a brief introduction and bibliography.

MACHIAVELLI. G. Inglese, 'Critica teatrale della *Mandragola*', *La Cultura*, 39: 127–31, refutes some of the opinions contained in R. Alonge, 'La riscoperta rinascimentale del teatro', pp. 5–118 of *Storia del teatro moderno e contemporaneo*, ed. Roberto Alonge and Guido Davico Bonino, 1: *La nascita del teatro moderno. Cinquecento e Seicento*, T, 2000, according to which the desire for children, triggering the action of the *Mandragola*, makes Nicia and Lucrezia the heroic actors of a necessary action they would otherwise morally condemn. G. Bardin, 'Machiavelli reads Boccaccio: *Mandragola* between *Decameron* and *Corbaccio*', *ItQ*, 149–150: 5–26.

RUZANTE. M. Canova, '1516–1531: ipotesi sull'attività teatrale del Ruzante', *RELI*, 15, 2000: 37–66, reassesses the chronology of Ruzante's theatrical *œuvre*.

5. PROSE

For the novella in general see the vol. of conference papers *Favole parabole istorie* noted above under THEATRE. C. Lucas-Fiorato, 'Le coffre: fonctions narratives d'un objet dans quelques nouvelles de la Renaissance', *ChrI*, 63–64, 2000: 161–80. An interesting aspect of the 15th-c. novella is analysed in J. Rawson, 'Marrying for love: society in the Quattrocento novella', Panizza, *Women*, 421–37, while Boccaccio as 16th-c. model for the *cornice* is discussed in M. Picone, 'Riscritture cinquecentesche della cornice del *Decameron*', *Versants*, 38, 2000: 117–38. F. Pignatti, 'La novella esemplare di Sebastiano Erizzo', *FC*, 25, 2000: 40–68, reassesses the *Sei giornate* (1567). The 15th-c. miracle story features in R. Chavasse, 'The Virgin Mary: consoler, protector and social worker in Quattrocento miracle tales', Panizza, *Women*, 138–64.

The dialogue is represented by V. Cox, 'Seen but not heard: the role of women speakers in Cinquecento literary dialogue', *ib.*, 385–400; G. Aquilecchia, 'Aretino's *Sei giornate*: literary parody and social reality', *ib.*, 453–62; C. La Charité, 'Du *Dialogo de la bella creanza de le donne* (1539) à l'*Instruction pour les jeunes dames* (1572) de Marie de Romieu, ou quand le paradoxe fait l'opinion', *RHR*, 28:103–12; P. Cherchi, 'La " Selva" de *I Marmi* doniani', *EL*, 26.1:3–40; M.-D. Couzinet, 'Mythe, fureur et mélancolie. L'inspiration historique dans les *Dialoghi della istoria* (1560) de Francesco Patrizi', *NRSS*, 19.1:21–36; and by various Bruno items noted under HUMANISM, above.

Raffaele Morabito, *Lettere e letteratura*, Alessandria, Orso, 196 pp., traces the history of letter-writing, seeing it as an experimental activity with no set rules. The study examines the relationship of letter-writing to other literary genres. It sets out the different categories of letters, tackles the question of literary models and the phenomenon of creating collections, assesses the impact of printing, and looks at the series of works dedicated to the writing of letters. Also on epistolography are D. Robin, 'Humanism and feminism in Laura Cereta's public letters', Panizza, *Women*, 368–84, M. Schuller, 'Le temps et l'espace dans les lettres d'Alessandra Macenghi Strozzi', *REI*, 46, 2000:163–88, and M. Kennedy Ray, 'Un'officina di lettere: le *Lettere di molte valorose donne* e la fonte della "dottrina femminile"', *EL*, 26.3:69–92.

Biography in the late Cinquecento is explored in C.-G. Dubois, 'L'individu comme moteur historiographique: formes de la biographie dans la période 1560–1600', *NRSS*, 19.1, 83–106. The little-known phenomenon of women's historiography, in the form of chronicles by Sisters Giustina Niccolini, Orsola Formicini, Fiammetta Frescobaldi, and Caterina Guarneri da Osimo, is addressed in K. Lowe, 'History writing from within the convent in Cinquecento Italy: the nun's version', Panizza, *Women*, 105–21, while a celebrated feminist appropriation of the 16th-c. vernacular treatise on women is analysed in A. Chemello, 'The rhetoric of eulogy in Lucrezia Marinella's *La nobilità et l'eccellenza delle donne*', *ib.*, 463–77.

Raul Mordenti, *I libri di famiglia in Italia*, II. *Geografia e storia*, Ro, Storia e Letteratura, 242 pp., is the long-awaited sequel to *Filologia e storiografia letteraria*, 1985, and is organized in three parts. The first section reviews research since the first volume, analyses the salient features of the *libri* as a literary genre, sets out the mechanisms whereby they were written and survived, and finally addresses the problem of the nature of *Ricordanze*. The second section examines the tradition in Tuscany, Northern, Central, and Southern Italy and that pertaining to religious minorities such as Jews and Protestants. The third section traces the origins of the genre, the evolution from business notes, and the transition from oral transmission to the authority of the written text. It covers the transformation of such texts into literature, their links to genealogy, biography, and autobiography, and the way in which the genre eventually declined. In the

appendix are the texts of eight papers delivered at a conference in
Rome in 1997. These include: L. Pandimiglio, 'Quindici anni (circa)
con i libri di famiglia' (115–30); G. Ciappelli, 'I libri di famiglia a
Firenze. Stato delle ricerche e iniziative in corso' (131–40); and
E. Irace, 'Dai ricordi ai memoriali: libri di famiglia in Umbria tra
Medioevo ed età moderna' (141–62).

BANDELLO. Carlo Godi, *Bandello: narratori e dedicatori della seconda
parte delle 'Novelle'*, Ro, Bulzoni, 642 pp., is the second volume (after
Narratori e dedicatori della prima parte delle 'Novelle', 1996) of an historical
and philological study that takes us to novella 2.59. It gives details of
the various figures in the text as well as their socio-cultural backgrounds, which does much to allow us to appreciate the world in
which the characters operate. The bibliographical data might have
been presented in a clearer fashion and to print the index to the MSS
in a separate booklet is, to say the least, eccentric. T. E. Mussio,
'Bandello's *Timbreo and Fenicia* and *The Winter's Tale*', *CDr*, 34,
2000:211–44.

BEMBO. Pietro Bembo, *'Prose della volgar lingua'. L'editio princeps del
1525 riscontrata con l'autografo Vaticano latino 3210*, ed. Claudio Vela,
Bo, CLUEB, cxxiv + 334 pp., is a meticulous critical edition of the
1525 text (Venice, Tacuino) which gives an insight into Bembo's
thinking as he made emendations to the MS in preparing it for
publication. The justification for using the earliest edition, instead of
those of 1538 or 1544, is that the 1525 editon had a greater impact at
the time on Italian culture. R. Righi, 'Una lettera inedita attribuita al
Bembo e un indizio per il suo epistolario', *SPCT*, 62:119–30,
discusses five letters in the Bologna Archivio di Stato and produces
evidence to identify the writer of the one yet unpublished letter as
Bembo and the addressee as Ranuccio Farnese, who had just been
appointed Cardinal. The text of the hitherto unpublished letter is also
given.

GARZONI. Paolo Cherchi, *L'alambicco in biblioteca: distillati rari*, ed.
Francesco Guardiani and Emilio Speciale, Ravenna, Longo, 2000,
371 pp., gathers 25 essays including 'Il "Klendario" di Garzoni,
riflessioni sul concetto di tempo e l'enciclopedia' (173–88) and
'Onomastica e critica testuale, il caso della *Piazza Universale* di Tomaso
Garzoni' (189–205). Tomaso Garzoni, *L'hospidale de' pazzi incurabili /
L'hospital des fols incurables*, ed. Adelin Charles Fiorato, trans. François
de Clarier, Paris, Honoré Champion, 453 pp., has an introduction
which assesses G.'s humanist themes, aspects of the novella and satire,
and his contribution to the debate on the nature and manifestations
of madness. There follows a transcription of the text of the *editio
princeps* of 1586 with useful notes and a facing French translation.

MACHIAVELLI. Geoff R. Berridge, Maurice Keens-Soper, and Thomas G. Otte, *Diplomatic Theory from Machiavelli to Kissinger*, Houndmills, Palgrave, ix + 216 pp., contains essays by Berridge on Machiavelli and Guicciardini. For Machiavelli diplomacy was an instrument to be used in the strategy of deception, particularly by the private citizen to increase his *reputazione*; otherwise, he is seen as having had no real interest in diplomacy, whereas Guicciardini is shown to have had long-term considerations in view where he advocated the training and deployment of ambassadors and the need to keep faith whenever possible. E. Nuzzo, 'Le "cose umane" tra "mutazioni" e "ordini" in Machiavelli. Rappresentazioni concettuali e figure metaforiche', *Archivio di storia della cultura*, 13, 2000: 3–26. F. Verrier, 'Lecture paradoxale des *Discours sur la première décade de Tite-Live* sub specie feminae: des exemples aux métaphores', *REI*, 47: 179–91, studies the sex-related language of the *Discorsi* to conclude that they are populated by 'women and viragos . . . and, among men, by 'androgynes and eunuchs'. J. Céard, 'Le prix des leçons de l'histoire: Machiavel, lecteur d'Hérodien', *NRSS*, 19.1: 9–20. M. C. Figorilli, ' "Odio" e "rovina" in Machiavelli: una lettura del II libro delle *Istorie fiorentine*', *FLI*, 104, 2000: 373–87. G. Cadoni, 'Il "profeta disarmato". Intorno al giudizio di Machiavelli su Girolamo Savonarola', *La Cultura*, 39: 239–66.

STRAPAROLA. D. Pirovano, 'Una storia editoriale cinquecentesca: *Le piacevoli notti* di Giovan Francesco Straparola', *GSLI*, 177, 2000: 540–69.

SEICENTO

By Letizia Panizza, *Royal Holloway College, London*, and Domenico Chiodo, *University of Turin*

1. General

L. Russo, 'La letteratura seicentesca e i dialetti', *Belfagor*, 56: 165–74, is a reprint of an important 1960 article, as relevant today as it was then, asserting that this 'secolo malfamato' was 'rivoluzionario', for here is the divide between the two great epochs of Italian literature, early and modern. In was in this century, furthermore, that regional or dialect literatures came to the fore, a phenomenon recognized by Croce and De Sanctis in the 19th c. and now taken for granted. Another characteristic of the Seicento baroque is sketched in C. Ossola, ' "Homo inchoatus, homo perfectus": figure dell'abbozzo in età barocca', *LItal*, 53: 337–46: that of a predilection for the imperfect and the incomplete in nature and art. The image of an 'abbozzo' or 'sketch' is used to describe both God's work in creation and the writer composing novels and essays in which aphorisms abound.

As if in answer to Russo, *I luoghi dell'immaginario barocco*, ed. Lucia Strappini, Na, Liguori, 2001, 610 pp., an impressive collection of 45 essays on the Baroque by Italian critics and scholars covering all aspects of cultural life in the Seicento, makes us wonder why this century could ever have been judged disparagingly. There are sections, discussed below, on theatre, institutions, opera, history of the book, the love of collecting, and narrative. Two general essays deal with issues of place. A. Pauly, 'Claves para una comprensión del controvertido debate sobre el barroco' (5–20), sees the debate unleashed by Galileo over Ariosto ('dice cose') against Tasso ('dice parole') as the *locus* of all later oppositions between Renaissance and Baroque, reason and nature, classical and romantic, and reviews Italian, French, German, and Spanish criticism. G. Benzoni, 'Barocco in laguna' (21–28), discusses the ways Venice and the Veneto region can and cannot be characterized as a 'place' of the Baroque.

The political significance of the cult of relics is examined in two articles. M. Rossi, 'Francesco Bracciolini, Cosimo Merlini e il culto mediceo della Croce: ricostruzioni genealogiche, figurative, architettoniche', *StSec*, 42: 211–76, with 20 pls, brings together the 1612 pilgrimage of Grand Duke Cosimo II, with his wife Christine of Lorraine, to the reliquary of the True Cross at Lucignano in the figure of a monumental 'Tree of Life' (part of a grand tour of his territory); the fabrication of a genealogy for Cosimo whereby he was descended from Godfrey of Bouillon, who procured the wood of Christ's cross placed in the monument; also a great spectacle with the Tree of Life allied to the Medici; and finally an epic by Francesco Bracciolini dedicated to Cosimo II, legitimizing the Medici dynasty precisely by its association with the Cross. M. L. Doglio, ' "Grandezze" e "meraviglie" della Sindone nella letteratura del Seicento', *FC*, 25, 2000:418–41, illustrates a similar tying together of a sacred relic, in this case the Holy Shroud (the 'Sindone') of Turin, the object of many works in Latin prose and verse beginning in 1581, and the destiny of the House of Savoy. The legends constructed gave the House a key role in bringing the Shroud from Jerusalem, a pious act which guaranteed divine protection for the dynasty.

GENDER STUDIES. Giuliana Morandini, *Sospiri e palpiti. Scrittrici italiane del Seicento*, Genoa, Marietti, 262 pp., vindicates Italian women writers of prose and poetry of the 17th and early 18th c., as well as women painters, arguing (like Russo) that modern sensibility (the 'sighs and heartbeats' of the title) developed then. She brings the eye of the novelist and psychologist to her perceptive essay on the accomplishments of women during this fruitful era in a great variety of genres, styles, and subject matter (only in the 19th c. would women be as creative), and illustrates her observations with short selections which include hitherto unknown poetry by women members of Arcadia. There is a bibliography of mainly Italian critical literature. S. Kolsky, 'Moderata Fonte, Lucrezia Marinella, Giuseppe Passi: an early seventeenth-century feminist controversy', *MLR*, 96:973–89, seeks an answer to why Marinella, in her famous 1600 answer to Passi's diatribe against women, did not mention Fonte's dialogue defending women which, though written earlier, was published the same year. He suggests that Marinella perhaps thought that Fonte had not gone far enough in attacking misogyny. N. Costa-Zalessow, 'Tarabotti's *La semplicità ingannata* and its twentieth-century inter-preters, with unpublished documents regarding its condemnation to the *Index*', *Italica*, 78:314–25, looks at the reception of the rebel nun Tarabotti, forced to live in a convent in 17th-c. Venice against her will. She defends T.'s biographer Emilio Zanette (condescending to Tarabotti and other women writers of the age) by setting up a dubious and mutually-exclusive polarity between Zanette (a 'historian', and therefore of sound judgement) and his critics (who are 'feminists', and therefore not historical). She also gives a summary of the condemna-tion, which she has brought to light and will publish separately, of T.'s book to the Index. By the same author, 'Fragments from an autobiography: Petronilla Paolini Massimi's struggle for self-assertion', *ItQ*, 147–148:27–36, adds to our knowledge of the troubled life of this poet and member of Arcadia whose aristocratic father was murdered for political reasons and who as a child was married for her property to the cruel Francesco Massimi, 29 years her senior. Costa-Zalessow has found passages from her lost memoirs in a life of Massimi by the last surviving descendent. D. Valentini, 'Artemisia's legacy in contemporary cinema', *FoI*, 34, 2000:519–25, discusses the controversy surrounding a 1997 film of Agnes Merlet about the court case of the painter Artemisia Gentileschi, raped by her art tutor. Taking into account Anna Banti's 1947 fictional treatment, and the published records of the trial, she considers the film to depart too much from the known historical accounts.

BIBLIOGRAPHY. F. Barcia, 'Per una bibliografia dei tacitisti italiani (secoli XVI–XVII)', *FC*, 25, 2000:302–15, lists 35 publications — versions, selections, commentaries of Tacitus's history of the Roman Empire, beginning with the Justus Lipsius edition of 1574. With the ban on Machiavelli's analysis of power, political theorists turned to Tacitus to understand contemporary Italy. L. De Venuto, 'La biblioteca di un notaio roveretano: Giovanni Battista Passerini (†1687)', *AARA*, 250, 2000:171–89, gives a picture of the notary's books, comprising solely legal texts. The jurist most frequently represented was Prospero Farinacci, Italy's famed Renaissance writer of law. Botero and Lipsius were also named among the moderns. The correspondence of two bibliophiles is documented in A. Mirto, 'Antonio Magliabechi e Carlo Dati: lettere', *StSec*, 42:381–434, revealing the cultural ties of Tuscany with the European book market and republic of letters in general from 1658, when Magliabechi was already the Medici librarian, to Dati's death in 1676.

2. POETRY

The premature decease of Giorgio Fulco has undoubtedly been a major loss for Seicento studies, and he has now been commemorated in the best possible way: his most significant periodical and miscellany articles have been gathered in the volume Giorgio Fulco, *La 'meravigliosa' passione. Studi sul barocco tra letteratura ed arte*, Ro, Salerno, xv + 530 pp. The collection also includes a valuable unpublished lecture, *La corrispondenza di Giovan Battista Marino dalla Francia*, presented at the conference *Le siècle de Marie de Médicis* (Collège de France, Paris, 20–22 January 2000), which cites new epistolary evidence and proposes new hypotheses for the dating of M.'s works and a general reorganization of the *corpus* edited by Guglielminetti. Also dedicated to Fulco's memory is the important contribution: M. Slawinski, 'Poesia e commercio librario nel primo Seicento: su alcune edizioni mariniane ignote o poco note', *FC*, 25, 2000:316–34, which adds fresh items to Giambonini's monumental Marino bibliography: a

Parma edition of *Lira III* (Anteo Viotti, 1616, discovered at the Oxford–Codrington Library), a copy (identified at Birmingham University) of the Bonino edition of the *Rime boscareccie* which were considered lost, and an eight-page pamphlet, printed at Terni in 1631, which has been found at the Bodleian Library and which reproduces a number of Marino texts under the title *Ottave*. The information is spiced with interesting observations on 17th-c. editorial practice and its effects on poetic production itself.

Gian Piero Maragoni, *Il gusto dell'agro. Diporti boscherecci e pescatori*, Varese, 65 pp., gathers three articles devoted to bucolic compositions by Giovan Battista Bergazzano, Paolo Zazzaroni, and Scipione Caetano. The volume carries a postface by Andrea Battistini. An entirely different genre, the mock-heroic, is addressed in a miscellany presented by Giorgio Bárberi Squarotti: *Teoria e storia dei generi letterari. Il poema eroicomico*, T, Tirrenia, 115 pp., obviously containing various contributions of 17th-c. interest, albeit all devoted to the interpretation of just two works, Tassoni's *La secchia rapita* and Francesco Bracciolini's *Lo scherno degli Dei*. For our field of interest I note: M. Sarnelli, 'Commistioni dei generi e polemiche poetico-religiose nel classicismo tardorinascimentale e barocco' (9–36); M. Boaglio, 'Le burlesche metamorfosi di Elena. Proemio e parodia nei poemi eroicomici del Seicento' (37–58); G. P. Maragoni, 'Il sorriso di Afrodite. Rilievi sull'uso del mitologico nella letteratura eroicomica del Seicento' (59–66); R. Rinaldi, ' "Con cambio secco": geometrie del Tassoni' (67–74); L. Montella, 'Il poema eroicomico e *La secchia rapita* di Tassoni (I canto)' (75–84).

Other studies address the geography, rather than the genre features, of the Baroque: N. Zago, 'La letteratura in Sicilia tra Cinquecento e Seicento', *Siculorum Gymnasium*, 52: 1165–78, affording in contrast a very brief summary of the island's literary activity in the centuries in question and identifying Scipione Errico of Messina as the foremost figure for 17th-c. Sicily. But the most important contribution in this context is *Tre catastrofi. Eruzioni, rivolta e peste nella poesia del Seicento napoletano*, ed. Giancarlo Alfano, Marcello Barbato, and Andrea Mazzucchi, Na, Cronopio, 2000, 161 pp., an anthology of poetic texts by 17th-c. southern literati (18 authors, 60 compositions) devoted to the eruptions of Vesuvius, Masaniello's revolt, and the 1656 plague. The volume also includes an introductory essay by Giancarlo Alfano. Another natural catastrophe to affect the Naples region, a disastrous cloudburst, is the subject of a curious composition brought to light in M. Rinaldi, ' "La curiosità che in me predomina". In margine ad un opuscolo dimenticato (1606) di Francesco Imperato', *Aevum*, 75: 705–13. The work is an epistle in *sdruccioli*, somewhat mediocre to judge from the specimens provided in the article, composed by Francesco Imperato, son of the celebrated Neapolitan naturalist Ferrante, and printed in an extremely rare pamphlet discovered in the British Library. M. Scalabrini, 'Un inedito travestimento secentesco del *Baldus*', *RLettI*, 19:173–79, reports an unpublished *ottava rima* translation of Folengo's macaronic poem by Gregorio Porrini, preserved in MSS at the Palatina in Parma and the Estense in Modena. L. Giachino, 'Tra celebrazione e mito. Il *Tempio* di Cinzio Aldobrandini', *GSLI*, 178:404–19, describes the anthology of lyric verse edited by Giulio Segni and dedicated to the powerful cardinal in 1600, a volume as rich in its printing qualities and illustrious authorship as it is poor in its poetic merits, which the writer makes an unconvincing attempt to highlight.

BARTOLI. B. Basile, 'Daniello Bartoli poeta?', *SPCT*, 62:37–47, addresses the authorship of some unattributed lines of verse quoted in Bartoli's *Uomo di lettere*: at the end of a 'who-done-it' narrative they are identified as the work of B. himself, who as a member of the Society of Jesus was forbidden to write verse in the vernacular. However, the 'thriller' is one where the 'culprit' is known from the outset: the attribution was already given not only in the *Bibliothèque de la Compagnie de Jésus*, but also in reference works by Ferrarese literati, by Mazzuchelli, and even by Quadrio.

CAMPANELLA. F. Giancotti, 'Tommaso Campanella: le poesie della *Scelta* e la loro disposizione', *StSec*, 42:3–57, continues from *StSec*, 41:3–25, a lengthy supplement to his edition of C.'s *Poesie* which promises, when finished, to be a substantial exegetical contribution. At the same time, the complexities of C.'s verse still call for interpretative contributions, even at the level of lexis, as is demonstrated by P. Luparia, 'Proposte di correzioni e aggiunte al GDLI', *Lo Stracciafoglio*, 1.2:65–67, which brilliantly elucidates the neologism *bombasso*, '[up]roar', not 'tyrant' as misunderstood by Firpo and all subsequent commentators.

CESARINI. T. Bonaccorsi, ' "Clausos rerum aperire sinus". L'esperimento di un poeta linceo: Virginio Cesarini' *BrC*, 7:51–76, sets out to illustrate C.'s Latin elegy on the ruins of Anzio (briefly discussed some years ago by Ezio Raimondi). She rightly stresses two points: C.'s constant reference to the Lucretian model of sapiential poetry and the complementary nature, within his intellectual make-up, of austere academic commitment as a Linceo and vocation as a poet. The edition of the text (accompanied by an Italian translation) is unfortunately marred by misinterpreting contracted forms dictated by metrical considerations as abbreviations and eliminating them: this means that C.'s elegant couplets do not always scan.

DOTTI. G. Bárberi Squarotti, 'Bartolomeo Dotti: l'arte del sonetto morale', *RLettI*, 19:79–104, identifies the rhetorical device of anti-thesis as the stylistic hallmark of Marino's and Marinist poetry, and also of one of the last representatives of the literary baroque, Bartolomeo Dotti, some of whose sonnets (from his *Rime*, 1689) he analyses.

GALILEI. Galileo Galilei, *Rime*, ed. Antonio Marzo, Ro, Salerno, 111 pp., offers the scientist's modest *corpus* of verse in volume form: it was already available, albeit without commentary, in the *Edizione Nazionale* of G.'s works. Of limited interest to students of 17th-c. poetry, its value perhaps lies mainly in the light it sheds on the personality of the illustrious Pisan, whose insensitivity to poetry was displayed in his *Considerazioni al Tasso*. G. Baffetti, 'Fra distanza e passione. Una poetica dell'occhio "patetico"', *LItal*, 53:49–62, enlarges the discussion about Galileo's negative critique of the *Gerusalemme liberata* to more general issues of Galileo's poetics.

LALLI. Ilaria Cappellini (ed.), 'Giovan Battista Lalli, *Rime del Petrarca trasformate*', *Lo Stracciafoglio*, 2.3:26–45, brings to light a parody of Petrarch (publ. 1638) by a writer better known for the mock-epics *Moscheide* and *Franceide*, and his parody of Virgil, *L'Eneide travestita*. Slight and uneven, it nonetheless achieves witty pungency in the rewriting of some of the best-known poems of the *Canzoniere*.

MARINO. V. Guercio, 'Ancora sui "baci di carta"': Marino, Guarini, Fenaruolo', *StItal*, 24, 2000:5–47, contributes to critical discussion of the 'kiss' section of *La lira*, particularly by extending the list of sources to a *canzonetta* by Girolamo Fenaruolo, a little-known 16th-c. author. We also note Guercio's edition, with commentary, of the 'Lugubri' section of *La lira* in a piecemeal re-edition of *La lira* that seems destined to continue indefinitely: Giambattista Marino, **Rime lugubri*, ed. Vincenzo Guercio, Modena, Panini, 1999, 272 pp. C. Serra, 'Un elogio secentesco del Cavalier Marino. Dagli *Elogii d'Huomini Letterati* di Lorenzo Crasso', *RLettI*, 19.2–3:61–75, gives a virtually diplomatic transcription of the eulogy in question, followed by a Latin epigram by Giuseppe Battista and a *canzone* by Antonio Bruni which likewise mark Marino's decease. T. E. Mussio, **Galileo, the new Endymion: progress and knowledge in G. B. Marino's *Adone*', *ItQ*, 147–148:15–26.

MICHIEL. L. Giachino, 'La sensualità in barocco. L'esperienza lirica di Pietro Michiel tra erotismo e concettismo', *QVen*, 33:69–108, is a reading of the lyric verse of Loredan's closest associate in the Incogniti academy. Among its most original and interesting features G. identifies 'un'aria disinvolta e talora blasfema', a kind of transposi-tion 'in direzione arguta e artificiosa' of the Venetian academy's libertine themes, and not very convincingly concludes with a judgement on the 'bifrontismo' of M.'s work as a poet, which is said to fluctuate between Marino's 'sensualism' and Chiabrera's 'grace'.

RADESCA. Enrico A. Radesca, **I quattro libri di canzonette, madrigali e arie alla romana*, ed. Marco Giuliani, Lucca, LIM, 2000, lxi + 116 pp., includes a critical edition of the texts set to music.

REGIO. A. Cerbo, 'La *Sirenide* di Paolo Regio', *BrC*, 7:77–106, affords information both on the author (bishop of Vico Equense and a typical Counter-Reformation church *letterato*) and on his work, a *poema spirituale* inspired by Dante's *Commedia*. C. underlines R.'s relations with the late-16th-c. Neapolitan *ambiente*: Bruno, Campanella, Quattromani, and particularly Giulio Cortese, of whose Accademia degli Svegliati he was a leading member.

RINALDI. L. Giachino, ' "Dispensiera di lampi al cieco mondo". La poesia di Cesare Rinaldi', *StSec*, 42:85–124, pursues a personal illustration of 17th-c. lyric collections by turning to the *œuvre* of an author who has often been pointed to as a precursor of Marino and the baroque style. The result may not be brilliant at the level of critical understanding, but the concluding bibliography of Rinaldi's works is useful.

RINUCCINI. Ottavio Rinuccini won a place in Italian literary histories thanks to Benedetto Croce, who recognized him as Italy's first real librettist and already pointed out, alongside his output of verse for music, an interesting lyric collection (publ. Florence 1622) which might have been expected to attract more attention among students of baroque poetry. Particularly welcome, therefore, is D. Boggini, 'Per un'edizione critica delle *Poesie* di Ottavio Rinuccini', *RLettI*, 19.2–3:11–60, which closely analyses two partly autograph MSS of the *Poesie* (Palatini 249 e 250 at the Florentine Biblioteca Nazionale Centrale). The poems they contain cover 'un ampio arco di tempo che va dagli esordi poetici del Fiorentino [...] al 1613', but in a version earlier than the 1622 printed text.

3. DRAMA

I luoghi dell'immaginario barocco, noted above, has eight contributions relevant in this context: A. Gareffi, 'L'età dell'oro della pastorale. Ancora sull'*Adelonda di Frigia*' (31–41), making the point that the author of this play, Federico Della Valle, rewrites the Golden Age as coming about with Christianity (Adelonda, a pagan Amazon, marries the Christian Almaro and converts: the pair find happiness living in the 'vera fede'); R. Ciancarelli, ' "Dialoghi fecondi" tra studiosi e uomini di teatro. Studi teatrali seicenteschi tra esperienza e conoscenza' (43–47), showing how theatre criticism knew how to adapt a text for production and the demands of live performance;

L. Strappini, 'Il valore dell'esempio nella drammaturgia barocca' (49–63), concerned with the assimilation of tragic hero to exemplary (Catholic) martyr punished for religious or political belief, a typology promoted especially by the Jesuits in missionary activity; A. Blundo, 'Il *Crispus* di Bernardino Stefonio dai collegi gesuiti alle scene dei comici dell'arte' (65–80), advancing this 1601 play as a prototype of the Jesuit theatre in which pagan culture is overcome by and fused with Christian values: it became so popular as to be adapted by actors of the 'commedia dell'arte'; M. Sarnelli, 'Riflessioni preliminari sulla problematica dell'eroe innocente nella drammaturgia manieristico-barocca' (81–93), developing in different ways the theme of the innocent hero, object of intense scrutiny in the commentaries on Aristotelian tragedy; N. Michelassi, 'Il *Trionfo della povertà*' (95–115), with 11 pls, some in colour, of stage sets, an original study of a manuscript containing designs for staging a religious drama, dated 1630, in a Florentine academy originating from the confraternity of St John the Evangelist: the article links the play (typically, but unfortunately, the text is incomplete) to the wider context of 'popular' spectacle in Florence meant to edify; M. P. Pagani, 'Il sacro spettacolo di Sant'Alessio' (117–22), turning to a similar drama about a Roman saint put on in the Barberini palace in Rome in 1639 (text by Giulio Rospigliosi, music by Stefano Landi); F. Piccinini, 'Carnevale di Roma del 1656: un carosello a palazzo Barberini' (123–33), illustrating further lavish Papal support, together with the Roman nobility, for spectacle, particularly in the year indicated because of the arrival of Queen Christine of Sweden; and finally, F. Angelini, 'Variazioni su Giuditta' (135–45), looking at the representations of this Old Testament warrior-heroine, who slays an enemy for her faith, in plays, opera, and painting.

PASTORAL DRAMA, COMEDY, TRAGEDY. The pastoral is represented by further contributions. Guidubaldo Bonarelli, *Filli di Sciro*, ed. Raffaele Manica, Manziana, Vecchiarelli, 13 + 172 pp., is an adequately introduced anastatic reprint of the 1607 edition of the genre's 'third' masterpiece (after the *Aminta* and *Pastor fido*), which gave rise to heated debate over the legitimacy of the female protagonist's 'double love', a feature central to the plot. Grazia Distaso, *Scenografia epica. Il Trionfo di Alfonso. Epigoni tassiani*, Bari, Adriatica, 1999, 108 pp., has a final chapter dealing with 'Tipologie della pastorale post-tassiana nel regno di Napoli' and thus affording an overview of the genre (limited, however, to southern authors) between the end of the Cinquecento and the mid-Seicento.

T. Stein, 'Quando Olindo diventa Aminta. Aspetti della fortuna teatrale di un episodio tassesco', *StSec*, 42:59–84, analyses three early-17th-c. dramatic versions of the episode of Olindo and Sofronia in the *Gerusalemme liberata*. With the partial exception of the first, the authors in question, Giovanni Villifranchi, Tobia De Ferrari, and Giovan Antonio Gessani, are very minor figures whose works now have only curiosity value. A. Colombo, 'Una commedia di un comico dell'arte: *L'inavertito* di Nicolò Barbieri tra oralità e scrittura', *Acme*, 44.2 : 101–42, analyses the linguistic texture of the comedy put on at Turin in 1629 by one of the leading early-17th-c. actor-managers. I also note N. Buommino, *Lo specchio nel teatro di Giovan Batista Andreini*, Ro, Lincei, 2000, 135 pp. *Teatri barocchi. Tragedie, commedie, pastorali nella drammaturgia fra '500 e '600*, ed. Silvia Carandini, Ro, Bulzoni, 2000, xxx + 602 pp., is a weighty tome gathering the proceedings of three conferences organized by the Associazione Sigismondo Malatesta. Despite the title it includes only a few items of interest to the student of Italian baroque theatre. The section devoted to tragedy has R. Tessari, 'La *Iudit* di Della Valle: pitture di "sperati diletti"' (109–24). The sections on comedy and pastoral drama are given over, respectively, to Bruno's *Candelaio* and to the *Aminta* and *Pastor Fido*. However, S. Mamone, '*Andromeda e Perseo*. Cicognini, Adimari & Co. sulle scene di accademia a Firenze al tempo di Cosimo I' (407–38), in investigating the staging of the two *favole piscatorie*, provides an interesting cross-section (marked by a mixture of court display and academic semiprofessionalism) of practice in Florentine stage entertainment current in the second and third decades of the 17th-c.

OPERA. Maria Grazia Accorsi, *Amore e melodramma. Studi sui libretti per musica*, Modena, Mucchi, 391 pp., brings together a series of already published essays devoted to the libretto. Over a time span running from the birth of music drama in the first decades of the Seicento down to the Romantic era, she passes from a relatively little-known author such as Benedetto Ferrari to more familiar figures such as Francesco de Lemene or a celebrity like Metastasio. She premises the volume with the hitherto unpublished paper, ' "Gravità e dolcezza" nell'*Euridice* di Ottavio Rinuccini', presented to the Paris conference *Euridice 1600–2000* (October 2000). In this lengthy contribution, rather than an analysis of the Rinuccini work, she conducts an in-depth investigation of 16th-c. theorizing on the dialectically oppositional (Ciceronian) pair *gravitas* and *suavitas*, with reference to the whole tradition of the Renaissance treatise, from Bembo to Tasso, and to its influence on music theory, on an author like Giuseppe Zarlino, or on Alessandro Guarini's writings on the relationship between poetry and music.

Two editions of libretti have also appeared: Ridolfo Campeggi, *L'Aurora ingannata*, ed. Paola Confalonieri, *Lo Stracciafoglio*, 2.3 : 12–25, *intermezzi* written to accompany the 1608 production of *Filarmindo*;

Giovan Francesco Busenello, *Didone*, ed. Monica Anchieri, *ib.*, 2.4:25–43, which presents the comic parts of the libretto set to music by Francesco Cavalli: a curious revisitation of the Dido legend which, rather than ending with the queen's suicide, concludes with her desecrating marriage to Iarbas. M. G. Genesi, 'La fioritura di accademie letterario-musicali a Codogno tra il 1580 e il 1650 circa', *Archivio storico lodigiano*, 119, 2000[2001]:63–98, details the prolific musical settings of religious and secular poetry produced by four academies in this small Lombard town. The investigation was prompted by the author's discovery, in Vienna, of a madrigal collection by Francesco Ugoni of the 'Accademia dei Novelli', dated 1616.

I luoghi dell'immaginario barocco, already noted, includes a section of five essays on opera: A. L. Bellina, 'Un "nuovo cammin". Intorno all'*Euridice* di Peri' (231–40), studying the problems surrounding the setting to music of the first Italian opera for which the entire score is extant; C. Micocci, 'Il mito come avventura, l'avventura come mito' (241–59), analysing the relationship between myth and novel, for which the plot is an essential ingredient, in the development of the new *melodramma*; A. Frattali, 'Lo scherzo barocco nel secolo del "recitar cantando"' (261–72), bringing out baroque interest in tying together poetry and music with jokes and humour; B. Nestola, 'Musica per le accademie e accademie per musica' (273–83), a succint survey of the numerous academies whose dominant interest was the production and performance of music for singing and instruments; and finally, L. Zoppelli, 'Il teatro dell'umane passioni: note sull'antropologia dell'aria secentesca' (285–91), giving a theoretical purpose to the popularity of the individual character's 'aria' in the social and psychological construction of the 'baroque' personality.

THEATRES. S. Vuelta Garcìa, 'Accademie teatrali nella Firenze del Seicento: l'Accademia degli Affinati o del Casino di San Marco', *StSec*, 42:357–78, continues an investigation of theatre organization in Medici Florence conducted by others in earlier numbers of the journal. Its subject is the Accademia degli Affinati, whose activity was sponsored by Prince Leopold and initiated c. 1650 with a particular interest in the experiments of contemporary Spanish theatre, which the Academy's leading dramatist, Pietro Susini, either imitated or, in the case of Calderón, translated.

4. PROSE

Three first-rate studies ranging from the general to the specific head the list of recent books on Seicento prose. Lucinda Spera, *Il romanzo italiano del tardo Seicento, 1670–1700*, pref. Alberto Asor Rosa, F, La

Nuova Italia, 2000, 223 pp., is a comprehensive analysis of the Italian
novel in the *late* Seicento, a period described by Asor Rosa as 'l'anello
mancante' in the history of the Italian novel. She first gleans a poetics
of the novel from the prefaces, dedicatory letters, and the like, of
individual novels (there is no literary-critical survey of the era). She
finds that authors lose control of their own work; that they dedicate
their novels to an elite, not a middle class as has been supposed; that
by now fiction is entirely in prose though maintaining distant
connections with the epic; that there is insistence on some kind of
'aderenza al vero storico', or at least verisimilitude; and at the same
time a large role is given to the reader's entertainment, procured by
varietas and the *curiositas* of the events narrated.

A second main section looks at models and motifs. These novels
mix genres, and engage both with the ancient (classical and Christian)
and the modern (contemporary history); some are mirrors of society
(the Brusoni trilogy on Venice is singled out); others are epistolary
novels (Marana's *Esploratore turco* looks at events in contemporary
Europe through a Muslim's eyes); in others there is a strong authorial
presence (as in Francesco Fulvio Frugoni's *Heroina intrepida*), not to
mention a 'realistic' historical novel by Gregorio Leti about a love
affair involving the Gonzaga dynasty. An extremely useful bibliography of the novels published in this period, and of new editions of
earlier novels, and another one of studies on Seicento Italian narrative
make this a highly recommendable text for reference and teaching
alike.

La novella barocca, ed. Lucinda Spera, Na, Liguori, 422 pp., is a
major study of the novella which shows that this typical Italian prose
genre continued to flourish in the Seicento. Of particular relevance is
Spera's own contribution: a 'repertorio bibliografico' of 481 editions
of novelle, some by the same author (Tommaso Costo's *Il Fuggilozio*
enjoyed 17 editions). The contributors are well-known literary
scholars: D. Conrieri (with 'Fortuna della novella del Seicento', a
valuable critical survey of studies on the 17th-c. novella), D. Capaldi
and G. Ragone (with 'La novella barocca: un percorso europeo', a
177-page essay, the longest in the volume, on the development of
modern European narrative by means of the novella), F. Tarzia (with
'Il cunto di tutti i cunti. Giambattista Basile e la proposta del modello
fiabesco'), F. Di Pietro (with 'Francesco Belli e l'uso della tradizione
in una prospettiva di consumo'), L. Strappini (with 'L'arte di predicar
bene: il valore dell'elemento narrativo nella predicazione italiana del
XVII secolo'), as well as L. Spera.

I luoghi dell'immaginario barocco, noted above, offers six essays on the
baroque novel. D. Conrieri, 'Sulla collocazione storica della narrativa
secentesca' (501–11), considers the 1620s and especially the 1630s as

the period of the consolidation and expansion of the baroque novel. Landmarks are G. F. Biondi's *L'Eromena* of 1624, the first of a trilogy completed in 1632; Francesco Pona's *La lucerna* of 1625; G. B. Manzini's *Cretideo* of 1637; and Matteo Peregrini's prescriptive manual of baroque wit and therefore style, *Delle acutezze*, of 1639. It is in this period that justifications of a 'poetic prose' appear — hence the need for elaborate rhetorical tropes hitherto the province of poetry, and the search for new forms and combinations of genres. R. Paternostro, '*L'Amorosa Clarice* o dell'inattualità di un romanzo barocco' (513–35), focuses on the religious, or at least spiritually uplifting, novel of Ferdinando Donno, published in 1625, and the difficulties encountered at the time in categorizing it, as it was unlike anything that had appeared before. P. provides a structural analysis of the novel and its metaphors. L. Spera, '*Ex ignoto notus*: alcune riflessioni sul moderno nei romanzi del Seicento' (537–46), seeks aspects of the modern as defined by Seicento authors, especially the Incogniti, presided over by the indefatigable promoter of new novels and their publication, Giovan Francesco Loredan. He not only encouraged an individual anti-rhetorical style, but also promoted traditional genres like the novella. Spera links the motto of the Incogniti given in the title to the cultivation of Pseudo-Dionysus and his negative theology, of Platonic derivation, about God and His attributes being unknowable and incomprehensible, and therefore inexpressible. All humans can do is say what He is not and remain silent. N. Cannizzaro, 'Guido Casoni, padre degli Incogniti' (547–60), looks at a neglected author in Venetian letters (1561–1642), whose vast literary network made him a central cultural figure in his day. Only late in life did he become acquainted with Loredan and the Incogniti. His own fondness for Pseudo-Dionysus may have inspired the motto of the Incogniti discussed in the previous article. R. Colombi, 'Introspezione e analisi nel romanzo d'amore della prima metà del Seicento' (561–74), examines five novels by Biondi, Donno, Assarino, Della Lenguaglia, and Morando, and provides an anatomy of the psychological novel of this half-century. Finally, G. Ragone, 'Genesi della novella barocca in Italia, dalle *Ejemplares* agli Incogniti' (575–88), gives persuasive evidence for the impact of Spanish 'Siglo de Oro' masterpieces like Cervantes' *Don Quijote* and *Novelas ejemplares*, and the anonymous progenitor of the picaresque novel, *Lazarillo de Tormes*, on the Italian Seicento. (The publisher Barezzo Barezzi in Venice, specialized in arranging Italian translations of Spanish material: Cervantes in 1626 and 1627; *Lazarillo* in two parts, 1622 and 1635.) These Spanish authors added strength to the production in Italian of fiction that was witty and entertaining, and without ulterior edifying motives.

H. Albani, 'Invitation à la lecture des romans baroques: quelques pages traduites de Biondi et de Marini', *ChrI*, 63–64, 2000:251–72, provides French readers with excerpts and contextualization of *Eromena* by G. F. Biondi, a 'prototype' of the baroque novel, and *Il Calloandro* by G. A. Marini, the 'crown'.

Translations of fiction with religious content enjoyed favour in the Seicento. J. Miszalska, 'La traduzione polacca dell'*Adamo* di G. F. Loredano', *StSec*, 42:165–86, offers a broad view of the penetration of Italian culture in Poland in the Renaissance — Padua was the university Poles regarded as their own, and numerous novels by Incogniti can be found in Polish libraries — before concentrating on Krzysztof Piekarski. He chose Loredan's novel for religious reasons, to the point of censoring its erotic features. Miszalska's comparison of selected passages of the Italian and Polish proves the point. D. Conrieri, 'La traduzione portoghese della *Maria Maddalena* di Anton Giulio Brignole Sale', *StSec*, 42:125–63, studies the translations from Italian of the friar, preacher, and chaplain to king Pedro II, Antonio Lopes Cabral, and finds that Brignole Sale's novel was prized for its encouragement of a sentimental devotion in which copious tears were seen as a sign of grace.

5. THOUGHT

Although Bruno belongs to the previous century, R. Marchi, 'Ovidio Montalbani e Giordano Bruno. Teoria del minimo e aspetti della cultura matematica, medica e astrologica nella Bologna del '600', *BrC*, 6, 2000:553–60, treats the reception of Bruno in Bologna university circles by focusing on the physician and ecclesiastical censor Montalbani. He was able to combine 'radical' Bruno views about progressing in natural philosophy from the minute to the grand, about the use of the telescope, and even about the centrality of the sun, with traditional Catholic teaching. A. Maggi, ' "Il secondo albero della vita": l'esaurirsi del pensiero rinascimentale nel *Mondo magico degli eroi* di Cesare della Riviera', *ib.*, 7:107–26, unravels the complexities of a philosopher who stands at the end of a long line of Renaissance Neoplatonists combining alchemy and natural magic into a closed hermetic discourse, which claims nevertheless to express orthodox Christian doctrine. Della Riviera's heroes of the *Mondo magico* (1603, 1605) are those who know how to ascend the steps of contemplation, using the image of the Tree of Life of the Garden of Eden. By the operations of natural magic, they will be able to find the 'second tree', situated in a geographical Paradise which can make one immortal. R. Palmer, 'Iconographies of Calabrian Philosophy, c. 1570–1700', *NRLett*, 20.2, 2000:7–53, takes the unusual approach of studying the woodcut and engraved iconography of the title-pages of the works of Calabrian natural philosophers because of their rich meanings. Calabria was part of Magna Grecia, associated with the Pythagorean school, a favourite of the natural philosophers considered here. Palmer deconstructs the portraits and emblems for T. Campanella, Paolo Antonio Foscarini (a Carmelite anti-Copernican cosmologist), Marco Aurelio Severino (a physician), Tommaso Cornelio (natural philosopher and follower of Descartes), Elia Astorini (a Platonist and an atomist), and Giacinto Gimma (founder of an Academy with Pythagorean interests). This kind of interpretation, Palmer concludes, 'reveals the seminal importance of emblematic invention for early modern mythologising of academic endeavour'. Another unusual method of scientific argument is offered by E. Zinato, 'Ironia, parodia, dissimulazione nei *Discorsi* di Giovanni Alfonso Borelli', *FC*, 25, 2000: 335–58. A rationalist physician, Borelli used rhetorical strategies inspired by Lucian in his polemical dialogues of 1649 to undermine current beliefs in the humours and astrological influences as causes of the plague.

On ethical and political issues, G. L. Betti, 'Trattatistica civile nel Seicento: la corte e il cortigiano', *StSec*, 42:277–98, gives a fine analysis of new thinking about the role of the courtier, now called 'il savio di corte', after the election of Urban VIII. Castiglione's educated adviser to the prince is revived, and so are Stoic moral precepts according to Seneca, himself a moral philosopher at corrupt Nero's court. The leader is Matteo Peregrini, whose *Savio in corte* of 1624 establishes the framework. The 'savio' serves his prince and serves God; he has a paradoxical role: blind obedience to the prince, to whom he is also friend and companion, and dedication to public life. For G. B. Manzini, the more rigorously Stoic 'savio' lives apart from the court, which by definition is corrupt, yet is committed to the public good. G. Capponi is a severe critic of the court, while at Bologna Camillo Baldi composes a code of behaviour for the courtier. Virgilio Malvezzi and Agostino Mascardi at Rome focus on the role of the man of letters in serving the prince. G. Cozzi, 'Scoperta dell'Anabattismo: lo stupore ammirato di Gregorio Barbarigo ambasciatore veneto', *SV*, 40, 2000: 235–38, completes Cozzi's article of the same title in the previous issue by giving the transcription of the letter from Barbarigo to Sarpi about the Anabaptists.

CAMPANELLA. *Compendio di filosofia della natura*, ed. Germana Ernst, introd., trans., and ann. Paolo Ponzio, Santarcangelo di Romagna, Rusconi, 1999, 261 pp., is a critical edn of a hitherto unpublished summary by C. of his own natural philosophy, composed about 1620 in Latin and entitled *Physiologiae Compendium*. The 'biology of nature' extends to astronomy, biology, medicine, and psychology. While drawing from Plato and Aristotle, C. sought also to distinguish himself from them, and did likewise with the moderns such as Copernicus, Tycho Brahe, and especially Galileo. He accepts (against the ancients and the Church) what Galileo had shown by means of the telescope, i.e. that the moon and heavenly bodies are not eternal, but corruptible like the earth, modifies the hypothesis of the infinity of worlds by postulating many systems within one great system, and, while denying the movement of the earth the status of certain knowledge, tentatively allows the planets to revolve around the sun to receive their *virtus* or innate force, and, at the same time, revolve around a fixed earth. Accompanied by a bibliography of primary and secondary sources on C.'s philosophy of nature, this new edition is a clear and succinct introduction to his scientific doctrines. Tommaso Campanella, *Universalis philosophiae seu Metaphysicarum rerum juxta propria dogmata, partes tres, libri 18*, XIV: *De immortalitate animae*, ed., introd., and ann. Teresa Rinaldi, Bari, Levante, 2000, xxii + 209 pp., with Italian trans. facing Latin original, deals with an issue central to C.'s philosophy and theology. In another series comprising modern critical editions of C. is: Tommaso Campanella, *Theologia: De conservatione et gubernatione rerum liber Vi*, ed. Maria Muccillo, Padua–Ro, CEDAM, 2000, 136 pp.

Tommaso Campanella, *Lettere (1595–1638)*, ed. Germana Ernst, Pisa–Ro, IEPI, 2000, 171 pp., brings together 38 Latin and Italian letters not included in Spampanato's edition of 1927 and previously scattered in diverse publications. Addressed to philosophers, theologians and men of letters, to princes and to popes, they document Campanella's far-flung European relationships. They range from the original dedicatory letter to Gasparo Schoppe of one of C.'s most important polemical theological works, *Atheismus trionfatus*, to a desperate note from C., 'carcerato 25 anni nel Castel Novo', to the Viceroy of Naples pleading for the 222 ducats owed to him for his keep but never delivered. 'Si more de fame . . . ed è nudo', he says of himself, speaking humbly in the third person. For a dose of C.'s satirical polemics, we now have *Censure sopra il libro del padre Mostro 'Ragionamenti sopra le litanie di Nostra Signora'*, ed. Antonino Terminelli, Ro, Ediz. Monfortane, 1998, 123 pp. Exasperated by the censorship of his own books, caused in large part, C. was convinced, by Nicolò Riccardi, Master of the Sacred Palace and nick-named 'Father Monster', C. decided to turn the tables. Picking out a long list of propositions from Riccardi's book on the Litany of the Blessed Virgin Mary, C. commented on them, and censured them as erroneous, absurd, and in some cases heretical. G. Ernst, 'Segni, virtù e onore nell'opuscolo *De' Titoli* di Tommaso Campanella', *FC*, 25, 2000: 281–301, introduces and supplies a modern critical edition of a letter/discussion concerning honorific titles dated 4 April, 1624, requested by a young member of the Papal staff, Virginio Cesarini. Titles bestow status and prestige, and define public functions; but C. wants to give the Pope titles that are his alone, and not shared by secular rulers.

Looking at themes, J. L. Fournel, 'Le contrôle des mariages et de naissances dans la pensée politique de Campanella', *ib.*, 209–20, relates the well-known prescription to hold wives and property in common, and to use a form of eugenics to produce healthy citizens for the Utopian *City of the Sun*, to wider political problems in C.'s political thought. A far more rewarding analysis of the same theme is afforded by M. Isnardi Parente, 'Tommaso Campanella e la *Repubblica* di Platone', *Archivio storico per la Calabria e la Lucania*, 66, 1999[2000]:93–112, in which she places C.'s *City of the Sun* in the context of Utopian literature of the 16th and 17th c. in Italy, going back first to the sources: Plato, Aristotle, Diogenes Laertius, and Diodorus Siculus. Beginning with Ficino in the Renaissance, Plato's views on sharing wives and property, on the equality of the sexes, and on sexual pleasure, were carefully suppressed. The extent to which C. follows Plato and links him with acceptable religious doctrine on these suspect issues is shown with fine discriminations.

C.'s antagonistic relationship with Venice is explored in G. Benzoni, 'Campanella e Venezia: qualche appunto, qualche spunto', *FC*, 25, 2000:263–80, a dense historical-cultural analysis of the 1606 tract *Antiveneti*, which denounced the anti-papal policy of the alleged capital of heresy and wickedness. For Benzoni, however, the main target was Paolo Sarpi, and not, as others have argued, Giovanni Marsilio.

SEGNERI. **Paolo Segneri: un classico della tradizione cristiana*, ed. Rocco Paternostro and Andrea Fedi, Stony Brook NY, Forum Italicum Publishing (Fililibrary, 15), 1999, 488 pp. P. Fasoli, 'Paolo Segneri e l'oratoria sacra secentesca', *FoI*, 35:261–71, examines the major themes and issues of the above book, which fills an 'inexplicable gap' in our knowledge of this Jesuit master of Italian 17th-c. oratory famed as a moralist, philosopher, spiritual adviser, papal orator, missionary preacher, and consummate stylist whose works were combed by the Accademia della Crusca. In the aim of persuasion, preaching becomes theatre, especially for the Jesuits. Segneri had a vast following in other countries and in later centuries.

TESAURO. Two major studies of T.'s key philosophical work have appeared. D. Aricò, 'Prudenza e ingegno nella *Filosofia morale* di Emanuele Tesauro', *StSec*, 42:187–208, shows how T. sought to combine difficult subject matter and a pleasing style, by uniting poetry and history, and practical prudence and speculation, by means of aphorisms: of a Stoic frame of mind, he judged that for life at court practical ethics was more important than analysis. By the same author, 'Il colore delle passioni. La *Filosofia morale* del Tesauro tra gli aforismi di Salvator Rosa', *FC*, 25, 2000: 359–417, makes persuasive new connections between Rosa and Tesauro. Rosa, who often chose philosophers and hermits as subjects for his paintings, studied ancient and modern political writers, and leaned towards Stoic philosophy, also wrote some 200 aphorisms taken from Tesauro's popular work of moral philosophy. Tesauro had used the aphorism to express his political thought based on Machiavelli, Guicciardini, Bodin, and Botero: Rosa's selections follow Tesauro closely, but make them his own, as the author shows by ample use of parallel texts. M. Maggi, 'La biblioteca del Tesauro. L'inventario del 1675, con un saggio di identificazione e un inedito', *LItal*, 53: 193–246, studies the library of the Jesuit to conclude that his books represent a 'strumento di lavoro per l'uomo di lettere più che creazione di bibliofilo'.

SETTECENTO

By G. W. SLOWEY, *Senior Lecturer in Italian, University of Birmingham*
(This survey covers the years 2000 and 2001)

I. GENERAL

Maria Augusta Morelli Timpanaro, *Autori, stampatori, librai: per una storia dell'editoria in Firenze nel secolo XVIII*, F, Olschki, 1999, 772 pp., is a major contribution to work in the area, bringing together a number of studies published in recent years, some of them revised and expanded. There is also one important new item, 'Contributo per un'indagine su Antonio Maria Ristori, libraio fiorentino (1707–1785) e sulla sua famiglia' (231–354). T. Olivieri, 'L'editoria sarda nel Settecento', *StS*, 41, 2000:53–69, discusses Piedmontese attempts to legislate for printing in Sardinia, while pointing out that the first part of the century produced little of any cultural value. Later printers such as Bonaventura Porro realized the importance of printing the results of scientific research from the university and work on the Sardinian language. The article also refers to the importance of printers such as Giuseppe Piattolo at Sassari. *Editoria libraria in Italia dal Settecento a oggi: biografia 1980–1998*, ed. Luca Clerici et al., Mi, Mondadori, 2000, 271 pp., deals with more than 500 entries divided into eleven categories. Susanna Corrieri, **Il torchio fra palco e tromba: uomini e libri a Livorno nel Settecento: introduzione di Maria Gioia Tavoni*, Modena, Mucchi, 2000, 222 pp. M. G. Tavoni, 'Di un flop editoriale nella Bologna del Settecento: Giovanni Battista Roberti alle prese con Petronio Dalla Volpe', *Il Carrobbio*, 26, 2000:137–56, is concerned with the period between 1751 and 1773 when R. was teaching at Bologna and discusses the problems that arose over the printing of the various volumes of the *Raccolta di varie operette*, including in an appendix R.'s *Lettera allo stampatore Petronio Dalla Volpe*.

A number of items deal with the importance of travel in the Settecento. Lorenzo Fabbri, *Descrizione del viaggio fatto da Lorenzo Fabbri nell'anno 1772 da Forlì a Londra: dedicato a sua Eccellenza il Signor Marchese Andrea Albicini*, ed. Furio Luccichenti, Mi, Ferrero, 1999, 245 pp. has a useful introduction which points out the rarity of diaries by Italians travelling abroad and also that Fabbri's diary, perhaps because he was of limited education and experience, is full of minor details of everyday travel. Again on Italians abroad, though this time a more educated traveller, we have M. Rebecchi, 'Paolo Andreini, un viaggiatore illuminato tra il Settecento e l'Ottocento', *Acme*, 54, 2:143–67, which gives much information on an intrepid traveller and early aeronaut, whose diaries of his travels in Europe and America give a very clear indication of his enlightened concerns and approach to everything he saw. He was critical of government and Church, and his scientific and mineralogical interests occasioned much discussion. R. Rabboni, 'Una vendemmia erudita di Angelo Maria Bandini: l'odeporico di Lombardia e Piemonte', *SPCT*, 60, 2000:95–114, analyses Bandini's diary of his journeys and also attempts to counter previously rather negative assessments of its value. M. Dell'Aquila, 'L'Ofanto nelle relazioni dei viaggiatori stranieri in Puglia tra Sette e Ottocento', *RLettI*, 19, 2–3:133–42, examines how foreign travellers such as Johann Hermann von Riedesel, and later Edward Lear, viewed the antiquities of the area. *L'immagine della Sicilia nell'Italia del Settecento*, introduction and notes by Carlo Ruta, Palermo, Edibisi, 2000, 127 pp., contains texts by 18th-c. Italian travellers, including Lazzaro Spallanzani. On a slightly different sort of journey we have A. R. Capoccia, 'Per una lettura delle *indipetae* italiane del Settecento: "indifferenza" e desiderio di martirio', *NRLett*, 2000.1:7–43, which examines some of the thousands of letters in the Jesuit archive in Rome and analyses the question of the desire of priests to further the apostolic mission to the Indies.

G. Santangelo, 'Meli e il "secolo dei lumi"', *Resta Vol.*, 1, 601–23, looks at Meli's interest in masonic and Enlightenment culture. G. Ricuperati, 'Non Swedenborg, ma Giannone. Sulla scoperta di un autografo parziale del *Triregno* nell'Archivio dell'Inquisizione', *RSI*, 112, 2000:75–137, traces the travels of a Giannone MS that brought it to the Inquisition archives in Rome. The article also deals with anti-Giannone writings, particularly those opposing his *Istoria civile*, and goes on to discuss Emanuel Swedenborg's work on the new Jerusalem, before concluding with a detailed description of the various Giannone MSS in the Inquisition Archives and an assessment of their importance for a new edition of the *Triregno*. *Gelehrsamkeit in Deutschland und Italien im 18. Jahrhundert / Letterati, erudizione e società scientifiche negli spazi italiani e tedeschi del '700*, ed. Giorgio Cusatelli et al., Tübingen, Niemeyer, 1999, xv + 312 pp. Pier Massimo Prosio, *'Impegno civile e società nella letteratura in piemontese del Settecento: dall'Arpa discordata al Calvo'*, *StP*, 27, 1998:315–22.

Since the second centenary of the setting up of revolutionary republics in Italy in the period 1796–99, a number of items have appeared dealing with different aspects of the period. Desmond Gregory, *Napoleon's Italy*, Associated University Presses, 242 pp., looks at Napoleon's impact on Italy in the fields of politics and war, but also includes a chapter on 'The awakening of national sentiment'. *Napoleonic Italy. Historical, literary and artistic perspectives*, ed. Eileen

A. Millar, Glasgow, Glasgow University Press, 2000, xxii + 137 pp., includes: M. G. Broers, 'Napoleonic Italy: nationalism, anarchy and collaboration' (1–27), which sees the states of the ancien régime in Italy as increasingly incapable of preserving order, while the Jacobin republics were unable to do anything except collaborate with the French, so that 'the search for an Italian national identity, in political terms, came after the event'; J. Lindon, 'The *libero scrittore* under Napoleon: from Alfieri to Foscolo' (29–58), which traces Alfieri's reaction to the first French invasion and Foscolo's career as the leading dissident under Napoleon; E. A. Millar, ' "L'uom fatale" or "il tiranno": changing literary attitudes to Napoleon in Italy' (59–92), which draws on the work of Monti, Cesarotti, and Cuoco, largely favourable to Napoleon, and contrasts it with that of opponents such as Foscolo; J. Kenworthy-Browne, 'Napoleon and Canova' (95–113), which deals with the work undertaken by Canova for Napoleon and members of his family. J. Lindon, 'Italy 1799', *RoS*, 18, 2000: 11–19. E. Di Rienzo, 'Neogiacobinismo e movimento democratico nelle rivoluzioni d'Italia (1796–1815)', *StS*, 41, 2000: 403–31, discusses the move to action which characterized Italy in this period, looking at various historical interpretations and using Foscolo as a 'personaggio esemplare'. On the same topic is M. Ceretti, 'La diffusione della pubblicistica antigiacobina in Italia e la testimonianza delle fonti nelle *Vicende memorabili di tempi suoi* di Alessandro Verri', *RSI*, 112, 2000: 138–88, which traces the rise of anti-French propaganda, particularly after 1796, in the context of the development of political journalism, and draws, as an example, on Verri's *Vicende*, with its wide use of sources. Inevitably, the Neapolitan 1799 experience figures importantly. R. De Lorenzo, 'Accademismo e associazione a Napoli tra "desideri" riformistici e "passioni" giacobine', *Clio*, 36, 2000: 443–66, looks especially at the part played by Carlo Lauberg, who headed the provisional government in Naples in 1799, and deals with his links to various scientific academies, his connection with freemasonry, and his ideas of social improvement. L. Gaeta, 'La costituzione della Repubblica Napoletana del 1799 e il lavoro', *StSen*, 112, 2000: 187–225, offers material which is useful for the history of legislation on work, drawing as it does on comparisons between Naples and other Italian republics in the 1790s, with an appendix containing the text of the projected Naples decree and those of other states. A. Di Benedetto, 'La rivoluzione napoletana del 1799: il vescovo Natale e il "Catechismo repubblicano" a lui attribuito', *GSLI*, 177, 2000: 71–86, presents the biography of this figure of the short-lived Neapolitan republic, to whom is attributed a catechism drawn up on republican principles, according to the rule of law and in defence of freedom and equality. On the city generally is *Naples in* *the Eighteenth-Century. The Birth and Death of a Nation State*, ed. Girolamo Imbruglia, Cambridge, CUP, 2000, ix + 208 pp., which contains the following items: M. G. Maiorini, 'The capital and the provinces' (4–23), looking at the relationship between Naples and its territories, particularly in the matter of the judiciary and politics; G. Montroni, 'The Court: power relations and forms of social life' (22–43), demonstrating the power of the court in relation to the sovereign, and also dealing with the images of power and the development of political languages; B. Salvemini, 'The arrogance of the market: the economy of the kingdom between the Mediterranean and Europe' (44–69), which is principally concerned with the development of markets, pointing out the failure of 18th-c. reformers to regenerate the southern economy; G. Imbruglia, 'Enlightenment in eighteenth-century Naples' (70–94), which highlights the difference between Naples and the rest of Europe, drawing on the work of Antonio Genovesi and discussing the problems caused by the general backwardness of political awareness, though finding honourable exceptions in Filangieri's *Scienza della legislazione* and Pagano's *Saggi politici*; A. M. Rao, 'The feudal question, judicial systems and the Enlightenment' (95–117), which discusses issues affecting the transformation of feudalism, pointing out how the language of Enlightened reform was at odds with that of lawyers who clung to existing political structures; E. Chiesi, 'Intellectuals and academies' (118–34), which draws on Saverio Mattei's *Dissertazione dell'utilità o inutilità delle accademie* to examine the decline of private academies and the rise of state-supported organizations and the links between these and freemasonry, treating the Reale Accademia delle Scienze as an example of the way in which bureaucracy and private interests could stifle intellectual debate; R. Di Benedetto, 'Music and Enlightenment' (135–53), which treats the lively debate on music in Naples in the 1770s, drawing widely on Antonio Planelli's *Dell'opera in musica* as well as Saverio Mattei's many writings on the subject, concluding that reform in music parallels reform in society and politics; A. Schnapp, 'Antiquarian studies in Naples at the end of the 18th century. From comparative archaeology to comparative religion' (154–66), which discusses how antiquarian finds in Isernia were influential in discussion of the pagan heritage of Christianity, and which looks at the anthropological studies of figures such as Andrea de Jorio; A. De Francesco, 'How not to finish a revolution' (167–82), which deals with Vincenzo Cuoco's *Saggio storico sulla rivoluzione di Napoli* and his *Frammenti di lettere a Vincenzio Russo*, and compares these with Mario Pagano's constitutional project. *La Repubblica napoletana: diari, memorie, racconti*, ed. Mario Battaglini, Mi, Guerini, 2000, 2 vols, 318, 317 pp., includes texts by Stendhal and Foscolo. *Leggi, atti, proclami ed altri *documenti della Repubblica napoletana, 1798–1799*, ed. Mario Barraglini and Augusto Placanica, 4 vols, Cava de' Tirreni, Di Mauro, 788, 690, 710, 237 pp. Maurizio Torrini, **'Scienza e istituzioni scientifiche a Napoli nel Settecento'*, pp. 7–19 of *Gli scienziati e la rivoluzione napoletana del 1799, giornata di studio, 23 novembre 1999*, Na, Italo Cernia, 2000. Olindo Pacia, **Giulio Nicolò Torno: un teologo e giurista del Settecento napoletano*, Na, Liguori, 1999, xxiii + 265 pp. Roberto Tufano, **Michele Torcia: cultura e politica nel secondo Settecento napoletano*, Na, Jovene, 2000, lxviii + 266 pp.

T. Calogero, 'L'istruzione pubblica nella Toscana di Pietro Leopoldo', *RST*, 46, 2000: 3–41, discusses Peter Leopold's *Regolamento Generale per tutte le Scuole Pubbliche del Granducato* of 1788, which it sees as the last stage in an education policy begun at the abolition of the Jesuits in 1773. The article identifies the main themes of the reform as centralization of education and uniformity in the provision of books and teaching methods, while pointing out that the *Regolamento* was never realized. Other aspects of Church–State relations in this area of Italy are dealt with in M. L. Trebiliani, 'Crisi di rapporti Stato–Chiesa nella Repubblica di Lucca', *RSCI*, 54, 2000: 71–89, analysing an apparently minor matter of jurisdiction that led to grave disturbances which highlighted conflicts of interest between Church and State. *Memorie dell'Istituto Veneto di Scienze, Lettere ed Arti*, 89, 2000, 470 pp., is entirely devoted to E. Ivetic, 'Oltremare. L'Istria nell'ultimo dominio veneto', which examines aspects of Venice's overseas territories, addressing itself particularly to the differences between rural and urban environments in all aspects of social and economic life. Paolo Ulvioni, **Atene sulle lagune: Bernardo Trevisan e la cultura veneziana tra Sei e Settecento*, Venice, Ateneo Veneto, 2000, 171 pp. **Vita privata e pubblica nelle provincie venete: memorie e avvenimenti storici dell'Archivio dei conti Degli Azzoni Avogadro*, ed. Giampietro Berti and Pietro Del Negro, Treviso, Canova, 1998, 207 pp., is a useful reprint of the 1954 edition. Mario Gecchele, **Fedeli sudditi e buoni cristiani: la rivoluzione scolastica di fine Settecento tra la Lombardia austriaca e la Serenissima*, Verona, Mazziana, 2000, 571 pp. Mario Taccolini, *Per il pubblico bene: la soppressione di monasteri e conventi nella Lombardia austriaca del secondo Settecento*, Ro, Bulzoni, 2000, 377 pp., discusses amongst other matters the impact of the suppression of the convents on education. **Il cerchio della vita: materiali di ricerca del Centro Studi Lazzaro Spallanzani di Scandiano sulla storia della scienza del Settecento*, ed. Walter Bernardi and Paola Mancini, F, Olschki, 1999, vii + 358 pp. *Saggi scientifici e letterari dell'Accademia di Padova*, 3 vols (in 4 tomes), Venice–Padua, Accademia Galileiana di Scienze, Lettere ed Arti, 2000, cxvi + 531, lxii + 496 and 462, cxxviii + 297 pp., is a facsimile reprint of the 1786, 1789, and 1794 editions. M. C. Zorzoli, **Docenti dell'università di Pavia tra Sei e Settecento: gli uomini, le idee, la facoltà di giurisprudenza tra diritto locale ed erudizione', *ASMC*, 6, 2000: 360–90. Fulvio De Giorgi, *Vita culturale e intenti educativi a Rovereto dal Settecento riformatore alla restaurazione*, Mi, I.S.U. Università Cattolica, 1999, 166 pp. *L'affermazione di una società civile e colta nella Rovereto del Settecento. Atti del Seminario di studio, Rovereto 9 ottobre, 3–4 dicembre 1998*, ed. Mario Allegri, Rovereto, Accademia Roveretana degli Agiati, 2000, 318 pp.

L'arte per i giubilei e tra i giubilei del Settecento: arciconfraternite, chiese, artisti, ed. Elisa Debenedetti, Ro, Bonsignori, 1999–2000, 2 vols, 297, viii + 324 pp. Stefano Pierfederici, *Il grande giubileo del 1750. Pellegrini, poveri e confraternite nella Roma del Settecento*, F, Libri Atheneum, 2000, 153 pp. *Roma negli anni di influenza e dominio francese, 1798–1814: rotture, continuità, innovazioni tra fine Settecento e inizio Ottocento*, ed. Philippe Boutry et al., Na, ESI, 2000, 454 pp., contains the proceedings of a conference held in Rome in 1994. Stefania Nanni, *Roma religiosa nel Settecento: spazi e linguaggi dell'identità cristiana*, Ro, Carocci, 2000, 185 pp. Stefano Ferrari, *Giuseppe Dionigio Crivelli (1693–1782): la carriera di un agente trentino nella Roma del Settecento*, Trent, Società di Studi Trentini, 2000, 169 pp. A. and C. Small, 'South Italy, England and Elysium in the 18th century', *Antiquaries Journal*, 79, 1999: 301–45, discusses a complex of interconnecting tunnels at Avigliano and inscriptions at two entrances in 18th-c. lettering, one referring to Inferno, the other to Elysium. The complex was probably constructed about 1762 by Carlo Corbo for rituals of the mystical, somewhat unorthodox, Neapolitan freemasonry of the time, and it can be compared to the tunnels at West Wycombe, where Italian freemasonry was apparently parodied.

L'Abruzzo nel Settecento, ed. Umberto Russo and Edoardo Tiboni, Pescara, Ediars, 2000, 717 pp. Salvatore Barbagallo, *Società e patriziato a Gallipoli nel Settecento, introduzione di Bruno Pellegrino*, Galatina, Congedo, 148 pp.

2. Prose, Poetry, Drama

Giovanna Scianatico, *Neoclassico*, Ro, Editalia, 2000, 173 pp., has an introductory essay outlining some of the themes and problems associated with the concept of neoclassicism, followed by a series of 17 brief items on major Italian figures. Adriana Chemello and Luisa Ricaldone, *Geografie e genealogie letterarie. Erudite, biografe, croniste, narra-trici, épistolières, utopiste tra Settecento e Ottocento*, Padua, Poligrafo, 2000, 252 pp., brings together a number of studies on Piedmontese and Veneto women, including Luisa Bergalli, Diodata Saluzzo, Isabella Teotochi Albrizzi, Isabella Mosconi Contarini, Ottavia Negri Velo, Giuseppina di Lorena Carignano, and Lucia Caterina Viale. A. Di

Ricco, 'Poesia e etica del pubblico nel *Caffè* e dintorni', *Carpi Vol.*, 375–91, looks at the links between poetry and Enlightenment, especially in the writings of Pietro Verri, drawing comparisons with Saverio Bettinelli and Parini. Marco Cerruti, *La guerra e i lumi nel Settecento italiano*, T, Thélème, 2000, 156 pp., contains discussions mainly on Parini, and the anthology of texts, edited by Bianca Danna, has selections from Muratori, Compagnoni, the two Verri brothers, and Sebastiano Franci. *Nuove ragioni dell'anti-illuminismo in Francia e in Italia*, ed. Lionello Sozzi et al., Pisa, ETS, 209 pp., contains the proceedings of a conference held in Turin in May 1998. Patrizia Delpiano, **Gli alberi del sapere: vecchia e nuova mappa delle conoscenze fra Settecento e Ottocento*, T, Paravia, 2000, 93 pp. Arnaldo Di Benedetto, *Dal tramonto dei lumi al Romanticismo. Valutazioni*, Modena, Mucchi, 2000, 292 pp., collects the following essays, some of which, separately published, are noted elsewhere in this section: 'Immagine dell'idillio nel secolo XVIII: Bertola e le poetiche della poesia pastorale' (9–37); 'Aspetti e carattere della *Buccolica* di Giovanni Meli' (39–61); 'Per Vittorio Alfieri' (63–73); 'La "repubblica" di Vittorio Alfieri' (75–118); ' "Il nostro gran Machiavelli": Alfieri e Machiavelli' (119–140); 'Le occasioni di un anniversario: Vittorio Alfieri tra Parini e Goethe (e oltre)' (141–71); 'La Rivoluzione Napoletana del 1799: il vescovo Natale e il *Catechismo Repubblicano* a lui attribuito' (173–202); ' "La sua vita stessa è una poesia": sul mito romantico di Torquato Tasso' (203–42); ' "Le rovine d'Atene": letteratura filellenica in Italia tra Sette e Ottocento' (243–76).

A. Bellio, 'Favole alla lettera. Bettinelli scrive al Bertola', *RLettI*, 19:103–31, contains eight unpublished letters in which Bettinelli shows his great support for Italian language and culture, and demonstrates his influence on Bertola's *Saggio sopra la favola*. R. Currò, 'La malattia dei letterati: immaginazione e malinconia nel Settecento', *Italianistica*, 30:325–40, in analysing 18th-c. notions on the effects of melancholy draws heavily on Muratori in such works as *Della forza della fantasia umana*. B. M. Bocazzi, 'Casanova e Algarotti: un incontro settecentesco in margine al *Newtonianismo per le dame*', *SV*, 39, 2000:123–33, discusses Casanova's frequently dismissive comments about Algarotti and Voltaire as well as his own interests in Newton's ideas. *Il carteggio tra Amaduzzi e Corilla Olimpica, 1775–1792*, ed. Luciana Morelli, pref. Enza Biagini and Simonetta Merendoni, F, Olschki, 2000, 460 pp., contains over 400 letters with rich information on the poetic and political atmosphere in Rome, as well as some unpublished and unknown compositions by Corilla Olimpica. Mariasilvia Tatti, *Le tempeste della vita: la letteratura degli esuli italiani in Francia nel 1799*, Paris, Campion, 1999, 375 pp., in spite of its title looks at Italians in France in the years either side of 1799, although concentrating on those exiles who left Italy after the collapse of the various republics in the wake of Austro-Russian military successes in 1799. The introduction sets the context in which to situate the interchange between Italy and France and also the conflicts which grew around the time of the new Cisalpine Republic in Lombardy. The author draws particularly on the experiences of Giambattista Casti, Gaetano Rossi, Vincenzo Monti, and Giuseppe Compagnoni, and adds in appendices letters by Casti and unpublished letters and poems by Luigi Cerretti. S. Verhulst, 'Leopardi e la prosa scientifica di Francesco Maria Zanotti', *RSF*, 56:393–413, deals mainly with Zanotti's *Della forza de' corpi che chiamano viva* of 1752, which was well used by Leopardi, and touches on the *Della forza attrattiva delle idee* (1747), which is critical of Locke's thinking. G. Dell'Aquila, 'Sulla *Vita di Francesco Petrarca* scritta da Ludovico Antonio Muratori', *RLettI*, 19:77–99, analyses Muratori's somewhat ambivalent attitude to Petrarch as shown in the *Perfetta poesia italiana* and *Riflessioni sopra il buon gusto intorno le scienze e le arti*, and examines in detail the *Vita di Francesco Petrarca* which shows Muratori's great admiration for Petrarch. The text of the *Vita* is included. Emilia Mirmina, **Il Settecento in Friuli: letteratura italiana e cultura nella Patria del Friuli e nel Friuli imperiale*, Padua, CLEUP, 1998[1999], 189 pp. Gian Paolo Romagnani, **'Sotto la bandiera dell'istoria': eruditi e uomini di lettere nell'Italia del Settecento: Maffei, Muratori, Tartarotti*, Sommacampagna, Cierre, 1999, xiv + 271 pp. Marco Cerruti, *Il piacer di pensare: solitudini, rare amicizie, corrispondenze intorno al 1800*, Modena, Mucchi, 2000, 149 pp., explores interesting literary byways. **Metamorfosi dei lumi: esperienze dell'io e creazione letteraria tra Sette e Ottocento*, ed. Simone Carpentari, Alessandria, Orso, 2000, 338 pp. Nino Borsellino and Walter Pedullà, **Il secolo riformatore. Poesia e ragione nel Settecento*, Mi, Motta, 1999, 744 pp. Vito Moretti, **Le forme dell'identità: dall'Arcadia al decadentismo*, Ro, Studium, 219 pp., contains material on the Settecento. *Lord Charlemont's 'History of Italian Poetry from Dante to Metastasio'. A Critical Edition from the Autograph Manuscript*, ed. George Talbot, 3 vols, Lewiston, Mellen, 2000, li + 589, 406, 398 pp., an edition of the Royal Irish Academy's manuscript history of Italian poetry, 1786–1799, by James Caulfield, Lord Charlemont, is indicative of the increasing interest in Italian literature in late 18th-c. Britain and is exceptional in devoting a large section to pre-Arcadian and Arcadian poets. On the same subject is G. Talbot, 'The historical background and intellectual context of Lord Charlemont's manuscript *History of Italian Poetry from Dante to Metastasio*', *ISt*, 54, 1999:85–101, which discusses the influences on Charlemont and his sources, ranging from early Dante commentators to writers such as Crescimbeni and Muratori, as well as acknowledging Baretti's work.

La Milano del Giovin signore: le arti nel Settecento di Parini, ed. Fernando Mazzocca e Alessandro Morandotti, Mi, Skira, 1999, 256 pp., catalogues an exhibition held at Milan's Museo del Risorgimento in 1999–2000. Paola Pimpinelli, *I riti della poesia nell'Arcadia perugina*, Perugia, Volumnia, 2000, 271 pp., includes a transcription of the entire text of the memoirs of the academy by Serafino Siepi (1776–1829). Tiziana Matteucci, **L'apocalisse in Arcadia*, F, Atheneum, 139 pp. F. Marri, 'Lettere di Giovanni De Gamerra', *StMus*, 29, 2000:71–183 and 293–454, discusses De Gamerra's dramatic and poetic production, some of which is defined as unreadable, but devotes the major part of this substantial contribution to his letters, which illustrate his links with major figures of the Enlightenment period and which are transcribed in full. **'Dolce dono graditissimo': la lettera privata dal Settecento al Novecento*, ed. Maria Luisa Betri and Daniela Maldini Chiarito, Mi, Angeli, 2000, 474 pp. Alberto Beniscelli, **Le passioni evidenti: parola, pittura, scena nella letteratura settecentesca*, Modena, Mucchi, 2000, 290 pp. Corrado Viola, **Tradizioni letterarie a confronto: Italia e Francia nella polemica Orsi-Bouhours*, Verona, Fiorini, xvii + 444 pp. Gian Paolo Marchi, *Luoghi letterari, Verona, Fiorini, xiii + 162 pp., collects essays including some on the Settecento.

Homerus, 'Iliade'. Traduzione del cav. Vincenzo Monti, ed. Arnaldo Bruni, vol. 2 (in three tomes), Bo, CLUEB, 2000, lxxvii + 308, viii + 590, and viii + 720 pp., is an exhaustive edition, not only of the translation itself, amongst the most influential of the period, but also of all the manuscript and printed tradition. Still in the field of translation is Cornelio Bentivoglio D'Aragona, *La Tebaide di Stazio*, ed. Renzo Rabboni, Ro, Salerno, 2000, 876 pp., one of the most important poetic translations of the 18th c., which exerted strong influence on both Alfieri and Foscolo.

Storia del teatro moderno e contemporaneo, ii: *Il grande teatro borghese Settecento-Ottocento*, ed. Roberto Alonge, T, Einaudi, 2000, xiv + 1248 pp., is organized in two sections, one dealing with the broad evolution of theatre and the other looking at the everyday reality of the theatrical world. Paola Trivero, *Tragiche donne. Tipologie femminili nel teatro italiano del Settecento*, Alessandria, Orso, 2000, 156 pp., draws on the stage depiction of characters such as Merope in Alfieri, Maffei, and Voltaire to illustrate the affective range of female figures under the headings of *madre*, *matrigna*, and *mogli e amanti*, and to show how in Alfieri the emotions become much more 'private' and interiorized through the use of soliloquy. The writer draws on the characters of Alfieri's Rosamunda and Clitennestra, as well as on the tragedies of Alessandro Pepoli, as examples of a movement towards *dramma borghese*, and goes on to examine the work of Martello, Pansuti, Ippolito Pindemonte, and Monti. Paola Luciani, *Le passioni *e gli affetti. Studi sul teatro tragico del Settecento*, Pisa, Pacini, 1999. Laura Riccò, *'Parrebbe un romanzo': polemiche editoriali e linguaggi teatrali ai tempi di Goldoni, Chiari, Gozzi*, Ro, Bulzoni, 2000, 302 pp., is divided into five sections, the first and fifth of which are new, while all the others are substantially revised versions of essays published earlier. The first section, entitled ' "Intieramente rifatta" ' (11–34), examines the arguments over the legal position of the Venetian Bettinelli and the Florentine Paperini editions and the theatrical consequences of this dispute, and also looks at Chiari's editorial suggestions for his own work; the fifth section, 'L'officina fiabesca' (217–84), examines the development of a personal theatrical language in Gozzi through the writing of the *fiabe*, and looks at the role of Sacchi as Truffaldino in *Il corvo* alongside the development and modification of the role of the *zanni* in Gozzi's work. Sections 2, 3, and 4 are respectively titled 'Gare editoriali fra Goldoni e Chiari' (35–103), 'Lo scrittoio teatrale' (105–45), and 'Fra scritto e non scritto' (149–215). Beatrice Alfonzetti, *Congiure. Dal poeta della botte all'eloquente giacobino (1701–1800)*, Ro, Bulzoni, 302 pp., collects various essays dealing with the treatment of conspiracy on the stage, from works by Gravina and Pansuti in Naples to the dramas of Alfieri. J. Misan-Montefiore, 'Le théâtre italien du Settecento vu par les revues françaises de la restauration', *RHT*, 207, 2000:223–34, analyses the response to Metastasio, Goldoni, Gozzi, and Alfieri in periodicals such as the *Revue encyclopédique* and the *Revue de Paris*, where Gozzi's *Fiabe* were received with widespread admiration. B. A. Naddeo, 'Urban Arcadia: representations of the "dialect" of Naples in linguistic theory and comic theatre, 1696–1780', *ECS*, 35:41–65, examines notions of local language and identity, drawing on Gravina's *Della ragion poetica* and Vico's *Scienza nuova* to demonstrate their belief that spoken language gave access to the basic beliefs and customs of a people. The article examines theatre production in Neapolitan, illustrating the extravagant use of deliberate (or invented) plebeian forms which were intended to offer a version of the urban environment as free of cares, other than those of love; it finishes with a discussion of the debate on dialect by writers such as Galiani (*Del dialetto napoletano*) and his opponents, Luigi Serio (*Lo vernacchio*), Vincenzo Porcelli, and Pagano. Still on the subject of Naples is F. Cotticelli, 'Teatro e scena a Napoli tra Viceregno e Regno nel Settecento', *Italica*, 77:214–23, which looks at the way in which the San Carlo and San Bartolomeo theatres, together with the Real Cappella, gave artistic life to the city, which was seen by the revolutionary authorities at the end of the century as a genuine instrument of teaching and propaganda. C. Barbolani, 'Un alfieriano militante in Spagna: Antonio Saviñón', *GSLI*, 177, 2000:570–93, discusses the translation of Alfieri's work into Spanish at the beginning of the Ottocento, and traces Alfieri's influence on Saviñón, who translated a number of his tragedies. B. Anglani, 'I dialoghi dell'assenza. Il carteggio tra l'abate Galiani e Madame d'Epinay', *AFLLSB*, 13, 1999:269–93, draws on Galiani's correspondence after his departure from Paris in 1769 to illustrate his feelings of exile, and the way in which he seems in these letters to be creating a kind of literary fiction. **Alessandro Malaspina e Fabio Ala Ponzone: lettere dal Vecchio al Nuovo Mondo (1788–1803)*, ed. Dario Manfredi, Bo, Il Mulino, 1999, 487 pp. Vincenzo Ferrone, *I profeti dell'illuminismo: le metamorfosi della ragione nel tardo Settecento italiano*, Ro–Bari, Laterza, 2000, viii, 468 pp., is an enlarged and updated version of the 1989 edition. Fabio D'Astore, **Dall'oblio alla storia: manoscritti di salentini tra Sette e Ottocento*, Galatina, Congedo, 155 pp. Maria Grazia Melchionda, **Il mondo muliebre nel Settecento*, Venice, IV, 2000, viii + 172 pp. **Il mondo vivo: aspetti del romanzo, del teatro e del giornalismo nel Settecento italiano*, ed. Ilaria Crotti, Piermario Vescovo, and Ricciarda Ricorda, Padua, Il Poligrafo, 235 pp.

D. Delpero, 'Il *Giornale Enciclopedico di Milano (1782–1797)* e *La Gazzetta Enciclopedica di Milano (1780–1802)*: due nuove fonti per la storia della musica milanese', *FMI*, 4, 1999:55–111, points out that most of the references to music in these periodicals are to theatre performances and gives extensive appendices of items. L. Tufano, 'La musica nei periodici scientifici-letterari napoletani della fine del XVIII secolo', *StMus*, 30:129–80, deals with the important writings on music which appeared in such periodicals as *Scelta Miscellanea*, *Giornale Enciclopedico di Napoli* and *Atti della Reale Accademia delle Scienze e Belle Arti*, highlighting in particular the large number of items on Metastasio. C. Bongiovanni, 'Note sulla tradizione musicale dell'oratorio *Sant'Elena al Calvario* di Pasquale Anfossi', *RMI*, n.s. 5:29–54, deals with Anfossi's 1771 setting of Metastasio's oratorio. L. E. Lindgren, 'An intellectual Florentine castrato at the end of the Medicean era', pp. 139–63 of *'Lo stupor dell'invenzione'. Firenze e la nascita dell'opera*, ed. Pietro Gargiulo, F, Olschki, xvii + 173 pp., looks at the career of Gaetano Berenstadt who, apart from being a much-sought-after singer, also established a book dealership and published various works. There is an appendix with a selection from his letters.

L'opera buffa napoletana, I: *Il periodo delle origini*, ed. Maria Teresa Colotti, Ro, Benincasa, 1999, xi + 353 pp., includes the annotated texts of three comic libretti in Neapolitan dialect by Nicola Corvo, Nicola Gianni, and Francesco Antonio Tullio. *L'opera buffa napoletana*, II: *Il periodo della sperimentazione*, ed. Maria Teresa Colotti, Ro, Benincasa, 300 pp., includes the annotated texts of three comic libretti in Neapolitan dialect by Carlo De Palma, Bernardo Saddumene, and Francesco Oliva. Melania Bucciarelli, **Italian Opera and*

European Theatre, 1680–1720: Plots, Performers, Dramaturgies, Turnhout, Brepols, 2000, xxiv + 227 pp.

L. Pancino, 'Le opere di Vivaldi nel raffronto fra libretti e partiture, v: *Orlando Furioso, Atenaide*', *ISV*, 21, 2000:5–32, examines the evidence of libretti, including that of Ristori's 1714 *Orlando Furioso*, and concludes that the extant libretto and score for *Atenaide* are sufficiently different not to be referring to the same performance. M. White, 'Biographical notes on the "figlie di coro" of the Pietà contemporary with Vivaldi', *ib.*, 75–96, looks at the records of 124 singers of the period, showing their great versatility and offering the possibility of further studies on the more important figures. J. A. Rice, 'The Roman intermezzo and Sacchini's *La contadina in corte*', *COJ*, 12, 2000:91–107, looks at the history of this important dramatic and musical sub-genre, drawing on work by Benedetto Micheli, using in particular Sacchini's *La contadina in corte* as an example. *Il tempo di Niccolò Piccinni: percorsi di un musicista del Settecento*, ed. Clara Gelao and Michele Sajous D'Oria, Bari, Adda, 2000, xv + 207 pp., accompanied an exhibition held in Bari. Ian Woodfield, *Opera and Drama in Eighteenth-Century London*, Cambridge, CUP, 339 pp., though primarily concerned with the cultural and commercial aspects of Italian opera in London, has a chapter on 'The English community in Rome' (93–104). On similar ground *Italian Opera in Late Eighteenth-Century London*, ii: *The Pantheon Opera and its Aftermath*, ed. Judith Milhous et al., Oxford, Clarendon Press, 883 pp., has a wealth of information on production, finances, and so on. *Tra Settecento e Novecento. Omaggio a Bertola e Di Rocco: temi, versi e ritmi fra letteratura e musica. Atti del Convegno, Supino, 29 novembre 1998 — Castellini, 13 dicembre 1998*, ed. Dante Cerilli, Foggia, Bastogi, 2000, 162 pp.

3. INDIVIDUAL AUTHORS

ALFIERI. Anna Barsotti, *Alfieri e la scena: da fantasmi di personaggi a fantasmi di spettatori*, Ro, Bulzoni, 255 pp., gathers together collected writings in part already published. Pietro Seddio, *Alfieri e le sue tragedie*, Marigliano, LER, 1999, 311 pp., is the first vol. of a projected work in three volumes. G. Semola, 'Alle radici della *Mirra*', *CLett*, 28, 2000:589–606, examines the Ovidian basis of A.'s tragedy, showing how he concentrates on the human and psychological elements in the drama, omitting the fabulous aspects of Ovid. The article emphasizes the complexity of A.'s portrayal of Mirra, claiming also that in other works there is an autobiographical element in A.'s picture of the 'eroe e tiranno'. F. Spera, 'Lettura del *Polinice* di Vittorio Alfieri', *Velli Vol.*, ii, 617–34, discusses the significance of A.'s choice of the most horrific myth of the tragic genre. G. Bárberi Squarotti, 'La lotta con Dio: il *Saul* alfieriano', *Resta Vol.*, I, 625–52, discusses interpretations of divine anger and the relevance of Saul's kingly authority.

F. Danelon, 'Il *Divorzio* e il tema del matrimonio in Alfieri', *Velli Vol*, II, 635–61, points out that most comic aspects of marriage are common on the 18th-c. stage, but that A.'s last comedy presents elements which seem to foreshadow 19th-c. themes and problems. The article draws on incidents and descriptions in the *Vita* to show how A. indicates a new way of conceiving marriage as a state in which 'la scelta individuale e la finalità eudemonistica incominciano ad affermarsi'. S. Costa, 'Per una poetica del "riso": Alfieri comico', *RLI*, 105:5–18, looks at A.'s comedies, talking of an ambivalence in the presentation of characters and situations where the classical heroes are redimensioned for the purpose of comedy, while political criticism and the awareness of human hypocrisy are never far away. B. Anglani, 'Alfieri tragicomico, e la profanazione dell'eroico', pp. 401–20 of *Teatro, scena, rappresentazione dal Quattrocento al Settecento*, ed. Paolo Andrioli et al., Galatina, Congedo, 2000, 453 pp., emphasizes the inseparable nature of the tragic and comic sides of A.'s writing, pointing to the parodistic elements in the *Vita* and detailing aspects of A.'s struggle against bourgeois values. A. Barsotti, 'Alfieri attore di se stesso', *Carpi Vol.*, 109–26, traces A.'s performances and readings of his own works, explaining how his contemporaries found his style exaggerated, though A. himself saw it as a challenge to established theatre practice. By the same writer is 'Alfieri e il teatro tragico', pp. 189–240 of *Storia del teatro moderno e contemporaneo*, II, noted above, which concerns itself primarily with the theatre aspects of A.'s work, demonstrating A.'s wish to test his pieces by reading them to the public before they were printed. The author devotes an important part of the essay to A. as actor and producer, though she points out that it is not always possible to be sure what public A. had in mind. The essay ends with a discussion of the way in which A.'s plays illustrate on the stage an 'azione interiore'. G. Santato, 'La vita e i viaggi. Il tempo e lo spazio nell'Alfieri viaggiatore', *GSLI*, 177, 2000:337–60, sets A.'s journeys in the context of 18th-c. travel, discussing the great impression which England made on him and detailing the stages of his conversion to the idea of Tuscan as the literary language. The writer points out how for A. the idea of time is the idea of the future and posterity is the poet's ultimate goal, while distance is an obstacle to be overcome with the notion of arriving 'nello spazio senza tempo del mito letterario'.

Studi Italo-Tedeschi, 20, 1999, is devoted entirely to A. and includes the following articles: R. Scrivano, 'L'Europa di Alfieri nella *Vita*' (1–18), which examines the way in which A. viewed himself in the context of his knowledge of Europe; E. Kanduth, ' "La Vita" — un viaggio: bilancio alfieriano del 1799' (19–38), which deals principally with the second part of the *Vita*, critical of Napoleon and the French, and also discusses A.'s own proposal to withdraw from literary life; R. Reisinger, 'Vittorio Alfieris Reisen: ideologische Suche und romantische Flucht?' (39–62), which analyses A.'s contacts with social groups during his first journey abroad in 1767 and the lines of thought he developed at this time, characterizing him as a proto-romantic; H. Felten, 'Vittorio Alfieri: il viaggio come messa in scena della malinconia' (63–77), which asserts that for all his travelling, A. never really left Piedmont, but treated Europe in his imagination as a literary experience; U. Schultz-Buschhaus, 'Alfieri e la "nobiltà dell'arte" ' (78–91), which discusses A.'s criticism of nobility seen as a social institution, but also looks at his criticism of what he called 'literary nobility', which included figures such as Metastasio; D. Gorret, 'Il volteresco rito franco. Per una lettura della Satira Settima' (92–103), which attaches to Voltaire much of the blame for the years of terror of the French Revolution, allowing parallels to be drawn with the *Misogallo*; A. Di Benedetto, 'Interesse di Goethe per Alfieri' (104–14), which points out that while A. never mentions Goethe in his writings, Goethe was certainly aware of A.'s work, even commissioning a translation of *Saul* for performance in Weimar, though his approach was not uncritical; M. A. Terzoli, 'Confessioni e verità. Note sulla *Vita* dell'Alfieri' (115–50), which begins with an embroidered story of A.'s death and goes on to examine A.'s accuracy of narration in the *Vita* as he attempts to exercise control through his projection of the image which succeeding generations will have of him; G. Santato, 'Lo spazio e il tempo nell'Alfieri viaggiatore. Dal concerto europeo alla fuga nella classicità' (151–65), where the author talks about the way in which A.'s writing is directed towards a view of his life, a kind of personal myth, as a preparation for the future Italy to accept him as its poet and prophet; D. Winter, 'Die literarisierende Freundschaftdarstellung in Vittorio Alfieris *Vita*' (166–84), which deals with narrative techniques used to describe friends, seeing them as part of a literary cult of friendship; A. Fabrizi, 'Alfieri e la musica' (185–99). Id., 'Su un epigramma alfieriano', *GSLI*, 178: 113–15, examines possible sources, and influences, of an anti-papal epigram. A. Di Benedetto, 'Le occasioni di un anniversario: Vittorio Alfieri tra Parini e Goethe', *GSLI*, 177, 2000:168–85, discusses the relationship between A. and Parini, with A. in 1783 seeking Parini's advice on works such as *Filippo*, but it also points out A.'s reservations on the value of Parini's satire. The article also talks of Goethe's interest in A.'s work while stressing the differences in their cultural worlds, concluding that A. is a less complex figure than

Goethe. Id., ' "Il nostro gran Machiavelli": Alfieri e Machiavelli',
CLett, 28, 2000:71–84, traces the importance of Machiavelli for
writers such as the Encyclopedists in France and the Verri brothers,
while emphasizing A.'s more balanced approach, seeing the influence
of Machiavelli in such A. works as *La congiura de' Pazzi*, and also in
Della tirannide and *Del principe e delle lettere*. Id., 'Dimore della poesia:
Alfieri', *ib.*, 29:33–53, looks at the history of dwellings associated
with A., from Palazzo Alfieri in Asti, where he was born, to homes in
Turin and Florence. Aris D'Anelli, *La malinconia del signor conte: Vittorio
Alfieri da Asti, malato non immaginario*, T, Piazza, 1999, 122 pp., attempts
a psychological and physiological analysis of A., though the result is
somewhat lightweight. V. Colombo, 'Su alcune lettere ritrovate di
Vittorio Alfieri a Luisa Stolberg', *StIt*, 23, 2000:133–45, presents
letters which cast fresh light on the couple's attempts to recover their
books and manuscripts from France. Id., 'Una lettera sconosciuta di
Vittorio Alfieri alla sorella Giulia', *ib.*, 26:63–70, presents a letter
written in July 1784 from Siena.

ALGAROTTI.　Francesco Algarotti, *Saggio sopra la pittura*, ed. William
Spaggiari, Ro, Izzi, 2000, 99 pp., has an introduction which links the
work (1756) with A.'s *Discorso sopra la pittura* of 1755, and discusses
A.'s aristocratic perspective on art, while pointing out that A. was
open to new ideas and examining his links with Tiepolo.

ASTORE.　*Francesco Antonio Astore: l'intellettuale e il patriota. Atti del
Convegno di studi, Casarano, 30 settembre–2 ottobre 1999*, ed. Gino Rizzo
and Fabio D'Astore, Galatina, Congedo, 354 pp. Giuliana Iaccarino,
Francesco Antonio Astore e i lumi del Settecento, Galatina, Congedo, 2000,
155 pp.

BAFFO.　*Baffo osceno*, ed. Marco Dotti, Ro, Stampa alternativa,
125 pp., offers the poems with a literal translation from the Venetian
by Ludovico Mian and includes the introduction written for a 19th-c.
edition by Apollinaire.

BALESTRIERI.　Domenico Balestrieri, *Rime milanesi per l'Accademia
dei Trasformati*, ed. Felice Milani, Parma, Fond. Pietro Bembo –
Guanda, cxxxii + 533 pp., includes a substantial introduction.

BARTOLO.　Domenico Bartolo, *Lo colascione scordato*, ed. Rosa
Troiano, Salerno, Edisud, 2000, 150 pp., edits B.'s Neapolitan poem
with an interesting introduction.

BECCARIA.　*Cesare Beccaria. La pratica dei lumi: IV. giornata Luigi Firpo.
Atti del convegno, Fondazione Luigi Firpo, 4 marzo 1997*, ed. Vincenzo
Ferrone and Gianni Francioni, F, Olschki, 2000, vi + 181 pp.,
contains the following items: G. Francioni, 'Notizie dal cantiere
dell'edizione nazionale beccariana' (1–12); G. Zagrebelsky, 'La legge
secondo Beccaria e le trasformazioni del tempo presente' (13–22);

M. G. Di Renzo Villata, 'Beccaria e gli altri tra ieri e oggi' (23–47); M. R. Di Simone, 'Riflessioni sulle fonti e la fortuna di Cesare Beccaria' (48–62); C. Capra, 'Il gruppo del *Caffè* e le riforme' (63–78); A. Burgio, 'L'idea dell'eguaglianza tra diritto e politica nel *Dei delitti e delle pene*' (79–98); G. Imbruglia, 'Riformismo e illuminismo. Il *Dei delitti e delle pene* tra Napoli e l'Europa' (99–126); E. Tortarolo, '"Opinione pubblica" e illuminismo italiano. Qualche appunto di lettura' (127–38); R. Pasta, '*Nugae Academicae*: divagazioni su Beccaria, le riforme e l'illuminismo' (139–71). A. J. Draper, 'Cesare Beccaria's influence on English discussions on punishment, 1764–1789', *HEI*, 26, 2000:177–99, assesses the impact of B.'s thinking on William Eden's *Principles of Penal Law (1771)* and on the fourth volume of William Blackstone's *Commentaries on the Laws of England* (1765–69), and discusses the way Jeremy Bentham developed B.'s ideas.

BERTOLA. *Un Europeo del Settecento. Aurelio de' Giorgi Bertola riminese*, ed. Andrea Battistini, Ravenna, Longo, 2000, 466 pp., is a major contribution to studies on Bertola, consisting of the proceedings of a conference held in Rimini in 1998, and divided into four sections. The first section is entitled *Da Rimini a Pavia, e da Pavia all'Europa* and contains the following items: M. Cerruti, 'Un riminese in Europa' (17–24), which deals with B.'s burning interest in travel right from his youth; G. Giarrizzo, 'Aurelio de' Giorgi Bertola massone' (25–35), which attempts to cast light on B.'s links with freemasonry and the effect of this on his literary output; M. F. Turchetta, 'Le lettere di Aurelio Bertola a Giovanni Cristofano Amaduzzi: un'autobiografia in forma epistolare' (37–60), which deals with B.'s twenty-year correspondence with a man he considered his ideal teacher; G. Polimeni, '"De la visata Atene i chiari ingegni": incontri e vita accademica negli anni pavesi di Aurelio Bertola' (61–76), looking at B.'s academic career in Pavia and examining his contacts with writers such as Carlo Ravizza; A. Fabi, 'Il carteggio Bertola–Vanetti' (77–117), taking up again the theme of B. as assiduous correspondent; L. Ricaldone, 'Aurelio de' Giorgi Bertola e la gentildonna. Con un appendice di lettere inedite' (119–50), tracing in B.'s letters to various women, amongst whom Maria Fortuna and Isabella Teotocchi Albrizzi, his ideas of love and life. The second part of the volume, entitled *Tra estetica e gusto*, contains: A. Piromalli, 'Aurelio Bertola: dal classicismo al neoclassicismo e oltre' (153–65), which deals with central aesthetic notions influencing B.'s ideas on art; C. Leri, 'Saggio sopra la grazia nelle lettere e nelle arti' (167–85), dealing with this important essay by B.; T. Scappaticci, 'Tra retorica ed estetica' (167–99), analysing various of B.'s writings on literature to illustrate his ability, while observing rules, to innovate in his thinking; A. Di

Benedetto, 'Immagini dell'idillio nel secolo XVIII' (201–16), examining other European writings in poetry as the basis for B.'s own ideas about Arcadian poetry; S. Contarini, 'La "gradatio" patetica: Bertola e Sulzer' (217–35), on B.'s contacts with Johann Georg Sulzer, the Swiss mathematician, whose *Teoria generale delle belle arti* had wide influence; A. Battistini, 'La sensibilità pittoresca della linea serpentina' (237–62), examining the influence on B. of William Hogarth's *Analysis of Beauty*; G. Cusatelli, 'Bertola e Gessner: proposta per una fonte dell'*Elogio*' (263–68), on the influence of Tasso on B. in his writing of the *Elogio di Gessner*. The third section has the title *I testi* and contains the following articles: A. Di Ricco, 'Le *Notti clementine*' (269–86), dealing with B.'s lines on the death of Clement XIV which brought him poetic fame; F. Fedi, 'Un ciclo poetico: le parti del giorno' (287–98), on poetry from B.'s period in Naples; G. Scianatico, 'Paesaggi campestri' (299–303), a brief note on the *Lettere campestri*; E. Mattioda, 'Monodramma e melodramma' (305–15), examining B.'s links with music; D. Tongiorgi, 'Un'opera accademica negli anni della crisi' (317–26), which discusses the writing of *Della filosofia della storia*. The fourth part is entitled *Al di là delle Alpi* and contains these items: M. and A. Stäuble, 'Sul Reno: dalla realtà all'immaginazione' (329–44), which emphasizes the literary structure of B.'s account of his journey; J. Lindon, 'Il "Reno pittorico" di Bertola e i suoi prodromi inglesi' (345–54), linking B.'s presentation of his 'picturesque journey' with the notion and genre of 'picturesque travel' founded by William Gilpin; G. Antonelli, 'Lingua e stile di Aurelio Bertola viaggiatore' (355–400), which presents various aspects of the use of language in Bertola; R. Unfer Lukoschik, 'Salomon Gessner fra Aurelio de' Giorgi Bertola ed Elisabetta Caminer Turra' (401–24), which concerns itself with the response of B. and Caminer to German literature, pointing out the different approach of the two in translating Gessner's poetry; E. Bonfanti, 'Bertola e la letteratura tedesca' (425–36), which looks at B.'s *Idea della bella letteratura alemanna*.

BIANCHI. Antonio Bianchi, *Il filosofo veneziano*, ed. Anco Marzio Mutterle, Padua, Editoriale Programma, 2000, 204 pp., the first edition of this work since 1770, is part of that cult of the philosophical novel, intended to educate, which we see in works such as Chiari's *La filosofessa italiana*. The editor describes B.'s novel as 'formalmente innovativa e ideologicamente reazionaria'.

CALOPRESE. R. A. Syska-Lamparska, 'Gregorio Caloprese e il Petrarca', *Della Terza Vol.*, 165–97, after discussing and dismissing C.'s view (reported by one of his students) that Petrarch is as corrupting an influence as Aretino, proceeds to examine C.'s links with the Investiganti, a group interested in philosophical and scientific research, and points out that in his major work on the poetry of Della Casa, C. praises Petrarch as an example of the 'buoni poeti'. The writer further discusses C.'s analysis of poetic values and style, asserting that his radical modification of the concept of Platonism brings it closer to the real.

CALZABIGI. Ranieri de' Calzabigi, *Alceste, Orfeo ed Euridice*, ed. Fabiano Licciardi, Palermo, Novecento, 2000, 208 pp. S. Badano, 'Echi biblici e religiosi nella *Lulliade* di Ranieri Calzabigi', *LItal*, 52, 2000:585–610, discusses the use of reference to the Bible and Islamic sources for satirical purposes in the *Lulliade*, with mention of C.'s parody of the *Risposta di Santigliano* of Metastasio.

CAMPAILLA. Tommaso Campailla, *L'Adamo*, ed. Giovanni Rossino, Verona, Fiorini, 1998, is a facsimile reprint of the 1737 edition with an essay by Corrado Dollo.

CARLI. C. Abbona, 'Le "lettere americane" di Gian Rinaldo Carli tra lumi ed "ammassi di sogni"', *GSLI*, 177, 2000:241–51, covers 56 letters sent by C. to his cousin, Girolamo Gravisi, between 1777 and 1779 which, according to the author, are an expression of C.'s 'Utopian' phase of thought. The letters are a mix of science and imagination, 'di lumi e di sogni', though the author also points out that at times C.'s ideas cannot be called enlightened.

CARMIGNANI. L. Frassineti, 'Paralipomeni nella storia del teatro italiano del Settecento: la *querelle* sugli spettacoli nella Firenze dei Lorena e la *Polissena* di Giovanni Carmignani', *Ariel*, 15, 2000:47–86, discusses this single tragedy by C., better known as a lawyer and writer on Alfieri, which ran into some trouble when it was performed in 1788 as not conforming sufficiently to Peter Leopold's strict regulations for theatre production, and talks of the role in theatre censorship of the *Osservatrice fiorentina*, which was particularly critical of C.'s play.

CASANOVA. Alain Buisine, *Casanova l'européen*, Paris, Tallandier, 442 pp., aims to illustrate the interior force which drove C. to be always on the move, demonstrating how he was as much at home with nobility and intellectuals as he was with cheats and adventurers. The book ends with a chapter on the 'false' C. of Fellini's film. **Giacomo Casanova: tra Venezia e l'Europa*, ed. G. Pizzamiglio, F, Olschki, vi + 350 pp., is the proceedings of a conference held at the Fondazione Cini in Venice in 1998. *L'Intermédiaire des Casanovistes*, 18, has the following articles of interest: J.-H. Roy, 'Fashioning identities: Casanova's encounter with la Charpillon' (1–9), which examines C.'s London adventure with Marianne Charpillon; B. Aleksić, 'Deux lettres dédommageantes de Premislas Zanovich à Casanova' (11–22), examining these two letters which seem to cast light on C.'s part in the Lord Lincoln card scandal which led to C.'s expulsion from Florence in 1771; F. Luccichenti, 'Casanova e gli ebrei' (23–33), which points to evidence of C.'s prejudiced approach in his writings. **Giacomo Casanova e le ostetriche: un capitolo di storia della medicina del 18. secolo*, ed. Romano Forleo and Federico Di Trocchio, T, Centro Scientifico, 2000, 144 pp. **Giacomo Casanova tra Venezia e l'Europa*, ed. Gilberto Pizzamiglio, F, Olschki, vi + 350 pp., gathers the proceedings of the conference held in 1998 at the Fondazione Cini. G.-D. Toubiana, **'Duel et substitution chez Casanova'*, *Littératures*, 40, 1999:151–56. J. Stagl, **'Zur Theorie des Schwindlers: Casanovas Soliloque d'un penseur'*, *RF*, 112, 2000:225–35.

CASTI.   Giovan Battista Casti, *Novelle galanti*, ed. Lucia Rodler, Ro, Carocci, 256 pp.

CESAROTTI.   Melchiorre Cesarotti, *Le poesie di Ossian*, ed. Enrico Mattioda, Ro, Salerno, 2000, xli + 948 pp., includes an excellent introduction as well as an extensive bibliography, and the texts of C.'s *Discorso* and *Osservazioni* on Ossian. G. Baldassarri, 'L'"originale" di *Fingal*. Postilla su Cesarotti e le stampe inglesi del 1762', *Resta Vol.*, I, 537–59, discusses the English text of Ossian used by C. for his translation.

CHIARI.   Pietro Chiari, *La schiava cinese; Le sorelle cinesi*, ed. Marco Catucci, Ro, Vecchiarelli, 1999, 182 pp., publishes two of the important plays by Chiari written as part of his disputes with Goldoni in 1753. Carlo Alberto Madrignani, *All'origine del romanzo in Italia. Il 'celebre Abate Chiari'*, Na, Liguori, 2000, 354 pp., begins from a historical rather than a textual perspective in approaching C.'s *La filosofessa italiana* (1753) and other works, also examining the contemporary critical attitude to C. in the context of his great public success.

CONFORTO.   G. G. Stiffoni, 'Per una biografia di Nicola Conforto (Napoli 1718–Madrid 1793): documenti d'archivio, libretti conservati nella Biblioteca Nacional di Madrid, fonti musicali manoscritte e a stampa', *FMI*, 4, 1999:7–54, gives a great deal of information, especially on C.'s collaboration with Metastasio, whose last work, *La Nitteti* (1755), C. produced for the court in Madrid.

CRUDELI.   Maria Augusta Morelli Timpanaro, *Per Tommaso Crudeli nel 250° anniversario della morte, 1745–2000*, F, Olschki, 2000, 120 pp., deals with C.'s Florentine background, describing in great detail his connections within the literary and cultural circles of the period, but, perhaps of greater importance, offering items by C. unpublished, or at least largely unknown, until now, including the MS of his celebrated ode composed on the occasion of a concert by the musician Farinello at the Teatro della Pergola in 1734. Tommaso Crudeli,

L'arte di piacere alle donne e alle amabili compagnie, ed. Marco Catucci, Ro, Quiritta, 2000, xliv + 38 pp., in the past has often been attributed to Crudeli, but Catucci suggests that it is by an 'Anonimo del secolo 18.' Renzo Rabboni, *Monsignor il dottor mordi graffiante: le rime inquisite di Tommaso Crudeli, preface by Guido Baldassarri, Udine, Istituto di studi storici Tommaso Crudeli, 2000, xi + 490 pp.

DANDOLFO. E. Stizzo, 'Un commediografo napoletano del '700, Gioacchino Dandolfo', *CLett*, 29:535–50, discusses the problems in dating D.'s work, given the absence of autobiographical material, in spite of his editorial success. The author asserts that D. presents not the crude, rough figures of Neapolitan life, but the wise 'rustego' and claims that D.'s writing bases itself increasingly on the daily reality of Naples.

DA PONTE. Lorenzo Da Ponte, *Memoirs*, trans. Elisabeth Abbott, ed., ann., and introd. Arthur Livingston, preface by Charles Rosen, NY, New York Review of Books, 2000, xxxii, 472 pp., is a reprint of the 1929 edition. G. Da Pozzo, 'Strategia del racconto nelle *Memorie di Lorenzo Da Ponte*', *Resta Vol.*, 1, 653–73, asserts that it is evident from the way in which he writes that Da P. was well aware of other 18th-c. autobiographies, particularly that of Casanova.

I. Bonomi, 'Novità e tradizione nella lingua dei libretti mozartiani di Da Ponte', *Velli Vol*, II, 597–616, analyses Da P.'s compositional technique, demonstrating how his ability to follow what Mozart wants is anything but passive and illustrating how he creates an extremely personal theatrical language. R. Andrews, 'From Beaumarchais to Da Ponte: a new view of the sexual politics of *Figaro*', *MusL*, 82:214–33, as well as analysing aspects of the relationship between the Count and Countess also has an interesting discussion of Cherubino as 'thematically central to the action while remaining dramaturgically on the margins'. C. R. Russell, 'Lorenzo Da Ponte's *Don Giovanni*', *Della Terza Vol.*, 227–37, discusses the parts of his libretto which Da P. took from Giuseppe Bertati's earlier libretto for Gazzaniga, as well as looking at other possible sources for the material, in particular Andrea Cicognini's *Il convitato di pietra*. Paolo Spedicato, *La sindrome di Sheherazade: intertestualità e verità in Lorenzo Da Ponte, Na, ESI, 2000, 196 pp.

DENINA. G. Ricuperati, 'Ipotesi su Carlo Denina, storico e comparatista', *RSI*, 113:107–37, discusses the problems raised by D.'s vast range of interests by examining the approach of various historians, and concludes with comments on D.'s interest in the idea of nation which, according to the author, 'il cosmopolita Denina aveva cercato di superare'. *Carlo Denina fra Berlino e Parigi (1782–1813): giornata di studio, Torino, Accademia delle Scienze, 30 novembre

2000, ed. Marco Cerruti and Bianca Danna, Alessandria, Orso, 211 pp.

FONTANINI. Giusto Fontanini, *L'Aminta di Torquato Tasso: difeso e illustrato da Giusto Fontanini con alcune osservazioni d'un accademico fiorentino*, ed. Andrea Gareffi, Manziana, Vecchiarelli, 2000, cxliii + 391 pp., is a facsimile reprint of the 1730 edition with a lengthy introduction and additions to Fontanini's index by Gareffi.

GALIANI. V. Giannantonio, 'La topica erudita, la commedia spagnoleggiante e il *Socrate immaginario* dell'abate Galiani', *CLett*, 29:637–54, considers G.'s only work for the theatre, which discards the vogue current at the time for everyday life in order to present a mythological version of optimism, against a background which satirizes false philosophy. The work is set in the context of theatrical reform, moving from a localized view of a comic theatre which is *zanni*-based to a more literary presentation of themes.

GIRALDI. Maria Augusta Morelli Timpanaro, *Il cavalier Giovanni Giraldi (Firenze 1712–1753) e la sua famiglia*, F, Olschki, 98 pp., is concerned particularly with G.'s very important library, some of which has ended up in the Biblioteca Magliabechiana.

GOLDONI. In the *Edizione Nazionale*, published by Marsilio in Venice, the following new titles have appeared: Carlo Goldoni, *L'avventuriero onorato*, ed. Bianca Danna, 336 pp.; *La buona madre*, ed. Anna Scannapieco, 382 pp.; *I due pantaloni*, ed. Franco Vazzoler, 354 pp.; *L'amore paterno*, ed. Andrea Fabiano, 2000, 256 pp.; *Il filosofo inglese*, ed. Paola Roman, 2000, 293 pp. Other editions of texts include: Carlo Goldoni, *La locandiera*, Mi, La Spiga, 2000, 76 pp.; Id., *Il ventaglio: con un profilo storico del teatro occidentale*, ed. Anna Crisi, Na, Liguori, 2000, 197 pp.; Id., *Trilogia della villeggiatura*, ed. Carlo Pedretti, Mi, Rizzoli, 2000, 346 pp.; Id., *Le baruffe chiozzotte; La locandiera*, ed. Carlo Pedretti, Mi, Fabbri, 331 pp.; Id., *Commedie*, ed. Carmelo Alberti, Ro, Salerno, lxxv + 861 pp.

Maggie Günsberg, *Playing with Gender: the Comedies of Goldoni*, Leeds, Northern Universities Press, 274 pp., is an excellent and most welcome volume which covers a wide range of topics including gender and class, but also food and fashion, highlighting the author's emphasis on the patriarchal ideal of women to be found in G. and also its subversion. Giorgio Padoan, *Putte, zanni, rusteghi. Scena e testo nella commedia goldoniana*, ed. Ilaria Crotti et al., Ravenna, Longo, 345 pp., collects together a number of previously published articles. Ilaria Crotti, *Libro, mondo, teatro. Saggi goldoniani*, 2000, 284 pp., contains seven essays which have already appeared since 1989, though in expanded form, and one new paper, '"Lettor carissimo": strategie di lettura e modelli di destinatario' (11–44). Franco Fido, *Nuova guida a Goldoni*, T, Einaudi, 2000, xi + 341 pp., offers the 1977 edition with the addition of other material, some of which has appeared elsewhere since then. There are two new essays, 'Tempo della città, tempo del teatro: cronotipi goldoniani' (194–204) and (245–57) the one also published (see below) in *Della Terza Vol.* There is also an appendix which contains six unpublished letters. M. Pieri, *ʻ "Grandi intrecci" e "grandi passioni": dittici e trilogie in Goldoni', *Italiana*, 2000, 9 : 173–94. *Problemi di critica goldoniana*, 7, 2000, contains: A. Fabiano, 'Due lettere inedite del Goldoni al *Journal de Paris*' (7–11); Piermario Vescovo, 'Momolo a Varsavia (Postilla a una postilla goldoniana)' (13–23); Anna Scannapieco, 'Scrittoio, scena, torchio: per una mappa della produzione goldoniana' (25–242); Piermario Vescovo, 'Parigi e Siviglia: spazio e tempo in commedia tra Sei e Settecento e in Goldoni: primi appunti' (243–87). F. Fido, 'La sinderesi di Giacinta: ancora sulle *Villeggiature* di Goldoni', *Della Terza Vol.*, 199–208, observes that the absence of true love in the trilogy seems to lead to the paradox of a proliferation of weddings, and that Giacinta's marriage and departure for Genoa are not intended or expected by G. to arouse the sympathies of the audience. F. Márquez Villanueva, 'Perspectiva hispana de Don Juan en Goldoni y Molière', *ib.*, 209–225, talks of Goldoni finding some of the details of Molière's play out of place dramatically, even though he was a great admirer of the French playwright. In particular, the ending with the return of the stone statue is changed in Goldoni, and the author points out that G., unlike Molière, seemed to be unaware that the encounter with the statue in the Spanish tradition represented 'uno de los grandes momentos dramáticos de todos los tiempos', going on to claim that G.'s handling of the myth is not far short of sabotage. **Memorie di Goldoni e memoria del teatro*, ed. Franco Angelini, Ro, Bulzoni, 2000, 182 pp., contains papers from a conference in Rome in 1993. Epifanio Ajello, **Carlo Goldoni: l'esattezza e lo sguardo*, Salerno, Edisud, 246 pp. Siro Ferrone, **Carlo Goldoni: vita, opere, critica, messinscena*, F, Sansoni, 212 pp.

GOZZI. Carlo Gozzi, *Novelle*, ed. Ricciarda Ricorda, Venice, Marsilio, 147 pp., is the first new edition for more than 100 years. It includes the 11 novelle from the 1774 edition with the addition of *La novella del Marchese Gradasso di Vesuvio* and two shorter works. Id., *L'augellino belverde*, F, Cesati, 100 pp., has an introduction by Antonella Del Gatto. Id., Carlo Gozzi, *La guerra dei due Carli: con 'Scrittura contestativa al taglio della tartana' e 'Il teatro comico all'Osteria del Pellegrino'*, ed. Sandro Bajini, Vicenza, Teatro Olimpico, 2000, 221 pp. Edoardo Sanguineti, **L'amore delle tre melarance: un travestimento fiabesco dal canovaccio di Carlo Gozzi*, Genoa, Il Melangolo, 143 pp.

John Louis DiGaetani, *Carlo Gozzi. A Life in the Eighteenth-Century Venetian Theatre, an Afterlife in Opera*, Jefferson, NC, McFarland, 2000,

209 pp., offers what its author claims as the first full biography in English or Italian of Gozzi. It deals with the main events of his life including his dispute with Goldoni, and analyses G.'s own plays. However, the notion of 'afterlife in opera' in the title is misleading in that, apart from the odd paragraph and some illustrations, there is no proper discussion of the fate of G.'s work in the hands of Prokofiev, Puccini, or Busoni, let alone Wagner. Nearly all quotations are in English with no indication of the Italian original. M. Corti, 'Tra "riso democraziano" ed echi classici: le novelle in prosa di Carlo Gozzi', *GSLI*, 178:64–83, examines the composition and editorial vicissitudes of the short stories, dealing with the presence of the 'io' narrator and the presentation of settings and characters based on real life.

LUNELLI SPINOLA.   Allegra Alecevich, *Una dama in Parnaso: una cheraschese illustre: Benedetta Clotilde Lunelli Spinola (1700–1774),* Cherasco, Città di Cherasco, 140 pp.

MALASPINA DI SANNAZZARO.   Luigi Malaspina Di Sannazzaro, *Dizionario di false credenze antiche e moderne,* ed. Fausto Barbagli e Cesare Repossi, Mi, Aisthesis, 2000, 135 pp.

MANFREDI.   A. Donnini, 'Eustachio Manfredi rimatore', *GSLI*, 178:205–57, looks at the edition of M.'s *Rime* of 1713 and others of previous years, examining Petrarchesque elements and pointing out that many of these compositions can be read in a moral key, since they were written for or addressed to nuns. The writer also looks at the great influence of Tasso on Manfredi.

MARCHESE.   Giulio Rosa, *'Di Fedra il cieco furor': passione e potere nella tragedia del Settecento: il 'Crispo' di Annibale Marchese: con l'edizione del testo,* Salerno, Edisud, 2000, 255 pp.

MARTINELLI.   C. Sodini, 'Vincenzio Martinelli. Un cosmopolita toscano del '700', *RST,* 46, 2000:61–106, is a continuation of the study, previously noted, begun in *RST,* 45, 1999:85–139. It starts with an analysis of M.'s *Lettere familiari e critiche,* which demonstrate his great interest in the Italian language and his defence of the culture of his native land. The article goes on to discuss his antagonism with Carlo Francesco Badini which eventually caused M. to return to Italy, as well as his differences with Voltaire, especially over Voltaire's negative judgement of Dante, before dealing with M.'s *Istoria del governo d'Inghilterra* (1776) which attempts to explain the rise of England's constitutional monarchy. The writer also examines *La Istoria della Casa de Medici,* which was never published, identifying large sections taken from previous histories of the Medici and judging M. 'un autore che, piccatosi di essere uno storico, fu sempre e soltanto un letterato'.

MASCHERONI.   Lorenzo Mascheroni, *Opere,* 5 vols, Bergamo, Moretti & Vitali, 2000, comprises: *Oltre il dolce Parrasio,* ed. Matilde Dillon

Wanke; *Invito a Lesbia Cidonia*, ed. Irene Botta, which is also published separately (see below); *Nel turbine de' pubblici affari*, ed. Duccio Tongiorgi; *Memorie analitiche*, ed. Luigi Pepe; *Geometria del compasso*, ed. Giorgio Mirandola. Id., *L'Invito: versi sciolti di Dafni Orobiano a Lesbia Cidonia*, ed. Irene Botta, Bergamo, Moretti & Vitali, 2000, lvii + 49 pp. **Lesbia Cidonia e i 'vincitor del tempo eterni libri': per Cesare Repossi*, ed. Franca La Vezzi and Fabio Gasti, Pavia, Tipografia Commerciale Pavese, 1999, 19 pp. *Catalogo delle lettere e delle opere di Lorenzo Mascheroni*, ed. Francesco Tadini et al., Bergamo, Secomandi, 1999, 490 pp.

MATTEINI. M. Valbonesi, 'Un epigono di Parini: Giosuè Matteini', *Italianistica*, 29, 2000:435–41, deals with M.'s *L'oracolo di Pistoia*, tracing its debt to Parini's *Il giorno*.

METASTASIO. Aurelio de' Giorgi Bertola, *Osservazioni sopra Metastasio*, ed. Gian Piero Maragoni, Manziana, Vecchiarelli, 75 pp. Alberto Beniscelli, *Felicità sognate: il teatro di Metastasio*, Genoa, Il Melangolo, 2000, 181 pp., examines M.'s poetic development from his days in Rome and Naples to his time in Vienna, emphasizing the great variety of his dramatic constructions, 'in apparenza iterate e tuttavia sempre diverse', which fulfil his 'antitragica aspirazione alla felicità'. The book also discusses M.'s debt to Racine and well as Corneille and Tasso, going on to analyse his interest in the tragic potential of ideological confrontation while praising his ability to produce convincing dialogue. P. Gibellini, 'Metastasio e la mitologia', *CLett*, 29:459–81, deals with M.'s debt to Gravina and his writing on Greek theatre, demonstrating how much he drew on classical sources for his plays. The article shows how far M. moved away from any magic or pagan inspiration, indicating his use of the gods and other classical elements to praise his sovereign patrons, and claims that 'l'evento tragico-mitico è evocato per esser poi esorcizzato' in order to remove irrational excess. Also on M. we have *Musica e Storia*, 9.1, most of which is devoted to seminars of the Fondazione Levi on Metastasio's *Passione* and its influence: B. Bertoli, 'Rilettura biblica della *Passione* di Pietro Metastasio' (55–74); J. Herczog, 'Oscillazioni di un genere sul crinale tra letteratura e melodrama: l'interpretazione musicale del primo "componimento sacro" del Metastasio' (75–94); E. Sala Di Felice, 'Vienna: devoto esordio metastasiano' (95–114); C. Campa, 'Hasse e Hiller tra primo e secondo Settecento e la determinazione dell'affetto sacro in musica: i *Beiträge zu wahren Kirchenmusik*' (115–44); A. L. Bellina, 'Affetti sacri e profani. Un'aria di paragone' (145–56); R. Mellace, 'Il pianto di Pietro: fortuna del tema e strategie drammaturgiche tra gli oratori viennesi e la *Passione* metastasiana' (157–75); S. Stroppa, 'Il pianto sospeso. Per un Metastasio ricondotto a se stesso' (177–98); B. Brumana, 'Fortuna e modelli compositivi della *Passione* tra Jommelli, Paisiello e Morlacchi' (199–224); E. Grossato, 'Presenza della *Passione* metastasiana nella Venezia musicale della prima metà del Settecento' (225–44); G. Mangini, '"Dove sono? dove corro?"'. Echi ottocenteschi della *Passione* (245–63); G. Morelli, 'Indagine sul titolo mendace della *Passione 1730*' (265–96).

MONTI. A. Colombo, 'Littérature et enjeux politiques: autour de Vincenzo Monti traducteur "républicain" de Perse (Milan, 1803)', *REI*, 46, 2000: 269–83, is concerned with M.'s translation of Persius' Satires, where M. sees Persius's as seeking the truly free man and the new morality of which the prince is to be the defender. The writer interprets M.'s version as a justification for Napoleon's political stance. L. Frassineti, 'L'autografo superstite delle lezioni pavesi di Vincenzo Monti', *SFI*, 58, 2000: 199–214, relates to M.'s lectures in Pavia between 1802–1804 on eloquence and poetry, pointing out where passages were censored by M.'s immediate family. Angelo Romano, *Vincenzo Monti a Roma*, Manziana, Vecchiarelli, 290 pp., gathers writings mainly published for the first time. Id., 'Rassegna montiana', *LItal*, 53: 106–34, is an extensive review of editions of Monti and writings on him between 1980 and 2000.

MURATORI. C. Viola, 'Alle origini del metodo muratoriano: appunti sul *De graecae linguae uso e praestantia*', *StSec*, 42: 299–356, discusses writings which form part of M.'s Milan years, although this particular work was not published until 1771, seeing it as a work which begins M.'s writings on methodology and emphasizing how even his early work illustrates that M. already had very clear ideas. Id., 'Muratori e le origini di una celebre *querelle* italo-francese', pp. 63–90 of *Studi di letteratura italiana in onore di Francesco Mattesini*, ed. Enrico Elli and Giuseppe Langella, Mi, Vita e Pensiero, 2000, lvi + 700 pp., is concerned with M.'s involvement in the Bouhours–Orsi dispute over the quality of Italian poetry, drawing on an unpublished work by M., *La conversazione di Mirtillo e d'Elpino*, in order to demonstrate how M., rather than remain trapped in a rather sterile French vs Italian dispute, attempts to widen the discussion, especially in his later work, *Della perfetta poesia italiana*.

PAOLINI MASSIMI. N. Costa-Zalessow, 'Una prosa e due poesie dimenticate di Petronilla Paolini Massimi', *FoI*, 34, 2000: 468–82, suggests the addition of various items to Virginio Emanuele Laurini's 1963 edition of P.M.'s work, and talks of evidence of narrative skill in a MS in the Vatican library.

PARINI. Licia Badesi, *Rivisitando la vita di Giuseppe Parini*, Rimini, Luisè, 1999, 131 pp., is a basic biography with no great pretensions to literary analysis. Guido Bustico, *Bibliografia di Giuseppe Parini*, F, Olschki, viii + 180 pp., is a welcome facsimile reprint of the 1929 edition. *Parini e le arti nella Milano neoclassica*, ed. Graziella Buccellati and Anna Marchi, Mi, Hoepli, 2000, xl + 234 pp., documents P.'s activities in the period between 1771 and 1793 and contains Parini texts with introductory essays by Gennaro Barbarisi, Fernando Mazzocca, and Silvia Morgana.

There are various collections celebrating the bicentenary of P.'s death. *RLettI*, 17, 1999, 634 pp., devotes the whole of parts 2 and 3, consisting of 58 articles, to P. with the title *Attualità di Giuseppe Parini: poesia e impegno civile*, ed. Giorgio Baroni. Likewise, *Quaderni di Acme*, 2000, 1225 pp., ed. Gennaro Barbarisi, devotes both volumes to the proceedings of two P. conferences held in Milan on November 8–10, 1999, and December 14–16, 1999, with the titles *Letteratura e società* and *La musica e le arti*. *Le buone dottrine e le buone lettere: Brescia per il bicentenario della morte di Giuseppe Parini, 17–19 novembre 1999*, ed. Bortolo Martinelli, Carlo Annoni, and Giuseppe Langella, Mi, Vita e Pensiero, xiv + 335 pp. *Interpretazioni e letture del Giorno. Gargnano del Garda (2–4 ottobre 1997)*, ed. Gennaro Barbarisi and Edoardo Esposito, Bo, Cisalpino, 1999, 701 pp. O. Pasquinelli, *'Un profilo di Giuseppe Parini nel secondo centenario della morte'*, *Cristallo*, 42.1, 2000:63–77.

F. Tancini, ' "Bongusto" e "bel mondo" nel *Mezzogiorno* del Parini', *Velli Vol.*, ii, 561–85, discusses the terms as used in P.'s polemic against the attitudes of the nobility as 'sintomo di squilibrio interiore'. F. Fido, 'Le "altre" odi di Parini e la sindrome del non finito', *Italica*, 77, 2000:14–25, starts from Dante Isella's 1975 edition of P.'s odes to discuss what should appear in a critical edition and argues for the inclusion of three compositions which do not appear in any other editions. F. Savoia, 'Parini librettista: *Ascanio in Alba*', *RLI*, 104, 2000:388–419, discusses what the author describes as a work in the style of Metastasio from a writer who is ethically so different, and also looks at P.'s description of the festivities for the wedding of Ferdinand of Austria with Maria Beatrice d'Este in 1771, pointing out P.'s emphasis on the 'democratic' moments and showing how the work fits in with P.'s career and other writings. On the same topic is G. Barbarisi, 'La "perpetua allegoria" dell'*Ascanio in Alba*', *Resta Vol.*, i, 561–79, which examines some of the themes prominent in this work. *Parini e la musica*, with texts by Matteo Sartorio, Mi, Museo teatrale alla Scala, 1999, 31 pp.

S. Morgana, 'L'*Agnoletta* del Parini tra riscrittura e sperimenta-zione', *Velli Vol.*, ii, 527–41, discusses P.'s earliest prose work, supposedly based on Pietro Fortini's *Agnellino*, pointing out the similarities, but also suggesting that there are substantial differences. G. Benvenuti, 'Due sonetti e un manoscritto pariniano', *ib.*, 511–26, presents two sonnets which P. contributed to the volume in celebration of the canonization of S. Girolamo Miani in 1766, together with variations on one of them contained in a MS in the Biblioteca Ambrosiana. G. Savarese, 'Gli sciolti di Parini al *Mosè della Lombardia. Per l'occasione e cronologia dei versi al Consigliere Barone De Martini'*, *ib.*, 587–96, dates these compositions to the early months of 1786. In the same vol. is also G. Carnazzi, 'Parini e la satira "cui Giovenal la sferza diè"' (543–59), dealing with the influence of Horace on P.'s satire, while detailing passages, especially in the Odes, which can be shown to be influenced by Juvenal. C. Annoni, 'Parini, poesia della secolarizzazione e fine della storia', *RLI*, 104, 2000:49–75, talks of P.'s poetry as celebrating and encouraging the secularization of the Christian discourse about society, as it parodies ideas of Catholicism in such works as *Alla moda*. The article further characterizes *Il giorno* as 'la parodia del cattivo esistente' and *Alla musa* as the celebration of the 'bella vincitrice'. C. Annoni, 'Le passioni fanno traviare: Parini, Manzoni e la *Colonna infame*', pp. 91–126 of *Studi di letteratura italiana in onore di Francesco Mattesini*, noted under MURATORI, offers some thoughts on an early composition by P., examining also the explanation of it given in the *Storia della colonna infame* by Manzoni. **L'Ambrosiana e Parini. Manoscritti e documenti sulla cultura milanese del Settecento*, ed. Guido Carnuzzi, Bo, Cisalpino, 1999, 128 pp. Italo Rocco, **Aneddoti pariniani di Giuseppe Giusti*', *Silarus*, 207, 2000:76–77.

PES.   Gavino Pes, *Tutti li canzuni: le straordinarie rime d'amore e di gelosia del Catullo gallurese del Settecento*, introd. and trans. Giulio Cossu, Cagliari, Torre, 335 pp., is a reprint of the 1981 edition.

PIAZZA.   Aldo Maria Morace, **Un romanziere del Settecento: Antonio Piazza*, Reggio Calabria, Pontari, 1999, 206 pp.

PIMENTEL.   Eleonora de Fonseca Pimentel, **Una donna tra le muse. La produzione poetica*, ed. Daniela De Liso et al., Na, Loffredo, 1999, 320 pp. Few works of this Neapolitan writer have survived. One which has, the sonnet *Sull'erruzione vulcanica del Monte Vesuvio*, is examined in D. De Liso, 'Un sonetto inedito di Eleonora de Fonseca Pimentel', *CLett*, 28, 2000:577–87, which also points out the link with Leopardi's *La ginestra*.

PINDEMONTE.   Ippolito Pindemonte, *Lettere a Isabella (1784–1828)*, ed. Gilberto Pizzamiglio, F, Olschki, 2000, lxxviii + 413 pp., contains letters to Isabella Teotochi Albrizzi, some published for the first time. The editor illustrates the closeness of the friendship between the two, based on shared ideas about literature and life, though he also points out that the almost non-existence of Isabella's replies sometimes makes the terms of their discussion difficult to establish clearly.

QUADRIO. F. Arato, 'Quadrio e la letteratura universale', *Belfagor*, 56:545–60, examines some of Q.'s compositions, dating from both before and after he left the Jesuits in 1741, as well as discussing Q.'s criteria in his *Della storia e della ragione di ogni poesia*.

VERRI, A. G. Cartago, 'Dai manoscritti alla stampa: varianti di "ortografia" negli articoli di Alessandro Verri per *Il Caffè*', *Acme*, 53.3, 2000:39–81, looks principally at V.'s *Di Giustiniano e delle sue leggi* in conducting a detailed analysis of corrections and alterations between manuscript and printed edition.

VERRI, P. Pietro Verri, *Memorie*, ed. Enrica Agnesi, Modena, Mucchi, 272 pp., gathers together a wide range of V.'s autobiographical writings between 1771 and 1789, some of them appearing for the first time. Giorgio Panizza and Barbara Costa, *L'Archivio Verri, Parte Seconda. La 'Raccolta Verriana'*, Mi, Fondazione Raffaele Mattioli per la Storia del Pensiero Economico, 2000, 348 pp., follows the previous part, published in 1997, dealing with the letters of major members of the Verri family, including Pietro and Alessandro.

VICO. Giambattista Vico, *'De nostri temporis studiorum ratione' di Giambattista Vico: prima redazione inedita dal ms. XIII B 55 della Biblioteca Nazionale di Napoli: indici e ristampa anastatica dall'edizione Napoli 1709*, ed. Marco Veneziani, F, Olschki, 2000, lxi + 440 pp., gives Vico's text in Latin with the commentary in Italian and contains a facsimile reprint of the Naples 1709 edition. Silvia Caianiello, *Catalogo vichiano internazionale. Censimento delle prime edizioni di Vico nelle biblioteche al di fuori d'Italia*, Na, Guida, 2000, 181 pp. Also on Vico bibliography is F. Ratto, 'Riviste vichiane: panorama internazionale di studi su Giambattista Vico', *RStI*, 18.1, 2000:198–218, which reviews issues of *New Vico Studies* from 1997 to 1999.

Leo Catana, **Vico and Literary Mannerism: a Study in the Early Vico and his Idea of Rhetoric and Ingenuity*, NY, Lang, 1999, xii + 142 pp. Giuseppe Mazzotta, **The New Map of the World: the Poetic Philosophy of Giambattista Vico*, Princeton U.P., 1999, xiii + 267 pp. Id., 'Vico's Istoria della poesia', *Italiana*, 2000, 9:157–60. Alain J.-L. Busst, *L'Orphée de Ballanche: genèse et signification. Contribution a l'étude du rayonnement de la pensée de Giambattista Vico*, Bern, Lang, 1999, 343 pp., discusses the influence of V. on the 19th-c. French thinker Pierre-Simon Ballanche. **Momenti vichiani del primo Settecento*, ed. Gilberto Pizzamiglio and Manuela Sanna, Na, Guida, 165 pp., collects papers presented to a seminar held in Pisa in 1999. G. De Miranda, 'Fino a "convincere chicchessia". Vico, i suoi contatti romani e i complessi rapporti con il mondo ecclesiastico', *Intersezioni*, 21:169–74, discusses V.'s links with elements in the Roma Curia and the events surrounding the initial suspension of the printing of the *Scienza Nuova* by the Holy Office. D. S. Cervigni, 'Vico's beginnings and ends: variations on the theme of the origin of language', *AnI*, 18, 2000: 13–28, claims that it is not just what V. says about the origin of language as a written expression or its metaphorical and political essence that is new, but also the way in which he says it, stating that 'his method, Socratic rather than Cartesian, is that of irony'.

New Vico Studies, 17, 1999, contains: I. Berlin, 'The reputation of Vico' (1–5); P. Burke, 'Vico disparaged?' (7–10); J. Mali, 'Sensus communis and Bildung: Vico and the rehabilitation of myth in Germany' (11–33); E. Morera, 'Vico and antifoundationalism' (35–51); S. Samuelson, 'Joyce's *Finnegans Wake* and Vico's mental dictionary' (53–66); F. Connelly, 'Embodied meaning: Giambattista Vico's theory of images' (67–83); D. P. Verene, 'On translating Vico: the Penguin Classics edition of the *New Science*' (85–107). *New Vico Studies*, 18, 2000, has the following articles: D. R. Kelley, 'Vico and the archeology of wisdom' (1–19); B. K. Axel, 'Who fabled: Joyce and Vico on history and constraint' (21–37); O. Remaud, 'The rhythm of history: nature, language, and politics in Vico's *Scienza nuova*' (39–55); J. Ashley, 'Vico and postmodern reflection' (57–69); T. I. Bayer, 'The future of Vico studies: Vico at the millennium' (71–76); M. Cherchi, 'A note on Vico's typology of language' (77–93); D. P. Verene, 'A note on Vico and Yeats' (95–99). *BCSV*, 30, 2000, contains the following items: G. Fulco, 'Precisazioni e interrogativi per un ammiratore di Vico' (13–15); L. Bianchi, ' "E contro la pratica de' Governi di Baile, che vorrebbe senza Religioni poter reggere le Nazioni": note su Bayle nella corrispondenza di Vico' (17–30); M. Sanna, 'Vico e lo "scandalo" della "metafisica alla moda lockiana" ' (31–50); A. Stile, ' "La corpulenza del Padre Malebranche" ' (51–60); P. Totaro, 'Il "lezzo di ser Benedetto": motivi spinoziani nell'opera di Biagio Garofalo' (61–76); R. Mazzola, ' "Le scrivo ciò che non ho potuto confidare alle stampe": Vico e Giacco' (77–92); M. Conforti, 'Echi dell'Accademia Medinaceli nell'epistolario vichiano' (93–108); M. Rascaglia, 'Gli interlocutori di Vico nei manoscritti della Biblioteca Nazionale di Napoli' (109–24); F. Piro, 'I presupposti teologici del giusnaturalismo moderno nella percezione di Vico' (125–49); F. Lomonaco, 'Piero Piovani e il Centro di studi vichiani' (153–75); C. Del Zotto, '*Marginalia* su due versioni danesi della *Scienza nuova "terza"* ' (177–84); R. Ruggiero, 'Le rivendicazioni di Tacito. In margine alle *Vici vindiciae*' (185–97); R. Mazzola, 'Vico e l'antica sapienza italica' (199–211); A. M. Damiani, 'La secolarizzazione politica nella *Nuova scienza*' (213–29); G. Calasso, 'Ancora sul Vico di Venturi' (231–33).

ZENO. V. Grohavaz, 'In margine ad alcuni postillati di Pier Caterino Zeno', *Aevum*, 74, 2000: 763–76, briefly describes Z.'s activities as editor of the *Giornale de' letterati d'Italia* and details marginalia from various of his works, with reference to Cicogna's study of them.

OTTOCENTO

POSTPONED

NOVECENTO

By ROBERTO BERTONI, *Senior Lecturer in Italian, Trinity College Dublin* and
CATHERINE O'BRIEN, *Professor of Italian, National University of Ireland, Galway*

I. GENERAL

Ugo M. Olivieri, *Un canone per il terzo millennio*, Mi, B. Mondadori,
274 pp., sees 20th-c. Italian literature as characterized by multiple
canons, takes into account the models offered both by critics and by
the educational system, and argues that the individual prevailed over
social trends and movements at the end of the millennium (contributors include: R. Bigazzi, B. Bongiovanni, P. Cataldi, R. Ceserani,
S. De Matteis, G. Ferroni, R. Luperini, G. Luti, F. Marenco,
C. Mazzacurati, F. Orlando, C. Ossola, M. Palumbo, and M. Sarpi).
Still on the 20th-c. canon, G. Petronio, 'Un bilancio del secondo
Novecento', *Problemi*, 116–17:22–27, proposes a list of canonical
books which includes Edoardo De Filippo's *Napoli milionaria* and
Primo Levi's *Se questo è un uomo*, and concludes that the presence of
deep ethical and social values is perhaps the appropriate criterion to
identify good literature. A reflection on the canon and periodization
in modern Italian literature is also present in R. Luperini, 'Estraneità
e tramonto dell'esperienza nella autocoscienza del moderno', *Allegoria*, 36:5–17, which identifies writers' 'self-awareness of modernity'
with perception of the metropolis, a sense of distance from the past,
disassociation of man from nature, and doubts on the meaning of life
(e.g. in Luigi Pirandello's *Il fu Mattia Pascal*), then subdivides 20th-c.
Italian literature into three periods: (i) the avantgarde in the 1910s
and 1920s; (ii) consolidation of a modern literary tradition down to
the 1960s; (iii) postmodernism, or a period when the avantgarde
becomes obsolete and loses its transgressive character. A canon based
on avantgarde writers is offered in Edoardo Sanguineti, *Atlante del
Novecento italiano. La cultura letteraria*, Lecce, Manni, 128 pp., which
includes photographs of a number of Italian writers by Giovanni
Giovannetti and an interview (conducted by Erminio Risso) where
S. sees the Italian *Novecento* characterized by fragmentation of the self,
subconscious experience, and awareness of language. He also highlights the importance of Pirandello, Svevo, the Crepuscolari, the
Futurists, and Palazzeschi in the first decades of the 20th c., but also
includes less well explored authors such as Vittorio Rata. He relies on
Antonio Gramsci in his discussion of cultural hegemony, political
perspectives, and philosophical convictions, and refines his notion of
style in relation to ideology and experience of life. Gian Mario
Anselmi, *Profilo storico della letteratura italiana*, F, Sansoni, x + 411 pp.

Assumpta Camps, *Historia de la Literatura Italiana Contemporánea*, II, Barcelona, PPU, 399 pp., covers the period 1945 to the present (vol. I, 1861–1945, was published in 2000). Some essays are about Italian literature in the 1980s and 1990s. For an 'alternative canon' see R. Carnero in *Sentieri narrativi del Novecento*, below. *Storia della letteratura italiana. Il Novecento. Scenari di fine secolo*, ed. Nino Borsellino and Lucio Felici, Mi, Garzanti.

Nicola Merola, *Un Novecento in piccolo. Saggi di letteratura contemporanea*, Catanzaro, Rubbettino, 2000, 246 pp., offers a general profile of the century together with various outlines of authors considered representative of the 20th c. such as Ungaretti, Gadda, Montale, Malaparte, Moravia, Luzi, Pierro, Zanzotto, Giudici, Bonaviri, Camilleri, Malerba, Neri, Vassalli, Tabucchi, Selva, Siti, Busi, and others. Romano Luperini, *Insegnare la letteratura oggi*, Lecce, Manni, 2000, 192 pp., examines the theoretical, ideological, and empirical problems facing those who currently teach Italian literature in the 'scuole medie superiori' in Italy. Pietro Gibellino, **Il calamaio di Dionisio: il vino nella letteratura italiana moderna*, Mi, Garzanti, 184 pp.

Marco Belpoliti, *Settanta*, T, Einaudi, 306 pp., focuses on the relationship between biography and society by discussing topics (e.g. the kidnapping and death of Aldo Moro) which were relevant to the lives and work of a number of writers including Leonardo Sciascia, Pier Paolo Pasolini, and Italo Calvino. *Sentieri narrativi del Novecento*, ed. Roberto Carnero and Giuliano Ladolfi, Novara, Interlinea, 100 pp., contains the following essays: G. Zaccaria, 'Oltre il neorealismo' (9–20); M. Guglielminetti, 'Pavese: l'ultimo dei classici?' (213–30), mainly on P.'s concept of myth; G. Baldi, 'Ordine e caos nell'opera di Gadda' (31–40), on the relationship between language, philosophy, and existential motives in G.'s work; E. Affinati, 'Appunti fenogliani' (41–42); E. Palandri, 'Calvino oltre il neorealismo' (43–48); R. Carnero, 'Per un canone alternativo: il caso Silvio D'Arzo' (49–62), exploring D.'s realism and psychological themes, in particular in *Casa d'altri*, and reviewing critical work on D.; N. Balestrini, 'La Neoavanguardia italiana degli anni Sessanta' (63–72), highlighting the novelty of the neoavantgarde as compared to early 20th-c. modernism; G. Baldissone, 'Tempo in frantumi, tempo di novelle. La novella italiana da Calvino ai giorni nostri' (73–86); and R. Carnero, 'La nuova narrativa italiana dal postmoderno al pulp' (87–98), which surveys some Italian novels in the 1980s and 1990s, highlights the influence of Pier Vittorio Tondelli on recent generations of writers, selects as representative of the 1980s Enrico Palandri, Andrea De Carlo, Daniele Del Giudice, and Aldo Busi, and enlists Giuseppe Culicchia and Enrico Brizzi for the 1990s together with Flavio Santi, Nicola Lecca, Guido Conti, and Carmine Abate for the last few years. G. Luti, 'Filosofia e letteratura in Italia nel primo Novecento', pp. 53–66 of *Modelli e stili di conoscenza nella scienza e nell'arte del Novecento*, F, Olschki, 2000, xii + 188 pp., examines neo-idealism, ethics, and irrationalism in some early 20th-c. Florentine journals (such as *Il Leonardo* and *La Voce*) and their reflection on the contemporary crisis of traditional structures in Italian fiction. G. Tellini, 'Sul romanzo italiano del Novecento' (pp. 67–84 of the same volume), illustrates some traits of the Italian 20th-c. novel, e.g. oblique narrations, antiheroic protagonists, and multiple structures. Vittorio Spinazzola, *La modernità letteraria*, Mi, Il Saggiatore, 2000, 560 pp., is about literature and the reading public ('I diritti del lettore', 11–66), publishing ('La funzione dell'editore', 67–128), a number of writers (including Nanni Balestrini, Carlo Cassola, Carlo Levi, and Pier Paolo Pasolini) viewed from a sociological angle (129–390), and popular and mainstream literature (391–543). Michele Sarfatti, *Gli ebrei nell'Italia fascista. Vicende, identità, persecuzione*, T, Einaudi, 2000, xii + 388 pp. *Studi in onore di Umberto Mariani. Da Verga a Calvino*, ed. Anthony G. Costantini and Franco Zangrilli, F, Cadmo, 2000, 217 pp.

The following entries are on literary theory. Loredana Chines and Carlo Varotti, *Che cos'è un testo letterario*, Ro, Carocci, 126 pp., is a manual on literary concepts including poetic form, narratology, and intertextuality. Mario Perniola, *L'arte e la sua ombra*, T, Einaudi, 2000, 122 pp., discusses the arts in general, including literature, and argues that contemporary styles, even when commercial and characterized by a 'psychotic' (extreme and violent) realism, reveal an enigmatic and paradoxically shining 'shadow' which constitutes the deep nature of art but is doomed to remain hidden in the background. Ferdinando Amigoni, *Il modo mimetico-realista*, Ro–Bari, Laterza, 90 pp., reviews the realist theories of Aristotle, Gyorgy Lukács, Erich Auerbach, Roland Barthes, Gérard Genette, Thomas G. Pavel, and other critics, and examines a number of novels including Carlo Emilio Gadda's *Quer pasticciaccio brutto de via Merulana*. Cesare Segre, *Ritorno alla critica*, T, Einaudi, 282 pp., collects previously published essays with the addition of unpublished material on points of agreement and disagreement between Primo Levi and Jean Améry (55–66), and an introd. (vii–xi) where the stagnation of criticism is lamented, and the need for serious interpretation of texts advocated. Gianni Turchetta, *Situazioni romanzesche: aspetti della comunicazione narrativa*, Mi, Unicopli, 220 p., investigates the possibility for survival and renewal of narrative theory in the context of changes in our perception of life and texts caused by contemporary technology.

On the broader field of cultural studies: *Italian Cultural Studies*, ed. Graziella Parati and Ben Lawton, Boca Raton, Bordighera Press,

250 pp., includes general essays by I. Kakandes, R. West (on the place of literature in Italian cultural studies), M. Galli Stampino, J. Buttigieg (on Antonio Gramsci and Francesco De Sanctis), and N. Pireddu (on Antonio Gramsci's and Paolo Mantegazza's approach to cultural politics and ethnology), essays by S. Carletti on the literary market and by R. M. Dainotto on 'the importance of being Sicilian', and other essays by A. W. B. Randolph, N. Hester, S. P. Hill, N. Bouchard, G. Lombardi, and D. Orlandi.

G. Luti, 'Per la storia letteraria del Novecento: il problema della periodizzazione', *RLI*, 104, 2000: 368–72, discusses the problem of dividing 20th-c. literary movements and developments into particular periods of time. M. Cerruti, ' "Leggere" nel Novecento', *ON*, 25.1: 169–84, suggests various ways of interpreting Novecento literary developments in Italy. Some aspects of Italian surrealism are considered in Silvana Cirillo, *Nei dintorni del surrealismo*, Ro, Lithos, 2000, 155 pp., which examines work by a number of authors including Corrado Alvaro, Dino Buzzati, Antonio Delfini, Tommaso Landolfi, Luigi Malerba, and Alberto Savinio. R. Luperini, 'Riflettendo sulle date: alcuni appunti sul neorealismo in letteratura', *Allegoria*, 37: 125–32, rather than looking at neorealism as a single organic movement, suggests various ways of interpreting divergent forms of neorealism that appeared between 1930 and 1955. G. Luti, 'Il dibattito sul neorealismo nelle riviste letterarie del dopoguerra', *NA*, 2218: 179–96, reviews the approach to neorealism of *Il Politecnico*, *Officina*, *Il Menabò*, *Il Verri*, and other journals, and concludes that the legacy of neorealism is still valid but requires an infusion of new life. **Manifesti futuristi: arte e lessico*, ed. Stefania Stefanelli, Livorno, Sillabe, 119 pp. Silvana Cirillo, **Nei dintorni del surrealismo: Alvaro, Buzzati, De Chirico, Delfini, Landolfi, Malerba, Savinio, Zavattini*, Ro, Lithos, 2000, 155 pp.

The cultural impact of journals in the years 1895–1923 is explored in a series of articles: Giuseppe Langella: 'La parabola delle avanguardie (1895–1923) — Il secolo delle riviste', *Poesia*, 147: 47–52, which looks in particular at the influence exerted by *Il Convito*, *Il Marzocco*, and *La Critica* in those years; 'Lo *Sturm und Drang* fiorentino', *ib.*, 148: 47–50, indicating the role played by *Medusa*, *Hermes*, and *Il Regno* at that time; 'Apprendisti stregoni', *ib.*, 149: 61–64, discussing the varying idealistic stances adopted in the pages of *Leonardo*; 'Fermenti religiosi', *ib.*, 150: 55–58, outlining the many journals (such as *Luce e ombra*, *Ultra*, *La Nuova Parola*, *Cultura sociale*, *L'Ateneo letterario-artistico*, *Athenea*, *Studi religiosi*, *Rivista storico-critica delle scienze teologiche*, *Nova et vetera*, *Coenobium*, *Rinnovamento*, *Torre*, and *San Giorgio*) that supported distinctive religious ferments in the same period; 'Saldi principî', *ib.*, 151: 53–56, discussing the contribution made by *Vita e pensiero* and *L'anima* to Italian culture in those years; 'Il partito degli intellettuali', *ib.*, 152:65–68, looking at the contribution made by figures such as Papini, Prezzolini, and Croce to the intellectual discourse; 'Dalla *Voce* all'Unità', *ib.*, 153:55–59; 'Riviste di poesia', *ib.*, 154:43–46, examining the role played by journals such as *La riviera ligure, L'eroica, Cronache latine, Il campo, La rassegna latina, La vita letteraria, Poesia*, and *Lirica*; 'Saper leggere', *ib.*, 156:57–61, detailing the role played by De Robertis's *Saper leggere* in the ongoing discourse on poetry and prose at that time. M. Di Gesù, 'Una avanguardia postmoderna?', *Italianistica*, 30:117–36, argues that the neo-avantgarde has close connections with postmodernism, and indeed constitutes its predecessor, and that an understanding of the neo-avantgarde allows better understanding of contemporary literature.

AnI, 19, ed. Dino S. Cervigni and entitled *Literature, criticism and ethics*, includes an introd. by C. (7–24), who partly links the issue to the events of 11 September 2001, and a number of essays on 20th-c. Italian literature and ethics from a variety of angles: C. Klopp (93–102) reflects on 'the return of the spiritual' after recent political changes in Italy with reference in particular to Bufalino, Tabucchi, and Celati; A. Casadei (103–18) observes that, especially in the 20th c., difficulties in considering the moral values of literature occurred which were due to the importance attached to textuality over content, but that co-operation between author and reader in modern literature may contribute to identify ethical aspects; and he gives examples from the work of several writers including Vitaliano Brancati, Giuseppe Pontiggia, Camilla Baresani, Diego De Silva, and Walter Siti; N. Bouchard (119–36) concentrates on Vincenzo Consolo's claim that his work has an 'ethical status' while his 'aesthetic practice' belongs in the amoral post-rationalist approach of postmodernity, and it is through his experimental narrative structures that he confronts moral truths and conflicts (see also 'La strategia del coro' under CONSOLO) below; S. Shankman (137–52) writes on 'ethics, transcendence and the other' in Marco Polo's *Il Milione* and Italo Calvino's *Le città invisibili*; A. M. Jannet (153–70) considers 'A matter of injustice: violence and death in Antonio Tabucchi'; T. E. Peterson (171–88) discusses ethics and pathos in Giuseppe Ungaretti's work; N. Pireddu (190–214) builds on the relationship between literature and science, and in particular on Martin Heidegger's concept of *techne*, in order to examine the ethical questions posed in a tech-nological era by Primo Levi's *La chiave a stella* and Daniele Del Giudice's *Atlante occidentale*, and concludes that these two writers do not abolish myth, or unmask the false neutrality of technology, but rather 'show that it is possible to re-enchant the world through technology itself'; R. Gordon (215–34) maps out Primo Levi's 'ordinary virtues' which constitute the foundation of his ethical preoccupations; S. Parussa (235–44) writes about 'Literature in question: figuring Auschwitz and redefining literature in the post-Holocaust theatre' (235–44); G. Gaeta (245–54) examines the ethical and political implications of Nicola Chiaromonte's views on intellectuals and society; A. Montani (255–68) analyses Giorgio Manganelli's 'etica dell'intelligenza', questions Manganelli's claim to an amoral and lying kind of literature, and shows how this writer's morality consists in his acceptance of the metaphorical and existential dimension of Hell; and F. Parmeggiani (269–83) meditates on 'Morselli e il tempo' especially in relation to eternity and the end of history.

Some essays include geographical aspects or deal with metaphorical and actual travel. *Tirature 01*, ed. Vittorio Spinazzola, Mi, Fond. Mondadori, 304 pp., includes a section (10–95) on a sociological geography of literature, and in particular on city, country, and other types of settings in modern Italian fiction. Vittorio Spinazzola, *Itaca, addio: Vittorini, Pavese, Meneghello, Satta: il romanzo del ritorno*, Mi, Il Saggiatore, 256 pp., is a study of time, syntax, autobiography, and other aspects of narrative journeys to the native lands where the authors examined rediscover their roots, test their degree of nostalgia for the archaic realities where they came from but are also aware of an existential progress towards the modern society which they embrace willingly in spite of their sympathy for the past. Gaia De Pascale, *Scrittori in viaggio. Narratori e poeti italiani del Novecento in giro per il mondo*, T, Bollati Boringhieri, 248 pp., is partly devoted to travel in general (9–17) and mostly to specific Italian authors travelling to the U.S.A., Latin America, India, and European countries. A particular aspect of the geography of literature is regional identity as in *La letteratura romanesca del secondo Novecento*, ed. Franco Onorati and Marcello Teodonio, Ro, Bulzoni, 337 pp., which contains the proceedings of a 1998 conference held in Rome.

Giosuè Salvatore Ciccia, **Il pessimismo nella storia della letteratura italiana contemporanea*, Soveria Mannelli, Rubbettino, 211 pp. *SpR*, 15, 2000, is entitled 'The prostitute in Italian society, art and literature', and includes essays by N. Castronuovo on Alberto Moravia's *La romana* and by E. Giordano on Stefano D'Arrigo's *Horcynus Orca*. L. Terruzzi, 'I nomi e la critica: un decennio di studi di onomastica letteraria in Italia', *Italianistica*, 30:365–92, surveys recent work on literary names, and identifies some of their structural and intertextual functions.

Other essays focus on various aspects of the history of criticism. Alberto Casadei, *La critica letteraria del Novecento*, Bo, Il Mulino, 210 pp., is a repertoire of schools of thought in criticism, with brief descriptions of most theories and more detailed treatment of certain critics such as Roland Barthes and Harold Bloom. Massimiliano Capati, *Il maestro abnorme. Benedetto Croce e l'Italia del Novecento*, F, Pagliai Polistampa, 2000, 166 pp., re-evaluates C.'s thought and his influence on Italian culture in spite of a recent decline in his popularity. *Giacomo Debenedetti: l'arte del leggere*, ed. Emilio Jona and Vanni Scheiwiller, Mi, Scheiwiller, 135 pp., contains papers from a conference on D. held in Biella in 1996. A. Borghesi, 'Cronaca di un'interpretazione mancata: il critico Debenedetti e lo scrittore Mussolini', *ParL*, 33–34–35:3–34, highlights D.'s view of literature as independent from politics and his isolation from Turin academic circles, and argues that D.'s article favourable to Benito Mussolini was the only compromise he made with Fascism. R. S. Dombrowski, 'Timpanaro in retrospect', *Italica*, 78:337–50, re-appreciates T.'s work after his death. On publishing: *Tutti i nostri mercoledì*, Bellinzona, Casagrande, 140 pp., an interview between Giulio Einaudi and Paolo Di Stefano, reviews E.'s career as a publisher and intellectual.

A number of essays focus on writers and politics. Arcangelo Leone De Castris, *Intellettuali del Novecento: tra scienza e coscienza*, Venice, Marsilio, 174 pp. Angelo D'Orsi, *Intellettuali nel Novecento italiano*, T, Einaudi, 374 pp., includes an introd., 'Gli intellettuali e l'etica della responsabilità' (3–36), where the intellectual question is seen as fundamental in the 20th c., and interpretations by Benda, Gramsci, and others are also reviewed. Intellectuals, though at times significantly engaged, appear to have been on the whole powerless in influencing politics or inadequate in their responsibilities towards society. There are also chapters on Giovanni Gentile, Marino Parenti, and Fascist culture (37–69), Aldo Capitini (70–145), Edoardo Persico (146–253), and Carlo Levi (254–356). See also 'La strategia del coro' under CONSOLO, below.

On women writers: Anna Folli, *Penne leggère. Neera, Ada Negri, Sibilla Aleramo. Scritture femminili italiane fra Otto e Novecento*, Mi, Guerrini e Associati, 256 pp., wonders if there is such a thing as 'letteratura al femminile' and how it is connected to life, and then examines the controversial relationship between works produced by women and their critical reception. On women's writing: Paola Azzolini, *Il cielo vuoto dell'eroina: scrittura e identità femminile nel Novecento italiano*, introd. Marina Zancan, Ro, Bulzoni, 239 pp. *Donne: due secoli di scrittura femminile in Sardegna 1775–1950. Repertorio bibliografico*, ed. Franca Ferraris Cornaglia, introd. by Laura Pisano, Cagliari, CUEC, 355 pp. In S. Branciforte, *'In a different voice: women writing World War II', *Della Terza Vol.*, 433–42, a feminine perpective of the War is found and studied in the writings of Renata Viganò and Liana Millu. *A History of Italian Women's Writing in Italy*, ed. Letizia Panizza and

Sharon Wood, CUP, 2000, 361 pp., provides a widely comprehensive assessment of the work of Italian women writers from 1350 to the closing years of the twentieth century. Essays which cover the latter include: S. Patriarca, 'Journalists and essayists' (151–63); L. Kroha, 'The novel, 1870–1920' (164–76); A. L. Lepschy, 'The popular novel, 1850–1920' (177–89); L. Re, 'Futurism and Fascism, 1914–1945' (190–204); A. Hallamore Caesar, 'The novel, 1945–1965' (205–17); A. Giorgio, 'The novel, 1965–2000' (218–37); C. O'Brien, 'Poetry, 1870–2000' (238–53); A. O'Healy, 'Theatre and cinema, 1945–2000' (254–66); S. Wood, 'Aesthetics and critical theory' (267–81). Both the 'Bibliographical guide to women writers and their work', ed. P. Morris (282–337) and the bibliography (338–50) offer useful updated references to individual women and cultural movements of the time.

2. POETRY

Il pensiero dominante. Poesia italiana 1970–2000, ed. Franco Loi and Davide Rondoni, Mi, Garzanti, 442 pp., is a collection of more than 150 poets whose work, over the last 30 years, has caught the attention of these two anthologists for a variety of reasons. The introduction (7–19) provides a brief sketch of developments in the 20th c. and an updated biography is presented for each poet. Oreste Macrì, *Realtà del simbolo. Poeti e critici del Novecento italiano*, pref. Anna Dolfi, Trento, La Finestra, xli + 649 pp. *Poesia del Novecento in Italia e in Europa*, ed. Edoardo Esposito, Mi, Feltrinelli, 2000, 2 vols, xx + 370, xx + 324 pp. G. Cavallini, ' "La scintilla che dice": su alcune sinestesie nella poesia italiana contemporanea', *CLett*, 29:345–53. N. Gardini, 'Considerazioni sullo stilnovismo novecentesco: il modello della *Vita Nova*', *Italianistica*, 29, 2000[2001]:445–50. R. Galaverni, 'Seguendo il luogo dei poeti', *NArg*, 12, 2000:288–334. M. M. Pedroni, 'Poesia ciclistica delle origini. Betteloni, Cannizzaro, Gozzano, Pascoli, Stecchetti', *Versants*, 40:185–206, outlines the role assigned to the bicycle in works by these poets. Francesco M. Chiancone, **Incontri con la poesia: Cesare Angelini, David M. Turoldo, Giuseppe Ungaretti, Ada Negri, Trilussa*, Pavia, Ponzio, 1999, 157 pp. *Poesia italiana dell'Ottocento e Novecento. Antologia personale di Vittorio Gassman*, Ro, Sossella, 2000, 176 pp., includes four CD-Roms to present the texts and readings of the most important poems of these centuries, which are recited by Gassman.

Several articles explore contrasting intertextual links between poets: S. Prandi, 'Montale, Sereni, Erba: i segni e la morte', *REI*, 46, 2000:209–30; R. de Rooy, 'Osservazioni su narratività e poesia moderna. Il secondo Montale *versus* il grande Caproni', *Moderna*, 2.2, 2000:123–36; F. Ricci, 'Sulle tracce del *tu*. Percorsi intertestuali nella

poesia di Luzi e di Montale', *SPCT*, 63:165–86; G. Bonacci
Gazzarrini, 'Tre poeti: Montale, Caproni, Luzi, nella patria dell'anima', *Cenobio*, 50:206–19. P. Pellini, 'Pretesto Montale, Ungaretti: la
divulgazione nelle università', *Il Ponte*, 57.4, 132–40, questions the
rejection by Italian academics of volumes by Enrico Testa on Montale
and Andrea Cortellessa on Ungaretti, and wonders if they will ever
find favour with university departments of Italian in Italy now that
the three year *laurea breve* is an integral part of university syllabuses.
R. Bettarini, 'Palazzeschi e Moretti', *RLI*, 104, 2000:448–50.
F. D'Alessandro, 'Sergio Solmi e Vittorio Sereni: un'amicizia poetica
novecentesca (con una conversazione inedita di V. Sereni)', *Italianistica*, 30:95–114, details the intellectual friendship between S. and
Sereni, and presents the hitherto unpublished text of Sereni's tribute
to S. which appeared in November 1982, one year after his death.
R. Manica, 'Debenedetti e Solmi', *NArg*, 15:164–75, identifies
affinities that united the two men in thought and written word. Pablo
Echaurren, *Vite di poeti. Campana, Majakovskij, Pound*, T, Bollati
Boringhieri, 2000, 109 pp., deals with anecdotes that characterize the
heroic lives of these poets for the author (poet, painter, and writer).
M. Pieracci Harwell, 'Una religione del sud', *CV*, 56:133–42,
examines the theme of destiny (which she equates with the 'religione
del sud') in certain poems by Enzo Agostino and Mario Luzi. Maria
Sabrina Titone, *Cantiche del Novecento. Dante nell'opera di Luzi e Pasolini*,
F, Olschki, 226 pp.

Baci ardenti di vita. Poeti contro la pena di morte, ed. Michelangelo
Camilliti e Donato Di Poce, Como, Lietocollelibri, 54 pp., collects
the reactions in prose and poetry of a number of contemporary poets
opposed to the death penalty. Paola Bianco, *Tra ermetismo e realismo.
La poesia siciliana da Quasimodo a Cattafi e ad Aliberti*, Foggia, Bastogi,
1999, 117 pp.

Some attention has also been paid to recent Italo-American poetry:
M. Marazzi, 'Poesia degli italoamericani', *Poesia*, 149:52–59, looks at
such poetry in the early years of the 20th c. and pays particular
attention to the work of Riccardo Cordiferro (1875–1940); Id.,
'Poesia degli italoamericani', *Poesia*, 151:58–69, outlines the particular dimensions of the poetry of the 'molisano' Arturo Giovannitti
(1884–1959). A. Ciccarelli, 'Writing (from) abroad: Italian writing in
the United States', *Italica*, 78:221–46, focuses on two books of poetry
(Luigi Fontanella's *Round Trip*, 1991, and Alessandro Carrera's *La
sposa perfetta — The Perfect Bride*, 1997) together with two works of
fiction (Paolo Valesio's novella *S'incontrano gli amanti*, 1993, and Franco
Ferrucci's novel *Lontano da casa*, 1996). P. Bartoloni, 'Poetry of
bilingualism: a review of Daniele Pieroni's *Passi esornativi e una
palinodia*', *FoI*, 35:568–74.

On dialect poetry: G. Turra, 'Senc che gnesuni pi romài intenz. Poesia e dialetto in Luciano Cecchinel', *QVen*, 33:143–72. Paola Campanile, **Pignarûl: suoni, colori, parlata valtellinese e friulana*, Venice, Marsilio, 113 pp., is a collection of poems, some in Valtellinese or Friulan.

3. NARRATIVE, THEATRE.

Margherita Ganeri, *Il romanzo storico in Italia. Il dibattito critico dalle origini al postmoderno*, Lecce, Manni, 168 pp., reconstructs old and recent debates on the historical novel, and investigates its complex status as a literary genre partly to be ascribed to popular literature and partly to serious fiction. Also on the historical novel, M. Jansen, 'History as a peripheral event? "Marginal" historical novels by three Italian writers: Loy, Pazzi, and Tabucchi', *Text*, 29:151–61, observes that postmodernist writers of historical novels, as Umberto Eco notes, construct and deconstruct history to the point that literature becomes 'invented historiography'; she ascribes renewed interest in the historical novel partly to the decline of ideology, and goes on to examine Roberto Pazzi's 'symbolical truth' in *Cercando l'imperatore*, Rosetta Loy's sense of history as a 'series of missed opportunities', and Antonio Tabucchi's existentialist and ontological philosophy, combined with his dimension of reality as a field of open possibilities. Niva Lorenzini, *Le maschere di Felicita. Pratiche di riscrittura e travestimento da Leopardi a Gadda*, Lecce, Manni, 160 pp., explores some aspects of intertextuality including parody, rewriting of previous texts, quotations, and repetition in a number of modern Italian writers including Guido Gozzano, Giorgio Caproni, and Carlo Emilio Gadda.

Based on social anthropology applied to literature, R. Nisticò, 'Ernesto De Martino e la teoria della letteratura', *Belfagor*, 56:269–86, argues that some theories of the Italian anthropologist Ernesto De Martino on tragic expression and rituals could be used to create an anthropological and existential theory of literature.

On the novel in general is **La cultura del romanzo*, ed. Franco Moretti, T, Einaudi, 919 pp. Geno Pampaloni, *Scritti letterari*, ed. Giuseppe Leonelli, T, Bollati Boringhieri, 544 pp., affords a survey of P.'s work as a critic by gathering his reviews and essays on numerous writers (including Calvino, Gadda, Luzi, Montale, and Fortini), and ends with an historical itinerary through 20th-c. Italian literature.

On comic fiction: Walter Pedullà, *Le armi del comico*, Mi, Mondadori, 314 pp., shows how farce questions conformism and comedy catches readers by surprise and disrupts their ordinary expectations, and also discusses a number of authors including Achille Campanile, Aldo Palazzeschi, Luigi Pirandello, Luigi Malerba, and Stefano Benni.

On detective fiction: Luca Crovi, *I delitti di carta nostra. Una storia del giallo italiano*, Bo, Punto Zero, 2000, 127 pp., is a repertoire of authors and stories from Emilio De Marchi's *La mano nera* (1883) to the novels of Carlo Lucarelli and his contemporaries. *SpR*, 16, 104 pp., a special issue entitled 'Il giallo', includes the following articles: G. Traina, 'Appunti sulla più recente letteratura poliziesca italiana' (5–16), on Umberto Eco's *Il nome della rosa*, Carlo Lucarelli, Andrea Camilleri, Sandrone Dazieri, and others; A. Di Grado (33–35) and J. Vizmuller-Zocco (36–43) on Camilleri; M. Chu (45–58) on Lucarelli's use of language and stereotypes from the angle of post-colonial critical theory; G. Adamo, 'Inizi e fini del romanzo giallo' (59–89), on thrillers' semantic, stylistic, and rhetorical aspects.

M. Jansen, 'Verso il nuovo millennio: rappresentazione dell'apocalisse nella narrativa italiana contemporanea (Benni, Busi, Vassalli)', *Narrativa*, 20–21:131–50, sees Stefano Benni, Aldo Busi, and Sebastiano Vassalli, in spite of differences in their style, as similar moral writers inside the framework of postmodernism but, in the case of Benni in particular, at the same time close to the Enlightenment and partly indebted to the praise of reason in Leonardo Sciascia's *Candido* and to the combined apocalyptic and comic dimensions of Umberto Eco's *Il nome della rosa*.

Marco Ariani and Giorgio Taffon, *Scritture per la scena*, Ro, Carocci, 320 pp., is a history of Italian theatre, including recent authors and in particular Dario Fo, Edoardo Sanguineti, and Giuliano Scabia. General information on various levels is given in *Teatro in Italia '98: cifre, dati, novità della stagione di prosa 1997–98*, Ro, SIAE, 1999, xxvi + 358 pp. *I fuoriscena: esperienze e riflessioni sulla drammaturgia nel sociale*, ed. Claudio Bernardi, Benvenuto Cuminetti, and Sisto Dalla Palma, Mi, Euresis, 358 pp, examines some social uses of theatre. Sisto Dalla Palma, **Il teatro e gli orizzonti del sacro*, Mi, Vita e Pensiero, 206 pp. *Il teatro di regia alle soglie del terzo millennio*, Ro, Bulzoni, 404 pp., includes essays by L. Cavaglieri on Luca Ronconi (35–52), by M. Cambiaghi on Luigi Squarzina (107–28), by D. Ruocco on Mario Missiroli (143–55), and others by A. Bentoglio, A. Camaldo, M. Covecchi, and A. Piletti Franzini. *Intervista sul teatro*, Palermo, Sellerio, 175 pp., is an interview by Luciano Lucignani with Vittorio Gassman.

4. INDIVIDUAL AUTHORS

ARBASINO. *Alberto Arbasino*, ed. Marco Belpoliti and Elio Grazioli, Mi, Marcos y Marcos (*Riga*, 18), 410 pp., includes texts by Arbasino (23–88) and interviews with him (89–141), together with published and previously unpublished essays on his work by Pietro Citati, Mario Fortunato, Giuliano Gramigna, Angelo Guglielmi, Nico Orengo,

Geno Pampaloni, Giuliano Scabia, and several other contributors. It constitutes a positive reappraisal of his work on the occasion of his 70th birthday. *La scrittura infinita di Alberto Arbasino*, ed. Elisabetta Cammarata, Cinzia Lucchelli, and Clelia Martignani, Mi, Interlinea, 1999, 125 pp., includes a previously unpublished text by A. on Ennio Flaiano, and three essays on A.'s novel *Fratelli d'Italia*: C. Martignani, 'Arbasino, la coscienza della complessità' (7–22), highlights antinaturalism, narrative procedures, and encyclopedic interests; C. Lucchelli, 'Sull'elaborazione culturale e stilistica di *Fratelli d'Italia*' (23–68), studies constant and variable aspects in the different versions of the novel; and E. Cammarata, 'Il rinnovamento dell'edizione '93' (69–110), analyses the structure and themes (travel, society, individuality, and family) of the 1993 version.

BALDINI. Raffaello Baldini, *Page Proof*, ed. Daniele Benati, Boca Raton, Bordighera Press, 54 pp., is a translation by A. Bernardi of B.'s Romagnol dialect play *Carta canta*. Benati also includes an interview with B. (1–9) and an assessment of his dialect writing (41–50).

BARICCO. Claudio Pezzin, *Alessandro Baricco*, Sommacampagna, Cierre, 114 pp. E. Bellavia, 'La lingua di Alessandro Baricco', *ON*, 25.1:135–68.

BARILLI. A. Castronovo, 'Stilista con idee — Bruno Barilli', *Belfagor*, 56:595–600.

BASSANI. Alberto Toni, *Con Bassani verso Ferrara*, Mi, Unicopli, 110 pp., is about the reality of Fascism in Ferrara and in B.'s work.

BERNARI. R. Capozzi, 'Arti visive e nuova oggettività nel primo Bernari', *FoI*, 35:140–62.

BERTI SABBIETTI. D. Fabiani, 'L'universo poetico di Rosa Berti Sabbietti: un itinerario nella luce', *QFLR*, 15, 2000:55–80.

BERTOLUCCI. G. Palli Baroni, 'La "patria poetica" di Attilio Bertolucci', *NArg*, 14:354–65, looks at the centrality of Parma and the surrounding countryside in B.'s poetry. Mariagiulia Castellari, *Attilio Bertolucci. La trama dei giorni da ricordare*, Faenza, Mobydick, 105 pp., examines the concept of time in B.'s poetry both in terms of a vital, existential drive, and as an aspect of the literary rhythm that flows in his texts.

BETOCCHI. G. Falaschi, 'Luigina Stefani nell'officina di Betocchi', *Belfagor*, 56:363–70, recounts difficulties faced by S. in 1984 while attempting to compile the complete ed. of B.'s poems, *Tutte le poesie*, and at the same time *La biblioteca e l'officina di Betocchi* (Bulzoni 1994), which provides detailed descriptions of the Betocchi poetry archives and a critically edited selection of 40 texts from B.'s œuvre. P. Turroni, 'Betocchi e Campana: riconoscimento di un maestro', *LetP*, 31.2:3–9, details B.'s acute critical presentation of C.'s poetry together with his efforts to have C.'s work fully appreciated.

BETTI. J. C. de Miguel, 'Progressione drammaturgica in Ugo Betti: da *Frana allo scalo nord* a *Corruzione al palazzo di giustizia*', *StIt*, 24, 2000:95–109.

BIAMONTI. E. Fenzi, 'Toponomastica e antroponomastica in Biamonti', *Il nome nel testo*, 2–3, 2000–01:61–76, shows how real and imagined place names in B.'s novels partly reflect the Franco-Ligurian border and partly an interaction between reality and myth.

BIANCIARDI. Irene Gambacorti, **Luciano Bianciardi: bibliografia 1948–1998*, F, Società Editrice Fiorentina, 339 pp.

BIGIARETTI. L. Fontanella, 'Parasurrealismo espressionista di Libero Bigiaretti', pp. 89–101 of *Libero Bigiaretti: la storia, le idee, la scrittura*, ed. Alfredo Luzi, Fossombrone, Metauro, 282 pp., examines expressionistic and surrealistic influences in B.'s short fiction from *Uccidi e muori* to *Abitare altrove*.

BIGONGIARI. T. O'Neill, 'Bigongiari verso il nuovo millennio', *Italica*, 78:247–55, reviews three books (two by Bigongiari) that contain critical evaluations of B. together with a selection of his letters, essays, and unpublished poems. In his assessment of B. the author places him on the same poetic level as Seamus Heaney. Piero Bigongiari, *La poesia pensa. Poesie e pensieri inediti*, F, Olschki, 1999, ix + 302 pp., includes the poems and thoughts (3–238); E. Del Lungo, 'Introduzione' (ix-x); E. Biagini, 'Prefazione, (xi–xxii); A. Noferi, 'Teoria, poesia e "confessione" nell'ultimo Bigongiari' (241–59) and P. F. Iacuzzi, 'L'ipotesto, laboratorio della "mens divinior"' (261–70), and 'Note ai testi' (271–97).

BILENCHI. C. Nesi, 'Dodici lettere inedite di Franco Calamandrei a Romano Bilenchi', *Autografo*, 42:125–48.

BO. *Carlo Bo – Giuseppe De Luca, Carteggio 1932–1961*, ed. Marta Bruscia, Ro, Storia e Letteratura, 1999, xx + 313 pp. S. Pautasso, 'Carlo Bo e la poetica del diario', *Poesia*, 148:17–20, details the 'diaristic' dimension to B.'s writing in prose and poetry.

BONAVIRI. Franco Musarra, *Scrittura della memoria. Memoria della scrittura. L'opera narrativa di Giuseppe Bonaviri*, Leuven–F, Leuven U.P., 1999, 131 pp. *Minuetto con Bonaviri*, ed. Roberto Bertoni, Dublin, Trinity College – T, Trauben, 100 pp., includes: R. Bertoni, 'Minuetto con Bonaviri' (15–65), an interview conducted by the two editors in which Bonaviri underlines the importance of autobiography in his work, offers a biological interpretation of art, gives his views on language, dreams, allegories, symbols, and texts such as the fragments of the pre-Socratics and the *Upanishad*; S. Zappulla Muscarà, 'L'incantevole mondo di Giuseppe Bonaviri' (9–13) on B.'s magic realism combined with lyricism; and R. Bertoni, 'Trasposizioni

letterarie (Note su alcuni aspetti dell'opera di Giuseppe Bonaviri)'
(66–97), on B.'s poetics of the sacrality of writing, the fantastic, and
intertextuality. Id., 'A non insular islander: presentation of Giuseppe
Bonaviri on the occasion of his visit to Ireland', *Italia & Italy*, 10, 5–7,
highlights the importance of history, myth, and folklore in B.'s work.
Carmine Di Biase, *Bonaviri e l'oltre. L'opera intera*, Na, ESI, 364 pp.,
articulates the concept of 'oltre' in B.'s work as a terrain stretching
beyond everyday life into the cosmic, a circular vision of the self,
time, and space, a passage from reality to dream and from the
material to the immaterial universe, and a journey into interiority.
Other aspects are grouped under the headings: time, cosmos, poetry,
myth, fable, essays, and analogy.

BONTEMPELLI. L. Fontanella, *'La poesia di Massimo Bontem-
pelli: tra crepuscolarismo e sperimentalismo futurista', *Della Terza
Vol.*, 307–12, briefly reappraises B.'s one verse collection, *Purosangue –
L'Ubriaco*, written 1916–18.

BORGESE. Luciano Parisi, *Borgese*, T, Tirrenia, 2000, 96 pp.,
includes a number of previously published articles but some of these
are re-elaborated, and the whole volume constitutes a monographic
work on B. where his spiritual, political, and literary itineraries are
examined and reconstructed.

BRAMBILLA. C. Annoni, 'La lentezza dell'essere e il gioco del
pallone. Studi su *Viola come il sangue* di Alberto Brambilla', *Cenobio*,
50 : 36–44.

BRANCATI. Massimo Schilirò, **Narciso in Sicilia. Lo spazio autobiografico nell'opera di Vitaliano Brancati*, Na, Liguori, 220 pp.

BUZZATI. *Studi buzzatiani*, 5, 2000, includes two studies by
F. Linari on the diary form in B.'s work and by G. Sandrini on the
intertextual influence of Giacomo Leopardi on B., essays by T. Bertol-
din, S. Basili, and A. Brambilla, a 1998 bibliography by M. Gallina,
and a number of articles on various topics. C. Gaiba, 'La porta
socchiusa. Il realismo di Dino Buzzati', *Intersezioni*, 21 : 335–48,
observes that B.'s fiction is based on a series of variations on a limited
number of themes (such as time and solitude) portrayed through
imagery (e.g. the wind, mountains, and animals), and argues that his
fantastic stories are not particularly inventive but that their literary
value rests mainly on a disquieting proximity between fantasy and
daily life. A. Gramone, 'Dino Buzzati's journalism: reporting from
the borderline', *Neohelicon*, 27 : 179–89, identifies a borderline terrain
between literature and journalism, and reality and fantasy, in B.'s
articles for *Il corriere della sera* published as 'Cronache terrestri'. Pietro
Biaggi, **Buzzati: i luoghi del mistero*, Padua, Messaggero, 142 pp.

CALVINO. Alberto Asor Rosa, *Stile Calvino*, T, Einaudi,
xiv + 170 pp., includes five previously published essays and an introd.

in which C.'s work is seen as highly innovative but at the same time linked to the classics, as a balanced attempt to combine reason and fantasy, the individual and the cosmos, positive and negative aspects of the human condition, and as a system of literary values interwoven with a responsible sense of ethics and social commitment. Mario Lavagetto, *Dovuto a Calvino*, T, Bollati Boringhieri, 150 pp., presents some previously published texts together with three unpublished essays on C.'s minimalism (87–113), *Lezioni americane* (117–33), and interest in Balzac (34–48), and sees C. as an experimental writer different from (or perhaps even alien to) but more advanced than the avantgarde.

A number of essays are on specific works by Calvino: A. Battistini, 'Le città visibili e invisibili di Italo Calvino', *EL*, 26.2:21–38, identifies some relations between the cities imagined in *Le città invisibili* and some of the cities experienced by C. in real life (Genoa, New York, Paris, Turin, and Venice), and concludes that in his work the concept of city stands for knowledge, existence, and human fears and aspirations in a modern society. A. Camps, 'Principio senza fine: l'iper-romanzo di Italo Calvino', *AnI*, 18, 2000:309–26, is about fragmentation, nothingness, and narrative strategies in *Se una notte d'inverno un viaggiatore*. Nunzio Li Fauci, *Marcovaldo e altri soggetti pericolosi*, Ro, Meltemi, 168 pp., reflects on the roles of reader and writer in C.'s *Marcovaldo*. C. Nocentini, 'Sense of self and familiarity with places in Italo Calvino's "La nuvola di smog"', *Journal of Mediterranean Studies*, 10, 2000:173–82, highlights C.'s problematic literary rendering of autobiographical places, such as the Sanremo landscape of sea, city, and hills, then focuses on the theme of moving to new places in 'La nuvola di smog'. Francesca Salvemini, **Il realismo fantastico di Italo Calvino*, Ro, Edizioni Associate, 71 pp.

CAMILLERI. **Andrea Camilleri*, ed. Giovanni Capecchi, Fiesole, Cadmo, 2000, 125 pp. Simona Demontis, *I colori della letteratura: un'indagine sul caso Camilleri*, Mi, Rizzoli, 292 pp., identifies narrative procedures (in particular typology of characters, intertextual reference and types of plot), sees C.'s implicit readers in part as a broad popular audience but also as a well-read public (especially in the stories set in the 19th-c.), and analyses his language in relation to standard Italian, dialect, and innovative language experiments. Armando Vitale, *Il mondo del commissario Montalbano. Considerazioni sulle opere di Andrea Camilleri*, Caltanissetta, Terzo Millennio, 124 pp.

CAMPANA. A. Mastropasqua, 'Citazione e allegoria nella *Genova* di Dino Campana: la costellazione Nietzsche–Baudelaire', *Avanguardia*, 15:73–88.

CAMPANILE. Giorgio Cavallini, *Estro inventivo e tecnica narrativa di Achille Campanile*, Ro, Bulzoni, 98 pp., shows how narrative structures contribute to comic effects in C.'s work.

CAMPO, C. P. Pòlito, 'Lettere a Mita di Cristina Campo rivisitate dalla Harwell', *CV*, 56:63–70, details Campo's intellectual background, her friendship with 'Mita', her predilection for Russian literature, and the intrinsic value of Harwell's friendship for her both as a poet and person. S. Carando, 'Davanti alla tomba di Cristina Campo: "il vero" e "la verità" ', *CV*, 56:355–60, considers the 'vero' or starkness of the inscription on Campo's tomb at the Certosa in Bologna and contrasts it with the immediacy or 'verità' of emotion in C.'s writings.

CAMPO, R. G. A. Viazmenski, 'Cinema as negotiation in Rossana Campo's *L'attore americano*', *Italica*, 78:203–20, notes how the female voice and experience dominate in C.'s novels and how women characters interact with life and society. Some filmic aspects of C.'s work are also examined.

CAPRONI. R. Scarpa, 'Tecniche reticenti nella poesia di Giorgio Caproni', *LS*, 36:189–202, provides an analysis of intuitions and allusions prevalent in C.'s poetry. C. Caracchini, 'Il linguaggio poetico nell'opera di Giorgio Caproni: a caccia di significato', *StCrit*, 15, 2000:151–66.

CASCELLA. S. Zafferani, 'Il peso della leggerezza. Sulla poesia di Anna Cascella', *Kamen*, 9.1, 2000:103–117, has a helpful bibliography (127–32) on this poet; P. Febbraro, 'La poesia di Anna Cascella. Una lettura in forma di discorso', *ib.*, 9.1, 2000:119–25, is based on an analysis of poems taken from Cascella's *Tesoro da nulla* (1990).

CELATI. G. Iacoli, 'Per una teoria della geografia letteraria nel postmoderno. Celati: paesaggi, derive', *Intersezioni*, 21:109–34, argues that C.'s nostalgia for the meaningful traits of a lost pre-industrial world is the foundation of a postmodern Utopia which consists in adopting both local and global perspectives, taking an oblique look at things, illustrating changes in geographical and social landscapes, and showing an awareness of difficulties in the interpretation of reality.

CHIARA. E. G. Caserta, *'Motivi dominanti e personaggi in *Una spina nel cuore* di Chiara', *Della Terza Vol.*, 405–12, harks back to a 1993 article published in *CJIS* (see *YWMLS*, 56:602).

CONSOLO. 'La strategia del coro. Intervista a Vincenzo Consolo', *Versodove*, 13:68–71, is an interview conducted by A. Di Prima where C. notes that politically committed and artistically developed writers are often marginalized. He reiterates the ethical value of literature linked to the value of aesthetics, highlights the importance of experimental language in a mass society, and advocates the need for serious research in criticism. See also *Colpi di penna, colpi di spada* under SCIASCIA, below.

CULICCHIA. L. Rorato, 'La realtà metropolitana del 2000: *Ambarabà* di Giuseppe Culicchia e *City* di Alessandro Baricco', *Narrativa*, 20–21:243–61.

D'ARZO. R. Carnero, '"E domani sarà lunedì". I racconti per ragazzi di Silvio D'Arzo', *RLI*, 104:451–62, evaluates D.'s stories for children as being some of his most stylistically perfect works.

DE ANGELIS. F. Ermini, 'Fuori luogo. Radice ed erranza in Milo De Angelis, Giampiero Neri, Ida Travi', *Testuale*, 28–29, 2000:49–58.

DE FILIPPO. Angelo Puglisi, *In casa Cupiello. Edoardo critico del populismo*, Ro, Donzelli, 117 pp., argues against D.'s *populismo* and in favour of his adherence to truth in his political and realist dimensions.

DE LIBERO. G. Lupo, 'Dalla *Genesi* all'*Apocalisse*: De Libero poeta biblico', *ON*, 25.1:87–133, assesses the echoes of the Bible in De L.'s poetry.

DE LUCA. M. Spunta, 'Struck by silence: a reading of Erri De Luca's *I colpi dei sensi*', *Italica*, 78:367–86.

DE PADOVA. E. N. Girardi, 'L'opera poetica di Michele De Padova', *Testo*, 42:91–128.

DE SIGNORIBUS. S. Morando, '"ti offro la parola che va da sola/ – fratello – ". Nota a margine di *Principio del giorno* di Eugenio De Signoribus', *Nuova Corrente*, 127:127–34, is a reference to De S.'s conviction that words are a link rather than a barrier between poet and reader.

DI BIASIO. A. Zambardi, 'Il percorso poetico-narrativo di Rodolfo Di Biasio', *Il Veltro*, 44, 2000:426–40.

ECO. F. Ferrucci, 'Eco e Manzoni', *NArg*, 13:142–50, illustrates Alessandro Manzoni's influence on E.'s novels (especially at the levels of a compatible concern for the historical novel and a search for an authentic language), but also detects their divergent approaches to the aesthetics of the baroque and the world vision of Catholicism. G. Corrado, 'Sulle trace dell'infinito: il *Baudolino* di Umberto Eco', *Il Ponte*, 57.4:109–15. T. Stauder, 'Un colloquio con Umberto Eco intorno a *Baudolino*', *LetP*, 110–11:3–14.

FENOGLIO. Peter Cooke, *Fenoglio's Binoculars, Johnny's Eyes*, NY, Lang, 2000, 160 pp., examines F.'s narrative procedures, his depiction of the Resistance movement, and his pessimistic approach to the subsequent history of Italy. Gabriele Pedullà, *La strada più lunga. Sulle tracce di Fenoglio*, Ro, Donzelli, 170 pp., reappraises F.'s work in the light of his novel *Una questione privata* and discusses his existential and psychological concerns in eight chapters entitled 'Nomi', 'Libri', 'Tempi', 'Oggetti', 'Sguardi', 'Silenzi', 'Morti', and 'Muri'.

FO. *Dario Fo: Stage, Text and Tradition*, ed. Joseph Farrell and Antonio Scuderi, Carbondale, South Illinois U.P., 2000, 222 pp., includes the editors' introd., where the political nature of F.'s work and his relationship with tradition are highlighted (1–19), P. Puppa, 'Tradition, traditions and Dario Fo' (181–96), which, among other things, shows how F. rigidly divides political enemies from friends but where complexity is rescued by flights of fantasy and humour, and essays by B. Holm, R. Jenkins, J. Lorch, C. Maeder, T. Mitchell, W. Valeri, and S. Wood (this last on Franca Rame) which by and large trace a reading itinerary through F.'s (and Rame's) work. J. Farrell and A. Scuderi, 'The poetics of Dario Fo', *Italia & Italy*, 10, 42–44, maintains that F.'s work is not only influenced by contemporary history and politics but must also be seen in the context of the theatrical tradition. Joseph Farrell, *Dario Fo and Franca Rame: Harlequins of the Revolution*, London, Methuen, 308 pp., is not only a sympathetic biography of F. and R., but also an overall study of their work which explores especially the links between creative texts and politics, the influence of authors such as Ruzante and Molière on F., and the active role played by F. and R. in recent Italian social history. E. Jaffe-Berg, 'Lingual interventions in Dario Fo', *QI*, 21.1, 2000: 29–46, is on F.'s *grammelot* as related to the history of theatre and contemporary performances.

FRABOTTA. K. Jewell, 'Frabotta's Elegies: theory and practice', *MLN*, 116: 177–92, analyses the value of gender in achieving a poetic voice in F.'s poetry.

GADDA. Federico Bertoni, *La verità sospetta. Gadda e l'invenzione della realtà*, T, Einaudi, 304 pp., analyses G.'s themes, style, and ideas in search of a reality underlying the surface of things and indicated by signs contained in matter, the human body, and language. R. S. Dombrowski, **'Gadda's creative bodies: on the theory and practice of the grotesque'*, *Della Terza Vol.*, 375–96. M. Bertone, 'Il curioso caso Gadda–Conrad', *ib.*, 397–403, explores the links between G.'s creative writing (with borrowings from Conrad) and his work on the translation of *The Secret Agent* (publ. 1953).

The Edinburgh Journal of Gadda Studies, 1 (http://www.arts.ed.ac.uk/italian/gadda/is), an Internet journal which can be read on line in full, includes the following articles: L. Lugnani, 'Racconto ed esperienza umana del tempo'; F. G. Pedriali, 'Il vettore, la cartolina, lo stemma. Da *Meditazione* a *Pasticciaccio*'; R. Stracuzzi, 'Retorica del racconto nel *Pasticciaccio*'; C. Savettieri, '*Incipit sub specie aeternitatis*'; R. Lampugnani, 'Lexicalisation of a scatological image in *La cognizione*: "Hacer una pera" revisited'; B. Vassileva, 'Confounding and doubling the self. Sharing the role of the protagonist in *La cognizione*'; and A. Sarina, '*L'incendio di via Keplero*. "Studio 128" e "racconto inedito"'.

On *La cognizione del dolore*: C. Fagioli, 'Per una nuova edizione critica della *Cognizione del dolore*', *Allegoria*, 36:38–64, is on the genesis of the novel in relation to its publishing history. On *Quer pasticciaccio brutto de via Merulana*: F. G. Pedriali, 'Symmetries in Gadda's *Quer pasticciaccio*', *Italica*, 78:176–92. R. A. Rushing, ' "La sua tragica incompiutezza": anxiety, mis-recognition and ending in Gadda's *Pasticciaccio*', *MLN*, 116:130–49, argues that the lack of endings in some of G.'s texts is to be attributed more to his theories of narrative than to flaws in his writing and then compares *Quer pasticciaccio brutto de via Merulana* to Luca Ronconi's film adaptation. *La letteratura in scena: Gadda e il teatro*, ed. Alba Andreini and Roberto Tessari, Ro, Bulzoni, 321 pp., contains papers from a 1996 conference held in Turin on 'Il *Pasticciaccio* da Gadda a Ronconi'.

GATTO.   *Catalogo delle lettere ad Alfonso Gatto* (1942–1970), ed. G. Lavezzi et al., pref. G. Pentich, Pavia, Tipografia Commerciale Pavese, 2000, includes 1500 letters sent by 565 people to G. over a 30-year period. Paola Greco, *Alfonso Gatto prosatore*, Lecce, Pensa Multi Media, 2000, 2000 pp., examines G.'s prose writing from 1932 to the 1970s. **Alfonso Gatto: diario di un poeta*, ed. Francesco D'Episcopo, Na, ESI, 135 pp.

GINZBURG.   L. Fontanella, 'Natalia Ginzburg. A voice of the twentieth century', pp. 33–45 of *Natalia Ginzburg. A Voice of the Twentieth Century*, ed. Angela M. Jeannet and Giuliana Sanguinetti Katz, Toronto U.P., 250 pp., highlights the relationship between fiction and memory in G.'s narrative work, particularly in *Le voci della sera* and *Lessico famigliare*.

GIUDICI.   A. Bertoni, ' "Nell'orma di una fuga il rotto filo'. La poesia dell'ultimo Giudici', *FC*, 24, 1999:472–85. S. Ramat, 'Giovanni Giudici. I versi della vita', *Poesia*, 146:2–14, outlines the most significant moments in G.'s poetry in the 2000 'Meridiano' edition of his collected work.

GIUNTINI.   M. Pieracci Harwell, 'Il tempo e le sue ceneri', *CV*, 56:345–53, looks at the 'gioco del tempo' together with the descent into the individual conscience in Giuntini's 2001 collection *La fabbrica del tempo*.

GOVONI.   S. Bertani, 'Il metro rinnovato di Corrado Govoni (1924)', *Testo*, 42:143–58.

GOZZANO.   C. Fabbian, 'Gozzano, la Signorina Felicita e la "perplessità crepuscolare"', *American Journal of Italian Studies*, 62:75–89, analyses the determination to change the language and imagery of poetry together with the irony and pain present in G.'s early poem 'La Signorina Felicita ovvero La Felicita'. M. Raso,

'Gozzano e Petrarca', *Avanguardia*, 13:27–46, underlines intertextual links that point to the impact of P.'s lyrics on G.'s writing. C. Della Coletta, 'The white lies of Guido Gozzano's second-hand India', *RStI*, 18.1, 2000:86–114. L. Angioletti, 'A proposito di Guido Gozzano', *Testuale*, 28.7, 2000:27–30. Guido Gozzano, *Tutte le poesie, ed. Andrea Rocca, Mi, Mondadori, xlvi + 802pp., seems to be merely a reprint of the 1980 edition.

JACOBBI. S. Ramat, 'Ruggiero Jacobbi. Le immagini del mondo', *Poesia*, 155:25–26, outlines the broad thematics in J.'s poetry twenty years after his death.

JACOROSSI. L. Picchi, 'Il male oscuro di Marcello Jacorossi', *CV*, 56:125–32, gives a clear outline of existential anxiety in J.'s work.

JAHIER. G. Ungarelli, 'Il ferroviere Jahier', *Belfagor*, 56:663–82, gives an account of the author's three meetings with J. and the latter's employment as a railway inspector in Bologna.

LA CAPRIA. M. Onofri, 'Sull'ultimo La Capria', *NArg*, 16:284–96, calls upon Voltaire's *candeur*, combined with Palazzeschi's and Sciascia's candid attitudes in interpreting L.'s recent essays on society and literature.

LANDOLFI. R. Turchi, 'Tommaso Landolfi come Rimbaud', *LetP*, 31.2, 2000:93–6. Leonardo Cecchini, *Parlare per le notti: il fantastico nell'opera di Tommaso Landolfi* (*Études Romanes*, 51), Copenhagen, Museum Tusculanum Press, 148 pp., surveys Tzvetan Todorov's and other critics' theories, ascribes L.'s work to the fantastic genre, examines the main themes in his experimental texts (in particular 'inconsistenza della realtà' and 'impotenza della letteratura'), and highlights reference to 19th-c. models and to Freud's psychoanalysis. C. Martignoni, 'Landolfi e la modernità. Registri e strutture delle prime raccolte', *StCrit*, 16:75–98, shows how the repetitions and estranging procedures of L.'s early texts soon gave way to a more cerebral and thoughtful narrative mode.

LAROCCHI. A. Rossi, 'Note su "Questa parola" di Marica Larocchi', *Testuale* 28–29, 2000:72–77, examines her 'fare e operare con le parole'.

LEVI, C. *Prima e dopo le parole. Scritti e discorsi sulla letteratura*, ed. Gigliola De Donato and Rosalba Galvagno, Ro, Donzelli, 338 pp., contains essays by L. on literature and society. V. Zaccaro, 'Un inedito di viaggio di Carlo Levi', *RLettI*, 19.2–3:279–94, presents some 1971 notes of L.'s journey from Germany to Italy, and relates them to the theme of travel in L.'s work.

LEVI, P. *Primo Levi: il mestiere di raccontare, il dovere di ricordare*, ed. Ada Neiger, Pesaro, Metauro, 128 pp., includes essays by Eraldo Affinati, Ferdinando Camon, Carmen Covito, and Giovanni Tesio. L. Emmett, ' "L'uomo salvato dal suo mestiere": aspects of *Se questo è un uomo* revisited in L's *Il sistema periodico*', *ItS*, 56:115–28, looks into autobiography, micro- and macro-history, structure, narrative tone, and ethical values, and shows that there is continuity between L.'s earlier and later work. Judith Kelly, *Primo Levi: Recording and Reconstruction in the Testimonial Literature*, Leicester, Troubador, 2000, 104 pp. A. Cavaglion, 'Dostoevskij presso Primo Levi', *Belfagor*, 56:429–36.

LOY. G. Minghelli, 'What's in a word? Rosetta Loy's search for history in childhood', *MLN*, 116:162–76, examines the twofold voice of the author as a child and historian narrator in *La parola ebrea* and concludes that this novel is about the absence of childhood and the presence of history.

LUZI. Mario D'Angelo, *La mente innamorata. L'evoluzione poetica di Mario Luzi (1935–1966)*, Chieti, Noubs, 2000, 126 pp., looks at the meaning of individual texts and tries to balance his earlier with his later writing. G. De Marco, '"Oltre i confini/del desiderio e del dolore" si ritesse la trama di "una lunga storia umana". Codicillo all'ultimo Luzi', *CLett*, 29:317–43. Giorgio Cavallini, *La vita nasce alla vita. Saggio sulla poesia di Mario Luzi*, Ro, Studium, 2000, 119 pp. L. Gattamorta, 'Eliot e Luzi: impersonalità e intersoggettività della lingua naturale', *The Italianist*, 20, 2000:193–228.

LUZZI. G. Isella, 'Il "predario" poetico di Giorgio Luzzi', *FoI*, 34, 2000:191–97.

MAGRIS. Y. Aversa, 'Il teatro di Claudio Magris: *Stadelman* e *Le voci*', *LetP*, 110–11:14–26. A. Brambilla, 'Passeggiando nel "giardino" di Claudio Magris', *Testo*, 42:159–70, examines the image of 'giardino', and argues that *Microcosmi* shows the quintessential literary aspects of M.'s work.

MALAPARTE. *Curzio Malaparte: il narratore, il politologo, il cittadino di Prato e dell'Europa*, ed. Renato Barilli and Vittoria Baroncelli, Na, CUEN, 2000, 390 pp.

MALERBA. R. Capozzi, 'Incontro con Malerba', *RStI*, 18.1, 2000:145–55. R. Glynn, 'Fiction as imprisonment in Luigi Malerba's *Il fuoco greco*', *MLR*, 97:72–82, notes similarities between historical and literary discourse in relation to postmodernism, examines *Il fuoco greco* as a fictional metahistorical narrative and a detective story concerned with the relationship between truth and reality, and concludes that in M.'s text 'history and fiction are portrayed as one and the same: history is fictive and fiction is historical'.

MALFAIERA. G. Niccolai, 'Convincenti ragioni', *Il Verri*, 15:112–18, analyses Anna Malfaiera's anthology *E intanto dire* (1999) and does 'poetic justice' to her work, which is frank and often blunt in her assessment of life and living.

MANCINELLI. M. Jansen, 'Laura Mancinelli e i casi "molto strani" del Capitano Flores', *Incontri*, 15.3–4, 2000:176–82, identifies some

typical traits in M.'s fiction, namely reference to the medieval world
through some names of characters reminiscent of chivalric narrrative,
ambiguities, and escapist intentions, but also intelligent parody of the
genre of detective fiction.

MANGANELLI. *La penombra mentale. Interviste e conversazioni
1965–1990*, ed. Roberto Deidier, Ro, Editori Riuniti, 2000, 237 pp.,
includes a number of interviews given by M. *Giorgio Manganelli
ascoltatore musicale*, ed. Paolo Terni, Palermo, Sellerio, 86 pp., is the
transcript of four radio interviews held in 1980 by Terni on the theme
of music. M. maintains, among other things, that the language of
music is pure form and consequently less dependent on meaning than
literature, musical variations are freer than literary variations, and
art in general is based on the interplay of anguish (or a sense of death)
and games. Giorgio Manganelli, *Il vescovo e il ciarlatano. Inconscio, casi
clinici, psicologia del profondo. Scritti 1969–1087*, ed. Paolo Trevi, Ro,
Quiritta, 110 pp., collects a number of essays by M. on Sigmund
Freud, Carl Gustav Jung, Ernst Bernhard, dreams, and the relationship between psychoanalysis and literature, and includes Trevi's essay
'Come si diventa uno scrittore: lo spazio psichico di Giorgio
Manganelli' (87–106) where relevant episodes in M.'s life and his
views on psychoanalysis are reconstructed. 'Dossier Giorgio Manganelli', pp. 33–55 of *Il Caffè illustrato*, 1, includes a previously
unpublished 'Intervista a Dio Onnipotente' by M. (33–37), M. Mari,
'La maniera di Manganelli' (38–45) where oxymora and the language
and structures of essay-writing are highlighted in M.'s fiction, and a
'Fotobiografia' (46–55), containing photographs and comments provided by Lietta Manganelli.

MANNA. V. Esposito, 'La poesia di Gennaro Manna: tra angoscia
esistenziale e urgenza metafisica', *RStI*, 17.2, 1999:233–41.

MANZI. S. Wright, 'Luigi Manzi: la poesia come perfetta coin-
cidenza di anima e forma', *ItQ*, 147–48:53–64, outlines the work of
a Roman poet (b. 1945) who opts for a personal dimension rather
than conforming to editorial and critical necessities. His lyricism is
inspired by the Graeco-Latin tradition, Leopardi, and French 20th-c.
poets. 'Conversazione con Luigi Manzi', *ib.*, 65–91, sees the author
questioning Manzi on his method of composition and on contemporary Italian poetry together with an outline of themes and developments in his work.

MARAINI. P. Guida, 'La ricostruzione dell'io nell'itinerario
poetico di Dacia Maraini', *Italica*, 78:74–89. J. Cannon, *Voci* and the
conventions of the *giallo*', *ib.*, 193–202, sees M.'s novel *Voci* as a
detective story (comparable to Sciascia's fiction) which partly breaks
the convention of the detective genre through use of humanly

developed female characters instead of androgynous female detectives, identification of investigators with their victims, and the absence of triumphant ratiocination. L. A. Salsini, 'Maraini addresses Tamaro. Revising the epistolary novel', *Italica*, 78 : 351–66, argues that in *Dolce per sé* M. creates 'a feminist poetics for the epistolary text' in that its heroine is liberated from the isolation which is common in epistolary texts, and this also applies, to a certain extent, to Susanna Tamaro in *Va' dove ti porta il cuore*.

MARIN.   M. Cecovini, B. Maier, and G. Baroni, 'Carteggi con Biagio Marin', *RLettI*, 19.2–3 : 301–72.

MARINETTI.   M. Mascia Galateria, 'Tipologia e dinamica dei carteggi di Marinetti', *Avanguardia*, 13 : 103–26, examines the direct and often extreme enthusiasm frequently present in M.'s work. F. Livi, 'Villes, voyages, mirages: F. T. Marinetti, 1902–1909', *RLI*, 105 : 19–34, argues that M.'s second manifesto, 'Tuons le clair de lune' (April 1909), makes explicit reference to well known literary memoirs of great adventures of conquest and discovery when it proposes to conquer the world with its new ideas and also crystallizes the passion for discovery in M.'s writings.

MARNITI.   Andrea Guastalla, *Il respiro della vita. Invito alla lettura di Biagia Marniti*, Ro, Studium, 212 pp., provides a critical introduction to M.'s work. It also includes heretofore unpublished letters from Alba de Céspedes to M. and a 'carteggio' Marniti–Ungaretti (1954–1957) which details the encouragement given by U. to M. in the early stage of her career.

MENEGHELLO.   Luigi Meneghello, *Le carte: materiali manoscritti inediti 1963–1989 trascritti e ripuliti nei tardi anni Novanta*, Mi, Rizzoli, 1999–2001, is now complete with III: *Anni Ottanta*, 486 pp.

MERINI.   E. Biagini, 'Nella prigione della carne: appunti sul corpo nella poesia di Alda Merini', *FoI*, 35 : 442–56.

MONTALE.   N. Scaffai, 'Gli *Ossi di seppia* come "libro-vita". Lettura macrotestuale della prima raccolta montaliano', *Italianistica*, 30 : 33–67, attempts to show how *Ossi di seppia* (esp. its final sections) bears the appearance of a 'life-book' in which an exemplary life-curve is described. Tommaso Arvigo, *Guida alla lettura di Montale. Ossi di seppia*, Ro, Carocci, 247 pp. P. Sica, 'Il "fanciullo invecchiato", la "poesia fisiologica" e la "civiltà meccanica": il senso dell'età umana, dell'arte e della società negli *Ossi di seppia* di Eugenio Montale', *MLN*, 116 : 150–61. A. Fabrizi, 'Montale fuori di casa', *RLettI*, 19.1 : 183–93, provides an analysis of *Fuori di casa* (1969), M.'s third prose work. G. Ferrara, 'Da Eugenio e Montale', *Atelier*, 17 : 12–16, considers the manner in which M. defines his role as poet and person in certain poems and prose passages. S. Yoeb II, 'Una lettura de "L'angelo nero" di Eugenio Montale', *Archivi del nuovo*, 6–7 : 141–47, offers a critical analysis of this key poem from *Satura II*. F. De Rosa, 'Dal quarto al quinto Montale', *Italianistica*, 29, 2000[2001]:395–421. J. Butcher, 'Le ultime poesie di Eugenio Montale. Intervista ad Andrea Zanzotto', *AnI*, 19:327–32.

L. Blasucci, 'Su un aspetto del leopardismo montaliano (lettura di "Fine dell'infanzia")', pp. 239–50 of *Studi per Umberto Carpi. Un saluto da allievi e colleghi pisani*, ed. Marco Santagata and Alfredo Stussi, Pisa, ETS, 2000, offers a reading of the poems that open 'Meriggi e ombre' where the author appraises M.'s treatment of the clash between 'infanzia' and 'età adatta' that is so vital a part of Leopardi's poetics. P. Sica, 'The feminine in Eugenio Montale's juvenile work: "Sensi e fantasmi di un adolescente" ', *RStI*, 18.2, 2000:236–49, explores the construction of femininity in M.'s early work and shows how the female subject is a source of love, sustenance, and inspiration. In Paolo De Cano, *Journey to Irma. Una approssimazione all'ispiratrice americana di Eugenio Montale*, Foggia, Matteo De Meo, 1999, 390 pp., part I deals with the Brandeis family and Irma's literary interests (the 'versi leggeri' pubblished in *Harper's Bazaar* and the *New Yorker*, her involvement with medieval literature), while part II looks at cultural influences, and especially the 'dantismo montaliano' that resulted from the Montale-Irma-Dante encounter in Florence. Éanna Ó Ceallacháin, *Eugenio Montale. The Poetry of the Later Years*, Oxford, Legenda, 199 pp., shows how M.'s poetry from *Satura* onwards has deep links with the historical and ideological context of the time. After a useful introduction to M.'s poetry (1–18), various aspects of the poet's later work are examined in a series of insightful chapters: 'Mosca and her predecessors' (19–52), '*Satura*: the poetry of public discourse' (53–81), 'The poet's persona: isolation and withdrawal' (82–121), 'L'Altro' (122–48), 'Memories: "Fummo felici un giorno" ' (149–75), and the appendix 'Montale's women' (177–83), which gives a brief account of the principal female figures in M.'s poetry. *Catalogo delle lettere di Eugenio Montale a Maria Luisa Spaziani (1949–1964)*, ed. G. Polimeni, pref. M. Corti, Pavia, Tipografia Commerciale Pavese, 1999, contains 315 letters of a literary nature sent by M. to Maria Luisa Spaziani. On his relationship with her and on other strands of his private life, see G. Cecchetti, *'Sull'altro Montale', Della Terza Vol.*, 351–59.

Angelo Marchese, *Montale. La ricerca dell'altro*, Padua, Messaggero, 2000, 368 pp., outlines the 'itinerario di ricerca' pursued by M. throughout his career as a poet. His poetry as 'testimonianza' is briefly evoked in L. Rebay, *'Montale testimone del Novecento', Della Terza Vol.*, 361–65, Roberto Orlando, *Applicazioni montaliane*, Lucca, Pacini Fazzi, 179 pp. P. Dyerval Angelini, 'Montale: alcune osservazioni per tentare di tradurlo in francese', *LetP*, 31.2,

2000:27–45, details certain difficulties and traps the successful translator must overcome when translating M. into French. This article is based on the translation by the author of M.'s *Poèmes choisis 1916–1980* (Gallimard, 1991).

MORETTI. A. I. Villa, 'Moretti, Maeterlinck e il simbolismo. Attrazioni e repulsioni del primissimo Moretti critico (con due testi dispersi)', *Archivi del nuovo*, 4–5, 1999[2000]:47–68, details the impact of two articles ('Degeneration' by Nordau and 'What is Art?' by Tolstoy published in the 'Faro romagnolo' between 1903 and 1907) on Moretti's initial attraction to symbolism. V. Petrocchi, 'Spigolature morettiane: partecipazione ad *Atys*', *ib.*, 6–7:111–28, discusses the presentation of some of M.'s writings in prose and poetry published in *Atys* by the English poet Edward Augustine Storer (who founded this avantgarde journal in Rome in 1918–21). It also included 'The Vagrant' which Storer dedicated to M., together with other poems, dedicated by one to the other, which echo similar ideas. S. Gola, 'Dalla finestra di casa Moretti... La presenza del mare nella produzione morettiana', *ib.*, 129–40. M. Raccanello, 'La traduzione d'autore. Il caso di Marino Moretti', *ConLet*, 34, 2000:387–404, examines M.'s translation of Guy de Maupassant's *Une vie* as a rewritten version of the original French text where M. reorganized punctuation and syntax, omitted some passages, reduced repetition, and injected his personal style into the French novel.

MORSELLI. B. Pischedda, 'Morselli: una *Dissipatio* molto postmoderna', *FAM*, 19, 2000:163–89, sees *La coscienza di Zeno* as a model for *Dissipatio H. G.*, then moves on to describe some of M.'s metanarrative procedures, his combination of 19th- and 20th-c. literary techniques, and his adoption of multiple registers.

NICCOLAI. D. Alesi, 'Appunti sulla nuova stagione letteraria di Giulia Niccolai', *Avanguardia*, 15:16–24, outlines the ever-changing spiral of words, images, and ideas in N.'s recent work.

NOVENTA. R. Damiani, 'Noventa e Montale tra reciproci malintesi', *LItal*, 53:413–21, outlines misunderstandings that characterized N.'s and M.'s relationship over the years, particularly N.'s criticism of what he regarded as M.'s inability to speak clearly to his readers and M.'s hostile reaction to this criticism. E. Capodaglia, 'Leopardi con gli occhi di Noventa', *Kamen*, 9.2, 2000:7–30, outlines the impact of L.'s poetry on that of Noventa particularly its emphasis on the 'valore e onore' of poetry. P. M. Forni, *Il pane di Noventa', *Della Terza Vol.*, 367–74, offers a close reading of N.'s most oft-quoted lyric, 'El saòr del pan', to set against the superficial critical clichés of many who cite it.

OLDANI. A. Anelli, 'Il senso delle figure in *Latitudine* di Guido Oldani', *Testuale*, 28–29, 2000:78–83.

ONOFRI *Carteggi Cecchi–Onofri–Papini (1912–1917)*, ed. Carlo D'Alessio, Mi, Bompiani, 2000, 221 pp., looks at the Cecchi–Onofri correspondence from 1912–1914 and that of Onofri–Papini between 1916–1917 and offers interesting insights on the entire 'esperienza vociana'. M. Vigilante, ' "Temi e non poemi" di Arturo Onofri: il complesso passaggio verso l'ultima fase poetica', *CLett*, 29:525–34.

ORELLI. P. Pellini, 'Il san buco e i sentieri da capre. Sulla poesia di Giorgio Orelli', *EL*, 26.3:93–106, examines the work of the Ticinese poet, particularly his three main collections: *L'ora del tempo* (1962), *Sinopie* (1977), and *Spiracoli* (1989). He pays particular attention to Luciano Anceschi's definition of him as 'Orelli lombardo della Svizzera' and P. V. Mengaldo's definition of his 'fissità araldica'. P. De Marchi and S. Ramat, 'Un arcobaleno allegro e muto. Per gli ottant'anni di Giorgio Orelli', *Poesia*, 151:3–7.

ORTESE. A. Gramone, 'Travelling through the I: Anna Maria Ortese's melancholic cities', *RoS*, 19:95–108, notes the recurrence of the words *malinconia* and *sole* in O.'s work, and, through reference to Julia Kristeva, Sigmund Freud, and other writers concerned with melancholy, examines O.'s melancholic and saturnine subjectivity, her sense of existential emptiness and spatial enclosure, ambivalence between isolation from and challenge of the outside world, and awareness of a permanent exile combined with a desire to return home as a traveller and, metaphorically, also as a writer.

PALAZZESCHI. P.'s correspondence in four vols, all publ. 1999–2001, Ro, Storia e Letteratura — F, Università degli Studi, comprises: *Carteggio*, I: *1904–1924*, ed. Simone Magherini, 527 pp.; *Carteggio*, II: *1935–1939*, ed. Marco Roncalli, 1499 pp.; *Carteggio*, III: *1940–1962*, ed. Francesca Serra, 479 pp.; *Carteggio*, IV: *1963–1974*, ed. Laura Diafani, xl + 503 pp. *Scherzi di gioventù e d'altre età. Album Palazzeschi (1885–1974)*, ed. Simone Magherini and Gloria Manghetti, pref. Gino Tellini, F, Pagliai Polistampa, 301 pp., consists of an assortment of P. papers (letters, book dedications, and the like) for which the editors suggest different critical interpretations.

G. Palermo, 'Il poeta, il teppista e il saltimbanco . . . Due parole su Aldo Palazzeschi e le arti figurative', *Archivi del nuovo*, 6–7:75–104, looks at texts written by P. to Boccioni, Rosai, and De Pisis (whom he befriended over the years) which record encounters with P. and the impressions made by these three artists on him. S. Magherini, 'L'invenzione del poeta illetterato: per uno studio delle fonti letterarie del primo Palazzeschi (1903–1907)', *Avanguardia*, 17, 2001:91–105. An appendix (106–10) also contains 'Palazzeschi lettore alla Biblioteca del Gabinetto G. P. Vieusseux di Firenze (1903–1907)', which details books consulted by P. in the library at that time.

E. Guerrini, 'Omaggio a Palazzeschi, geniale "homo ludens" del Novecento', *Il Ponte*, 57.4, 116–30, details papers presented at a conference in Florence in February 2001 to commemorate the life and work of Palazzeschi. L. Baldacci, 'Palazzeschi: problemi aperti', *RLI*, 105:35–44, discusses problems regarding P.'s standing as a writer which still exist 27 years after his death. G. Tellini, 'Palazzeschi: l'officina dello scrittore', *ib.*, 45–56, despite P.'s assertion that 'le biblioteche non so neanche dove stiano di casa', shows that P. was a frequent visitor to the Gabinetto Vieusseux Library in Florence, had almost 1,500 books in his own collection, was well acquainted with the writings of others, and paid great attention to what he wrote himself. Aldo Palazzeschi, *L'incendiario*, ed. Giuseppe Nicoletti, Mi, Mondadori, 122 pp. F. Curi, 'Palazzeschi e le due avanguardie', *Poetiche*, 2:193–221, highlights P.'s disposal of old models, and his literary legacy to the neo-avantgarde through Edoardo Sanguineti's interpretation of P. as a non-futurist writer, Alberto Arbasino's appropriation of P.'s 'parlato' style, and debts of other modern writers to Palazzeschi. Sibyl Siegrist Staubli, **Palazzeschi romanziere: fra sperimentalismo e tradizione. Lettura semiotica delle Sorelle Materassi e interpretazione storica*, Bern, Lang, 272 pp.

PASOLINI. A. Gibellini, 'Pasolini in una poesia di Andrea Zanzotto', *NArg*, 13:348–53. Giacomo Jori, *Pasolini*, T, Einaudi, 146 pp., gives a general analysis of P.'s work and has an accompanying videocassette. Pier Paolo Pasolini, *Per il cinema. Sceneggiature, scritti, interviste*, ed. Walter Siti and Franco Zabagli, Mi, Mondadori, 2 vols, 120, 3357 pp., includes essays by Bernardo Bertolucci, Mario Martone, and Vincenzo Cerami, and a biographical 'Cronologia' of P. by Nico Naldini. Id., *Teatro*, ed. Walter Siti and Silvia De Laude, Mi, Mondadori, 114, 1266 pp., includes interviews by Stanislas Nordey and Naldini's 'Cronologia'.

General essays on Pasolini: Gianni Biondillo, *Pasolini: il corpo della città*, introd. Vincenzo Consolo, Mi, Unicopli, 120 pp., discusses the theme of geographical and existential space in P.'s work from Friuli to Rome and beyond Rome to other places visited by P. **Corpi/Körper: Körperlichkeit un Medialität im Werk von Pier Paolo Pasolini*, ed. Peter Kuon, Frankfurt, Lang, 191 pp. F. Vighi, 'Pasolini con Adorno: fascismo rivisitato', *ISt*, 56:129–47, is about P.'s broad concept of Fascism, including his preoccupations with irrationalism and the authoritarian politics of neocapitalism, which is then compared to Theodor W. Adorno's theories. The essay concludes with P.'s view of *mimesis* founded on the experience of the human body. Guido Zingari, *Il pensiero in fumo. Giordano Bruno e Pasolini: gli eretici totali*, Genoa, Costa & Nolan — Mi, Editori Associati, 112 pp., discusses the mental framework shared by Bruno and P., one of intellectual heresy. This is attributed to their radical non-conformist views and to the fact that both writers advocated freedom from institutions and free ethics. P., in particular, aimed his Utopian critique against the intolerance of society. B. Pischedda, 'Petrolio, *Una significativa illeggibilità*', *StN*, 59:161–85, observes that *Petrolio*, though structurally experimental, has a nostalgic content, and also identifies some intertextual reference to Gustave Flaubert, Carlo Emilio Gadda, and other writers.

PARISE. E. Del Tedesco, '*L'odore del sangue* di Goffredo Parise: storia di un matricidio', *ParL*, 27–28–29, 2000:134–45. Id., 'Goffredo Parise. Nascita di una narrativa e iniziazione poetica', *StN*, 59:135–59, examines poetry in P.'s early work.

PARRONCHI. 'Un testimone dell'Italia "simbolista". Intervista ad Alessandro Parronchi', ed. L. Toppan, *REI*, 46, 2000:253–58.

PAVESE. A. Bianchi, ' "Tre vite e una sola morte". La trilogia delle macchine di Cesare Pavese', *LetP*, 31.2, 2000:11–26. *ChrI*, 68, is a special issue on Pavese and includes: P. Abbrugiati, 'Il mestiere per vivere: Pavese travailleur infatigable pour l'éditeur Einaudi' (7–30); G. Bosetti, '*Addenda* sur la mythopoiétique de Pavese et sur la poésie' (31–42); D. Ferraris, 'Pavese et l'image de la réussite' (43–61); M. Gallot, 'Pavese: paese et paesaggio' (63–76); P. Laroche, 'Le réel de l'écriture' (77–88); G. Romanelli, 'La "parola nuova" nella ricerca letteraria di Cesare Pavese' (89–102); J.-C. Vegliante, 'Rythme du vers, rythme de la prose dans quelques pages de Pavese' (103–25). G. Crafa, 'La presenza di Shelley nella formazione di Cesare Pavese', *CLett*, 29:675–90. Vittoriano Esposito, *Poetica e poesia di Cesare Pavese*, Foggia, Bastogi, 114 pp., includes some unpublished essays on P.'s poetry written between 1950s and the 1970s. One of these, 'La poetica di Pavese' (13–23), focuses on P.'s conception of 'poesia-racconto' and on his interest in symbols and myth. Roberto Gigliucci, *Cesare Pavese*, Mi, B. Mondadori, 214 pp., gives an account of P.'s life and works and an analysis of some key concepts, pays special attention to the interaction between textual and biographical aspects, and surveys works and concepts in alphabetical order as in a hypertext.

PICCOLO. S. Verdino, 'Lucio Piccolo – "Il barone magico" ', *Poesia*, 153:25–31, offers a reappraisal of P.'s poetry to mark the centenary of his birth. Lucio Piccolo, *Canti barocchi e gioco a nascondere*, Mi, Scheiwiller, 131 pp., is a collection of his poems, with bibliography, to mark the centenary of his birth.

PIOVENE. L. Parisi, 'I romanzi di Guido Piovene', *Testo*, 41:87–114, traces P.'s development from an initial philosophical and moral interest in indefiniteness and ambiguity in the first novels to a second period (beginning just after World War II) based on rejection of ambiguities and a need for the truth, and finally to a third phase (from the *Le furie* to *Le stelle fredde*) where ways to reject lies and bad faith are explored and some 'estasi laiche' appear which may in fact reveal a hidden religious sensibility.

PIRANDELLO. Corrado Donati, *Luigi Pirandello nella storia della critica*, Fossombrone, Metauro, 228 pp., surveys P. criticism from the early 20th c. to the present both in Italy and abroad. *Pirandello e la parola*, ed. Enzo Lauretta, contains papers from the 1999 P. conference held at Agrigento. A. Frabetti, *'Pirandello a Parigi. L'interpretazione del teatro pirandelliano in Francia nei primi anni Venti', *FC*, 24, 1999:375–426. Emma Grimaldi, *Come un quadro sottosopra: aspetti e problematiche del femminile in alcune opere di Pirandello*, Cava de' Tirreni, Avagliano, 236 pp. L. Kroha, *'Pirandello's poetics of paradox: representing the unrepresentable', *Della Terza Vol.*, 321–39. R. Pupino, 'Nomi e anonimi di Pirandello. Qualche esempio', *Il nome nel testo*, 2–3, 2000–01:61–76, argues that P.'s most anonymous characters are the embodiment of 'maschere nude' or 'apparenze', and spiritual entities created by their author in order to question the poetics of realism. Franco Zangrilli, *Il bestiario di Pirandello*, Fossombrone, Metauro, 168 pp., identifies frequent use of animal imagery in P.'s fiction, as symbols expressing the themes of primitiveness, work, femininity, vendetta, death, and time. Margherita Ganeri, *'Pirandello romanziere*, Soveria Mannelli, Rubbettino, 258 pp. F. Secchieri, *'Due note pirandelliane', *StIt*, 25:75–84. On P. and poetry: A. Barsotti, 'Praga–Pirandello: un nodo gordiano', *Ariel*, 16.1:93–126.

PIZZUTO. Antonio Pizzuto, *Ultime e penultime*, ed. Gualberto Alvino, Na, Cronopio, 282 pp. also contains a note by Contini on Pizzuto's late writings.

POLA. S. Boato, 'Marco Pola. "Il poeta di Trento"', *Poesia*, 148:53–59, discusses the marginalization of this poet who writes in both Italian and Trentino dialect.

PONTIGGIA. M. Forti, 'Pontiggia, su personaggi "nati due volte"', *NA*, 2219:160–85.

PRATOLINI. Piergiovanni Permoli, *Pratolini. Una città, un quartiere, un amore*, F, Chegai, 80 pp., gathers Permoli's reflections on P. and some letters exchanged by the two men.

PREZZOLINI. Olga Ragusa, *Gli anni americani di Giuseppe Prezzolini: il Dipartimento d'italiano e la Casa italiana della Columbia University*, F, Le Monnier, ix + 91 pp., introd. Paolo Bagnoli, includes a text in English by P.

QUASIMODO. M. C. Albonico, 'Salvatore Quasimodo interprete di Virgilio', *RLettI*, 19.1:123–70, offers a comparative evaluation of Q.'s *Fiore delle Georgiche* and corresponding passages in Virgil's writings. L. Angioletti, 'Proposta per una lettura di Salvatore Quasimodo', *Testuale*, 28.7, 2000, 23–26. A. Gendrat, 'La scrittura del *nostos* nelle prime raccolte poetiche di Salvatore Quasimodo', *Versants*, 39, 181–220, analyses Q.'s links with classical culture in *Ed è subito sera* (1942). G. Finzi, 'Salvatore Quasimodo. Il muro di odio non ancora caduto', *Poesia*, 152:19–25, shows how the 'muro di odio' (referred to by Quasimodo in his Nobel acceptance speech in 1959) was an integral part of his life as poet and individual.

RAGAZZONI.   Ernesto Ragazzoni, *Buchi nella sabbia e pagine invisibili. Poesie e prose*, ed. Renato Martinoni, T, Einaudi, 2000, lviii + 336 pp., provides an ample selection of R.'s poems together with critical and biographical material on the poet. M. Pedroni, 'Il giullare lirico. Rileggendo Ernesto Ragazzoni', *Versants*, 39, 161–80, details light and serious tones and the reasons for these in R.'s poetry.

REBORA.   S. Lurati, 'Clemente Rebora, poeta mistico', *RELI*, 14, 1999:75–104, examines the 'tensione mistica' in R.'s poetry and the subsequent 'annullamento dell'io in Dio' apparent in certain poems where this anxiety is paramount. *La musica in Leopardi nella lettura di Clemente Rebora*, ed. Gualtiero De Santi and Enrico Grandesso, Venice, Marsilio, 128 pp., includes the following essays: G. Guglielmi, 'Il Leopardi "mal noto" e la nuova poesia' (15–23); F. Foschi, 'Note su Leopardi e la musica' (25–32); G. De Santi, 'L'idea di musica da Madame de Staël a Leopardi a Rebora' (33–65); A. Colasanti, 'Clemente Rebora: una leggera stonazione' (67–85); M. Raffaeli, 'Una noterella metrica' (87–89); E. Capodaglio, 'Il puro suono' (91–104); D. Marchi, 'Canto del sacrificio muto. Silenzio, chiave, ritmo, tempo/istante nella nozione di canto reboriano' (105–13); A. Folin, 'Il Leopardi reboriano tra contingente ed eterno' (115–23). C. Riccio, 'L'accadere tragico: forma matura della poesia reboriana', *CLett*, 29:655–74. I. Ceccon, 'Parabola della critica reboriana. Rassegna di studi', *LItal*, 53:562–95. N. Trotta, 'Lettere di Clemente Rebora a Enzo Ferrieri', *RLettI*, 19.2–3:215–28. P. Montini, 'L'amicizia Rebora–Don Orione', *CV*, 56:293–308.

RÈPACI.   B. Zaczek, 'L'ovario di Ochette: fascism and female sexuality in Leonida Rèpaci's *Il deserto del sesso*', *RStI*, 18.1, 2000:116–25.

RIDOLFI.   D. Della Terza, 'Roberto Ridolfi', *Belfagor*, 56:683–98.

RUFFATO.   P. Cataldi and N. Bonifazi, 'Origini e strappi in Cesare Ruffato', *Testuale*, 28–29, 2000:59–71.

SABA.   A. Cadioli, 'Il "romanzetto" di *Trieste e una donna*', *Moderna*, 2.2, 2000:71–92. Umberto Saba, *Tutte le prose*, ed. Arrigo Stara, introd. Mario Lavagetto, Mi, Mondadori, lxxxii + 1530 pp., is an expanded edition of a work first published in 1964.

SANESI.   M. Scrignòli, 'Per la poesia *senza data* di Roberto Sanesi', *Poesia*, 153:15–16; V. Guarracino, 'Sanesi, "poeta del secolo scorso" ', *ib.*, 16–22. A. Hutchinson, 'Remembering Roberto Sanesi', *Italia & Italy*, 11–12:44–45.

SANGUINETI. E. Zinato, 'Con le spalle al futuro: il Chierico organico di Sanguineti', *Allegoria*, 37:117–22, details the ideological tendentiousness in S.'s 28 essays on Italian literature from the 13th to the 20th century where everything is examined in terms and language that have an unmistakably contemporary dimension. F. Curi, 'Maschere, pagliacci, ciarlatani. *Cataletto 12* di Sanguineti', *Poetiche*, 1:43–72, traces the development of the 'artista da saltimbanco' through the figures of Gozzano, Corazzini, Moretti, and Palazzeschi to the image of the clown in S.'s *Cataletto* (section 10) where S. compares himself to a 'scuoiatura del coniglio'. N. Lorenzini, 'Sanguineti fra Faust e Tristano: la parola all'inferno', *Il Verri*, 16:109–21, outlines the intertextual bonds that link S.'s work particularly to Goethe's *Faust*. The author also highlights Leopardi's fascination for Faust in his *Dialogo di Tristano e di un amico* (1832) and shows how S.'s *Novissimum Testamentum* (1986) echoes the nothingness of life and the feeling of destruction within life itself.

SATTA. V. Spinazzola, 'Al cimitero di Nuoro', pp. 191–245 of his *Itaca, addio: Vittorini, Pavese, Meneghello, Satta: il romanzo del ritorno*, Mi, Il Saggiatore, 256 pp., examines the opposition between nature and culture, the relationship between life and death, the ambiguities of the author's necessity for memory and wish for oblivion, and the interaction between the Sardinian and Italian languages, revealing the psychological laceration of the narrator, and concludes that *Il giorno del giudizio* constitutes an inquest into the value of life and an attempt to interrogate the archaic Sardinian world vis-à-vis modernity.

SAVINIO. P. Italia, 'Un'"Officina ferrarese" durante la guerra. L'apprendistato letterario di Alberto Savinio', *Archivi del nuovo*, 4–5, 1999[2000]:5–45, assesses the impact made on Savinio by figures such as Govoni, De Pisis, Soffici, Carrà, and the De Chirico brothers whom he met in Ferrara from 1915 onwards. It pays special attention to their influence on his formation as a writer and to his particular use of Greek and Latin words together with unusual archaic words in his poetry. U. Piscopo, 'Alberto Savinio — la lingua materna', *Il Ponte*, 57.4, 142–48, cites S.'s use of Biblical, Greek, and Latin sources in his use of Italian.

Thomas Bernet, *L'ironie d'Alberto Savinio à la croisée des discours. Lecture sémiotique de l'Introduction à una vie de Mercure et d'Achille enamouré mêlé à l'Evergète*, Bern, Lang, 1999, 246 pp., provides a semiotic analysis of S.'s use of irony in *Introduction à une vie de Mercure* (first published in the Parisian journal *Bifur* in 1929) and *Achille énamouré mêlé à l'Evergète* (also published in Paris in 1933). *Un'amicizia senza corpo. La corrispondenza*

Parisot–Savinio 1938–1952, ed. Giuditta Isotti Rosowsky, Palermo, Sellerio, 1999, 252 pp., shows that this correspondence was totally centred on literary and artistic topics. In it Henri Parisot becomes S.'s alter ego when he details his artistic creativity and outlines his plans for the future. M. Szalai, 'Alberto Savinio és az "önmaga tükörképévé vált ember"', *Italianistica debreceniensis*, 6, 1999:172–82. G. Caltagirone, 'Dagli *Exitus illustrium virorum* alla tanatografia novecentesca. *Narrate, uomini, la vostra storia* di Alberto Savinio', *Moderna*, 2.1, 2000:99–108. M. Moroni, 'The sacerdotal individual in Alberto Savinio's *Infanzia di Nivasio Dolcemare*', *RStI*, 18.2, 2000:198–210. 'Le muse di Alberto Savinio', *Antologia Vieusseux*, 16–17, 2000, includes the following articles presented at a 1999 conference on Savinio: F. Sanvitale, 'Prolusione per Alberto Savinio' (61–69); A. Debenedetti, 'Il signor Betti' (71–77); P. Italia, 'Sul dorso del Centauro' (79–102); M. Sabbatini, 'Ermafroditismo linguistico. Gli esordi di Savinio scrittore' (103–11); A. Tinterri, 'L'avventura colorata di Alberto Savinio' (113–18); M. Bucci, 'Alberto Savinio scenografo da Milano a Firenze' (119–34); M. De Santis, 'Savinio compositore per la radio' (135–52).

P. Italia, 'Savinio, Soffici e la politica culturale del fascismo nei primi anni Venti: *Il Nuovo Paese* e il *Corriere Italiano*', *NRLI*, 3, 2000:389–450, examines articles of literary, historical, and political interest written by S. in the early 1920s in these newspapers when responsible for their 'terza pagina'. Mussolini appointed S. their editor, and the articles presented include the first regular cinema reviews to appear in Italian newspapers and give an overview of Fascist cultural politics before the introduction of the 1923 publishing laws.

SBARBARO. Pasquale Guaragnella, *Il matto e il povero. Temi e figure in Pirandello, Sbarbaro, Vittorini*, Bari, Dedalo, 2000, 238 pp. Camillo Sbarbaro, *Pianissimo*, ed. Lorenzo Pollato, Venice, Marsilio, 166 pp., offers a stylistic and bibliographical analysis of this 1914 collection of S.'s poetry.

SCIASCIA. *Colpi di penna, colpi di spada* (Quaderni Leonardo Sciascia, 6), ed. Valentina Fascia, Mi, La Vita Felice, 238 pp., includes a dedication to Tom O'Neill and an essay by G. Traina on O'Neill's work in general, particularly his contribution to S. criticism (185–94), O'Neill's 1996 essay on Lampedusa, Sciascia, and Consolo (195–214), essays by Vincenzo Consolo, on S.'s balanced approach to language (11–17), R. Castelli on *Candido* (21–42), G. Panella on S. and Borges (43–66), V. Fascia on S. and Savinio (151–70), and other texts by A. Cinquegrani, M. D'Alessandro, A. Girardi, G. Petitti, A. Primo, F. Vancini, and A. Vecellio. I. R. Morrison, 'Leonardo Sciascia's *Candido* and Voltaire's *Candide*', *MLR*, 97:59–71, surveys criticism on both texts, then compares them and finds that similarities prevail over differences. On S.'s reception outside Italy: A. Camps, 'Una fortuna disuguale: Leonardo Sciascia in Spagna', *Revista de Literatura Comparada*, 5, 2000: 1–8.

SCIALOJA. F. Galluzzi, 'Il ritmo del corpo. Pittura e scrittura di Toti Scialoja', *Italianistica*, 29, 2000[2001]: 451–59.

SERENI. F. Moliterni, 'Forma e sapere tragico nel luogo della lirica. Giorgio Caproni e Vittorio Sereni', *CLett*, 29: 89–114. L. Wittman, 'Vittorio Sereni o l'istinto della gioia', *FoI*, 35: 403–31.

SERRA. A. Castronuovo, 'Serra e Cardarelli. Breve storia d'un acerbo rapporto', *LetP*, 31.2, 2000: 97–110, argues that the antipathy which divided these poets sprang from their divergent concepts of what literary criticism stood for in addition to harsh judgments each made about the other's poetry.

SILONE. Maria Nicolai Paynter, *Ignazio Silone. Beyond the Tragic Vision*, Toronto U.P., 2000, 288 pp. Y. Saito, 'Silone: "falsità", "doppiezza". Una voce in difesa', *Il Ponte*, 57.9: 112–36. Giuseppe Tamburrano, Gianna Granati, and Alfonso Isnelli, **Processo a Silone: la disavventura di un povero cristiano*, Manduria, Lacaita, 161 pp.

SINISGALLI. *Poesia*, 147, offers a number of articles to commemorate the 30th anniversary of S.'s death. They include: S. Ramat, 'Leonardo Sinisgalli. Poeta al servizio di due muse' (19), F. Vitelli, 'Sinisgalli poeta' (19–20); R. Aymone, 'Sinisgalli prosatore' (21–22); G. Lupo, 'Sinisgalli e le riviste tecnico-industriali' (23); G. Appella, 'Sinisgalli, l'arte e *Civiltà delle macchine*' (24–25).

SLATAPER. A. I. Villa, 'S. Slataper poeta: *In bicicletta* (1905)', *RLettI*, 19.2–3: 187–94.

SOFFICI. V. Trione, 'L'arte perenne: la riflessione critica di Ardengo Soffici nel dopoguerra', *Avanguardia*, 16: 49–78, looks at S.'s art and writings in order to examine S.'s conviction that the artist had to 'lavorare dentro la realtà' to discover its enigmatic dimension, to immerse oneself in it and become its reflection. G. Bárberi Squarotti, 'Il paesaggio di Soffici', *CLett*, 29: 303–15. A. Pietropaoli, 'Soffici e l'avanguardia', *Poetiche*, 2: 223–63, is about S.'s articles on Futurism, his interest in Apollinaire, and the 'enigma' of S.'s construction rather than spontaneous creation of his own brand of avantgarde poetics. See also SAVINIO, above.

SVEVO. M. Bresciani Califano, 'Svevo e il nuovo romanzo europeo: la strategia dell'anti-eroe', pp. 84–100 of *Modelli e stili di conoscenza nella scienza e nell'arte del Novecento*, F, Olschki, 2000, 188 pp., sees Svevo against the background of early 20th-c. scientific pluralism and sense of relativity.

TABUCCHI. J. Cannon, '*Requiem* and the poetics of Antonio Tabucchi', *FoI*, 35: 100–09. *Dedica a Antonio Tabucchi*, ed. Claudio

Cattaruzza, Pordenone, Associazione Provinciale per la Prosa, 240 pp., includes a letter to T. by Dacia Maraini (11–13), an interview conducted by Carlos Gumpert (17–105), and essays by L. Stegagno Picchio on travel, lightness, and other themes (109–16); R. Bodei on identity and re-experiencing other people's life through the writing of fiction (117–40); R. Ceserani on intertextuality and enigmas in *Il filo dell'orizzonte* (141–56); and B. Ferraro on various motifs in T.'s fiction (157–80). There are also biographical texts by D. Benati, C. and I. Feltrinelli, and J. Heralde (185–200). R. Ceserani, 'Bussando alla porta di Antonio Tabucchi', *Il Ponte*, 57.4:100–08, argues that in T.'s work continuity prevails over dramatic changes from one phase to the next, that T. uses equally complex structures both in his short and longer fiction, and that his stories may be seen as postmodernist thanks mainly to sophisticated literary procedures and existential elusiveness. Claudio Pezzin, *Antonio Tabucchi*, Sommacampagna, Cierre, 115 pp., illustrates changes in narrative perspective, metanarrative techniques, allegories, interpretation of clues leading to new clues, and chronological developments in T.'s work.

Antonio Tabucchi: geografía de un escritor inquieto / Antonio Tabucchi: Geography of a Restless Writer, ed. Maria José de Lancastre, Lisbon, Fundação Calouste Gulbenkian and Centro de Arte Moderna – Acarte, 360 pp., contains the proceedings of a Colloquium on T. held in April 1999, with essays by J. Blanco on T. as a critic of Fernando Pessoa (235–60), R. Bodei on subjectivity and vagueness of spatial dimensions in T.'s work (155–71), F. Brizio-Skov on 'Tabucchi microhistorian and metahistorian' (63–88), R. Ceserani on *Il filo dell'orizzonte* (195–207), B. Ferraro on T.'s reception outside Italy and his interweaving of art and writing (49–61), P. Mauri on otherness in T.'s work (37–48), and also essays by D. Benati, M. Bertone, B. Comment, A. Chrysostomides, C. Gumpert, F. Lopes, C. Meckel, A. Mega Ferreira, E. Prado Coelho, S. Vecchio, and T. Wada.

P. Diffley, 'The figure of the detective in the novels of Antonio Tabucchi', pp. 98–112 of *Crime Scenes: Detective Narratives in European Culture since 1945*, ed. Anne Mullen and Emer O'Beirne, Amsterdam–Atlanta, Rodopi, 2000, xiv + 325 pp., sees detectives in T.'s fiction as characters on a quest for the identity of others and themselves, conveyors of metanarratives as well as epistemological, existential, and cognitive values, and ultimately as functional to illustrate the writer's relationship with reality which moves from subjectivity in the 1980s (in *Notturno indiano* and *Il filo dell'orizzonte*) to an assertion of the objective importance of reality over dreams in the 1990s (in *Requiem* and especially in *La testa tagliata di Damasceno Monteiro*). A. Camps, 'Para un estudio de la recepción de la obra de Tabucchi en España', *RLLCGV*, 8:149–75. F. Brizio Skov, 'Antonio Tabucchi e il ruolo dell'intellettuale', *Incontri*, 16.3–4:180–93, identifies T.'s view of a committed intellectual who sees reality from a variety of perspectives, interrogates the enigmas of history, and is not aligned with any party in particular.

TAMARO. Claudio Pezzin, *Susanna Tamaro*, Sommacampagna, Cierre, 2000, 109 pp., considers T.'s novels from *La testa fra le nuvole* to *Anima Mundi*, identifies two phases in her work (the second phase starting with *Va' dove ti porta il cuore*), examines the themes of interiority, blindness, fate, birth, and death, predominance of biological over historical factors, aggressiveness, love, family, and 'discesa nel cuore', highlights the importance of the diary, letter forms and monologues in her work, and identifies a metaphysical tension and a spiritual tendency that is mainly Christian in origin but also based on Zen Buddhism. See also L. A. Salsini under MARAINI, above.

TARTAGLIA. G. Cattaneo, '*Tre ballate* di Ferdinando Tartaglia', *NA*, 2218:238–43.

TESSA. Mauro Novelli, *I 'Saggi lirici' di Delio Tessa*, Mi, Ediz. universitarie di Lettere, Economia, Diritto, 254 pp.

TIMPANARO. S. Landucci, 'Sebastiano Timpanaro: leopardiano del XX secolo', *NA*, 2217:229–44, details echoes of Leopardi's poetry in T.'s verse.

TOBINO. *NArg*, 14.2, includes an interview conducted by G. van Straten (254–58), and essays on T. by R. Manica (259–69) on T.'s life and work, E. Affinati (270–83) who appreciates T.'s modernity in spite of his old-fashioned style, and M. Zappella (284–97) on activity as a psychiatrist.

TOMASI DI LAMPEDUSA. Bruno Caruso, *Il Gattopardo e i racconti di Giuseppe Tomasi di Lampedusa, disegni di Bruno Caruso*, Palermo, Fond. Federico II — Soveria Mannelli, Rubbettino, 118 pp.

TOZZI. E. Saccone, *' "Fede", "fiducia", "sfiducia", "sospetto", nel *Podere* di Federigo Tozzi', *Della Terza Vol.*, 341–50. D. Garofano, *'Ipotesi su un testo tozziano: "Barche capovolte" ', *StIt*, 23, 2000:97–111.

TUSIANI. A. Molendini, 'Il difficile processo di identificazione di un italo-americano: Joseph Tusiani', *Quaderni*, 19, 1997[2000]: 217–40. A. Serrao, 'Two languages, two lands: l'io diviso e ritrovato di Joseph Tusiani', *Italica*, 78:410–13.

UNGARETTI. F. Livi, 'Ungaretti: autobiografia e memoria letteraria. *Giorno per giorno* e *La lampe de terre* de Henri Thuile', *LItal*, 53:354–76, shows how T.'s poems (written after his wife's death in 1911) were a source of comfort and inspiration that helped U. come to terms with his grief when writing *Giorno per giorno* (1940–46) to commemorate the death of his son Antonietto. M. Nota, 'Ungaretti: "un grumo di sogni" ', *ChrI*, 65:97–112. *Narrativa*, 19, includes selected papers on U. given at a conference in Paris in December 2000. They include: E. R. La Forgia, 'Tra il deserto e il mare: Ungaretti e l'Egitto' (5–23); J. C. Vegliante, 'Ancora sul "sogno africano" di Giuseppe Ungaretti' (25–37); R. Gennaro, 'Ungaretti tra italianità e fascismo (da nuovi documenti)' (39–59); Id., 'Documenti' (60–70), reports published in Belgian papers on lectures given by U. (March 1926) together with an interview given to the daily newspaper *Midi* (17 March 1926); F. Musarra, 'Alcune osservazioni sui costituenti ritmici nella poesia di Ungaretti' (71–88); J. C. Vegliante, 'Ritmo e semantica della parola in qualche esempio ungarettiano' (89–97); M. Nota, 'Notes sur *Il Taccuino del Vecchio*' (99–120); A. Dolfi, 'Ungaretti, Leopardi e il paradigma del moderno' (121–33); G. Andreotti, 'Conoscenza e sentimento del nulla' (135–44); P. Montefoschi, 'Ungaretti, il Brasile, le traduzioni e il modernismo brasiliano' (145–55).

Giuseppe Ungaretti, *Lettere a Giuseppe Prezzolini 1911–1969*, ed. Maria Antonietta Terzoli, Ro, Storia e Letteratura — Lugano, Dipartimento dell'Istruzione e Cultura del Cantone Ticino, 2000, 119 pp. A. Lang, 'The sound of silence: word of exile and liberation in Ungaretti's desert', *RLMC*, 53, 2000:323–36. T. E. Peterson, 'The ethics and pathos of Ungaretti's *Ragioni d'una poesia*', *AnI*, 19:171–88. C. Mileschi, 'Le temps de Ungaretti', *ChrI*, 65:77–96. C. Brook, 'Giuseppe Ungaretti: translator of William Blake', *FoI*, 35:368–82. D. Glenn, 'The redemption of historical time in Ungaretti's *Il dolore*', *The Italianist*, 20, 2000:121–55.

VITTORINI. Guido Bonsaver, **Elio Vittorini: The Writer and the Written*, Leeds, Northern Universities Press, 2000, 262 pp.

ZANZOTTO. A. Gibellini, 'Pasolini in una poesia di Andrea Zanzotto', *NArg*, 14:348–53, discusses Z.'s 1992 poem 'Fora par al Furlán' (Attraverso il Friuli) where Z. creates an imaginary conversation with the dead Pasolini. N. Gardini, 'Linguistic dilemma and intertextuality in contemporary Italian poetry: the case of Andrea Zanzotto', *FoI*, 35:432–41. *Poesia*, 154, offers three short articles on Z.'s new collection *Sovrimpressioni* (Mi, Mondadori): S. Ramat, 'Andrea Zanzotto – *Sovrimpressioni*' (17); N. Gardini, 'L'altra parte della cosa. Una lettura del nuovo Zanzotto' (18–20); A. Cortellessa, ' "Nel folto del finire senza fine". Sul nuovo Zanzotto' (21–31).

ROMANIAN STUDIES*

LANGUAGE

POSTPONED

LITERATURE

By Mircea Anghelescu, *Professor of Romanian Literature in the
University of Bucharest*

1. Works of reference and of general interest

Although few wide-ranging works have recently been initiated, and
those that have are late in coming to completion, volumes have
continued to be published in the series of dictionaries which were
started several years earlier. *Dicţionarul scriitorilor români*, coordinated
by the late professors Mircea Zaciu and Marian Papahagi, and by
Aurel Sasu (see *YWMLS*, 60:510), has now reached vol. III, *M–Q*,
Albatros, 973 pp. which deals with approximately 450 writers,
breaking out of the original exclusion of the Romanian diaspora from
a work planned pre-1989 under Communist censorship and including
several literary exiles, important writers abroad (impossible to even
mention before 1989) such as Norman Manea, Gabriela Melinescu,
and Petru Popescu. On the other hand, it lists too few of the writers
from the old Romanian provinces and Bessarabia, whom one could
never have mentioned as 'Romanian writers' before 1989, but whose
names could have easily been found in Mihai Cimpoi's 'open history':
the names of Gheorghe Madan, George Meniuc, and Constantin
Popovici, for example, are missing. Some scoria can also be found
which are difficult to explain in view of the prolonged period of
gestation: the entry for the Romanian-American writer Peter Neagoe
fails to list in its bibliography the only monograph on the author
(Denise-Claude Le Goff, *Peter Neagoe. L'homme et l'œuvre*, Lang, 1988);
Ioana Orlea, b. 21 April 1936, the entry notes (p. 545) that she was
'beginning with 1947 secretary, mechanical drawing specialist and
medical secretary' (i.e. beginning at 11 years old!); the entry for Ion
Omescu ignores the fact that he is now deceased, etc.

Published in recognition of the importance of Romanian writers of
the diaspora, *Dicţionar al scriitorilor români din Statele Unite şi Canada*, ed.
Aurel Sasu, Albatros, 313 pp., includes 109 names, some of them well
known: among others Eliade, Manea, Popescu, Codrescu (the latter

---

* The place of publication of books is Bucharest unless otherwise stated.

two having written for a long time only in English). It is more difficult to understand why the notion of 'writer' seems to have so extended as to cover a series of linguists who have never published any kind of literature as such, e.g. G. Vrabie.

Publication of *Dicţionar analitic de opere literare româneşti*, has continued with III, *M–P*, ed. Ion Pop, Cluj-Napoca, Casa Cărţii de Ştiinţă, 440 pp., listing 185 more or lesser known titles, according to a preference already established in the previous volumes: many contemporary works by authors barely on the threshold of notoriety are present here, whereas several well-known items of earlier literature are ignored — not only literature as belles-lettres, but also studies and critical articles which have proved to be landmarks in the evolution of public taste, a field completely overlooked by the authors (Macedonski's *Mişcarea literară în cei din urmă zece ani*, Gherea's *Personalitatea şi morala în artă*, Maiorescu with *O cercetare critică* etc.). The selected texts and information are however very carefully researched.

Eugen Simion, *Ficţiunea jurnalului intim*, 3 vols, Univers enciclopedic, 289, 341, 432 pp., debates, especially in vol. 3, the 'diary-type' writings (daily notes, either memoirs or travel notes) of Romanian literature, beginning with the 18th c. but paying special attention to the 20th c.: Lovinescu, Rebreanu, Eliade, Sebastian, Radu Petrescu, I. D. Sârbu, Steinhardt, Zaciu.

Alexandru Alexianu, *Istoria poeziei culte româneşti, 1570–1830*, ed. by Mircea Coloşenco, 4 vols, Majadahonda, 478, 495, 493, 495 pp., has been published from the late author's MS with, as a preface, a 1979 report by professor I. C. Chiţimia (himself now deceased) conceived with a view to publishing certain editions which for political reasons were not feasible at that time: Alexianu had been a high official of the Antonescu regime (governor general of Bessarabia) during the war. The book is not a history proper, but the vast and certainly valuable annotated anthology, often naively annotated, of a lover of poetry and old books — self-taught in the field — accompanied by historical excursions into the period. The notes sometimes contain erroneous references, and there are several mistakes long since corrected by literary history: it seems likely that in some cases they were completed by the editor without any specification to that effect. In fact, the entire edition lacks a minimal critical apparatus: there is no proper preface, no note on the edition, no note on the author, no bibliography, and it is disfigured by numerous printing mistakes.

A bibliography of the periodical publications of Transylvania has been authored by Nae Antonescu, *Reviste din Transilvania*, Oradea, Biblioteca revistei 'Familia', 350 pp.

2. MONOGRAPHS, PERIOD SYNTHESES, CRITICISM

OLD ROMANIAN LITERATURE

Two volumes in the 'popular books' series, edited by the philology department of the Institute for Linguistics of the Romanian Academy, present philological editions of virtually unknown texts: *Palia istorică*, Fundaţia Naţională pentru Ştiinţă şi Artă, 254 pp., vol. 4 of the series 'The oldest popular books in Romanian literature', with a historical and philological study by Alexandra Moraru and Mihai Moraru, contains several apocrypha referring to the Old and New Testament of the early 17th-c. MS 469 at the Library of the Romanian Academy. This MS was part of the thesaurus sent to Moscow in 1916 and could not be researched until 1957. *Alexie, omul lui Dumnezeu, Lemnul crucii*, and *Disputa lui Isus cu Satana*, respectively ed. and introd. Maria Stanciu-Istrate, Emanuela Timotin, and Liliana Agache, form the fifth volume of the previously mentioned series, Fundaţia Naţională pentru Ştiinţă şi Artă, 250 pp. *Fiziolog. Bestiar*, ed. Cătălina Velculescu and Vasile Guruianu, with an excursus by Manuela Anton, Cavallioti, 101 pp. + 7 pls, presents the *Fiziolog* as transcribed by Costea Dascălul of Şcheii Braşovului in 1693 from MS 1436 at the Library of the Romanian Academy. Ion Istrate, *Primul Occident. Începuturile poeziei şi teatrului în cultura română*, Piteşti, Paralela 45, 153 pp., deals with the autochthonous hymn-writing tradition, the poetry of Miron Costin, Dosoftei's 'enigma' in the 17th c., etc. Dan Horia Mazilu, *O istorie a blestemului*, Iaşi, Polirom, 429 pp., also touches on the study of certain literary figures (excommunication, the curse and curse books, etc.), and the curse as a form of protection for the library and the book. Id., *Recitind literatura română veche*, III ('Genurile literare'), Universităţii, 2000, 748 pp., is the last volume of a series, launched in 1994, concerning chronicles and chroniclers, travel notes (Constantin Cantacuzino, Nicolae Milescu), philosophical novels and texts (Udrişte Năsturel, Cantemir, etc.). Gheorghe Mihăilă, *Langue et culture roumaines dans l'espace sud-est europeen*, Academiei, 711 pp., contains several studies dealing with relations between the old Romanian historiography of the 15th–17th c. and Byzantine-Slavonic historiography, and also with writers of the 15th–16th c. such as Neagoe Basarab, Mihail Moxa, Grigore Ţamblac, etc.). Alexandru Ofrim, *Cheia şi psaltirea. Imaginarul cărţii în cultura tradiţională românească*, pref. Irina Nicolau, Piteşti, Paralela 45, 362 pp., is a piece of research on the interference of village and urban traditional culture, rejecting the definition of orality as 'the absence of writing' and insisting on the presence of books and writing in popular creations (books and symbolic gestures, the magic of writing and books, the beneficial action of reading, bibliomancy, divination through books, etc.).

A piece of global research on the books printed in Alba-Iulia by the beginning of the 18th century is provided by Eugen Pavel, *Carte şi tipar la Bălgrad (1567–1702)*, Cluj-Napoca, Clusium, 380 + xxi pp. The first chapter, 'Etape în istoria tiparului românesc de la Alba-Iulia', suggests some modifications to cultural history, to the history of printing, etc. — works published by Coresi without specification of place are here said to have been printed in Alba-Iulia — and chapter v discusses the 'Evoluţia normelor literare în tipăriturile bălgrădene'. Radu Ştefan Vergatti (who has also published as Radu Ştefan Ciobanu), *Nicolae Spătarul Milescu. Viaţa, călătoriile, opera*, Paideia, 1998, 298 pp. + 4 w/o. plates. Mircea Vasilescu, *'Iubite cetitoriule…'. Lectură, public şi comunicare în cultura română veche*, Piteşti, Paralela 45, 186 pp., studies 'roads of literary communication in the 16th–18th centuries', the foreword in old books, etc.

EIGHTEENTH CENTURY

Demetrii Principis Cantemirii Incrementorum et Decrementorum Aulae Othmanicae sive Aliothmanicae Historiae a Prima Gentis Origine ad Nostra Usque Tempora Deductae Libri Tres, ed. Dan Sluşanschi, pref. Virgil Cândea, Timişoara, Amarcord, 550 pp., is a critical edition of the Latin text with notes, indexes, and an English preface. Mihai Mitu, *Oameni şi fapte din secolul al XVIII-lea românesc*, Atos, 1999, 271 pp., contains several important studies on Ion Budai-Deleanu, Chesarie of Râmnic, and Alexandru Moruzi. N. A. Ursu, 'Traducerile ierodiaconului Gherasim de la Episcopia Romanului', *Anuarul Institutului de istorie 'A. D. Xenopol'* (Iaşi), 37, 2000: 127–44.

NINETEENTH CENTURY

Vasile Ciocanu, *Contribuţii istorico-literare*, Fundaţiei Culturale Române, 281 pp., brings together studies devoted especially to 19th-c. Moldavian writers: Stamati, Hâjdău, Kogălniceanu, Conachi, etc. Ioana Drăgan, *Romanul popular în România. Literar şi paraliterar*, Cluj, Casa Cărţii de Ştiinţă, 214 pp., conducts a statistical examination of the popular novel in Romania between 1831–1918 and outlines a potential typology of the popular novel. Ion Bogdan Lefter, *Mic dicţionar de scriitori bucureşteni din secolul XIX, sau despre cum se trăia altădată fala de a reprezenta Capitala*, Piteşti, Paralela 45, 111 pp.

ALECSANDRI. Victor Durnea, 'Orizonturi ale creaţiei şi ale vieţii în corespondenţa lui V. Alecsandri', pp. 7–76 of D.'s *Orizonturi regăsite*, Iaşi, Junimea, 1999.

CARAGIALE. Ion Luca Caragiale, *Opere*, iii, ed. Ştefan Ilin and Constantin Hârlav, Univers enciclopedic, 1238 pp., gathers his journalism; Marin Bucur, *I. L. Caragiale. Lumea operei*, III, ed. Ştefan Ion Ghilimescu, Piteşti, Paralela 45, 271 pp., is the last volume of a monograph begun in 1989 but left unfinished at the author's death in 1994. Gelu Negrea, *Anti-Caragiale*, Cartea românească, 196 pp., despite its title, is an essay arguing the case for the ground-breaking function of Caragiale's writing, and also stressing the symbolic value of *writing* in its work: 'his characters ... write and read with the same voluptuousness they use for speaking'.

CREANGĂ. Mircea Bertea, *Creangă înainte de Creangă*, Cluj-Napoca, Dacia, 285 pp.

EMINESCU. Mihai Cimpoi, *Critice. Fierăria lui Iocan*, Craiova, Fundaţia 'Scrisul românesc', 205 pp., includes *inter alia*: 'Eminescu şi abisul receptării', ' "Preot deşteptării noastre" ', 'Eminescu şi bolile culturii româneşti', etc.. Ion Derşidan, *Monologul dramatic eminescian*, Cluj-Napoca, 200 pp. Ion Funeriu, *M. Eminescu: lecturi infidele*, Academiei, 20 pp., is the text of a lecture. Constantin Georgescu, *Eminescu şi editorii săi*, 2 vols, Floare albastră, 2000, 446, 318 pp. Dan Mănucă, *Opinii literare*, Cartea românească, 164 pp., includes studies such as 'Un bilanţ negativ: Eminescu şi Lenau', 'Feţele unui epistolar', 'Mai este actual Eminescu?', etc. Ion Stanomir, *Reacţiune şi conservatorism. Eseu asupra imaginarului politic eminescian*, Nemira, 333 pp.

HASDEU. Bogdan Petriceicu Hasdeu, *Scrieri politice. 1869–1902*, ed. and ann. Ionel Oprişan, 2 vols, Saeculum I.O., 494, 473 pp.

HELIADE RĂDULESCU. Mircea Anghelescu, *Echilibru între antiteze. Heliade, o biografie*, Univers enciclopedic, 313 pp.

ODOBESCU. Florentin Popescu, *Romanul vieţii şi operei lui Alexandru Odobescu*, Constanţa, Ex Ponto, 319 pp., reconstructs the writer's life with some romance elements and with an interpretation of his *œuvre*, whose documentation stops at the year 1989.

PANN. Anton Pann, *Spitalul amorului*, ed. Doina Prisecaru, foreword Petre Florea, Centrul de conservare şi valorificare a tradiţiei, 52 pp.

TWENTIETH CENTURY

Nae Antonescu, *Reviste literare interbelice*, Cluj-Napoca, Dacia, 295 pp. Eva Behring, *Scriitori români din exil: 1945–1989. O perspectivă istorico-literară*, trans. (from German) Tatiana Petrache and Lucia Nicolau, rev. the author and Roxana Sorescu, Fundaţiei Culturale Române, 258 pp., constitutes a previously unpublished book, with chapters on 'Cronologia şi durata exilului literar', 'Identitatea culturală şi conşti-inţa de sine', 'Probleme fundamentale ale exilului scriitoricesc', and analytical texts on Eliade, Caraion, Goma, Manea, Ţepeneag. Lucian Boz, *Scrisori din exil*, ed. Mircea Popa, Cluj-Napoca, Dacia, 254 pp., consists of letters to and from Ştefan Baciu, Cioran, Eliade, Ionescu, and others. Maria-Luiza Cristescu, *Politici ale romanului românsc contemporan*, Cartea românească, 245 pp. Alina Ciobanu-Tofan, *Spiritus loci. Variaţiuni pe o temă*, Chişinău, Gunivas, 208 pp., concerns Bessarabian literature between the wars and in more recent times. Vitalie Ciobanu, *Vals pe eşafod*, Chişinău, Cartier, 281 pp., contains important essays on 'Valorile în societatea contemporană', 'Complexele culturilor din Europa Centrală', 'Proza basarabeană' etc. Caius Dobrescu, *Inamicul impersonal*, Piteşti, Paralela 45, 271 pp., comprises essays on the survival of ancient mental patterns in culture and literature. Constantin Eretescu, *Feţele lui Ianus. America văzută de aproape*, Fundaţiei Culturale Române, 238 pp., gathers essays on the Romanian-American cultural interference. Vasile Igna, *Subteranele memoriei. Pagini din rezistenţa culturii, 1944–1954*, Universal Dalsi, 406 pp., combines an anthology and an introductory study on the involvement of Romanian writers and intellectuals in the defence of democratic culture, and on the communist repression that followed. *Scriitori români din anii '80–'90. Dicţionar bio-bibliografic*, ed. Ion Bogdan Lefter, III, *P-Z*, Piteşti, Paralela 45, 310 pp., includes 147 writers born between 1944 and 1975. *În căutarea comunismului pierdut*, Piteşti, Paralela 45, 332 pp., assembles studies by P. Cernat, I. Manolescu, A. Mitchievici, and I. Stanomir, attempting to reconstitute the political and social context of the official culture of the years 1945–1989. Emil Manu, *Reviste româneşti de poezie*, Curtea veche, 367 pp., is a revised edition of the 1972 book, with additions that include some personal recollections. Irina Petraş, *Panorama criticii literare româneşti. Dicţionar ilustrat 1950–2000*, Cluj-Napoca, Casa Cărţii de Ştiinţă, 669 pp., is useful and well researched — including a great number of critics, essayists, literary historians (sometimes even linguists or philosophers with no connection to literary criticism) — but very uneven and sometimes failing even to observe its own guidelines. Emil Pintea, *'Gândirea'. Indice bibliografic adnotat*, Cluj-Napoca, Echinox, 1998, 599 pp., is a complete and very accurate bibliography of the famous journal *Gândirea*, of a traditionalist-orthodox orientation, published between 1921 and 1944. Marian Popa, *Istoria literaturii române de azi pe mâine*, 2 vols, Fundaţia Luceafărul, 1229, 1273 pp. (index of names vol. 2, pp. 1225–73), is the most voluminous history of Romanian literature since World War II, with ample excursions into the political situation of each period, references to the press and to documents of the Communist Party, the Writers' Union etc. Its abundant biographical information, some useful, some trivial, and a very uneven commentary, with anti-Semitic overtones at times, make this book very difficult to categorize. Press comments (Dan C. Mihăilescu in *Litere, arte, idei*, February 2002) have noticed similarities to the denunciations of writers published in *Cartea neagră a securităţii*. Virgil Nemoianu, *Tradiţie şi libertate*, Curtea veche, 534 pp., gathers essays selected from the Romanian press — on literary and cultural phenomena and books — and several interviews — on globalism and multiculturalism, the canon, modernity, 'the pleasures of exile' etc. Ion Pop, *Viaţă şi texte*, Cluj-Napoca, 328 pp., gathers various essays on exiled authors, among whom Ţepeneag, Sanda Stolojan, Nicolae Balotă etc., and on the poetry of the '80s. Cornelia Ştefănescu, *Destinul unei întîlniri: Marcel Proust şi românii*, Elion, 238 pp. Mircea Vasilescu, *Mass-(co)media. Situaţii şi moravuri ale presei de tranziţie*, Curtea veche, 186 pp., are essays from the journal *Dilema*, placed under the sign of Caragiale's own journalism.

BART. On Bart, alias Eugen P. Botez: Constantin Mohanu, *Jean Bart. Viaţa şi opera*, Biblioteca Bucureştilor, 402 pp.

BLAGA. *V. Băncilă–Lucian Blaga: corespondenţă*, ed. Dora Mezdrea, Muzeul Literaturii române — Muzeul Judeţean Brăila, 294 pp.

BOTTA. Giovanni Rotiroti, *Dan Botta, între poiesis şi aisthesis*, Constanţa, Pontica, 230 pp.

BREBAN. Nicolae Breban, *Stricte amintiri literare*, Cluj-Napoca, Dacia, 198 pp., consists of portraits of writers and polemical articles. Liviu Maliţa, *Nicolae Breban. Monografie*, Braşov, Aula ('Canon' series), 109 pp.

BUZURA. Ion Simuţ, *Augustin Buzura. Monografie*, Braşov, Aula ('Canon' series), 93 pp.

ELIADE. Ofelia Ichim, *Pădurea interzisă. Mit şi autenticitate în romanele lui Mircea Eliade*, Iaşi, Alfa, 228 pp.; Gheorghe Glodeanu, *Coordonate ale imaginarului în opera lui Mircea Eliade*, Cluj-Napoca, Dacia, 244 pp.

FUNDOIANU. *Cahiers Benjamin Fondane*, 4, 2000–01, ed. Monique Jutrin and Leon Volovici, includes: O. Salazar-Ferrer, 'Fondane, lecteur de Nietzsche' (23–31); M. Jutrin, 'Fondane lisant Bachelard en 1943' (32–40); M. Finkenthal, 'Fondane et la psychanalyse' (54–55); H. Lenz, 'Felix Aderca, un ecrivain novateur' (67–79), with some letters from Fundoianu to Aderca translated by L.

GOGA. Octavian Goga, *Opere*, 1, ed., ann., and comm. Ion Dodu Bălan, introd. Eugen Simion, Univers enciclopedic, lix + 1350 pp., contains the writer's poetry, dramatic writing, and memoirs.

HORIA. Crenguţa Gânscă, *Vintilă Horia: al zecelea cerc*, Cluj-Napoca, Dacia, 104 pp.

IONESCU. Marta Petreu, *Ionescu în ţara tatălui*, Cluj-Napoca, Biblioteca Apostrof, 175 pp.; see also Lucian Boz, *Scrisori din exil*, mentioned above.

IVASIUC. Ion Bogdan Lefter, *Alexandru Ivasiuc, ultimul modernist*, Piteşti, Paralela 45, 184 pp., is an expanded version of the 1987 monograph.

LOVINESCU, E. Eugen Lovinescu, *Sburătorul. Agende literare*, V: *1936–1939*, ed. Monica Lovinescu and Gabriela Omăt, ann. Alexandru George, Margareta Feraru, and Gabriela Omăt, Fundaţia Naţională pentru Ştiinţă şi artă, 718 pp.

LOVINESCU, M. Monica Lovinescu, *La apa Vavilonului*, II: *1960–1980*, Humanitas, 275 pp., the second volume of her memoirs, has useful indexes of names (265–75).

MANOLESCU. Nicolae Manolescu, *Literatura română postbelică. Lista lui Manolescu*: I, *Poezia*; II, *Proza. Teatrul*; III, *Critica. Eseul*, Braşov, Aula, 429 + 348 + 444 pp., is the first selection of the pre-1989 literary chronicles of the most respected literary critic of his time.

MARINO. Constantin M. Popa, *Adrian Marino. Monografie*, Braşov, Aula ('Canon' series), 109 pp.

NAUM. Ion Pop, *Gellu Naum. Poezia contra literaturii*, Cluj-Napoca, Casa Cărţii de Ştiinţă, 196 pp.

PANDREA. Previously unpublished texts by Petre Pandrea have appeared in the journal *Caiete critice*, 2001, 7–12, and also memoirs by the writer's daughter, Nadia Marcu Pandrea, and an essay by Eugen Simion.

PETRESCU. Cipriana Petre, *Didascalia în opera lui Camil Petrescu*, Cluj, Idea Design, 183 pp., has a foreword by Sanda Golopenţia. Previously unpublished texts (his B.A. thesis, his philosophy studies) are introduced by M. Ilovici in *Manuscriptum*, 31 : 35–47.

PREDA. Rodica Zane, *Marin Preda. Monografie*, Braşov, Aula ('Canon' series), 109 pp.

REBREANU. Gheorghe Glodeanu, *Liviu Rebreanu. Ipostaze ale discursului epic*, Cluj-Napoca, Dacia, 264 pp.

SADOVEANU. Izabela Sadoveanu, *Cărţi şi idei*, I, ed., pref. and ann. Margareta Feraru, Fundaţia Naţională pentru Ştiinţă şi Artă, XXV + 334 pp., comprises articles and chronicles.

SEBASTIAN. Iordan Chimet, *Dosarul Mihail Sebastian*, Universal Dalsi, 330 pp.

SIMION. Andrei Grigor, *Eugen Simion. Monografie*, Braşov, Aula ('Canon' series), 93 pp.

SELEJAN. Ana Selejan, *Retorica vulnerabilităţii. O monografie a poeziei lui Radu Selejan*, Cartea românească, 161 pp.

STEINHARDT. Nicolae Steinhardt, *Eu însumi şi alţi câţiva*, Cluj-Napoca, Dacia, 352 pp. *Amintiri despre N. Steinhardt*, a reader by Arşavir Acterian, edited by Fabian Anton, Cluj-Napoca, Dacia, 108 pp.

ŢEPENEAG. Dumitru Ţepeneag, *Războiul literaturii încă nu s-a încheiat*, ed. Nicolae Bârna, Alfa, 2000, 282 pp., collects his interviews. See also *Un român la Paris*, in Ion Pop, *Viaţă şi texte*, noted above.

VINEA.   Ion Vinea, *Opere*, IV, ann. and comm. Elena Zaharia-Filipaş, Fundaţia Naţională pentru Ştiinţă şi Artă, 405 pp., a critical edition, contains the first part of the 'journalism' section, between the years 1913–1919.

VISSARION.   Victor Petrescu and Ştefan Ion Ghilimescu, *I. C. Vissarion. Între uitare şi dăinuire*, Târgovişte, Biblioteca & Pandora, 187 pp., also contains previously unpublished correspondence from Gala Galaction, Eugen Lovinescu, Gheorghe Topîrceanu, etc.

VOINESCU.   Alice Voinescu, *Scrisori din Costeşti*, ed., ann. and introd. Constandina Brezu, Albatros, 171 pp., comprises letters from the period of her forced domicile between 1951 and 1953, and her inquiry deeds from the S.R.I. archives.

VORONCA.   Ilarie Voronca, *Plante şi animale*, Icare-Vinea, 40 pp., with drawings by Constantin Brâncuşi, is an anastatic edition of the volume published in 1929.

XI. RHETO-ROMANCE STUDIES

By INGMAR SÖHRMAN, *Göteborg University*

1. BIBLIOGRAPHICAL AND GENERAL

Maria Iliescu, Guntram A. Plangg, and Paul Videsott, *Die vielfältige Romania. Dialekt — Sprache — Überdachungssprache. Gedenkschrift für Heinrich Schmid (1921–1999)*, San Martin de Tor, ICLMR — Vich (Vigo di Fassa), Istitut Cultural Ladin 'Majon di Fasegn' — Innsbruck, Institut für Romanistik, 234 pp., a *Festschrift* in honour of the founding father of both Rumantsch Grischun and Ladin Dolomitan, gathers interesting articles on Ladin, Romansh, and other Romance varieties, written by a series of renowned researchers, and also includes Schmid's own bibliography (16–20). E. N. Mámsurova, 'Acerca de las llamadas "lenguas minoritarias" del grupo románico', *Sot la nape*, 53.1:33–42, *inter alia* draws attention to oft-neglected Russian contributions to the study of Rheto-Romance, including Friulan, and also to Russian investigation into other minority Romance languages such as Catalan, Galician, and Occitan.

2. FRIULAN

BIBLIOGRAPHICAL AND GENERAL. Giorgio Faggin, 'Testimonianze sulla lingua friulana', *Ladinia*, 23, 1999[2001]:183–89, a follow-up to his 1989 article in *Ladinia*, 13, presents comments (including bibliographical references) on Friulan as a language. 'Oparis di Manliu Michelutti pe Societât Filologjiche Furlane fin al 1996', *Sot la nape*, 53.2:119–22, compiles a bibliography of the recently deceased scholar's publications.

PHONOLOGY AND MORPHOLOGY. L. Spinozi Monai, 'Analisi comparata del tipo tardo latino *scriba, -anis* e di tipi analoghi dell'area slavo-romanza', *Ce fastu?*, 77:7–22, rejects the suggestion that the late Latin introduction of an extended stem in the plural may be due to Slav influence in favour of that of the disappearing lengthened vocative *scribanu*. In J. B. Trumper, 'Quattro percorsi culturo-linguistici a zigzag: ricuarts di une visite a Udin. ("Arglwydd Llewelyn, lyw pedeirieith". Dal bardo Llygad Gwr ca. nel 1260 d.C.)', *ib.*, 151–200, the rather enigmatic title does not reveal that the article re-examines some untypical Indo-European consonantal clusters, connecting Friulan BILITE ('weasel') and the toponym BILIGNE with the spread of the Celtic 'wolf' lexeme associated with the wolf god Belenos. A most useful basic grammar for Friulan is

Fausto Zof, *Gramatiche pratiche de lenghe furlane*, Pasian di Prât, 1999, 255 pp.

ONOMASTICS AND LEXIS. G. Ellero, '"Ararûl"', *Sot la nape*, 53.2:123–26, is a short etymological article. C. Malaguti, 'Sappada/Plodn. Origini di un nome', *ib.*, 51–55, gives a plausible explanation as to how the river name Piave/Plodn <Lat. PLAVIS, by being attached to the German preposition *zum*, might have given the toponym Sappada. C. C. Desinan, 'Toponimi di "guerra" in Friuli', *ib.*, 53.1:89–94, an overview of the toponymical evidence connected to 'war' and its cognates, shows that, although many are Italian, there are some interesting Friulan toponyms, e.g. 'Tana dai Disertôrs', which point to historical realities. Id., 'Prediali a Udine', *ib.*, 53.2:47–50, and 'Alcuni prediali tardivi in Friuli', *ib.*, 53.3–4:53–55, gives brief accounts of several toponyms. M. Buligatto, 'Annotazioni sul toponimo "Ronchi dei legionari"', *ib.*, 49–52, briefly discusses one name mentioned in Desinan's earlier article (see above) on 'war toponyms'. Id., 'La cognomizzazione del titolo gastaldo', *ib.*, 53.2:59–64, investigates the distribution in Friuli of surnames deriving from *gastaldo*, e.g. Castaldi, Gastaldin, Gastaldello, etc. Elwys De Stefani, *Contributo all'onomastica familiare friulana. Cognomi della Carnia: approcci e sondaggi archivistici ed etimologici*, Basel, Universität Basel, 626 pp., is a clear and detailed presentation of a field that has been thoroughly investigated. The etymological analyses seem well founded, and the documentation is extremely rich, enhancing the value of the contribution. Id., 'Storia e gente del Friuli attraverso i cognomi', *Ce fastu?*, 76, 2000[2001]:1175–95.

SOCIOLINGUISTICS AND LANGUAGES IN CONTACT. W. Cisilino, 'La tutele de minorance furlane de Regjon Autonome Friûl–Vignesie Julie', *ib.* 53.2:93–100, deals with the official recognition of Friulan in the region in 1996 and in Italy as a whole in 1999 and the question how these rights should be used. In continuation of this article, Id., 'Fondis pe redazion di une leç di politiche lenghistiche de Regjon Autonome Friûl Vignesie Julie a pro dal furlan', *ib.*, 53.3–4:57–65, looks at the background and future prospects of language policy in Friuli. G. Ellero, 'Letteratura e autonomia', *ib.*, 53.2:7–11, underlines the critical mass that is necessary for a region to produce a living literature and stresses the need for a unified language in Friuli. He questions the existence of a young Friulan literature and asks whether there is a future for a language that is not vitalized by a strong literature.

3. LADIN

BIBLIOGRAPHICAL AND GENERAL. [Anton Vian,] *Gröden, der Grödner und seine Sprache*, Bolzano, Raetia, 1998 (but distributed later), 208 pp., to mark Val Gardena's thousand years reproduces in facsimile a classic which describes the region, its people, and the language, and includes some short Ladin texts. Its linguistic value lies in the fact that it gives a good idea of the language of Val Gardena and how it was viewed in the mid 1850s. The book was published anonymously in 1864 (as written by 'ein Einheimischen'), but it is well known that Anton Vian was the author. Though interesting in itself, the facsimile would have gained in value had there been a short introduction to the book's content, reception, and use. R. Bauer and H. Goebl, 'Arbeitsbericht 11 zum ADL-I', *Ladinia*, 23, 1999[2001]: 281–301, presents a final report on the work of the first part (7 vols) of the monumental *Atlant linguistich dl ladin dolomitich y di dialec vejins*. This series of articles should be of interest to any frequent user of the atlas. H. Goebl, 'Der ALD-I im Ziel. Ein Rückblick auf der zweite Halbzeit', pp. 171–87 of Maria Iliescu et al., *Die vielfältige Romania* cit., sums up the atlas project. Marco Forni and Helga Alton, *Publicazions dl Istitut Ladin 'Micurà de Rü': Articuli publichei te 'Ladinia' 1977–1998 partii su per argumēnc. Articuli publichei te 'Lingaz y cultura' (1979–1985). Lista publicazions dl Istitut Ladin 'Micurà de Rü'*, San Martin de Tor, ICMLR, 2000, 47 pp. Heinrich Schmid, **Criteri per la formazione di una lingua scritta comune della Ladinia dolomitica*, San Martin de Tor, ICLMR — Vich, Istitut Cultural Ladin 'Majon di Fasegn', 2000, 152 pp., is a translation by N. Chioccetti from the original German.

PHONOLOGY AND MORPHOLOGY. Rut Bernardi, *Curs de gherdëina*, San Martin de Tor, ICLMR, 1999, 255 pp., albeit written as a course book, also serves as a basic grammar and gives a good idea of modern Val Gardena Ladin. H. Böhmer, 'Sprachliche Stereotypen im Comelico. Ein Beitrag zur subjektiven Dialekterkennung', *Ladinia*, 23, 1999[2001]: 191–207, contrasts her own results with those of Tagliavini (1926) in presenting the peculiarities of the Comelico dialect in order to show why it should be considered a Ladin dialect. The argumentation is wide-ranging and convincing. Marco Forni, *La ortografia dl ladin de Gherdëina cun i ponc dla ortografia che ie unic scemplifichei*, San Martin de Tor, ICLMR, 57 pp., sets out to simplify the spelling of Val Gardena Ladin, which many have considered too complicated. The orthography and spelling changes are clearly presented, and the book also contains some morphosyntactic recommendations. The Val Badia variety of Ladin is well described in Tone Gasser, *Gramatica ladina por les scores*, Bolzano, Istitut Pedagogich Ladin — San Martin de Tor, ICLMR, 2000, 237 pp., which, in spite of its modest size provides a clear presentation of the morphology and also the basic syntax. In Hans Goebl, 'Giovan Batista Pellegrini und Ascolis Methode der "particolar combinazione". Eine Besprechungsaufsatz',

Ladinia, 23, 1999[2001]:139–81, the great *Atlant linguistich dl ladin dolomitich y di dialec vejins* is used to re-evaluate the methods of Ascoli and Pellegrini. Tables, maps, and the geo-typological discussion clearly show how the old scholars have been misunderstood and the need for a meticulous investigation differentiating basic notions like 'specific' vs 'general', 'quantity' vs 'quality', etc. Erwin Valenti et al., *Gramatica dl ladin standard*, Vich, Istitut Cultural Ladin — San Martin de Tor, ICLMR — Bulsan, 140 pp., presents the unified Ladin written language within the SPELL (Servisc de Planificazion y Elaborazion dl Lingaz Ladin) project. The book is the result of large-scale collaboration on the part of the main Ladin cultural organizations. After some introductory notes by Otto Gsell on how the work has been carried out and what considerations have guided the authors in creating a unified morphology, there is a very brief description of Ladin phonology and orthography. Basic syntactical structures and fairly detailed morphological description alternate. There is a good account of Ladin word formation. On the whole, the grammar provides a sound basis for the unification of Ladin which is needed if a revitalization of the language is to take place. The project includes a dictionary which remains to be published. To judge from F. Chiocchetti, 'Tendenze evolutive nella morfologia nominale ladino-fassana: il plurale maschile in *-es*', pp. 151–70 of Maria Iliescu et al., *Die vielfältige Romania* cit., the standardization of Ladin would seem to be leading to standardization of the various Ladin dialects: the masculine plural in Fassano is tending to move in a west-Romance direction and use *-es* < Lat. -os, while in Val Gardena *-i* is standard, albeit mostly realized as a palatalization.

ONOMASTICS AND LEXIS. The SPELL project generates not only books on standardized Ladin Dolomitan but also books on the different dialects, such as the new *Dizionario Italiano–Ladino Fassoano / Dizionèr Talian–Ladin Fascian*, Vich, 1999. Otto Gsell, 'Johannes Kramer, ETYMOLOGISCHES WÖRTERBUCH DES DOLOMITENLADIN-ISCHEN (EWD), Bd. VIII, T-Z. unter mitarbeit von Klaus-Jürgen Fiacre, Ruth Boketta, Ute Mehren, Hamburg, Buske, 1996, S. 413', *Ladinia*, 23, 1999[2001]:223–59, albeit only a review article should be mentioned here since its many addenda, comments, and corrections must be of the utmost interest to any user of Kramer's work. Giovanni Mischì, *Wörterbuch Deutsch–Gadertalisch / Vocabolari Todësch–Ladin (Val Badia)*, San Martin de Tor, ICLMR, CD-ROM, + 40-p. booklet, augments the dictionary published in book form in 2000 and adds instructions and orthographic rules. This represents an improvement. The new work is easy to use, and it goes both ways, which its predecessor did not. It constitutes a most valuable modern tool for anyone dealing with Ladin. A multilingual reality clearly emerges from K. Odwarka and H. P. Pohl, 'Die Namen des Kalser Tales (am Grossglockner)', *Ladinia*, 23, 1999[2001]: 209–21, where the authors show that 8% of the toponyms in the region are pre-Roman, 30% Romance (Ladin), 7% Slavic, and 55% German. P. Videsott, 'Die Adaptierung des Lohnwortschatzes in *Ladin Dolomitan*', pp. 201–21 of Maria Iliescu et al., *Die vielfältige Romania* cit., suggests a standardized word formation system applied to loan words but based on ongoing linguistic discussion. Id., *Ladinische Familiennamen / Cognoms ladins*, Innsbruck, Wagner, 2000, 373 pp., is a detailed onomastic study with etymological explanations, involving the toil of going through the parish register (1605–1784) at Enneberg / La Pli de Mareo.

SOCIOLINGUISTICS AND LANGUAGES IN CONTACT. Rut Bernardi, 'Ladin Dolomitan als Sprache der Literatur — kann man auf Ladin Dolomitan Literatur schreiben?' pp. 135–49 of Maria Iliescu et al., *Die vielfältige Romania* cit., discusses the interesting problem whether a newly created unified language can rapidly become the artful tool of writers, and she gives a positive answer to a much debated question. A general view of the sociolinguistic situation in the Ladin parts of the Dolomites, with special regard to the education system, is given in *La minoranza ladina: aspetti culturali ed educative. Atti del Convegno, Ortisei, maggio 2000*, ed. Roland Verra, Bolzano, Istitut Pedagogich Ladin, 2000, 102 pp. A good description and evaluation of the implantation of Ladin Dolomitan is given in Id., 'Das Ladin Dolomitan: Probleme und Perspektiven', pp. 185–200 of Maria Iliescu et al., *Die vielfältige Romania* cit.

4. SWISS ROMANSH

BIBLIOGRAPHICAL AND GENERAL. Joachim Lengert, *Romanische Phraseologie und Parömiologie*, Bd 1, Tübingen, Narr, 1999, xl + 1112 pp., a vast bibliography, comprises references to most of what has been written on phraseology in Romansh, French, and Italian. Georges Lüdi et al., *Die Sprachenlandschaft Schweiz*, Tübingen, is a presentation of the linguistic situation of Switzerland dealing with all four national languages and their present status and use. H. Siller-Runggaldier and P. Videsott, 'Rätoromanische Bibliographie 1985–1997', *VR*, 59, 2000: 276–77, continue their thorough bibliographical documentation. A most interesting and varied collection of articles is presented in *Italica–Raetica– Gallica. Studia linguarum litterarum artiumque in honorem Ricarda Liver*, ed. Peter Wunderli, Iwar Werlem, and Matthias Grünert, Tübingen, Francke, xxvi + 718 pp. The articles extend over linguistic and cultural tendencies throughout the Romance field but focus on Romansh. Juliana Tschuor,

'Publicaziuns', *ASR*, 114:303–06, gives the annual Romansh bibliography extended because of an earlier curtailment.

PHONOLOGY AND MORPHOLOGY. Wolfgang Eichenhofer, *Historische Lautlehre der Bündnerromanischen*, Tübingen, Francke, 1999, 575 pp., provides a systematic description of historical phonology in Romansh. Although not all dialectal varieties have been included, there is at least one representative variety from each linguistic region, so that we are given a very good overview of the phonological development of Romansh in its varieties.

MORPHOSYNTAX. A short Vallader grammar and orthography is given in Jachen Andry, **Ün pêr tschögns davart ortografia, morfosintaxa e lexic dal vallader*, 2000, 63 + 15 pp., which are exercises for language laboratory use. The fairly parallel development of Latin CUM in Surselvan and Romanian is comparatively studied in M. Iliescu, 'Die "logisch-semantische" Präposition "mit" im Surselvischen und Rumänischen', pp. 87–99 of Maria Iliescu et al., *Die vielfältige Romania* cit. Her conclusion is that CUM/CU is a logical-semantic preposition different from grammatical and deictic prepositions. D. Varga, 'La subordination en *vallader* rhétoroman de la Basse-Engadine', *RLiR*, 257–58:169–96, explains how Vallader subordination is organized in two phases, complementation and then integration.

ONOMASTICS AND LEXIS. Part 3 of the Romansch etymological dictionary, *LIR (Lexic istoric retic)*, *Cuira–Friaul* has been published by Adolf Collenberg and his group in *ASR*, 114:121–66. Hans Danuser, **Flurnamenkarte Langwies 1 : 15,000*, Arosa, 2000. Wolfgang Eichenhofer, **"Stammt bündnerromanisch 'béča' aus BĀCA'*, *VR*, 59, 2000:116–19. Felix Giger, Carli Tomaschett, Marga Annastina Secchi, Claudio Vincenz, and Kuno Widmer have published three more fascicules of *Dicziunari Rumantsch Grischun*: 138, LASCHAR–LATROCINI, 139, LATROCINI–LAVETSCH, and 140, LAVETSCH–LAZOIRA. All were published at Chur in 2000. The complicated semantic and syntactic changes that the verb ADUNARE and its participle have undergone, comparing them with parallel constructions in French and Italian, are analysed in G. Hilty, 'ADUNATUS', pp. 75–86 of Maria Iliescu et al., *Die vielfältige Romania* cit. R. Liver, 'Die Etymologie von fr. *trouver* und die bündnerromanischen Reflexe von TROPUS und TROPARE', *VR*, 60:117–27, discusses the controversial etymology of *trouver* and suggests some reflections of this etymon in Romansh. The same author highlights unique Latin borrowings in Romansh in her article 'Extravagante Neologismen im Bündnerromanischen', pp. 121–32 of Maria Iliescu et al., *Die vielfältige Romania* cit. The two words she describes are MULTIFARI and EXPECTORAR. How a Latin word might come to Romansch through Lombard is shown in G. Hoyer, 'Davart la plazza dal pled latin FETA en rumantsch. In pled bregagliot "Fex" en la toponimia da l'Engiadin'Ota', *ASR*, 114:7–13, which elaborates meticulously on different names for batrachians and how only Sutsilvan and Surmiran have kept a supposedly Late Latin *QUATTERPEDIAS, while the other varieties have borrowed other words related to concepts like 'water' and 'rain'. She also gives a brief description of traditional beliefs connected with these animals. Tables and maps illustrate clearly her thesis in G. Hoyer, 'Les désignations de la salamandre et du triton dans les parlers germaniques de la Romania Submersa des Alpes centrales', *ib.*, 15–78. G. Plangg, 'Vorarlberger Familiennamen II', *Monfort*, 52, 2000:264–70, continues his work in the field of onomastics. A. Spescha, *'La personificaziun dell'aura', *Calender Romontsch*, 141, 2000: 297–316. A new Engadin dictionary has made a timely appearance: *Dicziunari puter–Deutsch / Wörterbuch Deutsch–puter*, ed. Gion Tscharner, Chur, LMV, 2000, xxxvi + 910 pp.

SOCIOLINGUISTICS AND LANGUAGES IN CONTACT. An empirical study of the effects of language immersion in Romansh schools is presented in R. Cathomas, 'Zur Wirksamkeit des immersiven Unterrichts an den bündnerromanischen Schulen in der Schweiz', pp. 179–97 of *Les langues minoritaires en contexte / Minderheitensprachen im Kontext*, ed. Anna-Alice Dazzi Gross and Lorenza Mondada, Neuchâtel, Institut Linguistique, 1999. W. Cisilino, 'Lenghe e dirit', *Sot la nape*, 53.1:95–99, discusses linguistic rights in the Graubünden and the consequences of the semi-official status of Romansh that was given in early 1996. A.-A. Dazzi Gross and M. Gross, 'Erfahrungen mit der gesamtbündnerromanischen Schriftsprache Rumantsch Grischun', pp. 53–73 of Maria Iliescu et al., *Die vielfältige Romania* cit., sums up the consequences of implementation of unified Romansh and future prospects. A gender analysis of Romansh is carried out in A.-A. Dazzi Gross and E. Caduff, ' "La directurs curaschusa . . ." oder Die Gleichberechtigung im Rätoromanischen', pp. 47–61 of *Sprachliche Gleichstellung von Frau und Mann in der Schweiz / La féminisation de la langue en Suisse / La femminilizzazione della lingua in Svizzera / ö L'egualtad linguistica da dunna ed om en Svizra*, ed. Daniel Elmiger and Eva Lia Wyss, Neuchâtel, Institut Linguistique, 2000. A fair résumé of language planning in the Romansh case is given in M. Gross, '*Rumantsch Grischun*. Planification de la normalisation', pp. 95–105 of *Les langues minoritaires en contexte / Minderheitensprachen im Kontext* cit.

3

CELTIC LANGUAGES

I. WELSH STUDIES

LANGUAGE

By DAVID THORNE, *Professor of Welsh Language and Literature,
University of Wales, Lampeter*

1. GENERAL

Xavier Delamaree, *Dictionnaire de la langue gauloise – une approche
linguistique du vieux-celtique continental*, Paris, Errance, 352pp., presents
a concise and dependable overview of the language.

2. GRAMMAR

G. R. Isaac, 'Colli sillafau mewn Brythoneg', *SC*, 34:105–18, revisits
the traditional theories regarding the loss of syllables in Brythonic
and suggests that factors other than accentuation and morphology
need to be considered. N. Sturzer, 'How Middle Welsh expresses the
unexpected', *CMCS*, 37–54, discusses the use of grammatical constructions in Middle Welsh in order to convey that an event is
unexpected or remarkable.

3. ETYMOLOGY AND LEXICOGRAPHY

G. R. Isaac, *SC*, 34:271–4, has notes on Leubrit, Loubrit from the
Book of Llandâf, on stanza 6 of the Juvencus poems and on *crees, oet re
rereint* from the Black Book of Carmarthen. E. Poppe, *ib.*, 275–78, has
notes on *y gadw, paratoi llong idaw, ac a neidyawd y neill hanner idi* in the
Welsh Life of St David. Parts 56, 57, 58 of GPC (ed. G. A. Bevan)
cover TEITHI–TORTH, TORTH–TRINIAF, TRINIAF–TWRSTNEIDDRWYDD
respectively. Ceri Jones, *Dweud eich Dweud: Geiriadur o Idiomau Cymraeg*,
Llandysul, Gomer xvii + 268 pp., is a valuable and well-presented
guide to colloquial and idiomatic Welsh. The bulk of the book is an
alphabetical list of the main grammatical features of Welsh but also
has an interesting, though elementary, section on the registers of the
language. Alun Rhys Cownie, *A Dictionary of Welsh and English Idiomatic
Phrases*, Cardiff, Univ. of Wales Press, xvii + 299pp., consists of 12,000
idioms arranged in alphabetical order, with translations, regional

variations and cross referencing. P. Schrijver, *EC*, 31:157–60, has notes on OW *guogaltou* (glosses to *Martianus Capella*) and on OW *tarnetor*, *niritarnher* (Computus fragment). Id., *ib*., 147–55, has notes on geminate spellings in the OW glosses. Geiriadur Ar-lein Cymraeg-Saesneg, Saesneg-Cymraeg Prifysgol Cymru Llanbedr Pont Steffan/ The University of Wales, Lampeter On-line Welsh-English, English-Welsh Dictionary, is a dynamic digital dictionary of over 100,000 headwords; it is accessed on http://www.e-addysg.com/geiriadur/

4. SOCIOLINGUISTICS

Dylan Phillips and Catrin Thomas, *Effeithiau Twristiaeth ar yr Iaith Gymraeg yng Ngogledd Orllewin Cymru/The Effects of Tourism on the Welsh Language in North-West Wales*, UWCASWC, iv + 111 pp., is a bilingual volume presenting a detailed analysis of the relationship between tourism, in-migration and language use in an area of Wales which is a stronghold of the Welsh language as well as a popular tourist area. Gwenfair Parry, *'Nid Iaith Fain mohoni': Y Gymraeg ym Mangor a Chaernarfon yn ystod y Bedwaredd Ganrif ar Bymtheg*, UWCASWC, 54 pp., is a detailed analysis of the situation of the Welsh language in Bangor and Caernarfon in the 19th c. and shows how commerce, education, in-migration, the church, and the influence of the gentry aided the march of bilingualism to the detriment of the Welsh language. M. E. Jones, 'Little Wales beyond Wales: the struggle of Selattyn, a Welsh parish in Shropshire', *NLWJ*, 31:129–34, records how the little parish of Selattyn near Oswestrey campaigned for centuries to maintain its Welshness and for a more central place for the Welsh language in the parish church.

EARLY AND MEDIEVAL LITERATURE

By JANE CARTWRIGHT, *Lecturer in Welsh, University of Wales, Lampeter*

G. R. Isaac, 'Mydr a pherformiad yr Hengerdd', *Dwned*, 7: 9–26, sheds new light on rhythmical, syllabic patterns in the Hengerdd and warns against focusing on the accent as the basis for metrics in early poetry. He also proposes a *terminus post quem* of *c.* 950 for 'Pais Dinogad'. Id., 'Myrddin, proffwyd diwedd y byd: ystyriaethau newydd ar ddatblygiad y chwedl', *LlC*, 24: 13–23, considers the etymology of the name Myrddin and discusses the character's associations with Caerfyrddin (Carmarthen) and the Old North. Id., 'Englynion *Geraint fab Erbin* yn Llyfr Du Caerfyrddin', *SC*, 34: 273–74, takes the word *crees* to mean 'body' rather than 'skin' (*cnes*) and provides notes on certain lines in the *englynion* concerning Geraint in the Black Book.

N. A. Jones, 'Trafodaethau ar waith Beirdd y Tywysogion: Llyfryddiaeth 1988–99', *LlC*, 24: 24–32, is a sequel to 'Discussions on the work of the Gogynfeirdd: a Bibliography', *SC*, 22–23: 42–48. Here Jones provides a bibliography on the poetry of the Gogynfeirdd which covers work published between 1988 and 1999. Id., 'Llywarch ap Llywelyn a Llywarch Brydydd y Moch', *LlC*, 24: 161–64, discusses problems relating to authorship and dating and suggests that there may have been two, or even three, poets known as Llywelyn Fardd amongst the Gogynfeirdd. B. J. Lewis, 'Adeiladu cerdd: cyfuniadau geiriol yng nghanu crefyddol y Gogynfeirdd', *LlC*, 24: 33–51, carefully examines the language employed by the Gogynfeirdd and the frequency with which familiar phrases or particular combinations of words recur in their poetry. R. M. Andrews, 'Galar tad am ei fab: "Marwnad Dygynnelw" gan Gynddelw Brydydd Mawr', *LlC*, 24: 52–60, examines the only extant Welsh elegy written by a father to his son which belongs to the Gogynfeirdd period. Id., 'Nodiadau', *LlC*, 24: 159–61, provides an alternative modern Welsh translation for one of the lines in 'Marwysgafn Feilyr Brydydd' and suggests that *cyngor* (advice) should be altered to *cynnor* (door frame/post) in her own edition of 'Marwnad Llywelyn ap Gruffudd' by Gruffudd ab yr Ynad Coch. R. Davies, 'Iolo Goch, Rhosier Mortimer a *Piers Plowman*', *LlC*, 24: 164–69, provides historical notes on the connections between Walter Brugge, Phylip ap Morgan, Rhosier Mortimer and Iolo Goch.

UWCASWC continues its pioneering work on Middle Welsh poetry and makes available the work of a further four 15th-c. poets in two volumes. *Gwaith Gwerful Mechain ac Eraill*, ed. Nerys Ann Howells,

Aberystwyth UWCASWC, xvi + 192 pp., edits the poetry of Gwerful Mechain, the only female poet from medieval Wales by whom a substantial corpus of poetry has survived. As well as providing editions of the poetry, Howells also establishes the poetic canon for Gwerful and places her poetry in its wider literary context. She demonstrates that Gwerful Mechain wrote religious and prophetic poetry as well as erotic and light-hearted verse and she moved in the same literary circles as Dafydd Llwyd of Mathafarn, Ieuan Dyfi and Llywelyn ap Gutun. *Gwaith Syr Phylib Emlyn, Syr Lewys Meudwy a Mastr Harri ap Hywel*, ed. M. Paul Bryant-Quinn, Aberystwyth UWCASWC, xix + 164 pp., provides editions of the work of three poets from South Wales who were all professionally affiliated to the church. As well as fine religious poetry to Christ and the Virgin Mary, the volume also contains poetry of a more humorous nature such as the satirical verse Syr Phylib Emlyn and Syr Lewys Meudwy composed for each other and a *cywydd* by Mastr Harri warning the poet Ieuan Tew that he is far too old to win the affection of the young girl he has fallen in love with. J. Hunter, 'A new edition of the Poets of the Nobility', *CMCS*, 41: 55–64, discusses the contribution made by UWCASWC's *Cyfres Beirdd yr Uchelwyr* and reviews six volumes of poetry in the series. Although Hunter warmly welcomes the series and acknowledges the important contributions made by the individual editors, he criticizes the series' failure to adopt a theoretical approach to editorial practice. The traditional editorial techniques adopted, according to Hunter, lead to certain poems which are not considered to be the legitimate work of the poet in question being 'relegated to ghettoes at the end of the privileged bodies of accepted poetry'. M. P. Bryant-Quinn, 'Ailystyried "Englynion yr Offeren" gan Ddafydd ap Gwilym', *Dwned*, 7: 27–42, provides a new edition of Dafydd ap Gwilym's 'Englynion yr Offeren' and demonstrates that the poem focuses specifically on the *Anima Christi*. He also suggests that the extant text may be incomplete and that it may have been composed for a specific occasion such as the consecration of a new cross or the celebration of a religious feast. *Dafydd ap Gwilym: His Poems*, trans. Gwyn Thomas, Cardiff, Univ. of Wales Press, xxviii + 318 pp., provides superb English translations of the complete poems of Dafydd ap Gwilym. The translations are based on *Gwaith Dafydd ap Gwilym*, ed. Thomas Parry, Cardiff, Univ. of Wales Press, 1952. In addition, translations of a further six poems which have since been added to the canon are also included. M. E. Owen, 'Manion? Meddygol', *Dwned*, 7: 43–63, demonstrates that poets, such as Dafydd Nanmor, were familiar with the Welsh medical texts. She edits and discusses a series of *englynion* by Dafydd Nanmor which associate the signs of the zodiac with various parts of the body. The content of the poetry demonstrates Dafydd Nanmor's familiarity with a medical tractate found in BL Add 14912 which appears to have been in the poet's possession, since it bears his signature. The article also includes a series of metaphors describing the penis which Owen associates with Dafydd ap Gwilym's 'Cywydd y Gal'. Marged Haycock, ' "Defnydd hyd Ddydd Brawd'': rhai agweddau ar y ferch ym marddoniaeth yr Oesoedd Canol', in *Cymru a'r Cymry 2000 / Wales and the Welsh 2000*, ed. Geraint H. Jenkins, xv + 162 pp. (41–70), sheds new light on various aspects of women's history in medieval Wales by discussing references to sewing, embroidery and weaving in Welsh poetry. B. O. Huws, 'Y bardd a'i noddwr yn yr Oesoedd Canol diweddar', *Cof Cenedl*, 16: 1–32, analyses the relationship between poet and sponsor in the late medieval period and beyond, focusing on the three poems which Guto'r Glyn composed for Hywel ab Ieuan Fychan and his family. The poems are preserved in two manuscripts which belonged to Hywel's descendants. E. Roberts, 'The impact of the Cistercians on Welsh life and culture in north and mid Wales', *Transactions of the Denbighshire Historical Society*, 50: 13–23, is a historical article which includes a discussion on the relationship between Cistercian monasteries and the production and patronage of Welsh literature. A. T. E. Matonis, 'A case study: historical and textual aspects of the Welsh Bardic Grammar', *CMCS*, 41: 25–36, traces the development of the Welsh bardic grammar and discusses the various recensions. S. Harper, 'So how many Irish men went to Glyn Achlach? Early accounts of the formation of *Cerdd Dant*', *CMCS*, 42: 1–25, discusses the relationship between *cerdd dant* and *cerdd dafod* drawing on sources from the middle ages as well as the 16th c. and 17th c. In particular she emphasizes the connections between Ireland and Wales and highlights Irish influence on the development of *cerdd dant*.

Peter Wynn Thomas's innovative new edition of *Peredur* is made available on the web: www.cardiff.ac.uk/cymraeg/peredur. The edition is based on the White Book of Rhydderch and includes sections on editorial methodology, the language of *Peredur*, vocabulary and detailed notes. R. M. Jones, 'Cenedlaetholdeb a llenyddiaeth y de-ddwyrain', *LlC*, 24: 1–12, examines the role played by Gwent in the development of the concept of nationalism in medieval Welsh literature. He proposes that *Breuddwyd Macsen*, *Cyfranc Lludd a Llefelys* and the Three Romances originated in Gwent. A. Hall, 'Gwŷr y Gogledd? Some Icelandic analogues to *Branwen Ferch Lŷr*', *CMCS*, 42: 27–50, compares the Second Branch of the *Mabinogi* with Germanic narratives and provides some interesting Scandinavian parallels. *150 Jahre 'Mabinogion' — Deutsch-Walisische Kulturbeziehungen*, ed. Bernhard Maier and Stefan Zimmer, Tübingen, Max Niemeyer, x + 283 pp.*

E. Poppe, 'Three textual notes on the Welsh Life of Saint David', *SC*, 34: 275–78, provides notes on three separate sentences which occur in *Hystoria o Uuched Dewi*. J. Cartwright, 'Santesau Ceredigion', *Ceredigion*, 14: 1–36, discusses hagiographical traditions associated with the female saints of Ceredigion. R. I. Daniel, 'Gwobrwyau gwrando'r offeren', *Y Cylchgrawn Catholig*, 13: 14–15, edits a religious text which enumerates the twelve rewards of listening to mass devoutly.

LITERATURE SINCE 1500

By A. Cynfael Lake, *Lecturer in Welsh, University of Wales Swansea*

D. M. Smith, 'Cyfieithu'r *Marchog Crwydrad*: testun llenyddol / crefyddol', *LlC*, 24:61–78, examines the Welsh version of *The Voyage of the Wandering Knight*. He also attempts to define the relationship between the five MSS copies and to account for the variant readings. Goronwy Wyn Owen, *Rhwng Calfin a Böhme*, Cardiff, Univ. of Wales Press, 211 pp., studies in detail Morgan Llwyd's beliefs which were in essence, he maintains, thoroughly Calvinistic. R. G. Gruffydd and R. J. Roberts, 'John Dee's additions to William Salesbury's dictionary', *THSC*, 2000 [2001]:19–43, list the (predominantly English) words written on one extant copy of Salesbury's *Dictionary in Englyshe and Welshe* (1547). P. Bryant-Quinn, 'To preserve our language: Gruffydd Robert and Morys Clynnog', *JWRH*, 8:17–34, sees Robert's Grammar as one instrument of the Counter-Reformation. Ceri Davies, *John Davies o Fallwyd*, Caernarfon, Pantycelyn, 103 pp., describes J.D.'s most important works, his Grammar of 1621 and Dictionary of 1632, and sets both in their native and humanistic context. He also outlines his long-standing relationship with William Morgan and his own involvement between 1588 and 1620 in the translation of the Scriptures into Welsh.

   N. Lloyd, 'Cyfraniad hynafiaethwyr oes y Stiwartiaid i ddiwylliant ein cenedl', *Cof Cenedl*, 16:33–63, shows that efforts by 17th-c. patriotic antiquarians to sustain traditional beliefs regarding Brutus and Arthur rested on feeble ground, but that their real contribution was the safeguarding in manuscripts of much valuable material which would otherwise have disappeared. J. G. Jones, 'Rowland Vaughan o Gaer-gai a'i gyfieithiad o *Eikon Basilike* (1650)', *Y Traethodydd*, 156:18–40, contemplates Vaughan's motives for translating *Eikon Basilike* and considers the translation in the light of other works which he translated. Id., 'Phylipiaid Ardudwy: Aspects of their bardic contribution in late-sixteenth and seventeenth-century Wales', *JMHRS*, 13:313–47, surveys the poetry of Siôn Phylip and other members of his family and outlines its social significance. *Y Canu Mawl i Deulu Penrhos*, ed. Dafydd Wyn Wiliam, Llangefni, p.p., 42 pp., provides an edited version of 15 poems composed between 1550–1740 to four families in the vicinity of Holyhead.

   A. C. Lake, 'Cywydd marwnad gan Siôn Ceri', *Dwned*, 7:83–92, discusses a recently discovered elegy by Siôn Ceri. I. Daniel, 'Y ffynhonnau yng nghanu'r Cywyddwyr', *ib.*, 7:65–81, lists some of the characteristics of the poems to holy wells. Nia Powell, 'Women and strict-metre poetry in Wales', *Women and Gender in Early Modern Wales*, ed. Michael Roberts and Simone Clarke, Cardiff, Univ. of Wales Press, 2000, 129–58, tracks female poets and accounts for their paucity. "Of those women we can identify, most were related to, married to or were the lovers of male poets". C. Charnell-White, 'Barddoniaeth ddefosiynol Catrin ferch Gruffudd ap Hywel', *Dwned*, 7:93–120, analyses two series of *englynion* by one such figure. One piece, composed during the early years of the Reformation, conveys Catrin's Catholic sympathies. N. M. Jenkins, ' "A'i gyrfa megis Gwerful": bywyd a gwaith Angharad James', *LlC*, 24:79–112, sheds light on Angharad's life and works, and offers an edited version of her 10 extant poems. H. Williams, 'Rhagor am William Owen, Y Chwaen-wen', *Y Traethodydd*, 156:156–64, touches upon Owen's manuscripts and hymn-writing and offers interesting biographical details.

G. Thomas, 'Gweledigaethau y Bardd Cwsg The Visions of the Sleeping Bard (1703)', *ZCP*, 52:200–10, draws parallells between Ellis Wynne's visions and contemporary descriptions of death and hell. Dafydd Wyn Wiliam, *Cofiant Lewis Morris 1742–65*, Llangefni, p.p., 188 pp., the second volume in the study of the life and works of Lewis Morris, covers the years spent in Cardiganshire. A. R. Jones, ' "Put it in a Welsh dress": Poetical translations by Lewis Morris', *NLWJ*, 31:345–56, draws attention to Welsh translations by Morris, including a collection of five love poems found in one of his manuscripts. Id., 'Canu caeth Lewis Morris', *LlC*, 24:113–30, comments on some of Lewis Morris's strict poems. Emrys Jones, 'The age of Societies', *The Welsh in London 1500–2000*, ed. Id., Bodmin, Univ. of Wales Press, 54–87, sketches the activities of the Cymmrodorion and Gwyneddigion societies. *Pleser a Gofid*, ed. Nia Tudur, Bangor, Department of Welsh, 137 pp., is a newly-edited annotated version of one of Twm o'r Nant's later interludes. S. Rosser, 'Jonathan Hughes a gwerineiddio llenyddiaeth y ddeunawfed ganrif', *Y Traethodydd*, 156:235–44, describes J.H. as a poet who served the common people, and she contrasts his role with that of the professional poet who had traditionally been associated with the ruling gentry class. Id., 'Gwerthu cerddi Saesneg', *Tu Chwith*, 15:88–91, suggests English influence on one ballad by Ellis Roberts. T. Jones, 'Hiwmor yn y baledi', *Canu Gwerin*, 24:3–16, outlines some comic themes in 18th-c. ballads. C. Evans, 'Y faled a therfysgoedd Beca yn ne orllewin Cymru, 1839–43', *JPHS*, 10:62–70, brings to notice two ballads, by Richard Williams and Dafydd Jones, concerning the Becca riots. Both make known their conservative and cautious viewpoints. E. W. James, 'Golwg ar rai o gerddi a baledi Cymraeg Troed-y-rhiw', Edwards, *Merthyr a Thaf*, 94–129, describes two contrasting popular genres connected with Troed-y-rhiw, namely the verses sung by the plough-boys to the oxen in pre-industrial times, as recorded by Benjamin Thomas, and the ballads printed by William Jones in the village in the 1870–80s. Id., 'Watching the white wheat and that hole below the nose: the English ballads of a late-nineteenth-century Welsh jobbing-printer', Rieuwerts, *Ballad Heritage*, 177–94, examines the few English ballads from the same press and their affinity with Welsh ballads. Id., 'Ballad implosions and Welsh folk stanzas', Constantinescu, *Ballad*, 101–17, sees the pieces known as *hen benillion* as "a source of possible lost ballad literature in Wales". Huw Walters, 'Cerddi ymddiddan ynghylch ymfudo i Awstralia', *NLWJ*, 31:381–400, shows that ballads concerning emigration to Australia date from the mid-19th c., and two ballads debating the pros and cons of emigration and composed by two relatives are discussed. E. G. Millward, 'Nodyn ar ddwy gerdd gan Jac Glan-y-gors', *Canu Gwerin*, 24:42–49, considers likely English prototypes for two poems by Glan-y-gors.

E. G. Millward, 'Rhagor o nofelau'r bedwaredd ganrif ar bymtheg', *LlC*, 24:131–48, lists a selection of novels published between 1795–1900. In spite of regular condemnatory comments on the moral dangers faced by those exposed to the genre, a steady stream of fiction appeared during the course of the 19th c. Id., 'Merthyr Tudful: tref y brodyr rhagorol', Edwards, *Merthyr a Thaf*, 9–56, describes the Merthyr literary societies of the 19th c. and their activities, and suggests that the temperance-motivated Cymmrodorion were quite radical in their choice of competitions for their *eisteddfodau*. B. F. Roberts, 'Mab ei dad: Taliesin ab Iolo Morganwg', *ib.*, 57–93, argues that Taliesin was instrumental not only in conveying and promoting but also defending his father's ideas. Huw Walters, 'Beirdd a phrydyddion Pontypridd a'r cylch yn y bedwaredd ganrif ar bymtheg: arolwg', *ib.*, 252–301, surveys the poetic activity in the Pontypridd area during the 19th c. He draws attention to the works of the most important figures and notes that under the influence of Caledfryn in the second part of the century the poets became more ambitious and sought to compose strict as well as free metre poems. H. T. Edwards, 'Talhaiarn: Swyddogaeth bardd', *Y Traethodydd*, 156:165–71, sees Talhaiarn as a protagonist of Victorian ideals which were so detrimental to the Welsh language and culture, yet, paradoxically, the welfare and future of the language were also a source of concern for him. M. Ellis, 'Detholiad o lythyrau John Jones ('Tegid'; 1792–1852)', *JMHRS*, 13:355–71, contains transcripts of 12 letters sent by Tegid to his literary acquaintances. H. T. Edwards, 'Llef dros y ganrif fwyaf', Jenkins, *Cymru*, 71–86, sets forth the viewpoints of commentators on 19th-c. literature. Dafydd Glyn Jones, *Agoriad yr*

Oes, Tal-y-bont, Y Lolfa, 285 pp., explores identity and historiography in a series of essays. The comments on Robert Jones, Rhos-lan, Emrys ap Iwan and Thomas Williams are of special interest. B. O. Huws, 'Y ddau Garneddog: golwg ar rai o lythyrau olaf Carneddog', *LlC*, 24:149–58, describes Carneddog's correspondence with his literary friends in North Wales following his removal to Leicestershire. *Dramâu Gwenlyn Parry*, Llandysul, Gomer, 379 pp., a complete collection of G.P.'s plays, also contains personal anectodes by Annes Gruffydd and brief comments on some of the characteristics of the works. *Cerddi Gwenallt*, ed. Christine James, Llandysul, Gomer, 674 pp., is a much-welcomed complete edition of all Gwenallt's poems. Most of the poems appeared in collections prepared by the poet himself and published during his lifetime; the others were collected by the editor from printed sources and from personal papers. The introduction provides a valuable framework for an appreciation of Gwenallt's work and the notes in the last section (these account for a third of the volume) include not only textual explanations to assist the modern reader but also, for each individual poem, souces, variants and details of critical studies. The hitherto neglected prose works of Waldo Williams have been collected and edited by Damian Walford Davies in *Waldo Williams Rhyddiaith*, Cardiff, Univ. of Wales Press, 414 pp. The editor argues that the prose works complement and shed important light on ideas and themes in the poetry. H. Gruffudd, ' "Y Llen", Dyfnallt Morgan: diwedd perfformans?', Edwards, *Merthyr a Thaf*, 172–91, sets the eisteddfod poem 'Y Llen' in its sociolinguistic context. M. W. Thomas, 'Caethiwed Branwen: agweddau ar farddoniaeth Alun Llywelyn-Williams', *ib.*, 393–414, explores the theme of guilt in the poet's works and suggests that his war experiences compelled him to question his earlier beliefs and values. Rh. Reynolds, 'Poetry for the air: *The minister*, *Sŵn y gwynt sy'n chwythu* and *The dream of Jake Hopkins* as radio odes', *WWR*, 7:78–105, analyses the themes and style of three works commissioned for radio transmission. W. I. Cynwil Williams, *Gwilym R. Jones*, Llandybïe, Barddas, 228 pp., is an interesting addition to the 'Bro a Bywyd' series. Alan Llwyd, 'Gweddnewidio Gwyn Thomas', *Barddas*, 262, 4–11; *ib.*, 263:4–8; *ib.*, 264:4–9, explores themes in G.T.'s poems and in particular the tension between powers of good and evil. G. Davies, 'Adennill Tir', Edwards, *Merthyr a Thaf*, 227–51, discusses the background and themes of his collection of poems, *Adennill Tir*. T. J. Jones, 'Cusanau eironig', *Taliesin*, 112:125–38, compares original Welsh poems by Menna Elfyn and English renderings and sees fundamental flaws in the former. *Gweld Sêr*, ed. M. Wynn Thomas, Cardiff, Univ. of Wales

Press, 253 pp., contains thirteen essays examining American influences on Wales in general and on Welsh literature in particular. Id., 'Ewtopia: cyfandir dychymyg y Cymry', Jenkins, *Cymru*, 99–118, outlines an analysis of European influences on Welsh litterateurs. Id., 'Dylanwadau: Dylan Thomas a llenorion Cymraeg', *Taliesin*, 112:13–29, analyses the mixed reactions by Welsh-speaking poets and critics to D.T.'s work, and suggests that his work challenged their preconceptions of style and their views concerning the poet's social role. H. T. Edwards, 'Yr Eisteddfod Genedlaethol ym Merthyr Tudful 1881 ac 1901', Edwards, *Merthyr a Thaf*, 130–57, emphasises the importance of the two *eisteddfodau* held in 1881 and 1901, the former representing the final attempt made in the 19th century to place the institution on a permanent footing. Id. also outlines the importance of the 1901 eisteddfod in 'The Merthyr National Eisteddfod of 1901', *MerH*, 13:19–26.

Glanmor Williams, 'Stephen Hughes (1622–1688): "Apostol Sir Gâr"; "The Apostle of Carmarthenshire"', *CarA*, 37:21–30, refers to Hughes's publishing ventures and his efforts to publish *Canwyll y Cymru* in particular. Huw Walters, 'Ar drywydd *Lamp y Cymro*', *ib.*, 37:69–72, describes the only issue of a periodical designed to facilitate the learning of English. M. Evans, 'Papur Pan', *Y Traethodydd*, 156:142–55, notes Evan Pan Jones's involvement with two journals, *Y Celt* and *Cwrs y Byd*, which he used to promote his views on land nationalization. Aled Jones and Bill Jones, '*Y Drych* and American Welsh identities, 1851–1951', *NAJWS*, 1:42–58, sketch four periods in the development of *Y Drych*, America's most enduring Welsh periodical, and look in detail at its 150 year history in *Welsh Reflections: Y Drych & America 1851–2001*, Llandysul, Gomer, 198 pp. *Y Drych*, they argue, 'sent out powerful messages to remind all its readers that they were still Welsh, and that the greatest of all the opportunities offered by the United States was their ability to remain Welsh, in language, faith and culture'. B. O. Huws, 'Pennod yn hanes cyhoeddi llyfrau Cymraeg rhwng y ddau Ryfel Byd', *WBS*, 4:50–64, describes the efforts of Gwallter Llyfnwy to publish material of a popular nature in the 1930s.

II. BRETON AND CORNISH STUDIES

By HUMPHREY LLOYD HUMPHREYS, formerly *School of Modern Languages, University of Wales, Lampeter*

1. BRETON

Parlons du breton!, ed. E. Morin, Rennes, Ouest France, 192 pp., 290 pictures, 26 maps, (+ CD), is designed to accompany a now peripatetic exhibition launched from the Musée de Bretagne — an idea of F. Broudic, produced and elaborated by the association Buhez. The collaboration of recognized specialist authors of twenty concise presentations of specific linguistic, literary, social, economic, and political aspects of the history of Breton and the richness and relevance of the illustrations should guarantee a wide public. Y. de Boisanger, 'Défense et illustration de la langue bretonne', *Bull. de l'Association bretonne*, 109:569–82, provides a concise overview of the language, while B. Massiet du Biest, 'Le fonds en langue bretonne de la Société Polymathique', *Bull. et Mémoire de la Société Polymathique du Morbihan*, 127:309–19, is an introduction to a learned society's collection of material.

Klask, Rennes, PUR, still hesitates between being a series or a periodical. Vol. 5, F. Favereau (ed.), *Le Bilinguisme précoce en Bretagne, en pays celtiques et en Europe atlantique*, 1999, 317 pp., consists of colloquium papers on the problems of the restorative teaching of minority languages no longer spoken by the present school intake. Half of these papers deal with Breton, some being very brief reports. J. Stephens (35–45) discusses problems arising from certain morphosyntactic features of Breton and Welsh; N. Davalan, (97–118), with more sustained documentation, interferences affecting the mastery of the various present tenses of the Breton verb *beza(ñ)*; G. Mercier et al., (125–38), reports on activities of the Breton speech synthesis project; J.-D. Robin, (139–57) describes the administrative context of the training and recruitment of teachers of Breton; F. Broudic, (179–92), analyses the 20th-c. decline of Breton speaking among the young. Vol. 6, J. Guyot, M. Ledo Andión, R. Michon, *Production télévisée et identité culturelle en Bretagne, Galice et pays de Galles / Produerezh skinwel hag identelezh sevenadurel e Breizh, Galiza ha Kembre*, 2000, 190 pp., is a general comparative report, of which just a fifth deals specifically with the Breton situation. Vol. 7, returning to a less thematic periodical format, has a number of articles touching sociolinguistic themes: R. Coadic, 'Langue et Modernité' (45–49); J.-D. Robin, 'L'enseignement (des mathématiques) en breton est-il une gageure?' (73–96); E. Vallerie, 'Ar veaj misterius da enez ar skiantoù' (97–104);

with G. Guével; 'Hinouriezh' (105–15) providing as a linguistic example a technical text on meteorology.

In *La Pierre en Basse-Bretagne – usage et représentations*, ed. J.-Y. Eveillard, Brest, Cahiers de Bretagne Occidentale, 18, CRBC, UBO, B. Tanguy, 'La pierre dans le paysage toponymique en Basse-Bretagne', provides an illustrated inventory of terms relating to stones, (5–26). P. Pondaven and M. Madeg, *Renabl anoiou lehiou arvor Gorre Leon: Trelez, Gwinevez, Ploueskad, Kleder, 1. Etre an Aod Veur ha Kanol ar Porz Nevez*, Brest, Ar Skol Vrezoneg – Emgleo Breiz, 225 pp., is the ninth volume of the continuing detailed inventory of the coastal toponymy of Léon in the north-west (see *YWMLS*, 51:560). M. Madeg, *Eul leoriad lesanoiou euz Bro-Dreger ha Bro-Ouelo*, Brest, Ar Skol Vrezoneg – Emgleo Breiz, 123 pp., pursues nicknames, another interest to which the author has contributed a number of informal publications.

J. Le Dû, *Nouvel Atlas linguistique de la Basse-Bretagne*, 2 vols, ix + maps 1–294, v + maps 295–601, Brest, CRBC, UBO, is a long awaited and highly important corpus of dialect data, with a coverage some three times denser than P. Le Roux's *ALBB*, which is generally vindicated as to dependability, significantly supplemented where common maps are concerned and sometimes corrected. The traditional commonsense, but expensive, practice of locating transcriptions on a map base has been followed and the adoption of IPA, long used in monographs, will be generally appreciated. It is unfortunate that there is no Breton index to the forms recorded and it is hoped that one will be made available in a subsequent publication, with thematic sub-indexes of individual phonic or grammatical phenomena. Computerized analysis and production of summary distribution maps is being considered as well as a CD-ROM.

Rh. Hincks, *Cwrs Llydaweg Sylfaenol*, 1, Lessons and Exercises, 362 pp., 2, Key to Exercises, Grammatical Index, Vocabularies, 85 pp., Aberystwyth, Prifysgol Cymru, n.d., is a generally sound foundation course. Particularly useful are the grammatical index and the list of lexical gallicisms commoner than or completely replacing the 'pure Breton' words. Id., *Yr Iaith Lenyddol fel Bwch Dihangol yng Nghymru ac yn Llydaw / Literary Language as a Scapegoat in Wales and in Brittany*, Aberystwyth, Univ. of Wales, 41 pp., might be considered a pamphlet, albeit well documented. The author's idealization of the literary standards of both languages is at least as romantic as any idealization of folk speech, and is too ready to play down often justified native-speaker dissatisfaction.

M. Menard and I. Kadored, *Geriadur brezhoneg An Here*, Plougastell-Daoulaz, An Here, lxii + 1436 pp., is a much expanded, unillustrated, version of J.-Y. Lagadec and M. Menard's *Geriadur . . . of 1995* (see *YWMLS*, 57:612). There are some 20,000 headwords, doubling the inventory of the original; the new material consists of established traditional vocabulary, a larger selection of derivatives, and further neologisms. There is no information on the currency of individual items and the IPA transcriptions have been somewhat modified. The Bibliothèque bretonne continues its steady publication of important early lexicographical documents. N° 10 is *Le* Nomenclator *latin-français-breton de Guillaume Quiquer de Roscoff (1633)*, ed. G. Le Menn, Saint-Brieuc, 2000, Skol, 398 pp.: vol. 1, presentation (7–41), text (42–396); vol. 2, general index with modern spellings for headwords. N° 11 is *Le Vocabulaire breton du* Catholicon *(1499) – le premier dictionnaire imprimé breton-français-latin de Jehan Lagadeuc*, Id., Saint-Brieuc, Skol, 205 pp.; this is an index in modern spellings to the Breton words therein. *Geriaoueg ha notennoù yezh Yeun ar Gow*, ed. H. ar Bihan and D. gKervella, Rennes, 2000, Hor Yezh, 152 pp., is a glossary of the more unusual words and expressions used by the author as well as lists he compiled of legal and slate-mining terms used in his district.

Anjela Duval – Oberenn glok, ed. R. Koadig (= Coadic) et al. Louergad, Mignoned Anjela et al., 2000, 1281 pp., 'Pennadoù skrid' (19–147); 'Barzhonegoù' (155–783, including 30 pp. each of notes and translations); 'Komz plaen' (787–1240), is a monumental tribute to the famous 'peasant poetess', containing her complete poetic and prose work and commemorative, biographical, and critical articles by numerous authors. A specific aspect of the same author's work is discussed by J. Le Lay, 'La bretonnité dans l'œuvre d'Anjela Duval', in *Bull. de l'Association bretonne*, 109:121–27. J. Gibson, *Tem ar marv en oberennoù Per Denez*, Mouladurioù Hor Yezh, 102 pp., is a critical presentation of the theme of death in Denez's prose fiction. P. Le Besco, *Trajedi santez Julit ha sant Sir he mab (édition commentée)*, Brest, Ar Skol Vrezoneg – Emgleo Breiz, 376 pp., presents an 18th-c. dramatic text (123–213), with a chiefly linguistic introduction (1–122) and a fully referenced glossary (215–317). In *Chroniqueurs et historiens de la Bretagne du Moyen Age au milieu du XXe siècle*, ed. N.-Y. Tonnerre, Rennes, PUR/Institut Culturel de Bretagne, 244 pp., we should note J.-P. Piriou, 'Une source historique méconnue : la tradition littéraire des Bretons d'Armorique' (35–42).

Hélias et les siens, ed. J.-L. Le Cam, Brest, CRBC, UBO, 258 pp. (Kreiz 15 — Actes du Colloque de Quimper), contains a number of articles directly concerned with Breton. F. Broudic, 'L'évolution sociolinguistique de la Bretagne et l'évolution personnelle de P.-J. Hélias par rapport à la langue bretonne: parallélisme ou divergence?' (125–41); F. Favereau, 'Le jeu du bilinguisme chez Pierre-Jakez Hélias' (143–61); D. Giraudon, 'Le tire-lire à l'alouette' (163–72), discussing traditional microtexts; G. Goyat, 'Le collectage des chansons en pays bigouden' (53–69); R. Calvez, 'Hélias et les siens?' (247–56). Twelve other contributions contribute to our overall understanding of the author and his work. J.-P. Piriou, *Anatole Le Braz: essai bibliographique*, Rennes, Terre de Brume-PUR, 1999, 367 pp., is an engaging presentation of one of the big names in republican Bretonism, an important collector who, however, published little in Breton.

Material published in *Hor Yezh* will be grouped here for convenience. H. Seubil gKernaudour, 'An Tabut etre ar mestr-a-di hag ar marmiton', 225:5–31, is an 18th-c. farcical interlude of 200 lines, while Id., 'Ar Miliner hag ar bouloñjer', 226:5–32, is a twelve-stanza northeastern song of 1820 in which the miraculous new food plant, the potato, is seen as a threat by a miller and a baker. Both pieces are given in their original form, accompanied by a peurunvan version; there are detailed notes on provenance and language, and a full glossary. Breton versions of lecture notes by L. Fleuriot present notes on Breton and Welsh diphthongs (228:5–13), and the evolution of certain points of morphology and syntax (ib.: 14–34). An interesting item is the uncommented facsimile of *'An Trede Amprest brezel'* featuring government publicity for a war loan in 1917, (227:45–51). 'Notennoù yezh' consist of lexical 'notes' often elaborate and substantial by G. ar (= Le) Menn (unless another author is named), which it seems appropriate to list here individually: *Hor Yezh*, 225:50. *ruz-poazh* (39–40); 51. *lindag* pe **linenn-dag* (40–43); 52. *drouklazhet* (43–46); 53. *eskemmez* (46–49); 54. the surname *Godu* (49–51); 55. *diallen* (51–52 – D. gKervella); 56. *mantokiñ* (52 – C. Cochin; see *Hor Yezh*, 221). Id., 226:57. *herberc'h* pe **herberj?* (33–38); 58. *anbrun*: peseurt plantenn eo? (39); 59. *bremañ-soudenn* etc. (40–44); 60. *moliac'h* etc. (45–47); 61. *pagn* (48–49); 62. *eizhvetez* (49–50); 63. *Ingrañchoù* (50); 64. *lavienneg* etc. (51–56); 65. *lindag* (56 – P.-Y. Kersulec, see Id., 225:40–43, above). Id., 227:66. *ezeviñ* (33–35); 67. *kabiez* (35–37); 68. *kerc'henn* 37–39). Id., 228:70. *ayaouic!* (1746) (49–53); 71. *dop(es)* (53–54); 72. Old Breton *gloiat(ou)*, Modern Breton *glaouetenn* (54–55); 73. Middle Breton *touser an courzou* (55–57); 74. Old Breton *poer* (57–58).

II. CORNISH

CS, 9 contains three lexicographical articles. A. Hawke, 'A rediscovered Cornish-English vocabulary', presents with full commentary two short 17th-c. lists totalling 114 items (83–114); N. J. A. Williams, '"A modern and scholarly Cornish-English dictionary": Ken George's *Gerlyver Kernewek Kemmyn* (1993)', backs up concise general criticisms with fully documented corrections for some 500 words (247–311); N. Kennedy, pp. 312–18, '*Gerlyver Sawsnek-Kernowek*', is a shorter review article assessing N. J. A. Williams's own dictionary (312–18). (see *YWMLS*, 62:548). C. Penglase, 'The future indicative in the early modern Cornish of Tregear', *EC*, 34:215–31, continues (see *YWMLS*, 62:547) his careful and very useful examination of the translation of Bonner's *Homilies* (*c.* 1555), easily the most substantial Cornish prose text. Simple to variously composite in form, seven tenses, including a 'recent future' [*sic*], are exemplified, each being described morphosyntactically and characterized semantically. Some points will obviously be difficult to assess precisely until the author's overall analysis of the entire system of twenty-five indicative tenses becomes available.

   B. Murdoch, 'The *MORS PILATI* in the Cornish *RESURREXIO DOMINI*', *Celtica*, 23, 1999:211–26, points out that this theme, rare in European drama, is absent from English material. The originality and the dramatic sophistication of the work are emphasized, with the expected penetration and breadth of vision. A number of titles with a provenance rarely concerned with Celtic studies have recently come to my attention, but unseen, will only be noted here. *S. Higgins, *Medieval Theatre in the Round: the multiple staging of religious drama in England*, Camerino, 1994, *Laboratorio degli studi linguistici*, special number, 168 pp. *S. Higgins, ' "Creating the creation": the staging of the Cornish medieval play *Gwryans an Bys*, or the Creation of the World', *European Medieval Drama*, 1,1996:161–88. *G. J. Betcher, 'A reassessment of the date and provenance of the Cornish *Ordinalia*', *Comparative Drama*, 29.4, 1996:436–52. *E. S. Newlyn, 'The Middle Cornish interlude:genre and tradition', *Comparative Drama*, 30.2, 1996:266–81. *S. L. Joyce and E. S. Newlyn (ed. of Cornwall section), *Records of Early English Drama* (Cornwall; Dorset), Toronto, 1999, Toronto UP and Brepols, 719 pp.

III. IRISH STUDIES

EARLY IRISH

By KEVIN MURRAY, *Department of Early and Medieval Irish, University College, Cork*

1. LANGUAGE

E. P. Hamp, *Ériu* 51: 59–62, 'Reading Old Irish writing: making complex mechanisms effortless – well, somewhat', makes an individual contribution to the problem of reading O Ir. in order 'to recover, as completely as possible, all the sound features of the text'. G. R. Isaac, *ib.*, 63–68, 'The most recent model of the development of absolute and conjunct flexion', points out some of the problems, particularly with regard to the theory of the particle **es*, in the derivation of absolute verbal forms in Celtic. E. Roma, *ib.*, 107–57, 'How subject pronouns spread in Irish: a diachronic study and synchronic account of the third person + pronoun pattern', is a long and detailed article on pronouns. P. Ó Néill, *ib.*, 159–80, 'Irish observance of the three Lents and the date of the St Gall Priscian (MS 904)', is a fascinating study of the St Gall Priscian and concludes that this 'manuscript was begun in October 850 and completed in August 851'. E. P. Hamp, *ib.*, 181–82, has a note on '*(h)uile*'; P.-Y. Lambert, *ib.*, 189–92, discusses 'Gaulish *souxtu*: Early Irish *suacht*'; P. Schrijver, *ib.*, 195–99, 'Non-Indo-European surviving in Ireland in the first millennium AD', is a perceptive note utilizing linguistic evidence to argue for the survival of a non-IE language in Ireland until after AD 500. K. H. Schmidt, *ZCP* 52: 137–53, 'Die altirischen Glossen als sprachgeschichtliches Dokument', focuses on the linguistic history of the Old Irish glosses P. Russell, *Peritia*, 14: 406–20, '*Graece . . . Latine*: Graeco-Latin glossaries in early medieval Ireland', notes that 'material similar to that which is attested in Laon MS 444 was a source for the vernacular glossaries', while there is a short language note by K. Murray, *ib.*, 15: 377–78, on '**Eterrí* "intermediate king, subordinate king"?'.

2. LITERATURE

J. Carey, *Ériu* 51: 183–87, 'The address to Fergus's stone', offers an edition, translation and discussion of the difficult *roscad* from *Do Fhallsigud Tána Bó Cúalnge*, a text analysed and edited by K. Murray in 'The finding of the *Táin*', *CMCS* 41: 17–23. M. Herbert, *SH*, 31:27–35, 'The legend of St Scothíne: perspectives from early

Christian Ireland', examines 'the association of Saint Scothíne with legends of a submarine Otherworld habitation'. U. Mac Gearailt, *ib.*, 71–85, '*Togail Troí*: An example of translating and editing in medieval Ireland', argues that 'the Irish version of the story of Troy reflects a large degree of independent writing by Irish authors at some remove from Latin literary sources'. P. Ó Riain, *ib.*, 221–42, 'The Martyrology of Óengus: the transmission of the text', shows how complex was the transmission of this important work in its three main phases. P. J. Smith, *Peritia* 15 : 108–44, '*Mide maigen Clainne Cuind*: a medieval poem on the kings of Mide', presents a comprehensive edition of the Middle Irish poem 'Mide, homestead of Conn's descendants'. D. Ó Corráin, *ib.*, 311–20, 'Some cruxes in *Críth gablach*', explains some of the poorly understood technical terms of this important tract.

The Individual in Celtic Literatures, ed. J. F. Nagy, Four Courts Press, Dublin, 2001, is the first volume of the CSANA yearbook. A. M. O'Leary, 'Mog Ruith and apocalypticism in eleventh-century Ireland', analyses the importance of Mog Ruith in Irish history (51–60). C. McKenna, 'Apotheosis and evanescence: the fortunes of Saint Brigit in the nineteenth and twentieth centuries' (74–108), examines the evolution of modern scholarship on Saint Brigit. E. Johnston, 'The salvation of the individual and the salvation of society in *Siaburcharpat Con Culaind*' (109–25), building particularly on the work of J. F. Nagy, focuses on the 'representation of Irish elite groups . . . and the mediation of knowledge' in this tale of Cú Chulainn's phantom chariot.

D. A. Bray, *Peritia*, 14: 282–96, 'Suckling at the breast of Christ: a spiritual lesson in an Irish hagiographical motif', examines the motif of holy men suckling infants in Irish hagiography. C. Bourke, *ib.*, 15: 373–76, 'On the *Imirce Ciaráin*', suggests that *Imirce Ciaráin*, 'hitherto regarded as the title of a lost voyage tale, is . . . the proper name of a manuscript'. E. Johnston, *ib.*, 14: 421–28, 'Íte: patron of her people?', looks at the representation of St Íte in various sources. The same author looks at the 'dossiers of two female saints . . . [to see] . . . whether we can identify female aspirations and female voices in the literary celebration of their careers' in 'Powerful women or patriarchal weapons? Two medieval Irish saints', *ib.*, 15: 302–10.

3.   OTHER (Collections of essays, *Festschriften* etc.)

In *Ní Chatháin Vol.*, the language contributions include W. Meid, 'Zu irisch *grád* "Liebe"' (298–99); G. Mac Eoin, 'The four names of St Patrick' (300–11). K. H. Schmidt, 'On the linguistic background of the personal pronouns of Old Irish' (289–94). S. Zimmer, 'The making of myth: Old Irish *Airgatlám*, Welsh *Llaw ereint*, Caledonian

Ἀργεντοκόξος᾽ (295–97), highlights an example of how linguistic misunderstandings may lead to the creation of new mythological details. P. Ó Néill, 'The Old Irish glosses of the *prima manus* in Würzburg, m.p.th.f.12: text and context reconsidered' (230–42), re-examines and re-edits the oldest glosses in Irish, the early stratum present in Würzburg. Turning to matters literary, T. Charles-Edwards, '*Tochmarc Étaíne*: a literal interpretation' (165–81), contributes an in-depth analysis of The Wooing of Étaín. D. W. Evans, 'The learned borrowings claimed for *Táin Bó Fraích*' (182–94), reconsiders some of the conclusions reached by James Carney concerning the Cattle-raid of Fráech finding them unconvincing. K. Murray, '*Baile in Scáil* and *Echtrae Chormaic*' (195–99), briefly compares two medieval Irish tales. E. Bhreathnach, 'Two contributors to the Book of Leinster: Bishop Finn of Kildare and Gilla na Náem Úa Duinn' (105–11), considers the origins and affiliations of two of the compilers of the important twelfth-century manuscript, the Book of Leinster. M. Herbert, 'The Life of Martin of Tours: a view from twelfth-century Ireland' (76–84), looks at a 12th-c. homily on St Martin and shows how this vernacular work 'reinforces the view that hagiographical accounts of Martin provided a "lexicon of images" which could be reconstructed and adapted in accordance with changing circumstances'.

The late Prof. Brian Ó Cuív's *Catalogue of Irish Language Manuscripts in the Bodleian Library at Oxford and Oxford College Libraries*, part 1: descriptions, Dublin Institute for Advanced Studies, xl + 324 pp., has been published a little over a year after his death. This book fills a major lacuna in Irish studies. Though a thorough review of the work will not be possible until the publication of part 2 of this catalogue (indexes and plates), it is clear that this volume is consistent with Prof. Ó Cuív's standards of rigorous scholarship.

Saints and Scholars: Studies in Irish Hagiography, ed. J. Carey, M. Herbert and P. Ó Riain, Dublin, Four Courts Press, xii + 418 pp., is a collection of twenty-two essays divided into six distinct groupings, viz. (i) The Columban tradition; (ii) Traditions of other Irish saints; (iii) Irish saints and Brittany; (iv) Irish saints' Lives in continental Europe; (v) Approaches to the study of Irish hagiography; (vi) Hagiographical scholarship: from 17th-c. beginnings to contemporary projects. With regard to work on the vernacular, we may note in particular two contributions: J. Carey, 'Varieties of supernatural contact in the Life of Adamnán' (49–62) and P. Russell, 'Patterns of hypocorism in early Irish hagiography' (237–49).

In *Irland und Europa im früheren Mittelalter: Texte und Überlieferung / Ireland and Europe in the Early Middle Ages: Texts and Transmissions*, ed. P. Ní Chatháin and M. Richter, Dublin, Four Courts Press, x + 400 pp., W. Meid, ' "Freundschaft" und "Liebe" in keltischen Sprachen' (1–5), examines further the terms for friendship and love in the Celtic languages. M. McNamara, 'Apocryphal infancy narratives: European and Irish transmission' (123–46), looks at 'the non-canonical accounts of the birth and upbringing of Mary and of the birth and infancy of Christ'. P. Kelly, 'The Rule of Patrick: textual affinities' (284–95), employs detailed textual analysis to suggest that *Ríagail Pátraic* may be 'more akin to a *cáin* than a monastic rule'. E. Poppe, 'The Latin quotations in *Auraicept na nÉces*: microtexts and their transmission' (296–312), believes that the evidence adduced in his study points towards 'a close and active interaction of various branches of Latin and vernacular learning in early medieval Ireland'. D. Edel, 'Stability and fluidity in the transmission of narrative texts: the delineation of characters in *Táin Bó Cúailnge*' (313–25), makes a plea for increased co-operation between the philological and literary approaches to early Irish literature. P. J. Smith, 'Early Irish historical verse: the evolution of a genre' (326–41), discusses the developments in historical verse in Ireland from the 7th c. to the 12th c. M. J. Enright, 'Fires of knowledge: a theory of warband education in medieval Ireland and Homeric Greece' (342–67), examines aspects of 'warrior groupings in pre-state chieftainship societies'.

MODERN IRISH

POSTPONED

IV. SCOTTISH GAELIC STUDIES

By SHEILA M. KIDD, *Lecturer in Celtic, University of Glasgow*

G. Jones, 'Beagan mu'n stad ghlotasach ann an Gàidhlig Ceann a Deas Earraghaidheil', *SGS*, 20, 2000:201–11, suggests, based on the evidence of a single informant from Jura, that the glottal stop is found in more environments in Jura Gaelic than has previously been found in studies of the Gaelic of Islay, Gigha, or Arran. Two articles by R. A. V. Cox examine the Norse influence on Gaelic: 'The phonological development of Scottish Gaelic uinneag "window" and related questions', *ib.*, 212–21, suggests that the remodelling of this Old Norse loan-word by using the Gaelic suffix –*óc* may have taken place in a bilingual environment; 'Maintenance of the Norse legacy in Scottish Hebridean nomenclature', *SSLF*, 631:45–52, demonstrates that the islands' Norse names are phonologically well preserved and that in terms of onomastic function they have been used innovatively in a Gaelic context. C. Ó Baoill, 'Of Mar', *SGS*, 20, 2000:165–69, considers the genitive forms of this place name and concludes that in its modern form, 'Màrr', can be traced back to the *Annals of Ulster*, and that where scholars have accepted Mair as the genitive this is in fact based on a misreading of the manuscript form. R. G. Wentworth, 'An dàrnacha beum ann an òrain na Gàidhlig', *ib.*, 117–46, demonstrates that some of the problems which arise in analysing vernacular stressed verse in Gaelic can be resolved by taking secondary stress into account, given that syllables with secondary stress can rhyme with those with primary stress.

The creation of the new Scottish Parliament and its significance for the future of Gaelic has prompted two articles by Wilson McLeod: 'A' Ghàidhlig anns an 21mh linn: sùil air adhart', *LCC*, 31:90–109, while offering a historical perspective on the shrinking of the Gaelic speaking community focuses on specific problems affecting the language at present, such as the lack of direction to language planning; 'Gaelic in the New Scotland: Politics, Rhetoric and Public discourse', Flensburg, European Centre for Minority Issues, <www.ecmi.de/jemie/download/JEMIE02MacLeod28-11-01.pdf>, discusses the position of Gaelic in the wake of the creation of the Scottish Parliament, drawing specific attention to the problems facing the language both at the level of the Scottish Executive and the level of the community.

Gaelic Identities: Aithne na nGael, ed. Gordon McCoy with Maolcholaim Scott, Belfast. The Institute for Irish Studies – Iontaobhas ULTACH, 2000, ix + 161 pp. includes: M. Herbert, 'Ireland and

Scotland: the foundations of a relationship', (19–27), an overview of the early histories of Ireland and Scotland with emphasis placed on the commonalities of Christianity, language and literature; D. E. Meek, 'God and Gaelic: the Highland churches and Gaelic cultural identity' (28–47), draws on Richard Niebuhr's models (*Christ and Culture*, 1952) in his examination of the multifaceted influence of the Church on Gaelic culture and language; T. Caimbeul, 'The Politics of Gaelic Development in Scotland', (53–66), considers the dynamics of the Gaelic revival of the last 20 years; R. Dunbar, 'Legal and Institutional Aspects of Gaelic Development', (67–87), is on a similar topic, but with more detailed discussion of the issue of secure status for Gaelic; P. Morgan, 'The Gael is dead; long live the Gaelic: the changing relationship between native and learner Gaelic users', (126–32), explores some of the complexities associated with the terms, 'native speaker' and 'learner', and argues that the main tension affecting the present-day language, is one between revitalization at a community level and revival at a more national level; K. MacKinnon, 'Neighbours in persistence: prospects for Gaelic maintenance in a globalising English world', (144–55), compares the situations of Gaelic and Irish, with a particular focus on the varying use of Gaelic in specific domains, and concludes that Gaelic's future lies in people's need for a language of their own in addition to English.

D. N. Dumville, '*Cethri Prímchenéla Dáil Riata*', *SGS*, 20, 2000:170–91, discusses this tract and its relationship to other genealogical manuscripts and by comparing six manuscript versions of the text examines further the four descent-groups. C. Downham, 'An imaginary Viking-raid on Skye in 795?', *ib.*, 192–96, concludes that the only reference to this supposed raid can in fact be put down to scribal error and that *Sc(r)í*, taken to mean Skye, should in fact read *sccríne* (shrine). T. O. Clancy, 'A Gaelic polemic quatrain from the reign of Alexander I, ca, 1113', *ib.*, 67–87, provides an analysis of this verse which offers an insight into the contemporary political situation, with the lordship over the south of Scotland being disputed between Alexander I and his brother David. M. Newton, 'Gaelic sources for *Ruaig Beinn Todhaig*', *ib.*, 156–64, discusses variant forms of a poem about Griogair Odhar Àrd who fought in this early 17th-c. battle. A. Gunderloch, 'Donnchadh Bàn's *Òran do Bhlàr na h-Eaglaise Brice* – literary allusion and political comment', *ib.*, 97–116, considers the background to this, the first composition by Donnchadh Bàn Mac an t-Saoir, and compares two versions, one with Jacobite leanings and one which is more Whig oriented. In addition, by demonstrating parallels with the ballad *Duan na Ceàrdaich*, she reveals how the poet used the ballad as a means of adding another level of meaning to his song. W. Gillies, 'Alexander Carmichael and Clann Mhuirich', *ib.*,

1–66, studies a group of texts relating to the MacMhuirich bardic family. He demonstrates that this material represents a literary cycle and shows how these learned poets retained a heroic status in popular Gaelic tradition down to the 20th c. S. Kidd, 'Social control and social criticism: the nineteenth century *còmhradh*', *ib.*, 67–87, discusses the origins of the *còmhradh*, or dialogue, which became the foremost genre in 19th-c. Gaelic prose writing, and discusses the change in its use over the course of the century from a means of promoting passive acceptance of clearance to a tool for encouraging criticism of landlords. I. C. Smith, 'On Gaelic and Gender', *SSR*, 2.1:9–14, explores both the influences which shaped him and the male-dominated nature of both Gaelic and Scottish literature until very recent times. M. MacLeod, 'Language and bilingualism in the Gaelic poetry of Iain Crichton Smith', *ib.*, 2.2:105–13, traces the progression from the poet's perception of Gaelic as an obstacle to true self-knowledge to his final acceptance of the language.

Michael Newton, *We're Indians Sure Enough: The Legacy of the Scottish Highlanders in the United States*, Auburn, Saorsa Media, 311 pp., offers valuable insights into an area of Highland emigrant history which to date has been greatly overshadowed by studies of the mass emigration to Canada in the 19th c. This book draws heavily on Gaelic sources, particularly song and poetry, and explores various aspects of Gaels' experiences in the United States such as the American Revolution and the goldrush and discusses their assimilation into English-speaking American society. *Brìgh an Òrain. A Story in Every Song*, ed. John Shaw, Montreal & Kingston, McGill-Queen's U.P., 2000, xxvii + 432 pp. is a very useful collection of traditional Gaelic material from Canada. It contains a far from exhaustive selection of the songs and tales recorded by the editor from the repertoire of the late Lauchie MacLellan of Broad Cove, Nova Scotia whose forebears had left Morar in the early 19th c. In addition to the 48 songs and nine tales, with the editor's translations and notes, the volume includes autobiographical material based on recordings of MacLellan. Equally valuable is a section entitled 'Gaelic Singing and Broad Cove Parish' which contextualizes the songs and demonstrates how fundamental song has remained in emigrant Gaelic settlements such as Broad Cove. *An Lasair. Anthology of 18th Century Scottish Gaelic Verse*, ed. Ronald Black, Edinburgh, Birlinn, xlii + 533 pp. is a very welcome contribution to the study of 18th-c. Gaelic literature, expanding significantly the existing canon of verse for the period. Some 63 poems with translations are included and also very full notes on poets, background to poems, and textual explanation where necessary. The introduction looks at the criticism of 18th-c. Gaelic literature from the contemporary ceilidh-house audience to the writing-based criticism of the Victorian period and finally to the maturing of criticism in the 20th c. The editor places much emphasis on the rhetoric of the panegyric code as a key to understanding the poetry.

4

GERMANIC LANGUAGES

I. GERMAN STUDIES

LANGUAGE

By CHARLES V. J. RUSS, *Reader in the Department of Language and Linguistic Science, University of York*

I. GENERAL

SURVEYS, COLLECTIONS, BIBLIOGRAPHIES. Two volumes treat aspects of the history of *Germanistik*: *150 Jahre Germanistik in Wien: Außeruniversitäre Frühgermanistik und Universitätsgermanistik*, ed. P. Wiesinger and D. Steinbach, Vienna, Praesens, 246 pp., and M. S. Batts, *Fünfzig Jahre IVG. Die Geschichte der Internationalen Vereinigung für Germanische Sprach- und Literaturwissenschaft*, with a postscript by P. Wiesinger, Vienna, Praesens, 2000, 80 pp. Also noted: **Deutsch in Estland und Ungarn. Beiträge zur Germanistik und Fachdidaktik*, ed. W. Ulrich (Folia Didactica, 6), Frankfurt, Lang, 154 pp. *National Varieties of German outside Germany. A European Perspective*, ed. G. Hogan-Brun (GLCS, 8), 275 pp., gives a wider focus to German and contains the following: G. Hogan-Brun, 'The landscapes of German across Europe: an ecolinguistic perspective' (13–32); S. Barbour, ' "Deutsch" as a linguistic, ethnic and national label: cultural and political consequences of a multiple ambiguity' (33–48); S. Wolff, 'German as a minority language: the legislative and policy framework in Europe' (49–66); F. Rash, 'Outsiders' attitudes towards the Swiss German dialects and Swiss Standard German' (67–101); V. Martin, 'The German language in Austria' (103–19); P. Nelde and J. Darquennes, 'German in old and new Belgium' (121–38); G. Newton, 'The use of German in the Grand Duchy of Luxembourg' (139–60); A. Alcock, 'From tragedy to triumph: the German language in South Tyrol 1922–2000' (161–94); K. M. Pedersen, 'German as first language and minority second language in Denmark' (195–220); J. Broadbridge, 'Alsatian: a living variety? A sociolinguistic study of southern Alsace' (221–42); and P. Stevenson, 'The multilingual marketplace: German as a Hungarian language' (243–58).

A volume that takes stock of the German language at the beginning of a new millennium is *Die deutsche Sprache zur Jahrtausendwende. Sprachkultur oder Sprachverfall?*, ed. K. M. Eichoff-Cyrus and R. Hoberg

(Duden. Thema Deutsch, 1), Mannheim. Dudenverlag, 2000, 344 pp., which contains the following articles: J. A. Bär, 'Deutsch im Jahr 2000. Eine sprachhistorische Standortbestimmung' (9–34); K.-H. Best, 'Unser Wortschatz. Sprachstatistische Untersuchungen' (35–52); K. M. Eichhoff-Cyrus, 'Vom Briefsteller zur Netikette: Textsorten gestern und heute' (53–62); P. Schlobinski, 'Chatten im Cyberspace' (63–79); J. Eichhoff, 'Sterben die Dialekte aus?' (80–88); H.-R. Fluck, 'Fachsprachen: zur Funktion, Verwendung und Beschreibung eines wichtigen Kommunikationsmittels in unserer Gesellschaft' (89–106); E. Neuland, 'Jugendsprache in der Diskussion: Meinungen, Ergebnisse, Folgerungen' (107–24); O. Schily, 'Sprache und Politik' (125–28); G. Stötzel, 'Wandel im öffentlichen Sprachgebrauch seit 1945' (129–42); E. Elitz, 'Sprache in den Medien — die Wortverdreher GmbH' (143–54); G. Pflug, 'Mediensprache zwischen Neugier und Moral' (155–69); A. Conrad, 'Bilder erschlagen die Wörter. Sprachliche Verpflichtungen eines Fernsehjournalisten' (170–76); M. Hellinger, 'Feministische Sprachpolitik und politische Korrektheit — der Diskurs der Verzerrung' (177–91); M. Dietrich, ' "Gerechtigkeit gegenüber jedermann" — "Gerechtigkeit gegenüber allen Menschen". Sprachliche Gleichbehandlung am Beispiel der Verfassung des Landes Niedersachsen' (192–223); B. Stuckard, 'Sprachliche Gleichbehandlung — (k)ein Thema für Frauenzeitschriften?' (224–46); M. W. Hellmann, 'Divergenz und Konvergenz: sprachlich-kommunikative Folgen der staatlichen Trennung und Vereinigung Deutschlands' (247–75); W. Oschlies. ' "Anslus, blic krig, drang nach osten . . ." Germanismen in der politischen Mediensprache des postkommunistischen Osteuropas' (276–88); H. D. Schlosser, '525 Jahre "Unwort". Gesamt-, West- und Ostdeutsches im Spiegel der Sprachkritik' (289–302); R. Hoberg, 'Sprechen wir bald alle Denglisch oder Germeng?' (303–16); A. Greule, ' "Deutsch fürs Leben." Fünfhundert Jahre Sprachratgeber' (317–29); and U. Förster, 'Die Gesellschaft für deutsche Sprache. Ein geschichtlicher Überblick' (330–40).

K. Fischer-Hupe, *Victor Klemperers 'LTI. Notizbuch eines Philologen'* (Germanistische Linguistik. Monographien, 7), Hildesheim, Olms, 561 pp., is a very detailed analysis of the genesis of the book and how its publication was received after 1945. K. is unusual in that he was a Jewish scholar of French literature. His work on German has never been mentioned in *YWMLS*. An English translation of the book has been done by M. Brady: *The Language of the Third Reich. LTI — Lingua Tertii Imperii. A Philologist's Notebook*, London, Athlone Press, 2000, 296 pp. F.-H. uses original documents from archives and private collections for her investigation. Some of these are presented in an appendix. The volume is heavily footnoted, with many quotations.

F.-H. discusses the long stage of material gathering during the Third Reich (real cloak-and-dagger stuff) and then a short period of putting together and writing up. After the genesis of the work, its reception and editions, those produced in West and East Germany, are discussed. Emphasis is placed on its reception by linguists — interesting since K. was a scholar of literature. Account is given of translations, reviews, and letters to newspapers. Eight commentaries on the work are given, treating such angles as K.'s 'encyclopedic style', his linguistic usage, etc. A help for readers of the original work is the chapter giving a commentary on particular places, with background information on people, books, and words. F.-H. has provided an index of words and concepts which is lacking in the original work. All in all this is a commentary on a work which treats the language of a period in German history of which many still today have had first-hand experience. However, no linguist of that time has produced a work actually compiled during the Third Reich. One almost needs the original work bound in with this study to appreciate its significance. There are also companion volumes of diaries which could illuminate things more and of which K.-H. makes use (V. Klemperer, *Tagebücher*, ed. W. Nowojski and G. Jäckel, 4 vols, Berlin, 1995–99).

In *Sprachsituation und Sprachkultur im internationalen Vergleich. Aktuelle Sprachprobleme in Europa*, ed. J. Scharnhorst (SST, 18), 1995, 291 pp., a number of contributions deal with language situation and language cultivation in a number of European countries, of which the following deal with German: H. Löffler, 'Zur Sprachsituation in der Schweiz (47–68); A. Trabold, 'Das Handbuch zur "Förderung der sprachlichen Kultur in der Bundesrepublik Deutschland"' (197–206); H. Schönfeld, 'Das Berlinische zwischen Kontinuität und Wandel' (207–26); O. Rösch, 'Deutsch-Deutsch-Deutsches Rußlanddeutsche in Berlin' (227–50); and E. Ising et al., 'Podiumsgespräch zur Sprachsituation in Berlin' (251–91). Also noted: H. Bister-Broosen and R. Willemyns, 'Europe's linguistic diversity and the language policy of the European Union', *Rauch Vol.*, 713–22; H. D. Schlosser, 'Die Sprachmauer', *LBer*, 185:115–22; H. P. Althaus, 'Distanz und Nähe. Deutschjüdische Wissenschaftler und das Jiddische', *ZGL*, 29:23–39.

INTERDISCIPLINES. General aspects of using German in everyday language are treated in *Wiegand Vol.*: H. P. Althaus, 'Sprache im Alltag, Sprachwissenschaft und Kunst' (3–18); A. Gardt, 'Beeinflußt die Sprache unser Denken? Ein Überblick über Positionen der Sprachtheorie' (19–40); G. Harras, 'Alltag, Lebenswelt, Lebensform und Sprache. Ein Gespräch' (41–56); U. Hass-Zumkehr, 'Sprache im Alltag als Konstruktion von Lexikografie und Sprachwissenschaft' (57–70); K. Mudersbach, 'Wie der Mensch im Alltag folgert. Ein Gegenvorschlag zur formalen Logik' (71–96); C. Thimm, 'Sprache interpersonal und medial — methodische Perspektiven' (97–113); W.-A. Liebert, 'Gehirn und Geistestätigkeit im Spiegel von Laienmodellen. Ein linguistischer Streifzug durch Alltag, Populärwissenschaft und HipHop-Kultur' (173–86); T. Roelcke, 'Fachsprachen im Alltag. Probleme und Pespektiven der Kommunikation zwischen Experten und Laien' (219–32); B. Schaeder, 'Fachsprache im Alltag: Anleitungstexte' (233–48); and A. Linke, 'Zur allmählichen Verfertigung soziokultureller Konzepte im Medium alltäglichen Sprachgebrauchs' (373–88). Items on forensic linguistics include H. J. Künzel, 'Eine Datenbank regionaler Umgangssprachen des Deutschen (DRUGS) für forensische Anwendungen', *ZDL*, 68:129–54, and H. Kniffka, 'Eine Zwischenbilanz aus der Werkstatt eines "forensischen" Linguisten: zur Analyse anonymer Autorschaft', *LBer*, 185:75–104.

Psycholinguistic items include: C. von Stutterheim, 'Hörerorientierung in der Kommunikation. Psycholinguistische Evidenz pro und contra', *Wiegand Vol.*, 467–84; M. Ripfel, 'Störungen des Spracherwerbs und der Sprachentwicklung bei Muttersprachlern durch veränderte gesellschaftliche Bedingungen', *ib.*, 573–90; W. Reinecke, 'Logogenmodell und Faktorenmatrix des Spracherwerbs. Anmerkungen zu ihren komplementären Potenzen', *Fest. Helbig*, 159–67, and H. Wode, 'Wann beginnt L2–Erwerb?', *Fest. Menke*, 945–60. Multilingualism is treated in K. Braunmüller, 'Verdeckte Mehrsprachigkeit', *Fest. Menke*, 117–28. Items on teaching German as a foreign language include: D. Rösler, 'Das sprachliche Reinheitsgebot im Fremdsprachenunterricht', *Jones Vol.*, 399–410; P. R. Portmann-Tselikas, 'Schreibschwierigkeiten, Textkompetenz, Spracherwerb. Beobachtungen zum Lernen in der zweiten Sprache', *DaF*, 38:3–13; T. Zuchewicz, 'Befähigung zum wissenschaftlichen Schreiben in der Fremdsprache Deutsch', *ib.*, 14–20; C. Dürscheid, 'Alte und neue Medien im DaF-Unterricht', *ib.*, 42–47; C. Z. Bolognini, 'Historie und Ideologie in interkultureller Kommunikation', *ib.*, 47–50; K. Kleppin, 'Motivation. Nur ein Mythos? (1)', *ib.*, 219–26; K. Blex, 'Zur Wirkung von Instruktionsmaßnahmen auf den Fremdsprachenerwerb (Studien 1983–1997)', *ib.*, 226–33; D. Blei and D. Spaniel, 'Lehr- und Lernwelten. Ein Beitrag zum europäischen Jahr der Sprachen 2001', *ib.*, 233–40; L. Götze, 'Normen — Sprachnormen — Normtoleranz', *ib.*, 131–33; B. Lindemann, 'Zum universitären Übersetzungsunterricht im Bereich DaF (am Beispiel Norwegen)', *ib.*, 153–59; P. Ecke, 'Simulationen im Unterricht Deutsch als Fremdsprache', *ib.*, 159–66; A. Satzger, 'Fachsprachenforschung — Akzente und Perspektiven', *ib.*, 166–73. On the same subject are D. Blei, 'Aspekte historiographischer Forschung zum Deutschen als Fremdsprache', *Fest. Helbig*, 41–51, and R. M. Queen, 'Bilingual intonation patterns: evidence of language change from Turkish-German bilingual children', *LSo*, 30:55–80.

Relations between language and literature are discussed in I. J. Hueck, 'Dichtung und Rechtssprichwörter im Recht — Poetry and proverbs in law in European and German history', *Rauch Vol.*, 723–30; G. Lerchner, 'Sprache der Nähe — Sprache der Distanz. Zu textstrategischen Funktionalisierungen alltagssprachlicher und literatursprachlicher Redekonstellationen', *ZGer*, 11:7–15; M. Hoffmann, 'Dichtersprache und Gebrauchssprache im Varietätenraum', *ib.*, 16–35; U. Fix, 'Die Ästhetisierung des Alltags — am Beispiel seiner Texte', *ib.*, 36–53; G. Yos, 'Gespräche in künstlerischen Texten im Spannungsfeld von mündlicher und schriftlicher Kommunikation', *ib.*, 54–70; and H. Poethe, ' "Simple storys." Das Alltägliche im Poetischen', *ib.*, 71–87. Also noted: W. Wilss, **Translating and Interpreting in the 20th Century* (Benjamin Translation Library, 29), Amsterdam, Benjamins, 1999, xiii + 256 pp.; A. Dreischer, **Sie brauchen micht nicht immer zu streicheln . . .' Eine diskursanalytische Untersuchung zu den Funktionen von Berührungen in medialen Gesprächen* (Arbeiten zur Sprachanalyse, 39), Frankfurt, Lang, 332 pp.; **Mediensprache und Medienlinguistik. Festschrift für Jörg Hennig*, ed. D. Möhn et al. (Sprache in der Gesellschaft. Beiträge zur Sprachwissenschaft, 26), Frankfurt, Lang, 388 pp.; W. D. Klein, 'Die Bezeichnungen für Filmtypen im Deutschen. Eine Untersuchung zur Lexik der Mediensprache', *DSp*, 28, 2000:289–312; and K. Luttermann, 'Gesetzesinterpretation durch Juristen und Laien: ein rechtslinguistischer Beitrag zum Nötigungstatbestand', *LBer*, 186:157–74.

GENERAL LINGUISTICS, PRAGMATICS, AND TEXT LINGUISTICS. General linguistic items include: K.-P. Konerding, 'Sprache im Alltag und kognitive Linguistik: Stereotype und schematisiertes Wissen', *Wiegand Vol.*, 151–72. Pragmatics is the subject of K. R. Wagner, **Pragmatik der deutschen Sprache*, Frankfurt, Lang, 495 pp. Acquisition of German features in K. Stromswold and K. Zimmermann, 'Acquisition of *nein* and *nicht* and the VP-internal subject stage in German', *LaA*, 8, 1999–2000:101–28. Contrastive textual studies include C. Fandrych, ' "Dazu soll später noch mehr gesagt werden." Lexikalische Aspekte von Textkommentaren in englischen und deutschen wissenschaftlichen Artikeln', *Jones Vol.*, 375–98; E. W. B. Hess-Lüttich, 'Rhetoric of dialogue in German philosophy, literature, and linguistics', *Rauch Vol.*, 491–501; S. Wichter, 'Diskurs und Vertikalität', *Wiegand Vol.*, 249–64; A. Lehr, ' "Überdosis Sprache." Ein Panoptikum sprachreflexiver Äußerungen in Pressetexten', *ib.*, 321–48; A. Storrer, 'Getippte Gespräche oder dialogische Texte? Zur kommunikationstheoretischen Einordnung der Chat-Kommunikation', *ib.*, 439–66; U. Püschel, 'Stilistik — Theorie für die Praxis', *ib.*, 563–72; B. Kelle, 'Regionale Varietäten im Internet — Chats als Wegbereiter einer regionalen Schriftlichkeit?', *DSp*, 28, 2000:357–71; B. Schönherr, 'Paraphrasen in gesprochener Sprache und ihre Kontextualisierung durch prosodische und nonverbale Signale', *ZGL*, 29:332–63; F. Krier, 'Diskursorganisation in den Debatten des Deutschen Bundestages', *DSp*, 29:97–121; S. Schmidt-Knaebel, 'Zur Typologie des psychotherapeutischen Dialogs, II: das Behandlungsgespräch im Rahmen der psychodramatischen Methode aus linguistischer Sicht', *ZGer*, 11:88–104; U. Schröter, 'Öffentliche Meinung versus gestirnte Nacht. Wortverbindungen in Text und Lexikon', *Sprachwissenschaft*, 26:121–43; É. Sáfár, **Persuasive Texte. Eine vergleichende Untersuchung sprachlicher Argumentationsstrategien* (Metalinguistica, Debrecener Arbeiten zur Linguistik, 8), Frankfurt, Lang, 200 pp.; S. Goes, **Das "nicht" war zu leise!' Untersuchungen zur kommunikativen Verarbeitung von Abweichungen in Gesprächen* (Göttinger Beiträge zur Linguistik, 1), Göttingen, Duehrkohp & Radicke, 355 pp., with transcripts on a CD; H.-R. Beck, **Politische Rede als Interaktionsgefüge: Der Fall 'Hitler'* (LA, 436), x + 225 pp.; K. Birkin, **Bewerbungsgespräche mit Ost- und Westdeutschen: Eine kommunikative Gattung in Zeiten des gesellschaftlichen Wandels* (LA, 441), ix + 251 pp.; B. Rossbach, 'Skizze einer semiotisch-linguistischen Theorie narrativer Texte', *ZDL*, 68:308–25; and I. Mummert and G. Pommerin, 'Ansätze einer kreativitätsorientier Textanalyse und Textüberarbeitung (II)', *DaF*, 38:143–52. Also noted: P. Godglück, 'Gestus und Formel. Anmerkungen zum Verhältnis von Hand- und Sprachhandlungen und ihrer Geschichte', *LiLi*, 31:82–97.

Fest. Lerchner contains a number of items on textual analysis: A. Schwarz, 'Die Freude am Guten und Bösen: zum Verhältnis der Textsorte Prosaroman und Schwankroman' (155–68); O. Bykova, 'Textsortenspezifische Relevanz der Ethnokonnotation' (169–81); U. Fix, 'Das Rätsel. Bestand und Wandel einer Textsorte. Oder: warum sich die Textlinguistik als Querschnittsdisziplin verstehen kann' (183–210); T. Roelcke, 'Prototypischer und stereotypischer Textsortenwandel. Überlegungen zur Gattungsgeschichte des literarischen Experiments' (211–42); I. Kühn, '"Die Vorrede könnte Blitzableiter sein." Variationen von Musterrealisierungen im gesellschaftlichen Kontext' (407–34); and G. Schuppener, '"Tempora mutantur." Der Wandel des Zeitverständnisses in Begrifflichkeit und Text' (453–74).

2. HISTORY OF THE LANGUAGE

The division of the history of German into periods is the subject of **Periodisierung. Die zeitliche Gliederung der deutschen Sprachgeschichte*, ed.

T. Roelcke (Dokumentation Germanistischer Forschung, 4), Frankfurt, Lang, 437 pp., which reproduces many of the seminal papers from the past on this subject. M. Durrell illustrates the intertwining of nationalism and linguistic history in 'Nationalism and the history of the German national language: Theodor Frings's theories of the origin of standard German', *Jones Vol.*, 195–212. Items of general interest include H. Klatte, 'Tagungsbericht Symposion "Die Volkssprachen als Lerngegenstände in Europa im Mittelalter und der frühen Neuzeit" (Bamberg, 18./19. Mai 2001)', *Sprachwissenschaft*, 26:233–38; A. Mihm, 'Oberschichtliche Mehrsprachigkeit und "Language shift" in den mitteleuropäischen Städten des 16. Jahrhunderts', *ZDL*, 68:257–87; H. Elsen, 'Formen, Konzepte und Faktoren der Sprachveränderung', *ZGL*, 29:1–22; J. Macha, 'Figurenrede in erzählender Literatur: eine Erkenntnisquelle für die Sprachgeschichte?', *Fest. Menke*, 473–85; J. Erben, 'Zur Frage der Einschätzung von Textsorten als Entstehungs- oder Verbreitungsort sprachlicher Neuerungen', *Fest. Lerchner*, 147–54.

A number of aspects of historical syntax appear in *Historische germanische und deutsche Syntax. Akten des internationalen Symposiums anläßlich des 100. Geburtstages von Ingerid Dal, Oslo, 27.9.–1.10.1995*, ed. J. O. Askedal (Osloer Beiträge zur Germanistik, 21), Frankfurt, Lang, 1998, 385 pp., which contains the following contributions: H.-W. Eroms, 'Ingerid Dals "Kurze deutsche Syntax" auf historischer Grundlage. Entdeckungen und Einsichten bei der Neubearbeitung' (9–23); S. Sonderegger, 'Dichterische Wortstellungstypen im Altgermanischen und ihr Nachleben im älteren Deutsch' (25–47); J. A. Hawkins, 'A typological approach to Germanic morphology' (49–68); K. Donhauser, 'Das Genitivproblem und (k)ein Ende? Anmerkungen zur aktuellen Diskussion um die Ursachen des Genitivschwundes im Deutschen' (69–86); W. Abraham, 'Grammatische Miszellen für Ingerid Dal' (87–132); S. Dentler, 'Gab es den Präteritumschwund?' (133–47); J. E. Härd, 'Rahmenstruktur und Objektfeld' (149–63); Rosemarie Lühr, 'Konzessive Relationen' (165–92); A. Greule, 'Zwischen Syntax und Textgrammatik: die Parenthese bei Otfrid von Weißenburg' (193–05); K. Keinästö, 'Die Antwortpartikeln *Ja* und *Neyn* im mittelhochdeutschen Prosa-Lancelot. Historische Syntax und Textgeschichte' (207–29); J. O. Askedal, 'Zur Syntax infiniter Verbalformen in den Berthold von Regensburg zugeschriebenen deutschen Predigten. Vorstufe der topologischen Kohärenz-Inkohärenz-Opposition?' (231–59); K. E. Schöndorf, 'Zur Geschichte und Verbreitung der Fügung *ich kam gegangen* in der Germania' (261–70); R. P. Ebert, 'Verbstellungsveränderungen bei Jugendlichen im 16. Jahrhundert' (271–85); A. Betten, 'Zur Textsortenspezifik der

Syntax im Frühneuhochdeutschen. Anmerkungen zu ihrer Berück-
sichtigung in neueren deutschen Standardwerken und Skizze einiger
Forschungsdesiderata' (287–95); M. Rössing-Hager, 'Satzformen des
Übergangs und des Neueinsatzes in frühneuhochdeutscher Prosa.
Eine Fallstudie' (297–314), and K. Braunmüller, 'Wortstellungs-
typologische Untersuchungen zu den Kontaktsprachen der Hansezeit
(Mittelniederdeutsch, Dänisch, Schwedisch)' (315–34).

   Rauch Vol. contains a number of items on Germanic: W. Abraham,
' "Jespersen's cycle": the evidence from Germanic' (63–70); C. M.
Barrack, '*Mother* reveals why intervocalic coronals misbehave'
(71–74); L. Forester, 'On the semiotics of Germanic alliterative verse'
(81–91); Y. Kleiner, '*Fernassimilation*: Germanic palatal umlaut and
breaking' (93–106); A. Liberman, 'The English *F*-word and its kin'
(107–20); A. L. Lloyd, 'The "shaping" of German *Farbe*: cathedral
renovations and the rebuilding of an etymology' (121–28); E. C.
Polomé, 'Some comments on the vocabulary of emotion in Germanic'
(129–40); and P. Valentin, '*Wirdhu* and the Germanic passive'
(141–46). Also noted: D. Schürr, 'Zu Schrift und Sprache der
Inschrift auf Helm B von Negau: "Germanizität" und inneralpine
Bezüge', *Sprachwissenschaft*, 26 : 205–31.

   Gothic is represented by: G. W. Davis, 'Mini-sound changes and
etymology: Gothic *bagms, mathl*, and *auhns*', *Rauch Vol.*, 147–54; F. van
Coetsem, 'On borrowing in Gothic: broadening the research methodology', *ib.*, 155–61; and T. L. Markey, 'A child of necessity: Gothic
ē-genitives', *JEGP*, 100 : 57–67.

   Old Saxon features in J. E. Cathey, 'Interpretatio Christiana
Saxonica: redefinition for reeducation', *Rauch Vol.*, 163–72; D. A.
Krooks, 'Selections from an English translation of the *Heliand*', *ib.*,
173–82; G. R. Murphy, '*Mid alofatun*: secular beer, sacred ale', *ib.*,
183–88; S. Suizuki, 'Anacrusis in the meter of *Heliand* ', *ib.*, 189–99;
and T. Klein, 'Altsächsisch oder altniederländisch? Zur Heimat des
Helianddichters', *Fest. Menke*, 375–84.

   OHG fields the following items: M. R. Barnes, 'Old High German
umlaut', *Rauch Vol.*, 239–46; W. Harbert, '*Erino portun ih firchnussu*', *ib.*,
256–68; T. E. Hart, 'Influence of early music theory on the syntax of
Otfrid's five book design: a preliminary report', *ib.*, 269–84; B. R.
Page, 'On Notker's *Anlautgesetz*', *ib.*, 305–09; P. W. Tax, 'Die
althochdeutschen "Consolatio"-Glossen in der Handschrift Einsiedeln 179': 'Grundtext- oder Glossenglossierung? Ein neuer systema-
tischer Ansatz', *Sprachwissenschaft*, 26 : 327–58; H. Tiefenbach, 'Zu
den althochdeutschen Griffelglossen der Handschriften Clm 6300,
6312 und Vatikan Pal. lat. 1631', *ib.*, 26 : 93–111; N. R. Wolf,
'Sprachgeschichte als Textsortengeschichte? Überlegungen am
Beispiel von Latein und Althochdeutsch', *Fest. Lerchner*, 1–10;

R. Bergmann, 'Zeile und Zwischenraum. Zur althochdeutschen Glossenüberlieferung', *ib.*, 11–21, and R. Grosse and I. Köppe, '"Kulturelles Gedächtnis" im historischen Wortschatz. Sachinformation im Althochdeutschen Wörterbuch', *ib.*, 33–60.

There are numerous items on Middle Low German and later in *Fest. Menke*: H. Blosen, 'Ein mittelniederdeutsches "Speculum humanae salvationis" in dänischem Gebrauch' (71–88); R. Damme, 'Zum mittelniederdeutsch-lateinischen Vokabular in der Kieler Handschrift "Cod. Bord. 111 quart"' (143–63); J. Fligge et al., 'Die niederdeutschen Handschriften der Stadtbibliothek Lübeck nach der Rückkehr aus kriegsbedingter Auslagerung: Forschungsbilanz nach einem Jahrzehnt (mit einer Liste aller niederdeutschen Handschriften' (183–237); V. Honemann, 'De Schevekloth. Wie der Bischof von Hildesheim seine Feinde verspottete. Ein Beitrag zu den Formen politischer Kommunikation in der Frühen Neuzeit' (357–73); E. Neuss, 'Auf der Suche nach einer Schreibnorm. Urkundenkopien des 17. Jahrhunderts' (535–44); S. Pavidis, 'Zur Sprache der Rigaer Schragen in der zweiten Hälfte des 15. Jahrhunderts' (581–89); R. Peters, 'Die westfälischen Texte des 13. Jahrhunderts' (591–602); I. Rösler, '*Kum, wi suupen eens tosamen, Schnack mi doch wat nÿes vör*. Ein politisches Bauerngespräch aus dem Jahre 1718' (625–37); K. E. Schöndorf, 'Kausale, konditionale und konzessive Sätze in den niederdeutschen Bibelfrühdrucken' (732–50); I. Schröder, 'Niederdeutsche Gelegenheitsdichtungen in den Vitae Pomeranorum' (351–69); E. Skvairs, 'Variation im Formelbestand und Identität des Ausstellers: eine Sprachkontaktstudie zu russisch-deutschen Rechtstexten des 14.–17. Jahrhunderts' (809–22); I. ten Venne, 'Zum Schreibsprachenwechsel vom Nieder- zum Hochdeutschen in Wittenberg' (893–90); U. Weber, '*Hermannus bekande, dat he sodanne breue all, wo wol id twyerleye schrifft gestalt were, mit siner hand — vnde de so vorwandelt — geschreuen hedde*. Zu echten und gefälschten Schriftstücken ungeübter Schreiber aus Spätmittelalter und Frühneuzeit' (907–18), and V. Winge, 'De denscke Kroneke — der niederdeutsche Saxo' (919–28). Also noted: P. H. Listen, 'Middle Low German adverbial *-liken, -likes, -lik*', *Rauch Vol.*, 295–304.

Items on Martin Luther include T. Francis, ' "Schyr van worde tho worde" or "Reyne sprake"? How "pure" was the 1534 "Bugenhagen" translation of Luther's Bible into Low German?', *Jones Vol.*, 60–81; W. Besch, 'Wider den Stachel löcken (lecken)', *Rauch Vol.*, 247–56; and R. P. Ebert, 'Zur Verbstellung in Luthers Schriften', *Sprachwissenschaft*, 26:309–326. Also noted: I. T. Piirainen, 'Graphematische Variation aus der Sicht des Zentrums und der Peripherie: das älteste Stadtbuch von Neusohl/Blanská Bystice', *NMi*, 102:77–83; J. Fuhrmann, **Theorie und Praxis in der Gesetzgebung des*

Spätmittelalters in Deutschland am Beispiel der Ingelheimer Schöffensprüche, Frankfurt, Lang, 172 pp.; S. Heimann-Seelbach, 'Pragmalinguistische Aspekte deutscher Fachprosa-Übersetzungen: Nicolaus Italicus — Magister Hainricus — Johannes Hartlieb', *Fest. Lerchner*, 93–111; E. Skála, 'Deutsche Fachprosa in Böhmen in der Epoche des Humanismus', *ib.*, 113–23; H. Wellmann, 'WAHRHAFFTIGE NEWE ZEITTUNG. Zu den Anfängen der deutschen Presse in der Mirakelliteratur', *ib.*, 243–60; J. Schwitalla, 'Wandlungen eines Mediums. Sprachliche Merkmale öffentlicher Briefe von Laien in der Reformationszeit', *ib.*, 261–79; R. Metzler, '*So ruestet euch mit waffen wider den Türcken*. Martin Luthers und Georg Agricolas Schriften für den Krieg gegen die Türken', *ib.*, 297–319, and V. Hertel, 'Textsortenbenennungen im Deutschen des 16. Jahrhunderts', *ib.*, 321–36.

The 17th c. is represented by A. Gardt, 'Die Kategories des Worts in der deutschen Sprachwissenschaft des 17. und 18. Jahrhunderts', *Jones Vol.*, 31–59; F. van der Lubbe, 'Bellin, Halbichhorst, Aedler: towards a history of purism in the Deutschgesinnete Genossenschaft', *ib.*, 82–100; S. Watts, '"Wer kan wider eines gantzen Landes Gewohnheit?" Justus Georg Schottelius as a dialectologist', *ib.*, 101–14; R. L. Kyes, 'Language attitudes in sixteenth and seventeenth-century Germany', *Rauch Vol.*, 285–93. The 18th c. is represented by I. Reiffenstein, 'Frauenbriefe des 18. Jahrhunderts als sprachgeschichtliche Quellen', *Fest. Lerchner*, 281–96; B. Uhlig, 'Die Rezension — Eine Textsorte des 18. Jahrhunderts in Deutschland', *ib.*, 337–65; C. J. Wells, 'Aspects of archaism in Adelung', *Jones Vol.*, 133–63; C. V. J. Russ, '*Caffee, Casse, Comanto*: borrowed words in the letters of Frau Dorothea Schiller', *ib.*, 164–78; and J. West, 'The state of the German lexicon around 1800: evidence from Scheller's *Handlexicon*', *ib.*, 179–94.

Aspects of the history of purism in the 19th and 20th cs feature in A. W. Stanforth, '"One Latin word, one Greek remark, and one that's French": purism in Modern English and German and the *Allgemeiner Deutscher Sprachverein*', *Jones Vol.*, 213–29; J. L. Flood, 'The London branch of the *Allgemeiner Deutscher Sprachverein*', *ib.*, 230–53; F. Rash, 'The *Schweizerischer Verein für die deutsche Sprache* and linguistic purism in twentieth-century German-speaking Switzerland', *ib.*, 254–77; and U. Püschel, '"Polizeiliche Tages-Mittheilungen." Etwas über den Journalisten Kleist und die "Berliner Abendblätter"', *Fest. Lerchner*, 367–83.

The language of National Socialism is treated by G. Horan, '"Frauenkraft and Mutterwille": female identity in National Socialist discourse', *Jones Vol.*, 278–300.

3. ORTHOGRAPHY

The new spelling features in J. M. Zemb, 'Welche Rechtschreibreform ist liberaler, die französische oder die deutsche?', *Sprachwissenschaft*, 26:473–88; J. E. Mogensen, 'Die neue deutsche Rechtschreibung. Probleme bei der Umsetzung in zweisprachigen Wörterbüchern mit Deutsch und Dänisch', *DaF*, 38:214–19; P. Suchsland, 'Soll man Kopf stehend und freudestrahlend Eis laufen? Linguistische Fußangeln der neuen deutschen Rechtschreibung', *Fest. Helbig*, 209–26; J. Rivers and C. Young, 'Wer beherrscht die deutsche Sprache? Recht, Sprache und Autorität nach der Rechtschreibreform 1996', *ZDL*, 68:173–90; and J. E. Mogensen and E. Møller, 'Die Neuregelung der Getrennt- und Zusammenschreibung im Deutschen. Gedanken und Vorschläge am Beispiel der Lexikographie', *ZGL*, 29:242–60. Also noted: F. Domahs et al., 'Silbische Aspekte segmentalen Schreibens — neulinguistische Evidenz', *LBer*, 185:13–30; J. Ossner 'Das <h>-Graphem im Deutschen', *ib.*, 187:325–52; M. Neef and B. Primus, 'Stumme Zeugen der Autonomie — Eine Replik auf Ossner', *ib.*, 353–78; J. Ossner, 'Worum geht es eigentlich? — Replik auf die Replik von M. Neef und B. Primus', *ib.*, 379–82; W. Wolski, 'Kriterien der Beurteilung von Rechtschreibmaterialien für die Grundschule', *Wiegand Vol.*, 591–616; J.-M. Zemb, 'Ein Wort? Hypothese beziehungsweise Hyperthese: nicht alles, was zusammengeschrieben wird, ist ein Wort', *Sprachwissenschaft*, 26:1–19, and E. Seidelmann, 'Orthoepie der *e*-Laute und die Morphemik des Deutschen,' *Fest. Menke*, 777–89.

4. PHONOLOGY

A pleasing development is that several items deal with the rather neglected area of German intonation: P. Gilles, 'Die Intonation der Weiterweisung. Ein Beitrag zur konversationsanalystisch orientierten Erforschung von Regionalintonantion am Beispiel des Hamburgischen und Berlinischen', *DSp*, 29:40–69; J. Peters, 'Steigend-fallende Konturen im Berlinischen', *ib.*, 122–47; D. M. Chun, 'Intonation in German as iconic symbol', *Rauch Vol.*, 323–34; K. G. Goblirsch, 'Consonant strength and syllable structure in Swedish and Bavarian', *ib.*, 335–44; S.-T. Yu, 'Multi-strata Lexikon vs. Constraintranking: Degemination im Deutschen', *LBer*, 186:129–56; M. Hoshii, 'Wortakzent im Japanischen und im Deutschen. Erwerbsprobleme bei japanischen Deutschlernern', *DaF*, 38:37–42. Also noted: N. Gutenberg, **Einführung in Sprechwissenschaft und Sprecherziehung*, Frankfurt, Lang, 340 pp.

5. MORPHOLOGY

Inflectional studies include: H. Clahsen et al., 'The mental representation of inflected words: an experimental study of adjectives and verbs in German', *Language*, 77:494–509; J. Kilbury, 'German noun inflection revisited', *JL*, 37:339–54; and P. Schlobinski, '*knuddel — zrueckknuddel — dich ganzdollknuddel*. Inflektive und Inflektivkonstruktionen', *ZGL*, 29:192–218. Derivational morphology is illustrated by D. Möhn, 'Konfixe auf -*o*, heteronyme und homonyme Lexemverwandtschaften. Ein lexikologischer Versuch zum Euro', *Fest. Menke*, 505–13; S. S. Shin, 'On the event structures of -*ung* nominals in German', *Linguistics*, 39:297–320; K. Willems, 'Produktivität, syntaktische Struktur und Norm. Deskriptive Normregularitäten transparenter nominaler Wortbildungsmuster und kontrastive Wortbildungsforschung', *ZGL*, 29:143–66; I. Barz, 'Kompositionsstrukturen', *Fest. Helbig*, 15–28; W. Motsch, 'Zur semantischen Grundlage deverbaler Nomen', *ib.*, 149–57; J. Schröder, 'Alles gut bedacht — Präfixverben im gegenwärtigen Deutsch', *ib.*, 169–75; and M. Schröder, 'Wortbildung in Textkomplexen', *Fest. Lerchner*, 385–405.

6. SYNTAX

General items include: G. Öhlschläger, 'Grammatiken für den Alltag', *Wiegand Vol.*, 187–218; U. Schmitz, 'http://www.ellipsen.de', *ib.*, 423–38; L. Götze, 'Eine funktionale Grammatik für Deutsch als Fremdsprache', *Fest. Helbig*, 81–94; E. Tschirner, 'Lernergrammatiken und Grammatikprogression', *ib.*, 227–40; M. Kaltenbacher, **Universal Grammar and Parameter Resetting in Second Language Acquisition* (EH, XIV, 386), 248 pp.; and K. Fischer, 'Noch immer: Ergänzungen und Angaben', *Sprachwissenschaft*, 26:239–68. Word classes are represented by G. Rauh, 'Wortarten und grammatische Theorien', *ib.*, 21–39; and H. Wellmann, 'Die Wortarten im Aufbau der Grammatik — damals und heute', *Fest. Helbig*, 241–57. Also noted: J.-M. Zemb, 'Amicus grammaticus . . .', *Sprachwissenschaft*, 26:113–20; A. Kathol, 'Positional effects in a monostratal grammar of German', *JL*, 37:35–66.

Items dealing with the whole sentence include: M. Steinbach, 'A theory of predicates', *LBer*, 185:105–14; K. Poncin, 'Präferierte Satzgliedfolge im Deutschen: Modell und experimentelle Evaluation', *ib.*, 186:175–204; C. Felser and L. Rupp, 'Expletives as arguments: Germanic existential sentences revisited', *ib.*, 187:289–324; and K. Baldauf, **Prädikate und Prädikationen in Gegenstandsbeschreibungen*.

Satzsemantische Analyse und stildidaktische Anwendung, ed. I. Pohl and K.-E. Sommerfeldt (SST, 37), xx + 463 pp.

Valency features in R. Hinkel, 'Der "Protagonist" und seine "Mitspieler". Was die Verbvalenz im DaF-Unterricht leisten kann (1)', *DaF*, 38:20–28; J. Kubczak, 'Nachdenken über *verletzen* und die Folgen oder: eine Valenzgruppe "in Not"', *Fest. Helbig*, 133–47; H. Schumacher, 'Von *verletzen* zu *verletzbar* und *Verletzung*. Zu einigen Aspekten des Zusammenhangs der Valenz von Verben, Adjektiven und Substantiven', *ib.*, 177–87; K.-E. Sommerfeldt, 'Textsortenwandel und Valenz', *ib.*, 189–99; and K. Keinästö, **'Unberechtigtes Altes umstoßen und berechtigtes Neues einführen.' Franz Kern als Vorläufer der deutschen Dependenzgrammatik. Eine Fallstudie zur deutschen Grammatographie am Ende des 19. Jahrhunderts* (Finnische Beiträge zur Germanistik, 5), Frankfurt, Lang, 125 pp.

Syntax of the noun phrase includes: E. Mallén, 'Binding conditions on case morphology in noun phrases', *Rauch Vol.*, 345–54; K. Schwabe and K. von Heusinger, 'On shared indefinite NPs in coordinative structures', *JSem*, 18:241–68; M. Hundt, 'Grammatikalisierungsphänomene bei Präpositionalobjekten in der deutschen Sprache', *ZGL*, 29:167–91; D. Weber, **Genus. Zur Funktion einer Nominalkategorie exemplarisch dargestellt am Deutschen* (EH, I, 1808), 152 pp.

Items on syntax of the verb phrase include J. O. Askedal, 'On the grammatical status of the subjunctive in reported speech in German', *Rauch Vol.*, 311–21; W. Abraham, 'Syntax and semantics of modal verbs in German and their diachronic root: soft aspectual and robust finiteness constraints', *Wiegand Vol.*, 113–29; A. Speyer, 'Ursprung und Ausbreitung der AcI-Konstruktion im Deutschen', *Sprachwissenschaft*, 26:145–87; J. Sabel, 'Das deutsche Verbum infinitum', *DSp*, 29:148–75; C. Dürscheid, 'Verbsyntax und Rollensemantik', *ib.*, 176–85; G. Starke, 'Partizipialgruppen mit Textbezug', *Fest. Helbig*, 201–07; W. Abraham, Werner and J. Conradie, **Präteritumschwund und Diskursgrammatik: Präteritumschwund in gesamteuropäischen Bezügen. Areale Ausbreitung, heterogene Entstehung, Parsing sowie diskursgrammatische Grundlagen und Zusammenhänge*, Amsterdam, Benjamins, xii + 148 pp.; R. Musan, 'The present perfect in German: outline of its semantic composition', *NLLT*, 19:355–401; J. O. Askedal, 'Zur Frage der Auxiliarisierung einiger deutscher Verben mit Infinitiv im Lichte der Grammatikalisierungstheorie', *Fest. Helbig*, 1–13; and M. Hennig, 'Werden die doppelten Perfektbildungen als Tempusformen des Deutschen akzeptiert?', *ib.*, 95–107.

Other word classes are discussed in: C. Di Meola, 'Vom Inhalts- zum Funktionswort: Grammatikalisierungspfade deutscher Adpositionen', *Sprachwissenschaft*, 26:59–83; H. Haider, 'Adverb placement — Convergence of structuring and licensing', *TL*, 26,

2000:95–134; S. Günther, '*wobei* (. . .) *es hat alles immer zwei seiten*. Zur Verwendung von *wobei* im gesprochenen Deutsch', *DSp*, 28, 2000:313–41; T Leuschner, ' "*. . . wo immer* es mir begegnet, . . . *wo* es *auch* sei.*"* Zur Distribution von "Irrelevanzpartikeln" in Nebensätzen mit *w- auch/immer*', *ib.*, 342–56; G. Scheibl, 'Zur Unterscheidung thetisch-kategorisch in deutschen *es*-Konstruktionen', *ib.*, 372–95; D. Nübling, 'Von *oh mein Jesus!* zu *oje!* Der Interjektionalisierungspfad von der sekundären zur primären Interjektion', *ib.*, 29:2–45; W. Abraham, 'Gibt es im Deutschen ein Klasse von Präpositionen mit Doppelrektion?', *ib.*, 63–75; S. Alatorzew, '*Während* — Präposition und Konjunktion zum Ausdruck gleichzeitiger Handlungen', *ib.*, 76–83; and T. Balci and F. Kanatli, 'Das Problem der Kasuswahl nach Wechselpräpositionen', *DaF*, 38:28–31.

Contrastive studies noted: S. H. Seong, 'On word order in German and Korean', *Rauch Vol.*, 355–66; C. Di Meola, 'Synchronic variation as a result of grammaticalization: concessive subjunctions in German and Italian', *Linguistics*, 39:133–50; and E. Gärtner, 'Zur Beschreibung komplexer Sätze in brasilianischen Gebrauchsgrammatiken', *Fest. Helbig*, 67–80.

Historical items include: V. Harm, 'Zur Herausbildung der deutschen Futurumschreibung mit werden + Infinitiv', *ZDL*, 68:288–307; and V. Ágel, 'Gegenwartsgrammatik und Sprachgeschichte. Methodologische Überlegungen am Beispiel der Serialisierung im Verbalkomplex', *ZGL*, 29:319–31.

7. SEMANTICS

General articles include J. Kilian, 'Kritische Semantik. Für eine wissenschaftliche Sprachkritik im Spannungsfeld von Sprachtheorie, Sprachnorm, Sprachpraxis', *ZGL*, 29:293–318; M. Schulz, 'Einzelwortbeschreibung und Wortschatzbeschreibung', *Sprachwissenschaft*, 26:41–58; R. Schützeichel, 'Textgebundenheit als Prinzip der Bedeutungsermittlung', *Fest. Lerchner*, 23–32; M. Kammerer, 'Verstärkungsbildungen im Deutschen. Versuch einer phänomenologischen Bestimmung', *Wiegand Vol.*, 293–320; P. R. Lutzeier, 'Die Rolle lexikalischer Daten im Alltag für das Strukturgerüst im Lexikon', *ib.*, 409–22; H. Blühdorn, 'Generische Referenz. Ein semantisches oder ein pragmatisches Phänomen?', *DSp*, 29:1–19; R. Wiese, 'The structure of German vocabulary: edge marking of categories and functional considerations', *Linguistics*, 39:95–116; S. Ramharter, 'Das semantische Wettbewerbsmodell', *LBer*, 186:205–36; and J. V. Istjagin, 'Die konnotative Ambiguität ethnokonnotierter lexikalischer Einheiten', *DaF*, 38:31–37.

Modal particles feature in L. Lemnitzer, ' "Wann kommt er denn nun endlich zur Sache?" Modalpartikel-Kombinationen — Eine korpusbasierte Untersuchung', *Wiegand Vol.*, 349–72; U. Nederstigt, 'Prosody: a clue for the interpretation of the additive focus particles *auch* and *noch*', *LBer*, 188:415–40; M. Dalmas, 'Fakten und Effekte. Wozu gebraucht man eigentlich *tatsächlich* und Co?', *Fest. Helbig*, 53–65; and M. Smirnova, 'Fragesätze in Widerspruchsfunktion. Ein semantisch-pragmatischer Beschreibungsansatz', *DSp*, 29:46–63,

Lexicographical studies are represented by H. Bergenholtz, 'Proskription, oder: so kann man dem Wörterbuchbenutzer bei Textproduktionsschwierigkeiten am ehesten helfen', *Wiegand Vol.*, 499–520; R. H. Gouws, 'Der Einfluß der neueren Wörterbuchforschung auf einen neuen lexikographischen Gesamtprozeß und den lexikographischen Herstellungsprozeß', *ib.*, 521–46; A. Holderbaum and J. Kornelius, 'Kollokationen als Problemgrößen der Sprachmittlung', *ib.*, 533–46; P. Kühn, ' "BLUME: ist Kind von Wiese": Bedeutungserläuterungen in der Lernerlexikographie', *ib.*, 547–62; H. Bergerová, 'Das Elend der Phraseographie und kein Ende. Diesmal am Beispiel deutsch-tschechischer Wörterbücher', *Fest. Helbig*, 29–40; G. Kempcke, 'Ein neues Wörterbuch "Deutsch als Fremdsprache" ', *ib.*, 121–32; H. E. Wiegand, 'Artikel einsprachiger Lernerwörterbücher, Textgestaltwahmehmung und Suchbereichsstrukturen. Plädoyer für übersichtliche Printwörterbücher im Zeitalter der neuen Medien', *ib.*, 259–81; and A. Mikeleitis-Winter, 'Wörterbuchtexte im Wandel?', *Fest. Lerchner*, 73–91. The *Deutsches Wörterbuch*, Stuttgart, Hirzel, continues on its way with vol. 3, fasc. 1, cols 1–160, 1999, *Antagonismus-appellieren*, and vol. 3, fasc. 2, cols 161–320, *appellieren-Arzneiglas*, 2000. Contrastive studies include E. Gombocz, 'An der "Schnittfläche" von Synchronie und Diachronie — Probleme bei der Erstellung einer deutsch-ungarischen Wortfamiliensammlung', *DSp*, 29:84–90; J. P. L. Zulategui, **Fraseología contrastiva del alemán y el espanol. Teoría y práctica a partir de un corpus bilingüe de somatismos*, ed. G. Wojtak (Studien zur romanischen Sprachwissenschaft und interkulturellen Kommunikation, 4), Frankfurt, Lang, viii + 255 pp.; H. Walter and V. Mokienko, **Russisch-Deutsches Jargon-Wörterbuch*, Frankfurt, Lang, 579 pp.; **Von der mono- zur bilingualen Lexikografie für das Deutsche*, ed. J. Korhonen (Finnische Beiträge zur Germanistik, 6), Frankfurt, Lang, 386 pp.; and W. Wang, **Zweisprachige Fachlexikographie. Benutzungsforschung, Typologie und mikrostrukturelle Konzeption* (Angewandte Sprachwissenschaft, 8), Frankfurt, Lang, 334 pp.

The trends of development in modern German lexis are featured in *Neues und Fremdes im deutschen Wortschatz. Aktueller lexikalischer Wandel*, ed. G. Stickel (Institut für Deutsche Sprache. Jahrbuch, 2000), Berlin,

de Gruyter, 388 pp., which contains the following contributions:
H. H. Munske, 'Fremdwörter in deutscher Sprachgeschichte: Integration oder Stigmatisierung?' (7–29); A. Gardt, 'Das Fremde und das Eigene. Versuch einer Systematik des Fremdwortbegriffs in der deutschen Sprachgeschichte' (30–58); H. E. Wiegand, 'Fremdwörterbücher und Sprachwirklichkeit' (59–88); D. Herberg, 'Neologismen der Neunzigerjahre' (89–104); A. Kirkness, 'Europäismen/Internationalismen im heutigen deutschen Wortschatz. Eine lexikographische Pilotstudie' (105–30); U. Busse, 'Typen von Anglizismen: von *der heilago geist* bis *Extremsparing* — aufgezeigt anhand ausgewählter lexikographischer Kategorisierangen' (131–55); I. Barz, 'Interferenzen beim Wortschatzausbau. Zum Zusammenspiel verschiedener Nominationsverfahren' (156–71); W. Wilss, 'Substantivische Wortbildungen in der deutschen Gegenwartssprache' (172–82); P. Eisenberg, 'Die grammatische Integration von Fremdwörtern. Was fängt das Deutsche mit seinen Latinismen und Anglizismen an?' (183–209); G. Augst, 'Gefahr durch lange und kurze Wörter? Lang- und Kurzwortgefahr? LKW-Gefahr?' (210–38); P. Schlobinski, 'Anglizismen im Internet' (239–57); N. Janich and A. Greule, '. . . *da weiß man, was man hat.* Verfremdung zum Neuen im Wortschatz der Werbung' (258–79); and J. Schiewe, 'Aktuelle wortbezogene Sprachkritik in Deutschland' (280–96). Also noted: A. Gardt, 'Zur Bewertung der Fremdwörter im Deutschen (vom 16. bis 20. Jahrhundert)', *DaF*, 38:133–43; F. Debus, 'Überfremdung der deutschen Sprache? Frage des englisch-amerikanischen Einflusses', *ib.*, 195–204; and H.-G. Schmitz, 'Anglizismen, Anglizismenkritik und neudeutsche Sprachwissenschaft', *Fest. Menke*, 707–31.

Historical studies include I. Förster et al., 'Beiträge zum Deutschen Wörterbuch. Aus der Arbeit am neuen [10]Paul', *ZGL*, 29:219–41; V. Harm, 'Gibt es eine Monosemierungstendenz in der Wortgeschichte des Neuhochdeutschen?', *ZGL*, 29:364–80; R. Eckhardt, 'On the underlying mechanics of certain types of meaning change', *LBer*, 187:31–74; and R. Niedballa, **Bord und Borte. Entwicklungsgeschichtliche Untersuchung eines Wortschatzelements* (EH, I, 1795), 435 pp.

Several items in *Jones Vol.* deal predictably with borrowing: L. Lipka, '*Handy, Mobbing, Friseur, Парикмахер* und *rascacielos*. Lehnwörter, Scheinentlehnung und Lehnübersetzungen in europäischen Sprachen sowie im Japanischen' (301–19); A. Kirkness, 'Anglicisms, borrowings and pseudo-borrowings in German: *-ical* revisited' (320–33); D. N. Yeandle, 'Types of borrowing of Anglo-American computing terminology in German' (334–60); and S. Barbour, 'Defending languages and defending nations: some perspectives on the use of "foreign words" in German' (361–74). Also noted: A. Kolwa, **Internationalismen im Wortschatz der Politik. Interlexikologische*

Studien zum Wortschatz der Politik in neun EU-Amtssprachen sowie im Russischen und Türkischen (Arbeiten zur Sprachanalyse, 38), Frankfurt, Lang, xi + 423 pp.; M. Besse, 'Das Verhältnis von Erb- und Lehnwörtern in der Fachsprache der Winzer. Am Beispiel des Dachbereichs "Rebe" ', *LiLi*, 31 : 37–81; M. Lilienkamp, **Angloamerikanismus und Popkultur. Untersuchungen zur Sprache in französischen, deutschen und spanischen Musikmagzinen* (BRA, 76), xxvi + 600 pp.; S. Kreuzer, 'Von *Ave* bis *Zores*. Hebräische und semitische Wörter in unserer Sprache', *LiLi*, 31 : 98–115; and R. Kössling, ' "Humanitas — das schönste Wort der lateinischen Sprache." Joachim Camerarius' lateinisch-griechischer Wortschatz der menschlichen Körperteile — ein Zeugnis renaissancehumanistischer Sprachkultur und Bildungsvermittlung', *Fest. Lerchner*, 61–72.

Metaphorical usage is dealt with by M. Beisswenger, 'Stoibers Kreuzzug und der Canossa-Gang des Bundestrainers. Spuren von Geschichtlichem in metaphorischen Wendungen der Alltagssprache', *Wiegand Vol.*, 129–50.

Among studies of individual words noted were P. Lutzeier, 'Words and concepts: some empirical tools, exemplified for the concept "kultiviert" ', *Jones Vol.*, 1–16; K.-D. Ludwig, 'Was (noch) nicht im Wörterbuch steht. Oder: was ist Bimbes?', *Wiegand Vol.*, 389–408; and E. König, 'From expressions for body parts to reflexive anaphors: semantic change in the development of intensifiers', *Rauch Vol.*, 503–17. Also noted: D. Schmützer, 'Mir fehlen die Worte! Zum sprachlichen Umgang mit Sexualität in der Öffentlichkeit', *Fest. Bauer*, 429–42.

Semantic change features in the following: M. Rein, 'Zur Bedeutungsbreite des Wortes *bekehren* und zur Bezeichnungskonkurrenz im Rahmen des Konzeptes "bekehren" im früheren Althochdeutschen', *LiLi*, 31 : 7–79; P. Koch, 'Bedeutungswandel und Bezeichnungswandel. Von der kognitiven Semasiologie zur kognitiven Onomasiologie', *ib.*, 121 : 7–36; and T. Vennemann gen. Nierfeld, 'Zur Etymologie von dt. *Balz*', *Sprachwissenschaft*, 26 : 425–31.

Popular etymology is discussed by P. Godglück, 'Eigenwissen und Fremdverstehen. Über die sogenannten Volksetymologien', *LiLi*, 31 : 136–49.

8. DIALECTS

General items include K. Ebner, 'Dialektale Elemente im regionalen Standard. Anmerkungen zur Lexikographie', *Fest. Bauer*, 49–60; W. V. Davies, 'Standardisation and the school: norm tolerance in the educational domain', *LBer*, 188 : 393–414; H. Bassler and H. Spiekerman, 'Regionale Varietäten des Deutschen im Unterricht Deutsch als

Fremdsprache (1)', *DaF*, 38:205–14; and E. Piirainen, 'Phraseologie und Arealität', *ib.*, 240–43.

Representing Low German is **Niederdeutsch. Sprache und Literatur einer Region*, ed. U. Föllner, Frankfurt, Lang, 198 pp., a collection of essays. *Fest. Menke* also contains numerous articles on various aspects of Low German: H.-W. Appel, 'Zur Variation zwischen kurzen *o* und *u* in niedersächsischen Dialekten' (19–29); U. and I. Bichel, 'Zwei Gedichte Klaus Groths auf dem Weg zu seinem "Quickborn"' (57–69); L. M. Eichinger, 'Regiolektales Sprechen in Hans Jakob Christoffel von Grimmelshausens "Simplicius Simplicissimus". Nicht zuletzt am Beispiel des Niederdeutschen' (165–82); U. Föllner, 'Protokolle des Plattdütschen Vereens to Magdeborg. Ein Sprachverein vor 100 Jahren' (249–57); L. de Grauwe, 'Eigenständigkeit einst und jetzt. Zu einigen Parallelen in Geschichte und Gegenwart des "Flämischen" und des Niederdeutschen' (299–313); R. Herrmann-Winter, 'Niederdeutsches in pommerschen Zeitschriften des späten 18. und frühen 19. Jahrhunderts' (331–40); K. J. Kohler, 'Überlänge im Niederdeutschen?' (385–414); D. Lele-Rozentile, 'Niederdeutsches in der lettischen Folklore' (415–28); U.-T. Lesle, 'Plattdeutsch zwischen gestern und morgen: Geschichtsbeschleunigung und die Suche nach der *identitas*' (429–49); P. Martens, 'Niederdeutsche Dialekt-Varianten in Hamburg' (487–503); F. Möller, 'Niederdeutsch im Buchhandel 1990 bis 2000' (515–25); D. Nerius, 'Zur Funktion und Struktur der Schreibung des Niederdeutschen' (527–34); U. Scheuermann, '"Wie heißt oder heißen in Ihrer Mundart . . . ?" Das Original und seine Wiederholung nach sechs Jahrzehnten am Beispiel von Elliehausen GÖ / Göttingen-Elliehausen' (639–57); C. Schuppenhauer, 'Wissenschaft, die Glauben schafft? Wider die leichtfertige Re-Ideologisierung des Niederdeutschen' (771–76); and D. Stellmacher, 'Zu den Kurzverben im Niederdeutschen' (861–66). Also noted: **Berlinisch heute. Kompetenz — Verwendung — Bewertung*, ed. H. Schönfeld (SST, 36), 191 pp.

Fest. Bauer contains a number of contributions on Bavarian dialects: G. W. Baur, 'Karl Weinhold als Anreger und Förderer von Matthias Lexers Kärntischem Wörterbuch' (23–30); L. M. Eichinger, '*Der-*, aspektuelles Präfix und bairisches Shibboleth' (61–88); F. Eiselt, 'Wort- und sachkundliche Anmerkungen zum "Steirischen Wortschatz" von Unger-Khull' (93–112); P. Ernst, '*Grant* und *grantig*' (113–122); E. Gabriel, 'Die Bildung des Partizips Präteriti im tirolischen Lechtal' (123–64); E. Glaser, 'Funktion und Verbreitung der Partikel *fai*' (165–90); H. Goebl, 'Die Germanismen im ladinischen Sprachatlas ALD-I' (191–210); O. Gschwantler, 'Diphthongvarianten in den Varietäten der Mundart von Brixen im Thale und Umgebung' (211–44); M. Hornung, 'Mundartwörterbücher als

Ausdruck der Identitätssuche sprachlicher Minderheiten' (245–50); P. A. Jorgensen, 'Die Dialektnotation in der Wienermundartdichtung' (251–68); H. Klausmann, 'Der Fernpass — Grenze und Brücke zwischen zwei oberdeutschen Mundarträumen' (269–88); S. Kloferová, 'Die Struktur der Benennung im Sprachkontakt (anhand des "Tschechischen Sprachatlas"' (289–302); F. Patocka, 'Anmerkungen zum Gebrauch der Partikel auch im bairisch-österreichischen Dialektraum' (303–16); G. A. Plangg, 'Zu romanisch-deutschen Erb- und Lehnwörtern in Westösterreich' (317–24); H. D. Pohl, 'Kärntner Speisen (und Verwandtes) diesseits und jenseits der deutsch-slowenischen Sprachgrenze' (325–42); R. Post, 'Die hochalemannische Siedlungsmundart von Saderlach/Banat und ihre Interferenzen aus dem Österreichischen' (343–54); I. Reiffenstein and P. Mauser, 'Pischelsdorf. Zur Geschichte von bairisch *Bischolf*' (355–66); M. Renn, 'Zu laut gebrüllt, bayerischer Löwe? Beobachtungen aus ostschwäbischer Sicht zur "Expansion" des Bairischen. Illustriert an Beispielen der Gastronomie im Ostallgäu und im nordwestlichen Tirol' (367–82); A. R. Rowley, 'Bairisch mit *A*-' (383–94); H. Scheuringer, 'Vom sprachlichen Nachhall vergangener Zeiten. Die Binnensprachinsel Nasswald im südöstlichen Niederösterreich' (421–28); E. Seidelmann, 'Bildungsweisen der Kollektiva in zimbrischer und Kärntner Mundart' (443–56); H. Tatzreiter, 'Dialektales in einem standardsprachlichen Text. Vorkommen und Funktion' (463–80); H. Tyroller, 'Kodifizierung der zimbrischen Sprache von Lusern und der mochenischen des Fersentales (Projektbeschreibung)' (481–500); and P. Wiesinger, 'Zu neuen historischen Belegen des 12. Jahrhunderts für die bairischen Wochentagsnamen und zur Herleitung von ahd. *pherintag*/frühmhd. *pherntag* "Freitag"' (501–20). Also noted: H. Tiefenbach, 'Ein Frühbeleg für das bairische Präfix *der-*', *Sprachwissenschaft*, 26:417–24.

Alemannic is represented by P. Dalcher, 'Wie das Schweizerische Idiotikon mit den Kinderreim-Wörtern umgeht', *Fest. Bauer*, 31–48; H. Christen, 'Ein Dialektmarker auf Erfolgskurs: Die /l/-Vokalisierung in der deutschsprachigen Schweiz', *ZDL*, 68:16–26; and A. Kraehenmann, 'Swiss German stops: geminates all over the word', *Phonology Yearbook*, 18:109–46.

Low German is treated by R. K. Seymour, ' "Elefanteneier" — A tale as told in the Westfalian dialect of Nienberge', *Rauch Vol.*, 367–78, and P. Gilles et al., 'Perzeptuelle Identifikation regional markierter Tonhöhenverläufe. Ergebnisse einer Pilotstudie zum Hamburgischen', *ZDL*, 68:155–72.

Work on West Central German includes S. Müller-Dittloff, *Interferenzen des Substandards im Westmitteldeutschen am Beispiel von Idar-Oberstein. Eine kontrast- und fehleranalytische Untersuchung* (*ZDL* Beihefte,

117), Stuttgart, Steiner, 375 pp. M.-D. offers an interesting view on the dialect situation by examining over 1100 essays by school pupils and compares them with the local and regional dialect. Even though the pupils are providing written material, this contains enough evidence to show dialect influence. The volume presents a detailed description of phonology, grammar, word formation, and vocabulary which is valuable in itself. M.-D. also contrasts the pupils' usage by means of error analysis. She highlights direct traces of dialect intereference, hypercorrection, and error correction, whereby an existing contrast is wrongly interpreted. There is much in the detailed analysis which is familiar to historical linguists, but the data are set out in tables and pie-charts easy to read and interpret. They show that mistakes which were determined by substandard usage accounted for about a third of all mistakes. The types of mistake were spread over a wide range, including confusing past and perfect tenses, <d> and <t>, use of the definite articles with names, mixing up of strong and weak verbs. Comparative studies in Bingen and Wittlich produced similar results. This volume contains a very wide range of dialect material. Also noted: D. Nübling, 'Wechselflexion Luxemburgisch-Deuts ch kontrastiv: ech soen — du sees/si seet vs. ich sage, du sagst, sie sagt. Zum sekundären Ausbau eines präsentischen Wurzelvokalwechsels im Luxemburgischen', *Sprachwissenschaft*, 26:433–72; K.-H. Mottausch, 'Zur Geschichte der Substantivflexion im Südhessischen um Lorsch-Worms', *ZDL*, 68:1–15, and S. Grosse, 'Zur literarischen Form der gesprochenen Sprache im Ruhrgebiet', *Fest. Lerchner*, 435–52.

East Central German is represented by U. Hirschfeld, 'Phonetische Merkmale des Sächsischen und das Fach Deutsch als Fremdsprache', *Fest. Helbig*, 109–120.

Speech islands are represented by W. Schabus, 'Emblematisierung der Dialekte und Sprachpolitik in den landlerisch-sächsischen Dörfern Siebenbürgens', *Fest. Bauer*, 395–420; R. Srámek, 'Zu den lexikalischen Elementen deutscher Herkunft der Stadt Brünn', *ib.*, 457–62; and J. M. Fuller, 'The principle of pragmatic detachability in borrowing: English-origin discourse markers in Pennsylvania German', *Linguistics*, 39:351–70.

Dialect vocabulary features in P. Seidensticker, 'Myrica Gale L., der Gagel. Ein apokryphes Lemma im "Promptuarium Medicine"', *ZDL*, 68:27–42; and J. Kiss, 'Zum Problem der Klassifizierung von Dialektwörtern', *ZDL*, 68:43–50. Dialect dictionaries include *Senslerdeutsches Wörterbuch*, ed. C. Schmutz and W. Haas, Freiburg (Switzerland), Paulusverlag, 2000, 729 pp., which treats the vocabulary of the dialect in the area between Freiburg and Berne, the so-called *Senslerbezirk*.

9. ONOMASTICS

General onomastic concerns feature in R. Wimmer, 'Eigennamense-
mantik auf der Basis des Alltagssprachgebrauchs', *Wiegand Vol.*,
265–80; E. Eichler, ' "Abtrünnige" Toponymie', *Fest. Bauer*, 89–92;
N. R. Wolf, 'Ethnymisches. Beobachtungen zu Übernamen in
Unterfranken', *ib.*, 521–32; T. Vennemann gen. Nierfeld, 'Germania
Semitica + *abr-* "strong", with a reflection on Abraham/Theoderic',
ib., 85–92; and Id., 'Germania Semitica + *aflal* (OE *athel-*, G *Adel*)
"nobility". With an appendix on Gk. ñAtlaV', *ib.*, 189–204.

Place names are illustrated by H. Blume, 'Rautheim, Rennelberg,
Rügen. Drei Braunschweiger Ortsnamen', *Fest. Menke*, 89–100;
M. Carstensen, ' "Amsel, Drossel, Fink und Star . . ." Tier- und
Vogelbezeichnungen in Orts- und Siedlungsnainen Schleswig-
Holsteins', *ib.* 129–41; H. Tiefenbach, 'Beobachtungen zum
Corveyer Namengut des 9. und 10. Jahrhunderts', *ib.*, 867–78.

MEDIEVAL LITERATURE

By NIGEL W. HARRIS, *University of Birmingham*

1. GENERAL

Medieval Germany: An Encyclopaedia, ed. John M. Jeep, NY, Garland, xxxviii + 928 pp., is a monumental work of reference. Its 647 alphabetically ordered entries encompass many aspects of political and social history, as well as language, literature, art and architecture, music, philosophy, theology, education, and 'daily life'; and, pleasingly, there is considerable coverage of Dutch literature and culture. Prominent among the contributors of literary articles are G. H. M. Claasens, A. Classen, R. H. Firestone, F. G. Gentry, E. R. Haymes, H. P. Heinen, E. R. Hintz, S. Jefferis, W. C. McDonald, J. A. Rushing, and S. C. Van D'Elden. Most entries are admirably clear and concise, although the accompanying bibliographies are in some cases thin. One could also argue that late-medieval literary culture and the works of Latin authors are somewhat under-represented. Quibbles such as these, however, are dwarfed by the sheer scale of the volume's achievement.

The second fascicle of the supplementary 11th vol. of *Die deutsche Literatur des Mittelalters. Verfasserlexikon*, ed. Kurt Ruh et al., Berlin, de Gruyter, 321–640 cols, contains, along with corrections and additions, many entirely new articles. Several of these deal with chronicles, plays, and medical and legal literature; but there is also new material on 'Glaubensbekenntnisse' (G. Steer) and 'Heiltumbücher' (F. Eisermann), and, of course, a wide range of authors. These include Heinrich von Coesfeld, Heinrich von Isernia, and Andreas and Vinzenz Grüner (all by F. J. Worstbrock); and three notable Humanists in Marsilio Ficino (S. Limbeck), Wessel Gansfort, and Dietrich von Pleningen (both by Worstbrock). *Deutschsprachige Literatur des Mittelalters. Studienauswahl aus dem 'Verfasserlexikon' (Bd. 1–10)*, ed. Burghart Wachinger, Berlin, de Gruyter, 1108 cols, is a selection of some 83 *Verfasserlexikon* articles. With commendable pragmatism, W. restricts his choice largely to authors and works which are likely to interest undergraduates. Hence Latin texts are excluded, and there is also little on non-mystical religious literature, historiography, or scientific and specialist literature. By contrast, the canonical OHG and MHG authors are well represented, as are short narratives and *Fastnachtspiele*.

Beutin, *Literaturgeschichte*, is a revised and expanded edition of this much used literary history (see *YWMLS*, 51:623, 54:648). It includes entirely new chapters on the periods between 1890 and 1920, and since 1989; other chapters have been revised to take greater account of the broader European cultural context. In the case of B. Lutz's contribution on medieval literature (1–56), this entails above all a five-page introductory sketch of medieval and pre-medieval European history.

The *Katalog der deutschsprachigen illustrierten Handschriften des Mittelalters*, vol. III, fasc. 4, ed. Norbert H. Ott and Ulrike Bodemann, 241–366 pp., continues its description of illustrated MSS and printed books of vernacular chronicles. This fascicle encompasses Austrian chronicles by Leopold von Wien and Ottokar von Steiermark, Gallus Öhem's *Chronik der Reichenau*, and the *Schwäbische Chronik* and *Gmünder Chronik* of Thomas Lirer. A. Otto, *Mediaevalia*, 20:227–55, examines a heterogeneous group of 15th-c. miscellany MSS, for which he establishes a common origin in a workshop such as that of Diebolt Lauber; and U. Weber, *Fest. Menke*, 907–18, analyses some late-medieval and early modern MSS written by unpractised hands. C. Meier, *FmSt*, 34, 2000:338–92, surveys the iconographical representation of various medieval conceptions of authorship; and in Suntrup, *Tradition*, 227–55, she studies medieval colour codes and allegories, especially those developed in relation to liturgy, heraldry, and courtly love.

In *GLM*, 38:50–54, E. A. Overgaauw summarizes and comments on the Deutsche Forschungsgemeinschaft's new proposals for cataloguing and providing information about medieval MSS on the internet; and R. Giel, *ib.*, 39:34–40, describes specifically the online database *Manuscripta Mediaevalia* <www.manuscripta-mediaevalia.de>. This initiative is also the subject of a notice by J. Bove, *ZDA*, 130:495–96, which is one of the first eight contributions to a new series called 'Mittelalter-Philologie im Internet'. Other projects described in vol. 130 include: the MS census known as the 'Marburger Repertorium zur Überlieferung der deutschen Literatur des Mittelalters' <www.marburger-repertorien.de> (J. Heinzle and K. Klein, 245–46); a database of medieval German autographs <www.uni-muenster.de/Fruehmittelalter/Projekte/Autographen/Abfrage.html> (V. Honemann, 247–48); a catalogue of MSS from the Diocesan and Cathedral Library in Cologne <www.ceec.uni-koeln.de> (P. Sahle, 370–74); an inventory of the MSS formerly in the City Archive in Kaliningrad (Königsberg) <www.bis.uni-oldenburg.de/kbg_hss_archiv> (R. G. Päsler, 374–75); details of copies of the six printed editions of the 'Straßburger Heldenbuch' <www.geocities.com/walter.kofler/> (W. Kofler, 376); the multi-purpose medieval gateway <www.mediaevum.de> (J. Hamm et al., 492–93); and the extraordinarily useful 'Mittelhochdeutsche Begriffsdatenbank' <mhdbdb.bgsu.edu> (H. P. Pütz and K. M.

Schmidt, 493–94). Moreover, J. Fligge et al., *Fest. Menke*, 183–237, discuss the LG MSS from Lübeck which have been returned there from the former GDR and USSR since 1989.

Wolfgang Milde, *Mediaevalia et Lessingania. Kleine Schriften*, ed. Wolfgang Maaz et al. (Spolia Berolinensia, 19), Hildesheim, Weidmann, xii + 390 pp., reprints some 24 of M.'s essays from between 1971 and 1998. Along with pieces on medieval and early modern libraries and their catalogues, and on Lessing, there are several dealing with medieval MSS, including M.'s important 1982 article on the Wolfenbüttel *Erec* fragments (see *YWMLS*, 44 : 749).

T. Bein, Nutt-Kofoth, *Text*, 81–98, surveys past and present approaches to editing medieval German texts, with particular reference to differing concepts of textual variance. In *Editio*, 15, H.-G. Roloff (25–36) discusses problems associated with editing translated texts from 1400–1750; and M. E. Dorninger (197–204) continues her critical bibliography of works dealing with editorial questions, this time covering publications from 1997. In *Schröder Vol.*, F. Debus (161–78) discusses attempts, especially by 19th-c. scholars, to reconstruct MHG works from post-medieval MSS; and K. Gärtner (273–88) evaluates the potential of the computer as tool and medium for the editing of medieval texts. S. Kranich-Hofbauer, *Firchow Vol.*, 217–30, pleads for an 'historical-diplomatic' approach to editing late-medieval works, arguing specifically against the normalization of analogous graphemes.

Verführer, Schurken, Magier, ed. Ulrich Müller and Werner Wunderlich (Mittelalter-Mythen, 3), St Gall, UVK, 990 pp., is an even thicker and more wide-ranging volume than its predecessors in this series (see *YWMLS*, 61 : 592–93). Save for an arguable shared status as outsiders who oppose and sometimes threaten society, the subjects it treats have little in common; and the contributors themselves use diverse methodological approaches. Nevertheless the book is a mine of up-to-date and generally well documented information. Its 60 chapters include studies of temptresses such as Eve (M. Hubrath), Venus (U. Müller), Dido (M. Mecklenburg), Helen of Troy (A. Classen), and, less predictably, Agnes Bernauer (J. L. Flood); male seducers are represented by the likes of Don Juan (J. Manuel López de Abaida and D. Studer) and Lancelot (U. Müller); the many scoundrels range from Eulenspiegel (W. C. McDonald) and Markolf (R. Brandt and H. Wuth) to Judas Iscariot (M. Dorninger) and Mordred (S. Schmidt); and the roll-call of magicians encompasses Merlin (U. Müller), Klingsor (R. Krohn), and even Albertus Magnus (L. Petzoldt). There are also several chapters on figures such as Everyman (S. Schmidt), Cundry (K. Pappas), and the Pied Piper of

Hamelin (W. Wunderlich), whom one would not necessarily have anticipated meeting in this company.

Brian Murdoch, *Adam's Grace. Fall and Redemption in Medieval Literature*, Cambridge, Brewer, 2000, xii + 205 pp., is a remarkably erudite study of the use of Adam, and other Adam-figures, to illuminate through literature such fundamental Christian themes as the Fall, redemption, and the universality of original sin. M. deals in turn with apocryphal lives of Adam, and with Adamic analogues and motifs in the legends of Gregorius, Parzival, and several lepers (including Hartmann's Heinrich).

Bettina Mattig-Krampe, *Das Pilatusbild in der deutschen Bibel- und Legendenepik des Mittelalters* (GB, 9), 252 pp., surveys developments in the presentation of Pontius Pilate in vernacular religious literature from the 9th to the 14th centuries. Whilst one can distinguish easily enough between biblical epics (from *Der Heliand* to *Die Erlösung*) which focus on Pilate's role in the Passion narrative, and legends (often based on the *Gospel of Nicodemus*) which also describe other aspects of his putative biography, M.-K. shows that it is impossible to speak of clear trends in his presentation and evaluation either within genres or at specific periods. Rather, Pilate remains, as in the New Testament, a complex and ambivalent figure, whose characterization varies considerably according to the viewpoints of individual authors and the precise nature of their source material. L. de Grauwe, *LB*, 90:161–79, examines the presentation of Pilate in the *Redentiner Osterspiel* and other Easter plays.

Verena Holzmann, '...*Ich beswer dich wurm vnd wyrmin* ...' *Formen und Typen altdeutscher Zaubersprüche und Segen* (WAGAPH, 36), 322 pp., is the first comprehensive survey of the more than 300 German charms and blessings from the 9th to the 16th cs which appear in modern editions. H. begins with a lucid introduction to the beliefs underlying these short texts, and then lists and prints them all, giving brief details of their date and MS tradition. She orders them according to four categories (command, narrative, parable, and prayer), the differences between and within which she explains in detail.

David N. Yeandle, '*Schame*' *im Alt- und Mittelhochdeutschen bis um 1210. Eine sprach- und literaturgeschichtliche Untersuchung unter besonderer Berücksichtigung der Herausbildung einer ethischen Bedeutung*, Heidelberg, Winter, xxv + 264 pp., is a meticulous study of *schame* in all its aspects (positive and negative, ethical and non-ethical, prospective and retrospective, physical and psychological, concerned with oneself and with others). Composite chapters on OHG and early MHG texts are followed by individual chapters devoted to Hartmann, Herbort von Fritzlar, Ulrich von Zatzikhoven, the *Nibelungenlied*, *Parzival*, *Wigalois*,

Tristan, Willehalm and *Titurel*, and Walther von der Vogelweide. Y.'s conclusions rely heavily on his division of references to *schame* into clear-cut categories which are by definition debatable; but his approach yields significant gains. Particularly convincing is his stress on the importance of *schame* as a positive ethical concept, and on the seminal importance of *Parzival* in formulating and propagating its role as a 'slôz ob allen siten'.

C. Stephen Jaeger, *Die Entstehung höfischer Kultur. Vom höfischen Bischof zum höfischen Ritter* (PSQ, 167), 389 pp., is a translation, by Sabine Hellwig-Wagnitz, of J.'s important 1985 volume *The Origins of Courtliness* (see *YWMLS*, 48:682). The text has not been updated, but there is new prefatory material by Horst Wenzel and by J. himself.

Peters, *Text*, contains several essays on the applicability of contemporary theories to the study of medieval literature. Reacting to the tenets of 'New Philology', K. Grubmüller (8–33) demonstrates a desire on the part of numerous medieval authors to assert and protect the thematic and formal integrity of their works; and B. Quast (34–46) argues that this desire is particularly strong in the case of authors of didactic or normative texts. J. Heinzle (198–214) reassesses the value for *Altgermanisten* of Norbert Elias's theory of civilization; and U. Friedrich (245–67) essays a discourse-analytical survey of literary constructions of the relationship between knight and horse. Meanwhile E. Brüggen (546–74) problematizes the distinction often drawn between 'fictional' and 'non-fictional' medieval literature; and F. Bezner (575–611) recommends a pragmatic, interdisciplinary approach to the study of medieval literary theories such as the *integumentum*. Elsewhere C. Brinker-von der Heyde, *DUS*, 53.2:55–64, discusses, from a medievalist's perspective, the debate surrounding the definition and usefulness of the terms *Kultur* and *Kulturwissenschaften*.

In Kellner, *Kommunikation*, P. Strohschneider (1–26) examines the relationship between literary communication and social interaction in medieval Germany, in the light especially of his concept of 'institutionality'; and B. Kellner (153–82) finds hints of a consciousness of literary tradition, and of an accepted canon, in both heroic epic and courtly romance. Meanwhile V. Honemann, *Das Mittelalter*, 6.1:19–30, discusses various forms of symbolic communication described in medieval German literature; and M. Schumacher, *DUS*, 53.6:8–15, evaluates the (generally non-prescriptive) guidelines for the practice of conversation found in medieval and early modern texts.

Other studies of a general nature include: Burghart Wachinger, *Erzählen für die Gesundheit. Diätetik und Literatur im Mittelalter* (SKHAW, 23), Heidelberg, Winter, 44 pp., a survey of both medical-dietetic and narrative literature in which stories are ascribed a balancing or therapeutic function; E. Feistner's discussion (*ZDA*, 130:253–69) of the characteristics of legends, fairy-tales, and forms which combine the two; I. Bennewitz's bibliography (*JIG*, 32:64–96) of scholarly works dealing with family and gender roles in medieval and other literature; and N. Harris's account (*FMLS*, 37:429–40) of recent research into the teaching of medieval German literature at American universities.

OTHER WORKS. *Juden in Europa. Ihre Geschichte in Quellen.* 1: *Von den Anfängen bis zum späten Mittelalter*, ed. Julius H. Schoeps and Hiltrud Wallenborn, Darmstadt, Primus, viii + 309 pp., is the first of a planned series of five collections of fundamental documents on the history of European Jewry, translated into NHG and aimed mainly at the non-specialist. It includes edicts of Frederick II and Charles IV, an excerpt from the *Sachsenspiegel*, texts by Jewish authors regulating community life in Worms, Speyer, and Mainz, and several chilling accounts of pogroms.

Jörg W. Busch, *Certi et veri cupidus. Geschichtliche Zweifelsfälle und ihre Behandlung um 1100, um 1300 und um 1475. Drei Fallstudien* (MMS, 80), 278 pp., is an absorbing and successful attempt to revise the traditional view that medieval historians were less inclined than their Humanist or modern counterparts to investigate or refute dubious statements found in their sources. On the basis of detailed discussion of three issues that generated historiographical controversy at distinct points during the Middle Ages, B. discerns a remarkable degree of continuity not only in historians' concern for demonstrably accurate truth, but also in the methods they adopted to pursue it. He also points, however, to the influence on late-medieval historiography of a gradually growing awareness of disparities between different historical periods and contexts.

Ludger Körntgen, *Königsherrschaft und Gottes Gnade* (Vorstellungs-welten des Mittelalters, 2), Berlin, Akademie, 540 pp., discusses perceptions of the sacred nature of kingship under the Ottonian and early Salian emperors, and stresses that these were not used merely to legitimize their rule, but also to generate socio-political action. K.'s sources include depictions of emperors in liturgical MSS (where their function is to remind readers of the Emperor's role and of his need for intercession).

Knut Görich, *Die Ehre Friedrich Barbarossas. Kommunikation, Konflikt und politisches Handeln im 12. Jahrhundert*, WBG, x + 638 pp., is a detailed but readable study of Barbarossa's (and his contemporaries') concept of honour, especially in so far as it motivated political action and was expressed in symbol and gesture. G. discusses the role played by honour in such political conflicts as the investiture controversy, as well as in Barbarossa's dealings with the law and with money. Relatively little use is made of literary parallels, though there is an interesting brief analysis of the 'rash boon' motif in *Iwein*. W. Haubrichs, *DB*, 105, 2000: 128–38, examines concepts of honour prevalent in early medieval society, drawing attention to their relational and legal orientation. Meanwhile Barbarossa's role as mediator is analysed in Hermann Kamp, *Friedensstifter und Vermittler im Mittelalter*, WBG, x + 384 pp., an innovative study of peacemaking and arbitration as practised in the Empire between the 7th and 15th cs, in which K. lays particular emphasis on the increasing institutionalization of these processes in the High Middle Ages. F. Shaw, *German History*, 19: 321–39, examines the medieval origins of the myth identifying Frederick II as an undead 'Last Emperor', before discussing the 19th-c. transference of this myth to Barbarossa.

In Haupt, *Endzeitvorstellungen*, H. Schulte Herbrüggen (49–93) surveys medieval and Renaissance expectations of the last times; P. Dinzelbacher (95–131) discusses the uncomfortable co-existence in medieval thought of the doctrines of a general and an individual judgement; J. Semmler (133–45) examines the nature and extent of fears that the world would end in the year 1000; W. G. Busse (179–96) discusses the fear occasioned by medieval people's association of the end of the world with natural catastrophes; H. J. F. Brall-Tuchel (197–228) surveys references to Gog and Magog in a variety of OHG and MHG texts; and H. Finger (251–70) considers the relationship between heresy and apocalyptic ideas in the 12th- and 13th-c. Rhineland. In *Fest. Brunner*, 391–402, R. Sprandel examines individual and collective responses to the Black Death. Also noted: *Recht und Verfassung im Übergang vom Mittelalter zur Neuzeit. Bericht über Kolloquien der Kommission zur Erforschung der Kultur des Spätmittelalters 1996 bis 1997*, ed. Hartmut Boockmann et al. (AAWG, 239), 520 pp.

2. GERMANIC AND OLD HIGH GERMAN

Ottar Grønvik, *Über die Bildung des älteren und des jüngeren Runenalphabets* (Osloer Beiträge zur Germanistik, 29), Frankfurt, Lang, 118 pp., argues that the older runic alphabet, with its evident indebtedness to the Norse phonemic system, was devised in Denmark between 180 and 200 AD, quite possibly by a single chieftain. He then traces its development into the younger, reduced *furthak* found in the recently discovered inscription from Ribe (*c.*720–30). G.'s careful analysis identifies the Viking period as one of significant change also in the matter of the (increasingly loose) relationship between phonemes and their graphemic representation. M. K. Dahm, *ABÄG*, 55: 15–20, postulates the influence of the Latin cursive 'p' on the development of the p-rune; and U. Schwab, *SM*, 42:797–839, discusses recent publications on runes and runic inscriptions.

Eckhart Meineke and Judith Schwerdt, *Einführung in das Althochdeutsche* (UTB, 2167), Paderborn, Schöningh, 350 pp., is an outstandingly thorough introduction to the subject. It begins with a survey of the Indo-European and Germanic foundations of OHG, and ends with a detailed but generally approachable treatment of OHG phonology, morphology, word formation, and syntax. In between there is an introduction to OHG literature (including glosses) which usefully provides photographs of some 16 MS pages.

The multi-volume *Althochdeutsches Wörterbuch*, ed. Rudolf Grosse et al., Berlin, Akademie, has spawned four fascicles in 2000 and 2001 (together constituting vol. IV, cols 1301–1620). These cover the alphabetical ground between 'houga' and 'inni'. Meanwhile A. Greule, *Fest. Ruberg*, 237–44, considers some of the purposes and possibilities of his *Syntaktisches Verbwörterbuch zu den althochdeutschen Texten des 9. Jahrhunderts* (see *YWMLS*, 61:601); and M. Rein, *LiLi*, 122:7–79, surveys the meanings and implications of OHG *bikêran*, and other terms relating to conversion which it superseded.

A great deal of work has been done on OHG glosses. Claudia Wich-Reif, *Studien zur Textglossarüberlieferung. Mit Untersuchungen zu den Handschriften St. Gallen, Stiftsbibliothek 292 und Karlsruhe, Badische Landesbibliothek St. Peter perg.87* (GB, 8), 383 pp., begins with a painstaking analysis of these two closely related MSS, followed by both a diplomatic and an annotated parallel edition of excerpts from them. W.-R. identifies certain features overlooked by previous scholars, such as seven 'new' vernacular glosses and some Latin ones to Priscian's *Institutio de arte grammatica*; and she postulates that the MSS have a common, late 9th-c. Rhenish-Franconian/Alemannic source. W.-R. then turns to define the characteristics of *Textglossare* more generally: their prime function, she contends, is to elucidate a specific Latin text, principally in Latin, but also on occasion by translating particular lemmata into the vernacular. Her work concludes with a list of some 166 MSS with OHG or OS glosses which fit this definition. H. Tiefenbach, *Sprachwissenschaft*, 26:93–111, examines several OHG dry point glosses recently published by E. Glaser (see *YWMLS*, 58:720–21) and by M. McCormick. P. W. Tax, *ib.*, 327–416, prints, elucidates, and assesses the 220 OHG glosses found in Einsiedeln 179, a 10th-c. MS containing Boethius's *De consolatione Philosophiae* and a Latin commentary on it. He concludes that, contrary to common belief, the OHG glosses frequently render the commentary, rather than the *Consolatio* itself — a finding which has potentially significant consequences, not least for lexicographers.

In Bergmann, *Glossen*, E. Hellgardt (261–96) compares semantic, morphological, and syntactical features of OHG, OS, and Old English interlinear glosses on the Psalms. H. Tiefenbach (325–51) discusses various problems associated with OS glosses, not least the difficulty of defining exactly what one is. C. Moulin-Fankhänel (353–79) surveys the OHG glosses in MSS formerly in the Cathedral Library at Würzburg; H. U. Schmid (381–92) explores perceived differences between the vocabulary of OHG glosses and 'literary' works; R. Grosse (393–410) discusses the use of conjunctions and prepositions in OHG glosses; and L. Voetz (411–27) argues that the so-called *St. Pauler Lukasglossen* are not in fact glosses, but rather constitute an interlinear version of their Latin source. Furthermore N. Henkel (429–51) discusses the functions of OHG glosses which appear in the form of a few letters, rather than whole words; C. Cigni (453–73) argues that both the Latin and the OHG glosses of Walafrid Strabo's *Hortulus* were intended for use in schools; S. Blum (475–84) demonstrates that the OHG glosses of Canon Law texts sometimes offered surprisingly free renderings appropriate to the vernacular cultural context; and M. Baldzuhn (485–512) examines MSS of Avianus's fables with OHG glosses, suggesting that those intended for oral exploitation in schools are often the most lightly glossed. E. Langbroek (513–28) discusses cases of problematic relationships between Latin lemmata and OHG glosses; W. Wegstein (529–35) presents evidence for dating the *Summarium Heinrici* to no later than 1101; and S. Stricker (551–73) examines the Latin verses and German interlinear glosses of the *Versus de volucribus*.

The *Heliand* is discussed by E. S. Dick, *Firchow Vol.*, 23–30, who examines its strategies of cultural and semantic transfer; by H. Haferland, *DVLG*, 95:237–56, who discerns the influence of Germanic heroic poetry on its narrative conception and structure; and by T. Klein, *Fest. Menke*, 375–84, who raises the fundamental issue of whether its language can be described as OS.

W. Haubrichs, *Fest. Ruberg*, 99–112, assesses the extent to which direct speech used in Otfrid's *Evangelienbuch* reflects contemporary oral usage; J. Schneider, *Firchow Vol.*, 343–58, discusses the historical-political context in which the work was composed; and W. Kleiber, *Schröder Vol.*, 115–41, examines the use of initials to separate groups of strophes in Otfrid's own MS of it.

Two articles in *Firchow Vol.* are concerned with Notker Labeo: A. A. Grotans (101–17) speculates on how his works might have been composed and copied, and identifies the scribal hands of the St Gall and Zürich MSS of them; and P. Ochsenbein (299–315) prints and comments on 25 short texts from as far apart as the 11th and 17th cs which discuss Notker's life and works. Meanwhile in Bergmann,

Glossen, 575–85, A. Schwarz suggests that Notker could be said to 'deconstruct' the texts he translates.

Essays on other OHG subjects: R. Schmidt-Wiegand, *Firchow Vol.*, 335–42, discusses examples of vernacular legal terms in Carolingian capitularies; H. Fromm, *Fest. Brunner*, 1–14, considers possible reasons for the 'gap' in OHG literature after *c.* 900; and W. Haubrichs, *Schröder Vol.*, 143–59, outlines the MS tradition of Latin lives of St George, on which the OHG *Georgslied* depends.

3. MIDDLE HIGH GERMAN

GENERAL. Beate Hennig et al., *Kleines Mittelhochdeutsches Wörterbuch*, 4th rev. edn, Tübingen, Niemeyer, xxvi + 503 pp., appears in a fourth edition only eight years after the publication of the first (see *YWMLS*, 55:710, 57:665, 60:584). This in itself bears testimony to its reliability and user-friendliness. The present edition revises and slightly expands its immediate predecessor, in the light of comments from reviewers and other users. E. Meineke, *Firchow Vol.*, 653–74, surveys existing MHG dictionaries and makes recommendations for future ones; and K. Gärtner and R. Plate, *Fest. Ruberg*, 247–56, describe two current lexicographical projects. One involves the preparation of online and CD-ROM versions of four existing MHG dictionaries (see *YWMLS*, 62:597; the CD-ROM is introduced in detail by T. Burch and J. Fournier, *ZDA*, 130:306–18). The other seeks to create, by *c.* 2022, a new four-volume *Mittelhochdeutsches Wörterbuch*. In Moser, *Verarbeitung*, R. Plate and U. Recker (169–83) discuss the information technology used in connection with this latter project; and Y. Yokoyama (159–68) describes the computer-assisted concordance to Wirnt von Gravenberg's *Wigalois* which was prepared as part of it. Also in Moser, *Verarbeitung*, Y. Koga (107–15) reports on work to create a bilingual MHG/Japanese dictionary; F. Debus (117–28) outlines the principles on which his forthcoming dictionary of names in MHG literature is based; I. Lemberg (129–47) discusses the role of information technology in the preparation of the *Deutsches Rechtswörterbuch*; P. Sappler (149–58) describes problems encountered when compiling the indices to the *Repertorium der Sangsprüche und Meisterlieder*; and S. Moser (185–98) gives details of the database constructed as part of his study of early NHG noun derivations. Meanwhile T. Klein (83–103) describes the processes involved in creating a MHG grammar from texts scanned into a computer; and C. M. Sperberg-McQueen (3–22) discusses various aspects of the relationship between information technology and philology.

Johannes Singer, *Mittelhochdeutscher Grundwortschatz*, 3rd rev. edn (UTB, 2253), Paderborn, Schöningh, x + 170 pp., is both fuller and easier to use than earlier editions. There is now at least one textual example (from Hartmann, the *Nibelungenlied*, or Walther) for each of the 698 lemmata; the layout of the entries is clearer; and the notes for the user are more helpful. Not least because of its excellent summary of MHG grammar, this is now an outstandingly useful volume for students.

JOWG, 12, 2000, subtitled 'Bilanz der Spätmittelalterforschung', features numerous articles that assess the current state of research into a particular subject and suggest lines of future inquiry. H. Brunner (1–20) begins with a general survey of late-medieval research by Germanists. Areas subsequently covered are editorial methodology (K. Kranich-Hofbauer, 49–64) and textual variance (M. J. Schubert, 35–47); vernacular MS culture (C. Bertelsmeier-Kierst and J. Wolf, 21–34); heroic epic and *Spielmannsdichtung* (W. Kofler, 95–105, and S. Kerth and E. Lienert, 107–22); *Mären* and their thematization of relationships between the sexes (M. Schnyder, 123–34); *Minnereden* (W. Achnitz, 137–49); late *Spruchdichtung* and early *Meistersang* (J. Rettelbach, 185–201); religious dawn songs (M. Derron and A. Schnyder, 203–16); *Volkslieder* (A. Classen, 217–28); Yiddish literature (W. Röll, 259–71); accounts of the life of Jesus (K.-E. Geith, 273–89); sermons (R. D. Schiewer, 291–309); 14th-c. German Bible translations (F. Löser, 311–23); vernacular medical literature (B. Schnell, 397–409); magic and its literary presentation (F. Fürbeth, 411–22); and the theory and practice of *geblümte Rede* (G. Hübner, 175–84). Moreover J. Goheen (163–74) considers research into late-medieval concepts of memory, with special reference to gnomic texts; both M. Ankermann (339–51) and W. Beutin (353–63) examine the relationship between mysticism and science; G. Blaschitz (381–96) discusses the interface between Germanic philology and *Realienkunde*; and C. Brinker-von der Heyde (65–81) assesses the potential of interdisciplinary research linking literary studies with intellectual history and anthropology. J. Janota, *BGDSL*, 123:397–427, surveys the entire field of late-medieval literature in one article.

Annette Volfing, *John the Evangelist in Medieval German Writing. Imitating the Inimitable*, OUP, x + 273 pp., is an important and original study of the ways in which the fourth Evangelist is presented and instrumentalized in MHG literature. Both devotional and poetological uses of John are explored, with special reference throughout to the question of imitation, be it the *imitatio sancti* enjoined in homiletic and similar contexts, or the *imitatio auctoris* problematized in narrative and lyric poetry. A substantial introductory chapter discusses the construction of the John-figure in Latin accounts of his biography and in the liturgy of his two saint's days. V. then turns to vernacular devotional works, analysing first a selection of sermons (in which John is typically perceived as a mirror reflecting Christ in both his writings and his person), and then the little known *Johannes-Libelli* (*c.* 1400). Finally she considers the poetological uses of John in both biblical epic and *Meisterlieder*. For all their differences, the narrative or lyrical personae who preside over these works share an intrinsically ambivalent view of John, who for them is both role-model and rival. J. F. Hamburger, Peters, *Text*, 296–327, discusses various presentations of John's virginity in medieval literature and art.

Other general or comparative studies: in *Fest. Ruberg*, R. Voss (21–34) discusses the concept of a person's name as presented in courtly literature, and S. Obermaier (45–60) considers various models of the relationship between hidden and obvious meanings of texts. In *Firchow Vol.*, J. C. Frakes (85–100) examines the motif of women watching men from windows in *Das Nibelungenlied, Die Klage, Kudrun,* and the narratives of Wolfram; and S. C. Van D'Elden (407–23) evaluates the claims to literacy or illiteracy made by the narrators of works by Hartmann, Wolfram, Hildegard, and Ulrich von Lichtenstein. Elsewhere W. G. Rohr, Görner, *Traces,* 47–87, analyses the meanings of *klâr* and its derivatives in various 12th-c. texts; S. Kerth, *Fest. Brunner,* 267–89, studies *Das Wachtelmäre* and other examples of MHG nonsense literature; I. Bennewitz, *JIG,* 32, 2000:8–18, discusses family structures and relationships presented in MHG literature; S. Müller, Kellner, *Kommunikation,* 51–71, points to motifs common to *Daz himelrîche* and other works as diverse as *Kudrun, Dukas Horant,* and the lyrics of Der von Kürenberg; E. Gössmann, *DB,* 105, 2000:49–57, examines gender-specific metaphors used by a number of authors, including Hildegard and Gertrud von Helfta, to illuminate divine and human nature; R. Peters, *Fest. Menke,* 591–601, comments on several 13th-c. Westphalian texts; A. Classen, *Spiewok Vol.,* 89–118, discusses the presentation of bereavement and grieving in MHG literature, especially in *Die Klage* and *Der Ackermann aus Böhmen;* Id., *SM,* 42:565–604, assesses the importance of money in Walther von der Vogelweide, Boppe, Der Stricker, Oswald von Wolkenstein, and *Fortunatus;* and W. Röcke, Hubrath, *Zwickau,* 145–66, studies descriptions of monsters and portents in late-medieval and early modern literature.

EARLY MIDDLE HIGH GERMAN LITERATURE

Robert G. Sullivan, *Justice and the Social Context of Early Middle High German Literature* (Studies in Medieval History and Culture, 5), NY, Routledge, xviii + 186 pp., illuminates the socio-historical content of early MHG religious literature from between roughly 1050 and 1200 by examining its concept of justice (*reht*). S. argues that this concept, which owes much to patristic and medieval Latin notions of *iustitia*, is concerned less with legal than with moral and social categories, emphasizing as it does not just impartial and corruption-free jurisdiction, but also favour and mercy towards the poor. As such it depends fundamentally on the perception of a divinely-inspired ordering of society, in which everyone has his 'due'. S. concludes that this perspective on justice constitutes both a reaction to the poverty and venality of contemporary society, and an intriguing precursor of the aristocratic code of courtly virtues.

C. Mackert, *ZDA*, 130:143–65, describes a forgotten 19th-c. copy by Heinrich Schreiber of a page from the lost 'Straßburg-Molsheimer-Handschrift', which shows received wisdom on the codex to be in need of revision; E. Hellgardt, *Firchow Vol.*, 149–60, points to apparent contradictions in the montage structure of Williram von Ebersberg's *Expositio in Cantica Canticorum*, and assesses the implications of Williram's use of the first person pronoun; M. Moser, *Spiewok Vol.*, 253–60, dicusses realistic and fantastic elements in the *Merigarto*; E. Nellmann, *ZDA*, 130:377–91, investigates textual contamination in the 'Vorauer Handschrift' of the *Kaiserchronik*; M. Schulz, Kellner, *Kommunikation*, 73–88, discusses ways in which the 'Kemenatenszene' of *König Rother* prefigures the work's harmonious ending; W. Hoffmann, *ZDP*, 120:345–60, argues for a return to the traditional view of Genelun in the *Rolandslied* as a self-centred traitor; and S. M. Johnson, *Firchow Vol.*, 187–94, edits, translates into English, and comments on the religious-didactic poem *Die Wahrheit*. O. Neudeck, *Euphorion*, 95:287–303, discusses ways in which forms of symbolic communication are presented and ironized in *Herzog Ernst (B)* and in the *Nibelungenlied*; R. Luff, *Euphorion*, 95:305–40, seeks to reconstruct the contours of an oral performance of the former work; and K.-P. Ebel, *FmSt*, 34, 2000:186–212, discusses its thematization of the peaceful resolution of conflict.

There are three full-length volumes devoted to Hildegard von Bingen. Barbara Beuys, *'Denn ich bin krank vor Liebe'. Das Leben der Hildegard von Bingen*, Munich, Hanser, 376 pp., is a popular biography. B.'s awareness of contemporary scholarship on Hildegard is not always sophisticated; her description of certain aspects of her life (for example her childhood and relationship with Richardis) are decidedly speculative; and her strong emphasis on Hildegard's progressiveness and modernity is not consistently convincing. On the other hand, this is a generally solid and highly readable account of Hildegard's life, which will have wide appeal. Viki Ranff, *Wissen und Weisheit bei Hildegard von Bingen* (MGG, 1.17), 443 pp., is a scholarly analysis of

Hildegard's thought written from a philosopher's perspective. R. studies the meanings and implications of the terms *scientia* and *sapientia* as they occur (apparently some 2,600 times between them) in Hildegard's works. These concepts emerge as more central to her theological and anthropological ideas than has hitherto been recognized, not least in that the similarities and differences between divine and human wisdom can be seen as paradigmatic for the relationship between God and his rational creatures more generally. R. also illuminates the linguistic means by which Hildegard conveys precise philosophical ideas; and she demonstrates that the abbess was both profoundly influenced by ancient, patristic, and medieval philosophy, and able to express herself in philosophically rigorous terms. Berndt, *Angesicht*, contains numerous essays on Hildegard. Several deal with her relationship to aspects of her spiritual and cultural context: F. J. Felten (27–86) discusses her views on contemporary reform movements, the circumstances of her own monastic life, and her coenobitic ideal; G. Iversen (87–113) studies her descriptions of the celestial hierarchies in the light of other contemporary perceptions of them; and F. Staab (157–79) and U. Vones-Liebenstein (213–40) examine her relationship to Cistercian spirituality and the *ordo canonicus* respectively. More specifically on Hildegard's own works, J. van Banning (243–68) and B. Mayne Kienzle (299–324) study her Gospel homilies, the former from a theological perspective and the latter focusing on her exegesis of the parable of the Prodigal Son; R. Berndt (269–90) explores her theology of vision, and H. B. Feiss (291–98) the Christology of the *Scivias*; C. J. Mews (325–42) discusses her use of reports of her visions to communicate views on the need for Church reform; J. Schröder (343–74) examines her treatment of the Book of Ezekiel in her visionary writings; and A. Schavan (17–23) considers her conception of human nature. Two pieces by L. Moulinier deal with the scientific writings attributed to Hildegard: the first (115–46) questions her authorship of *Causae et curae*, and the second (545–59) considers her presentation of magic, psychology, and 'soul-sickness' in that work and in the *Physica*. Meanwhile, M. Enders (461–501) discusses Hildegard's notably anthropomorphic concept of nature. Hildegard's reception and influence are studied by A. Einarsson (377–400), who sees her imagery as a key to understanding the Icelandic *Raudulfs Thattr*; by M. Embach (401–59), who discusses the transmission of her works in MSS and, especially, early printed editions; by E. Stein (577–91), who examines the reception of her visions in and via the much copied *Pentachronon* of Gebeno von Eberbach; by J. C. S. Paz (561–76), who surveys medieval discussions of her sanctity; and by W. Lauter (503–43), who catalogues no fewer than 82 relics and reliquaries devoted to her. Elsewhere R. Hilde-brandt, Bergmann, *Glossen*, 537–50, describes his planned new edition of Hildegard's *Physica*; and S. El Kholi, *Euphorion*, 95:257–62, comments on two of her letters (Storch 163 and 163R).

MIDDLE HIGH GERMAN HEROIC LITERATURE

'*Ortnit und Wolfdietrich D*'. *Kritischer Text nach MS Carm. 2 der Stadt- und Universitätsbibliothek Frankfurt am Main*, ed. Walter Kofler, Stuttgart, Hirzel, 451 pp., is the first edition of the so-called 'a' version of *Ortnit/Wolfdietrich D*, based on MS b, copied in Alsace around 1420. Editing a text of more than 2,800 *Nibelungenstrophen* is a Herculean task, which K. performs creditably. His text, intended to complement rather than replace editions of other versions, maintains a judicious balance between comprehensibility and fidelity to the base MS, though his use of a different typeface for material added from MS c is irritating. His introduction clarifies the work's convoluted origins and textual history, describes its MSS, and considers its internal contradictions.

There are several short studies of the *Nibelungenlied*. M. Jönsson, *SN*, 73:223–37, sees its author's presentation of dilemmas confronting the characters as a means of distancing himself from the fatalistic quality of his source; T. Robin, *RG*, 30, 2000:1–16, examines its narrative technique, stressing in particular affinities to drama; U. Schulze, *Fest. Brunner*, 161–80, discusses its reception and instru-mentalization of motifs from Walther von der Vogelweide; K. Wilson and D. P. Beistle, *GN*, 32:14–17, point to its innovative treatment of the heroic water-crossing topos; I. Cavalié, *ZDP*, 120:361–80, surveys interpretations of Siegfried's aggressive arrival at Worms; and E. R. Haymes, *Fest. Brunner*, 447–61, examines aspects of MS n which arguably reflect recollections of oral performances on the part of its scribe. Furthermore, A. Classen, *Neophilologus*, 85:565–87, interprets the *Nibelungenlied* and *Klage* in the light of sociological theories concerning communication and communicative action; K. Stack-mann, *ZDP*, 120:381–93, considers the implications for editorial theory of Joachim Bumke's remarkable synoptic edition of the *Klage*; E. Lienert, *ZDA*, 130:127–42, examines its presentation of dead heroes and their posthumous reputation; and N. Watanabe, *DB*, 107:115–25, discusses the differing concepts of *list* that inform the presentation of Kriemhild in the *Klage* and in *Der Rosengarten zu Worms A*. In *ASNS*, 238:241–59, E. Lienert sees the challenge and relevance of heroic epic in the problematic nature of its textuality and in its depiction of war, history, and heroism; and in Cramer, *Frauenlieder*, 151–61, H. Sievert analyses the *Wechsel* sung by the protagonists of *Karl und Galie* (141, 23–30, 49–56).

Joseph M. Sullivan, *Counsel in Middle High German Arthurian Romance* (GAG, 690), vi + 148 pp., is the first comprehensive study of counsel in romances from between roughly 1185 and 1290. S.'s definition of counsel (*rât*) is a very broad one, encompassing for example non-verbal aid and the promptings of God, the Devil, or one's own heart; but he concentrates especially on political advice given by and to individuals. A substantial introduction surveys the situations in which counsel is given, the status and personal qualities of those who participate in them, and differences in the presentation of counsel in romance as against epic. This is followed by three 'case studies', dealing with *Erec*, *Iwein*, and the *Prosa-Lancelot*. S. stresses throughout the role of counsel scenes in establishing character and generating narrative action, but also sees them as loci of comment on the function and value of advice in contemporary aristocratic society. The bulk of S.'s chapter on *Iwein* appears also in *Neophilologus*, 85:335–54.

Bernhard Öhlinger, *Destruktive 'unminne'. Der Liebe — Leid — Tod — Komplex in der Epik um 1200 im Kontext zeitgenössischer Diskurse* (GAG, 673), xxviii + 196 pp., discusses love's relationship with suffering, illness, combat, and death in six central MHG narratives: *Eneit*, *Erec*, *Parzival*, *Willehalm*, *Tristan*, and the *Nibelungenlied*. Ö. discerns in these works a powerful and intrinsically physical form of love which, when lost or unrequited, can have destructive or even fatal consequences. He then evaluates this concept of love against the background of contemporary theological attitudes, and concludes that, not least in its anti-Augustinian attempt to re-unite the erotic with the sacred, it is likely to have been regarded, if expressed unequivocally, as subversive or even heretical. The resultant need for veiled discourse is seen by Ö. as lying behind the ambiguous and frequently perplexing religious allusions of both Gottfried and Wolfram — a thesis that most readers will probably find intriguing rather than ultimately persuasive.

M. Chinca and C. Young, Peters, *Text*, 612–44, use examples from *Erec*, *Iwein*, and *Tristan*, and the work of Pierre Bourdieu, to problematize and develop aspects of Walter Haug's analysis of medieval vernacular literary theory (see *YWMLS*, 47:641, 59:662). T. Reuvekamp-Felber, *ZDP*, 120:1–23, surveys the author/narrator's statements about himself in prologues and epilogues by Hartmann, Wolfram, and Rudolf von Ems, stressing their dependence on considerations of genre and plot. W. McConnell, *Firchow Vol.*, 255–68, claims that both Gottfried and Wolfram address the dichotomy between the feminine and the masculine prevalent in their society, and propose a vision of ultimately androgynous wholeness which has its origin in Celtic perspectives.

Elisabeth Lienert, *Deutsche Antikenromane des Mittelalters* (Grundlagen der Germanistik, 39), Berlin, Schmidt, 223 pp., is an expert, lucid, and full introductory guide to German treatments of the *matière de Rome*. Separate chapters deal in turn with romances on Alexander, Aeneas, Troy, and Apollonius; these are framed by an introduction which defines the genre and examines its presentation of antiquity, and by a concluding discussion of its coherence and literary historical importance. There are excellent general and work-specific bibliographies. In *Fest. Brunner*, 129–46, L. surveys the involvement of women in warfare in a variety of romances. On Veldeke's *Eneit*, A. Volfing, *OGS*, 30: 1–25, discusses the hero's alleged sodomy and the author's concept of *rehtiu minne*; C. Kottmann, *SN*, 73:71–85, examines the tension between Classical traditions (especially polytheism) and medieval cultural norms; and T. S. Weicker, *ZDA*, 130: 1–18, discusses the work's origins, suggesting in particular that Veldeke's account of the theft of a MS is fictitious. On Herbort von Fritzlar's *Liet von Troye*, H. Mayer, *Firchow Vol.*, 245–54, considers the narrator and his comments; and M. Siebel-Achenbach, *GRM*, 51:267–83, compares Herbort's presentation of Helen with that in Benoît de Sainte-Maure's *Roman de Troie*.

HARTMANN VON AUE

Arthurian Romances, Tales, and Lyric Poetry. The Complete Works of Hartmann von Aue, trans. and comm. Frank Tobin, Kim Vivian, and Richard H. Lawson, University Park PA, Pennsylvania State U.P., xiv + 329 pp., unites for the first time in one volume prose translations of all of Hartmann's works, including the *Klagebüchlein* and all the lyrics, even those of questionable authenticity. Existing renderings of most of the works are not exactly thin on the ground, and the new volume does not entirely supersede these. Its translations, introductory material, and footnotes are, however, both scholarly and accessible; it has up-to-date bibliographies; and its format is convenient and handsome. G. Wolf, Peters, *Text*, 215–44, applies Pierre Bourdieu's concepts of 'habitus' and 'field' to the interpretation of *Erec* and *Iwein*; and K. Ridder, *DVLG*, 75:539–60, discusses Hartmann's reflections on the relationship between fictionality and authorship in the two romances. Specifically on *Erec*, W. Mieder, *MJ*, 36:45–76, examines Hartmann's use of proverbs and their thematic significance; E. Schmid, *Fest. Brunner*, 109–27, compares the differing models of marriage informing Chrétien's and Hartmann's versions; and W. C. McDonald, *LB*, 90:403–18, contends that the unnamed 'vrouwe' on Erec's shield (l.2313) forges a link between Enite and Mary (via Hartmann's putative reception of Geoffrey of Monmouth). On *Iwein*, F. Wenzel, Keller, *Kommunikation*, 89–109, assesses what the opening scene reveals about both aristocratic communication and courtly narrative culture; in the same volume, B. Quast (110–28) discusses the narrative models used to present courtly civilization, nature, and the hero's liminality; S. Heimann-Seelbach, *Euphorion*, 95: 263–85, analyses dilemmas faced by characters which they cannot resolve with reference to conventional ethical categories; N. Kaminski, *OGS*, 30: 26–51, perceives a conflict for control of the hero between Lûnete and (a homoerotically motivated) Gawein, supported respectively by Frau Minne and the narrator; and A. Hausmann, Peters, *Text*, 72–95, interprets the differing versions of Laudine's kneeling before Iwein.

Hartmann von Aue, *Der arme Heinrich*, ed. Hermann Paul and Kurt Gärtner (ATB, 3), 17th rev. edn, xxxviii + 63 pp., is not significantly different from the 16th edition (see *YWMLS*, 58: 733), though some details have been amended in the light of reviewers' comments, and the bibliography has been updated. R. A. Boggs et al., Moser, *Verarbeitung*, 211–29, describe a forthcoming multimedia edition, with supporting materials, of *Der arme Heinrich*. C. Brinker-von der Heyde, *JIG*, 32, 2000: 45–63, examines the structure of and relationships within the nuclear families described in Hartmann's legend and in *Helmbrecht*; and A. Classen, *StSp*, 11: 166–86, assesses the relationship between spiritual and worldly love in *Der arme Heinrich*, the letters of Abelard and Heloïse, and the writings of Hadewijch.

WOLFRAM VON ESCHENBACH

Joachim Bumke, *Die Blutstropfen im Schnee. Über Wahrnehmung und Erkenntnis im 'Parzival' Wolframs von Eschenbach* (Hermaea, n.s., 94), Tübingen, Niemeyer, vi + 205 pp., is a characteristically penetrating study, which begins with a detailed analysis of the scene of the blood drops on the snow that opens Book VI of *Parzival*, interpreted in the light of ancient and medieval theories of perception and knowledge. The focus then broadens into a discussion of Parzival's failings of perception and cognition more generally. B. sees these as resulting from the intrinsic, *tumpheit*-related inability of his senses, imagination, memory, and reason to work together — an inability which he never fully overcomes. B. goes on to suggest that issues of knowledge, perception, and learning are also problematized through the role of the comparably 'unlearned' narrator, whose frequently unreliable and self-contradictory interventions are used both to mock the procedures of more apparently sophisticated authors such as Hartmann, and to create an open narrative which the interpreter is challenged to unravel. B. summarizes many of his arguments in Peters, *Text*, 355–70. W. Haug, *BGDSL*, 123:211–29, argues that the prologue of *Parzival* seeks to prepare its audience for a differentiated, open narrative which transcends conventional categories of black and white; L. P. Johnson, *Fest. Brunner*, 181–98, examines Wolfram's presentation of various aspects of Parzival's early life against the background of Chrétien's *Perceval*; T. Tomasek, *Fest. Menke*, 879–91, discusses the implications of the image of the narrator naked in a bath (115,29–116,4); E. Nellmann, *ZDP*, 120:421–25, interprets the difficult lines (177,18–24) describing Gurnemanz's quadripartite heart; F. M. Dimpel, *ZDP*, 120:39–59, discusses the conflicts between love and knighthood depicted in the Gawain and Orgeluse episodes; and H. Lähnemann and M. Rupp, *BGDSL*, 123:353–78, analyse the narrative function of parenthetical structures in *Parzival*.

Wolfram von Eschenbach: 'Willehalm'. Abbildung des 'Willehalm'-Teils von Codex St. Gallen 857 mit einem Beitrag zu neueren Forschungen zum Sangallensis und zum Verkaufskatalog von 1767, ed. Bernd Schirok (*Litterae*, 119), Göppingen, Kümmerle, 2000, lii + 139 pp., does exactly what its title says. The black-and-white photographs of the MS's text of *Willehalm* (on which the now standard edition by Heinzle is based — see *YWMLS*, 56:747) is preceded by a discussion of articles published on the codex since the late 1980s, and by a fascinating analysis of its description in an 18th-c. sales catalogue. W. Röcke, *ZGer*, n.s. 2:274–91, explores the relationship between laughter and violence in *Willehalm*; and U. Liebertz-Grün, *GRM*, 51:385–95, interprets the Gardeviaz fragment of *Titurel* as an open metanarrative.

GOTTFRIED VON STRASSBURG

Patrizia Massadi, *Autorreflexionen zur Rezeption: Prolog und Exkurse in Gottfrieds 'Tristan'* (Quaderni di Hesperides, Serie Saggi, 2), Trieste, Parnaso, 2000, 253 pp., argues that the prologue of *Tristan* and its various excursuses (including the digression on literature and the allegorical interpretation of the *Minnegrotte*) constitute an intricate continuum structured along the lines of a contemporary Latin sermon — with the stanzaic part of the prologue comprising the *thema* and *distinctiones*, which are then subjected to *dilatatio* in the stichic part of the prologue and in the (carefully positioned) excursuses. M. claims that the principal theme of this continuum is the importance of the sympathetic reception of love stories, and that it reaches a climax in the so-called '*huote*'-*Exkurs*, in which the 'noble hearts' in the audience are offered an ideal form of love which is denied to the work's protagonists. This is of course far-fetched, but M. argues her case with conviction and no little perspicacity.

Peter K. Stein, *Tristan-Studien*, ed. Ingrid Bennewitz et al., Stuttgart, Hirzel, iv + 520 pp., comprises a modestly revised version of Stein's previously unpublished *Habilitationsschrift* (*Tristan in den Literaturen des europäischen Mittelalters*, Salzburg 1983), and his long 1979 essay *Die Musik in Gottfrieds von Strassburg 'Tristan'* (see *YWMLS*, 42:727), here offered as a memorial to him. The 300–page *Habilitationsschrift* is a magisterial survey of the entire Tristan tradition, with innumerable (partially updated) bibliographical references and much discussion of earlier research. S.'s coverage encompasses Celtic and other pre-literary motifs, the French, German, Norse, and Middle English verse texts, and prose versions in French, Italian, various Iberian languages, English (Malory), Greek, Russian, and Serbo-Croat. Elsewhere J.-M. Pastré, *Spiewok Vol.*, 261–78, interprets the French and German Tristan texts in the light of Lévi-Strauss's concepts of forgetting, misunderstanding, and indiscretion; E. Nellmann, *ZDP*, 120:24–38, studies the presentation of Brangäne in Gottfried, Eilhart, and the Carlisle fragments of Thomas, concluding that Gottfried used both of the other authors as sources; and G. Eifler, *Fest. Ruberg*, 113–30, points to the differing narrative perspectives of Gottfried and Thomas (in the Carlisle fragments). Specifically on Gottfried, M. Oswald, Kellner, *Kommunikation*, 129–52, shows, with reference to the *Brautwerbung* and to the Gandîn episode, how he presents art as legitimizing itself through integration into institutionalized social norms; M. Schausten, *BGDSL*, 123:24–48, analyses his use of biographical and autobiographical statements made by characters to establish and develop his hero's identity; W. Röll, *Fest. Brunner*, 199–209, suggests that he uses literary allusions, especially to Hartmann and Virgil, to shed light on the imperfect nature of the lovers' life in the *Minnegrotte*; R. H. Firestone, *Firchow Vol.*, 67–84, examines the concept of *saelde* and its derivatives in *Tristan*; U. Störmer-Caysa, *Poetica*, 33:51–68, discusses Gottfried's presentation of time and of kept or missed appointments; and U. Liebertz-Grün, *GRM*, 51:1–20, reads his work as an open, ambiguous 'meta-romance', in which a double-tongued narrator both proposes and debunks contemporary courtly discourses.

OTHER ROMANCES AND SHORTER NARRATIVES

Alison Williams, *Tricksters and Pranksters. Roguery in French and German Literature of the Middle Ages and the Renaissance* (IFAVL, 49), 2000, viii + 236 pp., studies literary scoundrels who can be categorized as tricksters (those who deceive for material gain) and pranksters (whose prime purpose is to entertain). Figures from German literature whom W. discusses include Pfaffe Amis and the Pfarrer vom Kalenberg, Reinhart Fuchs, Eulenspiegel, and various female protagonists of *Schwänke*. She is especially strong in her interpretations of the extent of Amis's victims' complicity in their own deception, and of the differences of tone and moral intention between Heinrich's *Reinhart Fuchs* and the *Roman de Renart*; and she demonstrates throughout how the transgressive, potentially destructive behaviour of tricksters often has the paradoxical effect of reinforcing social stability. Her book is also refreshing in its genuinely critical and constructive use of theoretical insights, in this case from Bakhtin, Bergson, and Freud.

Maryvonne Hagby, *'man hat uns fur die warheit ... geseit.' Die Strickersche Kurzerzählung im Kontext mittellateinischer 'narrationes' des 12. und 13. Jahrhunderts* (Studien und Texte zum Mittelalter und zur frühen Neuzeit, 2), Münster, Waxmann, x + 359 pp., is an original and valuable study of the complex intertextual relationships between Der Stricker's short narratives and various forms of Latin exempla. H. identifies Latin sources (often fables) for at least a quarter of Der Stricker's stories; his adaptations of these are, however, often free, and tend to emphasize their fictionality whilst clarifying and accentuating their didactic message. Moreover H. finds evidence of Der Stricker in turn being used as a source in 14th-c. Latin collections. Her book throws into consistent relief the German poet's learning and literary talent, as well as the perhaps surprising coherence of his *œuvre*. J. Margetts, *Fest. Brunner*, 227–48, establishes that much of the information on precious stones retailed in Der Stricker's *Von den edelen Steinen* is derived from Latin encyclopaedias; and H. Ragotzky, *BGDSL*, 123:49–64, discusses the complex relationships between Der Stricker's *Mären* and the didactic epimythia which often conclude them.

R.Chamberlain, *MGS*, 24, 1999:8–17, interprets Ulrich von Zatzikhoven's presentation of the dragon Elidiâ in *Lanzelet* as an example of the use of fantastic elements to imply spiritual meaning. A. Classen, *ABÄG*, 55:75–93, discusses issues arising out of recent publications on *Mauritius von Craûn*; and T. Bulang, Kellner, *Kommunikation*, 207–29, reads *Mauritius* as thematizing problems of courtly communication and interaction. There are three articles on Heinrich von dem Türlin's *Diu Crône*: G. Shockey, *ABÄG*, 55:127–45, argues that Heinrich, influenced by contemporary jurisprudence, attempts to reconstruct Arthur's court as an ideal of stability and the rule of law; M. Meyer, Peters, *Text*, 529–45, applies James Phelan's theory of 'literary character', as well as psychological perspectives, to an analysis of the figures of Artus and Gawein; and S. T. Samples, *Arthuriana*, 11.4:23–38, examines the role of the 'problem women'

Amurfina and Giramphiel, and the contrasting degrees to which they are integrated into Arthurian society. In addition, B. Schirok, *ZDA*, 130:166–96, discusses questions of editorial principle raised by Werner Schröder's recent edition of Ulrich von dem Türlin's *Arabel* (see *YWMLS*, 61:617).

There are two new monographs on the *Prosa-Lancelot*. Thordis Hennings, *Altfranzösischer und mittelhochdeutscher 'Prosa-Lancelot'. Übersetzungs- und quellenkritische Studien*, Heidelberg, Winter, xii + 452 pp., sheds new light on the relationship between the German romance and its French source. Painstakingly detailed comparison of five substantial parallel sections from the first part of the *Prosa-Lancelot* and the *Lancelot propre* yields two main insights. First, the German author worked from a MS of a strikingly independent, now lost, French version, whose text was similar to that of the hitherto little studied MS O. Secondly, his rendering of this version is a notably literal translation (of high quality), rather than an 'adaptation courtoise'. Essentially, H. has identified and convincingly reconstructed a missing link between the French and German traditions. She summarizes many of these points in *BGDSL*, 123:379–96, suggesting also that the German translation might have been made for the Count Palatine of the Rhine. Judith Klinger, *Der mißratene Ritter. Konzeptionen von Identität im 'Prosa-Lancelot'* (FGÄDL, 26), 528 pp., is a densely argued and theory-informed discussion of the many complex forms of personal identity thematized in the romance. Its three main sections deal successively with Lancelot as Arthurian knight, lover, and seeker after the Grail (and hence himself). Lancelot emerges as an ambivalent and inconsistent figure, whose identity is not the product of any intrinsic individuality, but rather is constructed by means of various, not always obviously compatible, narrative strategies. K. Speckenbach, *Fest. Ruberg*, 131–42, discusses parallels in the presentation of Lancelot's amorous relationship with Ginover and of his friendship with Galahot. K. Philipowski both re-assesses (*WW*, 51:165–82) the relationship between freedom, predestination, and heredity in the *Prosa-Lancelot*, and suggests (*DVLG*, 75:363–86) that its poetic structure is undermined and demystified by the use of allegory and personification.

Sebastian Coxon, *The Presentation of Authorship in Medieval German Narrative Literature 1220–1290*, OUP, x + 254 pp., is a distinguished and wide-ranging study of the varied ways in which 13th-c. narrative poets thematized their own authorship. The corpus of texts covered comprises all the narratives of Rudolf von Ems and Konrad von Würzburg, as well as some 17 heroic epics and 52 *Mären*. These are analysed against the background both of the techniques of self-presentation used by the canonical *Blütezeit* poets, and of such pertinent 13th-c. developments as the social diversification of literary culture and the rise of lay literacy. The picture which emerges is an immensely complex and in some respects surprising one: Rudolf's espousal of numerous strategies of self-assertion from both Latin and vernacular sources, and not least the portraits of him which feature in several MSS, contrast markedly with Konrad's often cursory references to himself and his patrons, and superficial disconnectedness from MHG literary traditions. Moreover the heroic epics and short stories which C. discusses evince not just the authorial anonymity and self-effacement one would expect to find in these genres, but also, especially in the case of the *Mären*, elements of an authorial self-consciousness more normally associated with romance. C.'s book is notable not least for its sensitivity to the tensions between 'original' texts and their MS transmission, and for its judicious use of Foucault's theory of 'author-function'. Also on Rudolf and Konrad: S. Zöller, *ZDA*, 130:270–90, re-evaluates Dieter Kartschoke's view of *Der gute Gerhart* as a study of the human conscience; and E. Feistner, *Fest. Brunner*, 291–304, examines the themes of eating and table manners in Konrad's narratives, amongst which she numbers *Die halbe Birne*.

Anne Wawer, *Tabuisierte Liebe. Mythische Erzählschemata in Konrads von Würzburg 'Partonopier und Meliur' und im 'Friedrich von Schwaben'*, Cologne, Böhlau, 2000, x + 257 pp., examines these two romances against the background of mythic analogues in which the love of a male protagonist and a woman with supernatural characteristics is hindered by a taboo. *Partonopier und Meliur* is compared especially to the Greek legend of Amor and Psyche, and *Friedrich von Schwaben* to the Irish *Echtra Airt*. Detailed textual analysis reveals that both German works are much more indebted to mythic narrative structures than are, say, the canonical Arthurian romances, but that they also develop and adapt these in ways that reflect high medieval preoccupations. This is true, for example, of the consistent foregrounding of questions of individual love in both romances, of *Partonopier und Meliur*'s transformation of what is originally a *Mädchentragödie* into a *Knabentragödie*, or of *Friedrich von Schwaben*'s emphasis on the theme of poverty caused by a divided inheritance. M. Schulz, *ABÄG*, 55:147–92, reads *Friedrich von Schwaben* as a didactic work dealing with the importance of honour and loyalty for the consolidation of political power.

In Nolte, *Helmbrecht*, F. P. Knapp (9–24) examines Wernher's presentation of the betrayal of class and homeland against the background of other contemporary Bavarian-Austrian works; H. Kästner (25–43) draws fascinating and suggestive parallels between the themes of *Helmbrecht* and contemporary Franciscan social and legal thought; and U. Seelbach (45–69) examines links between *Helmbrecht* and the Hildemar strophes of Neidhart, as well as updating (83–116) his 1981 bibliography (see *YWMLS*, 43:762–63).

Heinrich von Neustadt, *Leben und Abenteuer des großen Königs Apollonius von Tyrus zu Land und zur See*, trans. and ed. Helmut Birkhan, Berne, Lang, 463 pp., is the first modern translation of *Apollonius von Tyrland*. B.'s version is highly readable, the volume is handsomely produced (including for example all 109 miniatures from the Vienna MS C), and there are over 100 pages of explicatory material. All in all, the task of making *Apollonius* more readily available could hardly have been better performed, and one hopes the book will attract the wide non-specialist audience it deserves. D. Huschenbett, *Fest. Brunner*, 305–31, interprets and translates the closing sections (5949–6045) of Albrecht's *Jüngerer Titurel*. C. Wand-Wittkowski, *Poetica*, 32, 2000:227–49, sees Reinfried von Braunschweig as a 'new' type of hero, motivated by curiosity and avoiding the conventional pattern of crisis followed by rehabilitation; and A. Classen, *Seminar*, 37:95–112, discusses the often idealized presentation of women, marriage, and relationships between the sexes in *Reinfried*.

Studies of other late-medieval narratives: B. Kellner, Peters, *Text*, 268–95, surveys the relationship between the human and the demonic in Latin and vernacular Melusine stories (including that of Thüring von Ringoltingen); J. H. Winkelman, *ABÄG*, 55:223–38, discusses the relationship between late-medieval erotic insignia and *Mären* such as *Das Nonnenturnier*, *Gold und Zers*, and *Der Rosendorn*; C. Fasbender and C. Kropik, *Euphorion*, 95:341–55, present two radically different readings of *Das Nonnenturnier*, both of which they consider intrinsic to the work's texture and intention; J. Sander, Kellner, *Kommunikation*, 231–48, examines the construction of common authorship as a unifying factor in the corpus attributed in Cgm 270 to Heinrich Kaufringer; R. Schlechtweg-Jahn, *FCS*, 26, 2000:142–57, examines the roles of the author, the narrator, and dialogue in Hermann von Sachsenheim's *Die Mörin*; G. Kornrumpf, *Fest. Brunner*, 473–85, edits and introduces *Der Herr von Braunschweig*, a brief prose narrative in Jörg Stuler's *Historienbuch* (*c*.1479); and D. Huschenbett, *ZDA*, 130:431–34, contends that *Fortunatus* was written in Augsburg.

LYRIC POETRY

Schwob, *Entstehung*, is centred around the three leaves from an illustrated lyric MS (Budapest, National Library, Cod. Germ. 92, *c*.1300, from Austria/Bavaria), which were rediscovered in 1985. These fragments, known as Bu, are described by G. Kornrumpf (165–85), who also discusses their relationship to *Minnesang* MSS B and C, and the likely common source *BuBC. C. Bertelsmeier-Kierst (37–46) places Bu in the context of other Bavarian-Austrian lyric MSS, and suggests that it originated in Regensburg. A. Vizkelety (303–14) argues that Bu's iconography, but not its scribal hands, link it with a group of MSS produced around 1300 by the 'Meister der Münchner Weltchronik'; and M. Roland's comparison (207–22) of Bu's illustrations both to other works of the 'Meister' and to MS C leads him to date the fragments to the first decade of the 14th c. Meanwhile A. Hausmann (65–77) contends that the stanzas ascribed in Bu to Rudolf von Rotenburg were attributed in their (loose-leaf) source to Reinmar der Alte. The volume also contains essays on other lyric MSS: W. Hofmeister (79–106) surveys gaps left by the principal scribe of MS C, and discusses the ways in which these were filled; M. Siller (255–80) examines the 'Sterzinger Miszellaneen-Handschrift', arguing that it did not originate in the Southern Tyrol; C. Edwards (47–64) surveys the vernacular secular lyrics copied in MSS from the Benedictine monastery of Kremsmünster; and M. Schiendorfer (223–41) discusses opportunities and problems associated with attempts to reconstruct the lost 15th-c. song MS of Heinrich Laufenberg. Essays with a slightly broader perspective include F.-J. Holznagel's typology (107–30) of vernacular lyric MSS from the 12th-14th cs, T. Bein's plea (15–36) that literary historians should react more positively and creatively to MS attributions of stanzas or songs to more than one author, and U. Müller's assessment (187–206) of the value of jottings inserted in lyric MSS. In *ZDA*, 130:392–430, U. Peters compares the illustrations of German lyric MSS with those of their Provençal and French counterparts.

Alongside treatments of individual poets (discussed below), Cramer, *Frauenlieder*, contains several contributions of a more general nature. I. Kasten (3–18) surveys research into *Frauenlieder*, and suggests as a future project the elaboration of a 'Poetologie der weiblichen Stimme'; U. Wyss (163–69) censures the tendency of earlier scholars to view *cantigas de amigo* and their German equivalents as close to nature, and hence to the origins of Western love poetry; T. Cramer (19–32) outlines the difficulty of distinguishing between *Frauen-* and *Männerstrophen*, suggesting that acknowledging the 'andro-gyny' of many poems and stanzas opens up new interpretative possibilities; S. Obermaier (33–48) compares the roles played by the male and female first-person speakers of *Frauenlieder* and classical *Minnesang*; E. Schmid (49–58) identifies stylistic and rhetorical devices used by poets to distinguish between male and female speakers; and J. Margetts (59–67) shows how such distinctions can be drawn also on the basis of syntax. Meanwhile I. Bennewitz (69–84) considers the tendency of poets such as Reinmar and Neidhart to place erotic and obscene discourse in the mouths of female speakers; and N. R. Wolf (85–93) traces an increased use of dialogue in *Frauenlieder* by later medieval poets such as the Mönch von Salzburg and Oswald von Wolkenstein.

Hinderer, *Lyrik*, has a new publisher since its first edition (see *YWMLS*, 45:643), and also a new chapter on 'Lyrik heute'. U. Müller's contribution on the Middle Ages (20–48) has, however, been reproduced unaltered save for an updated bibliography. Jan-Dirk Müller, *Minnesang und Literaturtheorie*, ed. U. von Bloh et al., Tübingen, Niemeyer, viii + 246 pp., collects nine of M.'s essays published between 1984 and 2001. These are linked by a consistent attempt to apply the insights of literary theory to the study of MHG lyric poetry, especially that of Walther von der Vogelweide, Ulrich von Lichtenstein, and Neidhart. The latter is the subject of the most recent essay (233–44), which also appears in *Schabert Vol.*, 334–45. In it, M. interprets Neidhart's treatment of dialogue in his *Sommerlieder* as a sign of his rejection of the gender roles of conventional *Minnesang*.

H. Tervooren, *Fest. Brunner*, 15–47, examines traces of the Song of Songs and of Marian poetry in various examples of *Minnesang*; N. Henkel, Ragotzky, *Liedinterpretation*, 13–39, outlines the problems posed by stanzas which stand alone in some MSS, but in others form part of longer songs; L. Lieb, Kellner, *Kommunikation*, 183–206, discusses the function of the topos of the seasons in *Minnesang*; R. Schnell, Peters, *Text*, 96–149, argues that the shift from oral to written reception of *Minnelieder* typically entailed a different and narrower perception of the poetic 'I'; and F. J. Worstbrock, Ragotzky, *Liedinterpretation*, 75–90, postulates a lost vernacular *Minnesang* tradition emphasizing nature and joy, which had parallels in the Latin *Carmina Burana* and decisively influenced Neidhart.

The 'Carmina Burana': Four Essays, ed. Martin H. Jones (King's College London Medieval Studies, 18), Exeter, Short Run, 2000, x + 109 pp., contains pieces by experts in four different fields. A. J. Duggan (1–13) discusses the MS's social and intellectual context, with special reference to contemporary student culture; P. Dronke (25–40) examines the Latin songs, singling out CB 85, 120, 165, 131, and 177 as examples of the collection's amorous and satirical material; C. Edwards (41–70) surveys the MS's German texts, assessing its glosses, aphorisms, dramas, and excerpts from St John's Gospel and the *Eckenlied*, as well as the lyrics; and J. Walworth (71–83) examines its pictures and their relationships to the groups of poems they accompany. In Cramer, *Frauenlieder* (267–80), Edwards accounts for the more extensive use of *Frauenstrophen* in the MS's German and macaronic songs than in its purely Latin ones. In *MJ*, 36, D. Schaller (77–93) essays a typology of its Latin love lyrics on the basis of generic and formal criteria; and D. A. Traill, *ib.*, 95–112, offers a new edition (with translation and commentary) of CB 60 and 60a. Moreover, in *Fest. Brunner*, 211–26, J. Janota discusses the refrains of the bilingual love songs, especially CB 179–85.

In Schwob, *Entstehung*, 143–63, P. Kern compares Kürenberg 7,1, 7,10, 8,33, and 9,5 as transmitted in MSS C and Bu; and H. Tervooren (291–301) interprets the variant MS readings of *ber* and *eber* in Kürenberg, 8,9. T. Reuvekamp-Felber, Peters, *Text*, 377–402, discerns numerous elements of fictionality, and few of ritual, in Kürenberg's songs. Meanwhile T. Neukirchen, *GRM*, 51 : 285–302, discusses the strophes attributed to the Burggraf von Rietenburg, stressing their coherence and literary-historical importance, whereas J. Janota, Schwob, *Entstehung*, 131–42, suggests a common authorship for these strophes and for those attributed to the Burggraf von Regensburg. In *Fest. Brunner*, U. Meves (49–72) re-examines the documentary evidence relating to the biography of Ulrich von Gutenberg; D. Klein (73–93) assesses the interplay between the discourse of love and that of crusading propaganda, especially in songs by Hausen and Johansdorf; T. Ehlert (95–107) discusses ways in which Hartmann's lyrics both construct and ironically deconstruct the concept of *hohe Minne*; and R. Fisher, *ABÄG*, 55 : 61–74, addresses textual and translation problems of Wolfram's *Ez ist nû tac*, and considers its use of alienation techniques.

Hans Irler, *Minnerollen — Rollenspiele. Fiktion und Funktion im Minnesang Heinrichs von Morungen* (Mikrokosmos, 62), Frankfurt, Lang, 310 pp., interprets the poetic 'I' of Morungen's songs as oscillating between and creatively combining the roles of wooer, poet, and 'mediator' of love. The latter has the function of expressing joy and admiration for the lady on behalf of the audience, and is presented by I. as one of several devices used by Morungen to thematize the complex interaction between the poet's voice, his lady, and his audience which is intrinsic to *Minnesang*. For all the diverse relationships between poetry and reality which they suggest, Morungen's songs emerge as a surprisingly coherent whole, linked by a strong sense of the poet's individuality, and by a pervasive, and strikingly modern, degree of openness and ambiguity. D. Hirschberg, Ragotzky, *Liedinterpretation*, 40–56, discusses Morungen's concept of *herzeliebe*.

There are several essays on Walther von der Vogelweide. G. Hahn, *Fest. Brunner*, 147–60, discusses the coherence of his *œuvre*; C. Ortmann, Ragotzky, *Liedinterpretation*, 57–74, analyses the roles played by the singer and the concept of *werdekeit* in his 'Palästinalied'; J. Ashcroft, Cramer, *Frauenlieder*, 95–102, examines his songs with female speakers, emphasizing in particular their dialogicity and poetological motivation; W. Hoffmann, *LJb*, 42:9–42, surveys his *Altersdichtung*, paying particular attention to the 'Reuelied' (122,24); and M. Chinca, Hutchinson, *Landmarks*, 9–30, discusses the MS transmission of his 'Elegy', which he goes on to interpret as a 'kaleidoscope of lamentation'.

Jörn Bockmann, *'Translatio Neidhardi'. Untersuchungen zur Konstitution der Figurenidentität in der Neidhart-Tradition* (Mikrokosmos, 61), Frankfurt, Lang, 395 pp., is concerned with the construction of Neidhart's identity in all the songs attributed to him, and in the 15th-c. 'Schwankroman' *Neithart Fuchs*. B. examines first the names ascribed to Neidhart, which, with their consistently negative overtones, do not facilitate a clear distinction between author and protagonist. Then he analyses Neidhart's interaction with other characters in the songs of MSS R and c, again concluding that the relationships described are inconsistent, polyvalent, and multi-functional. Finally, a detailed discussion of *Neithart Fuchs* shows that it too constructs a protagonist who is both courtier and rascal, and who as such, for all his invariable application of *list*, remains ultimately ambivalent. I. Bennewitz et al., Hubrath, *Zwickau*, 19–54, survey the transmission of the *Neithart Fuchs* corpus, describe the principles of the forthcoming Salzburg Neidhart edition in which it will be printed, and interpret its 'Welt-Lauf-Lied' z 38/h. The contribution made by information technology to this project is described by U. Müller and A. Weiss in Moser, *Verarbeitung*, 201–09. Cramer, *Frauenlieder*, contains two comparative studies of the mother-daughter dialogues in Neidhart's *œuvre* and in the *cantigas de amigo*. E. Koller (103–22) constructs a typology of these; and V. Millet (123–32) sees Neidhart's originality above all in the roles he gives to his narrators. Moreover J.-D. Müller, Ragotzky, *Liedinterpretation*, 91–102, finds in Neidhart MS c narrative elements which suggest 15th-c. reception of these poems in written form; and G. Shockey, *NMi*, 102:469–81, discusses the peasant women presented in 'Sommerlied' 14.

Helmut Tervooren, *Sangspruchdichtung* (SM, 293), 2nd rev. edn, x + 150 pp., is a modestly revised and updated edition of this thorough and reliable survey (see *YWMLS*, 57:685). D. Peil, *Fest. Ruberg*, 35–44, discusses reflections on language in *Spruchdichtung*, especially by Reinmar von Zweter and Der Meissner; A.M. Rasmussen, Ashley, *Conduct*, 106–34, shows how critical understanding of the *Winsbecke* poems has been influenced by 19th-c. paternalistic values; H.-J. Behr, *Fest. Brunner*, 249–65, compares and contrasts Freidank's *Bescheidenheit* and Hermann Bote's *Köker*, with special reference to the modes of reception envisaged by the two poets; and U. Müller and F. V. Spechtler, Ragotzky, *Liedinterpretation*, 135–57, discuss the strophes composed by Friedrich von Sonnenburg in response to the Pope's offer to crown Rudolf von Habsburg (1274–75). On the basis of its animal images, R.-H. Steinmetz, *ASNS*, 238:260–79, argues that Frauenlob's 'Lied 4' invites a reading on both a secular and a spiritual level; P. Strohschneider, Peters, *Text*, 482–505, analyses communicative strategies in the complex known in the 'Kolmarer Liederhandschrift' as *Der Oberkrieg*; and F. V. Spechtler, Schwob, *Entstehung*, 281–90, argues, on the basis of an examination of the 'Mondsee-Wiener Handschrift', that the Mönch von Salzburg may have learnt new poetic and musical forms in Prague.

Die Lebenszeugnisse Oswalds von Wolkenstein. Edition und Kommentar. II : *1420–1428, Nr. 93–177*, ed. Anton Schwob et al., Vienna, Böhlau, xxvi + 379 pp., continues the diplomatic edition, begun in 1999, of all the surviving documents pertaining to Oswald's life. These are arranged chronologically, and each is accompanied by a detailed commentary providing background information and linguistic elucidation. The value of this edition for the interpretation of Oswald's uniquely self-absorbed poetry can hardly be overstated. Two contributions to *Firchow Vol.* are based on it. A. Schwob (359–67) discusses a vernacular *Wappenbrief* issued to Oswald in 1419 by Duke Przemkos von Troppau; and U. M. Schwob (369–84) finds clues to the nature of the relationships within the Wolkenstein family in documents up to the year 1419. Moreover in Cramer, *Frauenlieder*, 133–40, U. M. and A. Schwob compare the images of women found in these documents with those constructed in Oswald's songs. In the same volume, K. Helmkamp (141–49) examines questions of gender and genre in the *Wechsel* Kl. 56 and 107; and in Schwob, *Entstehung*, 243–54, A. Schwob discusses the origins, date, structure, and purpose of Oswald's song MS A. There are also two articles on Oswald by B. Wachinger. In Ragotzky, *Liedinterpretation*, 103–17, he highlights the audacity of the Marian allusions in the dawn songs; and in *Fest. Brunner*, 403–22, he analyses four songs from Klein's edition (Kl. 126, 131–2, 134) which do not appear in the two MSS whose compilation the poet oversaw. In addition, M. Schumacher, *BGDSL*, 123:252–73, interprets Kl. 6, with special reference to its indebtedness to contemporary 'contemptus mundi' perspectives; S. Hartmann, *ZDP*, 120:60–77, uses recent research to illuminate the historical background to Oswald's honouring by the French Queen (in Kl. 19); and V. Mertens, Peters, *Text*, 329–44, brings various theoretical perspectives to bear on the interpretation of Kl. 75.

Friederike Niemeyer, *'Ich, Michel Pehn.' Zum Kunst- und Rollenverständnis des meisterlichen Berufsdichters Michel Beheim* (Mikrokosmos, 59), Frankfurt, Lang, 398 pp., is a lucidly written investigation of Beheim's concept of art and his role as a poet, which, N. argues, evolved significantly in the course of his career. Benefiting from the relatively easy datability of many of Beheim's songs, N. begins with a chronological survey of his creative life, which she sees as consisting of three phases (*c.* 1435–52, 1452–*c.* 1465, 1466–*c.* 1472), the parameters of which reflect changes in the poet's location and material circumstances. Her subsequent discussion of individual works limits itself almost entirely to Beheim's songs dealing with love, art, and his own biography, and hence concentrates mainly on the first two of these periods. N. shows above all that the locus of Beheim's reflection on and experimentation with the nature of the poetic 'I' shifted from love poems to those dealing more explicitly with art, and that, in line with this, the contours of the 'I' became less abstract and apparently more firmly rooted in actuality.

Albrecht Classen, *Deutsche Liederbücher des 15. und 16. Jahrhunderts* (Volksliedstudien, 1), Münster, Waxmann, 354 pp., is a valuable inventory and study of the contents of some 20 song collections. Perhaps inevitably, C. concentrates mainly on 16th-c. corpora, but also covers four from the 15th c.: the *Ältere Augsburger Liederbuch*, the *Haager* and *Rostocker Liederhandschriften* and, of course, the *Liederbuch der Clara Hätzlerin*. Each is allotted a separate chapter, in which the title or incipit of each song is listed with brief explanatory comments, and the collection as a whole described and characterized. S. Gade, *BGDSL*, 230–51, examines the instrumentalization of a versified passage from the *Lucidarius* in a song in 'Regenbogens langer Ton'. In *Fest. Brunner*, K. Stackmann (463–72) prints and comments on a riddle, in Der junge Meissner's 'erster Ton', which appears in Heidelberg, Cpg 355 (15th c.), and E. Klesatschke and B. Taylor (487–512) list and discuss some 29 *Meisterlieder* categorized as either 'Loica' or 'Equivoca'. Finally, E. Langbroek and A. Roeleveld, *ABÄG*, 55: 193–221, edit and discuss the MLG poem *Van der hymmeluart marien* from the 15th-c. Wolfenbüttel, MS Cod. Guelf. Helmst. 1084.

DIDACTIC, DEVOTIONAL, AND RELIGIOUS LITERATURE

Thomasin von Zerklaere, *Der Welsche Gast*, ed. Raffaele Disanto (Quaderni di Hesperides, Serie Testi, 3), Trieste, Parnaso, 334 pp., is a new edition of Thomasin's text, based on MS A, and incorporating both the variants of MS G and the material from that MS added to the text of A by its 19th-c. editor Heinrich Rückert. D. reproduces the text of A far more faithfully than did Rückert, and corrects numerous errors in his predecessor's critical apparatus. As such his volume represents a worthwhile complement to the earlier edition; but one regrets that he fails to take full account of the work's MS tradition. C. Del Zotto, *RCCM*, 43: 267–92, analyses exempla from both the Aesopic and the zoological traditions in *Der Welsche Gast*.

Rudolf Kilian Weigand, *Der 'Renner' des Hugo von Trimberg. Überlieferung, Quellenabhängigkeit und Struktur einer spätmittelalterlichen Lehrdichtung* (WM, 35), 2000, x + 403 pp., exemplifies the merits of the so-called 'überlieferungsgeschichtlich' approach to the study of frequently copied late-medieval texts. W.'s investigation, the first really thorough one, of the *Renner*'s 65 (mainly 15th-c.) textual witnesses enables him to identify a total of seven versions — two authorial and five later adaptations. Some of these had a primarily regional sphere of distribution, but all appear to have been read predominantly by lay people. Moreover W.'s examination of Hugo's sources reveals a perhaps surprising degree of dependence on the author's own *Solsequium* and *Registrum multorum auctorum*, from which Hugo adopted not just didactic material, but also an essentially open structure — one of the causes, no doubt, of the *Renner*'s textual variability. D. Buschinger, *Spiewok Vol.*, 51–72, also discusses the *Renner*, with special reference to its comments on society and morality.

A. E. Wright, *'Hie lert uns der meister.' Latin Commentary and the German Fable 1350–1500* (MRTS, 218), xxxii + 293 pp., is an outstanding study of the Latin commentaries found in MSS that transmit the fables of Avianus and the Anonymus Neveleti, and their influence on late-medieval German fable collections. W. begins by surveying a number of little known Latin commentaries, and then documents and assesses the contribution made by them to the 'vernacularization' of fables in late-medieval Germany. With particular reference to Boner's *Edelstein*, the *Magdeburger Äsop*, the *Nürnberger Prosa-Äsop*, and the fables of Michael Beheim, he demonstrates that this impact was much greater than has hitherto been realized, and affected not just individual narratives and their moralizations, but also structural and programmatic features of entire collections. In many cases W. is able to identify the source MSS used by German fabulists with remarkable precision; and he also discusses occurrences of bilingualism in fable collections as diverse as the *Edelstein*, the *Nürnberger Prosa-Äsop*, and the uniquely complex *Breslauer Äsop*. R.-H. Steinmetz, *Fest. Menke*, 847–59, points to analogies between the 1498 *Reynke de vos* and late-medieval fable collections such as the *Magdeburger Prosa-Äsop*.

Petra Busch, *Die Vogelparlamente und Vogelsprachen in der deutschen Literatur des Mittelalters und der frühen Neuzeit* (*Poetica*, Beihefte, 24), Munich, Fink, 427 pp., is the first substantial study of two closely related late-medieval textual traditions. *Vogelparlamente* and *Vogelsprachen* are short texts in which pairs of birds speak brief rhyming stanzas; in the former, however, the birds offer advice to a king, whereas in the latter their utterances are of a more general moral-didactic nature. B. begins by describing and analysing all the relevant surviving MSS, postulating complex and at times highly speculative relationships between them. She then traces the genesis and development of the two traditions, concentrating especially on the work to which both can ultimately be traced back, the mid-14th-c. *Vogelparlament* of Ulrich von Lilienfeld. Some of B.'s conclusions are questionable, but she succeeds in establishing that both the MHG and MLG *Vogelparlamente* circulated mainly in lay aristocratic circles, whereas the exclusively MLG *Vogelsprachen* were intended mainly for a broad-based urban audience.

Meister Eckhart, *Deutsche Predigten. Eine Auswahl*, ed. and trans. Uta Störmer-Caysa (UB, 18117), 222 pp., is a welcome newcomer to Reclam's series of bilingual (MHG/NHG) editions of medieval texts. S.-C. prints and translates twelve sermons (Quint 2, 5b, 6, 9, 12, 20a, 38, 44, 52, 60, 70, and 78), which together form a coherent conspectus of Eckhart's vernacular homilies. Particularly laudable features of S.-C.'s work are her use, where possible, of recent editions, and her provision of some 76 pages of commentary, bibliography, and introductory material. Burkhart Mojsisch, *Meister Eckhart. Analogy, Univocity and Unity*, trans. Orrin F. Summerrell, Amsterdam, Grüner, xvi + 220 pp., is an English version of M.'s 1983 volume on Eckhart as a philosopher (*M.E. Analogie, Univozität und Einheit*). The opportunity has wisely been taken to allow M. to revise and update his original text in the light of recent research.

Helena Stadler, *Konfrontation und Nachfolge. Die metaphorische und narrative Ausgestaltung der 'unio mystica' im 'Fliessenden Licht der Gottheit' von Mechthild von Magdeburg* (DLA, 35), 210 pp., is an at times opaque study of the poetic and narrative strategies Mechthild uses to describe the simultaneously close and distant relationship, based on the participants' essential similarity and dissimilarity, which exists between God and the mystical soul. S. argues that metaphor, composed as it is of comparison and paradox, is an ideal means of expressing such a relationship; and she draws particular attention to Mechthild's metaphor of God as a vessel, whose contents are poured continually into a smaller vessel which then overflows — a vivid illustration of the combination of confrontation with and imitation of the divine which characterizes her concept of mystic union. S. goes on to explore in detail the paradox that this 'unio mystica' is also associated with the soul renouncing God's presence, waiting on him, and preparing itself for him. S. S. Poor, *JMEMS*, 31:213–50, interprets Mechthild's use of LG as the product of various theological and socio-political factors, and explores the differing attitudes towards female authorship evinced in the MS tradition of *Das fließende Licht*. In *JOWG*, 12, 2000, H. Fielmann (365–79) discusses the applicability of Ricarda Huch's historiographical methodology to the study of Gertrud von Helfta, and F.-J. Schweitzer (325–38) examines the relationship between asceticism and the heresy of the free spirit in writings by beghards and their opponents. A. Classen, *StSp*, 10, 2000: 182–204, examines the narrative strategies deployed in Seuse's autobiography; and S. Altrock and H.-J. Ziegeler, Peters, *Text*, 150–81, show how illustrated MSS and printed texts transformed the image of the author presented in the text of his *Exemplar*.

Heinrich von Nördlingen e Margarethe Ebner: Le Lettere (1332–1350), ed. Lucia Corsini (Medioevo Tedesco, Studi e Testi, 9), Pisa, E.T.S., 453 pp., reprints Philipp Strauch's 1882 edition of these authors' correspondence (the vast majority of the letters are by Heinrich), alongside a new Italian translation of them. This parallel text is preceded by introductory material by C. and by D. Bremer Buono which discusses medieval mysticism, the lives and works of Heinrich and Margarethe, and Heinrich's language; and it also features an impressively scholarly commentary. One regrets, however, that the opportunity was not taken to revise or replace Strauch's text.

The 'Vita' of Margaret the Lame by Friar Johannes O.P. of Magdeburg, trans. and comm. Gertrud Jaron Lewis and Tilman Lewis, Toronto, Peregrina, 187 pp., is the first translation into any vernacular of this originally Latin text from *c.* 1260–70. It is a saint's life with a difference: no miracles are described, and Margaret's death is dealt with only peremptorily; rather, the author is concerned primarily with her inner life and mystical experiences, and loses no opportunity to indulge in homiletic asides.

Three major publications have appeared on another saint's life with a difference, Bruder Hermann's *Yolanda von Vianden*. None of these, however, is able to take full advantage of the sensational rediscovery, in 1999, of the so-called 'Codex Mariendalensis' (MS M, *c.* 1325), the only medieval MS known to transmit Hermann's text. Bruder Hermann, *Yolanda von Vianden. Moselfränkischer Text aus dem späten 13. Jahrhundert*, ed. and trans. Gerald Newton and Franz Lösel (Beiträge zur Luxemburgischen Sprach- und Volkskunde, 21), Luxembourg, Institut Grand-Ducal, 1999, 186 pp., offers a lightly amended version of the text of John Meier's 1889 edition (based on a 17th-c. transcription of M by Alexander Wiltheim), along with a careful and accurate translation of Hermann's work — the first into German prose. The volume's introduction begins with discussion (by N.) of the work's textual history, previous translations, and language, and continues with an examination (by L.) of its historical context, author, religious purport, prologue, and characters. Michèle Backes, *Yolanda von Vianden und die religiöse Frauenbewegung ihrer Zeit* (Beiträge zur Luxemburgischen Sprach- und Volkskunde, 28), Luxembourg, Institut Grand-Ducal, 2000, 194 pp., assesses Hermann's text against the background of contemporary trends in spirituality and, in particular, of several Latin vitae of holy women, including works by Thomas of Cantimpré and Jacques de Vitry. Hermann's life of Yolanda emerges as remarkably different from these, not least in its lack of emphasis on miracles, stigmata, or mystical experiences. B. argues that it frequently reflects Dominican interests and perspectives, and that it was written with a specific, probably local audience in mind. A summary of B.'s monograph appears on pp. 150–55 of Berg, *Yolanda*, a volume which also contains 13 other papers. In these, A. Heinz (125–38) focuses, like Backes, on the extent to which Hartmann's *Yolanda* reflects contemporary religious ideas and practices; K. Gärtner (35–51) offers preliminary impressions of the relationship between MS M, Wiltheim's transcript, and Meier's edition; and R. Christmann (26–38) also incorporates some readings from M into her discussion of the work's language. H. Völker (52–63) finds suggestively few traces of the influence of French culture, toponyms, and general vocabulary on *Yolanda*; and J. Kramer (75–87) similarly discerns only very general typological similarities between *Yolanda* and contemporary French saints' lives. Relationships between *Yolanda* and other works are also studied by W. G. Rohr (13–25), who examines allusions to *Tristan, Parzival, Willehalm*, Walther von der Vogelweide (L 48,38), and *Das Häslein*; by F. Lösel (88–95), who discusses the role of the female protagonist and of the author in *Yolanda* and in *Der arme Heinrich*; by E. de Domínguez (139–49), who argues that Hermann's construction of Yolanda owes much to accounts of virgin martyrs such as St Catherine and St Agnes; and by G. Newton (64–74), who compares this construction of her with that of Wiltheim in his Latin *Vita venerabilis Yolandae* (1674). An historical perspective is provided by J. Milmeister (96–101), who investigates the controversy surrounding the 'real' Yolanda's entry into the Mariental convent, and by M. Margue (105–24), who demonstrates that Hermann's references to the convent's poverty are the product of literary stylization. Finally C. Hollerich (102–04) discusses the work's multifunctionality; and A. Rapp and U. Leuk (156–66) describe an approach to teaching it in schools, using, along with other media, a website <gaer27.uni-trier.de/CLL/welcome.html>.

Other work on legends includes M. Backes's discussion (Keller, *Kommunikation*, 249–60) of the genesis of the *Freiburger Magdalenenbuch* and the socio-historical functions of its various redactions, and reports by K. Klein (*ZDA*, 130:58–62) and W. Williams-Krapp (*ib.*, 302–05) of recently discovered fragments of Reinbot von Durne's *Georg* and the *Niederdeutsche Legenda Aurea* respectively. Meanwhile J. Eming, *ZDP*, 120:394–412, argues that in medieval Judas vitae, and notably in *Das alte Passional*, the introduction of the motif of incest paradoxically makes the betrayer into a more rounded, even heroic figure.

WernerJ. Hoffmann, *Konrad von Heimesfurt. Untersuchungen zu Quellen, Überlieferung und Wirkung seiner beiden Werke 'Unser vrouwen hinvart' und 'Urstende'* (WM, 37), 2000, x + 465 pp., is a meticulous study which valuably complements H.'s and Kurt Gärtner's 1989 edition of these verse re-tellings of material from the New Testament Apocrypha (see *YWMLS*, 51:659). H. begins by establishing the precise identity of Konrad's sources, which in the case of the *Urstende* is a version of the Gospel of Nicodemus preserved in only one Salzburg MS. Konrad's adaptations are shown to be notable above all for their freedom and for their consistent determination to concentrate only on 'essential' elements. H.'s examination of their MS tradition is particularly fruitful in the case of the *Hinvart* (preserved in ten MSS), but also encompasses a productive study of those parts of the sparsely transmitted *Urstende* that have survived in MSS of Heinrich von München's *Weltchronik*. The book concludes with a detailed account of Konrad's influence on later authors. B. Quast, *BGDSL*, 123:65–77, discusses Konrad's characterization, in the *Urstende*, of his 'werc' as a form of artefact, whose individuality is closely bound up with that of its author.

B. Haupt, Haupt, *Endzeitvorstellungen*, 147–78, considers the *Linzer Entecrist* against the background of both its direct source and its more general historical-theological background; K. Gärtner and R. Plate, *Fest. Brunner*, 333–45, edit and discuss the material concerning the history of heathen lands (especially Troy) in the so-called *Leipziger Schluß* of the *Christherre-Chronik*; and N. A. Bondarko, *LiLi*, 122:80–135, examines the function of orchards and palm trees in providing structural frameworks for 13th-c. religious texts in prose.

Falk Eisermann, *'Stimulus amoris'. Inhalt, lateinische Überlieferung, deutsche Übersetzungen, Rezeption* (MTU, 118), x + 649 pp., is a monumental study of the textual history of this much copied Franciscan ascetic treatise, the first version of which, probably written by James of Milan, dates from *c.*1300. E. identifies and describes some 500 Latin and 58 German MSS transmitting the text (or 'Textfamilie', as E. prefers): there are four main Latin redactions, each of which had taken a clearly defined shape by the mid-14th c., and five German translations, which vary considerably in quality and approach, but which all originated in the second half of the 14th c. The *Stimulus* was used by an enormously wide range of readers and authors (including Ludolf von Sachsen, Heinrich von St. Gallen, and Johannes von Tepl); but the spheres of influence of individual versions can in several cases be clearly circumscribed. Moreover, for all its variability, the *Stimulus* tradition as a whole is united by its title and its frequent (erroneous) attribution to a single author, namely St Bonaventure.

Albertanus de Brescia: 'De amore Dei et proximi' in der Übersetzung Heinrich Hallers, ed. Erika Bauer (Analecta Cartusiana, 18), Salzburg, Institut für Anglistik und Amerikanistik der Universität, 135 pp., edits Haller's text along with the three other previously unpublished parts of Innsbruck, Universitätsbibliothek, MS 641 (dated 1466 and written in Haller's own hand). These include his translation of an excerpt from the *Stimulus amoris* (along with a brief treatise on the love of God, and a comparably short work in which a father gives advice to his son). A well-organized introduction discusses Haller and his working environment at the Charterhouse in Schnals (Southern Tyrol), Albertanus's *De amore Dei*, and, especially, the relationship between it and Haller's translation.

Two monographs by Ernst Haberkern contain first editions of late-medieval theological texts. E.H., *Richard von St. Viktor: 'Benjamin minor', deutsch. Ein neu aufgefundenes Handschriftenfragment* (GAG, 685), 2000, 131 pp., edits, translates, and introduces the text of a fascinating four-leaf fragment from the collection of Gerhard Eis. Copied in the Nuremberg area early in the 15th c., it transmits part of a German adaptation of Richard of St Victor's *Benjamin minor* which appears to have been used by Johann von Indersdorf in his *Von dreierlei Wesen des Menschen*. H.'s conscientious edition and translation are combined with detailed discussion of Richard, his work and its biblical basis, and with a thorough analysis of the German MS's linguistic features. There is rather less on the content of the German adaptation, however, and H.'s facsimile of the fragment is of disappointing quality. E.H., *Das 'Beichtbüchlein' des Thomas Peuntner nach den Heidelberger, Münchner und Wiener Handschriften* (GAG, 696), 260 pp., makes available one of the few hitherto unpublished works by this notable representative of the later 'Vienna School', albeit in an edition which takes account of only 20 of its 37 known MSS. That said, H.'s base MS, Vienna, CPV 2828 (dated 1464) is obviously a reliable one. His introduction deals with Peuntner's life and works, the structure, content, and style of the *Beichtbüchlein*, and late-medieval catechetical and confessional literature more generally.

Heinrich Kalteisen OP: Drei Basler Predigten. Übersetzung vom Frühneuhochdeutschen ins Neuhochdeutsche, trans. Helga Haage-Naber (GAG, 691), 102 pp., provides modern German versions of the three Kalteisen sermons (V, VII, and X) published by H.-N. in 2000 (see *YWMLS*, 62:630). The introductory material from the earlier volume is re-ordered but otherwise unchanged. Other work on sermons includes C. Roth's detailed introduction, with textual examples, to the little known early 15th-c. sermon cycle of Johannes Bischoff (*ZDA*, 130:19–57); R. Schiewer's investigation (*MSS*, 45:40–57) of the preachers' names contained in the postil generally attributed to

Hartwig of Erfurt; J. Splett's analysis (*Fest. Menke*, 823–45) of the relationship between the *Bremer Evangelistar* and the glossed Gospel MSS of the so-called *Heidelberger Typ*; and W. Frey's discussion (*Fest. Brunner*, 431–45) of the conception of life as a pilgrimage, especially as presented in the sermons of Johannes Geiler von Kaysersberg.

Christoph Fasbender, *Von der Widerkehr der Seelen Verstorbener. Untersuchungen zur Überlieferung und Rezeption eines Erfolgstextes Jakobs von Paradies* (Jenaer Germanistische Forschungen, 13), Heidelberg, Winter, x + 384 pp., studies the textual history of *De apparitionibus animarum separatarum*, a treatise on apparitions from the dead written in 1454 by the Erfurt Carthusian Jakob von Paradies. F. prints the Latin text from Jakob's autograph, and describes and analyses its over 90 MSS and 13 printed editions. He establishes that it circulated widely in reformed Benedictine houses, and was also owned by a large number of secular priests and university students. Perhaps surprisingly, it underwent little variation in the course of its MS transmission. More significant levels of textual change, and a notably wide range of apparent functions, are however observable in the work's three German adaptations: a printed edition by Konrad Fyner (Esslingen, *c.* 1478), an adaptation by the Benedictine Thomas Finck (in Cgm 6940, *c.* 1490), and Georg Antworter's *Belehrung über das Beschwören von Geistern* (in a Bamberg MS dated 1482). F.'s volume is laced with astute and provocative observations both on the literary culture of 15th-c. Germany and on scholarly orthodoxies old and new.

Susanne Rischpler, *'Biblia Sacra figuris expressa.' Mnemotechnische Bilderbibeln des 15. Jahrhunderts* (WM, 36), 231 pp., is an innovative study of 15th-c. mnemonic pocket Bibles which couple large numbers of carefully coded pictures (ten per MS page) with brief captions or statements taken from a biblical *Summarium*. R. describes the known witnesses to this tradition (five MSS and five printed editions), establishes that they were almost certainly intended for use by clerics, and discusses their structure, pictorial code, mnemonic techniques, and sources. Her findings are tested and developed in a series of detailed page-by-page analyses of chapters from a diverse range of biblical books. R.'s well argued monograph, which contains several handsome plates, makes one wish for a facsimile edition of at least one of the MSS she discusses.

H. Blosen, *Fest. Menke*, 71–88, discusses an illustrated MLG *Speculum humanae salvationis* in Copenhagen, Gl. kgl. Sam. 80 fol. (*c.* 1440), and offers an edition, with commentary, of its prologue; G. Roth, *ZDA*, 130:291–97, introduces a West German adaptation of Dirc van Delft's *Tafel van der Kersten Ghelove* found in two 15th-c. MSS; and V. Honemann, Suntrup, *Tradition*, 75–95, examines the piety and religious practices of the seemingly conventional 'late-medieval' knight Florian Waldauf von Waldenstein, and of the Humanist Heinrich Bebel.

Tydeman, *Stage*, contains (351–420) a group of 44 documents concerning plays and their performance in the German-speaking lands between 1400 and 1550, selected, translated, and introduced by J. E. Tailby. These include, alongside excerpts from and outlines of religious and secular plays, texts as diverse as council minutes, an episcopal authorization, and an account of the collapse of a wall during the Bautzen St Dorothy play of 1413, which killed 33 people.

Dieter Trauden, *Gnade vor Recht? Untersuchungen zu den deutschsprachigen Weltgerichtsspielen des Mittelalters* (APSL, 142), 2000, vi + 465 pp., is a major monograph on late-medieval vernacular drama. T. begins by surveying the MSS and printed texts said by previous scholars to contain Last Judgment plays; from these, he singles out a corpus of 12 witnesses (from the 15th or 16th cs, nearly all Alemannic) which preserve texts likely to be similar to a lost 'original' version. The themes and structure of the plays within this corpus are then assessed against the background of medieval legal, moral, theological, and catechetical traditions. Both in their theological undergirding and in their manifest intention to edify the uneducated, the plays reveal a surprisingly consistent indebtedness to Dominican thought — a finding which T. is careful not to overplay, but which raises tantalizing questions about the origins and purposes of late-medieval religious drama more generally.

LB, 90, contains papers given at a symposium at Louvain in April 2000 on medieval German religious drama. Many of these focus on the *Redentiner Osterspiel*. U. Obhof (1–10) describes and discusses the MS in which it is transmitted (Karlsruhe, Badische Landesbibliothek, 369, dated 1464); I. Rösler (11–28) and L. Draye (43–51) study aspects of its language, and D. Stellmacher (29–41) its 1991 translation into modern LG by Dieter Andresen; E. Ukena-Best (181–214) assesses its presentation of *superbia*, the Devil, and hell, and K. Scheel (215–32) that of the 'knights' who guard Christ's tomb; and J. Nowé (325–59) examines its stage directions, both explicit and implicit, and their relevance to modern productions of the play. Moreover C. Kuné (233–48) discusses the depiction of John the Baptist in Limbo in the *Redentiner* and other Easter Plays, and E. Simon (53–74) assesses the evidence suggesting that plays with religious themes were performed in late-medieval Lübeck. C. Dauven-van Knippenberg (309–23) examines the use of dialogic structures, and especially of personal pronouns, to create a polarity of good and evil in the *Frankfurter Passionsspiel* of 1493; M. Straeter (263–95) discusses 'volkstümlich' elements in medieval German Christmas plays; and H. Linke (75–126) problematizes the frequently drawn but unmedieval distinction between 'religious' and 'secular' drama.

Spiewok Vol. includes three articles on religious drama: G. Borgnet (23–50) discusses the three structural blocs of the fragmentary *Wiener Passionsspiel*, and their treatment of earlier traditions; C. Kuné (197–218) analyses the negative stage directions in the *Heidelberger Passionsspiel* and related plays; and A. Touber (311–29) sees traces of Franciscan thought and iconography in the presentation of the crucifixion in the *Donaueschinger Passionsspiel*. G. Ehrstine, Peters, *Text*, 414–37, recommends, and gives examples of, a culturally-informed 'philology of the stage'; and E. E. DuBruck, *FCS*, 26, 2000:1–20, surveys recent research into late-medieval drama.

SCIENTIFIC AND SPECIALIZED LITERATURE

Frühneuhochdeutsches Glossenwörterbuch. Index zum deutschen Wortgut des 'Vocabularius Ex quo', ed. Klaus Grubmüller et al. (TTG, 27), xii + 889 pp., completes the edition of this frequently copied 15th-c. glossary, some 12 years after the appearance of its first five volumes. In contrast to the *Vocabularius* itself, this new, remarkably comprehensive index has alphabetically arranged German (rather than Latin) lemmata, listing first the early NHG and then the (many fewer) MLG forms which appear in the edition proper, alongside the Latin terms they were originally intended to translate or elucidate. As such the volume provides an enormously valuable resource for all who work with 15th-c. texts, particularly the many German ones translated from Latin. Elsewhere R. Damme, *Fest. Menke*, 143–63, describes and evaluates a late 15th-c. MLG–Latin vocabulary found in Kiel, Cod. Bord. 111. quart.

Marialuisa Caparrini, *Un Manuale di tedesco per italiani del XV secolo: Lo 'Sprachbuch' di Meister Jörg* (GAG, 694), xvi + 212 pp., introduces and edits an early 15th-c. manual compiled by a schoolmaster, originally from Nuremberg, who appears to have taught German to Italian merchants at a school near the 'Fondaco dei Tedeschi' in Venice. His work comprises a thematically-arranged glossary, a section on the morphology of adjectives, pronouns and verbs, and a set of three model dialogues; throughout, Italian forms and their German equivalents are presented in parallel columns. C.'s edition transcribes two MSS now in Florence: Magl. IV 66, dated 1467, transmits the entire work, whereas Ashb. 352, dated 1457, is a three-page fragment. Her lucid and thorough introduction deals with various historical, codicological, and linguistic matters. *Europäische Reiseberichte des späten Mittelalters. Eine analytische Bibliographie*, ed. Werner Paravicini (Kieler Werkstücke, D, 5), Frankfurt, Lang, 563 pp., is the second edition of this useful work of reference, first published in 1994 (see *YWMLS*, 56:771). A reprint of the first edition is supplemented by some 35 pp. of additional material, including many new bibliographical references, and a list of reviews of the first edition — corrections suggested in which are also incorporated. W. Baum, *JOWG*, 12, 2000:423–37, describes how contact with the East broadened the perspectives of Westerners between the 12th and 15th cs; K. Niehr, *GJ*, 2001:269–300, discusses the perception and description of unfamiliar phenomena in Bernhard von Brydenbach's *Peregrinationes in terram sanctam* and other pilgrimage reports; and M. Bärmann, *Daphnis*, 30:1–36, finds evidence of the reception of the *Basler Alexander* and of Mandeville's *Travels* in the late 15th-c. *Familienbuch der Herren von Eptingen*. Meanwhile N. Miedema, Suntrup, *Tradition*, 51–72, points to the interplay of tradition and innovation in geographical descriptions of Germany published in Nuremberg between roughly 1450 and 1550; K. Ridder and J. Wolf, *Firchow Vol.*, 317–34, examine Strasbourg MS 2119 (*c*.1450, from Nuremberg), a new-style 'urban encyclopaedia' containing texts and excerpts with a primarily historical and geographical orientation; and B. Schnell, *Fest. Brunner*, 369–90, edits and introduces a 14th-c. *Gedihte von der physionomie* found in the *Hausbuch des Michael de Leone*.

Constantin Hruschka, *Kriegsführung und Geschichtsschreibung im Spätmittelalter* (Kollektive Einstellungen und sozialer Wandel im Mittelalter, n.s. 5), Cologne, Böhlau, 445 pp., investigates the extent to which the perspectives on war evinced in late-medieval chronicles were influenced by changes in the purpose and practice of warfare. H. considers various forms of hostility presented in Latin chronicles written by clerics between 1378 and 1438 which were also translated into German. The main authors discussed are Andreas von Regensburg and Hermann Korner, as well as the compilers of the *Chronica episcoporum Monasteriensium*. Whilst, inevitably, each chronicle presents war significantly differently, H. demonstrates that they share certain characteristics: an essentially negative, non-participant's view of combat is typically combined with a concern for legal issues, and an awareness of the increasing importance of both territory and national consciousness. *Das Mittelalter*, 5.2, 2000, contains several studies of the reception and instrumentalization of historiography in the later Middle Ages. B. Studt (31–48) traces the reception of Alexander von Roes's *Memoriale* in German and Latin texts of the 15th c., and

S. Weigelt (71–85) that of Johannes Rothe's *Thüringische Landeschronik* in the 15th and 16th cs; U. Andermann (87–104) analyses German Humanist historians' sometimes uncritical treatment of Classical sources; and R. Schmid (115–38) discusses the production and functions of the official chronicles of Swiss cities. A. Rapp, Moser, *Verarbeitung*, 247–61, describes a computer-assisted project to edit 13th-c. and 14th-c. documents from the Archbishopric of Trier (see also <gaer27.uni-trier.de/Urkunden/welcome.htm>).

Joëlle Fuhrmann, *Theorie und Praxis in der Gesetzgebung des Spätmittelalters in Deutschland am Beispiel der Ingelheimer Schöffensprüche*, Berne, Lang, 172 pp., is an unusual and stimulating monograph which focuses on the little studied pronouncements of the 15th-c. lay judges of Ingelheim (Rheinhessen). Following a lucid historical introduction, F. assesses the *Ingelheimer Schöffensprüche*'s perspectives on women, children, and marriage, as well as on property, inheritance, and criminal law, alongside those of several comparable vernacular legal codes. She finds the tenor of the Ingelheim documents to be relatively liberal, even 'modern', a fact which she attributes to the increasing influence, in this part of the Empire, of Canon and Roman Law, and of Humanism. There are also three articles on the *Sachsenspiegel*: R. Schmidt-Wiegand, *Fest. Ruberg*, 257–62, discusses its presentation of persons exercising their right to silence in court; M. Dobozy, *Firchow Vol.*, 31–40, finds in it traces of an oral juridical tradition; and U. Schulze, Peters, *Text*, 47–71, discusses the nature of textual variance in it and other legal works. Meanwhile U.-D. Oppitz and K. Klein, *ZDA*, 130:298–301, present two newly discovered fragments of Bruder Berthold's *Rechtssumme*; and N. Schnitzler, Hubrath, *Zwickau*, 169–94, examines the authorship, textual history, contents, and purpose of the 14th-c. *Zwickauer Rechtsbuch*.

OTHER LATE-MEDIEVAL LITERATURE

'*Die Historia von den sieben weisen Meistern und dem Kaiser Diocletianus.*' *Nach der Gießener Handschrift 104*, ed. Ralf-Henning Steinmetz (ATB, 116), xxx + 86 pp., is, remarkably, the first modern edition of any of the eight 15th-c. German prose versions of the story of the seven sages. The text presented reproduces faithfully the flavour of the sole MS which preserves it (written *c.* 1464), but is rendered easily readable not least by the inclusion of modern punctuation. S.'s introduction and commentary situate this version and its individual exempla within the complex tradition of which it is part. K. Skow-Obenaus, *FCS*, 26, 2000:169–82, identifies misogyny as a pervasive theme which unifies the frame-story of *Die sieben weisen Meister* with the exempla it encloses.

Der 'Gute Gerhart' Rudolfs von Ems in einer anonymen Prosaauflösung und die lateinische und deutsche Fassung der Gerold-Legende Albrechts von Bonstetten, ed. Rudolf Bentzinger et al. (DTM, 81), viii + 184 pp., provides exemplary editions of two short prose works from the later 15th c. Both appear in recently rediscovered Weimar MSS formerly in the possession of Georg Spalatin (1484–1545), who is likely to have been interested mainly in the light they arguably shed on aspects of Saxon history. The introduction to the present volume, however, concentrates on codicological, literary, and linguistic matters; particularly valuable are the sections that discuss the relationships between the prose reduction of *Der gute Gerhart* and Rudolf's original, and between the Latin and German versions of the life of St Gerald.

Michael Mareiner, *Mittelhochdeutsche Minnereden und Minneallegorien der Prager Handschrift R VI Fc 26.* II: '*Standhaftigkeit in der Liebesqual*', *Wörterbuch und Reimwörterbuch* (EH, I, 1807), 436 pp., supplements M.'s recent edition of this 15th-c. discourse on love (see *YWMLS*, 62:625). It is an absolutely complete concordance and glossary of the words and rhymes found in that edition. One admires M.'s meticulousness, but wonders whether he might have proceeded a little more selectively: few readers, for example, will require NHG translations of 'bitter', 'boum', or 'blenden'. L. Lieb, Peters, *Text*, 506–28, discusses the poetics of *Minnereden*, emphasizing particularly their use of repetition.

The Letters of the Rožmberk Sisters: Noblewomen in 15th-Century Bohemia, trans. and introd. John M. Klassen et al., Cambridge, Brewer, x + 134 pp., makes available, in English translation, some 70 letters written between the 1440s and 1482 by (or in a few cases concerning) Perchta and Anéžka, the daughters of the long-time leader of the Catholic-Austrian party in Bohemia, Ulrich von Rožmberk, whose career and that of his powerful family is painstakingly described in K.'s introduction. Roughly a quarter of the letters were written in German, the rest in Czech. Much of their interest resides in the very different perspectives expressed by the unmarried Anéžka and the unhappily married Perchta, whose concept of herself in relation to her family is the principal subject of the essay that concludes the volume.

Sabine Drücke, *Humanistische Laienbildung um 1500. Das Übersetzungswerk des rheinischen Humanisten Johann Gottfried* (Palaestra, 312), Göttingen, Vandenhoeck & Ruprecht, 490 pp., is an immensely valuable study of the 17 German translations of works by ancient authors and Renaissance Humanists made by the Oppenheim priest Johann Gottfried between 1489 and 1494. D.'s summary of Gottfried's biography indicates not only that he was tutor to the Dalberg family, but also that he had considerable contact with the Heidelberg circle of Humanists. The works he selected for translation represent a wide range of periods and genres, but have in common an indebtedness to Aristotle's system of moral philosophy. D.'s investigation of Gottfried's sources and techniques of translation is based on a detailed analysis of three examples, by Cicero, Leonardo Bruni, and Pseudo-Isokrates. His renderings of these works (alongside the Latin originals) appear in a substantial appendix; they evince an approach to translation that owes much to the literal approach of Niklas von Wyle, along with a solicitous concern for comprehensibility. One hopes D.'s volume will stimulate further study of the still inadequately understood Humanist aim of involving non-Latinate readers in their ambitious educational programme.

Nina Hartl, *Die 'Stultifera Navis'. Jakob Lochers Übertragung von Sebastian Brants 'Narrenschiff'* (Studien und Texte zum Mittelalter und zur frühen Neuzeit, 1), 2 vols, Münster, Waxmann, 305 + 373 pp., is an overdue and most welcome study of this enormously influential Latin adaptation of the *Narrenschiff*. Its value resides primarily in H.'s provision of the first modern edition of substantial sections of Locher's work (nearly half of the chapters it shares with Brant's, plus all of its additional material), along with a careful NHG translation and an elucidatory commentary. One is also grateful, however, for H.'s introduction to Locher and the 15th-c. editions of the *Stultifera Navis*, and for her detailed analysis of the priorities and techniques of his didactic, humanistically oriented adaptation. A. Classen, *FCS*, 26, 2000:52–65, interprets Brant's *Narrenschiff* as a document of social and intellectual history.

Other articles on late-medieval works: in *Fest. Brunner*, N. R. Wolf (359–68) examines linguistic features of the *Hausbuch des Michael de Leone*, and O. Riha (423–30) lists and discusses research into Heinrich Wittenwiler's *Ring* published between 1988 and 1998; A. Hrubý, *Firchow Vol.*, 177–86, discusses eschatological motifs in the *Ackermann aus Böhmen*; A. Classen, *JEGP*, 100:377–405, surveys the varied *œuvre* of the Nuremberg Carthusian Erhart Gross, with special reference to his *Witwenbuch*; and T. Ehlert, *Firchow Vol.*, 41–65, considers the relationship between the *Küchenmeisterei* printed in Nuremberg around 1485 by Peter Wagner, and two earlier 15th-c. MS collections of recipes.

GJ contains several articles relevant to late-medieval German literary culture. L. Hellinga (20–26) approaches the early history of printing as a form of cultural history; C. Hust (60–67) examines an invoice detailing the costs of producing a 14th-c. antiphonal; R. Schartl (83–86) discusses the involvement of Fust and Gutenberg in two cases tried by the 'Frankfurter Schöffengericht' in 1446–47; K. Emmrich (87–94) assesses the possible contribution of four Mainz

clerics to the spread of printing to Rome; P. Amelung (95–97) refutes
D. Mauss's claim (see *YWMLS*, 62:635) that the rubricator 'P.W.'
was the same person as the scribe Peter von Urach; C. Reske (98–103)
surveys what is known about Anton Koberger and his Nuremberg
printing shop; M. K. Duggan (104–17) outlines the involvement of
15th-c. conciliarists in the preparation of an ordinary suitable for
printing; H. D. Saffrey (143–64) discusses the foundation of the
Cologne Confraternity of the Rosary in 1475, and the various printed
texts associated with it; J. A. Dane (165–67) argues that Hans
Schaur's 1497 and 1500 printed editions of Bartholomaeus Metlin-
ger's *Regiment der Kindheit* do not constitute two editions in the accepted
sense; and J. L. Flood (172–82) examines the printed book as a
commodity in the 15th and early 16th cs. Other work on early printed
material includes A. Simon's discussion (*OGS*, 30:52–79) of woodcuts
depicting women in Michael Furter's 1493 print of *Der Ritter vom Turn*
(showing how these consistently reflect a male-dominated agenda);
R. Schlusemann's examination (*Fest. Menke*, 659–75) of the career of
the Lübeck printer Johann Koelhoff; and F. Eisermann's study
(Suntrup, *Tradition*, 99–128) of how the production and distribution
of letters of indulgence in the 15th c. exploited the possibilities of new
technology in ways that decisively influenced the Protestant
reformers.

THE SIXTEENTH CENTURY

By MARK TAPLIN

1. GENERAL

Die deutsche Literatur: Biographisches und bibliographisches Lexikon. Reihe II: *Die deutsche Literatur zwischen 1450 und 1620. Abteilung A: Autorenlexikon,* ed. Wilhelm Kühlmann, Hans-Gert Roloff, and Johann Anselm Steiger, Tübingen, Frommann-Holzboog, continues with Vol. 2, fasc. 6–10, 401–814 pp., and Vol. 3, fasc. 1–5, 385 pp. Together the two latest instalments of this ongoing reference work contain 92 entries, including those for such important figures as Bonifatius Amerbach, Nikolaus von Amsdorff, and Jakob Andreae. Articles consist of a short biography of the individual concerned and a survey of his literary activities. In each case writers' published works (including edited and translated material) are listed, with full typographical details, library locations, and title page illustrations. Where appropriate, reference is also made to manuscript works and other unpublished sources, such as correspondence.

Das Berliner Modell der Mittleren Deutschen Literatur, ed. Christiane Caemmerer et al. (*Chloe*, 33), Amsterdam, Rodopi, 2000, vi + 494 pp., takes as its point of departure Hans-Gert Roloff's critique of the traditional periodization of early modern German literature. Roloff questions the usefulness of such categories as humanism, the baroque, and the early enlightenment, and proposes their replacement with the overarching concept of 'Mittlere Deutsche Literatur', covering the years 1450 to 1750. Together with the editors of the present volume, he argues that works produced during this period are the product of a unified literary culture characterized by Latin-German diglossia, increasing standardization of the vernacular, intensive engagement with the Classics, a 'Literaturkonzept, das von der Lehr- und Lernbarkeit erprobter Mittel und Verfahrensweisen zur erfolgreichen Artikulation zeitbedingter humaner Probleme und deren Lösungen ausgeht', and experimentation with new literary forms and media. Contributions of interest include B. Becker-Cantarino, 'Renaissance oder Reformation? Epochenschwellen für schreibende Frauen und die Mittlere Deutsche Literatur' (69–87), which identifies the Reformation, rather than the Renaissance, as the catalyst for literary activity by women during the early modern period; U. Seelbach, on the reception of medieval German literature in the 16th, 17th, and early 18th cs (89–115); G. van Gemert, 'Zur Verwertung mittelalterlichen Literaturguts im geistlichen Schrifttum der Frühen Neuzeit' (117–35), which stresses the continuities between late medieval and early modern Catholic devotional literature; F. von Ingen, 'Die Entwicklung des protestantischen Märtyrerbuchs' (137–52); W. Kühlmann, on the treatment of witchcraft in two Latin poems by Paul Schede Melissus (153–74); J.-M. Valentin, on the development of the theatre in Strasbourg during the half century following Johannes Sturm's departure from the city (175–89); H.-J. Bachorski, 'Wie der Narr ins Irrenhaus kommt. Diskursdifferenzierung im 16. und 17. Jahrhundert' (273–98), which charts the transition from medieval to modern conceptions of madness; and P. Sprengel, on Gerhard Hauptmann's portrayal of Luther as an icon of nationalism and antipapalism (419–41).

Christine Bachmann, *Wahre vnd eygentliche Bildnus. Situationsbezogene Stilisierungen historischer Personen auf illustrierten Flugblättern zwischen dem Ende des 15. und der Mitte des 17. Jahrhunderts* (Mikrokosmos, 58), Frankfurt, Lang, 300 pp. The subject of this revised doctoral thesis is the 'Bild des Menschen, das auf Flugblättern erkennbar ist'. Through an analysis of 88 *Flugblätter*, B. provides evidence of the continuity of early modern approaches to biography with the medieval Latin *vita* and other forms of exemplary literature. In the texts and images that B. considers, political and religious leaders tend to be portrayed less as individuals than as representatives of ideal types which recapitulate themes from Christian salvation history (an association reinforced by the deployment of biblical and other familiar motifs). As B. shows, these stylizing techniques were crucial to the effectiveness of the *Flugblätter* as propaganda. Thus Protestant authors drew on images familiar to their readers from traditional hagiography in order to demonstrate Luther's saintliness and prophetic calling, while Catholics retaliated by portraying the reformer as a negative exemplar of drunkenness and sensuality. By the second half of the 16th c., the figure of Luther had acquired a normative authority in Protestant circles that led to its being used for openly political purposes (B. provides examples of Luther's appearance in support of the rival claims of the Ernestine and Albertine branches of the Saxon ruling house). More generally, *Flugblätter* functioned as instruments of social control: sensationalizing biographies of witches and murderers warned readers of the dangers of challenging the established order, while in the life of the faithful widow Elisabeth Schramm women were presented with an alternative, positive model of Protestant piety and wifely devotion. Only with the emergence of a secular understanding of history alongside traditional Christian eschatology — a change that B. associates with the end of the Thirty Years War — did biography begin to take on a more recognizably 'modern' character. *Gebetsliteratur der Frühen Neuzeit als Hausfrömmigkeit. Funktionen und Formen in Deutschland und den Niederlanden*, ed. Ferdinand von Ingen and

Cornelia Niekus Moore (WoF, 92), 323 pp., aims to refocus scholarly attention on the neglected genre of the prayer book by highlighting its role in devotional life between the Reformation and the Enlightenment. The 15 articles contained in the volume offer an insight into the diverse uses for which prayer books were designed during this period: as catechetical manuals, as tools for instilling social discipline, and as aids to private devotion. Attention is also given to the structural and stylistic features of the genre. For the 16th c., useful contributions include J. Wallmann, 'Zwischen Herzensgebet und Gebetbuch. Zur protestantischen deutschen Gebetsliteratur im 17. Jahrhundert' (13–46), which considers the development of the Protestant prayer book in the light of Luther's ambivalent attitude towards set prayer; C. Niekus Moore, on the use of Lutheran prayer books for children to encourage the memorization and internalization of religious practice (113–29); A. Baumann, on the apologetic function of patristic texts in the prayer books of Andreas Musculus (227–58); and A. de Reuver, 'Stellung und Funktion des Gebets in Calvins Theologie. Eine Skizze' (259–90), which examines Calvin's understanding of prayer in the context of his soteriology. Bibliographical details for 50 printed and manuscript volumes held at the Herzog August Bibliothek, including some private prayer books used by members of the ducal family of Braunschweig-Lüneburg, are appended.

Kulturgeschichte Ostpreußens in der Frühen Neuzeit, ed. Klaus Garber, Manfred Komorowski, and Axel E. Walter (FN, 56), 2000, xxi + 1025 pp., focuses on six main topics: library holdings in Königsberg (Kaliningrad); ducal Prussia in the early modern period; the university of Königsberg during the same period; music and the arts in East Prussia; the image of Prussia in historiography and literature; and the literary history of East Prussia. Items of interest include W. Kühlmann and W. Straube, 'Zur Historie und Pragmatik humanistischer Lyrik im alten Preußen: von Konrad Celtis über Eobanus Hessus zu Georg Sabinus' (657–736), with the text of two poems by Eobanus Hessus and five by Sabinus; A. Mentzel-Reuters, 'Von der Ordenschronik zur Landesgeschichte — Die Herausbildung der altpreußischen Landeshistoriographie im 16. Jahrhundert' (581–637); and the contribution by A. Sanjosé, which examines three texts (a collection of epigrams by Andreas Lobwasser, an anonymous history of the Osiandrist controversy, and a German dramatization of the *History of Francesco Spiera*) as examples of 'bourgeois' literature in 16th-c. Königsberg (799–814).

Adelige und bürgerliche Erinnerungskulturen des Spätmittelalters und der Frühen Neuzeit, ed. Werner Rösener (Formen der Erinnerung, 8), Göttingen, Vandenhoeck & Ruprecht, 2000, 228 pp., contains papers presented at a colloquium held in Giessen in November 1994. Of particular interest to contributors are the ways in which late medieval and early modern German chronicles reflect the tension between urban and rural élites during this period. B. Mauer, 'Patrizisches Bewußtsein in Augsburger Chroniken, Wappen- und Ehrenbüchern', *ib.*, 163–76, considers the use by the Augsburg patriciate of family history to legitimize and cement its pre-eminence within civic life. T. Fuchs, *ib.*, 205–26, notes the increased emphasis in late 16th-c. and 17th-c. Hessian historiography on the local ruling house's alleged descent in the male line from Charlemagne. Albrecht Classen, *Frauen in der deutschen Literaturgeschichte. Die ersten 800 Jahre: Ein Lesebuch* (Women in German Literature, 4), NY, Lang, 2000, xix + 337 pp., includes texts by Argula von Grumbach (*Antwort*) and Ottilia Fenchlerin (*Liederbuch*). J. L. Flood, 'The printed book as a commercial commodity in the fifteenth and early sixteenth centuries', *Gutenberg-Jb.*, 76:172–82, suggests reasons for the success or failure of some early German printers. I. Bezzel, *ib.*, 183–89, sheds light on the publishing history of three Latin works with the unusual imprint 'Impressum Noriburgo. A. B. 1502'. V. Mertens, Hubrath, *Zwickau*, 3–18, considers the interplay between text and performance in songs, plays, and sermons held at the Ratsschulbibliothek Zwickau.

2. HUMANISM AND THE REFORMATION

Deutschland und Italien in ihren wechselseitigen Beziehungen während der Renaissance, ed. Bodo Guthmüller (Wolfenbütteler Abhandlungen zur Renaissanceforschung, 19), Wiesbaden, Harrassowitz, 2000, vi + 394 pp., takes as its theme German-Italian cultural relations in the later Renaissance. The volume contains contributions relating to music, painting, architecture, and sculpture as well as literature. Relevant articles include B. Roeck, 'Kulturtransfer im Zeitalter des Humanismus: Venedig und das Reich' (9–29), which offers some explanations (confessional conflict, the rise of princely states and corresponding economic and political decline of the *Reichsstädte*) for the failure of cities such as Augsburg to adopt wholesale Italian forms and styles; J. Glomski, on the role played by three German-trained scholars (Rudolf Agricola Jr, Valentin Eck, and Leonard Cox) in transmitting Italian Neo-Latin literary currents to Cracow (31–44); K. Heitmann, 'Machiavelli und die "antica bontà" der Deutschen' (61–101), which notes similarities between the image of the German people in Machiavelli and in works by the northern humanists Conrad Celtis and Heinrich Bebel (in both cases there is an emphasis on the Germans' love of liberty and piety, but also their divisions); A. Aurnhammer, 'Ariost in Deutschland um 1600' (127–51); A. Noe, 'Die Rezeption italienischer Literatur über die Verbreitung der

Vokalmusik' (153–57), which discusses the collections of Georg, Philipp Eduard, and Friedrich Fugger; and B. Marx, on the role of Florence as a cultural model for the court of Dresden under the Electors Augustus and Christian I, including correspondence and inventories of gifts received from the Grand Duke of Tuscany during the 1580s (211–97).

Deutsche Landesgeschichtsschreibung im Zeichen des Humanismus, ed. Franz Brendle et al. (Contubernium, 56), Stuttgart, Steiner, 293 pp., considers the impact of humanism on the development of local/regional historiography in German-speaking lands during the 16th c. Items of interest include U. Muhlack, 'Die humanistische Historiographie. Umfang, Bedeutung, Probleme' (3–18), which discerns a tension within humanist historiography between historicism and the desire to imitate Classical models; U. Andermann, on the works of the Hamburg humanist Albert Krantz (51–67); A. Schmid, 'Die Kleinen Annalen des Johannes Aventinus aus dem Jahre 1511' (69–95), which considers Aventinus's *Annales ducum Bavariae* to be an example of medieval rather than humanist historiography; C. Bauer and C. Kummer, on the Würzburg chronicler Lorenz Fries (97–111; 113–22); B. Stettler, 'Aegidius Tschudi. "Vater der Schweizergeschichte"' (123–33), which assesses the significance of Tschudi's work for subsequent Swiss historiography; B. Richter, on the historical works of Kaspar Brusch (135–44); F. Brendle, on Martin Crusius's Lutheran reinterpretation of the medieval history of Swabia (145–63); W. Ziegler, on the treatment of late medieval movements for church reform in humanist historiography (189–200); M. Ott, on the use of Roman inscriptions by Konrad Peutinger and Johannes Aventinus (213–26); S. Rau, 'Stadthistoriographie und Erinnerungskultur in Hamburg, Köln und Breslau' (227–57); and M. Klein, 'Zur württembergischen Historiographie vor dem Dreißigjährigen Krieg' (259–78).

N. Miedeme, Suntrup, *Tradition*, 51–72, discusses Conrad Celtis's project for a *Germania illustrata* and subsequent attempts to realize it in Nuremberg during the first half of the 16th c. H. Freytag, *Fest. Ruberg*, 61–74, considers attempts by humanist writers such as Petrus Vincentius to associate the name Lübeck with the Polish 'liubice', meaning 'crown'.

Wilfried Kettler, *Die Zürcher Bibel von 1531: Philologische Studien zu ihrer Übersetzungstechnik und den Beziehungen zu ihren Vorlagen*, Berne, Lang, 521 pp., explores the 'übersetzerische Eigenart' of the Zurich Bible by comparing selected chapters of the work with the Hebrew and Greek originals, with Luther's translations of the same texts (some, though not all, of which were available to the Zurichers), and with the corresponding passages in the Greek Septuagint and Latin Vulgate. In an informative, if not particularly groundbreaking, introductory section, K. places the Zurich Bible translation in the context of the Zurich *Prophezei* or *lectiones publicae*, emphasizing its basic character as a *Gemeinschaftswerk*. As the author notes, of the eight scholars who participated in the early work of the *Prophezei*, only Leo Jud was charged with translating a specific portion of the biblical text (the Apocrypha). The bulk of the study is given over to detailed analysis of selected biblical texts, eight from the Old Testament and four from the New. Of these, half were translated with the assistance of the Luther Bible and half without reference to Luther. K.'s examination confirms that the team of exegetes at the *Prophezei* followed closely Luther's pre-existing translations, where available. More surprising, perhaps, is his conclusion that, when translating texts independently of Luther, the Zurichers tended to choose a 'freer' rendering of the original Hebrew than their Wittenberg rival — underlining the point that Luther's approach to translation was more nuanced than is sometimes assumed. Heribert Smolinsky, **Deutungen der Zeit im Streit der Konfessionen: Kontroverstheologie, Apokalyptik und Astrologie im 16. Jahrhundert* (Schriften der philosophisch-historischen Klasse der Heidelberger Akademie der Wissenschaften, 20), Heidelberg, Winter, 53 pp. J. Hamm, *Fest. Brunner*, 513–40, considers 16th-c. and early 17th-c. literary treatments of the so-called massacre of Weinsberg, a notorious atrocity carried out during the German Peasants War. H. shows how this episode was used both to demonstrate the cruelty of the rebellious peasantry and as an exemplary warning of the fate of those who sought to overthrow their lawful masters. Appended to the article are two songs commemorating the massacre and drawings depicting the execution of two of the peasant leaders. H. Ehmer, 'Die evangelische Bewegung in den vorderösterreichischen Landen: Pfarrer, Mönche und Laien unter dem Einfluß der Reformation', *ZWL*, 60:363–94, includes a consideration of *Flugschriften*, sermons, and other works by Sebastian Lotzer, Johann Eberlin von Günzburg, the Rothenburg cleric Andreas Keller, and Johann Zwick. J. L. Flood, *Fest. Menke*, 239–48, discusses the role of the English reformer Robert Barnes in dealing with an outbreak of sweating sickness in Lübeck in 1529. M. Hubrath, Hubrath, *Zwickau*, 125–44, surveys the development of the printing industry in Zwickau between 1523 and 1550, placing particular emphasis on Zwickau's role as a centre for the production of Protestant school drama.

3. GENRES

DRAMA AND DIALOGUE

E. Vijfvinkel, *Spiewok Vol.*, 331–42, compares the portrayal of Christ in the surviving 16th-c. versions of the *Luzerner Osterspiel* with his depiction in the related *Donaueschinger Passionsspiel* (*c.* 1480). V. explains the greater emphasis in the former on Christ's dignity as a response to Reformation criticism of the passion play as a genre.

PROSE AND VERSE

Daniel Guggisberg, *Das Bild der "Alten Eidgenossen" in Flugschriften des 16. bis Anfang 18. Jahrhunderts (1531–1712): Tendenzen und Funktionen eines Geschichtsbildes*, Berne, Lang, 2000, xvi + 845 pp. This revised doctoral thesis considers the use of historical references and motifs in Swiss *Flugschriften* published between the second Kappel peace and the second war of Villmergen, a period dominated by conflict between rival Catholic and Protestant blocs within the *Eidgenossenschaft*. In part I of the study, G. attempts to define the term *Flugschrift* and offers some preliminary observations on the propaganda function of historical allusion in early modern texts. In part II, he catalogues some 123 *Flugschriften* (15 of which date from the 16th c.) and identifies nine distinct historical motifs within this corpus. The results of this analysis are summarized in tabular form at the end of the chapter. In part III, G. applies the same quantitative approach to a group of 12 *Flugschriften* published around the first war of Villmergen (1656). Overall, the study highlights the way in which early modern pamphleteers sought to 'instrumentalize' history for political purposes. By appealing to the example of the *Alte Eidgenossen* (Wilhelm Tell, Bruder Klaus, etc.), Catholic and Protestant writers were able to appropriate for their respective confessions the ideals of freedom, unity, and martial virtue on which the medieval Swiss Confederation was believed to have been founded. Manuel Braun, *Ehe, Liebe, Freundschaft: Semantik der Vergesellschaftung in frühneuhochdeutschen Prosaromanen* (FN, 60), 390 pp., relates changes in the portrayal of marriage, love, and friendship in texts published between 1474 and 1557 to changes in wider society during this period. In the anonymous *Fortunatus* (1509), B. discerns evidence of the collapse of medieval institutions and moral codes (a process that he terms 'Ausdifferenzierung'), as well as a foreshadowing of future developments (the Reformation, early modern state-building, the breakthrough of capitalism). Half a century later, the novels of Georg Wickram offer the prescription for a new social order founded on the moral-theological discourse of humanists and Protestant divines, with patriarchal marriage as its centrepiece. B. contrasts this with the late medieval discourse of love, as reflected in such works as Elisabeth von Nassau-Saarbrücken's *Hug Schapler*, Wilhelm Ziely's *Olwier und Artus*, and Veit Warbeck's *Die schöne Magelone*. According to B., the enhanced status of friendship in Wickram's novels is also a product of

'Ausdifferenzierung': in this case, the decline of traditional social networks like the extended family and the guild.

Albrecht Classen, *Deutsche Liederbücher des 15. und 16. Jahrhunderts* (Volksliedstudien, 1), Münster, Waxmann, 354 pp., analyses a representative selection of late medieval and early modern song books, including both published and manuscript works. C. provides a brief overview of each collection, together with a summary of the contents of the songs that appear within it (some of which are cited in full or in part). In his introduction, he reviews the historical development of the *Volkslied*, arguing for the retention in academic discourse of this catch-all term but noting the variety of sub-genres (ballads, love songs, drinking songs, *Türkenlieder*, etc.) that it encompasses. Appended to the volume are a thematic index of the songs listed and a select bibliography of *Liederbücher* from the 15th, 16th, and 17th cs. K. H. Marcus, *SCJ*, 32:723–41, considers the post-Reformation history of hymnody and hymnals in Basle, which alone of the Swiss Reformed cities resisted Zwingli's prohibition of congregational singing. Particular weight is attached to the contribution made by the Basle organist and professor of music Samuel Mareschal, who adapted the Lobwasser psalter for use in the city's churches. M. identifies in Mareschal's hymnal a synthesis of Lutheran and Calvinist musical traditions which testifies to the (relatively) open and pluralist religious climate in Basle during much of the 16th c. H. Brunner, Ragotzky, *Liedinterpretation*, 118–34, offers a typology of the 16th-c. German *Lied*, based on an examination of the largest contemporary song collection, Georg Forster's five-volume work *Frische teutsche Liedlein*. I. Simon, 'Zum Humanismus in Münster und zu den Sprichwortsammlungen von Johannes Murmellius (1513) und Antonius Tunnicius (1514)', *NdW*, 40, 2000:47–75. F. Wittchow, 'Eine Frage der Ehre: das Problem des aggressiven Sprechakts in den Facetien Bebels, Mulings, Frischlins und Melanders', *ZGer*, 11:336–60.

4. OTHER WORK

Die Praktiken der Gelehrsamkeit in der Frühen Neuzeit, ed. Helmut Zedelmeier and Martin Mulsow (FN, 64), vii + 361 pp., challenges the post-Enlightenment view of early modern learning as a form of decadent humanism. Z. and M. argue that the key to understanding this alien intellectual culture is to identify its underlying principles, methods, and institutional supports — in other words, to reconstruct its 'kulturelle Praxis'. For that reason, the focus of the essays published here is less on texts *per se* than on the conditions under which texts were produced, edited, disseminated, and received. The following

items are of particular interest: H. Zedelmeier, 'Lesetechniken. Die
Praktiken der Lektüre in der Neuzeit' (11–30), which distinguishes
between three kinds of reading prevalent in the early modern
period — devotional reading, confined to a domestic setting,
'gelehrtes Lesen', concerned primarily with the memorization of
knowledge, and 'politisches Lesen', a specialized variant of the second
type adapted to the specific circumstances of courtly society;
R. Häfner, 'Synoptik und Stilentwicklung: die Pindar-Editionen von
Zwingli/Ceporin, Erasmus Schmid und Alessandro Adimari'
(97–121); and E. Tortarolo, on the limited effectiveness of censureship
in early modern Europe (277–94). M. Mulsow, *ib.*, 307–47, considers
reactions to Melchior Goldast's unauthorized edition of Lipsius's
oration *De duplici concordia* and places the work in the context of
Goldast's wider polemical activity (307–47).

P. O. Müller, *Deutsche Lexikographie des 16. Jahrhunderts: Konzeptionen
und Funktionen frühneuzeitlicher Wörterbücher* (TTG, 49), xx + 668 pp.,
offers a comprehensive typology of dictionaries published in German-
speaking Europe during the 16th c. in which German features as a
'systematische Wörterbuchsprache'. M. identifies seven distinct forms
of lexicography for the early modern period, each of which is dealt
with in a separate chapter. Information is provided on the sources,
content and publishing history of the more than 100 works that meet
M.'s criteria for inclusion (set out in chapter II). Consideration is also
given to the 'paratextual' material published with the dictionaries
(prefaces, dedications, indexes, etc.), which shed light on the motivations of authors and their target audiences. For M., the most striking
feature of 16th-c. lexicography is its conscious rejection of the late-
medieval lexicographical tradition, most apparent in the humanist
polemic against the *Gemmae vocabulorum* (denounced as *sordidae gemmae*)
that had previously served as aids in the teaching of Latin. The 16th c.
also witnessed a notable shift towards the production of multilingual,
as opposed to exclusively bilingual Latin-German dictionaries. As
M. explains, the reasons for this were both practical (to assist
foreigners in learning German) and patriotic (to demonstrate the
much-vaunted *copia verborum* of German and hence its superiority to
the Romance languages). The study also highlights the role of 16th-c.
lexicographers as a force for linguistic standardization, through their
emphasis on 'sprachlandschaftsübergreifender Wortschatz' at the
expense of local forms. E. Bastress-Dukehart, 'Family, property, and
feeling in Early Modern German noble culture: the Zimmerns of
Swabia', *SCJ*, 32 : 1–19, evaluates the *Zimmern Chronicle* (1565–67) as
a source for the study of late-15th-c. and early-16th-c. noble attitudes
towards such questions as inheritance, honour, and kinship.

C. Göttler, *GR*, 76:121–42, identifies in late-15th-c. and early-16th-c. depictions of the miraculous Mass of St Gregory allusions to the contemporary practice of indulgences. M. Beer, *SCJ*, 32:931–51, examines the early modern concept of the family as delineated in the correspondence of the Nuremberg burgher Linhard Tucher. G. Quarg, *Gutenberg-Jb.*, 76:224–47, supplies details of nine newly rediscovered volumes from Cologne that once formed part of the *Bibliotheca Palatina*. W. Röcke, Hubrath, *Zwickau*, 145–68, discusses the eschatological interpretation of monstrous births and prodigies in works by the Zwickau doctor Jobius Fincelius and others. G. Fichtner, 'Disput mit Leonhart Fuchs: die frühesten medizinischen Thesendrucke in Tübingen', *Medizinhistorisches Journal*, 36:111–83. W. Klose, 'Ab wann gab es Stammbücher?', *LiLi*, 122:161–63. I. T. Piirainen, 'Graphematische Variation aus der Sicht des Zentrums und der Peripherie: das älteste Stadtbuch von Neusohl/Banská Bystrica', *NMi*, 102:77–83.

5. Individual Authors and Works

BEBEL, HEINRICH. V. Honemann, ' "Spätmittelalterliche" und "humanistische" Frömmigkeit: Florian Waldorf von Waldenstein und Heinrich Bebel', Suntrup, *Tradition*, 75–97.

BOCER, JOHANNES. L. Mundt, 'Johannes Bocers Ankündigungen von Aeneis-Vorlesungen an der Universität Rostock 1560–1563: ein Beitrag zur akademischen Vergil-Rezeption im 16. Jahrhundert', *WRM*, 25:103–21.

BULLINGER, HEINRICH. F. Mauelshagen, *Zwingliana*, 28:75–117, describes a hitherto unnoticed collection of 77 short works (mostly single-page prints) bequeathed by B. to his son Rudolf, who subsequently passed them on to the Zurich antiquary Johann Jakob Wick. U. B. Leu, *ib.*, 119–63, provides information on the recipients of copies of B.'s history and refutation of Anabaptism, *Der Widertöufferen ursprung* (1560).

CELTIS, CONRAD. Peter Luh, *Kaiser Maximilian gewidmet: Die unvollendete Werkausgabe des Conrad Celtis und ihre Holzschnitte* (EH, XXVIII, 377), 459 pp. + 58 pls, offers an in-depth analysis of 12 illustrations published with the first (and, in the event, only) volume of the planned edition of C.'s complete works (1502). By drawing on C.'s writings and correspondence, and on the work of pupils such as Jakob Locher, Joachim Vadian, and Johannes Aventinus, L. is able to identify the classical and medieval sources for the iconography of the woodcuts. Together, he argues, they form a kind of humanist manifesto, giving visual expression to key aspects of C.'s thought (for example, his conception of the poet's role in society and his patriotic belief in the *translatio sapientiae* from Italy to Germany). Each of the illustrations discussed in the study is reproduced in an appendix. L. also provides lucid summaries of the poetical works contained in the 1502 volume, including the *Amores*, the *Norimberga*, and the *Germania generalis*, which he relates to C.'s long-term project for a *Germania illustrata*.

CHYTRAEUS, DAVID. **David Chytraeus (1530–1600): Norddeutscher Humanismus in Europa. Beiträge zum Wirken des Kraichgauer Gelehrten*, ed. Karl-Heinz Glaser and Steffen Stuth, Ubstadt-Weiher, Vlg Regionalkultur, 2000, 195 pp.

CRUCIGER, ELISABETH. M. J. Haemig, 'Elisabeth Cruciger (1500?–1535): the case of the disappearing hymn writer', *SCJ*, 32:21–44, offers several explanations for the reluctance of learned writers, in particular, to credit C. with authorship of the hymn 'Herr Christ, der einig Gottes Sohn': C.'s gender; the condemnation of her husband and son in the intra-Lutheran disputes of the 1570s; and, above all, a decline in apocalyptic expectation from the early 17th c. onwards which affected perceptions of women's proper religious role.

DÜRER, ALBRECHT. J. Jacoby, *BHR*, 43:47–62, links the iconography of D.'s so-called Jabach altarpiece to contemporary approaches to the treatment of syphilis. In an appendix to the article, J. considers four possible options for the original location of the altarpiece.

FEICHTER, VEIT. *Die Schriften des Brixner Dommesners Veit Feichter (ca. 1510–1560). I: Das Brixner Dommesnerbuch*, ed. Andrea Hofmeister-Winter (IBKG, 63), 521 pp., contains a wealth of detail on Catholic liturgical practice during the early modern period. In her introduction, H.-W. provides a detailed description of the manuscript on which the edition is based, a short biography of F. (verger at Brixen cathedral between 1547 and 1560), some observations on F.'s language, and a topography of the Brixen cathedral complex. The text itself is presented as a 'dynamic edition', H.-W.'s aim being to avoid standardization where possible and to render all steps in the editorial process transparent to the reader. This is supported by the inclusion of a CD-ROM containing a facsimile of F.'s manuscript and a searchable electronic transcript of the work.

FISCHART, JOHANN. U. Seelbach, *Daphnis*, 29, 2000:464–583, assesses the contribution made by earlier F. scholarship to identifying F.'s sources in the *Geschichtklitterung*, *Eulenspiegel reimenweis* and *Catalogus catalogorum*.

FLACIUS ILLYRICUS, MATTHIAS. Martina Hartmann, *Humanismus und Kirchenkritik: Matthias Flacius Illyricus als Erforscher des Mittelalters* (Beiträge zur Geschichte und Quellenkunde des Mittelalters, 19), Stuttgart, Thorbecke, 336 pp., assesses F.'s pioneering role in the recovery and transmission of medieval religious texts. H. shows how

F. was able, through his connections with humanists, clerics, and printers throughout central Europe, to build up a unique library of manuscripts (listed in appendix 1), many of which he subsequently published either as stand-alone editions or in the context of his apologetic work, the *Catalogus testium veritatis*. The study highlights F.'s selective use of this material, which was intended to confer historical legitimacy on the Reformation critique of the papacy and to provide Protestants with an answer to the Catholic taunt, 'Where was your church before Luther?' (hence F.'s interest in late medieval heretical groups such as the Hussites and Waldenses). At the same time, the Croatian exile's historiographical method — which involved the reproduction of whole texts, rather than just short citations — is compared favourably with that of the authors of the *Magdeburg Centuries*, a work that he inspired but (contrary to popular belief) did not actually help to write. H. concludes that, despite his essentially confessional approach, F. may justly be regarded as the founder of modern *Mediävistik*.

FORTUNATUS. D. Huschenbett, *ZDA*, 130:431–34, makes the case for *F*.'s having been written as well as published in Augsburg, partly on the basis of links between Cyprus (the birthplace of the novel's hero) and Augsburg, where the cult of the Cypriot St Afra enjoyed considerable popularity during the medieval period.

FRISCHLIN, NIKODEMUS. W. Ludwig, *Daphnis*, 29, 2000:413–64, is the first detailed analysis of F.'s verse epic *Wirtembergicarum nuptiarum Libri VII*. L. highlights F.'s use of motifs and structures derived from both Vergil's *Aeneid* and the *Aeneid* supplement of Maffeo Vegio. Id., *ZWL*, 60:139–51, provides evidence for F.'s authorship of two Latin distichs engraved on a goblet awarded to Duke Ludwig of Württemberg by the University of Tübingen on the occasion of his wedding in 1575.

LALEBUCH. R. Kalkofen, 'Die verkehrten Welten im *Don Quijote* (1605/1615) und im *Lalebuch* (1597)', *ColH*, 29, 1999:159–97.

LINK, HIERONYMUS. S. Kerth, Hubrath, *Zwickau*, 79–110, considers three songs by L. commemorating contemporary political events (the text of two of the songs is appended).

LOTICHIUS SECUNDUS, PETRUS. P. Lebrecht Schmidt, ' "... unde utriusque poetae elegans artificium admirari licebit": zur Ovid-Rezeption (am. 2.6) des Petrus Lotichius Secundus (el. 2,7)', pp. 304–19 of *Traditio latinitatis: Studien zur Rezeption und Überlieferung der lateinischen Literatur*, ed. Joachim Fugmann, Martin Hose, and Bernhard Zimmermann, Stuttgart, Steiner, 2000, 378 pp.

LUTHER, MARTIN. M. Luther, **Annotierungen zu den Werken des Hieronymus*, ed. Martin Brecht and Christian Peters (Archiv zur Weimarer Ausgabe der Werke Martin Luthers, 8), Cologne, Böhlau,

2000, 279 pp. Timothy Dost, *Renaissance Humanism in Support of the Gospel in Luther's Early Correspondence: Taking all Things Captive*, Aldershot, Ashgate, vii + 244 pp. W. T. Cavanaugh, *JMEMS*, 31:585–605, considers L.'s critique of the Catholic doctrine of the sacrifice of the Mass.

MELANCHTHON, PHILIPP.   S. Brauer, *EG*, 56:309–24, assesses the impact of the first edition of M.'s *Loci communes* (1521). B. relates the work's 'dynamischer Charakter' to M.'s rejection of scholastic theology — pre-eminently the *Sentences* of Peter Lombard — in favour of an approach consistent with Luther's emphasis on the Word and the process of salvation.

MÖLLER, MARTIN.   G. Butzer, 'Rhetorik der Meditation: Martin Möllers "Soliloquia de Passione Iesu Christi" und die Tradition der eloquentia sacra', pp. 57–78 of *Meditation und Erinnerung in der Frühen Neuzeit*, ed. Gerhard Kurz (Formen der Erinnerung, 2), Göttingen, Vandenhoeck & Ruprecht, 2000, 405 pp., highlights M.'s application of techniques of affective rhetoric to meditation, placing him at the head of a tradition that includes such 17th-c. Lutheran writers as Matthäus Meyfart and Catharina Regina von Greiffenberg.

OPORINUS, JOHANNES.   Carlos Gilly, *Die Manuskripte in der Bibliothek des Johannes Oporinus: Verzeichnis der Manuskripte und Druckvorlagen aus dem Nachlass Oporins anhand des von Theodor Zwinger und Basilius Amerbach erstellten Inventariums* (Schriften der Universitätsbibliothek Basel, 3), Basle, Schwabe, 216 pp., provides a much-needed supplement to the works currently available on O., one of the most important printers of the mid-16th c. and a key figure in the cultural life of Basle during its golden age. The inventory that is edited here for the first time lists 456 titles, most of them manuscripts, and provides a snapshot of part of O.'s library at the time of his death (a catalogue of O.'s printed works, which numbered close to 4,000 and were auctioned to pay off his debts, was published in 1571). Full bibliographical details, often illustrated with citations from correspondence and other contemporary sources, are provided for each entry; the current location of 110 manuscripts and seven printed works is also noted. In his introduction, G. sets out the historical background to the composition of the inventory, which was drawn up by O.'s relatives Amerbach and Zwinger before his property could be confiscated by the Basle authorities, and provides an overview of its contents. As G. notes, most of the items listed are manuscripts that O. planned to publish in the near future. In the main, O. seems to have discarded the manuscripts for texts that had already appeared in print — hence the absence of authors such as Paracelsus and Celio Secundo Curione from the inventory.

PARACELSUS. *Der Frühparacelsismus. Erster Teil*, ed. Wilhelm Kühlman and Johannes Telle (Corpus Paracelsisticum, 1; FN, 59), viii + 732 pp., is the first of four projected volumes devoted to the early reception of P.'s thought and works, and contains 39 documents illustrating the so-called Paracelsian revival of the mid-16th c. These include letters by the astronomer Georg Joachim Rheticus and the Danzig-born Neo-Latin poet Alexander von Suchten, together with 25 dedicatory epistles by the physician Adam von Bodenstein, who between 1560 and 1576 oversaw the publication of more than 40 editions of P.'s works. The volume charts the beginnings of a concerted campaign, centred on Basle but with support from as far away as East Prussia, to replace the bankrupt Aristotelianism and Galenism of the universities with P.'s doctrine of the 'Tria Prima' (sulphur, mercury, and salt). In Bodenstein's letters, P. is depicted as a new Hippocrates, the restorer of ancient learning (specifically, of the Hermetic *prisca philosophia*) after a long period of decadence and decline. Care is also taken to demonstrate P.'s theological orthodoxy, in response to charges of atheism and Arianism that had been levelled against him. Each document published in the volume is accompanied by extensive explanatory notes and a short summary of contents; in the case of Latin texts, a modern German translation is supplied. The volume also includes a comprehensive bibliography and a set of user-friendly indices.

ROTH, STEPHAN. R. Metzler, 'Die Bibliothek des Zwickauer Stadtschreibers Stephan Roth (1492–1546): ein erster Überblick', Hubrath, *Zwickau*, 111–23.

RÜTE, HANS VON. *Sämtliche Dramen*, ed. Friederike Christ-Kutter et al. (Schweizer Texte, n. F. 14), 3 vols, Berne, Haupt, 2000, 879 + 342 pp., brings together R.'s plays in a critical edition for the first time. Volumes 1 and 2 of the work present R.'s *Fasznachtspil* (1532), the biblical dramas *Joseph* (1538), *Gedeon* (1540), *Noe* (1546), and *Goliath* (1555), and *Ein Kurtzes Osterspiel* (1552); the anonymous *Elsli Trag den Knaben*, which is sometimes attributed to R., is not included owing to its recent publication elsewhere. Volume 3 contains extensive background material, including a reconstruction of R.'s biography, essays on his use of language and music (song has an important dramatic function in the work of R. and other contemporary Swiss playwrights), and explanatory notes on the individual plays. Guidance on the structure and likely staging of each piece is also provided. Thematically, R.'s work is shown to be rooted in the political and religious circumstances of his home city of Berne during the Reformation and post-Reformation years — a fact which explains the primarily domestic appeal of the plays. R.'s treatment of the biblical subject matter of *Gedeon*, for example, is informed by local experience of the Reformation and iconoclasm; it also contains allusions to Berne's subsequent conquest of the Pays de Vaud. Similarly, *Ein Kurtzes Osterspiel* reflects the tension between Lutheran, Calvinist, and Zwinglian sympathizers within the Bernese church.

SACHS, HANS.   H. Kugler, 'Meisterliederdichtung als Auslegungskunst: zur impliziten Poetik bei Hans Sachs', *Fest. Brunner*, 541–57, describes S. as practising a 'Poesie nach Maß und Zahl' and links this to both S.'s artisanal background and a more general early modern tendency to measure literary quality in quantitative terms. N. Holzberg, *ib.*, 559–68, compares works by S. and the Italian religious exile Olympia Fulvia Morata. J. Rettelbach, Hubrath, *Zwickau*, 55–77, discusses genre distinctions in S.'s work.

SEITZ, ALEXANDER.   G. Möncke, *Gutenberg-Jb.*, 76:190–93, considers a previously unknown work by S., the *Declamatio in laudem artis medicae* (Basle, 1528), in which S. highlights the physical dangers of enforced celibacy for women (the syndrome known as *Suffocatio matricis*).

STAUPITZ, JOHANN VON.   B. Hamm, *AR*, 92:6–42, provides a useful introduction to S.'s life, works, and theology, with particular emphasis on his relationship with Luther.

STURM, JOHANNES.   V. Montagne, 'Jean Sturm et Valentin Erythraeus ou l'élaboration méthodique d'une topique dialectique', *BHR*, 61:477–509, considers the treatment by S. in his *Partitiones dialecticarum* of the notion of decorum, and the presentation of S.'s argument in tabular form by Valentin Erythraeus. The author situates S.'s pedagogical method in the context of humanist reflection on Melanchthon's *genus didascalicon* and argues that it can be summed up in three words: 'parler', 'imiter', and 'mémoriser'.

VADIAN, JOACHIM.   G. Alicke, *Daphnis*, 29, 2000:379–412, tracks V.'s edition of Pomponius Mela's *De chorographia* (1518) through successive printings. A. regards the work as an essential precursor to V.'s own *Epitome trium terrae partium* (1534). D. Demendt, 'Vadians Stellung zu Jan Hus und Hieronymus von Prag', *Zwingliana*, 28:165–82.

WICKRAM, GEORG.   A. Schulz, 'Texte und Textilien: zur Entstehung der Liebe in Georg Wickrams *Goldfaden* (1557)', *Daphnis*, 30:53–70, notes the marginalization of sexuality in W.'s novel as compared with medieval examples of the *Liebesroman*, and relates this to the 'verstärkte Sozialdisziplinierung der Frühen Neuzeit'. S. argues that in the *Goldfaden* the centre of interest is transferred from the body of the hero's beloved, Angliana, to signs (a ring, items of clothing, the golden thread itself), with love presented in terms of a 'semiotischer Prozeß'.

THE SEVENTEENTH CENTURY
POSTPONED

THE CLASSICAL ERA
POSTPONED

THE ROMANTIC ERA

By BIRGIT RÖDER, *University of Reading*

I. GENERAL STUDIES

Romantik, ed. Vera Alexander and Monika Fludernik (Literatur, Imagination, Realität, 26), Trier, Wissenschaftlicher Vlg, 2000, has articles on German, English, American, and Italian literature, and includes C. Liebrand, 'Punschrausch und *paradis artificiels*: E. T. A. Hoffmanns *Der goldene Topf* als romantisches Kunstmärchen' (33–50), who first sets out the problematic nature of the supposed dichotomy of the Volksmärchen/Kunstmärchen in 18th and 19th-c. Germany in order to show that H.'s story is a self-conscious romanticizing of the world which subverts the distinction between natural and artistic/ artificial, and between conscious and unconscious processes; F. Vonessen, 'Zwei Philosophien der Sprache: von Hamann und Herder zu Schelling und Jacob Grimm' (105–18), explaining the rejection of Herder's linguistic theory (reason creates language) by Hamann (language must precede reason), following the dispute historically through Schelling, who in 1861 suggested a new essay competition to recapitulate Herder's prize winner, and Jacob Grimm. Vonessen ends by agreeing with Heidegger that 'Die Sprache ist das Haus des Seins'; C. Karpenstein-Essbach, 'Romantische Ironie und das Denken der Marktwirtschaft' (167–80) taking an ironic look at Romantic irony, the phenomenon of modernity which Carl Schmitt and Georg Lukács failed to appreciate in the earlier part of the 20th c. Along the way she presents the (not quite convincing) comparison of Romantic irony with the economic marketplace.

Thomas Böning, *Alterität und Identität in literarischen Texten von Rousseau & Goethe bis Celan & Handke* (Rombach Wissenschaften: Reihe Litterae, 83), Freiburg, Rombach, 368 pp., explores the relationship between the Other and constructions of subjectivity. Focusing almost exclusively on theoretical issues, only two texts — F. Schlegel's *Lucinde* and Kleist's *Marquise von O . . .* — are discussed at any length. Silvio Vietta, *Ästhetik der Moderne. Literatur und Bild*, Munich, Fink, 317 pp., sets out to define the character of aesthetic theories in the modern era, and notes the particular significance of those current around 1800 to an understanding of contemporary developments. One chapter is devoted exclusively to a discussion of Romantic aesthetics (with a particular emphasis on Novalis and Caspar David Friedrich). Harm-Peer Zimmermann, *Ästhetische Aufklärung. Zur Revision der Romantik in volkskundlicher Absicht*, Würzburg,

Königshausen & Neumann, 647 pp., is an attempt to view Romanticism within the context of contemporary 'Alltagskultur' as a form of aesthetic Enlightenment. The first part of the book examines the philosophical underpinning of such a reading, whilst in the second part Adam Müller's theoretical writings are considered as precursors of modernist texts.

Katrin Seebacher, *Poetische Selbstverdammnis. Romantikkritik der Romantik* (Rombach Wissenschaften: Reihe Cultura, 13), Freiburg, Rombach, 2000, 285 pp., is a fascinating study. Building on Walter Benjamin's interpretation of the Romantic concept of art, S. suggests that Romantic literary criticism should not be seen as something separate from Romantic literature, and argues that an imminent critique of many Romantic works is already present within the work itself. Accordingly, such a critique should not be seen as a judgement of literary quality, but rather as an extended reflection on the nature of the Romantic project. To be a Romantic artist is to engage critically with the product of artistic creativity. Central to S.'s study is an analysis of Tieck's novel *Titan*; works by E. T. A. Hoffmann and Jean Paul are also considered.

Lothar Pikulik, *Signatur der Zeitenwende: Studien zur Literatur der frühen Moderne von Lessing bis Eichendorff*, Göttingen, Vandenhoeck & Ruprecht, 222 pp., contains a collection of essays spanning 25 years in which P. puts forward various texts from the Classical and Romantic eras as precursors of a literary modernism. Central to almost all of the essays is the concept of 'Schwellenüberschreitung'.

H. Börsch-Supan, 'Die romantische Strömung in der Berliner Kunst', *Schriften der Internationalen Arnim-Gesellschaft*, 3:97–122, explores the influence of Romantic ideas on the circle of writers and artists in Berlin with a view to identifying the defining characteristics of Berlin Romanticism. Among others, the architect, Karl Friedrich Schinkel, and the painter, Carl Blechen, are singled out for special consideration, and B.-S. argues that both were anxious to make good the keenly felt deficiencies of Berlin as a cultural milieu. The article contains some 13 illustrations. H. Kurzke, 'Romantik und Konservatismus', *Aurora*, 61:55–66, considers Romanticism and conservative political ideology as two types of 'traditionalism' in which religion plays a crucial role. Also noted: R. Fischer, *'Recht, Poesie, Geschichte — Friedrich Carl von Savigny und der Kreis der Marburger Romantiker', *ib.*, 67–82; U. Hentschel, *'Reisen in die Schweiz und ihre literarischen Grundlagen 1815–1840', *ib.*, 119–38.

THEMES. Paul Schulte, *Solgers Schönheitslehre im Zusammenhang des Deutschen Idealismus*, Kassel U.P., 371 pp., seeks to analyse the essential nature of beauty as defined by Kant, Schiller, Wilhelm von Humboldt, Schelling, Solger, Schleiermacher, and Hegel by drawing attention to similarities and differences in the theories of these writers. Although Solger's concept of beauty is the focal point of S.'s treatment, he offers a detailed overview of the development of theories of beauty from the time of the Enlightenment to the publication of Hegel's *Vorlesungen über die Ästhetik*.

Stephan K. Schindler, *Eingebildete Körper. Phantasierte Sexualität der Goethezeit* (Stauffenburg Colloquim, 49), Tübingen, Stauffenburg, 222 pp., traces the operation of specific discourses of sexuality in a variety of literary figures, ranging from Goethe's Werther to E. T. A. Hoffmann's often unstable Romantic protagonists, and concludes that although in the wake of 'Empfindsamkeit' spiritual love has replaced physical love, the female body (whether real or imaginary) remains the object of male desire. Ultimately the male subject is plunged into a hallucinatory vision of auto-eroticism.

Das Denken der Sprache und die Performanz des Literarischen um 1800, ed. Stephan Jaeger and Stefan Willer (Stiftung für Romantikforschung, 11), Würzburg, Königshausen & Neumann, 2000, 256 pp., is a collection of deconstructive readings of mostly German texts. The editors set the context with their introductory chapter, 'Einleitung. Das Denken der Sprache und die Performanz des Literarischen um 1800' (7–30). Thinking *about* language is always also thinking *in* language, they state, and thus they bring together linguistic theory and actual linguistic performance in literary works. Linguistic theory and literary texts around 1800 also tended to be cross-referential, and the connections continue to be found today in the works of writers such as Jacques Derrida and Judith Butler. S. Metzger, ' "schroffabbrechend". Vom poetischen Skalpell und der Denkform der Konjektur am Beispiel Hölderlins', *ib.*, 31–54, discusses conjectural thinking in Herder, Friedrich Schlegel, and Hölderlin. The concept of organicism brings together biology and poetry, not by making them the same, but because both discourses exhibit disruptions, disturbances and denials. R. André, 'Hölderlins Auf-Gabe und die Ode Blödigkeit', *ib.*, 55–74, gives a close, deconstructive reading of Hölderlin's ode, which sees the poem as a gift. T. Schultz, 'Der "papierne Kitt" und der "zarte Schmelz". Eine Opposition im Zeichen der Null', *ib.*, 75–94, speaks of 'representation' in both political and poetic senses of the word, and comes to the conclusion that Novalis's politics are not so conservative after all. A. Klawitter, 'Eisenfeile. Das Fragment als symbolische Form', *ib.*, 131–50, discusses the fragments of Novalis and Friedrich Schlegel, which deconstruct language. A. von Kempen, 'Eiserne Hand und Klumpfuß. Die forensische Rede in den Fällen Götz und Adam', *ib.*, 151–70, compares Goethe's Götz and Kleist's Adam, both of whom show the impossibility of ending the (legal) 'Prozeß' or of judging truth. R. Petzoldt, 'Das Spiel spielt sich selbst. Ludwig Tiecks verkehrte Welt', *ib.*, 171–90, deconstructs the 'play within the play' of German Romantic comedy. S. Jaeger, 'Das Rauschen der Blätter. Die Vollführung lyrischen Ausdrucks in der deutschen und englischen Romantik (Eichendorff, Brentano, Shelley)', *ib.*, 191–212, reads poems of the German Spätromantik alongside the English High Romantic poet Shelley as self-reflexive expressions of the attempt to find both the origins of language in general as well as the origins of the particular poem. D. Kremer, 'Fenster', *ib.*, 213–28, studies the motif of the window in Tieck, Hoffmann, and Arnim, which ranges from narcissism to voyeurism and which manifests the Romantic distance from realistic referentiality. K. van Eikels, 'Zwei Monologe. Die Poetik der sprechenden Sprache bei Heidegger und Novalis', *ib.*, 229–44, ends the volume in a kind of general survey in answer to the question raised in the introduction: the relationship of thought to language, dealt with here specifically with reference to Heidegger and Novalis.

Die Stadt in der europäischen Romantik, ed. Gerhart von Graevenitz (Stiftung für Romantikforschung, 11), Würzburg, Königshausen & Neumann, 2000, 287 pp., is not purely literary in its coverage, and includes C. Zimmermann, 'Raum in Bewegung — Bewegung im Raum. Beispiele aus London, Paris und Hamburg' (17–32), a demographic account which includes several contemporary descriptions of various European cities; R. Schlögl, 'Romantische Frömmigkeit der katholischen Stadtbürger' (33–54), taking an historical approach to Romantic religiosity, focusing on programmatic writing, letters, and sketches (rather than poetry) and then moves on to study testaments, obituaries, and inventories of personal book collections; U. Frevert, 'Stadtwahrnehmungen romantischer Intellektueller in Deutschland' (55–78), covering a wide range of city descriptions from approximately 1790–1840, taking brief, casual references from letters rather than aestheticised accounts or descriptions as her source, although she does focus on the writings of intellectuals. She discusses the city as 'mobility' and as 'the locus of experience', as a place distinct from the country. City living had different implications for women than for men, and in the Romantic city the beginnings of modernity can be found; U. Landfester, 'Um die Ecke gebrochen. Kunst, Kriminalliteratur, und Großstadttopographie in E. T. A. Hoffmanns Erzählung *Das Fräulein von Scuderi*' (109–26), which takes the story as an early example of the close link of a particular city with the detective novel, similar to Holmes in Baker Street and Lord Peter Wimsey in Picadilly Circus, London; K. Stierle, 'Progressive Universalpoesie und progressive Universalstadt. Friedrich Schlegel und Victor Hugo' (183–94), which ties in F. Schlegel's theory, A. W.

Schlegel's popularization of it, and Hugo's *Notre Dame de Paris*; H. Brüggemann, 'Luftbilder eines kleinstädtischen Jahrhunderts. Ekstase und imaginäre Topographie in Jean Paul' (127–82).

W. Schlink, 'Heilsgeschichte in der Malerei der Nazarener', *Aurora*, 61:97–118, contains six illustrations which are used to explore the iconographic tradition of the Nazarene group of Romantic painters. C. J. Minter, ' "Die Macht der dunklen Ideen": a Leibnizian theme in German psychology and fiction between the late Enlightenment and Romanticism', *GLL*, 54:114–36, examines Tieck's *William Lovell* and Jean Paul's *Titan* in the light of the theory of obscure perceptions at the turn of the 19th c. S. Eickenrodt, 'Ungeheure Sympathie', *JFG*, 2000:87–105, analyses the transformation of the ideal of friendship during the Romantic period. Together with a number of theoretical essays on the nature of friendship by Schleiermacher, Kant, Adam Smith, E. also analyses Tieck's novellas *Der Runenberg* and *Die Freunde*. Tieck is seen as celebrating the friendship of two individuals not in terms of a bond of virtue between two people, but rather in terms of a Romantic version of the 'Eucharist'. R. Borgards and H. Neumeyer, 'Der Mensch in der Nacht — die Nacht im Menschen. Aufgeklärte Wissenschaften und romantische Literatur', *Athenäum*, 11:13–39, explores the motif of 'die Nacht' and draws parallels with selected works of the German, English, and French Romantics; M. Bergengruen, ' "Anliegen unserer Leiber." Friedrich Heinrich Jacobi und der formative Widerspruch', *ib.*, 41–58, analyses Jacobi's philosphical views as reflected in his dialogues. B. explores three forms of dialogue: verbal exchanges (as with Lessing), written exchanges (as with Mendelssohn), or the fictional exchanges of Jacobi. H.-G. von Arburg, 'Gotthilf Schuberts *Die Kirche und die Götter* (1804) — ein frühromantischer Roman in literatur- und medizinhistorischer Sicht', *ib.*, 93–121, examines the reciprocal influence of theories of medicine and aesthetics. Also noted: W. Wiethölter, *'Ursprünglicher Gedanken — Wiederholung. Zum Phänomen frühromantischer Zyklik', *DVLG*, 75:587–656.

GENRES. *Mein Herz war ganz erfüllt. Romantische Reisebriefe*, ed. Gisela Henckmann, 2 vols, Berlin, Aufbau, 264, 334 pp., is a wide-ranging selection of letters by all the prominent Romantic authors (both male and female) and is divided up on geographical lines, each letter accompanied by colour reproductions of works of art by German Romantic painters. The result is a kaleidoscopic collection of Romantic travel writing, the first of its kind in this form. Two beautifully prepared volumes with illustrations that perfectly complement the selection of texts.

Gedichte der Romantik, ed. Wolfgang Frühwald, Stuttgart, Reclam, 532 pp., is an extensive collection which has the merit of incorporating a number of poems by women writers of the Romantic period (Dorothea Schlegel, Sophie Mereau-Brentano, Karoline von Günderode, Helmina von Chézy, Bettine von Arnim, und Luise Hensel) in the Romantic poetic canon. Also noted: **Fünfzig Gedichte der Romantik*, ed. Dietrich Bode, Stuttgart, Reclam, 85 pp.

2. INDIVIDUAL AUTHORS

ARNIM, BETTINE VON. Lisabeth M. Hock, *Replicas of a Female Prometheus. The Textual Personae of Bettina von Arnim* (NASNCGL, 27), xx + 260 pp., is a study of the development of the 'Bettine-personality' in A.'s six major works. Drawing on feminist theories of positionality, H. relates this development both to the real-life personality of the author and the development of her ideas on gender and politics.

ARNIM, L. A. VON. K. Peter, 'Deutschland in Not: Fichtes und Arnims Appelle zur Rettung des Vaterlandes', *Schriften der Internationalen Arnim-Gesellschaft*, 3 : 3–22, offers a clear outline of the political context of Berlin Romanticism. In addition, P. analyses F.'s *Reden an die deutsche Nation* in detail, and underlines the extent to which A. was influenced by Fichte. Taking Arnim's novel *Armut, Reichtum, Schuld und Sühne der Gräfin Dolores* as an example, P. demonstrates a number of parallels between the thought of F. and A., especially in respect of their attitudes towards, Jews, education, marriage, and morality in general. However, A. emerges not as a straightforward imitator of F., but rather as an independent author in his own right who shares the same ideals of German nationalism. K. Feilchenfeldt, 'Arnim und Varnhagen: literarisch-publizistische Partnerschaft und Rivalität im Kampf um die "deutsche Nation" 1806–1814', *ib.*, 23–39, explores the private and professional relationship between A. and V. F. also comments on their reactions to and reviews of each other's works. Ultimately F. concludes that the two authors are 'auf widerspruchs-volle Weise miteinander verbunden'. J. Knaack, 'Achim von Arnim, der Preußische Correspondent und die Spenersche Zeitung in den Jahren 1813 und 1814', *ib.*, 41–51, describes Arnim's work for the above newspaper and considers such aspects as the newspaper's statistics, the dates and forms of publication, the aims of the editors, the newspaper's commentary on, and representation of, contemporary events, as well as the shifts in the paper's ideological positioning as seen against a background of contemporary political developments. U. Landfester, 'Die Kronenwächterin: Ludwig von Arnim und Bettine von Arnims politisches Werk', *ib.*, 53–70, approaches the two writers' collaborative projects independently of their private relationship as married partners. H. Baumgart, 'Arnims "Judengeschichte": eine biographische Rekonstruktion', *ib.*, 71–94, explores an event in A.'s early life when Moritz Izig, who felt insulted as a result of A's anti-Jewish remarks, succeeded in getting the not altogether blameless A. involved in a scandal that ended in a challenge to a duel, a bout of fisticuffs and, ultimately, a court case. B. notes that the episode is alluded to in A.'s *Die Versöhnung in der Sommerfrische*. R. Paulin, 'Arnim und Tieck', *ib.*, 171–79, notes that although A. and T. have a number of biographical features in common, their correspondence and literary works confirm that they have very different views on a variety of issues, but most notably on social-political matters, where T. is revealed to be a profound sceptic. H. Schwinn, 'Paralleltexte: zu den kleinen Arbeiten Arnims und Brentanos 1810/11', *ib.*, 201–21, discusses the shorter writings of the two authors and emphasizes that each of these texts can only be interpreted with reference to its *Gegentext*.

Sheila Dickson, 'The body — some body — any body: Achim von Arnim and the Romantic chameleon', *GQ*, 74:296–307, investigates the influence of A.'s views on Romantic theories of science and perception on the presentation of the body (and above all on the presentation of the interaction of 'Körper' and 'Geist') in his short prose fiction.

BRENTANO, CLEMENS. K. Hasenpflug, 'Fraternale Kunstproduktion und romantische Kunstkritik: Clemens Brentanos Gedicht *O wie so oft*', *Schriften der Internationalen Arnim-Gesellschaft*, 3:183–99, discusses the genesis, intertextual structure, and interpretation of the above poem. Stefan Hoffmann, 'Brentano mit McLuhan. Über die romantische Aufhebung unreiner Medien. Eschatologische Strukturen in der Medientheorie', *Athenäum*, 11:123–38, explores the eschatological implications of the dialectical relationship between 'Unifizierung und Differenzierung' in Romantic and 20th-c. theories of communication.

DE LA MOTTE FOUQUÉ, FRIEDRICH. W. G. Schmidt, 'Der ungenannte Quellentext. Zur Wirkung von Fouqués *Held des Nordens* auf Wagners *Ring*-Tetralogie', *Athenäum*, 11:159–91, argues that W.'s *Ring* is based on F.'s novel although the composer never actually cites it directly as a source. E. Müller-Adams, 'Die Fremdheit des Weiblichen', *JFG*, 2000:43–60, interprets Undine as the archetype of the threatening 'Wasserfrau', linking it in the process to other literary figures such as Lorelei, Melusine, and the Sirens.

EICHENDORFF, JOSEPH VON. Ursula Regener, *Formelsuche. Studien zu Eichendorffs lyrischem Frühwerk* (UDL, 110), 192 pp., offers a chronological analysis of E.'s early poetry and, with reference to the author's biography, identifies a number of stages of development spanning an early engagement with existing models of poetic form, a lyrical treatment of adolescent crises, the development of a quasi-religious poetic which culminates in a poetics of 'Unbehagen' that points towards an aesthetic of modernity. *Joseph von Eichendorff. Fünfzig Gedichte*, ed. Hartwig Schultz, Stuttgart, Reclam, 77 pp., is an anthology which includes some of the author's lesser known poems.

Joseph von Eichendorff. Aus dem Leben eines Taugenichts: Lektüreschlüssel, ed. Theodor Pelster, Stuttgart, Reclam, 87 pp., is a handy reference including a brief biography and an interpretation of the work.

Joseph von Eichendorff, *Sämtliche Werke* — Historisch kritische Ausgabe, Vol. IV: *Dichter und ihre Gesellen*, ed. Volkmar Stein, Tübingen, Niemeyer, xi + 607 pp., which follows the orthography of the original first edition published by Duncker und Humblot in 1834 in Berlin. This excellent volume is completed by an extensive collection of notes as well as a comprehensive critical apparatus, and as such, represents an indispensable tool for Eichendorff-scholars.

S. von Steinsdorff, 'Eichendorff und die Romantik in Berlin 1809/ 1810', *Schriften der Internationalen Arnim-Gesellschaft*, 3 : 153–69, offers a chronologically structured account of E.'s sojourn in Berlin and his experiences there, beginning with his arrival in the city, his meeting with Arnim and Brentano, and ending with E.'s written account of his reactions to his stay there. J. Osinski, 'Eichendorffs Kulturkritik', *Aurora*, 61 : 83–96, interprets E.'s nationalism as a blend of cosmopolitanism and German melancholy, whilst at the same time viewing it as a critique of French culture.

GRIMM, JACOB AND WILHELM. *Brüder Grimm Gedenken*, 14, is divided into three sections: a history of the beginnings of *Germanistik* in Switzerland and the influence of the Grimm brothers; research into the Grimms' library; and a study of the selected correspondence of the two brothers. It contains: S. Sonderegger, 'Jacob Grimm und die Frühgeschichte der Germanistik in der Schweiz' (1–45), outlining the chronological development of Swiss *Germanistik* from its beginnings at the time of the Reformation up to the founding of the University of Zurich in 1833, and emphasizing the influential role of the brothers G. who corresponded with all the leading scholars of the day; F. Hinze, 'Die Benutzung einiger lituanistischer Werke durch Jacob Grimm' (89–101), drawing attention to Jacob G.'s interest in the languages and culture of the Baltic regions; U. Schröter, 'Zur Geschichte der Germanistik im 19. Jahrhundert am Beispiel des Briefwechsels zwischen Rudolf von Raumer und Jacob und Wilhelm Grimm' (161–75), discussing the correspondence between R. and the brothers G., in which a number of linguistic issues — in particular matters relating to the *Deutsches Wörterbuch* (1838) — feature prominently; H. Fiedler-Rauer, 'Zwei Bittschriften Alexander Vollmers an

Jacob Grimm und König Maximilian II von Bayern' (176–90), discussing those letters in which the impoverished V. appears in a somewhat idiosyncratic light, but is nonetheless presented as a conscientious scholar; A. McTigue, 'Die "Kinder- und Hausmärchen" der Brüder Grimm in irisch-gälischer Übersetzung' (191–214), drawing attention to the fact that even as early as the late 18th c. there was an interest in preserving the Gaelic language, a tendency which is also evident somewhat later in the works of the brothers G. The article also contains a chronological list of the 'Kinder- und Hausmärchen' that have been translated into Irish Gaelic.

HEBEL, JOHANN PETER. *Johann Peter Hebel*, ed. Heinz Ludwig Arnold (Text und Kritik, 151), Munich, Text + Kritik, 109 pp., contains the following: J. Knopf, ' ". . . und hat das Ende der Erde nicht gesehen." Heimat, die Welt umspannend — Hebel, der Kosmopolit' (3–10), drawing on the author's observations on astronomy, Jews, and the concept of 'Heimat', as well as on his literary works, in order to present a picture of H. as a convinced humanist and cosmopolitan thinker; G. Bevilacqua, ' ". . . wie sind die Worte richtig gesetzt." Zwei unveröffentlichte Hebel-Kommentare Ernst Blochs' (11–22), containing transcriptions of two hitherto unpublished commentaries by B. first broadcast by the Südwestfunk in 1969, and dealing with two of H.'s 'Kalendergeschichten'. B. notes a number of stylistic parallels in the writing of both Bloch and H.; Y.-G. Mix, 'Mediale und narrative Interdependenz. Zur Raum- und Zeitsemantik in Johann Peter Hebels Kalendertexten' (23–31), drawing attention to the way in which scholars have all too often ignored the social, religious, and cultural resonances of the period in which H.'s 'Kalendergeschichten' were written; C. Pietzcker, 'Wie der HebelFrieder und der ZundelPeter dem Consistorio auf ein Kurzes entwichen und dem geneigten Leser den Boden unter den Füßen wegstahlen. Eine literarische Lumpengeschichte' (32–46), exploring the literary devices H. deploys in order to elicit the reader's sympathy for the fictional thieves and rogues depicted in his works; A. Geisenhanslüke, 'Barocke Aufklärung. Tod und Vergänglichkeit in Hebels "Alemannischen Gedichten" und "Kalendergeschichten" ' (47–60), exploring the extent to which H.'s representations of death are a blend of Baroque and Enlightenment models in so far as at times death appears as an allegorical figure, whilst at others, remembrance and the overcoming of death are closely linked; A. Stadler, ' "Und wemme nootno gar zweytusig zehlt, isch alles z'semme g'keit." Zu einem Vers aus Peter Hebels Gedicht *Die Vergänglichkeit* im Jahre 2001' (61–68), reproducing H.'s poem — which is written in allemanisch — and is followed by an essay setting the work in its social and political context; J. A. Steiger, ' "... und fällt deswegen auch in Gottes Sprache." ' Johann Peter Hebels Kalendererzählung *Baumzucht* als Beispiel biblischer Volksaufklärung' (69–81), examining the influence of biblical models on the language of H.'s texts. S. traces the presence not only of direct allusions to the Bible (especially when the narrator comments on the events of the story), and argues that, in addition, H. succeeds in capturing something of the discursive style of the Lutheran Bible; R. Gillett, 'Hebel der Briefeschreiber. Prolegomena' (82–95), which begins with an outline of the history of the publication of H.'s letters, and ends by suggesting that, having been largely ignored by scholars to date, H.'s correspondence merits further scrutiny.

HOFFMANN, E. T. A. Dirk Baldes, *Das tolle Durcheinander der Namen: Zur Namengebung bei E. T. A. Hoffmann* (SBL, 72), 205 pp., interprets the names H. gives his characters as symbolizing the 'Prinzip der Mehrdeutigkeit' in his *œuvre*. In both the fairy tales and in *Die Elixiere des Teufels*, the fact that the same characters are often referred to by different names is a deliberate stylistic device on H.'s part designed to remind the reader of the inherent instability of personal identity. Aurélie Hädrich, *Die Anthropologie E. T. A. Hoffmanns und ihre Rezeption in der europäischen Literatur im 19. Jahrhundert*, (EH, 1, 1802), 501 pp., is a very wide-ranging study that seeks to offer an explanation of the reasons for H.'s extraordinary success in the 19th and 20th cs in Europe (and, above all, in France). Hädrich concludes that it is the multiplicity of levels of meaning and H.'s 'Verschlüsselungssymbolik' that has made his works into forerunners of European literary modernism. Henriett Lindner, *"Schnöde Kunststücke gefallener Geister." E. T. A. Hoffmanns Werk im Kontext der zeitgenössischen Seelenkunde* (Würzburger Wissenschaftliche Schriften, 367), Würzburg, Königshausen & Neumann, 352 pp., draws on writings by Herder, Schubert, Mesmer, as well as on contemporary treatises on psychology and psychiatry, and argues that H.'s *œuvre* should be seen as situated on the border of psychology, therapy (*Seelenkunde*), and literature. H.'s deep knowledge and continual interest in theories of madness prompted him to offer a literary treatment of such a theme, whereby, with no little irony, individual madness serves as an example of the collective insanity of society as a whole.

E. T. A. Hoffmann. *Das Fräulein von Scuderi*, with a commentary by Barbara von Korff-Schmising (BasisBibliothek, 22), Frankfurt, Suhrkamp, 149 pp., is a new edition of the novella which offers a great deal of background material relating to the genesis and reception of the story, as well as to interpretative approaches both in film and in critical literature. There is also a useful index.

H. Steinecke, '"Frohe Aspecten zur literarischen Laufbahn?"' E. T. A. Hoffmann in Plock 1802–04', *E. T. A. Hoffmann-Jahrbuch*, 9:7–21, concludes that even in Plock H. had begun to develop a literary style of his own. I. Schroeder, 'Das innere Bild und seine Gestaltung. Die Erzählung *Der Sandmann* als Theorie und Praxis des Erzählens', *ib.*, 22–33, interprets the 'Parallelität' of narrator and protagonist as a narrative device enabling the reader to gain access to both the 'innere' and 'äußere Welt'. M. Rohde, 'Zum kritischen Polenbild in E. T. A. Hoffmanns *Das Gelübde*', *ib.*, 34–41, explores the representation of Poland in *Das Gelübde* and concludes that H. offers a much more critical view of Poland than critics have acknowledged hitherto. R. Perlwitz, 'Signifikante Mittelaltererfindung in E. T. A. Hoffmanns *Der Kampf der Sänger*', *ib.*, 42–54, draws attention to anachronistic elements in H.'s representation of the Middle Ages and argues that for H. the Middle Ages is not to be seen as a utopian realm to be rediscovered in a Romantic sense but rather as an idealized age now lying irrevocably in the past. G. Sasse, 'Die Karnevalisierung der Wirklichkeit. Vom "chronischen Dualismus" zur "Duplizität des irdischen Seins" in E. T. A. Hoffmanns *Prinzessin Brambilla*', *ib.*, 55–69, interprets the love relationship between Giacinta/Brambilla and Giglio/Chiapperi as a symbol of H.'s view that the world is a blend of fantasy and reality. J. Gunia and D. Kramer, 'Fenster-Theater. Teichoskopie, Theatralität und Ekphrasis im Drama um 1800 und in E. T. A. Hoffmanns *Des Vetters Eckfenster*', *ib.*, 70–80, draws attention to the way in which H. makes use of especially striking visual means in order to shape the unrelated scenes on the marketplace to a coherent whole, as well as to the extent to which, in this respect, he is indebted to Hogarth und Chodowiecki's series of engravings. J. Petzel, 'Ritter und Bürger oder einige Gedanken zur Dürer-Rezeption von Fouqué und E. T. A. Hoffmann', *ib.*, 81–90, compares the representation of Dürer in the works of both authors and concludes that in H.'s work, Dürer represents a mediator between the nobility and 'Bürgertum' whose art has its roots in the ordinary people (Volk). M. Orosz, '"Das verworrene Gemisch fremdartiger Stoffe." Intertextualität und Authenzität bei E. T. A. Hoffmann', *ib.*, 91–124, examines a broad range of H.'s literary works and concludes that H.'s narrative technique involves the inclusion and parody of intertextual elements drawn from his own and other literary works. O. argues that whilst H.'s work remains rooted in the Romantic aesthetic, it none the less anticipates the aesthetics of postmodernism. C. Caduff, 'Die Kunst-Paare "Maler-Modell" und "Komponist-Sängerin" in literarischen Texten der Romantik und der Gegenwart', *ib.*, 125–48, analyses the relationship between the (female) muse and (male) artist in, amongst others, a number of H.'s stories. C. notes that whereas in Romantic literature woman is transformed from an object of physical attraction into an aesthetic figure, in modern literature the reverse is the case: the artistic Ideal is reduced to the status of a sexual object.

B. Röder, ' "Ich sah aus tiefer Nacht feurige Dämonen ihre glühenden Krallen ausstrecken." The problem of the Romantic ideal in E. T. A. Hoffmann's *Don Juan*', *ColGer*, 34:1–14, offers a new interpretation of this story whereby 'der kluge Mann' emerges as the critic of an unbridled Romanticism that renders the realization of art in the material world impossible — a position that H. ultimately rejects. W. Crisman, 'The noncourtship in E. T. A. Hoffmann's *Der Sandmann*', *ib.*, 15–26, offers a psychoanalytic reading of the novella in which he highlights what he regards as Clara's destructive influence on Nathanael's development and argues that she represents a partial and unsuccessful substitution for the mother.

C. Caduff, 'Das Landschaftsbild und die Instrumentalmusik', *GRM*, 50:399–413, argues that the surge in interest in both landscape painting and instrumental music that took place in both genres towards the end of the 18th c. constitutes an attempt to articulate the ineffable. C. draws a comparison between Diderot's descriptions of Vernet's salon paintings and H.'s commentaries on Beethoven's instrumental music, and notes that both authors arrive at, and try to overcome, the discursive limits of art and music criticism.

HÖLDERLIN, F. H. Beatrix Langner, *Hölderlin und Diotima*, Frank-furt–Leipzig, Insel, 228 pp., is a poetic treatment — though one based on extensive research — of the precarious love relationship between H. und Suzette Gontard, the model for the figure of Diotima in *Hyperion*. S. Bernofsky, 'Hölderlin as translator: the perils of interpretation', *GR*, 76:215–33, examines the ways in which H.'s *modus operandi* as a translator (above all in his engagement with the text of Sophocles's *Oedipus Tyrannus*) reflects the poet's more general concern with questions of interpretation and semantic mediation. K. Barkemeyer, 'Listening to the voice of/as the other: Friedrich Hölderlin and the deconstruction of the "German Nation" ', *ib.*, 234–53, investigates instances of alterity in H.'s presentation of 'Gesang' in the hymn *Der Mutter Erde*.

KLEIST. Seán Allan, *The Stories of Heinrich von Kleist. Fictions of Security*, NY, Camden House, xii + 243 pp., explores the way in which the ideological interests of a male aristocratic élite lie thinly concealed behind the metaphysical concepts that underpin the worlds in which the novellas take place. Moreover, it is precisely this over-reliance on such allegedly 'transcendent' notions that constitutes an obstacle to genuine human progress. *Heinrich von Kleist. Leben und Werk im Bild*, ed. Eberhard Siebert, Frankfurt, Insel, 252 pp., is a welcome supplement to more conventional biographical material and contains an extensive collection of documents and illustrations relating to K.'s life and work. Dirk Grathoff, *Kleist: Geschichte, Politik, Sprache*, Wiesbaden, Westdeutscher Vlg, 2000, 250 pp., is a revised edition of the volume published under the same title in 1999, and contains 16 essays covering aspects of K.'s life and individual works. *Heinrich von Kleist 1777–1811. Chronik seines Lebens und Schaffens*, ed. Wolfgang Barthel, Frankfurt (Oder), Kleist-Gedenk- und Forschungsstätte, 111 pp., is an accessible, concise introduction to K.'s life and works. The volume includes a large number of illustrations. *Heinrich von Kleist 1777–1811. Leben, Werk, Wirkung, Blickpunkte*, ed. Wolfgang Barthel and Hans-Jochen Marquardt, Frankfurt (Oder), Kleist-Gedenk- und Forschungsstätte, 2000, 330 pp., is a lavishly illustrated catalogue of the permanent exhibition at the Kleist museum in Frankfurt (Oder). It begins with a detailed survey of K.'s life, and is followed by a series of essays on the author's literary works, including K.'s use of language, and his political views.

Kätchen und seine Schwestern. Frauenfiguren im Drama um 1800, ed. Günther Emig and Anton Philipp Knittel (Heilbronner Kleist-Kolloquien, 1), Kleist-Archiv Sembdner der Stadt Heilbronn, 2000, 199 pp., includes the following: G.-L. Fink, ' "Das Kätchen von Heilbronn" oder "das Weib, wie es seyn sollte." Ein Rittermärchenspiel' (9–37), discussing K.'s ideal woman as derived from works such as Boccaccio's Griselda and Wilhelmine Karoline von Wobeser's novel *Elisa, oder das Weib, wie es sein soll*; G. Neumann, 'Erkennungsszene und Opferritual in Goethes *Iphigenie* und in Kleists *Penthesilea*' (38–80), bringing together anthropological work on sacrifice (Walter Burkert, Victor Turner) to discuss the two works in the context of their origins in Greek tragedy. Iphigenie and Penthesilea both demonstrate the 'unlivability' of the social order, the former by substituting for it a discourse of humanitarianism, the latter by reverting to barbarism; S. Doering, 'Himmelstochter, Höllenbraut. Bilder des Weiblichen bei Schiller und Kleist' (105–20), which maintains that K. depicts the 'heavenly' qualities in Kätchen as something other-worldly, but that his 'Höllenbraut' character, Kunigunde, is merely humanly evil: unlike Schiller and other contemporaries, K. evidently felt no need to call upon mythological material to depict outrageously evil female characters; I. Kurdi, 'Der Engel, der der Teufel ist. Zum Engel/Teufel-Motif im Werk von Kleist' (121–28), which refers to *Die Marquise von O . . ., Der Findling, Das Kätchen von Heilbronn, Der zerbrochene Krug*, and Lessing's *Nathan der Weise*; G. Brandstetter, ' "Eine Tragödie von der Brust heruntergehustet." Darstellung von Katharsis in Kleists *Penthesilea*' (81–104).

A. Weigel, 'Das imaginäre Theater Heinrich von Kleists. Spiegelungen des zeitgenössischen Theaters im erzählten Dialog *Über das Marionettentheater*', *BKF*, 14:21–114, is a very detailed essay dealing with the relationship between the theatrical landscape of K.'s day, the author's personal background and the publication of the essay *Über das Marionettentheater*. As well as offering a number of insights into the contemporary theatre, the essay explores K.'s criticism of August Wilhelm Iffland in some detail. M. Beckmann, 'Das Geheimnis der "Marquise von O . . ."', *ib.*, 115–54, offers a new interpretation of the novella which emphasises the aesthetic function of the anagrams in the text. M. Bohn, 'Kommunikationsproblematik in Heinrich von Kleists *Die Verlobung in St. Domingo*. Zur Vielfalt der Kommunikationsstörungen', *ib.*, 155–95, explores the problem of communication on a linguistic and non-linguistic level in the story. H. F. Weiss, 'Eine unbekannte Fassung der *Germania-Ode* in Heinrich von Kleists', *ib.*, 97–212, reports on the discovery of a hitherto unknown draft of the *Germania-Ode* in the unpublished correspondence of the Prinzessin von Solms. This version is published for the first time here. E. Siebert, '"Grüne Gläser" und "Gelbsucht". Eine neue Hypothese zu Kleists "Kantkrise"', *ib.*, 213–24, suggests that the text which was responsible for K.'s so-called 'Kant-Krise' was Sebastian Mutschelle's *Versuch einer solchen faßlichen Darstellung der kantischen Philosophie, daß hieraus das Brauchbare und Wichtige derselben für die Welt einleuchten möge*. H. Häker, 'Kleist auf Rügen', *ib.*, 225–34, explores the question of when K. visited the island of Rügen with his sister Ulrike, and suggests a date of 1800. Id., 'Nachrichten vom Offizierscorps der königlichen preussischen Armee von 1806', *ib.*, 235–64, offers a compilation of information relating to the genealogy and ranks of the Prussian army published in 1828. The names of the officers listed are compared with the names that appear in K.'s fictional works. W. Ort, 'Ein intriquer & unruhiger Geist. Auskunft aus Frankfurt (Oder) und Magdeburg über Heinrich Zschokke', *ib.*, 265–72, portrays K.'s close friend in a much more positive light than many previous critics have done hitherto.

B. Fischer, 'Kleist und die Romantik', *Schriften der Internationalen Arnim-Gesellschaft*, 3:135–51, seeks to define K.'s position *vis-à-vis* Romanticism more clearly. To this end F. explores the relationship between K.'s scepticism and his concept of irony. K. emerges as a 'Spielverderber' of Romantic aesthetics since he always places questions of literary 'Praxis' above questions of abstract aesthetics. *Gewagte Experimente und kühne Konstellationen. Kleists Werk zwischen Klassizismus und Romantik*, ed. Christine Lubkoll and Günter Oesterle (Stiftung für Romantikforschung, 12), Würzburg, Königshausen &

Neumann, 333 pp., contains the following contributions: the introduction by C. Lubkoll, G. Oesterle, and S. Waldow sets out the agenda for the volume, namely an exploration of K.'s relationship to the asethetics of German Classicism and Romanticism. This is followed by D. Grathoff, ' "Wenn die Geister des Äschylus, Sophokles und Shakespear sich vereinigten." Antike und Moderne im Werk Heinrich von Kleists' (21–33) who argues that K. regards his reception of classical antiquity as rooted in the Shakespearian tradition, and, as such, far more advanced than that typical of French and German neoclassical authors; W. Hinderer, 'Immanuel Kants Begriff der negativen Grössen, Adam Müllers Lehre vom Gegensatz und Heinrich von Kleists Ästhetik der Negation' (35–62), offering an analysis of *Die Marquise von O . . .* to show how K. develops a negative aesthetics through the use of contradiction — a stylistic tendency that is also discernible in his other works; G. von Graevenitz, 'Die Gewalt des Ähnlichen. Concettismus in Piranesis "Carceri" und in Kleists *Erdbeben in Chili*' (63–92), a very interesting essay comparing P.'s engravings with narrative structures in K.'s work (here G. illustrates his thesis with an extended discussion of *Das Erdbeben in Chili*). As a result of the distortion of space and perspective, the emotions of the reader/spectator oscillate between 'Gefühle des Erhabenen' and 'Gefühle des Entsetzlichen'; G. Neumann, '*Die Verlobung in St. Domingo*. Zum Problem literarischer Mimesis im Werk Heinrich von Kleists' (93–117), who interprets the novella as a love story that is doomed by successive failures of perception, and above all, by a fatal misreading of the revolutionary movement of world history; C. Lubkoll, 'Soziale Experimente und ästhetische Ordnung. Kleists Literaturkonzept im Spannungsfeld von Klassizismus und Romantik (*Die Verlobung in St. Domingo*)' (119–35), concluding that at almost every level, K.'s story confirms the author's radical political and aesthetic scepticism; J. Pfeiffer, 'Die Konstruktion der Geschlechter in Kleists *Penthesilea*' (187–98), analysing gender identity in *Penthesilea* and reading the play as an example of a 'Kulturvernichtungsphantasie größten Ausmaßes'. In P.'s view the Amazon state is not to be seen as an alternative to structures of patriarchal authority since it is, effectively, underpinned by essentially the same type of legal structure; M. Nutz, ' "Erschrecken Sie nicht, es läßt sich lesen." Verstörung und Faszination in Diskurskontexten — zur Rezeptionsgeschichte von Kleists *Penthesilea*' (199–223), offering an overview of contemporary and present-day readings of K.'s play; G. Brandstetter, 'Inszenierte Katharsis in Kleists *Penthesilea*' (225–48), exploring the way in which K. distances himself from classical models of catharsis, and substitutes in its place a version of catharsis consisting of two components; first, an 'inszenierte Katharsis', and second, an 'Affekt des Ekels';

D. Ottmann, ' "Das stumme Zeichen." Zum dramatischen Requisit in Kleists *Prinz Friedrich von Homburg*' (249–76), investigating K.'s use of stage props (notably the glove, the laurel wreath, and the Elector's chain of office) and in particular, the way in which he uses them at times to demonstrate 'die Einheitlichkeit der dargestellten Person', and at others to call that same unity into question.

J. Hibberd, 'Kleist's "Berliner Abendblätter" and the Peninsular War', *GLL*, 54:219–33, describes K.'s attempt to outwit the censor, inform his readers about the course of the struggle against French domination, and argue for an anti-Napoleonic attitude. K. Müller-Salget, 'Heinrich von Kleists Briefwerk. Probleme der Edition eines mehrfach fragmentierten Torsos', Bauer, *Edition*, 115–31, outlines the difficulties inherent in producing an edition of K.'s correspondence given such problems as the uncertainty over the dating of a number of letters, the fact that many are incomplete, that in some cases the original manuscript is missing, as well as the difficulties in ordering the material in the corpus. This is followed by a psychological analysis of K.'s correspondence, above all its egocentric character, which M.-S. interprets as a mechanism for the construction of a sense of personal identity. The essay includes seven reproductions of hand-written extracts from K.'s letters.

NOVALIS. 2001 was the 200th anniversary of Novalis's death and saw the following publications: Winfried Freund, *Novalis* (DTV Portrait), Munich, DTV, 159 pp., a biography containing a large number of contemporary illustrations. Though somewhat compressed, it is clearly written, and represents a good introduction to the life and works of N. Jürgen Daiber, *Experimentalphysik des Geistes. Novalis und das romantische Experiment*, Göttingen, Vandenhoeck & Ruprecht, 330 pp., portrays N. as a literary author who seeks to combine literary and scientific methodology in his work. C. Weder, 'Moral interest and religious truth: on the relationship between morality and religion in Novalis', *GLL*, 54:291–309, refers to N.'s notion of the indirect pursuit of goals and claims that — as in the discourse of the Enlightenment — a close link between morality and religion can be found in N.

RICHTER, JEAN PAUL. Julia Cloot, *Geheime Texte. Jean Paul und die Musik*, Berlin–NY, de Gruyter, 346 pp., analyses the form and function of the descriptions of music in J.P.'s texts. In the first part of her study C. explores questions of musical aesthetics and argues that J.P. had a detailed knowledge of contemporary musical developments. In the second part of her study, particular texts are analysed in terms of musical theory, with the result that she uncovers a series of 'geheime Texte', which might serve as an inspiration for 'erklingende Musik'. Paul Heinemann, *Potenzierte Subjekte — Potenzierte*

Fiktionen. Ich-Figurationen und ästhetische Konstruktionen bei Jean Paul und Samuel Beckett (Saarbrücker Beiträge zur vergleichenden Literatur- und Kulturwissenschaft, 16), Würzburg, Königshausen & Neumann, 422 pp., compares the complex constructions of subjectivity in the work of the two authors. Central to H.'s analysis is the author's sense of self-consciousness, as well as the search for new aesthetic forms in which the resistance of the creative process to closure is reflected.

Jean Pauls Persönlichkeit in Berichten der Zeitgenossen, ed. Eduard Berend, Weimar, Böhlau, xiii + 490 + xvi pp., is an important and wide-ranging collection of eye-witness accounts of encounters with J.P. Though first published in 1956, the volume has been out of print for decades. Numerous entries, detailed notes and a helpful index of names and topics make this an indispensable tool for anyone interested in aspects of J.P.'s biography.

Jahrbuch der Jean Paul Gesellschaft, 35–36, contains, amongst others, the following articles: P. Sprengel, 'Jean Pauls Antiklassizismus — Ein Rezeptionsphänomen?' (33–45), suggesting that we are wrong to see J.P. as an implacable opponent of Neoclassiscism. Neither Goethe nor J.P. himself sees him as such and there are no indications of such an antagonistic position in his work. As a result S. suggests that J.P.'s alleged hostility to Neoclassical aesthetics owes more to subsequent generations of scholars than to the author himself; H. Pfotenhauer, 'Das Leben schreiben — Das Schreiben leben. Jean Paul als Klassiker der Zeitverfallenheit' (46–58), seeing J.P.'s writing as a struggle against the passing of time and death. Exploring a range of works from various early compositions (*Grönländische Prozesse, Über die Schriftstellerei*) to J.P.'s posthumously published work, P. highlights what he terms as the author's obsessive desire to achieve literary immortality, a project in which writing is viewed as a weapon against the transitory nature of human existence; M. Schmitz-Emans, 'Der *Komet* als ästhetische Programmschrift — Poetologische Konzepte, Aporien und ein Sündenbock' (59–92), exploring the representation of Cain in J.P.'s fragmentary novel. In the process S.-E. compares J.P.'s figure with other literary treatments of Cain in the works of Byron, Coleridge, and Erasmus, and relates it to the tradition of the figure of the scapegoat. In J.P.'s work, Cain is, however, viewed more sympathetically, and, on account of his attitude of defiance belongs with such literary figures as Ahasuerus, Prometheus, and Faust; H.-W. Schmidt-Hannisa, '"Der Traum ist unwillkürliche Dichtkunst" — Traumtheorie und Traumaufzeichnung bei Jean Paul' (93–113), which underlines the importance of dreams for an understanding of J.P.'s *œuvre*; however, S.-H. notes that J.P. does not integrate his own dreams directly into his literary works, since he wishes to maintain his position as an autonomous, self-conscious author deliberately shaping his own material; B. Hunfeld, 'Glanz der Unebenheit. Aus Jean Pauls "Arbeitsloge" des *Hesperus*' (151–64) examining the preliminary drafts of J.P.'s *Hesperus* from both a formal and thematic perspective, considers the accompanying notes and drafts as a record of the creative process, that is as a description of the process of 'Entwerfung'; J. Cloot, 'Musikalische Landschaft' (165–88), examining the significance of music in J.P.'s work and concludes that its function is to embody the infinite by finite means. At the same time music is to be seen as a means of extending the action of the story at its climax, and thereby of overcoming the passing of time; E. Dangel-Pelloquin, 'Küsse und Risse: Jean Pauls Osculologie' (189–204), who traces the motif of the kiss in J.P.'s work, and notes that it is not the meeting of the lovers' lips, but rather their parting that is foregrounded. Accordingly, the significance of the kiss is not so much its expedition of plot, but rather the way in which it triggers a process of reflection about a lost state of paridisical innocence; B. Buschendorf, '"Um Ernst, nicht um Spiel wird gespielt." Zur relativen Autonomie des Ästhetischen bei Jean Paul' (218–37), who discusses the extent to which J.P.'s work is rooted in the Romantic tradition insofar as he is an adherent of transcendent metaphysics. At the same time, however, B. argues that J.P. remains critical of such absolute metaphysics, and argues for the close connection between art and social reality, and against the notion of an aesthetic realm wholly divorced from the concerns of the material world; J. Glotz, 'Blicke Jean Pauls auf Schiller' (238–50), focusing on J.P.'s *Vorschule* and considering the extent to which J.P. is influenced by S., as well as the extent to which the classical S. is, in turn, influenced by J.P.'s literary criticism. In spite of a number of clear-cut differences, G. argues that J.P. should not be seen as an opponent of Neoclassicism; S. Eickenrodt, 'Horizontale Himmelfahrt. Die optische Metaphorik der Unsterblichkeit in Jean Pauls *Komet*' (267–92), who analyses the motif of the eye/seeing (Erkennen) and the motif of flying/hovering (Transzendieren) in connection with the theme of immortality in J.P.'s *Komet*; U. Japp, 'Die narrative Instanz des Humoristen in *Dr. Katzenbergers Badereise*' (293–304), who puts forward a number of theories of humour and represents these in a series of quasi-mathematical functions. Also in this volume are J. P. Reemtsma, '*Komet*' (10–31); D. Grünbein, '*Ein sarkastisches Kind*' (32–33); T. Wirtz, 'Konstruiertes Leben. Bayle-Spuren im Werk Jean Pauls' (114–50); B. Sick, 'Jean Pauls unveröffentlichte Satiren- und Ironiehefte (1782–1803)' (205–17); R. Simon, 'Versuch über einige Rahmenbedingungen des literarischen Charakters in Jean Pauls "Flegeljahren"' (251–66); K. Wölfel, 'Schoppe' (305–20).

W. W. Schnabel, 'Erzählerische Willkür oder säkularisiertes Strukturmodell? Jean Pauls "Leben des vergnügten Schulmeisterlein Maria Wutz in Auenthal" und die biographische Form', *Athenäum*, 11:139–58, views *Wutz* as a conventional biographical model which J.P. extends and develops in order to achieve a new and unforeseen aesthetic impact.

SCHLEGEL, AUGUST WILHELM. E. Behler, 'Die frühromantische Sprachtheorie und ihre Auswirkung auf Nietzsche und Foucault', *Athenäum*, 11:193–214, is concerned, above all, with S.'s *Briefe über Poesie, Silbenmaß und Sprache*, in which language does not have a purely descriptive function, but is shown to be intimately bound up with other human discourses. This view of language is exploited by N. and F., who both develop it subsequently into a full-blown philosophical position.

SCHLEGEL, DOROTHEA. Barbara Becker-Cantarino, 'Dorothea Veit-Schlegel als Schriftstellerin und die Berliner Romantik', *Schriften der Internationalen Arnim-Gesellschaft*, 3:123–34, explores V.-S.'s role as a collaborator with, and translator for her husband. The second part of the article offers an interpretation of *Florian* and explores, in particular, V.-S.'s concept of love.

SCHLEGEL, FRIEDRICH. Andreas Barth, *Inverse Verkehrung der Reflexion. Ironische Textverfahren bei Friedrich Schlegel und Novalis* (Neues Forum für allgemeine und vergleichende Literaturwissenschaft, 14), Heidelberg, Winter, 392 pp., is a wide-ranging study that presents a number of interesting insights grouped around three main topics. In the first section, B. retraces the development of the debate concerning 'Selbstbewußtsein' in early Idealistic philosophy from Kant to the 'Wende in der Kunst' in the writings of the early German Romantics. This is followed by an analysis of theoretical writings on Romantic Irony by S. und N., as well as a study of the use of the same in a selection of poetic works. In the final section the material in the first two sections is drawn together and situated within the context of intellectual developments generally and the problem of irony is traced back to sections of Kant's *Kritik der Urteilskraft*.

Birgit Rehme-Iffert, *Skepsis und Enthusiasmus. Friedrich Schlegels philosophischer Grundgedanke zwischen 1796 und 1805*, Würzburg, Königshausen & Neumann, 160 pp., is a fascinating and highly readable study which argues that S.'s writings are not merely an unstructured set of self-contradictory aphorisms, but that there is a structural principle underpinning them that is clearly discernible which R.-I. terms 'Wechselerweis'. This term refers to an authorial attitude located between the extremes of a yearning for the infinite, and a position of scepticism *vis-à-vis* the possibility of attaining such a goal. The book contains a number of diagrams designed to illustrate the formal structures of S.'s writing. M. Chaouli, 'Friedrich Schlegels Labor der Poesie', *Athenäum*, 11:59–70, compares S.'s concept of 'Poesie' with contemporary developments in the natural sciences. B. Frischmann, 'Friedrich Schlegels Platonrezeption und das hermeneutische Paradigma', *ib.*, 71–92, is a critical discussion of S.'s reception of Plato in which the author defends S. against the charge that his interpretation of Plato is ahistorical. On the contrary our view of Plato's philosophy owes much to S.'s reception of the Greek philosopher's work.

TIECK, LUDWIG. Achim Hölter, *Frühe Romantik — frühe Komparatistik: gesammelte Aufsätze zu Ludwig Tieck* (Helicon, 27), Frankfurt, Lang, 239 pp., is a collection of essays by the author spanning some 15 years, which, with the one following exception have already been published in a variety of journals: 'Ludwig Tieck als Komparatist' (231–38), is a very brief article which considers T.'s life and works in order to suggest that he might be seen as a scholar of comparative literature *avant la lettre*. I. Meyer, 'Ludwig Tiecks *Des Lebens Überfluß*: Zur Dekomposition eines narrativen Zeit-Raumes', *Seminar*, 37:189–208, begins her essay with an overview of the critical reception of T.'s novella. Proceeding from an analysis of the work's narrative structures, M. offers her own interpretation, concluding that in it T. not only undermines the notion of the idyll, but also ironises the very genre of the novella itself.

VARNHAGEN, RAHEL LEVIN. *Rahel Levin Varnhagen. Briefwechsel mit Robert Ludwig*, ed. Consolina Vigliero, Munich, Beck, 1014 pp., contains for the first time a complete, critical edition (with commentary) of the correspondence between V. and her brother, the poet and publisher, Robert Ludwig, an edition which is based on the original hand-written manuscripts to be found in the Jagellonian Library in Krakow. The correspondence offers not only a lively picture of contemporary society, but also reveals an intimate and touching relationship between brother and sister. Almost half of the volume is devoted to an extensively researched — and most helpful — critical apparatus. *"Ich will noch leben, wenn man's liest." Journalistische Beiträge aus den Jahren 1812–1829*, ed. Lieselotte Kinshofer (Forschungen zum Junghegelianismus, 5), Frankfurt, Lang, 287 pp., is a collection of all V.'s texts that were published during her lifetime. In addition the volume includes those extracts from her correspondence and diaries that were published by her husband after her death. As well as providing a number of interesting insights into the world of this writer — who emerges as a music and literary critic worthy of some attention — the volume contains a detailed chapter on the sources of V.'s writings and, as such, represents a welcome contribution to Varnhagen-scholarship.

Rahel Levin Varnhagen: Studien zu ihrem Werk im zeitgenössischen Kontext,
ed. Sabina Becker (Saarländische Schriftenreihe zur Frauenforschung, 13), St. Ingbert, Röhrig, 285 pp., contains the following
contributions: S. Becker, 'Gelebte "Universalpoesie": Rahel
Varnhagen und die frühromantische Gesprächs-und Gesellgkeitskul-
tur' (17–51), which analyses V.'s correspondence, and concludes that
her preference for the epistolary genre and other 'fragmentary modes'
of writing underlines her status as a true representative of early
German Romanticism; U. Landfester, 'Durchstreifungen. Die Ordnung des Werks in Rahel Levin Varnhagens Schriften' (53–79), which
identifies 'produktive Durchstreichung' as a key discursive strategy in
V.'s writings, and explores its contribution to constructions of female
subjectivity; D. Barnouw, 'Einzigartig. Rahel Varnhagen und die
deutsch-jüdische Identität um 1800' (81–117), describing the influence on V. of her contemporary social and intellectual environment
(not least the Jewish cultural milieu represented by the salon of
Henriette Herz, as well as the thought of Moses Mendelssohn,
Marcus Herz, Ephraim Veitel, Samuel Levy, and David Friedländer).
Accordingly B. sees V.'s work as a blend of both individual and
collective responses to the events of her time; L. Weissberg, 'Zur
Pathologie des Salons. Regina Frohberg, Rahel Varnhagen, Karl
August Varnhagen und der *Schmerz der Liebe*' (119–61), which begins
with a discussion of the novel *Schmerz der Liebe* by Regina Frohberg
(Rebecca Friedländer), a close friend of V. The novel explores the
difficulties of being both Jewish and a woman, and considers salon
culture not as a social event, but rather as a compensatory mechanism
for dealing with frustrated female sexuality. Accordingly W. argues
that the salon should be seen as a symbol of real and metaphorical
sickness that reflects the oppression of women and Jews; J. A. Kruse,
'Gewonnen und verloren. Rahel Varnhagen und Heinrich Heine'
(163–99), describing the relationship between the 50-year-old V. and
H., who was half V.'s age at the time he made her acquaintance.
Whilst the relationship between the two was hardly conventional, in
K.'s opinion it nonetheless represented a successful German-Jewish
synthesis; J. Eder, 'Rahel Varnhagen und das junge Deutschland'
(201–30), which examines the reception of V. by the writers of
'Junges Deutschland'. Whilst authors such as Börne, Wienbarg,
Mundt, Laube, and Gutzkow recognise V. for the remarkable woman
she was, they do not really engage with her views on various topics
(for example, on the significance of Goethe, on the reception of Saint-
Simonist thought, and, above all, on woman's future role in society);
as a result, they fail to celebrate the worth of V.'s work for their own
and future generations; C. Schulze, ' "Jene urtheilt eigentlich nicht,
sie hat den Gegenstand." Rahel Varnhagens Goethe-Rezeption in

der Interpretation von Käte Hamburger' (231–58), describing the life and work of V. as depicted in the revised edition of Käte Hamburger's essay of 1968. In that essay H. plays down the social ramifications of V.'s Jewish background and attempts, in the spirit of the Enlightenment and Neoclassicism, to engage with V. 'the individual'; K. Feilchenfeldt, 'Weibliche Autorschaft und das Briefgenre. Rahel-Varnhagen-Philologie im Zeichen der Nachlaß-Edition aus dem Krakauer Depot' (259–85), which analyses the correspondence between V. and Pauline Wiesel. In the process F. comes to the conclusion that V.'s reputation as a female author owes less to her having adopted a genuinely feminine discourse, and more to her husband's posthumous editing of her letters. In carefully selecting what to publish and what to omit, V.'s husband contributed greatly to V.'s status as a female writer.

B. Hahn, ' "Eine Impertinenz" ': Rahel Levin liest Achim von Arnim', *Schriften der Internationalen Arnim-Gesellschaft*, 3 : 223–31, examines how Rahel Levin reads *Des Knaben Wunderhorn*, and why she was to refer to this collection as an 'Impertinenz'. In the process Hahn uncovers a series of phallic motifs, as well as traces of an anti-semitic tendency in the collected corpus of lyrics.

WACKENRODER. Alexandra Kertz-Welzel, *Die Transzendenz der Gefühle: Beziehungen zwischen Musik und Gefühl bei Wackenroder/Tieck und die Musikästhetik der Romantik* (SBL, 71), 326 pp., focuses on *Herzensergießungen eines kunstliebenden Klosterbruders* and *Phantasien über die Kunst* in order to explore the reciprocal relationship between music and feeling. In so far as both works emphasize the sensuality of music and its capacity to release ecstatic feelings they are programmatic for the new Romantic aesthetics. There is also a chapter discussing Schopenhauer's reception of the works of the two authors. W. Crisman, 'Which Galatea? Complicating while clarifying Wackenroder's key passage', *GN*, 32 : 148–53, discusses the origins of Christian and pagan images of femininity in W.'s *Herzensergießungen eines kunstliebenden Klosterbruders*.

LITERATURE, 1830–1880

By BARBARA BURNS, *Lecturer in German, University of Strathclyde*

1. GENERAL

REFERENCE WORKS AND GENERAL STUDIES. *Neue deutsche Biographie*, ed. Historische Kommission bei der Bayerischen Akademie der Wissenschaften, Berlin, Duncker & Humblot, has added vol. 20: *Pagenstecher–Püterich*, xvi + 816 pp. The *Österreichisches biographisches Lexikon*, ed. Österreichische Akademie der Wissenschaften, Vienna, has reached vol. 11: *Schwarz–Seidl*, 120 pp. Eda Sagarra, *Germany in the Nineteenth Century. History and Literature*, NY–Washington, Lang, 306 pp., combines a very readable historical account of political, social, and economic developments in Germany with a well-informed overview of literary activity at the time. The volume makes reference to a wide range of both male and female 19th-c. writers, with Fontane and Heine receiving special attention as eloquent commentators on their age. Of particular interest is a chapter on the German book trade and the rising popularity of journals. Volker Meid, **Reclams Lexikon der deutschsprachigen Autoren*, Stuttgart, Reclam, 1007 pp.

THEMES. There is a substantial body of writing on themes relating to women's studies. Jennifer Cizik Marshall, *Betrothal, Violence, and the 'Beloved Sacrifice' in Nineteenth-Century German Literature*, NY–Washington, Lang, 265 pp., is a well-illustrated survey which reflects the discourses of social anthropology and psychoanalysis. After outlining the theoretical basis of her approach, M. examines a selection of works by Storm, Keller, Raabe, Meyer, and Fontane, and discerns a progression from the physical violence against women exemplified in E. T. A. Hoffmann's work and characteristic of the Romantic period to the more subtle, psychological type of violence associated with Realism and typified in the private realm of patriarchal marriage depicted by Fontane. Anja Restenberger, *Effi Briest: Historische Realität und literarische Fiktion in den Werken von Fontane, Spielhagen, Hochhuth, Brückner und Keuler*, Frankfurt–Berlin, Lang, 274 pp., bears witness to the growing interest in recent years in the historical figure of Elisabeth von Ardenne, the story of whose disgrace separately inspired Fontane and Spielhagen to create their respective novels *Effi Briest* and *Zum Zeitvertreib*. Although Restenberger covers familiar ground in her introductory comments on marriage, adultery, and the tradition of the duel in 19th-c. society as well as in her analysis of *Effi Briest*, the central body of her study, which is devoted to Fontane and Spielhagen, offers interesting perspectives on their very different approaches to the same subject matter. A final section on adaptations of the motif by three 20th-c. authors adds a stimulating modern angle. Rita Morrien, *Sinn und Sinnlichkeit. Der weibliche Körper in der deutschen Literatur der Bürgerzeit*, Cologne–Weimar, Böhlau, x + 389 pp., has analyses of works by Keller and Ida Hahn among others. Sigrid Nieberle, *FrauenMusikLiteratur: Deutschsprachige Schriftstellerinnen im 19. Jahrhundert*, Stuttgart–Weimar, Metzler, 267 pp., is a Munich dissertation examining the association between music and female identity in 19th-c. women's writing. The opening chapters position the discussion within the gender studies arena, and address among other things the function of salon culture, the issue of dilettantism and the relationship between music and language. The main body of the volume focuses on musical motifs in selected texts by authors including Bettina von Arnim, Fanny Lewald, Johanna Kinkel, and Marie von Ebner-Eschenbach. L. Tate, 'The culture of literary *Bildung* in the bourgeois women's movement in imperial Germany', *GSR*, 24:267–81.

Eric Downing, *Double Exposures: Repetition and Realism in Nineteenth-Century German Fiction*, Stanford U.P., 2000, ix + 338 pp., is a highly erudite and complex study that engages with the narrative theories of Jacobson and Barthes, Horkheimer and Adorno, and Freud and Lacan in the process of examining the operation of repetition in literary realism. Individual chapters offer close, original readings of Stifter's *Der Hochwald* and the preface to *Bunte Steine*, Keller's *Sieben Legenden*, Storm's *Viola tricolor*, Meyer's *Die Hochzeit des Mönchs*, and Raabe's *Stopfkuchen*. Burghard Damerau, *Gegen den Strich: Aufsätze zur Literatur*, Würzburg, Königshausen & Neumann, 2000, 134 pp., contains chapters on Raabe, Heyse, and C. F. Meyer. Renate Bürner-Kotzam, *Vertraute Gäste — Befremdende Begegnungen in Texten des bürgerlichen Realismus*, Heidelberg, Winter, 237 pp., is a stimulating Berlin dissertation which investigates the role of the guest in Realist texts as messenger, mediator, parasite, detective, or therapist. Following a thorough discussion of the historical and theoretical background, there are individual chapters on Storm's *Immensee* and *Ein Doppelgänger*, Raabe's *Die Innerste*, *Zum Wilden Mann*, and *Unruhige Gäste*, and Stifter's *Zwei Schwestern* and *Der Hagestolz*. Christof Forderer, *Ich-Eklipsen: Doppelgänger in der Literatur seit 1800*, Stuttgart–Weimar, Metzler, 284 pp., is an ambitious study of the *doppelgänger*-motif spanning two centuries and a range of European authors. The focus on German writers largely predates our period, but includes some discussion of Nietzsche's *Die Geburt der Tragödie*. Erich Meuthen, *Eins und doppelt oder Vom Anderssein des Selbst. Struktur und Tradition des deutschen Künstlerromans*, Tübingen, Niemeyer, 343 pp., studies a range of authors from Goethe to Thomas Mann. Two chapters fall into our period: 'Vom doppelten Ursprung der Kunst. Eduard Mörike: *Maler Nolten*' (154–73), and

'Die weiße Wolke — oder: Das Ende der Kunstperiode. Gottfried Keller: *Der grüne Heinrich*' (174–94). Jutta Krienke, *'Liebste Freundin! Ich will dir gleich schreiben . . .'. Zur Ausbildung des unmittelbaren Erzählens am Beispiel der Verwendung des Briefes in der Kinderliteratur des 19. Jahrhunderts (Anna Stein, Elise Averdieck, Ottilie Wildermuth, Tony Schumacher)*, Frankfurt–Berlin, Lang, 309 pp., is a Cologne dissertation. The work contains a substantial first section examining the social and cultural context of the 19th-c. letter form and its use in literature for stylistic and didactic purposes, followed by well-informed analyses of works by eight writers of children's literature in which the letter mode is exploited in various ways. Mererid P. Davies, *The Tale of Bluebeard in German Literature from the Eighteenth Century to the Present*, OUP, 279 pp., claims to be the first monograph in any language on the history of Bluebeard and offers an exposition that is both scholarly and readable. D. traces the shifts in meaning and interest in the Bluebeard tale across two centuries of German literature, presenting the narratives as a seismograph of gender politics and cultural identity. Of particular interest is her examination of Eugenie Marlitt's novella 'Blaubart' (1866), the first German Bluebeard text published by a woman. There is also a comprehensive bibliography and index.

Heinrich Detering, *Herkunftsorte. Literarische Verwandlungen im Werk Storms, Hebbels, Groths, Thomas und Heinrich Manns*, Heide, Boyens, 236 pp., challenges the postmodern notion of the death of the author and analyses the way in which the writers in question drew on their Schleswig-Holstein origins in the creation of literary models. Georg Leisten, **Wiederbelebung und Mortifikation: Bildnisbegegnung und Schriftreflexion als Signaturen neoromantischer Dichtung zwischen Realismus und Fin de Siècle*, Bielefeld, Aisthesis, 2000, 247 pp., is a Tübingen dissertation. Susan Bernstein, **Virtuosity of the Nineteenth Century: Performing Music and Language in Heine, Liszt and Baudelaire*, CUP, 1999, 252 pp.

E. Schwarz, 'Das Bild der Juden in deutschen und französischen Romanen des ausgehenden 19. Jahrhunderts', Goltschnigg, *Literatur*, 92–114. D. Heinze, 'Fremdwahrnehmung und Selbstentwurf: die kulturelle und geschlechtliche Konstruktion des Orients in deutschsprachigen Reiseberichten des 19. Jahrhunderts', pp. 45–91 of *Beschreiben und Erfinden. Figuren des Fremden vom 18. bis zum 20. Jahrhundert*, ed. Karl Hölz, Frankfurt, Lang, 2000, 240 pp. C. Haug, ' "Reiselectüre" — eine populäre Buchreihe des Stuttgarter Verlagskonzerns Adolf Kröner: Reisebibliotheken als buchgeschichtliche Gattung des 19. Jahrhunderts', *Aus dem Antiquariat*, 2000:220–34. Rolf Krauss, **Photographie und Literatur: zur photographischen Wahrnehmung in der deutschsprachigen Literatur des neunzehnten Jahrhunderts*, Ostfildern–Ruit, Cantz, 2000, 172 pp., is a Stuttgart dissertation. Roderich Billermann, **Die 'métaphore' bei Marcel Proust: Ihre Wurzeln bei Novalis,*

Heine und Baudelaire, ihre Theorie und Praxis, Munich, Fink, 2000, 479 pp.
H. Schanze, 'Transformationen der Topik im 19. Jahrhundert:
Novalis, Droysen, Nietzsche, Fontane', pp. 367–75 of *Topik und
Rhetorik: Ein interdisziplinäres Symposium*, ed. Thomas Schirren and Gert
Ueding, Tübingen, Niemeyer, 2000, xxxi + 766 pp. Burkhard
Meyer-Sickendiek, **Die Ästhetik der Epigonalität: Theorie und Praxis
wiederholenden Schreibens im 19. Jahrhundert. Immermann — Keller —
Stifter — Nietzsche*, Tübingen–Basle, Francke, 352 pp., is a Göttingen
dissertation with analysis of Immermann's *Die Epigonen*, Stifter's *Der
Nachsommer*, and Keller's *Der grüne Heinrich. Schmerz in Wissenschaft,
Kunst und Literatur: il dolore nella scienza, arte e letteratura*, ed. Elena
Agazzi, Hürtgenwald, Pressler, 2000, 288 pp., has chapters on
Büchner and Storm. *(K)ein Kanon: 30 Schulklassiker neu gelesen*, ed.
Klaus-Michael Bogdal and Clemens Kammler, Munich, Oldenburg,
2000, 180 pp., includes examinations of Droste-Hülshoff's *Die Juden-
buche*, Fontane's *Effi Briest* and Storm's *Der Schimmelreiter*.

LYRIC. *Landmarks in German Poetry*, ed. Peter Hutchison,
Berne–Oxford, Lang, 2000, 218 pp., has interpretations of 12 major
poems dating from the Middle Ages to the 20th c., and includes T. J.
Reed on Heine's *Deutschland. Ein Wintermärchen* (135–50). Friedrich
Sengle, *Moderne deutsche Lyrik: von Nietzsche bis Enzensberger, 1875–1975*,
Heidelberg, Winter, 414 pp., is a general commentary rather than an
anthology, and has sections on over 50 poets spanning a century of
German lyric. The volume begins towards the end of our period, but
identifies the poetry of Nietzsche as marking a turning point. *Deutsche
Lyrik von den Anfängen bis zur Gegenwart*, ed. Walter Killy et al., 10 vols,
Munich, DTV, 4080 pp., is a reprint of *Epochen der deutschen Lyrik*
which appeared in the 1970s. Of interest for this period is vol. 8,
Gedichte 1830–1900.

NARRATIVE PROSE. *'Realismus'? Zur deutschen Prosa-Literatur des 19.
Jahrhunderts*, ed. Norbert Oellers and Hartmut Steinecke (*ZDP*, 120,
Sonderheft), contains V. C. Dörr, 'Idealistische Wissenschaft. Der
(bürgerliche) Realismus und Gustav Freytags Roman *Die verlorene
Handschrift*' (3–33); V. Nölle, 'Beichten und ihre "Bruchstellen" in
Erzählungen von Grillparzer, Keller und Joseph Roth' (34–53);
M. Lepper, '"[. . .] vor mein inneres Auge drängten abwechselnd
sich zwei öde Orte [. . .]." Gedächtnistopographie bei Theodor
Storm' (54–72); P. C. Pfeiffer, 'Geschlecht, Geschichte, Kreativität:
zu einer neuen Beurteilung der Schriften Marie von Ebner-
Eschenbachs' (73–89); S. Becker, 'Literatur als "Psychographie".
Entwürfe weiblicher Identität in Theodor Fontanes Romanen'
(90–110); C. Blasberg, 'Das Rätsel Gordon oder: warum eine der
"schönen Leichen" in Fontanes Erzählung *Cécile* männlich ist'
(111–27); J. Osborne, 'Theodor Fontanes *Stine* — ein "Schauspiel für

Männer"?' (128–52); R. Zeller, 'Die Moral im "Prachtschmiede der Dichtung". Zu C. F. Meyers *Angela Borgia*' (153–76); H. Ohl, 'Spielhagens Spätwerk und das Fin de Siècle. Figuren und Motive' (177–97); W. Thürmer, 'Die schöne Verwirklichung des Scheins. Zur Abstraktionsdynamik sozio-ökonomischer Prozesse in die poetische Konkretion der Österreich-Novelle *Conte Gasparo* Ferdinand von Saars' (198–218); M. Swales, 'Gedanken über eine mögliche Geburt des psychoanalytischen Realismus aus dem Geist weltlicher Unbeschreibbarkeit' (219–21).

Travelers in Time and Space / Reisende durch Zeit und Raum. The German Historical Novel / Der deutschsprachige historische Roman, ed. Osman Durrani and Julian Preece (ABNG, 51), Amsterdam–NY, Rodopi, ix + 473 pp., has six relevant chapters: G. Mühlberger and K. Habitzel, 'The German historical novel from 1780 to 1945: utilising the Innsbruck database' (5–23); F. Krobb, ' "Zeitgemäß, an der Hand der Geschichte": Bertold Auerbach und der deutsch-jüdische historische Roman des 19. Jahrhunderts' (25–38); J. S. Chase, 'Half-faded pictures: *Die Judenbuche* as historical fiction' (39–47); H. Hughes, 'The material world: a comparison between Adalbert Stifter's historical novel *Witiko* and Robert Bresson's film *Lancelot du Lac*' (199–208); S. Neuhaus, 'Zeitkritik im historischen Gewand? Fünf Thesen zum Gattungsbegriff des historischen Romans am Beispiel von Theodor Fontanes *Vor dem Sturm*' (209–25); C. Ujma, 'Zwischen Rebellion und Resignation: Frauen, Juden und Künstler in den historischen Romanen Fanny Lewalds' (283–99). J.-H. Bae, *Erfahrung der Moderne und Formen des realistischen Romans. Eine Untersuchung zu soziogenetischen und romanpoetologischen Aspekten in den späten Romanen von Raabe, Fontane und Keller*, Würzburg, Königshausen & Neumann, 2000, 198 pp., is a Göttingen dissertation with analysis of Raabe's *Stopfkuchen*, Fontane's *Frau Jenny Treibel*, and Keller's *Martin Salander*. Elias O. Dunu, **Modernisierungsprozesse und Literatur: Bedrohte Lebensräume in deutschsprachigen und subsaharischen Erzähltexten des 19. und 20. Jahrhunderts*, Hanover, Revonnah, 2000, 345 pp., includes analysis of Immermann's *Die Epigonen*, Stifter's *Der beschriebene Tännling*, Keller's *Das verlorene Lachen* and Raabe's *Pfisters Mühle*. Wolfgang Rath, **Die Novelle: Konzept und Geschichte*, Göttingen, Vandenhoeck & Ruprecht, 2000, 366 pp.

DRAMA. Anneliese Muchinke-Bach, *Das 'dramatische Bild' als existentielle Exposition in der deutschen Tragödie vom 17. bis 19. Jahrhundert*, Frankfurt–Berlin, Lang, 1999, 218 pp., includes Büchner, Grabbe, and Hebbel among the authors studied. Gabriele Clemens, **'Erziehung zu anständiger Unterhaltung.' Das Theaterspiel in den katholischen Gesellen- und Arbeitervereinen im deutschen Kaiserreich; eine Dokumentation*, Paderborn, Schöningh, 2000, 427 pp.

MOVEMENTS AND PERIODS. Gregor Reichelt, *Fantastik im Realismus. Literarische und gesellschaftliche Einbildungskraft bei Keller, Storm und Fontane*, Stuttgart–Weimar, Metzler, 237 pp., is a well-executed Konstanz dissertation which will serve as a valuable reference tool for students. The first half of the book provides a detailed survey of the theoretical background to the subject, and this is followed by four chapters on individual works, namely Keller's *Romeo und Julia auf dem Dorfe* and *Der grüne Heinrich*, Storm's *Der Schimmelreiter*, and Fontane's *Effi Briest*. There is a useful bibliography devoted almost entirely to studies on the fantastic. J. Becker, 'Wie modern ist der Poetische Realismus? Diskurs- und systemtheoretische Überlegungen', pp. 15–30 of '*Unverdaute Fragezeichen'. Literaturtheorie und textanalytische Praxis*, ed. Holger Dauer, St. Augustin, Gardez!, 1998, 198 pp. U. Fülleborn, '"Erweislose" Wirklichkeit: Frührealismus und Biedermeierzeit', pp. 102–27 of Ulrich Fülleborn, *Besitz und Sprache: offene Strukturen und nicht-possessives Denken in der deutschen Literatur; ausgewählte Aufsätze*, ed. Günter Blamberger, Munich, Fink, 2000, 439 pp.

Michael Perraudin, *Literature, the 'Volk' and the Revolution in Mid-Nineteenth Century Germany*, NY–Oxford, Berghahn, 242 pp., is a wide-ranging and instructive study which highlights the emergence in the 1830s and 1840s of a class of the disaffected mass poor that became a strong political force and increased the expectation of revolution. Individual chapters explore the impact of this social reality on the work of Heine, Büchner, Eichendorff, Gotthelf, Nestroy, Grillparzer, Stifter, Mörike, and Storm, and challenge the assumption that this literary period was marked by a disengagement on the part of writers from issues of public concern. '*Dürfen's denn das?'. Die fortdauernde Frage zum Jahr 1848*, ed. Sigurd Paul Scheichl and Emil Brix, Vienna, Passagen, 1999, 293 pp., includes F. Fellner, 'Die "Sündflut" der Pressefreiheit. Die Wiener Zeitungen im Revolutionsjahr 1848' (39–46); G. Mühlberger, 'Die Revolution von 1848 in Österreich im Spiegel des historischen Romans' (205–23); S. P. Scheichl, '1848 — kein Datum der österreichischen Literaturgeschichte' (225–36). N. K. Streitler, 'Panorama, Zoom, Nahaufnahme. Bildsequenzen im historischen und Abenteuerroman des Vormärz — mit einigen Ausblicken auf den bürgerlichen Realismus', *CEtGer*, 39, 2000:89–106. *Satire, parodie, pamphlet, caricature en Autriche à l'époque de François-Joseph*, ed. Gilbert Ravy and Jeanne Benay, Mont-St. Aignan, Rouen U.P., 1999, 263 pp., includes J. Benay, 'Les revues satiriques viennoises du *Vormärz* à l'ère libérale (1846–62). Entre *Kobold* et *Eulenspiegel'* (9–38); W. A. Coupe, '*Kikeriki* und die Minderheiten in der Donaumonarchie' (61–88); S. Frybes, 'Formes et figures de la satire viennoise et du grotesque en Galicie' (105–14); D. Goltschnigg, 'Das essayistische

Pamphlet als Strafprozeß — Kraus über Heine' (115–31); F. Kreissler, 'Der Wiener Spaziergänger. Le promeneur viennois Daniel Spitzer' (133–51); L. Pasteur, 'Bourgeois, prolétaires et justice sociale dans les publications de la social-démocratie autrichienne à l'époque de François-Joseph' (195–206); G. Stieg, '*Häuptling Abendwind*. Selbstzerstörung durch Selbstzensur' (245–53); M. Walle, 'Les Autrichiennes dans l'imagerie populaire et la caricature au XIXème siècle' (255–63).

Vormärzliteratur in europäischer Perspektive III: Zwischen Daguerreotyp und Idee, ed. Ian Hilton and Martina Lauster, Bielefeld, Aisthesis, 2000, 381 pp., completes the series and has material on Heine, Gutzkow, and Stifter. Dominik Westerkamp, *Pressefreiheit und Zensur im Sachsen des Vormärz, Baden-Baden, Nomos, 1999, xiv + 180 pp. P. Stein, 'Strukturwandel oder Kommunukationsrevolution? Literarisch-publizistische Öffentlichkeit im Umbruch der Revolution von 1848/49', *IJBAG*, 11–12, 1999–2000: 25–53. H. Lengauer, 'Ausübung der Freiheit: zur Rolle der Schriftsteller in Revolution (1848) und Zivilgesellschaft', pp. 41–53 of *Der Schriftsteller und der Staat. Apologie und Kritik in der österreichischen Literatur. Beiträge des 13. Polnisch-Österreichischen Germanistentreffens, Kazimierz Dolny 1998*, ed. Janusz Golec, Lublin, Wydawn. Uniw. Marii Curie-Sklodowskiej, 1999, 292 pp. J. Sonnleitner, '"Freiheit ist ja was Schreckliches." Notizen zu Staat und Dichter im österreichischen Vormärz', *ib.*, 27–40. K.-H. Götze, 'Die Entstehung der deutschen Literaturwissenschaft als Literaturgeschichte: Vorgeschichte, Ziel, Methode und soziale Funktion der Literaturgeschichtsschreibung im deutschen Vormärz', pp. 167–226 of *Germanistik und deutsche Nation 1806–1848*, ed. Jörg Jochen Müller et al., Stuttgart, Metzler, 2000, x + 383 pp.

LITERARY LIFE, JOURNALS, AND SOCIETIES. There have been two publications on the literary periodical *Die Gartenlaube*: Birgit Waldmeister, *Die Bilderwelt der 'Gartenlaube': Ein Beitrag zur Kulturgeschichte des bürgerlichen Lebens in der zweiten Hälfte des 19. Jahrhunderts*, Würzburg, Bayerische Blätter für Volkskunde, 1998, 336 pp., and Kirsten Belgum, *Popularizing the Nation. Audience, Representation, and the Production of Identity in 'Die Gartenlaube', 1853–1900*, Lincoln, Nebraska U.P., 1998, xxx + 237 pp. Gerd Eversberg, *Im Kreise der Dichter. Wilhelm Petersen (1835–1900) und seine Freundschaft mit Storm, Keller, Heyse, Groth u.a.; eine Ausstellung zum 100. Todestag*, Husum, Theodor-Storm-Gesellschaft, 2000, 96 pp. U. Tanzer, 'Anti-clericalism in literary journalism of the Liberal era: Ferdinand Kürnberger, Friedrich Schlögl, Daniel Spitzer and Ludwig Anzengruber', pp. 65–78 of *Catholicism and Austrian Culture*, ed. Ritchie Robertson and Judith Beniston, Edinburgh U.P., 1999, xiii + 191 pp.

REGIONAL LITERATURE. Szabolcs Boronkai, *Bedeutungsverlust und Identitätskrise. Ödenburgs deutschsprachige Literatur und Kultur im 19. Jahrhundert*, Berne–Berlin, Lang, 335 pp., is a Budapest dissertation which gives a well-informed account of the gradual decline in German literary and cultural activity during the 19th c. in a Hungarian town situated near the Austrian border. B. examines the role of the town's German-speaking theatre, and considers the artistic themes and preoccupations of eight local writers of the period, most notably Moritz Kolbenheyer (1810–84), who for 12 years conducted a correspondence with Hebbel. The work offers discerning insights into the process of political, social, and ideological change resulting in the loss of a culture which was perceived as belonging ultimately to neither of the two nations. *Literatur in Westfalen*, ed. Walter Gödden, Bielefeld, Aisthesis, 2000, 329 pp., has entries on Georg Weerth and Hoffmann von Fallersleben among others. F. Szász, 'Mehrsprachigkeit in einer gemeinsamen Kultur. Sprachgebrauch bei Literaten in/aus Ungarn zwischen zwei Revolutionen (1848–1918)', pp. 103–11 of *Schriftsteller zwischen (zwei) Sprachen und Kulturen. Internationales Symposion, Veszprém und Budapest, 6.–8. November 1995*, ed. Antal Mádl and Peter Motzan, Munich, Südostdeutsches Kulturwerk, 1999, 412 pp. W. Kessler, 'Stand und Probleme einer Literaturgeschichte Pommerns', *CGS*, 6, 1998:35–43, covers the period from 1815 to 1938.

2. INDIVIDUAL AUTHORS

ALEXIS. Janny Dittrich, *Willibald Alexis in Arnstadt. Geschichts- und literaturwissenschaftliche Untersuchungen über ein Dichterleben in der zweiten Hälfte des 19. Jahrhunderts*, Frankfurt–Berlin, Lang, 158 pp., is a fairly short but informative work focusing on A.'s 20-year period of residence in Arnstadt at the end of his literary career (1851–71). Written from the perspective of an historian, the study documents the impact of the 1848 revolution on Arnstadt and contains much biographical information on A., but also includes a chapter on the two late works written by A. in Arnstadt, the novel *Dorothee* and the novella *Ja in Neapel*.

ANNEKE, MATHILDE FRANZISKA. G. Schäfer, ' "Das Weib im Conflict mit den sozialen Verhältnissen": Mathilde Franziska Anneke (1817–1884)', pp. 249–64 of *Perspektiven der Frauenforschung. Ausgewählte Beiträge der 1. Fachtagung Frauen-/Genderforschung in Rheinland-Pfalz*, ed. Renate von Bardeleben and Patricia Plummer, Tübingen, Stauffenberg, 1998, xvi + 285 pp.

ASSING, LUDMILLA. N. Gatter, ' "Letztes Stück des Telegraphen. Wir alle haben ihn begraben helfen . . ." Ludmilla Assings journalistische Anfänge im Revolutionsjahr', *IJBAG*, 11–12, 1999–2000 : 101–20.

ASTON, LOUISE. M. S. Boehmer, 'Cuerpo, belleza y relaciones de poder en una escritora alemana del siglo XIX: Louise Aston', pp. 208–23 of *El cuerpo en la lengua y literatura alemanas: 'Ein weites Feld'*, ed. Brigitte E. Jirku, Valencia U.P., 1998, 260 pp.

BECHSTEIN, LUDWIG. Susanne Schmidt-Knaebel, *'Man muß doch jemand haben, gegen den man sich ausspricht.' Ludwig Bechsteins Briefe an Dr. Ludwig Storch*, Aachen, Shaker, 2000, 222 pp.

BÖRNE, LUDWIG. *Briefwechsel des jungen Börne und der Henriette Herz*, ed. Ludwig Geiger, Eschborn, Klotz, 2000, 201 pp., is a reprint of the Oldenburg und Leipzig edition of 1905.

BÜCHNER. The long-anticipated new Marburg edition of B.'s work has begun to appear: *Sämtliche Werke und Schriften, historisch-kritische Ausgabe mit Quellendokumentation und Kommentar*, ed. Burghard Dedner et al., WBG, commenced with vol. 3, *Dantons Tod*, 4 vols, 2000, 1607 pp., followed by vol. 5, *Lenz*, 526 pp. These impressive folio volumes contain meticulous detail and will remain the standard work for the foreseeable future. R. Nutt-Kofoth and B. Plachta, 'Schlechte Zeiten — gute Zeiten für Editionen? Zur Bedeutung der Marburger B.-Ausgabe für gegenwärtige Editionsphilologie', *Editio*, 15 : 149–67, concerns the mixed response to the edition in the popular press.

Georg Büchner — Woyzeck. Faksimile, Transkription, Emmendation und Lesetext, ed. Enrico de Angelis, Munich, Saur, 289 pp., documents and discusses the notoriously difficult *Woyzeck* manuscripts. The volume includes 46 facsimiles of originals together with their transcriptions, as well as various drawings and photographs. The editorial process of producing an emended version is explained, and the work ends with a complete reading text, free of annotation. There is an accompanying CD-ROM which enables users to search easily for words. Werner Weiland, *Büchners Spiel mit Goethemustern. Zeitstücke zwischen der Kunstperiode und Brecht*, Würzburg, Königshausen & Neumann, 192 pp., is a meticulously researched and clearly presented study of B.'s exploitation of works by Goethe which would have been familiar to readers of the time. Weiland substantiates the already established allusions linking *Danton's Tod* with *Egmont* and *Lenz* with *Werther*, and further contends that B. divided *Faust I* into two, creating the comedy *Leonce und Lena* by a critical updating of the early part of the action, and the disturbing social drama *Woyzeck* from the so-called 'Gretchentragödie'. The book is thoroughly annotated, and represents an interesting contribution to B. scholarship. Daniel Müller

Nielaba, *Die Nerven lesen. Zur Leit-Funktion von Georg Büchners Schreiben*, Würzburg, Königshausen & Neumann, 154 pp., ponders the interface between science and art in B.'s writing, in particular the manner in which his literary work manifests a critical response to contemporary findings in the discipline of physiology. The volume is divided into three substantial parts, the first on *Leonce und Lena*, the second on *Danton's Tod* and the third on *Lenz* and *Woyzeck*. The study represents a highly intelligent and rigorous piece of scholarship, but one feels constrained to remark that the complexity of the discourse may render it impenetrable to many students. Theresia M. Guntermann, *Arbeit — Leben — Sprache: eine diskursanalytische Untersuchung zu Texten Georg Büchners im Anschluss an Michel Foucault*, Essen, Die Blaue Eule, 2000, 259 pp., is a Munich dissertation.

Georg Büchner und die Moderne. Texte, Analysen, Kommentar. 1: *1875–1945*, ed. Dietmar Goltschnigg, Berlin, Schmidt, 616 pp., is the first of three substantial volumes documenting B. reception in the literary and political world. A collection of 125 chronologically presented texts by writers from the late 19th c to the Nazi period, each fully annotated, offers a fascinating overview of changing responses to B. over the 70-year period in question. David G. Richards, *Georg Büchner's 'Woyzeck'. A History of its Criticism*, Rochester, Camden House, xiv + 167 pp., is the first review of *Woyzeck* scholarship in English, and offers a comprehensive survey of the diverse critical approaches to this pivotal but problematic drama. Richards adopts a chronological approach, with individual chapters relating to distinct phases in the development of *Woyzeck* criticism from the 19th c. to the present. A full chapter is devoted to the significance of W. Lehmann's publication in 1967 of a new historical-critical edition. Richards has done justice to the huge task of collating the most important findings from a century of critical writing on *Woyzeck*; his analysis both accentuates the stature of this highly influential work in the history of German literature, and provides serious students of Büchner with a detailed and accessible research tool. Seiji Osawa, *Georg Büchners Philosophiekritik: eine Untersuchung auf der Grundlage seiner Descartes- und Spinoza-Exzerpte*, Marburg, Tectum, 1999, 231 pp., is a Marburg dissertation. Pierre Silvain, *Le brasier, le fleuve. Georg Büchner*, Paris, Gallimard, 2000, 142 pp. Liselotte Werge, *'Ich habe keinen Schrei für den Schmerz, kein Jauchzen für die Freude . . .'. Zur Metaphorik und Deutung des Dramas 'Dantons Tod' von Georg Büchner*, Stockholm, Almqvist & Wiksell, 2000, 299 pp. Theo Buck, *Riß in der Schöpfung: Büchner-Studien* II, Aachen, Rimbaud, 2000, 185 pp.

M. Niazi, 'Rhetorical *inventio* and revolutionary predication in *Danton's Tod*', *MDLK*, 93:36–52, draws on Aristotle's *Topics* to examine the speeches of Robespierre, Danton, and St. Just. S. Stern,

'Truth so difficult: George Eliot and G. B., a shared theme', *MLR*, 96:1–13, concerns the postulated influence of B.'s *Lena* on a three-page discourse on 'truth' in Eliot's *Adam Bede*. R. Drux, ' "Aussterben" als Innovation. "Die abgelebte moderne Gesellschaft" in den Dramen G. Bs.', *MDLK*, 93:300–17. B. Dedner et al., 'Französischsprachiges in Bs Schriften', *Editio*, 15:37–51. N. Pethes, ' "Er meinte, er müsse den Sturm in sich ziehen . . .": Lacan mit B. und die imaginäre Zeit des Erzählens', pp. 151–78 of *Lektüren des Imaginären: Bildfunktionen in Literatur und Kultur*, ed. Erich Kleinschmidt and Nicolas Pethes, Cologne, Böhlau, 1999, vi + 231 pp. U. Roth and G. Stiening, 'Gibt es eine Revolution in der Wissenschaft? Zu wissenschafts- und philosophiehistorischen Tendenzen in der neueren B.-Forschung', *ScPo*, 4, 2000:192–215. J. Hermand, 'Extremfall B.: Versuch einer politischen Verortung', *MDLK*, 92, 2000:395–411. S.-M. Weineck, 'Sex and history, or is there an erotic utopia in *Dantons Tod*?', *GQ*, 73, 2000:351–65. H. Schlemmer, 'Text und Sprache — G. B.: "Es war einmal ein arm Kind . . ." ', pp. 542–51 of *Literatur im interkulturellen Dialog. Festschrift zum 60. Geburtstag von Hans-Christoph Graf v. Nayhauss*, Berne–Berlin, Lang, 2000, 575 pp. I. Fellrath, ' "Le dieu de l'amitié": zu einer Schülerschrift G. Bs', *GRM*, 50, 2000:239–44. 'G. B.: das endlose Drama', pp. 101–15 of Gerhart Baumann, *Skizzen*, Freiburg, Rombach, 2000, 193 pp. U. Tanzer, 'Literarische Antworten auf das Zeitphänomen des Weltschmerzes: Vorschläge für einen fächerüber-greifenden Literaturunterricht am Beispiel von G. Bs *Leonce und Lena* und Johann Nestroys *Der Zerrissene*', pp. 143–54 of *Fächerübergreifender Literaturunterricht: Reflexionen und Perspektiven für die Praxis*, ed. Günter Bärnthaler and Ulrike Tanzer, Innsbruck, Studien-Vlg, 1999, 220 pp. N. Sorrentino, 'Metafore della morte nel *Dantons Tod*. Ancora sulla modernità di B.', *Annalia*, 8, 1998:91–111.

BURCKHARDT.   L. Gossman, 'The *Existenzbild* in B.'s art historical writing', *MLN*, 114, 1999:879–928. J. R. Lupton, 'B. in love: a response to Lionel Gossman', *ib.*, 929–32. Alfred Berchtold, *Jacob Burckhardt*, Lausanne, L'Age d'homme, 1999, 198 pp.

BUSCH.   *Wilhelm Busch: Da grunzte das Schwein, die Englein sangen*, ed. Robert Gerbhardt, Frankfurt, Eichborn, 2000, 381 pp. 'W. Bs schwarzer Humor', pp. 135–52 of Peter Nusser, *Unterhaltung und Aufklärung: Studien zur Theorie, Geschichte und Didaktik der populären Lesestoffe*, Frankfurt–Berlin, Lang, 2000, 213 pp. E. C. Hirsch, ' "Es saust der Stock, es schwirrt die Rute . . .": was mir W. B. eröffnet hat', *Satire*, 2000:27–34. C. Galway, 'Wann hatte W. B. Geburtstag?', *GN*, 31, 2000:14–18.

CARRIERE, PHILIPP MORITZ.   W. Bunzel, ' "Muth und Opferkraft für die Idee". Briefe Moritz Carrieres an Arnold Ruge und Theodor Echtermeyer (1839/41)', *IJBAG*, 8–9, 1996–97:39–73.

DAHN. H. Rölleke, 'Ich durfte nur die Harfe sein. Felix Dahns unveröffentlichtes Gedicht "Wolfram von Eschenbach"', *ZDA*, 130:197–201.

DAUMER, GEORG FRIEDRICH. S. Ihm, 'Antike Fundstellen zu Daumers *Polydora*. Hellas I–III', *Euphorion*, 94, 2000:435–49.

DROSTE-HÜLSHOFF. Bernd Völkl, *A.v.D.-H.*, *'Die Judenbuche'* (Reclams U.-B., Lektüreschlüssel für Schüler, 15305), Stuttgart, Reclam, 52 pp. Rüdiger Nutt-Kofoth, **Letzte Gaben von Annette von Droste-Hülshoff (1860). Zum editionsphilologischen Umgang mit einer frühen Nachlassedition*, Berne–Berlin, Lang, 1999, vol. 1: *Untersuchung*, 602 pp.; vol. 2: *Beigabe*, 292 pp. L. Köhn, ' "Seele fordernd stehn die Formen da": *Des Arztes Vermächtniß* als poetologische Verserzählung', Köhn, *Literatur*, 39–54. H.-J. Koppitz, 'A. v. D.-H. und Wilhelm Tangermann', *Kölnischer Geschichtsverein: Jahrbuch*, 71, 2000:133–43. W. Gössmann, 'Selbsterkundung: das dichterische Ich der Droste', Gössmann, *Literatur*, 140–57. G. Tytler, 'The presentation of Herr von S. in *Die Judenbuche*', *GQ*, 73, 2000:337–50.

Droste-Jahrbuch, 4, 1997–1998[2000], contains H. Koopmann, ' "Nicht fröhnen mag ich kurzem Ruhme." Zum Selbstverständnis der D. in ihren Dichtergedichten' (11–33); R. Böschenstein, 'Die Boa. Die Darstellung von Aggression in den Gedichten der D.' (35–65); P. Deselaers, ' "O laß mich schauen deinen Friedensbogen / Und deine Sonne leucht in meine Nacht!" Zum christlichen Selbstverständnis der A. v. D.-H.' (67–80); J. Guthrie, 'Von der Nächstenliebe zum Verbrechertum: Schiller, D. und die Ballade' (81–102); G. Bauer Pickar, ' "Läßt walten die verborg'ne Kraft!" Ds Lyrik aus heutiger amerikanischer Sicht' (103–26); O. Niethammer, 'Grenze, Spiegelung und anonymes Schreiben: Diskussion ausgewählter, vornehmlich feministischer Interpretationsansätze zur Lyrik der D. (1990–1998)' (127–40); J. Linder, 'Der Drostesche "Spiritus familiaris des Roßtäuschers": eine Ballade' (141–57); R. Nutt-Kofoth, 'Eine Abschrift fremder Hand von A. v. D.-Hs Jugendgedicht "Das befreyte Deutschland". Präzisierungen zu Überlieferung und Entstehung des Gedichts aufgrund eines neu eingesehenen Textträgers' (159–63); W. Woesler, 'Kindheit und Jugend der Dichterin A. v. D.-H.' (165–86); R. Nutt-Kofoth, 'Kein poetologisches Werk der D.: zu Gestalt und Rezeption der Ausgabe *Letzte Gaben* von 1860' (189–207).

EBNER-ESCHENBACH. *M. v. E.-E. Kritische Texte und Deutungen*, ed. Karl Konrad Polheim and Carsten Kretschmann, Tübingen, Niemeyer, has added *Zweiter Ergänzungsband. Briefwechsel mit Theo Schücking: Frauenleben im 19. Jahrhundert*, ed. Edda Polheim, 515 pp. This is an interesting and informative volume which comprises more than the title suggests. The work falls into three parts illuminating various facets of both women's lives. The first 150 pages contain E.-E.'s correspondence with Theo Schücking, daughter of Levin Schücking, and this is followed by a 200–page section incorporating a selection of Theo Schücking's other writings, letters she exchanged with eleven women writers including Fanny Lewald, Betty Paoli, and Hermine Villinger, and the text of E.-E.'s short story 'Die eine Sekunde'. The final part analyses aspects of Theo Schücking's literary work, as well as exploring E.-E.'s experience of life in Rome, her attitudes towards salon culture, and her views on the women's movement. L. N. Polubojarinova, '"Episteln von keiner Prophetin": der Brief im Schaffen M. v. E.-E.', Arlt, *Interkulturelle Erforschung*, 183–90. L. N. Polubojarinova, 'Hundegeschichten für Kinder und Erwachsene: *Krambambuli* M. v. E.-E., 'Kaschtanka' Anton Tschechows, 'Der weiße Pudel' Alexander Kuprins', *Fest. Kliewer*, 169–81. E. Schwarz, 'Jüdische Gestalten bei M. v. E.-E. und Ferdinand von Saar', Goltschnigg, *Literatur*, 115–32.

EYTH, MAX.   H. Thomé, 'Der schwäbische Ikarus: zur Psychologie des Erfinders in Max Eyths *Der Schneider von Ulm*', pp. 149–59 of *Modernisierung und Literatur. Festschrift für Hans Ulrich Seeber zum 60. Geburtstag*, ed. Walter Göbel, Tübingen, Narr, 2000, xv + 335 pp.

FELDER, FRANZ MICHAEL.   H. Sander, 'Rede zum Andenken an den Dichter Franz Michael Felder', *Allmende*, 19, 1999:113–23. N. Loacker, 'Der Sinn von Schoppernau: zu Franz Michael Felders Selbstbiographie', *ib.*, 124–38.

FONTANE.   *Meine liebe Mete: Ein Briefgespräch zwischen Eltern und Tochter*, ed. Gotthard Erler, Berlin, Aufbau, 584 pp., publishes the correspondence between F. and his daughter. *Theodor Fontane. Sie hatte nur Liebe und Güte für mich: Briefe an Mathilde von Rohr*, ed. Gotthard Erler, Berlin, Aufbau, 2000, 424 pp. *Theodor Fontane and the European Context. Literature, Culture and Society in Prussia and Europe*, ed. Patricia Howe and Helen Chambers, Amsterdam, Rodopi, 270 pp., publishes the proceedings of the Interdisciplinary Symposium at the Institute of Germanic Studies, University of London, in March 1999. The volume offers many new perspectives on F., placing him alongside a range of European writers and approaching his work from the background of other disciplines including philosophy, sociology, and art history. It contains R. Böschenstein, 'F.'s writing and the problem of "reality" in philosophy and literature' (15–32); N. Bachleitner, 'Of grieving girls and suicidal soldiers: T. F. and Ferdinand Saar' (33–41); P. J. Bowman, 'Schach von Wuthenow: interpreters and interpretants' (43–62); Y. Chevrel, 'T. F. and France: a problematic encounter' (63–75); H. Ester, 'Problems of translation, arising from the context of F.'s works' (77–84); B. Everett, 'Night air: *Effi Briest* and other novels by F.' (85–94); I.-S. Ewbank, 'Hedda Gabler, Effi Briest and "the Ibsen effect"' (95–104); H. V. Geppert, 'Prussian decadence: Schach von Wuthenow in an international context' (105–17); B. Hardy, 'Tellers and listeners in Effi Briest' (119–35); P. Howe, ' "A visibly-appointed stopping-place": narrative endings at the end of the century' (137–51); H. Kuzmics, 'Aristocracy and bourgeoisie in late nineteenth-century Prussia and England: comparing processes of individualisation in F. and Trollope' (153–66); J. Legrand, 'F. and Stendhal: mediators of a European idea of intellectual nobility' (167–79); W. J. McCormack, 'Haunted realism: Beckett through F.' (181–96); D. Mugnolo, 'T. F. and the nineteenth-century Italian novel: a contrastive comparison' (197–205); T. M. de Oliveira, 'F.'s *Effi Briest* and Eça de Queiró's *O Primo Basilio*: two novels of adultery in the context of European realism' (205–15); A. Stillmark, 'F. and Turgenev: two kinds of realism' (217–29); G. Weiss-Sussex, 'F.'s and Georg Hermann's Berlin: relationships with contemporary Berlin painting' (231–52); M. Zubiaurre, 'Panoramic views in F., Galdós and Clarín: an essay on female blindness' (253–63).

Thomas Grimann, *Text und Prätext. Intertextuelle Bezüge in Theodor Fontanes 'Stine'*, Würzburg, Königshausen & Neumann, 368 pp., is a lengthy Heidelberg dissertation in which the author undertakes an elaborate examination of the connections between *Stine* and the Passion story, Mozart's *Die Zauberflöte*, and Shakespeare's *The Winter's Tale*. Although interesting initially and meticulously researched throughout with keen attention to developing an appropriate methodological approach, the study is ponderous and repetitive and will be of significant use only to those with the most particularized interest. *Fontane und die bildende Kunst. SMPK, Staatliche Museen zu Berlin, Nationalgalerie*, ed. Claude Keisch, Berlin, Henschel, 1998, 335 pp., is a catalogue accompanying the exhibition from 4 September to 29 November 1998. Volker Müller, *Der Weg nach Sanssouci*, Würzburg, Königshausen & Neumann, 147 pp., is a collection of anecdotes and impressions of the Fontane centenary in 1998. Written by a journalist with a speculative interest in F.'s enduring popularity, the volume brings together rather random accounts of meetings with scholars at lectures and conferences and visits to locations which were significant in F.'s life and work. Self-indulgently written and lacking any critical apparatus, this is not a book for an academic library. Hang-Kyun Jeong, **Dialogische Offenheit. Eine Studie zum Erzählwerk Theodor Fontanes*, Würzburg, Königshausen & Neumann, 256 pp., is a Wuppertal dissertation. Jens Erik Classen, *'Altpreussischer Durchschnitt'? Die Lyrik Theodor Fontanes*, Frankfurt–Berlin, Lang, 2000, 331 pp. *Interpretationen. Gedichte von Theodor Fontane*, ed. Helmut Scheuer, Stuttgart, Reclam, 291 pp., has commentaries by a range of writers on 16 poems; each chapter is concluded with a short bibliography. Michael Bohrmann,

T. F., '*Unterm Birnbaum*' (Reclams U.-B., Lektüreschlüssel für Schüler, 15307), Stuttgart, Reclam, 81 pp. **Vermißte Bestände des Theodor-Fontane-Archivs. Eine Dokumentation*, Potsdam, Theodor-Fontane-Archiv, 1999, 245 pp. J. Preece, 'Fear of the foreigner: Chinese, Poles and other non-Prussians in T. F.'s *Effi Briest*', Thomas, *German Studies*, 173–95. A. Bennholdt-Thomsen, 'Bilder statt Leben. Zu Fs *Oceane von Parceval*', Fest. *Janz*, 149–60. P. Frank, 'Im Rausch der Sinne. T. Fs englische Reisebücher (1854/60) im Spiegel kulturgeschichtlicher Wahrnehmungstheorien', pp. 109–31 of *Praxisorientierte Literaturtheorie. Annäherung an Texte der Moderne*, ed. Thomas Bleitner, Bielefeld, Aisthesis, 1999, 306 pp. G. Erler, 'Plädoyer für Emilie: Frau Fontane als Briefschreiberin', *Brandis Vol.*, 898–901. H. Pfotenhauer, 'T. F.: *Der Stechlin*', pp. 227–47 of *Lektüren für das 21. Jahrhundert. Schlüsseltexte der deutschen Literatur von 1200 bis 1990*, ed. Dorothea Klein and Sabine Schneider, Würzburg, Königshausen & Neumann, 2000, 303 pp., offers an interesting introduction to F.'s last novel and has four plates reproducing paintings referred to in the narrative. H. Ragg-Kirkby, ' "Alles ist wie Opferstätte": society and sacrifice in the works of T. F.', *OGS*, 29, 2000:95–130. L. Köhn, 'Die Schrecken des Modernen: Fs Begründung realistischer Erzählprosa; *Aus den Tagen der Okkupation* (1871)', Köhn, *Literatur*, 67–97. *Theodor Fontane: Mit Fontane durch Frankreich und Flandern*, ed. Otto Drude, Frankfurt–Leipzig, Insel, 2000, 130 pp. H. Müller-Michaels, 'Normendiskurse in Fs späten Romanen', *DUB*, 53, 2000:94–102. T. Pelster, 'T. F., *Mathilde Möhring*: Vorschläge für die Erarbeitung eines Berliner Zeitromans', *ib.*, 103–12. M. Harmat, 'Eisenbahnen: Zivilisationskritik und Kulturskepsis in *Anna Karenina* und *Effi Briest*', Segebrecht, *Europa*, 190–98. N. Mecklenburg, ' "Weiber weiblich, Männer männlich": Fs Reden mit fremden Stimmen', pp. 137–49 of *Kultur Sprache Macht: Festschrift für Peter Horn*, ed. John K. Noyes, Frankfurt–Berlin, Lang, 2000, 404 pp. Id., 'Zur Poetik, Narratologie und Ethik der Gänsefüßchen: T. F. nach der Postmoderne', pp. 165–85 of *Instrument Zitat: über den literarhistorischen Nutzen und institutionellen Nutzen von Zitaten und Zitieren*, ed. Klaus Beekman and Ralf Grüttemeier, Amsterdam, Rodopi, 2000, 443 pp. W. Jens, 'Immortal William: über die Wallfahrt Fs zu Shakespeare', *Shakespeare-Jahrbuch*, 136, 2000:11–23. 'Kontrastierung mit anderen Autoren: F. als Erzähler', Gössmann, *Literatur*, 208–26. W. Rieck, 'Die Hohenzollern auf dem Königsthron im Urteil T. Fs', pp. 349–68 of *Studia niemcoznawcze: Studien zur Deutschkunde*, ed. Lecha Kolago, Warsaw, Inst. Germanistyki, 2000, 570 pp. Kenneth Attwood, *Fontane und das Preußentum*, Flensburg, Baltica, 2000, 361 pp.

Fontane-Blätter, 71, contains W. Rasch, 'Zwei unbekannte Theaterkritiken T. Fs. Mit einem Geburtstagsgruß für Otfried Keiler zum

70. Geburtstag' (10–16); Id., 'Am Lethestrom — Erinnerungen von Ottomar Beta an T. F.' (17–25); M. E. Brunner, '"Man will die Hände des Puppenspielers nicht sehen" — Wahrnehmung in *Effi Briest*' (28–48); M. Joch, 'Auf Sie und Sie mit der dominanten Fraktion. Ein sozioanalytischer Nachtrag zu *Frau Jenny Treibel*' (50–63). *Fontane-Blätter*, 72, contains W. Rasch, 'Eine unbekannte Rezension Fs von Karl Heigels *Neuen Novellen* (1873)' (10–13); Id., 'Am Lethestrom (II) — Karl Bleibtreus Erinnerungen an F.' (14–22); B. Gerth and M. Horlitz, '"... meine Theilnahme bleibt immer dieselbe." Briefe Mathilde von Rohrs an Paul Heyse und Wilhelm Hertz' (23–39); M. Masanetz, 'Vom Leben und Sterben des Königskindes. *Effi Briest* oder der Familienroman als analytisches Drama' (42–93); R. Selbmann, 'Von Birnbäumen und Menschen. Eine neue Sicht auf Fs Ballade *Herr von Ribbeck im Havelland*' (94–108); S.-A. Jørgensen, '*Der Schleswig-Holsteinische Krieg im Jahre 1864.* Gattung und Gesinnung' (109–21).

FRANÇOIS. B. Burns, 'Morality and psychology in L. v. F.'s crime story *Judith, die Kluswirtin*', *FMLS*, 37 : 58–69.

FRANZOS. L. Cybenko, 'Die Literaturlandschaft Galiziens und das Werk von Karl Emil Franzos: zum Problem der Datenrecherchen in Bibliotheken und Archiven von L'viv/Lemberg', Arlt, *Interkulturelle Erforschung*, 157–77.

FREILIGRATH. F. Vassen, 'Löwenritt und Tigersang: Ferdinand Freiligraths und Georg Weerths Exotismus im Vor- und Nachmärz', *IJBAG*, 11–12, 1999–2000 : 197–223.

FREYTAG. H.-J. Lieder, '"... sonst kann ich ja mit Niemand weiter sprechen": die Briefe von Arthur Scholtz im Nachlaß G. F.', *Brandis Vol.*, 883–97. G. V. Essen, 'Die Rückgewinnung der Geschichte in G. Fs "Ahnen"-Galerie', Essen, *Geschichten*, 162–86. P. Pregiel, 'Das Bild der Germanen in G. Fs *Ingo*', *Historisches Jahrbuch*, 120, 2000 : 182–98. M. Baisch and R. Lüdeke, 'Das Alte ist das Neue: zum Status des historisch-kritischen Wissens in G. Fs *Die verlorene Handschrift* und A. S. Byatts *Possession*', pp. 223–251 of *Text und Autor: Beiträge aus dem Venedig-Symposium 1998 des Graduiertenkollegs 'Textkritik' München*, ed. Christiane Henkes, Tübingen, Niemeyer, 2000, vi + 253 pp.

GOTTHELF. Bernhard von Rütte and Cécile von Rütte-Bitzius, *Jeremias Gotthelfs jüngere Tochter 1837–1914: ein Lebensbild*, Berne, Haller, 1999, 133 pp. R. Steinlein, 'J. G., *Der Knabe des Tell* (1846): ein Sonderfall deutschsprachiger geschichtserzählender Jugendliteratur im 19. Jahrhundert', Rutschmann, *Nebenan*, 125–58. H. P. Holl, '"... Wursts Ding im Leibe ...": Gs Seitenhiebe gegen den Sprachdidaktiker Raimund Jakob Wurst (1800–1845)', pp. 235–49 of *Sprachsplitter und Sprachspiele: Nachdenken über Sprache und Sprachgebrauch. Festschrift für*

Willy Sanders, ed. Jürg Niederhauser and Stanislaw Szlek, Berne–Berlin, Lang, 2000, 275 pp.

GRABBE. 'Verführer und Übermensch: zu Gs *Don Juan und Faust*', pp. 207–22 of P. Michelsen, *Im Banne Fausts: Zwölf 'Faust'-Studien*, Würzburg, Königshausen & Neumann, 2000, 237 pp.

GRILLPARZER. Konrad Schaum, *G.-Studien*, Berne–Berlin, Lang, 316 pp., is a collection of old and new essays by the author on various aspects of G.'s work. The study reflects a traditional style of literary criticism and is divided into two parts, the first examining aesthetic and cultural issues such as the relationship between drama and history in G.'s work, his conception of fate and tragedy, and his approach to human psychology and cultural criticism. The second part consists of indvidual analyses of the following works: *Das goldene Vließ, König Ottokars Glück und Ende, Ein treuer Diener seines Herrn, Des Meeres und der Liebe Wellen, Ein Bruderzwist in Habsburg*, and *Das Kloster bei Sendomir*. Nicoletta Dacrema, **F. G., disegni e problemi*, Geneva, Marietti, 2000, 141 pp. J. Pizer, ' "Last Austrians" in "turn of the century" works by F. G., Joseph Roth, and Alfred Kolleritsch', *GQ*, 74:8–21, has analysis of G.'s *Libussa*. H. Gronemeyer, 'F. Gs Locke in Armenien. Zum Schicksal der Autographen-Sammlung Hermann Kiewy', *Brandis Vol.*, 569–76. K. Wimmer, 'Médée à Delphes. La fin de la trilogie *La Toison d'or* de F. G.', *CEtGer*, 39, 2000:119–27. M. Klańska, 'Der Mensch und die Macht im Drama *König Ottokars Glück und Ende* von F. G.', pp. 11–26 of *Der Schriftsteller und der Staat. Apologie und Kritik in der österreichischen Literatur. Beiträge des 13. Polnisch-Österreichischen Germanistentreffens, Kazimierz Dolny 1998*, ed. Janusz Golec, Lublin, Wydawn. Uniw. Marii Curie-Sklodowskiej, 1999, 292 pp. B. Hoffmann, 'Die Kakophnie des Absoluten am Ende der Kunstperiode: F. Gs *Der arme Spielmann*', pp. 36–51 of *Die Musik, das Leben und der Irrtum: Thomas Bernhard und die Musik*, ed. Otto Kolleritsch, Vienna, Universal, 2000, 249 pp. S. P. Schleichl, ' "Kaum schön, von schwachem Geist und dürft'gen Gaben": was können wir über Erny in Gs "Treuem Diener seines Herrn" wissen?', pp. 183–99 of *Käthchen und seine Schwestern: Frauenfiguren im Drama um 1800: Internationales Kolloquium des Kleist-Archivs Sembdner, 12. und 13. Juni 1997 in der Kreissparkasse Heilbronn*, ed. Günther Emig and Anton P. Knittel, Heilbronn, Kleist-Archiv Sembdner, 2000, 198 pp. Alessandra Schininà, **'Ich wäre tot, lebt' ich mit dieser Welt': Franz Grillparzer in seinen Tagebüchern*, St. Ingbert, Röhrig, 2000, 140 pp.

GROTH. *Jahresgabe der K.G.-Gesellschaft*, 43, contains J. Wieske, 'Texte zum Leben K. Gs auf Fehmarn in den Jahren 1847–1853' (55–60); J. Kühl, 'Ich habe große Fußtouren dazu umsonst unternommen. K. G. und die Mathematik. Teil 2' (61–74); U. Bichel and I. Bichel, 'Vor 150 Jahren. K. G. im Jahre 1851' (75–106). J. Meyer,

'*Ein Tribut* zum Geburtstag. K. Gs plattdeutsche Ballade zum Schillerfest 1859', *Brandis Vol.*, 872–82.

GRÜN, ANASTASIUS. A. Janko, 'A. G. und die Slowenen: eine ambivalente Beziehung', pp. 117–25 of *Zur Geschichte der österreichisch-slowenischen Literaturbeziehungen*, ed. Andreas Brantner et al., Vienna, Turia & Kant, 1998, 415 pp. D. Scharmitzer, '"Der Landtagsfeldwebel hat schon seinen Säbel geschärft"': Briefe von Karl Deschmann an A. G.', *ib.*, 127–58. A. Janko, 'Deutsche Kultur und Bildung für Slowenen: kulturpolitische Auseinandersetzung A. Gs mit seinem Geburtsland Krain', Segebrecht, *Europa*, 144–50.

GUTZKOW. *Gutzkows Werke und Briefe. Kommentierte digitale Gesamtausgabe. Eröffnungsband*, ed. Gert Vonhoff and Martina Lauster, Münster, Oktober, 392 pp., introduces the enterprising and ambitious 'Editionsprojekt Karl Gutzkow' which aims to publish the works of G. both in book form and in an internet version at <www.gutzkow.de>. The purpose and methodology of the project are outlined, and interested scholars are encouraged to participate in the ongoing project through the interactive possibilities afforded by the digital medium. The volume includes an annotated selection of texts by G., and an accompanying CD gives accesss to the first stage of the work completed by the autumn of 2001.

HACKLÄNDER. R. H. Krauss, '"Reisen im neuen Styl." Die Eisenbahn im Werk Friedrich Wilhelm Hackländers (1816–77)', *LiLi*, 31:9–31.

HAHN-HAHN. E. Biedermann, '"Kein Thee im Mondschein unter den Linden." I. H.-Hs und Ida Pfeiffers Reiseberichte über Schweden', *Fest. Fritz*, 87–108.

HEBBEL. *H.Jb.*, 56, contains U. Fülleborn, '"Er ist Dein Eigenthum": Der Ring des Gyges und das Problem des Besitzdenkens im Drama F. Hs' (9–29); M. Ritzer, 'Bruderträume: das Individuationsmodell in Hs Märchen *Die Einsamen Kinder*' (31–55); K. Guthke, 'Goethes Weimar und Hs "Welt"' (57–81); M. Durzak, '"Außer der Bernauerin ist Niemand naß geworden." Hs problematischer Beitrag zur Geschichte des bürgerlichen Trauerspiels in *Agnes Bernauer*' (83–102); C. Kretschmann, 'Haben oder Sein. Zur Konfiguration von Hs Lustspiel *Der Rubin*' (103–37); R. Möller, '"Warm verköpen" — Brandstiftungen in Wesselburen zur Zeit F. Hs' (139–67); H. Thomsen, 'Theaterbericht' (185–94). M. Reich-Ranicki, 'Die Kammern der Mädchen werden nicht verschlossen', pp. 75–78 of *Frankfurter Anthologie: Gedichte und Interpretationen*, ed. Marcel Reich-Ranicki, Frankfurt–Leipzig, Insel, 2000, 298 pp. P. Schnyder, 'André Gide traducteur de Friedrich Hebbel: un texte inédit', *RZLG*, 24, 2000:89–109.

HEINE. The *Säkularausgabe* of H.'s *Werke, Briefwechsel, Lebenszeugnisse*, has added vol. 8K, *Über Deutschland 1833–1836: Aufsätze über Kunst und Philosophie. Kommentar*, ed. R. Francke, Berlin, Akademie, 813 pp. Olaf Hildebrand, *Emanzipation und Versöhnung. Aspekte des Sensualismus im Werk Heinrich Heines unter besonderer Berücksichtigung der 'Reisebilder'*, Tübingen, Niemeyer, vi + 365 pp., is a scholarly and perceptive study which identifies sensualism as a defining aesthetic principle throughout H.'s literary career. The first part of the book is devoted to a close reading of the *Reisebilder* and illustrates the significance of this concept for the poet before his Paris exile. In the second part the author examines the religious and political notions emanating from H.'s focus on sensualism; he considers the poet's conflict with Ludwig Börne in which the contrast between the spiritual and the sensual is defined in terms of an opposition of the Nazarenic and the Helennic; and finally through analysis of H.'s late poems the writer demonstrates the poet's enduring emphasis on a type of sensualism that seeks a pantheistic reconciliation of mind and matter. This book may not make easy reading for students, but will contribute to the literary-theoretical debate on Heine. Kai Neubauer, *Heinrich Heines heroische Leidenschaften: Ein Beitrag zur Anthropologie der Sinnlichkeit von Bruno bis Feuerbach*, Stuttgart, Metzler, 2000, 215 pp., is a Düsseldorf dissertation which traces the roots of H.'s sensualism back to the Renaissance interest in both Neoplatanism and Epicureanism. The work advances similarities in H.'s thought to that of Giordano Bruno, the founder of modern pantheism, as well as to that of Feuerbach.

Die französische Heine-Kritik. 2: *Rezensionen und Notizen zu Heines Werken aus den Jahren 1835–1845*, ed. Hans Hörling, Stuttgart–Weimar, Metzler, 446 pp., is the second of three volumes covering the period 1830–56. It contains some 220 contemporary articles, reviews, and short press items by writers including prominent figures such as Hector Berlioz, Théophile Gautier, Franz Liszt, Edgard Quinet, and George Sand. Both the scale and quality of H. reception in the Paris press alone attests to the recognition the poet enjoyed in France during his lifetime, and this series illuminates lesser-known aspects of H.'s influence outside his own country. Apart from giving the dates and sources, the entries are not annotated, as a German commentary on all three volumes will appear separately. *Heinrich Heine, cittadino d'Europa / Heinric Heine als Europäer*, ed. Alida F. Piccioni, Milan, Nuova Italia, 1999, 136 pp., contains some 10 articles by Italian and German scholars. *Heine voyageur. Textes réunis et présentés par Alain Cozic*, Toulouse U.P., 1999, 234 pp. *La poésie de Heinrich Heine: Sous la direction de Michel Espagne et Isabelle Kalinowski*, Paris, CNRS, 2000, 168 pp.

Markus Joch, *Brüderkämpfe: zum Streit um den intellektuellen Habitus in den Fällen Heinrich Heine, Heinrich Mann und Hans Magnus Enzensberger*, Heidelberg, Winter, 2000, vii + 483 pp., is a Berlin dissertation. Michael Magner, *Heinrich Heines 'De L'Allemagne' (1855) als jüdischer Gegenentwurf zur romantischen Poetik*, Bonn U.P., 1999, 242 pp., is a Bonn dissertation. Bettina F. Freelund, *Midrash, Aggada, und Shibboleth: Heine's Jewish Anti-Canon*, Ann Arbor, Mich., Bell & Howard, 2000, 208 pp.

'*Die Emanzipation des Volkes war die große Aufgabe unseres Lebens': Beiträge zur Heinrich-Heine Forschung anläßlich seines zweihundertsten Geburtstags 1997*, ed. Wolfgang Beutin, Hamburg, von Bockel, 2000, 343 pp., includes F. Schuh, 'H. Hs Stellung zu den Traditionen der Griechisch-Römischen Antike oder H. H. — Bruder im Apoll' (31–60); A. Ruiz, '"Hier ist heiliger Boden": deutsche Freiheitspilger und politische Emigranten in Paris von der Revolution von 1789 bis H. H.' (73–88); J. Dvořák, 'Ästhetik und politische Ökonomie: H. H., Karl Marx und der Saint-Simonismus' (89–104); W. Beutin, '"Die Literaturgeschichte ist die große Morgue, wo jeder seine Toten aufsucht, die er liebt oder womit er verwandt ist": H. H. als Historiker der Literatur' (105–15); G. Martens, 'Hs Taufe und ihre Spuren in den Gedicht-Zyklen *Nordsee* I und II' (119–32); E. Reichert, 'H. über Luther und die Reformation' (133–36); A. Post-Martens, 'Hs *Himmelreich auf Erden*' (137–50); C. Höpfner, '1848: Hs Rückkehr zu Gott?' (151–68); A. Sroka, 'Hs Haltung zu Katholizismus und Renaissance' (169–87); T. Bütow, '*Almansor*: H. und der Islam' (189–96); W. Beutin, '"... daß ich die gute protestantische Streitaxt mit Herzenslust handhabe ...": H. H. und die Geschichte des Unglaubens' (197–213); H.-J. Benedict, 'Wenn Christus noch kein Gott wäre, würde ich ihn dazu wählen: H. Hs heitere Religionskritik' (215–34); B. Witte, 'Demokratie braucht Erinnerung — zum Beispiel an die Revolution von 1848 und an H. H.' (243–51); P. Stein, 'Zu den Widersprüchen in der Rezeptionsgeschichte H. Hs' (253–66); A. Berger, 'H. und seine Zeitgenossen: Strömungen und Auseinandersetzungen im deutschen Liberalismus des Vormärz' (267–85); G. Wagner, 'Hs Modernität: Aspekte seiner Positionierung in der ästhetischen Kultur des 19. Jahrhunderts' (287–99); W. Beutin, '"Denn ich glaube an den Fortschritt, ich glaube, die Menschheit ist zur Glückseligkeit bestimmt ...": Hs politische Gedankenwelt in ihrer Zeit' (301–13); H. Beutin, '"Diese Cleopatra ist ein Weib. Sie liebt und verrät zu gleicher Zeit": Kritisches zur Darstellung von Frauen in Hs Werk' (315–29).

H.-Jb., 40, contains J. A. Kruse, 'Hs Zukunft: ambivalente Perspektiven' (1–15); S. Borchardt, 'Sphinx fatal. Die Sphinxfrau in

Heines Lyrik' (16–45); M. Ansel, 'Die Bedeutung von Hs "Romantischer Schule" für die hegelianische Romantik-Historiographie im
19. Jahrhundert' (46–78); M. Hallensleben, 'Hs "Romanzero" als
Zeit-Triptychon: Jüdische Memorliteratur als intertextuelle Gedächt-
niskunst' (79–93); H. Boenisch, 'H., Arnold, Flaubert and the cross-
channel link: implicit connections textual and technological'
(94–106); B. Balzer, '"Ich müsste eigentlich im Exil sterben." Der
Heine-Essay von Max Aub' (107–28). J. Harskamp, 'The artist and
the swallow-tail coat. H., Baudelaire, Manet and modernism in art',
Arcadia, 36:89–99. P. Waldmann, 'H. H. im Spiegel der Poetik
Martin Deutingers', *Compass*, 4:53–70. D. Pfaff, 'H. H. im Spiegel
der Poetik Martin Deutingers', pp. 167–84 of *Erzählen und Moral.
Narrativität im Spannungsfeld von Ethik und Ästhetik*, ed. Dietmar Mieth,
Tübingen, Attempto, 2000, 286 pp. S. Weigel, 'Zum Phantasma der
Lesbarkeit: Hs *Florentinische Nächte* als literarische Urszene eines
kulturwissenschaftlichen Theorems', pp. 245–57 of *Lesbarkeit der
Kultur: Literaturwissenschaften zwischen Kulturtechnik und Ethnographie*, ed.
Gerhard Neumann and Sigrid Weigel, Munich, Fink, 2000, 520 pp.
K. Evans-Romaine, 'Pasternak and the Russian reception of H.',
pp. 252–76 of *Cold Fusion: Aspects of the German Cultural Presence in Russia*,
ed. Gennady Barabtarlo, NY, Berghahn, 2000, vii + 310 pp.
R. Stauf, 'Interkulturelle Kopfgeburten: deutsch-französische Plan-
spiele am Beispiel Hs und Börnes', pp. 289–303 of *Nation als Stereotyp:
Fremdwahrnehmung und Identität in deutscher und französischer Literatur*, ed.
Ruth Florack, Tübingen, Niemeyer, 2000, vi + 344 pp. N. Reeves,
'From shanks's pony to Pegasus: the poetic vehicles of H. H., ironic
cosmopolitan and metapoet', pp. 19–32 of *Cosmopolitans in the Modern
World: Studies on a Theme in German and Austrian Literary Culture*, ed.
Suzanne Kirkbright, Munich, Iudicium, 2000, 220 pp. S. Wolting,
' "Land zwischen Rußland und Frankreich": mit H. H. nach Polen
und zurück', pp. 163–80 of *Oberschlesische Dialoge: Kulturräume im
Blickfeld von Wissenschaft und Literatur*, ed. Bernd Witte, Frankfurt–Ber-
lin, Lang, 2000, 292 pp.

    HEYSE. *Paul Heyse. Ein Schriftsteller zwischen Deutschland und Italien*,
ed. Roland Berbig and Walter Hettche, Frankfurt–Berlin, Lang,
321 pp., publishes the proceedings of a German-Italian conference
on Heyse. The volume represents a milestone in H.-research, for it is
the first such collaborative work on this author whose prodigious
reputation faded after his death and has only slowly been revived and
re-evaluated in the last 20 years. Contributors from both Germany
and Italy for the most part investigate aspects of H.'s preoccupation
with Italian art and literature, although there are also a few articles
on other subjects. The book finishes with a most useful H.-
bibliography covering the years 1852–2000. The contents are:

R. Bertazzoli, 'Die Rolle von P. H. in der italienischen Literaturwelt' (9–18); G. Häntzschel, 'Zum kulturgeschichtlichen Ort P. Hs als Literaturvermittler' (19–29); R. Bertozzi, 'P. H. als Übersetzer und Vermittler der italienischen Literatur in Deutschland' (31–52); W. Hettche, 'P. Hs *Novellen vom Gardasee*' (53–62); M. Galli, 'Hs *Italienische Novellen* als Makrotext' (62–75); R. Hillenbrand, 'Hs sogenannte Falkentheorie' (77–86); A. Fattori, '"Bürger zweier Welten"? Italien in Hs Lyrik' (87–100); J. John, '"Ich armer idealistischer Thor . . .". Zum Dichterbild in P. Hs Spruchbüchlein. Zugleich ein Beitrag zum Thema Epigonalität' (101–18); H. Gottwald, 'P. Hs *Mythen und Mysterien*' (119–33); H.-A. Koch, 'Märchentheater gegen Alltagswirklichkeit. Ein gemeinsames Rezept von Gozzi und H.' (135–49); J. Mahr, '"Das Leben darstellen." P. Hs Romane' (151–62); G. Rovagnati, '"Zur Lektüre für unreife Jugend soll das Buch freilich nicht empfohlen werden". P. Hs Übersetzung der *Mandragola* von Niccolò Machiavelli' (163–76); M. Bernauer, 'Zweierlei Moderne. P. H. und Italo Svevo' (177–92); H. Häntschel, 'Martha's Briefe an Maria. P. Hs Engagement für eine Modernisierung der Mädchenbildung in Bayern' (193–203); H. O. Horch, 'Jüdische Spuren in P. Hs Leben und Werk' (205–18); R. Berbig, 'Das gelobte Land Italien. P. Hs italienische Tagebuchnotizen 1852/53 im Kontext der Italien-Aufzeichnungen von Franz Kugler, Friedrich Eggers und Theodor Fontane' (219–41); K. Koebe, 'Die "höchste Ehrung, die einem Schriftsteller zuteil werden kann"? Der Nobelpreisträger P. H.' (243–54); R. Hillenbrand, 'Heyseana aus Heidelberg und Nürnberg. Sieben Briefe von P. H. sowie je einer von Geibel und Lenbach an H.' (255–65); R. Hillenbrand, 'Tagebuchverse von P. H.' (267–75); R. Hillenbrand, 'Nachlese zur H.-Sekundärliteratur' (277–320). B. Mullan, 'From Bavaria to Berlin. Stations in P. H's career as a patriotic dramatist', *Euphorion*, 95:129–65. R. Hillenbrand, 'Wahrheit und Dichtung in P. Hs *Salamander*', *ib.*, 167–80.

HORTER, JOHANN TRAUGOTT. H. Kraja, 'Aus den Forschungen von J. T. H. "Die Pastoren"', pp. 317–39 of *Sammeln, Erforschen, Bewahren. Zur Geschichte und Kultur der Oberlausitz. Ernst-Heinz Lemper zum 75. Geburtstag*, Görlitz, Oberlausitzische Ges. der Wiss., 1999, 569 pp.

IMMERMANN. *Immermann Jahrbuch*, 2, contains C. Immermann, 'Zur Feier des Geburtstages. Herausgegeben von P. Hasubek' (9–24); F. Schüppen, 'An den Rändern des bürgerlichen Realismus. Künstler, Liebe und Gesellschaft in "Petrarca"-Tragödien bei I. (1822) und Peter Hille (1896)' (25–40); H. Pöschl, '"Erotische Pädagogik". Is Deutung des Pygmalion-Stoffes' (41–56); T. Spreckelsen, '"Das so prächtige Sachen unter den Gelehrten vermodern!" Liebe, Tod und

Literatur in K. Is "Tristan und Isolde" ' (57–70); G. Schandera et al., 'I. in der DDR. Zur Rezeptionsgeschichte zwischen 1945 und 1990' (71–98); D. Göttsche, 'Der Zeitroman zwischen 1815 und 1830. Ein vergessenes Kapitel aus der Geschichte des deutschen Romans' (99–135).

KELLER. G. K., *Der grüne Heinrich*, ed. Helmuth Nürnberger, Düsseldorf, Artemis & Winkler, 2000, 839 pp., is a reprint of the 1879–80 edition. *Gottfried Keller. Schön ist doch das Leben! Biographie in Briefen*, ed. Peter Goldammer, Berlin, Aufbau, 330 pp., is an attractively presented collection of letters and diary entries spanning K.'s entire adult life which shed light on his search for artistic identity, his position in the social and cultural life of Zürich, and his contact with influential writers and thinkers of his day. As the book is designed to broaden the appeal of K. to a wider, younger readership than has previously been the case, critical apparatus is kept to a minumum, but Goldammer does intersperse the letters with helpful pieces of supplementary information, and there is a detailed index of names including some biographical data. The volume offers a fascinating insight into an author who emerges as a superb letter-writer possessed of a lively, humorous personality and a remarkable gift for narrative. Rolf Selbmann, *Gottfried Keller. Romane und Erzählungen*, Berlin, Schmidt, 192 pp. takes account of recent research and spans K.'s literary career with individual chapters on *Der grüne Heinrich*, *Die Leute von Seldwyla*, *Sieben Legenden*, *Züricher Novellen*, *Das Sinngedicht*, and *Martin Salander*. There is also a detailed bibliography. I. Denneler, 'Heinriche und andere Namensvettern. Zu G. Ks Prosa', Denneler, *Namen*, 69–79, concerns the significance of names in K.'s *Der Landvogt von Greifensee* and *Der grüne Heinrich*. G. Kaiser, 'Experimentieren oder erzählen? Zwei Kulturen in G. Ks *Sinngedicht*', *JDSG*, 45:278–301. J. Dyck, ' "Jugend hat keine Tugend". Zu Heirat und Sexualität in Ks *Romeo und Julia auf dem Dorfe*', Fest. *Pietzcker*, 173–78. P. Villwock, ' "Unter Streitverhältnissen": ein neu entdeckter Brief G. Ks zu *Die Leute von Seldwyla*', *Text*, 2000:84–97. W. Morgenthaler, 'Wann sind G. Ks *Leute von Seldwyla* entstanden? Zu einigen Datierungsfragen der "zweiten vermehrten Auflage" ', *ib.*, 99–110.

KOLBENHEYER, MORITZ. S. Boronkai, 'Wandlungen und Abwandlungen der ungarndeutschen Identität. Anhand von Leben und Werk des M. K. 1810–1884', *JUG*, 1998:147–61.

KUGLER, FRANZ. *Franz Kuglers Briefe an Emanuel Geibel*. ed. Rainer Hillenbrand, Frankfurt–Berlin, Lang, 466 pp., publishes 95 letters dating from 1839–57 which afford a penetrating insight into K.'s artistic and cultural interests. There are many references to other writers of the period whom he greatly influenced, including Burckhardt, Fontane, Storm, and his son-in-law Heyse, as well as first-hand accounts of revolutionary developments in Berlin. The volume includes a comprehensive critical introduction to K.'s life and work, has a number of relevant appendices, and is well indexed.

LAUBE, HEINRICH. A. Detken, 'Die Demimonde-Stücke und ihr Stellenwert im Spielplan Ls am Wiener Stadttheater', pp. 165–99 of *Theaterinstitution und Kulturtransfer* II. Fremdkulturelles Repertoire am Gothaer Hoftheater und an anderen Bühnen, ed. Anke Detken, Tübingen, Narr, 1998, 260 pp. K.-H. Göttert, ' "Die Rhetorik blühte noch"': zur Einschätzung des Vortrags in H. Ls Schriften zum Parlament und zum Theater', pp. 343–57 of *Rhetorica movet. Studies in Historical and Modern Rhetoric in Honour of Heinrich F. Plett*, ed. Peter L. Oesterreich and Thomas O. Sloane, Leiden, Brill, 1999, vii + 545 pp.

LENAU. *Lenau-Jb.*, 26, 2000, includes M. Wagner, 'N. L. und der Wein: eine Motivzusammenstellung' (5–41); K. Harer, 'N. A. Mel'-gunov in Wien 1840–41: Nachtrag zu "N. L. und der 'Brief eines russischen Literaten an H. Koenig'"' (53–56); M. Ritter, 'L.-Bibliographie 2000: Erscheinungen aus den Jahren 1998 und 1999 mit Nachträgen aus früheren Jahren' (135–36). **Nikolaus Lenau — heute gelesen*, ed. Gudrun Heinecke, Vienna, Braumüller, 2000, xiv + 151 pp. U. Abraham, 'Wassermythen und Waldesträume. Die archetypische Symbolsprache in der Naturlyrik N. Ls', pp. 237–56 of *Bildersprache verstehen*, ed. Ruben Zimmermann, Munich, Fink, 2000, 391 pp. R. G. Bogner, 'L. eroticus, Stifter neuroticus, Grillparzer tristis. (Re-)Konstruktion der Lebenswege dreier österreichischer Schriftsteller des 19. Jahrhunderts in neueren fiktionalen Dichterbiographien', Zimmermann, *Fakten*, 57–76. E. Stajèeva, ' "Der Triumphwagen des Wahnbefangenen"': ein Lenau-Porträt von Theodor Trajanov', pp. 265–76 of *70 Jahre Germanistik in Bulgarien*, ed. Ruska Simeonova and Emilia Staitscheva, Sofia, 'St. Kliment Ohridski' U.P., 1999, 507 pp. B. Deliivanova, 'Spezifik und Leistungsvermögen der epischen Form in *Faust* von N. L.', *ib.*, 387–93.

LEWALD. E. Berner, ' "Meine Tochter ist noch ein völliges Kind" — Emanzipationsansätze der deutschen Vormärzpublizistin F. L.: eine Beschreibung in lexikalisch-semantischen Feldern', pp. 97–116 of *Bausteine zu einer Geschichte des weiblichen Sprachgebrauchs*, vol. 4, *Fragestellungen, Methoden, Studies. Internationale Fachtagung Potsdam, 12.–15.9.1999*, ed. Gisela Brandt, Stuttgart, Heinz, 2000, 241 pp.

LILIENCRON. B. Burns, 'The influence of Ivan Turgenev's *Sportsman's Sketches* on the stories of D. v. L.', *OL*, 56: 106–20.

LORM, HIERONYMOUS. J. Veselý, 'H. L. und Adalbert Stifter', Fialová-Fürstová, *Mährische Literatur*, 94–102.

LUDWIG. M. Schönemann, 'Die blaue Blume des Apollonius Nettenmair. Zu O. Ls *Zwischen Himmel und Erde*', *SGGed*, 8, 2000: 173–80.

MARX, KARL. R. Sperl, 'Die editorische Dokumentation von Übersetzungen in der Marx-Engels-Gesamtausgabe', *Editio*, 14, 2000: 54–71.

MENDELSSOHN BARTHOLDY, FELIX. *Mendelssohn-Studien*, 11, 1999, includes C. Hellmundt, 'Anton Christanell und seine Beziehungen zu Felix Mendelssohn Bartholdy' (77–102); R. Elvers, 'Durchgerutscht. Einige Bemerkungen zur Ausgabe des Briefwechsels zwischen Fanny Hensel und Felix Mendelssohn Bartholdy' (131–43); T. Schinköth, '"Es soll hier keine Diskussion über den Wert der Kompositionen angeschnitten werden." Felix Mendelssohn Bartholdy im NS-Staat' (177–205).

MEYER. *Conrad Ferdinand Meyer. Fünfzig Gedichte*, ed. Dietrich Bode, Stuttgart, Reclam, 79 pp. *C. F. Meyer: Die Wirklichkeit der Zeit und die Wahrheit der Kunst*, ed. Monika Ritzer, Tübingen–Basle, Francke, 293 pp., marks the 100th anniversary of M.'s death in 1988 and reappraises his position in a European context as a contemporary of Wagner, Nietzsche, and Bismarck and a critical observer of the *Gründerzeit*. It contains M. Ritzer, 'Rätsel des Daseins und verborgene Linien. Zu C. F. Ms literarischer Philosophie' (9–33); H. Kaiser, 'Unzeitgemäße Zeitgenossenschaft. *Huttens letzte Tage* gelesen im Blick auf den frühen Nietzsche' (35–50); J. Söring, 'Wagner — Meyer — Nietzsche' (51–72); M. Engel, 'Der literarische Traum im Spätrealismus am Beispiel C. F. Ms' (73–92); K. S. Guthke, 'Lebenskunst, Sterbenskunst. C. F. M. und die Kultur des letzten Wortes in Europa' (93–125); C. Laumont, 'Grenzgefechte des Realismus. C. F. M. und Gustave Flaubert — Aspekte eines Vergleichs' (127–45); I. Denneler, '*incognito* — Überlegungen zum Historismus und Ästhetizismus C. F. Ms' (147–66); M. Andermatt, 'C. F. M. und der Kulturkampf. Vexierspiele im Medium historischen Erzählens' (167–90); P. Sprengel, 'Zwischen Ästhetizismus und Volkstümlichkeit. C. F. Ms Gedichte für Rodenbergs *Deutsche Rundschau*' (191–203); E. Pulver, '"Es mußte in Gottes Namen ein Entschluß gefaßt sein." C. F. M. im deutsch-französischen Spannungsfeld' (205–20); D. Müller, 'Kunstwelt und Heimat. Die imaginären Museen C. F. Ms und Gottfried Kellers' (221–35); P. Rusterholz, 'Scherz und Ernst der Fiktion in C. F. Ms Novellen' (237–50); P. M. Lützeler, 'Oszillierende Charaktere. Intertext und Zitat in C. F. Ms *Jürg Jenatsch*' (251–68); P. A. Bloch, 'Der Teil und das Ganze. C. F. Ms Gedicht "Der römische Brunnen" im Spiegel seiner Varianten' (269–90).

M. Boudinaud, 'L'implicite dans le discours du diplomate chez C. F. M.', *CEtGer*, 39, 2000: 107–18. W. Schönau, 'Das Drama des unbegabten Kindes. Zu C. F. Ms Novelle *Das Leiden eines Knaben'*, Fest. Pietzcker, 179–91. W. Taraba, 'C. F. Ms *Jürg Jenatsch*: Geschichte in der Geschichte', pp. 551–69 of *De consolatione philologiae: Studies in Honour of Evelyn S. Firchow*, ed. Anna Grotans, 2 vols, Göppingen, Kümmerle, 2000, 773 pp.

MEYSENBUG. G. Schwarz, 'Malwida von Meysenbug — Porträit einer Idealistin', pp. 31–49 of *Die Frau als Kulturschöpferin. Zehn biographische Essays*, ed. Katharina Kaminski, Würzburg, Königshausen & Neumann, 2000, 235 pp.

MÖRIKE. Ulrich Kittstein, *Zivilisation und Kunst: Eine Untersuchung zu Eduard Mörikes 'Maler Nolten'*, St. Ingbert, Röhrig, 329 pp., is a perceptive and scholarly study which offers a significant contribution to the resurgence of critical interest in this dark and difficult text. The discussion of the problems of the artist and of the themes of hypochondria, identity crisis, and madness is placed in the context of Norbert Elias's theory of civilisation, and includes substantial appraisal of the role of poetry in the novel which has traditionally been overlooked. Thomas Wolf, *Brüder, Geister und Fossilien. Eduard Mörikes Erfahrungen der Umwelt*, Tübingen, Niemeyer, vi + 178 pp., brings together three self-contained essays on M.'s problematic relationship with his brothers, two of whom had criminal records; on his association with the physician and writer Justinus Kerner who nurtured M.'s interest in spiritualism and the occult; and on his pursuits in later life as an amateur geologist whose passion for fossil-collection assumed quasi-religious proportions. Despite the apparent incongruity in combining such disparate topics, the overall achievement of this volume is to illuminate some known but neglected aspects of M.'s life and thought, and thereby to reveal a more faithful picture of the writer than has emerged in the past. Leif Ludwig Albertsen, **Mörikes Metra*, Flensburg, Futura, 1999, 79 pp. Karin de LaRoi-Frey, **Mörike von A bis Z*, Leinfelden–Echterdingen, DRW, 2000, 139 pp. F. Meyer, 'E. M. als politischer Dichter', *DVLG*, 75:387–421, challenges the notion of M.'s work as purely idyllic and unpolitical, and examines evidence of his critical reflection on contemporary politics found in the *Feuerreiter, Der alte Turmhahn*, the fragments of two dramas, and *Maler Nolten*. R. Seidel, 'Schwäbische Kunde. Probleme der Kommunikation zwischen Autor und Leser in fiktionalen M.-Biographien der achtziger Jahre. Mit einer Quellenbibliographie zur literarischen Verarbeitung der M.-Figur im 20. Jahrhundert', Zimmermann, *Fakten*, 77–99. Angela Spanaus, *'Zurückblickende Wehmut': die Welt der Stimmungen bei Eduard Mörike*, Trier, WVT, 1999, 357 pp., is a Wuppertal dissertation.

MÜLLER, FOOKE HOISSEN. *Fooke Hoissen Müller. Sämtliche Gedichte*, ed. Menso Folkerts, Aurich, Ostfriesische Landschaft, 1998, cxxxiii + 430 pp., publishes the complete poetic works of this almost forgotten northern German poet (1798–1856). The volume includes both poems in *Hochdeutsch*, sometimes reminiscent of Immermann or Heine, and poems in *Plattdeutsch*, composed in the latter part of his life.

NESTROY. The HKA of N.'s *Sämtliche Werke*, ed. Jürgen Hein et al., Vienna, Deuticke, has added *Stücke*, 24.1: *Zwey ewige Juden und Keiner*, ed. John R. P. McKenzie, 2000, xviii + 406 pp.; *Stücke*, 24.2: *Der Schützling*, ed. John R. P. McKenzie, 2000, xvi + 431 pp.; *Stücke*, 25.1: *Die schlimmen Buben in der Schule. Martha*, ed. Friedrich Walla, 2000, xv + 354 pp.; and *Stücke*, 30: *Mein Freund, Der gemüthliche Teufel*, ed. Hugo Aust, xvi + 639 pp. The 200th anniversary of N.'s birth this year has been celebrated in two major exhibitions for which substantial catalogues have been produced, and has triggered the publication of proceedings of the last three N. symposia in Vienna. Birgit Pargner and W. Edgar Yates, *Nestroy in München: eine Ausstellung des Deutschen Theatermuseums, 28. September 2001 — 6. Januar 2002*, Vienna, Lehner, 304 pp. *Die Welt steht auf kein' Fall mehr lang: Johann Nestroy zum 200. Geburtstag: Katalog zur 277. Sonderausstellung des Historischen Museums der Stadt Wien gemeinsam mit der Wiener Stadt- und Landesbibliothek: Historisches Museum, Karlsplatz, 6. Dezember — 27 Jänner 2002*, Vienna, Historisches Museum, 299 pp. *Der unbekannte Nestroy: Editorisches, Biographisches, Interpretatorisches: Beiträge zum Nestroy-Symposium im Rahmen der Wiener Vorlesungen, 16–17 November 1994*, ed. W. Edgar Yates, Vienna U.P., 116 pp. *'Bei die Zeitverhältnisse noch solche Privatverhältnisse': Nestroys Alltag und dessen Dokumentation: Beiträge zum Symposium im Rahmen der Wiener Vorlesungen, 19–20 März 1997*, ed. W. Edgar Yates, Vienna U.P., 148 pp. *Hinter den Kulissen von Vor- und Nachmärz: Soziale Umbrüche und Theaterkultur bei Nestroy: Beiträge zum Nestroy-Symposium im Rahmen der Wiener Vorlesungen, 23 Februar 2001*, ed. H. Christian Ehalt et al., Vienna U.P., 153 pp. Renate Wagner, **Nestroy zum Nachschlagen: Sein Leben — sein Werk — seine Zeit*, Graz–Vienna, Styria, 264 pp. Walter Schübler, **Nestroy. Eine Biographie in 30 Szenen*, Salzburg, Residenz, 318 pp. J. Hein, ' "Übersetzen's aus Frankreich a Stuck . . .". J. N. als übersetzender Bearbeiter', *Editio*, 14, 2000: 72–87.

Nestroyana, 21, contains B. Pargner and W. E. Yates, 'Adolf Bäuerle im Briefwechsel mit Charlotte Birch-Pfeiffer und Christian Andreas Birch. Sieben unveröffentlichte Briefe' (5–17); F. Walla, 'Wiederfindung und Wiederverwertung. Nachträge zu *Prinz Friedrich* und *Glück, Mißbrauch und Rückkehr*' (18–25); A. Böhn, 'Geometrisierung, Serialität und Komik bei N.' (26–33); J. Danielczyk and E. Fuhrich, 'Wiedergefundener N.-Brief in den Marischka-Beständen' (34–38); R. Theobald, ' "Bei dem Abschluß mit hervorragenden Talenten . . .". Ein unbekannter Brief des Direktors N.' (39–41); H. Jarka, 'N. im Exil' (42–71); A. Thomasberger, 'N.: ein Lehrer Hofmannsthals?' (72–79); H. J. Koning, 'Die Welt als Labyrinth bei Dürrenmatt und N.' (80–89); J. Danielczyk, 'Ferdinand Raimunds "Notizen Buch"' (101–05); R. Theobald, 'Neues von Franz Wiest. Ns Erzfeind im Kollegen-Klatsch' (106–10); F. Walla, '"Des Kaufmanns und des Gatten Ehre." Paul Lacroix als Quelle für Ns *Der alte Mann mit der jungen Frau* und *Mein Freund*' (111–23); I. Pangerl, 'Kultursponsoring durch das Kaiserhaus. Ein N.-Fund im Haus-, Hof- und Staatsarchiv' (124–31); U. Helmensdorfer, '*Berlin wird Weltstadt*. David Kalisch — ein preußischer N.? Versuch einer Annäherung' (132–49); J. Hein, '"Und wir haben gedacht, es ist eine Posse von N." Eine Reminiszenz bei Karl Emil Franzos' (150–52); G. Stieg, 'Fünf Abendwinde' (153–63).

NIETZSCHE. Duncan Large, *Nietzsche and Proust. A Comparative Study*, OUP, 298 pp., is a scholarly exposition on the previously neglected affinities between N. and Proust. The author reads Proust's novel *A la recherche du temps perdu* in the light of the great Nietzschean themes, and examines N.'s philosophy in terms of the Proustian issues of time and transcendence. A comprehensive bibliography and index complete this erudite work. Ralf Witzler, *Europa im Denken Nietzsches*, Würzburg, Königshausen & Neumann, 229 pp. *Zur Wirkung Nietzsches: Der Deutsche Expressionismus, Menno Ter Braak, Martin Heidegger, Ernst Jünger, Thomas Mann, Oswald Spengler*, ed. Hans Ester and Meindert Evers, Würzburg, Königshausen & Neumann, 143 pp., publishes contributions by six Dutch scholars to a conference held at the University of Nijmegen in 2000 on the influence of N. on the 20th c. The volume identifies connections with N. in prominent writers and thinkers who were heirs to his philosophy, tracing his impact on the ideas of Expressionism through National Socialism to post-modernism. Manfred Eger, *Nietzsches Bayreuther Passion*, Freiburg, Rombach, 598 pp., is a substantial and illuminating study on the complex relationship between N. and Wagner. E. takes issue with an entire corpus of scholarship that has perpetuated the orthodoxy of myths initiated by N. himself in defence of his break with Wagner. Careful revision of the evidence, E. claims, suggests that N.'s neurotic projection of his own weaknesses on to Wagner contributed to their estrangement. This places the association between the two men in a different light and brings fresh impetus to both Wagner and N. studies. Michael Steinmann, *Die Ethik Friedrich Nietzsches*, Berlin, de Gruyter, 2000, x + 257 pp. Laurence Lampert, *Nietzsche's Task: An Interpretation of 'Beyond Good and Evil'*, New Haven–London, Yale U.P., x + 320 pp. *Nietzsche*, ed. John Richards and Brian Leiter, OUP, 379 pp., is a collection of 13 previously published articles. The volume aims to bring together some of the most important recent philosophical writings on N., and covers topics such as N.'s views on truth and knowledge, his teachings on the eternal recurrence and will to power, his critique of morality, and his genealogical method. Johann Prossliner, *Friedrich Nietzsche: Also sprach Zarathustra*, ed. Volker Gerhardt, Berlin, Akademie, 2000, xi + 408 pp. *Licht wird alles, was ich fasse: Das Lexikon der Nietzsche-Zitate*, ed. Johann Prossliner, Munich, DTV, 415 pp. Bruno Hillenbrand, *Nietzsche: Wie ihn die Dichter sahen*, Göttingen, Vandenhoeck & Ruprecht, 2000, 160 pp.

H. Cancik and H. Cancik-Lindemaier, 'Ns *Mysterienlehre*', pp. 59–73 of *Mystique, mysticisme et modernité en Allemagne autour de 1900 / Mystik, Mystizismus und Moderne in Deutschland um 1900*, ed. Moritz Bassler and Hildegard Châtellier, Strasburg U.P., 1998, 328 pp. Elisabeth M. Weijers, *Nietzsche als versteller. Hoe het lichaam wordt wat het is*, Kampen, Agora, 2000, 271 pp. E. Kleinschmidt, 'Überlegungen zu einer amnestischen Kulturtheorie in F. Ns *Also sprach Zarathustra*', *Arcadia*, 36:100–17. B. R. Wheeler, 'Modernist reenchantments 1: from liberalism to aestheticized politics', *GR*, 74:223–36, begins with an examination of N.'s anti-liberalism. N. Rennie, ' "Schilderungssucht" and "historische Krankheit": Lessing, N., and the body historical', *GQ*, 74:186–96, examines the connection between Lessing's *Laokoon* and N.'s essay 'Vom Nutzen und Nachteil der Historie für das Leben'. M. Lackey, 'Atheism and sadism: N. and Woolf on post-God discourse', *PLit*, 24, 2000:346–63. A. Camion, ' "Die ewige Wiederkehr des Gleichen": retour sur quelques interprétations de la figure nietzschéene', *CEtGer*, 39, 2000:9–16. J. Darmaun, 'Le sens de l'histoire selon la deuxième *Considération intempestive* de N.', *ib.*, 17–28. A. R. García, 'La ilusión imposible. La estética en El nacimiento de la tragedia de Nietzsche', *CHA*, 610:79–86. Y. Guéneau, 'Politique, religion (et "Lumières") chez N.', *RevA*, 32, 2000:263–78. P. Bridgwater, 'Edward Carpenter and N.', Thomas, *German Studies*, 196–223. B. Scheer, 'Das Verhältnis von Ästhetik und Ethik im Denken Ns', pp. 51–68 of *Etho-Poetik. Ethik und Ästhetik im Dialog: Erwartungen, Forderungen, Abgrenzungen*, ed. Bernhard Greiner and Maria Moog-Grünewald, Bonn, Bouvier, 1998, xv + 218 pp. F. Lönker, 'N.: *Vom deutschen Mythologen zum europäischen Freigeist*', Essen, *Geschichten*, 187–200. G. Streim, 'Die "intimste Sprache" der "Modernität". Ns Décadence-Kritik im ästhetikgeschichtlichen Kontext', *Fest. Janz*, 120–31. B. Hillebrand, 'N., Benn und der Postmodernismus. Perspektivismus und Relativismus in heutiger Sicht', pp. 175–98 of *Il cacciatore di silenzi. Studi dedicati a Ferruccio Masini*, ed. Paolo Chiarini et al., Rome, Istituto Italiano di Studi Germanici, 1998, viii + 469 pp. P. Pütz, ' "Arischer" Frevel und "semitische" Sünde. Ns Prometheus-Konzeption', pp. 145–60 of *Prometheus. Mythos der Kultur*, ed. Edgar Pankow and Günter Peters, Munich, Fink, 1999, 248 pp. E. Behler, 'Translating N. in the United States: critical observations on *The Complete Works of Friedrich Nietzsche*', pp. 125–46 of *Translating Literatures — Translating Cultures. New Vistas and Approaches in Literary Studies*, ed. Kurt Mueller-Vollmer and Michael Irmscher, Berlin, Schmidt, 1998, xviii + 214 pp. Peter Stücheli, *Poetisches Pathos. Eine Idee bei Friedrich Nietzsche und im deutschen Expressionismus*, Berne–Berlin, Lang, 1999, 235 pp., is a Zurich dissertation. B. Biebuyck, 'N.'s curse on Christianity. Explorations of the power of creative metaphor', pp. 190–217 of *Faith and Fiction. Interdisciplinary Studies on the Interplay between Metaphor and Religion. A Selection of Papers from the 25th LAUD Symposium of the Gerhard Mercator University of Duisburg on 'Metaphor and Religion'*, ed. Benjamin Biebuyck, Frankfurt, Lang, 1998, 253 pp. 'Fiktionalisierung des Faktischen und Faktifizierung der Fiktion: Anmerkungen zur Autobiographie im Hinblick auf Goethe, Stendhal und N.', pp. 309–42 of Thomas Böning, *Alterität und Identität in literarischen Texten von Rousseau und Goethe bis Celan und Handke*, Freiburg, Rombach, 368 pp.

Nietzsche-Studien, 30, contains G. Abel, 'Bewußtsein — Sprache — Natur. Ns Philosophie des Geistes' (1–43); H.-J. Gawoll, 'N. und der Geist Spinozas: die existentielle Umwandlung einer affirmativen Ontologie' (44–61); D. R. Johnson, 'N's early Darwinism. The "David Strauss" essay of 1873' (62–79); H. Siemens, 'Agonal configurations in the *Unzeitgemässe Betrachtungen*. Identity, mimesis and the *Übertragung* of cultures in N.'s early thought' (80–106); M. Brusotti, 'Wille zum Nichts, Ressentiment, Hypnose. "Aktiv" und "reaktiv" in Ns *Genealogie der Moral*' (107–32); O. Dier, 'Die Verwandlung der Wiederkunft' (133–74); D. Havemann, 'Evangelische Polemik. Ns Paulusdeutung' (175–86); P. Greanet, 'The richest poverty: the encounter between Zarathustra and truth in the *Dionysos-Dithyramben*' (187–99); E. Eilon, 'N.'s principle of abundance as guiding aesthetic value' (200–21); E. Dufour, 'La physiologie de la musique de N.' (222–45); G. Moore, 'Hysteria and histrionics. N., Wagner and the pathology of genius' (246–66); H.-J. Pieper, 'Die Philosophie Robert Musils im Spannungsfeld der Theorien Ns und Machs' (267–94); P. Pütz, 'N. und der Antisemitismus' (295–304); J. Golomb and R. Wistrich, 'N.'s politics, fascism and the Jews' (305–21).

Nietzscheforschung, 8, includes G. Wohlfart, 'Artisten-Metaphysik. Der antike Boden von Ns Philosophie' (33–41); V. Ebersbach, 'N. im Garten Epikurs' (43–61); V. Riedel, 'N. und das Bild einer "dionysischen Antike" in der deutschsprachigen Literatur des 20. Jahrhunderts' (63–87); H. J. Schmidt, 'Von "Als Kind Gott im Glanze gesehn" zum "Christenhaß"'? Ns früh(st)e weltanschauliche Entwicklung

(1844–64), eine Skizze' (95–118); E. Marsal, 'Der Sansculotte Jesus Christ. Die Christologie des Pfortaschülers F. N. als eigenständige Rezeption des zeitgenössischen theologischen Spektrums' (119–36); J. Kjaer, 'Ns Auseinandersetzung mit dem Christentum in seiner Naumburger und Portenser Zeit' (137–56); V. Ebersbach, 'N. — ein Grieche unter Römern. Vorchristliche Fundamente in Nietzsche Kritik am Christentum' (157–87); K. Jauslin, 'Was der Löwe nicht vermochte: etwas für Kinder und Kindesköpfe. Über Fritz Nietzsches *Naumburger Festungsbuch*' (189–203); R. Ziemann, 'Ewiges Ziel und falsche Begriffe. Zu F. Ns Prometheus-Drama' (205–17); R. G. Müller, 'Erkenntnis und Erlösung. Über Ns Umgang mit vorchristlich-griechischem Gedankengut vor dem Hintergrund seiner christlichen Herkunft' (219–32); J. Pestlin, 'N. im Völkischen Beobachter. Eine Bestandsaufnahme' (235–48); H. Schneppen, 'N. und Paraguay: der Philosoph als Bauer?' (249–65); H. Völkerling, 'Im Schatten von Georg Brandes. Der Däne Konrad Simonsen in seinem Briefwechsel mit Elisabeth Förster-Nietzsche' (267–74); J. Hengst, 'Endspiel eines "Schreibthier"-Lebens. Metamorphose, Apotheose und Parodie in Ns letztem Brief an Jacob Burckhardt' (275–90); S. Dietzsch, 'N. und Ariadne' (291–306); H.-M. Gerlach, 'Wege der N.-Kritik — Jaspers, Bloch, Lukács' (307–13); V. Gerhardt, 'Ns Alter-Ego. Über die Wiederkehr des Sokrates' (315–32); C. Gentili, 'Die radikale Hermeneutik F. Ns' (333–36).

PAOLI. *Betty Paoli. Was hat der Geist denn wohl gemein mit dem Geschlecht?*, ed. Eva Geber, Vienna, Mandelbaum, 202 pp., with an essay by Karin S. Wozonig, presents the achievements and dilemmas of P.'s unconventional career as both a lyricist and the first German-speaking female journalist.

PREŠEREN, FRANCE. *France Prešeren. Deutsche Dichtungen*, ed. Wilhelm Baum, Klagenfurt, Kitab, 1999, 136 pp.

PRUTZ, ROBERT. S. Tschopp, 'Von den Aporien politischen Dichtens im Vormärz: Robert Eduard Prutz', *Euphorion*, 95 : 39–67.

RAABE. *The Odin Field*, trans. Michael Ritterson, Rochester, Camden House, xxx + 177 pp., is the first translation into English of R.'s historical novel *Das Odfeld* (1889), set during the Seven Years' War. Ritterson has succeeded in creating a highly readable English version of the work of an author whose prose is often complex and laden with archaisms and abstruse cultural allusions. Many of the references and foreign-language quotations are elucidated in a substantial section of notes, and a helpful introduction presents the salient aspects of R.'s life and work as well as tracing the genesis and reception of *Das Odfeld*. This translation will make a significant text accessible to a much wider readership, and represents a welcome contribution to R. studies which have been gaining momentum in recent decades. J. C. Marshall, 'W. R.'s apothecary: two texts tracing the pharmako-logy of the wild man', *ColGer*, 34:27–40, examines connections between *Zum Wilden Mann* and *Unruhige Gäste*.

Raabe-Jb., 42, contains H.-J. Schrader, 'Autorfedern unter Preß-Autorität. Mitformende Marktfaktoren der realistischen Erzähl-kunst — an Beispielen Storms, Rs und Kellers' (1–40); K. E. Laage, 'Sylt-Spiegelungen in Rs *Deutscher Mondschein* und Storms *Sylter Novelle*. Beobachtungen zur Regionalität in der Dichtung des Poetischen Realismus' (41–49); P. Goldammer, 'Die deutsche Reichshauptstadt als "ungemütliches Großnest". W. Rs Berlin' (50–66); W. Hettche, 'Die Motti zu W. Rs Roman *Die Kinder zu Finkenrode*' (67–78); S. R. Fauth, 'Schopenhauers Philosophie als dominanter Hypotext in Rs Erzählung "Höxter und Corvey"' (79–118); H. Rölleke, 'Vom "40jährigen Dintenjubiläum", dem "armen Heinrich" und dem "Abdruck eines drolligen Aufsatzes". Ein bislang unveröffentlichter Brief W. Rs an Carl Schultes' (119–25); H. Detering, 'Grobe Grellheiten, drollige Verse. Zwei Briefe Hermann Hesses über W. R.' (126–29); S. S. Tschopp, 'Kunst und Volk. Robert Eduard Prutz' und Gottfried Kellers Konzept einer zugleich ästhetischen und populären Literatur' (130–46). J. Pizer, 'Vienna as the Heart of Darkness: W. R.'s "Lesser-Germany" politics', pp. 1–18 of *Austria in Literature*, ed. Donald G. Daviau, Riverside CA, Ariadne, 2000, xii + 326 pp.

REUTER, FRITZ. *Fritz Reuter, Neubrandenburg, 1848*, ed. Christian Bunners (Beiträge der F.-R.-Gesellschaft; 9), Hamburg, von Bockel, 2000, 111 pp., contains W. Rieck, 'F. R. und Neubrandenburg' (9–28); A. Hückstädt, 'Neubrandenburg und die Neubrandenburger in Leben und Werk F. Rs' (29–49); A. Hückstädt, '"Freut euch, ihr Mecklenburger!" — Mecklenburg im Jahre 1848. Eine unbekannte Revolutionsgeschichte des Neubrandenburger Zeitzeugen Franz Boll' (61–76); U. Bichel, 'Johann Heinrich Voss, F. R. und die Idylle' (77–87); C. Bunners, '"... denn kemen wi woll up den rechten Weg." Maßstäbe des Menschlichen in F. Rs "Dörchläuchting"' (89–103); H.-G. Quadt, 'Betrachtungen zu *Kein Hüsung*' (105–09). G. Schmidt-Henkel, '"... denn Bezüge gibt's überall und Bezüge sind das Leben". F. R. und Theodor Fontane — mit einer ein-führenden Abschweifung zu Wilhelm Busch', *Fest. Fritz*, 53–63.

RÜCKERT. The HKA of R.'s works, ed. Hans Wollschläger and Rudolf Kreutner, Göttingen, Wallstein, has added *Liedertagebuch*. *Werke der Jahre 1846–1847*, vol. 1, ed. Rudolf Kreutner et al., Göttingen, Wallstein, 443 pp. The fact that the current volume spans only two years of R.'s later work bears witness to the phenomenal productivity of this neglected artist. R. was the most prolific 19th-c. poet, writing almost 10,000 short poems, largely dismissed in the past as 'Altersverse', in the last 20 years of his life alone. This edition, which publishes much of his work for the first time, at last does justice to the scale of his *oeuvre* and will lend fresh impetus to R. studies. The volume begins with a detailed month-by-month summary of R.'s activities in 1846–47, followed by the 257 poems that form the main body of the text. The chronological presentation of the poems, of which often several were composed on any given date, allows the reader to observe the course of the poet's introspective musings over the period in question. The next section has 70 pages of letters from R. to various correspondents, including several to his wife from whom he was separated during each winter semester while lecturing in Oriental Studies in Berlin. The study concludes with some 60 pages of editorial comment and notes on the poems and letters. J. M. Fischer, 'F. Rs *Kindertodtenlieder*', *Merkur*, 54, 2000: 1233–36.

SAAR. J. Stüben, 'Poetische Reflexionen über Völker und Staaten Europas im Werk von F. v. S.', Segebrecht, *Europa*, 54–70.

SACHER-MASOCH, LEOPOLD. Karin Bang, **Elsk mig! En studie i Leopold von Sacher-Masochs masochisme*, Copenhagen, Reitzel, 1998, 303 pp.

SACHER-MASOCH, WANDA. K. Gerstenberger, '"Das Mysterium der Liebe." Geschlechterkämpfe und Begehren bei Wanda von Sacher-Masoch', pp. 103–19 of *Frauen — Körper — Kunst. Literarische Inszenierungen weiblicher Sexualität*, ed. Karin Tebben, Göttingen, Vandenhoeck & Ruprecht, 2000, 272 pp.

SCHEFFEL, JOSEPH VICTOR V. J. Matoni, 'Ekkehard, ein bürgerlicher Held', pp. 147–57 of *Der einsame Held*, ed. Wilhelm G. Busse and Olaf Templin, Tübingen, Francke, 2000, 229 pp.

SCHIFF. Mamiko Ikenaga, **Die Ghettogeschichten von Hermann Schiff und Hermann Blumenthal*, Frankfurt–Berlin, Lang, 2000, ix + 361 pp., is a Düsseldorf dissertation.

SCHOPENHAUER. W. v. Löhneysen, 'Aus dem Nachlaß Arthur Schopenhauers', *Brandis Vol.*, 859–71.

SCHUMANN, ROBERT. A. W. Lemke, 'Robert Schumann und Johanna Kinkel. Musikalische Stimmen der Revolution von 1848/49', *IJBAG*, 11–12, 1999–2000: 179–96.

SEALSFIELD. W. Kriegleder, 'Die Gestaltung des "Chaos zum Ganzen und zum Einklang". Monosemierung als künstlerisches Prinzip in C. Ss Roman *Der Virey und die Aristokraten oder Mexiko im Jahre 1812*', Fialová-Fürstová, *Mährische Literatur*, 103–22. A. Měšt'an, 'Heutiger Stand der Forschung über den deutschsprachigen amerikanischen Autor C. S. aus Poppitz in Mähren', *ib.*, 123–28. J. P. Strelka, 'C. S. und die Freimaurerei', *Germanoslavica*, 6, 1999: 31–40.

SPYRI. *Johanna Spyri. Wenn die Heimat ruft: Geschichten, die das Leben schrieb*, Basle, Brunnen, 234 pp., is a collection of little-known stories from the early period of S.'s writing career, published to coincide with the centenary of her death this year. K. Spinner, 'Semiotik des Essens und Trinkens in J. Ss *Heidi*', pp. 431–40 of *Lese-Zeichen: Semiotik und Hermeneutik in Raum und Zeit. Festschrift für Peter Rusterholz zum 65. Geburtstag*, ed. Henriette Herwig, Tübingen, Francke, 1999, xvi + 499 pp. R. Schindler, 'Form und Funktion religiöser Elemente in J. Ss Werken', Rutschmann, *Nebenan*, 173–99.

STIFTER. The HKA of S.'s *Werke und Briefe*, ed. Alfred Doppler et al., Stuttgart, Kohlhammer, has added vol. IV.2: *Der Nachsommer: eine Erzählung*, ed. Wolfgang Frühwald and Walter Hettche, 1999, 269 pp., and vol. V.5: *Witiko: Apparat*, vol. 2, ed. Alfred Doppler and Wolfgang Wiesmüller, 429 pp. Mathias Mayer, *Adalbert Stifter. Erzählen als Erkennen*, Stuttgart, Reclam, 279 pp., offers a useful overview of S.'s entire writing career. It has five to eight pages of analysis on each story, and longer sections on *Der Nachsommer* and *Witiko*. There are also brief commentaries on S.'s non-fictional publications, and the volume finishes with some 40 pages of bibliography and an index of names. Michael Wild, *Wiederholung und Variation im Werk Adalbert Stifters*, Würzburg, Königshausen & Neumann, 169 pp., is a Freiburg dissertation which traces the changing form and function of repetition in S.'s work through close textual analysis of eight works spanning his writing career. Although familiar ground is perhaps inevitably revisited, it is a competent and useful study on a contentious aspect of S.'s style. Frank Schweizer, *Ästhetische Wirkungen in Adalbert Stifters 'Studien'. Die Bedeutung des Begehrens und der Aneignung im Rahmen von Adalbert Stifters ästhetischem Verfahren (unter Abgrenzung zu Gottfried Keller)*, Frankfurt–Berlin, Lang, 256 pp., is a Stuttgart dissertation in which the author challenges the traditional claim that S.'s work is devoid of references to sexual desire. The study ends with a 70–page exploration of the same theme in Keller by way of comparison. Axel Fliethmann, *Stellenlektüre: Stifter — Foucault*, Tübingen, Niemeyer, x + 184 pp., is a Cologne dissertation which presents an analysis of S.'s *Der Nachsommer* and Foucault's *Les mots et les choses*. The approach is grounded in the theory of deconstruction, and spans philosophy, psychoanalysis, and linguistics as well as literary criticism. Robert Ruprecht, *Subtile Signale. Beobachtungen zur Syntax bei Adalbert Stifter*, Berne–Berlin, Lang, 269 pp., examines two published versions of S.'s *Der Hagestolz* and his late story *Der Waldbrunnen* with the aim of demonstrating the significance of the largely syntactic changes made by S. in the process of review. Informed by the author's background in linguistics, the work focuses on the presentation of textual alterations and statistical data rather than on literary interpretation, and contains a multitude of tables and graphs likely to be meaningful only to a minority of readers.

C. Begemann, 'A. S.: *Der Nachsommer*', pp. 203–25 of *Lektüren für das 21. Jahrhundert. Schlüsseltexte der deutschen Literatur von 1200 bis 1990*, ed. Dorothea Klein and Sabine Schneider, Würzburg, Königshausen & Neumann, 2000, 303 pp., is a very readable commentary highlighting the significance of this now neglected novel. It includes eight illustrative plates. A. Doppler, 'A. S. als Briefschreiber. Dargestellt vor allem an den Briefen an Amalia Stifter', Bauer, *Edition*, 133–46. H. Blaukopf, 'Ss literarischer Protokollsatz. Ein Mittel zur Darstellung der "wirklichen Wahrheit"', pp. 9–26 of *Fiction in Science — Science in Fiction. Zum Gespräch zwischen Literatur und Wissenschaft*, ed. Wendelin Schmidt-Dengler, Vienna, Hölder-Pichler-Tempsky, 1998, 137 pp. P. Kelemen, 'Metaphorische Konstruktionen und Leserrollen in A. Ss *Bergkristall* (1852)', *Neohelicon*, 27, 2000: 165–85. G. Fieguth, ' "eine Sammlung von allerlei Spielereien und Kram für die Jugend": A. S., *Bunte Steine*', *Fest Kliewer*, 183–98. P. Becher, ' "Unser sudetendeutscher Klassiker . . .": Aspekte der deutschböhmischen Stifterrezeption 1918–38', *Brücken*, 7, 1999: 167–86.

STORM. M. Wenzel, 'Kein "Winkel" in der Geschichte. Die trügerische Idylle in T. Ss Erzählung *Waldwinkel*, pp. 149–68 of *Geschichtserfahrung im Spiegel der Literatur. Festschrift für Jürgen Schröder zum 65. Geburtstag*, ed. Cornelia Blasberg and Franz-Josef Deiters, Tübingen, Stauffenburg, 2000, xii + 459 pp. W. Palaver, 'Hauke Haien — ein Sündenbock? T. Ss *Schimmelreiter* aus der Perspektive der Theorie René Girards', Tschuggnall, *Religion*, 221–36. G. D'Onghia, 'Le ambivalenze prospettiche nell'ultima novella di S.', *Cultura tedesca*, 1999: 183–99. D. Jackson, 'T. Ss *Zerstreute Kapitel*', *Berliner Hefte*, 2000: 123–43.

STSG, 50, contains G. Eversberg, 'Region und Poesie. T. Ss Entwicklung zum Schriftsteller' (7–21); R. Morrien, 'Arbeit "in Kontrasten" — Künstler — und Vaterschaft in T. Ss Novelle *Eine Malerarbeit*' (23–35); D. Jackson, '*Ein Bekenntnis* — T. Ss frauenfreundliche Abrechnung mit einem mörderischen romantischen Liebesideal' (37–63); S. Bendel, 'Hochzeit der Gegensätze oder Suche nach dem Weiblichen? Wasser- und Feuerimaginationen in T. Ss *Regentrude*' (65–79); W. Lagler, ' "Ich grüße Sie auf dem letzten Lappen Papier." T. Ss Briefwechsel mit Rudolph von Fischer-Benzon' (81–101); D. Lohmeier, 'Neue Briefe aus der Storm-Familie in der Landesbibliothek. Mit drei Briefen Paul Heyses an Do Storm vom Juli 1888' (103–09); H. Borzikowsky, ' "Ich möchte dem Mann das gönnen." Rudolph Christian Ström — Photograph und Porträtist der Storm-Familie' (111–17); G. Eversberg, 'Eine bisher unbekannte Photographie von T. S.' (119–23); E. Jacobsen, 'S.-Bibliographie' (125–35).

Storm-Blätter aus Heiligenstadt, 2000, contains P. Goldmann, 'Miniatur-maler oder realistischer Novellist. T. S. in deutschen Konversa-tionslexika' (4–11); R. Fasold, 'Geschwisterliebe und Heimatsehnsucht in Texten T. Ss' (12–30).

WAGNER. Nike Wagner, *The Wagners. The Dramas of a Musical Dynasty*, trans. Ewald Osers and Michael Downes, London, Weiden-feld & Nicolson, 2000, xix + 327 pp., is written by the great-granddaughter of R. W., and offers an inside account of the family's troubled history and of the internecine disputes that have surrounded the Bayreuth Festival. The author presents a critical appraisal of her family's remarkable position in the nation's cultural identity and of its association with right-wing ideology. Marc A. Weiner, **Antisemiti-sche Fantasien: Die Musikdramen Richard Wagners*, Berlin, Henschel, 2000, 477 pp., is a translation by Thies Henning of *Richard Wagner and the anti-Semitic Imagination* (1995). Jens M. Fischer, **Richard Wagners 'Das Judentum in der Musik': eine kritische Dokumentation als Beitrag zur Geschichte des Antisemitismus*, Frankfurt–Leipzig, Insel, 2000, 380 pp. Mary A. Cicora, **Wagner's 'Ring' and German Drama: Comparative Studies in Mythology and Drama*, Westport, CT, Greenwood, 1999, viii + 186 pp. Bernd Zegowitz, **Richard Wagners unvertonte Opern*, Frankfurt–Berlin, Lang, 2000, 305 pp., is a Heidelberg dissertation. M. Owen Lee, **Wagner: The Terrible Man and his Truthful Art. The 1998 Larkin-Stuart Lectures*, Toronto U.P., 1999, x + 102 pp. A. Anderson, 'The tragic crisis for Wotan in W.'s *Der Ring des Nibelungen*', *AUMLA*, 95:35–53. H. G. Walther, 'R. W. und der (antike) Mythos', pp. 261–80 of *Antike Mythen in der europäischen Tradition*, ed. Heinz Hoffmann, Tübingen, Attempto, 1999, 303 pp. J. Rettelbach, 'Der Einzug der Meistersinger in die Oper', pp. 615–32 of *Vom Mittelalter zur Neuzeit. Festschrift für Horst Brunner*, ed. Dorothea Klein, Wiesbaden, Reichert, 2000, x + 752 pp. S. Friedrich, 'Die romantische Utopie in R. Ws "Kunstwerk der Zukunft"', Tschuggnall, *Religion*, 391–410. J. Führer, '"Deutschester Mensch" und europäisches Genie: "Der Fall Wagner"', pp. 85–97 of *Steinbruch: deutsche Erinnerungsorte. Annä-herung an eine deutsche Gedächtnisgeschichte*, ed. Constanze Carcenac-Lecomte, Frankfurt–Berlin, Lang, 2000, 300 pp. C. Öhlschläger and C. Pornschlegel, 'Welttheaterwelt: zur Struktur des Performativen im *Gesamtkunstwerk* R. Ws', pp. 171–217 of *Szenographien: Theatralität als Kategorie der Literaturwissenschaft*, ed. Gerhard Neumann, Freiburg, Rombach, 2000, 471 pp. L. VanEynde, 'Le temps, l'autre et la fantasmagorie: lecture de *Der fliegende Holländer* de R. W.', *EG*, 55, 2000:39–60.

WANGEMANN, THEODOR HERMANN. T. Hemme, 'Ein Reise-Jahr in Südafrika. Darstellungemechanismen und Bekehrungsstrategien

eines deutschen Missionars im 19. Jahrhundert', *AGGSA*, 26–27,
1998–99[2000]: 135–49.

ZSCHOKKE.　*'Guten Morgen, Lieber!' Der Briefwechsel Heinrich Zschokkes
mit seinem Verleger Sauerländer*, ed. Werner Ort, Berne–Berlin, Lang,
594 pp., contains all 367 letters exchanged between Z. and his
publisher. Much more than business correspondence, the letters offer
a fascinating insight into the private realms of both men, including
their political views. The volume is fully annotated and indexed, and
brings to light a large amount of previously unknown material.

LITERATURE, 1880–1945

By MALCOLM HUMBLE, *formerly Lecturer in German, University of St Andrews*

I. GENERAL

REFERENCE WORKS AND GENERAL STUDIES. Ingo Stoehr, *Literature of the Twentieth Century From Aestheticism to Postmodernism*, Rochester, NY, Camden House, 450 pp., is the first volume to appear of an important projected series. It takes as its background the paradigmatic transition from aestheticism and modernism to postmodernism. While the pattern is familiar from shorter works dealing with phases and movements and from the series of literary histories which have appeared in German in recent decades, this is the first lengthy survey in English which spans the whole century and links these develop-ments to a consideration of the political and social changes in Germany and Austria. The book achieves a good balance between appropriate emphasis on major works in all genres and broad generalizations about their place in these trends. It is particularly valuable for its account of the most recent developments following the convergence of East and West German literature and unification, in which a preoccupation with multicultural, global, and feminist issues combines with a renewed confidence in story-telling. Theo Stammen, *Literatur und Politik. Studien zu ihrem Verhältnis in Deutschland* (Spectrum Politikwissenschaft, 20), Würzburg, Ergon, 304 pp., assembles previously published essays, including pieces on Heinrich and Thomas Mann, Rudolf Kassner, Ernst Cassirer, Brecht, Elias Canetti, and Victor Klemperer. Bruno Hillebrand, *Was denn ist Kunst? Essays zur Dichtung im Zeitalter des Individualismus*, Göttingen, Vandenhoeck & Ruprecht, 430 pp. Margarita Pazi, *Staub und Sterne. Aufsätze zur deutsch-jüdischen Literatur*, ed. Sigrid Bauschinger and Paul Michael Lützeler, Göttingen, Wallstein, 300 pp., collects essays from the years 1981 to 1994. Marcel Reich-Ranicki, *Die Meister des zwanzigsten Jahrhunderts: Arthur Schnitzler — Robert Musil — Alfred Döblin — Thomas Mann — Kurt Tucholsky — Franz Kafka — Bertolt Brecht*, DVA, 250 pp.

THEMES. *Urgeschichten der Moderne. Die Antike im 20. Jahrhundert*, ed. Bernd Seidensticker and Martin Vöhler, Stuttgart, Metzler, 250 pp. *Commodities of Desire. The Prostitute in Modern German Literature*, ed. Christiane Schönfeld, Rochester, NY, Camden House, 262 pp.

NARRATIVE. Brigitte Bergheim, *Das gesellschaftliche Individuum: Untersuchungen zum modernen deutschen Roman*, Tübingen, Francke, 150 pp. Roger Kingerlee, *Psychological Models of Masculinity in Döblin, Musil and Jahnn: Männliches, Allzumännliches* (SGLL, 27), xviii + 391 pp., traces the portrayal of the central figures of *Berlin Alexanderplatz*, *Der Mann ohne Eigenschaften*, and *Perrudja* against the background of the developing psychology of male sexuality and identity in the work of Nietzsche, Mach, Magnus Hirschfeld, Freud, Jung, and Adler as received by their authors, and shows how they delivered a critique of masculinity and patriarchy which countered the misogynism of the *Freikorps* writers examined in Theweleit's *Männerphantasien*. Atsushi Imai, **Das Bild des ästhetisch-empfindsamen Jugendlichen. Deutsche Schul- und Adoleszensromane zu Beginn des 20. Jahrhunderts*, Wiesbaden, Deutscher Universitätsverlag, x + 206 pp. *Der Romanführer*, 36, ed. Hans-Christian Plesske (Deutschsprachige Prosa im Dritten Reich, ii: L-Z), Stuttgart, Hiersemann, 311 pp.

DRAMA. Marianne Streisand, **Begriffsgeschichte und Entdeckung der 'Intimität' auf dem Theater um 1900*, Munich, Fink, 377 pp. **Theatralität und die Krise der Repräsentation. DFG-Symposion 1999*, ed. Erika Fischer-Lichte (Germanistische Symposien. Berichtsbände, 22), Stuttgart, Metzler, 600 pp.

LYRIC. Walter Hinderer, *Geschichte der deutschen Lyrik. Vom Mittelalter bis zur Gegenwart*, 2nd enlarged edn, Würzburg, Königshausen & Neumann, 720 pp., extends the 1983 Reclam edition with a contribution by Theo Elm ('Lyrik heute') and an updated bibliography. Dieter Hoffmann, *Arbeitsbuch deutschsprachige Lyrik 1880–1916: Vom Naturalismus bis zum Expressionismus* (Uni-Taschenbuch, 2199), 450 pp. Id., *Arbeitsbuch deutschsprachige Lyrik 1916–1945: Vom Dadaismus bis zum Ende des Zweiten Weltkriegs* (Uni-Taschenbuch, 2200), 450 pp. Friedrich Sengle, *Moderne deutsche Lyrik. Von Nietzsche bis Enzensberger (1875–1975)* (BNL, 179), ii + 414 pp., drawn from the author's *Nachlass*, offers accounts of 50 poets with interpretations set against their historical background. S. Neuhaus, 'Gebrauchslyrik. Vorüberlegungen zum Studium einer vernachlässigsten Gattung', *LWU*, 34:99–116. Ulrike Stadler-Altmann, **Das Zeitgedicht der Weimarer Republik, mit einer Quellenbibliographie zur Lyrik im ersten Drittel des 20. Jahrhunderts, 1900–1933* (GTS, 69), vii + 860 pp.

MOVEMENTS AND PERIODS. Roger Bauer, *Die schöne Décadence. Geschichte eines literarischen Paradoxons* (Das Abendland, n.F., 28), Frankfurt, Klostermann, 422 pp., although it deals with its topic as an international, mainly French, phenomenon, tracing its course in three phases, contains sections on Nietzsche, Thomas Mann, George, Bahr, Schnitzler, Hofmannsthal, and Altenberg. Georg Leisten, **Wiederbelebung oder Mortifikation. Bildnisbegegnung und Schriftreflexion als Signaturen neoromantischer Dichtung zwischen Realismus und Fin de Siècle*, Bielefeld, Aisthesis, 247 pp. Hans Richard Brittnacher, **Erschöpfung und Gewalt. Opferphantasien in der Literatur des Fin de siècle*, Cologne, Böhlau, 392 pp. *Jahrhundertwende. Studien zur Literatur der Moderne. Zum*

70. Geburtstag von Gotthart Wunberg, ed. Stephan Dietrich, Tübingen, Narr, xii + 371 pp., assembles previously published essays by Wunberg. *Literatur um 1900. Texte der Jahrhundertwende neu gelesen*, ed. Cornelia Niedermeier and Klaus Wagner, Cologne, Böhlau, 208 pp., includes essays on Josef Popper-Lynkeus, *Phantasien eines Realisten*, Ernst Haeckel, *Die Welträtsel*, Sigmund Freud, *Die Traumdeutung*, H. S. Chamberlain, *Die Grundlagen des 19. Jahrhunderts*, Georg Simmel, *Die Philosophie des Geldes*, Hofmannsthal, *Das Erlebnis des Marschalls von Bassompierre*, Schnitzler, *Leutnant Gustl*, Beer-Hofmann, *Der Tod Georgs*, George, *Der Teppich des Lebens*, H. Mann, *Im Schlaraffenland*, and Scheerbart, *Rakkáx der Billionär*. U. Spörl, 'Mystisches Erleben, Leben und Schreiben um 1900. Überlegungen zu den Grenzen der Literaturwissenschaft', *KulturPoetik*, 1:214–30. P. Duesberg, 'Der Zeitgeist als übersteigerte Zeitwahrnehmung. Über den Modernisierungsprozess in der Literatur um 1900', *ZDP*, 120:183–206. G. Hübinger, 'Politik mit Büchern und kulturelle Fragmentierung im Deutschen Kaiserreich', *GR*, 76:290–307. B. Han, ' "Seefahrer auf unbekannten Meeren." Zu Martin Bubers Essaysammlung 'Die Gesellschaft" ', *ib.*, 308–18. M. Werner, 'Provincial modernism: Jena as publishing program', *ib.*, 319–34. K. Barndt, 'Railroads for locomotives of the mind: tracking culture and crisis in the S. Fischer Verlag', *ib.*, 335–48. Jan Steinhaussen, '*Aristokraten aus Not' und ihre 'Philosophie der zu hoch hängenden Trauben'. Nietzsche-Rezeption und literarische Produktion von Homosexuellen in den ersten Jahrzehnten des 20. Jahrhunderts: Thomas Mann, Stefan George, Ernst Bertram, Hugo von Hofmannsthal u.a.* (Ep, 326), 520 pp., attempts to show that works by these authors, especially those responding to Nietzsche, were linked by a secret homosexual discourse evident in common themes and motifs. *Zur Wirkung Nietzsches: Der deutsche Expressionismus. Meno ter Braak, Martin Heidegger, Ernst Jünger, Thomas Mann, Oswald Spengler*, ed. Hans Ester and Meindert Evers, Würzburg, Königshausen & Neumann, 180 pp., contains six contributions. Nancy C. Michael, **Elektra and Her Sisters. Three Female Characters in Schnitzler, Freud and Hofmannsthal* (Austrian Culture, 11), NY, Lang, 141 pp. **Paris? Paris? Bilder der französichen Metropole in der nicht-fiktionalen deutschsprachigen Prosa zwischen Hermann Bahr und Joseph Roth*, ed. Gerhard R. Kaiser and Erika Tunner (Jenaer germanistische Forschungen, n. F., 11), Heidelberg, Winter, 480 pp. Beate Horn, **Prosa im Simplicissimus: Zur Entwicklung literarischer Gattungen im Kontext von Zeitschrift, Bild und Satire* (RBDSL, B.75), 378 pp.

Krobb, *Literaturvermittlung*, contains, after an introduction by the editors: J. Fischer, ' "Märchen aus Irlands Gauen." Irisches und dessen Vermittlung im Kaiserreich' (23–44); G. von Glasenapp, ' "Eine neue und neuartige Epoche." Ostjüdische Literatur in deutsch-jüdischen Zeitschriften und Almanachen vor dem Ersten Weltkrieg' (45–60); R. G. Decloedt, 'Kontakte zwischen niederländisch- und deutschsprachigen Autoren. Persönliche Bekanntschaften und Begegnungen um die Jahrhundertwende' (61–74); F. Krobb, '"- denn Begriffe begraben das Leben der Erscheinungen." Über einen Versuch, den Dandy in die deutsche Literatur einzubürgern' (75–92); C. Girardi, 'Pierrotdichtungen im deutschen Sprachraum um 1900' (93–112); J. Beniston, 'Claudel als Dichter der Ekstase. *L'Annonce faite à Marie* im deutschen Sprachgebiet' (147–66), and contributions on Marie Herzfeld, Broch and Hanns Heinz Ewers (see below). The collection adds up to an original survey of the cosmopolitan context of German literature around 1900, with attention to publishing activities, translations, personal contacts, and international themes.

G. Moore, 'The super-hun and the super-state: allied propaganda and German philosophy during the First World War', *GLL*, 54:310–30. L. Tate, 'The culture of literary *Bildung* in the bourgeois women's movement in imperial Germany', *GSR*, 24:267–82. Thomas Anz, *Literatur des Expressionismus* (SM, 329), 200 pp. *Expressionismus am Bodensee. Literatur und bildende Kunst*, ed. Städtische Wessenberg-Galerie Konstanz, Eggingen, Isele, 128 pp.

Fähnders, *Prosa*, includes M. Bassler, 'Absolute Prosa' (59–78); C. Kanz, 'Geschlecht und Psyche in der Zeit des Expressionismus' (115–46); H. van den Berg, 'Fiktional-narrative Prosa im dadaistischen Projekt' (211–33). (See also under individual authors.) U. Hentschel, 'Der Expressionimus — eine gesteigerte (Früh)Romantik?', *LitL*, 24:137–51. C. Novero, 'Dada Diets: dysfunctional physiologies of devouring', *Seminar*, 37:1–20. C. Schneider, ' "Bestien des Aufruhres." Eine Untersuchung zur stilistischen Besonderheit der Fronterzählungen der späten zwanziger Jahre am Beispiel von Carl Paul Hiesgens', *LitL*, 24:152–64. *Jahrbuch zur Kultur und Literatur der Weimarer Republik*, 6, ed. Sabina Becker, Munich, Text + Kritik, 312 pp., includes articles on Doderer, Döblin, Ernst Jünger, Kracauer, Lasker-Schüler, and Weimar films. Jürgen Brokoff, *Die Apokalypse in der Weimarer Republik*, Munich, Fink, 200 pp., includes studies of the writings of Benjamin, Hitler, and Ernst Jünger. Vibeke Rützou Petersen, *Women and Modernity in Weimar Germany. Reality and its Representation in Popular Fiction*, Oxford, Berghahn, 200 pp., draws on a wide range of texts, with particular attention to the novels of Vicki Baum, in order to explore women as readers, their fictional representation and their significant place in Weimar Republic society. Kerstin Barndt, *Sentiment und Sachlichkeit. Der Roman der neuen Frau in der Weimarer Republik* (Literatur — Kultur — Geschlecht), Cologne, Böhlau, 296 pp. Helga Karrenbrock, *Märchenkinder — Zeitgenossen.*

Untersuchungen zur Kinderliteratur der Weimarer Republik, 2nd enlarged edn, Stuttgart, Metzler, 210 pp. Tatjana Röber, **'Die neuen Methoden der Betrachtung.' Subjektivitäts- und Wahrnehmungskonzepte in Kulturtheorie und 'sachlichem' Theater der 20er Jahre,* 2 vols, St. Ingbert, Röhrig, 582 pp. *Berlin — Wien — Prag. Moderne, Minderheiten und Migration in der Zwischenkriegszeit. Modernity, Minorities and Migration in the Inter-War Period,* ed. Susanne Marten-Finis and Matthias Uecker, Berne, Lang, 293 pp., comprises selected papers from a conference held in Belfast in 2000, which examine metropolitan culture, several from the perspective of Jewish studies. Authors included are Kraus and Kisch. Martin Travers, *Critics of Modernity: The Literature of the Conservative Revolution in Germany, 1890–1933* (GLC, 35), xiv + 256 pp., consists of studies of Benn, Bronnen, Ernst von Salomon, George, Hans Grimm, Ernst Jünger, and Löns, with attention also to minor figures and intellectual contexts. J. Todd, 'The price of individuality. E. R. Curtius' exclusion from the *George-Kreis', GRM,* 51:431–46. K. Führer, 'German cultural life and the crisis of national identity during the depression, 1929–1933', *GSR,* 24:461–86. G. Ulrich Grossmann and H. Uslar, 'Gleichgeschaltet im DAF-Konzern. Die Büchergilde Gutenberg unter nationalsozialistischer Herrschaft. Mit einer Bibliographie', *Marginalien,* 164.4:40–70. S. Röttig, 'Die Kiepenheuer-Bücherei 1936–1941', *ib.,* 163.3:15–29. H. Galle, 'Volk ans Gewehr. Groschenhefte im Dienste der Propaganda', *Buchhandelsgeschichte,* 2001.3:B92–101. J. P. Barbian, 'Zwischen Dogma und Kalkül. Der Herder Verlag und die Schrifttumspolitik des NS-Staates', *ib.,* 2001.4:B145–50. Zlata Fuss Phillips, *German Children's and Youth Literature in Exile 1933–1950: Biographies and Bibliographies,* Munich, Saur, 318 pp. Norbert Hopster, Petra Josting, and Joachim Neuhaus, **Kinder- und Jugendliteratur 1933–1945. Ein Handbuch,* Vol. 1. *Bibliographischer Teil mit Registern.* Vol. 2. *Darstellender Teil,* Stuttgart, Metzler, 1165, 1040 pp. Carsten Könneker, **'Auflösung der Natur. Auflösung der Geschichte.' Moderner Roman und NS-'Weltanschauung' im Zeichen der theoretischen Physik,* Stuttgart, M & F, 466 pp. Günter Hartung, *Deutschfaschistische Literatur und Ästhetik. Gesammelte Studien,* Leipzig U.P., 378 pp. Gaetano Biccari, **'Zuflucht des Geistes'? Konservativ-revolutionäre, faschistische und nationalsozialistische Theaterdiskurse in Deutschland und Italien 1900–1944* (FMT, 28), Tübingen, Narr, 319 pp. Theodor Verweyen, **Bücherverbrennungen. Eine Vorlesung aus Anlaß des 65. Jahrestages der 'Aktion wider den undeutschen Geist',* Heidelberg, Winter, 237 pp. *Literatur im Dritten Reich. Texte und Dokumente,* ed. S. Graeb-Könneker, Stuttgart, Reclam, 424 pp. *Theatre and War 1933–1945. Performance in Extremis,* ed. Michael Balfour, Oxford, Berghahn, 208 pp., includes essays on Fascist aesthetic propaganda in Germany, cultural 'sustenance' for the troops at the front and interned German refugees in the UK, and cabarets as a currency for survival in Jewish concentration camps.

H. Schneider, ' ". . .es sind ja so Viele . . ." Das Neue Deutsche Theater Prag: Hoffnung der Vertriebenen', *ZGer*, 11 : 142–48. *Jüdische Emigration. Zwischen Assimilation und Verfolgung, Akkulturation und jüdischer Identität*, ed. Claus-Dieter Krohn et al. (Exilforschung, 19), 294 pp., has contributions dealing with Nazi policy towards Jewish exiles and the later effects of the Jewish emigration: J. Matthäus, 'Abwehr, Ausharren, Flucht. Der Centralverein deutscher Staatsbürger jüdischen Glaubens und die Emigration bis zur "Reichskristallnacht" ' (18–40); S. Meinl, ' "Shalom — meine Heimat". Stationen der Flucht aus Deutschland' (41–64); G. A. Eakin-Thimme, 'Deutsche Nationalgeschichte und Aufbau Europas. Deutschsprachige jüdische Historiker im amerikanischen Exil' (65–79); J. Franke, ' "De véritables 'boches'." Französische und emigrierte deutsche Juden im Paris der dreißiger Jahre' (80–105); A. Klugescheid, ' "His Majesty's most loyal enemy aliens." Der Kampf deutsch-jüdischer Emigranten in den britischen Streitkräften 1939–1945' (106–27); W. Benz, 'Illegale Einwanderung nach Palästina' (128–44); M. Bauer, 'Paradies, Fegefeuer, Hölle. Exil und Holocaust in Rumänien' (145–67); K. E. Schirp, 'Presse als Brücke zwischen Heimat und Exil. Das Seminario Israelita in Buenos Aires' (168–88); H. Embacher, 'Eine Heimkehr gibt es nicht? Remigration nach Österreich' (187–209); H. O. Horch, 'Exil und Messianismus. Manès Sperbers Romantrilogie *Wie eine Träne im Ozean* im Kontext deutsch-jüdischer Exilliteratur' (210–26); S. Braese, 'Nach-Exil. Zu einem Entstehungsort westdeutscher Nachkriegsliteratur' (227–53); B. van der Lühe, 'Zeitzeugen der Shoah im Offenen Kanal Berlin. Verfolgung und Exil in der Zeit des NS als Gegenstand einer medienpraktischen Unterrichtseinheit. Ein Projekt an der Technischen Universität Berlin in Kooperation mit dem Offenen Kanal Berlin' (254–74).

Valérie Robert, *Partir ou rester? Les intellectuels allemands devant l'exil 1933–1939*, Paris, Sorbonne U.P., 438 pp. Edgar Banzig, *Internationale Lyrik zum spanischen Bürgerkrieg (1936–1939). Ästhetische und politische Tendenzen in Gedichten von Rafael Alberti, Erich Arendt, Paul Eluard, Stephen Spender und anderen*, St. Ingbert, Röhrig, 399 pp., Bettina Englmann, *Poetik des Exils* (UDL, 109), vii + 450 pp., includes studies of the novels of Döblin, Veza Canetti, and Soma Morgenstern. D. Schiller, 'Die Expressionismus-Debatte — Eine "wirkliche, nicht dirigierte Diskussion"?', *Exil*, no. 1 : 77–90. M. E. Humble, 'The renegade in German exile literature', *OL*, 56 : 56–74. M. G. Krob, 'Paris through enemy eyes: the *Wehrmacht* in Paris 1940–1944', *JES*, 31 : 3–28. R. Andress, 'Deutschsprachige Schriftsteller auf Mallorca

(1931–36) — ein ungeschriebenes Kapitel in der deutschen Exilforschung', *GSR*, 24 : 115–43. Reinhard Andress, '*Der Inselgarten*' — *das
Exil deutschsprachiger Schiftsteller auf Mallorca, 1931–1935*, Amsterdam–
Atlanta, GA, Rodopi (APSL 144), 197 pp., is a study, based on
unpublished sources, of this previously neglected area of the German
diaspora, with chapters on Thelen, Kessler, Blei, Otten, Martha Brill,
Erich Arendt, Klaus Mann, and Herbert Schlüter. While concentrating on the circumstances of their stay, it also analyses works it
inspired. Tom Ambrose, *Hitler's loss. What Britain and America Gained
from Europe's Cultural Exiles*, London, Owen, 232 pp., is a wide-ranging
study, including cinema, art, literature, theatre, music, opera,
architecture, and science, without the apparatus of scholarship.
Deutschsprachige Exilliteratur seit 1933, 3: *USA*, ed. John M. Spalek and
Konrad Feilchenfeldt, vol. 2, Munich, Saur, 500 pp., completes in 27
contributions the survey of emigrants not assigned to earlier volumes
on California and New York. While of the academics, publicists,
authors of children's literature, and translators represented only a
few (e.g. Erika Mann, Alfred Kantorowicz, Wilhelm Herzog, Leopold
Schwarzschild) have found a place in histories of 20th-c. literature,
the human interest in the stories of even the minor and unknown
figures is considerable. **L'Homme et la cité allemande au XXe siècle.
Souffrance et résistance*, ed. Françoise Kropper and Jean-Marie Paul,
Nancy U.P., 365 pp. Norman David Thau, **Romans de l'impossible
identité. Etre Juif en Europe occidentale 1918–1940*, ed. Jean-Marie
Valentin (Contacts, 3; Études et Documents, 52), Berne, Lang,
xii + 457 pp. *Aufbruch ins 20. Jahrhundert. Über Avantgarden*, ed. Heinz
Ludwig Arnold (TK Sonderband), Munich, Text + Kritik, 312 pp.,
deals with its subject as represented mainly in the German-speaking
area, and includes contributions on its relation to political move-
ments, the *Jugendbewegung*, theatre, film, publishers and periodicals,
Hanover, fashion, Socialist Realism and the fifties, together with
short pieces on Hugo Ball and Emmy Hennings, Benn, Schwitters,
Friedrich Glauser, Else Lasker-Schüler and Carl Einstein. W. Adam,
'Literaturgeschichte als Gemeinschaftsprojekt: Neue Quellen zur
Fachgeschichte der Germanistik in der ersten Hälfte des zwanzigsten
Jahrhunderts', *Euphorion*, 95.4: 357–422. **Das literarische Berlin im 20.
Jahrhundert. Mit aktuellen Adressen und Informationen*, ed. Silvio Vietta,
Stuttgart, Reclam, 275 pp.

SWITZERLAND, AUSTRIA, PRAGUE, AND HUNGARY.   U. Amrein, 'Die
Signatur der Grossstadt in der deutschsprachigen Schweizerliteratur
um 1900', *JDSG*, 45 : 302–19. *Rethinking Vienna 1900*, ed. Steven Beller
(Austrian History, Culture and Society, 3), Oxford, Berghahn,
xi + 292 pp., contains ten contributions reflecting the controversies
which have emerged from the seminal work of Carl E. Schorske,

especially his 'failure of liberalism' thesis, on *fin-de-siècle* Vienna. While they examine the culture in all its aspects, including the work of Freud, Herzl, and Popper, they also illuminate literature in the narrow sense with insights into Schaukal, Schnitzler, Kraus, and other writers. Eoin Bourke, *The Austrian Anschluss in History and Literature, Galway, Arlen House, 2000, 138 pp.

Österreich-Konzeptionen und jüdisches Selbstverständnis. Identitäts-Transfigurationen im 19. und 20. Jahrhundert, ed. Hanni Mittelmann and Armin A. Wallas (CJ, 35), 340 pp., assembles the papers given at a symposium held in Jerusalem in 2000. Authors treated include Beer-Hofmann and Weinheber, along with composers and artists. Eicher, *Grenzüberschreitungen*, contains T. Eicher, ' "Grenzüberschreitungen" der österreichischen Literatur um 1900' (9–28); D. G. Daviau, 'Die Rezeption der österreichischen Literatur der Jahrhundertwende in den Vereinigten Staaten, 1987–1999. Ein Bericht' (53–80); M. Reffet, 'Der Impressionismus als dominante Stilrichtung der deutschsprachigen Literatur der Jahrhundertwende' (81–94); R. Görner, 'Ringstraße oder Square. Junges Wien und Dandysmus' (95–110); F. Hackert, 'Ansichten zum europäischen Kaffeehaus' (111–34); R. Innerhofer, 'Technische Zukunftsbilder in der österreichischen Literatur um die Jahrhundertwende' (157–76). (See also below under ALTENBERG, PERUTZ, and RILKE.)

From Perinet to Jelinek. Viennese Theatre in its Political and Intellectual Context, ed. W. E. Yates, Allyson Fiddler, and John Warren (British and Irish Studies in German Language and Literature, 28), Oxford, Lang, 290 pp., has 20 essays, with introduction, on two hundred years of theatre, relating playwrights, plays and institutions to the political and intellectual context. Relevant to this section are R. Vilain, 'The sublime and the ridiculous: dramatic Wagner parodies in Vienna' (103–14); W. E. Yates, 'The rise and fall of the one-act play' (115–26); G. J. Carr, 'Corridors of power and whispered plots: the banning of Otto Stoessl's and Robert Scheu's *Waare* in 1897/ 1898' (127–42); A. W. Barker, 'Interior monologue, monodrama and the *Palais Stoclet*: Marie Pappenheim's libretto for Schoenberg's *Erwartung*' (143–54); J. Stewart, 'Egon Friedell and Alfred Polgar: cabaret in Vienna at the turn of the last century' (155–66); E. E. Smith, ' "Aber ich hab sie nit kennt, die Weiber": female autonomy unleashed in Karl Schönherr's *Der Weibsteufel*' (167–78); J. Beniston, 'Max Mell in the First Republic: the acceptable face of Catholic drama?' (179–90); J. Warren, 'Viennese theatre criticism between the wars' (191–202); L. A. Huish, ' "Eine typisch altösterreichisch-ungarische Mischung": the reception of Horváth's plays in Vienna, 1931–37' (203–14); S. Aichhorn, '*Vineta* von Jura Soyfer oder Die Avantgarde auf der Kellerbühne' (215–28); U. Tanzer, 'Das Spiel von Geld und Moral. Hugo von Hofmannsthals und Felix Mitterers *Jedermann*-Bearbeitungen' (229–42). A. A. Wallas, 'Drama der Revolution — Theater der Revolution? Revolutionäre Österreich-Konzeptionen im Theater der frühen Ersten Republik', *FMT*, 16:111–34. **Brücken nach Prag. Deutschsprachige Literatur im kulturellen Kontext der Donaumonarchie und der Tschechoslowakei. Festschrift für Kurt Krolop zum 70. Geburtstag*, ed. Klaas-Hinrich Ehlers et al., 2nd rev. edn, Frankfurt, Lang, 505 pp. René Geoffroy, **Ungarn als Zufluchtsort und Wirkungsstätte deutschsprachiger Emigranten (1933–1938/39)* (SDLNZ, 45), 485 pp.

MISCELLANEOUS. Edgar Wind, *Experiment and Metaphysics. Towards a Resolution of the Cosmological Antinomies*, trans. Cyril Edwards, introd. Matthew Rampley, EHRC, 148 pp., is the *Habilitationsschrift* of the eminent art historian. It is a significant addition to Kant criticism and looks forward to Wind's later work; its translation coincides with its republication in German.

2. INDIVIDUAL AUTHORS

ALTENBERG, PETER. *Semmering 1912. Ein altbekanntes Buch und ein neuentdecktes Photoalbum*, ed. Leo A. Lensing and Andrew Barker, Vienna, Eichbauer, 349 pp., adds to a new edition of the book of sketches of A.'s favourite holiday haunt two essays by the editors and colour reproductions of relevant items from A.'s collection of postcards with transcriptions of his comments. A. Honold, 'P. As "Ashantee." Eine impressionistische cross-over-Phantasie im Kontext der exotischen Völkerschauen', Eicher, *Grenzüberschreitungen*, 135–56.

ANDREAS-SALOMÉ, LOU. Chantal Gahlinger, **Der Weg zur weiblichen Autonomie: Zur Psychologie der Selbstwerdung im literarischen Werk von Lou Andreas-Salomé* (EH, 1, 1800), 494 pp. '. . .*als ich kam heim zu Vater und Schwester.' Lou Andreas-Salomé — Anna Freud Briefwechsel*, ed. Daria A. Rothe and Inge Weber, 2 vols, Göttingen, Wallstein, 907 pp.

BAHR, HERMANN. *Hermann Bahr — Mittler der europäischen Moderne: Hermann Bahr Symposion, Linz 1998*, ed. Johann Lachinger (Jb. des Adalbert Stifter Instituts des Landes Oberösterreich, 5), Linz, Adalbert Stifter Institut, 232 pp.

BALL-HENNINGS, EMMY. Bärbel Reetz, *Emmy Ball-Hennings. Leben im Vielleicht. Eine Biographie* (ST 3240), 400 pp., is based on unpublished documents.

BARLACH, ERNST. K. Lazarowicz, 'Der werdende Gott. Zum Theodizee-Problem in Bs Sündflut', *FMT*, 16:169–86.

BARTELS, ADOLF. M. Przybilski, 'A. B. und das Nibelungenlied', *ASNS*, 238:79–89.

BEER-HOFMANN, RICHARD. R. B.-H., *Der Briefwechsel mit Paula 1896–1937*, ed. Richard M. Sheirich and Andreas Thomasberger (Werke in 8 Bänden, 8), Paderborn, Igel, 480 pp.

BENJAMIN, WALTER. Helmut Kaffenberger, **Orte des Lesens — Alchemie — Monade. Studien zur Bildlichkeit im Werk Walter Benjamins* (Ep, 364), 230 pp. Markus Steinmayr, **Mnemotechnik und Medialität: Walter Benjamins Poetik des Autobiographischen* (EH, 1, 1788), 266 pp. Rolf J. Goebel, **Benjamin heute. Großstadtdiskurs, Postkolonialität und Flanerie zwischen den Kulturen*, Munich, Iudicium, 191 pp. Karl-Heinz Heber, **Zerstörung und Restitutio. Zum Verständnis der religionsphilosophischen, messianischen und mystischen Dispositionen in den Schriften Walter Benjamins*, Frankfurt, Lang, 216 pp. K. Ebeling, 'Die geheime Geschichte der Menschheit. W. B. und das Erbe des Surrealismus', *WB*, 47 : 485–506. P. Garloff, 'Monarchie, Demokratie, Dekonstruktion — Eine kulturwissenschaftliche Neulektüre von Bs *Zur Kritik der Gewalt*', *DVLG*, 75 : 329–59. M. Bullock, 'In a *Blauer Reiter* frame: Walter Benjamin's intentions of the eye and Derrida's specters of Marx', *MDLK*, 93 : 177–95. M. Mack, 'Between Kant and Kafka: B.'s notion of law', *Neophilologus*, 85 : 257–72. U. Steiner, 'Von Bern nach Muri. Vier unveröffentlichte Briefe W. Bs an Paul Häberlin im Kontext', *DVLG*, 75 : 463–90. K. Garber, 'Antiklassische Ästhetik aus empfindsamem Geist. Bs Kunsttheorie zwischen Symbolismus und Allegorismus', *Fest. Hohendahl*, 245–56. S. Bub, 'Himmel, Wolken und Nebel im Passagen-Werk. Zu B. und Baudelaire', *ASNS*, 238 : 61–71. J. Fürnkäs, 'Bs Gedächtnis', *DB*, 106 : 24–40.

BENN, GOTTFRIED. G. B., '*Hernach.' Briefe an Ursula Ziebarth, mit Nachschriften von U. Z. und einem Kommentar von Jochen Meyer*, Göttingen, Wallstein, 504 pp. Michael Braun, **'Hörreste, Sehreste.' Das literarische Fragment bei Büchner, Kafka, Benn und Celan*, Cologne, Böhlau, 312 pp. Fritz J. Raddatz, **Gottfried Benn: Leben — niederer Wahn. Biographie*, Berlin, Propyläen, 320 pp. Hans Dieter Schäfer, **Herr Oelze aus Bremen. Gottfried Benn und Friedrich Wilhelm Oelze*, Göttingen, Wallstein, 48 pp. Thomas Keith, **Nietzsche-Rezeption bei Gottfried Benn*, Cologne, Teiresias, 130 pp. N. Beaupré, 'Double guerre. G. B., médecin — et écrivain? de deux guerres', *Germanica*, 28 : 61–74. M. Schramm, 'G.Bs "Welle der Nacht" — absolute Dichtung?', *ZDP*, 120 : 571–89. M. Preiss, 'G. Bs Rönne-Novellen', *Fähnders, Prosa*, 93–113.

BERGENGRUEN, WERNER. S. Ward, 'W. B.'s *Am Himmel wie auf Erden*: the historical novel and "Inner Emigration"', *ABNG*, 51 : 301–12.

BLOCH, ERNST. '*Wir haben das Leben wieder vor uns.' Ernst Bloch Wieland Herzfelde Briefwechsel 1938–1949*, ed. Jürgen Jahn, Frankfurt, Suhrkamp, 390 pp.

BLUM, KLARA. *Klara Blum. Kommentierte Auswahledition*, ed. Zhidong Yang, Vienna, Böhlau, 652 pp.

BOLDT, PAUL. E. Scheiffele, '"Ihr jugendlichen Sonnen! Fleischern Licht!" Junge Frauen in P.Bs Lyrik', *GRM*, 51 : 419–30.

BORCHARDT, RUDOLF. M. Neumann, '"Res alienae sunt, verba mea" — Rudolf Borchardts "Idyllische Elegie" und ihre französische Vorlage', *JDSG*, 45 : 344–58.

BRECHT, BERTOLT. Wolf Kienast, **Kriegsfibelmodell. Autorschaft und 'kollektiver Schöpfungsprozess' in Brechts Kriegsfibel*, Göttingen, Vandenhoeck & Ruprecht, 336 pp. *Brecht-Handbuch*, 1. *Stücke*. 2. *Gedichte*, ed. Jan Knopf, Stuttgart, Metzler, xvii + 661, 448 pp., marks the first stage of a revised and much extended edition in four volumes and an index of the two-volume publication of 1980/1984, which will contain over 250 entries by more than 50 authors on phases of B.'s career, stylistic developments, individual works, etc. Volker Kaiser, **Risus Mortis. Strange Angels. Zur Lektüre 'Vom armen B.B.' Eine Studie zu Brecht und Benjamin* (Mannheimer Studien zur Literatur- und Kulturwissenschaft, 24), St. Ingbert, Röhrig, 151 pp. Kyung-Boon Lee, **Musik und Literatur im Exil. Hanns Eislers dodekaphone Exilkantaten* (Exilstudien, 9), Frankfurt, Lang, 294 pp. Christine Arendt, **Natur und Liebe in der frühen Lyrik Brechts* (HBG 35), 296 pp. P. Peters, 'B. und die Stimme der Nachrichten', *WB*, 47 : 352–73. B. Philipsen, 'Die Kälte weckt sie. B., die Tragödie und die Verleugnung des Politischen', *ib.*, 22–52. E. Horn, 'Die Regel der Ausnahme. Revolutionäre Souveränität und bloßes Leben in Bs *Maßnahme*', *DVLG*, 75 : 680–709. A. Combes, 'La longue marche de Schwejk d'une guerre mondiale à l'autre: de la reécriture du "Piscator-Kollektiv" (1927–28) au *Schwejk im Zweiten Weltkrieg* de B. (1943)', *Germanica*, 28 : 133–64. H. Drügh, 'Schwimm-Stil. Zum Verhältnis von (Populär-)Kultur und literarischem Text in Bs Gedicht "Vom Schwimmen in Seen und Flüssen"', *Hofmannsthal Jb.*, 9 : 261–90.

Brecht Yearbook, 26 contains J. Hillesheim and E. Wizisla, '"Was macht Deine Dichteritis?" B. B. im Bregenzer Land' (3–14); S. Suschke, 'Geniales Kind im Mörderhaus' (35–46); B. K. Tragelehn, 'Der Fall G/B' (47–60); A. Stephan, 'Zurück in die Zukunft des politischen Theaters? Soeren Voima schreiben mit *Das Kontingent* Bs *Maßnahme* weiter' (followed by an interview with S. V) (61–80); H. Maclean, 'Gestus in Performance: B. and Heiner Müller' (81–100); U. Garde, '"Never in body and seldom in spirit": Australian productions of B.'s plays and their reviews from 1945 to 1998' (101–26); D. Varney, 'Performing sexual difference: a feminist appropriation of B.' (127–42); M. Mumford, 'Gestic masks in B.'s theater: a testimony to the contradictions and parameters of a realistic aesthetic' (143–72); D. Müller Nielaba, 'Wie Dichten *Lesen* schreibt.

Zur Poetologie der Intertextualität beim jungen B., am Beispiel der Ballade "Das Schiff"' (173–90); R. Kaufmann, 'B.'s autonomous art, or more late modernism!' (191–212); B. Englmann, '"Es gibt eine Überlieferung, die Katastrophe ist." Erinnerungskultur versus "Kult der Erinnerung" in B. Bs *Lukullus*-Texten' (213–34); D. Ostmeier, 'B. B. and the internet' (235–56); A. Oestmann, 'From chaos to transformation: Brechtian histories *Im Dickicht der Städte*' (257–76); M. Statkiewicz, 'B.'s (non)philosophical theater' (277–94); J. K. Lyon, 'B.'s sources for *Furcht und Elend des III. Reiches*: Heinrich Mann, personal friends, newspaper accounts' (295–306); H.-A. Walter, 'Hier wird Brecht gespuckt oder "*Kim*: konnte nicht ermittelt werden." Die skandalöse Kommentierung von Bs Briefen' (307–15).

BROCH, HERMANN.   *Hermann Broch — Annemarie Meier-Graefe. Briefwechsel 1950–51*, ed. Paul Michael Lützeler, Frankfurt, Suhrkamp, 390 pp. *Hermann Broch 1886–1951 — eine Chronik*, ed. Paul Michael Lützeler (*MaM*, 94), 95 pp. Claus Caesar, **Poetik der Wiederholung. Ethische Dichtung und ökonomisches Spiel in Hermann Brochs Romanen 'Der Tod des Vergil' und 'Die Schuldlosen'* (Ep, 352), 200 pp. Sayd Ahmad Fathalla Abouzid, **Hermann Brochs Romane als Epochenanalyse und Zeitkritik: Zum Verhältnis von Erzählstrukturen und Argumentationsformen in der modernen deutschsprachigen Prosa* (EH, I, 1801), 307 pp. Paul Michael Lützeler, **Kulturbruch und Glaubenskrise. Hermann Brochs 'Die Schlafwandler' und Matthias Gränewalds Isenheimer Altar* (Kontakte 10), Tübingen, Francke, 117 pp. John Hargraves, **Music in the Works of Broch, Kafka and Mann* (SGLLC), 240 pp., examines the views on music of Friedrich Schlegel and Schopenhauer in relation to Broch's *Der Tod des Vergil*, T. Mann's *Zauberberg* and *Doktor Faustus*, and Kafka's *Josefine die Sängerin* and *Forschungen eines Hundes*. Joseph P. Strelka, *Poeta Doctus. Hermann Broch* (Edition Patmos, 6), Tübingen, Francke, vii + 157 pp. R. Halsall, 'The individual and the epoch: H. B.'s *Die Schlafwandler* as a historical novel', *ABNG*, 51:227–42. Id., 'Zur Kierkegaard-Rezeption H. Bs', Krobb, *Literaturvermittlung*, 131–46. F. Wefelmeyer, 'Geschichte als Verinnerlichung. H. B's *Der Tod des Vergil*', *ABNG*, 51:243–62.

CANETTI, ELIAS.   Michael Mack, **Anthropology as Memory. Elias Canetti's and Franz Baermann Steiner's Responses to the Shoah* (CJ, 34), vii + 230 pp. C. Liebrand, 'Jahrhundertproblem im Jahrhundertroman. Die "Frauenfrage" in Canettis *Blendung*', *TMJb*, 14:27–48.

DODERER, HEIMITO VON.   *Heimito von Doderer* (TK 150), 113 pp., contains L.-W. Wolff, 'Auf dem Weg zur Strudlhofstiege' (3–16); J. Busche, '"Edithas süße, verfälschte Sprache"' (17–21); R. Koch, 'Sieben Variationen über H. von D.' (22–29); G. Sommer, 'Der Fall Bachmann. Zu einem Brief H. von Ds an seinen Lektor Horst

Wiemer' (32–36); U. Japp, 'Mikrologie der Wut. Affektive Aufgip-felungen in H. von Ds Kurzprosa' (37–47); C. Deupmann, 'Ein fragwürdiges Kapitel. Erzählte Gewalt und gewalthaftes Erzählen bei H. von D.' (48–56); S. Martus, '"Ein Mord den jeder begeht." Der schwierige 'Fall Gütersloh" (57–68); A. Meier, '"In die eigne Mitte." Zu H. von Ds Drakentophilie' (69–78); G. Sommer, '"So also raunten die beiden dort auf dem Sande umher." Zur Darstellung von Sport und Spiel in den Werken H. von Ds' (79–89); D. Weber, 'Der Lavendelduft herrscht. Eine Hommage an H. von D. aus dem Jahr 1962' (90–92). *'*Schüsse ins Finstere.*' *Zu Heimito von Doderers Kurzprosa*, ed. Gerald Sommer and Kai Luehrs-Kaiser (Schriften der Heimito von Doderer-Gesellschaft, 2), Würzburg, Königshausen & Neumann, 296 pp., includes a bibliography of secondary literature on D.'s short fiction and speeches made at the award of the H. von D. prize. Eugen Banach, **Stifter und Doderer. Harmonik in erzählender Prosa* (Harmonikales Denken, 2), Vienna, Braumüller, 104 pp.

DÖBLIN, ALFRED. Gabriele Sander, *Alfred Döblin*, Stuttgart, Reclam, 400 pp. Oliver Jungen, *Döblin, die Stadt und das Licht* (Cursus. Texte und Studien zur deutschen Literatur, 15), Munich, Iudicium, 200 pp., examines Döblin's Berlin works from a new perspective, in relation to light as metaphor, motif and myth, drawing on poststruc-turalism and discourse theory. S. Becker, 'Zwischen Frühexpressio-nismus, Berliner Futurismus, "Döblinismus" und "neuem Naturalismus": A. D. und die expressionistische Bewegung', Fähn-ders, *Prosa*, 21–44. E. Kobel, '"bald im luft, bald im keller, nie auf erden." Kaiser Ferdinand der Andere in Ds *Wallenstein*', *JFDH*, 237–62. G. Sander, 'Alfred Döblins Roman "Berge, Meere und Giganten" — aus der Handschrift gelesen. Eine Dokumentation unbekannter textgenetischer Materialien und neuer Quellenfunde', *JDSG*, 45:39–69. M. Dufresne, 'De l'anéantissement à l'autodestruc-tion: d'Armand Mercier dans "Die Schlacht! Die Schlacht!" à Friedrich Becker dans "November 1918" et Edward Allison dans "Hamlet oder Die lange Nacht nimmt ein Ende" d'A. D.', *Germanica*, 28:13–30.

EDSCHMID, KASIMIR. H. Schlösser, 'Eine unfassbare Sehnsucht nach Glühendem.' Über K. E. und seine expressionistische Novellis-tik', Fähnders, *Prosa*, 147–63.

EHRENSTEIN, ALBERT. J. Drews, '"Trostlosigkeit, durch Kalauer unerträglich gemacht." A. Es *Tubutsch*', Fähnders, *Prosa*, 45–57.

EINSTEIN, CARL. **Carl-Einstein-Kolloquium 1998. Carl Einstein in Brüssel: Dialog über Grenzen*, ed. Roland Baumann and Hubert Roland (BBL, 22), 314 pp. S. Kyora, 'C. Es *Bebuquin*', Fähnders, *Prosa*, 79–92.

E. Kleinschmidt, 'Das Rauschen der Begriffe. Produktive Beschreibungsproblematik in C. Es "Kunst des 20. Jahrhunderts"', *WB*, 47:507–24.

EISNER, KURT. Bernhard Grau, *Kurt Eisner, 1867–1919. Eine Biographie*, Munich, Beck, 651 pp., gives attention to E.'s work on Nietzsche, his political journalism, and his relation to Marburg neo-Kantianism.

EWERS, HANS HEINZ. S. Stockhorst, 'Populäre Literaturvermittlung nach 1900. Selbst- und Fremdbilder in den Reiseberichten von H. H. E.', Krobb, *Literaturvermittlung*, 167–81.

FALLADA, HANS. M. Kuhnke, '"...welch eine ungeahnte Welt eröffnete sich mir." F. als Büchersammler', *Marginalien*, 162.2:28–48.

FEUCHTWANGER, LION. **Lion Feuchtwanger. A Bibliographic Handbook*, ed. John M. Spalek and Sandra Hawrylchak, 3. *Secondary Literature*. 4. *Reviews and Critical Literature about Individual Works*, Munich, Saur, 400, 420 pp. C. Heine Taxeira, 'L. F.: *Der falsche Nero*. Zeitgenössische Kritik im Gewand des historischen Romans: Erwägungen zur Entstehung und Rezeption', *ABNG*, 51:79–90.

FLEISSER, MARIELUISE. *Briefwechsel*, ed. Günther Rühle, Frankfurt, Suhrkamp, 740 pp. Elfo Hartenstein and Annette Hülsenbeck, *Marieluise Fleisser: Leben im Spagat*, Dortmund, Edition Ebersbach, 166 pp. Ingrid Eden, Hiltrud Häntzschel, and Reinhard Markner, *'Diese Frau ist ein Besitz.' Marieluise Fleisser und die literarischen Szenen ihrer Zeit* (*MaM*, 96), 160 pp., documents her personal and professional relations with a wide range of contemporaries.

FRANK, LEONHARD. W. Fähnders, 'Der Mensch ist gut . . . L. Fs Anti-Kriegs-Erzählungen', Fähnders, *Prosa*, 187–209.

FRIEDLAENDER, SALOMO. Mynona, *Das magische Ich. Elemente des kritischen Polarismus*, Bielefeld, Aisthesis, 302 pp.

GEORGE, STEFAN. *Stefan George: Werk und Wirkung seit dem 'Siebenten Ring'*, ed. Wolfgang Braungart, Ute Oelmann, and Bernhard Böschenstein, Tübingen, Niemeyer, xi + 456 pp., assembles papers given at the Bingen colloquium in 1998. **Verkannte Brüder? Stefan George und das deutsch-jüdische Bürgertum zwischen Jahrhundertwende und Emigration*, ed. Gert Mattenklott et al., Hildesheim, Olms, 287 pp.

CP, 51, has 19 essays on individual poems. W. Osthoff, 'Ergänzende Bibliographie der S. G.-Vertonungen 1895–200', *ib.*, 50:181–204. E. Osterkamp, 'Art history and humanist tradition in the Stefan George circle', *CC*, 23:211–30.

GOEBBELS, JOSEPH. D. Barnett, 'J.G.: expressionist dramatist as Nazi Minister of Culture', *NTQ*, 17:161–69.

HAUPTMANN, CARL. **Eberhard and Elfriede Berger, *Carl Hauptmann: Chronik zu Leben und Werk* (Sämtliche Werke. Supplementband, 1), Stuttgart, Frommann-Holzboog, 391 pp.

HERMANN, GEORG.   Godela Weiss-Sussex, *Metropolitan Chronicles. Georg Hermann's Berlin Novels 1897–1912* (SAG 379), 370 pp.

HERZFELD, MARIE.   S. Strümper-Krobb, 'Zwischen Naturalismus und Impressionismus. M. H. als Vermittlerin skandinavischer Literatur', Krobb, *Literaturvermittlung*, 131–46.

HERZL, THEODOR.   L. L. Albertsen, 'T. H. als reifer Dramatiker. Gedanken um sein Schauspiel *Das neue Ghetto*', *OL*, 56:37–55.

HESSE, HERMANN.   H.H., *Sämtliche Werke*, ed. Volker Michels, 8 vols, Frankfurt, Suhrkamp. Dominique Lingens, *Hermann Hesse et la musique* (Convergences, 20), Berne, Lang, x + 400 pp., based on unpublished sources, examines the role of music in H.'s life and work, especially as music critic and author of *Gertrud, Der Steppenwolf,* and *Das Glasperlenspiel.*

HILLE, PETER.   *Hille-Blätter*, 2001 contains R. Bernhardt, '"Vielleicht war er so eine Tyrannennatur." P. H. über Goethe' (5–49); K. Rosenberg, 'Das unordentliche Zimmer. P. H. und die Berliner Boheme' (51–79); R. Schepper, 'Eine Erwiderung zu Pierre G. Pouthiers Interpretation "Bin ich [. . .] daheim unter anderem Haupte": P. Hs Gedicht "Meernacht"' (99–111); F. Schuppen, 'Zu der Erziehungstragödie "Des Platonikers Sohn" von P.H. 1. Teil' (113–52).

HILLER, KURT.   *Schriften der Kurt Hiller-Gesellschaft*, vol. 1, Fürth, Klaussner.

HIRSCH, KARL JAKOB.   K. R. H., *Manhattan Serenade*, ed. Helmut Pfanner (Exil-Dokumente, 4), Berne, Lang, 159 pp.

HOFMANNSTHAL, HUGO VON.   *H. von H. und Marie von Gomperz, Briefwechsel*, ed. Ulrike Tanzer, Rombach, 240 pp. Christoph König, *Hofmannsthal: Ein moderner Dichter unter den Philologen* (Marbacher Wissenschaftsgeschichte, 2), Göttingen, Wallstein, 504 pp., based on unpublished sources, examines the *Habilitationsschrift* on Victor Hugo, H.'s relation to Goethe, the circle of scholars which formed around him (including Borchardt, Nadler, Benjamin, and C. J. Burckhardt) and the beginnings of research into his work. It devotes chapters to analyses of both versions of *Der Turm* and of *Die ägyptische Helena.* The approach is highly critical, aiming to reveal how H. claimed to have devised a new culture modelled on Goethe, but failed to realise it in his creative work; his resort to the terminology and support of contemporary scholarship became a means of hiding these deficiencies and directing his reception, as documented in later research. Ursula Renner, *'Die Zauberschrift der Bilder': Bildende Kunst in Hofmannsthals Texten* (Litterae, 55), Freiburg, Rombach, 594 pp., is more than an exhaustive account of H.'s relation to fine art, including Böcklin, the pre-Raphaelites (especially Millais), Leonardo's Mona Lisa, Giorgione, Palladio, Rodin, Van Gogh, Poussin, and the aesthetics of Nietzsche and Pater; it also traces the emergence of his own aesthetic through poems, *Der Tod des Tizian* and *Die Frau am Fenster* and other works, in which the primacy of subjectivity over abstraction is realised through non-verbal signs. *Richard Strauss, Hugo von Hofmannsthal: Frauenbilder*, ed. Ilija Dürhammer and Pia Janke, Vienna, Praesens, 320 pp. Françoise Salvan-Renucci, *'Ein Ganzes von Text und Musik.' Hugo von Hofmannsthal und Richard Strauss* (Dokumente und Studien zu Richard Strauss, 3), Tutzing, Schneider, 415 pp., examines the libretti with particular reference to the correspondence. E. Sauermann, 'Hs österreichischer Almanach auf das Jahr 1916 — ein Beitrag zur Geistesgeschichte oder zur Kriegspublizistik?', *DVLG*, 75:288–328. C. König, 'Artistenphilologie. Hs Elektra gegen Sophokles', *Euphorion*, 95:423–40. J. R. P. McKenzie, '"Wahrhaft das Sacrament": H.'s *Der Schwierige* and the sacrament of matrimony', *MLR*, 96:409–19. I. Mülder-Bach, 'Herrenlose Häuser. Das Trauma der Verschüttung und die Passage der Sprache in Hs Komödie "Der Schwierige"', *Hofmannsthal Jb.*, 9:137–62.

HORVÁTH, ÖDÖN VON. *Horváth: Einem Schriftsteller auf der Spur*, ed. Heinz Lunzer et al., Salzburg, Residenz, 160 pp.

HUCH, RICARDA. J. M. Skidmore, '"Nestorin der deutschen Literatur" or "Parasit Hitlers"? The early East German debate about R. H.', *GR*, 76:3–14.

JAHNN, HANS HENNY. Thomas Freeman, *The Case of Hans Henny Jahnn. Criticism and the Literary Outsider* (SGLLC/LCP), Rochester, NY, Camden House, 276 pp., provides the first survey of Jahnn criticism in all its variety, demonstrating its basis in an emotional reaction to the controversial themes and their depiction in his work. Joern Rauser, **'Über die Herbstwelten in der Literatur.' Alter und Altern als Themenkomplex bei Hans Henny Jahnn und Arno Schmidt* (EH, 1, 1810), 430 pp.

JANITSCHEK, MARIE. T. Klugsberger, 'Wissen und Leidenschaft. M. J.: *Esclarmonde* und Marie Najmájer: *Der Stern von Navarra*. Historische Romane zweier österreichischer Schriftstellerinnen der Jahrhundertwende', *ABNG*, 51:263–82.

JOHST, HANNS. R. Düsterberg, '"Gesegnete Vergänglichkeit." H.Js literarische "Vergangenheitsbewältigung"', *ZDP*, 120:590–611.

JUNG, FRANZ. H. Karrenbrock, 'Sprung aus der Welt. Zu F.Js expressionistischer Prosa', Fähnders, *Prosa*, 165–85.

JÜNGER, ERNST. E. J., *Politische Publizistik 1919–1933*, ed. Sven Olaf Berggötz, Stuttgart, Klett-Cotta, 850 pp. Steffen Martus, *Ernst Jünger* (SM 333), Stuttgart, Metzler, 269 pp., surveys the work from a literary rather than a political or philosophical perspective. Annette Rink, *Plutarch des Naturreichs: Ernst Jünger und die Antike*, Würzburg, Königshausen & Neumann, 250 pp., traces the wide range of references to Classical myth and antiquity, including Homer, Ovid, Alexander, Sulla, Prometheus, Hercules, and Clytemnestra, as a means of presenting J.'s reaction to modernity. Volker Mergenthaler, *Versuch, ein Dekameron des Unterstandes zu schreiben. Zum Problem narrativer Kriegsbegegnung in den frühen Prosatexten Ernst Jüngers*, (BNL, 183), 163 pp., examines in detail *In Stahlgewittern, Der Kampf als inneres Erlebnis*, and *Sturm* in relation to the paradoxical task of combining maximum authenticity with the subjectivity that is a precondition of narrative. L. Bluhm, 'Die "zitternde Nadel". Herkunft, Genese und Variation einer Nietzsche-Zuschreibung bei Thomas Mann, E. J. und Alfred Baeumler', *WW*, 51:48–55. D. Beltran-Vidal, 'De la tranchée au "Paris de la deuxième guerre": réflexion d'E. J. sur la guerre', *Germanica*, 28:75–86. H. Seferens, 'E. Js (allzu)williger Vollstrecker. Der SS-Intellektuelle Werner Best und die Doktrin des "heroischen Realismus"', *WB*, 47:594–615.

JÜNGER, FRIEDRICH GEORG. *'Inmitten dieser Welt der Zerstörung.' Friedrich Georg Jünger. Briefwechsel mit Rudolf Schlichter, Ernst Niekisch und Gerhard Nebel*, ed. Ulrich Fröschle and Volker Haase, Stuttgart, Klett-Cotta, 229 pp.

KAFKA, FRANZ. Joseph P. Strelka, *Der Paraboliker Franz Kafka* (Edition Patmos, 5), Tübingen, Francke, viii + 110 pp. Imke Keyer, *Jenseits der Spiegel kein Land: Ich-Fiktionen in Texten von Franz Kafka und Ingeborg Bachmann* (Ep, 343), x + 232 pp., considers a selection of stories by both authors in relation to difficulties in the construction of identity in modernity. *Franz Kafka: Eine ethische und ästhetische Rechtfertigung*, ed. Beatrice Sandberg and Jakob Lothe (Litterae, 85), Freiburg, Rombach, 304 pp. Elisabeth Schmidhäuser, *Kafka über Kafka. 'Der Process'* — *gelesen und gesehen*, Münster, LIT, 248 pp. K. Wagenbach, 'Ks Fabriken', *Fest. Bormann*, 163–69. P.-A. Alt, 'Erzählungen des Unbewussten. Zur Poetik des Traums in F. Ks Romanen', *Fest. Jacobs*, 153–74. N. Oellers, 'Notwendig, aber sinnlos: Ks Kampf ums Schloss, im Schnee', *ib.*, 175–90. H. Binder, 'Die Entdeckung Frankreichs. Zur Vorgeschichte von Ks und Brods Paris-Reisen', *Euphorion*, 95:441–82. S. Gustafson, 'Watching the subject: the mother's gaze in Dickens's *David Copperfield* and K.'s *Der Verschollene*', *MDLK*, 93:53–72. S. Grazzini, 'Das "Blumenfeld"-Fragment: vom Unglück verwirklichter Hoffnung. Noch einmal zur Frage der Komik bei F. K.', *ZDP*, 120:207–28. L. Vaughan, 'F. K.'s *Eine kaiserliche Botschaft* through an Hasidic prism', *GRM*, 51:151–58. R. Selbmann, 'Der Prozess ohne Gesetz: eine neue Deutung von Ks *Vor dem Gesetz* oder nur das alte Dilemma der Interpretation?', *WW*, 51:42–47. M. Ryan, 'K.'s *Die Söhne*: the range and scope of metaphor', *MDLK*, 93:73–86. P. Fenves, 'Continuing the fiction: from Leibniz's "Petite fable" to K.'s *In der Strafkolonie*', *MLN*,

116:502–20. K. Fickert, 'The failed epiphany in K.'s *In der Strafkolonie*', *GN*, 32:153–59. (See also BENN.)

KAISER, GEORG. Stephanie Pietsch, *'Noli me tangere.' Liebe als Notwendigkeit und Unmöglichkeit im Werk Georg Kaisers*, Bielefeld, Aisthesis, 341 pp.

KASCHNITZ, MARIE LUISE. *"Ein Wörterbuch anlegen." Marie Luise Kaschnitz zum 100. Geburtstag*, ed. Brigitte Raitz, with an essay by Ruth Klüger (*MaM*, 95), 108 pp., consists of a series of entries in alphabetical order covering all aspects of her life and career. *'Für eine aufmerksamere und nachdenklichere Welt.' Beiträge zu Marie Luise Kaschnitz*, ed. Dirk Göttsche, Stuttgart, Metzler, 210 pp.

KATZ, HENRY WILLIAM. Ena Pedersen, *Writer on the Run. German-Jewish Identity and the Experience of Exile in the Life and Work of Henry William Katz* (CJ, 33), vi + 197 pp.

KERR, ALFRED. A. K., *'So liegt der Fall.' Theaterkritiken 1919–1933 und im Exil*, ed. Günther Rühle, Frankfurt, Fischer, 1061 pp.

KEUN, IRMGARD. Hiltrud Häntzschel, *Irmgard Keun* (RoM, 50452), 159 pp. Stephanie Bender, *Lebensentwürfe im Romanwerk I. Ks*, Taunusstein, Driesen, 2000, 150 pp.

KEYSERLING, EDUARD VON. S. Henzel, '"Augen, die ihr Handwerk verstehen." E. von Ks Prosa als Paradigma literarischer Phänomenologie', *EG*, 56:325–42.

KLABUND. K., *Sämtliche Werke*, V. *Nachdichtungen und Übersetzungen. 1. Nachdichtungen aus dem Chinesischen, Japanischen und Persischen*, ed. Jutta Dahn-Liu, Amsterdam, Rodopi, 325 pp.

KLEMPERER, VICTOR. N. H. Donahue, 'At the heart of the matter. Deliberations on crisis in the diaries of V. K., 1933–1945', Bullivant, *Krisenbewußtsein*, 105–27.

KOLMAR, GERTRUD. Johanna Woltmann, *Gertrud Kolmar: Leben und Werk* (ST, 3254), 350 pp. B. Damerau, 'Männliches Bildnis: G. Ks poetisches Bild eines Geliebten', *ZGer*, 11:117–30.

KRACAUER, SIEGFRIED. Momme Brodersen, *Siegfried Kracauer* (RoM, 50510), 156 pp. M. Fleischer, 'The gaze of the *flâneur* in S. K.'s *Das Ornament der Masse*', *GLL*, 54:10–24. T. Hirai, 'S. K. und "die Geschichte — von den letzten Dingen" und die Sprache des "Vorraums"', *DB*, 106:12–23.

KRAUS, KARL. *'Verehrte Fürstin.' Karl Kraus und Mechtilde Licknowsky: Briefe und Dokumente*, ed. Friedrich Pfäfflin et al., Göttingen, Wallstein, 256 pp. *'Wie Genies sterben.' Karl Kraus und Annie Kalmar: Briefe und Dokumente*, ed. Friedrich Pfäfflin et al., Göttingen, Wallstein, 162 pp. *Karl Kraus und Die Fackel. Aufsätze zur Rezeptionsgeschichte / Reading Karl Kraus. Essays on the Reception of Die Fackel*, ed. Gilbert J. Carr and Edward Timms, Munich, Iudicium, 246 pp., contains G. J. Carr,

'The "young" K. and the "old" *Burgtheater*. Sources and interpretations' (23–39); P. Hawig, 'K. K. and Jacques Offenbach. Untersuchungen und Thesen zu einer Rezeption auf verschiedenen Ebenen' (40–54); P. Reitter, 'Mimesis, modernism and K. K.'s "Jewish question"' (55–73); E. Timms, '"True believers." The religious vision of a Jewish renegade' (74–87); A. Ribeiro, 'Nachwelt als diskursives Verfahren in der Fackel' (88–98); J. Johnson, 'The reception of K. K. by Schönberg and his School' (99–108); A. Janik, 'K. K. und die Entwicklung der analytischen Philosophie im 20. Jahrhundert' (109–19); C. Jäger, 'Unterwegs zum Ungedachten. K. Ks Aphorismen und die Denkbilder Benjamins und Blochs' (120–31); E. Lorenz, 'The significance of Albert Bloch's *Nachlass* for the understanding of K. K.'s work and biography' (132–46); K. Krolop, 'K.-K.-Rezeption in den böhmischen Ländern' (147–62); A. W. Barker, 'K. K., Friedrich Wolf and the response to February 1934' (163–72); H. Arntzen, 'Die K.-Rezeption nach 1945. Eine Typologie' (173–82); M. Rogers, 'Die Satire der Anspielung bei K. K. und das Problem der Anmerkung' (183–92); S. P. Scheichl, '"Wir wollen weniger zitiert und mehr gelesen sein." K. K. in Frankreich' (206–18); J. F. Bodine, 'K. K. and recent paradigms of literary criticism' (219–30); B. Dodd, 'K.K.'s reputation as language critic in the light of "linguistically grounded language criticism"' (231–46).

J. Pizer, 'The Kraus/Werfel polemic: the double as a sign of modernism's originality crisis', *ColGer*, 34:41–56. H. Yamaguchi, 'Das Zitat der visuellen Motive in K. Ks "Die letzten Tage der Menschheit"', *DB*, 106:4–11.

LAMPEL, PETER. Günter Rinke, *Sozialer Radikalismus und bündische Utopie: Der Fall Peter Lampel* (HBG, 31), 271 pp.

LANDAUER, GUSTAV. M. Baum, 'Der Jude G. L. und der Jude Jesus', *Mühsam-Magazin*, 9:59–69.

LASKER-SCHÜLER, ELSE. *Else Lasker-Schüler-Jahrbuch zur klassischen Moderne*, 1, ed. L. Bluhm and A. Meier, Trier, Wissenschaftlicher Vlg, 245 pp. Doerte Bischoff, *Ausgesetzte Schöpfung. Figuren der Souveränität und Ethik der Differenz in der Prosa Else Lasker-Schülers* (Hermaea, 95), Tübingen, Niemeyer, 560 pp. L. Blum, 'E. L.-S. beim kranken Nietzsche. Adnoten zu einer Legende', *WW*, 2000:325–28. H. M. Müller, '"Die Psalmen Davids neu zu schreiben in deinen Sand." Gedichte über das "Volk Israel" von E. L.-S., Gertrud Kolmar and Nelly Sachs', *GMon*, 53, 2000:45–59. D. Ostmeier, 'Beastly love: Gottfried Benn / E. L.-S.', *ColGer*, 33, 2000:43–74.

LERNET-HOLENIA, ALEXANDER. H. Barrière, 'Les deux conflits mondiaux dans les récits d'A. L.-H.: une guerre médiévale?', *Germanica*, 28:87–104.

LOERKE, OSKAR. T. Baginski, 'Traumerfahrung als Erkenntnisweg: O. Ls Gedicht "Die Hand"', *MDLK*, 93:145–58.

MANN, ERIKA. Gundel Mattenklott, 'Eigensinn und moralisches Engagement. Über E. Ms Kinderbücher', *ZGer*, 11:131–41.

MANN, HEINRICH. Ina-Gabriele Dahlem, **Auflösen und Herstellen. Zur dialektischen Verfahrensweise der literarischen Décadence in Heinrich Manns Göttinnen-Trilogie* (SDLNZ, 44), 260 pp. Britta Krengel, *Heinrich Manns Madame Legros. Revolution und Komik* (BSDL, 60), xii + 378 pp. M. Joch, 'Ein passiver Habitus. Überlegungen mit Bourdieu zu einem Motiv bei Flaubert und H. M.', *GRM*, 51:55–72. C. Simonin, 'Despotisme et chaos. H. M. et l'impérialisme allemand', *Germanica*, 28:31–43. M. Mattick, 'H. Ms Roman "Lidice" — Komik als Mittel, das Nicht-Fassbare darstellbar zu machen', *Exil*, no. 1:43–59.

MANN, KLAUS. James Robert Keller, *The Role of Political and Sexual Identity in the Works of Klaus Mann* (STML, 56), 216 pp., covers the full range of his writing in order to demonstrate the relation between his development as an anti-fascist and his sexual identity as a gay writer, in relation to differing conceptions of identity as developed by Erikson, Horney, Fromm, and more recent theories. Klaus's relations to his father and to Gide are compared with reference to *Unordnung und frühes Leid* and several stories by Klaus. L. Fitzsimmons, ' "Scathe me with less fire": disciplining the African German "Black Venus" in *Mephisto*', *GR*, 76:15–40. M. Jiménez, 'The black muse', *PhilP*, 47, 2000:74–81, compares Mann's *Mephisto* with István Szabó's film. G. M. Rösch, ' "I thought it wiser not to disclose my identity." Die Begegnung zwischen Klaus Mann und Richard Strauss im Mai 1945', *TMJb*, 14:233–48.

MANN, THOMAS. *Colleghefte, 1894–1895*, ed. Yvonne Schmidlin and Thomas Sprecher (TMS, 24), 218 pp. Michael Kämper-van den Boogaart, *Thomas Mann*, Berlin, Volk & Wissen, 160 pp. Reinhard Mehring, **Thomas Mann. Künstler und Philosoph*, Munich, Fink, 272 pp. Claudius Reinke, **Musik als Schicksal. Zur Rezeptions- und Interpretationsproblematik der Wagnerbetrachtung Thomas Manns*, Osnabrück, Rasch, 400 pp. Friedhelm Kröll, *Die Archivarin des Zauberers: Thomas Mann und Ida Herz*, Cadolzburg, Ars Vivendi, 200 pp., documents and provides a just appreciation of the crucial role of this devotee in M.'s life (as archivist and saviour of his library in 1933) and work (*Doktor Faustus*). Günther Schwarzberg, **Es war einmal ein Zauberberg. Thomas Mann in Davos — eine Spurensuche*, Göttingen, Steidl, 356 pp. Werner Wienand, **Größe und Gnade. Grundlagen und Entwicklung des Gnadenbegriffs im Werk Thomas Manns* (Studien zur Literatur- und Kulturgeschichte, 15), Würzburg, Königshausen & Neumann, 448 pp. Katrin Bedenig Stein, **Nur ein 'Ohrenmensch'? Thomas Manns Verhältnis zu den bildenden Künsten* (EH, 1, 1803), 351 pp. Michael Neumann, *Thomas Mann.*

Romane (Klassiker-Lektüren, 7), Berlin, Schmidt, 227 pp. Elke Kinkel, *Thomas Mann in Amerika. Interkultureller Dialog im Wandel? Eine rezeptions- und übersetzungskritische Analyse am Beispiel des Doktor Faustus* (Beiträge aus Anglistik und Amerikanistik, 10), Frankfurt, Lang, 300 pp. J. Neubauer, 'Am Scheideweg. T. M. und Hans Blüher, München 1919 (mit einem unveröffentlichten Brief Blühers an Mann)', *Fest. Bormann*, 171–83. S. Haupt, '"Rotdunkel." Vom Ektoplasma zur Aura. Fotografie und Okkultismus bei T. M. und Walter Benjamin', *ZDP*, 120:540–70. M. van Heeckeren, 'T. M.: Parteigänger oder Untergangsprophet der "Deutschen Ideologie"? Über das Verhältnis von Literatur und Zeitgeschichte im Frühwerk T. Ms', *Neophilologus*, 85:245–56. Y. Elsaghe, 'Die Jüdinnen in T. Ms Erzählwerk', *MDLK*, 93:159–76. Id., 'Kunigunde Rosenstiel. T. Ms späte Allegorie des jüdischen "Volks"', *GRM*, 51:159–72. Id., '"Gute Augen, [...] gute Rasse": zur Aufwertung des Schweizer-Stereotyps in T. Ms Spätwerk', *GQ*, 74:280–95. J. B. Berlin, '"Ihr Gedanke dieser Äusserung in Amerika noch eine weitere Publizität zu verschaffen, ist mir sehr sympathisch" — T. M's unpublished correspondence from 5 January 1936 to 3 May 1936 with Alfred A. Knopf and H. T. Lowe-Porter', *Euphorion*, 95:197–210. S. Pegatzky, 'Provozierendes Künstlertum. Drei neue Studien zu T. M', *LJb*, 42:387–94. R. Zimmermann, 'Dekadenz und Pose beim frühsten T. M. Zur Genese von T. Ms Personalstil', *Fest. Bender*, 419–42. J. Cölln, 'Gerichtstag der Literatur. Zur selbstreflexiven Konzeption von T. Ms Erzählsammlung "Tristan. Sechs Novellen"', *JDSG*, 45, 320–43. L. Köhn, 'Geburt der Sokrates-Tragödie aus dem Geist der Erzählung. T. M: *Der Tod in Venedig*', *Fest. Bender*, 443–67. J. Stoupy, 'La guerre — un jeu d'esprit: à propos des *Pensées de guerre* (1914) de T. M.', *Germanica*, 28:45–59. A. Kissler, '"Mein träumend Gefühl ..." T. Ms *Gesang vom Kindchen* als allegorische Dichtung und seine Beziehung zu Goethes *Hermann und Dorothea*', *Euphorion*, 95:211–36.

Christian Gloystein, *'Mit mir ist es was anderes.' Die Ausnahmestellung Hans Castorps in Thomas Manns Roman 'Der Zauberberg'* (Ep, 355), 220 pp., aims to show that the humanism formulated by Castorp in the 'Schnee' chapter can reasonably be taken, contrary to many previous interpretations, as the novel's central insight, which thanks to Castorp's special status is brought to life in a process in which the author frees himself from sympathy with death. W. Riedel, 'Literatur und Wissen. T. M: *Der Zauberberg*', *ASNS*, 238:1–18. Bernd-Jürgen Fischer, *Handbuch zu Thomas Manns 'Josephromanen'*, Tübingen, Francke, 880 pp. Maria Giebel, *Erzählen im Exil. Eine Studie zu Thomas Manns Joseph und seine Brüder* (EH, 1, 1806), iv + 196 pp. R. Wimmer, 'Goethe und das Gänsespiel. Anmerkungen zu T.Ms *Lotte in Weimar*', *Fest. Jacobs*, 205–18.

Thomas Mann, *Doktor Faustus, 1947–1997*, ed. Werner Röcke
(Publikationen zur *ZGer*, n.F. 3), Berne, Lang, 378 pp., contains the
papers given at a symposium held in Berlin in 1997 to commemorate
the 50th anniversary of the novel's publication. The essays are
marked by an interdisciplinary approach which allows a broad
historical sweep and a variety of political, literary, and musical
perspectives: H. R. Vaget, 'Fünfzig Jahre Leiden an Deutschland:
T. Ms *Doktor Faustus* im Lichte unserer Erfahrung' (11–34); G. Bollen-
beck, '*Doktor Faustus*: Das Deutungsmuster des Autors und die
Probleme des Erzählers' (35–57); S. Breuer, 'Wie teuflisch ist die
"konservative Revolution"? Zur politischen Semantik T. Ms'
(59–71); E. Lämmert, '*Doktor Faustus* — eine Allegorie der deutschen
Geschichte' (73–88); H. Münkler, 'Wo der Teufel seine Hand im
Spiel hat. T. Ms Deutung der deutschen Geschichte des 20.
Jahrhunderts' (89–107); H. Böhme, 'Der Affe und die Magie in der
"Historia von D. Johann Fausten"' (109–43); M. E. Müller, 'Die
Gnadenwahl Satans. Der Rückgriff auf vormoderne Pakttraditionen
bei T. M., Alfred Döblin und Elisabeth Langgässer' (145–65); J.-D.
Müller, 'Faust — ein Missverständnis wird zur Symbolfigur' (167–86);
W. Röcke, 'Teufelsgelächter. Inszenierungen des Bösen. Eine
musikgeschichtliche Annäherung an das Diabolische in T. Ms *Doktor
Faustus*' (187–206); D. Borchmeyer, 'Bescheidenheit contra Absolut-
heit der Kunst. Ein alternatives ästhetisches Modell in *Doktor Faustus*'
(207–62); I. van der Lühe, '"Es wird mein 'Parsifal'"': T. Ms *Doktor
Faustus* zwischen mythischem Erzählen und intellektueller Biographie'
(263–73); H. Danuser, 'Erzählte Musik. Fiktive Poetik in T. Ms *Doktor
Faustus*' (293–320); H. Osterkamp, '"Apocalipsis cum figuris." Composition als Erzählung' (321–43); K. Kropfinger, '"Montage" und
"Composition" im *Doktor Faustus* — Literarische Zwölftontechnik
oder Leitmotivik?' (345–67).

Gerhard Kaiser, *' . . .und sogar eine alberne Ordnung ist immer noch
besser als gar keine.' Erzählstrategien in Thomas Manns Roman Doktor Faustus*,
Stuttgart, Metzler, 220 pp. Inken Steen, *Parodie und parodistische
Schreibweise in Thomas Manns Doktor Faustus* (UDL, 105), vii + 208 pp.
Eva Bauer Licca, *Versteckte Spuren. Eine intertextuelle Annäherung an
Thomas Manns Roman 'Doktor Faustus'*, Wiesbaden, DUV, 309 pp. Elke
Kinkel, *Thomas Mann in Amerika. Interkultureller Dialog im Wandel? Eine
rezeptions- und übersetzungskritische Analyse am Beispiel des Doktor Faustus*
(Beiträge aus Anglistik und Amerikanistik, 10), Frankfurt, Lang,
300 pp. E. Downing, 'Paraphotography and the *Entwicklung* of *Bildung*
in T. M.'s *Doktor Faustus*', *GR*, 76:172–91. S.-H. Jang, 'Wer ist "die
kleine Seejungfrau" in T. Ms *Doktor Faustus*?', *WW*, 51:56–69.
S. Börnchen, 'Tritonus der Hoffnung — Ein fiktives Intervall in
T. Ms *Doktor Faustus*', *OL*, 56:334–54. R. Görner, 'Die Entstehung

des *Doktor Faustus*: T. Ms narrated poetics', *PEGS(NS)*, 70:46–55.
S. Matuschek, 'Dante, deutscher Dante und die Selbstbehauptung
gegen das Nationalgedicht in T. Ms *Doktor Faustus*', *LJb*, 42:271–85.
T. Klugkist, 'Die indirekte Autobiographie. Ein Nachtrag zu T. Ms
Doktor Faustus', *TeK*, 23:203–56.

M. Maar, 'Im Schatten des Calamus. Autobiographisches in T. Ms
indischer Novelle *Die vertauschten Köpfe*', *Merkur*, 55:678–85. *TMJb*,
14, contains U. Karthaus, '*Der Mann ohne Eigenschaften* und Hans
Castorp: Nachfahren *Fausts* und *Wilhelm Meisters*' (9–26); P. M.
Lützeler, 'Schlafwandler am Zauberberg. Die Europa-Diskussion in
Hermann Brochs und T. Ms Zeitromanen' (49–62); V. Neuhaus,
'Die Zaubertrommel' (63–68); M. Neumann, 'Die Irritationen des
Janus oder *Der Zauberberg* im Feld der klassischen Moderne' (69–86);
R. Bucheli, 'Max Rychner und T. M. Fast eine Freundschaft'
(87–104); H. Gildhoff, 'T. M. und die englische Sprache' (143–68);
E. Joseph, 'Ottilie und Hans Castorp im Spannungsfeld von Eros,
Humanität und mystischer Natur-Konnivenz. Über "Wahlverwandt-
schaften" in Goethes gleichnamigem Roman und T. Ms *Zauberberg*'
(169–88); H. M. Kaiser, 'Intertextuelles Spiel mit Wagner-Analogien:
T. Ms Burleske *Tristan* und *Der Ring des Nibelungen*' (189–212);
C. Könneker, 'Raum der Zeitlosigkeit. T. Ms *Zauberberg* und die
Relativitätstheorie' (213–24); J. Nordalm, 'T. Ms *Unordnung und frühes
Leid*, Erich Marcks und Philipp II von Spanien. Eine Beobachtung'
(225–32); F. Schössler, ' "Aneignungsgeschäfte." Zu T. Ms Umgang
mit Quellen in dem Roman *Königliche Hoheit*' (249–68); H. D.
Tschörtner, 'Nobelpreis für T. M. Gerhart Hauptmann schreibt
nach Stockholm' (269–72).

MAUTHNER, FRITZ. Katherine Arens, *Empire in Decline. Fritz
Mauthner's Critique of Wilhelminian Germany* (GLC, 37), ix + 222 pp.,
concentrates on the early novel cycle *Berlin W* (1886–90), the novels
Kraft (1894) and *Hypatia* (1892), the stories set in a Bohemia marked
by rising ethnic nationalism, and ends with two chapters on the
relation of Mauthner's philosophy to Hofmannsthal's *Ein Brief* and to
the entry of science into the public domain in the work of Ernst Mach,
Max Nordau's *Entartung*, and Ernst Haeckel's Monism. Mauthner
emerges as 'a voice of the loyal opposition to the German Empire'
whose language scepticism appears strikingly modern.

MAY, KARL. *Karl-May-Handbuch*, ed. Gert Ueding and Klaus
Rettner, 2nd rev. and enlarged edn, Würzburg, Königshausen &
Neumann, 620 pp., updates this survey of research. **Karl Mays 'Und
Friede auf Erden!'*, ed. Dieter Sudhoff and Hartmut Vollmer (Karl-
May-Studien 6), Oldenburg, Igel, 323 pp. T. Kramer, 'K. M. und
T. E. Lawrence. Bemerkungen zur Rezeption', *Fest. Hohendahl*,
331–54.

MEHRING, WALTER. W. M., *Reportagen der Unterweltstädte. Berichte aus Berlin und Paris 1918 bis 1933*, ed. Georg Schirmers, Oldenburg, Igel, 412 pp. M. Boussart, 'Die zwei Weltkriege in W. Ms Lyrik. Vom avantgardistischen Cabaret zur Elegie', *Germanica*, 28:119–31.

MENZEL, HERYBERT. M. Travers, ' "Selbstgefühl, Todeschicksal", and the end of "Parteidichtung": H. Ms *Anders kehren wir wieder* (1943)', *GLL*, 54:331–44.

MEYER-ECKHARDT, VICTOR. B. Hey'l, 'V. M.-Es Erzähltexte über die Französische Revolution 1924 bis 1951: zu Problemen der Gattungsgeschichte des historischen Romans im zwanzigsten Jahrhundert', ABNG, 51:91–110.

MÜHSAM, ERICH. *Mühsam-Magazin*, 9, contains H. J. Schönfeld, 'E. M. und Senna Hoy. Dokumente ihrer Bekanntschaft' (14–41); C. Knüppel, 'E. M. und die "Kurpfuscher" ' (42–46); Erich Mühsam, 'Kurpfuscher' (47–50); G. Heuer, 'Eine Postkarte aus Paris, "dem heißen, laut schlagenden Herzen Frankreichs". E. M. schreibt an Sigmund Freud' (51–58); E. Cutullé, 'Die Frau als Dämon' (70–80); U. Dittmann, ' "Eingeschreint in die Herzen aller freiheitlichen Kämpfer." E. M. aus der Sicht des Oskar Maria Graf — eine Collage' (81–103); B. Reetz, ' "Es handelt sich um einen Jugendfreund von mir, Erich Mühsam." Über die Briefe an Hermann und Ninon Hesse aus dem Nachlass von Emmy Ball-Hennings' (104–13); E. Hennings, 'Lebenslauf E. Ms und Brief an Ninon Hesse' (114–17).

MUSIL, ROBERT. Walter Fanta, *Die Entstehungsgeschichte des 'Mann ohne Eigenschaften' von Robert Musil* (LGGL, 49), 560 pp. Christian Kassung, *EntropieGeschichten. Robert Musils 'Mann ohne Eigenschaften' im Diskurs der moderen Physik* (Musil-Studien), Munich, Fink, 566 pp. Sebastian Seidel, *Dichtung gibt Sinnbilder. Die Sehnsucht nach Einheit. Das Lebensbaum-Mythologem und das Isis-Osiris-Mythologem in Robert Musils Roman 'Der Mann ohne Eigenschaften'* (New Yorker Beiträge zur Literaturwissenschaft, 3), Frankfurt, Lang, 230 pp. O. Pfohlmann, ' "Die Landschaft im Wagen suchen." Ein kritischer Bericht nach knapp vier Jahrzehnten psychoanalytischer Musil-Forschung', *IASL*, 26:119–83. L. Dietz, 'Unbekannte Essays von R. M. Versuch einer Zuweisung anonymer Beiträge im "Losen Vogel" ', *Hofmannsthal Jb.*, 9:33–136. J.-J. Pieper, 'Die Philosophie R. Ms im Spannungsfeld der Theorien Nietzsches und Machs', *Nietzsche-Studien*, 30:267–94. W. Lang, 'Zwischen Petersburg und Wien: der Zufall, oder Andrej Belyj und R. M.', *Arcadia*, 36:118–42. M. Eggers, 'Simultan übersetzen. Geschlechter- und Sprachdifferenzen und die Erzählstimme in Texten von Bachmann und M.', *WB*, 47:576–93. H. Kraft, 'Wer hätte schon Bilder "wegen ihrer Geschlechtlichkeit" und nicht "wegen ihres Kunstwertes"? Die Erzählung *Grauauges nebligster Herbst* von R. M.', *Fest. Bender*, 413–17. H. Madsen, ' "Es könnte ebenso anders sein . . .'' Zeitkritisches Abbild und utopisches Vorausbild in den Druckfahnenkapiteln des Romans *Der Mann ohne Eigenschaften* von R. M.', *LWU*, 34 : 3–18. (See also RILKE.)

PANIZZA, OSKAR. P. Brown, 'The continuing trials of O.P.: a century of artistic censorship in Germany, Austria and beyond', *GSR*, 24 : 533–56, concerns late-20th-c. performances of *Das Liebeskonzil.*

PAQUET, ALFONS. Sabine Brenner, Gertrude Cepl-Kaufmann, and Martina Thöne, **'Ich liebe nichts so sehr wie die Städte . . .' Alfons Paquet als Schriftsteller, Europäer, Weltreisender* (Frankfurter Bibliotheksschriften, 9), Frankfurt, Klostermann, 192 pp.

PERUTZ, LEO. H.-H. Müller, 'Literarische Phantastik oder Interpretationsprobleme? Zur Erzählkonzeption von L. P. — dargestellt an der Novelle ''Nur ein Druck auf den Kopf'' ', Eicher, *Grenzüberschreitungen*, 177–92.

PINTHUS, KURT. C. Spreizer, 'The old guard and the avant-garde: Karl Lamprecht, K. P. and literary expressionism', *GSR*, 24 : 283–302.

PLIVIER, THEODOR. P. Vaydat, 'T. P., romancier-reporter des deux guerres mondiales', *Germanica*, 28 : 105–18.

REMARQUE, ERICH MARIA. *Erich Maria Remarque* (TK 149), contains E. Hilsenrath, ' ''Lesen Sie mal den 'Arc de Triomphe.'' Erinnerung an E. M. Rs Roman' (1–7); J. Chambers II and T. Schneider, ' ''Im Westen nichts Neues'' und das Bild des modernen Kriegs' (8–18); B. Murdoch, 'Vorwärts auf dem Weg zurück. Kriegsende und Nachkriegszeit bei E. M. R.' (19–29); H. Schreckenberger, ' ''Durchkommen ist alles.'' Physischer und psychischer Existenzkampf in E. M. Rs Exilromanen' (30–41); T. F. Schneider, ' ''Ein ekler Leichenwurm.'' Motive und Rezeption der Schriften E. M. Rs zur nationalsozialistischen deutschen Vergangenheit' (42–54); J. Strümpl, 'Kammersymphonie des Todes. E. M. Rs ''Der Funke Leben'', Anna Seghers' ''Das siebte Kreuz'' und eine Gattung namens ''KZ-Roman'' ' (55–64); W. Fuld, 'Ein Treffen mit alten Bekannten. Zur Vorgeschichte des Romans ''Der Himmel kennt keine Günstlinge'' ' (65–68); H. Kloiber, 'Zwischen Schulstube und Internet. E. M. R. in der Didaktik' (69–78).

RILKE, RAINER MARIA. R. M. R., *Briefwechsel mit Auguste Rodin*, ed. Rätus Luck, Frankfurt, Insel, 500 pp. R. M. R., *'Paris tut not.' Briefwechsel mit Mathilde Vollmoeller*, ed. Barbara Glauert-Hesse, Göttingen, Wallstein, 272 pp.

A Companion to the Works of Rainer Maria Rilke, ed. Erika A. and Michael M. Metzger (SGLLC), 311 pp., contains, after an introduction by the editors: P. P. Brodsky, 'Colored glass and mirrors: life with R.' (19–39); J. Rolleston, 'The poetry and the politics of the young R., 1895–1902' (40–89); J. Ryan, 'R.'s early narratives'

(40–89); R. Freedman, '*Das Stunden-Buch* and *Das Buch der Bilder*: harbingers of R.'s maturity' (90–127); L. Ryan, 'Neue Gedichte — New Poems' (128–53); G. C. Schoolfield, '*Die Aufzeichnungen des Malte Laurids Brigge*' (154–87); K. S. Komar, 'Rethinking R.'s *Duineser Elegien* at the end of the millennium' (188–208); A. Keele, ' "Poesis and the great tree of being": a holistic reading of R.'s *Sonette an Orpheus*' (209–35); G. Bucher, 'R.'s poetry in the French language: the enigma of mythopoietic reversal' (236–63); K. S. Webb, 'R. and the visual arts' (264–88). Approaches to coverage and interpretation vary considerably, from detailed (even line-by-line) exegesis, as in the essays on the 'Dinggedichte', *Sonnets to Orpheus*, and *Malte*, to speculations on the meaning of the works for readers in a postmodern age. The cosmopolitan solitary is shown against the background of a developing modernistic culture, to which he substantially contributed with an unflinching view of suffering and death which belies the image of the ethereal mystic established by early critical assessments. All quotations are accompanied by exemplary translations.

Timothy J. Casey, *A Reader's Guide to Rilke's Sonnets to Orpheus*, Galway, Arlen House, 208 pp., begins with three short pieces on Rilke's life and work, the poem 'Orpheus, Eurydike, Hermes', and the *Duino Elegies*. The approach is basically thematic, so that Rilke's emphatic this-worldliness emerges clearly, thanks largely to judicious quotation from Rilke's own comments in letters, and each of the sonnets is given separate treatment. The author confronts the questionable aspects of the works noted by some earlier critics, the 'distrust of rationalising and moralising', but remains accessible to students coming to Rilke for the first time and to the general reader. Hajo Drees, *Rainer Maria Rilke: Autobiography, Fiction and Therapy* (STML, 60), x + 176 pp., surveys the autobiographical elements in R.'s work up to the *Duino Elegies*, with special attention to *Malte*, on the basis of theories of autobiography, R.'s aesthetics, and selected letters. Siglind Bruhn, **Musical Ekphrasis in Rilkes Marienleben* (IFAVL, 47), 235 pp. *Unreading Rilke. Unorthodox Approaches to a Cultural Myth* (SMGL, 92), ed. Hartmut Heep, 216 pp., offers critical readings based on recent literary theory and insights into R.'s psyche, his impact on Hollywood, Russian art, and other authors. It contains, besides an introduction H. Heep, 'R. M. Rs Frauen: Hass-Liebe auf den zweiten Blick' (11–18); H. Drees, 'Never mind Freud! Who needs psychoanalysis when you can write poetry? R. M. R's torture, therapy, and salvation' (19–34); H. Möller, ' "Ein Deutscher offenbar." Einige Bemerkungen zum Leben und Sterben eines Reiterfähnrichs' (35–42); E. L. Vines, 'R. and seeing in time and space' (43–52); I. Gilbert, 'From myth to language: childhood's narrative in R. M.

R.'s *Malte Laurids Brigge*' (53–60); E. W. B. Hess-Lüttich, 'Simultaneität und Sukzession. Zur (Hypertext?)Struktur der Zeit-Zeichen in Rs *Malte* und Prousts *Recherche*'(61–76); P. H. Stanley and J. Flaum, 'R.'s *Duino Elegies*: an alternative approach to the study of mysticism' (77–92); M. M. Gruettner, 'Zur Ökologie von Schöpfung und Verwandlung: Die achte *Elegie* von R. M. R.' (93–108); C. Hollender, 'The poet meets the mother of invention: the allegory of the tenth *Duino Elegy*' (109–24); L. Calvedt, '"Mitten im Schreiben sind wir mitten im Tod": death as an aesthetic phenomenon in R. and Handke' (125–36); J. S. Cushman, 'The avant-garde R.: Russian (un)orthodoxy and the visual arts' (137–48); K. S. Komar, 'R. in America: a poet re-created' (149–70).

Tina Simon, **Rilke als Leser. Untersuchung zum Rezeptionsverhalten. Ein Beitrag zur Zeitbegegnung des Dichters während des Ersten Weltkrieges* (EH, 1, 1785), 415 pp. G. Magnússon, 'Interpretation der 9. Elegie Rs im Licht jüdischer Gnosis', *TeK*, 23:159–202. Y.-G. Mix, 'R. M. R., Robert Musil und die Rezeption skandinavischer Literatur zur Zeit des *Fin de siècle*', *WW*, 51:375–87. R. Köhnen, 'Im Grenzverkehr der Künste. R., Rodin und Cézanne', Eicher, *Grenzüberschreitungen*, 193–228. G. Neumann, 'Rs Dinggedicht', *Fest. Bormann*, 143–61. E. Ziegler, 'Die "Herrin" der Insel. Die Verlegerin Katharina Kippenberg und R. M. R.', *Buchhandelsgeschichte*, 2001–02, B65–75.

ROTH, JOSEPH. Sebastian Kiefer, *Braver Junge — gefüllt mit Gift. Joseph Roth und die Ambivalenz*, Stuttgart, Metzler, 182 pp. Sidney Rosenfeld, *Understanding Joseph Roth*, Columbia SC, Univ. of South Carolina Press, xvii + 128 pp. M. Kämper-van den Boogaart, 'J. R. Eine offene Wunde in der Literaturgeschichte', *Fest. Hohendahl*, 93–114. I. Foster, 'J. R.'s *Radetzkymarsch* as a historical novel', *ABNG*, 51:357–70. J. Pizer, ' "Last Austrians" in "turn of the century" works by Franz Grillparzer, J. R., and Alfred Kolleritsch', *GQ*, 74:8–21. P. Saur, ' "Like a brother": J. R's symbolic siblings', *GN*, 32:3–14.

SCHAUKAL, RICHARD VON. M. Burri, 'Theodor Herzl and R. von S.: self-styled nobility and the sources of bourgeois belligerence in prewar Vienna', pp. 105–31 of *Rethinking Vienna 1900*, ed. Steven Beller (Austrian History, Culture and Society, 3), Oxford, Berghahn, xi + 292 pp.

SCHICKELE, RENÉ. D. Lamping, ' "Die Überwindung der Grenze." Deutsch-französische Grenzgänge in R. Ss Roman-Trilogie *Das Erbe am Rhein*', *Fest. Jacobs*, 191–203.

SCHNEIDER, REINHOLD. Ekkehard Blattmann, **Reinhold Schneider im Roten Netz. Der 'Fall Reinhold Schneider' im kryptokommunistischen Umfeld.* 1. *Text.* 2. *Materialien*, Frankfurt, Lang, viii + 958 pp. Ralf Schuster, **Antwort in der Geschichte: Zu den Übergängen zwischen den Werkphasen bei Reinhold Schneider* (MBSL, 51), 359 pp.

SCHNITZLER, ARTHUR. '*Sicherheit ist nirgends.' Das Tagebuch von Arthur Schnitzler*, ed. Ulrich von Bülow (*MaM*, 93), 160 pp. Bettina Marxer, **'Liebesbriefe, und was nun einmal so genannt wird.' Korrespondenzen zwischen Arthur Schnitzler, Olga Waissnix und Marie Reinhard: Eine literatur- und kulturwissenschaftliche Lektüre* (Ep, 362), 200 pp. Ruth Klüger, **Schnitzlers Damen, Weiber, Mädeln, Frauen*, pref. Hubert Christian Ehalt (Wiener Vorlesungen im Rathaus, 79), Vienna, Picus, 61 pp. A. W. Barker, 'Race, Sex and Character in S.'s *Fräulein Else*', *GLL*, 54: 1–9. G. Jackman, ' "Religiöse Nachwehen" in S.'s *Anatol*', *ib.*, 155–63. M. Pape, ' "Ich möcht' Jerusalem gesehen haben, eh' ich sterbe." Antisemitismus und Zionismus im Spiegel von A. Ss Roman *Der Weg ins Freie*', *JFDH*, 198–236. K. Fliedl, 'Ausbleibende Nachrichten. Ein Problem der Briefedition am Beispiel der Schnitzler-Beer-Hofmann-Korrespondenz', Bauer, *Edition*, 147–61.

SEIDEL, INA. A. Cardinal, 'I. S. From *Das Wunschkind* to *Lennacker*: strategies of dissimulation', *ABNG*, 51: 371–82.

SPITTELER, CARL. Philipp Theisohn, *Totalität des Mangels. Carl Spitteler und die Geburt des modernen Epos aus der Anschauung* (Ep, 344), 200 pp., analyses S.'s major epic works and his aesthetic writings in the context of changing conceptions of the epic in relation to the modern world.

STADLER, ERNST. A. Kramer, 'Heimatkunst und Moderne. Ein unbekanntes Gedicht von E. S.', *WW*, 51: 235–42.

SUTTNER, BERTHA VON. E. Biedermann, 'Eine Genossin des leibhaftigen Gottseibeiuns? Zu B. von Ss Briefwechsel mit Irma von Troll-Boristyàni 1886–1890', *ÖGL*, 45: 134–52.

TOLLER, ERNST. **Ernst Tollers Geburtsort Samotschin*, ed. Thorsten Unger and Maria Wojtczak (Schriften der Ernst-Toller-Gesellschaft, 3), Würzburg, Königshausen & Neumann, 80 pp., contains four essays linking T.'s birthplace to his autobiographical writings, his early years, and the literature of the eastern frontier areas.

TRAKL, GEORG. Alfred Doppler, **Die Lyrik Georg Trakls. Beiträge zur poetischen Verfahrensweise und zur Wirkungsgeschichte*, Salzburg, Otto Müller, 198 pp. Cornelia Ortlieb, **Poetische Prosa. Beiträge zur modernen Poetik von Charles Baudelaire bis Georg Trakl*, Stuttgart, Metzler, 300 pp. B. Neymeyr, 'Lyrisch-musikalische Kadenzen. Zur poetischen Figuration der Dekadenz in Ts Gedicht "Kleines Konzert" ', *Hofmannsthal Jb.*, 9: 241–60. E. Sauermann, 'Edition und Analyse von Ts Briefwechsel', Bauer, *Edition*, 163–86. A. Unterkircher, 'Der Briefwechsel Ludwig von Fickers mit Ludwig Wittgenstein und was ein Trakl-Brief damit zu tun hat', *ib.*, 205–16.

TUCHOLSKY, KURT. Stephanie Burrows, *Tucholsky and France* (BSD, 25/55), Leeds, Maney, 269 pp., combines biography and an analysis of the published journalism to show the extent to which T. was influenced by the French cultural and intellectual tradition and by his experience of France. It provides new insights into T.'s contacts with French freemasonry and literary, pacifist, and political circles. It considers his role in attempts to improve Franco-German relations through lectures and journalism. I. King, 'K. T. as prophet of European unity', *GLL*, 54.2: 164–72.

UNGAR, HERMANN. H. U., *Sämtliche Werke in drei Bänden*, 1: *Romane*, Paderborn, Igel, 352 pp.

VIEBIG, CLARA. C. Bland, 'Prussian, Rhinelander or German? Regional and national identities in the historical novels of C. V.', *ABNG*, 51:383–400. P. Colonge, 'Das Rheinland in C. Vs Romanwerk', *Fest. Jacobs*, 131–40.

WALDINGER, ERNST. C. Teissl, 'Ein Heimatdichter im Exil — E. W. (1896–1970)', *Exil*, no. 1:21–34.

WALSER, ROBERT. Marion Gees, *Schauspiel auf Papier. Gebärde und Maskierung in der Prosa Robert Walsers* (PSQ, 168), 192 pp. Kerstin Gräfin von Schwerin, *Minima Aesthetica. Die Kunst des Verschwindens. Robert Walsers ikrographische Entwürfe Aus dem Bleistiftgebiet* (EH, 1, 1814), 295 pp. Markus Schwahl, *Die Wirklichkeit und ihre Schwestern. Epistemologische Ideologiekritik und ihre ethnischen Implikationen im Werk Robert Walsers* (EH, 1, 1816), 268 pp. Elke Siegel, *Aufträge aus dem Bleistiftgebiet: zur Dichtung Robert Walsers*, Würzburg, Königshausen & Neumann, 184 pp. *Robert Walser. Herisauer Jahre 1933–1956*, ed. Peter Witschi (Herisauer Hefte), Herisau, 96 pp. S. Kammer, 'Gestörte Kommunikation. R. Ws Briefschreibspiele', Bauer, *Edition*, 229–45.

WEDEKIND, FRANK. **Kontinuität — Diskontinuität. Diskurse zu Frank Wedekinds literarischer Produktion (1903–1918)*, ed. Sigrid Dreiseitel and Hartmut Vinçon (Wedekind-Lektüren: Schriften der Wedekind Gesellschaft, 2), Würzburg, Königshausen & Neumann, 280 pp., assembles papers given at a symposium held in Darmstadt in 1999. H. Vinçon, 'Prolog ist herrlich! Zu F. Ws Konzept dramaturgischer Kommunikation', *Euphorion*, 95:69–82. E. Harris, 'Die Befreiung des Fleisches aus dem Stein. Pygmalion in F. Ws Erdgeist', *Fest. Bender*, 393–411.

WENGHÖFER, WALTER. *CP*, 50, publishes selected poems (41–50), and letters (51–63), followed by B. Pieger, ' "...zusammengezogen in Erwartung des Wortes." Der Dichter W. W.' (64–91).

WERFEL, FRANZ. **Jugend in Böhmen. Franz Werfel und die tschechische Kultur — eine literarische Spurensuche*, ed. Michael Schwidtal and Václav Bok, Vienna, Praesens, 220 pp.

ZUCKMAYER, CARL. Gunther Nickel, **Carl Zuckmayer und die Medien* (*Zuckmayer-Jb.*, 4), 2 vols, St. Ingbert, Röhrig, 800 pp.

ZWEIG, STEFAN. L. E. Mygdalis, 'S. Z. und Nikos Kazantzakis', *WW*, 5:243–47.

LITERATURE FROM 1945
TO THE PRESENT DAY

By JOANNE LEAL, *Lecturer in German, Birkbeck College, University of London*

1. GENERAL

*Digitale Literatur, ed. Heinz Ludwig Arnold (TK, 152), 137 pp. *Die freche Muse / The Impudent Muse. Literarisches und politisches Kabarett von 1901 bis 1999*, ed. Sigrid Bauschinger (Amherster Kolloquium, 20), Tübingen–Basle, Francke, 2000, 221 pp. C. D. Conter, ' "Alle Kommunisten sind Juden, alle Juden können Kommunisten werden." Über das Verhältnis von Juden und antifaschistischem Widerstand in der sozialistischen Literatur', *GMon*, 53, 2000: 279–73, considers the development of the depiction of the association of Jewish figures with antifascist resistance in the work of Friedrich Wolf, Bruno Apitz, Stephan Hermlin, and Jurek Becker amongst others. **Textual Responses to German Unification. Processing Historical and Social Change in Literature and Film*, ed. Carol Anne Costabile-Heming, Rachel J. Halverson, and Kristie A. Foell, Berlin–NY, de Gruyter, vi + 278 pp. Ioana Crâcium, **Die Politisierung des antiken Mythos in der deutschsprachigen Gegenwartsliteratur* (UDL, 102), 2000, ix + 349 pp. Iris Denneler, **Von Namen und Dingen. Erkundungen zur Rolle des Ich in der Literatur am Beispiel von Ingeborg Bachmann, Peter Bichsel, Max Frisch, Gottfried Keller, Heinrich von Kleist, Arthur Schnitzler, Frank Wedekind, Vladimir Nabokov und W. G. Sebald*, Würzburg, Königshausen & Neumann, 182 pp. F. Eigler, 'Engendering cultural memory in selected post-Wende literary texts of the 1990s', *GQ*, 74: 392–406.

 Das Jahrhundert Berlins: Eine Stadt in der Literatur, ed. Jattie Enklaar and Hans Ester (DK, 50), Amsterdam–Atlanta, Rodopi, 2000, 298 pp., contains a wide-ranging collection of essays, not all of which have the literary response to Berlin as their central concern. Essays focusing on the post-war period include H. Nijssen's interpretation of Johannes Bobrowski's *Auf den jüdischen Händler A. S. I, II* and *III* (117–30), and K. Gille's reconstruction of the debate about cultural politics in the GDR inspired by the first performance of Ulrich Plenzdorf's *Die neuen Leiden des jungen W.* (131–46). G. Labroisse addresses the reception of the work of Heiner Müller and insists on the centrality of his poetry to an understanding of his prose and plays (147–86). More obviously Berlin-centred articles include T. Kramer's exploration of the integration of socialist ideas in Christa Wolf's *Der geteilte Himmel* (187–202). G. Gemert examines what is described here as Peter Schneider's 'Mauer-Trilogie' (*Der Mauerspringer, Paarungen,* and *Eduards Heimkehr*) as a response to the division of Germany and its reunification and as an exploration of the problems these throw up for the '68 generation (203–22). M. Brosig analyses the autobiographical and literary connotations of Berlin in Brigitte Reimann's work, above all with regard to the theme of the quest for a home in both a geographical and a personal sense (223–42).

Petra Fachinger, *Rewriting Germany from the Margins. 'Other' German Literature of the 1980s and 1990s*, Montreal, McGill–Queen's U.P., 176 pp. *Flucht und Vertreibung in der deutschen Literatur*, ed. Sascha Feuchert (GANDLL, 21), 355 pp. *Schriftsteller als Intellektuelle. Politik und Literatur im Kalten Krieg*, ed. Sven Hanuschek, Therese Hörnigk, and Christine Malende (STSL, 73), 2000, viii + 339 pp. *Bestandsaufnahmen: Deutschsprachige Literatur der neunziger Jahre aus interkultureller Sicht*, ed. Matthias Harder, Würzburg, Königshausen & Neumann, 284 pp.

Schuld und Sühne? Kriegserlebnis und Kriegsdeutung in deutschen Medien der Nachkriegszeit (1945–1961), ed. Ursula Heukenkamp, 2 vols (ABNG, 50.1 and 50.2), 404, 405–827 pp. The 61 essays contained in these volumes represent the proceedings of a conference held in Berlin in 1999. The overarching theme of the contributions is the representation of war in various media in the post-war period and, as the title suggests, the emphasis is generally on the way in which questions of guilt and reparation have been explored in film, art, historiography, radio broadcasts, newspapers and magazines, school books and curricula, drama and prose. The first volume focuses on text-critical approaches with sections on individual war novels (by, amongst others, Gerd Gaiser, Heinrich Böll, Franz Fühmann, and Erich Maria Remarque); on the theme of Stalingrad, in several cases as it is represented in Theodor Plievier's novel of the same name; on the representation of the war-time experiences of children and young people; on the theme of the 'Heimkehrer'; and on 'Kriegserinnerungen', a section which includes S. Hoefert's examination of the war poems of Johannes Bobrowski, Peter Huchel, and Hanns Cibulka (341–52), H. Kloiber's reading of Elisabeth Langgässer's *Der Torso* (353–62), and I. Sellmer's analysis of Manès Sperber's *Die verlorene Bucht* (363–70). Contributions to the second volume, described as 'diskurskritisch', are contained in sections on the politics of memory; on images of Germany, notably here two essays on the reception of post-war German literature in France (M. George, 617–34) and Poland (W. A. Niemirowski, 643–58); and on differences in the representation of the war in its aftermath in East and West. This section includes illuminating studies by K. Hickethier (759–76) and P. Hoff (777–90) on the representation and interpretation of war in West and East German television programmes of the 1950s.

M. Hofmann, 'Literatur und kulturelle Differenz. Problemkonstellationen in Geschichte und Gegenwart', *WB*, 47:387–402. B. Linklater, ' "Philomela's revenge": challenges to rape in recent writing in German', *GLL*, 56:253–71. J. M. McNally, 'Shifting boundaries: an eastern meeting of East and West German "Kabarett" ', *ib.*, 173–90. E. Mitman, 'On the road to nowhere: utopian geography in postreunification literature', *Seminar*, 37:336–54. Barbara Oberwalleney, *Heterogenes Schreiben. Positionen der deutschsprachigen jüdischen Literatur (1986–1998)*, Munich, Iudicium, 230 pp. Birgit Patzelt, *Phantastische Kinder- und Jugendliteratur der 80er und 90er Jahre. Strukturen-Erklärungsstrategien-Funktionen*, Frankfurt, Lang, 274 pp. H. Peitsch, ' "Vereinigungsfolgen." Strategien zur Deligitimierung von Engagement in Literatur und Literaturwissenschaft der neunziger Jahre', *WB*, 47:325–51. Ingo Piel, *Die Judenverfolgung in autobiographischer Literatur. Erinnerungstexte nichtjüdischer Deutscher nach 1945* (EH, 1, 1789), 220 pp. Debbie Pinfold, *The Child's View of the Third Reich in German Literature. The Eye Among the Blind*, OUP, 293 pp. Edgar Platen, *Perspektiven literarischer Ethik. Erinnern und Erfinden in der Literatur der Bundesrepublik*, Tübingen–Basle, Francke, 291 pp. Mererid Puw Davies, *The Tale of Bluebeard in German Literature. From the Eighteenth Century to the Present*, OUP, xiv + 279 pp., explores the changing and often unconventional ways in which the Blaubart tale has been given literary expression since the 18th c. and includes a fascinating chapter on later-20th-c. re-workings of the story. It offers a brief overview of works by male authors in which the tale is used to 'describe or reassert a model of masculinity which is threatened by major changes', before focusing on a constrastive analysis of Unica Zürn's *Das Haus der Krankheiten*. Puw Davies reads this work as a response to the surrealist theory of Hans Bellmer (itself described 'as a kind of Bluebeard thinking') from a feminist subject position. Comparison of this work with others by Ingeborg Bachmann, Karin Struck and Elisabeth Reichart allows for insightful conclusions about the literary consequences of feminist appropriations of the Blaubart tale. E. Reichmann, 'Jüdische Figuren in österreichischer und bundesdeutscher Literatur der 1980er und 1990er Jahre — der schwierige Weg jüdischer und nichtjüdischer Autoren aus dem mentalen Ghetto', *GMon*, 53, 2000:237–50. Anja Restenberger, *Effi Briest: Historische Realität und literarische Fiktion in den Werken von Fontane, Spielhagen, Hochhuth, Brückner und Keuler*, Frankfurt, Lang, 274 pp. Alexander Ritter, *Deutsche Minderheitenliteratur. Regionalliterarische und interkulturelle Perspektiven der Kritik*, Munich, Südostdeutsches Kulturwerk, 428 pp. H. Ruch, ' "Es geht nicht um Christa Wolf" — Der deutsche Literaturstreit 1990/91', *MDG*, 47, 2000:396–422. Burkhard Schäfer, *Unberühmter Ort. Die Ruderalfläche im Magischen Realismus und in der Trümmerliteratur* (TSDL, 18), 392 pp. Anita Schilcher, **Geschlechts-rollen, Familie, Freundschaft und Liebe in der Kinderliteratur der 90er Jahre,* Frankfurt, Lang, 405 pp. R. Skare, ' "Real life within the false one." ' Manifestations of East German identity in post-reunification texts', *GMon*, 54:185–205, examines three works from the years 1996 and 1997 by Daniela Dahn, Hans-J. Misselwitz, and Thomas Rosen-löcher. Dagmar Spooren, **Unbequeme Töchter, entthronte Patriarchen. Deutschsprachige Bücher über Väter von Autorinnen*, Wiesbaden, Deutscher Universitäts-Verlag, 241 pp.

Das literarische Berlin im 20. Jahrhundert, ed. Silvio Vietta, Stuttgart, Reclam, 275 pp., provides a brief overview of Berlin's literary history until the end of the 19th c. before addressing a representative selection of 'die wichstigsten Autoren und Strömungen' of the 20th c. in chronologically ordered, thematically organized chapters. Each can offer little more than an overview of its subject but often contains useful contextualizing material. So, for instance, the chapter 'Theaterstadt Berlin' on Brecht and Heiner Müller (134–73), also offers brief histories of the city's most prominent theatres. The other chapters concerned with the post-war period take as their themes 'Die geteilte Stadt' (with a brief look at Christa Wolf's *Der geteilte Himmel* and Uwe Johnson's *Zwei Ansichten*, 174–200), and 'Berlin zwischen Mauerfall und Regierungsumzug' (201–20), which provides mainly biographical detail on Monika Maron, Jens Sparschuh, Durs Grünbein, Pieke Biermann, Richard Wagner, and Alexander Osang. The volume concludes with some helpful information on Berlin's various literary institutions and on literary Berlin in the Internet.

*Region-Literatur-Kultur. Regionalliteraturforschung heute, ed. Martina Wagner-Egelhaaf, Bielefeld, Aisthesis, 244 pp. Sabine Wilke, *Ambiguous Embodiment. Construction and Deconstruction of Bodies in Modern German Literature and Culture*, Heidelberg, Synchron, 2000, 237 pp.

AUSTRIA, SWITZERLAND. **Aug' um Ohr. Medienkämpfe in der österreichischen Literatur des 20. Jahrhunderts*, ed. Bernard Banoun, Arlette Camion, and Yasmin Hoffmann, Berlin, Schmidt, 248 pp. Eoin Bourke, *The Austrian Anschluss in History and Literature*, Galway, Arlen House, 2000, xx + 138 pp., represents the first contribution to a new series entitled 'Literature and Testimony' which, with an eye to the problems of teaching German literature 'in non-German places of learning', proposes to 'combine historical narrative and literary analysis' with a view to demonstrating how literary texts can 'spotlight, condense and illuminate historical conditions [. . .] in a more profound way than most other kinds of texts'. This volume succeeds in fulfilling those aims in part. Its retelling of the historical events surrounding the 'Anschluss', which focuses above all on the rise of anti-Semitism and its consequences for Austria's Jewish population, is detailed and informative but, with exceptions (the reading of Ernst Jandl's 'wien: heldenplatz' being one), too often literary works (by Stella Rotenberg, Ruth Klüger, Ilse Aichinger, Franz Werfel, and Erich Fried, amongst others) are treated as if they had the same status as the other documentary sources cited and, contrary to the stated intention, their literary specificity remains unregarded. M. Bunzl, 'Political inscription, artistic reflection: a recontextualization of contemporary Viennese-Jewish literature', *GQ*, 73, 2000: 163–70. M. Hussang, 'Weiße Flecken auf der literaturgeschichtlichen Landkarte: Vergangenheitsbewältigung und österreichische Gegenwartsliteratur', *GN*, 31, 2000: 2–7. Julia Neissl, *Tabu im Diskurs. Sexualität in der Literatur österreichischer Autorinnen*, Innsbruck, Studien Vlg, 336 pp.

G. Kaiser, ' ". . . ein männliches, aus tiefer Not gesungenes Kirchenlied . . .": Emil Staiger und der Zürcher Literaturstreit', MDG, 47, 2000: 382–94. Peter von Matt, *Die tintenblauen Eidgenossen. Über die literarische und politische Schweiz*, Munich, Hanser, 319 pp.

EAST GERMANY.   C. A. Costabile-Heming, '*Rezensur:* a case study of censorship and programmatic reception in the GDR', *MDLK*, 92, 2000: 53–67, examines the production histories of three works by Günter Kunert. Peter Davies, *Divided Loyalties. East German Writers and the Politics of German Division* (BSD, 24), 2000, 277 pp. A. Gilleir, 'Spuren einer weiblichen Opposition. Eine Interpretation von vergessener Literatur aus der DDR', *LitL*, 24:83–99. Karin R. Gürttler, *Die Rezeption der DDR-Literatur in Frankreich (1945–1990). Autoren und Werke im Spiegel der Kritik* (Kanadische Studien zur deutschen Sprache und Literatur, 45), Berne, Lang, 433 pp. D. Robb, 'The GDR *Singbewegung*: metamorphosis and legacy', *MDLK*, 92, 2000: 199–216, explores the history of political song in the GDR and its continued influence in the post-reunification period. Hans Joachim Schröder, *Interviewliteratur zum Leben in der DDR. Zur literarischen, biographischen und sozialgeschichtlichen Bedeutung einer dokumentarischen Gattung* (STSL, 83), 426 pp. A. Trebess, 'Zum Todesmotiv in der DDR-Literatur. Entwicklungen eines Tabu-Themas', *WB*, 47:70–91.

2. LYRIC POETRY

Holger Brohm, *Die Koordinaten im Kopf. Gutachterwesen und Literaturkritik in der DDR in den 1960er Jahren. Fallbeispiel Lyrik*, Berlin, Lukas, 292 pp. Ruth J. Owen, *The Poet's Role: Lyric Responses to German Unification by Poets from the GDR* (APSL, 147), xi + 366 pp. Friedrich Sengle, *Moderne deutsche Lyrik, von Nietzsche bis Enzensberger (1875–1975)* (BNL,

179), ii + 414 pp. S. Sperl, '*Stabat mater*: reflections on a theme in German-Jewish and Palestinian-Arab poetry', *CC*, 22, 2000:105–29.

3. DRAMA

Heidi Wunderlich, **Dramatis Persona: (Exit.)* — *Die Auflösung der dramatischen Figur als produktive Überschreitung*, Berlin, Logos, 225 pp., includes chapters on Heiner Müller's *Die Hamletmaschine* and Gisela von Wysocki's *Schauspieler Tänzer Sängerin*.

4. PROSE

Bettina Baumgärtel, **Das perspektivierte Ich. Ich-Identität und interpersonelle und interkulturelle Wahrnehmung in ausgewählten Romanen der deutschsprachigen Gegenwartsliteratur* (Ep, 335), 404 pp. S. Busch, 'Auch eine Form der "Vergangenheitsbewältigung": Die Darstellung von Juden und Judenvernichtung in Nachkriegsromanen von NS-Autoren', *GMon*, 53, 2000:419–33.

   Travellers in Time and Space. Reisende durch Zeit und Raum. The German Historical Novel. Der deutschsprachige historische Roman, ed. Osman Durrani and Julian Preece (ABNG, 51), 473 pp., is a volume of 29 essays, collecting the proceedings of a conference held at the University of Kent at Canterbury in 1998. Papers focusing on novels from the postwar period include D. Steuer's on Thomas Bernhard's *Auslöschung* (61–78), J. J. Long's on Dieter Kühn's *Beethoven und der schwarze Geiger* (111–28), M. Tait's on Stefan Heym's *Schwarzenberg* (331–42), and A. Herhoffer's comparative analysis of Christa Wolf's *Kassandra* and Peter Weiss's *Ästhetik des Widerstands* (343–56). Several essays explore in broader terms the development of the historical novel in the GDR. Amongst the most stimulating contributions are those offered by K. Habitzel and H. Uerlings. Habitzel's 'Der historische Roman der DDR und die Zensur' (401–22) provides a fascinating overview of East German censorship procedures before illustrating the intricacies and sometimes absurdities of the 'Druckgenehmigungsverfahren' at work in relation to three novels by Stefan Heym and one by Joachim Walther with reference to the files of the Ministry of Culture. Uerlings theme is 'Die Erneuerung des historischen Romans durch interkulturelles Erzählen' (129–54), and his wide-ranging essay provides a probing comparative analysis of Uwe Timm's *Morenga* and Hans Christoph Buch's *Die Hochzeit von Port-au-Prince* in which he demonstrates how multiple perspectives and intertextuality can function in a literary exploration of a non-European culture as a response to 'die Krise der Repräsentation' and at the same time unsettle European subject positions. Döblin's *Amazonas* trilogy is then read as a 'Vorbild' for the same kind of 'interkulturelles Erzählen' which allows for a problematization of 'die Kategorien europäischer Geschichtsschreibung'. Uerling also compares Franz Werfel's depiction of the Turkish massacre of the Armenians in *Die vierzig Tage des Musa Dagh* with Edgar Hilsenrath's treatment of the same theme in *Das Märchen vom letzten Gedanken*, before finally examining the way in which Ingeborg Bachmann's *Franza* novel 'die Verschränkung von kultureller und sexueller Differenz thematisiert'.

Dirk Frank, **Narrative Gedankenspiele. Der metafiktionale Roman zwischen Modernismus und Postmodernismus*, Wiesbaden, Deutscher Universitäts-Verlag, 255 pp. Erk Grimm, **Semiopolis. Prosa der Moderne und Nachmoderne im Zeichen der Stadt*, Bielefeld, Aisthesis, 354 pp. Christian Schärf, **Der Roman im 20. Jahrhundert* (SM, 331), 220 pp.

Elizabeth Snyder Hook, *Family Secrets and the Contemporary German Novel. Literary Explorations in the Aftermath of the Third Reich*, Rochester, NY, Camden House, x + 177 pp., offers readings of Christa Wolf's *Kindheitsmuster*, Thomas Bernhard's *Auslöschung*, Peter Schneider's *Vati*, Elfriede Jelinek's *Die Ausgesperrten* and Elisabeth Reichart's *Februarschatten* as a selection of novels representative of the work of 'two consecutive generations of writers who have explored the Nazi past within the context of the postwar family'. The works are taken to illustrate the ways in which questions of guilt and atonement for the past are confronted at the personal level of the relationship between parents and their children and to reveal the extent to which the Third Reich continues to act as a 'destabilizing force' within the family. In a detailed introduction, Snyder Hook identifies the many common features her chosen novels display: their focus on the complexities of memory and the difficulties of representing subjective experience; their depiction of the family as a unit which had acted as an instrument of Nazi ideology; their narrators' problematic search for a sense of identity and 'Heimat'. Despite this, the readings of the individual texts that follow, while they are thorough and often challenging, tend to remain unrelated to one another and the brief conclusion to the volume does little to draw attention to the significance of the very different ways in which these texts explore the consequences of the intersections between political and private pasts for identity, both personal and national, in the present.

5. INDIVIDUAL AUTHORS

AICHINGER, ILSE.   Annette Ratmann, **'Spiegelungen, ein Tanz': Untersuchungen zur Prosa und Lyrik I.As* (Ep, 342), 178 pp. K. Vloeberghs, 'Widerstände der Kreatur. Dialektik der Aufklärung in I. As Roman *Die größere Hoffnung*', *GM*, 53 : 7–20.

AMÉRY, JEAN.   'Literatur ohne Heimat. Hohenems, Voralberg und Österreich als literarische Topographien im Werk Jean Amérys', *WB*, 47:53–69.

ANDERSCH, ALFRED.   M. Uecker, ' "Das Verhältnis dieser Leute zu uns hat ja auch wirklich etwas Obzönes angenommen." Juden und Deutsche in A. As Roman *Efraim*', *GMon*, 53, 2000:491–505. R. W. Williams, ' "Geschichte berichtet, wie es gewesen. Erzählung spielt eine Möglichkeit durch." A. A. and the Jewish experience', *ib.*, 477–89.

APITZ, BRUNO.   T. Jung, 'Poetische Wahrheiten vor religiöser Folie in B. As Novelle *Esther*', *GMon*, 53, 2000:279–93.

ARTMANN, HANS CARL.   Michael Horowitz, **H. C. A. Eine Annäherung an den Schriftsteller und Sprachspieler*, Wien, Ueberreuter, 208 pp. Wieland Schmied, **H. C. A. 1921–2000. Erinnerungen und Essays*, Aachen, Rimbaud, 76 pp.

AUGUSTIN, ELISABETH.   H. Stern, 'Sprache zwischen Exil und Identität. Die Konstitution von Heimat durch Sprache bei E. A.', *GMon*, 53, 2000:77–93.

AUSLÄNDER, ROSE.   Kathrin M. Bower, *Ethics and Remembrance in the Poetry of Nelly Sachs and R. A.*, Rochester, NY, Camden House, 2000, 280 pp.

BACHMANN, INGEBORG.   **Einsam sind alle Brücken. Autoren schreiben über I. B.*, ed. Reinhard Baumgart and Thomas Tebbe, Munich, Piper, 160 pp. Peter Beicken, *Ingeborg Bachmann*, Stuttgart, Reclam, 168 pp., is a contribution to the series 'Literaturwissen für Schule und Studium', and as such provides the usual helpful bibliographical and biographical overview. The most impressive part of this slim volume, though, is its section on B.'s poetry which within limited space manages to offer relatively detailed readings of a surprising number of poems, both early and late as well as from the two collections, combining an indication of the state of critical thinking on B.'s poetry with the author's own illuminating analysis. The chapters on the essays, radio plays, and stories provide adequate overviews but at seven pages the section on the 'Todesarten' cycle is disappointingly brief. D. Burdorf, 'I. Bs *Enigma*. Textgenese und Intermedialität', *GRM*, 51:323–48. M. Eggers, 'Simultan übersetzen. Geschlechter-, Sprachdifferenzen und die Erzählstimme in Texten von B. und Musil', *WB*, 47:576–93. L. Friedberg, ' "A time yet to come . . .": translation and historical representation in I. B.'s poem "Night Flight / Nachtflug" ', *GQ*, 74:148–63. Doris Hildesheim, **I. B.: Todesbilder, Todessehnsucht und Sprachverlust in 'Malina' und 'Antigone'*, Berlin, Weissensee, 2000, 191 pp. Joachim Hoell, **Ingeborg Bachmann,*

DTV, 160 pp. A. Larcati, 'Unterwegs nach Böhmen. Zur topographischen Poetologie bei I. B.', *Sprachkunst*, 32:51–69. Katja Schmidt-Wistoff, **Dichtung und Musik bei I. B. und Hans Werner Henze. Der 'Augenblick der Wahrheit' am Beispiel ihres Opernschaffens*, Munich, Iudicium, 314 pp.

BAYER, KONRAD.   C. K. Stepina, 'K. B. und die Wiener Gruppe. Marginalien zu einer literarischen Provokation', *GN*, 31, 2000:139–47.

BECHER, JOHANNES R.   B. Robinson, 'Morphine as the *tertium quid* between war and revolution; or, the moon gland secrets poppy sleep over the western front of J. R. B.', *GQ*, 73, 2000:387–400.

BEHRENS, KATJA.   C. von Maltzan, ' "Die Angst davor, daß es rauskommt." Über das Schweigen von Opfern und Tätern bei K. B. und Bernhard Schlink', *GMon*, 53, 2000:463–76.

BECKER, JUREK.   J. S. Chase, 'Jurek the liar: humour and memory in B.'s *Jakob der Lügner*', *GMon*, 53, 2000:327–36. D. Rock, 'Questions of language, identity and Jewishness in J. B.'s works', *ib.*, 337–51. F. Schenke, 'Kommunisten, Schnorrer und Heimatlose. Jüdische Figuren in literarischen Texten von Peter Edel, Stephan Hermlin and J. B.', *ib.*, 315–25.

BERNHARD, THOMAS.   **Österreich und andere Katastrophen — T. B. in memoriam*, ed. Jeanne Benay and Pierre Béhar, St. Ingbert, Röhrig, 393 pp. P. Bozzi, 'Massengeschrei und Leerstelle: Zur Figur des Josef Schuster in T. Bs *Heldenplatz*', *GMon*, 53, 2000:251–64. G. Hens, 'Poetologie einer Dreieckbeziehung. Zu T. Bs Erzählung *Ja*', *ColGer*, 33, 2000:255–73. Matthias Konzett, *The Rhetoric of National Dissent in T. B., Peter Handke, and Elfriede Jelinek*, Rochester, NY, Camden House, 2000, 164 pp. Nikolaus Langendorf, **Schimpfkunst. Die Bestimmung des Schreibens in T. Bs Prosawerk* (EH, 1, 1815), 206 pp. Jonathan Long, *The Novels of T. B.*, Rochester, NY, Camden House, 180 pp., is a fascinating study which, taking issue with the notion of B. as a 'Geschichtenzerstörer', attempts to close a gap in existing scholarship by offering a detailed analysis of the narrative strategies in this author's work, with a view to exploring 'the *functioning* of form within the economy of each individual text'. The study focuses on those works which Long describes as B.'s 'most interesting and significant', amongst them *Frost, Verstörung, Das Kalkwerk, Korrektur, Wittgensteins Neffe, Alte Meister*, and *Auslöschung*, and considers above all the relationship between thematic and formal concerns within them, as well as the way in which they 'problematize questions of narrative representation and narrative transmission'. The analysis is able to demonstrate that while B.'s thematic range remains fairly limited, the formal devices he employs are much more varied, and thus this excellent study can highlight not only the changing nature of B.'s prose but also convincingly reveals him to be 'a skilled and highly self-aware storyteller'. J. J. Long, 'Resisting B.: women and violence in *Das Kalkwerk, Ja* and *Auslöschung*', *Seminar*, 37:33–52. S. Thabet, 'Choreographie des Alleinseins. Zur Poetik des Raumes in T. Bs erzählender Prosa', *WW*, 51:259–74. Id., ' "Meine Grundstücke sind meine Themen." Zur Darstellung des Raumes in T. Bs "Attaché an der französischen Botschaft" ', *Sprachkunst*, 31, 2000:17–36.

BEYER, MARCEL. E. Ostermann, 'Metaphysik des Faschismus. Zu M. Bs Roman *Flughunde*', *LitL*, 24:1–13.

BILLER, MAXIM. J. Chase, 'Shoah business: M. B. and the problem of contemporary German-Jewish literature', *GQ*, 74:111–31.

BIONDI, FRANCO. M. Kotsaftis, 'Fighting writing: the unruly literary *Stiefkind* F. B.', *GQ*, 74:67–79.

BOBROWSKI, JOHANNES. S. Egger, 'Die Mythologisierung von ostjüdischen Leben und Geschichte in der Lyrik J. Bs 1952–1962', *GMon*, 53, 2000:353–66. J. Joachimsthaler, ' "Kein Bild fügt sich dem anderen . . ." Zerbrechende Bildlichkeit in Bs früher Lyrik', *WB*, 47:221–40. J. P. Wieczorek, ' "Ein Wunder aller Wunder": J. B.'s Sarmatian poems to Jews', *GMon*, 53, 2000:367–78. John P. Wieczorek, *Between Sarmatia and Socialism. The Life and Works of J. B.* (APSL, 139), 2000, xii + 269 pp. See also CELAN, PAUL.

BÖLL, HEINRICH. W. Fehr, 'Zeitgeschichte und Literatur. Möglichkeiten mentalitätsgeschichtlicher Unterrichtskonzeption am Beispiel von H. Bs "Haus ohne Hüter" ', *DUS*, 53.5:12–24. R. Grimm, 'Zwei interTEXTetüden. Zu E. T. A. Hoffmanns *Der Artushof* und H. Bs *Wanderer kommst du nach Spa . . .*', *WW*, 51:352–61. S. Hermanns, ' "Die untrügliche Statistik hilft uns weiter . . ." Die Erinnerung an den Luftkrieg in H. Bs *Gruppenbild mit Dame*', *WW*, 51:248–58.

BORCHERT, WOLFGANG. Alexander Koller, *W. Bs 'Draußen vor der Tür'. Zu den überzeitlichen Dimensionen eines Dramas*, Marburg, Tectum, 2000, 115 pp.

BRINKMANN, ROLF DIETER. J. Röhnert, ' "Canneloni in Olevano": auch Brinkmann in Arkadien? Das Italien R. D. Bs in seinen Gedichten', *LitL*, 24:69–82.

CELAN, PAUL. M. Eskin, 'Answerable criticism. Reading C. reading Mandel'shtam', *Arcadia*, 35, 2000:66–80. S. Kiefer, 'Zwischen Mythos und "Mache". Notizen zum Handwerk P. Cs', *NRu*, 112.4:165–83. M. Pajević, 'Die Konzentration. Zur Bewegung des dichterischen Sprechens in der Poetik P. Cs', *WB*, 47:213–20. M. Pajević, 'The *stance* in the poetics of P. C.', *GLL*, 56:345–51. E. Petuchowski, 'Contrasts and realms of associations in P. C.'s "Assisi": some new considerations', *FMLS*, 37:70–90. Astrid Poppenhusen, *Durchkreuzung der Tropen. P. Cs 'Die Niemandsrose' im Lichte der traditionellen Metaphorologie und ihrer Dekonstruktion* (BNL, 184), 308 pp.

T. S. Presner, 'Traveling between Delos and Berlin: Heidegger and C. on the topography of "what remains" ', *GQ*, 74:417–29. F. Schössler and T. Tunkel, 'Utopie und Katastrophe — Paradoxale Strukturen in der Dichtung P. Cs', *LitL*, 24:122–35. J. Seng, 'Damit der Schrei der Opfer nicht verstummt. P. C. und der Dokumentarfilm *Nacht und Nebel'*, *NRu*, 112.2:166–72. Tobias Tunkel, *'Das verlorene Selbe.' P. Cs Poetik des Anderen und Goethes lyrische Subjektivität*, Freiburg im Breisgau, Rombach, 377 pp. J. P. Wieczorek, 'P. C. and Johannes Bobrowski: legitimacy and language', *GMon*, 47, 2000:191–212. B. Wiedemann, ' ". . . und sie auf meine Art entziffern." Zur Entstehung der Edition "Schwarzmaut" von Gisèle Celan-Lestrange and P. C.', *JFDH*, 263–97. See also SACHS, NELLY.

DELIUS, FRIEDRICH CHRISTIAN. K. von Oppen, ' "Wer jetzt schwarzweiss malt, hat keine Ahnung": F. C. D.'s *Die Birnen von Ribbeck* and the predicament of "Wendeliteratur" ', *GLL*, 56:352–65.

DÜRRENMATT, FRIEDRICH. P. A. Bloch, 'Ds Dramaturgie der Verkehrung', *ColH*, 29, 1999:105–44. Roland Harweg, *Situation und Text im Drama. Eine textlinguistisch-fiktionsanalytische Studie am Beispiel von F. Ds tragischer Komödie 'Der Besuch der alten Dame'* (BNL, 182), xvi + 374 pp. J. L. Plews, 'F. D.'s *Der Richter und sein Henker*: gluttony, victory, and justice', *MDLK*, 93:87–97. R. Wilczek, 'Gemälde als poetische Chiffren. Ein vernachlässigtes Detail in Ds frühen Kriminalromanen', *WW*, 51:70–78.

EDEL, PETER. See BECKER, JUREK.

ENZENSBERGER, HANS MAGNUS. Manon Delisle, *Weltuntergang ohne Ende: Ikonographie und Inszenierung der Katastrophe bei Christa Wolf, Peter Weiss und H. M. E.* (Ep, 346), 288 pp. A. Goodbody, 'Living with icebergs: H. M. E.'s *Sinking of the Titanic* as a post-apocalyptic text', *AUMLA*, 96:88–113. C. Nichols, 'Looking back at the end of the world: H. M. E. on 1989 and the millennium', *MDLK*, 92, 2000:412–44.

FASCHINGER, LILIAN. H. F. Pfanner, *'Magdalena Sünderin*: a contemporary picaresque novel by L. F.', *ColGer*, 33, 2000:163–75.

FASSBINDER, RAINER WERNER. G. Rühle, 'Die Gegenwart der Vergangenheit. Rückblick auf den Fassbinder-Konflikt', *GMon*, 53, 2000:507–25. G. Rühle, 'Trouble und der Versuch, Fs Stück *Der Müll, die Stadt und der Tod* aufzuführen', *ib.*, 527–36. M. Uecker, 'A fatal German marriage: the national subtext of F.'s *Die Ehe der Maria Braun*', *GLL*, 56:45–59. D. J. Vietor-Engländer, ' "Der Jud versteht sich auf sein Gewerbe." Why R. W. F.'s *Der Müll, die Stadt und der Tod* should not be performed in Germany. Misinterpretations, misunderstandings and controversies about this play', *GMon*, 53, 2000:536–48. F. Wefelmeyer, 'Die Ästhetik sich schließender Systeme. Judendarstellung bei R. W. F.', *GMon*, 53, 2000:549–65.

FICHTE, HUBERT. H. Kuroda, 'H. F. und griechische Klassik oder: "Unten werden die Schwarzen Ödipusse vorgeführt"', *DB*, 105, 2000:92–104.

FRIED, ERICH. P. O'Dochartaigh, 'E. F.'s *Höre, Israel!* — more than just shoes in the sand!', *GMon*, 53, 2000:191–205.

FRIES, FRITZ RUDOLF. See GRASS, GÜNTER.

FRISCH, MAX. C. H. Emden, '"Pro Memoria": M. Fs Poetik des Todes', *OGS*, 30:133–56. P. Hamm, 'Leben in der Frageform. M. F. — 10 Jahre nach seinem Tod', *Akzente*, 48:354–65. A. Nolte, '"Was kommt, das ist ja alles schon geschehen." Die Verwandlung von Motiven aus der Christus Passion in M. Fs *Andorra*', *NGR*, 15–16, 1999–2001:36–52.

FRISCHMUTH, BARBARA. **Barbara Frischmuth*, ed. Daniela Bartens and Ingrid Spöck, Vienna, Residenz, 304 pp.

GRASS, GÜNTER. D. Arendt, 'G. G. — ein Erzähler am "Faden des Zeitgeschehens" oder "Ich, das bin ich jederzeit"', *GRM*, 51:467–86. B. Balzer, 'Geschichte als Wendemechanismus: *Ein weites Feld* von G. G.', *MDLK*, 93:209–20. Michael Haase, **Eine Frage der Aufklärung. Literatur und Staatssicherheit in Romanen von Fritz Rudolf Fries, G. G. und Wolfgang Hilbig* (EALS, 13), 303 pp. K. F. Hilliard, 'Showing, telling, and believing: G. G.'s *Katz und Maus* and narratology', *MLR*, 96:420–36. C. Hummel, '"Gegen rhetorische Ohnmacht." Die Rezeption politischer Lyrik von G. G. aus den 60er Jahren', *WW*, 50, 2000:48–66. J. Preece, 'G. G., his Jews and their critics: from Klüger and Gilman to Sebald and Prawer', *GMon*, 53, 2000:609–24. K. H.-J. Bachorski, 'Wie die politische Furore einmal den literarischen Verstand vollends unterpflügte: die Primärrezeption von G. Gs Roman *Ein weites Feld*', *MDG*, 47, 2000:438–51. C. Petrescu, 'The narrative of apocalypse: Matthias Horx' *Es geht voran. Ein Ernstfall–Roman* und G. Gs *Die Rättin*', *NGR*, 15–16, 1999–2001:53–82.

GRÜNBEIN, DURS. A. Eshel, 'Diverging memories? D. G.'s mnemonic topographies and the future of the German past', *GQ*, 74:407–16. R. J. Owen, 'Science in contemporary poetry: a point of comparison between Raoul Schrott and D. G.', *GLL*, 56:82–96.

HANDKE, PETER. Alexander Au, **Programmatische Gegenwelt. Eine Untersuchung zur Poetik P. Hs am Beispiel seines dramatischen Gedichts 'Über die Dörfer'* (Heidelberger Beiträge zur deutschen Literatur, 10), Frankfurt, Lang, 228 pp. Petra Heyer, **Von Verklärern und Spielverderbern. Eine vergleichende Untersuchung neuerer Theaterstücke P. Hs und Elfriede Jelineks* (BSDL, 59), 388 pp. W. Kilmbacher, 'Ein "Plädoyer mit vielen erzählerischen Momenten" — Hs *winterliche Reise*', *ÖGL*, 45:65–78. See also BERNHARD, THOMAS and STRAUSS, BOTHO.

HÄRTLING, PETER. A. Waine, 'Little man, big man: masculinity and popular culture in P. H.'s *Hubert oder die Rückkehr nach Casablanca*', *FMLS*, 37 : 286–97.

HEIN, CHRISTOPH. F. Dieckmann, 'Indirekte Ortsaufklärung. C. Hs Roman *Willenbrock*', *Merkur*, 55 : 70–74. *C. H. in Perspective*, ed. Graham Jackman (*GMon*, 51), Amsterdam–Atlanta, Rodopi, 2000, 306 pp. M. Ossar, 'C. H.'s *Das Napoleon-Spiel* and the ludic principle', *GQ*, 2000 : 253–68. See also WOLF, CHRISTA.

HERMLIN, STEPHAN. See BECKER, JUREK.

HEYM, STEFAN. M. Tait, 'Belief in socialism: Jews, Jewishness and S. H.', *GMon*, 53, 2000 : 379–89. Meg Tait, **Taking Sides. S. H.'s Historical Fiction* (British and Irish Studies in German Language and Literature, 22), Oxford, Lang, 208 pp.

HILBIG, WOLFGANG. P. Cooke, 'The *Krimi* and the criminal state: W. H.'s *Eine Übertragung*', *MLR*, 96 : 1029–41. Paul Cooke, *Speaking the Taboo. A Study of the Work of W. H.* (APSL, 141), 2000, x + 247 pp., examines a selection of H.'s writings including *Die Weber, Eine Übertragung* and '*Ich*', in particular as an act of resistance to taboos which existed within the official 'Kulturpolitik' of the GDR. The study explores H.'s 'preoccupation with the nature of literature', including his engagement with the literary tradition of modernism, with Western 'Trivialliteratur' and with postmodern theory. At the same time it does justice to his understanding of his work as 'a vehicle for his social critique of the GDR and post-unification Germany', and his constant engagement with a social reality, above all with a view to uncovering those dimensions of it which are hostile to the establishment of a coherent sense of personal identity. A. Corkhill, 'Scarred landscapes: W. H.'s ecocritique', *AUMLA*, 96 : 173–88. R. J. Halverson, 'W. H.'s "*Ich*": narrating loss of voice, identity and self', *Seminar*, 37 : 244–54. G. Jackman, 'The quest for a new language: W. H.'s *Die Kunde von den Bäumen*', *GMon*, 47, 2000 : 247–71. See also GRASS, GÜNTER.

HILDESHEIMER, WOLFGANG. W. Lindemann, 'Negative Poetologie. Paradoxien des Schreibens in W. Hs *Vergebliche Aufzeichnugen*', *WW*, 2000 : 397–415.

HONIGMANN, BARBARA. A. R. Chédin, 'Nationalität und Identität. Identität und Sprache bei Lea Fleischmann, Jane E. Gilbert and B. H.', *GMon*, 53, 2000 : 139–51. P. Günther, 'Einfaches Erzählen? B. Hs "Doppeltes Grab"', *GMon*, 53, 2000 : 123–37. J. M. Peck, 'Telling tales of exile, (re)writing Jewish histories: B. H. and her novel *Soharas Reise*', *GSR*, 24 : 557–69.

JELINEK, ELFRIEDE. M. Bönnighausen, 'Sprachkörper und Körpersprache. E. Js *Nora* im Unterricht', *MDG*, 48 : 452–68. S. Henke, 'Pornographie als Gefängnis. E. Js *Lust* im Vergleich', *ColH*, 31,

2000:239–63. H. Kurzenberger, 'Die heutige Schaubühne als moralische Anstalt betrachtet. Über das Erbe der Aufklärung im postdramatischen Theater der E. J.', *FMT*, 15, 2000:21–30. A. Stricker, '"Er nicht als er" — Sie nicht als sie. Die "Selbst-Aufgabe" der E. J.', *Sprachkunst*, 32:71–92. E. L. Szalay, 'Of gender and the gaze: constructing the disease(d) in E. J.'s *Krankheit oder Moderne Frauen*', *GQ*, 74:237–58. See also HANDKE, PETER and BERNHARD, THOMAS.

JOHNSON, UWE. *Johnson-Jahrbuch*, vol. 8, ed. Ulrich Fries, Holgar Helbig, and Irmgard Müller, Göttingen, Vandenhoeck & Ruprecht, 238 pp. Michael Hofmann, *Uwe Johnson*, Stuttgart, Reclam, 247 pp., succeeds in its attempt to offer a 'grundlegende Einführung' to J.'s work. A detailed reading of *Jahrestage* forms the centrepiece of the study but individual chapters are also devoted to *Ingrid Babendererde. Reifeprüfung 1953*, *Mutmassungen über Jakob*, and *Das dritte Buch über Achim*. Further chapters touch on *Zwei Ansichten* and J.'s essays from the 1960s, 1970s and 1980s, including the 'Frankfurter Poetik-Vorlesungen', as well as Margarethe von Trotta's film version of *Jahrestage*. The analysis of the earlier novels certainly does justice to the author's aim to read them with regard to 'ihrem literarischen und historischen Eigenwert' but at the same time establishes the extent to which J.'s thematic and formal interests have remained constant in the course of his literary career. In particular, Hofmann is concerned to explore J.'s characteristic appropriation and combination of the 'Formenarsenal' of both 'Realismus' and 'literarische Moderne' in a way which serves to problematize the relationship between text and extra-literary reality, and to demonstrate how J. in so many of his works is concerned to articulate the individual's desire for identity, security, and 'Heimat' and at the same time to make clear why it is that in a post-Holocaust world such desires can never be realized. Hofmann draws on the aesthetic and literary theory of Schiller, Adorno, Benjamin, and Brecht to add a further, often illuminating, dimension to his thoughtful analysis of J.'s work. M. Kolb, 'Gesine Cresspahls Mecklenburg-Manhattan-Transfer und seine Konsequenzen: zwei un-heimliche Zeit-Räume in U. Js psychologischem Romanwerk *Jahrestage*', *MDLK*, 92, 2000:35–52. N. Mecklenburg, 'Ungeziefer und selektives Volk. Zwei Aspekte von New York in U. Js *Jahrestagen*', *GR*, 76:254–66.

KASER, NORBERT C. B. Sauer, '"ich verfasse briefe die sich blicken lassen koennen." Zum Briefwerk von n. c. k.', Bauer, *Edition*, 265–78.

KIPPHARDT, HEINAR. D. Barnett, 'Documentation and its discontents. The case of H. K.', *FMLS*, 37:272–85. D. Barnett, 'The Holocaust and documentary metadrama. H. K.'s *Bruder Eichmann*', *GMon*, 53, 2000:587–98.

KIRSTEN, WULF. P. Hamm, 'Gegenstandssüchtig. Über W. K.', *SuF*, 53:252–65.

KLEMPERER, VICTOR. R. H. Watt, ' "Du liegst schief, Genosse Klemperer." V. K. and Stalin on the language of a divided Germany in the 1940s and 1950s', *FMLS*, 37:252–71.

KLING, THOMAS. A. Anglet, 'Sekundäre Oralität und simulierte Medialität in T. Ks Gedichten', *WW*, 51:79–92.

KLUGE, ALEXANDER. C. Schulte, 'Die Lust aufs Unwahrschein-liche. A. Ks *Chronik der Gefühle*', *Merkur*, 55:344–50.

KLÜGER, RUTH. C. Finnan, 'Autobiography, memory and the Shoah: German-Jewish identity in autobiographical writings by R. K., Cordelia Edvardson and Laura Waco', *GMon*, 53, 2000:447–61.

KOEPPEN, WOLFGANG. Jörg Döring, *' . . .ich stellte mich unter, ich machte mich klein . . .' Wolfgang Koeppen 1933–1948*, Frankfurt, Stroem-feld, 358 pp. D. Basker, ' "Whose life is it anyway?" 'Jewish characters in W. K.'s post-war fiction', *GMon*, 53, 2000:637–49. S. Ward, 'German and Jewish identities in W. K.'s *Jakob Littners Aufzeichnungen aus einem Erdloch*', *ib.*, 651–63. Simon Ward, *Negotiating Positions. Literature, Identity and Social Critique in the Works of W. K.* (APSL, 146), vii + 150 pp.

KOLB, ULRIKE. B. Damerau, 'Muttersöhne. Die Konstruktion einer Art von Männern bei U. K.', *LitL*, 24:179–91.

KÖHLER, BARBARA. *Entgegenkommen. Dialogues with B. K.*, ed. Georgina Paul and Helmut Schmitz (*GMon*, 48) Amsterdam–Atlanta, Rodopi, 2000, 232 pp., grew out of a symposium held at the University of Warwick in 1997 and looks back over the poet's work since 1990 with a view to exploring its 'innate artistry' and its 'poetological concerns' rather than reading it only in the light of its GDR origins. Two essays (B. Dahlke, 45–62, and K. Leeder, 63–90) look further back to the poetry of the 1980s and its relationship to the GDR context in which it originated as well as to the work of various literary forebears such as Brecht, Hölderlin, Bachmann, and Celan. Amongst essays which offer overviews of larger sections of K.'s work (H. Schmitz on the poems from *Deutsches Roulette* to *Blue Box*, 127–46, and M. Littler and H. Owen on the Portuguese poems in *cor responde*, 147–74) are some which offer close readings of individual poems, like R. Thiel's analysis of 'Endstelle' from the collection *Deutsches Roulette* (91–126). Others focus on K.'s prose essays (K. Mey, 175–94) and on her text installations in the public sphere (A. Visser, 195–214). Issues that concern many of the contributors include the poet's exploration of subjectivity and identity, her poetic interaction with literary predecessors and gender issues. The volume ends with an article examining translation issues in the form of responses to the poem

'Rondeau Allemagne' from *Deutsches Roulette* and also records a discussion with the author about her work and poetics. As the first volume of critical essays on B. K. it represents a wide-ranging and welcome response to the work of the poet.

KÜHN, DIETER. **D. K. Ein Treffen mit dem Schriftsteller und seinem Werk*, ed. Ofelia Martí-Peña and Brigitte Eggelte, Berne, Lang, 219 pp.

KUNERT, GÜNTER. See WOLF, CHRISTA.

LANGE, HARTMUT. W. Hoffmann, 'Müller-Lengfeldts letzte Reise. Zur Interpretation von H. Ls Novelle *Die Bildungsreise*', *WW*, 51:420–34.

LEONHARD, RUDOLF. J. Ross, '"Leiden verpflichtet." Recast Jewish figures in R. L.'s post-war antifascist *Erzählungen*', *GMon*, 53, 2000:391–402.

LIND, JAKOV. *Writing after Hitler. The Work of J. L.*, ed. Andrea Hammel, Silke Hassler, and Edward Timms, Cardiff, Univ. of Wales Press, xiv + 222 pp. This collection of essays constitutes a successful attempt to go some way at least to doing justice to the literary variety of an author whose life and work range over not only several cultures but also several languages. S. Rosenfeld's opening contribution (5–28) provides a helpful introductory overview of the author's life and offers some illuminating readings of his fictional works, particularly several of the stories from the collection *Eine Seele aus Holz*, and is complemented by two further essays focusing on and historically contextualizing L.'s experiences in the Netherlands and Israel (J. Houwink ten Cate, 29–40, and M. H. Gelber, 41–56). The reception of L.'s work in Austria and Germany and Britain and the USA forms the subject of contributions by U. Seeber (113–36) and S. Hassler (137–57) respectively. While E. Eppler's article (158–76) explores the variety of languages and stylistic registers expressed in L.'s writing, the majority of articles attempt to explore his work in the context of writing after the Holocaust. W. Strickhausen (57–72), for instance, using L.'s autobiographical writings to read his fictions, demonstrates that the Holocaust is not only 'the underlying reference point to which all events before and afterwards are related' but argues that L.'s use of the grotesque is the consequence of his realization that the 'social, political and cultural predisposition which made Auschwitz possible' continued largely unchanged after 1945. In a sensitive and illuminating comparison of L.'s *Counting My Steps* and Ruth Klüger's *weiter leben*, in relation to the issue of gendered narrative, A. Hammel (177–92) reads the former as 'an assertion of [L.'s] individuality' which leads him to create a 'self-styled heroic persona', while Klüger's text, which can be seen to draw on 'feminist methods of reclaiming the past and rewriting women's lives', is concerned to institute dialogue 'both with the figures of her past and with the present-day reader'. E. Meidl, 'Between languages: J. L.'s novel *Travels to the Enu*', *AUMLA*, 93, 2000: 51–66. K. Thorpe, 'The invisible soldier — J. L.', *GMon*, 53, 2000: 207–19.

LOHER, DEA. A. Geisenhanslüke, 'Körper — Familie — Gewalt. Bemerkungen zum zeitgenössischen Theater am Beispiel von D. L. und Marius von Mayenburg', *MDG*, 48: 394–405. A. Ludewig, 'D. Ls Theaterstück *Adam Geist*', *FMT*, 15, 2000: 113–24.

MARON, MONIKA. Lennart Koch, *Ästhetik der Moral bei Christa Wolf und M. M. Der Literaturstreit von der Wende bis zum Ende der neunziger Jahre* (Schriften zur Europa- und Deutschlandforschung, 8), Frankfurt, Lang, 518 pp. E. Gilson, ' "Nur wenige kurze Augenblicke, die sicher sind." Zur konstruktivistisch inspirierten Darstellung des Erinnerns und Vergessens in M. Ms Familiengeschichte *Pawels Briefe*', *ColGer*, 33, 2000: 275–88.

MAYENBURG, MARIUS VON. See LOHER, DEA.

MEINECKE, THOMAS. G. Mecky, 'Ein Ich in der Genderkrise: zum Tomboy in T. Ms *Tomboy*', *GR*, 76: 195–214.

MITTERER, FELIX. E. Bourke, 'The figure of a Tyrolean Jew in F. M.'s *Kein schöner Land* ', *GMon*, 53, 2000: 265–77.

MONÍKOVÁ, LIBUŠE. M. Schwidtal, 'Kunst im Zeichen der Diktatur. L. Ms Roman *Der Taumel* ', *NDL*, 2000: 107–16.

MORGNER, IRMTRAUD. S. von der Emde, 'Places of wonder: fantasy and utopia in I. M.'s *Salman Trilogy*', *NGC*, 82: 167–92.

MÜLLER, HEINER. Jan-Christoph Hauschild, *H. M. oder Das Prinzip Zweifel. Eine Biographie*, Berlin, Aufbau, 619 pp. M. Hofmann, 'Geschichte als Katastrophe. H. Ms theatralisches Nachdenken über Deutschland aus heutiger Sicht', *MDG*, 48: 406–28. M. Griffen, 'Image and ideology in the work of H. M.', *MDLK*, 93: 426–50. A. Ichikawa, '*Germania Tod in Berlin* — Erinnerung an einen Staat und einen Autor', *DB*, 106: 81–92. H.-C. Stillmark, 'Hacks und M. — ein folgenloser Streit', *MDG*, 47, 2000: 424–36. H. L. Roddy, 'A revolutionary critique of individualism: H. M.'s *Mauser* in Texas', *MDLK*, 92, 2000: 184–98. See also WOLF, CHRISTA.

MÜLLER, HERTA. Grazziella Predoiu, *Faszination und Provokation bei H. M. Eine thematische und motivische Auseinandersetzung* (EH, 1, 1783), 235 pp. Although the author's overview of the 'Forschungsstand' in relation to H. M.'s writing suggests that she is unaware of some of the work being done outside the German-speaking world, her study offers a comprehensive examination of this author's prose work. She provides an overview of the development of Romanian-German literature since 1945 in order to explain the forms in which it emerged in the 1980s and to allow for a comparison of M.'s work with that of her contemporaries. In a chapter entitled 'Literarische Vorbilder und geistige Affinitäten' the author places M.'s writing in a broader German context by exploring her fiction's relationship to that of Thomas Bernhard and Franz Innerhofer, particularly in relation to the concept of the 'negativer Heimatroman'. The main part of the study explores two thematic strands in M.'s work, the countryside and the town, but also examines those themes which characterize M.'s work as whole, such as the confrontation with dictatorship, 'Heimat' and childhood. The final chapter on the linguistic characteristics of the texts explores whether it is M.'s language that helps to account for her work's appeal to a German reading public.

NADOLNY, STEN. Dieter Hoffmann, *Postmoderne Erzählstrukturen und Interkulturalität in S. N's Roman 'Selim oder Die Gabe der Rede'* (EH, 1, 1786), 178 pp.

NEUMANN, ROBERT. A. M. Jäger, ' "Man kann sterben — oder man attackiert." — R. N. und sein Roman *Der Tatbestand oder Der gute Glaube der Deutschen*', *GMon*, 53, 2000: 221–36.

ÖZDAMAR, EMINE SEVGI. S. Johnson, 'Transnational *Ästhetik des türkischen Alltags*: E. S. Ö.'s *Das Leben ist eine Karawanserei*', *GQ*, 74: 37–57.

PLESSEN, ELISABETH. See WOLF, CHRISTA.

REICHART, ELISABETH. V. Holler, 'Warum in die Ferne schweifen? Zur Rezeption von Gerhard Roths und E. Rs "Japanromanen" ', *Sprachkunst*, 31: 37–51.

REIMANN, BRIGITTE. H. L. Jones, ' "Volkseigen ist nicht einfach ein Wort, volkseigen — das ist eine Sprengladung": language and identity in B. R.'s *Die Geschwister*', *GMon*, 47, 2000: 213–28.

REITZ, EDGAR. H. Christians, 'E. R. *Die zweite Heimat* (1993) oder Epos und Avantgarde', *WB*, 47: 374–86.

REZZORI, GREGOR VON. I. Foster, 'Cultural cross-dressing: stereotypes in G. v. R.'s *Memoiren eines Antisemiten*', *GMon*, 53, 2000: 599–608.

RIEGER, FRANZ. M. Luserke, 'Über F. Rs Roman *Internat in L.* (1986)', *LitL*, 24: 116–21.

ROTENBERG, STELLA. D. McLaughlin, ' "Auf dass Auschwitz nicht das letzte Wort sei." The exile poet S. R.', *GMon*, 53, 2000: 182–89.

ROTH, GERHARD. See REICHART, ELISABETH.

SACHS, NELLY. S. Neuenfeldt, 'Verwandlung als ein poetisches Thema und Gestaltungsprinzip in der Lyrik von N. S.', *Sprachkunst*, 32: 27–50. Anita Riede, *Das 'Leid-Steine-Trauerspiel'. Zum Wortfeld 'Stein' im lyrischen Kontext in N. Ss 'Fahrt ins Staublose' mit einem Exkurs zu Celans 'Engführung'*, Berlin, Weissensee, 337 pp. See also AUSLÄNDER, ROSE.

SCHLINK, BERNHARD. K. Brazaitis, 'On re-reading *The Reader*: an exercise in ambiguity', *AUMLA*, 95: 75–96. W. C. Donahue, 'Illusions of subtlety: B. S.'s *Der Vorleser* and the moral limits of holocaust fiction', *GLL*, 56:60–81. See also BEHRENS, KATJA.

SCHMIDT, ARNO. K. Bayer, '"Sinnwendewippchen." Anmerkungen zu A. Ss "Etymtheorie"', *WW*, 51:275–92. *'Des Dichters Aug' in feinem Wahnwitz rollend . . .' Dokumente und Studien zu 'Zettel's Traum'*, ed. Jörg Drews and Doris Plöschberger (TK), 298 pp.

SCHNEIDER, PETER. C. Riordan, 'German-Jewish relations in the works of P. S.', *GMon*, 53, 2000:625–35.

SCHNEIDER, ROBERT. A. Imai, 'Spiel der Auflehnung gegen Gott. Versuch über R. S.: *Schlafes Bruder* (1992)', *DB*, 107:102–14.

SCHROTT, RAOUL. See GRÜNBEIN, DURS.

SCHULZE, INGO. C. Cosentino, 'I. Ss *Simple Storys* und die Tradition der amerikanischen short story', *GN*, 31, 2000:134–38.

SCHÜTZ, STEFAN. See WOLF, CHRISTA.

SEBALD, W. G. K. Hall, 'Jewish memory in exile: the relation of W. G. S.'s *Die Ausgewanderten* to the tradition of the *Yitzkor* books', *GMon*, 53, 2000:153–64. S. Harris, 'The return of the dead: memory and photography in W. G. S.'s *Die Ausgewanderten*', *GQ*, 74:379–91. R. Jeutter, ' "Am Rand der Finsternis." The Jewish experience in the context of W. G. S.'s poetics', *GMon*, 53, 2000:165–79. T. Wirtz, 'Schwarze Zuckerwatte. Anmerkungen zu W. G. S.', *Merkur*, 55:530–34.

SEGHERS, ANNA. J. Vogt, 'What became of the girl: a minor archeology of an occasional text by A. S.', *NGC*, 82:145–65. C. Wolf, 'Im Widerspruch. Zum 100. Geburtstag von A. S.', *SuF*, 53:18–30. E. Jonas-Märtin and L. Mertens, 'A. S. — Suche nach der eigenen Identität?', *GMon*, 53, 2000:403–17.

STRAUSS, BOTHO. Dorothee Fuss, **'Das Bedürfnis nach Heil.' Zu den ästhetischen Projekten von Peter Handke und B. S.*, Bielefeld, Aisthesis, 252 pp.

STREERUWITZ, MARLENE. V. Holler, 'Frauenleben. Zur Figurengestaltung in der Prosa von M. S.', *LitL*, 24:100–15.

SÜSKIND, PATRICK. E. Moffatt, 'Grenouille: a modern schizophrenic in the enlightening world of *Das Parfum*', *FMLS*, 37:298–313. R. Wilczek, 'Zarathustras Wiederkehr. Die Nietzsche-Parodie in P. Ss *Das Parfum*', *WW*, 2000:248–55.

TABORI, GEORGE. N. O. Eke, 'Das Schreckliche und das Komische. G. T. und die Shoah', *GMon*, 53, 2000:567–86. Jan Strümpel, **Vorstellungen vom Holocaust. G. Ts Erinnerungs-Spiele*, Göttingen, Wallstein, 2000, 208 pp.

TESCHKE, HOLGER. A. Kuhlmann, 'Revolutionsträume vor dem Mauerfall: Der DDR-Dramatiker H. T.', *GQ*, 74:58–66.

TIMM, UWE. S. Wilke, ' "Hätte er bleiben wollen, er hätte anders denken und fühlen lernen müssen": Afrika geschildert aus Sicht der Weißen in U. Ts *Morenga*', *MDLK*, 93:335–54.

VANDERBEKE, BIRGIT. R. Tamaru, 'Verlust der Basis oder Abwesenheit der Basis. Eine Analyse von B. Vs *Das Muschelessen* und *Gut genug* unter dem Aspekt der *gender*-Problematik', *DB*, 105, 2000:105–16.

VESPER, BERNWARD. G.-J. Berendse, 'Schreiben als Körperverletzung: Zur Anthropologie des Terrors in B. Vs *Die Reise*', *MDLK*, 93:318–34.

WAGNER, BERND. C. Cosentino, 'Programmiertes Schweigen oder schwellender Redestrom? Zur Authentizität des Schreibens in B. Ws Roman *Club Oblomow*', *GN*, 32:120–26.

WALSER, MARTIN. Dieter Borchmeyer, **M. W. und die Öffentlichkeit*, Frankfurt, Surhkamp, 70 pp. Martin Reinhold Engler, *Identitäts- und Rollenproblematik in M. Ws Romanen und Novellen*, Munich, Iudicium, 309 pp., is concerned to demonstrate continuity in W.'s work at the level of a constitutive theme: 'die Problematik der krisenhaften Identität'. To this end the study focuses mainly on the literary strategies used to delineate the identity crises of the main characters of a representative spread of novels from the five decades of W.'s literary career (although with detailed reference to several other works, both literary and essayistic) — *Ehen in Philippsburg, Halbzeit, Seelenarbeit, Brandung*, and *Die Verteidigung der Kindheit* — using W.'s own poetological statements as well as a range of sociological and psychological perspectives to illuminate the works in the light of W.'s concept of a 'Negativkarriere'. In doing so, the study successfully shows that W.'s 'Subjektutopie der Negatividentität' undergoes a substantial development in the course of his writing, particularly in the late 1970s when awareness of their own failure and the resulting withdrawal into 'Innerlichkeit' becomes the foundation of what is described here as the 'ironic existence' of W.'s later protagonists. A. Eshel, 'Vom eigenen Gewissen. Die Walser-Bubis-Debatte und der Ort des Nationalsozialismus im Selbstbild der Bundesrepublik', *DVLG*, 74, 2000:333–60, offers a reading of *Ein springender Brunnen* in the context of the dispute over the politics of memory in contemporary German culture. P. Kegelmann, 'Der Schriftsteller als Redner: zur Gedankenführung in M. Ws Friedenpreisrede', *Rhetorik*, 19, 2000:109–15. J. Kopperschmidt, 'Noch einmal M. W. und seine Paulskirchenrede. Oder: Versuch auf eine "Anstatt-Erwiderung" zu erwidern', *Rhetorik*, 19, 2000:103–08. K. Prümm, 'Selbstmächtiges Erinnern? M. Ws Konzept der Erinnerung in dem Roman *Ein springender Brunnen* (1998) und in seiner Rede nach der Verleihung des Friedenpreises des Deutschen Buchhandels (1998)', *MDG*, 47,

2000:452–61. W. Schaller, 'Verblendung und Einsicht. Literarisch vermittelte Handlungs- und Selbstdeutungsmuster der Protagonisten in M. Ws Romanen *Brandung* und *Finks Krieg*', *GM*, 53:21–45. S. Taberner, 'The final taboo? M. W.'s critique of philo-semitism in *Ohne einander*', *Seminar*, 37:154–66.

WEIL, GRETE. S. Backmann, 'Configurations of myth, memory, and mourning in G. W.'s *Meine Schwester Antigone*', *GQ*, 73, 2000:269–86. M. Mattson, 'Classical kinship and personal responsibility: G. W.'s *Meine Schwester Antigone*', *Seminar*, 37:53–72.

WEISS, PETER. Heewon Lee, *Kunst, Wissen und Befreiung. Zu P. Ws Ästhetik des Widerstands* (BBLI, 35), 317 pp. A. Solbach, 'Narzißtisches Bekenntnis bei P. W.: Strategien der Verleugnung in der autobiographischen Prosa', *LitL*, 24:14–36. See also ENZENSBERGER, HANS MAGNUS.

WOHMANN, GABRIELE. B. Pivert, 'Bilder in der Art von Hopper. Zum 70. Geburtstag von G. W.', *DeutB*, 31:192–204.

WOLF, CHRISTA. T. O. Beebee and B. M. Weber, 'A literature of theory: C. W.'s *Kassandra* lectures as feminist anti-poetics', *GQ*, 74:259–79. F. Eigler, 'Rereading C. W.'s "Selbstversuch": cyborgs and feminist critiques of scientific discourse', *GQ*, 73, 2000:401–15. A. Herhoffer, ' "Vor den Worten kommt die Angst": C. Ws Suche nach einer neuen Sprache', *GMon*, 47, 2000:229–46. L. Köhn, 'C. W.: *Till Eulenspiegel*. DDR-Moderne um 1970', *Eulenspiegel-Jb.*, 41:139–57. I. Nickel-Bacon, 'Methodenkompetenz konkret: C. Ws *Kassandra* als Beispiel für zwei methodisch begründete Lesarten', *DUS*, 53.6:88–96. K. Schuhmann, ' "Die arge Spur, in der die Zeit von uns wegläuft." Begegnungen mit Kleist im letzten Jahrhundertdrittel — C. W., Günter Kunert, Heiner Müller, Christoph Hein, Stefan Schütz, Elisabeth Plessen', *WB*, 47:418–32. B. Wagener, ' "Eines Tages, dachte ich, werde ich sprechen können, ganz leicht und frei." Die Utopie der neuen Sprache in C. Ws *Was bleibt*', *LWU*, 33, 2000:265–71. See also MARON, MONIKA and ENZENSBERGER, HANS MAGNUS.

II. DUTCH STUDIES

LANGUAGE

POSTPONED

LITERATURE

By WIM HÜSKEN, *Senior Lecturer, University of Auckland*

I. GENERAL

Traditionally, Dutch art has received wide international attention while very few people abroad have seemed to be interested in Dutch literature. However, things are gradually changing. Translations of Dutch texts into other European languages, though still very few in number, seem to attract the attention these texts deserve. This is not only true for medieval romances, plays, and mystical treatises but also for modern Dutch literature. In Germany in particular there seems to be a genuine curiosity regarding this relatively unknown field of studies. France, Italy, and the United Kingdom are not far behind either, as the following pages will show.

The current sociological approach in Dutch and Flemish literary research also makes its contribution to the wider academic world interesting from an interdisciplinary point of view. For example, *Beschaving: een geschiedenis van de begrippen hoofsheid, heusheid, beschaving en cultuur*, ed. P. den Boer (Nederlandse Begripsgeschiedenis, 3), Amsterdam U.P., vii + 360 pp., includes essays on the concept of civilization by literary historians who pay special attention to the diachronic development of the various terms used in literary texts to express the idea behind the concept: from medieval and 17th-c. *hoofsheid* (courtliness) and *heusheid* (courtesy) to *beschaving* (civilization) and *cultuur* (culture) in the 19th and 20th cs. For reasons as yet not fully understood, Dutch language users never embraced *civilisatie* as an acceptable equivalent for French and English 'civilisation'. Revisiting an earlier essay on this topic, the former Professor of medieval Dutch literature at the University of Utrecht, W. P. Gerritsen, concentrates in 'Hoofsheid herbeschouwd' (81–105) on the medieval concept of courtliness. E. K. Grootes, former Professor of Dutch Renaissance literature at the University of Amsterdam, studies 17th-c. courtesy in 'Heusheid en beleefdheid in de zeventiende eeuw' (131–45), while R. A. M. Aerts and W. E. Krul, 'Van hoge beschaving naar brede cultuur' (213–53), describe the transitional period during which the introduction of the term *cultuur* took place, replacing the old-fashioned term *beschaving*. Globalization and democratic movements eventually resulted in a victory of the term *cultuur* after World War II, as is shown by R. A. M. Aerts in 'Cultuur zonder beschaving: over het gebruik van cultuur sinds de Tweede Wereldoorlog' (287–318).

On a similar topic, *Beschaafde burgers: burgerlijkheid in de vroegmoderne tijd*, ed. Harald Hendrix and Marijke Meijer Drees (Utrecht Renaissance Studies), Amsterdam U.P., 129 pp., is a collection of essays on bourgeois mentality in early modern Dutch literature. 19th-c. views have heavily influenced our perception of the degree to which 17th-c. authors would have regarded their environment as bourgeois, as is shown by R. Aerts in 'De burgerlijkheid van de Gouden Eeuw: geschiedenis van een constructie' (5–22). M. Meijer Drees's essay, 'Zeventiende-eeuwse literatuur in de Republiek: burgerlijk?' (63–79), is directly related to 17th-c. literature. The works of Jacob Cats in particular are seen as typically bourgeois but, as Meijer Drees demonstrates, neither he nor any of his contemporaries used the term as a key concept in their works. The word *burgerlijk* rather referred to the ancient concept of a *societas civilis*, an orderly society.

Perspectieven voor de internationale neerlandistiek in de 21ste eeuw, ed. Gerard Elshout et al. (Handelingen Veertiende Colloquium Neerlandicum), Woubrugge, IVN — Münster, Nodus, 457 pp., considers the study of Dutch language and literature abroad in the 21st c. In 2000, Dutch was taught by 584 lecturers at 215 universities worldwide. The section on literature has nine contributions: A. J. Gelderblom and A. M. Musschoot, 'Veranderingen in een bedding van continuïteit: de literatuurgeschiedenis in een nieuw jasje' (151–68), discuss the concepts behind the forthcoming and eagerly awaited multi-volume history of Dutch literature, the first volume of which is to appear in print in 2003; H. Louwerse, 'Zwartrijders in de Nederlandse literatuur: het motief van de queeste in de migrantenliteratuur' (169–78), reviews novels by four Moroccan immigrant authors; H. Visser, 'Wat kan jeugdliteratuur bijdragen aan de kennis van het hedendaagse sociaal-culturele leven in Nederland en Vlaanderen' (179–88), discusses children's literature and its significance for our knowledge of the social lives of Dutch and Flemish young people; M. Vogel, 'Orde en onrust: "triviale" misdaadliteratuur als studieobject van de neerlandistiek' (189–200), looks at crime fiction as a new area of research in Dutch literary studies; R. Wolfswinkel, ' "Hier worden geen pruiken geleverd aan kaal geknipten vrouwen". Kappersetalage 1945' (201–09), wonders why there is hardly any difference in the way authors wrote about female collaborators shortly after World War II and how they are depicted in novels today; J. Fenoulhet, 'Plagiaat en de historische roman: de gevallen Boudier-Bakker en Du Perron' (211–16), studies Menno ter Braak's accusation of plagiarism against Ina Boudier-Bakker's historical novel *Vrouw Jacob* (1935) and his failing to do the same with Eduard du Perron's *Schandaal in Holland* (1939); W. Dharmowijono, 'Stille plunderaars: Chinezen in de verhalen van Beb Vuyk' (217–24), assesses the role of Chinese characters in short stories by Beb Vuyk; J. Skovbjerg, 'Over interpretatie van Lucebert. Tussen woord en beeld: "Visser van ma yuan" als ekfrasis' (225–32), attempts a pictorial interpretation of one of Lucebert's most famous poems; Finally, S. Vanderlinden and V. Staïesse, 'De zwaan en de boogschutter of de niet te kortwieken verbeelding' (233–44), concentrate on Hella Haasse's semi-autobiography, *Zwanen schieten* (1997).

*Kerven in een rots: opstellen over Nederlandse taalkunde, letterkunde en cultuur, aangeboden aan Jan W. de Vries bij zijn afscheid als hoogleraar Dutch Studies aan de Universiteit Leiden, ed. Berry Dongelmans, Josien Lalleman, and Olf Praamstra (Stichting Neerlandistiek Leiden, 7), Leiden, Stichting Neerlandistiek te Leiden, viii + 285 pp., is a Festschrift in honour of the former Professor of Dutch Studies at the University of Leiden. The volume includes six contributions on 17th-c. and 20th-c. literature. Michael Dingenouts et al., **Dall'autunno del Medioevo alle montagne dei Paesi Bassi: la letteratura nederlandese in traduzione italiana*, Milan, Iperborea, 119 pp., is a survey of Dutch literature in Italian translation and was published on the occasion of an exhibition on the topic, held in March 2001 at the Università Cattolica del Sacro Cuore in Milan.

*The Bookshop of the World: The Role of the Low Countries in the Booktrade, 1473–1941, ed. Lotte Hellinga et al., 't Goy-Houten, Hes–De Graaf, 332 pp., contains 21 contributions on various aspects of the Dutch book-trade from the earliest stages of printing in the Low Countries (e.g. M. Goris, 'Boethius's *Consolatio Philosophiae* and the early printing tradition' [49–54]) to the mid-20th c. (e.g. D. van Galen Last, 'The patriotic reaction in 1940–41 in the Netherlands and France: a comparative analysis' [298–308]). Special attention is paid to Anglo-Dutch relationships in book printing and some articles in this area are P. G. Hoftijzer, 'The English book in the seventeenth-century Dutch Republic' (89–107); F. Korsten, 'The Elzeviers and England' (131–43); and P. Arblaster, 'London, Antwerp and Amsterdam: journalistic relations in the first half of the seventeenth century' (145–50).

Jozef Janssens and Rik van Daele, **Reinaerts streken: van 2000 voor tot 2000 na Christus*, Leuven, Davidsfonds–Literair, 317 pp., is a review of 4000 years of stories related to foxes, paying special attention to the European *Renard* tradition. The book concentrates in more detail on medieval versions of the tale, the Dutch *Reynaert de Vos* in particular, but it also studies 20th-c. renderings by Stijn Streuvels, Louis Paul Boon, and others.

2. THE MIDDLE AGES

Marcel van der Voort, *Dat seste boec van serpenten: een onderzoek naar en een uitgave van boek VI van Jacob van Maerlants 'Der naturen bloeme'* (MSB, 75), 480 pp., studies Jacob van Maerlant's observations of serpents in Book VI of his encyclopaedic treatise, *Der naturen bloeme* (*c.* 1270). Maerlant's text, an adaptation of Thomas of Cantimpré's *Liber de natura rerum* (given in an appendix, in Latin as well as in Dutch translation), is best represented in a London manuscript from the first quarter of the 13th c. It is this version that Van der Voort presents in a critical edition of Maerlant's text, and in facsimile at the end of his book. Apart from a thorough account of the relationship between the 12 versions of the text, the author also discusses the general background of man's love-hate relationship with serpents and explanations of Maerlant's many remarks on the 35 different serpents he describes. Two further publications on Jacob van Maerlant are Martine Leonarda Meuwese, **Beeldend vertellen: de verluchte handschriften van Jacob van Maerlants 'Rijmbijbel' en 'Spiegel Historiael'*, n.p., 353 pp. + CD-ROM, on illuminated manuscripts of Maerlant's rhymed version of the Bible and his history of the world; and **Jacob van Maerlants 'Der naturen bloeme' und das Umfeld: Vorläufer — Redaktionen — Rezeption*, ed. Amand Berteloot and Detlev Hellfaier (Niederlande-Studien, 23), Münster, Waxmann, 311 + [36] pp. This collection of essays concentrates on various aspects of Maerlant's *Der naturen bloeme*. Contributions include P. Wackers, 'Die mittelniederländische enzyklopädische Tradition' (11–27); W. G. Rohr, 'Etymologie und Deutung der Natur bei Konrad von Megenberg und Jacob van Maerlant' (69–82); S. Bogaart, 'Die Tierwelt in zwei mittelniederländischen Enzyklopädien: Jacob van Maerlants *Der Naturen Bloeme* und die niederländische Übersetzung von Bartholomaeus' Anglicus *De proprietatibus rerum*' (83–103); A. Berteloot, 'Kalender, Leerseiten und Miniaturen: ein Streifzug durch die Detmolder Maerlant-Handschrift' (105–18); D. Hellfaier, 'Von Brügge nach Detmold: Anmerkungen zur Überlieferungsgeschichte der Detmolder Naturen-Bloeme-Handschrift' (119–34); M. Meuwese, 'Die Illumination der Detmolder *Der Naturen Bloeme*-Handschrift' (135–52), and H. P. Westgeest, 'De illustraties in de *Der Naturen Bloeme*-handschriften' (153–64), both on illustrations; H. Lengenfelder, 'Anmerkungen zu Bildern in Jacob van Maerlants *Der Naturen Bloeme*, Handschrift D' (165–84); W. P. Gerritsen, 'Maerlant als Dichter in *Der Naturen Bloeme*' (185–95), on Maerlant as poet of *Der Naturen Bloeme*; T. Schoonheim,

'Bronnen van Maerlants *Der Naturen Bloeme* in het licht van de geografie' (197–216), on geographical sources; M. van der Voort, 'Onderzoek naar het slangenboek in Maerlants *Der Naturen Bloeme*: een verslag' (217–31), once more on serpents; H. van Engen, 'Nicolaas van Kats en *Der Naturen Bloeme*' (233–52), on the man to whom Maerlant dedicated his book; K. H. van Dalen-Oskam, 'Experimentator en de anderen: over de bronverwijzingen in *Der Naturen Bloeme*' (253–65), on sources; G. H. M. Claassens, 'Leer van dit wrede dier: *Instructio morum* in Jacob van Maerlants *Der Naturen Bloeme*' (267–89), on moral implications; and W. J. J. Pijnenburg, '*Der Naturen Bloeme* en het belang daarvan voor de lexicografie van het Nederlands' (291–301), on the importance of the work for Dutch lexicography.

Erwin Mantingh, **Een monnik met een rol: Willem van Affligem, het Kopenhaagse Leven van Lutgart en de fictie van een meerdaagse voorlezing* (MSB, 73), 2000, 411 pp., reiterates the question of authorship of the *Life* of Saint Lutgart of Tongeren (1182–1246), attributed to Willem van Affligem. Mantingh identifies two candidates, the abbot of Affligem monastery and its prior. By comparing the style in both monks' works he arrives at the conclusion that it was the latter to whom this literary masterpiece should be attributed. Special attention is paid to medieval ways of reading and the relationship with the oral transmission of literature.

*Ruusbroec in meervoud: inhoudende de handelingen van het colloquium 'Langs gerechte wegen. Jan van Ruusbroec vandaag' van 27 november 1999 te Hoeilaart, ed. Luc Versluys, Hoeilaart, Ruusbroeccomité Groenendaal-Hoeilaart, 208 pp., publishes the proceedings of a colloquium on the greatest mystic author in the Low Countries of the 14th c., Jan van Ruusbroec: P. Mommaers, 'Heeft mystiek iets te maken met het gewone leven' (39–46), wonders whether mysticism is relevant for people living their ordinary lives; G. de Baere, 'Jan van Ruusbroec (1293–1381), een kritisch man van de kerk' (123–43), studies Ruusbroec's critical attitude towards the Church; H. Noë, 'Jan van Ruusbroec, beelden van toen en nu' (161–76), concentrates on imagery in his works; H. van Assche, 'Het na-leven van Ruusbroec' (177–204), discusses the influence of his works on later authors. Translated from the 1998 French edition, Claude-Henri Rocquet, **Ruusbroec: een inleiding tot zijn persoon en tijd*, Zoetermeer: Meinema, 2000, 112 pp., is a biography of the same mystic author, whose influence stretched far beyond the borders of the Low Countries. Hilde Noë, **In een verwonderen van al deser rijcheyt: het beeldgebruik in Jan van Ruusbroecs 'Dat rijcke der ghelieven'* (Antwerpse studies over Nederlandse literatuurgeschiedenis, 7), Leuven, Peeters, 326 pp., researches the use of images in one of his works. Jan van Ruusbroec, **Een spieghel*

der eeuwigher salicheit, ed. G. de Baere, introd. P. Mommaers, trans. into English A. Lefevere, trans. into Latin Laurentius Surius (Corpus Christianorum, continuatio mediaevalis, 108; Jan van Ruusbroec, Opera omnia, 8), Turnhout, Brepols, 489 pp., is an authoritative edition of his treatise, *Speculum aeternae salutis,* edited in English, Latin, and Middle Dutch.

Hans van Dijk et al., *Spel en spektakel: Middeleeuws toneel in de Lage Landen* (Nederlandse literatuur en cultuur in de Middeleeuwen, 23), Amsterdam, Prometheus, 401 pp., contains 15 essays on drama from the 14th to the mid-16th c. Two contributions aim at positioning Dutch medieval drama in an international context: C. Dauven-van Knippenberg, 'Duitstalig geestelijk toneel van de Middeleeuwen' (57–75), focuses on a comparison with German religious drama; and J. Koopmans, 'Toneelgeschiedenis rond de grens. Drama in de Noord-Franse steden' (83–97), looks at the situation on the linguistic border between French and Dutch. Other essays concentrate on topics such as the relationship between liturgy and drama: I. de Loos, 'Drama als liturgie — liturgie als drama' (35–56); the origin, meaning and function of proper names in three of the so-called *abele spelen*: W. Kuiper, 'Oorsprong, betekenis en functie van de eigennamen in de abele spelen *Esmoreit, Gloriant* en *Lanseloet van Denemerken*' (98–110); and H. Pleij, 'Spektaculair kluchtwerk. De strijd om de broek als theater' (263–81), examines the spectacular in performances of farces.

The relationship between Hiëronymus Bosch's paintings, his *Haywain* triptych and *Conjuror* in particular, and medieval Dutch literature is studied by Eric de Bruyn, **De vergeten beeldentaal van Jheronymus Bosch: de symboliek van de hoogwagen-triptiek en de Rotterdamse marskramer-tondo verklaard vanuit Middelnederlandse teksten,* 's-Hertogenbosch, ABC, Stichting Archeologie, Bouwhistorie en Cultuur, 552 pp. **Aan de vruchten kent men de boom: de boom in tekst en beeld in de middeleeuwse Nederlanden,* ed. Barbara Baert and Veerle Fraeters (Symbolae Facultatis Litterarum Lovaniensis, Ser. B, 25), Leuven U.P., 294 pp., publishes essays on the motif of the tree in medieval Dutch art and literature: B. Baert, ' "Totten paradise soe sult ghi gaen": de verbeelding over de herkomst van het kruishout' (18–47), concentrates on the theme of the Holy Cross and iconography, mainly related to *Dat Boec van den Houte*; R. Faesen, ' "Een boem die hadde wortele op wert ende den tsop neder wert": een mystieke boom bij Hadewijch en Ruusbroec' (48–65), looks at the theme of the inverted tree in Hadewijch's first vision and in Ruusbroec's treatise *Die gheestelike Brulocht*; V. Fraeters, ' "Een uytlegginge vanden boom mercurii": onderzoek naar de betekenis en de herkomst van de "arbor mercurialis" aan de hand van een Middelnederlandse rijmtekst' (66–95), reviews alchemy and the theme of the mercury tree as introduced in Joos Balbiaen's *Een uytlegginge vanden boom mercurij*. She also includes an edition of this text from the version in London, BL, MS Sloane 1255; R. Jansen-Sieben, 'De balsemboom: mythisch, medisch, magisch' (120–39), has a close look at balm trees in the works of Jacob van Maerlant; J. Koldeweij, 'De "bosboom" als beeld voor 's-Hertogenbosch' (140–65), studies the motif of the forest as a source for the name of the 's-Hertogenbosch Chamber of Rhetoric, 'Moyses-Bosch'; J. Oosterman, 'Ik breng u de mei: meigebruiken, meitakken en meibomen in Middelnederlandse meiliederen' (166–89), focuses on maypoles and folkloric traditions related to Spring celebrations; J. van der Meulen, 'Onze Lieve Vrouwe van de Droge Boom in Brugge: devotiebeeld en literaire traditie' (208–37), studies the theme of the dry tree in Bruges as reflected in the religious 'Ghilde vanden Droghen Boome' as well as in the Gruuthuse manuscript; D. van der Poel, 'Memorabele bomen: de minneboom als allegorische constructie in de Middelnederlandse wereldlijke letterkunde' (238–57), looks at love trees and their allegorical contexts; R. Vervoort, 'Duivelse bomen of toverbomen?: een onderzoek naar de betekenis van de boom op heksenvoorstellingen' (258–80), focuses on witchcraft and dead trees.

*Vanden levene Ons Heren, ed. Ludo Jongen and Norbert Voorwinden (Middelnederlandse tekstedities, 8), Hilversum, Verloren, 286 pp., is a new bilingual edition, including a translation into modern Dutch, of the first Middle Dutch life of Christ, composed *c.* 1250. The unknown author has received wide acclaim for being the creator of one of the most beautiful poems in medieval Dutch literature. The edition is based on a later manuscript of 1438 in which the complete text is preserved.

Diederic van Assenede, *Floris en Blancefloer*, ed. Ingrid Biesheuvel (Griffioen), Amsterdam, Querido, 103 pp., is an edition in modern Dutch translation of the famous love story, adapted from the French by Diederic van Assenede (*c.* 1230–90), concerning Blancefloer, the Christian daughter of a female slave at the court of the Moorish king Fenus, and the king's son Floris. Disapproving of their love and aiming to create a permanent separation between the couple, the king tells his son that Blancefloer has died, whereas in fact she has been sold by him to slave drivers. Seeing her son gradually pine away grieving the loss of his loved one, Floris's mother reveals the truth to him. The young man immediately starts a quest for his beloved Blancefloer and after long wanderings he eventually finds her. And all is well that ends well! **Fragmenten van de Roman van Heinric en Margriete van Limborch*, ed. Lieve de Wachter et al. (Antwerpse studies over Nederlandse literatuurgeschiedenis, 6), Leuven, Peeters, vii + 269 pp., publishes fragments of another popular text in the Low

Countries, a chivalric mixture of various genres of medieval love stories.

Dating back to the last quarter of the 15th c. are the three parts of a manuscript, presumably copied in Borgloon, in the Belgian province of Limburg: *Het handschrift-Borgloon: Hs. Amsterdam, Universiteitsbibliotheek (UvA), I A 24 l, m, n,* ed. Jos Biemans et al. (Middeleeuwse Verzamelhandschriften uit de Nederlanden, 5), Hilversum, Verloren, 2000, 286 pp., presents a complete edition of this heavily damaged manuscript. The two most important texts edited here are the fragments of *Jonathas ende Rosafiere* and the *Roelantslied,* the Dutch rendition of the *Song of Roland.* Further texts include songs and stories much in favour among the public over the period of Lent and the opening lines of Anthonis de Roovere's *Vander mollen feeste.*

Other text editions are: Segher Diengotgaf, **Trojeroman, naar het Wissense handschrift (Brussel, Koninklijke Bibliotheek, IV 927),* ed. Jozef Janssens and Ludo Jongen (Alfa), Amsterdam U.P., v + 93 pp.; **Un'artistica rappresentazione di Esmoreit, figlio del re di Sicilia,* ed. Fulvio Ferrari (Labirinti, 51), Trento, Dipartimento di Scienze Filologiche e Storiche, 185 pp., presenting the text of this play both in Dutch and in Italian; and **Het Hartebok: Hs. Hamburg, Staats- und Universitätsbibliothek, 102c in scrinio,* ed. Erika Langbroek et al. (Middeleeuwse verzamelhandschriften uit de Nederlanden, 8), Hilversum, Verloren, 222 pp.

3. The Rhetoricians' Period

Nelleke Moser, *De strijd voor rhetorica: poetica en positie van rederijkers in Vlaanderen, Brabant, Zeeland en Holland tussen 1450 en 1620,* Amsterdam U.P., 287 pp., reviews the position of Rhetoricians in the Low Countries. The central theme of the book is the question of how they justified their literary art in their works. While later criticised by a new generation of Renaissance poets, the Rhetoricians themselves compared their products with the works of contemporary artists and, subsequently, more often than not rejected these. In order to promote their own art they employed various tools in their plays and poems such as metaphors related to flowers, a theme introduced in a seminal strophic poem, a so-called *refereyn,* written by the official town poet of Bruges, Anthonis de Roovere (*c.* 1430–1482). Rhetoricians also claimed the art of rhetoric to be directly inspired by the Holy Spirit. Thus they drew a line of demarcation between their art and the activities of other poets not united in Chambers of Rhetoric. During the early stages of their development they compared themselves with musicians, for both music and poetry were regarded as reflecting the harmony of the heavenly spheres. In the mid-16th c., Rhetoricians started to place themselves on a higher level, claiming their works were not only agreeable from a musical point of view but that they also contained important messages educating readers and audiences in religion, social behaviour, and other areas. Furthermore, their plays not only proved the eternal truth of God's words but they also invited individual beholders to contemplate on their meaning. This, so they argued, gave Rhetoricians a status in life equivalent to the position of priests, and they regarded themselves as sent by God to save mankind.

Kamers, kunst en competitie: teksten en documenten uit de rederijkerstijd, ed. Johan Oosterman et al. (Griffioen), Amsterdam, Athenaeum–Polak & Van Gennep, 143 pp., is an anthology, in modern Dutch translation, of texts written in the context of the Chambers of Rhetoric. The edition not only contains literary works (strophic poems and extracts from a rhymed manual on how to compose them) but also archival documents related to the history and internal regulations of specific Chambers, stipends awarded to individual Rhetoricians, records of the prosecution of those who were accused of heresy, and bills banning plays and other activities traditionally displayed by these Chambers and their members.

Martine de Bruin et al., *Repertorium van het Nederlandse lied tot 1600*, Ghent, KANTL — Amsterdam, Meertens Instituut Koninklijke Nederlandse Akademie van Wetenschappen, 2 vols, 919 pp. + CD-ROM, offers a complete inventory of all Dutch songs preserved in print or in manuscript up to the year 1600. The result is an impressive list of 7621 texts on 1158 different melodies. The CD-ROM includes, among other things, transcriptions of about 2000 songs. *Dutch Occasional Poetry, 16th through 18th Centuries: A Genre Rediscovered*, ed. J. A. Gruys and Adèle Nieuweboer, Leiden, IDC, 935 microfiches, is an impressive edition of 3641 poems, including a catalogue on CD-ROM.

Een intellectuele activist: studies over leven en werk van Philips van Marnix van Sint Aldegonde, ed. Henk Duits and Ton van Strien, Hilversum, Verloren, 126 pp., contains papers read at a colloquium held in 1998, 400 years after Marnix's death, at the Free University of Amsterdam: H. Duits, 'Inleiding: Marnix zestig jaar later' (8–22), reviews 40 years of Marnix-scholarship, after the last official commemoration, in 1938, of Marnix's birth in 1540; G. Marnef, 'Burgemeester in moeilijke tijden: Marnix en het beleg van Antwerpen' (28–36), looks at Marnix's years as burgomaster of Antwerp, with special attention to the year 1585 when Antwerp surrendered to the Spanish; R. De Smet, 'Taal, context en conventie in Marnix' correspondentie' (37–50), studies the author's use of language in his correspondence; C. Augustijn, 'Marnix de theoloog' (51–58), discusses Marnix's theological views, and W. Frijhoff, 'Marnix over de opvoeding' (59–75), his ideas about education; L. F. Groenendijk writes about Marnix's catechism for childern, *Cort begrijp* (1599), in 'Marnix' kindercatechismus' (76–86); W. B. de Vries, 'Marnix als intellectuele tuinliefhebber' (87–95), reviews the intellectual lover of gardens; and T. van Strien, 'Marnix en de Nederlandse literatuur' (96–106), looks at Marnix's place in Dutch literature. Especially useful is a bibliography of six decades of scholarship on the man and his works, 'Bibliografie van de Marnix-studie 1940–2000' (107–21).

Simon Stevin, *Het burgherlick leven and anhangh*, ed. Pim den Boer, transl. Anneke C. G. Fleurkens, Utrecht, Bijleveld, 223 pp., is an edition given in facsimile as well as in modern Dutch translation of Stevin's *Vita politica* (1590). The treatise was a study of the then political situation analysed through mathematics. It attempted to remind the Dutch, still at war with the Spaniards, of their rights and duties.

4. THE SEVENTEENTH CENTURY

Jeroen Jansen, *Decorum. Observaties over de literaire gepastheid in de renaissancistische poëtica*, Hilversum, Verloren, 439 pp., studies a fundamental aspect of Renaissance poetics, its theories about *decorum*. The central question answered in this monograph is whether there is a transformation in the way *decorum* was applied to 17th-c. literature, changing from a serious concern regarding matters of content, notably related to the genre of farce, to appropriate ways of approaching audiences during the era of French Classicism in drama. The author includes many observations on French and Italian authors as well.

Charles van Leeuwen, *Hemelse voorbeelden: de heiligenliederen van Joannes Stalpart van der Wiele, 1579–1630* (Memoria), Nijmegen, SUN, 389 pp., concentrates on a collection of 541 religious poems, *Gulde-Iaers Feest-dagen*, posthumously published in 1634. Van Leeuwen studies the way the collection has been structured and the rationale behind this presentation, the historical context, sources of the songs and their musical settings, traditions related to the veneration of saints, and Roman Catholic spirituality. Whether all songs included in Stalpart's collection are originally his own is a question only marginally discussed. Van Leeuwen shows how Stalpart's songs — composed amidst a congregation of beguines in Delft, a town where Calvinism was perhaps not the sole denomination but certainly the only sanctioned faith for those who held official positions — reflected the ideals of a Contra-Reformational spirit.

Bert van Selm, *De Amadis van Gaule-romans: productie, verspreiding en receptie van een bestseller in de vroegmoderne tijd in de Nederlanden, met een bibliografie van de Nederlandse vertalingen*, ed. Berry Dongelmans et al. (Stichting Neerlandistiek Leiden, 8), Leiden, Stichting Neerlandistiek te Leiden, xii + 226 pp., is a posthumously published monograph on the many Dutch translations and adaptations of the popular story of *Amadis de Gaula*, how and where they were printed, distributed, and received in the Netherlands. Johan Koppenol, in his inaugural lecture as Professor of historical Dutch literature at the Free University of Amsterdam, *De schepping anno 1654: oudere letterkunde en de verbeelding*, Amsterdam, VU Boekhandel–Uitgeverij, 36 pp., looks at conceptions of the cosmos as reflected in Joost van den Vondel's tragedy *Lucifer* and Jacob Westerbaen's Arcadian poem *Ockenburgh*, both published in 1654.

Writing the History of Women's Writing: Toward an International Approach, ed. Suzan van Dijk, Lia van Gemert, and Sheila Ottway (Verhandelingen Koninklijke Nederlandse Akademie van Wetenschappen, Afd. Letterkunde, n.s., 182), Amsterdam, Royal Netherlands Academy of Arts and Sciences, xxii + 276 pp., contains the proceedings of a colloquium entitled 'Met of zonder lauwerkrans?', held in Amsterdam, 9–11 September 1998. M. A. Schenkeveld-van der Dussen, *De geheimen van het vrouwelijk hart: Nederlandse vrouwelijke auteurs over de liefde in lyriek en roman (1600–1840)* (Mededelingen van de Afdeling Letterkunde, Koninklijke Nederlandse Akademie van Wetenschappen, n.s. 64.3) Amsterdam, Koninklijke Nederlandse Akademie van Wetenschappen, 35 pp., reviews the theme of love in texts written by female authors.

Constantijn Huygens, *Nederlandse gedichten 1614–1625*, ed. Ad Leerintveld (Monumenta literaria neerlandica, 12.1, 12.2), The Hague, Constantijn Huygens Instituut, 2 vols, 390, 845 pp., is a new critical edition of the poetry written by one of the secretaries of the Prince of Orange up to and including the works published in his first collection, *Otia* (1625). The edition is based on Leerintveld's 1997 doctoral dissertation, *Leven in mijn dicht*. Constantijn Huygens, *Dingen*, ed. Jan P. G. Heersche et al. (Uitgaven Stichting Neerlandistiek VU, 34), Amsterdam, Stichting Neerlandistiek VU Amsterdam — Münster, Nodus, 307 pp., is an edition with translations into modern Dutch of epigrams on objects, arranged alphabetically from *asijn* (vinegar) to *zijde* (silk), united under the heading 'Dingen' (Things) in Huygens's collection of poetry, *Korenbloemen* (in manuscript and in editions of 1658 and 1672).

Frequently seen as one of many 17th-c. minor Dutch poets, Jacob Westerbaen (1599–1670) became a wealthy man after his marriage, in 1625, with Anna Weytsen, widow of the eldest son of the famous

'State Pensionary', Johan van Oldenbarneveldt. After the success of his first collection of poems, published in 1624, Westerbaen decided to dedicate the rest of his life to writing poetry and hunting. Jacob Westerbaen, *Gedichten*, ed. Johan Koppenol (Griffioen), Amsterdam, Athenaeum–Polak & Van Gennep, 165 pp., presents an anthology of his works in modern Dutch translation, with special attention to his political and religious poems.

Mainly meant for use in secondary schools, *Verhalen over verre landen: reizen op papier 1600–1800*, ed. Karel Bostoen et al. (Tekst en context, 5), Amsterdam U.P., 104 pp., presents fragments in modern Dutch translation from 17th-c. and 18th-c. travel journals. Special attention is paid to the accounts written by Gerrit de Veer, Willem Ysbrandt Bontekoe, Cornelis Stout, and Maria and Johanna Lammens. The final chapter deals with an imaginary travel story, Hendrik Smeeks's *Krinke Kesmes* (1708).

Born as the second child to Pieter Cornelis Hooft's second wife, Leonora Hellemans, Arnout Hellemans Hooft (1629–80), after having finshed his studies, went on his 'grand tour' through Europe. Accompanied by Reyer Anslo, an acclaimed poet himself, he left on 31 August 1649, travelling through the Holy Roman Empire, Switzerland, Italy, and France, returning home on 10 November 1651. *Een naekt beeldt op een marmore matras seer schoon: het dagboek van een 'grand tour' (1649–1651)*, ed. E. M. Grabowsky and P. J. Verkruijsse (Egodocumenten, 23), Hilversum, Verloren, 231 pp., is an edition of the diary Arnout kept during his journey. Brought up in a Calvinist milieu, the young man neverthless took a special interest in Catholicism. Italian women appear to have had a distinct attraction for him as well. Useful additions to this edition are appendices on the secret code he used when writing about his sexual adventures and on the various different monetary systems he encountered during his travels. *Predikant en toerist: het dagboek van Joannes Vollenhove, Engeland, 17 mei-30 oktober 1674*, ed. G. R. W. Dibbets, Hilversum, Verloren, 224 pp., is an edition of yet another diary kept by the Calvinist vicar and poet, Johannes Vollenhove (1631–1708), who accompanied a Dutch diplomatic delegation on its journey to England from 17 May to 30 October 1674. A few months earlier, on 19 February, the Peace Treaty of Westminster had been signed, concluding the third Anglo-Dutch war. Vollenhove seems to have been particularly impressed by the cultural attractions London offered foreign visitors in those days. In the introduction to this edition Dibbets includes a brief biography of Vollenhove's life and works.

Hendrik van 't Veld, *Beminde broeder die ik vand op 's werelts pelgrims wegen: Jan Luyken (1649–1712) als illustrator en medereiziger van John Bunyan (1628–1688)*, Utrecht, De Banier, 2000, 559 pp., studies the illustrations the poet and etcher Jan Luyken made for four of Bunyan's works and their influence on later illustrators. Van 't Veld also elaborates on Luyken's mystic concepts, inspired by Jacob Böhme, and his religious convictions in general.

5. THE EIGHTEENTH CENTURY

During the second half of the 18th c., 60 literary societies were active in the Netherlands. Marleen de Vries, **Beschaven! Letterkundige genoot- schappen in Nederland 1750–1800*, Nijmegen, Vantilt, 476 + [16] pp., identifies three different types: poetic, meditative, and linguistic. The common denominator of these societies was their aim to educate people and to impart higher levels of civilization. By the end of the century most societies became seriously involved in the political discussions of the day, related to patriotism and the French revolution. André Hanou, **Bewegende beelden: Pygmalion en het beeld van de literatuur van de Nederlandse Verlichting*, [Nijmegen], Vantilt, 31 pp., describes in this inaugural lecture as Professor of historical Dutch literature at the University of Nijmegen how and why the myth of Pygmalion was introduced into Dutch art and literature of the 18th c.

Pieter Langendijk, *Het wederzijds huwelijksbedrog*, ed. Anna S. de Haas (Griffioen), Amsterdam, Querido, 168 pp., is a new annotated edition of one of the most popular comedies of the early 18th c., written in 1714. In an essay following the text of the play, De Haas discusses the development of 18th-c. French classicist drama in the Netherlands in general, Langendijk's works, and this play in particular.

't Zoet der eenzaamheid: gedichten van Juliana Cornelia de Lannoy, ed. Pim van Oostrum (De amazone, 2), Amsterdam U.P., 127 pp., is an anthology of the works of one of the most widely acclaimed 18th-c. women writers, who was not only successful as a poet but also as a dramatist. Three areas of her poetic production are highlighted here: De Lannoy's defence of women as first-class literary authors, satire and irony as weapons used in the battle of the sexes, and gratitude toward our ancestors who fought for our freedom as an independent nation.

Aardenburg of De onbekende volksplanting in Zuid-Amerika: roman van Petronella Moens, ed. Ans Veltman-Van den Bos and Jan de Vet, Amsterdam U.P., 137 pp., is an abridged edition of a novel by Petronella Moens, *Aardenburg* (1817), in which an imaginary society in South America is described. When and where precisely the novel is situated remains unclear. More important for Moens, who, as a young child, lost her sight, were the moral lessons she wanted to teach her readers, especially in relation to love and marriage and the sense of public responsibility in a modern society, both guided and inspired by religion. Further notable points of discussion in this novel are education and slavery. Discussions related to the latter of the two areas had barely started in the Netherlands, even though trading slaves had recently, in 1814, been prohibited by King William I. In the debate about abolishing slavery Moens took a position somewhere in the middle: on the one hand the main character in her novel, Adolf Tavernier, refuses to hunt down escaped slaves but he does not want to encourage others to run away by improving the escaped slaves' conditions. In any case, Moens despised racism. At the time, her novel did not attract many readers and even today it is a curio rather than a masterpiece.

Een verdeelde Verlichting: stemmen uit de spectators, ed. Dorothée Sturkenboom (Griffioen), Amsterdam, Athenaeum–Polak & Van Gennep, 167 pp., is an anthology from a number of less well-known spectatorial papers, published between 1718 and 1799. The selection made by the editor concentrates on four areas: relations between men and women, power relations, natives and foreigners, and body and mind. One of the reasons why spectatorial papers disappeared by 1800 was, according to Sturkenboom, their overwhelming success. The new genre of the epistolary novel took over their position as moral teacher *par excellence*. **De Hollandsche Spectator, 11 september 1733–12 februari 1734: aflevering 196 t/m 240*, ed. José de Kruif (Duivelshoekreeks, 14), Leuth, Astraea, 385 pp., is a further volume (See *YWMLS*, 61:785) in the complete edition of *De Hollandsche Spectator*, the best known weekly paper in the Netherlands, written by Justus van Effen.

6. The Nineteenth Century

Korrie Korevaart, *Ziften en zemelknoopen: literaire kritiek in de Nederlandse dag-, nieuws- en weekbladen, 1814–1848*, Hilversum, Verloren, 499 pp., reviews literary criticism in newspapers and weekly magazines in the first half of the 19th c. By developing stronger commercial positions and expanding into opinion papers rather than merely publishing news, the social function of newspapers changed during this period. However, literary reviews did not reach full maturity until the 1830s. One of the reasons for this relatively late development was the existence of a special tax on newspapers as a result of which individual issues normally did not exceed four pages. The Belgian Revolution of 1830 was another cause for the radical changes that took place in Dutch newspapers. Only a third of all newspapers included literary reviews, more often than not including other articles on cultural topics as well. Consequently, they were more expensive and attracted bourgeois readers, as a result of which reviews tended to be relatively conservative. Some, such as *De Avondbode* and the *Bredasche Courant*, even received government funding. Most reviews appeared anonymously but it can be assumed that the world of poets and novelists largely overlapped the world of the reviewers. A majority of reviews concentrate on recent political events and matters of regional importance and aesthetic criteria were less dominant than ethical ones. A remarkable feature of this survey of literary reviews in the first half of the 19th c. is that works nowadays regarded as belonging to the canon of 19th-c. Dutch literature hardly figured in these reviews. Views held by modern literary historians about the way literature was received and the reasons for praising individual texts do not always seem to coincide with what can be deduced from the reviews studied in this monograph.

*Wie leert 't krekeltjen zijn lied? De poëtische oorspronkelijkheid van Willem Bilderdijk: negen beschouwingen over gedichten van Bilderdijk, ed. Piet Gerbrandy and Marinus van Hattum, Groningen, Passage, 2000, 144 pp., contains nine essays on Willem Bilderdijk's poetry by, among others, K. Fens, R. Bloem, R. Schouten, and M. J. G. de Jong. In more than one essay published here the conclusion is reached that, more often than not, Bilderdijk's revolutionary ideas were cast in a rather old-fashioned classicist style.

Maria-Theresia Leuker, **Künstler als Helden und Heilige: nationale und konfessionelle Mythologie im Werk J. A. Alberdingk Thijms (1820–1889) und seine Zeitgenossen* (Niederlande-Studien, 26), Münster, Waxmann, 369 + [16] pp., reviews the ways J. A. Alberdingk Thijm, prominent critic and writer of short stories, managed to advance the mythical dimensions of 17th-c. art and literature, notably in those men and women, Joost van den Vondel and Maria Tesselschade in particular, who converted to Roman Catholicism. Leuker compares Thijm's observations on the 'Muiderkring', to which, 19th-c. critics wrongly believed, not only Tesselschade belonged but also Vondel, with other 19th-c. publications, written by representatives from the liberal-Protestant camp.

P. J. Buijnsters and L. Buijnsters-Smets, **Lust en leering: geschiedenis van het Nederlandse kinderboek in de negentiende eeuw*, Zwolle, Waanders, 504 pp., present a history of 19th-c. Dutch children's books, including various genres of non-fiction, picture books, and translations. Two authors, Jan Gouverneur and Jan Schenkman, are given special attention in chapters dedicated to their respective lives and works.

*De gedichten van De Schoolmeester, ed. Marita Mathijsen (Griffioen), Amsterdam, Querido, 246 pp., is a new edition of poems written by Gerrit van de Linde (1808–58), who published his works under the pseudonym of 'De Schoolmeester', the school master. As a student of

theology Van de Linde fathered an illegitimate child with a young girl and also had a relationship with the wife of one of his professors. After he had been found guilty of these misdeeds, Van de Linde decided to flee to England where he started a boarding school. There he wrote his satirical poems which were, shortly after his death, collected into one volume by his friend, Jacob van Lennep.

Judit Gera, *Van een afstand: Multatuli's Max Havelaar tegendraads gelezen* (Taal en gender, 4), Amsterdam, Veen, 64 pp., presents a feminist interpretation of the famous novel by Multatuli (pseudonym of Eduard Douwes Dekker), *Max Havelaar* (1860), concentrating on his views related to colonialism and to the division of roles between men and women. *'Men moet van myn gestreken lans, een vlaggestok maken': brieven van Multatuli en Tine Douwes Dekker aan de redersfamilie Smit,* ed. Chantal Keijsper, Amsterdam, Lubberhuizen, 53 pp., is an edition of nine previously unpublished letters by Multatuli, written in 1868, and seven letters from his wife Tine, dated 1870, all addressed to the shipowner family Smit. The immediate cause for Multatuli's sending these letters was the argument he had with J. J. Rochussen, a well-known politician, about money. *Indonesien: Kontinuitäten und Diskontinuitäten in den politischen und gesellschaftlichen Strukturen des 19. und 20. Jahrhunderts,* ed. Bernd Schenk and Hans-Jürgen Fuchs (Kolonialismus und Literatur, 4; Mitteilungen der Internationalen Multatuli-Gesellschaft Ingelheim, 7), [Fernwald], Litblockín, 157 pp., publishes papers read at a colloquium held, in 1999, in Ingelheim (Germany) where Multatuli lived during the final years of his life.

Ada Deprez, Walter Gobbers, and Karel Wauters, *Hoofdstukken uit de geschiedenis van de Vlaamse letterkunde in de 19e eeuw* (Studies op het gebied van de Moderne Nederlandse Literatuur, 4), Ghent, KANTL, vol. 2, iii + 290 pp., covers three areas of special study related to 19th-c. Flemish literature: W. Gobbers, 'Kritiek en betoog. Recenserend, essayistisch en wetenschappelijk proza in de marge van de Vlaamse heropleving' (1–88), discusses the role literary criticism and scholarly discourse played in Flanders and the Flemish movement. Between 1830 and 1890, novelists and critics occupied the same position in the debate regarding the emancipation of Flanders's population and, consequently, literary critics were by no means objective in their value judgements. In addition, the glorification of beauty was not the main criterion for their praise or reprimand but literature's functionality. C. Berg, 'De Frans-Belgische literatuur en haar "Vlaamse school" (1830–1880)' (89–132), reviews the wide range of opportunities for an intricate system of French cultural life in a Flemish environment, notably in towns such as Bruges, Ghent, and Antwerp. Until now, French and Flemish literary circles have been researched as separate fields, mutually excluding one another.

Berg, on the other hand, pleads for contrasting and comparing the two since both functioned within the same geographical area and cultural context. J. J. M. Westenbroek, 'Guido Gezelle (1830–1899) en de West-Vlaamse school' (133–274), concentrates on the most important 19th-c. Flemish poet, Guido Gezelle, and a number of his colleagues, poets of West Flanders such as Hugo Verriest, Karel de Gheldere, and Albrecht Rodenbach. Gezelle never took an active part in the Flemish movement. Instead he was driven by the ambition to protect the Flemish language, reflecting its Roman Catholic background, from being infiltrated by the language as it was spoken and written in the north, with its strong Protestant foundation. The first volume of this history of Flemish literature in the 19th c. was published in 1999 (See *YWMLS* 61 : 786).

7. 1880 TO 1945

The implications of Darwin's theory regarding the origin of species by means of natural selection, as published in his famous book (1859), were only fully grasped by young Dutch literary authors around the year 1880. Many authors adopted the view that nature is cruel and, consequently, they started questioning the existence of God. Mary Kemperink, *Het verloren paradijs: de Nederlandse literatuur en cultuur van het fin de siècle*, Amsterdam U.P., 384 pp., presents a survey of how late 19th-c. and early 20th-c. authors dealt with these ideas in their works, including poetry and novels by a wide range of writers, among them Louis Couperus, Frederik van Eeden, Herman Gorter, Herman Heijermans, Hélène Lapidoth-Swart, Henriëtte Roland Holst-van der Schalk, and Albert Verwey. Kemperink includes observations on the role of the town in their narrative prose, the problem of race, different social ranks, gender and the idea of marriage, science, religion, art and, finally, the position of the artist in a modern society.

Maarten Klein, **Noodlot en wederkeer: de betekenis van de filosofie in het werk van Louis Couperus*, Maastricht, Shaker, 2000, xiv + 273 pp., traces the influence of philosophical movements and the works of various philosophers, such as Nietzsche and Ralph Waldo Emerson, on stories and novels written by Louis Couperus. Eventually Klein identifies narrative motifs derived from their theories related to, among other things, fate, friendship, and the Dionysus-Christ motif. Micky Cornelissen, **Poëzie is niet een spel met woorden: de criticus Willem Kloos temidden van zijn tijdgenoten*, Nijmegen, Vantilt, 234 pp., concentrates on the contribution Willem Kloos (1859–1938), one of the leaders of the 'Movement of 1880' (*Tachtigers*), made to the field of literary criticism between 1879 and 1900. Cornelissen compares Kloos's poetic concepts to the ones held by his contemporaries, eventually coming to the conclusion that he was not the revolutionary person many people believed him to have been.

Jan van der Vegt, **A. Roland Holst: biografie*, Baarn, De Prom, 2000, 735 + [40] pp., is a long-awaited biography of one of the most productive poets of the 20th c., Adriaan Roland Holst (1888–1976), whose *Een winter aan zee* (1937) is regarded as his best work. Léon Hanssen, **Menno ter Braak 1902–1940: Want alle verlies is winst: 1902–1930*, [Amsterdam], Balans, 2000, 556 pp., is the first volume of a two part biography of one of the most discussed critics of the inter-war period. In vol. 2, **Sterven als een polemist: 1930–1940*, [Amsterdam], Balans, 727 pp., Hanssen discusses the last ten years of Ter Braak's life. On 10 May 1940, the day German troops crossed the Dutch border and occupied the country, Ter Braak committed suicide, believing that life was no longer worth living now National Socialism would also dominate daily life in the Netherlands. Mels de Jong, *A. M. de Jong, schrijver: biografie*, Amsterdam, Querido, 462 pp., is a biography of an author who is mainly regarded as a writer of regional novels, a genre many critics still see as semi-literary rather than belonging to 'high' literature. De Jong's socialist views made him sympathize with the working classes, especially those who live in the country. In the 1970s, a television series based on his cycle of novels, *Merijntje Gijzens jeugd*, published between 1924 and 1928, led to revived popularity of De Jong's works. During the years leading up to World War II, De Jong had openly criticized and resisted National Socialism and the moment the Netherlands were overrun by the Germans, on 10 May 1940, he knew his life was in danger. After his neighbour, a member of the Dutch National Socialist party, had been wounded in a gunfight, De Jong was murdered in a revenge attack on 18 October 1943. Cees Slegers, **Antoon Coolen, 1897–1961: biografie van een schrijver*, n.p., 656 pp., is a biography of yet another author of regional novels whose works currently enjoy a revival. Ludo Stynen, **Lode Zielens: volksschrijver*, Tielt, Lannoo, 455 pp., is a biography of the Flemish novelist and writer of short stories, Lode Zielens (1901–44), who dedicated many of his works to describing the lives of Antwerp citizens, women in particular, belonging to the lower classes in society.

Jaap Grave, **Zulk vertalen is een werk van liefde: bemiddelaars van Nederlandstalige literatuur in Duitsland, 1890–1914*, Nijmegen, Vantilt, 360 + [8] pp., deals with the translation of Dutch literature into German and the role of intermediaries in this process. Harold van Dijk, **'In het liefdeleven ligt gansch het leven': het beeld van de vrouw in het Nederlands realistisch proza, 1885–1930*, Assen, Van Gorcum, x + 384 pp., studies the image of women in Dutch realist prose published between 1885 and 1930.

Sonja Neef, **Kalligramme: zur Medialität einer Schrift: anhand von Paul van Ostayens 'De feesten van angst en pijn'*, [Amsterdam], ASCA, 2000, 360 pp., studies the interaction between visual and poetic aspects of Paul van Ostayen's collection of poems, *De feesten van angst en pijn*, written between 1918 and 1921, and published in their handwritten multi-coloured calligraphic form. Further publications on Van Ostayen include Kathrin Koetz, **Die Prosa Paul van Ostaijens: stilistische, poetologische und philosophische Korrespondenzen mit dem Werk von Mynona (Salomo Friedländer)* (Niederlande-Studien, 24), Münster, Waxmann, 243 pp., and Geert Buelens, **Van Ostaijen tot heden: zijn invloed op de Vlaamse poëzie*, Nijmegen, Vantilt — Ghent, Koninklijke Academie voor Nederlandse Taal- en Letterkunde, 1302 pp., a detailed review of the huge influence the poet Paul van Ostayen (1896–1928) had, and still has, on 20th-c. Flemish poetry.

Martien J. G. de Jong, **Een klauwende muze: de tussenwereld van Maurice Gilliams* (Studies op het gebied van de Moderne Nederlandse Literatuur, 6), Ghent, KANTL, 138 pp., concentrates on the life and works of the Flemish author, Maurice Gilliams (1900–82). Special attention is paid to his diaries, the way Gilliams dealt with his critics, and his activities as a painter.

8. 1945 TO THE PRESENT DAY

Piet Calis, *Het elektrisch bestaan: schrijvers en tijdschriften tussen 1949 en 1951*, Amsterdam, Meulenhoff, 408 pp., is the concluding part of a four volume series on literary journals between 1941 and 1951 (see *YWMLS*, 61:792). In this volume the author concentrates on the role periodicals such as *Reflex*, *Cobra*, *Braak*, and *Blurb* played in the introduction of the so-called 'Fifties' Movement' (*Vijftigers*) in poetry, and the way some of the more established ones (*Libertinage* and *Podium*) reacted to the new generation of poets. Through interviews with and minute scrutiny of hundreds of letters exchanged between some of its major representatives, so far unpublished, Calis offers a fascinating picture of how modern Dutch literature was reshaped during the first years after World War II. Koen Hilberdink, *'Ik ben een vreemdeling. Ik sta apart': een biografie van Paul Rodenko (1920–1976)*, Amsterdam, Meulenhoff, 2000, 438 pp., is a biography of one of the most influential poets and critics of the 1950s who, however, did not belong to the generation of poets named after this era. Gerard Bes, **Hans Lodeizen 1924–1950: Liever liefde dan gedichten*, [Amsterdam], Balans, 343 + [16] pp. Thomas Vaessens, **De verstoorde lezer: over de onbegrijpelijke poëzie van Lucebert*, Nijmegen, Vantilt, 63 pp., studies the reception of Lucebert's (1924–94) poetry, claiming that his works should, instead of being approached from a modernist point of view, rather be seen as post-modern.

Marianne Vogel, *'Baard boven baard': over het Nederlandse literaire en maatschappelijke leven 1945–1960*, Amsterdam, Van Gennep, 294 pp., studies the influence of gender on the reception of novels written between 1945 and 1960, arriving at the obvious conclusion that male authors were better received and taken more seriously than their female colleagues.

Annick Cuynen, *'Ik houd er niet van, al te zeer begrepen te worden': de kunstenaar in het werk van Simon Vestdijk* (Studies op het gebied van de moderne Nederlandse literatuur, 5), Ghent, KANTL, 413 pp., studies Simon Vestdijk's (1898–1976) thoughts regarding artists as reflected in his novels, his poetry, and his critical essays. Artists are central to Vestdijk's works and reveal his ideas concerning the relationship between art and reality, and the artist's psyche.

Apollo in Brasserie Lipp: bespiegelingen over Willem Frederik Hermans, ed. Raymond J. Benders and Wilbert Smulders, [Amsterdam], De Bezige Bij — [The Hague], Willem Frederik Hermans Instituut, 251 pp., publishes essays on the life and the works of one of the most important post-war Dutch authors, Willem Frederik Hermans (1921–1995). Odile Heynders et al., *Omwikkel mij met uw verstand: drie beschouwingen over het werk van Willem Frederik Hermans*, Amsterdam, De Bezige Bij — The Hague, Willem Frederik Hermans Instituut, 2000, 93 pp., presents three prize-winning essays awarded by the WFH institute that was established to promote the dissemination of knowledge related to the life and the works of the author: O. Heynders, 'Visuele kracht en onmacht: over surrealistische gedichten van W. F. Hermans en Paul Éluard' (9–39), discusses surrealist themes in Hermans's poetry; J. van der Does, 'Een klassieke schoonheid: over thema's en dubbele bodems in *Au pair*' (41–69), analyses Hermans's novel *Au pair* (1985); G. Franssen, 'De geheime politie van het zwijgen en de zondebok: de literaire politiek van Willem Frederik Hermans' (71–92), concentrates on Hermans's literary politics.

Ria van den Brandt, Bert Vanheste, and Erik Borgman, *Louis Paul Boon en de verscheidenheid van de wereld*, Nijmegen, Vantilt, 111 pp., discuss the world picture of the Flemish author Louis-Paul Boon (1912–79). Marco Daane, *De vrijheid nog veroveren: Richard Minne 1891–1965* (Open domein, 39), Amsterdam–Antwerp, Arbeiders-pers, 552 pp., is a biography of the Flemish poet and writer of short stories and essays, Richard Minne, who published most of his narrative works as newspaper articles. Daane's monograph is only the third book ever written about the life and the works of Minne, a man whose poems and stories frequently confused their readers. According to Daane, the explanation for Minne's difficult personality can be found in the fact that, as a young man, he spent four years of his life as a farmer. Characteristic of his poetry is its simplicity of style. Minne sometimes does not even use one single adjective in a poem or only very common ones. This gave him the opportunity to concentrate more on his poems' contents and it allowed him fully to employ irony and sarcasm. Moving away from the intricate style of preceding generations of poets, Minne clearly introduced a new and refreshing style in Flemish poetry.

III. DANISH STUDIES*

LANGUAGE

By Tom Lundskær-Nielsen, *Senior Lecturer in Danish, Department of Scandinavian Studies, University College London*

(This survey covers the years 2000 and 2001)

1. General

R. Allan and T. Lundskær-Nielsen, 'Danish', pp. 184–89 of *Facts about the World's Languages*, ed. Jane Garry and Carl Rubino, NY, New England Publishing Associates, 896 pp., presents a very concise overview of different aspects of Danish. Other general presentations include: Thomas Andersen, Uwe Helm Petersen, and Flemming Smedegaard, **Sproget som ressource. Dansk systemisk funktionel lingvistik i teori og praksis*, Odense U.P., 350 pp. **Moderne lingvistiske teorier og færøsk*, ed. Kurt Braunmüller and Jógvan í Lon Jacobsen, *Nordisk Sprogråds skrifter*, Oslo, Novus, 249 pp. Catharina Grünbaum, *Nordisk språkförståelse — att ha och mista. En rapport baserad på fyra konferenser om nordisk språkförståelse — 'Det omistliga'*, Hanaholmen, Fondet for dansk-norsk samarbeid (Lysebu og Schæffergården). The same theme is addressed by J. Lund, 'Nordisk sprogsamarbejde — på nye betingelser', *Sprog i Norden*, Novus, 2000: 104–11, and in an even wider context (partly from a historical angle) by I. L. Pedersen, 'Sprogkontakt, sprogpåvirkning — og sprogpolitik', *ib.*, 34–44. The status of Danish in the past, present, and future is the subject of current debate, as seen in the following four publications: Pia Jarvad, **Det danske sprogs status i 1990'erne med særligt henblik på domænetab* (Dansk Sprognævns skrifter, 32), Gyldendal, 170 pp.; Ivar Gjørup, **Den sjette sans — sprog, skrift og liv gennem tre årtusinder*, Spektrum, 2000, 301 pp.; T. Kristiansen, 'Den danske sprogsituation ved århundredeskiftet — status og udviklingslinjer', pp. 43–81 of *'Speider over hav mot Danmark.' Landskonferancen for norsklærere i lærerutdanninga Schæffergården 12.–14. mai 2000*, Nord-Trøndelag, 2000; and E. Hansen, I. Kjær, and J. Lund, 'Styrk sproget', *Nyt fra Sprognævnet*, 2000.2: 1–6.

The notion of a standard language is the theme of the special issue of *Language Awareness*, 10.1, 'Changing representations of standardness in late modernity: the case of Denmark', ed. T. Kristiansen, Clevedon, Multilingual Matters, 71 pp. It has two articles by the

---

* The place of publication of books is Copenhagen unless otherwise stated.

editor: 'The notion of standard language in late modernity: introducing three studies of young Danes' perceptions and evaluations of standardness in language' (1–8), and 'Two standards: one for the media and one for school' (9–24). Four festschrifts for eminent senior Danish linguists have appeared: *To honour Eli Fischer-Jørgensen — Festschrift on the Occasion of her 90th Birthday, February 11th 2001*, ed. Nina Grønnum and Jørgen Rischel (Travaux du Cercle linguistique de Copenhague, 31), C. A. Reitzel, 297 pp.; **Den analytiske gejst — Festskrift til Uwe Geist på 60-årsdagen 23. september 2001*, ed. Lars Heltoft and Carol Henriksen, Roskilde U.P., 271 pp.; **Ord til Arne Hamburger på ottiårsdagen 11. juli 2001*, ed. Henrik Galberg Jacobsen and Jørgen Schack (Dansk Sprognævns skrifter, 31), Gyldendal, 217 pp.; *Sproglige åbninger: Festskrift til Erik Hansen 18. september 2001: E som Erik, H som 70*, ed. Pia Jarvad et al., Hans Reitzel, 472 pp. Erik Hansen is also congratulated in a shorter article by V. Sandersen, 'I anledning af..', *Nyt fra Sprognævnet*, no. 3 : 1–4. Edel Hildebrandt, *Ind med sproget*, Politiken, 187 pp. Jørn Lund, **Sproglig status. Syv kapitler om det danske sprog*, Hans Reitzel, 152 pp. Jacob Steensig, **Sprog i virkeligheden. Bidrag til en interaktionel lingvistik*, Aarhus U.P., 338 pp. **Tegn og betydning — Betydningsdannelse i filosofisk, biologisk og semiotisk perspektiv*, ed. Torkild Leo Thellefsen, Akademisk Forlag, 255 pp.

2. HISTORY OF THE LANGUAGE, PHONOLOGY, MORPHOLOGY, LEXIS, SYNTAX, SEMANTICS, AND PRAGMATICS

There is a revised edition of Allan Karker, **Dansk i tusind år. Et omrids af sprogets historie*, C. A. Reitzel, 282 pp. **Dansk sprog- og stilhistorisk tekstbase*, ed. Hanne Ruus et al., Institut for Nordisk Filologi, Copenhagen University. H. F. Nielsen, 'Skandinaviens ældste sproghistorie i komparativ belysning', pp. 56–63 of *Studier i Nordisk 1998–1999*, ed. Kjeld Kristensen, Selskab for Nordisk Filologi, 2000, 199 pp. Hans Frede Nielsen, **The Early Runic Language of Scandinavia: Studies in Germanic Dialect Geography*, Heidelberg, Winter, 2000, 445 pp., traces the earliest known stages of the language. I. L. Pedersen, 'Hvad er forklaringen på forklaringerne?', pp. 1–24 of *Studier i Svensk Språkhistoria*, ed. Lars-Erik Edlund, Umeå, Institutionen för litteraturvetenskap och nordiska språk vid Umeå Universitet, 2000, 456 pp. I. L. Pedersen and F. Gregersen, 'A la recherche du word order not quite perdu', pp. 393–431 of *Textual Parameters in Older Languages*, ed. Susan Herring et al., Amsterdam, Benjamins, 2000, 448 pp.

A major work on historical Danish prosody has been written by the Grand Old Lady of phonetics, Eli Fischer-Jørgensen, *Tryk i ældre dansk. Sammensætninger og afledninger* (Historisk-filosofiske meddelelser, 84),

806   *Danish Studies*

Det Kgl. Danske Videnskabernes Selskab–C. A. Reitzel, 516 pp.
Robert Zola Christensen, *Skrift og tale*, Lund, Studentlitteratur, 2000,
159 pp., focuses on the relationship between Danish spelling and
writing and standard pronunciation from both a diachronic and a
synchronic viewpoint. Jan Katlev and Hanne Steen Spliedt, *Hvorfor
siger vi sådan*, Politiken, 144 pp. M. H. Juul and C. Elbro, 'Når
bogstavets lyd af hænger af sammenhængen. Om tilegnelsen af
videregående af kodningsfærdighed', *Psykologisk Pædagogisk Rådgivning*,
38, no. 1:3–13. A. Gudiksen, '-vorn's lydlige form', *Danske Talesprog*,
no. 2:27–76; and Id., 'Orddannelse ved analogi', Widell, *Møde*,
113–21. M. H. Juul, 'Fra analfabet til avanceret ortografibruger. En
oversigt over de vanskeligheder man møder som bruger af dansk
ortografi', pp. 85–113 of *Danske Studier*, ed. Iver Kjær and Flemming
Lundgreen-Nielsen, C. A. Reitzel, 216 pp. V. Sandersen, 'Om
bogstavet *ø*, *Nyt fra Sprognævnet*, 2000.3:11–15. A. M. Ågerup,
'Euroen', *ib.*, 2000.4:1–4. *Erik Hansen — Glæden ved grammatik —
udvalgte artikler og af handlinger*, ed. Henrik Galberg Jacobsen and
Henrik Jørgensen, Hans Reitzel, 325 pp. Henrik Jørgensen, *Studien
zur Morphologie and Syntax der festlandskandinavischen Personalpronomina mit
besonderer Berücksichtigung des Dänischen* (Acta Jutlandica, 75.2; Humanities Series, 73), Aarhus U.P., 2000, 319 pp., discusses pronominal
forms in Norwegian and Swedish as well as in Danish.

Ny forskning i grammatik, ed. Jens Nørgård-Sørensen et al. (Fælles-
publikation 7, RASK Supplementary Vol. 11), Odense U.P., 2000,
305 pp., includes the following contributions: E. Hansen, 'Ante-
poneret adverbial' (73–86); E. Skafte Jensen, 'Sætningsadverbialer
og topologi med udgangspunkt i de konnektive adverbialer' (141–54);
H. Korzen, 'Frie prædikativer på dansk og fransk. En kontrastiv
analyse af en problematisk ledtype' (155–77); F. Sørensen, 'Om
steder via præpositioner i dansk' (259–67); and R. Therkelsen, 'Om
klassifikation af ledsætninger' (269–85). *Studier i Nordisk 1998–1999*,
Selskab for Nordisk Filologi, 2000, contains four relevant articles:
J. Schack, 'Ordmærker i dansk' (5–18); H. Jørgensen, 'Begrebet
"klisis" og dets anvendelse på analysen af de danske letled' (37–50);
O. Togeby, 'Lette led' (51–55); C. Hansen, 'Den danske vrede — en
sprog-billedlig brugervejledning for udlændinge' (100–111). M. H.
Andersen, 'Fremmedarbejdere, gæstearbejdere, nydanskere — og
perkere', *Nyt fra Sprognævnet*, no. 3:31–36. S. Beltoft, 'Din nisse', *ib.*,
49–52. L. Bernhardt and T. W. Knoth, 'Fra dativ-led til subjekt',
Sprint, 3–8. J. Bruntse, 'Fed? Nej, selvfed', *Nyt fra Sprognævnet*, no.
3:45–46. N. Davidsen-Nielsen, 'Hvad er apposition?' *ib.*, 6–10.
E. Engberg-Pedersen, 'The interrelationship of grammar, text type,
and age: expression of time relations and the pragmatic status of
event participants in Danish narratives', *Acta Linguistica Hafniensia*, 32,

2000:121–41. A. Hamburger, 'Valgfrihed', *Nyt fra Sprognævnet*, no. 3:26–27. E. Hjorth, 'Har man sine tvivl, eller kan man nøjes med én?', *ib.*, 22–25. H. Holmberg, 'Stavekontrol — kontrol af stavning?', *ib.*, 53–55. P. Jarvad, 'Vel er du Manden, men du er sku da itte helt søverin — Om ordet *suverän*', *ib.*, 2000.4:9–13. A. Jensen, 'Hvilken præposition bruger man efter *kontrol?*', *ib.*, 2000.2:7–10, and Id., 'Mor har haft repareret cyklen', *ib.*, no. 1:1–4. J. N. Jensen, 'Var det hundene han gik i? En grammatisk analyse af nogle danske idiomer', *ib.*, no. 3:17–22. A. Å. Jervelund, 'Den dag i dag og alt i alt', *ib.*, 41–44. B. Jørgensen, 'Ævred', *ib.*, 46–48. A. Karker, 'Når synsvinklerne kortslutter — Om ubetænksomhed i det sproglige udtryk', *ib.*, 2000.3:1–7. J. Kornbeck, 'Hvordan subsidiaritet blev til nærhed', *ib.*, 2000.4:5–9. O. Ravnholt, 'Flygtninge/indvandrere, et sammensat ord med skråstreg?', *ib.*, no. 3:28–31. M. Rathje, 'Eksponere og overeksponere', *ib.*, 37–41. V. Sandersen, 'Om dobbeltnægtelser i dansk', *ib.*, no. 1:6–8. T. Thrane, '*Sikke* et ord', *Hermes*, 27:85–137.

The 'comma' debate continues in the wake of the 'new comma' recommended by *Dansk Sprognævn*. *Nyt fra Sprognævnet*, no. 2, has the new comma as its theme, including a short article by N. Davidsen-Nielsen, 'Tidens tegn' (2–5), and two more substantial publications have appeared on the same topic: Celine Haastrup and Anne Riber Petersen, *Politikens bog om tegn og tegnsætning, Politiken, 192 pp.; and Kirsten Rask, Komma — de nye regler, Grafisk Litteratur, 48 pp. *Can you reach the salt? Pragmatikkens klassiske tekster, ed. Carol Henriksen, Roskilde U.P., 262 pp.

3. DIALECTOLOGY, CONTRASTIVE LINGUISTICS, BILINGUALISM, AND APPLIED LINGUISTICS

*Ømålsordbogen. En sproglig-saglig ordbog over dialekterne på Sjælland, Lolland-Falster, Fyn og omliggende øer, vol. 5 (Universitets-Jubilæets danske Samfunds skrifter, 550), Institut for Dansk Dialektforskning–C. A. Reitzel, 2000, 473 pp. Karen Margrethe Pedersen, *Dansk sprog i Sydslesvig. Det danske sprogs status inden for det danske mindretal i Sydslesvig 1–2, 2 vols, Aabenraa, Institut for Grænseregionsforskning, 2000, 302, 391 pp. Lise Horneman Hansen, Jysk — de-bøjning — en undersøgelse af svag præteritum[s]bøjning (Institutionen för nordiska språk vid Uppsala universitet, 54), Uppsala U.P., 237 pp.

Danske Talesprog, no. 1, Institut for dansk dialektforskning–C. A. Reitzel, 2000, contains the following articles: I. L. Pedersen, 'Fra folkemål til multietnolekt: kontinuitet eller brud?' (5–29); I. Ejskjær, 'Udtryk for (løbe) løbsk i danske dialekter' (31–59); A. Jensen, 'Det drejer sig om *kræng*. Et forsøg på at analysere en betydningsudvikling' (61–87); F. Køster, 'Træk af sproget i byerne på Fyn' (89–108);

R. Horak, '*Hvad mener du med dette begreb, kære kollega?* Parametre i kontrastiv terminologisk analyse af variationsbegreber' (109–42); P. Quist, 'Ny københavnsk "multietnolekt". Om sprogbrug blandt unge i sprogligt og kulturelt heterogene miljøer' (143–211). P. Quist has also written **Nydansk på Nørrebro', Mål & Mæle*, 2000, no. 7:3:5–10, and **Unge, identitet og sprog. Operationalisering af identitetsbegrebet i en empirisk undersøgelse', pp. 23–38 of **Ungdom, språk og identitet*, ed. Ulla-Britt Kotsinas, Anna-Brita Stenström and Eli-Marie Drange, Nordisk Ministerråd, 2000, 152 pp. I. Ejskjær, 'Nogle reliktord i danske dialekter', pp. 67–73 of *Dialekter och folkminnen. Hyllningsskrift till Mai Reinhammer den 17 maj 2000*, ed. Lennart Elmevik et al., Uppsala, Swedish Science Press, 2000, 294 pp. I. L. Pedersen, '"De måtte ud af sengen klokken var fem". Adverbielle ledsætninger med tomt konjunktionalfelt i danske dialekter', *ib.*, 223–30; and Id., 'Lille fag hvad nu? Et oplæg til en diskussion af nordisk dialektforsknings vilkår og muligheder', *ib.*, 257–76. Other articles by I. L. Pedersen include: 'Ungdomssprog — dialekt eller register? En oversigt over nyere, især nordisk, ungdomssprogsforskning', *Nordlyd*, 28, 2000:44–59; 'Urban and rural dialects of Slesvig: political boundaries in the millenial retreat of Danish in Slesvig', *IJSL*, 145, 2000:131–51; 'Bymålenes stilling i Danmark. En oversigt og diskussion', pp. 169–80 of *Våra Språk i tid og rum*, ed. Marianne Blomquist et al., Helsinki; and 'Talesprog som identitetsskaber og identitetsudtryk', *Nordlit*, 10:41–55. A. Gudiksen, 'Om forholdet mellem -*et* og -*ig* i de danske dialekter', *Folkemålsstudier. Meddelanden från Föreningen för nordisk filologi*, 39, 2000:127–40. T. Kristiansen, 'Findes Næstved-københavnsk?', *ib.*, 207–18. M. Maegaard, '"Jeg er da stolt af at jeg er sønderjyde — altså sådan forholdsvis". Om sprogbrug og sprogholdninger hos sønderjyske unge', *Danske Talesprog*, no. 2:77–166; and Id., 'Sprogholdninger hos sønderjyske unge', Widell, *Møde*, 217–26. K. M. Pedersen, 'Variation i valens', *ib.*, 277–286.

Ord & Sag, 20, 2000, features the following articles: J. Ejsing, 'Hvad vi kaldte hinanden i det gamle Salling' (6–12); K. M. Pedersen and V. Sørensen, 'Om øg, heste og andre bæster' (13–31); N. Dalsgaard, 'Haj ær da i sær faks — om et speciale fuldt af skældsord' (32–35); T. Arboe, 'Stunthoser, springtriller — og andre fodløse strømper' (36–53). *Ord & Sag*, 21, includes the following contributions: T. Arboe, 'Jyske kollektiver — et grammatisk fænomen under afvikling' (6–14); V. Sørensen, 'Midtøstjysk — et kort signalement af Klaus Moltesens dialekt' (28–31); N. Grøftehauge and V. Sørensen, 'Vil du ikke rende og hoppe — et spørgsmål om underforståelse og omtolkning' (32–45). *Sprog & Samfund*, 18.2, 2000, has two articles on dialect issues: J. Lund, 'Danske dialekter under afvikling' (8), and

G. Søndergaard, 'Dialekter og bykulturer' (9–12). M. H. Andersen, 'Engelsk i dansk: Sproglig normering. En undersøgelse af unge storkøbenhavneres holdninger til bøjning og stavning af engelske ord i dansk', *Sprog i Norden*, Novus, 129–36. H. Liedtke, 'Zum Anredesystem im Deutschen und im Dänischen', in **Die deutsche Sprache der Gegenwart. Festschrift für Dieter Cherubim zum 60. Geburtstag*, ed. Stefan J. Schierholz et al., Frankfurt, Lang, 2000. P. Quist, ***'Flersprogethed og flersprogede udtryk', *Daghøjskolen*, 15.2, 2000:29–32. Vibeke Winge, **Pebersvend og poltergejst. Tysk indflydelse på dansk*, Gyldendal, 2000, 120 pp. P. Colliander and D. Hansen, 'Når den fremmedsproglige kompetence svigter', *Sprint*, 9–21. Helle Pia Laursen, *Magt over sproget — om sproglig bevidsthed i andetsprogtilegnelsen*, Akademisk Forlag, 282 pp.

Dansk — vejen til integration (Modersmål-Selskabets årbog 2000), C. A. Reitzel, 2000, 141 pp., has Danish as a second language as its theme. Among the articles are: K. Lund, 'Interkulturel kommunikation — at navigere i misforståelser' (35–43); A. Tølle and J. Møller, 'Integreret tosprogethed — vejen til integration' (45–52); A. Holmen, 'Dansk som andetsprog er kommet for at blive' (69–76); N. Jørgensen, 'Perkerdansk og de sure gamle mænd' (109–17); A. Hermann, 'Det nye modersmål — banebryder for integration' (133–38). *Det er conversation 801 değil mi? Perspectives on the Bilingualism of Turkish Speaking Children and Adolescents in North Western Europe*, ed. Anne Holmen and Jens Normann Jørgensen (Copenhagen Studies in Bilingualism, Køge Series, K7), Danish University of Education, 2000, 229 pp., includes the following two contributions: J. Steensig, 'Notes on some uses of code-switches and other interactional devices in conversation 801' (9–30); and A. Holmen and J. N. Jørgensen, 'The interdependence of second language and bilingual development in successively bilingual school children' (137–57). Janus Møller, *Identitet og kodevekslen hos unge tosprogede med dansk-tyrkisk baggrund* (Copenhagen Studies in Bilingualism, Køge Series, K8), Danish University of Education, 2000, 156 pp. **En køn strid — sprog, magt og køn hos tosprogede børn og unge*, ed. Jens Normann Jørgensen et al. (Copenhagen Studies in Bilingualism, Køge Series, K10), Roskilde U.P., 142 pp. In *Sprogs status i Danmark år 2011*, ed. Anne Holmen and Jens Normann Jørgensen (Københavnerstudier i tosprogethed, 32), Danish University of Education, 2000, 161 pp., a number of linguists attempt to predict the position of languages in Denmark a decade hence. Articles include: E. Hansen, 'Normering og sprognævn' (7–20); T. Kristiansen, 'Normering og holdninger' (21–58); L. Brink, 'Engelsk i dansk — udvikling, status, normering' (59–73); A. Holmen and J. N. Jørgensen, 'Har vi en dansk sprogpolitik? Om holdninger til sproglig mangfoldighed i Danmark' (75–90); K. M. Pedersen, 'Dansk i

Sydslesvig — funktion, status og sprogpolitik' (91–126); H. Haber-
land, 'Kan dansk overleve som kultursprog?' (127–38); R. Phillipson,
'English, or no to English in Scandinavia?' (139–52); Id., 'En
sprogpolitik for Danmark' (153–61). Leif Becker Jensen, *Den sproglige
dåseåbner — om at formidle faglig viden forståeligt*, Roskilde U.P., 243 pp.
Ebbe Kyrø, *Skriv bedre*, Høst & Søn, 164 pp. *Danskbogen — danskfaget
i de pædagogiske uddannelser*, ed. Anne Petersen, Klim, 298 pp. Kirsten
Rask, *Skriv professionelt*, Grafisk Litteratur, 48 pp.

4. LEXICOGRAPHY, GRAMMARS, STYLISTICS, AND
RHETORIC

Retskrivningsordbogen, Ashehoug, Dansk Sprognævn, 749 pp., is the
third edition of this important work. In connection with its appearance, *Nyt fra Sprognævnet*, no. 4, is made up of articles commenting and
providing guidance on aspects of this new edition, in particular on
some of the changes from the second edition: E. Hansen, 'Lovens
bogstav' (1–2); A. Å. Jervelund, 'Nye opslagsord' (3–5); Id., 'Stregen
strøget!' (6–8); and Id., '*Postbuddet, publikummet* og *pyjamassen*. Dobbelt-
skrivning af konsonanter i bøjningsformer' (9–11); J. Schack,
'Ændringer i opslagsords staveform eller ordform' (12–17); and Id.,
'Ændringer i Retskrivningsreglerne' (18–20). The changes to spellings
and word forms are listed on pp. 21–23.

Among new dictionaries are: *Supplement til Ordbog over det danske
Sprog*, 4, ed. Henrik Andersson et al., Det Danske Sprog- og
Litteraturselskab–Gyldendal, 1492 cols. *Politikens Engelsk-Dansk
Idiomordbog*, ed. Gitte Hou Olsen, Politiken, 394 pp. *Politikens Etymolo-
gisk Ordbog. Danske ords historie*, ed. Jan Katlev, Politiken, 2000, 698 pp.
Politikens lille danske ordbog, ed. Pia Jarvad, Politiken, 179 pp. *Politikens
Retskrivningsordbog*, ed. Vibeke Appel et al., Politiken, 557 pp. + CD-
ROM. *Politikens Øresundsordbog*, ed. Jonny Sjöberg, Politiken, 2000,
125 pp. *Retskrivningsordbog*, ed. Jens Axelsen et al., Gyldendal, 752 pp.
Ordsprogsordbog. Dansk-Engelsk — Engelsk-Dansk, ed. Else Barlach, Gad,
219 pp. *Engelsk-Dansk/Dansk-Engelsk Ordbog*, Gyldendal, 904 pp. *Fork.
Ordbog. Fork., SMS-beskeder og Smileys i én bog*, ed. Christian Becker-
Christensen and Susanne Keiding, Politiken, 210 pp. *Bevingede Ord &
Aforismer. En citatordbog*, ed. Joachim Bo Bramsen, Politiken, 496 pp.
Institutionsnavne — dansk-engelsk, ed. W. Glyn Jones, Arne Juul, and
Jens Axelsen, Gyldendal, 243 pp. *Russisk-dansk Erhvervsordbog*, ed. Joel
Nordborg Nielsen and Galina Starikova, Akademisk Forlag, 120 pp.
Kirsten Rask, *Sprogrenserordbog — tal dansk!*, Hestnes, 2000, 47 pp.
Morten Thing, *Forsøg til en lille personlig jødisk ordbog* (Skriftserie for
Roskilde Universitetsbibliotek, 33), Roskilde Univ. Library, 2000,
106 pp. *LexicoNordica*, 8, ed. Henning Bergenholtz and Sven-Göran

Malmgren, Oslo, Nordisk forening for leksikografi i samarbeit med Nordisk språkråd, 313 pp. E. Hjorth, 'Åben, implicit og skjult normering i ordbogsarbejde', *Sprog i Norden*, Novus, 137–50.

Robin Allan, Philip Holmes, and Tom Lundskær-Nielsen, *Danish. An Essential Grammar*, London, Routledge, 2000, 200 pp., is a condensed version of the same authors' *Danish: A Comprehensive Grammar* (see *YWMLS*, 57:933), but with an extra chapter on pronunciation. Much shorter and very simple presentations are Ane Børup, Ulrik Hvilshøj, and Bolette Rud. Pallesen, *Dansk Basisgrammatik*, Gyldendal, 2000, 88 pp.; and Lis Hedelund, **Korrekt sprog og rigtige kommaer — nødtørftig grammatik for opgaveskrivere*, Roskilde U.P., 66 pp. A major new work of Danish grammar from a functional perspective is Ole Togeby, *Fungerer denne sætning? Funktionel dansk sproglære*, I-III, IV, V, 5 vols in 3, Aarhus U.P., 111, 212, 333 pp. **Ældres og yngres sprog: sprog eller barriere?*, Ældre-Forum, 2000, 41 pp., includes J. Lund, 'Sprog — en ledsager gennem tilværelsen' (10–15); and L. Brink, 'Kommunikationsproblemer mellem generationer' (16–26). J. Gabrielsen, 'Hvad er Topik? — et udblik over topikkens *retoriske* funktioner', *Sprint*, 22–33. D. Rasmussen, 'Teenageres persuasive strategier', *Rhetorica Scandinavica*, 13, 2000:45–61.

Hermes, 27, focuses on the theme of business rhetoric and contains the following articles: H. Nørreklit and C. K. de Wit, 'Sustainable communication practices in management control — are body and mind in conflict or convention?' (9–29); P. H. Andersen and A. E. Nielsen, 'Making friends with your money? A semiotic analysis of relationship communication strategies in the financial sector' (31–53); F. Frandsen and W. Johansen, 'The rhetoric of green hotels' (55–83); H. Hermann, 'Kommunikativ adfærd i virksomhedsrepræsentationer' (139–71); A. Grinsted, 'The discursive organization of research interviews' (173–92). J. Scheuer, 'Ledelsesmæssige idealer og sproglig virkelighed i medarbejdersamtaler', *Tidsskrift for Arbejdsliv*, 4:27–48; Id., 'Rytmisk tale og kaskaderespons — om dialogisk prosodi i en medarbejdersamtale', *Danske Talesprog*, no. 2:1–26. Knut Aspegren et al., **Basisbog i kommunikation med patienter og kolleger*, Munksgaard, 2000, 156 pp. Carol Henriksen, *Modeller for kommunikation og public relations*, Roskilde U.P., 90 pp. **Den kommunikerende organisation*, ed. Anne Katrine Lund and Helle Petersen, Samfundslitteratur, 2000, 167 pp. Mie Femø Nielsen, *Replik til journalistikken — mikroanalyse af medieinterviewet*. Akademisk Forlag, 270 pp. **Profil og offentlighed — pr for viderekomne*, ed. Mie Femø Nielsen, Samfundslitteratur, 373 pp. Kirsten Wandahl, **Skriv på dansk*, Akademisk, 2000, 100 pp. Ellen Bak Åndahl and Susanne Nonboe Jacobsen, **Skriv og bliv læst*, Børsen, 2000, 327 pp.

5. Onomastics

Peder Gammeltoft, *The Place-Name Element Old Norse 'bólstaðr' in the North Atlantic Area* (Navnestudier, 38), Institut for Navneforskning–C. A. Reitzel, 349 pp. Bent Jørgensen, *Stednavne i Vestsjællands Amt. Slagelse, Korsør, Skælskør, Slagelse Herred, Vester Flakkebjerg Herred, Øster Flakkebjerg Herred* (Danmarks Stednavne, 24), Institut for Navneforskning–C. A. Reitzel, 251 pp. Bent Jørgensen, Birgitte Brinkmann Thomasen, and Anita Mai Agerup, *Vejledning i retskrivning af vejnavne*, Dansk Sprognævn, 16 pp. B. Jørgensen, 'Stednavne i 2000', *Nyt fra Sprognævnet*, no. 1:4–5. Georg Søndergaard, *Danske for- og efternavne. Betydning. Oprindelse. Udbredelse*, Askholm, 2000, 344 pp.

LITERATURE

By JENS LOHFERT JØRGENSEN, *Lecturer in Danish, Department of German and Nordic Studies, The University of Iceland*

(This survey covers the years 1995–2001)

1. GENERAL

J. Erslev Andersen, 'En gestikulerende anonymos — Antagelser om modernisme, modus og modernitet', *Fest. Sørensen*, 203–20. Sune Auken, *Eftermæle. En studie i dansk dødedigtning fra Anders Arrebo til Søren Ulrik Thomsen*, Museum Tusculanum, Univ. of Copenhagen, 1998, 239 pp. Lise Christensen and Robert Zola Christensen, *Snylteren — Temporalitet og narrativ struktur i vandrehistorien*, Museum Tusculanum, Univ. of Copenhagen, 232 pp., is the first major academic work on urban myths in Denmark. It discusses the relationship between temporal variables and the narrative structure of this special genre of narration. In the first part of the book, the authors elaborate a theoretical model of three temporal variables, which is, in the second part, used to analyse a particular urban myth in 11 variables, thereby showing the stylistic, literary effects of certain linguistic choices of the narrators. P. Dahlerup, 'New Literarity. Betragtninger over litteraturhistoriegenren', *KKKK*, 92:95–108.

Dansk Forfatterleksikon. Biografier, ed. John Chr. Jørgensen, Rosinante, xvii + 599 pp., contains 800 biographical articles on Danish authors and is remarkable for its inclusion of a number of young authors as well as Faroese and Greenlandic authors. Each article concludes with a list of the author's most important works and the most important criticism on him/her. *Dansk forfatterleksikon. Værker*, ed. John Chr. Jørgensen, Rosinante, xv + 307 pp., is the first companion to Danish literature to be published. It includes *c.* 500 articles on single Danish, Faroese, and Greenlandic works from the 13th c. until the present day, and discusses their structure, themes, and genre as well as the critical response to them. Gads Forlag has published a number of literary introductions, works of reference, and companions in recent years, e.g. Johannes Fibiger and Gerd Lütken, *Litteraturens veje*, 1996, 472 pp., which is an outstanding introduction to Danish literary history; *Litteraturens tilgange — metodiske angrebsvinkler*, ed. Johannes Fibiger, Gerd Lütken, and Niels Mølgaard, 559 pp.; and Henrik Rasmussen, Kamilla Hygum Jacobsen, and Jeanne Berman Camara, *Gads litteraturleksikon*, 1999, 351 pp.

Per Krogh Hansen, *Karakterens rolle. Aspekter af en litterær karakterologi* (Skrifter for Center for Æstetik og Logik, 6), Medusa, 2000, 300 pp., is an attempt to place the role of the character centrally in literary theories orientated towards formal, functional, and structural aspects of texts. H. argues that these theories have neglected character and proposes a literary 'characterology', a methodology to analyse the role of the character. J. H. C. Jensen, 'Antropomorfismens reversibilitet. Perception og tekstualitet i lyrikken', *KKKK*, 91 : 49–64. An earlier issue of the same journal, 89, 2000, contains official opposition and opposition *ex auditorio* to Jørgen Holmgaard's doctoral thesis *Teoriens topik* by M. Pahuus, S. Kjørup, and O. Christensen, and H.'s responses to these. The discussion between H. and Kjørup continues in the subsequent volume, which also includes articles about literary topoi, e.g. S. A. Svenstrup, 'Gotiske steder. Fysiske, fænomenologiske og litterære rum i den gotiske tradition' (97–111), and K. Esmann Knudsen, 'Lysthuset. Haven som formidler af et indre rum' (113–28).

Læsninger i dansk litteratur, vols 1–5, ed. Poul Schmidt et al., Odense U.P., 1998–99, includes 103 new interpretations of Danish literary classics. Malan Marnersdóttir, *Analyser af færøsk litteratur*, ed. Jens Cramer, Århus, Modtryk, 175 pp., contains an overview of Faroese literary history and eight articles on central periods, authors and their works in Faroese literature, e.g. William Heinesen's *Tårnet ved verdens ende* and Gunnar Hoydal's *Stjernerne over Andes*. Niels Martinov, *Litterære ismer fra romantik til postmodernisme og magisk realisme*, Århus, Systime, 1998, 76 pp., is an overview of the most important literary movements in Denmark from romanticism onwards. Gemzøe, *Metafiktion*, is important as the first extensive theoretical work on metafiction in Denmark. In 11 articles, the contributors define metafiction theoretically, analyse the role it plays in literary, theatrical, and cinematic examples and investigate the relationship between metafiction and modernism. Throughout, the book focuses on the way in which metafiction is revealed through self reflection. The volume includes A. Gemzøe, B. Timm Knudsen, and G. Larsen, 'Om metafiktion' (9–28), A. Gemzøe, 'Metafiktionens mangfoldighed' (29–50), G. Larsen, 'Lille metafiktionsstudie. Om udsigelse og subjekt i metafiktion' (51–74), P. Stein Larsen, 'O nitroglycerin! Apostrofiske former i ny dansk lyrik' (171–98), and C. Falkenstrøm, 'Meta her og der. Om litterær selvrefleksion og ekspressionistisk lyrik' (199–219).

Erik A. Nielsen and Svend Skriver, *Dansk litterær Analyse*, Akademisk Forlag, DR Multimedie, 2000, 340 pp., is an introduction to interpretation at university level. The book is a revised version of the 1990 *Livsbilleder — om digtningens udtryksformer* I-II, updated with text examples and literary theories from the 1990s. It consists of introductory chapters on method and interpretation, and main chapters on the interpretation of epic, lyric, and dramatic texts. The last part of the book is an anthology of text examples. Furthermore, *Om Litteraturanalyse*, ed. Lis Møller, Århus, Systime, 1999, viii + 267 pp., is an introduction to interpretation at university level, including chapters covering analysis of theme, line of action, narration, figurative language, and form and prosody. Lars Ole Sauerberg, *Litteraturviden-skaben siden nykritikken. En kort introduktion*, Odense U.P., 2000, 185 pp., presents the movements in literary theory since New Criticism, during which time the field has gone through an explosive development, i.e. structuralism, reader-response theory, deconstruction, discourse theory, cultural studies, new historicism, post-structural psychoanalytical theory, gender studies, and postcolonial studies. C. Sestoft, 'Tekst og kontekst i litteraturhistorien eller litteratur som distinkt historisk praksis, *KKKK*, 92 : 109–22.

Et Spring ind i et Billede. Johannes V. Jensens mytedigtning, ed. Aage Jørgensen and Anders Thyrring Andersen, Odense U.P., 2000, 206 pp. *Heimur skáldsögunnar*, ed. Ástráður Eysteinsson, Reykjavik, Bókmenntafræðistofnun Háskóla Íslands, 342 pp. *Romanticism in Theory*, ed. Lis Møller and Marie-Louise Svane, Aarhus U.P., 272 pp. *Rudolf Broby-Johansen — en central outsider i det 20. århundrede*, ed. Olav Harsløf, Museum Tusculanum, 2000, 343 pp.

2. The Middle Ages

Ole Bruhn, *Tekstualisering. Bidrag til en litterær antropologi*, Aarhus U.P., 1999, 227 pp.

SAXO GRAMMATICUS. In *Tolv principper hos Saxo — en tolkning af Danernes Bedrifter*, Multivers, 1999, 358 pp., Sigurd Kværndrup, in contradiction to the tradition, maintains that Saxo based the first 12 of the 16 books of the *Gesta Danorum* on 12 'core ideas', i.e. symbolical principles for human thought and development, and for ethical action. Each core idea penetrates a single book, with the result that all 12 take on a character of unity, which brings *Gesta Danorum* close to being an allegorical novel.

3. The Seventeenth Century

Charlotte Appel, *Læsning og bogmarked i 1600-tallets Danmark* (Danish Humanist Texts and Studies, 23), Det Kongelige Bibliotek, Museum Tusculanum, 1009 pp., discusses the extent to which the Danish people had the possibility to read printed texts, and which types of texts were available in the 17th c., a time when the typographical medium was relatively new. It includes an investigation of the Danish people's ability to read and write, of the publishing industry in the 17th c., and of specific popular genres and works. Kim Lembek, *Den danske litterære verssatire 1652–1742 og dens europæiske baggrund* (Studier fra Sprog og Oltidsforskning, 333), Museum Tusculanum, Univ. of Copenhagen, 1999, 150 pp.

4. The Eighteenth Century

1700–tallets litterære kultur, ed. Frits Andersen, Ole Birklund Andersen, and Per Dahl, Aarhus U.P., 1999, 231 pp.

BRORSON, H. A.   Anne Marie Petersen, *Kom min due. Hans Adolph Brorson og hans salmer* (OUSSLL, 44), 2000, 128 pp., deals with the contradiction between the Lutheran conception of a merciful God and the inexorable demands of Pietism in B.'s psalms, considered in relation to his life and his age.

5. The Nineteenth Century

Flemming Conrad, *Smagen og det nationale. Studier i dansk litteraturhistorie-skrivning 1800–1861*, Museum Tusculanum, Univ. of Copenhagen, 1996, 480 pp.

ANDERSEN, H. C.   J. Bøggild, 'Det er ikke ramme alvor med den ramme — H. C. Andersens *Tante Tandpine*', *Fest. Sørensen*, 179–202. P. Christensen, 'Tand for tunge', *ib.* 253–78. Marie Davidsen, *Havde man ikke vor Herre, saa havde man Ingenting!* (OUSSLL, 41), 2000, 125 pp., sees A.'s fairy tales and stories as an opposition to contemporary life philosophy as it finds expression in the romantic novel of self discovery. This opposition reveals itself through a focus on the moment at the expense of extension in and of time, a focus that either fragments and collapses meaning or has the character of a sudden and meaningful change, i.e. a miracle.

BLICHER, ST. ST.   J. Bøggild, 'Fortællingens røde tråd — en læsning af St. St. Blichers Hosekræmmeren', *Spring*, 17: 175–93.

CLAUSSEN, S.   Dan Ringgaard's doctoral thesis *Den poetiske lækage. Sophus Claussens lyrik, rejsebøger og essayistik*, Museum Tusculanum, Univ. of Copenhagen, 2000, 536 pp., is an exploration of C.'s poetry in particular, which appears to be organized in three phases, i.e. the poetry of the 18th c., the poetry of the turn of the c., and the late work. These three phases are regarded as representing three general types of poetry and also three different poetic responses to what Ringgaard names 'the poetic leakage'. The poetic leakage is an aporia throughout C.'s work. On the one hand, his poems, with their rounded perfection, strove towards autonomy; on the other hand, this autonomy was constantly disturbed by the external world, partly because language refers to the external world, and partly due to C.'s interest in this world. The poetic leakage is one of Ringgaard's sources of fascination in *Den poetiske lækage*, which is a renewal of modern C. criticism, in part because he examines not only what the poems mean, but also how they mean it.

JACOBSEN, J. P.   J. Lohfert Jørgensen, 'Neikvæð færni í Frú Maríu Grubbe eftir J. P. Jacobsen', pp. 194–205 of *Heimur skáldsögunnar*, ed. Ástráður Eysteinsson, Reykjavik, Bókmenntafræðistofnun Háskóla Íslands, 342 pp. C. Madsen, *Om læsning. Kierkegaard, Kafka, Mallarmé og Jacobsen* (Afhandlinger fra Aarhus Univ.) Aarhus U.P., 1995, 200 pp. includes an interpretation of J.'s poem 'Arabesk til en Haandtegning af Michel Angelo' (122–84). Erik Østerud, *Theatrical and Narrative Space. Studies in Strindberg, Ibsen and J.P. Jacobsen*, Aarhus U.P. 1998, 152 pp., includes an interpretation of J.'s short story 'Mogens' (101–34).

KIERKEGAARD, S.   J. Elbek, 'Søren Kierkegaards acedia', *Spring*, 17 : 143–54. J. B. Jensen, 'Samtidigheden er det afgørende — om Søren Kierkegaards religiøsitet og dens konsekvenser', *ib.*, 132–42. *Romanticism in Theory*, ed. Lis Møller and Marie-Louise Svane, Aarhus U.P., 272 pp., approaches the question of romanticism and theory from different angles grouped under three headings: language and semiotics; image, imagery, imagination; and the Romantic Other. It includes, in addition to other contributions, I. W. Holm, 'The overgrown space: Romantic imagination and arabesque in Søren Kierkegaard's *The Concept of Irony*' (165–74). Pia Søltoft, *Svimmelhedens etik — om forholdet mellem den enkelte og den anden hos Buber, Lévinas og især Kierkegaard*, Søren Kierkegaard Forskningscenteret, G.E.C. Gads, 2000, 399 pp., discusses the ethics of K. based on the thesis that there is a strong correlation between the subject's relationship to him- or herself and to another, and between subjectivity and intersubjectivity in K.'s work, and is written against a perception of the fundamental solitude of the subjective in K.'s philosophy.

STUCKENBERG, V. AND I.   In *Afstandens mellemværende. Iscenesættelsens former hos Ingeborg og Viggo Stuckenberg og hos Vilhelm Hammershøi*, Odense U.P., 159 pp., Malene Rehr explores the love life of the Stuckenbergs as a conflict between soul and body, immortality and mortality, idealized perfection and reality in relation to the staging of love in their works. In the second part of the book, Rehr discusses the relationship between the Stuckenbergs transfiguration of love into art and the paintings of the contemporary artist Vilhelm Hammershøi.

6.   THE TWENTIETH CENTURY

50 years after the publication of the first edition of *Danske digtere i det 20. århundrede*, Gads Forlag and the Univ. of Southern Denmark are publishing a new edition in three volumes with new articles on the most important Danish authors of the 20th c. So far, vol. II, *Fra Morten*

Nielsen til Hans-Jørgen Nielsen. 'Virkelighedens udfordring'. *Dansk litteraur i perioden fra 1940–70*, 2000, 635 pp., and vol. III, *Fra Kirsten Thorup til Christina Hesselholdt*. *'Det formelle gennembrud.'*. *Dansk litteratur i perioden 1970–2000*, 664 pp., have been published. Jakob Hansen, *Litterære verdensbilleder. Menneske og natur hos Solvej Balle, Merete Pryds Helle og Niels Lyngsø*, Museum Tusculanum, Univ. of Copenhagen, 2000, 111 pp., is an investigation into the relationship between man and nature in Solvej Balle's *Ifølge loven*, Merete Pryds Helle's *Vandpest* and *Men Jorden står til evig tid*, and Niels Lyngsø's long poem 'STOF'. Hansen argues that the focus in these works is not existential but physiological and biological. This is revealed through the composition of the works, which appears as a model of the relationship between man and nature.

BALLE, S.   M. Ping Huang, 'Vendingens latter', *Passage*, 34, 2000:84–87, an issue devoted to humour.

BJELKE, H.   H. O. Jørgensen, 'Bjelke med omgivelser', *Passage*, 37:45–47, an issue devoted to the avant-garde.

BLIXEN, K.   Dag Heede, *Det Umenneskelige. Analyser af seksualitet, køn og identitet hos Karen Blixen* (OUSSLL, 48), 258 pp., is a new reading of B.'s work, which is seen as creating a fundamentally dehumanized universe that deconstructs traditional human 'master narratives' such as sexuality, gender, and identity, using 'queer', parodic, inverted, and exaggerated effects. In his provocative and inspirational book, Heede argues that the focus on B.'s life is due to criticism's inability to confront this dehumanization, which he regards as an undiscovered potential of the work. L. Hvarregaard, 'Fuglar í eigin líkkistum. Sagan Gestaboð Babette eftir Karen Blixen lesin með gleraugum sálgreiningarinnar', pp. 221–28 of *Heimur skáldsögunnar*, ed. Ástráður Eysteinsson, Reykjavik, Bókmenntafræðistofnun Háskóla Íslands, 342 pp. L. H. Kjældgaard, 'Genkendelsens gåde. 'Anagnorisis' i Karen Blixens "Alkmene" ', *Spring*, 17:155–74.

BOBERG, T.   M. Vinding, 'Glemslens erindring — om Thomas Bobergs *Sølvtråden* og rejsebogsgenren', *Spring*, 17:66–77.

BROBY-JOHANSEN, R.   *Rudolf Broby-Johansen — en central outsider i det 20. århundrede*, ed. Olav Harsløf, Museum Tusculanum, 2000, 343 pp., was published on the 100th anniversary of B.'s birth and portrays his influence on the fields of literature, painting, film criticism, politics, and the teaching of art. Among its nine articles are O. Harsløf, 'Myten om Broby' (11–41), and F. Klysner, 'Digteren Broby — mellem romantik og revolution' (102–33).

ERIKSEN, J. M.   J. Eriksen-Benrós, 'I magtens vertigo: parallelise-ring og forgrening i Jens-Martin Eriksens *Vinter ved daggry*', *Spring*, 17:89–103.

GROTRIAN, S. S. Iversen, 'Den gale vej? Sammenhænge og sammenfald i Simon Grotrians digtning', *Spring*, 17:50–58.

GRØNDAHL, J. C. P. Krogh Hansen, 'Prinsesser, prinser og prostituerede. M.s.h.p. J. C. Grøndahls kunst(ige) eventyr *Stilheden i glas*', Gemzøe, *Metafiktion*, 97–115. C. Krogholm Kristiansen, ' "Tynget af modernisme og melankoli" — Jens Chr. Grøndahls vej baglæns ud af modernismen', *ib.*, 117–41.

HANSEN, B. HR. N. Frydenbjerg Elf, 'Ét med avantgarden. Bo hr. Hansens fortsatte leg med et overstået fænomen', *Passage*, 37:55–65.

HEINESEN, W. B. Hansen, ' "et spring ind i et billede". William Heinesen — en moderne hjemstavnsfortæller', *Spring*, 17:194–208.

HELLE, M. PRYDS. M. Ping Huang, ' "Det er vandets vej" — en lyd af verden', *Passage*, 35, 2000:5–11, an issue devoted to the audial aspects of texts.

HESSELHOLDT, C. H. E. Breisnes, 'At kalde kærlighed for fisk & hjerte for hjerte — om Christina Hesselholdts trilogi, *Det enestående*', *Spring*, 17:78–88.

HØJHOLT, P. L. Bukdahl, 'Son of Per — Højholts personalefest: Kom som du i hvert fald ikke er!', *Passage*, 39:71–79. S. Hjerkegaard, 'Digtets nedsmeltning, lighedens afgrund — om Per Højholts digt "Tiltale" ', *Spring*, 17:43–49. C. Madsen, 'Poetisk erfaring som aberration og affirmation — Mallarmé, Friedrich og Højholt', *Fest. Sørensen*, 47–66. J. Smærup Sørensen, L. Bukdahl, and C. Dorph, 'Højttaler — holdt! Et stereofonisk Arena-interview med Per Højholt 1976 og 1999', *Passage*, 36, 2000:5–45, is a remarkable double interview over 23 years with the author.

JENSEN, J. V. *Et Spring ind i et Billede. Johannes V. Jensens mytedigtning*, ed. Aage Jørgensen and Anders Thyrring Andersen, Odense U.P., 2000, 206 pp., discusses through nine articles the nature of what J. characterized as 'myths', i.e. a short narrative form which he used throughout his work and defined in various — mutually contradictory — ways. A *leitmotif* in the articles is the viewpoint that the myths of J. are at one and the same time an expression of an experience of modernism and an attempt to come to an agreement with modernity. The book includes E. M. Christensen, 'Mytebegrebet i historisk antropologisk oversigt' (11–27); I. Holk, 'Johannes V. Jensen og mytismen. Bidrag til en ny genre- og stilhistorie' (69–80); F. Harrits, 'Et Spring ind i et Billede. Om Johannes V. Jensens mytedigtning belyst ud fra "Fusijama" og "Det røde Træ" ' (81–96); A. Gemzøe, 'Springets poetik. Mytens metamorfose' (139–60); and P. Bager, 'Kongens Fald: roman og myter' (161–88). F. Harrits, 'Fragilitas. Omkring Johannes V. Jensens "Vinternat"', *Fest. Sørensen*, 119–34. Steen Klitgård Povlsen, *Dødens værk. Fem kapitler om døden i moderne litteratur, litteraturteori og psykoanalyse*, Aarhus U.P., 2000, 476 pp., is an interpretation of the theme of death in a number of modernistic texts, inspired by poststructuralist psychoanalytical theory. Povlsen argues that there is a parallel between modernism and psychoanlysis, in that they both deal with fundamental experiences of loss, both offer an attempt to heal the loss through the use of language, and both fail to complete this healing. Through this thesis, Povlsen interprets, among other works, Johannes V. Jensen's *Kongens Fald*.

JUUL, P.   L. Korsbek, 'sagde jeg, siger jeg. Udsigelsen og den lyriske stemme hos Pia Juul', *Spring*, 17 : 26–42. L. Wedell Pape, 'Den omvendte verden. Turneringer i Pia Juuls *En død mands nys*', *Fest. Sørensen*, 221–33.

KNUTZON, L.   Birgitte Hesselaa, *Vi lever i en tid — Line Knutzons dramatik*, Borgens, 239 pp., is the first book on the works of the leading dramatist of the new generation of Danish dramatists. Positing the thesis that there is a correlation between Knutzon's innovations on stage and the development of modern society, H., through analyses of Knutzon's dramaturgy, character building, style, and dialogue, reveals recurrent themes in the work.

LARSEN, T.   S. Baggesen, 'Thøger Larsens italienske rejse', *Fest. Sørensen*, 303–24.

LAUGESEN, P.   A. Abildgaard Nielsen, 'Bladet fra munden. Om tekst, stemme og musik hos Peter Laugesen', *Passage*, 35, 2000 : 88–99.

LLAMBÍAS, P. H.   M. Holst, ' "Jeg hænger på en herreløs hest" — en dialog med Pablo Henrik Llambias', *Spring* 17 : 9–25. C. K. Kristiansen, 'Ustedets poetik. Pablo Henrik Llambías' *Rådhus*', *KKKK*, 90, 2000 : 35–52.

MADSEN, S. Å.   Anker Gemzøe, M*etamorfoser i Mellemtiden. Studier i Svend Åge Madsens forfatterskab 1962–1986* (Skrifter for Center for Æstetik og Logik. Aalborg Universitet, 3), Medusa, 1997, 563 pp.

MICHAEL, I.   Kristian Himmelstrup, *Den udødelige soldat og jeg. Ib Michael og hans forfatterskab*, Museum Tusculanum, Univ. of Copenhagen, 199 pp., is a guide to the versatile writings of M. It includes a biography, a reading of the six coherent phases in M.'s writing, and a discussion of the main characteristics of his work, e.g. the combining of opposite or different sources of inspiration, carnivalism and magic realism, and of the major themes, e.g. death and immortality, identity and the lack of the same.

NORDBRANDT, H.   T. Buchard, 'Guldpokalen mine herrer: om Henrik Nordbrandts digtning i kontrast til Thomas Bredsdorffs læsning, *Spring*, 17 : 122–131.

RIFBJERG, K.   P. Rye Hansen, 'Den "skandaløse" bevidsthed. Om psykoanalyse, agoni og allegori i Klaus Rifbjergs novelle "Bevidstheden" ', *KKKK*, 89, 2000 : 9–32.

SEEBERG, P.   Peter Vejrum, *Som et firben i solen. En undersøgelse af Peter Seebergs eftersøgning 1946–1999* (OUSSLL, 43), 2000, 117 pp., is an examination of S.'s work, which is described as a search based on a contradiction between nihilism and spirit. It is Vejrum's thesis that this contradiction has been maintained throughout the work and that development in S.'s writing has only been of an aesthetic nature.

THOMSEN, S. U.   D. Ringgaard, 'Poesien er ambulant — Poesi, form og svigtende modernisme i Søren Ulrik Thomsens digte', *Fest. Sørensen*, 93–117. *Spring*, 16, is devoted to T. and includes 20 articles covering all aspects of his work, including S. Auken and S. Skriver, 'Receptionen af Søren Ulrik Thomsens forfatterskab 1981–2000' (15–24), J. Erslev Andersen, 'Hjemfaldenhed og metafysik. om Søren Ulrik Thomsens *Hjemfalden*' (70–79), F. Stjernfelt, 'Ca. 15 formale aspekter i Søren Ulrik Thomsens digte' (121–35), and M. Stidsen, 'Thomsen mellem modernisme og postmodernisme' (137–49).

ØRNSBO, J.   S. H. Larsen, 'Metaforikken i Jess Ørnsbos *Tidebogen*', *Spring*, 17:59–65.

IV. NORWEGIAN STUDIES*

LANGUAGE

POSTPONED

LITERATURE SINCE THE REFORMATION

By ØYSTEIN ROTTEM, *Cand. phil., Copenhagen*

1. GENERAL

The primary objective of Per Thomas Andersen, *Norsk litteraturhistorie*, Universitetsforlaget, 614 pp., is to satisfy the need for a modern textbook for university students at first degree level, a literary history which encompasses Norwegian literature as a whole. In that regard the work fully answers the purpose. The book is handy, insightful, and well-written. The broad historical lines are drawn in a way that make them easy to follow, and the presentation of particular works and writers provides on several occasions new insights with respect to the themes treated. The presentations of old Norse literature and the period of baroque writing are the best parts, but good care is also taken of later periods. The work can also be recommended to advanced students, teachers, and university professors as well as non-academic readers.

2. THE SIXTEENTH TO THE NINETEENTH CENTURIES

INDIVIDUAL AUTHORS

DASS, P.   J. Haarberg, 'Den filologiske kommentar som litteraturvitenskapelig praksis. Og en kommentabel passasje hos Petter Dass', *Edda*, 269–79.

HOLBERG, L.   Lars Roar Langslet, *Den store ensomme. En biografi om Ludvig Holberg*, Press, 502 pp., presents a broad and many-facetted picture of the 'father of Danish-Norwegian literature'. Langslet describes H. as a lonely genius and tries to explain why he became such an asocial person. The intellectual endeavours and achievements of H. form, however, the main interest of Langslet. Like most others he regards the comedies as H.'s *chef d'oeuvre*, but in his biography he also seeks to upgrade other parts of H.'s work. Of special interest is his discussion of the political philosophy of H. In contrast to many others Langslet tends to regard H. as a rather conservative person.

---

* The place of publication of books is Oslo unless otherwise stated.

PRAM, CHR. Rolf Nyboe Nettum, *Christen Pram. Norges første romanforfatter*, Aschehoug, 223 pp., is an insightful and meticulous presentation of Pram's life and work. Pram played an important part in the intellectual life of his time, and this is the first book where his influence is fully recognized.

3. THE NINETEENTH CENTURY

INDIVIDUAL AUTHORS

ANDERSEN, T. S. Tingvold, 'Tryggve Andersen — sjel og samfunn i forfall', *Bøygen*, no. 4:30–34.

ASBJØRNSEN, P. CHR. Truls Gjefsen, *Peter Christen Asbjørnsen — '. . . diger og folkesæl'*, Andresen & Butenschøn, 483 pp., is a traditional biography where the tensions and conflicts in A.'s life and thought are given considerable attention. Most people know him only as the collector of Norwegian folk tales, but he was also concerned with many other matters, which G.'s biography covers, and A.'s strong fascination for folk tales is also explained.

BJØRNSON, B. K. Imerslund, 'Bjørnson og folkehøgskolen', *SS*, no. 2:68–77.

COLLETT, C. O. A. Kvamme, 'Tragedien i *Amtmandens Døttre*', *Bokvennen*, no. 2:38–43.

DYBFEST, A. O. Opstad, 'Syk kjærlighet — tanker om Arne Dybfests forfatterskap', *Bøygen*, no. 4:36–39.

GARBORG, A. *Norskrift*, 102, is devoted to the study of the writings of Garborg and contains the following articles: I. Aarstein, 'Tekstrevisjon i *Den burtkomne faderen*' (5–26); Ø. B. Haaland, 'Kristelig dekadanse i Arne Garborgs *Fred*' (27–55); E. Bjørhusdal, 'Ironi og ideologi i Arne Garborgs litteraturkritikk' (56–72); A. Skaret, 'Kristendomsbilde i to Arne Garborg-romanar. Ei samanlikning av Daniel Brauts og Gabriel Grams kristendomsoppfatning' (73–88); M. Vikingstad, 'Natur, erotisme og identitet i Arne Garborgs *Haugtussa*' (89–104); S. E. Karlsen, 'Ironi og intensjon i *Bondestudentar* og *Trætte mænd* — En sammenlikning' (105–28); U. Leirvåg, 'Arne Garborgs Kolbotnbrev og Knudaheibrev. Ei samanlikning av forteljeteknikk og tematikk' (129–46). J. Hellesnes, 'Garborg og Nietzsche', *NLÅ*, 17–23. S. Time, 'Om Garborg som polemikar', *ib.*, 24–44. M. Vikestad, 'Naturen i Arne Garborgs *Haugtussa*. Til 150-årsdagen for Arne Garborg', *Bokvennen*, no. 1:52–60. A. Solheim, 'Garborg og Tolstoj — og global etikk', *Samtiden*, no. 2:11–15. S. Time, 'Det nasjonale og det allmenne — om Arne Garborgs språk- og kulturfilosofi', *Mål og makt*, no. 1:4–11.

HAMSUN, K. Lars Frode Larsen: *Radikaleren. Hamsun ved gjennombruddet 1888–1891*, Schibsted, 544 pp., is a very well-documented study of the literary and political ideas of Hamsun at the time of his literary breakthrough. L. maintains that Hamsun looked upon himself as a radical writer who wished to promote the ideas of the liberal party Venstre. Although he argues his case convincingly he seems to overestimate the author's political commitments as compared to his literary goals. Debatable is also his definition of *Hunger* as an autobiographical work, and not as a novel, as which it is normally regarded. Harald S. Næss, *Knut Hamsuns brev. Supplementsbind*, Gyldendal, 327 pp. S. von Schnurbein, 'Failed seductions. Crises of masculinity in Knut Hamsun's *Pan* and Knut Faldbakken's *Glahn*', *ScSt*, 73:147–64. N. Rønhede, 'Pan. Af Løjtnant Thomas Glahns Papirer. Uden for Genre', *Edda*, 315–23. M. Žagar, 'Imagining the redskinned other. Hamsun's article "Fra en Indianerleir" (1885)', *ib.*, 385–95. M. Humpál, 'Den åpne avslutningen i Knut Hamsuns *Mysterier*', *NLÅ*, 45–51. K. M. Lindbach, 'Kulturelle identiteter i Hamsuns *Mysterier* og deres funksjon i romanen', *Nordlit*, no. 10:109–22. J. Langdal, 'Hamsun-spørsmålet og angsten for det enkle', *SS*, no. 1:24–36. D. Kovacs, 'Acting out: comparative analyses of Romantic realism in Stephen Crane and Knut Hamsun', *Nordlit*, no 9:63–78.

HANSEN, M.   Olaf Øyslebø, *Maurits Hansen som forteller. En studie av fortellemåter, språk og stil i de første romaner fra norsk miljø etter 1814*, Solum, 236 pp.

IBSEN, H.   Tom Eide, *Ibsens dialogkunst. Etikk og eksistens i 'Når vi døde vågner'*, Universitetsforlaget, 299 pp. *Ibsen Studies*, 1.2, contains the following articles: L. Møller, 'Repetition, return and doubling in Henrik Ibsen's major prose plays' (7–31); M. P. Sandberg, 'Ibsen and mimetic home of modernity' (32–58); I.-S. Ewbank, 'Ibsen in Wonderful Copenhagen 1852' (59–78); H. K. Sødal, 'Beautiful butterfly, Agnes mine? A new interpretation of Agnes in Henrik Ibsen's *Brand*' (79–93); T. Modalsli, 'Ibsen, Bjørnson and Bernhard Dunker, 1864–66' (94–106). A. Aarseth, 'Peer Gynt and Hegel's ideas on Egyptian art', *ScSt*, 73:535–46. L. P. Wærp, 'Overgangens figurasjoner. Doktordisputas, Universitetet i Tromsø 9. desember 2000. Førsteopponent Atle Kittang. Andreopponent Lis Møller. Svar fra doktoranden', *Edda*, 144–65. A. Nærø, 'Henrik Ibsens samtidsdramatikk. Noen refleksjoner om dramatisk objektivitet', *ib.*, 176–90. H. E. Aarseth, ' "Å omkalfatre utfall og intrige." Genrerefleksjon og metafiksjon i Ibsens *Kjærlighedens komedie*', *ib.*, 294–314. S. A. Skålevåg, 'Sannheter om sinnet — Ibsen og psykiatrien', *Nytt norsk tidsskrift*, 18:261–70. A. M. Rekdal, 'Henrik Ibsen og friheten som dilemma', *ib.*, 271–81. F. Engelstad, 'Henrik Ibsen som maktutreder', *ib.*, 281–96.

JÆGER, H.   To decide whether Ketil Bjørnstad, *Jæger. En rekon-struksjon*, Aschehoug, 758 pp., is a novel or a biography is no easy task, but for the most part the novelist Bjørnstad keeps to facts. The book is well-documented and presents a rather flattering picture of Jæger.

KROHG, CHR.   H. Fjørtoft, 'Idolatri og impresjonisme i Christian Krohgs *Albertine*', *Motskrift*, no. 2:47–55.

LIE, J.   Per Mæleng, *Marginalia. Feminiteten som undertekst. En litteraturvitenskapelig avhandling om Jonas Lies roman 'Familien på Gilje. Et interiør fra firtiårene' (1883)*, Trondheim, Norges teknisk-naturvitenskapelige Universitet, 265 pp.

VINJE, A. O.   In Olav Vesaas, *Å. O. Vinje. Ein tankens hærmann*, Cappelen, 523 pp., the picture of Vinje as an ironical man full of paradoxes is strengthened. Moreover, Vesaas describes him as a man who enjoyed rather than disliked making enemies. As a whole this is a very fine biography, written by a man born in the same district as Vinje.

WERGELAND, H.   H. O. Andersen, 'Wergelands stake', *SS*, no. 2:56–60.

AANRUD, H.   K. Imerslund, 'Harmonisk realisme? Om Hans Aanruds fortellinger', *NLÅ*, 52–67.

4. THE TWENTIETH CENTURY

GENERAL.   Jahn Thon, *Refleksjon — kritikk — protest. Forståelsesformer i unglitterære tidsskrifter: Heretica, Rondo og Profil*, Det historisk-filosofiske fakultet, Oslo Univ., 421 pp. B. Markussen, 'Romanens rom. Teoretiske perspektiver med eksempler fra Jarvoll, Kjærstad, Ørstavik og Lønn', *Edda*, 70–84. H. H. Wærp, ' "Det er jo bare Ord": Prosadikt i Norge, 1890–2000', *Norsk Litteraturvitenskapelig Tidsskrift*, no. 1:27–38. A. Dvergsdal, 'Om dramateksten som sådan — og om nyere norsk dramatikk i bokform', *Nordica Bergensia*, 24:67–86. J. Sejersted, 'Emnets poetiske Brugbarhed. Politisk lyrikk, noen innfall og les-ninger', *ib.*, 123–55. E. Vassenden, 'Spørsmålet om kraft. To slags billeddannelse i litteraturen', *Vagant*, no. 2–3:8–17, is a critical survey of the art of constructing images in modern Norwegian poetry and prose fiction. P. K. Hansen, ' ". . . i en eim av HB og sur rullings." En litterær turists ferieberetning fra de norske randområder', *ib.*, 29–37, deals with the 'dirty realism' of modern writers like Jonny Halberg, Kyrre Andreassen, and Frode Grytten.

INDIVIDUAL AUTHORS

ASKILDSEN, K.   H. Bache-Wiig, 'Thomas F. — en klok gammel gubbe? Billedvegring og billedbegjær i en novelle av Kjell Askildsen', *Norsk Litteraturvitenskapelig Tidsskrift*, no. 1:59–67.

BJØRNEBOE, J.   Sven K. Bjørneboe, *Onkel Jens. Et familieportrett av Jens Bjørneboe*, Aschehoug, 159 pp.

BREKKE, P.   Most of the articles in *Lenkede fugler som evig letter. Om Paal Brekkes forfatterskap*, ed. Ole Karlsen, LNU–Cappelen, 308 pp., are based on lectures given at the yearly poetry seminar in Flisa. The contributions are as follows: I. Stegane, 'Paal Brekke og den norske modernismen' (31–36); P. S. Larsen, 'Paal Brekke — moment til ei lyrikkhistorisk plassering' (37–62); T. Seiler, '*Som tror vi seirer ved å glemme* — Hukommelsens poetiske og politiske funksjon i Paal Brekkes lyriske forfatterskap' (63–83); A. Linneberg, ' "Krigen kom til oss. Det hendte oss bare." Avbrytelsens estetikk hos Paul Virilio og Paal Brekke' (84–106); Ø. Rottem, 'APOKALYPSE NÅ? — En lesning av diktsamlingen *Løft min krone, vind fra intet* som postkatastrofisk samtidskommentar og metapoetisk stunt' (107–122); A. G. Lombnæs, 'Modernitet og mening hos Arnulf Øverland og Paal Brekke' (123–35); M. Borkenhagen, ' "Ja vi skal våkne, vi vil ikke våkne." Om oppvåkningsmotivet i *Roerne fra Itaka*' (136–52); S. S. Karlsen, 'Dikt i kontekst: en lesning av "Der alle stier taper seg" ' (153–75); O. Karlsen, 'Paal Brekke og sonetten' (176–97); S. Jarvoll, 'En gjenlesning av Paal Brekkes *Det skjeve smil i rosa*' (198–211); I. Havnevik, 'Først og sist i Paal Brekkes lyriske forfatterskap' (212–34); S. Furuseth, ' "En forfriskende gjennomtrekk i den poetiske stuelummerhet"; Erling Christie leser Paal Brekke' (235–51); J. M. Steinveg, 'Krigen, eksilet — og Paal Brekkes roman *Aldrende Orfeus*' (252–70); H. H. Wærp, ' "*Don't touch me!*" — Paal Brekkes Indiareise' (271–89).

BRYNILDSEN, AA.   V. Roddvik, 'Aasmund Brynildsen og mystikken i Østkirken', *Dyade*, no. 1 : 12–31.

BØGE, K.   E. Stokke, 'Om kvinnespråkets problem i Karin Bøges roman *For alt jeg vet*', *NLÅ*, 139–48.

CHRISTENSEN, L. S.   Kåre Kverndokken, *Lars Saabye Christensen. Et forfatterskap*, Gyldendal, 72 pp.

DAHLE, G.   S. von der Poll, 'Apen som evangelist? Gro Dahles *Apens evangelium* i lys av 90–talls litteraturen i Norge', *TsSk*, no. 1 : 109–26.

FALKBERGET, J.   O. Nygaard, 'Historien som ideologi. Johan Falkbergets *Nattens brød*', *Dyade*, no. 1 : 2–10.

FOSSE, J.   L. Sætre, 'On the terms of words: masks of a Christian life', *Scandinavica*, 40 : 285–99. Id., 'Modernitet og heimløyse. Det moderne dramaets ironi: form og tematikk i *Namnet* av Jon Fosse', *NLÅ*, 149–78. A. Korpalska, ' "Det må vere enkelt og djupt, for å seie det dumt" ', *Nordica Bergensia*, 25 : 167–77.

GRIEG, N.   A. G. Bentzen, 'Fra Møhlenpris til Moskva. Nordahl Griegs vei til kommunismen', *Historisk tidsskrift*, 80 : 199–229.

GRYTTEN, F.   E. K. Narvhus, 'Ei bikube uten dronning. Estetiske og tematiske trekk i Frode Gryttens *Bikubesong*', *Norsklæraren*, no. 2 : 18–25.

GRØNDAHL, C.   I. Stegane, 'Cathrine Grøndahls lyrikk', *Nordica Bergensia*, 24 : 89–98.

GUNDERSEN, G. B.   J. Bjøndal, 'Fra diktingen er det ingen redning. Betraktninger omkring Gunnar Bull Gundersens modernistiske prosjekt', *Bøygen*, no. 4 : 40–44.

HAUGE, A.   Jan Inge Sørbø, *Angen av bork og ein brennande einerbusk. Om Alfred Hauges forfattarskap*, Gyldendal, 190 pp., is an insightful monograph on H.'s work which shows in a balanced and informative way the close relations between the writer's life and work.

HAUGE, O. H.   Ole Karlsen, *Fansmakt og bergsval dom. En studie i Olav H. Hauges romantiske metapoesi*. Doktordisputas ved Universitetet i Oslo 20. mai 2000. Førsteopponent Idar Stegane. Andreopponent Katherine Hanson. Svar fra opponenten', *Nordica Bergensia*, 25 : 200–49.

HOEL, S.   A. Schmeling, 'Vertrauen — Verrat — Verantwortung. Zeitkomposition und Aussage in Sigurd Hoels Roman "Møte ved milepelen"', *Nordica*, 18 : 185–213. A.-K. Skardhamar, 'Barneskildringer i nordisk litteratur i 1920– og 30–åra, med utgangspunkt i Pär Lagerkvist: *Gäst hos verkligheten* og Sigurd Hoel: *Veien til verdens ende*', *NLÅ*, 68–87.

HOFMO, G.   U. Langås, 'Gunvor Hofmo and Orphic inspiration', *Scandinavica*, 40 : 97–111. S. Furuseth, 'Versifikasjon og litterær betydning. En drøfting med utgangspunkt i Gunvor Hofmos lyrikk', *Motskrift*, no. 2 : 47–55.

JONSSON, T.   J. O. Gatland, 'The problem with "the other" in the poetry of Tor Jonsson', *Scandinavica*, 40 : 113–29. A. Säll, 'Vid tillvarons gräns. Om Tor Jonsson', *Horisont*, no. 1 : 34–39.

KITTELSEN, E.   L. Sætre, 'Det moderne som oppgåve hos Erling Kittelsen', *Prosopopeia*, no. 1 : 36–42.

KJÆRSTAD, J.   Bjarne Markussen, *Romanens optikk. En studie i Jan Kjærstads Rand og Svein Jarvolls 'En australiareise'*, Bergen U.P., 335 pp. Ø. Rottem, 'Romanen som fortelling og konstruksjon. Strøtanker om Jan Kjærstads poetikk', *Nordica Bergensia*, 24 : 39–46. H. H. Skei, 'Jan Kjærstads Wergeland-trilogi. Frå Samarkand til Lambaréné', *NLÅ*, 9–16.

KROG, H.   E. Tjønneland, 'Individualisert erindring i Helge Krogs essayistikk', *Nordica Bergensia*, 25 : 179–99.

LARSEN, G.   Randi Bård Størmer, *Gunnar Larsen*, Gyldendal, 452 pp.

LOE, E.   E. Tjønneland, 'Naiviteten i Erlend Loes *Naiv. Super. Regresjon eller estetisk utopi?*', *Edda*, 85–94. G. Bø, 'Erlend Loe — lattermild opprører', *Nordica Bergensia*, 24 : 47–66. E. S. Tønnesen,

'Dannelsesprosjekt i to generasjoner. En krysslesning av Dag Solstad og Erlend Loe', *NLÅ*, 121–38.

MELLI, A.   L. R. Waage, 'Å komme på kant med Vårherre — Analyse av en eksemplarisk novelle: *Tilfeldighetsmorderen* av Aleksander Melli', *Nordica Bergensia*, 24:25–38.

MYKLE, A.   Leif Johan Larsen, *Mønsteret og meningen. Agnar Mykles romaner om Ask Burlefot* (doctoral thesis), Trondheim, Norges teknisknaturvitenskapelige Universitet, 505 pp. R. Fuglestad, '"Å holde universet i sin hånd." Lykke og død i Agnar Mykles novelle "Apollon og Jahve"', *NLÅ*, 109–20.

SANDEMOSE, A.   K. A. Øverby, 'Aksel Sandemoses mesterverk. *Varulven*, en modernistisk roman?', *Bokvennen*, no. 3:42–49.

SOLSTAD, D.   Jan H. Landro, *Jeg er ikke ironisk. (Samtaler med Dag Solstad)*, Pax, 199 pp. T. Haugen, 'I tegnenes rike. Dekadente mønstre i Solstads forfatterskap', *Edda*, 48–69. E. Tjønneland, 'Meningstapet i Dag Solstads *Professor Andersens natt*: konflikten mellom eksistens og historiefilosofi', *Nordica Bergensia*, 24:99–122. S. Malkenes, 'Dag Solstad og fotball', *Vinduet*, no. 1:56–60. K. A. Nyhus, 'Tomhet, ensomhet og meningsbegjær. Dag Solstads forfatterskap med utgangspunkt i romanen *T. Singer*', *Prismet*, no. 4:144–49. A.-C. Aksnes, 'Fanget av bildet — Dag Solstads *Irr! Grønt!*', *Agora*, no. 2–3:218–42. K. Barfod, 'Solstad & Nielsen', *Spring*, København, no. 17:104–16.

VESAAS, T.   F. Hermundsgård, 'Tarjei Vesaas and German Expressionist theater', *ScSt*, 73:125–46. B. Ekern, 'Rytme, klang og polyfoni i Tarjei Vesaas' *Brannen*. Musikalsk komposisjon og estetikk i moderne litteratur', *Edda*, 324–34.

VOLD, J. E.   H. H. Wærp, '"Virkeligheten, den dusjen". Jan Erik Vold gjennom fire tiår', *Nordlit*, no. 9:97–130.

VAA, A.   Leif Mæhle, '*Fann eg dei stigar . . .*'. *Vandringar i Aslaug Vaas dikting*, Aschehoug, 206 pp.

ØRSTAVIK, H.   C. Hamm, 'Tåreperse eller språkkritikk? Hanne Ørstavik og den ukjente kvinnens melodrama', *Vagant*, no. 2–3:41–47.

AAMODT, B.   H. Gujord, 'Fra kameratskap til kvantefysikk. Bjørn Aamodts lyrikk fra søttitall til nittitall', *Nordica Bergensia*, 24:5–24.

V.   SWEDISH STUDIES

POSTPONED

5

SLAVONIC LANGUAGES*

I. CZECH STUDIES

LANGUAGE

By Marie Nováková and Jana Papcunová,
Ústav pro jazyk český Akademie věd České republiky, Prague

1. General and Bibliographical

GENERAL. Corpus linguistics is again a major topic: F. Čermák, *PLS*, 44:24–27, provides a basic characterization of corpus linguistics; Id., 'Český národní korpus: stav v roce 2001', Jarošová, *Slovenčina*, 121–35, describes the synchronic and diachronic parts of the Czech National Corpus; M. Křen, 'Český národní korpus — počítačové demonstrace', *ib.*, 136–41, brings further details on work with the corpus; J. Kocek and M. Kopřivová, *JazA*, 38.3:106–08, present detailed information on the whole project; Z. Hladká and K. Osolsobě, *PLS*, 44:63–70, elucidate the preparation of various Czech corpora. V. Dovalil, *SaS*, 62:176–84, deals with the language norm and varieties in the language, R. Blatná, Hladká, *Čeština*, III, 233–41, is on the relationship between the language variety and the language system, F. Daneš, *ib.*, 37–47, discusses changes in Czech during the process of globalization, and J. Kořenský, 'Čeština a čas', *ib.*, 65–72, is on the changes of means of expression. M. Šipková, *PLS*, 44:136–42, refers to the causes of differences between the norm of standard and common Czech; J. Panevová, *Termina 2000*, 40–47, comments on the so-called grammar-checker and its usage. Both the collective work of Anna Černá, Ivana Svobodová, Josef Šimandl, and Ludmila Uhlířová, *Na co se nás často ptáte: ze zkušeností jazykové poradny*, Prague, Scientia, 168 pp., and Jaroslava Hlavsová, *Čeština bez chyb: 333 slov, v nichž se často chybuje*, Prague, Víkend, 95 pp., provide information on how to avoid making mistakes in Czech. The collective volumes *Konec a začátek v jazyce a literatuře*, ed. Dobrava Moldanová, Marie Čechová, Josef Peřina, and Zora Millerová, Ústí nad Labem, Univ. J. E. Purkyně, 378 pp., *Naše a cizí v interetnické a interpersonální jazykové komunikaci*, ed. Irena Bogoczová, Jaroslav

---

* For languages using the Cyrillic alphabet names are transliterated according to the Library of Congress system, omitting diacritics and ligatures.

Hubáček, and Hana Srpová, Ostrava, Ostravská Univ., 326 pp., and *Čeština —jazyk slovanský*, ed. Pavlína Kuldanová and Ivana Gejgušová, Ostrava, Ostravská Univ., 152 pp., comprise a great number of contributions covering a wide spectrum of linguistic themes from grammar, word formation, and lexicology to stylistics, sociolinguistics, dialectology, language contacts, semantics, and pragmatics.

BIBLIOGRAPHIES. *Bibliografie české lingvistiky 1995*, compiled by Jana Papcunová and Alena Nejedlá, Prague, Ústav pro jazyk český AV ČR, 229 pp., continues in the series of linguistic bibliographies (the last one published in 1994, see *YWMLS*, 56:1005) and contains 1049 entries on Czech. Marie Nováková, *Bibliografie české onomastiky 1997–1998*, *Prague*, Ústav pro jazyk český AV ČR, 60 pp. (282 entries on the Czech onomastics). A personal bibliography of Adolf Erhart has appeared in *Erhart Vol.*, 14–23 (for the years 1951–2000) and of Vladimír Šaur in *SPFFPSU-D*, 1:10–22, covering the years 1960–98.

2. HISTORY OF THE LANGUAGE

A monograph by Naděžda Kvítková, *Staročeský text z kvantitativního hlediska*, Prague, Charles Univ., 124 pp., describes the processing of a word-frequency dictionary of *Staročeská kronika tak řečeného Dalimila* by means of a quantitative method. K. Kučera, 'The development of entropy and redundancy in Czech from the 13th to the 20th century: is there a linguistic arrow of time?', pp. 153–62 of *Text as a Linguistic Paradigm: Levels, Constituents, Constructs. Festschrift in honour of Luděk Hřebíček*, ed. Ludmila Uhlířová, Gejza Wimmer, Gabriel Altmann, and Reinhard Köhler, Trier, Wissenschaftlicher Vlg, 312 pp., presents the results of an experiment oriented on changes in entropy and redundancy of graphemes and phonemes. Id., *ČDS*, 9:78–81, comments on the building of a diachronic corpus on similar material from seven centuries and on the possibilities of its use for general study of the Czech vocabulary; L. Zimová, Hladká, *Čeština*, III, 299–310, analyses economy as a specific feature in grammars of the 16th and 17th cs; V. Koblížek, *Termina 2000*, 68–72, focuses on baroque medical terminology; A. Černá, *JazA*, 38.3:7–13, is on the vocabulary of medicine in *Slovník česko-latinský* (from 1562) by Tomáš Rešel; Z. Braunšteinová, *ib.*, 14–19, analyses Old Czech compounds with the first component *prvo-*; M. Vajdlová, *ib.*, 20–24, writes on verbal compounds in Old Czech; A. Stich, *Souvislosti*, 12:111–23, deals with the language of Šimon Lomnický z Budče; E. Pallasová, *PLS*, 44:116–20, writes on the Old Czech compound words in the *Hlaholská bible* from the 14th c.; B. Vykypěl, *ib.*, 162–72, discusses the expression *slečna* in Czech of 14th–17th cs; and M. Homolková, *Slavia*, 70:357–60, the Old Czech word *žizn*.

3. Phonetics and Phonology

V. Mistrová, *Čeština*, 11:107–08, is on problems of intonation in the case of lengthened vowels in final sentence position; I. Pavelková, *JazA*, 38.4:78–83, discusses the glottal stop in Czech, and M. Krčmová, Witosz, *Stylistyka*, 261–67, studies differences in acoustic segmentation of a non-official discourse.

4. Morphology and Word Formation

K. Gutschmidt, Hladká, *Čeština*, III, 107–15, examines the voice of a verb in Czech at the end of the 19th c. (on Slavonic background); K. Pala and I. Kopeček, *ib.*, 207–13, define basic types of syllabic segments and the system of morphological and phonological segmentation; J. Šimandl, *ib.*, 265–75, is on the main features of contemporary Czech morphology, especially the adaptation of loan words; P. Mareš, *PLS*, 44:58–64, deals with the questions of Czech declension and conjugation; O. Uličný, *ib.*, 89–94, compares standard and substandard functions of some morphological devices in Czech; J. Panevová, *ib.*, 81–88, covers reflexive pronouns in Czech; P. Karlík, *ib.*, 93–98, investigates morphosyntactic attributes of modal phasal verbs; K. Oliva, *SaS*, 62:200–07, and M. Komárek, *ib.*, 208–09, discuss the relationship of reflexive verbs and the structure of a sentence; N. Utěšená, *SPFFPSU-D*, 1:112–31, sketches some problems of verbs changing from one verb class to an other; M. Šulc, *JazA*, 38.3:117–28, elucidates animate -*a* in the acc. sg. of inanimate masculines; J. Mravinacová, *ib.*, 76–81, follows the problem cases of morphological adaptation of Anglicisms. Several articles in *ČDS*, 9, are based on material from the Czech National Corpus: J. Klímová (6–8) on derivation of diminutives; U. Lisowska (48–49) on gender variation in loan words; V. Petkevič (60–73) on morphological tagging of the Czech National Corpus. D. Hlaváčková, *SaS*, 62:62–70, is on the same topic, but based on material from spoken Czech in the region of Brno; M. Zuková, *NŘ*, 84:81–89, pays attention to word formation, namely of compound neologisms.

5. Syntax and Text

Hladká, *Čeština*, III, includes a number of studies concerned with syntactic themes: L. Uhlířová (29–35) on clitics in Czech on Slavonic background; J. Toman (73–79) on the position of clitics (based on a study by Václav Ertl from 1924); A. Svoboda (81–86) on clitics from the viewpoint of the functional perspective of an utterance; J. Bártová (99–106) on types of tautological constructions; P. Kosta (117–38) on

sentence negation in Czech; N. Nübler (147–53) on the valency of
the subject in Czech sentences; J. Panevová and V. Řezníčková
(139–46) analyse some positions of valency members of four Czech
verbs (*číst, prodávat, mluvit, předělávat*); K. Oliva jr. (163–72) on word
order; M. Straňáková-Lopatková (183–95) on some types of syntactic
homonymy; V. Petkevič (197–205) on nonprojective constructions in
Czech from the viewpoint of an automatic morphological disambigu-
ation of Czech texts; and E. Hajičová (173–81) on syntactic research
of the Czech National Corpus. J. Hoffmannová, *NŘ*, 84:113–20,
writes on the syntax of institutional dialogues from the pragmatic
viewpoint; J. Bártová, *ib.*, 121–25, on structures of the form *A is A*
(e.g. *hra je hra*) and their functions, meaning, and use; M. Jelínek,
Termina 2000, 48–53, deals with functions and types of syntactic
condenser in special texts; I. Kolářová, *SPFFPSU-D*, 1:137–46,
analyses some types of questions containing the verb *myslet*; B. Bedna-
říková, *ib.*, 132–36, focuses on the so-called third syntactical plane;
and M. Martinková, *LPr*, 11:16–28, analyses topic-focus articulation
in three different translations of the novel *A Farewell to Arms* by Ernest
Hemingway.

6. ORTHOGRAPHY

H. Tešnar, *SPFFPSU-D*, 1:95–111, discusses changes in Czech
orthography in the first half of the 19th c.; J. Šimandl, *ČDS*, 9:30–32,
draws attention to writing of capital letters in connection with the
internet, and M. Hrdlička, *Češtinǎř*, 11:110–11, analyses the *M/mloci*
in the novel by Karel Čapek from the orthographic point of view.

7. LEXICOLOGY AND PHRASEOLOGY

Jiří Rejzek, *Český etymologický slovník*, Voznice, Leda, 752 pp., is a
modern etymological dictionary focused on the common vocabulary.
F. Esvan, Hladká, *Čeština*, III, 155–61, discusses some pecularities of
the Czech *verba videndi*; F. Čermák, *ib.*, 223–32, writes on the types of
lexical combinations in Czech; K. Komárek, *NŘ*, 84:253–60,
investigates the vocabulary of the Czech bibles from the 20th c.;
M. Křístek, *PLS*, 44:102–07, is on the vocabulary of present-day
Czech from the stylistic point of view; B. Junková, Witosz, *Stylistyka*,
287–95, classifies lexical devices of Czech journalism according to
their origin; K. Pala, Jarošová, *Slovenčina*, 155–67, writes on the
building of the Czech lexical database for a new modern dictionary
of Czech; P. Smrž, *ib.*, 168–80, on the storage and processing of
electronic dictionaries; D. Svobodová, *ČJL*, 51:170–78, on loan
words (especially Anglicisms) in Czech; Z. Opavská, *JazA*,

38.3:54–58, on the processing of *nomina actoris* in monolingual dictionaries; P. Šmídová, *ib.*, 59–65, on hybrid compounds in Czech with the first component *mini-*; D. Svobodová, *ib.*, 70–75, on the adaptation of loan words from English; Z. Tichá, *ib.*, 82–86, on some tendencies in the new vocabulary; and L. Janovec, *ib.*, 93–97, on phraseologisms in present-day Czech. Contemporary Czech lexicology and lexicography also pay a great attention to the building of the Czech National Corpus: M. Šulc, *SaS*, 62:53–61, discusses the thematic point and representativeness of the Czech corpus; R. Blatná, *ČDS*, 9:8–9, is on phrasemes and variants of set phrases; M. Kopřivová, *ib.*, 19–21, on names composed of the noun *země* + *genitive of the noun* (e.g. *země tulipánů* = *Nizozemí*); F. Čermák, *ib.*, 27–30, on the meaning of the expression *konference*; R. Blatná, *ib.*, 32–35, on the meaning of the word *kočkopes* and its frequency; and P. Smetáková, *ib.*, 54–56, on the word *střecha* and its meanings.

Another comprehensive volume is *Termina 2000*, which comprises materials from two terminological conferences: J. Kraus (59–62) sums up the questions of special language and terminology in connection with the changes of the language situation at the end of the 20th c., and Id. (185–88) investigates terminology as a part of the national language and concentrates on borrowing of terms and their word formation; F. Čermák (31–36) on overlapping of terms and phrasemes (based on Czech botanic terms); O. Martincová (54–58) on Czech terminological norms; J. Damborský (96–99) on loanwords in Czech and Polish terminology; V. Holubová (157–60) on determinologization in Czech; R. Kocourek (196–203) on terminological Anglicisms and their characterization; M. Jelínek (204–11) on verbo-nominalization in special texts; A. Jaklová (277–80) on the relationship between terminology and slang expressions; in addition, there are many contributions concerning terminology in individual disciplines: Z. Kavková (93–95, body building); P. Loucká (131–34, natural sciences); L. Hums (135–37, economics); J. Bachmannová (144–46, folk terminology of bead making); J. Světlá (147–50, travel); J. Hubáček (166–68, administration); S. Machová (212–15, linguistics); I. Bozděchová (216–22, the European Union); J. Rambousek (244–50, geodesy); J. Bartošek (251–60, journalism); M. Grygerková (271–76, the church); M. Mlčoch (308–12, sports journalism). F. Stícha, *NŘ*, 84:126–32, writes on music terms in Czech.

8. SEMANTICS AND PRAGMATICS

F. Stícha, Hladká, *Čeština*, III, 87–97, follows the semantics of the identifiers *ten*, *tento* (based on material from the Czech National

Corpus); M. Hirschová, *ib.*, 243–49, is on the obscurity of the utterance content vs. the obscurity of its communicative function; J. Hoffmannová, *ib.*, 251–58, points out the specific properties of Czech verbal play; L Uhlířová, *ib.*, 215–21, deals with universal and specific features of electronic communication by the Language Service in the Czech Language Institute, and also, *NŘ*, 84:1–15, comments on basic features of electronic correspondence; J. Hoffmannová, *PLS*, 44:46–57, analyses various types of institutional dialogues (at the doctor's, in an old people's home or communication between students); she also, Gajda, *Złota*, 157–63, investigates both conflict and humorous communication in the Czech Parliament; M. Čechová, *ib.*, 55–62, draws attention to intertextuality as a condition of a successful communication; A. Jurman, *SaS*, 62:185–99, discusses the semantics of address and manifestations of politeness in present-day Czech and gives the results of a questionnaire investigation in Prague; M. Lašťovičková, *JazA*, 38.4:37–44, criticizes feminist suggestions on forms of address to God; L. Rejmánková, *Češtinář*, 11:129–36, writes on interactive and language competence; Z. Léblová, *JazA*, 38.1–2:5–17, on conflict dialogues in family communication. The collective volume *Obraz světa v jazyce: Sborník z 27. ročníku česko-polské meziuniverzitní konference v Praze 2000*, ed. Irena Vaňková, Prague, Charles Univ., 161 pp., contains several essays on Czech semantics and pragmatics: R. Blatná, 'K sémantice slova barva' (29–36); R. Myslivečková, A. Hudáková, and P. Vysuček, 'Barvy v českém znakovém jazyce' (63–77); J. Šlédrová, 'Mělký a plytký v češtině' (78–87); L. Římalová, 'Silný a slabý v češtině' (88–95); I. Nebeská, 'Některé mentální predikáty' (96–105); K. Skwarska, 'Tykání a jeho zdvořilejší protějšek v češtině' (137–45) (in comparison with Polish); similarly also J. Hoffmannová, 'Diskurz, dialog, konverzace: mezi stylistikou a pragmatikou', Witosz, *Stylistyka*, 23–31; O. Müllerová, 'Styl rozhlasového dialogu s hostem — mezi institucionální a soukromou komunikací', *ib.*, 268–77; A. Jaklová, 'První čechoamerická periodika z hlediska pragmatického', *ib.*, 278–86.

9.   Sociolinguistics and Dialectology

sociolinguistics. J. Valdrová, *Sociologický časopis*, 37:183–205, analyses the media projection of gender and in *NŘ*, 84:90–96, investigates newspaper headlines from the gender viewpoint; J. Nekvapil, *PLS*, 44:65–80, is on relationship of language management and an ethnic community in the Czech Republic; A. Macurová, *SaS*, 62:92–104, on sign language of the Czech deaf and dumb from the sociolinguistic point of view. L. Hašová, 'Zur Verwendung des

Ethnonyms der Tscheche/die Tschechen in Fernsehdiskussionen', pp. 108–13 of *Beiträge der Europäischen Slavistischen Linguistik: Polyslav*, vol. 4, ed. Katharina Böttger, Sabine Dönninghaus, and Robert Marzari, Munich, Sagner, 292 pp., is on the creation of a Czech ethnic stereotype; she also writes on code mixing in Czech, *JazA*, 38.4:52–57.

DIALECTOLOGY. S. Kloferová, *NŘ*, 84:171–74, focuses on the umlaut *ae* and its manifestations in the *Český jazykový atlas*; P. Jančák, *ib.*, 175–83, offers a characterization of Czech-Moravian and Czech-Silesian opposites in vocabulary; L. Čižmárová, *ib.*, 206–12, is on the dialectal morphology of a collective name of family; V. Šaur, Hladká, *Čeština*, III, 343–47, endeavours to find an answer (on the basis of Moravian dialectal material) to the question of whether dialects really die; Z. Holub, *Výběr*, 38:1–31, is on the South Bohemian dialect of Doudleby; Z. Hlubinková, *NŘ*, 84:199–201, on word formation of deadjectival words in East Moravian dialects; M. Ireinová, *ib.*, 202–05, analyses adjectival forms in common speech in the city of Jindřichův Hradec; G. Balowska, pp. 107–22 of *Studia nad współczesnymi językami i literaturami południowo- i zachodniosłowiańskimi*, ed. Władysław Lubaś, Mieczysław Balowski, Opole, Uniw. Opolski, 181 pp., deals with the semantics of the verb *czekać* in the works of Óndra Łysohorský; I. Bogoczová and M. Bortliczková, *ib.*, 91–106, discuss Czech-Polish dialects.

Luděk Bachmann, *Nářečí na Vysokomýtsku*, ed. Jarmila Bachmannová, Prague, Academia, 201 pp., describes and analyses the East Bohemian dialect in the second half of the 20th c. Zdeňka Sochová, *Lašská slovní zásoba*, Prague, Academia, 302 pp., presents a detailed analysis of the dialectal vocabulary. Silvestr Kazmíř, *Slovník valašského nářečí*, Vsetín, Malina, 517 pp., compiles a dictionary of Moravian-Wallachian dialect and also gives a survey of the grammar; and Josef Fabián, *Slovník nespisovného jazyka valaského*, Valašské Meziříčí, Valašské Athény, 133 pp., also collects Wallachian proverbs and idioms. Ivana Šmejdová, *Malý slovník krkonošských názvů*, Prague, Olympia, 166 pp., is a dictionary of dialectal geographical names.

SLANG. Zdeňka Tichá and Luboš Skopec, *Tři slangové slovníky*, Prague, Karolinum, 156 pp., contains dictionaries of sport, chess, and motor sport slang. Aleš Launer, *Slangové výrazy pro drogy: Anglicko-český výkladový slovník*, Prague, Academia, 164 pp., compiles Czech slang vocabulary of drugs with English equivalents. D. Svobodová, Hladká, *Čeština*, III, 291–98 analyses Anglicisms in Czech slang of graffiti writers, skateboarders, modern music lovers, and players of computer games.

A noteworthy work by Miroslav Červenka, *Dějiny českého volného verše*, Brno, Host, 248 pp., discusses the principle of rhythm in free verse and gives a characterization of Czech free verse from symbolism to the present day. František Všetička, *Tektonika textu*, Olomouc, Votobia, 269 pp., is devoted to the composition structure of Czech prose of the 1930s. N. Bermel, *NŘ*, 84:16–30, describes dialogues in modern Czech fiction; R. Blatná, *SaS*, 62:1–22, applies a mathematical and statistical approach to the analysis of the verse of Ivan Blatný; M. Těšitelová, *ib.*, 81–91, is a quantitative analysis of fiction, specifically of direct speech; S. Čmejrková, *PLS*, 44:28–45, investigates language and stylistic devices in advertising texts; P. Kaderka, *JazA*, 38.4:5–12, aims at revealing what is text, context, and discourse; V. Pfeffer, *SPFFPSU-D*, 1:161–63, defines the language of trivial (minor) literature; L. Binar, *ib.*, 164–71, sums up basic opinions and characterizations of present-day journalistic style; Z. Hladká, *NŘ*, 84:225–34, deals with the style of personal correspondence; M. Červenka and K. Sgallová, *ČL*, 49:254–81, investigate accentual rhythm in the most important Czech 19th-c. folk song collections; S. Bělánková, *Čeština*, 12:33–43, brings a characterization of the so-called photonovel; S. Pastyřík, *ib.*, analyses the language and style of the litany to St Zdislava by V. Fišerová.

    ASPECTS OF THE LANGUAGE OF INDIVIDUAL WRITERS. K. Dvořák, *ČJL*, 51:123–31, on the language of Karel Čapek; C. Maglione, *NŘ*, 84:74–80, on the language of stories of Petr Šabach; M. Jelínek, *PLS*, 44:74–89, on the style of dramatic texts of Václav Havel; J. Svobodová, *JazA*, 38.4:119–31, on the language in works of Jáchym Topol; M. Grygar, *Poláčkův Vol.*, 185–95, M. Křístek, *ib.*, 207–17, and P. Mareš, *ib.*, 218–25, analyse language, style, and multilingualism in the works of Karel Poláček; F. Všetička, *Stylistyka*, 10:443–49, writes on composition and style in *Hostinec U kamenného stolu* by Karel Poláček; I. Kolářová, *ib.*, 451–59, on sources of lexical humour in *Čisté radosti mého života* by Jan Šmíd. Jaroslava Janáčková et al., *Řeč dopisů, řeč v dopisech Boženy Němcové*, Prague, ISV, 198 pp., focus on the style of letters written by the authoress.

AOn, 41–42, contains contributions by L. Olivová-Nezbedová, 'Čeština a pomístní jména' (123–37); J. David, 'Několik poznámek k toponymům odvozeným z apelativ kobyla a kůň na území Čech' (34–42); P. Štěpán, 'Sufixy –nda a –anda v toponymii Čech' (203–15); J. Matúšová, 'Vztah toponym ze sbírky pomístních jmen v Čechách k řemeslné výrobě' (110–20); J. Malenínská, 'K úvahám o

metaforických přenosech v toponymii — anatomické topolexémy
*líce, *čelist, *kostrč, *řitka' (105–09); J. Jiskra, 'Jména vodních toků
ve Smrčinách', 97–103; J. Domański, 'Říční jméno Stěnava a jeho
paralely' (50–62); K. Severin, 'Voštice' (143–83); E. Michálek, 'K
staročeským biblickým překladům hebrejského Golgota a latinského
Calvaria' (121–22); S. Pastyřík, 'Před lexikografickým zpracováním
hypokoristických podob rodných jmen' (138–42); L. Michálková,
'Současná tyronyma — názvy sýrů' (193–202). The festschrift *Vlastní
jména v mluvnicích češtiny a v tradicích českého mluvnictví: Sborník k jubileu
Rudolfa Šrámka*, ed. Helena Kneselová and Ivana Kolářová, Brno,
Masaryk Univ., 67 pp., contains: M. Knappová, 'K dnešnímu stavu
české antroponomastiky' (9–16); P. Hauser, 'Vlastní jména v
příručních mluvnicích českého jazyka' (17–29); N. Kvítková, 'Antro-
ponyma v Dalimilově kronice' (39–44); J. Bartošek, 'Pojmenování
Česko — téma století' (57–62); S. Kloferová, 'Vlastní jména v
Českém jazykovém atlase' (63–64).

M. Vondrová and V. Blažek, Hladká, *Čeština*, III, 311–42, study
Slavonic archaisms and dialectal features in the toponymy of
Bohemia; L. Olivová-Nezbedová, pp. 76–80 of *Umělecká reflexe krajiny:
Tvář naší země - krajina domova*, vol. 4, Lomnice nad Popelkou, 83 pp.,
writes on minor place names as an evidence of the past of the country;
I. Lutterer, *ib.*, 81–93, is on the relationship of Czech toponyms to
human beings and nature. S. Pastyřík, *Češtinář*, 11:65–71, is on
compound names from the time of Magna Moravia, and also, *ib.*,
12:3–6, on the borrowing of first names from foreign languages and
their adaptation in the Czech language system; B. Prouzová, *ib.*,
43–46, analyses Czech hypocorisms; J. Abou el-Seoud, *NŘ*,
84:31–37, compares Czech and Arabic personal names; M. Harvalík,
JazA, 38.3:25–33, tries to define the correlation between minor place
names and common nouns; J. David, *ib.*, 34–39, is on folk etymology
and vulgarisms in Czech toponyms; I. Kolářová, *ib.*, 40–45, on a type
of chrematonyms (e.g. *Univerzita Pardubice*).

12. LANGUAGES IN CONTACT AND COMPARATIVE STUDIES

F. Uher, *ČJL*, 51:11–19, is on language globalization and on the
position of Czech in this process; J. Nekvapil, *Češtinář*, 11:72–84,
analyses interpersonal behaviour in an international company;
B. Karlssonová, pp. 125–28 of *Emigrace a exil jako způsob života*, ed.
Stanislav Brouček, Karel Hrubý, and Antonín Měšťan, Prague,
Karolinum, 193 pp., discusses bilingual education (Czech-Swedish)
in a family; L. Veselovská, Hladká, *Čeština*, III, 11–27, analyses Czech
derived nominals and English gerunds; M. Reslová, *JazA*,
38.3:148–53, is on the ways of expressing the English perfect in

Czech. D. Šlosar and M. Nekula, pp. 105–09 and 152–58 respectively, of *Češi a Němci: Dějiny — kultura — politika*, ed. Walter Koschmal,
Marek Nekula, and Joachim Rogall, Prague, Paseka, 473 pp., are
devoted to Czech-German language contacts and to Czech-German
bilingualism; J. Jodas, *ČMF*, 93:81–88, studies Bohemianisms in the
German speech of the city of Olomouc in the 1930s; Id., *SPFFPSU-
D*, 1:172–79, analyses Germanisms in several Czech dictionaries;
G. Engelhardt, *NŘ*, 84:235–44, follows Czech and German purism
and compares them. M. Sládková, *LPr*, 11:29–38, compares verbal
aspect in Czech and French. G. Neščimenko, Hladká, *Čeština*, III,
277–89, compares the language of Czech and Russian journalism;
S. Žaža, *Erhart Vol.*, 226–32, is on the functions of the verb *dát/dat'* in
Czech and Russian; Id., *SPFFPSU-D*, 1:55–64, on Czech equivalents
of the Russian adverbal infinitive; V. Šaur, *ib.*, 81–85, on relationships
between the standard language and dialects (a Czech-Bulgarian
comparison); I. Bogoczová, *ČJL*, 52:15–19, on interference in the
speech of bilingual pupils in the Czech-Polish border area; O. Bláha,
JazA, 38.3:138–43, on the future tense in Czech, Slovak, and Upper
Sorbian.

13. CZECH ABROAD

A. Jaklová, *NŘ*, 84:245–52, analyses the language and style of the
first Czech periodicals in America at the end of the 19th c.; and in
Stylistyka, 10:151–64, she studies comicality in contemporary Czech-
American periodicals; similarly, M. Šipková, *NŘ*, 84:192–98, is on
the language of the Czech-American weekly *Našinec* and on penetration of Anglicisms and Americanisms into its language. J. Bachmannová, *ib.*, 184–91, describes the condition of Czech dialects in
enclaves in Poland; G. Sokolová, *SaS*, 62:258–73, investigates the
question of mother tongue in ethnically mixed regions; M. Hádková,
Termina 2000, 304–07, describes typical features of spoken Czech
used by Vietnamese.

LITERATURE
POSTPONED

II. SLOVAK STUDIES
LANGUAGE
POSTPONED

LITERATURE
POSTPONED

III. POLISH STUDIES

LANGUAGE

By NIGEL GOTTERI, *University of Sheffield*

1. SURVEY

D. Szumska, 'Przegląd polskich prac językoznawczych z zakresu slawistyki ogłoszonych drukiem w roku 1997/98', *RicSl*, 45–46, 1998–99:265–76.

2. PHONETICS, PHONOLOGY, AND ORTHOGRAPHY

J. Rubach and G. Booij, 'Allomorphy and optimality theory: Polish iotation', *Language*, 77:26–60, argue that optimality theory 'predicts allomorphy in many [. . .] instances where lexical phonology would have cyclic rules [. . .] and has the effect of dramatically reducing the abstractness of underlying representations.' J. Rubach, 'Backness switch in Russian', *Phonology*, 17, 2000:39–64, draws brief comparisons with Ukrainian and Polish (45). P. Rutkowski, 'Wprowadzenie do fonologii generatywnej', *PJ*, no.1:12–30, takes illustrations from Polish and includes a useful bibliography (29–30). On orthography, see Z. Saloni, 'O pisowni *nie* — i może o innych sprawach', *PJ*, no.7:12–17; on punctuation, see A. Kowalska, 'O trudnościach w użyciu apostrofu w pisowni obcych nazw osobowych', *PJ*, no.4:33–41.

3. MORPHOLOGY AND WORD-FORMATION

S. Karolak, 'К вопросу о понятиях и терминах славянской аспектологии', *RLing*, 25:1–21. W. J. Sullivan and D. Bogdan, 'Tense, aspect, and the organization of Polish narrative', *Word*, 52:357–68, proposes an analysis of aspect in Polish which claims to break out of the binary mould and attempts thereby to do greater justice both to the derivational morphology of verbs and to the organization of spoken text. M. Krupa, 'Ewolucja normy w zakresie dopełniacza liczby mnogiej rzeczowników męskich miękkotematowych (na podstawie *Słownika ortoepicznego* S. Szobera i *Słownika poprawnej polszczyzny* pod red. W. Doroszewskiego)', *PJ*, no.4:22–32. M. Olejniczak, '30 lat słowotwórstwa gniazdowego (Rys historyczny)', *PJ*, no.6:15–31. A. Piotrowicz and M. Witaszek-Szymborska, 'O zestawieniach we współczesnej polszczyźnie (na przykładzie słowotwórstwa kosmetycznego)', *PJ*, 2000, no.10:34–44.

A. Szczaus, 'Funkcjonowanie słowotwórczych szeregów synonimicznych w świadomości językowej XVI-wiecznych pisarzy i leksykografów', *ib.*, 20–33. K. Waszakowa, 'Różnorodność i intensywność procesów przejmowania elementów obcych w słowotwórstwie współczesnej polszczyzny', *PJ*, no.6 : 2–14.

Zygmunt Saloni, *Czasownik polski*, Wa, WP, 256 pp., is an accessible reference work covering 12,000 verbs, and aiming to develop and extend Tokarski's 1951 *Czasowniki polskie*. Hanna Jadacka, *System słowotwórczy polszczyzny (1945–2000)*, Wa, PWN, 201 pp., claims to be the first synthesizing study of the development of the Polish word-forming system of the last half-century in the context of political developments. The chief material on which the book is based consists of neologisms (listed on pp. 169–201 and dating from 1945–64 and 1989–2000), which allow the author to trace trends in the word-forming system; among these are the increasing popularity of formations based on two stems, and a converse decline in popularity of straight suffixation.

4. Syntax

M. Gawełko, 'O roli strony biernej w polskim systemie językowym', *PJ*, 2000, no.8 : 50–59. R. Huszcza, 'Nie ma, żeby nie było — o segmentalnych wykładnikach tematyczno-rematycznej struktury zdania w polszczyźnie', *ib.*, 1–9. P. Rutkowska, 'Składnia polskich grup liczebnikowych: próba opisu formalnego', *ib.*, 10–28. M. Grochowski, 'On the word order of Polish synsyntagmatic lexemes', *SaS*, 61, 2000 : 138–44, in an interesting, if dense and breathless paper, concludes firstly that synsyntagmatic lexemes with a stable linear position precede the expression with which they enter into a syntactic connection and secondly that much work remains to be done on more subtle classifications of Polish conjunctions, particles, and adverbs.

Steven Franks and Tracy Holloway King, *A Handbook of Slavic Clitics*, New York, OUP, 2000, 424 pp., apply the methods of formal linguistics to a particularly appropriate area, and in the careful, scholarly manner for which Franks is known. Henryk Wróbel, *Gramatyka języka polskiego*, Kw, Spółka Wydawnicza "Od nowa", 335 pp., comes from one of the editor-authors of the multi-volume PAN Grammar, and draws on the experience of the writing and revision of the latter, on subsequent discussions, and on discoveries made as a result of computer implementations of its view of morphology, such as can be seen at < http : / / www.icsr.agh.edu.pl/ fleksbaz/ >. Clearly and accessibly written, the grammar covers phonetics and phonology (23–48), morphology in general (52–72), parts of speech, (73–81), inflexion (84–167), word-formation (170–218) and, in many ways the most innovative section, syntax (221–335). The great value of this volume is that it simultaneously both introduces its subject(s) at a level appropriate to Polish undergraduate linguists and distils for their teachers and older colleagues a long career of careful research, close observation, and mature and often collective reflection.

5. Lexicology and Phraseology

E. Breza, 'Wskrzeszony wyraz *sylabus*', *Polonistyka*, 54:410–11. R. Dulian, '1. *Market, hipermarket, supermarket*, czyli nowe zapożyczenia w języku polskim; 2. *Salon prasowy*, Tak czy nie!', *PJ*, no.5:75–77, finds *salon prasowy* risible. M. Łojek, 'Słownictwo homilii w świetle badań statystycznych', *PJ*, no.6:32–48. J. Mędelska and M. Marszałek, 'Twórzmy słownik "polskiego jezyka radzieckiego"', *PJ*, 2000, no.8:39–49. M. Nowak, 'Zawrotna kariera połączenia *dwa w jednym*', *PJ*, no.6:83–85. R. Ociepa, 'O współczesnych anglicyzmach w nazewnictwie zawodów i stanowisk służbowych', *ib.*, 49–55. A. Pięcińska, 'Nowe zjawiska w polskiej rzeczywistości widziane przez pryzmat języka: *sex-shop*', *PJ*, 2000, no.9:70–77; and her 'Nowe zjawiska w polskiej rzeczywistości widziane przez pryzmat języka: *grill, pager, notebook*', *PJ*, no.1:71–78, and her 'Nowe zjawiska w polskiej rzeczywistości widziane przez pryzmat języka: *fitness-club, snowboard, body, jogging, billboard*, (fachowiec od) *public relations*', *PJ*, no.2:67–76. D. Połowniak-Wawrzonek, 'Metafora POLITYKA TO WALKA ZBROJNA w polskiej frazeologii', *PJ*, no.2:4–21. M. Preyzner, 'Trudny orzech do zgryzienia. Nowa propozycja metodologiczna', *PJ*, no.4:49–50, examines reactions to contamination of and between literal and figurative expressions. J. Rejzek, 'K etymologii psl. **korenъ*', *Slavia*, 70:345–47. T. Rittel, 'Materiał historycznojęzykowy we współczesnej szacie metodologicznej (w kontekście książki Jana Ożdżyńskiego o słownictwie flisackim od XV do XVIII wieku)', *PJ*, no.5:2–16. E. Rudnicka, 'Sposoby opisu znaczeń i użyć przenośnych różnych jednostek leksykalnych w *Słowniku języka polskiego* pod red. M. Szymczaka (I)', *PJ*, no.3:2–18, and its continuation in *PJ*, no.4:5–21. T. Sudujko, 'Jednosegmentowe jednostki leksykalne o postaci *tak*', *PJ*, no.3:19–30.

6. Semantics and Pragmatics

A. Grybosiowa, 'Kilka refleksji na temat zasad (maksym) konwersacyjnych H. P. Grice'a', *PJ*, no.7:7–11. M. Łaziński, 'Pan ksiądz i inni panowie. Wtórna funkcja lekceważąca jednostki *pan*', *PJ*, 2000, no.8:29–38, and his 'Pan ksiądz i inni panowie. Wtórna funkcja lekceważąca jednostki *pan* (dokończenie)', *PJ*, 2000, no.9:19–28. M. A. Moch, 'Perswazja — wartości — wybór. O języku kampanii samorządowej 1998 roku', *PJ*, no.5:28–39. J. Nicpoń, 'Nagana jako edukacyjny akt mowy', pp. 333–38 of an issue of *Polonistyka*, 54:322–80, chiefly concerned with language and also including B. Stramek, 'Anglicyzmy w języku polskim' (347–49). E. Połubińska-Gałecka, 'Językowy obraz *ziemi* we współczesnej polszczyźnie', *PJ*, 2000, no.10:4–19, distinguishes seven or eight senses of *ziemia*. K. Sykulska, 'Kim jest bard? Współczesne rozumienie terminu', *PJ*, no.5:54–62.

7. SOCIOLINGUISTICS AND DIALECTOLOGY

M. Bugajski, 'Język polski na przełomie stuleci — uwagi o niektórych przyczynach obecnego stanu', *PJ*, no.7:1–6, finds that recent times have brought into question the appropriateness of the term *język literacki*, since the standard language is no longer principally to be found in literature; users of the term (and those who routinely use the term *literary language* in preference to *standard language* in English), may wish to point out in response that they never intended to limit their vision to the language of *literatura*, whether *piękna* or *naukowa*. M. Büthner-Zawadzka, 'Polska gwara wyścigowa', *PJ*, 2000, no.9:37–45. K. Geben, 'Kresowizmy pochodzenia białoruskiego w języku uczniów szkół polskich na Wileńszczyźnie', *ib.*, 46–61. Z. Greń, 'Socjolingwistyczne uzupełnienie i weryfikacja dialektologicznych badań arealnych (na przykładzie gwar cieszyńskich)', *SFPS*, 36, 2000:41–63; Id., 'Próba poszerzenia i weryfikacji badań językowych na Śląsku Cieszyńskim', *Slavia*, 70:11–24. A. Grybosiowa, '*Modern Polish?*', *PJ*, 2000, no.8:70–73, seems optimistic, but less so than many of the people she quotes when discussing the influence of (principally American) mass culture. I. Kamińska-Szmaj, 'Język wiadomości prasowych przed rokiem 1989 i po roku 1989', *PJ*, no.1:31–40, finds press language after 1989 more attractive, but less clearly delineated in terms of genre. A. Kondratiuk and S. Rudnicki, 'Sytuacja językowa we wsi Omylne na południowej Żytomierszczyźnie', *SFPS*, 36, 2000:65–82. On Iu. A. Labyntsev and L. L. Shchabinskaia, 'Литературное наследие "православных поляков"', *Slavianovedenie*, 2000, no.3:81–89, see *YWMLS*, 62:887. A. Majkowska, 'Deskrypcje nieokreślone w polszczyźnie mówionej', *PJ*, no.2:22–27. M. Michalik, 'Definicja językowo-kulturowa jako sposób diagnozy kompetencji lingwistycznej uczniów szkół specjalnych', *PJ*, no.5:17–27. K. Mosiołek-Kłosińska, 'Jak współcześni Polacy wyobrażają sobie piękną i bogatą polszczyznę', *PJ*, no.1:41–51, contains an introduction and sections on text types and cohesion, and continues into *PJ*, no.2:28–41, which covers style, correctness, and effectiveness. T. Piekot, 'System aksjologiczno-normatywny w socjolekcie kulturystów', *PJ*, no.5:40–53. R. Roszko, 'Nowomowa skomputeryzowanych wideofilmowców', *SFPS*, 36, 2000:97–107. R. S., 'Postawy Polaków wobec własnego języka', *PJ*, no.1:65–70. P. Szczotka, 'Próba wyznaczenia współczesnej granicy pomiędzy dialektem śląskim i małopolskim w Czadeckiem (Kisuce). (Z pogranicza językowego polsko-słowackiego)', *SFPS*, 36, 2000:135–55. B. Walczak, 'Uczniowski świat wartości w zwierciedle języka', *Polonistyka*, 54:627–28, is a review of Ryszard Jedliński, **Językowy obraz świata wartości w wypowiedziach uczniów kończących szkołę podstawową*, Kw, Wyd. Naukowe AP, 2000, 289 pp.

The stream of works on *kultura języka* continues with, for example, Jerzy Bralczyk, *Mówi się. Porady językowe profesora Bralczyka*, Wa, PWN, 233 pp.

8. INDIVIDUALS, WORKS, STYLISTICS

ĆWICZENIE KATECHISMOWE. H. Popowska-Taborska, '*Ćwiczenie Katechismowe* z 1758 roku na tle wcześniejszych druków kaszubskich', *SFPS*, 36, 2000:83–95.

LEŚMIAN. M. Klimczak, 'Funkcja neologizmów w kreowaniu poetyckiego obrazu świata Bolesława Leśmiana', *PJ*, no.4:42–48.

MARIAN TEXTS. R. Mazurkiewicz, 'Staroczeskie wzorce i analogie polskich średniowiecznych pieśni maryjnych', *Slavia*, 70:25–50.

MODERN POETRY. A. Rejter, 'Topos Arkadii a językowy obraz świata w polskiej poezji współczesnej', *PJ*, 2000, no.8:60–69.

NIZIURSKI. U. Szyszko, 'Porównania w metaforycznym opisywaniu ludzi przez dzieci i młodzież (na podstawie utworów Edmunda Niziurskiego)', *PJ*, no.3:43–49.

OLÁH IN TRANSLATION. A. Zoltán, 'Rekonstrukcja zaginionych fragmentów Bazylikowego przekładu *Athili* M. Oláha (1574)', *SSH*, 46:13–23, treats Cyprian Bazylik's 1574 Polish translation of Miklós Oláh's *Athila*, which latter was published in Basle in 1568, in Latin; the reconstruction is based on the original and on an old Belorussian manuscript. Bazylik translated *Hunni* as *Węgrowie*.

POETRY FOR CHILDREN. J. Kowalewska-Dąbrowska, 'Niektóre problemy związane z interpretacją toposu "świata na opak" w wybranych utworach poetyckich dla dzieci', *PJ*, 2000, no.9:5–18.

ROZMYŚLANIE PRZEMYSKIE. A. Przyborska, 'Archaizmy w tekście *Rozmyślania przemyskiego*', *PJ*, 2000, no.9:29–36.

9. POLISH AND OTHER LANGUAGES

S. Dubisz, 'Polska, Polonia, polonistyka a Europa', *PJ*, no.1 : 3–11. R. Laskowski, 'Rosyjskie *znat'*, polskie *wiedzieć, znać*', pp. 128–43 of *Слово в тексте и в словаре. Сборник статей к семидесятилетию академика Ю. С. Апресяна*, ed. L. L Iomdin and L.P Krysin, Moscow, Izdatel'stvo "Iazyki russkoi kul'tury", 2000, 648 pp. E. Siatkowska, 'Porównanie wpływu kontrreformacji na rozwój zachodniosłowiańskich języków literackich', *SlSl*, 35, 2000: 175–81. J. Siatkowski, 'Słowiańskie nazwy "myśliwego" w świetle materiałów Atlasu ogólnosłowiańskiego', *ib.*, 155–60. G. Szpila, 'Opis konotacyjny leksemów w analizie kontrastywnej frazeologizmów', *PJ*, no.3 : 31–42, examines *fly/mucha, bee/pszczoła, flea/pchła, wasp/osa, butterfly/motyl, hornet/szerszeń, moth/mól, gad-fly/bąk, marble-fly/giez, drone/truteń, locust/szarańcza, moth/ćma, beetle/chrząszcz,* and *cricket/świerszcz.* H. C. Trepte, 'Switching languages in émigré literature', *CanSS*, 33, 1999: 215–221, is concerned chiefly with Polish émigré writers and with what Juliusz Mieroszewski calls 'the price of Polish' (217). M. Kondratenko, 'Наименования природных явлений в польских и немецких говорах Силезии. Опыт сопоставительного анализа фрагментов языковой картины мира', *WSl*, 46 : 109–16. G. Sokolová, 'Mateřský jazyk v národnostně smíšeném prostředí', *SaS*, 62 : 258–73, deals with Czech, Polish, and Slovak in the Těšin and Ostrava regions, on which topic see also I. Bogoczová, 'Stylizace — druhá přirozenost (K jazykové komunikaci na Těšínsku)', *SlSl*, 61, 2000 : 18–29.

On translation and related matters, R. Uzar and J. Waliński, 'Analysing the fluency of translators', *IJCL*, 5, 2000: 155–66, deals with translations from Polish into English, but is couched in general terms and says nothing as yet about Polish. A. Legeżyński, 'Syndrom wieży Babel', *Polonistyka*, 54 : 566–70, is prompted by the appearance of *After Babel* in Polish: George Steiner, *Po wieży Babel. Problemy języka przekładu*, trans. O. and W. Kubiński, Kw, Universitas, 2000, 685 pp. An important Polish scholar's 1993 contribution to translation studies has now appeared in Polish: Elżbieta Tabakowska, *Językoznawstwo kognitywne a poetyka przekładu*, trans. A. Pokojska, Kw, Universitas, 188 pp., in which connection mention should also be made of the Polish version of *Kognitywne podstawy języka i językoznawstwa*, ed. E. Tabakowska, Kw, Universitas, 363 pp., and belatedly of Jerzy Świątek, *W świecie powszechnej metafory. Metafora językowa*, Kw, PAN Oddział w Krakowie, 1998, 125 pp.

Iwona Kienzler, *Słownik terminologii Unii Europejskiej angielsko-polski i polsko-angielski*, Gdańsk, IVAX, 199 pp., is small in size but encyclopaedic in approach; entries in the main section are ordered by English term, the Polish-English section functioning effectively as a Polish index to the main section, and a final entirely non-linguistic section giving sketches (in order of Polish name) of member and candidate member countries of the European Union.

10. ONOMASTICS

E. Breza, 'Nazwiska *Tąta, Tonta, Tontar(a)* i podobne', *PJ*, no.6:81–83; Id., 'Polskie nazwiska "taneczne" ', *SFPS*, 36, 2000:23–40. E. Rudolf-Ziółkowska, 'Uwagi o antroponimii ziemi łuckiej w XVII–XVIII wieku (na podstawie Albumu studentów Akademii Zamojskiej z lat 1595 — 1781', *ib.*, 109–19. J. Strzelecka, 'Księgi hipoteczne zreponowane jako źródło do badań antroponimii Starej i Nowej Warszawy', *ib.*, 121–34. M. Szembor, 'Popularne i oryginalne imiona nadawane w Gliwicach w latach 1990–1996', *PJ*, no.6:56–63. K. Wojtczuk, 'Formy typu *mini, super, agro-, auto*, jako tworzywo nazw firm siedleckich z lat 90', *PJ*, no.2:42–49.

Naming a child *Opieniek* is an abuse of parental power, according to the strong view expressed by the Polish Language Council, *PJ*, no.3:80, in an issue containing a number of announcements from the Council (63–80), including 'Opinia o wyrazie *leasing* (na zamówienie Kancelarii Sejmu RP)' (65–69). See also <http://www.rjp.pl/opinie/opinie.php> for the Council's recommendations.

LITERATURE

By JOHN BATES, *University of Glasgow*

1. GENERAL

The slightly loosely titled *Dawni pisarze polscy od początku piśmiennictwa do Młodej Polski. Przewodnik biograficzny i bibliograficzny. Tom I*, ed. Roman Loth, WSiP, 2000, 422 pp., covers the letters A-H. *Słownik literatury polskiej XX wieku*, ed. Marek Pytasz, Katowice, Videograf, 604 pp., actually takes the last decade of the 19th c. as its starting point, and divides the 20th into three parts: 1890–1918, 1918–1947, and 1947–1998. The invaluable *Słownik badaczy literatury polskiej*, ed. Jerzy Starnawski, Łódź, wyd. Uniwersytetu Łódzkiego, whose first volume appeared in 1994, has developed into second (1998, 506 pp.) third (2000, 426 pp.), and fourth volumes (363 pp.). Maria Bursztyn and Katarzyna Radzymińska, *Literatura polska. Słownik encyklopediczny*, Ww, Europa, 2000, 529 pp., is aimed primarily at school children. *Literatura polska w przekładach 1990–2000*, ed. Danuta Bilikiewicz-Blanc, Tomasz Szubiakowicz et al., Wa, Biblioteka Narodowa, 2000, 309 pp., is a useful bibliography. *RuLit*, 42:669–971, consists of a bibliography of articles published in the journal during the years 1960–2000.

Bolecki, *Genologia*, contains substantial theoretical contributions from leading critics as well as items devoted to individual authors, which are dealt with separately below. Jones, *Censorship*, contains a number of essays on individual Polish authors and issues from the 19th–20th cs, which are dealt with below. *Ciało i tekst. Feminizm w literaturoznawstwie — antologia szkiców*, ed. Anna Nasiłowska, IBL, 290 pp., is a compilation of leading Polish women critics and translations of French feminist criticism. *Krytyka feministyczna. Siostra teorii i historii literatury*, ed. Grażyna Borkowska and Liliana Sikorska, IBL, 2000, 360 pp., is a varied collection by leading scholars on, for example, Z. Nałkowska's *Dom kobiet*, A. Gruszecka and Polish homoerotic verse. *Modernizm i feminizm: postacie kobiece w literaturze polskiej i obcej*, ed. Eugenia Loch, UMCS, 276 pp., not only covers individual women writers from M. Komornicka to M. Gretkowska, but also discusses pregnancy in H. Sienkiewicz's *Trilogy*. *Pogranicza wrażliwości w literaturze i kulturze. Część II. Meandry wrażliwości XX wieku* (Rozprawy i studia 332), ed. Inga Iwasiów and Piotr Urbański, Szczecin, Uniwersytet Szczeciński, 1999, analyses D. Mostwin and L. Buczkowski among others. *Rola i miejsce kobiet w edukacji i kulturze polskiej. Tom 2*, Wiesław Zamrożek, Dorota Żołądź-Strzelczyk, Pń, Instytut Historii UAM, 335 pp., examines these issues within C. Norwid and N. Żmichowska's works, amongst others. The sixth volume of *Kobieta i praca. Wiek XIX i XX*, ed. Anna Żarnowska and Andrzej Szwarc, Wa, DiG, 2000, 401 pp., contains an essay by J. Zacharska, 'Nauczycielka w literaturze przełomu XIX i XX w.' (267–90), dealing with the issue in works by E. Orzeszkowa and others. *Dzieciństwo i sacrum. Studia i szkice literackie*, ed. Joanna Papuzińska and Grzegorz Leszczyński, Wa, Stowarzyszenie Przyjaciół Książki dla Młodych — Polska Sekcja IBBY, comprises two volumes: the first, published in 1998 (317 pp.) contains essays on K. Irzykowski's *Pałuba*, as well as on K. Filipowicz, A. Kamieńska, and others, while the second (2000, 183 pp.) includes a number of non-Polish authors such as A. de Saint-Exupéry, J. R. Tolkien, and C. S. Lewis. Ryszard Waksmund, *Od literatury dla dzieci do literatury dziecięcej (tematy – gatunki – konteksty)*, Ww, WUW, 2000, 443 pp., does not limit its focus to the Polish context.

Krzysztof Kurek, *Polski Hamlet. Z historii idei i wyobraźni narodowej* (Biblioteka Literacka Poznańska Studiów Polonistycznych 16), Pń, ABEDIK, 1999, 168 pp., deals specifically with the influence of Shakespeare's hero on J. Korzeniowski's *Bitwa nad Mozgawą* (chapter 3) and J. Słowacki's *Horsztyński* (chapter 4), as well as the impact of performances and their reception on other Polish writers. Wojciech Ligęza, *Jaśniejsze strony katastrofy. Szkice o twórczości poetów emigracyjnych*, Kw, Universitas, 265 pp., examines A. Wat, J. Wittlin, B. Obertyńska, M. Pankowski, and A. Janta. Eugenia Loch, *Wokół modernizmu: studia o literaturze XIX i XX wieku*, UMCS, 1996, 298 pp., deals with J. I. Kraszewski's novellas, Orzeszkowa's *Nad Niemnem*, S. Żeromski's Jewish heroes, and the role of romantic poetry in creating S. Wyspiański's leading protagonists, before turning to J. Iwaszkiewicz and J. B. Ożóg. Małgorzata Szulc Packalén, *Under två kulturers ok: allmogeskildringar i den polska och svenska 1800– och 1900– talslitteraturen* (Acta Universitatis Upsaliensis: Studia Slavica Upsaliensia 43), Uppsala U.P., 300 pp. Jan Poradecki, *Prorocy i sztukmistrze. Eseje o poezji polskiej XX wieku*, PWN, 1999, 263 pp., addresses leading late 20th-c. poets in the main. Jan Prokop, *Klerk i diabeł. Literatura, ideologia, mity*, Kw, Viridis, 1999, 125 pp., although dealing with Z. Herbert and A. Mickiewicz's *Pan Tadeusz*, devotes rather more space to the latter two issues than the first. Leszek Szaruga, *Literatura i życie. Ważniejsze wątki dyskusji literackich 1939–1989*, UMCS, 199 pp. Jan Tomkowski, *Pokolenie Gombrowicza: narodziny powieści XX wieku w Polsce*, Wa, Czytelnik, 193 pp., examines works by writers making their debuts in the inter-war period, such as T. Breza, before going on to consider post-war writers such as T. Parnicki and A. Kuśniewicz. Bożena Umińska, *Postać z cieniem. Portrety żydówek w polskiej literaturze od końca*

XIX wieku do 1939 roku, Wa, Sic!, 374 pp., a thorough and methodologically scrupulous analysis, examines the problem in relation to writers such as G. Zapolska, Iwaszkiewicz, B. Schulz, and W. Gombrowicz. Marta Wyka, *Punkty widzenia*. *Szkice krytyczne*, WL, 2000, 182 pp., deals with G. Herling-Grudziński, Herbert and T. Konwicki, New Wave writing (including E. Lipska) as well as French writers such as Malraux, Camus, and Gide. Andrzej Zawada, *Mit czy świadectwo? Szkice literackie*, Ww, WUW, 2000, 260 pp., contains essays on contemporary classics such as C. Miłosz, Herbert, Iwaszkiewicz, Wat, and Konwicki, as well as more recent writers.

Maski współczesności: o literaturze i kulturze XX wieku, ed. Lidia Burska and Marek Zaleski, IBL, 338 pp., is as panoramic as its title suggests, with contributions by leading critics on A. Stasiuk, the diaries of Nałkowska and M. Dąbrowska, the generation of 1968, and M. Jasnorzewska-Pawlikowska's correspondence. *Od romantyzmu do współczesności. W kręgu historii i dydaktyki literatury. Tom poświęcony Profesorowi Mieczysławowi Inglotowi z okazji 70. rocznicy urodzin*, ed. Władysław Dymek, Ww, WUW, 418 pp., comprises four sections: (i) literature and language teaching; (ii) history of literature; (iii) interpretations of individual texts, including works by Norwid, Miłosz, and Herling-Grudziński; (iv) a bibliography of Inglot's own works for the years 1950–2000. *Literackie Kresy i bedekery. Księga ofiarowana Profesorowi Bolesławowi Hadaczkowi*, ed. Katarzyna R. Łozowska and Ewa Tierling, Szczecin, Uniwersytet Szczeciński, 2000, 448 pp., deals with various authors including Mickiewicz. *Góry — Literatura — Kultura. Tom 4*, ed. Jerzy Kolbuszewski, Ww, WUW, 239 pp., considers, *inter alia*, the role of mountains in Mickiewicz's work. *Kanonada: Interpretacje wierszy polskich (1939–1989)*, ed. Aleksander Nawarecki with Dariusz Pawelec, Katowice, wyd. Uniwersytetu Śląskiego, 1999, 183 pp., focuses on the leading poets of the period. *Ze studiów nad literaturą rosyjską i polską: księga poświęcona pamięci profesora Bohdana Galstera*, ed. Jerzy Świdziński, Pń, wyd. Poznańskiego Towarzystwa Przyjaciół Nauk, 1999, 163 pp.

A. Fiut, 'Przypływy i odpływy chaosu', *Dialog*, 45.1, 2000:95–103, analyses the views of Miłosz and Gombrowicz in relation to theatre. W. Koschmal, 'Zur Evolution des 'vegetativen' Erzählens. Wacław Berent und Bruno Schulz', *ŻSP*, 60.2:337–60. P. Nowaczyński, 'Kłopoty z kogutem. Z dziejów poetyckiego obrazowania', *Twórczość*, 56.3, 2000: 106–12, examines the issue with reference to poets from J. Kochanowski to E. Bryll. B. Schultze, 'Prometeusz w Polsce: narodowy, ponadkulturowy i globalny ("Praca nad mitem" w polskiej literaturze 19. i 20. stulecia)', *RuLit*, 41, 2000:407–16. D. Wachna, 'Sposoby widzenia sztuki w *Wężach i różach* Zofii Nałkowskiej oraz *Przygodzie w nieznanym kraju* Anieli Gruszeckiej', *ib.*, 42:537–54.

M. Zaleski, '"Ludzie ludziom. . .?" "Ludzie Żydom. . .?" Świadectwo literatury', *RPN*, 13.1–2, 2000:80–85, deals with the question in terms of Nałkowska, H. Grynberg, and M. Bieńczyk's works.

2. From the Middle Ages up to Romanticism

The two works discussed in Barbara Milewska-Waźbińska's *W kręgu bohaterów spod Wiednia. Rzecz o dwóch łacińskich eposach staropolskich*, Wa, Uniwersytet Warszawski, Wydział Polonistyki Instytut Filologii Klasycznej, 1998, 218 pp., are J. Kaliński's *Viennis* and A. Ustrzycki's *Sobiesciados carminum libri quinque. Słownik sarmatyzmu. Idee, pojęcia, symbole*, ed. Andrzej Borowski, WL, 255 pp., an attractive volume, devotes some space to literature. Hanna Dziechcińska, *Pamiętniki czasów saskich. Od sentymentalizmu do sensualizmu*, Bydgoszcz, WSP, 1999, 147 pp. Joanna Zawadzka, *Kronika serc czułych. Stereotypy polskiej powieści sentymentalnej I połowy XIX wieku*, IBL, 1997, 212 pp., discusses the genesis and beginnings of Sentimentalism, stereotypes in relation to title, plot, and character, before turning to the sentimental sensibility, landscape, and the epistolary novel.

J. Błoński, 'Uparte trwanie baroku', *TD*, nos 3–4:183–89. R. Dąbrowski, 'Narracja i dialog w polskiej epopei oświeceniowej (*Wojna chocimska, Pułtawa, Jagiellonida*)', *RuLit*, 39, 1998:721–36. J. I. J. Van der Meer, 'Politics and Theatre in Late 18th Century Poland', *ZSP*, 60.1:151–74. J. Okoń, 'Św. Wojciech i *Bogurodzica* jako czynniki kształtowania polskiej świadomości narodowej (do początku renesansu w Polsce)', *RuLit*, 39, 1998:699–719; and his 'Postać Parysa w dramatach polskiego renesansu', *ib.*, 41, 2000:11–30.

INDIVIDUAL WRITERS

BOGUSŁAWSKI. M. Klimowicz, '*Cud albo Krakowiaki i górale* — sztuka rewolucyjna czy tylko wzywająca do powstania?', *Odra*, 40.12, 2000:52–56, concludes that the play is both.

DRUŻBACKA. Krystyna Stasiewicz, *Zmysłowa i elokwentna prowincjuszka na staropolskim Parnasie: rzecz o Elżbiecie Drużbackiej i nie tylko*, Olsztyn, Littera, 191 pp.

GOŚCIECKI. R. Krzywy, '"Muzy — Poetów boginie". Późnobarokowy supplement do staropolskiego mitoznawstwa. (O *Poselstwie wielkim* Franciszka Gościeckiego)', *RuLit*, 41, 2000:95–107.

KOCHANOWSKI. *Treny. The Laments of Kochanowski*, ed. and ann. Piotr Wilczek [Studies in Comparative Literature, 6], Oxford, Legenda, 75 pp., contains a bilingual text with Adam Czerniawski's translation of the cycle, an essay ('A Reading of Treny') by the same

(56–72), and is essentially a revamped and upgraded version of the 1996 Katowice edition.

LUBOMIRSKI. G. Trościński, 'Rękopiśmienne litteraria Stanisława Herakliusza Lubomirskiego w zbiorach Biblioteki Seminarium Duchownego w Sandomierzu', *RuLit*, 42:365–68. MORELOWSKI. J. Wójcicki, '*Ad Modum Sarbievii.* Wzorce Horacjańskie w praktyce twórczej Józefa Morelowskiego', *RuLit*, 40, 1999:693–704. WĘGIERSKI. J. I. J. Van der Meer, 'Women and the literary field of the Stanislavian Age (Węgierski's epigrams about the Five Elżbietas)', *WSl*, 46.2:201–24.

3. Romanticism

Zbigniew Przychodniak, *Walka o rząd dusz: studia o literaturze i polityce Wielkiej Emigracji* (Seria Filologia polska 67), Pń, wyd. Naukowe Adama Mickiewicza, 360 pp., considers M. Mochnacki's writings, Mickiewicz's journalism, as well as hitherto unknown texts by the two. Jerzy Starnawski, *W świecie olbrzymów. Studia o twórczości i recepcji czterech wielkich romantyków*, Przemyśl, wyd. Towarzystwa Przyjaciół Nauk w Przemyślu, 1998, 254 pp., gathers sketches from over 40 years. *Mickiewicz, Słowacki, Krasiński*, ed. Ewa Owczarz and Jerzy Smulski, Łowicz, Mazowiecka Wyższa Szkoła Humanistyczno-Pedagogiczna, 355 pp., is a wide-ranging collection by various hands. D. Danek, 'Obrazy wyjaskrawione i słabe światełka. Inne spojrzenie na romantyzm', *Twórczość*, 56.9, 2000:84–94, proposes a more psychoanalytical approach. L. Kaczyńska, 'Dramat romantyczny w teatrze współczesnym', *RuLit*, 42:137–52, raises, but ultimately leaves open, the question of the role of romantic drama in contemporary Polish society. R. K. Przybylski, 'Na romantyczną klasykę i tak jesteśmy skazani', *Dialog*, 46.5–6:161–66. E. Zarych, 'Problemy w badaniach nad wpływem filozofii niemieckiej — od Kanta do Hegla — na literaturę polskiego romantyzmu', *TD*, no. 2:52–77.

INDIVIDUAL WRITERS

KRASIŃSKI. J. Zieliński, 'Chrześniak Napoleona', *Dialog*, 46.5–6:167–78, maintains the continuing lofty status of K.'s *Nie-Boska komedia* as the most 'universal' of all Polish Romantic dramas. KRASZEWSKI. M. Rudkowska, 'Stanisław August Poniatowski — dekadencja władzy? Obraz ostatniego króla Polski w twórczości Józefa Ignacego Kraszewskiego', *RuLit*, 42:451–63.

MICKIEWICZ. Jarosław Marek Rymkiewicz, Dorota Siwicka, Alina Witkowska, and Maria Zielińska, *Mickiewicz. Encyklopedia*, Wa, Horyzont, 699 pp., is a major new work of reference by leading scholars. Katarzyna Leżeńska, *Kto jest kim w Panu Tadeuszu*, Wa, Prószyński i S-ka, 1999, 123 pp., is a colourful and well-illustrated popular guide. Marek Piechota and Jacek Lyszczyzna, *Słownik Mickiewiczowski*, Katowice, Książnica, 2000, 422 pp. Leszek Zwierzyński, *Wyobraźnia akwatyczna Mickiewicza*, Katowice, wyd. Uniwersytetu Śląskiego, 1998, 174 pp., discusses aquatic imagery and symbolism in *Sonety krymskie* and other works.
PL(W), 92.3, contains two essays on M.'s work: M. Riedaś-Grodzka, ' "Rozumienie szałem". *Oda do młodości* jako platoński lot ku idei' (5–29) and J. Erdman, 'Niebo gwiaździste w *Panu Tadeuszu* Adama Mickiewicza' (31–42). The same number also contains two articles on translations of certain works by M.: L. Pszczołowska, 'Potęga metrum. O puszkinowskim przekładzie *Czat*' (171–77) and M. Kowalski, 'O metodzie translatorskiej Paula Cazina w przekładzie *Pana Tadeusza*' (179–95). J. Bates, 'Adam Mickiewicz. Dziady (Forefathers)', Jones, *Censorship*, 1585–87. T. Chachulski, '*Dumania w dzień odjazdu* Adama Mickiewicza: tekst i jego tradycje', *PL(W)*, 92.1:203–20. A. Duda, 'Dziady Mickiewicza z perspektywy wiersza *Aryman i Oromaz*', *RuLit*, 40, 1999:605–20. G. Jankowicz, 'Dalekie okolice. Przestrzeń w *Konradzie Wallenrodzie*', *ib.*, 41, 2000:31–53. J. Kopczyński, 'Ja — Gustaw, czyli Mickiewicz według Białoszewskiego', *Dialog*, 46.5–6:179–93. M. Kuziak, 'Hermeneutyka tekstu literackiego w prelekcjach paryskich Adama Mickiewicza', *TD*, no. 2:191–206, and his 'Przemiany koncepcji narodowości w prelekcjach paryskich Mickiewicza', *RuLit*, 40, 1999:517–23. W. Owczarski, ' "Płynąć, płynąć i płynąć. . ." Woda jako temat wyobraźni Mickiewicza', *Twórczość*, 56.7, 2000:67–82. D. Siwicka, 'Historia trzeciego tysiąclecia według Adama Mickiewicza', *RPN*, 13.8, 2000:76–84. J. Skuczyński, 'III część *Dziadów*: między obrzędem ludowym a liturgią chrześcijańską', *RuLit*, 39, 1998:737–51. A. Sulikowski, 'Interpretacje trzech wierszy Mickiewicza. Do samotności, Do M. Ł. W dzień przyjęcia Komunii Św., Mędrcy', *ib.*, 42:211–27.

NORWID. Aleksandra Melbechowska-Luty, *Sztukmistrz. Twórczość artystyczna i myśl o sztuce Cypriana Norwida*, Wa, Neriton, 542 pp. + 16 pp. colour illus. M. Baran, 'Jaka czułość? O wierszu Norwida', *RuLit*, 41, 2000:477–86. D. Klimanowska, 'Balet i mistyka — Cypriana Norwida poetyka odblask tańca', *PrzH*, 45.2:53–66. K. Kwaśniewska, 'Czapski czyta Norwida', *RuLit*, 42:435–50. S. Sawicki, 'Norwid — od strony prawnuków', *TD*, no. 6:24–32. R. Gadamska-Serafin, 'Oblicza smutku w młodzieńczych lirykach Norwida', *RuLit*, 39, 1998:611–26. M. Wiater, 'O Norwidowskiej "istotnej i całej" postaci kobiecej', *ib.*, 753–62, and her 'Obrazy "ja" na przykładzie korespondencji Norwida', *ib.*, 42:421–33.

SŁOWACKI. *PL(W)*, 92.3, contains three essays on S.: M. Kuziak, 'Juliusz Słowacki w kręgu wczesnoromantycznej filozofii egzystencji. O antropologii muzycznej w twórczości poety' (43–64); J. Ławski, 'Metamorfozy świata poetyckiego *Marii* Malczewskiego w *Janie Bielskim* Słowackiego' (77–113); and M. Masłowski, 'Koncept roli w dramatach Słowackiego' (65–75). *Dialog*, 45.5, 2000, contains two essays on the play *Samuel Zborowski*: D. Jagła, 'Dramat Lucyfera' (109–25) and A. Kuligowska-Korzeniowska, 'Bezdnia możliwości. O transcrypcji scenicznej *Samuela Zborowskiego* Cezarego Jellenty' (126–37). G. Królikiewicz, 'Ruiny romantyczne inaczej: ironia, żart, karykatura', *RuLit*, 42:1–16, focuses on the issue in relation to *Beniowski* and *Fantazy*. M. Łapot, 'Juliusz Słowacki na warsztacie badawczym Czesława Zgorzelskiego', *ib.*, 40, 1999:621–31. E. Łubieńska, 'Sen i przebudzenie Anhellego', *ib.*, 41, 2000:623–42. M. Podraza-Kwiatkowska, 'Rozważania rocznicowe o Juliuszu Słowackim', *ib.*, 40, 1999:1–10.

4. FROM REALISM TO NEO-REALISM

Grażyna Borkowska, *Alienated Women: A Study on Polish Women's Fiction 1845–1918*, Budapest, CEU Press, 337 pp., is a fine translation by Ursula Phillips of Borkowska's seminal 1996 work. *Wiersze pozytywistów*, ed. Tadeusz Budrewicz, Katowice, Książnica, 2000, 181 pp., intended for students and school pupils, contains essays on the poetry of W. Gomulicki, M. Konopnicka, and A. Asnyk, and others. Iwona Loewe, *Konstrukcje analityczne w poezji Młodej Polski*, Katowice, wyd. Uniwersytetu Śląskiego, 2000, 140 pp., is a linguistic analysis.

A. Andrzejewska, 'Artysta młodopolska: biały i czarny mag', *RuLit*, 42:17–40. A. Makowski, '"Realizm" czy "tendencja"? O pojmowaniu realizmu w krytyce literackiej drugiej połowy XIX wieku', Bolecki, *Genologia*, 225–57, focuses primarily upon P. Chmielowski's criticism. G. Matuszek, 'Dojrzewanie i (czy) deprawacja. O "edukacyjnym" wątku w polskiej naturalistycznej dramaturgii', *RuLit*, 42:153–63, examines the theme with reference to works by Zapolska, Z. Wójcicka, and less well-known Polish naturalists. G. Ritz, 'Modernistyczna liryka kobieca. Od "nagiej duszy" do duszy kobiety', *Twórczość*, 56.1, 2000:57–80. M. Sadlik, '"W otchłani" miłości', *RuLit*, 42:183–98, focuses on the theme of love in the works of Młoda Polska writers, including Komornicka and K. Przerwa-Tetmajer. D. Trześniowski, '"A trwanie twoje jest, jak śmierć, na zawsze – coraz

straszniejsze i krwawsze . . .". Modernistyczny wizerunek Salome',
PL(W), 92.1:7–31, examines the Salome thread in the works of four
Polish modernists, J. Kasprowicz, K. Zawistowska, W. Wolski, and
A. Szandlerowski.

INDIVIDUAL WRITERS

BERENT. P. Bukowski, 'Autentyczność i amoralizm. Problemy indy-
widualnej tożsamości w *Czerwonym Pokoju* Augusta Strindberga i
Próchnie Wacława Berenta', *TD*, no. 2:78–100.

BRZOZOWSKI. A. Zawadzki, ' "Dusza eseistyczna". Miejsce eseju
w pisarstwie Stanisława Brzozowskiego', *RuLit*, 41, 2000:55–62.

BUJNICKI. P. Bukowiec, 'Zapomniany pamiętnik Kazimierza
Bujnickiego', *RuLit*, 41, 2000:595–601.

CHMIELOWSKI. Adam Makowski, *Metoda krytycznoliteracka Piotra
Chmielowskiego*, IBL, 272 pp.

KOMORNICKA. G. Ritz, 'Maria Komornicka: zagrożone autorstwo
a kategoria "gender" ', *PL(W)*, 92.1:33–51.

KRZYWICKI. S. Łucyk, 'Krytyka kultury wielkomiejskiej w pub-
licystyce Ludwika Krzywickiego', *PrzH*, 45.2:67–80.

MICIŃSKI. M. Kurkiewicz, '*Dęby czarnobylskie* Tadeusza Micińskiego: oryginalność cyklu', *RuLit*, 42:465–73. C. Suszka, 'W poszuki-
waniu utraconej jedni. O synkretyzmie kulturowo-religijnym w
twórczości Tadeusza Micińskiego', *ib.*, 165–82.

ORZESZKOWA. I. Wiśniewska, 'Listy Elizy Orzeszkowej do Ignacego i Julii Baranowskich (1897–1899)', *PL(W)*, 92.3:197–229 and
her 'Listy Orzeszkowej do Ignacego Baranowskiego (1900–1903)',
ib., 92.4:163–90.

PRUS. H. K. Kamiński, 'Bolesław Prus', Jones, *Censorship*,
1969–71. A. Kluba, 'Teoria Prusa', *RuLit*, 40, 1999:525–37.

ŚWIĘTOCHOWSKI. G. Borkowska, 'Arystokratyczny liberalizm
Aleksandra Świętochowskiego', *TD*, no. 2: 101–13.

S. WITKIEWICZ. T. Poller, 'Cztery żywioły w pismach tatrzańskich
Stanisława Witkiewicza', *Kultura współczesna*, 2000, nos 1–2:70–78.

ŻEROMSKI. Elżbieta Kalemba-Kasprzak, *Prometeusz z przepiórką.
Dramaty Stefana Żeromskiego: od Czarowica do Przełęckiego*, Pń, wyd.
Naukowe UAM, 2000, 340 pp. *RPN*, 14.2, contains two essays on Ż.'s
work: J. Szacki, 'Nasz Żeromski' (32–34) and A. Waśkiewicz, 'Drugie
życie Żeromskiego' (35–38), which largely reconsiders *Przedwiośnie* in
the light of the recent film version. Z. A. Adamczyk, 'Listy Ludwika
Szczepańskiego do Stefana Żeromskiego z 1897 roku', *PrzH*,
45.3:91–97. M. Czubaj, 'Żeromski a sprawy miejskie,' *Twórczość*,
56.4, 2000:46–70. W. Waszczuk, 'Role czytelnicze Stefana Żeromskiego w jego *Dziennikach*', *RuLit*, 40, 1999:539–52.

5. FROM 1918 TO 1945

Gułag polskich poetów. Od Komi do Kołymy, selected by Nina Taylor-Terlecka, London, Polska Fundacja Kulturalna, 181 pp., is an anthology with introductory essay (5–20). Paweł Rodak, *Wizje kultury pokolenia wojennego* [Monografie FNP], Ww, Funna, 2000, 361 pp. M. Gawin, ' "Wpadnij do Mieszkańskiej." O konflikcie między socjalistami a *Wiadomościami Literackimi* w latach trzydziestych', *RPN*, 13.1–2, 2000:38–43. S. Kryński, 'Zwariowane czy najsmutniejsze miasto. O *Andrzeju Paniku* Kurka i *Zwariowanym mieście* Wiktora', *RuLit*, 39, 1998:627–46. M. Młodkowska, 'Gettowe trajektorze. O zapisie osobistego doświadczenia w dziennikach z getta warszawskiego (Abraham Lewin, Rachela Auerbach, Janusz Korczak)', *TD*, no. 1:135–55. P. Rodak, ' "Kiedy ludzie będą braćmi ...". Portret *Płomieni* i *Drogi*', *Twórczość*, 56.8, 2000:73–92, concerns two literary journals of the German Occupation. T. Skórczewski, 'Czy krytyka literacka jest sztuką? Wokół jednej z wątków międzywojennych sporów o granice krytyki', *PL(W)*, 92.4:45–73. I. Warzecha, 'Motywy mickiewiczowskie w międzywojennej poezji wileńskiej', *PL(W)*, 92.3:115–33.

INDIVIDUAL WRITERS

BOY. H. Markiewicz, 'Larwy i pamflety. 90 lat sporów z Boyem i o Boya', *Twórczość*, 56.11, 2000:70–84.

BRZĘKOWSKI. P. Majerski, 'Boczny tor awangardowego eksperymentu (O powieściach Jana Brzękowskiego)', *RuLit*, 40, 1999:649–62.

CZUCHNOWSKI. P. Tański, ' "Wygnanie ptaków" w Londynie. Emigracyjna poezja Mariana Czuchnowskiego', *PL(W)*, 92.1:161–78.

GAŁCZYŃSKI. Kira Gałczyńska, *Zielony Konstanty*, Wa, KiW, 2000, 382 pp.

GOMBROWICZ. Jerzy Jarzębski, *Podglądanie Gombrowicza*, WL, 2000, 247 pp., collects previously published essays. H. Bereza, 'Goma', *Twórczość*, 56.7, 2000:83–87, concerns G.'s correspondence with the Argentinian writer Juan Carlos Gómez. E. Fiała: 'Homo transcendens w *Kosmosie* Gombrowicza', *PrzH*, 45.3:59–78; 'Księga lęków polskich, czyli *Trans-Atlantyk* Gombrowicza', *RuLit*, 40, 1999:569–80; and his 'O początkach i perspektywach psychoanalitycznej interpretacji literatury. Gombrowicz w optyce Freuda i Fromma', *PL(W)*, 92.4:75–96. S. Kryński, 'Artysta i reszta ludzkości. *Ferdydurke* jako (przy)powieść o artyście', *RuLit*, 41, 2000:545–61. L. Neuger, '*Kosmos* Witolda Gombrowicza. Genologiczne podstawy hipotez sensowności', Bolecki, *Genologia*, 160–72.

INGARDEN.   Bogdan Ogrodnik, *Ingarden*, Wiedza Powszechna, 2000, 340 pp.

IRZYKOWSKI.   B. Pawłowska-Jądrzyk, 'Przeciw aforystyczności. Świadomość językowa w *Pałubie* Karola Irzykowskiego', *TD*, no. 6:77–94.

IWASZKIEWICZ.   A. Fiut, 'Jak za szybą', *RuLit*, 42:41–56, deals with the portrait of Ukrainians in I.'s prose works. A. Pomorski, 'Wszyscy jesteśmy Azjaci', *Twórczość*, 56.2, 2000:74–94. T. Stefańczyk, 'Ciemne ścieżki i jasne polany (w dwudziestą rocznicę śmierci Jarosława Iwaszkiewicza)', *ib.*, 56.3, 2000:63–86.

LEŚMIAN.   P. Pietrych, 'Bolesława Leśmiana *Strój* – ballada (o) niejasności', *PL(W)*, 92.1:53–71. J. M. Rymkiewicz, 'Leśmian — dzieje geniusza', *Twórczość*, 56.5, 2000:56–92, and 56.6, 2000:70–82. A. Wiatr, 'Trochę inna Dziewczyna', *ib.*, 56.3, 2000:87–105, examines the poem *Dziewczyna* from the 1936 collection *Napój cienisty*.

NAŁKOWSKA.   M. Dernałowicz, 'Ostatnia młodość Nałkowskiej', *Twórczość*, 56.7, 2000:88–94, concerns N.'s diaries. A. Galant, 'Skradziony profil. Matka w *Dziennikach* Zofii Nałkowskiej', *RuLit*, 42:555–67.

PRZYBOŚ.   B. Kierc, 'Cel sfer', *Twórczość*, 56.11, 2000:58–69. R. Nycz, 'Wiersz jest jak "raca". Juliana Przybosia poetyka oświecenia a estetyka nowoczesna', *RuLit*, 42:261–69. R. K. Przybylski, 'Znawca sztuki nowoczesnej', *ib.*, 271–77.

NAPIERSKI.   T. Wójcik, 'Stefan Napierski. Przypomnienie pisarza', *Twórczość*, 56.10, 2000:50–76.

SAMOZWANIEC.   Anna Wojciechowska, *Magdaleny z Kossaków Samozwaniec widzenie świata*, Wa-Pń, PWN, 2000, 223 pp.

SCHULZ.   J. Jarzębski, 'Miasto Schulza', *TD*, no. 2:40–51. H. Schmid, 'Gleitmetapher, Scheinkausalität und theatralisches "als ob" in Bruno Schulz' *Wichura* (*Der Sturmwind*)', *ŻSP*, 60.2:361–403. A. Czabańska-Wróbel, 'Fantazmaty dzieciństwa. Glosa do *Wiosny* Schulza', *RuLit*, 42:57–66.

SEBYŁA.   *PL(W)*, 92.1, contains two essays on S.: A. Kluba, 'Niewyrażalność w świadomości artystycznej Władysława Sebyły. Analiza wypowiedzi krytycznych i tekstów poetyckich' (73–117), and B. Dąbrowski, 'Poeta egzystencji. Wątki egzystencjalistyczne w liryce Władysława Sebyły' (119–36).

TRZEBIŃSKI.   E. Janicka, 'Andrzej Trzebiński wobec ideologii Konfederacji Narodu', *Twórczość*, 56.8, 2000:93–102.

WAT.   W. Bolecki, 'Od "postmodernizmu" do "modernizmu" (Wat — inne doświadczenie)', *TD*, no. 2:29–39. W. Parnas, '"Antykwariat anielskich ekstrawagancji" albo "święty bełkot". Rzecz o *Piecyku* Aleksandra Wata', *TD*, no. 1:107–19. B. Przymuszała, '"Czas wzbogacony" w późnej liryce Aleksandra

Wata', *PL(W)*, 92.1:137–59. J. Zieliński, 'Dramat antysocrealistyczny. Zapomniany utwór teatralny Aleksandra Wata', *Dialog*, 45.12, 2000:123–32, deals with the play *Kobiety z Monte Olivetto*, written at the start of the 1950s and printed for the first time in the same issue (5–52).

WIERZYŃSKI. *Wspomnienia o Kazimierzu Wierzyńskim*, ed. Paweł Kądziela, Wa, biblioteka Więzi, 432 pp. + 16 pp. of photographs.

S. I. WITKIEWICZ. Jan Błoński, *Witkacy 2. Filozof —sztukmistrz — estetyk*, WL, 2000, 395 pp. + 22 plates. G. Tomassucci, 'Czterdziestu Mandelbaumów niepoprawnych politycznie', *Dialog*, 45.2, 2000:143–52, deals with W.'s attitudes to the Jewish question.

J. WITTLIN. M. Stępień, 'Inwalida pierwszej wojny światowej (o Józefie Wittlinie)', *RuLit*, 39, 1998:647–62.

6. 1945 TO THE PRESENT DAY

Przemysław Czapliński, *Wzniosłe tęsknoty. Nostalgie w prozie lat dziewięćdziesiątych*, WL, 270 pp., discusses, amongst others, Stasiuk, P. Huelle, S. Chwin, and I. Filipiak. Elżbieta Dutka, *Ukraina w twórczości Włodzimierza Odojewskiego i Włodzimierza Paźniewskiego*, Katowice, wyd. Uniwersytetu Śląskiego, 2000, 144 pp., analyses the image of the Ukraine in the two prose writers' works in terms of literary research, the literary tradition, and through memory, *inter alia*. Julian Kornhauser, *Postscriptum. Notatnik krytyczny*, WL, 1999, 192 pp., is an interesting volume of sketches involving self-reflection on the author's part about the development of Polish literature from the New Wave to the late 1990s. Dariusz Nowacki, *Zawód czytelnik: notatki o prozie polskiej lat 90*, Kw, Znak, 1999, 192 pp., consisting of three parts — the socio-political context, 'strolls' and 'rehearsals', finally analyses individual works by such authors as G. Musiał and J. Pilch.

Magdalena Piekara, *Bohater powieści socrealistycznej*, Katowice, Gnome, 164 pp., covers the representation of various aspects of the eponymous hero's life from love to laughter and death. *Opozycja w PRL. Słownik biograficzny 1956–1989. Tom I*, ed. Jan Skórzyński with Paweł Sowiński and Małgorzata Strasz, Wa, Ośrodek Karta, 2000, 436 pp., includes entries on J. Andrzejewski (14–16), S. Barańczak (23–25), J. Bocheński (44–46), J. Ficowski (79–80), M. Fik (81–82), and K. Orłoś (280–81). Bolecki, *Genologia*, contains three essays on matters relating to the politicization of Polish literature during the socialist realist period and after: K. Krasuski, 'Gatunkowe odmiany polskiej powieści neosocrealistycznej (neoprodukcyjnej)' (200–08); J. Smulski, 'Literatura polskiego socrealizmu. Kilka uwag o wybranych problemach genologicznych' (191–99); and G. Wołowiec,

'Samokrytyka pisarza jako gatunek wypowiedzi' (209–24). L. M. Bartelski, 'Nad rocznikami *Nowin Literackich*', *Twórczość*, 56.2, 2000:47–73. J. Bates, 'Drugi obieg (Second Circulation)', Jones, *Censorship*, 695–96. P. Michałowski, 'Szczeciński Zjazd — widmo i obrzeża socu', *TD*, no. 1:222–26.

H. Gosk, 'Funkcje materiału biograficznego w polskiej prozie lat dziewięćdziesiątych', *RuLit*, 40, 1999:553–67. T. Mizerkiewicz, 'Mityczne światy powieściowe', *ib.*, 41, 2000:681–97. M. Orski, 'Literackie targi', *Odra*, 41.1:65–69, which deals with the question of the 'necessity' of contemporary literature, presents a generally optimistic conclusion. K. Uniłowski, 'Sztuka cytatu: od powieści przez anty-powieść do metapowieści', Bolecki, *Genologia*, 173–90, takes for analysis contemporary Polish works by Białoszewski, R. Schubert, Buczkowski, and J. Limon. *Odra*, 40.10, 2000, presents correspondence between J. Giedroyć and M. Wańkowicz from 1950: 'Korespondencja Jerzego Giedroycia i Melchiora Wańkowicza' (39–51).

INDIVIDUAL WRITERS

ANDRZEJEWSKI. J. Bates, 'Jerzy Andrzejewski', Jones, *Censorship*, 56–58.

BARAŃCZAK. G. Gömöri, 'Stanisław Barańczak', Jones, *Censorship*, 180. J. Kandziora, '"To, co się wymyka". O prześwietlaniu idiomu w *Chirurgicznej precyzji* Stanisława Barańczaka', *TD*, no. 6:151–64.

BIAŁOSZEWSKI. A. Gleń, 'Początek myślenia bycia. Białoszewski-Heidegger', *RuLit*, 42:313–29.

BIEŃCZYK. M. Leciński, '"Likwidacja przewagi." Empatia i praca żałoby w *Tworkach* Marka Bieńczyka', *TD*, no. 1:156–66.

BOROWSKI. D. Kulesza, '*Kamienny świat* Tadeusza Borowskiego. Cykl. Narracja. Obrona *Pożegnania z Marią*', *RuLit*, 42:569–85.

K. BRANDYS. J. Trzcińska, 'Rastignac w krainie carów. O mowie przedmiotów w powieści Kazimierza Brandysa *Obywatele*', *RuLit*, 42:587–605. L. Wyrzykowska, 'O początkach drogi pisarskiej Kazimierza Brandysa', *ib.*, 41, 2000:709–21.

BUCZKOWSKI. S. Buryła, 'Między *Wertepami* a *Czarnym Potokiem*. Zagadnienia ewolucji prozy Leopolda Buczkowskiego', *TD*, no. 2:265–73.

CHWIN. A. Franaszek, 'Kamień i wino. Wokół pisarstwa Stefana Chwina', *Twórczość*, 56.12, 2000:58–82, deals mainly with C.'s recent novel *Esther*.

TKACZYSZYN-DYCKI. W. Forajter, 'Inwersje', *PL(W)*, 92.1: 179–201, is largely concerned with the writer's 1992 verse collection *Peregrynarz*.

FILIPOWICZ.   I. Furnal, ' "Nie jestem bezwolną kłodą drzewa".
Kornela Filipowicza przygody z istnieniem', *RuLit*, 42 : 607–22.
GRYNBERG.   D. Krawczyńska, ' "Twarzą w twarz, maską w maskę,
w potrzasku". O *Racoonie* Henryka Grynberga', *TD*, no. 6: 165–73.
HERBERT.   Julian Kornhauser, *Uśmiech sfinksa, O poezji Zbigniewa
Herberta*, WL, 164 pp. T. Garbol, 'Chrystus w poezji Zbigniewa
Herberta', *RuLit*, 42 : 199–210. J. Kornhauser, '*Hermes, Pies i Gwiazda*
– pamięć i wyobraźnia', *ib.*, 40, 1999 : 679–87. J . Rozmus, 'Przez
wielką szybę. O muzycznych i malarskich nieporozumieniach w
twórczości Zbigniewa Herberta', *ib.*, 41, 2000 : 433–57, and on a
similar theme is A. Wiatr, 'Zbigniewa Herberta przygody z muzyką',
Twórczość, 57.1 : 44–78.
HERLING-GRUDZIŃSKI.   Włodzimierz Bolecki, *Rozmowy w Neapolu*,
Wa, Szpak, 2000, 359 pp. Arkadiusz Morawiec, *Poetyka opowiadań
Gustawa Herlinga-Grudzińskiego. Autentyzm — dyskursywność — para-
boliczność*, Kw, Universitas, 2000, 269 pp. J. Gadyś, '*Dziennik pisany
nocą* jako dziennik pisarza', *RuLit*, 40, 1999 : 663–78. A. Morawiec,
'Przypowiastka o sensie ludzkiego cierpienia (Interpretacja opowia-
dania *Gusnący Antychryst* Gustawa Herlinga-Grudzińskiego)', *ib.*,
581–88. M. Rembowska, 'Związki międzytekstowe w opowiadaniach
Gustawa Herlinga-Grudzińskiego (rekonesans)', *ib.*, 41,
2000 : 661–80. L. Sokół, 'Herlinga-Grudzińskiego opowieść tea-
tralna', *Dialog*, 45.6, 2000 : 158–64, discusses the mini-novel *Biała noc
miłości*.
HŁASKO.   Dorota Suska, *Z problemów stylizacji językowej w opowiadaniach Marka Hłaski*, Częstochowa, WSP, 2000, 194 pp., a linguistic
analysis, considers colloquial style, criminal and drivers' jargon, as
well as Warsaw slang in H.'s work.
JANTA.   M. Stępień, ' "Wszystkie strony świata są moje" (O
Aleksandrze Jancie)', *RuLit*, 42 : 475–86.
KIJOWSKI.   W. Tomaszewska, 'Rola krytyki w kształtowaniu litera-
tury. Szkic o poglądach metakrytycznych Andrzeja Kijowskiego',
PL(W), 92.4 : 97–110.
KOZIOŁ.   A. Więckowski, 'Urszuli Kozioł znaki ognia', *Odra*, 40.3,
2000 : 94–97.
KRYNICKI.   J. Gontorow, 'Krynicki', *Odra*, 40.7–8, 2000 : 66–71.
LATAWIEC.   P. Łuszczykiewicz, 'Światło pod powieką. O poezji
Bogusławy Latawiec', *Odra*, 40.2, 2000 : 89–92.
LEM.   P. Czapliński, 'Stanisław Lem – spirala pesymizmu', *TD*,
no. 6 : 59–75. W. Kudyba, 'Lem-felietonista', *RuLit*, 42;487–98.
MARKIEWICZ.   H. Markiewicz, 'Mój życiorys polonistyczny – z
historią w tle', *Twórczość*, 57.7 : 54–69 and 57.8 : 54–69, is an interesting account of the vicissitudes of Polish literary scholarship in the
years 1946–92.

MIŁOSZ. Bożena Karnowska, *Miłosz i Brodzki. Recepcja krytyczna twórczości w krajach anglojęzycznych* [Badania Polonistyczne za Granicą, 6], IBL, 2000, 210 pp. *TD*, nos 3–4 is devoted almost exclusively to M.'s work, and contains essays by leading critics on various aspects and phases of the poet's creative work. These include: R. Nycz, 'Miłosz wśród prądów epoki: cztery poetyki' (7–17); M. Zaleski, 'Miłosz, poeta powtórzenia' (27–38); A. van Nieukerken, 'Czesław Miłosz wobec tradycji europejskiego romantyzmu' (39–56); and A. Nasiłowska, 'Kobiety w poezji Czesława Miłosza' (72–90). G. Gömöri, 'Czesław Miłosz', Jones, *Censorship*, 1598–1600. E. Kołodziejczyk, 'Podróż syna marnotrawnego. O motywie romantycznym w *Trzech zimach* Czesława Miłosza', *PL(W)*, 92.3:135–69 and her ' "Złączeni jednym węzłem dziedziczenia". Powinowactwa *Trzech zim* z poezją Oskara Miłosza', *RuLit*, 42:291–312. J. Olejniczak, 'Gatunek jako temat (przykład Czesława Miłosza)', Bolecki, *Genologia*, 67–76. R. Węgrzyniak, 'Miłosz i teatr', *Dialog*, 45.1, 2000:104–21. Z. Żrebiec, 'Spór o *Zniewolony umysł*. Polemika Gustawa Herlinga-Grudzińskiego z Czesławem Miłoszem', *RuLit*, 41, 2000:563–82.

MOSTWIN. Marian Stępień, *Trzecia wartość. O twórczości Danuty Mostwin*, Kw, wyd. Uniwersytetu Jagiellońskiego, 2000, 269 pp. + 60 photographs.

MROŻEK. J. Speina, 'Przestrzeń świata przedstawionego w opowiadaniach Sławomira Mrożka', *RuLit*, 41, 2000:643–59.

MYŚLIWSKI. *Dialog*, 45.10, 2000, contains two items devoted to M.'s dramatic works: M. Wawrzyniak, 'Metaforyczny realizm Wiesława Myśliwskiego' (118–23) and a discussion entitled 'Rozmowy Obywatel Pleksy' (124–31) about M.'s *Requiem dla gospodyni* printed in the same issue (5–47). H. Bereza, 'Suwerenność', *Twórczość*, 57.1:36–40, also concerns M.'s dramatic works.

PODSIADŁO. S. Stabro, 'Jacek Podsiadło a kontrkultura', *RuLit*, 42:331–46.

POŚWIATOWSKA. Grażyna Borkowska, *nierozważna i nieromantyczna. O Halinie Poświatowskiej*, WL, 202 pp.

U. Klatka, 'Listy Haliny Poświatowskiej do Adama Włodka (1957–1959)', *RuLit*, 42:499–509.

RÓŻEWICZ. S. Frącz, '*Unde Malum?* Tadeusza Różewicza', *Odra*, 40.10, 2000:54–58. A. Kaczyńska, 'Maski i karnawał u Goethego i Różewicza', *Dialog*, 45.2, 2000:99–104, compares Goethe's *Italienische Reise* and R.'s *Et in Arcadia ego*, and similarly, P. Lachmann, 'Goethe z odzysku,' *Twórczość*, 56.12, 2000:93–101.

SŁOBODZIANEK. M. Czata, 'Eschatologiczne gry Tadeusza Słobodzianka', *Dialog*, 45.9, 2000:131–43.

SZCZEPAŃSKI.   Beata Gontarz, *Pisarz i historia. O twórczości Jana Józefa Szczepańskiego* [Prace naukowe 1950], Katowice, wyd. Uniwersytetu Śląskiego, 176 pp.

SZYMBORSKA.   J. Blazina, 'Szymborska's Two Monkeys: The Stammering Poet and the Chain of Signs', *MLR*, 96:130–39. C. Cavanagh, '"Przepisywanie" Wielkiej Historii. Achmatowa, Szymborska i żona Lota', *TD*, no. 2:11–28.

TERLECKI.   A. Chomiuk, 'Powieść historyczna wobec zmian w historiografii. Przypadek Władysława Lecha Terleckiego', *RuLit*, 42:623–36. B. Górska, 'Teatr wyobraźni Władysława Terleckiego', *Odra*, 40.9, 2000:68–72, examines the radio plays.

TYRMAND.   Inga Iwasiów, *Opowieść i milczenie. O prozie Leopolda Tyrmanda* [Rozprawy i studia 436], Szczecin, Uniwersytet Szczeciński, 2000, 225 pp., is an important new study.

WIRPSZA.   '"Gry gatunkowe" na przykładzie poezji Witolda Wirpszy', Bolecki, *Genologia*, 77–85.

WOROSZYLSKI.   G. Gömöri, 'Wiktor Woroszylski', Jones, *Censorship*, 2556–57.

WYKA.   M. Krakowiak, 'Początek drogi (O debiucie krytycznoliterackim Kazimierza Wyki)', *RuLit*, 40, 1999:705–13.

ZIOMEK.   M. Juda-Mieloch, 'Literaturoznawca na ramionach gigantów. Figura autorytetu w późnych tekstach Jerzego Ziomka', *PL(W)*, 92.4:111–34.

IV. RUSSIAN STUDIES

LANGUAGE

POSTPONED

LITERATURE FROM THE BEGINNING TO 1700

POSTPONED

LITERATURE, 1700–1800

POSTPONED

LITERATURE, 1800–1848

By Boris Lanin, *Professor of Literature, Russian Academy of Education, Moscow*

1. General

A. V. Bogatyrev, *Схемы и форматы индивидуализации интенционального начала беллетристического текста*, Tver' State U.P., 197 pp., explores different methods of hermeneutic studies of text. This is the continuation of Bogatyrev's previous book *Элементы неявного смыслообразования* (1998). E. M. Thompson, *Imperial Knowledge: Russian Literature and Colonialism* (Contributions to the Study of World Literature, 99), Westport, CT, Greenwood Press, 2000, viii + 239 pp.; *Литературные мелочи прошлого тысячелетия: К 80–летию Г. В. Краснова*, Kolomna, Kolomna State Pedagogical Institute, 256 pp.; *Литературные салоны и кружки XIX века*, ed. N. L. Brodsky, Mw, Agraf, 496 pp.; K. V. Mochul'sky, *Великие русские писатели XIX века*, StP, Aleteia, 160 pp.; R. Iu. Danilevsky, 'Русская литературная мысль и наследие Г. Э. Лессинга', *RusL*, no.4:90–108; T. S. Grits, V. V. Trenin, and M. M. Nikitin, *Словесность и коммерция (Книжная лавка А. Ф. Смирдина)*, Mw, Agraf, 304 pp., is a reprint of a very interesting book which was edited by Victor Shklovsky and Boris Eikhenbaum and first published in 1929; A. M. Liubomudrov, 'О православии и церковности в художественной литературе', *RusL*, no.1:107–24; R. M. Lazarchuk, *Литературная и театральная Вологда 1770–1800–х годов. Из архивных разысканий*, Vologda, Legiia, 1999, 238 pp., reminds us of the names of Russian provincial writers, such as A. M. Brianchaninov, M. A. Zasodimsky, A. A. Zasetsky, A. V. Oleshev, A. A. Petrov, and others; the main chapter is devoted to M. N. Muraviev. O. N. Kulishkina, 'Русская афористика 1–й трети 19 века', *Vestnik of St Petersburg University*, 2000, ser. 2, no.3:90–7; P. V. Akul'shin, *П. А. Вяземский. Власть и общество в дореформенной России*, Mw, Pamiatniki Istoricheskoi Mysli, 238 pp.; A. L. Iastrebov, Mw, Agraf, 1999, 528 pp.; N. Ie. Mednis, *Венеция в русской литературе*, Novosibirsk, Novosibirsk State Pedagogical University, 1999, 391 pp. К. Iu. Lappo-Danilevsky, 'Лессинг и Винкельман в «Журнале изящных искусств»', *RusL*, no.2:105–17; S. V. Berezkina, 'Почему Федора Толстого прозвали «Американцем»?', *RusL*, no.3:92–95; N. A. Prozorova, 'К биографии А. И. Соколовой (Синее Домино)', *RusL*, 2000, no.4:159–74, is on Alexandra Ivanovna Sokolova ('Sinee Domino'), who published two excellent memoirs *«Из воспоминаний смолянки»*, and *«Встречи и знакомства»*; P. R. Zaborov publishes 'Из неизданной книги Ф. Д. Батюшкова «Около талантов» —«В семье Майковых', *RusL*, 2000, no.3:177–94; A. Tosi, 'Sentimental irony in early nineteenth-century Russian literature: the case of Nikolai Brusilov's *Bednyi Leandr*', *SEEJ*, 44,2000:266–86; A. V. Sharonova, 'О проблеме взаимоотношений редактора и авторов «Библиотеки для чтения»', *RusL*, 2000, no.3:83–96.

2. LITERARY HISTORY

Two extremely useful guides for scholars are *Russian Literature in the Age of Pushkin and Gogol: Poetry and Drama*, ed. C. A. Rydel (*Dictionary of Literary Biography*, Volume 205), Gale, Detroit–Washington, DC–London, 1999, xxvi + 449 pp.; and *The Cambridge Companion to the Classic Russian Novel*, ed. M. V. Jones and R. F. Miller, CUP, 1998. See also *A. A. V. V. Storia della civiltà letteraria russa*, ed. M. Colucci and R. Picchio, 2 vols, Turin, 1997, 789, 897 pp.; *A. A. V. V. Dizinario Chronologia*, UTET, Turin, 1997, 405 pp. Among Russian studies in literary history are V. Sh. Krivonos, *Русская литература XIX века*, Samara, Samara State Pedagogical University, 154 pp.; *История русской литературы XIX века: 1800—1830-е годы: В 2 ч.*, ed. V. N. Anoshkina and L. D. Gromova, 2 vols, Mw, VLADOS, 288, 256 pp.; *Литературоведческий сборник. Вып. 5/6*, Donetsk, Donetsk National University, 328 pp., with papers on Pushkin, Garshin, Karamzin, A.Sukhovo-Kobylin, and Chekhov; *Поэтика русской литературы: К 70-летию профессора Юрия Владимировича Манна: Сборник статей*, Mw, RGGU, 366 pp., papers by V. Markovich, S. Broitman, N. Tamarchenko, B. Egorov, and others; A. L. Zorin, *«Кормя двуглавого орла...»: Русская литература и государственная идеология в последней трети XVIII — первой трети XIX века* (Historia Rossica), Mw, Novoe Literaturnoe Obozrenie,

416 pp.; C. A. Ruud and S. A. Stepanov, *Fontanka 16: The Tsar's Secret Police*, Montreal–Kingston, McGill-Queens U.P., 1999, xvi + 394 pp.; *Литературные салоны и кружки: Первая половина XIX века*, ed. N. L. Brodsky, Mw, Agraf, 496 pp.

3. THEORY

GENERAL

W. M. Todd III, *The Familiar Letter as a Literary Genre in the Age of Pushkin* (Studies in Russian Literature and Theory), Evanston, IL, Northwestern U.P., 1999, xii + 230 pp., is a paper reprint of one of the most influential works in Slavic Studies (first publication in 1976).

Some interesting books have been published in Russian and Ukranian provincial publishing houses: *Проблемы целостного анализа художественного произведения, выпуск 2,* Borisoglebsk, Borisoglebck State Pedagogical Institute, 94 pp., collected papers on narration in works of Griboedov, Lermontov, Pushkin, Turgenev, L. Tolstoi, and Viazemsky; V. S. Vakhrushev, *Образ. Текст. Игра. Очерки по теории литературы,* Borisoglebsk, Borisoglebsk State Pedagogical Institute, 126 pp.; *Филологические исследования: сборник научных работ, выпуск 3,* ed. M. M. Girshman, Donetsk, Iugo-Vostok, 380 pp. — works by Iu. Borev, M. Girshman, A. Korablev, A. Domashenko, N. Tamarchenko, etc. Of some interest is T. A. Kitanina, 'Материалы к указателю литературных сюжетов (Сюжеты о соперниках и призраках)', *RusL*, 1999, no.3 : 205–19. One of the most impressive books of the last year is *Литературная энциклопедия терминов и понятий,* ed. A. N. Nikoliukin, Mw, Intelvak, 1600 pp.(!). V. M. Golovko, *Историческая поэтика русской классической повести,* Stavropol', Stavropol' State University, 205 pp.; V. A. Golovashin, *Русская пародия,* Tambov, MINTs, 74 pp. —history of parody in Russian literature of the 18th and 19th cs; V. V. Golovin, *Русская колыбельная песня в фольклоре и литературе,* Åbo Akademi U.P., 2000, 451 pp.; A. B. Pen'kovsky, *Нина: Культурный миф золотого века русской литературы в лингвистическом освещении,* Mw, Indrik, 1999, 520 pp.; E. G. Chernysheva, *Проблемы поэтики русской фантастической прозы 20–40-х годов XIX века,* Mw, Moscow State Pedagogical University, Prometei, 2000, 143 pp.; E. G. Chernysheva, *Мир преображенья: Мифологические и игровые мотивы в русской фантастической прозе 20–40-х годов XIX века,* Blagoveshchensk, Mw, Prometei, 1996, 109 pp.; V. I. Tiupa, *Аналитика художественного: Введение в литературоведческий анализ,* Mw, Labirint-MP, RGGU, 192 pp.

ROMANTICISM

Iu. Mann, *Русская литература 19 века: Эпоха романтизма*, Mw, Aspekt, 247 pp.; P. M. Austin, *The Exotic Prisoner in Russian Romanticism* (Middlebury Studies in Russian Language and Literature, 15), NY, Lang, 1997, xiv + 215 pp.; A. N. Girivenko, *Русский поэтический перевод в культурном контексте эпохи романтизма*, Mw, URAO, 2000, 234 pp.

POETRY

M. Wachtel, *The Development of Russian Verse: Meter and its Meaning* (Cambridge Studies in Russian Literature), NY, CUP, 1998, xii + 323 pp., is an extremely valuable study of Russian verse; E. K. Sobolevskaya, 'Минус-стих, его природа и онтологические основания (к вопросам метафизики стиха)', *RusL*, no.4:68–82, is an excellent study of one of the difficult terms in 20th-c. literary theory; N. S. Movnina, 'Идеальный топос русской поэзии конца 18 — начала 19 века', *RusL*, 2000, no.3:13–36; O. N. Grinbaum, *Гармония строфического ритма в эстетико-формальном измерении (на материале "онегинской строфы" и русского сонета)*, St Petersburg State U.P., 2000, 158 pp.; O. N. Grinbaum and G. Ia. Martynenko *Русский сонет и «золотая пропорция» ритма*, St Petersburg State U.P., 1999, 16 pp.

MEMOIRS

A. M. Skabichevsky, *Литературные воспоминания*, Mw, Agraf, 432 pp.; L. I. Nazarova, 'Воспоминания о Викторе Андрониковиче Мануйлове (1903–1987)', *RusL*, no.4:172–94; E. S. Khaev, *Болдинское чтение: Статьи, заметки, воспоминания*, Nizhnii Novgorod State U.P., 156 pp. – interesting works on Pushkin and Tiutchev.

GENDER STUDIES

L. P. Moiseeva, 'Проблема женской эмансипации в русской литературе 30–40-х годов XIX века', *ONS*, 2000, no.4:164–71.

COMPARATIVE STUDIES

O. Rikhterek, 'Чешское восприятие русской литературы в контексте 20 века', *RusL*, no.4:83–89, is mostly about Pushkin and Chekhov. *Landschaft und Lyrik: Die Schweiz in Gedichten der Slaven: Eine kommentierte Anthologie*, ed. Peter Brang, introd. Christoph Ferber, Basel, 1998, 733 pp.; R. Elfrath, *Der Deutsche als Charakter in der russischen Literatur des 19. Jhs — seine Funktion und sein Wandel in der Erzählstruktur* (Wissenschaftsskripten, Reihe 4: Slawische Sprach- und Literaturwissenschaft, 1) Gießen, 1998, 153 pp., explores the poetics of *Deutsche* in the works of Pushkin, Turgenev, L. Tolstoy and Chekhov; *Cold Fusion: Aspects of the German Cultural Presence in Russia*, ed. G. Barabtarlo (Studies in Slavic Literature, Culture, Society), NY, Berghahn, 2000, viii + 310 pp., has papers on E. T. A. Hoffmann's influence on Gogol, the role of Kantian ethics in the 'Legend of the Grand Inquisitor', and many others. G. Marinelli-König, *Russland in den Wiener Zeitschriften und Almanachen des Vormärz (1805–1848): Ein Beitrag zur Geschichte der österreichisch-russischen Kultur- und Literaturbeziehungen. Beiheft mit Nachträgen* (Sitzungsberichte, 654; Veröffentlichungen der Komission für Literaturwissenschaft, 18), Vienna, 1998, 129 pp.

4. Gogol

GENERAL

V. Sh. Krivonos, 'К проблеме пространства у Гоголя: Петербургская окраина', *Izv. RAN, SLI*, 2000, no.2:15–22; S. V. Aleksandrova, 'Повести Н. В. Гоголя и народная зрелищная культура', *RusL*, 1:50–65, a Bakhtinian study of Gogol's novellas; V. Otroshenko, 'Гоголиана', *Oktjabr'*, 2000, no.4:123–42. V. E. Vetlovskaya, 'Творчество Гоголя сквозь призму проблемы народности', *RusL*, 2:3–24, is interesting in some ways, but is just funny research, a hello from the 50s: the same phrases, the same ideological aspect —'narodnost'!

DEAD SOULS

A. Lounsbery, ' "Russia! What do you want of me?": the Russian reading public in *Dead Souls*', *SRev*, 60:367–89. L. I. Sazonova, 'Литературная родословная гоголевской птицы-тройки', *Izv. RAN SLI*, 2000, no.2:23–30, argues that the poetic formula 'troika-bird' has its roots in folk songs about Russian 'troika' and in Ezekiel's vision of God's glory; V. I. Glukhov, 'Сумароковский "след" . . . в "Мертвых душах" Гоголя', *RRe*, 2000, no.5:3–6.

STUDIES ON VARIOUS WORKS

A. Schönle, 'Gogol, the picturesque, and the desire for the people: a reading of *Rome*', *RusR*, 59:597–613; V. Sh. Krivonos, 'О смысле повести Гоголя «Рим»', *Izv. RAN, SLI*, no.6:14–26; B. I. Matveev,

'Приемы изображения в повести Н. В. Гоголя "Невский проспект"', *RRe*, 2000, no.2:11–19; C. Putney, *Russian Devils and Diabolic Conditionality in Nikolai Gogol's Evenings on a Farm near Dikanka* (Middlebury Studies in Russian Language and Literature, 15), NY, Lang, 1999, xiii + 250 pp.; E. Dryzhakova, 'Рискованная шутка Гоголя на чтениях «Ревизора»', *RusL*, 1:190–95.

Iu. Barabash, 'Сладкий ужас мщенья, или Зло во имя добра?', *VL*, no.3:31–65, is on the theme of revenge in Gogol's and Shevchenko's works. There are several works written by V. A. Voropaev: 'Последняя книга Гоголя (к истории создания и публикации «Размышлений о «Божественной Литургии»)', *RusL*, 2000, no.2:184–95; 'Лествица Николая Гоголя', *Literaturnaia Ucheba*, 2000, no.2:159–82; 'Подданный русского царя. Гоголь и Государь Николай Павлович', *Literaturnaia Ucheba*, no.2:140–51; 'Чей удел на земле выше? Из духовной биографии Гоголя', *Literaturnaia Ucheba*, no.3:103–29.

5. Pushkin

GENERAL

A Bibliography of Alexander Pushkin in English: Studies and Translations, ed. L. Leighton (Studies in Slavic Languages and Literatures, 12), Lewiston, NY, Mellen, 1999, xiii + 310 pp. — very helpful; S. Lominadze, 'Пушкин — поэт обыкновенного человека', *VL*, 2000, no.3:127–70; E. P. Chelyshev, 'Постижение русского национального гения', *VF*, 2000, no.1:71–83; *А. С. Пушкин: pro et contra. Личность и творчество Александра Пушкина в оценке русских мыслителей и исследователей. Антология*, comp. V. M. Markovich and G. E. Potapova, 2 vols, StP, RkhGI, 2000, 712, 733 pp.; V. I. Novikov, 'Культурные контексты этики Пушкина', *ONS*, no.6:176–88; N. A. Marchenko, *Приметы тихой старины: Нравы и быт пушкинской эпохи*, Mw, Izograf, EKSMO-Press, 368 pp.; M. G. Altshuller, 'Между двух царей (заметки о гражданской лирике Пушкина)', *RusL*, 1:11–32. The images of two tsars are in the focus of a very interesting study, V. I. Vlashchenko, 'Загадка "Метели"', *Russkaia Slovesnost'*, 2000, no.1:43–49.

V. N. Kasatkina, 'Романтическая муза А.С.Пушкина', *Russkaia Slovesnost'*, 2000, no.2:4–10, was followed by a book under the same title: V. N. Kasatkina (Anoshkina), *Романтическая муза Пушкина*, Mw, Moscow State University, 128 pp; W. Slater, 'The patriot's Pushkin', *SRev*, 58, 1999:407–27; B. M. Gasparov, *Поэтический язык Пушкина как факт истории русского литературного языка*, StP, Akademicheskii Proekt, 1999, 400 pp.; *Пушкин и Оренбургский край. Документы. Записи. Письма. Воспоминания. Исследования*, ed. A. G. Prokofieva, Orenburg, Orenburg State Pedagogical University, 2000, 239 pp.

Several works by Vladimir Nepomniashchy have been published this year: V. S. Nepomniashchy, *Да ведают потомки православных. Пушкин. Россия. Мы*, Mw, Sestrichestvo Vo Imia Elizavety, 400 pp.; *Лирика Пушкина как духовная биография*, Mw, Moscow State University PH, 240 pp.; *Московский пушкинист. IX*, ed. V. S. Nepomniashchy, Mw, Nasledie, 312 pp.; V. S. Nepomniashchy, *Пушкин: Избранные работы 1960–1990 гг*, 2 vols, I: *Поэзия и судьба*, II: *Пушкин. Русская картина мира*, Mw, Zhizn′ i Mysl′, 496, 496 pp.

New issues of *Михайловская Пушкиниана* were published by the Pushkin State Museum 'Mikhailovskoe'. Among the most interesting are *Выпуск 13. Пушкинская михайловская энциклопедия (материалы): Михайловское. Тригорское*, Mw, Berbum-M, 200 pp.; *Выпуск 14. По материалам конференции «У каждого времени свой Пушкин»*, Mw, Berbum-M, 168 pp.; *Выпуск 17. V. Iu. Koztin, «...Тот уголок земли»: Локус Михайловского в поэтическом творчестве А. С. Пушкина*, Mw, Berbum-M, 240 pp.; *Выпуск 18. V. G. Nikiforov, Земли родной минувшая судьба*, Mw, Berbum-M, 292 pp.; *Выпуск 19. A.V. Bukovsky, Псковская хроника: послессыльный период жизни и творчества А. С. Пушкина*, Mw, Berbum-M, 168 pp.; *Выпуск 20. Памяти С. С. Гейченко*, Mw, Berbum-M, 170 pp.

BIOGRAPHY

Perhaps the best biography published in the last decade is D. M. Bethea, *Realizing Metaphors: Alexander Pushkin and the Life of the Poet*, Madison, Wisconsin U.P., 1998, xviii + 224 pp. Among other valuable sources are *Хроника жизни и творчества А. С. Пушкина: В 3 т.: 1826–1837*, ed. G. I. Doldobanov (Pushkin v XX veke, 9), 1.2: *1829–1830*, II.1: *1831–1832*, Mw, IMLI RAN, Nasledie, 488, 424 pp. K. A. Rozova, *Подарок пушкиниста М. А. Цявловского*, Mw, Stroimaterialy, 334 pp.; V. Osipov, *Зима, весна, лето и Болдинская осень: Жизнь А. С. Пушкина в 1830 году*, Mw, Raritet, 430 pp.; S. T. Ovchinnikova, *А.С.Пушкин. Москва. Арбат: Летопись жизни А. С. Пушкина с 5 декабря 1830 г. по 15 мая 1831 г.*, Mw, Russkaia Kniga, 200 pp.

Two paradoxical and provocative books hav been written by Iu. Druzhnikov, *Смерть изгоя. По следам неизвестного Пушкина: роман-исследование*, Baltimore, Seagull Press, 320 pp.; and *Дуэль с пушкинистами: полемические эссе*, Mw, Khroniker, 335 pp.

See also V. I. Kuleshov, *А. С. Пушкин. Научно-художественная биография*, Mw, Nauka, 1997, 432 pp.; I. Surat, *Пушкин: биография и лирика. Проблемы. Разборы. Заметки. Отклики*, Mw, Nasledie, 1999, 240 pp.; A. P. Liusyi, *Pushkin, Tavrida, Kimmeriia*, Mw, Iazyki russkoi kul'tury, 2000, 248 pp. *Записки графа Федора Петровича Толстого*, ed. E. G. Chekunova and E. G. Gorokhova, Mw, RGGU, 319 pp.; O. Iu Zakharova, *Генерал-фельдмаршал светлейший князь М. С. Воронцов. Рыцарь Российской империи*, Mw, Tsentrpoligraf, 381 pp.; V. F. Kashkova, *«Утешен буду я любовью. . .»: Дневник пушкинского года*, Tver', Tverskoe Oblastnoe Knizhno-Zhurnal'noe Izdatel'stvo, 192 pp.; M. Romm, 'А. С. Пушкин 13 июня 1831 года', *Neva*, no.2:226–28. S. V. Berezkina, 'Пушкин в Михайловском. О духовном надзоре над поэтом (1824–1826)', *RusL*, 2000, no.1:3–21; G. V. Antiukhin, *«Края Москвы, края родные. . .»: Бабушка А. С. Пушкина – Мария Алексеевна*, Voronezh, SVP 'Voinskoe Sodruzhestvo', 24 pp.; A. M. Bessonova, *Родословная роспись потомков Абрама Петровича Ганнибала – прадеда Александра Сергеевича Пушкина*, StP, Bel'veder, 2nd revised edn; I. V. Danilov, *Прадед Пушкина Ганнибал*, StP, Media Press, 208 pp.; A. G. Bitov, *Вычитание зайца. 1825*, ed. Irina Surat, Mw, Nezavisimaia Gazeta, 367 pp., has illustrations by Alexandr Pushkin and Rezo Gabriadze — the famous Georgian director — and is an excellent book written by one of the best Russian prose writers, with brilliant style, imagination, and deep knowledge of Pushkin.

There is an excellent work that explores Pushkin's duel and death in semiological key: I. Reyfman, 'Death and mutilation at the duelling site: Pushkin's death as a national spectacle', *RusR*, 60:72–88. See also E. Gusliarov, *Все дуэли Пушкина*, Kaliningrad, Iantarnyi skaz, 96 pp; I. Efimov, 'A duel with the Tsar', *RusR*, 58, 2000:574–90; L. O'Bell, 'Writing the story of Pushkin's death', *SRev*, 58, 1999:393–406.

M. L. Gofman, *Невеста и жена Пушкина*, ed. I. F. Vladimirov, Mw, Nash Dom–L'Age d'Homme — Ekaterinburg, U-Faktoriia, 112 pp., includes several works by the famous Pushkinist who emigrated from the USSR in 1920s.

There are several papers about Pushkin's celebrations: F. A. Molok, 'Пушкинский юбилей 1937 года в русском зарубежье', *RusL*, 1999, no.4:143–52, and T. V. Evdokimova, 'Добавление к статье Ф. А. Молока 'Пушкинский юбилей 1937 года в русском зарубежье' по материалам коллекции Лидии и Сержа Варсано, хранящейся в Пушкинском кабинете ИРЛИ (Пушкинский Дом) РАН', *ib.*, 152–54; I. Surat, 'Пушкинский юбилей как заклинание истории', *NovM*, 2000, no.6:176–86; M. V. Zagidullina, *Пушкинский миф в конце XX века*, Cheliabinsk State U.P., 243 pp; E. Matveev, 'Пушкин после юбилея', *NSo*, 2000, no.6:281–82.

There are several works by Iurii Chumakov — one of the best specialists in 'Evgenii Onegin': Iu. N. Chumakov, 'Поэтика «Евгения Онегина»', *Izv. RAN SLI*, 2000, no.1:11–24; Id., *Стихотворная поэтика Пушкина*, StP, State Pushkin Theatre Center, 1999, 431 pp.; Id., *"Евгений Онегин" А. С. Пушкина. В мире стихотворного романа*, Mw., MSU PH, 1999, 128 pp. S. Dalton-Brown, *Pushkin's 'Evgenii Onegin'* (Critical Studies in Russian Literature), Bristol, Bristol Classical Press, 1997, 145 pp. E. I. Mazovetskaia, '«Евгений Онегин» на иврите', *RusL*, 1:187–89, publishes an old letter about translating 'Onegin' into Hebrew. A. M. Gurevich, *Сюжет «Евгения Онегина»*, Mw, Moscow State University, 112 pp.

Two works study the opening of 'Evgenii Onegin': N. V. Pertsov, 'Загадка начала «Евгения Онегина»', *Izv. RAN SLI*, 2000, no.3:25–30; N. I. Mikhailova, 'Мой дядя самых честных правил ... (Из наблюдений над текстом первой строфы «Евгения Онегина»)', *ib.*, 31–34, which reveals some literary ideas of the first stanza of Pushkin's novel. V. D. Rak, '«Обшикать Федру, Клеопатру...»', *RusL*, 2000, no.4:94–104. There three works about Tatiana Larina, O. P. Hasty, *Pushkin's Tatiana*, Madison, Univ. of Wisconsin Press, 1999, xvii + 269 pp.; M. I. Shapir, 'Как звали няню Татьяны Лариной? (Из комментариев к "Евгению Онегину")', *Izv. RAN SLI*, 2000, no.6: 62–63; S. A. Martianova, 'Татьяна Ларина в последней главе романа "Евгений Онегин"', *Russkaia Slovesnost*, 2000, no.1:36–42; V. I. Shirinkin, 'Восьмая глава «Евгения Онегина» в Перми', *RusL*, 2000, no.4:111–13; J. W. De Sherbinin, 'Pushkin's "flying creations": fowl play in *Evgenii Onegin*', *RusR*, 58, 2000:535–47; Iu. M. Nikishov, 'Пленник, Алеко, Онегин: родство и несходство братьев', *Izv. RAN SLI*, no.4:12–22.

STUDIES ON VARIOUS WORKS

P. Cavendish, 'Poetry as metamorphosis: Aleksandr Pushkin's *Ekho* and the reshaping of the Echo myth', *SEER*, 78, 2000:439–62; *Alexandre S. Pouchkine et le Monde Noir: 'Moia Afrika, Mon Afrique, My Africa'*, ed. D. Gnammankou, Paris, Présence Africaine, 1999, 287 pp.; S. Povartsov, '"Цареубийственный кинжал" (Пушкин и мотивы цареубийства в русской поэзии)', *VL*, no.1:88–116; E. Svenitskaya, '"Песни западных славян" Пушкина как художественное единство', *ib.*, 319–29; V. S. Listov, '"Восстань, восстань, пророк России ..." (к истолкованию спорной пушкинской строфы)', *Izv. RAN SLI*, no.4:47–50; N. I. Mikhailova,

'Из наблюдений над текстом стихотворения "Воспоминание" (Пушкин и Овидий)', *ib.*, 51–52. The article is concerned with a quotation from Ovid's 'Ex Ponto' discovered in Pushkin's poem 'Memory'.

R. Gregg, 'Germann the Confessor and the stony, seated countess: the moral subtext of Pushkin's *The Queen of Spades*', *SEER*, 78, 2000:612–24; N. Mikhailova, '"Пиковая дама означает тайную недоброжелательность . . .", *Oktjabr'*, no.6:178–84; S. Davydov, 'The Ace in the *Queen of Spades*', *SRev*, 58, 1999:309–28.

G. Krasukhin, 'Над страницами "Маленьких трагедий" Пушкина', *VL*, no.5:101–34; N. Eliseev, 'Моцарт и Сальери. Опыт истолкования', *Neva*, 2000, no.6:191–98; O. B. Zaslavsky, 'Пушкинский Сальери и тип творчества', *Izv. RAN SLI*, no.4:23–28; A. Kahn, *Pushkin's 'The Bronze Horseman'* (Critical Studies in Russian Literature), London, Bristol Classical Press, 1998, ix + 149 pp., suggests that for Pushkin there is no escape from history into the private world; V. Esipov, 'Что мы знаем Об Иване Петровиче Белкине?', *VL*, no.6:324–33; E. S. Afanasiev, '«Повести Белкина» А. С. Пушкина: ироническая проза', *RusL*, 2000, no.2:177–84; N. Prozhogin, '"Что в имени тебе моем?..". Не только о дате', *VL*, no.6:281–95; C. Dunning, 'Rethinking the canonical text of Pushkin's *Boris Godunov*', *RusR*, 60:569–91; K. I. Sharafadina, 'Загадка «Психеи, которая задумалась над цветком»: о неосуществленном пушкинском замысле прикнижной виньетки', *RusL*, 1999, no.3:72–83; V. P. Stark, 'Рецензия А. С. Пушкина на «Словарь о святых»', *ib.*, 2000, no.4:104–11; M. Schneider, *Postmeister und Stetionsaufseher: Eine Studie zur deutschen Puškin-Rezeption* (Vortrage und Abhandlungen zur Slavistik, 33), Munich, Sagner, 1997, 173 pp., is a study of German perception of Pushkin's 'Станционный смотритель' from 1837 to 1995 (24 translations of this story into German appeared during this period); *Пушкинская конференция в Стэнфорде. 1999: Материалы и исследования*, ed. D. Bethea, Mw, OGI, 512 pp.; A. P. Davydov, *«Духовной жаждою томим»: А. С. Пушкин и становление «срединной» культуры в России*, Novosibirsk, Sibirskii Khronograf, 242 pp.; M. N. Darvin, V. I. Tiupa, *Циклизация в творчестве Пушкина: Опыт изучения поэтики конвергентного сознания*, Novosibirsk, Nauka, 293 pp.

S. V. Berezkina, 'Мотивы матери и материнства в творчестве А. С. Пушкина', *RusL*, no.1:167–86; M. D. El'zon, '«Всяк сущий в ней язык . . .» (об источнике пушкинского наречия)', *ib.*, 189–90; I. V. Nemirovsky, 'О «Пророке» и Пророке', *RusL*, no.3:3–10; L. M. Lotman, 'Об альтернативах и путях решения текстологической «загадки» «Русалки» Пушкина', *RusL*, no.1 : 129–52; E. S. Rogover, 'Образы и мотивы «Медного всадника» Пушкина в русской прозе XX века', *RusL*, no.2 : 42–55. See also: V. P. Moskvin, '"Грозой снесенные мосты …"', *RRe*, no.3 : 3–6; S. A. Fomichev, 'К истолкованию пушкинского наброска «Критон, роскошный гражданин …»', *RusL*, no.4 : 114–18; K. I. Sharafadina, 'Игра «во вкусе rococo» в мадригале Пушкина «Красавице, которая нюхала табак» (1814)', *ib.*, 118–41; G. K. Valeev, 'Читая Пушкина: " …там люди, в кучах за оградой …"', *RRe*, 2000, no.4 : 104–10; N. Poliakova, 'Несчастные отцы и блудные дети', *Neva*, no.10 : 233–35, on Vyrin and Pliushkin. J. L. Morgan IV, 'Love, friendship, and poetic voice in Aleksandr Pushkin's Lycée elegies', *SRev*, 58, 1999 : 352–70; I. M. Helfant, 'Pushkin's ironic performances as a gambler', *ib.*, 371–92.

PUSHKIN AND OTHER WRITERS

E. G. Etkind, *Божественный глагол. Пушкин, прочитанный в России и во Франции*, Mw, Iazyki russkoi kul'tury, 1999, 600 pp., is a brilliant study, one of the best books by Etkind; D. Shengold, 'Adding to the "guest" list: Hugo's Hernani and Pushkin's Don Juan', *SRev*, 58, 1999 : 329–36; C. T. Nepomnyashchy, 'Pushkin's *The Bronze Horseman* and Irving's "The Legend of Sleepy Hollow": a curious case of cultural cross-fertilization?', *ib.*, 337–51; V. D. Rak, 'Раннее знакомство Пушкина с произведениями Байрона', *RusL*, 2000, no.2 : 3–25; A. A. Dobritsyn, 'Пушкин и Клод-Жозеф Дора (О возможном источнике стихотворения "Нет, я не дорожу мятежным наслажденьем …")', *Izv. RAN SLI*, no.6 : 59–61, poses the question of the influence which French 'poésie fugitive' had on Alexander Pushkin's late lyric poetry. Claude-Joseph Dorat's verse epistle, 'Au Marquis de ***' ('Toi qui de Beautés en Beautés …'), is discussed as one of possible literary sources of Pushkin's 'Net, ya ne dorozhu myatezhnym naslazhden'em …'(1830); I. Kresikova, *Цветаева и Пушкин: Попытка проникновения. Эссе и этюды*, Mw, RIF 'Roi', 168 pp.; F. Raskol'nikov, 'Место античности в творчестве Пушкина', *RusL*, 1999, no.4 : 3–25, and 'Загадки пушкинской «Сказки о Золотом Петушке»', *RLJ*, 54, 2000 : 79–94; R. Iu. Danilevsky, 'Миссия гения (Пушкин и Гете)', *RusL*, 1999, no.3 : 3–21; N. L. Dmitrieva, 'Роза у Пушкина и Тургенева', *RusL*, 2000, no.3 : 101–06; *A. C. Пушкин и мир славянской культуры: К 200-летию со дня рождения поэта*, ed. L. N. Budagova, Mw, Institut slavianovedeniia RAN, 2000, 277 pp.; A. Iu. Sergeeva-Kliatys, 'Странствователь и странник (К теме «Батюшков и Пушкин»)', *Izv. RAN SLI*, 2000, no.3 : 35–39, about connections between Pushkin's 'Pilgrim' and Batiushkov's tale 'Wanderer and stay at home'; V. D. Skvoznikov, 'К понятию "пушкинской традиции" (Пушкин и поздний Жуковский)', *Russkaia Slovesnost'*, no.6:2–9; E. Ginzburg, '«Я встретил вас» . . . «в подлунной стороне»: от Жуковского — через Пушкина — к Тютчеву', *CASS*, 35:439–51; D. P. Ivinskii, *Пушкин и Мицкевич: История литературных отношений*, Mw, Moscow State University, 2000; M. F. Murianov, *Пушкин и Германия*, Mw, Nasledie, 1999, 446 pp.; A. A. Zhirov, *Нащокин, Пушкин и другие*, Mw, Zvonnitsa-MG, 160 pp.; A. I. Reitblat, *Как Пушкин вышел в гении: Историко-социологические очерки о книжной культуре Пушкинской эпохи*, Mw, Novoe Literaturnoe Obozrenie, 336 pp.; T. I. Krasnova, 'А. С. Пушкин в Зарубежной России', *Vestnik of St Petersburg University*, 2000, ser. 2, no.2:76–82.

Also worthy of mention are: *Ежегодник Рукописного отдела Пушкинского Дома на 1996 год: Б .Л. Модзалевский: Материалы к научной биографии*, ed. I. G. Ivanova, StP, Dmitrii Bulanin, 608 pp.; T. I. Levicheva, *Письма А. С. Пушкина Южного периода: 1820–1824: Проблемы текстологии*, 2nd revd edn, Mw, Nauka, 391 pp.; S. K. Romaniuk, *В поисках пушкинской Москвы*, Mw, Profizdat, 256 pp. A. D. Gdalin, *Памятники А. С. Пушкину: История. Описание. Библиография*, Vol. 1, part 1, StP, Akademicheskii Proekt, 510 pp.; *Вацуриана*, ed. T. Selezneva, StP, 2001 — selected papers in honour and memory of Vadim Erazmovich Vatsuro; *Воронцовское общество: 1991—2001*, ed. V. N. Alekseev and V. A. Udovik, StP, Vorontsovskoe obschestvo, 44 pp.; N. Ramazanova, 'А. С. Пушкин и А. Ф. Львов. К истории создания "Народного гимна" ', *Neva*, no.2:214–9.; L. L. Bel'skaia, 'Пушкинские эпиграфы в русской поэзии', *RRe*, 2000, no.1:3–9; D. N. Medrish, 'Пушкинский образ в контексте народной культуры', *RRe*, 2000, no.5:110–16; A. L. Sobolev, *Автограф Пушкина*, Mw, Druzhinin, 1998, 84 pp.; L. S. Skepner, 'А. С. Пушкин в сознании поморов (конец 19–начало 20 века)', *RusL*, 2000, no.3:96–101.

PUSHKIN AS ARTIST AND ILLUSTRATOR

S. V. Denisenko and S. A. Fomichev, *Пушкин рисует. Графика Пушкина*, StP, Notabene — NY, Tumanov, 256 pp.; V. Udovik, 'М. С. и Е. К. Воронцовы в рисунках А. С. Пушкина', *Neva*, no.10:213–6. Of some interest is A. V. Kornilova, *Григорий Гагарин: Творческий путь*, Mw, Iskusstvo, 255 pp., is a biography of one of the most successful illustrators of Pushkin's works.

6. OTHER INDIVIDUAL AUTHORS

BATIUSHKOV. L. N. Maikov, *Батюшков, его жизнь и сочинения*, Mw, Agraf, 528 pp., a reprint of the 1896 edition, is still one of the best books about Batiushkov.

BELINSKY. G. Iu. Karpenko, *Возвращение Белинского: Литературно-художественное сознание русской критики в контексте историософских представлений*, Samara, Samarskii Universitet, 368 pp.; A. S. Kurilov, 'В. Г. Белинский о мировом значении А.С.Пушкина', *Russkaia Slovesnost'*, 2000, no.3:28–32; no.4:31–36.

BULGARIN. O. V. Sliadneva, 'Принципы редакторской и рекламной практики Фаддея Булгарина (на примере газеты «Северная пчела»)', *Vestnik of St Petersburg University*, 1999, ser. 2, no.3:72–77; N. N. Akimova, '«Северный архив» и его издатель', *RusL*, no.3:96–107, is a paper about F. Bulgarin. A very important publication is F. V. Bulgarin, *Воспоминания*, Mw, Zakharov, 784 pp. — a reprint of 1846–1849 writings.

BUNINA. W. Rosslyn, *Anna Bunina (1774–1829) and the Origins of Women's Poetry in Russia* (Studies in Slavic Language and Literature, 10), Lewiston, NY, Mellen, 1997, xviii, 360 pp.

CHAADAEV. There are several interesting works on Chaadaev: R. Aizlewood, 'Revising Russian identity in Russian thought: from Chaadaev to the early twentieth century', *SEER*, 78, 2000:20–43; *Чаадаев и Мамардашвили. Перекличка голосов, проблем и перспектив. Традиция и эволюция исторического взгляда в русской историософии*, Perm', 106 pp.; R. S. Cherepanova, 'Петр Чаадаев мифический и реальный', *ONS*, no.3:102–09; Iu. G. Oksman and V. V. Pugachev, *Пушкин, декабристы и Чаадаев*, ed. L. E. Gerasimova, V. S. Parsamova, and V. M. Selezneva, Saratov, Volga–Parokhod, 1999, 260 pp., is a valuable book including four papers by the famous Soviet scholar Iulian Oksman: 'Повесть о прапорщике Черниговского полка. (Неизвестный замысел Пушкина)', 'Воспоминания П. А. Катенина о Пушкине', 'Политическая лирика и сатира Пушкина', 'Пушкинская ода "Вольность". (К вопросу о датировке)', and seven papers by V. V. Pugachev ('Предыстория Союза благоденствия и пушкинская ода "Вольность"', 'Декабрист Н. И. Тургенев и пушкинская "Деревня"', 'Декабристы, "Евгений Онегин" и Чаадаев", "Кто победил 14-го декабря?" etc).

DERZHAVIN. A very useful source is G. R. Derzhavin, *Записки. 1743–1812. Полный текст*, Mw, Mysl', 2000, 334 pp. Polemics about Derzhavin's last piece were published in *RusL*: K. Iu. Lappo-Danilevsky, 'Последнее стихотворение Г. Р. Державина', *RusL*, 2000, no.2:146–58; with a response from M. D. El'zon, 'О пользе чтения стихов по горизонтали (к истолкованию последнего стихотворения Г. Р. Державина)', *ib.*, no.3:81–83; I. Mess-Beier, 'Карнавальный Державин', *RLJ*, 54, 2000:65–78.

GRIBOEDOV. S. Shtil'man, '"Про ум Молчалина"', *Russkaia Slovesnost*, no.6:10–15.

KOZLOV. V. Afanasiev, 'Жизнь и лира. Заметки о забытом поэте-классике Иване Ивановиче Козлове (1779–1840)', *Literaturnaia Ucheba*, 2000, no.4:84–90.

LERMONTOV. Biographical studies include A. Ochman, *Роковой поединок: Дуэль и гибель М. Ю. Лермонтова в отечественной литературе XX века*, Piatigorsk, 264 pp.; V. Obraztsov, '"Из чьей руки свинец смертельный . . .". Михаил Лермонтов, Николай Мартынов и злой рок', *NG*, July 31; *Лермонтовский заповедник Тарханы. Документы и материалы, 1701–1924*, ed. P. F. Frolov, Penza, State Lermontov Museum 'Tarkhany', 222 pp. On L.'s works, V. Golstein, *Lermontov's Narratives of Heroism* (Studies in Russian Literature and Theory. Evanston), Northwestern U.P., 1998. x + 244 pp.; A. M. Shteingol'd, E. M. Taborisskaya, 'Две рефлексии по поводу романа «Герой нашего времени» (предисловие Лермонтова и статья Белинского)', *RusL*, no.1:33–49; E. E. Naidich, 'Очерк Лермонтова «Кавказец» в свете полемики вокруг «Героя нашего времени»', *RusL*, no.4:141–48; A. A. Gerasimenko, *Божественный певец: к 160-летию со дня трагической гибели М. Ю. Лермонтова*, Mw, Piatigorsk, Tri L, 168 pp.; M. Kononenko, 'Неизвестный М. Ю. Лермонтов', *NSo*, no.7:257–68; V. Afanasiev, 'Печальный демон, дух изгнанья . . . Размышления над поэмой М. Ю. Лермонтова "Демон"', *Literaturnaia Ucheba*, 2000, no.3:98–107; G. V. Stadnikov, 'Лермонтов и Гете', *RusL*, 1999, no.3:22–31.

MIANDIN. A. V. Pigin, 'Повесть о бесе Зерефере в обработке И. С. Мяндина', *RusL*, 1:159–66, is a very interesting study of the forgotten Russian writer I. S. Miandin.

MURAVIEV. N. A. Khokhlova, *Андрей Николаевич Муравьев — литератор*, StP, Dmitrii Bulanin, 244 pp.

OZEROV. J. A. Cassiday, 'Northern poetry for a Northern people: text and context in Ozerov's *Fingal* ', *SEER*, 78, 2000:240–67.

PAVLOVA. M. Sendich, 'Karolina Pavlova's early poetry: the birth of a poet's craft', *RLJ*, 54, 2000:47–64.

RYLEEV. A. V. Arkhipova, 'О текстологии К. Ф. Рылеева (как печатать поэму «Наливайко»)', *RusL*, no.1:125–29.

SIPOVSKY. A. Iu. Veselova, 'Роман В. Новодворского (В. В. Сиповского) «Путешествие Эраста Крутолобова в Москву и Санкт-Петербург в 30-х годах XIX столетия» и русская литература 18–19 веков', *RusL*, no.3:107–16.

ZHUKOVSKY. *В. А. Жуковский в воспоминаниях современников. К. Н. Батюшков, П. А. Вяземский, А. И. Герцен, М. И. Глинка, Н. В. Гоголь, А. В. Кольцов, А. С. Пушкин, И. С. Тургенев, Н. М. Языков,* ed. O. B. Lebedeva and A. S. Ianuzhkevich, Mw, Nauka, Iazyki russkoi kul'tury, 1999, 726 pp.; O. B. Lebedeva, A. S. Ianuzhkevich, 'Неизвестные переводы В. А Жуковского из Гете', *RusL*, no.2:76–81; V. V. Sdobnov, 'Демоническая сфера в поэтическом мире В. А. Жуковского', *Russkaia Slovesnost'*, 2000, no.3:32–39.

LITERATURE, 1848–1917

By Boris Lanin, *Professor of Literature, Russian Academy of Education, Moscow*

1. General

Literary Journals in Imperial Russia, ed. D. A. Martinsen (Cambridge Studies in Russian Literature), CUP, 1997, xiv + 265 pp.; E. K. Sozina, *Сознание и письмо в русской литературе*, Ekaterinburg, Ural State U.P., 552 pp., follows Barthes's methodological tracks exploring works by Pushkin, Tiutchev, Herzen, Dostoevsky, Saltykov-Shchedrin, Aksakov, Tolstoy, and Leskov. A. Kara-Murza, *Знаменитые русские о Венеции*, Mw, Nezavisimaia Gazeta, 384 pp.; A. Kara-Murza, *Знаменитые русские о Риме*, Mw, Nezavisimaia Gazeta, 472 pp.: ample citations from Gogol, Turgenev, Nekrasov, and Voloshin; A. Kara-Murza, *Знаменитые русские о Флоренции*, Mw, Nezavisimaia Gazeta, 352 pp., with wide citations from Fonvizin, Apollon Grigoriev, Dostoevsky, Herzen, Kuzmin, Rozanov, Blok, Karsavin, Berdiaev, and others. P. Brooks, *Troubling Confessions: Speaking Guilt in Law and Literature*, Chicago U.P., 2000, x + 192 pp., is an excellent study on the role of confession in the Western cultural tradition based on several key texts, including Tolstoy's *Kreytzer Sonata*, and Dostoevsky's *Notes from the Underground* and *Brothers Karamazov*; E. Gollerbakh, *К незримому граду. Религиозно-философская группа 'Путь' (1910–1919) в поисках новой русской идентичности*, StP, Aleteia, 2000, 560 pp.; E. N. Penskaia, *Проблемы альтернативных путей в русской литературе. Поэтика абсурда в творчестве А. К. Толстого, М. Е. Салтыкова-Щедрина, А. В. Сухово-Кобылина*, Mw, Carte Blanche, 2000, 236 pp.; T. I. Pecherskaia, *Разночинцы шестидесятых годов XIX века: феномен самосознания в аспекте филологической герменевтики (мемуары, дневники, письма, беллетристика)*, Novosibirsk, Siberian Branch of Russian Academy of Sciences, Institute of Philology, 1999, 299 pp.; N. S. Prokurova, *Не сотвори зла: к проблеме преступления и наказания в русской художественной литературе и публицистике*, Mw, Academia, 342 pp.; N. S. Prokurova, *Вопросы судопроизводства в творчестве Ф. М. Достоевского, Л. Н. Толстого, А. П. Чехова*, Volgograd, Volgogradskii Komitet po Pechati, 1996, 51 pp.; M. F. Pianykh, 'Три богатыря: В. Л. Соловьев, Ф. Достоевский и Л. Толстой в прологе к российскому трагическому XX столетию', *Neva*, 2000, no.10:170–81.; *О ничтожестве литературы русской. Сборник статей*, ed. S. Gaier, StP, Aleteia, 2000, 224 pp., includes works by Pushkin, Dostoevsky, Tolstoy, Blok, Gorky, Abram Terts, and J. Brodsky.

L. A. Sugai, *Гоголь и символисты*, Mw, State Slavic Culture Academy, 1999, 374 pp.; *Среди великих: Литературные встречи*, ed. M. M. Odesskaia, Mw, RGGU, 445 pp., is on L. Tolstoy, Chekhov, Dostoevsky, and others; T. Broslavskaya, 'Письма из прошлого. И. Ф. Стравинский о М. К. Чюрленисе: параллели творческих судеб', *Neva*, 2000, no.1:226–31; E. I. Goncharova (publication), 'Письма З. Гиппиус к Б. Савинкову: 1908—1909 годы', *RusL*, no.3:126–62; A. M. Liubomudrov, 'Из эпистолярного наследия Б. К. Зайцева (по материалам петербургских архивов)', *ib.*, 162–87, publishes B. K. Zaitsev's letters to N. K. Mikhailovsky, V. S. Miroliubov, S. Iu. Kopel'man, and Z. I. Grzhebin from the St Petersburg archives; D. S. Noskova, 'А. Н. Майков: послесловие к циклу (по архивным материалам)', *RusL*, no.2000, no.2:195–99, is on A. N. Maikov's archives in Pushkinskii Dom (f. 168); P. A. Gaponenko, 'О языке поэмы А. Н. Майкова "Странник"', *RRe*, 2000, no.6:11–17; N. E. Miasoedova, 'Неопубликованная статья А. В. Майкова «Загадка святой Катерины»', *RusL*, no.2: 82–102; D. I. Pisarev, *Полное собрание сочинений и писем: В 12 т. Т. 3: Статьи и рецензии. 1861. Июнь — декабрь*, ed. G. G. Elizavetina, Mw, Nauka, 526 pp.; I. S. Aksakov, *Еврейский вопрос: Статьи из газет «День», «Москва» и «Русь». 1862 г. —1883 г.*, Mw, Sotsizdat, 160 pp.; S. M. Baluev, 'О политической публицистике П. И. Вейнберга («Современная летопись» в № 1 Библиотеки для чтения» за 1860 г.)', *VSPU*, 1.2:117–21; B. V. Mel'gunov, 'О первых юбилеях русских писателей (И. С. Тургенев, А. Н. Островский, Н. А. Некрасов)', *RusL*, no.4:148–53; A. N. Rozov, 'Заметки о церковной критике второй половины 19 – начала 20 века (образ священника в русской литературе)', *ib.*, 32–50.

2. Literary History

Русская литература рубежа веков (1890-е — начало 1920-х годов), книга 1, Mw, Nasledie, 960 pp.; E. V. Anisimov, *Императорская Россия. XIX — начало XX века*, StP, Norint, 32 pp., is a brochure written by one of the leading Russian historians, containing some interesting material on Russian literary life.

3. Theory

L. V. Karasev, *Вещество литературы*, Mw, Iazyki Slavianskoi Kul'tury, 400 pp., is on so-called 'ontological poetics' which is based on 'co-operation with text, close relationships between human being and text' — on Gogol, Dostoevsky, Chekhov, Bulgakov, and

Platonov; V. V. Fedorov, *Статьи разных лет*, Donetsk, 2000, 242 pp., is a selection of works by one of Bakhtin's most devoted followers; A. A. Korablev, *Поэтика словесного творчества. Системология целостности*, Donetsk State U.P., 224 pp.; *Язык, литература, эпос: К 100-летию со дня рождения академика В. М. Жирмунского*, ed. D. S. Likhachev, StP, Nauka, 443 pp.; V. V. Kozhinov, *Размышления об Искусстве, Литературе и Истории*, Mw, Soglasie, 816 pp.; A. Etoev, *Душегубство и живодерство в детской литературе*, StP, Krasnyi matros, 76 pp.; B. F. Egorov, *Структурализм. Русская поэзия. Воспоминания*, Tomsk, Vodolei, 512 pp.; S. Vaiman, *Неевклидова поэтика: Работы разных лет*, Mw, Nauka, 479 pp.; N. V. Guzhieva, '«Русские символисты» — литературно-книжный манифест модернизации', *RusL*, 2000, no.2:64–80.; S. G. Bocharov, *Сюжеты русской литературы*, Mw, Iazyki russkoi kul'tury, 1999, 632 pp. (for polemics over this book, see V. Nepomniashchii, 'О горизонтах познания и глубинах сочувствия', *NovM*, 2000, no.10:175–94). D. Gasperetti, *The Rise of the Russian Novel: Carnival, Stylization, and Mockery of the West*, DeKalb, IL, Northern Illinois U.P., 1998, ix + 260 pp. O. N. Kalenichenko, *Судьбы малых жанров в русской литературе конца XIX–XX века (святочный и пасхальный рассказы, модернистская новелла)*, Volgograd, Peremena, 2000, 231 pp. S. Z. Agranovich and I. V. Samorukova, *Двойничество*, Samara, Samarskii Univ., 132 pp., present 'counterpartship' as a literary archetype in three main modes: 'counterparts-antagonists', 'carnival pairs', and 'twins'. L. Zel'tser, *Выразительный мир художественного произведения*, Mw, E. Rakitskaia, 452 pp., discusses two main concepts, 'izobrazhenie' and 'vyrazhenie', illustrated on works by Turgenev, Saltykov-Schedrin, Ostrovsky, Chekhov, Gorky, and Bunin. A. M. Kelly, *Views from the Other Shore: Essays on Herzen, Chekhov, and Bakhtin*, New Haven, Yale U.P., 1999, ix + 260 pp.

Mochizuki, *Culture*, contains three important works: V. Grechko, 'Авангард и философия языка' (149–58); F. Osuka and T. Kibe, 'Трансформация концепции «символ» и «лингвистический поворот» в философии языка (теория языка Г. Г. Шпета и А. Ф. Лосева)' (211–32), S. Kitami and N. Kakinuma, 'Обоснование А. Белым и Вяч. Ивановым концепции символа' (233–58).

GENDER STUDIES. S. Grenier, *Representing the Marginal Woman in Nineteenth-Century Russian Literature: Personalism, Feminism, and Polyphony* (Contributions in Women's Studies, 185), Westport, Greenwood, x + 175 pp., is on images of marginal women in Russian literature from the very little-known Zhukova to Pushkin, Herzen, Tolstoy, and Dostoevsky; V. A. Smirnov, *Литература и фольклорная традиция:*

вопросы поэтики (архетипы «женского начала» в русской литературе XIX — начала XX века). Пушкин. Лермонтов. Достоевский. Бунин, Ivanovo, Iunona, 236 pp.

COMPARATIVE STUDIES. One of the most interesting books in this field is *The Gothic-Fantastic in Nineteenth-Century Russian Literature*, ed. N. Cornwell (Studies in Slavic Literature and Poetics), Amsterdam, Rodopi, 1999, 293 pp. See also O. B. Lebedeva, A. S. Ianushkevich, *Германия в зеркале русской словесной культуры 19 — начала 20 века* (Bausteine zur slavischen Philologie und Kulturgeschichte. N. F. Reihe A: Slavistische Forschungen, 30), Cologne–Weimar–Vienna, 2000, 274 pp. I. S. Emelianov, *Русско-якутские литературные связи в прозе (Конец 19 —начало 20 в)*, Novosibirsk, Nauka, 108 pp.

4. CHEKHOV

D. Reyfield, *Understanding Chekhov: A Critical Study of Chekhov's Prose and Drama*, London, Bristol Classical Press, 1999, xvii + 295 pp., is an updated and renewed version of his *Chekhov: The Evolution of His Art* (1975); V. I. Tiupa, *Нарратология как аналитика повествовательного дискурса («Архиерей» А.П. Чехова)*, Tver′ State U.P., 58 pp.; N. S. Prokurova, *Мечта – это Антон Павлович: психологический этюд*, Volgograd, Volgogradskii Komitet po Pechati, 1998, 46 pp.; *Альтшуллер А. Я. А. П. Чехов в актерском кругу: Воспоминания об А. Я. Альтшуллере*, ed. T. D. Zolotnitskaya, StP, Stroiizdat SPb, 224 pp.; C. A. Flath, 'Chekhov's underground man: "An Attack of Nerves"', *SEEJ*, 44, 2000:375–92; I. Gracheva, 'А. П. Чехов и И. М. Прянишников', *VL*, no.1:329–35; O. Iu. Starodubova, '"Мантифолия", или несколько слов о природе чеховского юмора', *RRe*, 2000, no.1:125–27; I. V. Gracheva, 'Глубины чеховского слова', *RRe*, 2000, no.3:20–25; I. V. Gracheva, 'Язык ассоциаций в творчестве А. П. Чехова', *RRe*, no.1:3–10; D. A. Kirjanov, *Chekhov and the Poetics of Memory* (Studies on Themes and Motifs in Literature, 52), NY, Lang, 2000, x + 193 pp.; M. Tugusheva, *О Чехове с любовью*, Mw, KRUK, 2000, 143 pp.

DRAMA. *The Cambridge Companion to Chekhov*, ed. V. Gottlieb and P. Allain, CUP, 2000, xxxiii + 293 pp., devotes 16 of its 17 contributions to Chekhov's drama. *Чеховиана. Полет «Чайки»*, ed. V. V. Gul′chenko, Mw, Nauka, 397 pp. S. Evdokimova, 'What's so funny about losing one's estate, or infantilism in *The Cherry Orchard*', *SEEJ*, 44, 2000:623–48; L. M. Borisova, 'Паузы и антипаузы в драматургии А. П. Чехова', *RRe*, no.1:11–18.

PROSE. S. P. Stepanov, 'О субъективации чеховского повествования', *RusL*, no.4:16–31; J. L. Conrad, 'Chekhov's 'Ionych' as commentary on Turgenev's prose', *RLJ*, 54,

2000:95–110; Iu. A. Bel'chikov, 'Авторское повествование в рассказе А. П. Чехова "Спать хочется"', *Russkaia Slovesnost'*, no.3:64–66; D. N. Medrish, 'Время и пространство в незавершенном романе А. П. Чехова', *RRe*, 2000, no.1:10–14; E. S. Afanasiev, 'Иронический эпос Чехова (о повести "Степь")', *Izv. RAN SLI*, no.6:27–33; E. S. Afanasiev, 'Пушкин – Чехов: ироническая проза', *RusL*, no.4:195–206.

5. DOSTOEVSKY

GENERAL. S. Belov, *Ф. М. Достоевский и его окружение: Энциклопедический словарь. В 2 т.*, 2 vols, StP, Rossiiskaia Natsional'naia Biblioteka, 573, 544 pp., a really unique study of enormous value — the result of life-long study!

Two works by Igor' Volgin: *Колеблясь над бездной. Достоевский и императорский дом*, Mw, Tsentr Gumanitarnogo Obrazovaniia, 1998, 656 pp.; 'Пропавший заговор. Достоевский и политический процесс 1849 года', *Oktjabr'*, 2000, no.3:56–143, is the last part of Volgin's large research; W. Kasack, *Dostojewski: Leben und Werk*, Frankfurt, Insel, 1998, 160 pp.; M. D. Gordin, 'Loose and baggy spirits: reading Dostoevskii and Mendeleev', *SRev*, 60:756–80; I. Zohrab, '«Европейские гипотезы» и «русские аксиомы»: Достоевский и Джон Стюарт Милль', *RusL*, 2000, no.3:37–52, is an excellent paper, a real discovery in Dostoevsky studies!

J. P. Scanlan, 'Dostoyevsky's arguments for immortality', *RusR*, 59, 2000:1–20; K. Nakamura, *Чувство жизни и смерти у Достоевского*, StP, Dmitrii Bulanin, 1997, 330 pp.; T. Mochizuki, 'Играя со словами классики: Достоевский в современной литературе', Mochizuki, *Culture*, 159–77; S. Olivie, 'Достоевский в наше время (о книге Д. Уолша «После идеологии. Возвращение к духовным основаниям свободы»)', *RusL*, 1999, no.3:118–26; Z. Price, 'Lukacs, Dostoyevsky, and the politics of art: Utopia in *The Theory of the Novel* and *The Brothers Karamazov*', *SEEJ*, 45:343–52; V. Terras, *Reading Dostoyevsky*, Madison, WI, Univ. of Wisconsin Press, 1999, 170 pp.; O. Meerson, *Dostoevsky's Taboos*, Dresden U.P., 1998, xvi + 232 pp.; M. M. Bakhtin, *Собрание сочинений: Т. 2. Проблемы творчества Достоевского, 1929. Статьи о Л. Толстом, 1929. Записи курса лекций по истории русской литературы, 1922–1927*, Mw, Russkie Slovari, 2000, 800 pp. See also R. Coates, *Christianity in Bakhtin: God and the Exiled Author*, CUP, 1998, xiii + 201 pp; *Человек есть тайна: Юбилейный сборник, посвященный 180-летию со дня рождения Ф. М. Достоевского*, ed. S. L. Vaaz, Saratov, Saratov State Social-Economical Univ., 329 pp.; A. B. Krinitsyn, *Исповедь подпольного человека: К антропологии Ф. М. Достоевского*, Mw,

Dialog–Moscow, MGU, Maks-Press, 372 pp.; G. M. Serdobintseva, *Идеал Достоевского*, Riazan', RINFO, 1999, 73 pp.; *Достоевский. Материалы и исследования. Т. 16: Юбилейный сборник*, ed. N. F. Budanova and I. D. Iakubovich, StP, Nauka, 447 pp.; F. Kautman, 'Борьба Масарика с Достоевским', *RusL*, no.1 : 222–46; B. Tarasov, 'Наши "старые" и "новые" силлогисты в зеркале мысли Достоевского', *NSo*, no.11 : 228–53; S. Lominadze, 'Перечитывая Достоевского и Бахтина', *VL*, no.2 : 39–58; G. Adelman, *Retelling Dostoyevsky: Literary Responses and Other Observations*, Lewisburg, Bucknell U.P., 2000, 273 pp.; A. Červeňák, *Dostojevského sny (Eseje a štúdie o snoch s Dostojevskom)*, Pezinok, Fischer, 1999, 199 pp., is a study about dreams in Dostoevsky's works (in Slovak); G. A. Time, 'Немецкий «миф» о Л. Толстом и Ф. Достоевском первой трети XX века (русско-немецкий диалог как опыт мифотворчества)', *RusL*, no.3 : 36–52; A. Vorontsov, 'Достоевский и идеал человека', *NSo*, no.11 : 254–74; V. Il'iashevich, 'Достоевский и Ревель' *ib.*, 276–84; V. A. Bachinin, 'Петербург — Москва — Петушки, или "Записки из подполья" как русский философский жанр', *ONS*, no.5 : 182–91; O. G. Dilaktorskaia, 'Крокодил в "Крокодиле" Ф. М. Достоевского', *Russkaia rech'*, 2000, no.4 : 11–18; *Достоевский. Материалы и исследования. Т. 16: Юбилейный сборник*, ed. N. F. Budanova and I. D. Iakubovich, StP, Nauka, 447 pp.; N. Perlina, 'Vico's concept of knowledge as an underpinning of Dostoyevsky's aesthetic historicism', *SEEJ*, 45 : 323–42, is part of a broader project 'Eternal plots in search of authors: Gogol, Dostoyevsky, Tolstoy from the Inferno to Resurrection', and is focused on 'Notes from the House of the Dead', and 'Diary of a Writer', on one hand, and Giambattista Vico's philosophical work 'The New Science', on the other; C. A. Flath, 'The *Passion* of Dmitrii Karamazov', *SRev*, 58, 1999 : 584–99; O. S. Soina, '"Пушкинская речь" Ф. М. Достоевского. Опыт современного прочтения', *Chelovek*, no.3 : 153–63; no.4 : 165–75.

M. Cadot, *Dostoïevski d'un siècle à l'autre, ou la Russie entre Orient et Occident*, introd. Rudolf Neuhäuser. Maisonneuve et Larose, 352 pp.; *Diagonales dostoïevskiennes. Mélanges en l'honneur de J. Catteau*, ed. M.-A. Albert, Paris-Sorbonne U.P., 428 pp. J. Hassine, *Proust à la recherche de Dostoïevski*, Paris, Nizet, 170 pp. P. Lamblé, *La Philosophie de Dostoïevski*, 2 vols, I: *Les Fondements du système philosophique de Dostoïevski*, II : *La Métaphysique de l'histoire de Dostoïevski*, Paris, L'Harmattan, 238, 208 pp. A. Lazari, *W Kręgu Fiodora Dostojewskiego: poczwiennictwo*, Lydz, Ibidem, 2000, 188 pp.

A RAW YOUTH. S. Fusso, 'Dostoevsky's comely boy: homoerotic desire and aesthetic strategies in *A Raw Youth*', *RusR*, 59, 2000 : 577–96;

I. Lunde, 'Ia gorazdo umnee napisannogo': on apophatic strategies and verbal experiments in Dostoyevskii's *A Raw Youth*', *SEER*, 79:264–89.

CRIME AND PUNISHMENT. J. Tucker, 'The religious symbolism of clothing in Dostoyevsky's *Crime and Punishment*', *SEEJ*, 44, 2000:253–65;J. Spiegel, *Dimensions of Laughter in 'Crime and Punishment'*, Cranbury, Susquehanna U.P., 2000, 168 pp., counts 250 laughs and 70 smiles in Dostoevsky's novel.

THE IDIOT AND THE DEVILS. Khoo Soon Vkha, 'Положительно прекрасный человек (тайна князя Мышкина)', *RusL*, no.2:132–47; B. A. French, *Dostoyevsky's 'Idiot': Dialogue and the Spiritually Good Life* (Studies in Russian Literature and Theory), Evanston, Northwestern U.P., xv + 242 pp.; C. Cravens, 'The strange relationship of Stavrogin and Stepan Trofimovich as told by Anton Lavrent'evich G-v', *SRev*, 59, 2000:782–801. *Dostoyevsky's 'The Idiot': A Critical Companion*, ed. L. Knapp (NorthWestern /AATSEEL Critical Companions to Russian Literature), Evanston, Northwestern U.P., 1998. viii + 274 pp., contains papers by R. F. Miller, N. Straus, D. Bethea, and L. Knapp. W.J. Leatherbarrow, 'Misreading Myshkin and Stavrogin: the presentation of the hero in Dostoevskii's *Idiot* and *Besy*', *SEER*, 78, 2000:1–19; T. Kasatkina, '"Идиот" и "чудак": синонимия или антонимия?', *VL*, no.2:90–103; *Dostoyevsky's 'The Devils': A Critical Companion*, ed. W. J. Leatherbarrow (AATSEEL Critical Companions to Russian Literature), Evanston, IL, Northwestern U.P., 1999, 165 pp. V. Vinokurov, 'The end of consciousness and the ends of consciousness: a reading of Dostoyevsky's *The Idiot* and *Demons* after Levinas', *RusR*, 59, 2000:21–37.

DOSTOEVSKY AND OTHER WRITERS. K. S. Korkonosenko, 'Полифонический роман Достоевского и агонический «руман» Унамуно', *RusL*, 1999, no.4:114–23; V. Serdiuchenko, 'Футурология Достоевского и Чернышевского', *VL*, no.3:66–84; V. Serdiuchenko, *Достоевский и Чернышевский: единство крайностей*, L'vov State U.P., 1999, 208 pp.; A. I. Batiuto, 'Белинский в восприятии Достоевского (1860–1870-е годы)', *RusL*, no.3:11–35; O. N. Kalenichenko, *Малая проза Ф. М. Достоевского, А. П. Чехова и писателей рубежа веков (новелла, святочный рассказ, притча)*, Volgograd, Peremena, 1997, 101 pp.; B. N. Tarasov, *Непрочитанный Чаадаев, неуслышанный Достоевский: христианская мысль и современное сознание*, Mw, Academia, 1999, 288 pp.; D. A. Badalian, 'А. С. Хомяков и Ф. М. Достоевский. К истории развития «идеи народности» в русской культуре 19 в.', *VSPU*, ser. 2, 1999, no.4:108–11; D. Offord, 'Beware the Garden of Earthly Delights: Fonvizin and Dostoyevskii on life in France', *SEER*, 78, 2000:625–42; F. F. Seeley, *Saviour or Superman? Old and New*

Essays on Tolstoy and Dostoyevsky, Nottingham, Astra, 1999, x + 147 pp., has some essays first published in Russian or Italian; L. A. Poliakiewicz, 'Chekhov's *The Island of Sakhalin* and Dostoyevsky's *Notes from a Dead House* as Penological Studies', *CASS*, 35:397–421.

6. TOLSTOY

G. Nabiev, *Человек в мире Л. Н. Толстого*, Mw, Dialog — MGU, 1999, 278 pp.; T. Kasatkina, 'Философия пола и проблема женской эмансипации в "Крейцеровой Сонате" Л. Н. Толстого', *VL*, no.4:209–22; V. Kantor, 'Лев Толстой: Искушение неисторией', *VL*, 2000, no.4:120–81; D. Rancour-Laferriere, *Tolstoy on the Couch: Misogyny, Masochism, and the Absent Mother*, New York U.P., 1998, viii + 270 pp., is an excellent psychoanalytic approach to *The Kreutzer Sonata* (1890); E. V. Petrovskaya, 'Гете и Руссо в творческом сознании молодого Толстого: «поэзия» и «правда»', *RusL*, no.1:80–92; *Л. Н. Толстой и А. П. Чехов. Рассказывают современники, архивы, музей . . .*, ed. A. S. Melkova, Mw, Nasledie, 1998, 391 pp., has 21 chapters in which various aspects of Tolsloy's and Chekhov's relations are analysed; P. Kolstø, 'A mass for a heretic? A controversy over Lev Tolstoi's burial', *SRev*, 60:75–95; I. Mardov, 'Лев Толстой: прозрение в мнимодушевность', *VL*, 2000, no.1:161–72; E. V. Belousova, 'Библия в восприятии Л. Н. Толстого', *Literaturnaia Ucheba*, 2000, no.1:124–58; G. Browning, 'Peasant Dreams in *Anna Karenina*', *SEEJ*, 44, 2000:525–36; V. Berezin, 'Слово о Хаджи- Мурате', *Oktjabr'*, no. 1:186–8; N. Burnasheva, 'Литературный источник трилогии Л. Н. Толстого?', *VL*, 2000, no.2:316–21; A. Pastor, 'У Толстого', *VL*, 2000, no.6:310–22; A. L. Tolstaya, 'Дневник 1903 года', *Oktjabr'*, no.9:169–77; N. P. Puzin, *Дом-музей Л.Н.Толстого в Ясной Поляне*, B.M., Iasnaia Poliana, 135 pp.; V. Remizov, '"Делай, что должно . . .": Государственному музею Л. Н. Толстого – 90 ЛЕТ', *Oktjabr'*, no.9:166–68. N. A. Es'kova, 'Еще раз о мире и мй ре и о "Войне и мире"', *RRe*, no.2:120–22; G. D. Udalykh, 'Дипломаты и дипломатия в романе Л. Н. Толстого "Война и мир". (Стилистические приемы изображения)', *RRe*, 2000, no.6:3–10; Iu. A. Ozerov, 'Москва и Петербург в романе Л. Н. Толстого "Война и мир"', *Russkaia Slovesnost'*, no.1:68–75.

DRAMA. S. A. Shul'tz, 'Драматургия Л. Н. Толстого как пограничный феномен', *RusL*, 2000, no.1:21–39; N. S. Avilova, 'Речевые портреты в пьесе Л.Н. Толстого "Плоды просвещения"', *RRe*, 2000, no.3:14–19.

TOLSTOY AND OTHER WRITERS. Z. Zafer, '«Анна Каренина» Л. Н. Толстого и «Джевдет Бей и его сыновья» Орхана

Памука', *RusL*, no.4 : 169–72; B. Bialokozowicz, 'Лев Толстой глазами Яна Бодуэна Де Куртенэ', *Slavianovedenie*, no.6 : 93–104; L. Gladkova, 'Об истинном искусстве. По переписке Л. Н. Толстого с Ф. Ф. Тищенко', *Oktjabr'*, 2000, no.9 : 173–77; E. Khan-Pira, 'Живой труп и мертвые трупы у Пушкина и Толстого', *RRe*, 2000, no.4 : 111–16.

7. TURGENEV

Two books are of great interest: V. N. Toporov, *Странный Тургенев (четыре главы): Чтения по истории и теории культуры, выпуск 20*, Mw, RGGU, 1998, 192 pp., is an excellent book full of new ideas and insights; G. B. Kurliandskaya, *Тургенев. Мировоззрение, метод, традиции*, Tula, Grif I K, 230 pp., is by one of the most distinguished researchers of Turgenev's prose. Among the most interesting topics of *Тургеневский ежегодник*, Orel, State Turgenev Museum, 117 pp., are Turgenev's ethics, the nihilistic character in Russian literature, a window as a symbol in Pushkin's and Turgenev's prose. V. Sh. Krivonos, 'Мотив стука в поэтике И.С. Тургенева', *Izv. RAN SLI*, 2000, no.5 : 32–37, considers the motive of knocking as a form of manifestations of the 'strange' in Turgenev's poetics. Special attention has been paid to an analysis of close connection of this motive with the theme of fate. See also O. L. Fetisenko, 'О датировке эпиграммы И. С. Тургенева «К нему читатель не спешит . . .»', *RusL*, 2000, no.2 : 201–03; *Библиотека И. С. Тургенева. Часть 1: книги на русском языке*, ed. L. A. Balykova, Orel, State Museum of Turgenev's Literature, 1994, 208 pp.; N. Chernov, *Спасско-Лутовиновская хроника. 1813–1883: Документальные страницы литературной и житейской летописи*, Tula, 1999, 445 pp.; S. L. Zhidkova, 'Тургеневы в Петровское время (комментарий к одному письму И. С. Тургенева)', *RusL*, 1999, no.3 : 83–92; N. S. Nikitina, 'Статья Тургенева «По поводу «Отцов и детей» и черновая рукопись романа', *RusL*, no.4 : 3–15; A. V. Stepanov, 'Висячие мосты тургеневского стиля. "Отцы и дети"', *Russkaia Slovesnost'*, 2000, no.5 : 66–70; T. V. Trofimova, 'О повести И. С. Тургенева «Несчастная»', *RusL*, no.1 : 195–205. There are several interesting works by P. Waddington: *Turgenev and Julian Schmidt: New or Neglected Materials*, Wellington, Whirinaki Press, 1998, 60 pp.; Id., *Turgenev and Pavlovsky: a Friendship and a Correspondence*, Pinehaven, 1998, 60 pp.; Id., *A Catalogue of Portraits of Ivan Sergeevich Turgenev (1818–83)*, Pinehaven, 1999, 73 pp.; Id., *Turgenev's Mortal Illness: From its Origins to the Autopsy*, Pinehaven, 1999, 103 pp.; Id., 'И. С. Тургенев. ‹Подготовительные материалы к роману «Дым»›',

RusL, 2000, no.3 : 106–43; *Ivan Turgenev and Britain*, ed. P. Waddington, Oxford–Providence, RI, Berg, 1995. x, 302 pp.

TURGENEV AND OTHER WRITERS. V. Gromov, *Под сенью Пушкина: Литературные очерки об И. С. Тургеневе и А. С. Пушкине*, Orel, 1999, 314 pp.; G. E. Potapova, '«Гетевское» и «пушкинское» в повести И. С. Тургенева «Фауст»', *RusL*, 1999, no.3 : 32–41; C. Richards, 'Occasional Critics: Henry James on Ivan Turgenev', *SEER*, 78 : 463–86; B. V. Mel'gunov, '«Мы вышли вместе...» (Некрасов и Тургенев на рубеже 40–х годов)', *RusL*, 2000, no.3 : 143–49; N. P. Generalova, 'Оправдание Человека. К трактовке финала «Фауста» Гете (И. С. Тургенев и А. А. Фет)', *RusL*, 1999, no.3 : 42–57; N. N. Mostovskaya, 'Memento mori у Тургенева и Некрасова', *RusL*, 2000, no.3 : 149–55; V. Aleksandrov, 'И. С. Тургенев и Ялмар Бойесен (Hjalmar Hjorth Boyesem)', *Literaturnaia Ucheba*, no.1 : 67–97; K. Sawada, 'И. С. Тургенев в Японии', *RusL*, 1999, no.4 : 108–14.

8. OTHER AUTHORS

ANNENSKY. A. N. Eliseeva, 'Вещь как символ в поэзии И. Анненского', *VSPU*, 1.2 : 112–16; G. Nikitin, 'Мир беспокойных цветов (к 145–летию со дня рождения И. Ф. Анненского)', *Literaturnaia Ucheba*, 2000, no.4 : 97–105.

APUKHTIN. N. G. Podlesskikh-Zhirkevich (publication), 'Новые материалы об А. Н. Апухтине из архива А. В. Жиркевича', *RusL*, 1999, no.3 : 126–63.

BAL'MONT. N. A. Molchanova, 'Аполлоническое и дионисийское начало в книге К. Д. Бальмонта «Будем как солнце»', *RusL*, no.4 : 51–67; P. V. Kupriianovsky, 'К. Д. Бальмонт в письмах к Л. М. Гарелиной-Бальмонт', *RusL*, 2000, no.1 : 143–56.

BLOK. Iu. M. Osipov, E. S. Zotova, *Последний поэт Империи: 120 лет со дня рождения А. А. Блока*, Rostov-na-Donu, Rostov State Economy U.P., 265 pp.; J. W. de Sherbinin, 'Poetry of the swamp: Blok's "folk" cycle *Bubble of the Earth*', *CSP*, 43 : 177–93; Choi Chzhon Sool, 'Лермонтовские реминисценции и аллюзии в лирике А. Блока', *RusL*, no.2 : 161–75; Choi Chzhon Sool, 'Стихотворение М. Лермонтова «Благодарность» в восприятии А. Блока', *RusL*, 2000, no.1 : 173–79; V. Esipov, '"И только высоко, у царских врат ..." (Об одном стихотворении Блока)', *VL*, no.4 : 331–37; A. Kazintsev, 'Жертва вечерняя. К 120–летию со дня рождения Александра Блока', *NSo*, 2000, no.11 : 228–41; A. N. Shustov, '«Письмо» или посвящение?', *RusL*, 1999, no.4 : 138–40, about Blok's 'Письмо' (1908); *Андрей Белый и Александр Блок. Переписка. 1903—1919. Переписка*, ed. A. Lavrov, Mw, Progress–Pleiada, 608 pp.

BUNIN. Th. G. Marullo, *If you see the Budha. Studies in the Fiction of Ivan Bunin*, Evanston IL, Northwestern U.P., 1998, 208 pp.

DANILEVSKY. B. P. Baluev, *Споры о судьбах России: Н. Я. Данилевский и его книга «Россия и Европа»*, Tver', Bulat, 2nd revd edn, 415 pp.

DRUZHININ. *А. В. Дружинин. Проблемы творчества. К 175-летию со дня рождения. Межвузовский сборник научных трудов*, ed. N. B. Aldonina, Samara State Pedagogical U.P., 1999, 197 pp.; S. Layton, 'Colonial mimicry and disenchantment in Alexander Druzhinin's "A Russian Circassian" and other stories', *RusR*, 60 : 56–71.

EVREINOV. An Chzien, 'Заметки о ранней драматургии Н. Н. Евреинова', *RusL*, 2000, no.1 : 156–73, is about N. N. Evreinov's early plays 'Фундамент счастья' (1902) and 'Красивый деспот' (1905).

FET. *А. А. Фет и русская литература: Материалы Всероссийской научной конференции «VI Фетовские чтения» (Курск — Орел, 1–5 2000 г.)*, ed. V. A. Koshelev and G. D. Aslanova, Kursk, Kursk State Pedagogical U.P., 2000, 366 pp.; V. A. Koshelev, '«Лирическое хозяйство» Афанасия Фета и обстоятельства ссоры Тургенева и Толстого', *RusL*, no.1 : 206–22; Iu. L. Vorotnikov, 'Образ качелей в творчестве А. А. Фета и Ф. Сологуба', *RusL*, no.2 : 25–33; N. V. Vulikh, 'А. А. Фет – переводчик од Горация', *ib.*, 117–22; I. A. Kuz'mina, 'Письма А. А. Фета П. И. Бартеневу (к истории перевода стихотворения Ф. И. Тютчева "Des premiers ans de votre vie...")', *RusL*, no.4 : 165–69; M. D. El'zon, 'Об источнике стихотворения А. А. Фета «The Echoes»', *RusL*, 2000, no.2 : 199–21; V. Afanasiev, 'Афанасий Фет: Поэзия и вера', *Literaturnaia Ucheba*, no.2 : 152–61; G. Nikitin, '"Не я, мой друг, а Божий мир богат ... 180 лет со дня рождения А. А. Фета"', *ib.*, 2000, no.5 : 170–79; V. Koshelev, 'О "тургеневской" правке поэтических текстов Афанасия Фета', *NLO*, no.2 : 157–91.

GARSHIN. *Vsevolod Garshin and the Turn of the Century: An International Symposium*, ed. P. Henry, V. Porudominsky and M. Girshman, 3 vols, Oxford, Northgate, 2000, xv + 275, 300, 248 pp., has a lot of contributions of different value.

GONCHAROV. E. Krasnoshchekova, *Иван Александрович Гончаров: Мир творчества*, StP, Pushkinskii Fond, 1997, 491 pp.; E. Krasnoshchekova, «Обрыв» И. А. Гончарова в контексте антинигилистического романа 60-х годов, *RusL*, no.1 : 66–79;

G. G. Bagautdinova, *Роман И.А.Гончарова «Обрыв»: Борис Райский – художник*, Ioshkar-Ola, Mari U.P., 103 pp.; V. I. Kholkin, 'Русский человек Обломов', *RusL*, 2000, no.2:26–63; T. B. Il'inskaya, 'Огюстен Тьерри в черновиках И. А. Гончарова («Обрыв» и воспоминания «В университете»)', *RusL*, no.2:122–32.

GOFMAN. E. M. Krapivina, 'Предсмертное письмо Виктора Гофмана', *RusL*, 2000, no.4:153–54, is a brief note about Victor Gofman's last letter.

GRIGORIEV. There are two new books: B. F. Egorov, *Аполлон Григорьев*. Mw, Molodaya gvardiia, 2000, 219 pp.; A. Grigoriev, *Письма*, ed. R. Vitager and B. Egorov, Mw, Nauka, 1999, 474 pp., the most complete selection of Grigoriev's letters with excellent commentaries.

GUMILEV. E. Iu. Raskina, 'ПространствоРоссии в поэтической географии Н. С. Гумилева', *RusL*, no.2:34–41; M. D. El'zon, '«Римские» или «рыжие»? (О неучтенном литературном источнике «Отравленной туники» Н. С. Гумилева)', *RusL*, no.3:205–06.

HERZEN. N. Bontadina, *Alexander Herzen und die Schweiz: Das Verhätnis des russischen Publizisten und Aristokraten zur einzigen Republik im Europa seiner Zeit*, (Slavica Helvetica), Berne, Lang, 1999, 510 pp.; S. Gurvich-Lishchiner, 'Диалог о стихии и культуре (Герцен и Блок)', *VL*, no.4:179–208.

IVANOV. L. M. Borisova, 'Трагедия Вячеслава Иванова в отношении к символистской теории жизнетворчества', *RusL*, 2000, no.1:63–77.

KIREIEVSKY. H. Slezkine, *Kireievski et Optino Poustyne*, ed. and introd. Jean P. Besse, Lavardac, Saint-Jean le Roumain, 254 pp.

KROPOTKIN. M. V. Mikhailova, 'Письма кн. Петра Алексеевича Кропоткина В. П. Жуку (К истории перевода книги П. А. Кропоткина «Идеалы и действительность в русской литературе)', *RusL*, 2000, no.3:157–69.

LEONT'EV. V. A. Kotel'nikov and O. L. Fetisenko publish 'Литературные автопортреты К. Н. Леонтьева («Для биографии К. Н. Леонтьева», «Список сочинений К. Леонтьева с характеристикой»)', *RusL*, no.2:147–61.

LESKOV. O. V. Evdokimova, *Мнемонические элементы поэтики Н.С.Лескова*, StP, Aleteia, 317 pp.; A. A. Kretova, *«Будьте совершенны» (Религиозно-нравственные искания в святочном творчестве Н. С. Лескова и его современников)*, Mw–Orel, 1999, 304 pp.; G. Safran, 'Ethnography, Judaism, and the art of Nikolai Leskov', *RusR*, 59:235–51. *Юбилейная международная конференция по гуманитарным наукам, посвященная 70–летию Орловского государственного университета: Материалы. Выпуск 1: Н. С. Лесков*, Orel, Orel State U.P., 274 pp.; I. V. Stoliarova publishes 'Рассказ Н. С. Лескова «Бессребреник»', *RusL*, 1999, no.3:101–11; S. I. Zenkevich publishes 'Неизвестный фельетон Н. С. Лескова', *RusL*, 1999, no.3:111–18; T. A. Iliashenko, 'Евангельские купели. Библеизмы у Н. С. Лескова', *RRe*, no.1:73–78; O. V. Evdokimova, '«Юношеские воспоминания» Н. С. Лескова о Киеве («Печерские антики»)', *RusL*, 2000, no.1:126–32;

NADEZHDIN. L. A. Shilov, '«Обновленный» Н. И. Надеждин и библиотекарь Публичной библиотеки Н. А. Шлегель', *RusL*, 1999, no.3:163–68.

OSTROVSKY. K. S. Rahman, *Ostrovsky: Reality and Illusion* (Birmingham Slavonic Monographs, 30), Birmingham U.P., 1999, 251 pp., is a very thorough study of Ostrovsky's plays (without *The False Dmitry, Vasily Shuisky*, and *The Snow Maiden*, though); A. I. Zhuravleva, M. S. Makeev, *Александр Николаевич Островский*, Moscow State U.P., 112 pp.; A. I. Noskov, 'А. Н. Островский в Симбирской губернии в 1849 году', *RusL*, 1999, no.3:93–101.

PISEMSKY. S. M. Baluev, 'К истории текста «Путевых очерков» А. Ф. Писемского', *RusL*, 2000, no.3:155–57; S. M. Baluev, 'Об оценке Н. А. Добролюбовым «Записок Салатушки» А. Ф. Писемского', *VSPU*, ser. 2, 2000, no.4:81–85; S. M. Baluev, 'Цитация в «Путевых очерках» А. Ф. Писемского', *ib.*, no.2:69–75; no.3:83–89; S. M. Baluev, '«Записки Салатушки» А. Ф. Писемского (ирония персонажа как отражение позиции автора)', *ib.*, 1999, no.4:73–82.

POLONSKY. L. A. Pronina, *Полонский и время*, Riazan', Poverennyi, 2000, 160 pp.

ROZANOV. T. A. Elshina, '« Философ в фельетонистах. . .» (В. В. Розанов)', *RusL*, 2000, no.3:194–202.

SALTYKOV-SHCHEDRIN. B. I. Matveev, 'Библеизмы в прозе М.Е. Салтыкова-Щедрина', *RRe*, no.2:3–12.

SLUCHEVSKY. A. Iu. Kozyreva, 'Цикл К. Случевского «Мефистофель»: художественное строение и философский смысл', *VSPU*, 1.2:117–21; E. Takho-Godi, *Константин Случевский. Портрет на пушкинском фоне*, StP, 2000, 400 pp.

SOLOGUB. A. D. Semkin, 'Евреинов и Сологуб. К истории постановки пьесы «Ванька-ключник и паж Жеан»', *RusL*, 2000, no.2:112–19; L. Heller, 'Фантазии и утопии Федора Сологуба: замечания по поводу «Творимой легенды»', *RusL*, 2000, no.2:119–27; V. Vavere, 'Федор Сологуб в Латвии', *ib.*, 127–35; J. Merill, 'The many "loves" of Fedor Sologub: the textual history of incest in his drama', *SEEJ*, 44, 2000:429–47.

SOLOVIEV. M. V. Maksimov edits four volumes of studies on Vladimir Soloviev's heritage: *Соловьевские исследования*, I: *Метафизика и теория познания Вл. Соловьева*, Ivanovo, IGEU; II: *Социальная философия и историософия Вл. Соловьева*, Ivanovo, IGEU (on Gerzen, Dostoevsky, Florovsky, D. Andreev, and Soloviev); III: *Соловьев и традиции отечественной и зарубежной мысли*, Ivanovo, IGEU (on Leontiev and Soloviev, Soloviev and "The Silver Age", etc.); IV: *Вл. Соловьев: литературное наследие. Эстетика. Критика*, Ivanovo, IGEU, on Tiutchev, Prishvin, and Soloviev. Among other valuable sources are P. Davidson, 'Vladimir Solov′ev and the ideal of prophecy', *SEER*, 78, 2000:643–70; C. Hooper, 'Forms of love: Vladimir Solov′ev and Lev Tolstoy on *Eros* and Ego', *RusR*, 60:360–80; *Вл. Соловьев: pro et contra. Личность и творчество Владимира Соловьева в оценке русских мыслителей и исследователей*, ed. V. F. Boikov, StP, RkhGI, 2000, 896 pp., an anthology with commentaries. J. D. Cornblatt, 'The truth of the words: Solovyov's *Three Conversations* speaks on Tolstoy's *Resurrection*', *SEEJ*, 45:301–21; *Соловьевский сборник: материалы международной конференции*, ed. I. V. Borisova and A. P. Kozyrev, Mw, Fenomenologiia–Germenevtika, 515 pp.; P. P. Gaidenko, *Владимир Соловьев и философия Серебряного века*, Mw, Progress–Traditsiia, 468 pp.; *В. С. Соловьев: жизнь, учение, традиции*, ed. O. B. Ionaitis, Ekaterinburg, Ural State U.P., 2000, 221 pp.; M. V. Maksimov, *Владимир Соловьев и Запад: Невидимый континент*, Mw, Prometei, 1998, 242 pp.

TIUTCHEV. Biographical work includes V. Kozhinov, *Пророк в своем отечестве: Федор Тютчев – история России, век 19-й*, Mw, Algoritm, Soloviev, 416 pp.; J. Dewey, 'Tiutchev and Amalie von Lerchenfeld: some unpublished documents', *SEER*, 79:15–30, an analysis of the previously unpublished letters and diaries of Count Maximilian Joseph von Lerchenfeld and of circumstances which can illuminate the Munich period of Tiutchev's life (1822–1826). I. V. Kozlik, *В поэтическом мире Ф. И. Тютчева*, Ivano-Frankovsk, *Plai*; Kolomyia, *BIK, 1997, 156 pp.;* B. N. Tarasov, 'Тютчев и Паскаль (антиномии бытия и сознания в свете христианской онтологии', *RusL*, 2000, no.3:53–74; no.4:26–45; *Анализ одного стихотворения. «О чем ты воешь, ветр ночной?..» Ф. И. Тютчева*, Tver′ State U.P., 72 pp., collected papers,.; Li Su-Yon, '«Бездна безымянная» в философской лирике Ф. И. Тютчева', *RusL*, no.4:162–65; Li Soo Ion, 'Традиция пушкинского «Пророка» в стихотворениях Ф. И. Тютчева «Безумие» и «Странник»', *RusL*, no.3:116–18.

TOLSTOY A. K. L. Kuklin, 'Субъективные заметки о российском стихотворце графе Алексее Константиновиче Толстом', *Neva*, 2000, no.8:172–95; O. N. Kulishkina, 'Козьма Прутков в истории русской афористики', *RusL*, no.4:153–62.

LITERATURE FROM 1917 TO THE PRESENT DAY

By BORIS LANIN, *Professor of Literature, Russian Academy of Education, Moscow*

1. GENERAL

The Routledge Companion to Russian Literature, ed. Neil Cornwell, London–NY, Routledge, x + 271 pp., has nine chapters devoted to the 20th c., some (but not all) of which had earlier appeared in *A Reference Guide to Russian Literature*, ed. Neil Cornwell, London, Fitzroy Dearborn, 1998. B. Paramonov, *След: Философия. История. Современность*, Mw, Nezavisimaia Gazeta, 528 pp. is a selection of brilliant essays on new trends in modern Russian culture. See also K. Ryzhov, *Россия: 600 кратких биографий*, Mw, Veche, 576 pp.

Two works about literature on the Internet are *Общество и книга: от Гутенберга до Интернета*, ed. A. P. Koroleva, Mw, Traditsiia, 280 pp., and A. Ageev, *Газета, глянец, Интернет: Литератор в трех средах*, Mw, Novoe Literaturnoe obozrenie, 512 pp. Also of interest is *Русские детские писатели XX века: Биобиблиографический словарь*, ed. G. A. Chernaia, 3rd revd edn, Mw, Flinta, Nauka, 512 pp. *L-критика: Ежегодник академии русской современной словесности. Вып. 2*, Mw, ARSS, OGI, 176 pp., contains papers by N. Eliseev, D. Bak, R. Arbitman, A. Latynina, M. Lipovetsky, and others.

M. Scheglov, *На полдороге: Слово о русской литературе*, Mw, Progress-Pleiada, 320 pp. includes this critic's works on Lev Tolstoi, Leonid Leonov, Alexandr Blok, Alexandr Grin, Fedor Dostoevskii, Sergei Esenin, Victor Nekrasov, V. Kardin's memoirs, and correspondence between V. Nekrasov and V. Turbin. I. K. Kuzmichev, *Введение в общее литературоведение XXI века*, Nizhnii Novgorod, NNGU, 324 pp., makes only brief mention of 'the twenty-first century' in this strange and out-of-date book.

B. Dubin, *Слово — письмо — литература: Очерки по социологии современной культуры* (Nauchnoe prilozhenie, 26), Mw, Novoe literaturnoe obozrenie, 412 pp., contains a selection of Dubin's works that have been previously published in journals.

2. LITERARY HISTORY

Among the most valuable works this year are E. G. Gershtein, *Память писателя: Статьи и исследования 30 — 90-х годов*, StP, Inapress, 672 pp.; S. Rassadin, *Русская литература: от Фонвизина до Бродского*, Mw, Slovo, 288 pp., M. Edel'shtein in 'Песнь методологической невинности', *NovM*, no.10 : 202–07 (a stern critique of the so called 'philological best-seller'). 'Нерасшифрованные послания' by Nikolai Pereiaslov; D. Kaliuzhnyi, and A. Zhabinskii, *Другая история литературы: от самого начала до наших дней*, Mw, Veche, is a fairly superficial compilation of dubious concepts on the history of literature. See also M. M. Golubkov, *Русская литература XX в. После раскола*, Mw, Aspekt Press, 267 pp. V. Kanashkin, *После тризны, или Поэтика самоистязания: Литература и власть*, Krasnodar, Sovetskaia Kuban', 256 pp., is written in an aggressive and nationalistic style. There is interesting material from the KGB archives in V. Shentalinskii, *Донос на Сократа*, Mw, Formika-S, 461 pp., including denunciations of Korolenko, Belyi, Berdiaev, Karsavin, Kol'tsov, Platonov, Pasternak, Mandel'stam.

On the Silver Age see S. M. Pinaiev, *Над бездонным провалом в вечность . . .: Русская поэзия Серебряного века*, Mw, Unikum-Tsentr, Pomatur, 256 pp., and *Северо-Запад: Историко-культурный региональный вестник: Сборник памяти В.А.Сапогова*: Cherepovets, Cherepovets State U.P., 2000, 256 pp., which contains papers on the Silver Age, Tsvetaeva, Mandel'shtam, Pasternak, and memoirs.

On literary culture see A. Brintlinger, *Writing a Usable Past: Russian Literary Culture, 1917–1937*, Evanston, Northwestern U.P., 2000, x + 253 pp., and V. V. Pozdeev, *«Третья культура»: проблемы формирования и эстетики*, Mw, MGOPU, 2000, 134 pp., on modern urban folklore, poetry, and culture. Of some interest are B. Kolonitskii, *Символы власти и борьба за власть: к изучению политической культуры российской революции 1917 года*, StP, Dmitrii Bulanin, 352 pp.; I. Murav'eva, *Век модерна: Панорама столичной жизни*, StP, Pushkinskii fond, 272 pp.

T. Mochizuki, *Culture*, includes papers by K. Eimermakher, D. Prigov, P. Toorop, B. Lanin, K. Numano, I. Kameyama, M. Suzuki, M. Yasukhara, N. Umetsu, V. Arseniev, S. Nishi, K. Tateoka, V. Grechko, T. Mochizuki, E. Vlasov, V. Smolensky, F. Osuka, T. Kibe, S. Kitami, N. Kakinuma, A. Genis, S. Lakoba, and T. Nakamura.

On modern literature see N. L. Leiderman and M. N. Lipovetskii, *Современная русская литература. В 3 тт. Книга 2. Семидесятые годы (1968–1986)*, Mw, URSS, perhaps the best book of this type in the last 30 years. See also S. P. Belokurova and S. V. Drugoveiko, *Русская литература: Конец XX века*, StP, Paritet, 512 pp., and L. N. Vorob'eva, *Современная русская литература. Проза — 1970–1990-е годы*, Samara, SGAKI, 183 pp.; L. Pann, *Нескучный сад: поэты и прозаики, 80-е–90-е. Заметки о русской литературе* конца XX века, Tenafly, N.J, Hermitage, 1998, 220 pp., is a unique collection of essays on Brodskii, Petrushevskaia, Siniavskii, Venedict Erofeev, Lev Loseff, Anatoly Naiman, Aleksei Tsvetkov, Vladimir Gandel'sman, Regina Derieva, Yuri Miloslavskii, Andrei Gritsman, Aleksandr Genis, Igor' Efimov, Sergei Gandlevskii, and Bakhyt Kenzheev.

POSTMODERNISM. M. Lipovetsky, 'Russian literary Postmodern-ism in the 1990s', *SEER*, 79:31–50, is mainly on the typology of Russian literary postmodernism, with the contention that Russian postmodernism has been represented by two trends: conceptualism and neo-baroque. V. Liutyi, 'Козье копытце', *NSo*, no.10:268–83, offers an analysis of two 'typical' postmodern texts: 'Медный кувшин Старика Хоттабыча' by Sergei Oblomov, and 'Чайка' by Boris Akunin. See also O. V. Bogdanova, *Современный литера-турный процесс: К вопросу о постмодернизме в русской литературе 70 — 90-х годов XX века*, St Petersburg State U.P., 252 pp.

THE EMIGRATION. There are two monographs: E. V. Tikhomi-rova, *Проза русского зарубежья и России в ситуации постмодерна*, Ivanovo, Ivanovo State U.P., 2000, 244 pp., and O. A. Buzuev, *Литература русского зарубежья Дальнего Востока: проблемы худо-жественного своеобразия (1917–1945 гг.)*, Mw, Moscow State Peda-gogical U.P., 121 pp. See also O. N. Mikhailov, *От Мережковского до Бродского. Литература русского зарубежья*, Mw, Prosveshchenie, 336 pp. An important collection is D. S. Merezhkovskii, *Царство Антихриста: Статьи периода эмиграции*, comp. and ed. O. G. Korostelev and A. N. Nikoliukin, StP, RkhGI, 656 pp.

Русская поэзия Китая: Антология, ed. V. Kreid and O. Bakich, Mw, Vremia, 720 pp., is a very interesting collection containing the lyrics of 58 Russian émigré poets, including Arsenii Nesmelov and Valerii Pereleshin. In similar fashion, *Диаспора: Новые материалы. Вып. 2*, ed. O. Korostylev, StP, Feniks, 752 pp., contains a paper by Vladimir Nabokov (1926), Vladimir Veidle's memoirs (previously written as scripts for 'Svoboda' radio), Teffi's letters to the Bunins, papers by R. Iangirov and F. Poliakov, and materials for a biblio-graphy of Vladimir Alloi's works. See also *Юбилейная международ-ная конференция по гуманитарным наукам, посвященная 70-летию Орловского государственного университета: Мате-риалы. Выпуск 2: Л.Н.Андреев, Б. К. Зайцев*, Orel, Orel State U.P., 284 pp.; D. K. Samin, *Самые знаменитые эмигранты России*, Mw, Veche, 480 pp.; O. Bakich, 'Мария Визи — поэт России, Китая и США', *RES*, 73:373–86; O. D. Volkogonova, *Н. А. Бердяев: Интеллектуальная биография*, Moscow State U.P., 112 pp.; W. Cowdenys, 'Глас вопиющего в литературной пустыне: З.А. Шаховская и русская эмиграция в Бельгии', *RES*, 73:151–66;

G. N. Slobin, 'The "homecoming" of the first wave diaspora and its cultural legacy', *SRev*, 60 : 513–29.

Two works by L. Livak are of great interest: 'Histoire de la littérature russe en exil: la "période héroïque" de la jeune poésie russe à Paris', *RES*, 73 : 133–49, argues that the so-called Paris period, 1921–1924, was as important for Russian émigré literature as its Berlin period; 'The Surrealist compromise of Boris Poplavsky', *RusR*, 60.2 : 89–108.

SOCIALIST REALISM.   Several significant papers were published in *RES*, 73.4: M. Aucouturier, 'La périodisation de la "literature soviétique": réflexions et propositions' (589–603), talks with A. Drawicz, S. Porȩmba, and M. Čudakova and offers a new periodization based on the notion of the 'literary generation'; G. Belaia, 'Имманентное сопротивление художественного текста' (605–17); some interesting documents are presented in A. Berelowitch, 'Les écrivains vus par l'OGPU' (619–36); M. Chudakova, 'К проблеме "et": феномен *советского писателя* как специфического аггломерата биографии и творчества' (637–50); E. Dobrenko, 'Надзирать — наказывать — надзирать: соцреализм как прибавочный продукт насилия' (667–712) on the so-called 're-forging' in Stalinist culture; H. Günther, 'Прощание с советским каноном' (712–18); L. Heller, 'Un pas en avant, deux pas en arriè ou comment on étudie le realisme socialiste soviétique', (719–38), a series of presuppositions which seem to underlie the methodology of studying Soviet culture in his work; M. Niqueux, 'Quels textes lisons-nous? Les classiques soviétiques au fil des revisions', (739–46), examining various editions of *Чапаев, Цемент, Разгром* and *Как закалялась сталь*; and the book *Литература факта* is discussed by M. Weinstein, 'Essau de lecture poéticienne de *La Littérature du fait (1929)*', (747–62).

See also *Аппарат ЦК КПСС и культура 1953–1957: Документы (Культура и власть от Сталина до Горбачева. Документы)*, ed. E. S. Afanas'eva, Mw, ROSSPEN, 808 pp., a very useful collection of documents with able commentary; T. M. Goriaeva, *Политическая цензура в СССР. 1917–1991 (Культура и власть от Сталина до Горбачева. Документы)*, Mw, ROSSPEN, 400 pp.; C. Depretto, 'La censure à la période soviétique, 1917–1953: état de la recherché', *RES*, 73 : 651–66; S. E. Reid, 'Socialist realism in Stalinist terror, the *Industry of Socialism* art exhibition, 1935–41', *RusR*, 60 : 153–84.

3. THEORY

М. М. Бахтин: pro et contra. Личность и творчество М. М. Бахтина в оценке русской и мировой гуманитарной мысли, ed. K. Isupov, vol.

1, StP, RkhGI, 552 pp., is a major edition. See also E. Lozowy, 'Satire et histoire: l'article encyclopédique de Bakhtine sur la satire dans le contexte de la critique littéraire soviétique des années 1920 et 1930', *CASS*, 35:375–94.

Литературные манифесты: От символизма до «Октября», ed. N. L. Brodskii and N. P. Sidorov, Mw, Agraf, 384 pp., is a reprint of an old and useful book. M. Epshtein, *Философия возможного*, StP, Aleteia, 334 pp., offers an interesting study of the methodology of research in culture and literature. See also L. V. Ovchinnikova, *Русская литературная сказка XX века (история, классификация, поэтика)*, Mw, Moscow State Open Pedagogical University, 122 pp.

CRITICISM

A. Schönle, 'Social power and individual agency: the self in Greenblatt and Lotman', *SEEJ*, 45:61–79; S. Lovell, 'Tynianov as sociologist of literature', *SEER*, 79:415–33; Z. M. Dinnershtein, *А.К.Воронский. В поисках живой воды*, Mw, ROSSPEN, 360 pp.

A. Kasymova writes about the interesting modern critic Nikita Eliseev in 'Номинатор, или Повествования Н. Е.', *Znamia*, no.4:232–36. There are two discussions of the nationalistic critic Vladimir Bondarenko: N. Eliseev, 'Красота дьявола', *NovM*, no.5: 167–78, and Al. Mikhailov, 'Значимая книга', *NSo*, no.12:268–9. There is also a long discussion about modern literature in *LitG*: see A. Latynina, 'Сумерки литературы', no.47, P. Basinskii, 'Литературные гадания', no.49, S. Kaznacheev, no.50–51, A. Varlamov, no.52. Two significant studies by Viktor Miasnikov are 'Бульварный эпос', *NovM*, no.11:150–58, and 'Технотриллер — здесь и сейчас' *Znamia*, no.10:175–85 (about I. Shtemler, S. Kaledin, Iu. Latynina, Iu. Dubov, B. Shirianov).

PROSE. K. Kokshenova, *Революция низких смыслов: о современной русской прозе*, Mw, Leto, 224 pp. M. Adamovich, in 'Юдифь с головой Олоферна', *NovM*, no.7: 165–74, offers the term 'pseudoclassics' for a trend in modern literature that includes N. Perumov, Peppershtein, Anufriev, A. Chernov, M. Verbitskii, V. Kuritsyn, D. Galkovskii, V.Sorokin, B.Shirianov, M. Gel'man, M. Frai, N. Gryzunova, and L. Goralik. O. Lebedushkina, 'Роман с немцем, или Русский человек на rendez-vous с Западом', *DN*, 9:161–72, analyses works by N. Sadur, M. Rybakova, K. Pleshakov, I. Murav'eva, and Ia. Mogutin.

There is an excellent article on modern Russian prose: V. Kaplan, 'Заглянем за стенку', *NovM*, no.9:156–70, has many penetrating insights, with sharp but fair conclusions. He speculates on Ie. Lukin,

S. Lukianenko, V. Krapivin, L. Kudriavtsev, E. Gevorkian, Iu. Latynina, T. Tolstaia, V. Khlumov, V. Pelevin, M. Veller.

POETRY. There are some valuable books: E. Etkind, *Проза о стихах*, StP, Znanie, 446 pp., V. Finkel', *Поэты рубежа*, Philadelphia [no publisher], 1999, 314 pp., on Joseph Brodsky, Inna Bogachinskaia, Vera Zubareva and Mikhail Iupp; M. Gasparov, *О русской поэзии: Анализы. Интерпретации. Характеристики*, StP, Azbuka, 480 pp; N. A. Turanina, *Именная метафора в русской поэзии начала XX века*, Orel State U.P., 2000, 110 pp. Of particular interest is S. Sandler, 'Scared into selfhood: the poetry of Inna Lisnianskaia, Elena Shvarts, Ol'ga Sedakova', *SRev*, 60:473–90. See also some interesting interviews: I. Lisnianskaya, 'Всего труднее быть самой собой', *Trud*, July 7 (interview with E. Konstantinova); E. Rein, 'Нельзя быть бывшим сенбернаром', *Obshchaia Gazeta*, September 6 (interview with T. Bek).

Among other publications are A. S. Karpov, *Неугасимый свет: Н. Гумилев, А. Ахматова, О. Мандельштам, М. Цветаева, Б. Пастернак, Н. Заболоцкий: очерки*, Mw, RUDN, 338 pp.; S. Zavialov, 'Оправдание поэзии', *NovM*, no.5:183–88, on the new generation of St Petersburg poets E. Fanailova, G. Dashevskii, and A. Skidan. Zavialov is challenged by V. Shubinskii, 'Кофий императрицы', *ib.*, 188–94, writing about Fanailova, Dashevskii, Skidan, Oleg Iur'ev, Nikolai Kononov, Viktor Efimov, and Igor' Bulatovsky.

L. G. Kikhney, *Akmeizm: Miroponimanie i poetika*, Mw, MAKS Press, 184 pp. Also V. Novikov, 'Nos habebit humus', *NovM*, no.6:167–78, writes about so called 'philological poetry', Alexandr Eremenko, Timur Kibirov, Maksim Amelin, Igor' Irteniev, Dmitrii Bykov, and Vera Pavlova. A. Uritsky makes observations on the anthology *Время Ч* in 'Поэты и время', *DN*, no.12:200–02; V. Gubailovsky in 'Три книги стихов', *DN*, no.11:150–52, writes about the poetry of A. Beliakov, Ia. Mogutin, and P. Ivanova.

Словарь языка русской поэзии XX века, 1: *A — B*, ed. V. P. Grigoriev, Mw, Iazyki slavianskoi kul'tury, 896 pp., V. V. Veidle, *Эмбриология поэзии*, Mw, LVS, 128 pp., M. Jacobson, and L. Jacobson, *Песенный фольклор ГУЛАГа как исторический источник: 1940–1991*, Mw, Sovremennyi Gumanitarnyi Universitet, 561 pp. See also V. Zhirmunskii, *Поэтика русской поэзии*, StP, Azbukaklassika, 496 pp. (a reprint).

MEMOIRS

One of the most interesting memoirs of this year is S. Frank, *Непрочитанное. . . Статьи, письма, воспоминания*, Mw, Moskovskaia shkola politologicheskikh issledovanii, 592 pp. See also

V. Nemirovich-Danchenko, *На кладбищах: Воспоминания и впечатления*, Mw, Russkaia Kniga, 544 pp. — interesting memoirs by famous prosewriter and famous director's brother; I. Dedkov, 'Новый цикл российских иллюзий. Из дневниковых записей 1985–1986 годов', *NovM*, no.11:119–42, no.12:147–65; A. Turkov, 'Там чудеса . . .' *Znamia*, no.11, <http://magazines.russ.ru/znamia/2001/11/tur.html> on V. Petelin and P. Vegin's memoirs as an ethical issue; A. Rubashkin 'Нет пророка в своем отечестве', *Neva*, no.10:157–60, writes about the scholars B. Putilov, V. Bakhtin, V. Vatsuro, V. Tunimanov, and A. Lavrov; V. Nekrasov, '*От слова "любить"* . . .' *Zvezda*, 8:88–94, memoirs on I. S. Sokolov-Mikitov (published by V. Kondyrev); V. Katanian, *Лоскутное одеяло: Дневники*, Mw, Vagrius, 528 pp., memoirs on Galich, Lilia Brik, and others; K. Bulychev, *Как стать фантастом: Записки семидесятника*, Cheliabinsk, Okolitsa, 325 pp.; A. Brusilovsky, *Студия*, StP, Letnii sad, 212 pp., memoirs on Ven. Erofeev, Oleg Tselkov, and others.

COMPARATIVE STUDIES

A. Etkind, *Толкование путешествий: Россия и Америка в травелогах и интертекстах*, Mw, Novoe Literaturnoe Obozrenie, 496 pp., is on the American roots of Russian nihilism, Freudo-marxism in America, 'metadialogue' between Pasternak and Nabokov; everything is written in brilliant story-teller's manner. *Айзек Азимов — американский писатель и ученый: Библиографический указатель 1959–2000. Биобиблиографические материалы. Творчество. Критика. Связь со Смоленщиной*, ed. I. Karpenchenkova, Smolensk, Smolenskaia oblastnaia Universal'naia Biblioteka, 223 pp.

S. V. Nikol'skii, *Над страницами антиутопий К.Чапека и М.Булгакова (поэтика скрытых мотивов)*, Mw, Indrik, 176 pp., is on utopian ideas in Chapek's and Bilgakov's works. V. Khazan, *Особенный еврейско-русский воздух: к проблематике и поэтике русско-еврейского литературного диалога в XX веке*, Jerusalem, Gesharim, Mw, Mosty Kul'tury, 432 pp., is on Bunin, Bal'mont, Babel', Esenin, Dovid Knut, Mandel'shtam, and Osorgin.

PROSE

A. Goldshtein, *Аспекты духовного брака*, Mw, NLO, 320 pp., is an excellent collection of essays mostly published in 'Zerkalo', 'Neprikosnovennyi Zapas', and other magazines, devoted to Sasha Sokolov, Leonid Dobychin, Milan Kundera, George Orwell, and others. K. Ragozina ironically writes about I. Stogoff and M. Elizarov in 'Пара слов о стареющих юношах', *Znamia*, no.11:219–20.

O. Slavnikova in 'Экспансия', *NovM*, no.6:179–85, analyses prose by Pavel Krusanov, Andrei Levkin, Sergei Nosov, Victor Lapitsky, and Alexandr Sekatsky. M. O. Chudakova, *Избранные работы*, I: *Литература советского прошлого* (Studia philologica), Mw, Yazyki Russkoi Kul'tury, 344 pp. M. Abasheva, *Литература в поисках лица*, Perm', 112 pp., is on Russian prose of the second half of the 20th c. T. A. Ponomareva, *Проза новокрестьян 1920–х годов: типология. Поэтика.* Mw, Moscow State Pedagogical University, 2000, 132 pp. V. I. Shul'zhenko, *Кавказ в русской прозе второй половины XX века: проблематика, типология персонажей, художественная образность*, Moscow State U.P., 122 pp.

POSTMODERNISM

R. Glintershchik, *Современные русские писатели-постмодернисты: очерки новейшей русской литературы*, Kaunas, Shviesa, 2000, 375 pp., has chapters on Venedict Erofeev, Dovlatov, Petrushevskaia, Akunin, Pelevin, and Sorokin.

GENDER STUDIES

I. Zherebkina, *Страсть: Женское тело и женская сексуальность в России*, StP, Aleteia, 336 pp., provides notes on Vera Zasulich, Marina Tsvetaieva, Nina Berberova, Lidiia Ginzburg, Lilia Brik, Zinaida Gippius, Sofiia Parnok, and others. *Женщины: свобода слова и свобода творчества*, ed. S. Vasilenko, Mw, Eslan, 189 pp. *Мифология и повседневность: гендерный подход в антропологических дисциплинах: Материалы научной конференции (19 — 21 февраля 2001 г.)*, ed. K. A. Bogdanov and A. A. Panchenko, StP, Aleteia, Institut Russkoi literatury (Pushkinskii Dom), 400 pp. W. Tomasik, 'The motif of male friendship in Stalinist mythology', *CanSP*, 43, 2000:67–74. E. Borenstein, *Men without Women: Masculinity and Revolution in Russian Fiction, 1917–1929*, Durham, Duke U.P., 2000, xi + 346 pp., is an illuminating study of the ways in which masculinization of early Soviet society influences Soviet prose: Babel, Bogdanov, and Platonov.

EPISTOLARY

Ю. Г. Оксман — К. И. Чуковский. Переписка, ed. A. L. Grishunin, Mw, Iazyki Slavianskoi Kul'tury, 174 pp.

4. INDIVIDUAL AUTHORS

AIGI. M. Kucherskaia reviews Aigi's new book *Продолжение отъезда* in 'Поэт Айги в "Проекте ОГИ"', *Izvestiia*, December 1.

AITMATOV. N. Kolesnikov, *Myth in the Works of Chingiz Aitmatov*, Lanham MD, U.P. of America, 1999, 133 pp.

AIZENBERG. M. Bondarenko, 'Жизнь в тексте, или По ту сторону Красных ворот' *Znamia*, no.4: 224–6.

AKHMADULINA. V. Gubailovsky, 'Нежность к бытию', *DN*, no.8: 189–96, is about Akhmadulina's new lyrics.

AKHMATOVA. *Анна Ахматова: pro et contra: Антология*, ed. S. Kovalenko, vol. 1, StP, RkhGI, 964 pp. D. V. Kupriianov and V. M. Vorobiev, *Ахматова и юмор*, Tver', Sozvezdie, 112 pp. See also M. Sinel'nikov, 'Дафнис и Хлоя', *MN*, no.31, July 31, on Akhmatov's biographical prose.

AKSENOV. Two works about his latest novel *Кесарево свечение*: A. Latynina, 'Этот жанр все-таки хорош своим несовершенством', *LitG*, no.31–32, August 8–14, and K. Gazarian 'Кукушкин карнавал', *Obshchaia gazeta*, no.31.

AKUNIN. G. Tsiplakov, 'Зло, возникающее в дороге, и Дао Эраста Фандорина', *NovM*, no.11 : 159–81, is one of the first really deep and interesting works on Boris Akunin.

ALESHKOVSKY, IUZ. E. Ponomarev, 'Прорезается душа . . . Диссидентское и общечеловеческое в текстах Юза Алешковского', *Zvezda*, no.7 : 191–99.

ALESHKOVSKY, P. V. Brougher, 'Werewolves and vampires, historical questions and symbolic answers, in Petr Aleshkovsky's *Vladimir Chigrintsev*', *SEEJ*, 45 : 491–505.

ASTAF'EV. N. L. Leiderman, *Крик сердца. Творческий облик Виктора Астафьева*, Ekaterinburg, AMB, 34 pp.

AVALIANI. A. Uritsky, 'Сестры зыбкость и цельность' *Znamia*, no.6 : 218–19.

AZOL'SKY. E. Ermolin, 'Люди бездны', *DN*, no.4 : 188–98.

BAITOV. L. Kostiukov, 'Существо дела', *Znamia*, no.10 : 219–20.

BELYI. I. Vishnevetsky, *Трагический субъект в действии: Андрей Белый* (Heidelberger Publikationen zur Slavistik: Literaturwissenschaftliche Reihe, 12), Frankfurt, Lang, 2000, v + 212 pp., G. Walker, 'Adumbrations of the end in Andrei Belyi's treatment of Africa', *RusR*, 60 : 381–403.

BERBEROVA. O. Ronen, 'Берберова (1901–2001)', *Zvezda*, no.7 : 213–20; N. L. Peterson, 'The private "I" in the works of Nina Berberova', *SRev*, 60 : 491–512.

BITOV. A. Bitov, 'Благодать безвременья', interview by L. Paikova, *Iskusstvo kino*, 5 : 73–81.

BOLMAT. S. Arutiunov in 'Комедия убийства', *Znamia*, no.6 : 219–21, writes about Sergei Bolmat's novel *Сам по себе*.

BRODSKY. There are two useful books about Brodsky: A. M. Ranchin, *"На пиру Мнемозины": Интертексты Бродского*, Mw,

Novoe Literaturnoe Obozrenie, 336 pp. — on motifs from Pushkin, Derzhavin, and Khodasevich, and the Roman theme in Brodsky's poetry; D. MacFadyen, *Joseph Brodsky and the Soviet Muse*, Montreal–Kingston, McGill-Queen's U.P., 2000, 209 pp., portrays the cultural, psychological, and political atmosphere in Leningrad of the 1950s and 1960s.; M. Iupp, 'Ося Бродский — легенда и факты', *LR*, no.30, July 27.

BULGAKOV. E. A. Iablokov, *Художественный мир Михаила Булгакова*, Mw, Iazyki Slavianskoi kul'tury, 424 pp.; M. Petrovsky, *Мастер и город: Киевские контексты Михаила Булгакова*, Kiev, Dukh i Litera, 367 pp. See also M. and E. Bulgakovs, *Дневник Мастера и Маргариты*, Mw, Vagrius, 558 pp.: many interesting things are selected in this book, some facts are really new.

BYKOV, D. There were very sharp debates on Bykov's novel *Оправдание*: see A. Kavtorina, 'Попытка оправдания, или Персонаж на дорогах истории', *Neva*, no.11: 187–201. E. Ivanitskaia evaluates this novel highly in 'Преступление и оправдание', *ib*., no.7: 210–15, and S. Khazagerova is very pessimistic about it in 'У них там были забавные представления о писательстве . . .', *Znamia*, no.9: 204–07.

CHERCHESOV. D. Bak 'Триста лет одиночества, или Вечность у реки', *NovM*, no.7: 187–90, is about Alan Cherchesov's most successful novel *Венок на могилу ветра*.

CHUDAKOV. The eminent scholar Alexandr Chudakov suddenly became the author of one of the best modern Russian novels *Ложится мгла на старые ступени* ('idyllic novel'). A. Marchenko gives an analysis of it in 'В начале жизни школу помню я', *NovM*, no.5: 195–200.

CHUKOVSKY. O. Kanunnikova, 'С кем протекли его боренья?..', *NovM*, no.11: 194–202 is on Kornei Chukovsky.

DOBYCHIN. R. C. Borden, 'The flogging angel: toward a mapping of Leonid Dobychin's *Gorod En*', *RusR*, 60: 259–74.

DOVLATOV. There are two books: V. Solov'ev, E. Klepikova, *Довлатов вверх ногами: Трагедия веселого человека*, Mw, Kollektsiia 'Sovershenno sekretno', 192 pp.; *О Довлатове*, comp. and ed. E. Dovlatova, Tver', Drugie Berega, 224 pp., has essays and memoirs by Iunna Morits, A. Ar'ev, Joseph Brodsky, A. Genis, V. Kamianov, and A. Zverev); the selection is devoted to what would have been Dovlatov's 60th birthday, but includes some materials that were written several years ago. See also D. Gillespie, 'The booze and the blues: laughter and the "real" world in the work of Sergei Dovlatov', *ASEES*, 15.1–2: 21–37.

DRUZHNIKOV. L. Zvonareva, V. Olbrykh, *Состоявшийся вне тусовки: Творчество и судьба писателя Юрия Дружникова. Опыт документального исследования*, Mw, ACADEMIA — Randevu AM, 160 pp.

DUDINTSEV. T. Domracheva, and Z. Vodopianova (comp.), 'Не хлебом единым. Трагическая судьба писателя [Владимира Дудинцева] и его романа', *Trud–7*, no.136, July 26.

EROFEEV VEN. There are two valuable works on Venedikt Erofeev: *Литературный текст: проблемы и методы исследования. Вып. 7. Анализ одного произведения: «Москва-Петушки»* *Вен.Ерофеева*, Tver' State U.P., 208 pp., with papers by I. Fomenko, G. Prokhorov, N. Veselova, Iu. Domansky, D. Stupnikov, O. Lekmanov, N. Pavlova, S. Broitman, Iu. Orlitskii, and A. Iablokov; and S. Steblovskaia, 'Веничка и Христос', *LR*, No. 31, August 3.

ESENIN. N. I. Shubnikova-Guseva, *Поэмы Есенина: От «Пророка» до «Черного человека»: Творческая история, судьба, контекст и интерпретация*, Mw, IMLI RAN, Nasledie, 688 pp., G. I. Averina, *Есенин и художники*, Riazan', Poverennyi, 2000, 112 pp.

FADEEV. *Александр Фадеев. Письма и документы из фондов Российского Государственного Архива литературы и искусства*, ed. N. I. Dikushina, Mw, Literaturnyi Institut, 359 pp.

FILIPPOV. Vasia Filippov is a rising star of modern Russian poetry, and its 'collective underconsciousness', and M. Bondarenko's paper 'Чтобы книга стала Телом', *Znamia*, no.8: 222–26, is the first critical study of his works.

GALICH. *Галич. Проблемы поэтики и текстологии*, ed. E. A. Krylov, Mw, Gosudarstvennyi kul'turnyi tsentr-muzei V.S.Vysotskogo, 230 pp.

GANDLEVSKY. Two works about this popular poet and prosewriter: M. Remizova, 'Не напрасно' *NovM*, no.4: 194–97, writes about first full selection of his works *Порядок слов* (Ekaterinburg, 2000), and L. Kostiukov, 'Свидетельские показания', *DN*, no.7: 181–84.

GANDEL'SMAN. L. Pann, in 'Доказательство в образах', writes about his book *Тихое пальто* in *NovM*, no.7: 194–99.

GOLIAVKIN. S. Ivanova, 'Я думал, я один такой . . .', *Znamia*, no.8: 226–27.

GORIN. *Григорий Горин, Воспоминания современников*, ed. L. Gorina and Yu. Kushak, Mw, EKSMO-Press, 368 pp.

GORKY. C. Marsh, 'Truth, lies and story-telling in *The Lower Depths*', *CanSP*, 43, 2000: 507–20, studies G.'s drama as a narrative. V. Baranov, *Беззаконная комета: Роковая женщина Максима Горького*, Mw, Agraf, 380 pp., is about Budberg-Zakrevskaia. *А. М. Горький и М.И.Будберг. Переписка. 1920–1936*, ed. V. S. Barakhov, Mw, INLI RAN, 544 pp.

GRANIN. About Granin's latest novel *Вечера с Петром Великим* see L. Lazarev, 'Это открывается нашим дням . . .', *Znamia*, no. 4:222–24.

GRIGORIEVA. See I. Znamenskaia, 'Я штопаю дыру в миропорядке', *DN*, no.7:215–17.

GUMILEV. V. Polushin, 'О происхождении Гумилева', *LR*, no.28, July 13.

IVANOV, VIACH. Two valuable works about Viacheslav Ivanov are: G. Janecek, 'Viacheslav Ivanov's "Alpine Horn" as a manifesto of Russian Symbolism', *SEEJ*, 45:30–44. S. S. Averintsev, '*Скворешниц вольных гражданин . . .': Вячеслав Иванов: путь поэта между двумя мирами*, StP, Aleteia, 167 pp.

IUR'EV. About Oleg Iur'ev's novel *Полуостров Жидятин*, see Miasnikov's 'Два полуострова — остров', *NovM*, no.4:188–91.

KATAEV. R. C. Borden, *The Art of Writing Badly: Valentin Kataev's Mauvism and the Rebirth of Russian Modernism* (Studies in Russian Literature and Theory), Evanston, IL, Northwestern U.P., 1999, 404 pp.

KASSIL'. K. A. Livers, 'The soccer match as Stalinist ritual: constructing the body social in Lev Kassil's 'The Goalkeeper of the Republic'', *RusR*, 60:592–613, is a very interesting study which sometimes corresponds with Alexandr Goldstein's and Vadim Rudnev's studies.

KHARMS. In A. Wanner, 'Russian minimalist prose: generic antecedents to Daniil Kharms's "Sluchai"', *SEEJ*, 45:451–72, the resulting disintegration is shown as the ultimate vanishing point of all minimalist art: the empty canvas, the white page, the protracted silence.

KHLEBNIKOV. R. Vroon and A. Hacker, 'Velimir Khlebnikov's "Perevorot v Vladivostoke": history and historiography', *RusR*, 60:36–55.

KOLKER. There are two works on Kolker's poetry: N. Basovsky, 'Уж если читать, так поэтов . . .', *Znamia*, no.6:221–23; and A. Mashevsky, 'Авангардизм традиционности', *NovM*, no.9:175–84.

KOTLIAR. T. Kasatkina, 'Простые вещи', *NovM*, no.6:198–205.

KOROLEVA. L. Anninsky recalls the poet Nina Koroleva in 'О безумном столетье моем', *DN*, No. 7:220–21.

KOVAL'. E. Grodskaia, 'Взгляд и Нечто', *Znamia*, no.12:211–13.

KRUSANOV. I. Klekh, '"Стрекозиные песни" Крусанова', *Znamia*, no.4:218–19, is on Pavel Krusanov and his novels 'Бессмертник', and 'Укус ангела'.

KUBLANOVSKY. V. Gubailovsky, 'Треснувший образец', *DN*, no.10: 113–21.

KUNIN. R. Salys, 'Three-rib circus: women and historical discourse in "Rebro Adama"', *RusR*, 60.4: 614–30.

LEVITANSKY. V. Kulle, 'Поэт личного стыда', *NovM*, no.11: 188–91, reflects on Levitansky's posthumous book ". . .*год две тысячи*" (2000).

LEVKIN. G. Ermoshina, 'Уходящий из кадра', *DN*, no.5: 204–05.

LICHUTIN. See M. Remizova, 'Козел отпущения', *NovM*, no.11: 186–88, on L.'s latest novel *Миледи Ротман*.

MAIAKOVSKY. B. Gorb, *Шут у трона Революции: Внутренний сюжет творчества и жизни поэта и актера Серебряного века Владимира Маяковского*, Mw, ULISS-MEDIA, 116 pp.

MAKANIN. G. S. Smith, 'On the page and the snow: Vladimir Makanin's *Anderground, ili Geroi nashego vremeni*', *SEER*, 79: 434–58.

MANDELSHTAM. N. A. Petrova, *Литература в антропоцентрическую эпоху. Опыт О Мандельштама*, Perm' State Pedagogical U.P., 311 pp. M.'s poetry is described as a link in Russian poetry's history: from Pushkin, Lermontov, Nekrasov, Tiutchev to Mandel'shtam, Maiakovsky, Pasternak, Tsvetaeva, and then to Brodsky. The author argues that M.'s poetry is a harmonic mixture of modernism and poetic realism. *Смерть и бессмертие поэта: Материалы международной научной конференции, посвященной 60–летию со дня гибели О. Э. Мандельштама, Москва, 28–29 декабря 1998 г.*, ed. M. Z. Vorobieva, Mw, RGGU, 320 pp.; V. Terras, 'The black sun: Orphic imagery in the poetry of Osip Mandelstam', *SEEJ*, 45: 44–89. See also selected memoirs in: *Осип и Надежда Мандельштамы в рассказах современников*, ed. O. Figurnov and M. Figurnov, Mw, Natalis, 2002, 544 pp.

MANUILOV. About Victor Manuilov's novel " Жернова" see E. Ermolin, 'Летят щепки', *NovM*, no.6: 191–94.

MELIKHOV. V. Miasnikov, 'Все те же мы', *DN*, no.6: 212–15.

MORITS. M. Kapustin, 'Громкое молчание прервано "КраДким курсом литераДуры"', *Obshchaia gazeta*, no.20: 7.

MOSHCHENKO. A. Smirnov, 'Путь к "Вишневому переулку"', *NovM*, no.11: 191–94.

NABOKOV. There are several excellent books, either studies or biographies. G. Khasin, *Театр личной тайны: Русские романы В. Набокова*, Mw, StP, Letnii Sad, 188 pp., is a phenomenological interpretation of Nabokov's texts. *Torpid Smoke: The Stories of Vladimir Nabokov*, ed. S. Kellman and I. Malin (Studies in Slavic Literature and Poetics, 35), Amsterdam, Rodopi, 2000, 246 pp., A. Zverev, *Владимир Набоков*, Mw, Molodaia Gvardiia, 453 pp., is a typical biography, using the traditional 'Zhizn' zamechatel'nykh liudei' series. L. N. Tselkova, *В. В. Набоков в жизни и творчестве*, Mw, Russkoe slovo, 128 pp.

NEKRASOV VS. L. Kostiukov, 'Ракурс. Робкие размышления о поэзии Всеволода Некрасова', *DN*, no.10:147–51.

NEZHNYI. V. Senderov 'Уход преподобного Симеона', *NovM*, no.4:191–94.

NOSIK. See A. Kuznetsova 'И я там был ...', *Znamia*, no.10:220–23, on Nosik's latest novel about Vasilii Zhukovskii *Царский наставник*.

NOSOV E. A speech by Alexandr Solzhenitsyn about Nosov's works that S. gave on his prize award ceremony is published in *NovM*, no.5:179–82. See also M. Remizova and T. Kravchenko, 'два новых классика', *NG*, April 25.

NOVIKOV. There are a lot of debates on Vladimir Novikov's last novel *Сентиментальный дискурс. Роман с языком*. The most interesting papers are D. Bavil'sky's 'Алиби', *Znamia*, no.4:220–22, and V. Miasnikov's 'И слово всегда буде(и) т мысль', *NovM*, no.5:200–03.

OKUDZAVA. *Творчество Булата Окуджавы в контексте культуры XX века*, comp. and ed. I. Rishina, Mw, Sol', 152 pp, is the materials of the 1st conference on Bulat Okudzhava (Peredelkino, November 19–21, 1999): papers by Vl. Novikov, L. Bakhnov, G. Belaia, Ia. Gordin, V. Kulle, Alexandr Kushner, M. Pozdniaev, Iu. Kariakin, L. Lazarev, S. Lominadze and others; Ia. Dukhan reviews the volumes of selected lyrics by Okudzhava: 'Гремят барабаны ...', *Neva*, no.10:203–04.

OLEINIKOV. T. Epstein, 'The dark and stingy Muse of Nikolai Oleinikov', *RusR*, 60.2:238–58.

OLESHA. Two new works: R. D. LeBlanc, 'Gluttony and power in Iurii Olesha's *Envy*', *RusR*, 60.2:220–37; M. Kanevskaya, 'The crisis of the Russian avant-garde in Iurii Olesha's *Envy*', *CanSP*, 44:475–493, analyses *Envy* as Olesha's perception of the destruction of the avant-garde in the mid-twenties and its replacement by a radically different aesthetic system (Socialist Realism).

PASTERNAK. V. Afiani and N. Tomilina, *«А за мною шум погони...» Борис Пастернак и власть. 1956 — 1972 гг.: Документы*, Mw, ROSSPEN, 432 pp., have some new materials about the publication of *Doctor Zhivago*; M. Swift, 'A self-conscious tale: Pasternak's *Povest'*', *CanSP*, 43, 2000:481–89, argues that 'Povest' is both self-reflective and self-reflexive, a self-conscious text.

PAVLOV. P. Basinsky, 'Переулок — не тупик', *NovM*, no.8:187–88.

PAVLOVA. V. Gubailovsky, 'Отрицая Платона', *NovM*, no.5 : 203–06.

PELEVIN. G. Nekhoroshev, ' Настоящий Пелевин. Отрывки из биографии культового писателя', *NG*, August 29 and 30.

PETKEVICH, INGA. V. Shpakov, 'Под сапогом Софьи Власьевны', *DN*, no.5 : 202–04.

PETKEVICH, IURII. A. Kuznetsova, 'Жизнь музыки', *Znamia*, no.12 : 213–14.

PIKUL'. A. Pikul', *Валентин Пикуль : из первых уст*, 3rd revd edn, Mw, Veche, AST, 432 pp.

PLATONOV. There are two new books on Platonov: K. A. Barsht, *Художественная антропология Андрея Платонова*, Voronezh U.P., 184 pp.; O. Meerson, *"Свободная вещь": Поэтика неостранения у Андрея Платонова*, 2nd revd edn, Novosibirsk, Nauka, 122 pp.

POPOV V. A. Melikhov, 'Победа над ужасом', *Znamia*, no. 9 : 219–20, is about Popov's latest novella *Ужас победы*.

PRIVGOV. I. Balabanova, *Говорит Дмитрий Александрович Пригов*, Mw, OGI, 168 pp., dialogues with Prigov, sometimes very deep and paradoxical.

PRISHVIN. Z. Ia. Kholodova, *Художественное мышление М.М.Пришвина: содержание, структура, контекст*, Ivanovo State U.P., 2000.

PRISTAVKIN. E. Scheglova writes about Pristavkin's new novel *Долина смертной тени* in 'Казнить нельзя — помиловать', *Znamia*, no.4 : 228–29.

RASPUTIN. D. Ol'shansky, ' Север без признаков Юга. Старая и новая проза Валентина Распутина', *NG*, August 29.

ROZHDESTVENSKY. *Словарь рифм Роберта Рождественского*, comp. and ed. A. Babkin, Tiumen', Iu. Mandriki, 352 pp.

RUBTSOV. N. Koniaev, *Николай Рубцов*, Mw, Molodaia gvardiia, 346 pp.

RYZHII. There are two papers on Boris Ryzhii, who committed suicide in 2001. N. Koliada 'По есенинскому следу', *Kulisa-NG*, no.8, May 18; A. Mashevsky, ' Последний советский поэт', *NovM*, 12 : 174–78.

RZHEVSKAIA. Two interesting works were published: D. Stakhov, 'О мести, понимании и прощении' *DN*, no.12 : 195–97, about her early prose, and N. Eliseev 'Между Оруэллом и Диккенсом', *NovM*, no.9 : 187–92, about her writings as a whole.

SHALAMOV. E. Lozowy, 'Variations hypostatiques — Les doubles fictionnels de Chalamov', *CanSP*, 43, 2000 : 461–79.

SEDAKOVA. M. A. Perepelkin, *Анализ лирического произведения*, Samara, Samarskii Univ., 108 pp., is a study of Olga Sedakova's poetry; A. Ulanov comments on both Sedakova's prose and poetry, in 'Переводчик с языка молчания', *Znamia*, no.11:217–19.

SENCHIN. M. Kucherskaia, 'Погружение в пустоту', *NovM*, no.10:189–92, is on Senchin's book *Афинские ночи*.

SERGEEV-TSENSKY. L. E. Khvorova *Эпопея С. Н. Сергеева-Ценского "Преображение России" в культурно-аксиологической парадигме русской литературы*, Moscow State Pedagogical U.P., 2000, 121 pp.

SHCHEPKINA-KUPERNIK. D. Rayfield, 'The forgotten poetess: Tatiana L'vovna Shchepkina-Kupernik', *SEER*, 79:601–37.

SHENBRUNN. A. Frumkina 'Сегодня. Завтра. Вчера', *NovM*, no.6:186–91, is on about Svetlana Shenbrunn's novel *Розы и хризантемы*.

SHEVCHUK. E. Reutov, 'Приближаясь к Ломброзо': *Znamia*, no.9:224–26.

SHVARTZ. There are several articles on Elena Shvartz: V. Shubinsky, 'Садовник и сад' *Znamia*, no.11:228–30; E. Svitneva compares her lyrics with jazz compositions: 'Координаты духа, или Дикопись в ритме свинга', *NovM*, no.9:189–92.

SIPOVSKY. A. Iu. Veselova, 'Роман В. Новодворского (В. В. Сиповского) «Путешествие Эраста Крутолобова в Москву и Санкт-Петербург в 30-х годах XIX столетия» и русская литература 18 — 19 веков', *RusL*, no.3:107–16.

SLAVNIKOVA. Olga Slavnikova is not only a critic but also a novelist. There are several papers about her novels: E. Ivanitskaia, 'Жизнь в петле', *DN*, no.10:163–65, V. Lipnevich, 'Долгое прощание, или 'О, Славникова!' *ib.*, 166–69, E. Ermolin, 'Время правды пришло', *NovM*, no.11:182–86.

SOLZHENITSYN. A. V. Urmanov, *Поэтика прозы А.И.Солженицына*, Moscow State Pedagogical U.P. V. Bondarenko, 'Цитатник Солженицына', *Zavtra*, no.29, July 17, is the only review of Solzhenitsyn's new book *Два века вместе*.

SOSNORA. A. Ariev, 'Ничей современник. Виктор Соснора: случай самовоскрешения', *VL*, no.3 <http://magazines.russ.ru/voplit/2001/3/ar.html> ; and A. Kuznetsova, 'Миракль', *Znamia*, no.11:221–23.

STRATANOVSKY. See V.Gubailovsky, 'Воскресение Шарикова', *NovM*, no.7:193–94.

SULEIMENOV. H. Ram, 'Imagining Eurasia: the poetics and ideology of Olzhas Suleimenov's *AZ I IA*', *SRev*, 60:289–312.

SUL'CHINSKAIA. One more excellent study by V. Gubailovsky, 'Обратная сторона жизни', *NG*, 20 April.

TRIFONOV. Two new publications: N. L. Leiderman and M. N. Lipovetskii, *От «советского писателя» к писателю советской эпохи:*

путь Юрия Трифонова, Ekaterinburg, AMB, 42 pp; T. Spektor, 'The Orthodox Christian subtext of Trifonov's allusions to Chekhov's "The Student" in *Another Life*', *SEEJ*, 45:473–89.

TSVETAEVA. A very interesting publication: M. Tsvetaeva, *Неизданное. Записные книжки: В 2 т. Т. 1: 1913–1919*, ed. E. B. Korkina and M. G. Krutikova, vol. 1, Mw, Ellis Lak, 2000, 560 pp. See also: J. L. Morgan, 'A portrait of the General as a young man: Marina Tsvetaeva's "Generalam dvenadtsatogo goda"', *RusR*, 60:205–19. See also U. Stock, 'Marina Tsvetaeva: the concrete and the metaphoric discourse of exile', *MLR*, 96:762–77, and S. Iu. Lavrova, *Художественно-лингвистическая парадигма идеостиля Марины Цветаевой*, Moscow State Pedagogical U.P..

TVARDOVSKII. N. L. Leiderman, *Творческая драма советского классика: Александр Твардовский в 1950–60-е гг*, Ekaterinburg, AMB, 40 pp.; A. L. Grishunin, *'Василий Теркин' Александра Твардовского*, Mw, Khudozhestvennaia Literatura, 77 pp.

VLADIMOV. Two works of considerable interest: L. A. Anninskii, *Крепости и плацдармы Георгия Владимова*, Moscow State U.P., 104 pp., and F. Ellis, 'Georgii Vladimov's *The General and His Army*: the ghost of Andrei Vlasov', *MLR*, 96:437–49.

VODENNIKOV. V. Gubailovsky's paper 'Стратегия поэтического успеха' is published in *NG*, May 24.

VOINOVICH. T. Novikov, 'The poetics of confrontation: Carnival in V. Voinovich's *Moscow 2042*', *CanSP*, 43, 2000:491–505, an elegant bakhtinian study of Voinovich's novel.

VOLKOV. A. Nesbet, 'In borrowed balloons: the Wizard of Oz and the history of Soviet aviation', *SEEJ*, 45:80–95, a fascinating research on Aleksandr Volkov.

VOLOS. Two works on Volos's novel *Недвижимость*: V. Miasnikov, ' Квартира — больше, чем жилье', *DN*, no.7: 204–07, and V. Gubailovsky, 'Книга о счастье', *ib.*, 207–09. See also A. Volos, 'Dolzhno preodolet' otchaianie', interview by N. Sirivlia, *Vremia novostei*, July 27.

VYSOTSKY. V. P. Izotov, *Словарь поэзии Высоцкого*, Orel, 58 pp., the 6th issue of this useful study (the 1st was published in Orel in 1999) in which 428 new words are commented. Id., *Высоцкий и рубеж тысячелетий*, Orel, 2000, 56 pp., contains 14 papers covering various aspect of Vysotsky's poetry.

ZAMIATIN. N. N. Komelik, *Творческое наследие Е. И. Замятина в контексте традиций русской народной культуры*, Tambov State U.P., 122 pp.

ZINOVIEV. A. Zinoviev interviews V. Poliakov in 'Спустившись с зияющих высот', *LitG*, no.33, August 15–21; O. Zinovieva, 'Трудный путь к "Зияющим высотам"', *Zavtra*, no.32, August

7 — a fragment from the book *Александр Зиновьев. Творческий экстаз*, written by Alexandr Zinoviev's wife.

ZORIN. N. Alexandrov, 'Школа трезвости', *DN*, no.5: 201–02.

V. UKRANIAN STUDIES
POSTPONED

VI. BELARUSIAN STUDIES
POSTPONED

VII. SERBO-CROAT STUDIES

LANGUAGE
POSTPONED

LITERATURE
POSTPONED

VIII. BULGARIAN STUDIES
POSTPONED

ABBREVIATIONS

I. ACTA, FESTSCHRIFTEN AND OTHER COLLECTIVE AND GENERAL WORKS

Actes (Barcelona): *Actes del Novè Col·loqui d'Estudis Catalans a Nord-Amèrica (Barcelona, 1998)*, ed. August Bover, Maria Rosa Lloret, and Mercè Vidal-Tibbits, PAM, 562 pp.

AIEO 6: Le Rayonnement de la civilisation occitane à l'aube d'un nouveau millénaire. Actes du 6e Congrès international de l'AIEO (Association Internationale d'Etudes Occitanes) (Vienne, 12–19 septembre 1999), ed. Georg Kremnitz, Barbara Czernilofsky, Peter Cichon, and Robert Tanzmeister, Vienna, Edition Praesens Wissenschaftsverlag, ix + 867 pp.

Aikhenvald, *Marking: Non-Canonical Marking of Subjects and Objects*, ed. Alexandra Y. Aikhenvald, R. M. W. Dixon, and Masayuki Onishi (Typological Studies in Language, 46), Amsterdam, Benjamins, xii + 362 pp.

Aleza, *Estudios: Estudios de filología, historia y cultura hispánicas*, ed. Milagros Aleza Izquierdo and Angel López Garcia, Valencia U.P., 2000, 239 pp.

Alvar, *Lyra: Lyra mínima oral: Los géneros breves de la literatura tradicional. Actas del Congreso Internacional (Alcalá de Henares, 1998)*, ed. Carlos Alvar, Cristina Castillo, Mariana Masera, and José Manuel Pedrosa, Alcalá U.P., 556 pp.

Andersen, *Actualization: Actualization. Linguistic Change in Progress*, ed. Henning Andersen (Current Issues in Linguistic Theory, 219), Amsterdam, Benjamins, [viii +] 250 pp.

Andrade, *Crioulos: Crioulos de base portuguesa. Actas do Workshop sobre Crioulos de Base Lexical Portuguesa*, ed. Ernesto d'Andrade, Maria Antónia Mota, and Dulce Pereira, Lisbon, APL, 2000, 257 pp.

APL 15: Actas do XV Encontro Nacional da Associação Portuguesa de Linguística (Faro, 29–30 de Setembro e 1 de Outubro de 1999), ed. Rui Vieira de Castro and Pilar Barbosa, Braga, Associação Portuguesa de Linguística, 2000, 642 pp.

Arlt, *Interkulturelle Erforschung: Interkulturelle Erforschung der österreichischen Literatur*, ed. Herbert Arlt and Alexandr W. Belobratow, St. Ingbert, Röhrig, 2000, 391 pp.

Ashley, *Conduct: Medieval Conduct*, ed. Kathleen Ashley and Robert L. A. Clark (Medieval Cultures, 29), Minneapolis, University of Minnesota Press, xx + 241 pp.

Baron, *Possession: Dimensions of Possession*, ed. Irène Baron, Michael Herslund, and Finn Sørensen (Typological Studies in Language, 47), Amsterdam, Benjamins, vi + 335 pp.

Bauer, *Edition: 'Ich an Dich.' Edition, Rezeption und Kommentierung von Briefen*, ed. Werner M. Bauer, Johannes John, and Wolfgang Wiesmüller (Innsbrucker Beiträge zur Kulturwissenschaft, Germanistische Reihe, 62), Universität Innsbruck, 278 pp.

Benoit-Dusausoy, *History: History of European Literature*, ed. A. Benoit-Dusausoy and Guy Fontaine, trans. Michael Wooff, London, Routledge, 2000, xxviii + 731 pp.

Berchtold, *Dragonetti: L'orgueil de la littérature: Autour de Roger Dragonetti*, ed. J. Berchtold and C. Lucken, Geneva, Droz, 1999, 126 pp.

Berg, *Yolanda: 'Man mohte schrîven wal ein bûch.' Ergebnisse des Yolanda-Kolloquiums 26–27 November 1999*, ed. Guy Berg (Beiträge zur Luxemburgischen Sprach- und Volkskunde, 31), Luxembourg, Institut Grand-Ducal, 166 pp.

Bergmann, *Glossen: Mittelalterliche volkssprachliche Glossen. Internationale Fachkonferenz des Zentrums für Mittelalterstudien der Otto-Friedrich-Universität Bamberg, 2. bis 4. August 1999*, ed. Rolf Bergmann et al. (Germanistische Beiträge, 13), Heidelberg, Winter, x + 610 pp.

Bernard-Griffiths, *Mélodrames: Mélodrames et romans noirs, 1750–1890*, ed. S. Bernard-Griffiths and J. Sgard, Toulouse-Le-Mirail U.P., 2000, 534 pp. + 4 pl.

Bernt, *Angesicht: 'Im Angesicht Gottes suche der Mensch sich selbst.' Hildegard von Bingen (1098–1179)*, ed. Rainer Berndt (Erudiri Sapientia, 2), Berlin, Akademie, 696 pp.

Bertaud Vol.: L'Histoire littéraire. Ses méthodes et ses résultats. Mélanges offerts à Madeleine Bertaud, ed. Luc Fraisse (HICL, 389), Geneva, Droz, xvi + 872 pp.

Bessière, *Commencements: Commencements du roman*, ed. Jean Bessière (Colloques, congrès et conférences sur la littérature comparée, 2), Paris, Champion, 216 pp.

Beugnot Vol.: Inventaire, Lecture, Invention: mélanges de critique et d'histoire littéraires offerts à Bernard Beugnot, ed. Jacinthe Martel and Robert Melançon, Montreal, Paragraphes, 1999, 447 pp.

Beutin, *Literaturgeschichte:* Wolfgang Beutin et al., *Deutsche Literaturgeschichte von den Anfängen bis zur Gegenwart*, 6th rev. edn, Stuttgart, Metzler, x + 721 pp.

Boitani, *Produzione: Lo spazio letterario del Medioevo, 2: Il Medioevo volgare, 1: La produzione del testo*, ed. Piero Boitani, Mario Mancini, and Alberto Varvaro, 2 vols, Rome, Salerno, 1999–2001, 745, 962 pp.

Bolecki, *Genologia: Genologia dzisiaj*, ed. Włodzimierz Bolecki and Ireneusz Opacki, Warsaw, IBL, 2000, 274 pp.

Borrego, *Cuestiones:* Julio Borrego Nieto, Jesús Fernández González, Luis Santos Río, and Ricardo Senabre Sempere, *Cuestiones de actualidad de la lengua española*, Instituto Caro y Cuervo — Salamanca U.P., 382 pp.

Brandis Vol.: Scrinium Berolinense. Tilo Brandis zum 65. Geburtstag, ed. Peter Jörg Becker, Wiesbaden, Reichert, 2 vols, 2000, 1–617, 618–1160 pp.

Bullivant, *Krisenbewußtsein: Literarisches Krisenbewußtsein. Ein Perzeptions- und Produktionsmuster im 20. Jahrhundert*, ed. Keith Bullivant and Bernhard Spies, Munich, Iudicium, 337 pp.

Burger, *Queering: Queering the Middle Ages*, ed. Glenn Burger and Steven F. Kruger (Medieval Cultures, 27), Minneapolis–London, University of Minnesota Press, xxiii + 318 pp.

Calboli, *Papers V: Papers on Grammar V*, ed. Gualtiero Calboli, Bologna, CLUEB, 2000, xii + 202 pp.

Carpi Vol.: Studi per Umberto Carpi, ed. Marco Santagata and Alfredo Stussi, Pisa, ETS, 2000, xxv + 710 pp.

Carvalho Vol.: Estudios dedicados a Ricardo Carvalho Calero, ed. José Luís Rodríguez, 2 vols, Santiago de Compostela, Parlamento de Galicia — Universidade de Santiago, 2000, 1007, 1044 pp.

Charpentier Vol.: La Poétique des passions à la Renaissance. Mélanges offerts à Françoise Charpentier, ed. François Lecercle and Simone Perrier, Paris, Champion, 428 pp.

CIEG 6: Actas do VI Congreso Internacional de Estudios Galegos: Un século de estudios galegos. Galicia fóra de Galicia (Universidad de La Habana, Facultad de Artes y Letras, Cátedra de Cultura Gallega, 17 a 21 de abril de 2000), ed. Dieter Kremer, 2 vols, Sada, Corunna, Ediciós do Castro — Galicien-Zentrum der Universität Trier xxi + 1039 pp.

CILPR 22: Actes du XXIIe Congres International de Linguistique et de Philologie Romanes, Bruxelles, 23–29 juillet 1998, ed. Annick Englebert, Michel Pierrard, Laurence Rosier, and Dan Van Raemdonck, 9 vols, I: *L'histoire de la linguistique, médiatrice de théories*, II: *Les nouvelles ambitions de la linguistique diachronique*, III: *Vivacité et diversité de la variation linguistique*, IV: *Des mots aux dictionnaires*, V: *Les manuscrits ne brûlent pas*, VI: *De la grammaire des formes à la grammaire du sens*, VII: *Sens et fonctions*, VIII: *Les effets du sens*, IX: *Contacts interlinguistiques*, Tübingen, Niemeyer, 2000, xii + 249, xii + 488, xii + 433, xiv + 628, x + 166, xii + 570, xiv + 733, x + 204, xii + 422 pp.

CISEHL 2: Actas del II Congreso Internacional de la Sociedad Española de Historiografía Lingüística (León, 2–5 de marzo de 1999), ed. M. Maquieira Rodríguez, M. D. Martínez Gavilán, and M. Villayandre Llamazares, Madrid, Arco Libros, 1024 pp.

Constantinescu, *Ballad: Ballad and Ballad Studies at the Turn of the Century. Proceedings of the 30th International Conference of the Ballad Commission of S.I.E.F., 15–20 August 2000, Bucharest, Romania / Balada şi studiile despre baladă la cumpăna dintre sedole. Actele celei de a 30-a Conferinţe Internaţionale a Comisei de balade din cadrul S.I.E.F., 15–20 August 2000, Bucureşti, România*, ed. Nicolae Constantinescu, Bucharest, Bucharest U.P. — Deliana, 248 pp.

Contreras Vol.: Features and Interfaces in Romance. Essays in Honor of Heles Contreras, ed. Julia Herschensohn, Enrique Mallén, and Karen Zagona (Current Issues in Linguistic Theory, 222), Amsterdam, Benjamins, xiv + 302 pp.

Cortijo, *Estudios: Estudios galegos medievais*, ed. Antonio Cortijo Ocaña, Giorgio Perissinotto, and Harvey L. Sharrer, Santa Barbara, CA, University of California at Santa Barbara, Department of Spanish and Portuguese, Centro de Estudios Galegos, 186 pp.

Cossy, *Progrès: Progrès et violence au XVIIIe siècle*, ed. Valérie Cossy and Deidre Dawson, Paris, Champion, 458 pp.

Cramer, *Frauenlieder: Frauenlieder — 'Cantigas de amigo'. Internationale Kolloquien des Centro de Estudos Humanísticos (Universidade do Minho), der Faculdade de Letras (Universidade do Porto) und des Fachbereichs Germanistik (Freie Universität Berlin), Berlin 6.11.98, Apúlia 28.–30.3.1999*, ed. Thomas Cramer et al., Stuttgart, Hirzel, 2000, xii + 391 pp.

De Robertis Vol.: Per Domenico De Robertis, ed. I. Becherucci, S. Giusti, and N. Tonelli, Florence, Le Lettere, 2000, 561 pp.

Delcourt, *Bibliothèque bleue: La Bibliothèque bleue et les littératures de colportage*, ed. Thierry Delcourt and Élisabeth Parinet (Études et rencontres de l'École des Chartes, 7), Paris-Troyes, École des Chartes-La Maison du Boulanger, 2000, 288 pp.

Della Terza Vol.: Studies for Dante: Essays in honor of Dante della Terza, ed. Franco Fido, Rena A. Syska-Lamparska, and Pamela D. Stewart, Fiesole, Cadmo, 1998, 514 pp.

Denneler, *Namen:* Iris Denneler, *Von Namen und Dingen. Erkundungen zur Rolle des Ich in der Literatur am Beispiel von Ingeborg Bachmann, Peter Bichsel, Max Frisch, Gottfried Keller, Heinrich von Kleist, Arthur Schnitzler, Frank Wedekind, Vladimir Nabokov und W. G. Sebald*, Würzburg, Königshausen & Neumann, 181 pp.

D'Hulst, *Going Romance 1999: Romance Languages and Linguistic Theory 1999. Selected Papers from 'Going Romance' 1999, Leiden, 9–11 December*, ed. Yves D'Hulst, Johan Rooryck, and Jan Schroten (Current Issues in Linguistic Theory, 221), Amsterdam, Benjamins, viii + 406 pp.

Dor, *Conjointure: Conjointure arthurienne. Actes de la 'classe d'excellence' de la Chaire Francqui 1998*, ed. Juliette Dor (Textes, Études, Congrès, 20), Louvain-la-Neuve, Université Catholique de Louvain, Publications de l'Institut d'Études Médiévales, 2000, 127 pp.

Dousteyssier-Khoze, *(Ab)Normalities: (Ab)Normalities*, ed. C. Dousteyssier-Khoze and Paul Scott (Durham Modern Language Series), Durham U.P., 180 pp.

Dubois Vol.: Histoire et littérature au siècle de Montaigne. Mélanges offerts à Claude-Gilbert Dubois, ed. François Argod-Dutard, Geneva, Droz, 416 pp.

Duffy, *Science: La Nature Dévoilée. French Literary Approaches to Science*, ed. Larry Duffy and Catherine Emerson, Hull, Hull Univ. Department of French, 2000, vi + 200 pp.

Edgington, *Crusades: Gendering the Crusades*, ed. Susan B. Edgington and Sarah Lambert, Cardiff, Univ. of Wales Press, xvi + 215 pp.

Edwards, *Merthyr a Thaf: Cyfres y Cymoedd: Merthyr a Thaf*, ed. Hywel Teifi Edwards, Llandysul, Gomer, 414 pp.

Eicher, *Grenzüberschreitungen: Grenzüberschreitungen um 1900. Österreichische Literatur im Übergang*, ed. Thomas Eicher (Übergänge. Grenzfälle. Österreichische Literatur in Kontexten, 3), Oberhausen, Athena, 254 pp.

Erhart Vol.: Grammaticus. Studia linguistica Adolfo Erharto quinque et septuagenario oblata, ed. Ondřej Ševčík and Bohumil Vykypěl, Brno, Masaryk Univ., 234 pp.

Esposito, *Dante: Dante e il Giubileo*, ed. E. Esposito, Florence, Olschki, 2000, 223 pp.

Essen, *Geschichten: Unerledigte Geschichten. Der literarische Umgang mit Nationalität und Internationalität*, ed. Gesa von Essen and Horst Turk, Göttingen, Wallstein, 2000, 505 pp.

Fähnders, *Prosa: Expressionistische Prosa. Aisthesis Studienbuch*, 1, ed. Walter Fähnders, Bielefeld, Aisthesis, 248 pp.

Fest. Bauer: Erträge der Dialektologie und Lexikographie. Festgabe für Werner Bauer zum 60. Geburtstag, ed. Herbert Tatzreiter, Maria Hornung, and Peter Ernst, Vienna, Praesens, 1999, 535 pp.

Fest. Bender: 'Das Schöne soll sein.' Aisthesis in der deutschen Literatur. Festschrift für Wolfgang F. Bender, ed. Peter Hesselmann, Michael Huesmann, and Hans-Joachim Jakob, Bielefeld, Aisthesis, 494 pp.

Fest. Bormann: Poesie als Auftrag. Festschrift für Alexander von Bormann, ed. Dagmar Ottmann and Markus Symmank, Würzburg, Königshausen & Neumann, 376 pp.

Fest. Brunner: Vom Mittelalter zur Neuzeit. Festschrift für Horst Brunner, ed. Dorothea Klein, Elisabeth Lienert, and Johannes Rettelbach, Wiesbaden, Reichert, 2000, x + 752 pp.

Fest. Dronke: Poetry and Philosophy in the Middle Ages. A Festschrift for Peter Dronke, ed. John Marenbon, Brill, Leiden, xi + 392 pp. + 4 pls.

Fest. Fritz: Stationen — Stationer. Festschrift für Axel Fritz, ed. Eva Lambertsson Björk and Elin Nesje Vestli, Halden, Høgskolen i Æstfold, 2000, 321 pp.

Fest. Helbig: Linguistik und Deutsch als Fremdsprache. Festschrift für Gerhard Helbig zum 70. Geburtstag, ed. Bernd Skibitzki and Barbara Wotjak, Tübingen, Niemeyer, 1999, xvi + 339 pp.

Fest. Hohendahl: Passagen. Literatur — Theorie — Medien. Festschrift für Peter Uwe Hohendahl, ed. Manuel Köppen and Rüdiger Steinlein, Berlin, Weidler, 374 pp.

Fest. Jacobs: Der europäische Roman zwischen Aufklärung und Postmoderne. Festschrift zum 65. Geburtstag von Jürgen C. Jacobs, ed. Friedhelm Marx and Andreas Meier, Weimar, Verlag und Datenbank für Geisteswissenschaften, 272 pp.

Fest. Janz: Der schöne Schein der Kunst und seine Schatten. Festschrift für Rolf Peter Janz zum 60. Geburtstag, ed. Hans Richard Brittnacher and Fabian Stoermer, Bielefeld, Aisthesis, 2000, 408 pp.

Fest. Kliewer: Aus 'Wundertüte' und 'Zauberkasten': über die Kunst des Umgangs mit Kinder- und Jugendliteratur. Festschrift zum 65. Geburtstag von Heinz-Jürgen Kliewer, ed. Henner Barthel, Frankfurt am Main–Berlin, Lang, 2000, 590 pp.

Fest. Lerchner: Sprachgeschichte als Textsortengeschichte. Festschrift zum 65. Geburtstag von Gotthard Lerchner, ed. Irmhild Barz, Ulla Fix, Marianne Schröder, and Georg Schuppener, Frankfurt, Lang, xii + 498 pp.

Fest. Menke: 'Vulpis Adolatio'. Festschrift für Hubertus Menke zum 60. Geburtstag, ed. Robert Peters et al. (Germanistische Beiträge, 11), Heidelberg, Winter, 976 pp.

Fest. Pietzcker: Jugend. Psychologie — Literatur — Geschichte. Festschrift für Carl Pietzcker, Würzburg, Königshausen & Neumann, 359 pp.

Fest. Richter: Begegnung der Zeiten. Festschrift für Helmut Richter zum 65. Geburtstag, ed. R. Fasold, C. Giel, V. Giel, M. Masanetz, and M. Thormann, Leipzig, Universitätsverlag, 1999, 419 pp.

Fest. Ruberg: 'Vox sermo res'. Beiträge zur Sprachreflexion, Literatur- und Sprachgeschichte vom Mittelalter bis zur Neuzeit. Festschrift Uwe Ruberg, ed. Wolfgang Haubrichs et al., Stuttgart, Hirzel, 291 pp.

Fest. Seebold: Grippe, Kamm und Eulenspiegel. Festschrift für Elmar Seebold zum 65. Geburtstag, ed. W. Schindler and J. Untermann, Berlin, de Gruyter, 1999, 415 pp.

Fest. Sørensen: Ekbátana — Festskrift til Peer E. Sørensen, ed. Carsten Madsen and Rolf Reitan, Århus, Institut for Nordisk Sprog og Litteratur, Klim, 2000, 332 pp.

Fialová-Fürstová, *Mährische Literatur: Mährische deutschsprachige Literatur. Eine Bestandsaufnahme. Beiträge der internationalen Konferenz Olmütz, 25.–28.4.1999*, ed. Ingeborg Fialová-Fürstová, Olomouc, Univerzitni Nakl, 1999, 288 pp.

Firchow Vol.: 'De consolatione philologiae'. Studies in Honor of Evelyn S. Firchow, ed. Anna Grotans et al., 2 vols (Göppinger Arbeiten zur Germanistik, 682), Göppingen, Kümmerle, 2000, xiv + 448, x + 449–775 pp.

Frajzyngier, *Reflexives: Reflexives, Forms and Functions*, ed. Zygmunt Frajzyngier and Traci S. Curl (Typological Studies in Language, 40), Amsterdam, Benjamins, 2000, xiv + 286 pp.

Gajda, *Złota: Złota księga*, ed. Stanisław Gajda, Opole, Uniwersytet Opolski, 367 pp.

Gemzøe, *Metafiktion: Metafiktion — selvrefleksionens retorik i moderne litteratur, teater film og sprog*, ed. Anker Gemzøe, Britta Timm Knudsen, and Gorm Larsen (Modernismestudier 1), Copenhagen, Medusa, 276 pp.

Gendre Vol.: Les Fruits de la saison: mélanges de littérature des XVIe et XVIIe siècles offerts au professeur André Gendre, ed. Philippe Tessier et al. (Recueil de travaux publiés par la Faculté des Lettres et Sciences humaines de l'Université de Neuchâtel, 48), Geneva, Droz, 2000, 510 pp.

Giorgi, *Perspectives: Perspectives de la recherche sur le genre narratif français du dix-septième siècle*, ed. Giorgetto Giorgi (Quaderni del Seminario di Filologia Francese, 8), Pisa, Edizioni ETS — Geneva, Slatkine, 2000, 303 pp.

Goltschnigg, *Literatur: Egon Schwarz, 'Ich bin kein Freund allgemeiner Urteile über ganze Völker': Essays über österreichische, deutsche und jüdische Literatur*, ed. Dietmar Goltschnigg and Hartmut Steinecke, Berlin, Schmidt, 2000, 282 pp.

Goodman, *Art: Art and Culture in the Eighteenth Century: New Dimensions and Multiple Perspectives*, ed. Elise Goodman, Newark, University of Delaware Press, 162 pp.

Görner, *Traces: Traces of Transcendency. Spuren der Transzendenz*, ed. Rüdiger Görner (London German Studies, 7), Munich, Iudicium, 256 pp.

Gössmann, *Literatur:* Wilhelm Gössmann, *Literatur als Lebensnerv: Vermittlung, Leselust, Schreibimpulse*, Düsseldorf, Grupello, 1999, 301 pp.

Grodek, *Ruse: Écriture de la ruse*, ed. Elzbieta Grodek (Faux titre, 190), Amsterdam, Rodopi, 2000, 455 pp.

Gutiérrez-Rexach, *Spanish Syntax: Current Issues in Spanish Syntax and Semantics*, ed. Javier Gutiérrez-Rexach and Luis Silva-Villar, Berlin–New York, Mouton de Gruyter, vi + 354 pp.

Hamesse, *Prologues: Les Prologues médiévaux: actes du Colloque international organisé par l'Academia Belgica et l'École française de Rome avec le concours de la F.I.D.E.M. (Rome, 26–28 mars 1998)*, ed. Jacqueline Hamesse (Textes et Études du Moyen Age, 15), Turnhout, Brepols, 2000, 691 pp.

Haupt, *Endzeitvorstellungen: Endzeitvorstellungen*, ed. Barbara Haupt (Studia Humaniora, 33), Düsseldorf, Droste, 383 pp.

Head, *Hagiography: Medieval Hagiography: An Anthology*, ed. Thomas Head (Garland Reference Library of the Humanities, 1942), New York-London, Garland, 2000, 834 pp.

Herman, *Manuscrit trouvé: Le Topos du manuscrit trouvé*, ed. Jan Herman and Fernand Hallyn (Bibliothèque de l'Information grammaticale, 40), Louvain–Paris, Peeters, 1999, 532 pp.

Hicks Vol.: 'Riens ne m'est seur que la chose incertaine'. Études sur l'art d'écrire au Moyen Age offertes à Eric Hicks par ses élèves, collègues, amies et amis, ed. Jean-Claude Mühlethaler and Denis Billiote, Geneva, Slatkine, xxiv + 323 pp.

Hinderer, *Lyrik: Geschichte der deutschen Lyrik vom Mittelalter bis zur Gegenwart*, ed. Walter Hinderer, 2nd rev. edn, Würzburg, Königshausen & Neumann, 708 pp.

Hladká, *Čeština,* III: *Čeština univerzália a specifika*, ed. Zdeňka Hladká and Petr Karlík, vol. III, Brno, Masaryk Univ., 347 pp.

Hubrath, *Zwickau: Literarisches Leben in Zwickau im Mittelalter und in der frühen Neuzeit. Vorträge eines Symposiums anläßlich des 500jährigen Jubiläums der Ratsschulbibliothek Zwickau am 17. und 18. Februar 1998*, ed. Margarete Hubrath and Rüdiger Krohn (Göppinger Arbeiten zur Germanistik, 686), Göppingen, Kümmerle, xii + 344 pp.

Hulk, *Inversion: Subject Inversion in Romance and the Theory of Universal Grammar*, ed. Aafke Hulk and Jean-Yves Pollock, OUP, vii + 215 pp.

Hutchinson, *Landmarks: Landmarks in German Poetry*, ed. Peter Hutchinson (British and Irish Studies in German Language and Literature, 20), Oxford, Lang, 2000, 218 pp.

ICHL 14: Historical Linguistics 1999. Selected Papers from the 14th International Conference on Historical Linguistics, Vancouver, 9–13 August 1999, ed. Laurel J. Brinton with Desirée Lundström (Current Issues in Linguistic Theory, 215), Amsterdam, Benjamins, xii + 389 pp.

Indursky, *Discurso: Discurso, memória, identidade*, ed. Freda Indursky and Maria do Carmo Campos, Porto Alegre, Sagra Luzzatto, 2000, 612 pp.

Jacob, *Lengua medieval: Lengua medieval y tradiciones discursivas en la Península Ibérica. Descripción gramatical — pragmática histórica — metodología*, ed. Daniel Jacob and Johannes Kabatek, Frankfurt, Vervuert, 000 pp.

Jarošová, *Slovenčina: Slovenčina a čeština v počítačovom spracovaní*, ed. Alexandra Jarošová, Bratislava, Veda, 194 pp.

Jenkins, *Cymru: Cymru a'r Cymry 2000 / Wales and the Welsh 2000. Trafodion Cynhadledd Milflwyddiant Canolfan Uwchefrydiau Cymreig a Cheltaidd Prifysgol Cymru / Proceedings of the Millennium Conference of the University of Wales Centre for Advanced Welsh and Celtic Studies*, ed. Geraint H. Jenkins, Aberystwyth, University of Wales Centre for Advanced Welsh and Celtic Studies, 162 pp.

Jones, *Censorship: Censorship: A World Encyclopedia*, ed. Derek Jones, 4 vols, London–Chicago, Fitzroy Dearborn, 2891 pp.

Jones Vol.: 'Proper Words in Proper Places'. Studies in Lexicology and Lexicography in Honour of William Jervis Jones, ed. Máire C. Davies, John L. Flood, and David N. Yeandle (Stuttgarter Arbeiten zur Germanistik, 400), Stuttgart, Heinz, xxiv + 420 pp.

Kellner, *Kommunikation: Literarische Kommunikation und soziale Interaktion. Studien zur Institutionalität mittelalterlicher Literatur*, ed. Beate Kellner et al. (Mikrokosmos, 64), Frankfurt, Lang, viii + 260 pp.

Kleiber Vol.: Sprachgeschichte, Dialektologie, Onomastik, Volkskunde. Beiträge zum Kolloquium am 3./ 4. Dezember 1999 an der Johannes Gutenberg-Universität Mainz. Wolfgang Kleiber zum 70. Geburtstag, ed. R. Bentzinger, D. Nübling, and R. Steffens (ZDL, Beiheft, 115), Stuttgart, Steiner, 437 pp.

Köhn, *Literatur:* Lothar Köhn, *Literatur — Geschichte: Beiträge zur deutschen Literatur des 19. und 20. Jahrhunderts, mit einer Einführung von Thomas Düllo*, Münster-Hamburg, Lit, 1999, v + 387 pp.

Kostecki, *Mecenat: Z dziejów mecenatu kulturalnego w Polsce*, ed. Janusz Kostecki, Warsaw, Biblioteka Narodowa, 1999, 421 pp.

Krause, *Heroine:* Kathy M. Krause, *Reassessing the Heroine in Medieval French Literature*, Gainesville, Florida U.P., 187 pp.

Kremer, *Onomastik: Onomastik: Akten des 18. Internationalen Kongresses für Namenforschung (Trier, 12.-17. April, 1993)*, ed. Dieter Kremer, 2 vols, Tübingen, Niemeyer, 2000, vii + 299, vii + 330 pp.

Krobb, *Literaturvermittlung: Literaturvermittlung um 1900. Fallstudien zu Wegen ins deutschsprachige kulturelle System*, ed. Sabine Strümper-Krobb and Florian Krobb, Amsterdam, Rodopi, 181 pp.

Lamíquiz Vol.: Lengua y Discurso: estudios dedicados al Profesor Vidal Lamíquiz, Madrid, Arco/ Libros, 2000, 000 pp.

L'Épistolaire: L'Épistolaire au XVIe siècle (Cahiers V.-L. Saulnier, 18), Paris, PENS, 256 pp.

Le Gonidec Vol.: Galice —Bretagne — Amérique latine: Mélanges offerts à Bernard Le Gonidec, ed. Xesús Lago Garabatos and Jean-Pierre Sánchez, Rennes, Université Rennes 2, Laboratoire Interdisciplinaire de Recherche sur les Amériques – Centre d'Études Galiciennes, 322 pp.

Lepschy, *Dictionaries: A Linguistics Round-table on Dictionaries and the History of the Language*, ed. Giulio Lepschy and Prue Shaw (UCL Centre for Italian Studies, Occasional Papers 4), London, UCL, 2000, vi + 127 pp.

Linehan, *Medieval World: The Medieval World*, ed. Peter Linehan and Janet L. Nelson, London-New York, Routledge, xix + 745 pp.

Losada Vol.: Professor Basilio Losada. Ensinar a pensar con liberdade e risco, ed. Isabel de Riquer, Elena Losada, and Helena González (Col·lecció Homenatges, 18), Barcelona, Universitat de Barcelona, 2000, 756 pp.

LSRL 30: Romance Syntax, Semantics and L2 Acquisition. Selected Papers from the 30th Linguistic Symposium on Romance Languages, Gainesville, Florida, February 2000, ed. Joaquim Camps and Caroline R. Wiltshire (Current Issues in Linguistic Theory, 216), Amsterdam, Benjamins, x + 246 pp.

Luongo, *Épopée: L'Épopée romane au Moyen Age et aux temps modernes: Actes du XIVe Congrès International de la Société Rencesvals pour l'Étude des Épopées Romanes (Naples, 1997)*, ed. Salvatore Luongo, Naples, Fridericiana Editrice Universitaria, 1027 pp.

Marchal, *Salons: Vie des salons et activités littéraires, de Marguerite de Valois à Mme de Staël*, ed. Roger Marchal, Nancy U.P., 343 pp.

Marietti, *Dante: Dante, poete et narrateur*, ed. M. Marietti and C. Perrus, Paris, Presses de la Sorbonne, 334 pp.

McWhorter, *Language Change: Language Change and Language Contact in Pidgins and Creoles*, ed. John McWhorter (Creole Language Library, 21), Amsterdam, Benjamins, 2000, viii + 503 pp.

Méchoulan, *Vengeance: La Vengeance dans la littérature d'Ancien Régime*, ed. Éric Méchoulan (Paragraphes, 19), Département d'Études Françaises, Université de Montréal, 2000, 189 pp.

Mochizuki, *Culture: Russian Culture on the Threshold of Centuries* / Русская культура на пороге нового века, ed. T. Mochizuki, Sapporo, Slavic Research Center, 370 pp.

Moser, *Verarbeitung: Maschinelle Verarbeitung altdeutscher Texte. 5. Beiträge zum fünften Internationalen Symposion Würzburg 4–6. März 1997*, ed. Stephan Moser et al., Tübingen, Niemeyer, x + 320 pp.

Ní Chatháin Vol.: Ogma: Essays in Celtic Studies in honour of Próinséas Ní Chatháin, ed. M. Richter and J.-M. Picard, Dublin, Four Courts Press, xvi + 329 pp.

Nolte, *Helmbrecht: Wernher der Gärtner, 'Helmbrecht'. Die Beiträge des Helmbrecht-Symposions in Burghausen 2001*, ed. Theodor Nolte and Tobias Schneider, Stuttgart, Hirzel, 119 pp.

Nutt-Kofoth, *Text: Text und Edition. Positionen und Perspektiven*, ed. Rüdiger Nutt-Kofoth et al., Berlin, Schmidt, 2000, 432 pp.

Offord, *Francophone Literatures:* Malcolm Offord, Laïla Ibnlfassi, Nicki Hitchcott, Sam Haigh, and Rosemary Chapman, *Francophone Literatures. A literary and linguistic companion*, London, Routledge, ix + 283 pp.

Orduna Vol.: Studia in honorem Germán Orduna, ed. Leonardo Funes and José Luis Moure, Alcalá de Henares U.P., 634 pp.

Orioles, *Plurilinguismo: Documenti letterari del plurilinguismo*, ed. Vincenzo Orioles, Rome, Il Calamo, 2000, 428 pp.

Paden, *Genres: Medieval Lyric. Genres in Historical Context*, ed. William D. Paden, Urbana–Chicago, Illinois U.P., 2000, 371 pp.

Panizza, *Women: Women in Italian Renaissance Culture and Society*, ed. Letizia Panizza, Oxford, Legenda, 2000, xxi + 523 pp.

Paravicini Bagliani, *Chasse: La chasse au Moyen Age. Société, traités, symboles* ed. Agostino Paravicini Bagliani and Baudouin Van den Abeele (Micrologus Library, 5), Turnhout, Brepols, 266 pp.

Peters, *Text: Text und Kultur. Mittelalterliche Literatur 1150–1450. DFG-Symposion 2000*, ed. Ursula Peters (Germanistische Symposien Berichtsbände, 23; DVLG, 'Sonderband'), Stuttgart, Metzler, xviii + 661 pp.

Phillips, *Second Crusade: The Second Crusade: Scope and Consequences*, ed. Jonathan Phillips and Martin Hoch, Manchester U.P., 256 pp.

Piastra, *Mariologia: Gli studi di mariologia medievale. bilancio storiografico. Atti del I Convegno Mariologico della Fondazione Ezio Franceschini con la collaborazione della Biblioteca Palatina e del Dipartimento di Storia dell'Università di Parma (Parma, 1997)*, ed. Clelia Maria Piastra, Tavarnuzze, Sismel — Florence, Edizioni del Galluzzo, xiv + 362 pp.

Pinchard, *Pour Dante: Pour Dante. Dante et l'Apocalypse: Lectures Humanistes de Dante*, ed. B. Pinchard, Paris, Champion, 488 pp.

Pintzuk, *Diachronic Syntax: Diachronic Syntax. Models and Mechanisms*, ed. Susan Pintzuk, George Tsoulas, and Anthony Warner, OUP, 2000, xii + 380 pp.

Poláčkův Vol.: Pátečníci a Karel Poláček. Sborník příspěvků ze sympozia Patečníci a Karel Poláček, ed. Pavel Janáček and Jan Tydlitát, Boskovice, Albert, 285 pp.

Pucci, *Sites:* Suzanne R. Pucci, *Sites of the Spectator: Emerging Literary and Cultural Practice in Eighteenth-Century France* (SVEC 2001:09), Oxford, Voltaire Foundation, 202 pp.

Ragotzky, *Liedinterpretation: Fragen der Liedinterpretation*, ed. Hedda Ragotzky et al., Stuttgart, Hirzel, 225 pp.

Rauch Vol.: Interdigitations. Essays for Irmengard Rauch, ed. Gerald F. Carr, Wayne Harbert, and Lihua Zhang, New York, Lang, xxi + 762 pp.

Regueira, *Estudios: Da gramática ó diccionario: estudios de lingüística galega*, ed. X. L. Regueira and A. Veiga (*Verba*, anexo 49), Santiago de Compostela, Univ. de Santiago, 311 pp.

Renzi Vol.: Current Studies in Italian Syntax. Essays offered to Lorenzo Renzi, ed. Guglielmo Cinque and Giampaolo Salvi, Oxford, Elsevier, xii + 326 pp.

Repetti, *Phonological Theory: Phonological Theory and the Dialects of Italy*, ed. Lori Repetti (CTL, 212), Amsterdam, Benjamins, 2000, x + 301 pp.

Resta Vol.: Studi di filologia e letteratura italiana in onore di Gianvito Resta, ed. Vitilio Masiello, Rome, Salerno, 2000, 2 vols, xvi + 712, 713–1527 pp.

Rieuwerts, *Ballad Heritage: Bridging the Cultural Divide: Our Common Ballad Heritage / Kulturelle Brücken: Gemeinsame Balladentradition. 28 Internationale Balladenkonferenz der SIEF-Kommission für Volksdichtung in Hildesheim, Deutschland, 19.–24. Juli 1998*, ed. Sigrid Rieuwerts and Helga Stein, Hildesheim, Olms, 2000, 520 pp.

Rigg Vol.: Anglo-Latin and its Heritage. Essays in Honour of A. G. Rigg on his 64th Birthday, ed. Sian Echard and Gernot R. Wieland, Brepols, Turnhout, xviii + 280 pp.

Rivara, *L'Oeuvre inachevée: L'Oeuvre inachevée*, ed. Annie Rivara and Guy Lavorel (Publications du C.E.D.I.C.), Lyons, Université Jean Moulin, 1999, 293 pp.

Rodríguez González Vol.: Eladio Rodríguez González: Día das Letras Galegas 2001, Santiago de Compostela, Departamento de Filoloxía Galega da Universidade de Santiago, 312 pp.

Roig Miranda, *Transmission: La Transmission du savoir dans l'Europe des XVIe et XVIIe siècles*, ed. Marie Roig Miranda, Paris, Champion, 2000, 542 pp.

Ruhstaller, *Tendencias: Tendencias en la investigación lexicográfica del español. El diccionario como objeto de estudio lingüístico y didáctico*, ed. Stefan Ruhstaller and Josefina Prado Aragonés, Huelva U.P., 2000, 571 pp.

Rutschmann, *Nebenan: Nebenan: der Anteil der Schweiz an der deutschsprachigen Kinder- und Jugendliteratur. Kolloquium in Rauischholzhausen vom 4. bis 7. Oktober 1998*, ed. Verena Rutschmann, Zurich, Chronos, 1999, 321 pp.

Schabert Vol.: Bi-Textualität. Inszenierungen des Paares. Ein Buch für Ina Schabert, ed. Annegret Heitmann et al., Berlin, Schmidt, 418 pp.

Schøsler, *Valence: La Valence, perspectives romanes et diachroniques (Actes du Colloque international tenu à l'Institut d'études romanes à Copenhague du 19 au 20 mars 1999)*, ed. Lene Schøsler (*ZFSL*, Beiheft 30), Stuttgart, Steiner, 131 pp.

Schröder Vol.: Zur Überlieferung, Kritik und Edition alter und neuerer Texte. Beiträge des Colloquiums zum 85. Geburtstag von Werner Schröder am 12. und 13. März 1999 in Mainz, ed. Kurt Gärtner and Hans-Henrik Krummacher (Abhandlungen der Akademie der Wissenschaften und der Literatur Mainz, Geistes- und sozialwissenschaftliche Klasse, 2000–02), Mainz, 2000, 308 pp.

Schwob, *Entstehung: Entstehung und Typen mittelalterlicher Lyrikhandschriften. Akten des Grazer Symposiums 13.–17.Oktober 1999*, ed. Anton Schwob and András Vizkelety (JIG, Reihe A — Kongressberichte, 52), Frankfurt, Lang, 328 pp.

Segebrecht, *Europa: Europavisionen im 19. Jahrhundert: Vorstellungen von Europa in Literatur und Kunst, Geschichte und Philosophie*, ed. Wulf Segebrecht, Würzburg, Ergon, 1999, 305 pp.

Sellier Vol.: Le rayonnement de Port-Royal. Mélanges en l'honneur de Philippe Sellier, ed. Dominique Descotes (Colloques, congrès et conférences sur le Classicisme, 2), Paris, Champion, 635 pp.

Sornicola, *Stability: Stability, Variation and Change of Word-Order Patterns over Time*, ed. Rosanna Sornicola, Erich Poppe, and Ariel Shisha-Halevy (Current Issues in Linguistic Theory, 213), Amsterdam, Benjamins, 2000, xxxii + 323 pp.

Spiewok Vol.: 'Pur remembrance.' Mélanges en mémoire de Wolfgang A. Spiewok, ed. Anne Berthelot (Wodan, 79), Greifswald, Reineke, viii + 342 pp.

Stellmacher, *Dialektologie: Dialektologie zwischen Tradition und Neuansätzen. Beiträge der internationalen Dialektologentagung, Göttingen, 19.–21. Oktober 1998*, ed. D. Stellmacher (ZDL Beiheft, 109), Stuttgart, Steiner, 1998, 437 pp.

Stephens, *Women's Writing: A History of Women's Writing in France*, ed. Sonya Stephens, CUP, 2000, ix + 314 pp.

Suárez, *Letras galegas: Letras galegas en Deusto. Dez anos de estudios galegos. 1991–2001*, ed. M. L. Suárez and I. Seoane, Deusto, Cátedra de Estudios Galegos–Univ. de Deusto, 210 pp.

Suntrup, *Tradition: Tradition and Innovation in an Era of Change — Tradition und Innovation im Übergang zur Frühen Neuzeit*, ed. Rudolf Suntrup and Jan R. Veenstra (Medieval to Early Modern Culture — Kultureller Wandel vom Mittelalter zur Frühen Neuzeit, 1), Frankfurt, Lang, 282 pp.

SVEC 2001:04: SVEC 2001:04. La diffusion de Locke en France — traduction au dix-huitième siècle —; lectures de Rousseau, Oxford, Voltaire Foundation, v + 364 pp.

SVEC 2001:10: SVEC 2001:10. From Letter to Publication. Studies on Correspondence and the History of the Book. With the Besterman Lecture 2000, Oxford, Voltaire Foundation, v + 295 pp.

SVEC 2001 : 12: SVEC 2001 : 12. Voltaire — Religion and ideology — Women's studies — History of the book — Passion in the eighteenth century, Oxford, Voltaire Foundation, vi + 476 pp.

Termina 2000: Termina 2000. Sborník příspěvků z 2. konference 1996 a 3. konference 2000, ed. Milan Žemlička, Prague, Galén, 320 pp.

Thomas, *German Studies: German Studies at the Millennium*, ed. Neil Thomas, Durham U.P., 1999, 280 pp.

Tollet, *Textes: Les Textes judéophobes et judéophiles dans l'Europe chrétienne à l'époque moderne*, ed. Daniel Tollet, Paris, PUF, 2000, xiii + 246 pp.

Tomlinson, *Theatre: French 'Classical' Theatre Today. Teaching, Research, Performance*, ed. Philip Tomlinson, Amsterdam–Atlanta, Rodopi, 307 pp.

Tschuggnall, *Religion: Religion — Literatur — Künste. Aspekte eines Vergleichs*, ed. Peter Tschuggnall, Anif/Salzburg, Müller-Speiser, 1998, 558 pp.

Tydeman, *Stage: The Medieval European Stage, 500–1550*, ed. William Tydeman, CUP, lxii + 720 pp.

Tyssens Vol.: Convergences médiévales: Epopée, lyrique, roman. Mélanges offerts à Madeleine Tyssens, ed. Nadine Henrard, Paola Morena, and Martin Thiry-Stassin (Bibliothèque du Moyen Age, 19), Brussels, De Boeck–Université, 646 pp.

Van den Heuvel Vol.: Humour, ironie et humanisme dans la littérature française. Mélanges offerts à Jacques Van den Heuvel par ses élèves et amis, ed. Philippe Koeppel (Colloques, congrès et conférences sur le dix-huitième siècle, 1), Paris, Champion, xvi + 271 pp.

Varela Vol.: A. Abuín et al., *Homenaje a Benito Varela Jácome*, Santiago de Compostela, Universidade, 629 pp.

Veiga, *Verbo: El verbo entre el léxico y la gramática*, ed. Alexandre Veiga, Víctor M. Longa, and JoDee Anderson, Lugo, Tris Tram, 231 pp.

Villar, *Religión : Religión, Lengua y Cultura prerromanas de Hispania, Actas del VIII Coloquio Internacional sobre Lenguas e Culturas Prerromanas de la Península Ibérica*, ed. Francisco Villar and María Pilar Fernández Álvarez, Salamanca U.P., 750 pp.

Widell, *Mode: Møde om Udforskningen af Dansk Sprog, Aarhus Universitet 12.–13. oktober 2000*, ed. Peter Widell and Mette Kunøe, Aarhus U.P., 299 pp.

Weiss, *Romance: Medieval Insular Romance. Translation and Innovation*, ed. Judith Weiss, Jennifer Fellows, and Morgan Dickson, Cambridge, Brewer, 2000, 196 pp.

Wiegand Vol.: Sprache im Alltag. Beiträge zu neuen Perspektiven in der Linguistik. Herbert Ernst Wiegand zum 65. Geburtstag gewidmet, ed. Andrea Lehr, Matthias Kammerer, Klaus-Peter Konerding, Angelika Storrer, Caja Thimm, and Werner Wolski, Berlin–New York, 2000, xii + 634 pp.

Wild, *Genre: Genre et Société. Actes du colloque sur 'L'émergence de genres nouveaux dans les sociétés européennnes des XVIe et XVIIe siècles'*, ed. Francine Wild, 2 vols, Nancy U.P., 2000, 280, 256 pp.

Wilson-Chevalier, *Fémynie: Royaume de Fémynie: pouvoirs, contraintes, espaces de liberté des femmes, de la Renaissance à la Fronde*, ed. Kathleen Wilson-Chevalier and Éliane Viennot (Colloques, congrès et conférences sur la Renaissance, 16), Paris, Champion, 1999, 304 pp.

Witosz, *Stylistika: Stylistyka a pragmatyka*, ed. Bozena Witosz, Katowice, Wydaw. Uniwersytetu Śląskiego, 388 pp.

Xornadas Lamas: Xornadas sobre Lamas Carvajal: Actas das xornadas realizadas pola Dirección Xeral de Promoción Cultural en Ourense os días 21 e 22 de outubro de 1999, Santiago de Compostela, Xunta de Galicia, Consellería de Cultura, Comunicación Social e Turismo, 234 pp.

Zimmermann, *Auctor: Auctor et Auctoritas. Invention et conformisme dans l'écriture moderne*, ed. Michel Zimmermann (Mémoires et Documents de l'Ecole des Chartes, 59), Paris, Ecole des Chartes, 593 pp.

Zimmermann, *Fakten: Fakten und Fiktionen. Strategien fiktionalbiographischer Dichterdarstellungen in Roman, Drama und Film seit 1970. Beiträge des Bad Homburger Kolloquiums, 21.–23 Juni 1999*, ed. Christian v. Zimmermann, Tübingen, Narr, 2000, vi + 352 pp.

II. GENERAL

abbrev.	abbreviation, abbreviated to
Acad., Akad.	Academy, Academia, etc.
acc.	accusative
AN	Anglo-Norman
ann.	annotated (by)
anon.	anonymous
appx	appendix
Arg.	Argentinian (and foreign equivalents)
AS	Anglo-Saxon
Assoc.	Association (and foreign equivalents)
Auv.	Auvergnat
Bel.	Belarusian
BL	British Library
BM	British Museum
BN	Bibliothèque Nationale, Biblioteka Narodowa, etc.
BPtg.	Brazilian Portuguese
bull.	bulletin
c.	century
c.	circa
Cat.	Catalan
ch.	chapter
col.	column
comm.	commentary (by)
comp.	compiler, compiled (by)
Cz.	Czech
diss.	dissertation
ed.	edited (by), editor (and foreign equivalents)
edn	edition
EPtg.	European Portuguese
fac.	facsimile
fasc.	fascicle
Fest.	Festschrift, Festskrift
Fin.	Finnish
Fr.	France, French, Français
Gal.-Ptg.	Galician-Portuguese (and equivalents)
Gasc.	Gascon
Ger.	German(y)
Gk	Greek
Gmc	Germanic
IE	Indo-European
illus.	illustrated, illustration(s)
impr.	impression
incl.	including, include(s)
Inst.	Institute (and foreign equivalents)
introd.	introduction, introduced by, introductory
It.	Italian
izd.	издание
izd-vo	издательство
Jb.	Jahrbuch
Jg	Jahrgang
Jh.	Jahrhundert
Lang.	Languedocien

Lat.	Latin
Lim.	Limousin
lit.	literature
med.	medieval
MHG	Middle High German
Mid. Ir.	Middle Irish
Mil.	Milanese
MS	manuscript
n.d.	no date
n.F.	neue Folge
no.	number (and foreign equivalents)
nom.	nominative
n.p.	no place
n.s.	new series
O Auv.	Old Auvergnat
O Cat.	Old Catalan
Occ.	Occitan
OE	Old English
OF	Old French
O Gasc.	Old Gascon
OHG	Old High German
O Ir.	Old Irish
O Lim.	Old Limousin
O Occ.	Old Occitan
O Pr.	Old Provençal
O Ptg.	Old Portuguese
OS	Old Saxon
OW	Old Welsh
part.	participle
ped.	педагогический, etc.
PIE	Proto-Indo-European
Pied.	Piedmontese
PGmc	Primitive Germanic
pl.	plate
plur.	plural
Pol.	Polish
p.p.	privately published
Pr.	Provençal
pref.	preface (by)
Procs	Proceedings
Ptg.	Portuguese
publ.	publication, published (by)
Ren.	Renaissance
repr.	reprint(ed)
Rev.	Review, Revista, Revue
rev.	revised (by)
Russ.	Russian
s.	siècle
ser.	series
sg.	singular
Slg	Sammlung
Soc.	Society (and foreign equivalents)
Sp.	Spanish
supp.	supplement

Sw.	Swedish
Trans.	Transactions
trans.	translated (by), translation
Ukr.	Ukrainian
Univ.	University (and foreign equivalents)
unpubl.	unpublished
U.P.	University Press (and foreign equivalents)
Vlg	Verlag
vol.	volume
vs	versus
W.	Welsh
wyd.	wydawnictwo

* before a publication signifies that it has not been seen by the contributor.

III. PLACE NAMES

B	Barcelona	NY	New York
BA	Buenos Aires	O	Oporto
Be	Belgrade	Pń	Poznań
Bo	Bologna	R	Rio de Janeiro
C	Coimbra	Ro	Rome
F	Florence	SC	Santiago de Compostela
Gd	Gdańsk	SPo	São Paulo
Kw	Kraków, Cracow	StP	St Petersburg
L	Lisbon	T	Turin
Ld	Leningrad	V	Valencia
M	Madrid	Wa	Warsaw
Mi	Milan	Ww	Wrocław
Mw	Moscow	Z	Zagreb
Na	Naples		

IV. PERIODICALS, INSTITUTIONS, PUBLISHERS

AA, Antike und Abendland

AAA, Ardis Publishers, Ann Arbor, Michigan

AAA, Archivio per l'Alto Adige

AAASS, American Association for the Advancement of Slavic Studies

AABC, Anuari de l'Agrupació Borrianenca de Cultura

AAC, Atti dell'Accademia Clementina

AAL, Atti dell'Accademia dei Lincei

AALP, L'Arvista dl'Academia dla Lenga Piemontèisa

AAM, Association des Amis de Maynard

AAPH, Anais da Academia Portuguesa da História

AAPN, Atti dell'Accademia Pontaniana di Napoli

AAPP, Atti Accademia Peloritana dei Pericolanti. Classe di Lettere Filosofia e Belle Arti

AARA, Atti della Accademia Roveretana degli Agiati

AASB, Atti dell'Accademia delle Scienze dell'Istituto di Bologna

AASF, Annales Academiae Scientiarum Fennicae

AASLAP, Atti dell'Accademia di Scienze, Lettere ed Arti di Palermo

AASLAU, Atti dell'Accademia di
    Scienze, Lettere e Arti di Udine
AASN, Atti dell'Accademia di
    Scienze Morali e Politiche di
    Napoli
AAST, Atti dell'Accademia delle
    Scienze di Torino
AAVM, Atti e Memorie
    dell'Accademia Virgiliana di
    Mantova
AAWG, Abhandlungen der
    Akademie der Wissenschaften in
    Göttingen, phil.-hist. Kl., 3rd
    ser., Göttingen, Vandenhoeck &
    Ruprecht
AB, Analecta Bollandiana
ABa, L'Année Balzacienne
ABÄG, Amsterdamer Beiträge zur
    älteren Germanistik
ABB, Archives et Bibliothèques de
    Belgique — Archief– en
    Bibliotheekswezen in België
ABC, Annales Benjamin Constant
ABDB, Aus dem Antiquariat.
    Beiträge zum Börsenblatt für den
    deutschen Buchhandel
ABDO, Association Bourguignonne
    de Dialectologie et
    d'Onomastique, Fontaine lès
    Dijon
ABHL, Annual Bulletin of Historical
    Literature
ABI, Accademie e Biblioteche
    d'Italia
ABN, Anais da Biblioteca Nacional,
    Rio de Janeiro
ABNG, Amsterdamer Beiträge zur
    neueren Germanistik,
    Amsterdam, Rodopi
ABNG, Amsterdamer Beiträge zur
    neueren Germanistik
ABor, Acta Borussica
ABP, Arquivo de Bibliografia
    Portuguesa
ABR, American Benedictine Review
ABr, Annales de Bretagne et des
    Pays de l'Ouest
ABS, Acta Baltico-Slavica
ABSJ, Annual Bulletin of the Société
    Jersiaise
AC, Analecta Cisterciensa, Rome
ACCT, Agence de Coopération
    Culturelle et Technique
ACer, Anales Cervantinos, Madrid

ACIS, Association for
    Contemporary Iberian Studies
ACo, Acta Comeniana, Prague
AColl, Actes et Colloques
Acme, Annali della Facoltà di
    Filosofia e Lettere dell'Università
    Statale di Milano
ACP, L'Amitié Charles Péguy
ACUA, Anales del Colegio
    Universitario de Almería
AD, Analysen und Dokumente.
    Beiträge zur Neueren Literatur,
    Berne, Lang
ADEVA, Akademische Druck- und
    Verlagsanstalt, Graz
AE, Artemis Einführungen,
    Munich, Artemis
AE, L'Autre Europe
AEA, Anuario de Estudios
    Atlánticos, Las Palmas
AECI, Agencia Española de
    Cooperación Internacional
AEd, Arbeiten zur
    Editionswissenschaft, Frankfurt,
    Lang
AEF, Anuario de Estudios
    Filológicos, Cáceres
AEL, Anuario de la Escuela de
    Letras, Mérida, Venezuela
AELG, Anuario de Literarios
    Galegos
AEM, Anuario de Estudios
    Medievales
AF, Anuario de Filología, Barcelona
AFA, Archivo de Filología
    Aragonesa
AfAf, African Affairs
AfC, Afrique Contemporaine
AFe, L'Armana di Felibre
AFF, Anali Filološkog fakulteta,
    Belgrade
AFH, Archivum Franciscanum
    Historicum
AFHis, Anales de Filología
    Hispánica
AfHR, Afro-Hispanic Review
AfL, L'Afrique Littéraire
AFLE, Annali della Fondazione
    Luigi Einaudi
AFLFUB, Annali della Facoltà di
    Lettere e Filosofia dell'Università
    di Bari

AFLFUC, Annali della Facoltà di Lettere e Filosofia dell'Università di Cagliari

AFLFUG, Annali della Facoltà di Lettere e Filosofia dell'Università degli Studi di Genova

AFLFUM, Annali della Facoltà di Lettere e Filosofia dell'Università di Macerata

AFLFUN, Annali della Facoltà di Lettere e Filosofia dell'Università di Napoli

AFLFUP(SF), Annali dellà Facoltà di Lettere e Filosofia dell'Università di Perugia. 1. Studi Filosofici

AFLFUP(SLL), Annali della Facoltà di Lettere e Filosofia dell'Università di Perugia. 3. Studi Linguistici-Letterari

AFLFUS, Annali della Facoltà di Lettere e Filosofia dell'Università di Siena

AFLLS, Annali della Facoltà di Lingua e Letterature Straniere di Ca' Foscari, Venice

AFLLSB, Annali della Facoltà di Lingue e Letterature Straniere dell'Università di Bari

AFLN, Annales de la Faculté des Lettres et Sciences Humaines de Nice

AFLS, Association for French Language Studies

AFP, Archivum Fratrum Praedicatorum

AFrP, Athlone French Poets, London, The Athlone Press

AG, Anales Galdosianos

AGB, Archiv für Geschichte des Buchwesens

AGF, Anuario Galego de Filoloxia

AGGSA, Acta Germanica. German Studies in Africa

AGI, Archivio Glottologico Italiano

AGP, Archiv für Geschichte der Philosophie

AH, Archivo Hispalense

AHCP, Arquivos de História de Cultura Portuguesa

AHDLMA, Archives d'Histoire Doctrinale et Littéraire du Moyen Âge

AHF, Archiwum Historii Filozofii i Myśli Społecznej

AHP, Archivum Historiae Pontificae

AHPr, Annales de Haute-Provence, Digne-les-Bains

AHR, American Historical Review

AHRF, Annales Historiques de la Révolution Française

AHRou, Archives historiques du Rouergue

AHSA, Archives historiques de la Saintonge et de l'Aunis, Saintes

AHSJ, Archivum Historicum Societatis Jesu

AHSS, Annales: Histoire — Science Sociales

AI, Almanacco Italiano

AIB, Annali dell'Istituto Banfi

AIBL, Académie des Inscriptions et Belles-Lettres, Comptes Rendus

AIEM, Anales del Instituto de Estudios Madrileños

AIEO, Association Internationale d'Études Occitanes

AIFMUR, Annali dell'Istituto di Filologia Moderna dell'Università di Roma

AIFUF, Annali dell'Istituto di Filosofia dell'Università di Firenze

AIHI, Archives Internationales d'Histoire des Idées, The Hague, Nijhoff

AIHS, Archives Internationales d'Histoire des Sciences

AIL, Associação Internacional de Lusitanistas

AILLC, Associació Internacional de Llengua i Literatura Catalanes

AION(FG), Annali dell'Istituto Universitario Orientale, Naples: Sezione Germanica. Filologia Germanica

AION(FL), Annali dell'Istituto Universitario Orientale, Naples: Sezione Filologico-letteraria

AION(SF), Annali dell'Istituto Universitario Orientale, Naples: Studi Filosofici

AION(SL), Annali dell'Istituto Universitario Orientale, Naples: Sezione Linguistica

AION(SR), Annali dell'Istituto Universitario Orientale, Naples: Sezione Romanza

AION(SS), Annali dell'Istituto Universitario Orientale, Naples: Sezione Slava

AION(ST), Annali dell'Istituto Universitario Orientale, Naples: Sezione Germanica. Studi Tedeschi

AIPHS, Annuaire de l'Institut de Philologie et de l'Histoire Orientales et Slaves

AIPS, Annales Instituti Philologiae Slavica Universitatis Debreceniensis de Ludovico Kossuth Nominatae — Slavica

AISIGT, Annali dell'Istituto Storico Italo-Germanico di Trento

AITCA, Arxiu informatizat de textos catalans antics

AIV, Atti dell'Istituto Veneto

AJ, Alemannisches Jahrbuch

AJCAI, Actas de las Jornadas de Cultura Arabe e Islámica

AJFS, Australian Journal of French Studies

AJGLL, American Journal of Germanic Linguistics and Literatures

AJL, Australian Journal of Linguistics

AJP, American Journal of Philology

AKG, Archiv für Kulturgeschichte

AKML, Abhandlungen zur Kunst-, Musik- und Literaturwissenschaft, Bonn, Bouvier

AL, Anuario de Letras, Mexico

AlAm, Alba de América

ALB, Annales de la Faculté des Lettres de Besançon

ALC, African Languages and Cultures

ALE, Anales de Literatura Española, Alicante

ALEC, Anales de Literatura Española Contemporánea

ALet, Armas y Letras, Universidad de Nuevo León

ALEUA, Anales de Literatura Española de la Universidad de Alicante

ALFL, Actes de Langue Française et de Linguistique

ALH, Acta Linguistica Hungaricae

ALHA, Anales de la Literatura Hispanoamericana

ALHa, Acta Linguistica Hafniensia

ALHisp, Anuario de Lingüística Hispánica

ALHist, Annales: Littérature et Histoire

ALit, Acta Literaria, Chile

ALitH, Acta Litteraria Hungarica

ALLI, Atlante Linguistico dei Laghi Italiani

ALM, Archives des Lettres Modernes

ALMA, Archivum Latinitatis Medii Aevi (Bulletin du Cange)

ALo, Armanac de Louzero

ALP, Atlas linguistique et ethnographique de Provence, CNRS, 1975–86

AlS, Almanac Setòri

ALT, African Literature Today

ALu, Alpes de Lumière, Fourcalquier

ALUB, Annales Littéraires de l'Université de Besançon

AM, Analecta Musicologica

AMAA, Atti e Memorie dell'Accademia d'Arcadia

AMAASLV, Atti e Memorie dell'Accademia di Agricultura, Scienze e Lettere di Verona

Amades, Amades. Arbeitspapiere und Materialien zur deutschen Sprache

AMal, Analecta Malacitana

AMAP, Atti e Memorie dell'Accademia Patavina di Scienze, Lettere ed Arti

AMAPet, Atti e Memorie dell'Accademia Petrarca di Lettere, Arti e Scienze, Arezzo

AMAT, Atti e Memorie dell'Accademia Toscana di Scienze e Lettere, La Colombaria

AMDLS, Arbeiten zur Mittleren Deutschen Literatur und Sprache, Berne, Lang

AMDSPAPM, Atti e Memorie della Deputazione di Storia Patria per le Antiche Province Modenesi

AMGG, Abhandlungen der Marburger Gelehrten Gesellschaft, Munich, Fink

AmH, American Hispanist

AMid, Annales du Midi
AmIn, América Indígena, Mexico
AML, Main Monographien
Literaturwissenschaft, Frankfurt,
Main
AMSSSP, Atti e Memorie della
Società Savonese di Storia Patria
AN, Академия наук
AN, Americana Norvegica
ANABA, Asociación Nacional de
Bibliotecarios, Arquiveros y
Arqueólogos
AnAlf, Annali Alfieriani
AnEA, Anaquel de Estudios Arabes
ANeo, Acta Neophilologica,
Ljubljana
ANF, Arkiv för nordisk filologi
AnI, Annali d'Italianistica
AnL, Anthropological Linguistics
AnM, Anuario Medieval
AnN, Annales de Normandie
AnnM, Annuale Medievale
ANPOLL, Associação Nacional de
Pós-graduação e Pesquisa em
Letras e Lingüística, São Paulo
ANQ, American Notes and Queries
ANS, Anglo-Norman Studies
ANTS, Anglo-Norman Text Society
AnVi, Antologia Vieusseux
ANZSGLL, Australian and New
Zealand Studies in German
Language and Literature, Berne,
Lang
AO, Almanac occitan, Foix
AÖAW, Anzeiger der
Österreichischen Akademie der
Wissenschaften
AOn, Acta Onomastica
AP, Aurea Parma
APIFN, Актуальные проблемы
истории философии народов
СССР.
APK, Aufsätze zur portugiesischen
Kulturgeschichte, Görres-
Gesellschaft, Münster
ApL, Applied Linguistics
APL, Associação Portuguesa de
Linguística
APPP, Abhandlungen zur
Philosophie, Psychologie und
Pädagogik, Bonn, Bouvier
APr, Analecta Praemonstratensia
AProu, Armana Prouvençau,
Marseilles

APS, Acta Philologica Scandinavica
APSL, Amsterdamer Publikationen
zur Sprache und Literatur,
Amsterdam, Rodopi
APSR, American Political Science
Review
APUCF, Association des
Publications de la Faculté des
Lettres et Sciences Humaines de
l'Université de Clermont-Ferrand
II, Nouvelle Série
AQ, Arizona Quarterly
AqAq, Aquò d'aquí, Gap
AR, Archiv für
Reformationsgeschichte
ARAJ, American Romanian
Academy Journal
ARAL, Australian Review of
Applied Linguistics
ARCA, ARCA: Papers of the
Liverpool Latin Seminar
ArCCP, Arquivos do Centro
Cultural Português, Paris
ArEM, Aragón en la Edad Media
ArFil, Archivio di Filosofia
ArI, Arthurian Interpretations
ARI, Архив русской истории
ARL, Athlone Renaissance Library
ArL, Archivum Linguisticum
ArLit, Arthurian Literature
ArP, Археографски прилози
ArSP, Archivio Storico Pugliese
ArSPr, Archivio Storico Pratese
ArSt, Archivi per la Storia
ART, Atelier Reproduction des
Thèses, Univ. de Lille III, Paris,
Champion
AS, The American Scholar
ASAHM, Annales de la Société d'Art
et d'Histoire du Mentonnais,
Menton
ASAvS, Annuaire de la Société des
Amis du vieux-Strasbourg
ASB, Archivio Storico Bergamasco
ASCALF, Association for the Study
of Caribbean and African
Literature in French
ASCALFB, ASCALF Bulletin
ASCALFY, ASCALF Yearbook
ASE, Annali di Storia dell'Esegesi
ASEES, Australian Slavonic and
East European Studies

ASELGC, 1616. Anuario de la
Sociedad Española de Literatura
General y Comparada

ASGM, Atti del Sodalizio
Glottologico Milanese

ASI, Archivio Storico Italiano

ASJ, Acta Slavonica Japonica

ASL, Archivio Storico Lombardo

ASLSP, Atti della Società Ligure di
Storia Patria

ASMC, Annali di Storia Moderna e
Contemporanea

ASNP, Annali della Scuola Normale
Superiore di Pisa

ASNS, Archiv für das Studium der
Neueren Sprachen und
Literaturen

ASocRous, Annales de la Société J.-J.
Rousseau

ASolP, A Sol Post, Editorial Marfil,
Alcoi

ASP, Anzeiger für slavische
Philologie

AsP, L'Astrado prouvençalo. Revisto
Bilengo de Prouvenco/Revue
Bilingue de Provence, Berre
L'Etang.

ASPN, Archivio Storico per le
Province Napoletane

ASPP, Archivio Storico per le
Province Parmensi

ASR, Annalas da la Societad
Retorumantscha

ASRSP, Archivio della Società
Romana di Storia Patria

ASSO, Archivio Storico per la Sicilia
Orientale

ASSUL, Annali del Dipartimento di
Scienze Storiche e Sociali
dell'Università di Lecce

AST, Analecta Sacra Tarraconensia

ASt, Austrian Studies

ASTic, Archivio Storico Ticinese

AŞUI, (e), (f), Analele Ştiinţifice ale
Universităţii 'Al. I. Cuza' din Iaşi,
secţ. e, Lingvistică, secţ. f,
Literatură

AT, Athenäums Taschenbücher,
Frankfurt, Athenäum

ATB, Altdeutsche Textbibliothek,
Tübingen, Niemeyer

ATCA, Arxiu de Textos Catalans
Antics, IEC, Barcelona

Ate, Nueva Atenea, Universidad de
Concepción, Chile

ATO, A Trabe de Ouro

ATS, Arbeiten und Texte zur
Slavistik, Munich, Sagner

ATV, Aufbau Taschenbuch Verlag,
Berlin, Aufbau

AtV, Ateneo Veneto

AUBLLR, Analele Universităţii
Bucureşti, Limba şi literatura
română

AUBLLS, Analele Universităţii
Bucureşti, Limbi şi literaturi
străine

AUC, Anales de la Universidad de
Cuenca

AUCP, Acta Universitatis
Carolinae Pragensis

AuE, Arbeiten und Editionen zur
Mittleren Deutschen Literatur,
Stuttgart–Bad Cannstatt,
Frommann-Holzboog

AUL, Acta Universitatis Lodziensis

AUL, Annali della Facoltà di Lettere
e Filosofia dell'Università di
Lecce

AUMCS, Annales Uniwersytetu
Marii Curie-Skłodowskiej, Lublin

AUML, Anales de la Universidad de
Murcia: Letras

AUMLA, Journal of the Australasian
Universities Modern Language
Association

AUN, Annali della Facoltà di Lettere
e Filosofia dell'Università di
Napoli

AUNCFP, Acta Universitatis Nicolai
Copernici. Filologia Polska,
Toruń

AUPO, Acta Universitatis
Palackianae Olomucensis

AUS, American University Studies,
Berne — New York, Lang

AUSP, Annali dell'Università per
Stranieri di Perugia

AUSt, Acta Universitatis
Stockholmiensis

AUTŞF, Analele Universităţii din
Timişoara, Ştiinţe Filologice

AUU, Acta Universitatis Upsaliensis

AUW, Acta Universitatis
Wratislaviensis

AVen, Archivio Veneto

AVEP, Assouciacien vareso pèr
l'ensignamen dòu prouvençou,
La Farlède
AVEPB, Bulletin AVEP, La Farlède
AvT, L'Avant-Scène Théâtre
AWR, Anglo-Welsh Review

BA, Bollettino d'Arte
BAAA, Bulletin de l'Association des
Amis d'Alain
BAAG, Bulletin des Amis d'André
Gide
BAAJG, Bulletin de l'Association des
Amis de Jean Giono
BAAL, Boletín de la Academia
Argentina de Letras
BaB, Bargfelder Bote
BAC, Biblioteca de Autores
Cristianos
BACol, Boletín de la Academia
Colombiana
BÄDL, Beiträge zur Älteren
Deutschen Literaturgeschichte,
Berne, Lang
BADLit, Bonner Arbeiten zur
deutschen Literatur, Bonn,
Bouvier
BAE, Biblioteca de Autores
Españoles
BAEO, Boletín de la Asociación
Española de Orientalistas
BAFJ, Bulletin de l'Association
Francis Jammes
BAG, Boletín de la Academia
Gallega
BAIEO, Bulletins de l'Association
Internationale d'Études
Occitanes
BAJR, Bulletin des Amis de Jules
Romains
BAJRAF, Bulletin des Amis de
Jacques Rivière et d'Alain-
Fournier
BALI, Bollettino dell'Atlante
Linguistico Italiano
BALM, Bollettino dell'Atlante
Linguistico Mediterraneo
BalS, Balkan Studies, Institute for
Balkan Studies, Thessaloniki
BAN, Българска Академия на
Науките, София

BAO, Biblioteca Abat Oliva,
Publicacions de l'Abadia de
Montserrat, Barcelona
BAPC, Bulletin de l'Association Paul
Claudel
BAPRLE, Boletín de la Academia
Puertorrigueña de la Lengua
Española
BAR, Biblioteca dell'Archivum
Romanicum
BARLLF, Bulletin de l'Académie
Royale de Langues et de
Littératures Françaises de
Bruxelles
BAWA, Bayerische Akademie der
Wissenschaften. Phil.-hist. Kl.
Abhandlungen, n.F.
BB, Biblioteca Breve, Lisbon
BB, Bulletin of Bibliography
BBAHLM, Boletín Bibliografico de
la Asociación Hispánica de
Literatura Medieval
BBB, Berner Beiträge zur
Barockgermanistik, Berne, Lang
BBGN, Brünner Beiträge zur
Germanistik und Nordistik
BBib, Bulletin du Bibliophile
BBL, Bayreuther Beiträge zur
Literaturwissenschaft, Frankfurt,
Lang
BBLI, Bremer Beiträge zur
Literatur- und Ideengeschichte,
Frankfurt, Lang
BBMP, Boletín de la Biblioteca de
Menéndez Pelayo
BBN, Bibliotheca Bibliographica
Neerlandica, Nieuwkoop, De
Graaf
BBNDL, Berliner Beiträge zur
neueren deutschen
Literaturgeschichte, Berne, Lang
BBSANZ, Bulletin of the
Bibliographical Society of
Australia and New Zealand
BBSIA, Bulletin Bibliographique de
la Société Internationale
Arthurienne
BBSMES, Bulletin of the British
Society for Middle Eastern
Studies
BBUC, Boletim da Biblioteca da
Universidade de Coimbra
BC, Bulletin of the 'Comediantes',
University of Wisconsin

BCB, Boletín Cultural y Bibliográfico, Bogatá

BCEC, Bwletin Cymdeithas Emynwyr Cymru

BCél, Bulletin Célinien

BCh, Болдинские чтения

BCLSMP, Académie Royale de Belgique: Bulletin de la Classe des Lettres et des Sciences Morales et Politiques

BCMV, Bollettino Civici Musei Veneziani

BCRLT, Bulletin du Centre de Romanistique et de Latinité Tardive

BCS, Bulletin of Canadian Studies

BCSM, Bulletin of the Cantigueiros de Santa Maria

BCSS, Bollettino del Centro di Studi Filologici e Linguistici Siciliani

BCSV, Bollettino del Centro di Studi Vichiani

BCZG, Blätter der Carl Zuckmayer Gesellschaft

BD, Беларуская думка

BDADA, Bulletin de documentation des Archives départementales de l'Aveyron, Rodez

BDB, Börsenblatt für den deutschen Buchhandel

BDBA, Bien Dire et Bien Aprandre

BDL, Beiträge zur Deutschen Literatur, Frankfurt, Lang

BDP, Beiträge zur Deutschen Philologie, Giessen, Schmitz

BEA, Bulletin des Études Africaines

BEC, Bibliothèque de l'École des Chartes

BelE, Беларуская энцыклапедыя

BelL, Беларуская лінгвістыка

BelS, Беларускі сьвет

BEP, Bulletin des Études Portugaises

BEPar, Bulletin des Études Parnassiennes et Symbolistes

BEzLit, Български език и литература

BF, Boletim de Filologia

BFA, Bulletin of Francophone Africa

BFC, Boletín de Filología, Univ. de Chile

BFE, Boletín de Filología Española

BFF, Bulletin Francophone de Finlande

BFFGL, Boletín de la Fundación Federico García Lorca

BFi, Bollettino Filosofico

BFLS, Bulletin de la Faculté des Lettres de Strasbourg

BFo, Biuletyn Fonograficzny

BFPLUL, Bibliothèque de la Faculté de Philosophie et Lettres de l'Université de Liège

BFR, Bibliothèque Française et Romane, Paris, Klincksieck

BFR, Bulletin of the Fondation C.F. Ramuz

BFr, Börsenblatt Frankfurt

BG, Bibliotheca Germanica, Tübingen, Francke

BGB, Bulletin de l'Association Guillaume Budé

BGDSL, Beiträge zur Geschichte der deutschen Sprache und Literatur, Tübingen

BGKT, Беларуская грамадска-культуральнае таварыства

BGL, Boletin Galego de Literatura

BGLKAJ, Beiträge zur Geschichte der Literatur und Kunst des 18. Jahrhunderts, Heidelberg, Winter

BGP, Bristol German Publications, Bristol U.P

BGREC, Bulletin du Groupe de Recherches et d'Études du Clermontais, Clermont-l'Hérault

BGS, Beiträge zur germanistischen Sprachwissenschaft, Hamburg, Buske

BGS, Beiträge zur Geschichte der Sprachwissenschaft

BGT, Blackwell German Texts, Oxford, Blackwell

BH, Bulletin Hispanique

BHR, Bibliothèque d'Humanisme et Renaissance

BHS(G), Bulletin of Hispanic Studies, Glasgow

BHS(L), Bulletin of Hispanic Studies, Liverpool

BI, Bibliographisches Institut, Leipzig

BibAN, Библиотека Академии наук СССР

BIDS, Bulletin of the International Dostoevsky Society, Klagenfurt

BIEA, Boletín del Instituto de Estudios Asturianos

BIHBR, Bulletin de l'Institut Historique Belge de Rome
BIHR, Bulletin of the Institute of Historical Research
BIO, Bulletin de l'Institut Occitan, Pau
BJA, British Journal of Aesthetics
BJCS, British Journal for Canadian Studies
BJECS, The British Journal for Eighteenth-Century Studies
BJHP, British Journal of the History of Philosophy
BJHS, British Journal of the History of Science
BJL, Belgian Journal of Linguistics
BJR, Bulletin of the John Rylands University Library of Manchester
BKF, Beiträge zur Kleist-Forschung
BL, Brain and Language
BLAR, Bulletin of Latin American Research
BLBI, Bulletin des Leo Baeck Instituts
BLe, Börsenblatt Leipzig
BLFCUP, Bibliothèque de Littérature Française Contemporaine de l'Université Paris 7
BLI, Beiträge zur Linguistik und Informationsverarbeitung
BLi, Беларуская літаратура. Міжвузаўскі зборнік.
BLJ, British Library Journal
BLL, Beiträge zur Literatur und Literaturwissenschaft des 20. Jahrhunderts, Berne, Lang
BLR, Bibliothèque Littéraire de la Renaissance, Geneva, Slatkine–Paris, Champion
BLR, Bodleian Library Record
BLVS, Bibliothek des Literarischen Vereins, Stuttgart, Hiersemann
BM, Bibliothek Metzier, Stuttgart
BMBP, Bollettino del Museo Bodoniano di Parma
BMCP, Bollettino del Museo Civico di Padova
BML, Беларуская мова і літаратура ў школе
BMo, Беларуская мова. Міжвузаўскі зборнік
BNE, Beiträge zur neueren Epochenforschung, Berne, Lang

BNF, Beiträge zur Namenforschung
BNL, Beiträge zur neueren Literaturgeschichte, 3rd ser., Heidelberg, Winter
BNP, Beiträge zur nordischen Philologie, Basel, Helbing & Lichtenhahn
BO, Biblioteca Orientalis
BOCES, Boletín del Centro de Estudios del Siglo XVIII, Oviedo
BOP, Bradford Occasional Papers
BP, Български писател
BP, Lo Bornat dau Perigòrd
BPTJ, Biuletyn Polskiego Towarzystwa Językoznawczego
BR, Болгарская русистика.
BRA, Bonner Romanistische Arbeiten, Berne, Lang
BRABLB, Boletín de la Real Academia de Buenas Letras de Barcelona
BRAC, Boletín de la Real Academia de Córdoba de Ciencias, Bellas Letras, y Nobles Artes
BRAE, Boletín de la Real Academia Española
BRAG, Boletín de la Real Academia Gallega
BRAH, Boletín de la Real Academia de la Historia
BrC, Bruniana & Campanelliana
BRIES, Bibliothèque Russe de l'Institut d'Études Slaves, Paris, Institut d'Études Slaves
BRJL, Bulletin ruského jazyka a literatury
BrL, La Bretagne Linguistique
BRP, Beiträge zur romanischen Philologie
BS, Biuletyn slawistyczny, Łódź
BSAHH, Bulletin de la Société archéologique et historique des hauts cantons de l'Hérault, Bédarieux
BSAHL, Bulletin de la Société archéologique et historique du Limousin, Limoges
BSAHLSG, Bulletin de la Société Archéologique, Historique, Littéraire et Scientifique du Gers
BSAM, Bulletin de la Société des Amis de Montaigne

BSAMPAC, Bulletin de la Société des Amis de Marcel Proust et des Amis de Combray

BSASLB, Bulletin de la Société Archéologique, Scientifique et Littéraire de Béziers

BSATG, Bulletin de la Société Archéologique de Tarn-et-Garonne

BSBS, Bollettino Storico–Bibliografico Subalpino

BSCC, Boletín de la Sociedad Castellonense de Cultura

BSD, Bithell Series of Dissertations — MHRA Texts and Dissertations, London, Modern Humanities Research Association

BSD, Bulletin de la Société de Borda, Dax

BSDL, Bochumer Schriften zur deutschen Literatur, Berne, Lang

BSDSL, Basler Studien zur deutschen Sprache und Literatur, Tübingen, Francke

BSE, Галоўная рэдакцыя Беларускай савеюкай энцыклапедыі

BSEHA, Bulletin de la Société d'Études des Hautes-Alpes, Gap

BSEHTD, Bulletin de la Société d'Études Historiques du texte dialectal

BSELSAL, Bulletin de la Société des Études Littéraires, Scientifiques et Artistiques du Lot

BSF, Bollettino di Storia della Filosofia

BSG, Berliner Studien zur Germanistik, Frankfurt, Lang

BSHAP, Bulletin de la Société Historique et Archéologique du Périgord, Périgueux

BSHPF, Bulletin de la Société de l'Histoire du Protestantisme Français

BSIH, Brill's Studies in Intellectual History, Leiden, Brill

BSIS, Bulletin of the Society for Italian Studies

BSLA, Bulletin Suisse de Linguistique Appliquée

BSLLW, Bulletin de la Société de Langue et Littérature Wallonnes

BSLP, Bulletin de la Société de Linguistique de Paris

BSLV, Bollettino della Società Letteraria di Verona

BSM, Birmingham Slavonic Monographs, University of Birmingham

BSOAS, Bulletin of the School of Oriental and African Studies

BSP, Bollettino Storico Pisano

BSPC, Bulletin de la Société Paul Claudel

BSPia, Bollettino Storico Piacentino

BSPN, Bollettino Storico per le Province di Novara

BSPSP, Bollettino della Società Pavese di Storia Patria

BSR, Bulletin de la Société Ramond. Bagneres-de-Bigorre

BsR, Beck'sche Reihe, Munich, Beck

BSRS, Bulletin of the Society for Renaissance Studies

BSSAAPC, Bollettino della Società per gli Studi Storici, Archeologici ed Artistici della Provincia di Cuneo

BSSCLE, Bulletin of the Society for the Study of the Crusades and the Latin East

BSSP, Bullettino Senese di Storia Patria

BSSPHS, Bulletin of the Society for Spanish and Portuguese Historical Studies

BSSPin, Bollettino della Società Storica Pinerolese, Pinerolo, Piemonte, Italy.

BSSV, Bollettino della Società Storica Valtellinese

BSZJPS, Bałtosłowiańskie związki językowe. Prace Slawistyczne

BT, Богословские труды, Moscow

BTe, Biblioteca Teatrale

BTH, Boletim de Trabalhos Historicos

BulEz, Български език

BW, Bibliothek und Wissenschaft

BySt, Byzantine Studies

CA, Cuadernos Americanos

CAAM, Cahiers de l'Association Les Amis de Milosz

CAB, Commentari dell'Ateneo di Brescia
CAC, Les Cahiers de l'Abbaye de Créteil
CadL, Cadernos da Lingua
CAFLS, Cahiers AFLS
CAG, Cahiers André Gide
CaH, Les Cahiers de l'Humanisme
CAIEF, Cahiers de l'Association Internationale des Études Françaises
CalLet, Calabria Letteraria
CAm, Casa de las Américas, Havana
CAm, Casa de las Américas, Havana
CanJL, Canadian Journal of Linguistics
CanJP, Canadian Journal of Philosophy
CanL, Canadian Literature
CanSP, Canadian Slavonic Papers
CanSS, Canadian–American Slavic Studies
CarA, Carmarthenshire Antiquary
CARB, Cahiers des Amis de Robert Brasillach
CarQ, Caribbean Quarterly
CAT, Cahiers d'Analyse Textuelle, Liège, Les Belles Lettres
CatR, Catalan Review
CAVL, Cahiers des Amis de Valery Larbaud
CB, Cuadernos Bibliográficos
CC, Comparative Criticism
CCe, Cahiers du Cerf XX
CCend, Continent Cendrars
CCF, Cuadernos de la Cátedra Feijoo
CCMe, Cahiers de Civilisation Médiévale
CCol, Cahiers Colette
CCU, Cuadernos de la Cátedra M. de Unamuno
CD, Cuadernos para el Diálogo
CDA, Christliche deutsche Autoren des 20. Jahrhunderts, Berne, Lang
CdA, Camp de l'Arpa
CDB, Coleção Documentos Brasileiros
CDi, Cuadernos dieciochistas
CDr, Comparative Drama
ČDS, Čeština doma a ve světě

CDs, Cahiers du Dix-septième, Athens, Georgia
CDU, Centre de Documentation Universitaire
CduC, Cahiers de CERES. Série littéraire, Tunis
CE, Cahiers Élisabéthains
CEA, Cahiers d'Études Africaines
CEAL, Centro Editor de América Latina
CEB, Cahiers Ethier-Blais
CEC, Conselho Estadual de Cultura, Comissão de Literatura, São Paulo
CEC, Cahiers d'Études Cathares, Narbonne
CECAES, Centre d'Études des Cultures d'Aquitaine et d'Europe du Sud, Université de Bordeaux III
CEcr, Corps Écrit
CEDAM, Casa Editrice Dott. A. Milani
CEG, Cuadernos de Estudios Gallegos
CEL, Cadernos de Estudos Lingüísticos, Campinas, Brazil
CELO, Centre d'Etude de la Littérature Occitane, Bordes.
CEM, Cahiers d'Études Médiévales, Univ. of Montreal
CEMa, Cahiers d'Études Maghrebines, Cologne
CEMed, Cuadernos de Estudios Medievales
CEPL, Centre d'Étude et de Promotion de la Lecture, Paris
CEPON, Centre per l'estudi e la promocion de l'Occitan normat.
CEPONB, CEPON Bulletin d'échange.
CER, Cahiers d'Études Romanes
CERCLiD, Cahiers d'Études Romanes, Centre de Linguistique et de Dialectologie, Toulouse
CEROC, Centre d'Enseignement et de Recherche d'Oc, Paris
CERoum, Cahiers d'Études Roumaines
CeS, Cultura e Scuola
CESCM, Centre d'Études Supérieures de Civilisation Médiévale, Poitiers
CET, Centro Editoriale Toscano

CEtGer, Cahiers d'Études Germaniques
CF, Les Cahiers de Fontenay
CFC, Contemporary French Civilization
CFI, Cuadernos de Filologia Italiana
CFLA, Cuadernos de Filología. Literaturas: Análisis, Valencia
CFM, Cahiers François Mauriac
CFMA, Collection des Classiques Français du Moyen Âge
CFol, Classical Folia
CFS, Cahiers Ferdinand de Saussure
CFSLH, Cuadernos de Filología: Studia Linguistica Hispanica
CFTM, Classiques Français des Temps Modernes, Paris, Champion
CG, Cahiers de Grammaire
CGD, Cahiers Georges Duhamel
CGFT, Critical Guides to French Texts, London, Grant & Cutler
CGGT, Critical Guides to German Texts, London, Grant & Cutler
CGP, Carleton Germanic Papers
CGS, Colloquia Germanica Stetinensia
CGST, Critical Guides to Spanish Texts, London, Támesis, Grant & Cutler
CH, Crítica Hispánica
CHA, Cuadernos Hispano-Americanos
CHAC, Cuadernos Hispano-Americanos. Los complementarios
CHB, Cahiers Henri Bosco
ChC, Chemins Critiques
CHCHMC, Cylchgrawn Hanes Cymdeithas Hanes y Methodistiaid Calfinaidd
CHLR, Cahiers d'Histoire des Littératures Romanes
CHP, Cahiers Henri Pourrat
CHR, Catholic Historical Review
ChR, The Chesterton Review
ChRev, Chaucer Review
ChrA, Chroniques Allemandes
ChrI, Chroniques Italiennes
ChrL, Christianity and Literature
ChrN, Chronica Nova
ChS, Champs du Signe

CHST, Caernarvonshire Historical Society Transactions
CHum, Computers and the Humanities
CI, Critical Inquiry
CiD, La Ciudad de Dios
CIDO, Centre International de Documentation Occitane, Béziers
CIEDS, Centre International d'Etudes du dix-huitième siècle, Ferney-Voltaire
CIEL, Centre International de l'Écrit en Langue d'Òc, Berre
CIEM, Comité International d'Études Morisques
CIF, Cuadernos de Investigación Filológica
CIH, Cuadernos de Investigación Historica
CILF, Conseil International de la Langue Française
CILH, Cuadernos para Investigación de la Literatura Hispanica
CILL, Cahiers de l'Institut de Linguistique de l'Université de Louvain
CILT, Centre for Information on Language Teaching, London
CIMAGL, Cahiers de l'Institut du Moyen Âge Grec et Latin, Copenhagen
CIn, Cahiers Intersignes
CIRDOC, Centre Inter-Régional de Développement de l'Occitan, Béziers
CIRVI, Centro Interuniversitario di Ricerche sul 'Viaggio in Italia', Moncalieri
CISAM, Centro Italiano di Studi sull'Alto Medioevo
CIt, Carte Italiane
CIUS, Canadian Institute of Ukrainian Studies Edmonton
CivC, Civiltà Cattolica
CJ, Conditio Judaica, Tübingen, Niemeyer
CJb, Celan-Jahrbuch
CJC, Cahiers Jacques Chardonne
CJG, Cahiers Jean Giraudoux
CJIS, Canadian Journal of Italian Studies
ČJL, Český jazyk a literatura

CJNS, Canadian Journal of Netherlandic Studies
CJP, Cahiers Jean Paulhan
CJR, Cahiers Jules Romains
CL, Cuadernos de Leiden
CL, Comparative Literature
ČL, Česká literatura
CLA, Cahiers du LACITO
CLAJ, College Language Association Journal
CLCC, Cahiers de Littérature Canadienne Comparée
CLCWeb, Comparative Literature and Culture, A WWWeb Journal, < http://www.arts.ualberta.ca/clcwebjournal/ >
CLE, Comunicaciones de Literatura Española, Buenos Aires
CLe, Cahiers de Lexicologie
CLEAM, Coleción de Literatura Española Aljamiado–Morisca, Madrid, Gredos
CLESP, Cooperativa Libraria Editrice degli Studenti dell'Università di Padova, Padua
CLett, Critica Letteraria
CLEUP, Cooperativa Libraria Editrice, Università di Padova
CLF, Cahiers de Linguistique Française
CLHM, Cahiers de Linguistique Hispanique Médiévale
CLin, Cercetări de Lingvistica
CLit, Cadernos de Literatura, Coimbra
ClL, La Clau lemosina
CLO, Cahiers Linguistiques d'Ottawa
ClP, Classical Philology
CLS, Comparative Literature Studies
CLSl, Cahiers de Linguistique Slave
CLTA, Cahiers de Linguistique Théorique et Appliquée
CLTL, Cadernos de Lingüística e Teoria da Literatura
CLUEB, Cooperativa Libraria Universitaria Editrice Bologna
CLus, Convergência Lusíada, Rio de Janeiro
CM, Cahiers Montesquieu, Naples, Liguori — Paris, Universitas — Oxford, Voltaire Foundation
CM, Classica et Mediaevalia

CMA, Cahier Marcel Aymé
CMar, Cuadernos de Marcha
CMCS, Cambrian Medieval Celtic Studies
CMERSA, Center for Medieval and Early Renaissance Studies, State University of New York at Binghamton. Acta
ČMF (PhP), Časopis pro moderni filologii: Philologica Pragensia
CMHLB, Cahiers du Monde Hispanique et Luso-Brésilien
CMi, Cultura Milano
CML, Classical and Modern Literature
ČMM, Časopis Matice Moravské
CMon, Communication Monographs
CMP, Cahiers Marcel Proust
CMRS, Cahiers du Monde Russe et Soviétique
CN, Cultura Neolatina
CNat, Les Cahiers Naturalistes
CNCDP, Comissão Nacional para a Comemoração dos Descobrimentos Portugueses, Lisbon
CNor, Los Cuadernos del Norte
CNR, Consiglio Nazionale delle Ricerche
CNRS, Centre National de la Recherche Scientifique
CO, Camera Obscura
CoF, Collectanea Franciscana
COJ, Cambridge Opera Journal
COK, Centralny Ośrodek Kultury, Warsaw
CoL, Compás de Letras
ColA, Colóquio Artes
ColGer, Colloquia Germanica
ColH, Colloquium Helveticum
ColL, Colóquio Letras
ComB, Communications of the International Brecht Society
ComGer, Comunicaciones Germánicas
CompL, Computational Linguistics
ConL, Contrastive Linguistics
ConLet, Il Confronto Letterario
ConLit, Contemporary Literature
ConS, Condorcet Studies
CORDAE, Centre Occitan de Recèrca, de Documentacion e d'Animacion Etnografica, Cordes

CorWPL, Cornell Working Papers in Linguistics
CP, Castrum Peregrini
CPE, Cahiers Prévost d'Exiles, Grenoble
CPL, Cahiers Paul Léautand
CPr, Cahiers de Praxématique
CPR, Chroniques de Port-Royal
CPUC, Cadernos PUC, São Paulo
CQ, Critical Quarterly
CR, Contemporary Review
CRAC, Cahiers Roucher — André Chénier
CRCL, Canadian Review of Comparative Literature
CREL, Cahiers Roumains d'Études Littéraires
CREO, Centre régional d'études occitanes
CRev, Centennial Review
CRI, Cuadernos de Ruedo Ibérico
CRIAR, Cahiers du Centre de Recherches Ibériques et Ibéro-Américains de l'Université de Rouen
CRIN, Cahiers de Recherches des Instituts Néerlandais de Langue et Littérature Françaises
CRITM, Cahiers RITM, Centre de Recherches Interdisciplinaires sur les Textes Modernes, Université de Paris X-Nanterre
CRLN, Comparative Romance Linguistics Newsletter
CRM, Cahiers de Recherches Médiévales (XIIIe–XVe siècles), Paris, Champion
CRQ, Cahiers Raymond Queneau
CRR, Cincinnati Romance Review
CRRI, Centre de Recherche sur la Renaissance Italienne, Paris
CRRR, Centre de Recherches Révolutionnaires et Romantiques, Université Blaise-Pascal, Clermont-Ferrand.
CrT, Critica del Testo
CS, Cornish Studies
CSAM, Centro di Studi sull'Alto Medioevo, Spoleto
ČSAV, Československá akademie věd
CSDI, Centro di Studio per la Dialettologia Italiana
CSem, Caiete de Semiotică

CSFLS, Centro di Studi Filologici e Linguistici Siciliani, Palermo
CSG, Cambridge Studies in German, Cambridge U.P.
CSGLL, Canadian Studies in German Language and Literature, Berne — New York — Frankfurt, Lang
CSH, Cahiers des Sciences Humaines
CSIC, Consejo Superior de Investigaciones Científicas, Madrid
CSJP, Cahiers Saint-John Perse
CSl, Critica Slovia, Florence
CSLAIL, Cambridge Studies in Latin American Iberian Literature, CUP
CSLI, Center for the Study of Language and Information, Stanford University
CSM, Les Cahiers de Saint-Martin
ČSp, Československý spisovatel
CSS, California Slavic Studies
CSSH, Comparative Studies in Society and History
CST, Cahiers de Sémiotique Textuelle
CSt, Critica Storica
CT, Christianity Today
CTC, Cuadernos de Teatro Clásico
CTE, Cuadernos de Traducción e Interpretación
CTe, Cuadernos de Teología
CTex, Cahiers Textuels
CTH, Cahiers Tristan l'Hermite
CTh, Ciencia Tomista
CTJ, Cahiers de Théâtre. Jeu
CTL, Current Trends in Linguistics
CTLin, Commissione per i Testi di Lingua, Bologna
CUECM, Cooperativa Universitaria Editrice Catanese Magistero
CUER MA, Centre Universitaire d'Études et de Recherches Médiévales d'Aix, Université de Provence, Aix-en-Provence
CUP, Cambridge University Press
CUUCV, Cultura Universitaria de la Universidad Central de Venezuela
CV, Città di Vita

CWPL, Catalan Working Papers in Linguistics
CWPWL, Cardiff Working Papers in Welsh Linguistics

DAEM, Deutsches Archiv für Erforschung des Mittelalters
DaF, Deutsch als Fremdsprache
DAG, Dictionnaire onomasiologique de l'ancien gascon, Tübingen, Niemeyer
DalR, Dalhousie Review
DanU, Dansk Udsyn
DAO, Dictionnaire onomasiologique de l'ancien occitan, Tübingen, Niemeyer
DaSt, Dante Studies
DB, Дзяржаўная бібліятэка БССР
DB, Doitsu Bungaku
DBl, Driemaandelijkse Bladen
DBO, Deutsche Bibliothek des Ostens, Berlin, Nicolai
DBR, Les Dialectes Belgo-Romans
DBr, Doitsu Bungakoranko
DCFH, Dicenda. Cuadernos de Filología Hispánica
DD, Diskussion Deutsch
DDG, Deutsche Dialektgeographie, Marburg, Elwert
DDJ, Deutsches Dante-Jahrbuch
DegSec, Degré Second
DELTA, Revista de Documentação de Estudos em Lingüística Teórica e Aplicada, Ŝao Paulo
DESB, Delta Epsilon Sigma Bulletin, Dubuque, Iowa
DeutB, Deutsche Bücher
DeutUB, Deutschungarische Beiträge
DFC, Durham French Colloquies
DFS, Dalhousie French Studies
DGF, Dokumentation germanistischer Forschung, Frankfurt, Lang
DgF, Danmarks gamle Folkeviser
DHA, Diálogos Hispánicos de Amsterdam, Rodopi
DHR, Duquesne Hispanic Review
DhS, Dix-huitième Siècle
DI, Deutscher Idealismus, Stuttgart, Klett-Cotta Verlag
DI, Декоративное искусство

DIAS, Dublin Institute for Advanced Studies
DiL, Dictionnairique et Lexicographie
DiS, Dickinson Studies
DisA, Dissertation Abstracts
DisSlSHL, Dissertationes Slavicae: Sectio Historiae Litterarum
DisSlSL, Dissertationes Slavicae: Sectio Linguistica
DisSoc, Discourse and Society
DK, Duitse Kroniek
DkJb, Deutschkanadisches Jahrbuch
DKV, Deutscher Klassiker Verlag, Frankfurt
DL, Детская литература
DLA, Deutsche Literatur von den Anfängen bis 1700, Berne — Frankfurt — Paris — New York, Lang
DLit, Discurso Literario
DLM, Deutsche Literatur des Mittelalters (Wissenschaftliche Beiträge der Ernst-Moritz-Arndt-Universität Greifswald)
DLR, Deutsche Literatur in Reprints, Munich, Fink
DLRECL, Diálogo de la Lengua. Revista de Estudio y Creación Literaria, Cuenca
DM, Dirassat Masrahiyyat
DMRPH, De Montfort Research Papers in the Humanities, De Montfort University, Leicester
DMTS, Davis Medieval Texts and Studies, Leiden, Brill
DN, Дружба народов
DNT, De Nieuwe Taalgids
DOLMA, Documenta Onomastica Litteralia Medii Aevi, Hildesheim, Olms
DOM, Dictionnaire de l'occitan médiéval, Tübingen, Niemeyer, 1996–
DosS, Dostoevsky Studies
DoV, Дошкольное воспитание
DPA, Documents pour servir à l'histoire du département des Pyrénées-Atlantiques, Pau
DPL, De Proprietatibus Litterarum, The Hague, Mouton
DpL, День поэзии, Leningrad
DpM, День поэзии, Moscow
DR, Drama Review

DRev, Downside Review
DRLAV, DRLAV, Revue de
Linguistique
DS, Diderot Studies
DSEÜ, Deutsche Sprache in
Europa und Übersee, Stuttgart,
Steiner
DSL, Det danske Sprog- og
Litteraturselskab
DSp, Deutsche Sprache
DSRPD, Documenta et Scripta.
Rubrica Paleographica et
Diplomatica, Barcelona
DSS, XVIIe Siècle
DSt, Deutsche Studien,
Meisenheim, Hain
DSt, Danske Studier
DT, Deutsche Texte, Tübingen,
Niemeyer
DteolT, Dansk teologisk Tidsskrift
DtL, Die deutsche Literatur
DTM, Deutsche Texte des
Mittelalters, Berlin, Akademie
DTV, Deutscher Taschenbuch
Verlag, Munich
DUB, Deutschunterricht, East
Berlin
DUJ, Durham University Journal
(New Series)
DUS, Der Deutschunterricht,
Stuttgart
DUSA, Deutschunterricht in
Südafrika
DV, Дальний Восток
DVA, Deutsche Verlags-Anstalt,
Stuttgart
DVLG, Deutsche Vierteljahresschrift
für Literaturwissenschaft und
Geistesgeschichte

E, Verlag Enzyklopädie, Leipzig
EAL, Early American Literature
EALS, Europäische Aufklärung in
Literatur und Sprache, Frankfurt,
Lang
EAS, Europe-Asia Studies
EB, Estudos Brasileiros
EBal, Etudes Balkaniques
EBM, Era Bouts dera mountanho,
Aurignac
EBTch, Études Balkaniques
Tchécoslovaques

EC, El Escritor y la Crítica,
Colección Persiles, Madrid,
Taurus
EC, Études Celtiques
ECan, Études Canadiennes
ECar, Espace Caraïbe
ECent, The Eighteenth Century,
Lubbock, Texas
ECentF, Eighteenth-Century Fiction
ECF, Écrits du Canada Français
ECI, Eighteenth-Century Ireland
ECIG, Edizioni Culturali
Internazionali Genova
ECL, Eighteenth-Century Life
ECla, Les Études Classiques
ECon, España Contemporánea
EconH, Économie et Humanisme
EcR, Echo de Rabastens. Les
Veillées Rabastinoises, Rabastens
(Tarn)
ECr, Essays in Criticism
ECre, Études Créoles
ECS, Eighteenth Century Studies
EdCat, Ediciones Cátedra, Madrid
EDESA, Ediciones Españolas S.A.
EDHS, Études sur le XVIIIe Siècle
EDIPUCRS, Editora da Pontífica
Universidade Católica de Rio
Grande do Sul, Porto Alegre
EDL, Études de Lettres
EDT, Edizioni di Torino
EDUSC, Editora da Universidade
de Santa Catarina
EE, Erasmus in English
EEM, East European Monographs
EEQ, East European Quarterly
EF, Erträge der Forschung,
Darmstadt, Wissenschaftliche
Buchgesellschaft
EF, Études Françaises
EFAA, Échanges Franco-Allemands
sur l'Afrique
EFE, Estudios de Fonética
Experimental
EFF, Ergebnisse der
Frauenforschung, Stuttgart,
Metzler
EFil, Estudios Filológicos, Valdivia,
Chile
EFL, Essays in French Literature,
Univ. of Western Australia
EFR, Éditeurs Français Réunis
EG, Études Germaniques

EH, Europäische
Hochschulschriften, Berne–
Frankfurt, Lang
EH, Estudios Humanísticos
EHF, Estudios Humanísticos.
Filología
EHN, Estudios de Historia
Novohispana
EHQ, European History Quarterly
EHR, English Historical Review
EHRC, European Humanities
Research Centre, University of
Oxford
EHS, Estudios de Historia Social
EHT, Exeter Hispanic Texts,
Exeter
EIA, Estudos Ibero-Americanos
EIP, Estudos Italianos em Portugal
EJJR, Études Jean-Jacques
Rousseau
EJWS, European Journal of
Women's Studies
EL, Esperienze Letterarie
El, Elementa, Würzburg,
Königshausen & Neumann
–Amsterdam, Rodopi
ELA, Études de Linguistique
Appliquée
ELF, Études Littéraires Françaises,
Paris, J.-M. Place — Tübingen,
Narr
ELH, English Literary History
ELin, Estudos Lingüísticos, São
Paulo
ELit, Essays in Literature
ELL, Estudos Lingüísticos e
Literários, Bahia
ELLC, Estudis de Llengua i
Literatura Catalanes
ELLF, Études de Langue et
Littérature Françaises, Tokyo
ELLUG, Éditions littéraires et
linguistiques de l'université de
Grenoble
ELM, Études littéraires
maghrebines
ELR, English Literary Renaissance
EMarg, Els Marges
EMH, Early Music History
EMus, Early Music
ENC, Els Nostres Clàssics,
Barcelona, Barcino
ENSJF, École Nationale Supérieure
de Jeunes Filles

EO, Edition Orpheus, Tübingen,
Francke
EO, Europa Orientalis
EOc, Estudis Occitans
EP, Études Philosophiques
Ep, Epistemata, Würzburg,
Königshausen & Neumann
EPESA, Ediciones y Publicaciones
Españolas S.A.
EPoet, Essays in Poetics
ER, Estudis Romànics
ERab, Études Rabelaisiennes
ERB, Études Romanes de Brno
ER(BSRLR), Études Romanes
(Bulletin de la Société Roumaine
de Linguistique Romane)
ERL, Études Romanes de Lund
ErlF, Erlanger Forschungen
ERLIMA, Équipe de recherche sur
la littérature d'imagination du
moyen âge, Centre d'Études
Supérieures de Civilisation
Médiévale/Faculté des Lettres et
des Langues, Université de
Poitiers.
EROPD, Ежегодник рукописного
отдела Пушкинского дома
ERR, European Romantic Review
ES, Erlanger Studien, Erlangen,
Palm & Enke
ES, Estudios Segovianos
EsC, L'Esprit Créateur
ESGP, Early Studies in Germanic
Philology, Amsterdam, Rodopi
ESI, Edizioni Scientifiche Italiane
ESJ, European Studies Journal
ESk, Edition Suhrkamp, Frankfurt,
Suhrkamp
ESoc, Estudios de Sociolingüística
ESor, Études sorguaises
EspA, Español Actual
ESt, English Studies
EstE, Estudios Escénicos
EstG, Estudi General
EstH, Estudios Hispánicos
EstL, Estudios de Lingüística,
Alicante
EstLA, Estudios de Lingüística
Aplicada
EstR, Estudios Románticos
EStud, Essays and Studies
ET, L'Écrit du Temps

ETF, Espacio, Tiempo y Forma, Revista de la Facultad de Geografía e Historia, UNED

EtF, Etudes francophones

EtH, Études sur l'Hérault, Pézenas

EthS, Ethnologia Slavica

ETJ, Educational Theatre Journal

ETL, Explicación de Textos Literarios

EtLitt, Études Littéraires, Quebec

EUDEBA, Editorial Universitaria de Buenos Aires

EUNSA, Ediciones Universidad de Navarra, Pamplona

EUS, European University Studies, Berne, Lang

ExP, Excerpta Philologica

EzLit, Език и литература

FAL, Forum Academicum Literaturwissenschaft, Königstein, Hain

FAM, Filologia Antica e Moderna

FAPESP, Fundação de Amparo à Pesquisa do Estado de São Paulo

FAR, French-American Review

FAS, Frankfurter Abhandlungen zur Slavistik, Giessen, Schmitz

FBAN, Фундаментальная бібліятэка Акадэміі навук БССР

FBG, Frankfurter Beiträge zur Germanistik, Heidelberg, Winter

FBS, Franco-British Studies

FC, Filologia e Critica

FCE, Fondo de Cultura Económica, Mexico

FCG — CCP, Fondation Calouste Gulbenkian — Centre Culturel Portugais, Paris

FCS, Fifteenth Century Studies

FD, Fonetică şi Dialectologie

FDL, Facetten deutscher Literatur, Berne, Haupt

FEI, Faites entrer l'infini. Journal de la Société des Amis de Louis Aragon et Elsa Triolet

FEK, Forschungen zur europäischen Kultur, Berne, Lang

FemSt, Feministische Studien

FF, Forum für Fachsprachenforschung, Tübingen, Narr

FF, Forma y Función

FFM, French Forum Monographs, Lexington, Kentucky

FGÄDL, Forschungen zur Geschichte der älteren deutschen Literatur, Munich, Fink

FH, Fundamenta Historica, Stuttgart-Bad Cannstatt, Frommann-Holzboog

FH, Frankfurter Hefte

FHL, Forum Homosexualität und Literatur

FHS, French Historical Studies

FIDS, Forschungsberichte des Instituts für Deutsche Sprache, Tübingen, Narr

FHSJ, Flintshire Historical Society Journal

FilM, Filologia Mediolatina

FilMod, Filologia Moderna, Udine –Pisa

FilN, Филологические науки

FilR, Filologia Romanza

FilS, Filologické studie

FilZ, Filologija, Zagreb

FiM, Filologia Moderna, Facultad de Filosofía y Letras, Madrid

FinS, Fin de Siglo

FIRL, Forum at Iowa on Russian Literature

FL, La France Latine

FLa, Faits de Langues

FLG, Freiburger literaturpsychologische Gespräche

FLin, Folia Linguistica

FLinHist, Folia Linguistica Historica

FLK, Forschungen zur Literatur- und Kulturgeschichte. Beiträge zur Sprach- und Literaturwissenschaft, Berne, Lang

FLP, Filologia e linguística portuguesa

FLS, French Literature Series

FLV, Fontes Linguae Vasconum

FM, Le Français Moderne

FMADIUR, FM: Annali del Dipartimento di Italianistica, Università di Roma 'La Sapienza'

FMDA, Forschungen und
Materialen zur deutschen
Aufklärung, Stuttgart — Bad
Cannstatt, Frommann-Holzboog
FMI, Fonti Musicali Italiane
FMLS, Forum for Modern
Language Studies
FMon, Le Français dans le Monde
FmSt, Frühmittelalterliche Studien
FMT, Forum Modernes Theater
FN, Frühe Neuzeit, Tübingen,
Niemeyer
FNDIR, Fédération nationale des
déportés et internés résistants
FNS, Frühneuzeit-Studien,
Frankfurt, Lang
FoH, Foro Hispánico, Amsterdam
FNT, Foilseacháin Náisiúnta Tta
FoI, Forum Italicum
FoS, Le Forme e la Storia
FP, Folia Phonetica
FPub, First Publications
FR, French Review
FrA, Le Français Aujourd'hui
FranS, Franciscan Studies
FrCS, French Cultural Studies
FrF, French Forum
FrH, Französisch Heute
FrP Le Français Préclassique
FrSoc, Français et Société
FS, Forum Slavicum, Munich, Fink
FS, French Studies
FSB, French Studies Bulletin
FSlav, Folia Slavica
FSSA, French Studies in Southern
Africa
FT, Fischer Taschenbuch,
Frankfurt, Fischer
FT, Finsk Tidskrift
FTCG, 'La Talanquere': Folklore,
Tradition, Culture Gasconne,
Nogano
FUE, Fundación Universitaria
Española
FV, Fortuna Vitrea, Tübingen,
Niemeyer
FZPT, Freiburger Zeitschrift für
Philosophie und Theologie

GA, Germanistische Arbeitshefte,
Tübingen, Niemeyer
GAB, Göppinger Akademische
Beiträge, Lauterburg, Kümmerle

GAG, Göppinger Arbeiten zur
Germanistik, Lauterburg,
Kümmerle
GAKS, Gesammelte Aufsätze zur
Kulturgeschichte Spaniens
GalR, Galician Review,
Birmingham
GANDLL, Giessener Arbeiten zur
neueren deutschen Literatur und
Literaturwissenschaft, Berne,
Lang
Garona, Garona. Cahiers du Centre
d'Etudes des Cultures
d'Aquitaine et d'Europe du Sud,
Talence
GAS, German-Australian Studies,
Berne, Lang
GASK, Germanistische Arbeiten zu
Sprache und Kulturgeschichte,
Frankfurt, Lang
GB, Germanistische Bibliothek,
Heidelberg, Winter
GBA, Gazette des Beaux-Arts
GBE, Germanistik in der Blauen
Eule
GC, Generalitat de Catalunya
GCFI, Giornale Critico della
Filosofia Italiana
GEMP, Groupement
d'Ethnomusicologie en Midi-
Pyrénées, La Talvèra
GerAb, Germanistische
Abhandlungen, Stuttgart,
Metzler
GerLux, Germanistik Luxembourg
GermL, Germanistische Linguistik
GeW, Germanica Wratislaviensia
GF, Giornale di Fisica
GFFNS, Godišnjak Filozofskog
fakulteta u Novom Sadu
GG, Geschichte und Gesellschaft
GGF, Göteborger Germanistische
Forschungen, University of
Gothenburg
GGF, Greifswalder Germanistische
Forschungen
GGVD, Grundlagen und Gedanken
zum Verständnis des Dramas,
Frankfurt, Diesterweg
GGVEL, Grundlagen und
Gedanken zum Verständnis
erzählender Literatur, Frankfurt,
Diesterweg

GIDILOc, Grop d'Iniciativa per un Diccionari Informatizat de la Lenga Occitana, Montpellier

GIF, Giornale Italiano di Filologia

GIGFL, Glasgow Introductory Guides to French Literature

GIGGL, Glasgow Introductory Guides to German Literature

GIP, Giornale Italiano di Psicologia

GJ, Gutenberg-Jahrbuch

GJb, Goethe Jahrbuch

GJLL, The Georgetown Journal of Language and Linguistics

GK, Goldmann Klassiker, Munich, Goldmann

GL, Germanistische Lehrbuchsammlung, Berlin, Weidler

GL, General Linguistics

GLC, German Life and Civilisation, Berne, Lang

GLCS, German Linguistic and Cultural Studies, Frankfurt, Lang

GLL, German Life and Letters

GLM, Gazette du Livre Médiéval

GLML, The Garland Library of Medieval Literature, New York –London, Garland

GLR, García Lorca Review

GLS, Grazer Linguistische Studien

Glyph, Glyph: Johns Hopkins Textual Studies, Baltimore

GM, Germanistische Mitteilungen

GML, Gothenburg Monographs in Linguistics

GMon, German Monitor

GN, Germanic Notes and Reviews

GoSt, Gothic Studies

GPB, Гос. публичная библиотека им. М. Е. Салтыкова-Щедрина

GPI, Государственный педагогический институт

GPSR, Glossaire des Patois de la Suisse Romande

GQ, German Quarterly

GR, Germanic Review

GREC, Groupe de Recherches et d'Études du Clermontais, Clermont-l'Hérault

GRECF, Groupe de Recherches et d'Études sur le Canada français, Edinburgh

GREHAM, Groupe de REcherche d'Histoire de l'Anthroponymie

Médiévale, Tours, Université François-Rabelais

GRELCA, Groupe de Recherche sur les Littératures de la Caraïbe, Université Laval

GRLH, Garland Reference Library of the Humanities, New York — London, Garland

GRLM, Grundriss der romanischen Literaturen des Mittelalters

GRM, Germanisch-Romanische Monatsschrift

GrSt, Grundtvig Studier

GS, Lo Gai Saber, Toulouse

GSA, Germanic Studies in America, Berne–Frankfurt, Lang

GSC, German Studies in Canada, Frankfurt, Lang

GSI, German Studies in India

GSl, Germano-Slavica, Ontario

GSLI, Giornale Storico della Letteratura Italiana

GSR, German Studies Review

GSSL, Göttinger Schriften zur Sprach– und Literaturwissenschaft, Göttingen, Herodot

GTN, Gdańskie Towarzystwo Naukowe

GTS, Germanistische Texte und Studien, Hildesheim, Olms

GV, Generalitat Valenciana

GY, Goethe Yearbook

H, Hochschulschriften, Cologne, Pahl-Rugenstein

HAHR, Hispanic American Historical Review

HB, Horváth Blätter

HBA, Historiografía y Bibliografía Americanistas, Seville

HBG, Hamburger Beiträge zur Germanistik, Frankfurt, Lang

HDG, Huis aan de Drie Grachten, Amsterdam

HEI, History of European Ideas

HEL, Histoire, Épistémologie, Language

Her(A), Hermes, Århus

HES, Histoire, Économie et Société

HeyJ, Heythrop Journal

HF, Heidelberger Forschungen, Heidelberg, Winter

HHS, History of the Human Sciences
HI, Historica Ibérica
HIAR, Hamburger Ibero-Amerikanische Reihe
HICL, Histoire des Idées et Critique Littéraire, Geneva, Droz
HIGL, Holland Institute for Generative Linguistics, Leiden
HisJ, Hispanic Journal, Indiana–Pennsylvania
HisL, Hispanic Linguistics
HistL, Historiographia Linguistica
HistS, History of Science
His(US), Hispania, Ann Arbor
HJ, Historical Journal
HJb, Heidelberger Jahrbücher
HJBS, Hispanic Journal of Behavioural Sciences
HKADL, Historisch-kritische Arbeiten zur deutschen Literatur, Frankfurt, Lang
HKZMTLG, Handelingen van de Koninklijke Zuidnederlandse Maatschappij voor Taalen, Letterkunde en Geschiedenis
HL, Hochschulschriften Literaturwissenschaft, Königstein, Hain
HL, Humanistica Lovaniensia
HLB, Harvard Library Bulletin
HLQ, Huntington Library Quarterly
HLS, Historiska och litteraturhistoriska studier
HM, Hommes et Migrations
HMJb, Heinrich Mann Jahrbuch
HP, History of Psychiatry
HPh, Historical Philology
HPos, Hispanica Posnaniensia
HPR, Hispanic Poetry Review
HPS, Hamburger Philologische Studien, Hamburg, Buske
HPSl, Heidelberger Publikationen zur Slavistik, Frankfurt, Lang
HPT, History of Political Thought
HR, Hispanic Review
HRef, Historical reflections / Reflexions historiques
HRel, History of Religions
HRev, Hrvatska revija
HRJ, Hispanic Research Journal
HRSHM, Heresis, revue semestrielle d'hérésiologie médiévale

HS, Helfant Studien, Stuttgart, Helfant
HS, Hispania Sacra
HSLA, Hebrew University Studies in Literature and the Arts
HSlav, Hungaro-Slavica
HSMS, Hispanic Seminary of Medieval Studies, Madison
HSp, Historische Sprachforschung (Historical Linguistics)
HSSL, Harvard Studies in Slavic Linguistics
HSt, Hispanische Studien
HSWSL, Hallesche Studien zur Wirkung von Sprache und Literatur
HT, Helfant Texte, Stuttgart, Helfant
HT, History Today
HTe, Hecho Teatral (Revista de teoría y práctica del teatro hispánico)
HTh, History and Theory
HTR, Harvard Theological Review
HUS, Harvard Ukrainian Studies
HY, Herder Yearbook
HZ, Historische Zeitschrift

IÅ, Ibsen-Årbok, Oslo
IAP, Ibero-Americana Pragensia
IAr, Iberoamerikanisches Archiv
IARB, Inter-American Review of Bibliography
IASL, Internationales Archiv für Sozialgeschichte der deutschen Literatur
IASLS, Internationales Archiv für Sozialgeschichte der deutschen Literatur: Sonderheft
IB, Insel-Bücherei, Frankfurt, Insel
IBKG, Innsbrucker Beiträge zur Kulturwissenschaft. Germanistische Reihe
IBL, Instytut Badań Literackich PAN, Warsaw
IBLA, Institut des Belles Lettres Arabes
IBLe, Insel-Bücherei, Leipzig, Insel
IBS, Innsbrücker Beiträge zur Sprachwissenschaft
IC, Index on Censorship
ICALP, Instituto de Cultura e Língua Portuguesa, Lisbon

ICALPR, Instituto de Cultura e
Língua Portuguesa. Revista
ICC, Instituto Caro y Cuervo,
Bogotà
ICLMR, Istitut Cultural Ladin
'Micurà de Rü'
ICMA, Instituto de Cooperación
con el Mundo Árabe
ID, Italia Dialettale
IDF, Informationen Deutsch als
Fremdsprache
IDL, Indices zur deutschen
Literatur, Tübingen, Niemeyer
IdLit, Ideologies and Literature
IEC, Institut d'Estudis Catalans
IEI, Istituto dell'Enciclopedia
Italiana
IEO, Institut d'Estudis Occitans
IEPI, Istituti Editoriali e Poligrafici
Internazionali
IES, Institut d'Études Slaves, Paris
IF, Impulse der Forschung,
Darmstadt, Wissenschaftliche
Buchgesellschaft
IF, Indogermanische Forschungen
IFAVL, Internationale Forschungen
zur Allgemeinen und
Vergleichenden
Literaturwissenschaft,
Amsterdam–Atlanta, Rodopi
IFC, Institutión Fernando el
Católico
IFEE, Investigación Franco-
Española. Estudios
IFiS, Instytut Filozofii i Socjologii
PAN, Warsaw
IFOTT, Institut voor Functioneel
Onderzoek naar Taal en
Taalgebruik, Amsterdam
IFR, International Fiction Review
IG, Information grammaticale
IHC, Italian History and Culture
IHE, Índice Histórico Español
IHS, Irish Historical Studies
II, Information und Interpretation,
Frankfurt, Lang
IIa, Институт языкознания
IIFV, Institut Interuniversitari de
Filologia Valenciana, Valencia
III, Институт истории искусств
IJ, Italian Journal
IJAL, International Journal of
American Linguistics

IJBAG, Internationales Jahrbuch
der Bettina-von-Arnim
Gesellschaft
IJCS, International Journal of
Canadian Studies
IJFS, International Journal of
Francophone Studies, Leeds
IJHL, Indiana Journal of Hispanic
Literatures
IJL, International Journal of
Lexicography
IJP, International Journal of
Psycholinguistics
IJSL, International Journal for the
Sociology of Language
IJSLP, International Journal of
Slavic Linguistics and Poetics
IK, Искусство кино
IKU, Institut za književnost i
umetnost, Belgrade
IL, L'Information Littéraire
ILASLR, Istituto Lombardo.
Accademia di Scienze e Lettere.
Rendiconti
ILen, Искусство Ленинграда
ILG, Instituto da Lingua Galega
ILing, Incontri Linguistici
ILTEC, Instituto de Linguistica
Teórica e Computacional, Lisbon
IMN, Irisleabhar Mhá Nuad
IMR, International Migration
Review
IMU, Italia Medioevale e
Umanistica
INCM, Imprensa Nacional, Casa
da Moeda, Lisbon
InfD, Informationen und Didaktik
INLF, Institut National de la
Langue Française
INIC, Instituto Nacional de
Investigação Científica
InL, Иностранная литература
INLE, Instituto Nacional del Libro
Español
InstEB, Inst. de Estudos Brasileiros
InstNL, Inst. Nacional do Livro,
Brasilia
IO, Italiano e Oltre
IPL, Istituto di Propaganda Libraria
IPZS, Istituto Poligrafico e Zecca
dello Stato, Rome
IR, L'Immagine Riflessa
IRAL, International Review of
Applied Linguistics

IRIa, Институт русского языка Российской Академии Наук
IrR, The Irish Review
IRSH, International Review of Social History
IRSL, International Review of Slavic Linguistics
ISC, Institut de Sociolingüística Catalana
ISI, Institute for Scientific Information, U.S.A.
ISIEMC, Istituto Storico Italiano per l'Età Moderna e Contemporanea, Rome
ISIM, Istituto Storico Italiano per il Medio Evo
ISLIa, Известия Академии наук СССР. Серия литературы и языка
ISOAN, Известия сибирского отделения АН СССР, Novosibirsk
ISP, International Studies in Philosophy
ISPS, International Studies in the Philosophy of Science
ISS, Irish Slavonic Studies
IsS, Islamic Studies, Islamabad
ISSA, Studi d'Italianistica nell'Africa Australe: Italian Studies in Southern Africa
ISt, Italian Studies
ISV, Informazioni e Studi Vivaldiani
IT, Insel Taschenbuch, Frankfurt, Insel
ItC, Italian Culture
ITL, ITL. Review of Applied Linguistics, Instituut voor Toegepaste Linguistiek, Leuven
ItQ, Italian Quarterly
ItStudien, Italienische Studien
IUJF, Internationales Uwe-Johnson-Forum
IULA, Institut Universitari de Lingüística Aplicada, Universitat Pompeu Fabra, Barcelona
IUP, Irish University Press
IUR, Irish University Review
IV, Istituto Veneto di Scienze, Lettere ed Arti
IVAS, Indices Verborum zum altdeutschen Schrifttum, Amsterdam, Rodopi

IVN, Internationale Vereniging voor Nederlandistiek

JAAC, Journal of Aesthetics and Art Criticism
JACIS, Journal of the Association for Contemporary Iberian Studies
JAE, Journal of Aesthetic Education
JAIS, Journal of Anglo-Italian Studies, Malta
JAMS, Journal of the American Musicological Society
JanL, Janua Linguarum, The Hague, Mouton
JAOS, Journal of the American Oriental Society
JAPLA, Journal of the Atlantic Provinces Linguistic Association
JARA, Journal of the American Romanian Academy of Arts and Sciences
JAS, The Journal of Algerian Studies
JASI, Jahrbuch des Adalbert-Stifter-Instituts
JATI, Association of Teachers of Italian Journal
JazA, Jazykovědné aktuality
JazLin, Jazykověda: Linguistica, Ostravska University
JazŠ, Jazykovedné štúdie
JAZU, Jugoslavenska akademija znanosti i umjetnosti
JBSP, Journal of the British Society for Phenomenology
JČ, Jazykovedný časopis, Bratislava
JCanS, Journal of Canadian Studies
JCHAS, Journal of the Cork Historical and Archaeological Society
JCL, Journal of Child Language
JCLin, Journal of Celtic Linguistics
JCS, Journal of Celtic Studies
JDASD, Deutsche Akademie für Sprache und Dichtung: Jahrbuch
JDF, Jahrbuch Deutsch als Fremdsprache
JDSG, Jahrbuch der Deutschen Schiller-Gesellschaft
JEA, Lou Journalet de l'Escandihado Aubagnenco

JEGP, Journal of English and
Germanic Philology
JEH, Journal of Ecclesiastical
History
JEL, Journal of English Linguistics
JES, Journal of European Studies
JF, Južnoslovenski filolog
JFDH, Jahrbuch des Freien
Deutschen Hochstifts
JFG, Jahrbuch der Fouqué
Gesellschaft
JFinL, Jahrbuch für finnisch-
deutsche Literaturbeziehungen
JFL, Jahrbuch für fränkische
Landesforschung
JFLS, Journal of French Language
Studies
JFR, Journal of Folklore Research
JG, Jahrbuch für Geschichte,
Berlin, Akademie
JGO, Jahrbücher für die Geschichte
Osteuropas
JHA, Journal for the History of
Astronomy
JHI, Journal of the History of Ideas
JHispP, Journal of Hispanic
Philology
JHP, Journal of the History of
Philosophy
JHR, Journal of Hispanic Research
JHS, Journal of the History of
Sexuality
JIAS, Journal of Inter-American
Studies
JIES, Journal of Indo-European
Studies
JIG, Jahrbuch für Internationale
Germanistik
JIL, Journal of Italian Linguistics
JILAS, Journal of Iberian and Latin
American Studies (formerly
Tesserae)
JILS, Journal of Interdisciplinary
Literary Studies
JIPA, Journal of the International
Phonetic Association
JIRS, Journal of the Institute of
Romance Studies
JJQ, James Joyce Quarterly
JJS, Journal of Jewish Studies
JL, Journal of Linguistics
JLACS, Journal of Latin American
Cultural Studies
JLAL, Journal of Latin American
Lore
JLAS, Journal of Latin American
Studies
JLH, Journal of Library History
JLS, Journal of Literary Semantics
JLSP, Journal of Language and
Social Psychology
JMemL, Journal of Memory and
Language
JMEMS, Journal of Medieval and
Early Modern Studies
JMH, Journal of Medieval History
JMHRS, Journal of the Merioneth
Historical and Record Society
JML, Journal of Modern Literature
JMLat, Journal of Medieval Latin
JMMD, Journal of Multilingual and
Multicultural Development
JMMLA, Journal of the Midwest
Modern Language Association
JModH, Journal of Modern History
JMP, Journal of Medicine and
Philosophy
JMRS, Journal of Medieval and
Renaissance Studies
JMS, Journal of Maghrebi Studies
JNT, Journal of Narrative
Technique
JONVL, Een Jaarboek: Overzicht
van de Nederlandse en Vlaamse
Literatuur
JOWG, Jahrbuch der Oswald von
Wolkenstein Gesellschaft
JP, Journal of Pragmatics
JPC, Journal of Popular Culture
JPCL, Journal of Pidgin and Creole
Languages
JPh, Journal of Phonetics
JPHS, The Journal of the
Pembrokeshire Historical Society
JPol, Język Polski
JPR, Journal of Psycholinguistic
Research
JQ, Jacques e i suoi Quaderni
JRA, Journal of Religion in Africa
JRG, Jahrbücher der Reineke-
Gesellschaft
JRH, Journal of Religious History
JRIC, Journal of the Royal
Institution of Cornwall
JŘJR, Jazyk a řeč jihočeského
regionu. České Budějovice,

Pedagogická fakulta Jihočeské univerzity

JRMA, Journal of the Royal Musical Association

JRMMRA, Journal of the Rocky Mountain Medieval and Renaissance Association

JRS, Journal of Romance Studies

JRUL, Journal of the Rutgers University Libraries

JS, Journal des Savants

JSCS, Journal of Spanish Cultural Studies

JSEES, Japanese Slavic and East European Studies

JSem, Journal of Semantics

JSFWUB, Jahrbuch der Schlesischen Friedrich-Wilhelms-Universität zu Breslau

JSH, Jihočeský sborník historický

JSHR, Journal of Speech and Hearing Research

JSL, Journal of Slavic Linguistics

JSoc, Journal of Sociolinguistics

JSS, Journal of Spanish Studies: Twentieth Century

JTS, Journal of Theological Studies

JU, Judentum und Umwelt, Berne, Lang

JUG, Jahrbuch der ungarischen Germanistik

JUS, Journal of Ukrainian Studies

JV, Jahrbuch für Volkskunde

JVF, Jahrbuch für Volksliedforschung

JVLVB, Journal of Verbal Learning and Verbal Behavior

JWCI, Journal of the Warburg and Courtauld Institutes

JWGV, Jahrbuch des Wiener Goethe-Vereins, Neue Folge

JWH, Journal of World History

JWIL, Journal of West Indian Literature

JWRH, Journal of Welsh Religious History

JZ, Jazykovedný zborník

KANTL, Koninklijke Akademie voor Nederlandse Taal- en Letterkunde

KASL, Kasseler Arbeiten zur Sprache und Literatur, Frankfurt, Lang

KAW, Krajowa Agencja Wydawnicza

KAWLSK, Koninklijke Academie voor Wetenschappen, Letteren en Schone Kunsten van België, Brussels

KB, Književni barok

KBGL, Kopenhagener Beiträge zur germanistischen Linguistik

Kbl, Korrespondenzblatt des Vereins für niederdeutsche Sprachforschung

KDC, Katholiek Documentatiecentrum

KDPM, Kleine deutsche Prosadenkmäler des Mittelalters, Munich, Fink

KGOS, Kultur- und geistesgeschichtliche Ostmitteleuropa-Studien, Marburg, Elwert

KGS, Kölner germanistische Studien, Cologne, Böhlau

KGS, Kairoer germanistische Studien

KH, Komparatistische Hefte

KhL, Художественная литература

KI, Književna istorija

KiW, Książka i Wiedza

KJ, Književnost i jezik

KK, Kirke og Kultur

KKK, Kultur og Klasse. Kritik og Kulturanalyse

KlJb, Kleist-Jahrbuch

KLWL, Krieg und Literatur: War and Literature

Klage, Klage: Kölner linguistische Arbeiten. Germanistik, Hürth-Efferen, Gabel

KN, Kwartalnik Neofilologiczny

KnK, Kniževna kritika

KO, Университетско издателство 'Климент Охридски'

KO, Книжное обозрение

KP, Книжная палата

KRA, Kölner Romanistische Arbeiten, Geneva, Droz

KS, Kúltura slova

KSDL, Kieler Studien zur deutschen Literaturgeschichte, Neumünster, Wachholtz

KSL, Kölner Studien zur Literaturwissenschaft, Frankfurt, Lang

KSt, Kant Studien

KTA, Kröners Taschenausgabe, Stuttgart, Kröner

KTRM, Klassische Texte des romanischen Mittelalters, Munich, Fink

KU, Konstanzer Universitäts-reden

KUL, Katolicki Uniwersytet Lubelski, Lublin

KuSDL, Kulturwissenschaftliche Studien zur deutschen Literatur, Opladen, Westdeutscher Verlag

KZG, Koreanische Zeitschrift für Germanistik

KZMTLG, Koninklijke Zuidnederlandse Maatschappij voor Taal- en Letterkunde en Geschiedenis, Brussels

KZMTLGH, Koninklijke Zuidnederlandse Maatschaapij voor Taal- en Letterkunde en Geschiedenis. Handelingen

LA, Linguistische Arbeiten, Tübingen, Niemeyer

LA, Linguistic Analysis

LaA, Language Acquisition

LAbs, Linguistics Abstracts

LaF, Langue Française

LAILJ, Latin American Indian Literatures Journal

LaLi, Langues et Linguistique

LALIES, LALIES. Actes des sessions de linguistique et de littérature. Institut d'Etudes linguistiques et phonétiques. Sessions de linguistique. Ecole Normale Supérieure Paris, Sorbonne nouvelle

LALR, Latin-American Literary Review

LaM, Les Langues Modernes

LangH, Le Langage et l'Homme

LArb, Linguistische Arbeitsberichte

LARR, Latin-American Research Review

LaS, Langage et Société

LATR, Latin-American Theatre Review

LatT, Latin Teaching, Shrewsbury

LB, Leuvense Bijdragen

LBer, Linguistische Berichte

LBIYB, Leo Baeck Institute Year Book

LBR, Luso-Brazilian Review

LC, Letture Classensi

LCC, Léachtaí Cholm Cille

LCh, Literatura Chilena

LCP, Language and Cognitive Processes

LCrit, Lavoro Critico

LCUTA, Library Chronicle of the University of Texas at Austin

LD, Libri e Documenti

LdA, Linha d'Agua

LDan, Lectura Dantis

LDanN, Lectura Dantis Newberryana

LDGM, Ligam-DiGaM. Quadèrn de lingüística e lexicografía gasconas, Fontenay aux Roses

LE, Language and Education

LEA, Lingüística Española Actual

LebS, Lebende Sprachen

LEMIR, Literatura Española Medieval y del Renacimiento, Valencia U.P.; http://www.uv.es/~lemir/Revista.html

Leng(M), Lengas, Montpellier

Leng(T), Lengas, Toulouse

LenP, Ленинградская панорама

LetA, Letterature d'America

LetD, Letras de Deusto

LETHB, Laboratoires d'Études Théâtrales de l'Université de Haute-Bretagne. Études et Documents, Rennes

LetL, Letras e Letras, Departmento de Línguas Estrangeiras Modernas, Universidade Federal de Uberlândia, Brazil

LetLi, Letras Libres, Mexico D.F.

LetMS, Letopis Matice srpske, Novi Sad

LetP, Il Lettore di Provincia

LetS, Letras Soltas

LevT, Levende Talen

Lex(L), Lexique, Lille

LF, Letras Femeninas

LFil, Listy filologické

LFQ, Literature and Film Quarterly

LGF, Lunder Germanistische Forschungen, Stockholm, Almqvist & Wiksell

LGGL, Literatur in der Geschichte, Geschichte in der Literatur, Cologne–Vienna, Böhlau

LGL, Langs Germanistische Lehrbuchsammlung, Berne, Lang

LGP, Leicester German Poets, Leicester U.P.

LGW, Literaturwissenschaft — Gesellschaftswissenschaft, Stuttgart, Klett

LH, Lingüística Hispánica

LHum, Litteraria Humanitas, Brno

LI, Linguistic Inquiry

LIA, Letteratura italiana antica

LIÅA, Litteraturvetenskapliga institutionen vid Åbo Akademi, Åbo Akademi U.P.

LiB, Literatur in Bayern

LIC, Letteratura Italiana Contemporanea

LiCC, Lien des chercheurs cévenols

LIE, Lessico Intellettuale Europeo, Rome, Ateneo

LiL, Limbă şi Literatură

LiLi, Zeitschrift für Literaturwissenschaft und Linguistik

LingAk, Linguistik Aktuell, Amsterdam, Benjamins

LingBal, Балканско езикознание – Linguistique Balkanique

LingCon, Lingua e Contesto

LingFil, Linguistica e Filologia, Dipartimento di Linguistica e Letterature Comparate, Bergamo

LingLett, Linguistica e Letteratura

LíngLit, Língua e Literatura, São Paulo

LinLit, Lingüística y Literatura

LINQ, Linq [Literature in North Queensland]

LInv, Linguisticae Investigationes

LiR, Limba Română

LIT, Literature Interpretation Theory

LIt, Lettera dall'Italia

LitAP, Literární archív Památníku národního písemnictví

LItal, Lettere Italiane

LitB, Literatura, Budapest

LitC, Littératures Classiques

LitG, Литературная газета, Moscow

LitH, Literature and History

LItL, Letteratura Italiana Laterza, Bari, Laterza

LitL, Literatur für Leser

LitLing, Literatura y Lingüística

LitM, Literární měsíčník

LitMis, Литературна мисъл

LitP, Literature and Psychology

LitR, The Literary Review

LittB, Litteraria, Bratislava

LittK, Litterae, Lauterburg, Kümmerle

LittS, Litteratur og Samfund

LittW, Litteraria, Wrocław

LiU, Література Україна

LivOS, Liverpool Online Series. Critical Editions of French Texts. Department of Modern Languages. University of Liverpool < http:// www.liv.ac.uk/www/french/ LOS/ >

LJb, Literaturwissenschaftliches Jahrbuch der Görres–Gesellschaft

LK, Literatur-Kommentare, Munich, Hanser

LK, Literatur und Kritik

LKol, Loccumer Kolloquium

LL, Langues et Littératures, Rabat

LlA, Lletres Asturianes

LLC, Literary and Linguistic Computing

LlC, Llên Cymru

LlLi, Llengua i Literatura

LLS, Lenguas, Literaturas, Sociedades. Cuadernos Hispánicos

LLSEE, Linguistic and Literary Studies in Eastern Europe, Amsterdam, Benjamins

LM, Le Lingue del Mondo

LN, Lingua Nostra

LNB, Leipziger namenkundliche Beiträge

LNL, Les Langues Néo-Latines

LNouv, Les Lettres Nouvelles

LoP, Loccumer Protokolle

LOS, Literary Onomastic Studies

LP, Le Livre de Poche, Librairie Générale Française

LP, Lingua Posnaniensis

LPen, Letras Peninsulares

LPh, Linguistics and Philosophy

LPLP, Language Problems and Language Planning

LPO, Lenga e Païs d'Oc, Montpellier

LPr, Linguistica Pragensia

LQ, Language Quarterly, University of S. Florida

LQu, Lettres québécoises

LR, Linguistische Reihe, Munich, Hueber

LR, Les Lettres Romanes

LRev, Linguistic Review

LRI, Libri e Riviste d'Italia

LS, Literatur als Sprache, Münster, Aschendorff

LS, Lingua e Stile

LSa, Lusitania Sacra

LSc, Language Sciences

LSil, Linguistica Silesiana

LSNS, Lundastudier i Nordisk Språkvetenskap

LSo, Language in Society

LSp, Language and Speech

LSPS, Lou Sourgentin/La Petite Source. Revue culturelle bilingue nissart-français, Nice

LSty, Language and Style

LSW, Ludowa Spółdzielnia Wydawnicza

LTG, Literaturwissenschaft, Theorie und Geschichte, Frankfurt, Lang

ŁTN, Łódzkie Towarzystwo Naukowe

LTP, Laval Théologique et Philosophique

LU, Literarhistorische Untersuchungen, Berne, Lang

LVC, Language Variation and Change

LW, Literatur und Wirklichkeit, Bonn, Bouvier

LWU, Literatur in Wissenschaft und Unterricht

LY, Lessing Yearbook

MA, Moyen Âge

MAASC, Mémoires de l'Académie des Arts et des Sciences de Carcassonne

MACL, Memórias da Academia de Ciências de Lisboa, Classe de Letras

MAe, Medium Aevum

MAKDDR, Mitteilungen der Akademie der Künste der DDR

MAL, Modern Austrian Literature

MaL, Le Maghreb Littéraire – Revue Canadienne des Littératures Maghrébines, Toronto

MaM, Marbacher Magazin

MAPS, Medium Aevum. Philologische Studien, Munich, Fink

MARPOC, Maison d'animation et de recherche populaire occitane, Nimes

MAST, Memorie dell'Accademia delle Scienze di Torino

MatSl, Matica Slovenská

MBA, Mitteilungen aus dem Brenner-Archiv

MBAV, Miscellanea Bibliothecae Apostolicae Vaticanae

MBMRF, Münchener Beiträge zur Mediävistik und Renaissance-Forschung, Bachenhausen, Arbeo

MBRP, Münstersche Beiträge zur romanischen Philologie, Münster, Kleinheinrich

MBSL, Mannheimer Beiträge zur Sprach- und Literaturwissenschaft, Tübingen, Narr

MC, Misure Critiche

MCV, Mélanges de la Casa de Velázquez

MD, Musica Disciplina

MDan, Meddelser fra Dansklærerforeningen.

MDG, Mitteilungen des deutschen Germanistenverbandes

MDL, Mittlere Deutsche Literatur in Neu- und Nachdrucken, Berne, Lang

MDLK, Monatshefte für deutschsprachige Literatur und Kultur

MDr, Momentum Dramaticum

MEC, Ministerio de Educação e Cultura, Rio de Janeiro

MedC, La Méditerranée et ses Cultures

MedH, Medioevo e Umanesimo
MedLR, Mediterranean Language Review
MedP, Medieval Perspectives
MedRom, Medioevo Romanzo
MedS, Medieval Studies
MEFR, Mélanges de l'École Française de Rome, Moyen Age
MerH, Merthyr Historian
MerP, Mercurio Peruano
MF, Mercure de France
MFDT, Mainzer Forschungen zu Drama und Theater, Tübingen, Francke
MFS, Modern Fiction Studies
MG, Молодая гвардия
MG, Молодая гвардия
MGB, Münchner Germanistische Beiträge, Munich, Fink
MGG, Mystik in Geschichte und Gegenwart, Stuttgart-Bad Cannstatt, Frommann-Holzboog
MGS, Marburger Germanistische Studien, Frankfurt, Lang
MGS, Michigan Germanic Studies
MGSL, Minas Gerais, Suplemento Literário
MH, Medievalia et Humanistica
MHJ, Medieval History Journal
MHLS, Mid-Hudson Language Studies
MHRA, Modern Humanities Research Association
MichRS, Michigan Romance Studies
MILUS, Meddelanden från Institutionen i Lingvistik vid Universitetet i Stockholm
MINS, Meddelanden från institutionen för nordiska språk vid Stockholms universitet, Stockholm U.P.
MiscBarc, Miscellanea Barcinonensia
MiscEB, Miscel·lània d'Estudis Bagencs
MiscP, Miscel·lània Penedesenca
MITWPL, MIT Working Papers in Linguistics
MJ, Mittellateinisches Jahrbuch
MK, Maske und Kothurn
MKH, Deutsche Forschungsgemeinschaft: Mitteilung der Kommission für

Humanismusforschung, Weinheim, Acta Humaniora
MKNAWL, Mededelingen der Koninklijke Nederlandse Akademie van Wetenschappen, Afd. Letterkunde, Amsterdam
ML, Mediaevalia Lovaniensia, Leuven U.P.
ML, Modern Languages
MLAIntBibl, Modern Language Association International Bibliography
MLIÅA, Meddelanden utgivna av Litteraturvetenskapliga institutionen vid Åbo Akademi, Åbo Akademi U.P.
MLIGU, Meddelanden utgivna av Litteraturvetenskapliga institutionen vid Göteborgs universitet, Gothenburg U.P.
MLit, Мастацкая літаратура
MLit, Miesięcznik Literacki
MLIUU, Meddelanden utgivna av Litteraturvetenskapliga institutionen vid Uppsala universitet, Uppsala U.P.
MLJ, Modern Language Journal
MLN, Modern Language Notes
MLQ, Modern Language Quarterly
MLR, Modern Language Review
MLS, Modern Language Studies
MM, Maal og Minne
MMS, Münstersche Mittelalter-Schriften, Munich, Fink
MN, Man and Nature. L'Homme et la Nature
MNGT, Manchester New German Texts, Manchester U.P.
MO, Monde en Oc. Aurillac (IEO)
ModD, Modern Drama
ModS, Modern Schoolman
MoL, Modellanalysen: Literatur, Paderborn, Schöningh–Munich, Fink
MON, Ministerstwo Obrony Narodowej, Warsaw
MosR, Московский рабочий
MoyFr, Le Moyen Français
MP, Modern Philology
MQ, Mississippi Quarterly
MQR, Michigan Quarterly Review
MR, Die Mainzer Reihe, Mainz, Hase & Koehler
MR, Medioevo e Rinascimento

MRev, Maghreb Review

MRo, Marche Romane

MRS, Medieval and Renaissance Studies

MRTS, Medieval and Renaissance Texts and Studies, Tempe, Arizona, Arizona State University

MS, Marbacher Schriften, Stuttgart, Cotta

MS, Moderna Språk

MSB, Middeleeuwse Studies en Bronnen, Hilversum, Verloren

MSC, Medjunarodni slavistički centar, Belgrade

MSG, Marburger Studien zur Germanistik, Marburg, Hitzeroth

MSHA, Maison des sciences de l'homme d'Aquitaine

MSISS, Materiali della Società Italiana di Studi sul Secolo XVIII

MSL, Marburger Studien zur Literatur, Marburg, Hitzeroth

MSLKD, Münchener Studien zur literarischen Kultur in Deutschland, Frankfurt, Lang

MSMS, Middeleeuse Studies — Medieval Studies, Johannesburg

MSNH, Mémoires de la Société Néophilologique de Helsinki

MSp, Moderne Sprachen (Zeitschrift des Verbandes der österreichischen Neuphilologen)

MSS, Medieval Sermon Studies

MSSp, Münchener Studien zur Sprachwissenschaft, Munich

MSUB, Moscow State University Bulletin, series 9, philology

MTCGT, Methuen's Twentieth-Century German Texts, London, Methuen

MTG, Mitteilungen zur Theatergeschichte der Goethezeit, Bonn, Bouvier

MTNF, Monographien und Texte zur Nietzsche-Forschung, Berlin — New York, de Gruyter

MTU, Münchener Texte und Untersuchungen zur deutschen Literatur des Mittelalters, Tübingen, Niemeyer

MTUB, Mitteilungen der T. U. Braunschweig

MUP, Manchester University Press

MusL, Music and Letters

MusP, Museum Patavinum

MyQ, Mystics Quarterly

NA, Nuova Antologia

NAFMUM, Nuovi Annali della Facoltà di Magistero dell'Università di Messina

NAJWS, North American Journal of Welsh Studies

NArg, Nuovi Argomenti

NAS, Nouveaux Actes Sémiotiques, PULIM, Université de Limoges

NASNCGL, North American Studies in Nineteenth-Century German Literature, Berne, Lang

NASSAB, Nuovi Annali della Scuola Speciale per Archivisti e Bibliotecari

NAWG, Nachrichten der Akademie der Wissenschaften zu Göttingen, phil.-hist. Kl., Göttingen, Vandenhoeck & Ruprecht

NBGF, Neue Beiträge zur George-Forschung

NC, New Criterion

NCA, Nouveaux Cahiers d'Allemand

NCEFRW, Nouvelles du Centre d'études francoprovençales 'René Willien'

NCF, Nineteenth-Century Fiction

NCFS, Nineteenth-Century French Studies

NCL, Notes on Contemporary Literature

NCo, New Comparison

NCSRLL, North Carolina Studies in the Romance Languages and Literatures, Chapel Hill

ND, Наукова думка

NDH, Neue deutsche Hefte

NdJb, Niederdeutsches Jahrbuch

NDL, Nachdrucke deutscher Literatur des 17. Jahrhunderts, Berne, Lang

NDL, Neue deutsche Literatur

NdS, Niederdeutsche Studien, Cologne, Böhlau

NDSK, Nydanske Studier og almen kommunikationsteori

NdW, Niederdeutsches Wort

NE, Nueva Estafeta

NEL, Nouvelles Éditions Latines,
 Paris
NFF, Novel: A Forum in Fiction
NFS, Nottingham French Studies
NFT, Német Filológiai
 Tanulmányok. Arbeiten zur
 deutschen Philologie
NG, Nevasimaia Gazeta
NG, Nordistica Gothoburgensia
NGC, New German Critique
NGFH, Die Neue Gesellschaft/
 Frankfurter Hefte
NGR, New German Review
NGS, New German Studies, Hull
NH, Nuevo Hispanismo
NHi, Nice Historique
NHLS, North Holland Linguistic
 Series, Amsterdam
NHVKSG, Neujahrsblatt des
 Historischen Vereins des Kantons
 St Gallen
NI, Наука и изкуство
NIJRS, New International Journal
 of Romanian Studies
NIMLA, NIMLA. Journal of the
 Modern Language Association of
 Northern Ireland
NJ, Naš jezik
NJb, Neulateinisches Jahrbuch
NJL, Nordic Journal of Linguistics
NKT, Norske klassiker-tekster,
 Bergen, Eide
NL, Nouvelles Littéraires
NLÅ, Norsk Litterær Årbok
NLD, Nuove Letture Dantesche
NLe, Nuove Lettere
NLH, New Literary History
NLi, Notre Librairie
NLLT, Natural Language and
 Linguistic Theory
NLN, Neo-Latin News
NLO, Novoe Literaturnoe obozrenie
NLT, Norsk Lingvistisk Tidsskrift
NLWJ, National Library of Wales
 Journal
NM, Народна младеж
NMi, Neuphilologische
 Mitteilungen
NMS, Nottingham Medieval Studies
NN, Наше наследие
NNH, Nueva Narrativa Hispano-
 americana
NNR, New Novel Review
NOR, New Orleans Review

NORNA, Nordiska
 samarbetskommittén för
 namnforskning, Uppsala
NovE, Novos Estudos (CEBRAP)
NovM, Новый мир
NovR, Nova Renascenza
NOWELE, North-Western
 European Language Evolution.
 Nowele
NP, Народна просвета
NP, Nouvello de Prouvènço (Li),
 Avignon, Parlaren Païs
 d'Avignoun
NQ, Notes and Queries
NR, New Review
NŘ, Naše řeč
NRE, Nuova Rivista Europea
NRe, New Readings, School of
 European Studies, University of
 Wales, College of Cardiff
NRF, Nouvelle Revue Française
NRFH, Nueva Revista de Filología
 Hispánica
NRL, Neue russische Literatur.
 Almanach, Salzburg
NRLett, Nouvelles de la République
 des Lettres
NRLI, Nuova Rivista di Letteratura
 Italiana
NRMI, Nuova Rivista Musicale
 Italiana
NRO, Nouvelle Revue
 d'Onomastique
NRP, Nouvelle Revue de
 Psychanalyse
NRS, Nuova Rivista Storica
NRSS, Nouvelle Revue du Seizième
 Siècle
NRu, Die Neue Rundschau
NS, Die Neueren Sprachen
NSc, New Scholar
NSh, Начальная школа
NSL, Det Norske Språk- og
 Litteraturselskap
NSlg, Neue Sammlung
NSo, Наш современник . . .
 Альманах
NSP, Nuovi Studi Politici
NSS, Nysvenska Studier
NSt, Naše stvaranje
NT, Навука і тэхніка
NT, Nordisk Tidskrift
NTBB, Nordisk Tidskrift för Bok-
 och Biblioteksväsen

NTC, Nuevo Texto Crítico

NTE, Народна творчість та етнографія

NTg, Nieuwe Taalgids

NTQ, New Theatre Quarterly

NTSh, Наукове товариство ім. Шевченка

NTW, News from the Top of the World: Norwegian Literature Today

NU, Narodna umjetnost

NV, Новое время

NVS, New Vico Studies

NWIG, Niewe West-Indische Gids

NyS, Nydanske Studier/Almen Kommunikationsteori

NYSNDL, New Yorker Studien zur neueren deutschen Literaturgeschichte, Berne, Lang

NYUOS, New York University Ottendorfer Series, Berne, Lang

NZh, Новый журнал

NZh (StP), Новый журнал, St Petersburg

NZJFS, New Zealand Journal of French Studies

NZSJ, New Zealand Slavonic Journal

OA, Отечественные архивы

OB, Ord och Bild

OBS, Osnabrücker Beiträge zur Sprachtheorie, Oldenbourg, OBST

OBTUP, Universitetsforlaget Oslo–Bergen–Tromsø

ÖBV, Österreichischer Bundesverlag, Vienna

OC, Œuvres et Critiques

OcL, Oceanic Linguistics

Oc(N), Oc, Nice

OCP, Orientalia Christiana Periodica, Rome

OCS, Occitan/Catalan Studies

ÖGL, Österreich in Geschichte und Literatur

OGS, Oxford German Studies

OH, Ottawa Hispánica

OIU, Oldenbourg Interpretationen mit Unterrichtshilfen, Munich, Oldenbourg

OL, Orbis Litterarum

OLR, Oxford Literary Review

OLSI, Osservatorio Linguistico della Svizzera italiana

OM, L'Oc Médiéval

ON, Otto/Novecento

ONS, Obshchestvennye Nauki i Sovremennost'

OPBS, Occasional Papers in Belarusian Studies

OPEN, Oficyna Polska Encyklopedia Nezależna

OPI, Overseas Publications Interchange, London

OPL, Osservatore Politico Letterario

OPM, 'Ou Païs Mentounasc': Bulletin de la Société d'Art et d'Histoire du Mentonnais, Menton

OPRPNZ, Общество по распространению политических и научных знаний

OPSLL, Occasional Papers in Slavic Languages and Literatures

OR, Odrodzenie i Reformacja w Polsce

ORP, Oriental Research Partners, Cambridge

OS, 'Oc Sulpic': Bulletin de l'Association Occitane du Québec, Montreal

OSP, Oxford Slavonic Papers

OSUWPL, Ohio State University Working Papers in Linguistics

OT, Oral Tradition

OTS, Onderzoeksinstituut voor Taal en Spraak, Utrecht

OUP, Oxford University Press

OUSL, Odense University Studies in Literature

OUSSLL, Odense University Studies in Scandinavian Languages and Literatures, Odense U.P.

OWPLC, Odense Working Papers in Language and Communication

PA, Présence Africaine

PAc, Primer Acto

PAf, Politique Africaine

PAGS, Proceedings of the Australian Goethe Society

Pal, Palaeobulgarica —
Старобългаристика
PAM, Publicacions de l'Abadia de
Montserrat, Barcelona
PAN, Polska Akademia Nauk,
Warsaw
PaP, Past and Present
PapBSA, Papers of the
Bibliographical Society of
America
PAPhS, Proceedings of the American
Philosophical Society
PapL, Papiere zur Linguistik
ParL, Paragone Letteratura
Parlem!, Parlem! Vai-i, qu'as paur!
(IEO-Auvergne)
PartR, Partisan Review
PaS, Pamiętnik Słowiański
PASJ, Pictish Arts Society Journal
PaT, La Parola del Testo
PAX, Instytut Wydawniczy PAX,
Warsaw
PB, Д-р Петър Берон
PBA, Proceedings of the British
Academy
PBib, Philosophische Bibliothek,
Hamburg, Meiner
PBLS, Proceedings of the Annual
Meeting of the Berkeley
Linguistic Society
PBML, Prague Bulletin of
Mathematical Linguistics
PBSA, Publications of the
Bibliographical Society of
America
PC, Problems of Communism
PCLS, Proceedings of the Chicago
Linguistic Society
PCP, Pacific Coast Philology
PD, Probleme der Dichtung,
Heidelberg, Winter
PDA, Pagine della Dante
PdO, Paraula d'oc, Centre
International de Recerca i
Documentació d'Oc, Valencia
PE, Poesía Española
PEGS(NS), Publications of the
English Goethe Society (New
Series)
PenP, Il Pensiero Politico
PENS, Presses de l'École Normale
Supérieure, Paris
PerM, Perspectives Médiévales
PEs, Lou Prouvençau à l'Escolo

PF, Présences Francophones
PFil, Prace Filologiczne
PFPS, Z problemów frazeologii
polskiej i słowiańskiej, ZNiO
PFSCL, Papers on French
Seventeenth Century Literature
PG, Païs gascons
PGA, Lo pais gascon/Lou pais
gascoun, Anglet
PGIG, Publikationen der
Gesellschaft für interkulturelle
Germanistik, Munich, Iudicium
PH, La Palabra y El Hombre
PhilosQ, Philosophical Quarterly
PhilP, Philological Papers, West
Virginia University
PhilR, Philosophy and Rhetoric
PhilRev, Philosophical Review
PhLC, Phréatique, Langage et
Création
PHol, Le Pauvre Holterling
PhonPr, Phonetica Pragensia
PhP, Philologica Pragensia
PhR, Phoenix Review
PHSL, Proceedings of the Huguenot
Society of London
PI, педагогический институт
PId, Le Parole e le Idee
PIGS, Publications of the Institute
of Germanic Studies, University
of London
PiH, Il Piccolo Hans
PIMA, Proceedings of the Illinois
Medieval Association
PIMS, Publications of the Institute
for Medieval Studies, Toronto
PIW, Państwowy Instytut
Wydawniczy, Warsaw
PJ, Poradnik Językowy
PLing, Papers in Linguistics
PLit, Philosophy and Literature
PLL, Papers on Language and
Literature
PL(L), Pamiętnik Literacki, London
PLRL, Patio de Letras/La Rosa als
Llavis
PLS, Přednášky z běhu Letní školy
slovanských studií
PL(W), Pamiętnik Literacki,
Warsaw
PM, Pleine Marge
PMH, Portugaliae Monumenta
Historica

PMHRS, Papers of the Medieval
Hispanic Research Seminar,
London, Department of Hispanic
Studies, Queen Mary and
Westfield College
PMLA, Publications of the Modern
Language Association of America
PMPA, Publications of the Missouri
Philological Association
PN, Paraulas de novelum, Périgueux
PNCIP, Plurilinguismo. Notizario
del Centro Internazionale sul
Plurilinguismo
PNR, Poetry and Nation Review
PNUS, Prace Naukowe
Uniwersytetu Śląskiego,
Katowice
PoetT, Poetics Today
PolR, Polish Review
PortSt, Portuguese Studies
PP, Prace Polonistyczne
PPNCFL, Proceedings of the Pacific
Northwest Conference on
Foreign Languages
PPr, Papers in Pragmatics
PPU, Promociones y Publicaciones
Universitarias, S.A., Barcelona
PQ, The Philological Quarterly
PR, Podravska Revija
PrA, Prouvenço aro, Marseilles
PraRu, Prace Rusycystyczne
PRev, Poetry Review
PRF, Publications Romanes et
Françaises, Geneva, Droz
PRH, Pahl-Rugenstein
Hochschulschriften, Cologne,
Pahl–Rugenstein
PrH, Provence Historique
PrHlit, Prace Historycznoliterackie
PrHum, Prace Humanistyczne
PRIA, Proceedings of the Royal
Irish Academy
PrIJP, Prace Instytutu Języka
Polskiego
Prilozi, Prilozi za književnost, jezik,
istoriju i folklor, Belgrade
PrilPJ, Prilozi proučavanju jezika
PRIS-MA, Bulletin de liaison de
l'ERLIMA, Université de Poitiers
PrLit, Prace Literackie
PRom, Papers in Romance
PrRu, Przegląd Rusycystyczny
PrzH, Przegląd Humanistyczny
PrzW, Przegląd Wschodni

PS, Проблеми слов'янознавства
PSCL, Papers and Studies in
Contrastive Linguistics
PSE, Prague Studies in English
PSGAS, Politics and Society in
Germany, Austria and
Switzerland
PSLu, Pagine Storiche Luganesi
PSML, Prague Studies in
Mathematical Linguistics
PSQ, Philologische Studien und
Quellen, Berlin, Schmidt
PSR, Portuguese Studies Review
PSRL, Полное собрание русских
летописей
PSS, Z polskich studiów
slawistycznych, Warsaw, PWN
PSSLSAA, Procès-verbaux des
séances de la Société des Lettres,
Sciences et Arts de l'Aveyron
PSV, Polono-Slavica Varsoviensia
PT, Pamiętnik Teatralny
PUC, Pontifícia Universidade
Católica, São Paulo
PUCRS, Pontífica Universidade
Católica de Rio Grande do Sul,
Porto Alegre
PUE, Publications Universitaires,
Européennes,
NY–Berne–Frankfurt, Lang
PUF, Presses Universitaires de
France, Paris
PUG Pontificia Università
Gregoriana
PUMRL, Purdue University
Monographs in Romance
Languages, Amsterdam —
Philadelphia, Benjamins
PUStE, Publications de l'Université
de St Étienne
PW, Poetry Wales
PWN, Państwowe Wydawnictwo
Naukowe, Warsaw, etc

QA, Quaderni de Archivio
QALT, Quaderni dell'Atlante
Lessicale Toscano
QASIS, Quaderni di lavoro
dell'ASIS (Atlante Sintattico
dell'Italia Settentrionale), Centro
di Studio per la Dialettologia
Italiana 'O. Parlangèli',
Università degli Studi di Padova

QCFLP, Quaderni del Circolo Filologico Linguistico Padovano
QDLC, Quaderni del Dipartimento di Linguistica, Università della Calabria
QDLF, Quaderni del Dipartimento di Linguistica, Università degli Studi, Firenze
QDLLSMG, Quaderni del Dipartimento di Lingue e Letterature Straniere Moderne, Università di Genova
QDSL, Quellen zur deutschen Sprach- und Literaturgeschichte, Heidelberg, Winter
QFCC, Quaderni della Fondazione Camillo Caetani, Rome
QFESM, Quellen und Forschungen zur Erbauungsliteratur des späten Mittelalters und der frühen Neuzeit, Amsterdam, Rodopi
QFGB, Quaderni di Filologia Germanica della Facoltà di Lettere e Filosofia dell'Università di Bologna
QFIAB, Quellen und Forschungen aus italienischen Archiven und Bibliotheken
QFLK, Quellen und Forschungen zur Literatur- und Kulturgeschichte, Berlin, de Gruyter
QFLR, Quaderni di Filologia e Lingua Romanze, Università di Macerata
QFRB, Quaderni di Filologia Romanza della Facoltà di Lettere e Filosofia dell'Università di Bologna
QFSK, Quellen und Forschungen zur Sprach- und Kulturgeschichte der germanischen Völker, Berlin, de Gruyter
QI, Quaderni d'Italianistica
QIA, Quaderni Ibero-Americani
QIGC, Quaderni dell'Istituto di Glottologia, Università degli Studi 'G. D'Annunzio' di Chieti, Facoltà di Lettere e Filosofia
QIICM, Quaderni dell'Istituto Italiano de Cultura, Melbourne
QILLSB, Quaderni dell'Istituto di Lingue e Letterature Straniere

della Facoltà di Magistero dell'Università degli Studi di Bari
QILUU, Quaderni dell'Istituto di Linguistica dell'Università di Urbino
QINSRM, Quaderni dell'Istituto Nazionale di Studi sul Rinascimento Meridionale
QJMFL, A Quarterly Journal in Modern Foreign Literatures
QJS, Quarterly Journal of Speech, Speech Association of America
QLII, Quaderni di Letterature Iberiche e Iberoamericane
QLL, Quaderni di Lingue e Letterature, Verona
QLLP, Quaderni del Laboratorio di Linguistica, Scuola Normale Superiore, Pisa
QLLSP, Quaderni di Lingua e Letteratura Straniere, Facoltà di Magistero, Università degli Studi di Palermo
QLO, Quasèrns de Lingüistica Occitana
QM, Quaderni Milanesi
QMed, Quaderni Medievali
QP, Quaderns de Ponent
QPet, Quaderni Petrarcheschi
QPL, Quaderni Patavini di Linguistica
QQ, Queen's Quarterly, Kingston, Ontario
QR, Quercy Recherche, Cahors
QRCDLIM, Quaderni di Ricerca, Centro di Dialettologia e Linguistica Italiana di Manchester
QRP, Quaderni di Retorica e Poetica
QS, Quaderni di Semantica
QSF, Quaderni del Seicento Francese
QSGLL, Queensland Studies in German Language and Literature, Berne, Francke
QSt, Quaderni Storici
QStef, Quaderni Stefaniani
QSUP, Quaderni per la Storia dell'Università di Padova
QT, Quaderni di Teatro
QuF, Québec français
QuS, Quebec Studies
QV, Quaderni del Vittoriale

QVen, Quaderni Veneti
QVer, Quaderni Veronesi di
  Filologia, Lingua e Letteratura
  Italiana
QVR, Quo vadis Romania?, Vienna

RA, Romanistische Arbeitshefte,
  Tübingen, Niemeyer
RA, Revista Agustiniana
RAA, Rendiconti dell'Accademia di
  Archeologia, Lettere e Belle Arti
RABM, Revista de Archivos,
  Bibliotecas y Museos
RAct, Regards sur l'Actualité
Rad, Rad Jugoslavenske akademije
  znanosti i umjetnosti
RAE, Real Academia Española
RAfL, Research in African
  Literatures
RAG, Real Academia Galega
RAL, Revista Argentina de
  Lingüística
RAN, Regards sur l'Afrique du Nord
RANL, Rendiconti dell'Accademia
  Nazionale dei Lincei, Classe di
  scienze morali, storiche e
  filologiche, serie IX
RANPOLL, Revista ANPOLL,
  Faculdade de Filosofia, Letras e
  Ciências Humanas, Univ. de São
  Paulo.
RAPL, Revista da Academia
  Paulista de Letras, São Paulo
RAR, Renaissance and Reformation
RAS, Rassegna degli Archivi di
  Stato
RASoc, Revista de Antropología
  Social
RB, Revue Bénédictine
RBC, Research Bibliographies and
  Checklists, London, Grant &
  Cutler
RBDSL, Regensburger Beiträge zur
  deutschen Sprach- und
  Literaturwissenschaft, Frankfurt–
  Berne, Lang
RBG, Reclams de Bearn et
  Gasconha
RBGd, Rocznik Biblioteki Gdańskiej
  PAN (Libri Gedanenses)
RBKr, Rocznik Biblioteki PAN w
  Krakowie

RBL, Revista Brasileira de
  Lingüística
RBLL, Revista Brasileira de Lingua
  e Literatura
RBN, Revista da Biblioteca
  Nacional
RBPH, Revue Belge de Philologie et
  d'Histoire
RBS, Rostocker Beiträge zur
  Sprachwissenschaft
RC, Le Ragioni Critiche
RCat, Revista de Catalunya
RČAV, Rozpravy Československé
  akademie věd, Prague, ČSAV
RCB, Revista de Cultura Brasileña
RCCM, Rivista di Cultura Classica e
  Medioevale
RCEH, Revista Canadiense de
  Estudios Hispánicos
RCEN, Revue Canadienne d'Études
  Néerlandaises
RCF, Review of Contemporary
  Fiction
RCL, Revista Chilena de Literatura
RCLL, Revista de Crítica Literaria
  Latino-Americana
RCo, Revue de Comminges
RCSF, Rivista Critica di Storia della
  Filosofia
RCVS, Rassegna di Cultura e Vita
  Scolastica
RD, Revue drômoise: archéologie,
  histoire, géographie
RDE, Recherches sur Diderot et sur
  l''Encyclopédie'
RDM, Revue des Deux Mondes
RDsS, Recherches sur le XVIIe
  Siècle
RDTP, Revista de Dialectología y
  Tradiciones Populares
RE, Revista de Espiritualidad
REC, Revista de Estudios del Caribe
RECat, Revue d'Études Catalanes
RedLet, Red Letters
REE, Revista de Estudios
  Extremeños
REEI, Revista del Instituto Egipcio
  de Estudios Islámicos, Madrid
REH, Revista de Estudios
  Hispánicos, Washington
  University, St Louis
REHisp, Revista de Estudios
  Hispánicos, Puerto Rico
REI, Revue des Études Italiennes

REJ, Revista de Estudios de
Juventud
REJui, Revue des Études Juives,
Paris
REL, Revue des Études Latines
RELA, Revista Española de
Lingüística Aplicada
RelCL, Religion in Communist
Lands
RELI, Rassegna Europea di
Letteratura Italiana
RELing, Revista Española de
Lingüística, Madrid
RelLit, Religious Literature
ReMS, Renaissance and Modern
Studies
RenD, Renaissance Drama
RenP, Renaissance Papers
RenR, Renaissance and Reformation
RenS, Renaissance Studies
RER, Revista de Estudios
Rosalianos
RES, Review of English Studies
RESEE, Revue des Études Sud-Est
Européennes
RESS, Revue Européenne des
Sciences Sociales et Cahiers
Vilfredo Pareto
RevA, Revue d'Allemagne
RevAl, Revista de l'Alguer
RevAR, Revue des Amis de Ronsard
RevAuv, Revue d'Auvergne,
Clermont-Ferrand
RevEL, Revista de Estudos da
Linguagem, Faculdade de Letras,
Universidade Federal de Minas
Gerais
RevF, Revista de Filología
RevHA, Revue de la Haute-
Auvergne
RevG, Revista de Girona
RevIb, Revista Iberoamericana
RevL, Revista Lusitana
RevLex, Revista de Lexicografía
RevLM, Revista de Literatura
Medieval
RevLR, Revista do Livro
RevO, La Revista occitana,
Montpellier
RevP, Revue Parole, Université de
Mons-Hainault
RevPF, Revista Portuguesa de
Filosofia
RevR, Revue Romane

RF, Romanische Forschungen
RFE, Revista de Filología Española
RFe, Razón y Fe
RFHL, Revue Française d'Histoire
du Livre
RFLI, Rivista di Filologia e
Letterature Ispaniche
RFLSJ, Revista de Filosofía y
Lingüística de San José, Costa
Rica
RFLUL, Revista da Faculdade de
Letras da Universidade de Lisboa
RFLUP, Línguas e Literaturas,
Revista da Faculdade de Letras,
Univ. do Porto
RFN, Rivisti di Filosofia
Neoscolastica
RFo, Ricerca Folklorica
RFP, Recherches sur le Français
Parlé
RFR, Revista de Filología Románica
RFr, Revue Frontenac
RG, Recherches Germaniques
RGand, Romanica Gandensia
RGCC, Revue du Gévaudan, des
Causses et des Cévennes
RGG, Rivista di Grammatica
Generativa
RGI, Revue Germanique
Internationale
RGL, Reihe Germanistische
Linguistik, Tübingen, Niemeyer
RGo, Romanica Gothoburgensia
RGT, Revista Galega de Teatro
RH, Reihe Hanser, Munich,
Hanser
RH, Revue Hebdomadaire
RHA, Revista de Historia de
America
RHAM, Revue Historique et
Archéologique du Maine
RHCS, Rocznik Historii
Czasopiśmiennictwa Polskiego
RHDFE, Revue Historique de Droit
Français et Étranger
RHE, Revue d'Histoire
Ecclésiastique
RHEF, Revue d'Histoire de l'Église
de France
RHel, Romanica Helvetica,
Tübingen and Basle, Francke
RHFB, Rapports — Het Franse
Boek
RHI, Revista da Historia das Ideias

RHis, Revue Historique
RHL, Reihe Hanser
Literaturkommentare, Munich,
Hanser
RHLF, Revue d'Histoire Littéraire
de la France
RHLP, Revista de História Literária
de Portugal
RHM, Revista Hispánica Moderna
RHMag, Revue d'Histoire
Maghrébine
RHMC, Revue d'Histoire Moderne
et Contemporaine
RHPR, Revue d'Histoire et de
Philosophie Religieuses
RHR, Réforme, Humanisme,
Renaissance
RHRel, Revue de l'Histoire des
Religions
RHS, Revue Historique de la
Spiritualité
RHSc, Revue d'Histoire des
Sciences
RHSt, Ricarda Huch. Studien zu
ihrem Leben und Werk
RHT, Revue d'Histoire du Théâtre
RHTe, Revue d'Histoire des Textes
RI, Rassegna Iberistica
RIA, Rivista Italiana di Acustica
RIa, Русский язык
RIAB, Revista Interamericana de
Bibliografía
RIaR, Русский язык за рубежом
RICC, Revue Itinéraires et Contacts
de Culture
RICP, Revista del Instituto de
Cultura Puertorriqueña
RicSl, Ricerche Slavistiche
RID, Rivista Italiana di
Dialettologia
RIE, Revista de Ideas Estéticas
RIEB, Revista do Instituto de
Estudos Brasileiros
RIL, Rendiconti dell'Istituto
Lombardo
RILA, Rassegna Italiana di
Linguistica Applicata
RILCE, Revista del Instituto de
Lengua y Cultura Españoles
RILP, Revista Internacional da
Língua Portuguesa
RIM, Rivista Italiana di Musicologia
RIndM, Revista de Indias
RInv, Revista de Investigación

RIO, Revue Internationale
d'Onomastique
RIOn, Rivista Italiana di
Onomastica
RIP, Revue Internationale de
Philosophie
RIS, Revue de l'Institute de
Sociologie, Université Libre,
Brussels
RiS, Ricerche Storiche
RITL, Revista de Istorie și Teorie
Literară, Bucharest
RivF, Rivista di Filosofia
RivL, Rivista di Linguistica
RJ, Romanistisches Jahrbuch
RKHlit, Rocznik Komisji
Historycznoliterackiej PAN
RKJŁ, Rozprawy Komisji Językowej
Łódzkiego Towarzystwa
Naukowego
RKJW, Rozprawy Komisji
Językowej Wrocławskiego
Towarzystwa Naukowego
RLA, Romance Languages Annual
RLaR, Revue des Langues Romanes
RLB, Recueil Linguistique de
Bratislava
RLC, Revue de Littérature
Comparée
RLD, Revista de Llengua i Dret
RLet, Revista de Letras
RLettI, Rivista di Letteratura
Italiana
RLex, Revista de Lexicología
RLF, Revista de Literatura
Fantástica
RLFRU, Recherches de Linguistique
Française et Romane d'Utrecht
RLH, Revista de Literatura
Hispanoamericana
RLI, Rassegna della Letteratura
Italiana
RLib, Rivista dei Libri
RLing, Russian Linguistics
RLiR, Revue de Linguistique
Romane
RLit, Revista de Literatura
RLJ, Russian Language Journal
RLLCGV, Revista de Lengua y
Literatura Catalana, Gallega y
Vasca, Madrid
RLLR, Romance Literature and
Linguistics Review

RLM, Revista de Literaturas
Modernas, Cuyo
RLMC, Rivista di Letterature
Moderne e Comparate
RLMed, Revista de Literatura
Medieval
RLMexC, Revista de Literatura
Mexicana Contemporánea
RLMod, Revue des Lettres
Modernes
RLModCB, Revue des Lettres
Modernes. Carnets
Bibliographiques
RLSer, Revista de Literatura Ser,
Puerto Rico
RLSL, Revista de Lingvistică şi
Ştiinţă Literară
RLT, Russian Literature
Triquarterly
RLTA, Revista de Lingüística
Teórica y Aplicada
RLV, Revue des Langues Vivantes
RLVin, Recherches Linguistiques de
Vincennes
RM, Romance Monograph Series,
University, Mississippi
RM, Remate de Males
RMAL, Revue du Moyen Âge Latin
RMar, Revue Marivaux
RMC, Roma Moderna e
Contemporanea
RMEH, Revista Marroquí de
Estudios Hispánicos
RMH, Recherches sur le Monde
Hispanique au XIXe Siècle
RMI, Rivista Musicale Italiana
RMM, Revue de Métaphysique et
de Morale
RMon, Revue Montesquieu
RMRLL, Rocky Mountain Review
of Language and Literature
RMS, Reading Medieval Studies
RMus, Revue de Musicologie
RNC, Revista Nacional de Cultura,
Carácas
RNDWSPK, Rocznik Naukowo-
Dydaktyczny WSP w Krakowie
RO, Revista de Occidente
RoczH, Roczniki Humanistyczne
Katolickiego Uniw. Lubelskiego
RoczSl, Rocznik Slawistyczny
ROl, Rossica Olomucensia
RoM, Rowohlts Monographien,
Reinbek, Rowohlt

RomGG, Romanistik in Geschichte
und Gegenwart
ROMM, Revue de L'Occident
Musulman et de la Méditerranée
RoN, Romance Notes
RoQ, Romance Quarterly
RORD, Research Opportunities in
Renaissance Drama
RoS, Romance Studies
RoSl, Роднае слова
RP, Радянський письменник
RP, Revista de Portugal
RPA, Revue de Phonétique
Appliquée
RPac, Revue du Pacifique
RPC, Revue Pédagogique et
Culturelle de l'AVEP
RPF, Revista Portuguesa de
Filologia
RPFE, Revue Philosophique de la
France et de l'Étranger
RPh, Romance Philology
RPL, Revue Philosophique de
Louvain
RPl, Río de la Plata
RPLit, Res Publica Litterarum
RPM, Revista de Poética Medieval
RPN, Res Publica nowa, Warsaw
RPol, Review of Politics
RPP, Romanticism Past and Present
RPr, Raison Présente
RPS, Revista Paraguaya de
Sociologia
RPyr, Recherches pyrénéennes,
Toulouse
RQ, Renaissance Quarterly
RQL, Revue Québécoise de
Linguistique
RR, Romanic Review
RRe, Русская речь
RRL, Revue Roumaine de
Linguistique
RRou, Revue du Rouergue
RRR, Reformation and Renaissance
Review
RS, Reihe Siegen, Heidelberg,
Winter
RS, Revue de Synthèse
RSBA, Revista de studii britanice şi
americane
RSC, Rivista di Studi Canadesi
RSCI, Rivista di Storia della Chiesa
in Italia

RSEAV, Revue de la Société des enfants et amis de Villeneuve-de-Berg

RSF, Rivista di Storia della Filosofia

RSH, Revue des Sciences Humaines

RSh, Радянська школа

RSI, Rivista Storica Italiana

RSJb, Reinhold Schneider Jahrbuch

RSL, Rusycystyczne Studia Literaturoznawcze

RSl, Revue des Études Slaves

RSLR, Rivista di Storia e Letteratura Religiose

RSPT, Revue des Sciences Philosophiques et Théologiques

RSR, Rassegna Storica del Risorgimento

RSSR, Rivista di Storia Sociale e Religiosa

RST, Rassegna Storica Toscana

RSt, Research Studies

RStI, Rivista di Studi Italiani

RT, Revue du Tarn

RTAM, Recherches de Théologie Ancienne et Médiévale

RTLiM, Rocznik Towarzystwa Literackiego im. Adama Mickiewicza

RTr, Recherches et Travaux, Université de Grenoble

RTUG, Recherches et Travaux de l'Université de Grenoble III

RUB, Revue de l'Université de Bruxelles

RUC, Revista de la Universidad Complutense

RuLit, Ruch Literacki

RUM, Revista de la Universidad de Madrid

RUMex, Revista de la Universidad de México

RUOt, Revue de l'Université d'Ottawa

RUS, Rice University Studies

RusH, Russian History

RusL, Русская литература, ПД, Leningrad

RusM, Русская мысль

RusMed, Russia Medievalis

RusR, Russian Review

RUW, Rozprawy Uniwersytetu Warsawskiego, Warsaw

RV, Revue Voltaire

RVB, Rheinische Vierteljahrsblätter

RVF, Revista Valenciana de Filología

RVi, Revue du Vivarais

RVQ, Romanica Vulgaria Quaderni

RVV, Romanische Versuche und Vorarbeiten, Bonn U.P.

RVVig, Reihe der Villa Vigoni, Tübingen, Niemeyer

RZLG, Romanistische Zeitschrift für Literaturgeschichte

RZSF, Radovi Zavoda za slavensku filologiju

SA, Studien zum Althochdeutschen, Göttingen, Vandenhoeck & Ruprecht

SAB, South Atlantic Bulletin

Sac, Sacris Erudiri

SAG, Stuttgarter Arbeiten zur Germanistik, Stuttgart, Heinz

SAH, Studies in American Humour

SANU, Srpska akademija nauka i umetnosti

SAOB, Svenska Akademiens Ordbok

SAQ, South Atlantic Quarterly

SAR, South Atlantic Review

SAS, Studia Academica Slovaca

SaS, Slovo a slovesnost

SASc, Studia Anthroponymica Scandinavica

SATF, Société des Anciens Textes Français

SAV, Slovenská akadémia vied

SAVL, Studien zur allgemeinen und vergleichenden Literaturwissenschaft, Stuttgart, Metzler

SB, Slavistische Beiträge, Munich, Sagner

SB, Studies in Bibliography

SBAW, Sitzungsberichte der Bayerischen Akad. der Wissenschaften, phil-hist. Kl., Munich, Beck

SBL, Saarbrücker Beiträge zur Literaturwissenschaft, St. Ingbert, Röhrig

SBL, Старобългарска литература

SBR, Swedish Book Review

SBVS, Saga-Book of the Viking Society

SC, Studia Celtica, The Bulletin of
the Board of Celtic Studies
SCB, Skrifter utgivna av Centrum
för barnkulturforskning,
Stockholm U.P.
SCC, Studies in Comparative
Communism
SCen, The Seventeenth Century
SCES, Sixteenth Century Essays
and Studies, Kirksville, Missouri,
Sixteenth Century Journal
SCFS, Seventeenth-Century French
Studies
SchG, Schriftsteller der Gegenwart,
Berlin, Volk & Wissen
SchSch, Schlern-Schriften,
Innsbruck, Wagner
SchwM, Schweizer Monatshefte
SCJ, Sixteenth Century Journal
SCL, Studii și Cercetări Lingvistice
SCl, Stendhal Club
ScL, Scottish Language
ScM, Scripta Mediterranea
SCN, Seventeenth Century News
SCO, Studii și Cercetäri de
Onomasticä
ScO, Scriptoralia, Tübingen, Narr
ScPo, Scientia Poetica
SCR, Studies in Comparative
Religion
ScRev, Scandinavian Review
ScSl, Scando-Slavica
ScSt, Scandinavian Studies
SD, Sprache und Dichtung, n.F.,
Berne, Haupt
SD, Современная драматургия.
SdA, Storia dell'Arte
SDFU, Skrifter utgivna genom
Dialekt- och folkminnesarkivet i
Uppsala
SDG, Studien zur deutschen
Grammatik, Tübingen,
Stauffenburg
SDL, Studien zur deutschen
Literatur, Tübingen, Niemeyer
SDLNZ, Studien zur deutschen
Literatur des 19. und 20.
Jahrhunderts, Berne, Lang
SdO, Serra d'Or
SDOFU, Skrifter utgivna av
Dialekt-, ortnamns- och
folkminnesarkivet i Umeå

SDS, Studien zur Dialektologie in
Südwestdeutschland, Marburg,
Elwert
SDSp, Studien zur deutschen
Sprache, Tübingen, Narr
SDv, Sprache und
Datenverarbeitung
SE, Série Esludos Uberaba
SeC, Scrittura e Civiltà
SECC, Studies in Eighteenth-
Century Culture
SECCFC, Sociedad Estatal para la
Conmemoración de los
Centenarios de Felipe II y
Carlos V
SEDES, Société d'Éditions
d'Enseignement Supérieur
SEEA, Slavic and East European
Arts
SEEJ, The Slavic and East
European Journal
SEER, Slavonic and East European
Review
SEES, Slavic and East European
Studies
SEI, Società Editrice
Internazionale, Turin
SELA, South Eastern Latin
Americanist
SemL, Seminarios de Lingüística,
Universidade do Algarve, Faro
SEN, Società Editrice Napoletana,
Naples
SEP, Secretaría de Educación
Pública, Mexico
SeS, Serbian Studies
SEz, Съпоставително
езикознание
SF, Slavistische Forschungen,
Cologne — Vienna, Böhlau
SFAIEO, Section Française de
l'Association Internationale
d'Études Occitanes, Montpellier
SFI, Studi di Filologia Italiana
SFIS, Stanford French and Italian
Studies
SFKG, Schriftenreihe der
Franz–Kafka–Gesellschaft,
Vienna, Braumüller
SFL, Studies in French Literature,
London, Arnold
SFL, Studi di Filologia e Letteratura
SFPS, Studia z Filologii Polskiej i
Słowiańskiej PAN

SFR, Stanford French Review
SFr, Studi Francesi
SFRS, Studia z Filologii Rosyjskiej i
Slowiańskiej, Warsaw
SFS, Swiss-French Studies
SFUŠ, Sborník Filozofickej Fakulty
Univerzity P. J. Šafárika, Prešov
SG, Sprache der Gegenwart,
Düsseldorf, Schwann
SGAK, Studien zu Germanistik,
Anglistik und Komparatistik,
Bonn, Bouvier
SGECRN, Study Group on
Eighteenth-Century Russia
Newsletter
SGEL, Sociedad General Española
de Librería
SGesch, Sprache und Geschichte,
Stuttgart, Klett-Cotta
SGF, Stockholmer Germanistische
Forschungen, Stockholm,
Almqvist & Wiksell
SGG, Studia Germanica Gandensia
SGGed, Studia Germanica
Gedanensia
SGI, Studi di Grammatica Italiana
SGLL, Studies in German
Language and Literature,
Lewiston-Queenston-Lampeter
SGLLC, Studies in German
Literature, Linguistics, and
Culture, Columbia, S.C.,
Camden House, Woodbridge,
Boydell & Brewer
SGP, Studia Germanica
Posnaniensia
SGS, Stanford German Studies,
Berne, Lang
SGS, Scottish Gaelic Studies
SGU, Studia Germanistica
Upsaliensia, Stockholm, Almqvist
& Wiksell
SH, Slavica Helvetica, Berne, Lang
SH, Studia Hibernica
ShAn, Sharq al-Andalus
SHCT, Studies in the History of
Christian Thought, Leiden, Brill
SHPF, Société de l'Histoire du
Protestantisme Français
SHPS, Studies in History and
Philosophy of Science
SHR, The Scottish Historical
Review

SI, Sprache und Information,
Tübingen, Niemeyer
SIAA, Studi di Italianistica
nell'Africa Australe
SiCh, Слово і час
SIDES, Société Internationale de
Diffusion et d'Édition
Scientifiques, Antony
SIDS, Schriften des Instituts für
deutsche Sprache, Berlin, de
Gruyter
Siglo XX, Siglo XX/20th Century
SILTA, Studi Italiani di Linguistica
Teorica ed Applicata
SiN, Sin Nombre
SINSU, Skrifter utgivna av
institutionen för nordiska språk
vid Uppsala universitet, Uppsala
U.P.
SIR, Stanford Italian Review
SISMEL, Società Internazionale
per lo Studio del Medioevo
Latino, Edizioni del Galluzzo,
Florence
SIsp, Studi Ispanici
SISSD, Società Italiana di Studi sul
Secolo XVIII
SJLŠ, Slovenský jazyk a literatúra v
škole
SKHAW, Schriften der phil.-hist.
Klasse der Heidelberger
Akademie der Wissenschaften,
Heidelberg, Winter
SkSt, Skandinavistische Studien
SKZ, Srpska Književna Zadruga,
Belgrade
SL, Sammlung Luchterhand,
Darmstadt, Luchterhand
SL, Studia Linguistica
SLÅ, Svensk Lärarföreningens
Årsskrift
SlaG, Slavica Gandensia
SlaH, Slavica Helsingensia
SlaL, Slavica Lundensia
SlavFil, Славянска филология,
Sofia
SlavH, Slavica Hierosolymitana
SlavLit, Славянските литератури
в България
SlavRev, Slavistična revija
SlaW, Slavica Wratislaviensia
SLeg, Studium Legionense
SLeI, Studi di Lessicografia Italiana

SLESPO, Suplemento Literário do Estado de São Paulo
SLF, Studi di Letteratura Francese
SLG, Studia Linguistica Germanica, Berlin, de Gruyter
SLI, Società di Linguistica Italiana
SLI, Studi Linguistici Italiani
SLIGU, Skrifter utgivna av Litteraturvetenskapliga institutionen vid Göteborgs universitet, Gothenburg U.P.
SLILU, Skrifter utgivna av Litteraturvetenskapliga institutionen vid Lunds universitet, Lund U.P.
SLinI, Studi di Lingua Italiana
SLit, Schriften zur Literaturwissenschaft, Berlin, Dunckler & Humblot
SLit, Slovenská literatúra
SLitR, Stanford Literature Review
SLIUU, Skrifter utgivna av Litteraturvetenskapliga institutionen vid Uppsala universitet, Uppsala U.P.
SLK, Schwerpunkte Linguistik und Kommunikationswissenschaft
SLL, Skrifter utg. genom Landsmålsarkivet i Lund
SLM, Studien zur Literatur der Moderne, Bonn, Bouvier
SlN, Slovenský národopis
SLO, Slavica Lublinensia et Olomucensia
SlO, Slavia Orientalis
SlOc, Slavia Occidentalis
SlOth, Slavica Othinensia
SlPN, Slovenské pedagogické nakladateľstvo
SlPoh, Slovenské pohľady
SlPr, Slavica Pragensia
SLPS, Studia Linguistica Polono-Slovaca
SLR, Second Language Research
SLRev, Southern Literary Review
SLS, Studies in the Linguistic Sciences
SlSb, Slezský sborník
SlSl, Slavica Slovaca
SlSp, Slovenský spisovateľ
SLu, Studia Lulliana
SLWU, Sprach und Literatur in Wissenschaft und Unterricht

SM, Sammlung Metzler, Stuttgart, Metzler
SM, Studi Medievali
SMC, Studies in Medieval Culture
SME, Schöninghs mediävistische Editionen, Paderborn, Schöningh
SMer, Студенческий меридиан
SMGL, Studies in Modern German Literature, Berne – Frankfurt – New York, Lang
SMI, Stilistica e metrica italiana
SMLS, Strathclyde Modern Language Studies
SMRT, Studies in Medieval and Reformation Thought, Leiden, Brill
SMS, Sewanee Medieval Studies
SMu, Советский музей
SMV, Studi Mediolatini e Volgari
SN, Studia Neophilologica
SNL, Sveučilišna naklada Liber, Zagreb
SNM, Sborník Národního muzea
SNov, Seara Nova
SNTL, Státní nakladatelství technické literatury
SÖAW, Sitzungsberichte der Österreichischen Akademie der Wissenschaften, phil.-hist. Klasse
SOBI, Societat d'Onomastica, Butlleti Interior, Barcelona
SoCR, South Central Review
SOH, Studia Onomastica Helvetica, Arbon, Eurotext: Historisch-Archäologischer Verlag
SoK, Sprog og Kultur
SopL, Sophia Linguistica, Tokyo
SoRA, Southern Review, Adelaide
SoRL, Southern Review, Louisiana
SOU, Skrifter utgivna genom Ortnamnsarkivet i Uppsala
SP, Sammlung Profile, Bonn, Bouvier
SP, Studies in Philology
SPat, Studi Patavini
SpC, Speech Communication
SPCT, Studi e Problemi di Critica Testuale
SPES, Studio per Edizioni Scelte, Florence
SPFB, Sborník Pedagogické fakulty v Brně

SPFFBU, Sborník prací Filosofické fakulty Brněnské Univerzity

SPFFBU-A, Sborník prací Filosofické fakulty Brněnské Univerzity, A - řada jazykovědná

SPGS, Scottish Papers in Germanic Studies, Glasgow

SPh, Studia philologica, Olomouc

SPi, Serie Piper, Munich, Piper

SPIEL, Siegener Periodicum zur Internationalen Empirischen Literaturwissenschaft

SPK, Studia nad polszczyzną kresową, Wrocław

SpLit, Sprache und Literatur

SpMod, Spicilegio Moderno, Pisa

SPN, Státní pedagogické nakladatelství

SPol, Studia Polonistyczne

SPR, Slavistic Printings and Reprintings, The Hague, Mouton

SpR, Spunti e Ricerche

SPRF, Société de Publications Romanes et Françaises, Geneva, Droz

SPS, Specimina Philologiae Slavicae, Munich, Otto Sagner

SPS, Studia Philologica Salmanticensia

SPSO, Studia Polono–Slavica– Orientalia. Acta Litteraria

SpSt, Spanish Studies

SPUAM, Studia Polonistyczna Uniwersytetu Adama Mickiewicza, Poznań

SR, Slovenská reč

SRAZ, Studia Romanica et Anglica Zagrabiensia

SRev, Slavic Review

SRF, Studi e Ricerche Francescane

SRL, Studia Romanica et Linguistica, Frankfurt, Lang

SRLF, Saggi e Ricerche di Letteratura Francese

SRo, Studi Romanzi

SRom, Studi Romeni

SRoP, Studia Romanica Posnaniensia

SRP, Studia Rossica Posnaniensia

SRU, Studia Romanica Upsaliensia

SS, Symbolae Slavicae, Frankfurt–Berne–Cirencester, Lang

SS, Syn og Segn

SSBI, Skrifter utgivna av Svenska barnboksinstitutet

SSB, Strenna Storica Bolognese

SSCJ, Southern Speech Communication Journal

SSDSP, Società Savonese di Storia Patria

SSE, Studi di Storia dell'Educazione

SSF, Studies in Short Fiction

SSFin, Studia Slavica Finlandensia

SSGL, Studies in Slavic and General Linguistics, Amsterdam, Rodopi

SSH, Studia Slavica Academiae Scientiarum Hungaricae

SSL, Studi e Saggi Linguistici

SSLF, Skrifter utgivna av Svenska Litteratursällskapet i Finland

SSLP, Studies in Slavic Literature and Poetics, Amsterdam, Rodopi

SSLS, Studi Storici Luigi Simeoni

SSMP, Stockholm Studies in Modern Philology

SSPHS, Society for Spanish and Portuguese Historical Studies, Millersville

SSR, Scottish Studies Review

SSS, Stanford Slavic Studies

SSSAS, Society of Spanish and Spanish-American Studies, Boulder, Colorado

SSSlg, Sagners Slavistische Sammlung, Munich, Sagner

SSSN, Skrifter utgivna av Svenska språknämnden

SSSP, Stockholm Studies in Scandinavian Philology

SST, Sprache — System und Tätigkeit, Frankfurt, Lang

SSt, Slavic Studies, Hokkaido

ST, Suhrkamp Taschenbuch, Frankfurt, Suhrkamp

ST, Studi Testuali, Alessandria, Edizioni dell'Orso

StB, Studi sul Boccaccio

StBo, Studia Bohemica

STC, Studies in the Twentieth Century

StCJ, Studia Celtica Japonica

STCL, Studies in Twentieth Century Literature

StCL, Studies in Canadian Literature

STCM, Sciences, techniques et civilisations du moyen âge à l'aube des temps modernes. Paris, Champion
StCrit, Strumenti Critici
StD, Studi Danteschi
StF, Studie Francescani
StFil, Studia Filozoficzne
STFM, Société des Textes Français Modernes
StG, Studi Germanici
StGol, Studi Goldoniani
StH, Studies in the Humanities
StI, Studi Italici, Kyoto
StIt, Studi Italiani
StL, Studium Linguistik
StLa, Studies in Language, Amsterdam
StLI, Studi di Letteratura Ispano-Americana
StLi, Stauffenburg Linguistik, Tübingen, Stauffenburg
StLIt, Studi Latini e Italiani
StLM, Studies in the Literary Imagination
StLo, Studia Logica
STM, Suhrkamp Taschenbuch Materialien, Frankfurt, Suhrkamp
StM, Studies in Medievalism
STML, Studies on Themes and Motifs in Literature, New York, Lang
StMon, Studia Monastica
StMus, Studi Musicali
StMy, Studia Mystica
StN, Studi Novecenteschi
StNF, Studier i Nordisk Filologi
StO, Studium Ovetense
StP, Studi Piemontesi
StPet, Studi Petrarcheschi
StR, Studie o rukopisech
StRLLF, Studi e Ricerche di Letteratura e Linguistica Francese
StRmgn, Studi Romagnoli
StRo, Studi Romani
StRom, Studies in Romanticism
StRu, Studia Russica, Budapest
StS, Studi Storici
StSec, Studi Secenteschi
StSem, Studia Semiotyczne
StSen, Studi Senesi
StSet, Studi Settecenteschi

StSG, Schriften der Theodor-Storm-Gesellschaft, Heide in Holstein, Boyens
StSk, Studia Skandinavica
STSL, Studien und Texte zur Sozialgeschichte der Literatur, Tübingen, Niemeyer
StSp, Studies in Spirituality
StT, Studi Tassiani
STUF, Sprachtypologie und Universalienforschung
StV, Studies on Voltaire and the 18th Century
STW, Suhrkamp Taschenbücher Wissenschaft, Frankfurt, Suhrkamp
StZ, Sprache im technischen Zeitalter
SU, Studi Urbinati
SUBBP, Studia Universitatis Babeş-Bolyai, Philologia, Cluj
SUDAM, Editorial Sudamericana, Buenos Aires
SuF, Sinn und Form
SUm, Schede Umanistiche
SUP, Spisy University J. E. Purkyně, Brno
SupEz, Съпоставително езикознание, Sofia
SV, Studi Veneziani
SVEC, Studies in Voltaire and the Eighteenth Century, Oxford, Voltaire Foundation (formerly *StV*)
SZ, Studia Zamorensia

TAL, Travaux d'Archéologie Limousine, Limoges
TAm, The Americas, Bethesda
TAPS, Transactions of the American Philosophical Society
TB, Tempo Brasileiro
TBL, Tübinger Beiträge zur Linguistik, Tübingen, Narr
TC, Texto Crítico
TCBS, Transactions of the Cambridge Bibliographical Society
TCERFM, Travaux du Centre d'Études et de Recherches sur François Mauriac, Bordeaux
TCL, Twentieth-Century Literature

TCLN, Travaux du Cercle Linguistique de Nice

TCWAAS, Transactions of the Cumberland and Westmorland Antiquarian and Archaeological Society

TD, Teksty Drugie

TDC, Textes et Documents pour la Classe

TEC, Teresiunum Ephemerides Carmeliticae

TECC, Textos i Estudis de Cultura Catalana, Curial — Publicacions de l'Abadia de Montserrat, Barcelona

TeK, Text und Kontext

TELK, Trouvaillen — Editionen zur Literatur- und Kulturgeschichte, Berne, Lang

TeN, Terminologies Nouvelles

TeSt, Teatro e Storia

TE(XVIII), Textos y Estudios del Siglo XVIII

TF, Texte zur Forschung, Darmstadt, Wissenschaftliche Buchgesellschaft

TFN, Texte der Frühen Neuzeit, Frankfurt, Keip

TGLSK, Theorie und Geschichte der Literatur und der Schönen Künste, Munich, Fink

TGSI, Transactions of the Gaelic Society of Inverness

THESOC, Thesaurus Occitan

THL, Theory and History of Literature, Manchester U.P.

THM, Textos Hispánicos Modernos, Barcelona, Labor

THR, Travaux d'Humanisme et Renaissance, Geneva, Droz

THSC, Transactions of the Honourable Society of Cymmrodorion

TI, Le Texte et l'Idée

TidLit, Tidskrift för Litteraturvetenskap

TILAS, Travaux de l'Institut d'Études Latino-Américaines de l'Université de Strasbourg

TILL, Travaux de l'Institut de Linguistique de Lund

TJ, Theatre Journal

TK, Text und Kritik, Munich

TKS, Търновска книжевна школа, Sofia

TL, Theoretical Linguistics

TLF, Textes Littéraires Français, Geneva, Droz

TLit, Travaux de Littérature

TLP, Travaux de Linguistique et de Philologie

TLQ, Travaux de Linguistique Québécoise

TLTL, Teaching Language Through Literature

TM, Les Temps Modernes

TMJb, Thomas Mann-Jahrbuch

TMo, O Tempo e o Modo

TMS, Thomas-Mann Studien, Frankfurt, Klostermann

TN, Theatre Notebook

TNA, Tijdschrift voor Nederlands en Afrikaans

TNT, Towarzystwo Naukowe w Toruniu

TOc, Tèxtes Occitans, Bordeaux

TODL, Труды Отдела древнерусской литературы Института русской литературы АН СССР

TP, Textual Practice

TPa, Torre de Papel

TPS, Transactions of the Philological Society

TQ, Theatre Quarterly

TR, Телевидение и радиовещание

TravL, Travaux de Linguistique, Luxembourg

TRCTL, Texte-Revue de Critique et de Théorie Littéraire

TRI, Theatre Research International

TRISMM, Tradition — Reform — Innovation. Studien zur Modernität des Mittelalters, Frankfurt, Lang

TrK, Трезвость и культура

TrL, Travaux de Linguistique

TrLit, Translation and Literature

TRS, The Transactions of the Radnorshire Society

TS, Theatre Survey

TSC, Treballs de Sociolingüística Catalana

TSDL, Tübinger Studien zur
deutschen Literatur, Frankfurt,
Lang
TSJ, Tolstoy Studies Journal
TSL, Trierer Studien zur Literatur,
Frankfurt, Lang
TSLL, Texas Studies in Literature
and Language
TSM, Texte des späten Mittelalters
und der frühen Neuzeit, Berlin,
Schmidt
TsNTL, Tijdschrift voor
Nederlandse Taal- en
Letterkunde
TSRLL, Tulane Studies in
Romance Languages and
Literature
TsSk, Tijdschrift voor
Skandinavistiek
TsSV, Tijdschrift voor de Studie van
de Verlichting
TSWL, Tulsa Studies in Women's
Literature
TT, Tekst en Tijd, Nijmegen, Alfa
TT, Travail Théâtral
TTAS, Twayne Theatrical Arts
Series, Boston–New York
TTG, Texte und Textgeschichte,
Tübingen, Niemeyer
TTr, Terminologie et Traduction
TUGS, Texte und Untersuchungen
zur Germanistik und
Skandinavistik, Frankfurt, Lang
TVS, Theorie und Vermittlung der
Sprache, Frankfurt, Lang
TWAS, Twayne's World Authors
Series, Boston–New York
TWQ, Third World Quarterly

UAB, Universitat Autònoma de
Barcelona
UAC, Universidad de Antioquia,
Colombia
UAM, Uniwersytet Adama
Mickiewicza, Poznań
UB, Universal-Bibliothek, Stuttgart,
Reclam
UBL, Universal-Bibliothek, Leipzig,
Reclam
UCLWPL, UCL Working Papers in
Linguistics
UCPL, University of California
Publications in Linguistics

UCPMP, University of California
Publications in Modern Philology
UDL, Untersuchungen zur
deutschen Literaturgeschichte,
Tübingen, Niemeyer
UDR, University of Dayton Review
UERJ, Universidade Estadual do
Rio de Janeiro
UFPB, Universidade Federal da
Paraiba
UFRGS, Univ. Federal do Rio
Grande do Sul (Brazil)
UFRJ, Universidade Federal do Rio
de Janeiro
UFSC, Universidade Federal de
Santa Catarina
UFSM, Universidade Federal de
Santa Maria
UGE, Union Générale d'Éditions
UGFGP, University of Glasgow
French and German Publications
UL, Українське
літературознавство, Lvov U.P.
UM, Українська мова і література
в школі
UMCS, Uniwersytet Marii Curie-
Skłodowskiej, Lublin
UMov, Українське мовазнавство
UNAM, Universidad Nacional
Autónoma de Mexico
UNC, Univ. of North Carolina
UNCSGL, University of North
Carolina Studies in Germanic
Languages and Literatures,
Chapel Hill
UNED, Universidad Nacional de
Enseñanza a Distancia
UNESP, Universidade Estadual de
São Paulo
UNMH, University of Nottingham
Monographs in the Humanities
UPP, University of Pennsylvania
Press, Philadelphia
UQ, Ukrainian Quarterly
UR, Umjetnost riječi
USCFLS, University of South
Carolina French Literature Series
USFLQ, University of South Florida
Language Quarterly
USH, Umeå Studies in the
Humanities, Stockholm, Almqvist
& Wiksell International
USLL, Utah Studies in Literature
and Linguistics, Berne, Lang

USP, Universidade de São Paulo

UTB, Uni-Taschenbücher

UTET, Unione Tipografico-Editrice Torinese

UTPLF, Università di Torino, Pubblicazioni della Facoltà di Lettere e Filosofia

UTQ, University of Toronto Quarterly

UVAN, Українська Вільна Академія Наук, Winnipeg

UVK, Universitätsverlag Konstanz

UVWPL, University of Venice Working Papers in Linguistics

UWCASWC, The University of Wales Centre for Advanced Studies in Welsh and Celtic

UZLU, Ученые записки Ленинградского университета

VAM, Vergessene Autoren der Moderne, Siegen U.P.

VAS, Vorträge und Abhandlungen zur Slavistik, Giessen, Schmitz

VASSLOI, Veröffentlichungen der Abteilung für Slavische Sprachen und Literaturen des Osteuropa–Instituts (Slavistiches Seminar) an der Freien Universität Berlin

VB, Vestigia Bibliae

VBDU, Веснік Беларускага дзяржаўнага ўніверсітэта імя У. І. Леніна. Серыя IV

VCT, Les Voies de la Création Théâtrale

VDASD, Veröffentlichungen der Deutschen Akademie für Sprache und Dichtung, Darmstadt, Luchterhand

VDG, Verlag und Datenbank für Geisteswissenschaften, Weimar

VF, Вопросы философии

VGBIL, Всесоюзная государственная библиотека иностранной литературы

VH, Vida Hispánica, Wolverhampton

VHis, Verba Hispanica

VI, Военно издателство

VI, Voix et Images

VIa, Вопросы языкознания

VIN, Veröffentlichungen des Instituts für niederländische Philologie, Erftstadt, Lukassen

ViSH, Вища школа

VIst, Вопросы истории

Vit, Вітчизна

VKP, Всесоюзная книжная палата

VL, Вопросы литературы

VLet, Voz y Letras

VM, Время и мы, New York — Paris — Jerusalem

VMKA, Verslagen en Mededelingen, Koninklijke Academie voor Nederlandse Taal- en Letterkunde

VMUF, Вестник Московского университета. Серия IX, филология

VMUFil, Вестник Московского университета. Серия VII, философия

VÖAW, Verlag der Österreichischen Akademie der Wissenschaften, Vienna

Voz, Возрождение

VP, Встречи с прошлым, Moscow

VPen, Vita e Pensiero

VR, Vox Romanica

VRKhD, Вестник Русского христианского движения

VRL, Вопросы русской литературы

VRM, Volkskultur am Rhein und Maas

VS, Вопросы семантики

VSAV, Vydavateľstvo Slovenskej akadémie vied

VSh, Вышэйшая школа

VSh, Визвольний шлях

VSPU, Вестник Санкт-Петербургского университета

VSSH, Вечерняя средняя школа

VV, Византийский временник

VVM, Vlastivědný věstník moravský

VVSh, Вестник высшей школы

VWGÖ, Verband der wissenschaftlichen Gesellschaften Österreichs

VySh, Вища школа

VysSh, Высшая школа

VyV, Verdad y Vida

VZ, Vukova zadužbina, Belgrade

WAB, Wolfenbütteler Arbeiten zur
Barockforschung, Wiesbaden,
Harrassowitz
WADL, Wiener Arbeiten zur
deutschen Literatur, Vienna,
Braumüller
WAGAPH, Wiener Arbeiten zur
germanischen Altertumskunde
und Philologie, Berne, Lang
WAiF, Wydawnictwa Artystyczne i
Filmowe, Warsaw
WaT, Wagenbachs
Taschenbücherei, Berlin,
Wagenbach
WB, Weimarer Beiträge
WBDP, Würzburger Beiträge zur
deutschen Philologie, Würzburg,
Königshausen & Neumann
WBG, Wissenschaftliche
Buchgesellschaft, Darmstadt
WBN, Wolfenbütteler Barock-
Nachrichten
WBS, Welsh Book Studies
WF, Wege der Forschung,
Darmstadt, Wissenschaftliche
Buchgesellschaft
WGCR, West Georgia College
Review
WGY, Women in German Yearbook
WHNDL, Würzburger
Hochschulschriften zur neueren
Deutschen Literaturgeschichte,
Frankfurt, Lang
WHR, The Welsh History Review
WI, Word and Image
WIFS, Women in French Studies
WJMLL, Web Journal in Modern
Language Linguistics
WKJb, Wissenschaftskolleg.
Institute for Advanced Study,
Berlin. Jahrbuch
WL, Wydawnictwo Literackie,
Cracow
WŁ, Wydawnictwo Łódzkie
WLub, Wydawnictwo Lubelskie
WLT, World Literature Today
WM, Wissensliteratur im
Mittelalter, Wiesbaden, Reichert
WNB, Wolfenbütteler Notizen zur
Buchgeschichte
WNT, Wydawnictwa Naukowo-
Techniczne
WoB, Wolfenbütteler Beiträge

WoF, Wolfenbütteler Forschungen,
Wiesbaden, Harrassowitz
WP, Wiedza Powszechna, Warsaw
WPEL, Working Papers in
Educational Linguistics
WPFG, Working Papers in
Functional Grammar,
Amsterdam U.P.
WRM, Wolfenbütteler Renaissance
Mitteilungen
WS, Wort und Sinn
WSA, Wolfenbütteler Studien zur
Aufklärung, Tübingen, Niemeyer
WSiP, Wydawnictwa Szkolne i
Pedagogiczne, Warsaw
WSJ, Wiener Slavistisches Jahrbuch
WSl, Die Welt der Slaven
WSlA, Wiener Slawistischer
Almanach
WSP, Wyższa Szkoła Pedagogiczna
WSp, Word and Spirit
WSPRRNDFP, Wyższa Szkoła
Pedagogiczna w Rzeszowie.
Rocznik Naukowo-Dydaktyczny.
Filologia Polska
WSS, Wiener Studien zur
Skandinavistik
WUW, Wydawnictwo Uniwersytetu
Wrocławskiego
WuW, Welt und Wort
WW, Wirkendes Wort
WWAG, Woman Writers in the Age
of Goethe
WWE, Welsh Writing in English. A
Yearbook of Critical Essays
WZHUB, Wissenschaftliche
Zeitschrift der Humboldt-
Universität, Berlin: gesellschafts-
und sprachwissenschaftliche
Reihe
WZPHP, Wissenschaftliche
Zeitschrift der pädagogischen
Hochschule Potsdam.
Gesellschafts- und
sprachwissenschaftliche Reihe
WZUG, Wissenschaftliche
Zeitschrift der Ernst-Moritz-
Arndt- Universität Greifswald
WZUH, Wissenschaftliche
Zeitschrift der Martin-Luther-
Universität Halle-Wittenberg:
gesellschafts- und
sprachwissenschaftliche Reihe

WZUJ, Wissenschaftliche Zeitschrift der Friedrich-Schiller-Universität Jena/Thüringen: gesellschafts-und sprachwissenschaftliche Reihe

WZUL, Wissenschaftliche Zeitschrift der Karl Marx Universität Leipzig: gesellschafts-und sprachwissenschaftliche Reihe

WZUR, Wissenschaftliche Zeitschrift der Universität Rostock: gesellschafts- und sprachwissenschaftliche Reihe

YaIS, Yale Italian Studies

YB, Ysgrifau Beirniadol

YCC, Yearbook of Comparative Criticism

YCGL, Yearbook of Comparative and General Literature

YDAMEIS, Yearbook of the Dutch Association for Middle Eastern and Islamic Studies

YEEP, Yale Russian and East European Publications, New Haven, Yale Center for International and Area Studies

YES, Yearbook of English Studies

YFS, Yale French Studies

YIP, Yale Italian Poetry

YIS, Yearbook of Italian Studies

YJC, Yale Journal of Criticism

YM, Yearbook of Morphology

YPL, York Papers in Linguistics

YR, Yale Review

YSGP, Yearbook. Seminar for Germanic Philology

YSPS, The Yearbook of the Society of Pirandello Studies

YWMLS, The Year's Work in Modern Language Studies

ZÄAK, Zeitschrift für Ästhetik und allgemeine Kunstwissenschaft

ZB, Zeitschrift für Balkanologie

ZBL, Zeitschrift für bayerische Landesgeschichte

ZbS, Zbornik za slavistiku

ZCP, Zeitschrift für celtische Philologie

ZD, Zielsprache Deutsch

ZDA, Zeitschrift für deutsches Altertum und deutsche Literatur

ZDL, Zeitschrift für Dialektologie und Linguistik

ZDNÖL, Zirkular. Dokumentationsstelle für neuere österreichische Literatur

ZDP, Zeitschrift für deutsche Philologie

ZFKPhil, Zborník Filozofickej fakulty Univerzity Komenského. Philologica

ZFL, Zbornik za filologiju i lingvistiku

ZFSL, Zeitschrift für französische Sprache und Literatur

ZGB, Zagreber germanistische Beiträge

ZGer, Zeitschrift für Germanistik

ZGKS, Zeitschrift der Gesellschaft für Kanada-Studien

ZGL, Zeitschrift für germanistische Linguistik

ZGS, Zürcher germanistische Studien, Berne, Lang

ZK, Zeitschrift für Katalanistik

ZL, Zeszyty Literackie, Paris

ZMS(FL), Zbornik Matice srpske za filologiju i lingvistiku

ZMS(KJ), Zbornik Matice srpske za književnost i jezik

ZMS(Sl), Zbornik Matice srpske za slavistiku

ZNiO, Zakład Narodowy im. Ossolińskich, Wrocław

ZnS, Знание — сила

ZNTSh, Записки Наукового товариства ім. Шевченка

ZNUG, Zeszyty Naukowe Uniw. Gdańskiego, Gdańsk

ZNUJ, Zeszyty Naukowe Uniw. Jagiellońskiego, Cracow

ZNWHFR, Zeszyty Naukowe Wydziału Humanistycznego. Filologia Rosyjska

ZNWSPO, Zeszyty Naukowe Wyższej Szkoly Pedagogicznej w Opolu

ZO, Zeitschrift für Ostforschung

ZPŠSlav, Zborník Pedagogickej fakulty v Prešove Univerzity Pavla Jozefa Šafárika v Košiciach-Slavistika, Bratislava

ZR, Zadarska revija
ZRAG, Записки русской
  академической группы в США
ZRBI, Зборник радова
  бизантолошког института,
  Belgrade
ZRL, Zagadnienia Rodzajów
  Literackich
ZRP, Zeitschrift für romanische
  Philologie
ZS, Zeitschrift für
  Sprachwissenschaft
ZSJ, Zápisnik slovenského
  jazykovedca
ZSK, Ze Skarbca Kultury

ZSL, Zeitschrift für siebenbürgische
  Landeskunde
ZSl, Zeitschrift für Slawistik
ZSP, Zeitschrift für slavische
  Philologie
ZSVS, Zborník Spolku
  vojvodinských slovakistov, Novi
  Sad
ZT, Здесь и теперь
ZV, Zeitschrift für Volkskunde
ZvV, Звезда востока
ZWL, Zeitschrift für
  württembergische
  Landesgeschichte

NAME INDEX

Hamp, E. P., 585
Hampe Martínez, T., 247
Hamsun, Knut, 823–24
Han, B., 735
Handke, Peter, 674, 725, 759, 770, 773, 780
Hankins, J., 446, 448
Hanley, C., 70
Hannibal, Abraham Petrovich, 868
Hanou, A., 795
Hansen, A. B., 32
Hansen, B., 819
Hansen, Bo hr., 819
Hansen, C., 806
Hansen, D., 809
Hansen, E., 804, 805, 806, 809, 810
Hansen, J., 818
Hansen, J. A., 340
Hansen, L. H., 807
Hansen, Maurits, 824
Hansen, P. K., 813, 819, 825
Hansen, P. R., 820
Hanska, Eveline Rzewuska, Madame, 169
Hanson, K., 827
Hanssen, L., 800
Häntschel, H., 717
Häntzschel, G., 717
Häntzschel, H., 746, 750
Hanuschek, S., 763
Harano, N., 60, 67
Harbert, W., 600, 915
Härd, J. E., 599
Harder, M., 763
Hardy, B., 709
Hardy, I., 67
Harer, K., 719
Hargraves, J., 744
Hârlav, C., 555
Harm, V., 606, 608
Harmat, M., 710
Harneit, R., 125
Harney, L. D., 258
Haroche-Bouzinac, G., 147
Harper, S., 573
Harras, G., 595
Harri ap Hywel, 572
Harris, C. J., 278, 289
Harris, E., 761
Harris, J., 36, 235
Harris, N., 614, 619
Harris, S., 780
Harrison, J., 262
Harrits, F., 819
Harrow, S., 192
Harskamp, J., 716
Harsløf, O., 815, 818
Harsting, P., 12

Hart, T. E., 600
Hartebok, 790
Hartenstein, E., 746
Hartl, N., 656
Härtling, Peter, 774
Hartmann von Aue, 55, 56, 616, 617, 620, 624, 625, 629, 630–31, 632, 633, 640, 647
Hartmann, M., 668
Hartmann, P., 144
Hartmann, S., 642
Hartung, G., 737
Hartwig von Erfurt, 650
Harvalík, M., 837
Harvell, T. A., 279
Harvey, R., 200, 223
Harweg, R., 772
Hasdeu, Bogdan Petriceicu, 556
Hasenohr, G., 66, 226
Hasenpflug, K., 680
Häslein, Das, 647
Hašová, L., 834
Haspelmath, M., 21
Hass-Zumkehr, U., 595
Hassine, J., 881
Hassler, S., 777
Hasty, O. P., 869
Hasubek, P., 717
Hatcher, A. G., 64
Hattum, M. van, 797
Hatungimana, J., 29
Haubrichs, W., 620, 622, 623, 912
Hauf, A. G., 306, 309, 310
Haug, C., 698
Haug, W., 629, 632
Hauge, Alfred, 827
Hauge, Olav H., 827
Haugen, T., 828
Haupt, B., 620, 648, 913
Haupt, S., 753
Hauptmann, Carl, 746
Hauptmann, Gerhard, 659, 755
Hausbergher, M., 443
Hauschild, J.-C., 778
Hauser, P., 837
Hausmann, A., 631, 638
Hausmann, F.-R., 18
Havel, Václav, 836
Havemann, D., 725
Havercroft, B., 202
Havnevik, I., 826
Hawcroft, M., 115
Hawig, P., 751
Hawke, A., 583
Hawkins, J. A., 599
Hawkins, P. S., 383
Hawrylchak, S., 746
Haxell, N. A., 177
Hayashi, C., 92

Haycock, M., 573
Hayes, J. L., 26
Haymes, E. R., 614, 628
Head, B. F., 319
Head, T., 913
Headley, J. M., 249
Heaney, Seamus, 383, 388, 528
Hebbel, Friedrich, 698, 700, 703, 713
Hebel, Johann Peter, 682–83
Heber, K.-H., 742
Hébert, Anne, 195, 197, 200–01
Hébert, F., 199
Hébert, P., 200
Hecquet, Philippe, 139
Hedelund, L., 811
Hedeman, A., 77
Heeckeren, M. van, 753
Heede, D., 818
Heep, H., 758
Heersche, J. P. G., 793
Hegel, Georg Wilhelm Friedrich, 385, 675, 676, 824, 850
Heidegger, Martin, 520, 674, 677, 723, 735, 772, 857
Heidelberger Passionsspiel, 652
Heigel, Karl, 711
Heijermans, Herman, 799
Heil, A., 406
Heimann-Seelbach, S., 602, 631
Hein, Christoph, 774, 782
Hein, J., 405, 722, 723
Heine, Heinrich, 694, 696, 698, 699, 701, 702, 714–16, 722
Heine Taxeira, C., 746
Heinecke, G., 719
Heinemann, E. A., 52
Heinemann, P., 689
Heinen, H. P., 614
Heinesen, William, 814, 819
Heinric en Margriete van Limborch, 789
Heinrich (author of Reinhart Fuchs), 634
Heinrich von Coesfeld, 614
Heinrich von Isernia, 614
Heinrich von Morungen, 640
Heinrich von München, 648
Heinrich von Neustadt, 630, 637
Heinrich von Nördlingen, 646
Heinrich von St. Gallen, 648
Heinrich von dem Türlin, 634
Heinrich von Veldeke, 629, 630
Heinsius, N., 7
Heintze, H., 384
Heinz, A., 647
Heinze, D., 698
Heinzer, F., 9
Heinzle, J., 615, 618, 632
Heiric of Auxerre, 9